THE SOCIOLOGY
OF PHILOSOPHIES

THE SOCIOLOGY
OF PHILOSOPHIES

A Global Theory
of Intellectual Change

RANDALL COLLINS

THE BELKNAP PRESS OF
HARVARD UNIVERSITY PRESS
Cambridge, Massachusetts, and London, England

Fourth printing, 2002

First Harvard University Press paperback edition, 2000

Library of Congress Cataloging-in-Publication Data

Collins, Randall, 1941–
The sociology of philosophies : a global theory of intellectual
change / Randall Collins.
p.   cm.
Includes bibliographical references and index.
ISBN 0-674-81647-1 (cloth)
ISBN 0-674-00187-7 (pbk.)
1. Knowledge, Sociology of.   2. Philosophy—History.
3. Comparative civilization.   4. Philosophers—Social networks.
I. Title.
BD175.C565   1998
306.4′2′09—dc21   97-18446

In every hair there are an infinite number of lions, and in addition all the single hairs, together with their infinite number of lions, in turn enter into a single hair. In this way the progression is infinite, like the jewels in Celestial Lord Indra's net.

Fa-tsang (T'ang Dynasty)

Homer was wrong in saying, "Would that strife might perish from among gods and humans." For if that were to occur, all things would cease to exist.

Heraclitus

Contents

COMPARATIVE HISTORY OF
INTELLECTUAL COMMUNITIES

Part I: Asian Paths

COMPARATIVE HISTORY OF
INTELLECTUAL COMMUNITIES

Part II: Western Paths

Figures, Maps, and Tables

FIGURES

MAPS

TABLES

Preface

The twentieth century is the first in which comprehending world history has become possible. Previous generations of scholars knew too little about other parts of the world beyond their own. Cosmopolitan historical research, beginning in the German university revolution around 1800, reached a critical mass in the early years of our own century. Then appeared the first great efforts to break out of a Eurocentric viewpoint and to sketch the shapes on a world scale: Weber, Spengler, Toynbee, Kroeber. Their work is judged of mixed quality today, not surprisingly for pioneering efforts; that it appeared simultaneously indicates it was based on an underlying shift in the means of intellectual production. The literature of that generation, in T. S. Eliot, Ezra Pound, James Joyce, and Hermann Hesse, shares the quality of opening a treasure chest of world culture; *The Waste Land* could quote from ancient India as well as pre-classical Greece, and Pound's *Cantos* extended the range of allusion from Renaissance Italian to medieval Chinese.

Two generations later, we are in a position to understand world culture much more deeply. Ironically, as scholarship has filled in more gaps and given firmer contours to what formerly was just coming into focus, we face new obstacles to understanding. We suffer from cognitive overload, from having amassed too much information to assimilate it. Disciplinary specialization and subspecialization are predictable in an academic profession that since 1960 has grown worldwide to a size dwarfing anything before. That is one reason why, since European universities expanded recently from elite to mass systems, doctrines have arisen attacking the very possibility of knowledge. Although the world is certainly not a text, today when several hundred thousand publications appear every year in the humanities and social sciences, and another million in the natural sciences, it may well feel as if we are drowning in a sea of texts.

Will we close our eyes on knowing world history at just the time when we have the resources to break out of our regional cultures? Practitioners of world comparisons are not entirely lacking; scholars such as Braudel, Needham, McNeill, and Abu-Lughod have continued to widen East-West perspectives, and Malraux opened the doors of a "museum without walls" of world art. Although contemporary Western scholars are often hedged in by historicist particularism, Asian scholars such as Shigeru Nakayama and Hajime Nakamura have made bold efforts at trans-parochial history from the other side. Further on in the twenty-first century, when economic linkage and intermigration will indeed produce a common world culture, educated people will likely be embarrassed to know so little about the intellectual history of other parts of the world than their own.

But how to deal with the practical problem? To be a literate person today is like living in the library of Jorge Luis Borges, where near-infinite corridors of books contain the universe but we lack a key to their contents. My strategy has been to focus on intellectual networks: the social links among those thinkers whose ideas have been passed along in later generations. I have chosen philosophers because theirs is the archetypal intellectual role, which goes back several thousand years in each of the world civilizations, and from which have branched off most of the specialized disciplines. My first labor has been to assemble such networks for China, India, Japan, Greece, the Islamic world, medieval Christendom, and modern Europe, over very long periods of time. Assembling these networks has become a little history of its own; I have been working on some parts of this project for over 25 years.

The networks are a mnemonic device, a way to keep track of the expanses of history outside the few places that are familiar to us all. The networks are also the basis of a theory; I am arguing that if one can understand the principles that determine intellectual networks, one has a causal explanation of ideas and their changes. In a very strong sense, networks are the actors on the intellectual stage. Networks are the pattern of linkage among the micro-situations in which we live; the sociology of networks penetrates deeply into the very shapes of our thought. The network dynamics of intellectual communities provides an internal sociology of ideas, taking us beyond the reductionism of traditional externalist sociology. The historical dynamics of social identities in networks, too, casts the question of canonicity in another light. We need not fall into a Platonism of eternal essences to avoid the polemical simplification of reputation to sociopolitical dominance; there is a social construction of eminence which does justice to the inner processes of intellectual life.

I have attempted to render names of historical places and persons in their most accessible forms. Chinese names are romanized following the Wade-Giles conventions. Indian names are generally given in their most familiar Sanskrit forms and, like Greek, Persian, Arabic, and Japanese names, are printed here

with a minimum of diacritical marks. The Sanskrit ṣ and ś have been phoneti-
cized as *sh*.

The century, the period of 100 years, is an arbitrary unit, based on the
conventions of our decimal system. It corresponds to nothing significant about
the long-term movement of social communities. The convention of referring
to centuries merely lulls us into misleading reifications such as "the seventeenth
century, the Century of Genius," or "the Golden Age of the Greeks, the fifth
century B.C." It would be theoretically more illuminating to describe intellectual history in terms of active generations, about 3 per hundred years. A
33-year period is the approximate length of an intellectual's creative work. By
the end of that time, a cohort of thinkers will be virtually replaced by a new
adult generation. Generational periods constitute a more or less minimal unit
for structural change in an intellectual attention space. It is useful to think of
Chinese intellectual chains as building up in 6 generations from Confucius to
Mencius and Chuang Tzu—the same distance as from Thales to Socrates and
Democritus. We ourselves are living 5 generations after Hegel (an early groping
world historian), and 10 generations after Descartes.

I will not be so bold as to rewrite familiar dates in a totally new system.
It is desirable at least to step outside the Western religious framework which
undergirds "Anno Domini" and "Before Christ," and the equally parochial
years since the hegira of Muhammad (A.H.), or the mythical Emperor Fu Hsi
who anchors Chinese chronology at the equivalent of 2698 B.C. I use the
notation B.C.E. (Before Common Era) and C.E. (Common Era), which, although
arbitrarily modeled on the Western calendar, represents an attempt by world
historians to establish a trans-parochial time frame. As much as possible, I
refer to time periods numerically—"the 300s B.C.E." or "the 1200s C.E.,"
avoiding the reification of centuries as nouns, although there is an almost
irresistible temptation to lapse into common usage in referring to our own
times.

The bibliography is far from short, but I have not covered the entire
specialized literature, even in the Western languages familiar to me. As W. K. C.
Guthrie wrote in introducing his *History of Greek Philosophy,* it seemed better
to finish the work in my own lifetime.

Acknowledgments

I an indebted to many individuals for their help in reading chapters or otherwise offering criticism, information, and advice: Joe Bryant, John Rist, Alexander Murray, Gerald Larson, Alexander Rosenberg, Alan Sica, Jean-Louis Fabiani, Johan Heilbron, Konrad Jarausch, Michael Mahoney, David MacGregor, Eiko Ikegami, Harrison White, Stephen Kalberg, Sal Restivo, Stephan Fuchs, Charles Bazerman, David Glidden, Alan Beals, David Bloor, Gene Anderson, Alexandra Maryanski, Karl Morrison, Shigeru Nakayama, Norbert Wiley, Michèle Lamont, Joan Richards, Johan Goudsblom, Murray Milner, Robert Wuthnow, Paul DiMaggio, Steve Fuller, David Kaufer, Charles Lemert, Wolfram Eberhard, Nikki Keddie, Nathan Sivin, Brian Copenhaver, Robert Westman, Judith McConnell, Jonathan Turner, and Sam Kaplan. I also thank participants for comments on colloquia at Uppsala, Amsterdam, Marseille, ENS, Harvard, Princeton, Virginia, Dayton, Riverside, UCLA, International Christian University, and Joetsu University. Jie-li Li, Anthony McConnell-Collins, Maren McConnell-Collins, and Pat Hanneman helped with network figures and maps. The map on page 576 is from *The Penguin Atlas of Modern History (to 1815)* by Colin McEvedy (Penguin Books, 1972), p. 33, © 1972 by Colin McEvedy, and is reproduced by permission of Penguin Books Ltd. Michael Aronson of Harvard University Press has been an endlessly patient and supportive editor, Amanda Heller a world-class manuscript editor. Donna Bouvier guided the project through production efficiently and supportively. The Swedish Consortium for Advanced Studies in Social Science kindly hosted me during part of this research. Not least, I wish to pay respects to the memory of my teachers, explorers of social-historical time and space: Talcott Parsons, Reinhard Bendix, Wolfram Eberhard, and Joseph Ben-David.

Introduction

Intellectual life is first of all conflict and disagreement. Teaching may give the opposite impression, when initiates relate to novices what we claim to know; but the forefront where ideas are created has always been a discussion among oppositions. This heartland of disagreement is difficult to avoid; to deny it is to exemplify it. This is not to say that no agreement ever happens. Leave aside the question of when and whether consensus arrives eventually upon particular points. Even at the height of discussion, the number of opinions is not multiplied as far as might be possible. Intellectual conflict is always limited by focus on certain topics, and by the search for allies. Not warring individuals but a small number of warring camps is the pattern of intellectual history. Conflict is the energy source of intellectual life, and conflict is limited by itself.

This book presents the dynamics of conflict and alliance in the intellectual networks which have existed longest in world history. This enterprise is situated in today's field of contending positions, in sociology, and in intellectual life generally. It too is framed by its nexus of disagreement. Some might say that the effort undermines itself; that this of all times in world history is the least appropriate for a comparative, global eye, seeking out the universal and fundamental. But opposites structure one another; I could equally well say that no time in history is better suited for the effort.

Let me lay out my approach by critically reflecting on some opposing views.

1. *Ideas beget ideas.* The tradition of intellectual historians is to enter into arguments and concepts, showing how one set of ideas leads to another. Such disciplinary custom proves nothing about what is possible or impossible as an explanation. The strongest argument against treating ideas in terms of anything other than themselves was put forward by Leibniz and restated by Searle. If one imagines a human brain enlarged to gigantic size, Leibniz says, and oneself entering among the machinery, one will see nothing that resembles an idea, no matter how closely one examines the structures of the brain (*Monadology* 17). Searle (1992) resurrects the point against computer models of artificial intelli-

1

gence, and by extension against any psychological or neurological theory which describes the mind as a computer. Computers are created by humans who have minds, and the inputs and outputs of computers are always interpreted by human consciousness. To suggest that a computer might think is only a *façon de parler*. It is we who project a homunculus into the computer, a human mind which decides how the pattern of electronic branchings is to be interpreted as meaningful ideas. Things and ideas are irreducible realms; there simply is no way to go from an external description of the one to the inner meanings of the other.

The Leibniz-Searle argument might seem to hold against sociological reductions of ideas as well; the observable economic and political behaviors of classes and states are not of the same kind as the ideas they purport to explain. Yet Leibniz points to a clue: the connection between ideas and the spatial world of human bodies is endlessly mysterious if these are truly distinct substances; ideas and bodies are correlated because they are aspects of a single kind of being. Naturally one will not find ideas amid the machinery of the brain or the computer if one is looking for an idea-thing amid material-things. Ideas are not thing-like at all, except insofar as we represent them in symbols written on materials such as paper, but are first of all communication, which is to say interaction among bodily humans. To enter into the physical brain (or inside the computer) is precisely the wrong way to perceive ideas; for ideas are in the process of communication between one thinker and another, and we perceive the ideas of another brain only by having them communicated to us. It is the same with oneself: one perceives one's own ideas only insofar as one is in a communicative mode. There is no thinking except as aftermath or preparation of communication. Thinkers do not antedate communication, and the communicative process creates the thinkers as nodes of the process.

The difficulty of reducing ideas to political economy is not found in this direction. Economic and political activity is not merely physical but mindful as well, above all because it is social. The force of the anti-reductionist point is that certain kinds of ideas which we are interested in explaining cannot be explained by referring to social action where that kind of communication does not take place. There are regions of sociological reduction where the explanation is crude and unsuccessful. Economic and political macro-structures do not explain much about abstract ideas, because such ideas exist only where there is a network of intellectuals focused on their own arguments and accumulating their own conceptual baggage train. It is the inner structure of these intellectual networks which shapes ideas, by their patterns of vertical chains across the generations and their horizontal alliances and oppositions. Reduction is an error not because we are making a primitive category mistake about ideas and things, but because we look for a pattern of communicative action that is too remote from the focus of attention where the intellectual action is going on.

2. *Individuals beget ideas.* Here too is a long-standing tradition, the cult of the genius or intellectual-hero. Put in those terms the concept seems old-fashioned. It persists, when stripped of the adulatory rhetoric that once surrounded it, because it is rooted in the categories through which we think about ourselves. Individuals are defined as the responsible agents in modern law and politics; the Goffmanian rituals of everyday life worship the autonomy and privacy of the individual self. The hero mode works just as well in the guise of the antihero: Wittgenstein in his leather jacket upsetting the rigidities of Cambridge high table represents the hero-leader as much as the marble bust of Aristotle or Newton. Efforts to revise the canon leave intact the category of individuals so honored; the very notion of the neglected thinker, the devalued woman philosopher or the Romanticist image of the artist creating in oblivion in a garrett, is that of the individual outside the ranks of the privileged individuals of the canon.

We arrive at individuals only by abstracting from the surrounding context. It seems natural for us to do this because the world seems to start with ourselves. But the social world had to be bracketed for us to arrive at the lonely individual consciousness; and indeed it is only within a particular tradition of intellectual practices that we have learned how to construct this pure individual starting point, like Descartes climbing into a peasant's stove and resolving to doubt everything that could be doubted. In the case of the ideas we are concerned with here, the ideas which have mattered historically, it is possible to demonstrate that the individuals who bring forward such ideas are located in typical social patterns: intellectual groups, networks, and rivalries.

The history of philosophy is to a considerable extent the history of groups. Nothing abstract is meant here—nothing but groups of friends, discussion partners, close-knit circles that often have the characteristics of social movements. Take the upsurge of German Idealism, from Kant to Hegel and Schopenhauer. The first thing to strike us should be the dates: all the major works are between 1781 (Kant's *Critique of Pure Reason*) and 1819 (Schopenhauer's *World as Will and Representation*)—38 years, the approximate length of a generation. There is a social core: Fichte, Schelling, and Hegel, who once lived together in the same house. Fichte takes the early lead, inspiring the others on a visit while they are young students at Tübingen in the 1790s, then turning Jena into a center for the philosophical movement to which a stream of the soon-to-be-eminent congregate; then on to Dresden in the heady years 1799–1800 to live with the Romantic circle of the Schlegel brothers (where August Schlegel's wife, Caroline, has an affair with Schelling, followed later by a scandalous divorce and remarriage). Fichte moves on to Berlin, allying with

Schleiermacher (also of the Romantic circle) and with Humboldt to establish the new-style university; here Hegel eventually comes and founds his school, and Schopenhauer lectures fruitlessly in competition. There is a good deal more to these connections: the analysis will occupy us in Chapter 12.

The point is not to extol Fichte; he plays a part in a structure, the typical role of organizational leader.[1] The moving from group to group, finding organizational resources and then moving on to set up centers elsewhere, is typical of persons in this structural position. The organizational leader is not necessarily the intellectual leader; a successful theory group is one in which both are present. This enables us to comprehend the role of Kant, who is the intellectual progenitor of Idealism, although he is also socially tangential, as well as a good deal older than the others. Nevertheless, in far-away Königsberg, a crescive network was forming, in which several members (Hamann, Kant's pupil Herder) got their creative fame before Kant himself. Kant initially was not an Idealist; his first *Critique* prohibits just the kind of philosophy that his followers went on to develop. Kant was playing in a different intellectual arena. His ideas were picked up and transformed into a billowing philosophical movement precisely when an organized group appeared. Kant's late work was turned Idealist by the presence of this movement. Here again the link is Fichte: he was the one member of the Idealists to make personal contact with Kant, and launched his own career on Kant's sponsorship.

Fichte, one may say, made Kant what he turned out to be for the history of philosophy. But this is not to substitute one hero for another; better to say "Fichte" made "Kant" what he turned out to be. "Fichte" is shorthand, a way of designating a social movement within the intellectual community. It is a movement which drew in new recruits, charged them with creative energy, and presented them with fruitful tasks in lines of thought then opening up. This movement has both an internal structure and external conditions at a second level of social causation. The Idealist movement emerged at just this time in the struggle to transform the German universities, which resulted in the autonomy of the philosophical faculty and the birth of the modern research university.

Dissidents are as much a part of the network structure as are favorites: here we find Schopenhauer hanging on the edge of the group, never able to break into it, and Schelling, once the movement's darling, later its embittered outcast. These patterns too are part of the field of structured possibilities, apportioned among participation at the core of the attention space, unrequited attraction and repulsion at the periphery. To see the development of ideas as the lengthened shadows of imposing personalities keeps us imprisoned in conventional reifications. We need to see through the personalities, to dissolve them into the network of processes which have brought them to our attention as historical figures.

Such structures anchor the development of philosophy in all historical regions. If we turn to ancient Greece, we find the history of philosophy can be recounted in terms of a series of interlinked groups: the Pythagorean brotherhood and its offshoots; Socrates' circle, which spawned so many others; the acute debaters of the Megara school; Plato's friends, who constituted the Academy; the breakaway faction that became Aristotle's Peripatetic school; the restructuring of the network that crystallized with Epicurus and his friends (very tight bonds here), withdrawing into their Garden community, and their rivals, the Athenian Stoics, with their revisionist circles at Rhodes and Rome; the successive movements at Alexandria.

Many parallels can be cited in China. I will mention just one: the Neo-Confucians of the Sung dynasty, the most important development of Chinese philosophy since the early Warring States. Like the German Idealists, the Neo-Confucians burst on the scene in two overlapping generations, in this case active around 1040 to 1100 via a group linked by personal ties. Those who became notable were the brothers Ch'eng Hao and Ch'eng I; their teacher Chou Tun-yi; their father's cousin Chang Tsai; and their neighbor Shao Yung. There were tensions and differences among the group, and various lines of disciples split off from them. Once again we see the organizing core: the Ch'eng brothers were instrumental in linking the others together, and it was through their movement that the earliest thinker, Chou Tun-yi, retrospectively acquired his reputation as a founder. (This relabeling parallels, in a degree, the experience of Kant.) The subsequent politics of the movement, as it split into rival factions and received its canonical formulation in the fourth generation by Chu Hsi and Lu Chiu-yüan, exemplify structured processes that are historically general.

In Europe such groups have structured the main intellectual movements from the 1600s to the present. The correspondence network formed by Marin Mersenne in Paris in the 1620s, and extended to England by Henry Oldenburg, was the organizing basis of what eventually became the French Académie des Sciences and the English Royal Academy in the 1660s. In a larger sense, the "invisible college" continued for more than 60 years, providing an organizational core for the founding generations of modern Western philosophy. Growth in the sheer size of the surrounding population or expansion in the total numbers of educated intellectuals does not outdate these concentrated groups who dominate attention at the innovative core. In our own times we find again two close-knit groups with major intellectual impact: the Vienna Circle of the 1920s and 1930s, whose subsequently scattered followers (and visitors, such as Ayer and Quine) dominated Anglophone philosophy through midcentury; and the Paris existentialists of the 1930s and 1940s, whose aftermath includes most of the famous names of the 1960s and 1970s.

Another pattern of creativity is intergenerational networks, chains of eminent teachers and pupils. Such are easy to illustrate from all portions of history, and the analysis of chains will occupy us in the chapters that follow. Here are a few of the famous ones: Thales-Anaximander-Anaximenes; Parmenides-Socrates-Plato-Aristotle-Theophrastus-Arcesilaus-Chrysippus; Panaetius-Posidonius-Cicero; Whitehead-Russell-Wittgenstein; or, to approach the present, Brentano-Husserl-Heidegger-Gadamer (as well as Heidegger-Marcuse and Heidegger-Arendt). Creativity is not random among individuals; it builds up in intergenerational chains.

The third characteristic of intellectual fields is structural rivalry. Intellectual work is almost always concentrated at the same time as other work of a similar degree of innovativeness and scope. The major philosophers appear in pairs or trios, rival positions developing contemporaneously with one another (i.e., they are active within the same generational span, approximately 35 years). We can take as emblematic that Heraclitus, the partisan of absolute flux, was contemporary (ca. 490–70 B.C.E.) with Parmenides, the partisan of absolute immobile Being. Epicurus and Zeno the Stoic established within five years of each other (306–301 B.C.E.) the two schools that were to dominate Hellenistic and Roman intellectual life for many centuries. In a later epoch, the leading Christian and pagan philosophers, Origen and Plotinus, emerged close together (ca. 220–50 C.E.), splitting off from the same teacher. In China ca. 340–300 B.C.E. Mencius, Chuang-tzu, and Hui Shih were contemporaries and rivals; centuries later (1170–1200 C.E.), the rationalist and idealist branches of Neo-Confucianism were championed by the acquaintances Chu Hsi and Lu Chiu-yüan. Nearer our own day, the logical positivists and the phenomenologists and existentialists not only were contemporary but developed some of their most memorable doctrines in opposition to the other. The pattern of contemporaneous creativity by opponents of comparable stature is nearly universal across history.

Such rivalries are not necessarily personal ones. Contemporary advocates of rival positions do not always direct their attacks against one another, or even pay attention to them. Epicurus and Zeno had their own agendas and argued mainly against philosophies and doctrines of preceding generations; explicit rivalry between their schools developed only in succeeding generations. At founding moments, spaces open up which are filled not merely by individuals but by a small number of intellectual movements which restructure the attention space by pressing in opposing directions. It is conflicts—lines of difference between positions—which are implicitly the most prized possessions of intellectuals. For this reason the history of philosophy is the history not so much of problems solved as of the discovery of exploitable lines of opposition.

Have we forgotten the individual? After all, not all intellectuals belong to these groups. Proud, isolated Heraclitus is not the only one of his kind. Some important intellectuals (though fewer) are isolated in time, without contemporaries of stature who can act as structural rivals. Besides these empirical objections, there is a more basic matter of principle. Creative intellectuals are generally introverts, not extroverts. Intellectual creativity is done not in group situations but by working alone, usually for many hours of the day. The contradiction is only apparent. Intellectual groups, master-pupil chains, and contemporaneous rivalries together make up a structured field of forces within which intellectual activity takes place. And there is a pathway from such social structures into the inner experience of the individual's mind. The group is present in consciousness even when the individual is alone: for individuals who are the creators of historically significant ideas, it is this *intellectual* community which is paramount precisely when he or she is alone. A human mind, a train of thinking in a particular body, is constituted by one's personal history in a chain of social encounters. For intellectuals, these are special kinds of social chains, and therefore special kinds of minds.

The sociology of mind is not a theory of how intellectuals are affected by "non-intellectual motives." To frame the question in this way is to assume that thinking normally takes places independently, in a pristine realm driven by nothing but itself. But thinking would not be possible at all if we were not social; we would have no words, no abstract ideas, and no energy for anything outside of immediate sensuality. The lesson of Chapter 1 is that thinking consists in making "coalitions in the mind," internalized from social networks, motivated by the emotional energies of social interactions. My concern is not with "non-intellectual motives" but to show what intellectual motives are.

That ideas are not rooted in individuals is hard to accept because it seems to offend against a key epistemological point. Here the question is analytically distinct from the propensity to worship intellectual heroes. It is assumed that objective truth itself depends on the existence of a pure observer or thinker, untrammeled by anything but insight into truth. The notion is that the social is necessarily a distortion, an alien intrusion in epistemology; if ideas are determined by social interactions, then they cannot be determined by truth. This objection comes so naturally that it is hard to think except within this dichotomy: either there is truth which is independent of society, or truth is social and therefore not objectively true. There are two prejudices here. One is the assumption that constructing an idealized individual, outside of the social, provides a vantage point that social networks cannot provide just as well. On the contrary: there is even more difficulty in connecting such a disembodied individual to the world than there is in connecting a social group to the world, since a group is already to some degree extended in the world of time and space.

The second prejudice or tacit assumption is that the criterion of truth exists in free-floating reality, along with the free-floating thinker-observer. But the very concept of truth has developed within social networks, and has changed with the history of intellectual communities. To say this is not automatically to assert either self-doubting relativism or the non-existence of objectivity. It is no more than a historical fact to say that we have never stepped outside of the human thought community; and the sociology of thinking implies that we never will step outside of it. The very notion of stepping outside is something developed historically by particular branches within intellectual networks; so are the polemics about the allegedly corrosive effects of a sociology of ideas. In the Epilogue I will argue at greater length that social construction of knowledge is realism, not anti-realism, and that it is a more secure defense of realism than the usual methods of asserting our prejudice in favor of objective reality.

3. *Culture begets itself.* A contemporary argument asserts the autonomy of culture. The epithet "reductionist" is taken as a self-evident refutation of that to which it can be applied. Yet there is no compelling evidence that culture is autonomous, that its forms and changes are explainable only in terms of itself.

Some sociologists make the anti-reductionist argument by pointing out that many cultural stances—ethnic consciousness, religious belief, political ideologies—are not correlated with social class and other familiar sociological variables. Culture is autonomous in the statistical sense that one cannot predict persons' culture from their social position. Instead, culture develops within its own channels; French neighborhoods which have supported the revolutionary left do so repeatedly from one historical period to the next; American upper-middle-class professionals contained both Progressives and their opponents. The hidden assumption here is to treat the social as if it referred to social class and a few other variables of traditional survey research, while leaving ethnicity, religion, ideology, and the like outside. This is a failure to think through the experienced reality which lies behind terms such as "ethnicity" or "political belief." Each of these is a type of social interaction, a specific form of discourse which has meaning for a particular social network, a set of interactions which marks off some persons as having a particular ethnic or religious or political identity from those who do not. Culture is not autonomous of society, because we never know anything under this term except from describing the kinds of things which happen in interaction. To say that culture is autonomous, that culture explains itself, is either inaccurate or superfluous: inaccurate if culture is defined in a fashion that excludes the social, for such culture has never existed; superfluous if defined broadly, for in that case culture is coextensive with the social, making cultural explanations sociological ones. At best the metaphor of the autonomously cultural points to distinctive regions, distinctive networks and zones of focal attention, within the social.

The argument is sometimes put more abstractly: culture is meta-social, the grounds which make the social possible. In tribal societies much behavior is structured by the rules of kinship; more generally, all social life consists in playing social games which are constituted by their rules. Often joined to this theory is the claim that such meta-structures are historically specific; different tribes, groups, historical epochs play different games, and live in irreducibly distinctive worlds. Applied to the history of ideas, this line of argument for irreducible cultural particularism takes the form that the limits and possibilities of thinking are given by language; the nature of a syntax determines what philosophy can be formulated in it. If this is so, then the philosophies of the world are hermetically sealed by the distinctiveness of languages such as Indo-European, Semitic, and Chinese.

In this argument it is the Chinese language, with its dearth of explicit syntax, which prevented philosophies from developing formal syllogistic logic and pursuing that route toward epistemology (Hansen, 1983). Time is elided because verbs lack tense. Nouns do not distinguish between singular and plural, abstract or concrete. Without the definitive article, most things appear as mass nouns (like "water" in English), with no distinct emphasis given to the particular ("the table"). Realms of philosophical consideration are cut off. What is constructed in the characteristic Chinese worldview is language-embedded. The same word can often be used as noun, adjective, or verb, giving the haunting multiple meanings of Chinese poetry, while avoiding the Greco-European style of philosophizing by piecing apart abstract distinctions. To this quality of language is due the centrality of concepts such as *Tao,* a distinctively Chinese blending of process and substance. For Chinese, no abstract metaphysics is possible; its worldview is sui generis in being simultaneously concrete and ethereal.

Yet a language is not static. New conceptual terms are produced by philosophical arguments; the development of philosophy is the development of its language. This is not to say that languages may not pose difficulties, and that time is not taken in their overcoming; but the pace of philosophical movement is rather slow in every part of the world, rarely making more than one conceptual step in any 35-year generation or so. The speed of conceptual transformation among Chinese philosophers in their most intense periods of debate, as in the years 365–235 B.C.E., is on a par with comparable periods elsewhere.

The argument as applied to Chinese is parochial. Other languages have their philosophical difficulties as well. The Greeks had no words to distinguish between "similar" and "identical"; both were rendered by *ömoios,* giving rise to early problems for Pythagoreans and Sophists (Guthrie, 1961–1982: 1:230). The copula is not present in Arabic; the Indo-European languages, however, have difficulty in distinguishing between the existential and copulative senses of "to be." Nevertheless, philosophers have made explicit the distinctions brought into focus by their debates. Ibn Sina was well aware of the absence of the copula and the difficulties it caused, and modified the verb "to exist" *(wajada)* to call attention to "existential propositions" *(wujudiyya)* in contrast to a long list of propositional types (Afnan, 1958: 97; Graham, 1978: 25–26). Medieval Latin philosophers used this Arabic philosophical capital to sharpen their sense of the different meanings of "to be," ringing on these a series of metaphysical changes based on the distinction between existence and essence, against the existing grain of the language.[2] Among the early Greeks, the idiom of adjective and article ("the unlimited," "the cold") made it natural to fail to distinguish between abstract and concrete; nevertheless, Aristotle overcame the difficulty with his armory of distinctions created upon reaching the vantage point of higher abstraction.

All philosophical communities start with concrete words in their common-sense meanings. In archaic China, *Tao* had only the concrete sense of a road or pathway; it started to take on the first of its many abstract meanings in the *Analects* as an intellectual community formed around Confucius. Like all languages, later Chinese pressed older concrete words into service as abstractions. It is the same with the Greeks: *aer* (fog, mist, darkness) was given the meaning of "substance" by Anaximenes; *logos* was a common Greek word with many meanings until a philosophical meaning was created for it by Heraclitus (Guthrie, 1961–1982: 1:124–126, 420–434). Chinese philosophers, when sustained by a dense enough argumentative network, extended and reinterpreted from the resources of their own language (such as clarifying by means of particles and explanations) to make the distinctions and reach the levels of abstraction which constituted the forefront of their debates; by the mid-200s B.C.E. the Mohists had broken through concrete words to explicit abstract distinctions, and formulated the rules of logical argumentation.

In short, language is no deus ex machina to account for philosophy. Neither is eternally fixed; both change, and the changes of the intellectual community are what move a language into more abstract and refined terms.

The general version of this argument, that every cultural activity is irreducibly shaped by its distinctive meta-rules, may be criticized in the same way. It is not historically true that cultural practices are fixed and changeless, although ethnographic descriptions which sample slices taken out of time may give this impression. Nor is it necessary in sociological theory to accept the premise that social activity is game-like, that it is shaped by rules at all. A different way of conceiving of social action will be presented in Chapter 1.

4. *Everything is fluid; it is impossible to fix any contours or sharpen any explanatory concepts.* The argument for the autonomy or particularistic flow

of culture is allied with a more general position variously labeled poststructuralist, postpositivist, or postmodernist. No general explanations are possible; there can be no general theory of ideas, sociological or otherwise. Yet paradoxically, postmodernism is itself a general theory of ideas. The theory has been accumulating in intellectual networks for several generations. One stream began in the phenomenological movement searching for the essences of consciousness, broadened by Husserl into a crisis of European science and by Heidegger into a crisis of lived meaning. Another stream came from Saussure's semiotics of language structure via formalist literary theory and Lévi-Strauss's search for the codes underlying every item of society and culture. Wittgensteinian analytical philosophy was eventually levied for contributions, yielding the argument that thought has fragmented into a plurality of language games. Popularizing the whole movement was the fusion with Marxism and Freudianism widespread among French intellectuals after 1960; then in a twist which snatched intellectual victory from political defeat came the shift to post-Marxism, spearheaded by disillusioned activists who turned the Marxian technique of ideological unveiling (and the allied technique of Freudian unveiling) against those grand narratives themselves.

These sets of overlapping movements have constituted a theory of ideas, converging on its reflexivity and its rejection of any fixed standpoint from which an explanation might be made. At the same time, postmodernism is itself an explanation. A good deal of its explanatory stance runs parallel to, or even derives from, the branch of sociology studying the social production of ideas. In Mannheim's and Scheler's generation this lineage was called the sociology of knowledge; around 1960 it became the research field of sociology of science, studying scientists' networks, publications, and careers; in the late 1970s it was deepened by micro-sociological ethnographers of everyday life into laboratory studies of the local social construction of scientific knowledge, and theorized by neo-Durkheimians such as David Bloor and the Edinburgh school. The widespread poststructuralist notion that the world is made up of arbitrary oppositions has its roots in classical sociology: Saussure was influenced by Durkheim's sociology of ideas, and by a different route the poststructuralists took over the theme of Lévi-Strauss (a pupil of Durkheim's nephew Marcel Mauss) of a binary code of oppositions, while repudiating the specifics of structuralist theory. Garfinkel's ethnomethodology, which was the paradigm for studying the local production of knowledge in scientific laboratories, comes from the same lineage of Husserlian phenomenology which in another network branch produced Derrida.[3]

Postmodernists radicalize the sociology of ideas in repudiating the possibility of general explanation, including the causal and dynamic principles of Marx, Durkheim, or Lévi-Strauss. Unmasking is turned back against itself.

Ideas cannot be explained by the social because nothing can be explained by anything, most centrally because the very fixing of thing-like boundaries is itself undermined by the unmasking. To turn reflexivity against itself in this way in some respects recapitulates previous stances of philosophical skepticism (such as the Pyrrhonian skeptics of the Hellenistic/Roman period); although postmodernism differs from Pyrrhonian quietism because it has acquired an aggressively moralizing and polemical stance in its alliances with a branch of radical feminists, gay liberation theorists, and ethnic/racial insurgents. Dissolving boundaries serves to attack privilege and to hold out the possibility of reconstructing social categories (if only provisionally and temporarily) in drastically different ways. On the most general theoretical level, we ought to recognize that postmodernism here is Durkheim's social determinism of categories radicalized into a fluid future from which his evolutionary directionality has been pulled out; it is Marx's sociology of ideologies cut adrift from his directionality of modes of production into a condition of permanent epistemological revolution.

One does not have to repudiate a general sociological understanding of the dynamics of historical paths in order to see that Durkheimian or Marxian unilinear evolutionism is too restrictive. To recognize that social beings are not thing-like does not commit us to holding that the processes which they are have no structure and no causal contours.

The topic of this book is a sociology of philosophies, which is to say the abstract conceptions produced by networks of specialized intellectuals turned inward upon their own arguments. This network displays definite social dynamics over the expanse of world history. This topic is not the same thing as the production of popular culture, such as the advertising, pop stars, tourist industry, personal apparel, electronic networks, and their multiplex intercombinations that make up the topics for postmodernist sociology of culture. There remains a distinction between intellectual networks and these commercial marketplaces, even today, and the distinction was even sharper at most times in past history. Postmodernist thinkers, like other intellectuals before them, live in a region of academic discourse that is generally unrecognized by most people outside their network. The generalized rhetoric of postmodernist critique tends to hold illegitimate the drawing of any analytical boundaries; but this is mere assertion.

One may claim that the personal is political, and that there is no rigid separation between what intellectuals do and the economic, political, ethnic, and gendered relations of the surrounding historical era. But the level at which such statements are true cannot be fixed in advance of research on the way intellectual networks operate. The personal is political, but the politics of intellectual practice, within the inwardly focused network of specialists, is not the same thing as the politics of gaining power in the state, or the politics of men and women in their homes or sexual encounters. Winning the focus of attention within the contests among philosophers is done with specifically intellectual resources, which are social resources specific to intellectual networks. There is abundant historical evidence that when players in this arena try to win their way solely with the weapons of external politics, they win the battle at the cost of their intellectual reputations in the long-term historical community. These are not the same game; and at those times in history when one game reduces to another, the intellectual game does not so much give in as disappear, to reappear only when an inner space becomes available for it again. Without an internal structure of intellectual networks generating their own matrix of arguments, there are no ideological effects on philosophy; we find only lay ideologies, crude and simple.

It is fashionable in some quarters to declare that there are no distinctions among internal and external, between micro and macro, the local and the far-flung and long-lasting. What gives force to such claims is that micro and macro, local and distant, are indeed connected; the macro is built out of chains of micro-encounters in local situations, and in some respects there is analytical primacy in the local rituals which constitute momentary reality in those chains, and charge up the symbols with significance which makes it possible for humans to maintain what continuity they can from one micro-local situation to another. This is not the same thing as dissolving all such concepts; one cannot formulate the relations between the micro-situational and the trans-local if one lacks concepts with which to designate them. Any sociology which attempts to abolish such terms soon finds itself smuggling the distinctions back in under other words.

Postmodernism is a radicalization of the sociology of ideas, under the impetus to some extent of disillusioned ex-Marxism, to some extent of the militant ideologies of newer social movements. In the academic world, its alliances with specialized departments of literary and cultural studies tend to reduce the explanatory focus of sociological theory. These several layers of intellectual politics do not make a sociology of philosophies impossible. They do make it one of a family of warring cousins; but conflict in intergenerational lineages is nothing anomalous; indeed, it is a main pattern of intellectual history.

If there is a kinship among all the branches of the sociology of ideas, does that mean that my sociology of philosophies, like all its kin, is reflexively self-undermining? Some branches of the family embrace the paradox willingly or even enthusiastically; others reject it. My own stance is that the sociology of philosophies is not a self-undermining skepticism or relativism; that it has definite historical contours, as well as a general theory of intellectual networks which, far from being self-undermining, is self-exemplifying and self-reinforcing. The argument is best made at the end of the book, in the Epilogue, after the full weight of the historical networks has been encountered.

The objection from the alleged skeptical or self-undermining consequences of the sociology of ideas is an epistemological objection. A different kind of objection is a moral one: that the sociology of ideas, with its general principles of social causation, is anti-humanistic. Individuals are nodes in networks of social interaction, human bodies where emotional energies accumulate and streams of idea-symbols crystallize into coalitions in the mind. Doesn't this denigrate us, reducing our lived experience to epiphenomena and our hard-fought human dignity to the totalitarian imposition of the group? I put the point harshly in order to deny that any such consequences follow.

Do we not have agency? It is a matter of analytical perspective. Agency is in part a term for designating the primitives of sociological explanation, in part a code word for free will. Do not human beings make efforts, strain every nerve or let themselves go lax, make decisions or evade them? Such experiences clearly exist; they are part of micro-situational reality, the flow of human life. I deny only that the analysis should stop here. One has the experience of will power; it varies, it comes and goes. Where does it come from? How do you will to will? That chain of regress comes to an end in a very few links. The same can be said about thinking. Are not one's thoughts one's own? Of course they are; yet why do they come into one's head at a certain moment, or flow out upon one's lips or beneath one's fingers in a certain sequence of spoken or written words? These are not unanswerable questions if one has a micro-sociological theory of thinking. To explain thinking is not to deny that thinking exists, any more than to explain culture is to deny that culture exists. Culture, on a macro-level, is the medium in which we move, just as thought and feeling are the medium of micro-local experience in our own conscious bodies. Neither of these is an end point, cut off by a barrier to further analysis.

To continue on, to understand how our emotions and thoughts are flows in sociological networks, does not deny our human condition. One can perceive all these levels simultaneously. You and I are *thus,* as particular individuals, with all our uniqueness, and yet uniquely constituted by the flows of emotion and thought within us and through us. The tension between the particular and local, and the surrounding links which are the social, and which define our very particularity: this is the human condition.

To pursue social causation everywhere, without privileged exemptions, does not mean that history is a rigid sequence. The social structure of the intellectual world, the topic of this book, is an ongoing struggle among chains of persons, charged up with emotional energy and cultural capital, to fill a small number of centers of attention. These focal points, which make up the cores of the intellectual world, are periodically rearranged; there is a limited amount of attention that can be distributed through the total intellectual network, but who and what is in those nodes fluctuates as old intellectual movements fade out and new ones begin. These nodes in the attention space are crescive, emergent; starting with small advantages among the first movers, they accelerate past thresholds, cumulatively monopolizing attention at the same time that attention is drained away from alternative nodes. The identities that we call intellectual personalities, great thinkers if they are energized by the crescive moment of dominant nodes of attention, lesser thinkers or indeed no one of note if they are not so energized, are not fixed. It is precisely because the social structure of intellectual attention is fluidly emergent that we cannot reify individuals, heroizing the agent as if each one were a fixed point of will power and conscious insight who enters the fray but is no more than dusted by it at the edge of one's psychic skin. This reified individuality can be seen only in the retrospective mode, starting from the personalities defined by known ending points and projecting them backwards as if the end point had caused the career. My sociological task is just the opposite: to see through intellectual history to the network of links and energies that shaped its emergence in time.

The first three chapters present the general theory. Chapter 1 lays out the theory of interaction ritual chains, which is the micro-core of the argument for the social predictability of intellectuals' thinking. Chapter 2 gives a theory of the network structure which determines the location of creativity, and compares the evidence of networks of Chinese and Greek philosophers over several dozens of generations. The subsequent chapters confront the theory with long-term segments of these intellectual networks and those of India, Japan, the medieval Islamic, Jewish, and Christian worlds, and the European West through the 1930s. Each chapter highlights a particular analytical theme. The chapters need not be read in any particular sequence, although Chapter 3, on ancient Greece, presents some central principles that figure in what follows. A brief summary of the analytical model is given in "Conclusions to Part I: The Ingredients of Intellectual Life." Chapter 15 presents the conclusions of the entire analysis in a sketch of the pathways along which intellectuals through their debates drive the sequence of ideas during long periods of time. The reader may find it useful as a road map of the book. The Epilogue draws epistemological conclusions from the whole argument.

THE SKELETON OF THEORY

CHAPTER 1

Coalitions in the Mind

Intellectuals are people who produce decontextualized ideas. These ideas are meant to be true or significant apart from any locality, and apart from anyone concretely putting them into practice. A mathematical formula claims to be true in and of itself, whether or not it is useful, and apart from whoever believes it. A work of literature, or of history, claims the same sort of status, insofar as it is conceived as art or scholarship: part of a realm that is higher, more valid, less constrained by particular occasions of human action than ordinary kinds of thoughts and things. Philosophy has the peculiarity of periodically shifting its own grounds, but always in the direction of claiming or at least seeking the standpoint of greatest generality and importance. This continues to be the case when the content of philosophy is to assert that everything is transient, historically situated, of local value only; for the relativistic statement itself is asserted as if it were valid. This is an old conundrum of the skeptical tradition, discussed at great length in Hellenistic philosophy. Skeptics in attempting to avoid making assertions implicitly stand on a meta-distinction among levels of assertion of varying force. This illustrates the sociological point admirably, for only the intellectual community has the kind of detachment from ordinary concerns in which statements of this sort are meaningful.

Intellectual products are felt, at least by their creators and consumers, to belong to a realm which is peculiarly elevated. They are part of Durkheim's "la vie sérieuse." We can recognize them as sacred objects in the strongest sense; they inhabit the same realm, make the same claims to ultimate reality, as religion. "Truth" is the reigning sacred object of the scholarly community, as "art" is for literary/artistic communities; these are simultaneously their highest cognitive and moral categories, the locus of highest value, by which all else is judged. As Bloor (1976) has pointed out about mathematics, intellectual truth has all the characteristics Durkheim stated for the sacred objects of religion: transcending individuals, objective, constraining, demanding respect.

What gives particular ideas and texts this sacred status? It is possible to state a sociological theory of very wide scope, which tells us the conditions under which symbols are generated and are felt to be morally and cognitively binding. This is the theory of interaction rituals. It connects symbols to social membership, and hence both to emotions of solidarity and to the structure of social groups. Such a theory, I will attempt to show, accounts for variations in solidarity and belief found across different social structures, and for the dynamics of individual lives. A specific form of this emotional energy is what we call creativity.

Our first theoretical problem is to show why intellectual products have their own kind of sacred status, different from the more ordinary sacred objects with which everyday life is also permeated and which hold together personal friendships, property relations, and authority structures. I must also show why the sacred objects of intellectuals under the guiding category of "truth" are different from the sacredness of religion proper in its moral community of faith. After this, I consider how intellectuals produce and circulate symbols in their own highly stratified communities.

General Theory of Interaction Rituals

Let us begin at the site of all action: the local situation. All events take place in a here-and-now as concrete and particular. The perspective of micro-sociology, which analyzes the structures and dynamics of situations, is all too easily interpreted as a focus on the individual actor or agent. But a situation is just the interaction of conscious human bodies, for a few hours, minutes, or even micro-seconds; the actor is both less than the whole situation and larger, as a unit in time which stretches across situations. The detached agent who makes events happen is as artificial a construction as the detached non-social observer, who represents the idealized vantage point of classical epistemology. The self, the person, is more macro than the situation (strictly speaking, the person is meso); and it is analytically derivative because the self or agent is constructed by the dynamics of social situations.

The local situation is the starting point of analysis, not the ending point. The micro-situation is not the individual, but it penetrates the individual, and its consequences extend outward through social networks to as macro a scale as one might wish. The whole of human history is made up of situations. No one has ever been outside of a local situation; and all our views of the world, all our gathering of data, come from here. Philosophical problems of the reality of the world, of universals, of other minds, of meaning, implicitly start with this situatedness. I will not pursue these epistemological problems here, except to note that if one refuses to admit anything beyond the local, one arrives at some version of skepticism or relativism; if one idealizes what happens in situations as the following of rules and uses these inferred rules as a tool for constructing the rest of the world, one arrives at a type of idealism.

In sociology, emphasis on the primacy of the local was introduced by symbolic interactionism and radicalized by ethnomethodology; as a research technique and as an explicit epistemology, the stance has been picked up by the branch of sociologists of science who study the local production of scientific knowledge in laboratory sites. To deny that anything exists other than the local is true in one sense, misleading in another. It is true that nothing exists which is not thoroughly local; if it did not exist locally, where could it possibly be found? But no local situation stands alone; situations surround one another in time and space. The macro-level of society should be conceived not as a vertical layer above the micro, as if it were in a different place, but as the unfurling of the scroll of micro-situations. Micro-situations are embedded in macro-patterns, which are just the ways that situations are linked to one another; causality—agency, if you like—flows inward as well as outward. What happens here and now depends on what has happened there and then. We can understand macro-patterns, without reifying them as if they were self-subsisting objects, by seeing the macro as the dynamics of networks, the meshing of chains of local encounters that I call *interaction ritual chains*.

The sociology of ideas (which as a research field has become concerned mainly with the sociology of scientific knowledge) encounters serious limits in understanding knowledge as a purely local construction. The significant ideas which are the topics of intellectual history are those which are carried trans-locally. Examining the local site of knowledge production misses what another branch of the sociology of science has been good at investigating: the groups of thinkers, the chains of network contacts, the rivalries between one segment of an argumentative community and another. Groups and chains face both inward and outward: inward because what we mean by an intellectual group is just that its members assemble face-to-face often enough to build up intense exchanges of ritual interaction, forging idea-emblems, identities, emotional energies that persist and sometimes dominate others; outward because chains are a way of referring to long-distance links across situations. How is this linking done? The impacts of situations both inward and outward are parts of the same process. Intensely focused situations penetrate the individual, forming symbols and emotions which are both the medium and the energy of individual thought and the capital which makes it possible to construct yet further situations in an ongoing chain.

"Interaction ritual" is Goffman's (1967) term, by which he calls attention to the fact that the formal religious rituals which Durkheim ([1912] 1961) analyzed are the same type of event which happens ubiquitously in everyday life. Religious rituals are archetypes of interactions which bind members into a moral community, and which create symbols that act as lenses through which members view their world, and as codes by which they communicate. There is a wealth of anthropological research which demonstrates the importance of rituals in tribal societies, and the power of their attendant category schemes to control what people take for granted and what they cannot even think about. In complex societies like our own, these category schemes take on a greater variety corresponding to the relations among groups in a stratified social order (Douglas, 1973); Bernstein (1971–1975) shows them embedded in the language of social classes. Goffman's (1959, 1971) ethnography of everyday life investigated more explicitly the Durkheimian mechanism of how social solidarity is produced. For Goffman, every fleeting encounter is a little social order, a shared reality constructed by solidarity rituals which mark its entering and its closing through formal gestures of greeting and departure, and by the little marks of respect which idealize selves and occasions.

Let us broaden this perspective still further. The ritualism of social encounters is variable; everything that happens can be arrayed on a continuum from the most intense production of social solidarity and sacred symbolism, down through the mundane and fleeting rituals of ordinary life, and down still further to encounters which produce no solidarity and no meaning at all. Understanding the source of this variability provides us with a key to the structuring of local encounters; interactions at different degrees along this continuum determine just how strongly are generated social symbols and emotions, which carry over into subsequent situations. A general theory of interaction ritual (which I abbreviate IR) is simultaneously a key to the sociology of individual thinking and emotion, and to the varied linkage from one local situation to another.

The following are the ingredients of any interaction ritual:

1. a group of at least two people is physically assembled;
2. they focus attention on the same object or action, and each becomes aware that the other is maintaining this focus;
3. they share a common mood or emotion.

At first glance, this seems to miss the core of the usual definition of "ritual"—stereotyped actions such as reciting verbal formulas, singing, making prescribed gestures, and wearing traditional costumes. These are the superficial aspects of a formal ritual, which have their social effect only because they ensure a mutual focus of attention. The same focus can occur implicitly in what we may call *natural rituals*. To the extent that these ingredients are sustained, they build up social effects:

4. The mutual focus of attention and the shared mood cumulatively intensify. Bodily motions, speech acts, and vocal micro-frequencies become attuned

into a shared rhythm. As micro-coordination becomes intense, participants are temporarily united in a shared reality, and experience a boundary or membrane between that situation and whoever is outside it.

5. As a result, the participants feel they are members of a group, with moral obligations to one another. Their relationship becomes symbolized by whatever they focused on during their ritual interaction. Subsequently, when persons use these symbols in discourse or thought, they are tacitly reminded of their group membership. Symbols are charged with social meaning by the experience of interaction rituals; and symbols run down and lose their compelling significance if such encounters are not reenacted within a period of time. Hence there is a fluctuation in the daily relevance of symbols. Symbols remind members to reassemble the group, whether by having another church service, another tribal ceremony, another birthday party, another conversation with a friend, another scholarly conference. The survival of symbols, and the creation of new ones, depends on the extent to which groups reassemble periodically.[1] Symbols which are sufficiently charged with feelings of membership carry the individual along certain courses of action even when the group is not present. Well-charged symbols become emblems to be defended against desecrators and outsiders; they are boundary markers of what is proper, and battle flags for the precedence of groups.

6. Individuals who participate in IRs are filled with emotional energy, in proportion to the intensity of the interaction. Durkheim called this energy "moral force," the flow of enthusiasm that allows individuals in the throes of ritual participation to carry out heroic acts of fervor or self-sacrifice. I would emphasize another result of group-generated emotional energy: it charges up individuals like an electric battery, giving them a corresponding degree of enthusiasm toward ritually created symbolic goals when they are out of the presence of the group. Much of what we consider individual personality consists of the extent to which persons carry the energy of intense IRs; at the high end, such persons are charismatic; a little less intensely, they are forceful leaders and the stars of sociability; modest charges of emotional energy make passive individuals; and those whose IR participation is meager and unsuccessful are withdrawn and depressed. Emotional energy (abbreviated EE) flows from situations when individuals participate in IRs to situations when they are alone. Encounters have an emotional aftermath; it is by this route that persons can pursue their interior lives and their individual trajectories, and yet be shaped by the nodes of social interaction. EE ebbs away after a period of time; to renew it, individuals are drawn back into ritual participation to recharge themselves.

All social life is an ecology of human bodies, coming together and moving apart across the landscape. Where individuals meet, their encounters have in varying degrees the qualities which generate interaction rituals. In principle, we can predict what will happen: how much solidarity will be generated in various situations, what kinds of symbols are created and how attached particular people are to them. These encounters produce an ongoing flow of social motivations, as people come away from each situation with a store of charged symbols (which can be called *cultural capital,* or CC), and with emotional energies. Persons are attracted to those situations in which they can make the best use of their previously acquired cultural capital and symbolic resources to focus discursive action and thereby generate further solidarity.[2] Individual lives are chains of interaction rituals; the meshing of these chains constitutes everything that is social structure in all its myriad shapes.

Consider now the peculiar kinds of interaction ritual chains that constitute the world of intellectuals.

The Interaction Rituals of Intellectuals

Intellectual groups have something in common with all social memberships. Every local group is attached to its symbols; but the nature of these symbols varies, and so does members' self-consciousness in relation to them. Isolated communities, where the same lineup of persons is recurrently thrown together, tend to reify their symbols as if they were concrete objects; at the extremes of self-subsistent tribes or deliberately separated cult communities, the emotional attachment to symbols is personified as magical or religious forces. At the other extreme of the continuum, encounters take place at the shifting nodes of far-flung networks, where a changing cast of characters negotiates fleeting relations with a mixture of cultural capitals. These patterns result in abstract symbols, which participants treat with detachment and reflexive awareness of their social relativity. Intellectuals are a peculiar combination of the intensely localistic and the detached and cosmopolitan, of Durkheimian mechanical and organic solidarity.

Intellectual sacred objects are created in communities which spread widely yet are turned inward, oriented toward exchange with their own members rather than outsiders, and which claim the sole right to decide reflectively on the validity of their ideas. Purely local groups such as the tribe or the circle of friends are primarily concerned with their own solidarity and identity; they do not make the kind of universalistic and transcendental claim for their symbols that intellectuals do for their "truth." Intellectuals are much more reflexively and self-analytically aware of their group identity than are lay groups. Intellectuals look on themselves from the abstract standpoint of historical, philosophical, or even sociological or psychological reflection. Artists have historically acquired a similarly haughty attitude about their art.

What is it about the social interactions of intellectuals that creates those abstractly decontextualized symbols which go under the guiding banner of "truth"? The distinctive IRs of intellectuals are those occasions on which intellectuals come together for the sake of their serious talk: not to socialize, nor to be practical. Intellectuals set themselves apart from other networks of social life in the act of turning toward one another. The discussion, the lecture, the argument, sometimes the demonstration or the examination of evidence: these are the concrete activities from which the sacred object "truth" arises.

There is a rival possibility. The distinctive activities of intellectuals are reading and writing; an "egghead" is someone whose nose is always in a book, someone always writing things that no one, perhaps, ever reads. Intellectuals' writings are not personal letters to an individual who will read them and respond. The lay viewpoint, if it is unabashed, sees this clearly enough, like the duke of Gloucester, upon being presented with a new volume of *Decline and Fall of the Roman Empire:* "Another damned, thick, square book! Always scribble, scribble, scribble! Eh, Mr. Gibbon?"

And indeed this is true. Intellectuals are especially oriented toward the written word. Especially in the modern world, they experience their creativity alone and on paper, though they may at some point report it orally. And if the earliest moments of creation may sometimes be vocal or mental, intellectuals nevertheless feel the compulsion to get their ideas on paper, and not only that but "in print." Whether anyone reads them or not,[3] there is a powerful symbolic payoff in getting one's works published; it moves them out of the realm of privacy and into the realm of the public (the intellectual public, that is, which alone counts). Intellectuals tend to feel that an idea has not fully entered into their reality until it is in the system of cross-referenced books and journals which constitutes the products of the intellectual community.

Nevertheless, although lectures, discussions, conferences, and other real-time gatherings would seem to be superfluous in a world of texts, it is exactly these face-to-face structures which are most constant across the entire history of intellectual life. Writing, of course, would have been less important in early intellectual history, since implements were expensive and the process of publication laborious. But after the printing revolution (around 1000 C.E. in Sung dynasty China; by 1450 in Europe), it should have been increasingly the case that intellectuals carry out their activities without ever meeting one another. There is no such trend. As we shall see in considerable detail throughout the following chapters, the basic form of intellectual communities has remained much the same for over two thousand years. Key intellectuals cluster in groups in the 1900s C.E. much as in the 400s B.C.E. The personal contacts between eminent teachers and later-to-be-eminent students make up the same kinds of chains across the generations. And this is so even though communications technology has become increasingly available, and the numbers of intellectuals have increased enormously from on the order of hundreds in Confucius' China, to the million scientists and scholars publishing today.

Intellectual life hinges on face-to-face situations because interaction rituals can take place only on this level. Intellectual sacred objects can be created and sustained only if there are ceremonial gatherings to worship them. This is what lectures, conferences, discussions, and debates do: they gather the intellectual community, focus members' attention on a common object uniquely their own, and build up distinctive emotions around those objects. But what is it that distinguishes such gatherings of intellectuals from any other kind of IR? One difference is in the structure of attention. The key intellectual event is a lecture or a formal debate, a period of time when one individual holds the floor to deliver a sustained argument on a particular topic. This is different from the give-and-take of sociable conversations, which typically cannot reach any complex or abstract level because the focus shifts too often. Intellectuals giving their attention for half an hour or more to one viewpoint, developed as a unified stream of discourse, are thereby elevating the topic into a larger, more encompassing sacred object than the little fragmentary tokens of ordinary sociable ties.

This gives us part of the answer. It is not enough, since there are other lay occasions on which one individual monopolizes the discourse. Controlling who gets to speak is the principal mode of enacting authority on the micro-level; any boss, chief, high-ranking officer, or authoritarian parent also can control such a one-way structure of discourse. Other IRs are closer to intellectual lectures: political speeches, sermons, entertainments, and commemorative addresses. A speaker holds the floor for fairly long periods—and, he or she hopes, the rapt attention of a large audience. These occasions have the ritual structure of public events or festive breaks in community routine, and thus are some way along the continuum toward the "transcendental" qualities that intellectual rituals have. Despite these similarities, intellectual IRs differ in the nature of their focus and in the relationship between speaker and audience. The intellectual IR consists not in giving orders or practical information but in expounding a worldview, a claim for understanding taken as an end in itself. The audience is in the stance of pure listeners, not subordinates nor participants in the moral community of faith which is invoked by religious ritual. Intellectual discourse focuses implicitly on its autonomy from external concerns and its reflexive awareness of itself.

What makes it possible for intellectuals to take this distinctive stance? Is it because intellectuals are especially immersed in reading and writing? The key intellectual ritual, the lecture, is one that has been prepared for by reading a relevant background of texts; and its contents are typically on the way to becoming published (if not there already). An intellectual IR is generally a situational embodiment of the texts which are the long-term life of the discipline. Lectures and texts are chained together: this is what makes the distinctiveness of the intellectual community, what sets it off from any other kind of social activity.

It is not surprising, then, that intellectual communities arose historically at the same time as public systems of writing. This can be said more precisely. It is not merely that an alphabet or ideograph system should be invented and put into use for keeping administrative or commercial tallies or making religious inscriptions. Such writing existed in Egypt and Mesopotamia, many centuries before the existence of an intellectual community. What is needed is a social arrangement for writing texts of some length and distributing them to readers at a distance, an autonomous network for intellectual communication. As Goody and Watt (1968), Havelock (1982), and others have pointed out, writing enables one to transcend the immediate present; it is a gateway to abstraction and generality. Intellectuals, as the community uniquely oriented toward writing—those who live for the production and passing on of texts—could only come into existence with the text-distribution structure. Their ideals of truth and wisdom are the central sacred objects of this structure. But a system of written communication is not enough. We see this in the early texts themselves. The breakthrough into intellectual abstraction in India is shown in the Upanishads, which depict dialogues among sages and lecture-like guidance by masters of disciples. In China the corresponding period is depicted in the *Analects* of Confucius, again in one-sided dialogues dominated by the master. In Greece the intellectual dialogue was made famous by Plato and imitated by succeeding generations. Structurally these are not ordinary conversations; rather they give a leading role to one speaker, who guides the sustained thread of argument throughout.

Without face-to-face rituals, writings and ideas would never be charged up with emotional energy; they would be Durkheimian emblems of a dead religion, whose worshippers never came to the ceremonies. Texts do not merely transcend the immediate particulars of the here-and-now and push toward abstraction and generality. To be oriented toward the writings of intellectuals is to be conscious of the community itself, stretching both backwards and forwards in time. Intellectual events in the present—lectures, debates, discussions—take place against an explicit backdrop of past texts, whether building upon them or critiquing them. Intellectuals are peculiarly conscious of their predecessors. And their own productions are directed toward unseen audiences. Even when they lecture to an immediate group, perhaps of personal students, disciples, or colleagues, the message is implicitly part of an ongoing chain, which will be further repeated, discussed, or augmented in the future.

Members of the audience in intellectual rituals are in a distinctively non-passive situation. It is a deep-seated part of intellectual structures that questions are asked, debates take place; polemics and denunciations also often occur, in a circulating structure that resembles equally the *kula* ring, the potlatch, and the vendetta. Even when intellectuals sit silently in the audience, they are conscious of their own part as members of this ongoing community. Their own ideas have been formed by the chain from the past; the situation before them is merely one more link in that formation. They will go on to incorporate these ideas in their own future creations and discourses—at least, they are sifting them through to see whether these are materials worthy to take in for this purpose.

The crucial focus of an intellectual group is the consciousness of the group's continuity itself as an activity of discourse, rather than the particular contents of its discussions. Lectures do not always convince; conferences rarely result in unanimity. The intellectual groups that I chart in this book each contained a range of opinion. Socrates' circle was taken up with debates; the network of the Neo-Confucians in Sung China had its internal divergences; leading members of intellectual circles, whether Jena-Weimar Idealists, the Vienna Circle, or the Paris existentialists, went in different directions. The ritual focus of group solidarity is not so much on the level of particular statements and beliefs, but on the activity itself. The focus is on a peculiar kind of speech act: the carrying out of a situation-transcending dialogue, linking past and future texts. A deep-seated consciousness of this common activity is what links intellectuals together as a ritual community.

This, then, is the intellectual ritual. Intellectuals gather, focus their attention for a time on one of their members, who delivers a sustained discourse. That discourse itself builds on elements from the past, affirming and continuing or negating. Old sacred objects, previously charged up, are recharged with attention, or degraded from their sacredness and expelled from the life of the community; new candidate sacred objects are offered for sanctification. By reference to texts past and texts future, the intellectual community keeps up the consciousness of its projects, transcending all particular occasions on which they were enacted. Hence the peculiar guiding sacred object—truth, wisdom, sometimes also the activity of seeking or research—as both eternal and embodied in the flow of time.

Life-Trajectories as Interaction Ritual Chains

The entire macro–social structure, of non-intellectuals as well, is anchored on ritual interactions. What we call structure is a shorthand way of describing repetitive patterns, encounters that people keep coming back to, a recycling of rituals. This larger structure has the feel of externality; it seems thing-like, compulsory, resistant to change. This sense of constraint arises in part because the major institutions as repetitive networks are based on their distinctive IRs, which have generated emotional commitments to their identifying symbols. It is characteristic of these intensely produced membership symbols that people reify them, treat them as things, as "sacred objects" in Durkheim's sense. Organizations, states, as well as positions and roles within them, are sacred objects in just this sense: reified patterns of real-life interaction, cognitively raised above the level of the merely enacted, and treated as if they were self-subsistent entities to which individuals must conform. This symbolic social structuring of the world extends even to physical objects by making them into property appropriated under the sanction of social groups.

As individuals move through this grid of encounters, they generate their own histories of ritual participation. We may call this an *interaction ritual chain*. Each person acquires a personal repertoire of symbols loaded with membership significance. Depending on the degree of cosmopolitanism and social density of the group situations to which they have been exposed, they will have a symbolic repertoire of varying degrees of abstraction and reification, of different generalized and particularized contents. This constitutes their *cultural capital* (CC).[4]

And they will have, at any point in time, a level of *emotional energy* (EE), by which I mean the kind of strength that comes from participating successfully in an interaction ritual. It is a continuum, ranging from a high end of confidence, enthusiasm, good self-feelings; through a middle range of lesser emotional intensity; on down to a low end of depression, lack of initiative, and negative self-feelings. Emotional energy is long-term, to be distinguished from the transient, dramatically disruptive outbursts (fear, joy, anger, etc.) which are more conventionally what we mean by "emotions."[5] Emotional energy is the most important kind of emotion for its effects on IR chains. It fluctuates depending on recent social experience: intense ritual participation elevates emotional energy, rejection from ritual membership lowers it; dominating a group situation raises emotional energy, being dominated lowers it; membership rituals within a high-ranking group give high amounts of emotional energy, membership rituals within a low-ranking group give modest emotional energy.

An individual's trajectory of action at any given moment depends on where that person is situated in relation to the local social structure, the networks in which one participates. From the individual's point of view, this is his or her opportunity structure. From the point of view of understanding the whole set of individuals, we need to know what the whole network looks like: How many other persons does each one have contact with, and how is each matched up with the others in cultural and emotional resources for carrying out IRs? How far is the network connected via intermediaries, and where is it broken into separate networks? Individuals are motivated to participate in rituals of highest solidarity, gravitating toward those encounters in which their repertoire of symbols and their level of emotions mesh with those of other persons so as to generate high degrees of solidarity, and away from those encounters in which they are subordinated or excluded. If the network is stratified, one attempts if possible to dominate one's ritual interactions; lacking the resources to do this, one attempts if possible to evade rituals in which one is subordinated.

In all this there are structural constraints. Where there exists competition for membership in egalitarian rituals, some individuals dominate attention because of their relatively higher CC and EE, while others are less attended to because they lack these resources. In groups stratified by property or coercive power, the constraints are even sharper; there is a limited amount of structural space in the ruling coalition, and there may be severe limits on the ability of the powerless to withdraw from being coerced. For intellectuals, there is a special kind of limitation on how much space there is at the top of the hierarchy of ritual attention, which I shall discuss presently as the "law of small numbers." In all these respects, the local macro-structure determines which ritual encounters will be relatively most attractive or unattractive to a given individual, and hence how that person will channel his or her cultural capital and emotional energy. It is possible that the whole structure might reach equilibrium, a point at which every individual has found the best solidarity payoff possible under the circumstances. More common is a constantly shifting round of negotiations from one encounter to another, like eddies propagated across a pond fed by many streams.

The model of IR chains may be extended inward, toward the intimate landscape of how individuals talk and think, moment by moment. We will return to this promise of a sociology of thinking. Since it is the thoughts of intellectuals that we are most concerned about, let us first take the various components of the IR chain—cultural capital, emotional energy, stratified network structures—and see how they apply to intellectual communities.

Intellectuals' Cultural Capital

Consider now the trajectory of an individual's career across the intellectual milieu as an IR chain. The intellectual world is a massive conversation, circulating cultural capital in intermittent face-to-face rituals as well as in writing. What makes one an intellectual is one's attraction to this conversation: to participate in the talk of its "hot center," where the ideas have the greatest sacredness, and if possible to attach one's own identity to such ideas so that one's ideas are circulated widely through the conversation, and one's personal reputation with it. The conversation of intellectuals is competitive, an implicit shouldering aside and grasping of one another to get as much into the focus of attention as possible. How does one succeed in this struggle for ritual centrality? One can make two kinds of claims: "My ideas are new" and "My ideas are important."

Creativity implies new ideas. These circumvent the possibility that others will ignore one's conversational overtures because they have already heard them before. But ideas cannot be too new, whatever their creativeness. Einsteinian general relativity theory, if plopped down in the midst of the Hellenistic intellectual community, would not make one successful, because the topic would be too far removed from what is recognizable. Successful ideas must be important, and importance is always in relation to the ongoing conversations of the intellectual community. Ideas are important because of their position in the scale of intellectual sacred objects. Symbols too have their careers, built up as they circulate in IR chains. New sacred objects may displace old ones, but the interaction rituals in which new symbols are consecrated use as ingredients the older sacred objects to assemble the group and focus its attention. Cultural capital includes paradigms in the Kuhnian sense, but also it includes the means of breaking down paradigms and substituting others in their place.

What makes some cultural capital worth more than others? At a minimal level, knowledge of the basic vocabulary of the field, of its concepts, its past successes, its best-known sacred objects. But this only brings one entry into the field. To reach a more eminent position, one must be aware of the center of current discussion, and of the symbolic ingredients that can get one the floor. In the modern sociology of science this is called the research front, but this term is a little too specific to a particular kind of innovation-oriented intellectual field. In many historical periods, the intellectual community is in a scholasticizing mode, worshipping exalted texts from the past which are regarded as containing the completion of all wisdom. Eminence here goes to those persons who make themselves the most impressive guardians of the classics.

Intellectual creativity comes from combining elements from previous products of the field. The references found in a paper are a rough indication of the cultural capital it draws upon. Derek Price (1975: 125) has calculated from citation patterns that in contemporary natural science, it takes on the average 12 "parent papers" to give birth to one "offspring paper." Turning the structure the other way, we can say that the most eminent intellectuals are those whose papers end up being cited the most; their ideas are "parents" to the greatest number of "offspring." Their ideas make it possible for other people to make their own statements. Here we encounter a complexity. Our common-sense image of a major intellectual, a great scientist, mathematician, or scholar, is someone who has produced an important discovery: the conception of Platonic Ideas, the theory of evolution, the fundamental theorem of the calculus. These are the great accomplishments of the field; without them, there would be nothing to teach novices or to broadcast for outsiders to admire. Within the intellectual community, however, great truths are most important if the community is in a scholasticizing mode, turned backwards toward its own past. When the community is oriented toward innovation, great truths are not so much an advantage as an obstacle. For if the truth is already discovered, there is little or nothing for the intellectuals who come afterwards to do; they can be teachers to the outside world, preservers and interpreters of the truth, but not discoverers in their own right.

The paradox is that for an intellectual community to be in a great creative age, it must be both making great discoveries and also overturning them, and not just once but over and again. The most successful intellectuals tend to be chained together across the generations. This implies that the cultural capital of each one is built on the accomplishment of his or her predecessors, but also goes beyond it in truly major ways. We are not dealing here simply with a Kuhnian paradigm, in the sense of an exemplar of successful research. Such exemplars include cognitive worldviews, which have already answered the major questions. The work they leave to do, in a host of "offspring papers," is minor, routine, a matter of adding details to what is already known in the large. Such work occupies the middle or lower-middle rungs of the ranking of intellectual eminence. The cultural capital which consists of having learned a powerful paradigm, then, cannot be the most valuable CC for one's own future success.

The most important CC is that which facilitates one's own discoveries. Above all, it locates the intellectual territory on which work can be done. It does not merely solve puzzles but creates them. Fermat's last theorem, tantalizingly holding out the claim for a proof, is perhaps a greater source of fame than his more definitive work; and it doubtless will have paid off greater eminence for Fermat than for anyone who eventually solved it. (This seemed to be the case when the problem was finally solved in 1994.) Great intellectual work is that which creates a large space on which followers can work. This implies that the imperfections of major doctrines are the source of their appeal. But there must be greatness on both sides: great doctrines, great imperfections. One reason why Plato was such a dominant figure in late antiquity is that the ambiguities in his doctrine of Ideas led to many elaborations, and even to the formation of divergent schools. His shifting theories of the soul, of immortality and reincarnation, were one source of his popularity and fruitfulness. Similarly, the Vienna Circle had already run into a major problem as soon as it was formed in the 1920s; its aggressive emphasis on the verifiability and empirical grounding of meaningful statements soon led to difficulties in expounding and verifying its own principles. But although the contradictions were to become the object of attack by its opponents, they provided a hidden social strength of the group, insofar as they gave materials for creative work to many members of the circle. If Schlick's original doctrine had proven simple to put into operation, the problems of philosophy would have immediately dissolved, and the group would have put itself out of business.

Intellectuals do not go looking for contradictions to propagate. They try to solve problems, not create them. The surface of the intellectual world, the sacred objects it focuses upon, and the structural underpinnings of the intellectual community do not line up symmetrically. Consciously and intentionally, intellectuals are oriented toward what they believe is the truth. They do not want to undermine their own truths, even though it is socially useful to have flawed truths which will keep their names alive in subsequent generations of creative workers. The crucial cultural capital, then, must be something into which intellectuals feel their way. What they learn that makes them eminent is an awareness of not only the great solutions of the past, the ingredients that they can put into their own creations, but also where the action next will be. They need to appropriate the puzzles which have the greatest significance for the future activities of their colleagues. This sense of how to relate to the intellectual field is the most important item of cultural capital individuals take from their teachers. This is one reason why there is a link from eminence to eminence in the chains across the generations.

Emotional Energy and Creativity

Emotional energy is the feature of creativity that most lends itself to psychological study. Its distribution, however, is socially patterned. We know from Derek Price's studies that the most eminent intellectuals—in this case, scientists of the mid-1900s whose work receives the most citations—are the most prolific publishers; and they are the individuals who stay in the field the longest, while others drop out. This evidence suggests that eminence is largely a matter of having access to a large amount of CC, and turning it over with the greatest rapidity, recombining it into new ideas and discoveries. This would make creativity a matter of sheer activity, of emotional energy in using cultural capital. The psychologist Dean Keith Simonton (1984, 1988) has shown that creative persons in a variety of fields produce large amounts of work, only portions of which receive recognition. Their formula for success seems to be to range widely and try out new combinations of ideas, some of which become selected for recognition by the intellectual community.

This picture is bolstered by many studies (summary in Collins, 1975:

273–274) which find that creative persons have a strong desire to make their own judgments; this in turn is typically related to childhood opportunities for independence and novel experience. Often too there is a period of physical or social isolation in which these young persons become introduced to a vicarious community of the mind. Their IR chains become detached from the local circulation of mundane culture and from its pressures for local conformity. The lowering of ritual density is a prerequisite for innovation; but it must also be linked to the intermittent support of the rituals of intellectual communities to give it content and energy. Such a career pattern from childhood onward shows the successive development of energies directed at independence and innovation; for some people this energy channels into the networks of an intellectual field, whereupon it is transformed upward or downward depending on the structural opportunities available.

"Emotional energy" describes well the surge of creative impulse that comes upon intellectuals or artists when they are doing their best work. It enables them to achieve intense periods of concentration, and charges them with the physical strength to work long periods of time. It is this feeling of creative ideas seeming to flow spontaneously that the Greeks attributed mythologically to visitations of the Muses or *daimones*.

Emotional energy alone is not enough: in the absence of sufficient cultural capital and related network position in an intellectual community, creative enthusiasm is more likely a prelude to frustrated ambitions and failure of recognition. Conversely, one might have the CC but lack the EE in that situation to be able to use it. This is apparent in more mundane situations, in conversations when one is unable to think of what one wanted to say, only to have it come rushing to mind after one has left the scene. This is what Rousseau called "l'esprit d'escalier," the clever remark that comes too late, when one is already descending the stairs. This happens because the power situation in the immediate interaction is unfavorable, reducing one's emotional energy and leaving one unable to have the confidence and initiative to use one's cultural capital to good social effect. This shortage of focused energy afflicts intellectuals in the form of writer's block. Here too the flow of energy comes from one's sense of where the opportunities are for forming favorable social alliances (in this case vicarious ones), and where these opportunities are blocked.[6]

The emotional energy specific to creative intellectual fields is not the same as the confidence and aggressiveness of persons in other arenas of social life. It is not the same as the emotional energy of the successful politician or the financial entrepreneur, of the sociability star or the sexual hotshot. Each of these is specific to a particular kind of social market, where the opportunities are especially good for certain people's particular kinds of cultural capital and emotional energy. There are distinctive kinds of cultural capital and hence of

related emotional energy for intellectual networks; and there are further spe-
cificities among fields, so that conditions that make persons creative in geology
will usually serve them little in literature or mathematics or music.

In the general model of IR chains, EE goes up or down depending on one's
immediate and recent experiences in interactions. This applies to intellectuals
as well. If intellectual life is constructed by rituals in which speakers become
centers of attention, and in which ideas and texts symbolize the continuity of
an intellectual community across time, we can expect that individuals' intellectual EE will be driven upward or downward by their type of contact with
these situations and sacred objects. The crucial variable is how closely one is
drawn into participation in these symbolic activities. The speaker at the seminar increases his or her emotional energy if the audience is responsive; so do
the listeners, if they have the personal cultural capital, and the trajectory of
their own intellectual projects, that makes their ideas mesh well with the line
being expounded. In the opposite direction, the inability to carry off the lecture
for that audience, or the inability to follow it, perhaps even the sense of having
one's ideas excluded, depresses one's EE. One's personal level of EE is like a
reservoir filled up or drained by the amount of experience one has with such
favorable or unfavorable situations, and by the balance between the two.

Flows of EE are cumulative over long as well as short periods of time. Since
possessing high emotional energy is one of the things that enables a person to
attract attention in a ritual interaction, and which affects creativity in general,
there is a tendency for persons who are already well started in EE to become
even more "energy-rich" over time. A high level of energy reaches a plateau
or goes into a reversal if one's career trajectory takes one into levels of
competition for attention in which one becomes overmatched. This occurs
when someone who has become famous within a particular research specialty
is propelled into a larger arena, perhaps interdisciplinary or in the eye of the
wider public, where one may not have the resources to match up with the
existing competition. The effect of starting with low levels of EE is likely to
be even more emphatically cumulative. Just as success breeds the ingredients
of success, failure breeds intellectual failure. Depression, writer's block, the
shifting of one's attention away from intellectual projects and back onto the
everyday world: these are typical pathways by which would-be intellectuals
fail to make a mark and drop out of the field. The majority of the intellectual
field at any time consists of persons who are in this transient position.

The core experiences of intellectuals are their immediate interactions with
other intellectuals. EE is also affected by vicarious experience of the intellectual
community. Since words, ideas, and texts are loaded with connotations of
membership in different segments of intellectual communities, the experience
of reading, even of thinking about intellectual topics, also affects one's emo-

tional energies. Reading and thinking are vicarious interaction rituals to the extent that an individual can take part in them, and thus can affect his or her level of emotional energy. This is true also for the experience of writing. Writing is a vicarious participation in the world of symbolic memberships: insofar as one is able to work out a satisfactory relationship among ideas, one is creating social coalitions including oneself. Successful writing builds up emotional energy. Even over a very short-run period of minutes or hours at one's desk, the process of writing can be a self-enhancing emotional flow.

High levels of creativity become crystallized in symbols, and in that form can circulate through the intellectual field, energizing whoever can most closely attach oneself to them. When a group has a high degree of agreement on the ideas put forward by some intellectual leader, that person becomes a sacred object for the group. Thus arise the cult figures of intellectual life: Confucius, Aristotle, Hegel, Marx, Wittgenstein. Such personalities, or even their names, become a shorthand for a whole system of ideas. Since intellectuals are highly aware of the cult heroes of the past, and must take some stance toward the incipient or established heroes of the present, the question arises within each intellectual's mind: Can I myself become one of these heroes, perhaps achieve eponymous fame after death? The motivation to make oneself a sacred object is an energizing force of intellectual careers. One of the reasons why there tends to be a chain from one highly creative intellectual to another is that the younger person draws energy from the older as just such a symbolic hero. It is not merely a matter of transmitting cultural capital from one generation to the next, since we are dealing here with creative departures rather than loyal discipleship. The protégé's consciousness is filled by the image of what it is to be an intellectual hero, by an ideal to emulate, even while one challenges the content of the master's ideas.

The flow of emotional energy helps explain a curious point which often comes up in creative lives. Persons who later become eminent are frequently linked together much earlier in their lives. Hegel and Schelling were schoolmates at Tübingen, along with the future poet Hölderlin, well before any of them had done anything to merit intellectual eminence. But the group already was beginning to generate a certain charisma. They engaged in intense intellectual discussions, the archetypal intellectual ritual. Some of their activities were explicitly ritualistic, such as an enthusiastic celebration of the French Revolution (Kaufmann, 1966: 8). These ritual interactions were accumulating emotional energy in advance of a specific creative direction. The cultural capital which gave shape to their EE came as the group encountered Fichte, who was already in contact with Kant and had begun to carry out the Idealist revolution in philosophy. It seems likely that it was precisely their emotional quality, their enthusiasm, that attracted Fichte, just then entering his first success, to travel across Germany in 1795 to meet with them. As the members of the group opened niches in the intellectual attention space, the success of one helped pull the others along. Among the former schoolmates, Schelling achieved creative fame first, with his *Philosophy of Nature* in 1797. He then used his influence to get Hegel a position at Jena, the hot center of the Idealist movement, and access to publishers. It was in trying to keep up with his old comrade that Hegel struggled to find his own niche in the intellectual world, finally breaking through in 1806 with *The Phenomenology of Spirit,* and in the process splitting with his old friend to take up different spaces in the intellectual world.

There are numerous other instances of this early, formative group structure in intellectual careers.[7] One gets the impression of a group, starting with the ingredients of talented young individuals and their available cultural resources, building up emotional energy through their intense intellectual interactions. The emotional energy at this time is free-floating; it can go in different directions, depending on how opportunities arise. As these individuals later work their way into specific intellectual networks, their energy turns to creativity. Looking back on them retrospectively, we identify them by their later products: we see them as incipient philosophers, novelists, poets, whatever the opportunity structure turns them out to be.

The Opportunity Structure

Moment by moment and situation by situation, each person is moving through a continuum of interaction rituals, real or vicarious, ranging from minimal to high intensity, which bring in a flow of cultural capital and calibrate their emotional energy up or down. These local situations are embedded in a larger structure: in this case the whole intellectual community, spreading as far as the networks happen to extend in that historical period. What cultural capital flows to any one individual depends on where that individual is located and what is nearby. Emotional energy fluctuates by local success or failure in interaction rituals, and that too depends on something beyond the individual, namely, the way one's own cultural capital and emotional energy matches up with that of the other persons with whom one comes into contact. Opportunities for solidarity or rivalry, and for being near the hot center or off on the dim periphery, are apportioned within the network as a whole. Cultural capital flows around these networks, benefiting most those persons who have access to it while it is still new. Emotional energy also flows around the networks, collecting in intense pools here and there, but ebbing away at times because of shifts in the attention space which may be far beyond the province of the individuals affected by it.

What any individual will do at any moment in time depends on local processes; but what flows into these local situations comes from farther away. Micro-action is affected by the macro-structure. The sheer numbers of persons in the field and the shape of their network connections is the macro-context within which any micro-situation is negotiated. A sociological theory can move in three directions from this point. (1) We can ask a still more macro-question: What larger social conditions determine whether intellectual networks will exist at all? This directs us to the macro-foundations of networks in political, religious, and educational organization. (2) We can concentrate on the shape of the network structure itself and its dynamics over time; this leads us to considerations of the internal stratification of intellectual networks, and to the principle of change through structural rivalry that I call the law of small numbers. (3) We can dig more deeply into the micro-level and ask how the individual reacts to being in various positions within a network.

The first question will occupy us in later chapters. Let us consider the second and third here.

Whatever the mode of eminence, some individuals always have more access than others to the cultural capital out of which it is produced. This does not depend on the characteristics of individuals. The opportunity structure focuses attention on some portions of the field and leaves others in the shadows. Cultural capital is apportioned around an attention space; the more valuable CC is that which can be used most successfully in the next round of competition for attention.

Imagine a large number of people spread out across an open plain—something like a landscape by Salvador Dalí or Giorgio de Chirico. Each one is shouting, "Listen to me!" This is the intellectual attention space. Why would anyone listen to anyone else? What strategy will get the most listeners? Two ways will work.

A person can pick a quarrel with someone else, contradicting what the other is saying. That will gain an audience of at least one; and if the argument is loud enough, it might attract a crowd. Now, suppose everyone is tempted to try it. Some arguments start first, or have a larger appeal because they contradict the positions held by several people; and if other persons happen to be on the same side of the argument, they gather around and provide support. There are first-mover advantages and bandwagon effects. The tribe of attention seekers, once scattered across the plain, is changed into a few knots of argument. The law of small numbers says that the number of these successful knots is always about three to six. The attention space is limited; once a few arguments have partitioned the crowds, attention is withdrawn from those who would start yet another knot of argument. Much of the pathos of intellectual life is in the timing of when one advances one's own argument.

The other way these intellectual attention seekers can get someone to listen is to find a topic someone else is talking about and agree with it, adding something which extends the argument. Not "No, you're wrong because . . ." but "Yes, and furthermore . . ." This transforms the relationship into teacher and favorite student. The plain full of dispersed egotists becomes clumped another way, into lineages of master-pupil chains.

It makes no difference whether persons pursue these strategies consciously or unconsciously. The outcome is the same either way. Of course one might reject the whole image as offensive to intellectual values, the pursuit of truth for its own sake. Very well; let us adopt this pursuit of truth as our starting point. Dispersed across an open plain are a number of persons pursuing truth. Why should anyone listen to what any particular individual among them says is the truth? The problem of forming a truth-recognizing community is exactly the same as the problem for attention seekers, and the rest follows as before.[8]

The two strategies and their associated social processes, forming arguments and forming lineages, go on simultaneously. It is because persons are in lineages, learning something from one another, that they have something to argue about; and what cultural capital they thereby possess influences who is attracted to joining the crowd on one side of an argument or another.

Consider now that everything that happens on the plain of intellectual attention seekers is experienced as interaction rituals varying from low to high intensity. All persons move toward those IRs in which they get the largest payoff in emotional energy, and away from those which are an energy drain. Whether they get energy boosts or losses depends on the lineup of CC and EE among whomever they come into contact with; and those other persons' CC and EE are affected in turn by their further contacts, and so on throughout the network. The structure should be regarded as a constrained market. To the extent that persons have access to one another, they can match up their CCs and EEs to their best advantage as an open bargaining process.[9] But the degree of access is itself variable. Individuals may have only limited contacts and must bargain for IR participation in an unfavorable matchup of CCs and EEs because particular persons are all who happen to be accessible. Here again the shape of the network, and where individuals happen to be within it, determines what they can do: what they think, and with what creative energy.

The most important network feature which affects the fate of its members is the stratification of the attention space. Each person is trying to get the best intellectual status membership he or she can, not only directly but vicariously. Everyone is attracted to thinking high-status ideas as well as associating with high-status persons. The problem is that negotiating alliances is a mutual process. One side, looking up the status ladder, might wish to make an alliance, while the other side, looking down, is less eager; the successful intellectual may welcome followers but is unlikely to give them much recognition in return.

The crunch is all the worse because the intellectual field is structured by rivalries. Opposing positions contend over domination, and even within a single position there is only a limited amount of attention to be split up among its proponents.

Each intellectual faces a strategic choice. One can go all out, try to be king of the mountain, which means trying to be alone or nearly alone at the center of one of the major intellectual positions. Or one might cut one's losses and aim for a more modest position: as loyal follower of some successful position; perhaps as an ancillary or collaborator to an active research front; perhaps as a specialist in some less recognized but also less competitive topic. Some individuals may be explicitly aware of these choices. But this process goes on whether they are aware of it or not. Individuals do not need to be calculating machines; they are unlikely to have sufficient information about the whole network in order to make a thorough calculation, and intrinsic limitations on cognitive capabilities narrow the possibilities in any case.[10] The flow of cultural capital and emotional energy in a network structure moves people around whether they like it or not. Initially most intellectuals aim unrealistically high, and are driven down emotionally by the structure. Whether or not someone starts out to be a follower or a narrow specialist, sometimes those are the opportunities that open up, while grander positions are denied. The flow of cultural capital is a long-term constraint; one's emotional energy adjusts to available circumstances more rapidly. By the same token, some people happen to be swept up into the structures that turn them from nameless ciphers into the great creative figures of their field.

The Totality of Intellectual Rituals and Sacred Objects

The intellectual world consists of all the interaction rituals which take place periodically across the landscape and of the flow of sacred objects—ideas and texts—which result from them. To envision the intellectual world this way is deliberately to challenge our prevailing conceptions of intellectual life, whether contemporary or historical. When we ourselves formulate "what is happening" in the intellectual world, we invariable impose an image of one or a few currents, typically distorted by partisanship. Intellectual historians may be less partisan because of greater distance, but their view remains partial, fitted around a few patterns and necessarily limited to a manageable number of names and themes. But the intellectual world is much bigger than that, and not so tightly focused. The most detailed evidence we have covers natural scientists, who make up only part of the intellectual world. In the 1970s there were approximately 1 million natural scientists publishing in any year and 110,000 social scientists (Price, 1986: 234).[11] If we go backwards in history, or laterally into less active fields, the numbers are smaller, but in every case the total active intellectual community is much bigger, and more diverse, than the simplified pictures that even the most assiduously detailed history presents. And even this is not far enough. Intellectual activity is intermittent. Today there are more than a million scientists who come in and out of activity every few years; the mass of the scientific community is in this intermittent class. Still larger is the surrounding fringe of students, would-be intellectuals, vicarious participants, intellectuals in transition in or out. This is the reality on which we impose our simplifications.

Imagine what it would be like to see through walls and even into people's minds. The social landscape would appear to us flickering with thoughts. If one walked everywhere throughout the corridors of a large university, hearing lectures and conversations and the inner conversations that constitute thinking, one's sensation would be of tremendous variety, even cacophony. There would be plenty of mundane, non-intellectual thoughts: people thinking about tasks they have to do, ruminating about their friends and enemies, plotting erotic or organizational politics; bitter obsessive thoughts, perhaps some rehearsing of lines and replaying of jokes, as well as scattered bits of words, phrases, images, the flotsam and jetsam of recent past exchanges of cultural capital. But some of these ideas would be glowing brightly with emotional significance, charged up by interaction rituals into sacred objects. These are the ideas that act as magnetic poles in intellectual thinking, that are the focus of the long and serious attention that is the activity of the intellectual world at its most intense.

There will be fewer of these highly charged ideas, but they are disproportionately influential, magnetically shaping lesser thoughts like iron filings within an individual mind, and exerting a pull across many people that makes them an intellectual group. But even these ideas are of many different sorts: not just in different corridors of the university but on the same hallway, in the same conversation, and sometimes in the same mind. If we extend the scope outward in time and space, the totality of sacred objects, both intense and mild, that makes up the intellectual world is massive: a diversity of thoughts that constitutes all the intellectual ploys, factions, specialties, and disciplines at a given time in history, and a diversity of such diversities when we move our focus of attention across the years—20, 50, 1,000 years ago and more. If we could come back 50 years in the future, or 250 years, it is a safe bet that a similar structure would be observed, but filled with other contents.

My point is not to be ironic, or pessimistic, or relativistic. I can well assume that many of these thoughts were and are valuable, as experiences worth having, even as truths. Many of them deserve to be sacred objects. The totality of knowledge today resembles Jorge Luis Borges's circular library, with endless volumes on endless shelves, and inhabitants searching for the master catalogue buried among them written in a code no one can understand. But we can also think of it as a magic palace of adventurously winding corridors with treasures in every room. It suffers only from surfeit, since new and greater treasures are always to be found.

Borges's image has the alienated tone characteristic of modern intellectuals; but the underlying problem is the inchoate democracy of it all, the lack of a master key. Much of the intellectual malaise of the early 1900s has this conservative undertone, a desire for stratification. But in fact democracy and stratification are both present in any active intellectual community. Even in my optimistic image of the magic castle of ideas, the people who live inside feel that there are outer and inner chambers—although they do not always know which is which, and they tend to inflate the status of their own chamber, hoping it is one of the inner ones. The whole has a structure which is independent of the numbers of people and ideas within it. There is only enough structural space for a limited number of inner chambers, no matter how much one expands the crowds in the antechambers.

What I refer to as the law of small numbers proposes that there is always a small number of rival positions at the forefront of intellectual creativity; there is no single inner chamber, but there are rarely more than half a dozen. This is particularly so in the realm of theory, and hence above all in philosophy. But segmental restructurings are also possible, especially as fields acquire empirical materials (which might include the texts of their own history). Then the magic palace can be split into different wings, even detached ones. Each discipline or specialty can have its own inner and outer rings, subject again to the law of small numbers, a limited democracy at the top, enhanced under some conditions by a high rate of change and by uncertainty in the fringes over where the center really lies.

This overall structure is the field of forces within which individuals act and think. Its structure is responsible for the stable patterns of ideas and of energies that make up intellectual routine; and it is when large-scale forces rearrange the inner chambers, vacating some and consolidating others, that recombination of ideas and intense flows of emotional energies occur which make up the episodes of heightened creativity.

Stratification within Intellectual Communities

The most thorough data we have on intellectual stratification concern scientific fields. There is good reason to believe that the basic structures are similar in philosophy and indeed in most of the humanistic (perhaps also the artistic) disciplines.[12]

Productivity is very unequally distributed among scientists. The chances of producing a large number of papers is inversely related to the square of the number of producers (Price, 1986: 38, 223); hence the number of scientists who produce a very large number of papers in vanishingly small. Derek Price (1986: 140) estimates that the degree of stratification is the same in all scientific fields, and has been of the same order since the takeoff of science at the time of the inception of the British Royal Society in the 1660s.

The shape of the community is a sharply narrowing pyramid: if we look at the population of scientists, the pyramid sits on a wide base of modest producers; if we look at the population of papers produced by those individuals, it is a pyramid with its nose pushed into the ground and its base to the sky. Of those who publish anything at all, the biggest group (75 percent) produce just one or two papers, adding up to 25 percent of all papers published. About one twentieth of the group publish half of all papers; they produce 10 or more papers per lifetime. The top two scientists out of 165 (1.2 percent) produce 50 or more papers, and thus produce one quarter of all the papers.

Authors in a particular field are divided into those who are continuously active (continuants) and those who are active only a short time (transients) (Price, 1986: 206–226). The transients are represented by only a quarter of the papers at any given time, but since they are coming and going every year, the floating population of transients makes up 75–80 percent of the total population of scientists. The "normal continuants" who publish fairly often for a while are 60 percent of the active population in any given year, but about 20 percent of the total floating population. And the core group of high producers who publish every year are 1–2 percent of the total floating population.

The levels of stratification among scientists are thus as follows:

scientific stars (small absolute numbers)
inner core—top producers (1–2 percent of total floating population)
outer core (20 percent of floating population)
transients—a few publications or one-shot producers (75–80 percent of
    floating population)
audience and would-be recruits (10 to 100 × size of floating population)

Career levels in the scientific world depend on passing a series of barriers: (1) one's first publication, which admits one into the scientific community as distinguished from laypersons (frequently this is the Ph.D. research); (2) one's next few publications, which put one in the intermediate group of transients or potential continuants; (3) five years of continuing publication, which puts one in the high-producing elite or core. Total productivity depends mainly on how long one stays active in research. Members of this core group (which makes up 20 percent of those who are active at any one time, but only 1–2 percent of the total floating population) produce 25 percent of all publications over their lifetimes.

The sheer amount of productivity across the whole community correlates well with the quality of the papers and the eminence of the individual scientist. We see this in the similar picture of stratification on the citation side. Half of the archive is cited in any year. About 75 percent of papers, if cited at all, are cited only once. Transients' papers are rarely cited, and if so, not very repeatedly (transients produce about 25 percent of the papers and get less than 5–10 percent of the citations). At the other end of the spectrum, about 1 out of 400 papers (less than 0.25 percent of the total) is cited 20 or more times per year. About 1 percent of papers receive about one third of the citations (Price, 1986: 73, 107–108, 230, 234, 261).

Notice that the papers are even more stratified than the authors. The high producers at the core of the field are indeed the most heavily cited; but since they produce (as we have seen) 25 percent of all papers, some few of their papers must be much more frequently cited than their other papers. Among the highest-producing publishers on record are the mathematicians Cayley (with 995 papers), Euler, and Cauchy, and the physicist Kelvin (with 660) (Price, 1986: 44; 1975: 176, 195). Their fame, however, rests on a small percentage of their work. This is inevitable if a small number of high producers are going to swamp the field.

Thus we arrive at yet a fourth level of stratification: leaders within the core, and indeed core activities among the activities of those leaders. If the total population is something like 1 million scientists producing 1 million papers per year, even the top 1–2 percent gives 10,000 to 20,000 scientists. They are the *crème* but not the *crème de la crème*. There must be further differentiation among these, to arrive at the Einsteins and the other heroes one reads about in histories of science. Data do not abound for other kinds of intellectuals; but the situation among scientists surely applies to all.

Stratification of Cultural Capital and Emotional Energy

Access by intellectuals to the core productive cultural capital is limited. Again, we know the most about the limiting structures among natural scientists; this gives us insight into the kinds of features that stratify any intellectual field.

Modern science is competitive and fast-moving; only the first person to publish a discovery gets credit. Hence the tendency for scientists to congregate around the popular research areas. There is a premium on speed, on getting out the crucial results before someone else does. Those who are tightly connected in social networks will have an advantage here. Evidence on informal communications, the circulation of pre-publications before formal publication, shows where this informal group is located. Membership in the social core network is correlated with being highly productive, in part because it facilitates rapid transmission of cultural capital.

Because of the proliferation of papers, if one relies entirely on reading the literature as an outsider, one is less likely to know where to look. A random overview through the literature by journal browsing, or worse yet by indexing and abstracting services (whether in print media or electronically on-line), which overload the channels rather than focusing them, will not lead one to the key cultural capital to follow up. Again, one needs the advantage of being intellectually and socially connected to the core.

In the research sciences, innovation depends on familiarity with the latest research technology (Price, 1986: 237–253). Such knowledge is usually tacit and informal, passed around by personal contact, rather than the subject of published papers. This is another resource monopolized by those close to the active core of the research community.

Do these structures make the modern research sciences more sharply stratified in comparison to non-science fields? Large numbers of scientists and a reliance on expensive, rapidly changing research technologies force the pace of intellectual competition. A smaller field, such as philosophy, or indeed any of the humanities, does not put such a premium on rapid access to a moving front of soon-to-be-outdated information or research equipment. Still, the degree of stratification of cultural capital may be roughly the same, in that the more slowly moving fields are also less differentiated into specialties; what competition does exist is all focused on the same central claims for intellectual importance. And here there is a crunch, a limited amount of attention space, which allows only a small number of intellectual positions to be recognized at any one time.

These processes affect the cumulation of EE both positively and negatively. At the top, individuals who have good access to cultural capital through their previous experience, their mentors, and their participation in core social networks have high EE. They are enthusiastically attached to their field, work very hard at exploiting their opportunities, and receive very high rewards in the form of recognition. They are best able to monitor the level of competition; although they may often have the experience of being forestalled in publication by a rival (as Hagstrom, 1965, shows), they also are able to beat others much of the time. They move on an accelerating (or high constant) level of EE. This is what gives them the reputation of being "creative" individuals.

At the low end there is a population which is transient. I would attribute their transience to their low EE, and that in turn to the weak structural position for access to crucial cultural capital. They appear as "the kind of person" who always has troubles—obstacles, distractions, family and financial difficulties—which just seem to keep them from ever getting their work done. This is where we find the familiar writer's block of failing intellectuals, the "dissertationitis" of advanced graduate students. I interpret their problem as a low level of EE specific to success in the intellectual field. Emotional energies reflect the distribution of cultural capital and network opportunities in the structure around them. These persons seem to be "Calamity Janes," because their level of EE for intellectual production is constantly being drained, leaving them unable to rise above non-intellectual obstacles.

The intellectual barriers in themselves are considerable. There are several hurdles to get over; passing the lowest may seem like a big deal when viewed from "downstream," from the outsider's viewpoint, but individuals with relatively modest cultural capital and emotional energy are likely to become demoralized when they discover there is yet another barrier beyond that, and another and another. Publishing one article makes one a recognized scientist or scholar, but only by putting one into the large transient community, most of whom are about to fall back out into inactivity; publishing two or a few articles gets one into the outer ring of the intellectually active world. And people publishing at these low levels of productivity tend to be those who are rarely cited (and in many cases not cited at all); hence the hoped-for payoff does not materialize. Even after publishing a few papers, the chance of much recognition, and much increment to one's EE, is not great, unless one is already linked into the core networks. Then come the further barriers: publishing several papers a year for five years, and finally getting into the top group of famous producers. The last is the killer: for the structure of the intellectual community seems to guarantee that such stars will always exist; but for the vast majority of practicing and would-be scientists and scholars, becoming such a star is an inaccessible goal. Experiencing these barriers is what causes the high level of transience, of dropping out from active research.[13] Even for individuals who make it through to the higher levels of intellectual success, there is a continuing struggle over a narrow competitive space. This motivates many even of the best equipped to drop their highest creative aspirations and settle for a follower role in some intellectual camp. The stratification of EE is more restrictive than the stratification of CC; it is the former which makes the apex of the intellectual world a narrow pyramid peak.

The Sociology of Thinking

Social structure is everywhere, down to the most micro level. In principle, who will say what to whom is determined by social processes. And this means that there is not only a sociology of conversation but a sociology of thinking. Verbal thinking is internalized conversation. The thinking of intellectuals, whether creative or routine, is especially accessible to this kind of analysis. That is because, unlike most ordinary thoughts, it leaves traces: both immediately, in writing, and more globally, in the structure of intellectual networks.

Language itself is the product of a pervasive natural ritual. The rudimentary act of speaking involves the ingredients listed at the outset of this chapter: group assembly, mutual focus, common sentiment; as a result, words are collective representations, loaded with moral significance. Durkheim stressed that we recognize sacred objects by the feeling of constraint and externality in dealing with them, and the outrage which automatically wells up when they are violated. This is the way we behave when someone misuses a word, commits a mispronunciation, or violates the grammar conventional in the group.

Words, like any other feature of cultural capital, have a history across IR chains. They are generated (or introduced to new individuals) in some interactional situation, and are loaded with the emotional significance corresponding to the degree of solidarity in that particular encounter. Once acquired as part of one's repertoire, they become means for negotiating further situations. A word smoothly accepted or awkwardly taken is a way of testing whether someone else will participate in further solidarity ritual with oneself; and words are attractors or repulsers which move one toward or away from particular encounters.

The same applies to other aspects of language besides vocabulary and pronunciation. The coordination of language acts between conversationalists, their deepening rhythmic entrainment in a particular occasion of talk, shapes the ongoing meaning of verbal gestures from one encounter to the next. Micro-situational coordination occurs on several levels: in the mutual anticipation and enactment of a grammatical structure, in the speech acts in which this grammar is socially embedded, in the emotional flows of personal relations, in the cognitive dimension of what is being talked about, in Goffmanian reframings. All these constitute the social action which gives meaning to talk. Language is not a closed social universe; it can be used to refer to things and to coordinate practical actions. Whether it does this or not, language works only because it conveys Durkheimian solidarity. This gives a sociological interpretation to the philosophical distinction between sense and reference (Dummett, 1978: 441–454). The reference of words is their pointing to something outside that segment of conversation; the sense of words (and of sentences, of talk in general) is their symbolic connection to social solidarity, that is, to their past histories and present usage in interaction ritual chains. Particular acts of discourse may not always have reference; but discourse cannot occur at all if it does not have an interaction ritual sense.

The Predictability of Conversations

It is because language has social sense (as well as sometimes an external reference) that conversations are in principle predictable. I say this even though Chomsky stressed the infinite varieties of sentences that can be spoken and recognized; and of course there are numerous practical difficulties of being in a position to predict just what people are going to say. Nevertheless, if we knew some general characteristics of any two individuals' cultural capital, emotional energies, and position within a market of possible interactions, we could predict many things about what they might say to each other. In situations where we are aware of many of these elements (e.g., cocktail parties with professional associates, and especially those among new acquaintances who share nothing but a common occupation), we often find that conversations are predictably stereotyped. And this is so even though we are usually limited to knowing only our own ritual ingredients, whereas full predictability would require us to know those on both sides.

In general, conversation is determined as follows. Individuals' positions in social markets (their previous success and current opportunities for negotiating membership in encounters of different degrees of social ranking) determine how much they are attracted to, repulsed by, or indifferent to any particular encounter that arises before them. Some combinations of people result in mutual motivation to continue the interaction they had last time; some persons are starved for interaction with others, especially of higher rank; other persons are satiated by interactions and indifferent to persons of lower rank. (I am not trying to be comprehensive about the structural possibilities here.)

The degree of network attraction that individuals feel will determine their choice of linguistic acts. They choose the words, phrasing, style of speech that will fit with the type of group membership they are attempting to negotiate. Their interlocutor does the same. Out of this negotiation, each person discovers from the symbols the other puts forth more about the implied web of group memberships that are being enacted. Over the course of the conversation, the membership stakes go up or down, and this changes the momentary motivation of the participants to go on with the conversation, to change its level of emotional commitment, or to terminate.

Conversation is determined as individuals choose their language acts to fit their market motivations. Each utterance is a ploy, suggesting a group membership context that is being invoked and a level of intimacy on which to have a personal relationship. The hearer sizes up what is being offered, feels some degree of attraction or repulsion because of prior resources and current market situation, and chooses a reply that is the counter-offer in this social negotiation. Utterances are chain-linked via their membership and intimacy implications; knowing an individual's position in social networks and hence his or her motivations, we could predict what that person will say next in response to each prior utterance.

I do not mean to imply that people usually engage in conscious deliberation, thinking through membership implications and choosing something from their repertoire to fit whatever membership and intimacy they would like to achieve.

When people talk, they are conscious mainly of *what* they are talking about (i.e., its reference) and only subliminally of the social motivations that determine what they say (i.e., its sense). It is only when people get caught in a situation where they have trouble either going ahead or extricating themselves that they become self-conscious, when they deliberately calculate what to say and what social effect it will have. Some people, of course, may do this quite a lot (uneasy adolescents in sexual negotiations, social climbers, politicians); their special network positions make them more self-conscious than normal.

The Predictability of Thinking

Thinking is, most centrally, internalized conversation. What we think about is a reflection of what we talk about with other people, and what we communicate with them about on paper. Combining this premise with the theory of emotional energy generated by interaction, we may say that what someone thinks about is determined by the intensity of recent experience in IRs, and by the interactions which one anticipates most immediately for the future.

Thinking is driven by the emotional loadings of symbols charged up by the dynamics of the markets for social membership. One's emotional energy at any given moment selects the symbols which give one an optimal sense of group membership. Thinking is a fantasy play of membership inside one's own mind. It is a maneuvering for the best symbolic payoff one can get, using energies derived from recent social interactions and anticipations of future encounters. Symbols are charged up with an intensity dependent on the degree of emotional solidarity actually occurring in a ritual situation. For this reason, immediately after a very intense ritual participation, one's mind remains full of impelling thoughts, symbols left over from that situation which hang with great force in one's consciousness. An exciting game leaves the crowd buzzing with a compulsion to talk about it for hours thereafter, and in the absence of real conversations, to think it over inside their heads. The same is true of a powerful political speech, an emotional religious service, or, on a more intimate level, a conversation which significantly shifts one's emotional energies.

A similar constraint comes from anticipated interactions. When one knows that certain kinds of encounters are coming up, the thoughts appropriate to the social relationships one wishes to negotiate—that is, the contents that would be called up by one's market motivation in that situation—come flooding into one's thoughts. A hypothesis: the more intense the motivational significance of an anticipated encounter, the more one's thoughts are filled by an imaginative rehearsal of the anticipated conversation. One is not usually conscious of this rehearsal as such; these contents are simply what one thinks about.

To catch the force of this social causality, let us imagine constructing an artificial intelligence (AI) that will think like a human. Instead of filling it with programs for information processing, we start from the outside in. Its key ability would to be carry out interaction rituals. Our sociological AI (let us call it an IR-AI) must be equipped with rudimentary ability to focus attention and share common emotional moods, then to store the results of each highly focused interaction as markers of social membership. Such an AI would have to be more than a computer with a monitor and keyboard; it must have a kind of body, capable of recognizing and producing emotions. The most natural way to do this is to give it an electronic ear and a voice box, capable of tuning in the rhythmic patterns of human speech and imitating them. Initially, then, our IR-AI would carry out IRs on the most rudimentary level, by synchronizing voice rhythms with its conversational partner. The focus of attention in the IR would simply be the vocal coordination itself; the content of those patterns where rhythmic resonance was best achieved would be stored as symbols of that moment of social solidarity. Such an IR-AI might well be conceived of as a baby, cooing rhythmically in interaction with its human parents.[14]

The aim is for the baby IR-AI to build up a conversational repertoire, following the ritualistic coordination of conversational turn taking. Its capacity to speak, its verbal repertoire, would be not programmed in but built up through its history of IRs. Our IR-AI would store speech patterns in memory, each ranked in order of its EE loading, a quantity varying with the intensity of rhythmic coordination in interaction. This would be its cultural capital. Just as in real humans and their IRs, the EE loading of symbols is greatest at the moment when the IR is taking place, then gradually fades away over succeeding days and weeks if it is not reused in another successful IR. Memories not tagged by ongoing social emotions fade out.

Follow our thought experiment to the point at which our IR-AI is capable of full-fledged conversation. The leap to thinking is simply to put the IR-AI in privacy, away from human contacts, and have it carry out conversations with itself. It is programmed to search its memory for partners it has recently conversed with, pulling out those with the highest EE rating by virtue of successful rhythmic coordination in those conversations. It searches through its repertoire of cultural capital for those topics that brought the best EE payoff, and uses them to construct the utterances of an internal conversation.

Such an IR-AI would be completely open. What conversations it makes with other people, and what inner conversation it has as its thinking, can fill any of the huge variety which is human discourse. What it talks about and hence what it thinks about will depend on whom it interacts with. For it to become a philosopher, it must converse with philosophers; to become a sociologist, it must converse with sociologists. How would it become a creative intellectual of the first rank? In the same way as a human: it would have to make network contact in the core circles of the previous generation of creative intellectuals, becoming introduced to the central lines of argument among rival groups. It must catch a sense of the crystallization points in the network playing out the law of small numbers as the focus of the attention space shifts. It would do this not by some form of super-sophisticated calculation of network positions, but by being part of the network, attuned through the shifting levels of EE in the items of CC that make up its flow of conversations. Our sociological artificial intelligence creates by constructing a new conversation that combines the cultural capital of several groups so as to maximize the EE level of each, uniting the separate conversational rituals into one intensely focused ritual commanding the attention of the network. It creates by making a new coalition in the mind.

The Inner Lives of Intellectuals

Intellectual life, like everything else, takes place in a series of embedded levels. Start at the center with a human body charged with emotions and consciousness. Around him or her is the intellectual network and its dynamics, the market opportunities for ideas which open up at particular times. Creativity comes to those individuals optimally positioned to take advantage of these opportunities. Since the situation is competitive, those who have the first chances acquire an entrenched advantage in creative eminence; others are constrained to become followers, or rivals taking the opposite tack from those already taken by the leaders. Some who come too late remain challengers who are squeezed out by the structure.

Surrounding the micro-core is the organizational base which makes it possible for intellectual networks to exist. The universities, publishers, churches, regal patrons, and other suppliers of material resources set the numbers of competitors in intellectual careers. Their organizational dynamics affect the underlying shape of the intellectual field; especially fateful are times of crisis, which rearrange career channels and provoke the reorganization of the attention space that underlies the epochs of greatest creativity.

Finally, there is the largest structure, the political and economic forces which feed these organizations. This outermost level of macro-causality does not so much directly determine the kinds of ideas created as give an impetus for stability or change in the organizations which support intellectual careers, and this molds in turn the networks within them.

At the center of these circles lies the creative experience: Hegel at his desk on the night of October 12, 1806, struggling to finish his *Phenomenology of Spirit* while the battle of Jena booms in the background. The intellectual alone, reading or writing: but he or she is not mentally alone. His or her ideas are loaded with social significance because they symbolize membership in existing and prospective coalitions in the intellectual network. New ideas are created as combinations or reframings of old ones; the intellectual's creative intuitions are feelings about what groups these ideas are appealing to and which intellectual antagonists are being opposed. The network structure of the intellectual world is transposed into the creative individual's mind. Creative flashes are the emotional energy that comes from imaginary interaction rituals.

Thinking is a conversation with imaginary audiences.[15] In the case of the creative intellectual, this is not just any imagined audience (like the Meadian "generalized other" in its most abstract sense). High degrees of intellectual creativity come from realistically invoking existing or prospective intellectual audiences, offering what the marketplace for ideas will find most in demand. This requires that the individual creator must know his or her audience well, through reading and above all through face-to-face contacts which ramify into the crucial junctures of the network. Successful interaction rituals bring increases in emotional energy, deriving from a favorable balance of resources vis-à-vis one's interlocutors: possessing the cultural capital that makes one accepted as a member of the group, and above all cultural capital which enables one to capture the center of attention within it. Creative intellectuals experience such interaction rituals inside their head. The emotional energy of success in these imaginary rituals is what constitutes creative energy: the capacity for sustained concentration, the sensation of being pulled along by the attraction of a flow of ideas. If the process is often accompanied by a feeling of exultation, it is because these are not merely any ideas but *ideas that feel successful*.

This does not mean that intellectuals must be self-conscious about whom their ideals will appeal to. They need not think about thought collectives at all; they can concentrate entirely on the reference of their thoughts—in philosophy, mathematics, sociology, whatever—and try to work out the ideas that seem to them best. The social sense of their ideas is present nevertheless, and it is this that guides them in constructing new idea combinations. Creative enthusiasm is nothing but the emotional energy specific to intellectuals who are in those crucial network positions where they have the cultural capital that will appeal to key audiences. It is the emotional side of anticipating how the intellectual community will restructure itself into new coalitions, using one's idea creations as new emblems of membership. To speak in Mead's idiom, intellectual creators have their generalized others lodged most firmly in the core of the intellectual community; their own thinking is an implicit conversation which reaffirms the existence of the concerns of other intellectuals. The creative intellectual, in playing with different ideas, is playing with different restructurings of the intellectual community, producing a new generalized other within his or her mind, in confidence that the intellectual network will reorganize itself around these ideas.

The external reference of ideas may also exist; I do not wish to deny whatever reality contents intellectual ideas may have, in addition to their social membership sense. (How could I, without undercutting the truth of my own ideas?) Human thought is double-sided. A thinker simultaneously finds the best path available through all these constraints and attractions. Ideas leap to one's mind and arrange themselves into arguments which represent the most emotionally energizing membership coalition available in one's network; in this very process one works out the best statement of empirical truth, of logical argument, of conceptual adequacy one can. The social construction of ideas is much deeper than a simple dichotomy between logic and evidence on one side and social constraints on the other. We shall see that logic is deeply social, an implicit reflection on the history of the intellectual operations themselves.

In the bulk of this book, as we examine the history of intellectual networks, we generally find that intimate materials on the micro-level of the sociology of thinking are not available; our telescope simply does not resolve to a fine enough focus. What we glimpse, at best, are the long-term contours of interactional chains and their products, the ideas which are famous because they have been carried along in the ongoing terms of argument. The weak resolution of the telescope makes it easy to slip back into reifying personalities, the personal names treated as noun substances who are the normal topics of intellectual historiography. But even where we necessarily peer at the past through a darkened lens, let us keep reminding ourselves to think analytically about the reality that once was these human lives: the flow of micro-situations that is the topic of our story.

There is a social causation of creativity, even at its intimate core—the contents of the new ideas that flash into the minds of intellectuals in their creative moments. The flux of interaction ritual chains determines not merely who will be creative and when, but what their creations will be.

CHAPTER 2

Networks across the Generations

High levels of intellectual creativity are rare. Why this is so is the result of structural conditions, not individual ones. A famous rhetoric has it that philosophies are lengthened shadows of great personalities. But psychologists' efforts to show conditions affecting creative personalities are underdetermined. Particular configurations, such as birth order among siblings, remoteness from one's father, a longing for love, bodily clumsiness (suggested by Sulloway, 1996; Scharfstein, 1980), surely occur much more frequently than major creative thinkers. Nor is it sufficient to have been born in an era of peace and support for intellectual activity, or to have experienced other low-level conditions for self-actualization (documented by Simonton, 1976; Kuo, 1986, 1988; Maslow, 1970). The rarity of creativeness also shows the limits of any externalist explanation by general conditions of the surrounding society; zeitgeist, political or material circumstances affect everyone, and such explanations cannot tell us why their creative agents are so few.

The Rarity of Major Creativity

Let us see how often notable philosophers appeared in China and in Greco-Roman antiquity. For the moment, let us take eminence as a matter of how much attention particular thinkers have received from later historians of philosophy. Figures 2.1 and 2.2 display segments of the networks which connect such philosophers with one another. (A modified version of Figure 2.1 appears in Chapter 4 as Figure 4.2, and a fuller version of Figure 2.2 appears as Figure 3.4 in Chapter 3.) The full sequence of networks for China from 535 B.C.E. to 1565 C.E. is shown in Figures 4.1 through 4.4 and 6.1 through 6.5; the sequence of Greek networks from 600 B.C.E. to 600 C.E. is in Figures 3.1, 3.2, and 3.4 through 3.8. Such networks will be the backbone of this book, interspersed throughout the following chapters. On these charts, the names of major philosophers are given in capitals (e.g. MENCIUS, CHUANG TZU, SOCRATES,

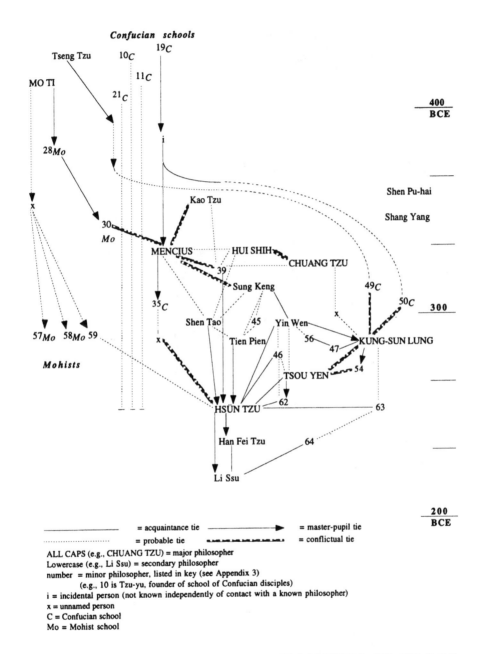

Confucian schools

Tseng Tzu
MO TI
28Mo
x
57Mo 58Mo 59
Mohists
10C 19C 11C 21C
i
Kao Tzu
30 Mo
MENCIUS HUI SHIH CHUANG TZU
39
Sung Keng
35C
Shen Tao 45 Yin Wen
Tien Pien 56
47 KUNG-SUN LUNG
49C 50C
x
46
TSOU YEN 54
62
HSÜN TZU 63
Han Fei Tzu 64
Li Ssu
Shen Pu-hai
Shang Yang

400 BCE
300
200 BCE

_____ = acquaintance tie   ————▶ = master-pupil tie
.... = probable tie   ▬▬▬▬▬ = conflictual tie

ALL CAPS (e.g., CHUANG TZU) = major philosopher
Lowercase (e.g., Li Ssu) = secondary philosopher
number = minor philosopher, listed in key (see Appendix 3)
        (e.g., 10 is Tzu-yu, founder of school of Confucian disciples)
i = incidental person (not known independently of contact with a known philosopher)
x = unnamed person
C = Confucian school
Mo = Mohist school

FIGURE 2.1. NETWORK OF CHINESE PHILOSOPHERS, 400–200 B.C.E.

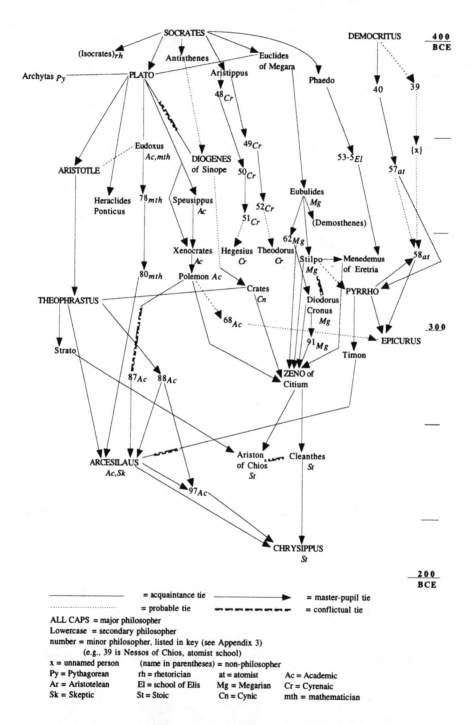

FIGURE 2.2. NETWORK OF GREEK PHILOSOPHERS FROM
SOCRATES TO CHRYSIPPUS

EPICURUS), and the names of secondary philosophers in initial capitals and lower case (Kao Tzu, Han Fei Tzu, Antisthenes, Speusippus). Minor thinkers are indicated by numbers, listed in the keys in Appendix 3.[1]

Set aside for the moment issues of changing canonicity, and whether we can distinguish between "reputation" and "creativity." These do not affect the central point which must begin our analysis: creative philosophers occur infrequently in the total scheme of historical time, even by the most generous criterion of creativity.

Consider all those philosophers who can be regarded as "major," as well as those who can be considered "secondary." Our Chinese sequence runs for 2,100 years, or 63 generations; the Greek sequence covers 1,200 years, or 36 generations.[2] Across the whole expanse of time, major philosophers appear about once a generation in Greece, once every two generations in China. Secondary philosophers are a little more frequent, but not much: in China there is one per generation on the average, in Greece two per generation. Even minor thinkers do not appear in overwhelmingly large numbers, averaging six or seven individuals who are contemporary during any given lifetime:

China

2,100 years	63 generations	
25 major philosophers	0.4 per generation	1 per 84 years
61 secondary philosophers	1.0 per generation	1 per 34 years
356 minor	5.7 per generation	1 per 6 years

Greece

1,200 years	36 generations	
28 major philosophers	0.8 per generation	1 per 43 years
68 secondary philosophers	1.9 per generation	1 per 18 years
237 minor	6.6 per generation	1 per 5 years

One might be tempted to make something of the fact that philosophers of the higher degrees of importance are about twice as common in Greece as in China. But this I think is not an important lesson. The higher ratio of Greek to Chinese philosophers at the more creative levels is due almost entirely to the 7 generations between 500 and 265 B.C.E., beginning with Heraclitus and Parmenides, and ending with Epicurus and Zeno the Stoic. This period includes 14 major and 31 secondary philosophers. Yet even here the concentration is not overwhelming: it averages 2 major philosophers and slightly fewer than 5 secondary philosophers active in any given period of 33 years, a total core community that could very easily form a small face-to-face group. Even if we bring in the minor figures, the maximum is still no more than 15 or 20 at a time. And this is as high a concentration of philosophical action as anywhere in world history.

The Chinese, too, had their hot spots. The 4 generations of the late Warring States period from 365 to 235 B.C.E. contain 5 major and 9 secondary philosophers, including Mencius, Hui Shih, Chuang Tzu, Kung-sun Lung, Tsou Yen, and Hsün Tzu. These are the most influential and sophisticated of the ancient philosophers. Moreover, this period contains two anonymous works whose authors rank at the top of philosophical creativity: the *Tao Te Ching*, attributed anachronistically to the (probably) mythical Lao Tzu; and the Mohist *Canons*, the high point of rationalist logic in all of Chinese history. These give us high creative densities of 2.33 major and 2.67 secondary figures per generation. The other concentrated period of philosophical creativity is in the Sung dynasty, especially the 3 generations of the Neo-Confucian movement from 1035 to 1165 C.E., and again from 1167 to 1200, which gives an average of 2.33 major and 1.33 secondary figures per generation.[3] The high-density periods of Chinese philosophy are about the same as those of Greece; the Greeks merely have more of them.[4]

Who Will Be Remembered?

We might regard the preceding exercise as based on nothing but subjective estimates of creative worth, arbitrarily imposing a historically situated standard that shifts from one epoch to another. Such issues are not to be passed by lightly with a show of numbers, since every measurement rests on the meaning of what is measured. In framing the topic, issues of method are issues of theory.

Canons are historically situated; but let us grasp the full implications. We cannot invoke as a foil a reservoir of "deserving" but unknown thinkers in the shadows throughout history, just as "creative" as the ones whose names were trumpeted, as if there were some trans-historical realm in which their achievement is measured. Ideas are creative because they hold the interest of other people. The very concept of creativity implies the judgment of one generation upon another. Shall we say that we are studying not creativity but reputation? The distinction arises from our tendency to heroize, to reify the individual apart from the context. Although it seems to violate our sense that causes ought to be antecedent to what we are explaining, the "creativity" of a particular philosopher is not established until several generations have passed, because it literally is a matter of how sharp a focus that individual's ideas become in the long-term structure of the networks which transmit ideas.

My sociological criterion for creativity is the distance across generations that ideas are transmitted. I have ranked philosophers in China and Greece according to how many pages of discussion they receive in various histories of philosophy. My ratings are based on composites of ratings from all sources.[5]

The reader is free to reassign the boundaries between the ranks and reanalyze; I doubt this would materially change our picture of the structural patterns in the networks.

The sources closest to the ancient philosophers were also attempting to make historical judgments as to what ideas were influential, and what ideas were worth remembering or combatting. Modern histories of Chinese philosophy rely ultimately on ancient sources such as the early historian Ssu-ma T'an (ca. 120 B.C.E.) and the criticism of schools in contemporary memory by Mencius, Hsün Tzu, Han Fei Tzu, and the *Chuang Tzu*. The modern histories, like their predecessors, often quote entire passages from these ancient sources, building on the amount of attention that earlier philosophers received from others closer in time. We cannot jump outside of history. But this is not a limitation on what we can understand of intellectual creativity; it is the nature of the beast. Intellectual greatness is precisely one's effect on the course of intellectual history, influencing generations downstream from one's own.

In my rankings, greatness is based on the degree to which a philosopher remains of interest to other thinkers across long periods of time. Canons do change, but only among those figures who have entered into the long-term chain of reputation in the first place. The first threshold is reputation that carries down beyond one or two generations. For this reason, the level of structural creativity is not easy to discern among one's own contemporaries. Plato in his own lifetime was no better known—and perhaps less so—than other offshoots of Socrates' circle such as Aristippus, founder of the Cyrenaic school, or Antisthenes, who pioneered the social iconoclasm that later became Cynicism. Aristotle made more of a stir in his own day; it is said that when he returned to Athens in triumph upon the victory of his patron Alexander the Great, he wore a gold crown and rings and was carried in a throne-like chair. Yet Aristotle had to flee for his life when Alexander died in 323 (Grayeff, 1974: 44–45). His philosophical doctrines, balanced carefully between materialism and the Platonic doctrine of Ideas, were propagated in pure form for only two generations, and for the next hundred years his school gave out under his name a much more materialist doctrine consisting largely of empirical science. There were more ups and downs to come. After the rediscovery of Aristotle's original texts and their propagation during the rearrangement of all the philosophical factions around 80–50 B.C.E., Aristotle's fame rose to moderate levels for some 600 years; yet his doctrines typically circulated in a syncretistic form under the dominance of Platonism. It was only in medieval Islam and Christendom that Aristotle became the master in his own right, "The Philosopher" *tout court,* reaching the height of reputation in the generations from 1235 to 1300 C.E. Again in the 1500s Aristotle's reputation was touted by one faction of the Humanists, enhancing his reputation yet again because he became the chief foil for attacks launching the self-consciously "modern" period of Western philosophy.

Socrates, by contrast, was heroized above all during the period when Cynics and Skeptics were popular, 400–300 B.C.E., that is to say, in the generations immediately following his death. He was claimed by many schools. The Cynics traced their lineage back to Socrates' associate Antisthenes, whom they regarded as the master of Diogenes of Sinope. The Megarian school, founded by Socrates' protégé Euclid[6] (or Euclides), carried on the tradition of questioning and debate, and pioneered methods of logic. From Socrates flowed the short-lived schools of Elis (founded by his pupil Phaedo) and of Cyrene (founded by Antisthenes); these too pursued Socrates' omni-questioning technique, now applied to questions of the value of life itself. To a considerable extent Plato propagandized his own doctrines, which derived more from Pythagorean and other sources than from Socrates, by attaching them to a famous figure, and thereby riding into the center of attention on the popularity of rival schools which at the time outshone his own. When Plato, in turn, rose to dominance (not as dialectics but as metaphysics, increasingly mixed with occultism) after 100 C.E., Socrates' fame dissipated; nor did it return among the Islamic or medieval Christian philosophers. For us moderns, Socrates' fame is largely an appendage of our interest in Plato.

One can tell similar stories of East Asia. Confucius, whose fame and doctrinal tradition built up over many generations, was not always treated as the symbolic property of the Confucian school. He appears as a rather "Taoist" sage in the *Chuang Tzu* stories (ca. 300 B.C.E.). And there are the up-and-down reputations of the "greats," such as Mencius (fl. ca. 300 B.C.E.), who was not elevated to the official Confucian canon until 40 generations later by the Neo-Confucians around 1050–1200 C.E. (Graham, 1958: xiv, 158).[7]

The dose of realism provided by the long-term view is a salutary (if unwelcome) antidote to our personal egotism, and to that projected egotism which we attach to our hero-ideals, the rare "genius" of generations past whom we pattern ourselves upon in our inner imagination. Intellectuals make their breakthroughs, changing the course of the flow of ideas, because of what they do with the cultural capital and emotional energy flowing down to them from their own pasts, restructured by the network of tensions among their contemporaries. The merit of their contributions, its "intrinsic worth" as well as "social impact," is a matter of how the structure develops after their own deaths. We intellectuals are truly eddies in the river of time—perhaps more so than other humans, because it is our business to attend to this connectedness across the generations.

Creativity, then, is for the long haul. Let us be clear what this means. The minimal unit of intellectual change is a generation, approximately 33 years. It takes at least that long for a significant change to take place in philosophical premises; and it takes at least another generation or two to see if the change has a structural impact on what later intellectuals can do. Sociologists can see this in our own discipline: we are clear on who are the classic sociologists (Weber, Durkheim, Mead, Simmel) of 1900–1930 or so, but the generation immediately after them was just in the process of winnowing down those names from a larger pool;[8] and in their own lifetimes and shortly after, their reputations were fluctuating and sometimes rather localized and minor. A creative work that receives attention for 5 or even 10 or 20 years may be only a minor fluctuation, too brief to be picked up in the long-term perspective of intellectual history. To get a sense of the magnitude of processes involved here, one might attempt to estimate how much space the "postmodernist" philosophers making a stir in the 1980s are likely to take up in the histories of philosophy that might be written two centuries, or even two generations, from now—and the same, of course, for today's participants in the future histories of sociology, or any other discipline. The sociological issue is to see the relationship between the human foreground of any particular generation (and indeed the still shorter periods of a few years or decades that make up the focus of an intellectual's immediate projects), and the vastly more impersonal, ruthlessly structured sequence of generations that is the realm of creativity we call historically "great."

What Do Minor Philosophers Do?

This viewpoint may leave us with a nagging doubt. Are we dealing only with fame, not with creativity itself? Is it not possible that there have been many creative individuals, buried in obscurity, who have simply not received credit for their advances? This is a powerful image because it sustains most of us intellectuals, who rarely get the credit we think we deserve. And, like a resurrection myth, it holds out a promise: retrospective discovery after our deaths. Let us see.

The instances of posthumous fame that we do know are never pure rags-to-riches stories. The most important case in Western philosophy is Spinoza, whose vogue came, about 100 years after his death, as the favorite of one faction in the Idealist controversies at the time of Kant. But Spinoza had a certain notoriety in his own day; he was well enough situated to be visited and plagiarized by Leibniz, and he began in the Cartesian network near its most active center. Nietzsche struggled in obscurity for 20 years before becoming famous during his last years of madness. Schopenhauer had a longer drought, and receiving fame only when he was very old, and mostly after his death. But both Nietzsche and Schopenhauer from early adulthood were well connected to major intellectual networks, and their conflicts with their compatriots are not at all contrary to the usual dynamics of creative network contact. And all of them were prolific publishers, a pattern correlated with eminence (Price, 1986; Simonton, 1988); they had the emotional energy and the cultural capital that is typical of creative success. Rediscoveries of "lost works" would not be possible at all unless there was some connection to the networks of the intellectual world so that they could be retrieved. And that means intellectuals must make those connections in their own lifetime, or their work will never make it after their death.

What about creative work that is just plain buried forever? Here it becomes relevant to know what intellectual life is like as one moves away from the center. As we get farther from the major figures on the network charts, it becomes increasingly characteristic for philosophers to develop the ideas of a lineage chief, to add criticisms, explications, and commentaries. They are not creative precisely because they are followers. This is quite common in the ranks of "secondary" figures, although this pool also includes figures who stand on their own, who fail to make the deep intellectual impact that would leave them in the historical first rank. A typical secondary figure of this independent sort would be Yang Chu (fl. 380 B.C.E.) in the generation after Mo Ti and before Mencius. Yang Chu broke through prevailing consensus by preaching the doctrine that the natural is not inherently moral or sociable, and that radical individualism is itself natural (Graham, 1978: 59). In Greece a comparable level of importance would be represented by Gorgias, the famous rhetor and Sophist; or Xenophanes, who attacked anthropomorphic polytheism; or Stilpo, the most acute of the Megarian logicians. These men were not epigones; some indeed were extremely eminent in their own day. Mencius declared, somewhat rhetorically, that "the words of Yang Chu and Mo Tzu fill the world" (*Mencius* 3b.9), and Gorgias in his day was perhaps more famous than Socrates. That these secondary figures differ from the major ones becomes apparent only in the long run, as their ideas are sifted over; some are very influential, but their ideas are too easily absorbed by the discourse of the next generation (as with those of Yang Chu and Xenophanes), others proving ephemeral because the network turns in a different direction (as with Gorgias).

No buried treasures here; perhaps we may find real treasures as we reassess their merits, but there is nothing buried about them. Can closet creativity then be lurking in the ranks of the minor figures? But minor figures are the typical epigones—loyal, scholarly, perhaps polemical against opponents. What they lack above all is originality and depth. Nor are minor figures necessarily obscure in their own day. Let Wang T'ung stand for many (224 in the key to Figure 6.2): a famous Confucian lecturer in the capital city of Ch'ang-an ca. 600 C.E., teacher of hundreds of students, including many of the politicians who founded the T'ang dynasty. His contemporaries were very impressed: "Since the time of Confucius there has been nobody like him . . . He perpetrated the *Odes* and the *History,* rectified the Rites and music, compiled the *First Classic* [i.e., chronicle of 289–589 C.E., in imitation of Confucius' *Spring and Autumn Annals*] and extolled the teaching in the *Changes.* With him, the great principles of the sages and all things that can be done in the world, have been brought to completion" (quoted in Fung, 1948: 2:407). Yet the modern historian Fung Yu-lan calls him a minor figure who produced unremarkable editions of the classics. Some of the other modern historians mention him (e.g., Needham, 1956: 452), others neglect him; his fame was ephemeral and without historical impact. There are hundreds more like him, in every part of the world: long lines of Stoic, Epicurean, Academic teachers—Diogenes of Babylon, Clitomachus, Apollodorus "the Tyrant of the Garden," and many others—whose names are not of much interest even to specialists. But these men wrote numerous books, packed lecture halls, were sent as ambassadors by their cities. The most eminent academics of today are cast in their mold.

Some persons get a minor level of attention in our histories, not so much because of their own fame but because they were associates of more important people, or happened to figure in some curious or noteworthy historical event. We know of associates of Confucius or Mencius who appear only as interlocutors in their dialogues, of bystanders in the Zen histories, of Philostratus (172 in Figure 3.5) who happens to have been a teacher of Cleopatra. On the China chart, the incidental figure (311 in Figure 6.4) above the Ch'eng brothers, connecting them to the preceding philosophers Chang Tsai and Chou Tun-I, is Ch'eng Hsiang, the father of these key Neo-Confucians. I preserve such figures in the charts because they sometimes have this facilitating effect; at times without them crucial linkages would not be made.[9]

Such figures give us a sense of the routine parts of the intellectual world, the minor leagues and sub-minor leagues on which major centers of network attention occasionally peak. If we like, we can push further. More specialized historians magnify the milieu with which they deal, and bring other minor or sub-minor figures into view. Li T'ung-hsuan (232 in Figure 6.2) is not even mentioned in the main histories of Chinese or Buddhist philosophy, but gets considerable space in Odin (1982) on Hua-yen philosophy. The magnifying glass, where available, sometimes shows us intellectuals possessing considerable skill in rearranging, systematizing, and popularizing a position; but it confirms our picture that creativity is rare. Such glimpses are useful, too, in understanding the barren periods on our chart. Is it just our unsympathetic bias that makes the Yuan and early Ming dynasties (1300–1450 C.E.) look so devoid of philosophy? No, the records are there; some figures can be dragged into the light (see, e.g., Dardess, 1983: 131–181, who shows us some Confucians absorbed in political reform), but they serve to confirm our impression of intellectual routine in philosophy proper.

Perhaps the outermost fringe of the intellectual world that we can grasp historically consists of persons who have no eminence at all, even in their own time, not even through incidental connections with the more famous. They show up in historical sources on ordinary life, and are sometimes brought to light by a historian such as Elizabeth Rawson (1985: 49), who would like to display the reading habits of ordinary people in the provinces, in this case landowners in the Roman countryside ca. 50 B.C.E. There were apparently many such people, from our adventitious sample, scattered here and there, not only reading but expounding Epicurean and Stoic ideas. We know we are in the intellectual provinces because the ideas are not only old but garbled. They stand in contrast even to those of our "minor" philosophers, who were after all persons of some importance in the intellectual networks of their own day. It is good to know about this fringe, for the sake of realism, and good to know, too, because it makes us understand ourselves. The horizontal spread of intellectual structures does not change much over the centuries; we too live in a mass of readers and would-be writers, reflecting old ideas without knowing what we are doing, dreaming of intellectual glory. Creative epochs are rarer than routine ones; and even at the best of times, the inner circles of the intellectual world are surrounded by peripheries upon peripheries, where most of us live.[10]

The Structural Mold of Intellectual Life: Long-Term Chains in China and Greece

It has been conventional in intellectual history to write in terms of "schools." Texts as far back as the Warring States period of ancient China (before 220 B.C.E.) spoke, somewhat rhetorically, of "the hundred schools" *(chia)* (see, e.g., *Chuang Tzu,* chap. 33). Diogenes Laertius (ca. 200 C.E.) grouped his biographies into Ionian and Italian schools or "successions." But at least four different things can be meant by "school."

The loosest meaning, that individuals have similar modes of thought, need not imply anything about their social organization. About 100 B.C.E. the official Han historian Ssu-ma T'an first grouped earlier Chinese philosophers into six "schools," among them the "Taoist school," for texts resembling the *Tao Te Ching.* But *Tao* was a term used in many different intellectual camps over the previous centuries, and the emergence of a tightly organized Taoist religion was to come in the centuries after. Such "schools of thought" are not very important unless they are based on more tangible structures.

A more rigorous use of the concept of school is to demonstrate intellectual influences among its members. This is the principal pursuit of intellectual historians. Nevertheless, I will not pursue "schools" of this sort. Transmission of intellectual influence certainly occurs, but it is not an explanation, in the sense of showing why, out of all the persons who could read or hear of an idea, a certain few become important by shaping their cultural capital in new directions. Left to itself, the tracing of "influences" implies an infinite regress, in which every thinker's ideas can always be traced back to yet another preceding influence. The channel that carries the energies of intellectual creativity is more than ideas floating in an atmosphere of influence, even if we can pin down such influence to the presence of a certain text in the personal library of a certain thinker; the central channel is the personal contact of face-to-face encounters. I will demonstrate the paramount importance of two further kinds of "schools" or "circles."

One of these involves chains of personal relationships, of which the most important are relationships between teachers and their pupils; besides these vertical ties are horizontal links of personal contacts among contemporaries.

Finally, a "school" can be literally an organization: a place where teaching takes place and authority and property are passed down through an explicit succession, as in the Platonic Academy, the Aristotelean Lyceum, or Chu Hsi's Neo-Confucian White Deer Hollow Academy. Here the doctrine is part of the organizational property and an emblem of its social identity.

Figures 2.1 and 2.2, as well as most of the other network figures in this book, illustrate the third type—chains of personal relationships. It is easy to recognize on these charts the fourth type as well—formally organized schools.[11]

What, then, do the Chinese and Greek network charts show? The first thing which should strike us is the extent to which the named figures, especially the major ones (printed in all capitals) are linked to other philosophers. These links are both vertical (master-pupil chains across the generations) and horizontal (links of acquaintanceship among contemporaries). For the important figures, these links are at all levels of eminence; the bigger stars are connected to more major and secondary figures than anyone else is, but to more minor figures as well.[12]

The most notable philosophers are not organizational isolates but members of chains of teachers and students who are themselves known philosophers, and/or of circles of significant contemporary intellectuals. The most notable philosophers are likely to be students of other highly notable philosophers. In addition to this vertical organization of social networks across generations, creative intellectuals tend to belong to groups of intellectual peers, both circles of allies and sometimes also of rivals and debaters.

For Greece, I have divided philosophers into dominant, major, secondary, and minor figures. Network links are calculated both backward (to predecessors and associates) and forward (to pupils).[13] Calling these the "upstream" and "downstream" sides of the networks, we find:

Greek philosophers	Upstream links	Downstream links
Dominant (8)	3.8	4.0
Major (20)	2.0	2.2
Secondary (68)	1.3	1.0
Minor (237)	0.7	0.4

The dominant philosophers have, on the average, considerably more predecessors and associates who are intellectually significant than other major philosophers do, and so on down the line. The disparities are even greater on the output side. Moreover, if we examine the network in regard to the eminence of those intellectuals to whom each one is linked, we find that the more eminent philosophers themselves tend to be more closely linked *to others at high levels of eminence*. Of 28 philosophers at the major and dominant levels, 18 (64 percent) are linked to others at those levels, compared to 33 of 68 (49 percent) secondary philosophers who are so linked. Generally speaking, the higher up in the ranking of eminence, the more connections: Socrates is directly connected with 3 other major philosophers and with 11 secondary ones; Plato is connected with 3 major and 6 secondary philosophers.

For Chinese philosophers, the pattern is similar:

Chinese philosophers	Upstream links	Downstream links
Dominant (9)	4.7	6.0
Major (16)	2.4	1.6
Secondary (61)	1.5	1.0
Minor (356)	1.0	0.4

Again, the philosophers who dominate long periods of intellectual life have by far the largest number of links to both predecessors and successors. Here we are dealing only with their immediate contacts, in their own generation and those just before and after. If we examine the chain extending backwards in time, we see that the more important the philosopher, the more eminent his contacts within successive links in the chain:

China: dominant philosophers (9):	*2 steps*	*4 steps*
Number of major or dominant philosophers upstream	2.1	3.3
Number of secondary philosophers upstream	1.9	3.0
Both kinds upstream	4.0	6.3
China: major philosophers (16):	*2 steps*	*4 steps*
Major or dominant philosophers upstream	0.8	1.4
Secondary philosophers upstream	1.6	2.5
Both kinds upstream	2.4	3.9

China: secondary philosophers (61):	*2 steps*	*4 steps*
Major or dominant philosophers upstream	0.6	1.0
Secondary philosophers upstream	1.0	1.7
Both kinds upstream	1.6	2.7

Two links typically cover one's own contemporaries plus the generation of one's mentors (although dense networks might use up 2 or more links in the present). Four links allow for a more complicated chain.[14] In Figure 2.1 Kung-sun Lung is connected to Mencius, in the previous generation, through several intermediaries; and Mencius himself connects back to Mo Ti 3 generations in the past.

The stars of Chinese philosophy existed in a neighborhood consisting of, on the average, 2 major and an additional 2 secondary philosophers within 2 links of themselves; going backwards or outwards 4 links, each was typically connected to more than 6 other important thinkers. Major philosophers who are not dominant stars are rather less well connected to other major philosophers (they have slightly less than 1 tie two steps away, and slightly more than 1 tie within 4 steps), although their connections to secondary thinkers are almost as good as the stars'. And secondary philosophers are connected backwards still more modestly, but above the level of minor philosophers.

The Greeks are much the same:

Greece: dominant philosophers (8):	*2 steps*	*4 steps*
Number of major or dominant philosophers upstream	1.8	3.9
Secondary philosophers upstream	4.1	8.3
Both kinds upstream	5.9	12.1
Greece: major philosophers (20):	*2 steps*	*4 steps*
Major or dominant philosophers upstream	0.9	2.2
Secondary philosophers upstream	1.0	2.7
Both kinds upstream	1.9	4.9
Greece: secondary philosophers (68):	*2 steps*	*4 steps*
Major or dominant philosophers upstream	0.7	1.6
Secondary philosophers upstream	1.5	2.9
Both kinds upstream	2.2	4.5

The immediate neighborhood of the most eminent Greek philosophers is much like that of their Chinese counterparts. These Greeks have even more connections with secondary figures than the Chinese do, so that within 4 links upstream they connect to an average of 12 significant philosophers. The ordinary major philosophers (non-stars) in both places have about the same kinds of connections. We do see, though, that secondary philosophers in Greece have rather better connections deep in their networks (4 links) than the secondary Chinese; in fact, Greek secondary philosophers have about the same number of deep links as ordinary major philosophers. This is because so many secondary philosophers are close downstream from the dominant Greeks, with their huge connections; secondary figures such as Crates the Cynic, Speusippus, or Antisthenes benefit from tying into the lineages behind Plato or Socrates. This high density of Greek philosophical networks in several periods is only partly matched in China, with the high network density around the time of the Chi-hsia Academy, and again with the "Dark Learning" group, the Ch'an lineages, and the Neo-Confucians.

The result of this continued density across the generations is that the important Greek philosophers inherit the intellectual capital and stimulation of a very large indirect community. Plato is within 2 links of Gorgias, and 4 links of Protagoras, Empedocles, Parmenides, and Pythagoras. Epicurus is 4 links from Democritus but also from Socrates; Arcesilaus, the skeptical reformer of the Academy, is 2 links from both Aristotle and Zeno the Stoic, and within 4 links of Socrates. Aristotle's deep network includes 6 major and 12 secondary philosophers; that of Chrysippus, the most acute of the Stoics, includes 7 majors and 10 secondaries. Eminence, it seems, breeds eminence, and the more densely the better.

The Importance of Personal Ties

What does it mean that eminent philosophers have the most ties vertically and horizontally, especially with other eminent philosophers? We might suspect some methodological artifacts. Perhaps we know of more connections of major philosophers with minor figures simply because more information is preserved about the stars, including the names of their pupils and associates. But recall that "minor" figures in the charts were typically rather notable persons in their own day, of independent if local standing. Figures whom we know about only because they are mentioned in the context of some other figure are not "minor" but incidental, a separate category not at issue here.

More serious is the possibility that what we consider to be the creative eminence of philosophers is merely the result of their having had a great many personal followers. The followers retrospectively create the eminence. Isn't it tautological to define persons as eminent when they are well connected in their intellectual communities, then argue that the cause of their eminence is this connection? The answer is no; there is less circularity than meets the eye. It can be shown that the model is not simply required by our implicit definitions.

For one thing, there are empirical exceptions. In the Greco-Roman world, the important isolates from chains of significant followers are Heraclitus, Philo of Alexandria, and the Skeptic Aenesidemus. In China, the major isolates are the anonymous author of the *Tao Te Ching,* and the Han dynasty philosopher Tung Chung-shu; and among secondary figures, the early "legalist" politicians Shen Pu-hai and Shang Yang (both fl. 350 B.C.E.), and the Han dynasty rationalist Wang Ch'ung. Moreover, there are a number of cases of "twilight" creativity, when the most distinguished achievements are made at the end of the line, lacking even minor pupils to carry them on. Augustine is the prime example in the Greco-Roman orbit; in Islam, Avicenna (Ibn Sina, fl. 1120). Hegel, who overrated the prevalence of the pattern that "the owl of Minerva flies at dusk," was apparently thinking of himself as an exemplar, but his own pupils proved him wrong.

It is also possible to conceive of a historical pattern in which eminent philosophers are not contemporaries, nor personally connected in chains, nor members of the same organizations, nor concentrated in the same places. That such structures are empirically found is not due to a conceptual tautology.[15]

I have argued that in a sense reputation is not really distinct from creativity; that what we consider intellectual greatness is having produced ideas which affect later generations, who either repeat them, develop them further, or react against them. It does not follow as a matter of definition that a great thinker is one who has a personal network of eminent followers; hypothetically, one's ideas could affect later generations without this personal transmission. Having said this, I would add that it is possible to assess whether some individuals received more retrospective eminence than they deserve, in the sense that they did not really produce the ideas which are later attributed to them.

This kind of renown is especially likely for originators of chains. Thales is traditionally regarded as the first Greek philosopher and the first mathematician; but it is not at all clear that he was a very innovative intellectual in his own right. He is counted as one of the "Seven Sages" of antiquity; but the oldest source that gives him this title is Plato, 200 years later.[16] The other "Sages" are not strictly what we would call philosophers, but primarily politicians who were known for their astute practical judgment and their pithy sayings. Solon, Thales' contemporary and probable acquaintance, was somewhat more of an intellectual in that he was both a law giver and a poet, but others such as Pittacus or Bias of Priene were simply famous politicians. As in these other cases, Thales was known for his political advice at a time when the city-states were undergoing major struggles over the establishment of democracy, and in which "tyrants"—who included a number of the "Sages"—played a role as arbiters, lawgivers, and setters of precedents. Thales seems to have played this role in Miletus. His special eminence in what became known as "philosophy" may well be due to the fact that he had some connection with Anaximander, the first writer of a book on cosmology, and he in turn with a third-generation thinker, Anaximenes.

Thales does not pose a serious problem since he is only a secondary figure by the long-term criterion of how much attention he gets in later histories; Anaximander, by contrast, is at least a borderline major figure. Confucius is perhaps more seriously overestimated. Along with Chu Hsi, he is the dominant figure in terms of attention received across the whole of Chinese thought. Much of his fame is as a cult figure, rather than for the content of what he actually taught. Confucius made an important breakthrough with his doctrine of how individuals should behave and states should be ordered by deference to traditional rituals and documents. But it is clear that "Confucianism" as a sophisticated position about human nature, moral issues, rationality, and cosmology was created by later philosophers of much greater intellectual complexity such as Mencius, Hsün Tzu, and Tung Chung-shu, not to mention the still greater metaphysical departures of the Neo-Confucians. What stuck to Confucius' name was primarily the ideology of attributing all intellectual virtue to the past, initially to the old documents themselves, and gradually to Confucius and eventually a canonized Mencius and even Chu Hsi.[17] It is clear that without the much later successes of the Confucian school, Confucius himself would have figured as of no greater importance than Mo Ti, or even Yang Chu or Shang Yang.

Mo Ti is probably overrated in the same sense; though he made an important new departure with his utilitarianism and ethical universalism, he is probably of greatest importance in having founded an organization which gradually turned from military to intellectual activities. The lesser-known figures who perfected Mohist logic four or five generations after Mo Ti are probably responsible for his position as a major figure in a long-term view of Chinese intellectual history. In the West a comparable case might be Pythagoras, perhaps most important as a founder of an organization which built up philosophical and mathematical doctrines to a high level, reflecting back retrospective glory on the founder.

What do such cases do to our overall assessment of network patterns? In my opinion they do not shake the theoretical results, and even reinforces them. Perhaps we should lower the ranking of some of these figures. But since they come early in the charts, and hence lack eminent predecessors (although Mo Ti and Pythagoras seem to be connected via minor or incidental figures to whatever eminent predecessors there were), to reduce their ranking would enhance the average connectedness among the truly eminent. And it makes sense that major philosophical creativity does not jump out of nowhere. For China, the takeoff generation is apparently that of Mencius, Hui Shih, and Chuang Tzu, just as in Greece it is the generation of Heraclitus and Parmenides.[18]

We might also question the significance of horizontal connections among major philosophers. That Socrates or Cicero knew virtually everybody of his day might be a trivial circumstance, simply the clubbing together of people who were already eminent, much in the same way that today movie stars and other celebrities are invited to meet one another, without any effect on how they happened to become famous in the first place. This is a possibility we can check. In many instances the contacts contributed something because they preceded later creative productions; this is the case with Cicero, and with Socrates' many contacts in his youth. For the most part, I would judge, contacts among the eminent are not simply the "clubbing together" phenomenon; the horizontal connections are substantively important. But it is not strictly a matter of "influence" in the conventional sense, where one person passes ideas to the other. We see this most graphically where persons are in close contact long before any of them becomes creative.[19] I suggest three processes, overlapping but analytically distinct, that operate through personal contacts. One is the passing of cultural capital, of ideas and the sense of what to do with them; another is the transfer of emotional energy, both from the exemplars of previous successes and from contemporaneous buildup in the cauldron of a group; the third involves the structural sense of intellectual possibilities, especially rivalrous ones.

These processes operate in all types of personal contacts, the vertical chains of masters and pupils as well as the horizontal contacts among contemporaries. Consider the question: Why are vertical ties so prevalent, and why are they correlated with the degree of eminence? One might answer that the chains pass along intellectual capital: Aristotle is eminent because he received such a good education from Plato, who in turn was well educated by his contacts with Socrates, Archytas, Euclid of Megara, and others. This is surely not the whole story, since the eminent figures of the younger generation make their reputation not by repeating their received cultural capital but by elaborating it in new directions. But granted the importance of these intellectual resources, why is it that they are so often received through personal contacts rather than more distantly from books?

For very early periods, of course, the latter was not possible. Strictly speaking, philosophy as we are considering it, in every culture area, only begins after the time when writing came into use. But it took some time before new ideas were typically circulated in writing. Confucius' sayings were written down as the *Analects* by the generation of his pupils (ca. 470–430 B.C.E.); and the texts known as the *Mo Tzu* and the *Chuang Tzu* clearly came after the lifetimes of their eponymous authors, although in the case of Chuang Tzu they certainly include some writing of his own. It is not that these thinkers claimed to teach only orally. Confucius is credited with writing the *Spring and Autumn Annals,* a historical work later subject to endless analysis for occult significances; and the books of Hui Shih, earlier than Chuang Tzu, are said to have filled several carts (*Chuang-Tzu,* chap. 33).[20] Similarly in Greece, Heraclitus, who shunned people generally, allegedly deposited his book in the temple of Artemis at Ephesus. Whereas Socrates is famous for his personal oral style, his contemporary Democritus is credited with 60 books, and by this time there was an open market for books.[21]

The significance of the breakthrough to writing is controversial. Eric Havelock (1982, 1986) goes so far as to argue that Plato's generation was the first to become oriented to written texts rather than oral recitations, and that philosophical abstractions were not possible until this transition was made. But the Greek philosophical community goes back some six generations before this, if in a context of a literacy still subordinate to oral ritualism. Havelock's argument does not apply well to the chronology of Chinese intellectuals, who were oriented to written symbols very early, and constituted a kind of cult of writing that began many generations before Confucius. The very identity of a scholar was his familiarity with books, although this was most characteristic of the earliest period (the rise of the Confucians around 500 B.C.E.), and again after the establishment of the unified dynasties (221 B.C.E.). In between, the importance of oral discourse increased, rather than decreased, as intellectual life was shaped especially by the face-to-face debate at courts during the Warring States period. Havelock overgeneralizes a model of primordial orality, which he conceives as conservative ritual embedded in and upholding the public social order; yet the oral discourse of an intellectual community need be neither concretized nor conservative.

In principle, soon after the early intellectual networks arose, one could acquire the important philosophical doctrines without personal contact with the author. Personal closeness gave some advantage, of course, in times of clumsy and slow channels of written publication. But it is striking, as we look across the whole span of known history, that the pattern of personal connections does not change in any significant degree from the most ancient times to the most recent. The personal chains are still there in late Greco-Roman antiquity just as they are near the beginning. Wang Yang-ming's network ca. 1500 C.E., when book publishing was quite a big business, is very little different from Mencius' 1,800 years earlier. The clincher is that the same kinds of networks exist in modern European philosophy, right up through the twentieth century (see Figures 10.1 through 14.1). We still see chains running from Brentano to Gadamer, Marcuse, and Arendt, and from Frege to Wittgenstein and Quine, and groups in Vienna, Paris, and elsewhere.[22] I would venture to predict that the importance of personal connections will not decline in the future, no matter what overlay of new communications technology is invented. E-mail, or any other form of communication which opens up a dispersed and defocused structure of communications, will not substitute for the focused chains which are the core of intellectual life.

What then is being passed through these personal chains? Intellectual capital, to be sure. The reason why books are not as valuable as personal contacts is that a general exposure to the ideas of the time is not sufficient for first-rate intellectual performance; what personal contact with a leading practitioner does is to focus attention on those aspects of the larger mass of ideas which constitute the analytical cutting edge. Of course, creative intellectuals of each new generation take off from this point in new directions. Personal contact with leaders of the previous generation can help here too, not so much in the substance as in the style of work; there is a transmission of emotional energy, and of a role model showing how to aim at the highest levels of intellectual work.

Emotional energy is intensified to high levels in the interaction rituals of everyday life by strongly focused group interactions. The experience of witnessing a famous teacher surrounded by pupils is a motivating one, even though, for reasons that we will see presently, few pupils get full benefit. The same experience occurs in horizontal group contacts. A group such as the "Seven Sages of the Bamboo Grove" is simultaneously building up the creative inspiration among all its members; without one another, their more extreme flights of fancy and iconoclasm would surely not have taken wing.

Contacts with opponents is just as emotionally intensifying as contact with one's allies, perhaps even more so. It is for this reason that intellectuals seem to be drawn to their opponents; they seek them out, like magnets tugging at each other's opposite poles. The intellectual world at its most intense has the structure of contending groups, meshing together into a conflictual super-community. The horizontal ties that meshed at Athens at the time of Socrates and his successors formed the same kind of structure that built up the excitement of the Chi-hsia Academy and its rivals during the Warring States, that existed among the Buddhist factions in the early T'ang, and again among the multiple schools of the Sung dynasty which crystallized in the Neo-Confucians. Intellectuals are excited by the flow of ideas, by the prospects for development, by their struggles with their enemies; and this is so even if they are looking backwards toward restoration of some ancient or even eternal ideal. The ritual density of interactions among intellectuals drives up their energy—all the more so when famous names come together, rival sacred objects embodied in actual persons, bathing their audience in the clash of their auras.

These energies are channeled in particular directions. Intellectual fields allow only certain possibilities to flourish at a given time. To know about these possibilities, to have a sense of what is opening up, it is crucial to be in the thick of things, and especially to be in contact with one's rivals. Thus, major intellectuals meeting one another do not necessarily communicate any intellectual capital; they may not learn anything at all substantive from one another. The fact that the rival Neo-Confucians Chu Hsi and Lu Chiu-yüan met and debated perhaps added nothing to each other's repertoire of ideas. But the very situation that brought them together must have involved a long-standing consciousness of a split in the intellectual field, and this in itself encouraged both Chu and Lu to develop such positions, expanding them into rival super-systems.

The Structural Crunch

At the level of the flow of ideas and emotions, there is a disparity between causes and effects. If contact with eminent forebears and contemporaries is important to creativity, as is living in a time when there are structural rivalries, there are nevertheless many more individuals who are exposed to these conditions than there are newborn intellectual stars. Confucius was reputed to have 1,000 pupils, Theophrastus (perhaps more accurately and less rhetorically) is credited with 2,000 (*DSB*, 1981: 13:328). Of these my charts list 11 of Confucius' pupils (1 borderline minor, the rest at minor rank or below), and 4 of Theophrastus' (1 major, 1 secondary). We know the names of some of Cicero's compatriots who studied with the same array of philosophers at Athens and Rhodes (Rawson, 1985: 6–13), but only Cicero reaped the intellectual and emotional resources to make himself famous in philosophy. We can be sure that for every major philosopher capable of transmitting significant cultural capital and emotional energy, there were many more pupils who had the opportunity to reinvest these resources than actually did so.

Does this mean that our sociological model is inevitably incomplete and needs supplementing with psychological, individual, and other idiosyncratic circumstances? It would seem prudent to admit that it does. But this sort of distinction would rest on a misunderstanding. Individuals do not stand apart from society, as if they are what they are without ever having interacted with anyone else. We could go into further detail about just what social experiences, what chains of interaction rituals of the sort described in Chapter 1, have generated their individuality.[23] The particularity of the individual is the particularity of the social path.

Let us put this question aside for the moment. The main theoretical problem is not that what I have said so far is too sociological, but that it is not sociological enough; it omits a key fact about the structure of intellectual networks. The structure of the intellectual world allows only a limited number of positions to receive much attention at any one time. There are only a small number of slots to be filled, and once they are filled up, there are overwhelming pressures against anyone else pressing through to the top ranks.

In addition to the necessary advantages of getting the most relevant cultural capital, of being in the situations that heighten one's emotional energy to a creative pitch, of becoming aware of structural possibilities as they open up, it is also necessary to be first. One must be in the lead, or else the structural possibilities, as far as the individual is concerned, begin to close down. Opportunities and encouragement, both objective and subjective, flow cumulatively to those few persons who get a head start down the structural channels; they dry up for others who may initially be not far behind. It is the sense of these forces flowing in the intellectual world that moves some people to drop out, to give up on intellectual dreams of eminence, or perhaps to stay in the field but settle for a subsidiary career as commentator or expositor, perhaps to retail others' ideas to a provincial audience, perhaps to go into politics or some other field where one's competition is not head-to-head with other intellectuals on their home turf.

Creativity is squeezed out of the structure, so to speak, through small openings. But these openings always have the size to let several thinkers through at a time; creative breaks seem to occur simultaneously in several directions. We see this pattern strongly in the network charts (Figures 4.1 through 4.4 and 6.1 through 6.5 for China, 3.1, 3.2, and 3.4 through 3.8 for Greece).

In China, major figures typically match up with major rivals in their generation: Mencius, Chuang Tzu, and Hui Shih; Kung-sun Lung overlapping (and debating) with Tsou Yen, and he in turn with Hsün-Tzu; the Buddhist stars Fa-tsang and Hui-Neng; the creative generations of neo-Confucianism, first with Chang Tsai, Shao Yung, and Chou Tun-I; then Chu Hsi and Lu Chiu-yüan. Secondary figures also appear in contemporaneous clusters. Some philosophers are matched with others of slightly lower rank, but complete isolates from significant competition are very few.

It is the same with the Greeks. The key figures come on the scene as rivals within the same generation: Parmenides and Heraclitus; the stars of the Sophistic movement, together with Socrates as well as Democritus; Aristotle and Diogenes the Cynic; Epicurus and Zeno the Stoic founding their rival schools at Athens within a few years of each other. When we include the secondary figures with the stars, the pattern of simultaneously appearing creativity becomes overwhelming.[24]

The structure of simultaneous and opposing creativity leads us on to the law of small numbers, and the struggle to divide the intellectual attention space, which will occupy us throughout the following chapters. Not only Greek and Chinese but also Indian, Japanese, Islamic, medieval Jewish and Christian, and modern European philosophers appear in tightly focused networks of rivals. Here we need take only the general point that the structural crunch is a pattern of both network density and creativity driven by conflict. The famous names, and the semi-famous ones as well who hold the stage less long, are those persons situated at just those points where the networks heat up the emotional energy to the highest pitch. Creativity is the friction of the attention space at the moments when the structural blocks are grinding against one another the hardest. The most influential innovations occur where there is a maximum of both vertical and horizontal density of the networks, where the chains of creative conflict have built up over an unbroken chain of generations.

The structural conditions which make this possible are the subject of the chapters that follow. Here I anticipate a fact which emerges from an overview of all the networks of world philosophy. The total number of philosophers who are significant in world history is approximately 135 to 500 persons: the smaller number if we take only the major figures in each world civilization, the intermediate one if we add the secondary figures.[25] The distribution of philosophers for all networks is shown in Table 2.1.

Even if we add the minor figures in all the networks discussed in this book, the total is still only 2,700, a tiny fraction of the population of the world over these generations (an estimated 23 billion people who lived between 600 B.C.E. and 1900 C.E.; calculated from McEvedy and Jones, 1978: 342–354). The intellectual world of long-term fame is much more sharply stratified than the economic-political structure of societies, even in those periods when ruling aristocracies were less than 5 percent of the populace. Moreover, before 1600 C.E. or later, disciplines were relatively little differentiated; after that date most of the scientific and scholarly fields branched off from the networks of philosophers, and the networks include many of the most famous founders of such fields. Hence this total ranging from 150 to fewer than 3,000 persons accounted for virtually all of the intellectual accomplishment in the "theoretical" fields of knowledge until quite recently—excluding the fields of literature, music, and the fine arts, which had their own networks.

For the reader of our own time, a question arises in looking over these networks: Where are the women? I have assembled these networks by collecting the names which have dominated attention among intellectuals over the last 25 centuries, and there are very few women among them. In China there were a few women among the religious Taoists; in the Islamic world some of the Sufi mystics; in medieval Christendom, where philosophy was based in

TABLE 2.1. DISTRIBUTION OF PHILOSOPHERS FOR ALL NETWORKS

Civilization	Generations	Major	Secondary	Total important (major + secondary)	Minor	Total
China (535 B.C.E.– 1565 C.E.)	63	25	61	86	356	440
Greece (600 B.C.E.– 600 C.E.)	36	28	68	96	237	330
India (800 B.C.E.– 1800 C.E.)	78	22	53	75	272	350
Japan (600–1935 C.E.)	40	20	36	56	157	210
Islam/Judaism (700–1600 C.E.)	27	11	41	52	420	470
Christendom (1000–1600 C.E.)	18	11	46	57	360	420
Europe (1600–1900 C.E.)	9	19	61	80	350	430
Totals	271	136	366	502	2,152	2,670

universities consisting exclusively of men, women had an intellectual role only in devotional religious movements and some of the secular courts. Does this mean that the history of world philosophy is simply the expression of a male viewpoint? Until very recently it has been overwhelmingly populated by males; yet it is hardly possible to lump it into one category as a male viewpoint. The basic structure of intellectual life is division among rival viewpoints. Maleness does not predict who will be an idealist or a materialist, rationalist or mystic, or any of the other lines of demarcation which have existed within philosophy.

Throughout world history, when women have been in the intellectual attention space it was most often as religious mystics. But mysticism is not a uniquely female form of thought, and most mystics have been men. The connection is organizational, not a matter of intrinsic mentalities; mysticism has been the part of the intellectual field which flourishes best outside of tightly organized lineages and hence has been most open to outsiders, and thus to women. The issue is not male and female mentalities, which would be a reductionist explanation, but social discrimination on the level of the material base. It is not individuals, whether male or female, let alone of any skin color, that produce ideas, but the flow of networks through individuals. Historically, in the times when women had access to the networks at the center of intellectual attention, they filled an array of philosophical positions (Waithe, 1987–1995). Among the Greeks, the Epicurean materialists were the lineage most open to women, and women philosophers were also found among the Cynics, who were iconoclastic about sexism as well as everything else. In late antiquity women appeared among the Platonic mathematicians. In the 1600s and 1700s, when European networks broke free from the monopolistic male universities, we find Anne Conway, a spiritual monist linked to the circle of Henry More, and Catherine Cockburn, who weighed in on the side of Locke and debated Shaftesbury and Hutcheson. In the 1800s, when women broke into the philosophical field, they included German Idealist sympathizers such as Madame de Staël and radical materialists such as Mary Ann Evans (George Eliot); in more recent times women appear in the networks alike of the analytical school as well as the Paris existentialists and structuralists. Leaders of feminist theory—Dorothy Smith in sociology, a pupil of the ethnomethodologist Harold Garfinkel, and thus a grandpupil of the network of Alfred Schutz and the phenomenologists; Julia Kristeva, in the Tel Quel circle with Derrida—recombine the cultural capital and emotional energy of the larger intellectual networks of the preceding generation.

Historians of the future, looking back at our times, will see the feminist movement as one of the forces reshaping intellectual life. But the intellectual field is never dominated by just one faction, whether feminist or masculinist; and it is predictable that as there are increasing numbers of women in the intellectual field with the overcoming of institutional discrimination, women will spread throughout the various positions which make up the dynamics of intellectual life. There is no deep philosophical battle between male and female mentalities because mentalities do not intrinsically exist. That opposition is put forward in the intellectual field today because the creative field always operates by oppositions; our current debates are another phase of the age-old dynamic.

The core of the networks that have dominated attention during the generations of recorded history, and that totals 100 or 500 or 2,700 names, was privileged over all the others who did not make it into the center of attention. To speak of this as a little company of genius would be to misread the sociological point entirely. It is the networks which write the plot of this story; and the structure of network competition over the attention space, which determines creativity, is focused so that the famous ideas become formulated through the mouths and pens of a few individuals. To say that the community of creative intellectuals is small is really to say that the networks are focused at a few peaks. The struggle of human beings to situate themselves high on such a peak, and the conditions which make those peaks few but interlinked, are the substance of the sociology of philosophies, and of intellectual life.

In this struggle almost all of us must fail. This wounds our intellectual egotism, and deflates the dream of glory, posthumous if need be, which is the symbolic reward of intellectual work. There simply is not room in the attention space for more than a few to get first-rate recognition at one time, and over the flow of generations still fewer who are remembered for the long-term influences which make them secondary reputations, let alone major thinkers. It is the fate of almost all intellectuals to be forgotten, most of us sooner than later.

Instead of taking this realization as depressing, it is possible to view it in a different light. All of us, from stars to bystanders, are part of the same field of forces. The network that links us together shapes and distributes our ideas and our energies. We are such stuff as Kant was made of, or Wittgenstein, or Plato; if we are sociologists, Weber and Mead are quite literally flowing through our minds, as Dilthey and Rickert, Wundt and James flowed through theirs; if mathematicians, we cannot think without thinking as part of the network, however remote, which is also the mind of Pythagoras or Newton. They, and we, are constituted by the oppositions and tensions among different parts of the network which make up the intellectual problems and hence the topics we think about. It is the same with our contemporaries, friends and rivals alike, and with those who will come after us in the future. The stars are few because the focus of attention in such a network is a small part of the whole. Those persons at the centers which become the focal points for us all are not intrinsically different from ourselves. We are all constituted of the same ingredients; we make one another what we are.

CHAPTER 3

Partitioning Attention Space:
The Case of Ancient Greece

Creative persons are typically linked to one another in chains, and appear as contemporary rivals. But is there not a sense in which networks of creativity beg the question? Another factor is presupposed that generates some creativity in the first place. The structural factors so far identified are part of the pattern in which creativity occurs. Within chains over time, creativity often increases. Secondary philosophers in an earlier generation give rise to major philosophers, and the biggest stars usually have major philosophers upstream. The process is not merely the transmission of cultural capital but its intensification.

Creativity involves new combinations of ideas arising from existing ones, or new ideas structured by opposition to older ones. Conflicts are the lifeblood of the intellectual world. This is rarely recognized by intellectuals in the heat of action. Their focus is on truth, and they attack their predecessors and compatriots for failing to arrive at it. The theme recurs across the millennia, from Heraclitus to the Vienna Circle to the foundationalist controversies of today. Kant's version was to complain about the sorry state of metaphysics, allegedly once queen of the sciences. This is a ritual incantation, a preparation for battle, for there is no previous period in which metaphysics rules serenely without disagreements.

The crucial feature of creativity is to identify an unsolved problem, and to convince one's peers of the importance of solving it. It is typical for intellectuals to create problems at the very moment they solve them. In India the issue of how to escape from the bonds of karma did not exist until the Buddhists proposed a means of escape. Epicurus made fear of the gods an issue at the same time that he propounded a solution to these fears. Kant discovered that science was threatened when he announced a Copernican revolution to end the threat.

A single philosopher in isolation rarely develops a new issue or a new way of resolving it; this usually happens to two or more philosophers in the same generation but rival lineages. The emergence of new problems is part of the transformation of the whole intellectual problem space. The underlying dynamic is a struggle over intellectual territory of limited size. Creativity occurs both as this space opens up and as it closes down; the result is two kinds of intellectual innovation, by opposition and by synthesis.

The Intellectual Law of Small Numbers

The structure of intellectual life is governed by a principle: *the number of active schools of thought which reproduce themselves for more than one or two generations in an argumentative community is on the order of three to six*. There is a strong lower limit; creativity can scarcely occur without rival positions, and almost always in any creative period there are at least three. There is also an upper limit; whenever there are more than about four to six distinct positions, most of them are not propagated across subsequent generations.

The principle is dynamic over time. Positions appear and disappear, grow stronger and weaker in adherents. The law of small numbers holds sway amid the flux. *Strong positions* (those which have dominant external support), subdivide in subsequent generations into as many as four or five factions. On the other side, *weak positions* (those that have a poor or declining external base) disappear, or amalgamate into others by syncretisms or syntheses. We may add a corollary: a second reason why positions become weak is that the entire attention space becomes overcrowded, violating the upper limits of the law of small numbers. This too is an incentive to reduce the number of positions by synthesis.

Why should this pattern exist? There are several aspects to the question. One is structural: Why should the number of self-sustaining groups be from three to six? There is also the dynamic issue: Why do schools rise and fall? Combining the two issues, When schools do rise and fall, why do they split or amalgamate?

The structural question has already been partially answered. There is a lower limit because intellectual creativity is a conflict process. If there is any creativity at all, there must be an organizational basis in the intellectual world such that there are at least two positions, and in fact there are usually at least three. If there is freedom to have more than one position, a third at least always seems available; a plague on both houses is always a viable intellectual strategy.[1]

The upper limit also derives from the structure of conflict. Even though new positions are largely structured by the negation of existing positions, any individual philosopher needs allies if his or her position is to be transmitted to anyone else and propagated across generations. Hence, proliferation of new positions above the level at which groups can still be relatively large and visible (i.e., above about six) is self-defeating. This does not mean that there cannot be periods when positions proliferate to very large numbers. The number got dangerously high in Plato's generation in Greece, when in addition to the Academy there were also the schools of Megara, Cyrene, Elis, Abdera, Cyzicus, the emerging Skeptic movement, Isocrates' school of rhetoric, and the remnants of the Pythagoreans. But most of these groups dropped out within a generation or two, leaving a structural limit of three to six. Conflict is limited by itself.

Why then do lineages appear in the first place, some proving successful, some proliferating, others declining? Because of changing external conditions of social life which provide material bases for intellectuals to work and publicize themselves. That is why, although ideas do not reduce to surrounding social conditions, nevertheless large-scale political and economic changes indirectly set off periods of intellectual change. We will trace both levels in a two-step process of social causality: the inner splits and alliances which take place as networks maneuver under the law of small numbers; and the outer changes in the material base, which trigger periods of inner realignment.

The Forming of an Argumentative Network and the Launching of Greek Philosophy

Look now at the shifting structure of Greek philosophy. The earliest philosophy gradually crystallizes out of a plethora of political "wise men" and questioners of the traditional religious beliefs in the generations around 600 B.C.E. Here external conditions are prominent: the democratic revolution and political reforms, the spread of literacy, and their effect in undermining the religious practices connected with traditional political life.[2] A crucial step follows: an intellectual community separates out by turning toward its own topics and standards of competition. The initial rounds of discussion are cosmological. Anthropomorphic deities once defined the categories of the natural world; the social conditions which undermined the old religious cults now open a new argument space. Into this vacuum step the first secular intellectuals. The community concerned with the topics of proto-philosophy begins to form among cosmological poets such as Alcman (late 600s) or even Hesiod (700s), introducing order into the disparate religious myths, depicting the rise of the cosmos as a genealogy of deities. In the generation of Pherecydes and Xenophanes, intellectuals reflectively distance themselves from the myths by reinterpreting or criticizing. Thales, later singled out as the "first philosopher" because he expressly recognizes the shifting of old cultural capital into a new problem space, declares that "all things are full of gods," and goes on to in-

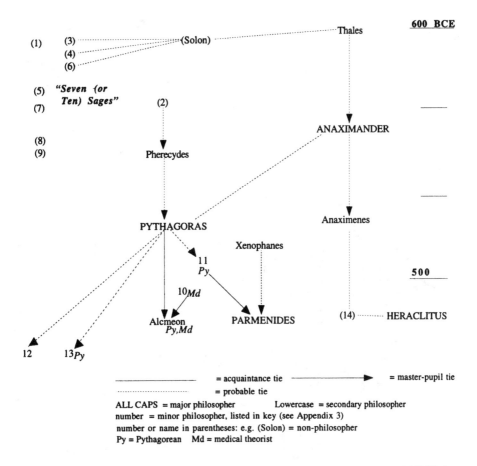

FIGURE 3.1. FORMING THE NETWORK OF GREEK PHILOSOPHERS,
600–465 B.C.E.

terpret them counter-anthropomorphically as ultimate constituents of nature. Heraclitus, who as a priest is a last remnant of the old pre-philosophical base, continues this play with concepts on the border of the secular and the divine as late as three generations into the secular intellectual community.

The first burst of creativity occurs in rivalry, not in unity. There are several candidates for the basic elements: the anthropomorphic gods themselves; various physical elements as prime *arche,* or a non-physical element such as the *apeiron;* the "unbounded" of Anaximander; or the numbers of the Pythagoreans, at first conceived as quasi-physical entities like the collections of pebbles used for calculation.[3] Personal lineages begin to appear from one leader to the next across the generations. We see three lineages in Figure 3.1,

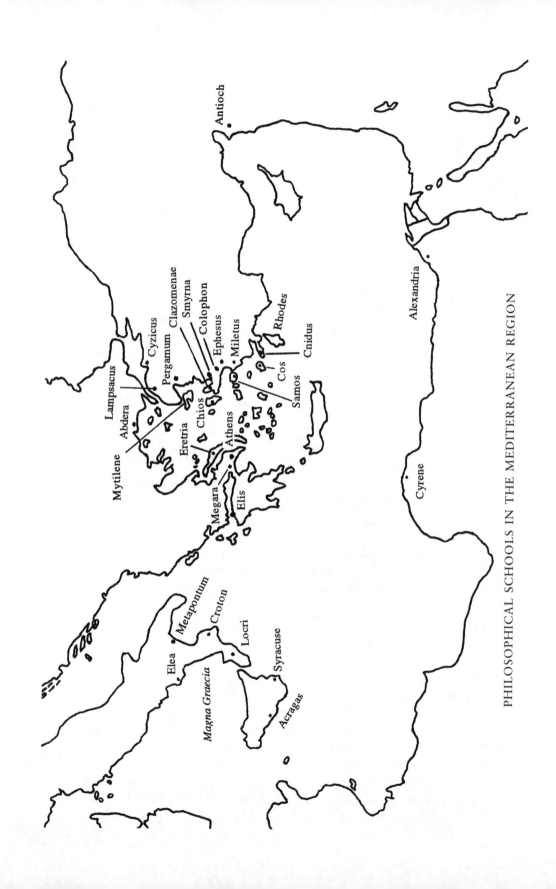

Antioch

Alexandria

Rhodes

Cnidus

Cos

Samos

Cyzicus

Clazomenae

Smyrna

Colophon

Pergamum

Ephesus

Miletus

Lampsacus

Abdera

Mytilene

Eretria

Chios

Athens

Megara

Elis

Cyrene

Metapontum

Croton

Locri

Elea

Magna Graecia

Syracuse

Acragas

PHILOSOPHICAL SCHOOLS IN THE MEDITERRANEAN REGION

deriving from Thales; from Pherecydes, possibly connecting with the "sage" Pittacus (2 in the key); and from Xenophanes.

This activity took place in what must have been a self-conscious community. Miletus, the largest city and major trading port on the Ionian coast, was only 20 miles from the island of Samos, where Pythagoras originated; Pherecydes was from Leros, an island 40 miles off Miletus; Heraclitus at Ephesus was in the next city north of Miletus, 30 miles away; Xenophanes at Colophon was another 15 miles inland, a day's journey from Ephesus; slightly farther up the coast was Clazomenae (home of Anaxagoras), with Sardis (home of the cosmological poet Alcman, who later migrated to Sparta) 20 miles inland. Even the systematizers of mythology were from this region: Homer is reputed to have lived (or at least his tradition was perpetuated) at Smyrna, a day's sail (20 miles) up the coast from Clazomenae, and Cyme, the home of Hesiod's father, was another 30 miles north.[4] Unquestionably the rival "cosmologists" knew about one another. In this network of towns, the bigger ones 30,000 to 65,000 in population, with a good deal of coastal travel, and intellectual life carried on in public recitations, it is unlikely that there would not have been much personal contact.[5] A competitive community of Ionian intellectuals existed, from the poets of around 700 B.C.E. onward, down through the next half-dozen generations.

External political forces broke up this local structure in the late 500s. Xenophanes left in the Persian conquest of Ionia in 545 (*DSB*, 1981: 14:536), Pythagoras perhaps 15 years later. The shift in philosophy that came with the move to Magna Graecia is not a matter of geographical determinism. The "Italian" or "Eleatic" schools were continuations of the Ionian networks; the "Italian" (actually Sicilian) Empedocles produced an eclectic combination four-element scheme (earth, air, fire, water) by recombining the material elements of Ionian cultural capital.[6] What was occurring was the crystallization of a new set of oppositions in the intellectual world. The element-seekers had become too numerous, with nothing to give precedence to one position or another. Empedocles' eclectic combination represents the kind of alliance on the material element front one might expect from the law of small numbers. In this Empedocles was extremely successful, boiling down the Ionian philosophies to a piece of cultural capital that was to prove enormously resilient over the next two thousand years.

A new opposition emerged against the whole movement of element-seeking. Characteristically, there was a two-pronged attack in the same generation. Heraclitus moved toward disowning the concrete level entirely; the constituents of the universe consist instead of a process, the flux, and also of a structure regulating and patterning it, the *logos*. Heraclitus was the first to break through and recognize a higher level of abstraction. The Pythagoreans, with their doctrine of number, might seem to present a parallel, but it is doubtful that the generation of Pythagoras himself viewed numbers in other than concrete terms; the doctrine of the numerical Forms is not clearly visible until four generations later, with Plato, although it may have emerged in the Pythagorean school itself in the intervening period.

Within Heraclitus' lifetime, Parmenides also crossed the border to a higher level of philosophical abstraction. His famous monism, based on logical arguments that Being cannot be itself if it admits of differentiation or change, is clearly a response to the element theories, and likely to Heraclitus as well (Guthrie, 1961–1982: 2:23–24). With this, the internal structure of the intellectual community was well launched on its autonomous path. Parmenides posed a puzzle—speaking more strictly, a deep trouble—for intellectuals to work upon. He thereby carved out a distinctive space that no longer owed anything to popular religious conceptions. Henceforward, when the border between philosophy and religion became salient, the philosophers would have their own autonomous contribution to make, and indeed could generate their own philosophical religions. Heraclitus too, with his concept of *logos,* provided an abstract tool that could be bent to many uses in this internal struggle within the intellectual world.

External factors impinged again on this increasingly complex intellectual community. The next two generations saw further democratic revolutions, the geopolitical upheavals of the Persian wars and their aftermath of Athenian imperialism. These events sent ambassadors and refugees traveling around the Greek world. In this milieu appeared traveling Sophists, typically men not as well based in private fortunes and political position as the earlier pre-Socratics. The search for livelihood was one impetus for the emergence of education for fees, and hence for the rise of the professional teacher and the organized school (Kerford, 1981). Political issues of the surrounding social milieu are prominent in the Sophists' doctrines, especially their discussions of *nomos* (law, custom) versus *physis* (nature), and of the source of moral and legal obligation. The Sophists became famous for teaching how to argue on either side of a question, making a living by selling a practical skill useful to citizens in the participatory law courts of the democratic city-states. But the Sophists were also heirs to internal developments in the intellectual community. They argued on the level of abstract principles, not concrete cases, and religious reifications for them were a thing of the past. Part of their shocking effect on laypeople was that they were an intellectual avant-garde; they attracted the usual hostility of laypersons whose loyalty was attached to reified sacred objects, directed against cosmopolitans operating at a higher level of abstraction.

The Sophists carved out a new stance within the intellectual field. This was the technique of deliberately playing at paradoxes, of confronting other intellectual positions with inconsistencies generated by a more abstract analysis. The cultural capital here came originally from Heraclitus' and Parmenides' breakthroughs, now shorn of ontological content. Heraclitus' doctrine was generally taken to consist of the flux, ignoring the *logos* which holds sway above it. Parmenides was regarded as the source of paradoxical statements about the impossibility of change. The two great opposites were united in arguing for the impossibility of an uncontradictory worldview. Parmenides directly taught the Sophists' network, while Heracliteans were noisy at Ephesus with their flaunted contradictions. One of their number, Cratylus, was reputed to have refused to speak at all, and could only gesture, to avoid contradicting himself (Guthrie, 1961–1982: 2:358); he shows up at Athens at the time of Socrates and Plato. This space in the intellectual lineup would be filled by the Megarians and the Skeptics long after the external political conditions which first made the Sophists possible had disappeared.

Down to the generation of Socrates, there are many contenders for intellectual attention, but essentially four positions maintain themselves longitudinally. The element-seekers divide into three long-standing schools: the atomists, who hold a strongly materialist stance and counter the arguments of Parmenides with a view of combinations of hard elements of Being moving in the void; at the other end, the Pythagoreans, who increasingly have moved to a conception of Number as an abstraction above the material level; in the middle, Empedocles' four-element doctrine is carried on especially in the schools of medicine in the theory of the four humors. The fourth position is that of paradoxing and relativism, a turf which includes the nature of argument itself, and some self-consciousness about the nature of logic and abstractions. In short, three substantive positions, and a fourth as "plague on all houses."

In the network (Figure 3.2) Socrates is a pivot; he is connected with virtually every chain prior to his time, often by debate, and from him flow most of the organized schools of the next generation. This network centrality is the source of his fame. Substantively I believe Socrates' originality is overrated. Contemporary accounts—especially that of Aristophanes, and apparently other dramatists (Guthrie, 1961–1982: 3:40)—depict him as another fast-talking exponent of the physical cosmologies, another member of the lineage of Anaxagoras; when he was condemned to death in 399 B.C.E. for impiety against literalist religion, it was on much the same charge as that on which Anaxagoras was expelled from Athens around 430. What is transmitted in the Platonic dialogues is to a large extent Plato's own sophistication about epistemology, and the theory of Forms seems to be Plato's generalization of Pythagorean number philosophy.

Nevertheless, if Socrates is only an emblem, he represents a crucial change in the structure of intellectual networks. What "Socrates" did (if in combina-

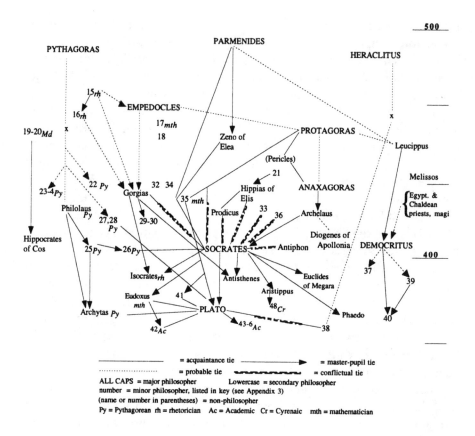

FIGURE 3.2. CENTRALIZATION OF THE GREEK NETWORK IN
ATHENS, 465–365 B.C.E.

tion with "Plato") was to recombine intellectual stances: where the Sophists
had worked this material from the relativistic (and politically liberal) side,
Socrates/Plato combined it with the transcendent ontology that came from the
Pythagoreans, and fortified it by grappling with the ontological puzzle bequeathed by Parmenides. Relativism and dialectic still anchor this position: in
Plato, it is that opposition by which the doctrine of Forms defines itself. In
Socrates, it is more likely that the dialectic itself remains central; though he
had ties to wealthy conservative patrons (and did not have to live the life of
commercial scrambling for which he scorned his Sophist rivals), he seems to
have balanced the possibility of eternal truths and standards against the arguments of relativism. Most of Socrates' offshoots in the next generation would
take some portion of the relativistic turf, especially Euclides at Megara, who
emphasized the intellectual side as logic; and Antisthenes, who taught that

distrust of intellectual positions should be a lived commitment, thus giving rise to Cynicism. We should also include Isocrates, another pupil of Socrates (and of the Sophist and rhetorician Gorgias), who repudiated philosophy entirely and set up a fee-taking educational system based on rhetoric alone. Isocrates is a Sophist gone respectable; for him arguing is just a technique, with no claims for or against truth or political significance per se.

For those followers who stayed within philosophy, Socrates' position can be regarded as upping the ante in the relativistic position; instead of the "naive dialectic" of the Sophists, Socrates and such followers as Euclides of Megara and Plato were now explicitly conscious of dialectic argument about the dialectic itself. It would be wrong to conclude that the intellectual field was completely taken over by dialectic and its higher forms, epistemology and value theory. Socrates' most important contemporary was Democritus, who produced the most comprehensive ontology yet, and on the materialist side. Structurally, Democritus and Socrates divide the field between rival ways of doing philosophy: the one a systematizer of prior ontological reflection (including apparently a good deal of mathematics from the Pythagoreans and elsewhere); the other an aggressive progenitor of a method for opening up new intellectual problems.

How Long Do Organized Schools Last?

What follows is obvious: we should look at the social conditions surrounding Plato and Aristotle, and perhaps at the founding of the Epicurean and Stoic schools, the twilight generation in which classic philosophy begins to fade. Thereafter, for readers schooled in the Western philosophical tradition, it is tempting to tune out until philosophy reawakens a millennium or more later. Plato and Aristotle are the great classics, and the maneuvers of the myriad schools which accompanied them, virtually down to the end of Greco-Roman antiquity, are historical marginalia.

The process of constituting a "classic" cannot be understood in this way. It was rather remote posterity that elevated Plato and Aristotle to the virtual exclusion of all others. Their elevation seems particularly fickle if we focus on their doctrines rather than merely their names. Aristotle's school moved away from his position virtually from the time of his death, and then in a few generations the school itself collapsed; thereafter, throughout antiquity and much of the Islamic and early Christian Middle Ages, "Aristotelean" philosophy was seen very piecemeal, distorted into a kind of Idealism. It was only with Averroës and his influence in Christendom around 1250 that Aristotle became "The Philosopher" familiar from our education. "Plato" was more continuously a famous name, but his Academy shifted the contents taught under it, changing drastically several times between emanationist religion and skepticism. The epistemological sharpness of the Platonic dialogues which moderns admire is a selective interpretation, and by no means the dominant one in the networks that succeeded Plato.

It is crucial to pursue these networks throughout antiquity, and not only for the sake of contrast, of highlighting the peaks against the valleys, and because of the premonition that the Hellenistic era better holds up the mirror to our own times than does the Golden Age of the founders. The essence of philosophical creativity lies not in the genius of individuals but in the structural realignments which take place under the law of small numbers. Here we confront an unanswered question: If expansion and contraction in the number of intellectual lineages structure the pattern of creativity, what explains the existence of the lineages themselves?

Schools of thought, grounded in intergenerational network lineages, are best able to reproduce themselves when they are based in organizations with material property and a hierarchy of offices. Shifts in this hard organizational backbone set off the realignments which in turn structure intellectual space under the law of small numbers. To demonstrate, let us take an overview of the pattern of organized schools across the entire Greco-Roman period (see Figure 3.3).

The first organized school in Greece was the Pythagorean brotherhood. This was a secret society, with internal ranks and religious practices (*DSB*, 1981: 11:219–220; Guthrie, 1961–1982: 1:173–181; Burkert, 1972). It also had a material reality, with its own buildings, such as the citadels in Crotona, Metapontum, and Locri in southern Italy (see Map 1). In this early phase, Pythagoras' own active lifetime (around 530–520 B.C.E.) and the next two generations, the brotherhood was explicitly political, ruling with the support of, and probably drawing membership from, the local aristocracy. The democratic rebellion which swept Magna Graecia around 450 B.C.E. burned their meetinghouses. The Pythagoreans withdrew to Tarentum, which was still held under Archytas' leadership when Plato visited him around 390 and again in 365 (*DSB*, 1981: 11:24–29). Others returned to the Greek mainland, where in Plato's day there was a Pythagorean center in Phlius, a small town in the Peloponnesus. In the late 400s Pythagoreans were out of politics and circulating in general intellectual life; Philolaus at Thebes was reputed to have published their secret doctrines (Guthrie, 1961–1982: 1:155).[7] The major intellectual innovations of the school, especially its discoveries in mathematics, apparently took place during this generation. By 350 the school had disappeared.

Around 470 another organized school seems to have existed in Abdera, comprising a succession of teachers from Leucippus and Democritus onwards (Guthrie, 1961–1982: 2:382). This too seems to have been more of a ritual

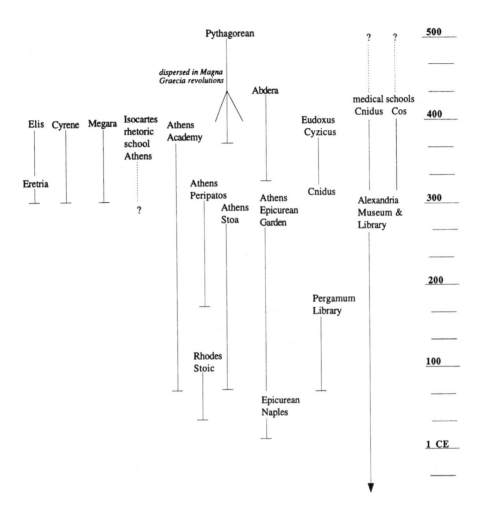

FIGURE 3.3. ORGANIZED SCHOOLS OF GREEK PHILOSOPHY,
600 B.C.E.–100 C.E.

brotherhood than a fee-taking school. It carried on for five generations down to around 330, including a branch at its mother city—Abdera being a colony—Teos, off the Ionian coast. Nausiphanes, teaching at Teos, connected Epicurus to this school.

Just after 400 B.C.E., the intellectual community discovered the school as an institutional structure that can be deliberately created. There was a huge outpouring of foundations, leading to a crisis in the attention space because it overflowed the limits of the law of small numbers. The schools were modeled, in part, on the Pythagoreans, as a religious fraternity living in common on endowed property. In another respect, these were the first schools of higher education, beyond the level of the elementary schooling of the youth cohort of the city-state, the *ephebes* who went through athletic and military drill together, along with some training in music and poetry (Marrou, 1964). The philosophical schools put on a formal and material foundation the commercial education in advanced subjects which the Sophists had pioneered.

The Academy, founded around 380 in Athens, was originally a park and public gymnasium outside the city; Plato subsequently purchased a garden and built houses for lodging students and visitors (*DSB*, 1981: 11:27). Members took their meals in common (following Pythagorean precedent) and were expected to contribute financially according to their means. Plato nominated his successor; subsequently the *scholarch* was elected. The organization was legally recognized as a religious fraternity dedicated to the Muses and thus as a property-conveying unit. The organization of the other schools founded at this time is less well known. There were famous schools at Megara, a day's journey from Athens; at Elis, near the site of the Olympic games in the northwest Peloponnesus (120 miles from Athens); more remotely, at the Greek colony of Cyrene on the African coast; and at Cyzicus, a colony of Miletus, on the Propontus (Sea of Marmara) in Asia Minor.

A different type of school was founded at the same time: Isocrates, like virtually all the other founders a pupil of Socrates, founded in Athens the first school of rhetoric (Marrou, 1964: 119–136, 267–281). Isocrates' school became the model for the dominant form of higher education in the Greek and Roman world, eclipsing in numbers the schools of philosophy. For centuries thereafter rhetoricians and philosophers were professional rivals over the territory of higher education (Marrou, 1964: 287–290). Another institutional development more closely tied to philosophy had taken place a generation earlier (in the late 400s), when Hippocrates founded his school of medicine on the island of Cos at the southeast corner of the Ionian coast, a reform movement at the traditional shamanistic medical center of the Asclepiads. The followers or associates of Hippocrates apparently soon split, with a rival medical school appearing at Cnidus, the neighboring port on the mainland (*DSB*, 1981: 6:422–424). Now the intellectual field was beginning to divide in yet another dimension than the rivalries under the law of small numbers: rhetoric and medicine eventually became professional specialties in their own right, fields of attention increasingly cut off from philosophy. But in the founding generations, these disciplines added to the struggle within the central attention space, aggravating the crisis of overcrowding. The medical schools were carriers of some of the main philosophical positions; and the rhetoricians overlapped with the activities of Aristotle's school, as Aristotle played off their concepts in a crucial component of his philosophical synthesis.

During the following generations, the crisis of the law of small numbers came to a head. The material bases of intellectual life drastically reorganized. Most of the schools which branched off from Socrates flourished for two or three generations and then died. The school at Elis was moved, in the third generation, by Menedemus to his home Eretria (on the island of Euboea, northeast of Athens) before it disappeared, and the school at Cyrene split into three branches in its third generation (Reale, 1985: 55–56, 39–42). The head of one branch, Theodorus "the atheist," was expelled from Cyrene, later garnered political support from the Ptolemys at Alexandria, and returned in triumph. The head of another branch was prohibited from lecturing by Ptolemy because his doctrine was moving students to commit suicide. The school at Megara, less melodramatic but sophisticated in logic, similarly flourished for three generations and then disappeared. Eudoxus' school at Cyzicus, which maintained visiting ties with the Academy, moved to Cnidus, apparently in response to Persian military advances; it produced a good deal of creativity, especially in mathematics and astronomy, but lapsed within two generations (*DSB*, 1981: 4:465–467). It was during this period, too, that the Pythagoreans and the Abdera school came to an end. We can add the two Hippocratic medical schools to the list of casualties.[8]

In the generations just before and after 300 B.C.E., there was a wave of reorganization. So many schools had died out that there was room for new ones to form by recombining their cultural capital. Aristotle founded his Lyceum in Athens, in imitation of the Academy, in 335. Epicurus founded his Garden community in 307, Zeno of Citium his Stoic school (after the Stoa, or "Porch," in Athens where he lectured), about 302. Of the older schools, only the Academy survived.

These four Athenian schools dominated intellectual life for two centuries. Now stability sets in, comfortably within the law of small numbers. In Figure 3.3 we see one other organized school, the Museum and Library at Alexandria. But this was no doctrinal rival to the four philosophies. The networks headquartered at Athens maintained overseas branches. The Peripatetics and Stoics had strong ties at Alexandria. The founding of the Museum and Library occurred under the influence of Demetrius of Phalerum, a pupil of Theophrastus and friend of Aristotle. Rivalry over geopolitical prestige was a motivating factor, while the successors to Alexander partitioned his empire.[9] Neither the Library nor the Museum was a teaching institution, thus leaving the Athens schools in command. But instruction in private schools also existed at Alexandria, and after the breakup of the Athens schools around 50 B.C.E., the syncretizing philosophies seem to have been based there to a considerable extent, down through 500 C.E. The Epicureans, too, had branches, but the intellectual leadership was firmly at Athens. Branch communities received directions by letter from the headquarters, and were expected to send contributions.[10]

The Peripatos had the rockiest history. The school weathered a wave of anti-Macedonian sentiment after the death of its patron Alexander the Great in 323, and prospered under Theophrastus. At Theophrastus' death, his manuscripts and those of Aristotle were removed to private hands in Skepsis, a small city in Asia Minor, possibly as the result of hard feelings over the succession of Strato as *scholarch* (Guthrie, 1961–1982: 6:59). Although the school's doctrine changed at that time, the school itself survived for six more generations. But after 100 B.C.E., we hear of no more *scholarchs* of the Peripatos.[11]

The end point for all the Athenian schools came shortly after 100 B.C.E., under the external shock of the Roman conquest.[12] Even earlier, the Stoic school was coming loose from its Athenian base. A library was founded at Pergamum around 190 B.C.E. by the Attilid kings in explicit rivalry with the Ptolemys in Egypt; another was created at Rhodes by around 100 (*OCCL*, 1937: 64). Panaetius first studied at the Library at Pergamum under its head, Crates the Stoic, around 165 (*EP*, 1967: 6:22). In the first generation after 100 B.C.E., Posidonius made the Stoic school at Rhodes far more famous than the school at Athens, where he himself had studied under Panaetius (Reale, 1985: 434). But after Posidonius, the Rhodes school lapsed, and the Stoa in Athens is heard from no more.

With each episode of change in the material base comes a new partitioning of intellectual space. One can readily see in Figure 3.3 the opening up of a field of intellectual organizations which took place around 400 B.C.E.; then a rearrangement of schools around 300, when most of the seven to nine schools existing at that time disappeared and were replaced by three or four others.[13] Organizational turning points are intellectual turning points as well. Long-lasting schools such as the Academy and the Peripatos shifted their doctrines each time in response to realignments of the entire field. Another big period of doctrinal shift occurred at the organizational turning point 100–50 B.C.E., when the formal schools were replaced by purely personal followings of philosophers.

Moreover, intellectual space can be filled by more than just formal organizations. Personal networks of masters, pupils, and compatriots are typically channeled within formal schools when these exist. The organizational pattern summarized in Figure 3.3 is reflected on the network level in Figures 3.2 through 3.5. The amount of fractionation in the attention space sometimes exceeds the numbers of formal schools that I have enumerated, and the splitting of informal networks also contributed to straining the law of small numbers. Informal networks dominated among most pre-Socratics; there was no actual school at Miletus, nor in my opinion at Elea or in Sicily. Most of these intellectuals were involved in politics and made their living from their private fortunes, in political office, or by making speeches or practicing medicine.[14] The Sophists continued this pattern, except that some of them, like Protagoras or Gorgias, became notorious for taking pupils for pay, which was regarded in aristocratic circles as a shocking innovation.[15] Socrates, who was not so very different from the other Sophists in his intellectual relationships, was very self-consciously respectable in that he lived off his wealthier friends as a guest; this same relationship of patron to client, glossed as his "amicus," was the prestigious form of intellectual support in Roman times as well (Rawson, 1985: 67). Isocrates' school set the model for the commercialized fee-taking pattern, which seems to have become respectable in Hellenistic times but was downgraded again for a while with the Roman conquest. By around 200 C.E., when official salaried positions were established for professors of rhetoric or philosophy, or for a municipal doctor, these too were considered respectable, since they did not involve selling one's services for fees (Jones, [1964] 1986: 1012–13; cf. Rawson, 1985: 170–171).

Although there are only two organized schools among the pre-Socratics, neither reaching back much before 500 B.C.E., Figure 3.2 shows some five or six personal chains, already reaching the limits of the law of small numbers. The school of Abdera (Figure 3.3) begins soon after the Miletus chain leaves off; one might say the intellectual "space" for a naturalist or materialist position was continuously filled by these two interrupted chains (if indeed there was no actual contact between them, as implied in the report that Leucippus was a native of Miletus). Other chains appear in the generations after 500, involving Heraclitus, Parmenides, Empedocles, Protagoras, and Anaxagoras.

The generation around 400 which sees the proliferation of organized schools—Megarian, Cyrenaic, Academic, and so on—is in fact even more crowded (Figure 3.4). The Cynics appear at this time, prefigured by Antisthenes and then epitomized by Diogenes of Sinope. This was far from being an organized school; indeed it might even be called an anti-school, with its doctrine of avoiding material possessions and social responsibilities of any kind. The Cynic movement adds to the pattern of intellectual rivalries of the 300s C.E.; for all its maverick qualities, it had the same life span as most of the other "minor" Socratic schools. Diogenes' follower Crates was the last "pure" Cynic. The whole movement covered only three generations, from Antisthenes, who lived on the whole a conventional lifestyle; through Diogenes, who radicalized the position from an intellectual one to a total commitment as a way of life; ending with Crates and his contemporaries. Other followers turned the Cynic stance into a formula for popular literature, writing plays, diatribes, and satires, which provided a basis of material support (Reale, 1985: 35–37). Cynicism caught the public eye more than any other philosophical

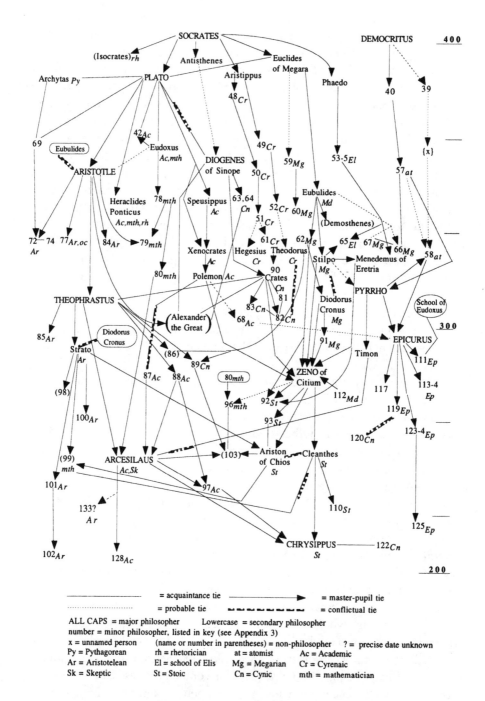

FIGURE 3.4. PROLIFERATION AND RECOMBINATION OF THE
GREEK SCHOOLS, 400–200 B.C.E.

position by its total commitment to living its doctrine, and the term "philosopher" conjured up more than anything else the image of the black-robed figure preaching in the streets, contemptuous of worldly things. Nevertheless, the movement disappeared around 300 B.C.E., the same time as most of its rivals.

The Skeptics, too, were a movement rather than a school. Again there were forerunners, before the famous expositor Pyrrho. The style of paradox making had been in the air ever since the followers of Heraclitus and of Parmenides around 450 B.C.E. The Megarian school of logicians incorporated many skeptical themes. Pyrrho seems most notable for making skepticism a full-fledged commitment; he allegedly refused to choose between alternatives, even in daily life, and was guided about by friends to keep him from hurting himself (D.L., 1925: ix, 61; cf. Frede, 1987: 181–183). Basing himself on a different intellectual content, he nevertheless ended up in practice in much the same position as the Cynics. His disciple Timon systematized the doctrine but did not attempt to live it. There were no more independent Skeptics in the following generation; instead, skepticism was taken over by one of the organized schools, the Academics, in the revolution carried out by Arcesilaus.

Adding the informal lineages to the formal schools reinforces the general pattern. They further heightened the competition for intellectual space in the 300s B.C.E., lasted for a few generations, and disappeared or amalgamated into the small number of factions which survived.

Small Numbers Crisis and the Creativity of the Post-Socratic Generation

The three generations from Socrates' students down through 300 B.C.E. were a time of structural crisis for the philosophical community. The law of small numbers was being seriously violated. At the outset, a new organizational form came into existence. Half a dozen formally organized schools rushed into this new space, while there were two older schools still operating (the Pythagorean and the Abderan); in addition, there appeared two lifestyle movements, unorganized anti-schools so to speak: Skeptics and Cynics. The new schools all had an initial burst of creativity, intellectual energy stirred up by the opening structural opportunities. They divided the cultural capital already available by applying it in divergent directions and elaborating explicitly against one another.

Euclides and the Megarian school appropriated Parmenides' metaphysics in a fairly pure form. They declared that Being is always unitary and "the sole good is that which is always one and alike and the same" (Reale, 1987: 281–282, 374). Euclides ethicized Eleatic metaphysics while explicitly grounding Socrates' ethical standards in an objective ontology. This was roughly the same turf that Plato staked out; hence it is not surprising to find the Megarian school polemicizing against Plato for breaking up pure Being into a plurality of Ideas, and later against Aristotle for his conception of potentiality as an additional dimension of Being. Across the next two generations, the Megarian school maintained a good deal of prominence. It backed away from the Eleatic metaphysics and placed increasing emphasis on developing formal logic and on the famous debating skills of members such as Stilpo and Eubulides, who was known as a paradoxer, and whose followers were known as Eristics for their contentiousness. This kept the Megarians in the public eye, but also moved them increasingly onto the same turf as the Skeptics and Cynics; late in the century they amalgamated with the Cynics and eventually with the Stoics.

Antisthenes, taking the other direction, played up the dialectical side of Socrates' method, with a special emphasis on opposing other schools of thought. He seems to have been a materialist, declaring against Plato that only the bodily exists; he held that pain is a good thing, citing hero stories of the deeds of Heracles (Reale, 1987: 367–370)—thus taking the opposite side from the hedonistic school of Aristippus. He also scorned intellectual debate by arguing that it is impossible for two men to contradict each other. Whether or not Diogenes was Antisthenes' pupil—Antisthenes rejected the practice, now followed by his rivals, of taking formal pupils—Diogenes went on to fill this slot in the intellectual world by making himself an exemplar of anti-conventionality in every respect. Diogenes took up the sophisticated position of being an intellectual's anti-intellectual, a mocker of all. His followers, to the extent that they were able to sustain themselves, did so by institutionalizing mockery as a literary form.

The Skeptics we have already noted. In some respects Pyrrho and Timon duplicated the turf that the Megarian logicians were already occupying, while jettisoning any positive doctrine such as Eleatic metaphysics; they made skepticism not just an epistemological argument but a lifestyle, which in turn brought them onto Cynic territory. It is not surprising that all three of these network lineages were unstable, though the core intellectual doctrine of skepticism was to have a long history in a series of new homes.

In the long run of the intellectual community, these schools became "minor"; in their day, however, they attracted the most attention of all. Their chosen turf overlapped most closely with lay concerns, and personalities such as Antisthenes, Diogenes, Crates, and Pyrrho dramatized themselves in the public eye.[16] This was also true of the famous Aristippus and his Cyrenaic school. Aristippus took the subjectivist line that only feelings exist for us; and he pushed this to an ethical conclusion, that the individual could control his own happiness. Aristippus was admired, like Socrates, for his gay serenity. The

Cyrenaics elaborated the intellectual position of hedonism, along with the ideal of the sage immune to worldly vicissitudes. This position was fraught with inner conflicts; but it was precisely these conflicts that contributed to the intellectual vitality of the school over the next several generations (Reale, 1987: 40–43, 384–386). Hegesias argued that the goal of life is pleasure, but that it is rarely attainable; therefore life is indifferent, and suicide is acceptable. His rivals opposed this scandalous doctrine with other sources of happiness in this world where pleasures are few and fleeting. Theodoris favored the inner condition of joy based on wisdom, defined as acting without regard to laws or conventions, indifferent even to torture and death. These dramatic arguments attracted a good deal of attention. They also had the effect of moving the Cyrenaics onto the same turf as the Cynics; after Hegesias, Anneceris, and Theodorus, the Cyrenaic school disappeared, and the technical core of its hedonistic ethics was appropriated by the Epicureans.

Holding a position between the other schools was Phaedo's at Elis. Advocating a doctrine of detachment, it was kept intellectually alive by controversies with other schools; in its final generation, Menedemus played against the Megarian doctrine of an unchanging good (also shared by other schools) by arguing that the good is wholly in the mind (Reale, 1987: 287–288).

Subject to overcrowding under the law of small numbers, some of these schools were bound to be short-lived. Against this background of competing schools, Plato and Aristotle put together the intellectual stances that were to win long-term eminence. Plato differs from the others, partly in breadth, and in holding to a core of serious intellectual activity for its own sake. He avoided the flamboyant lifestyle movements for a relatively conventional practice. Not that he was without political or religious projects; but discussion of these did not call for any radical dropping out from ordinary duties, powers, or property. In any case, competition for attention on that side of the field was already intense. As long as the relativistic dialectical schools were active, the Academy took the opposite pole, defending transcendent truths. Plato with his wide intellectual contacts drew every resource into defense of this position. The final collapse of the Pythagoreans in his own generation left him free to appropriate their doctrines, including mathematics as an exemplar of Forms, and (apparently) also their doctrine of transmigration, which Plato elaborated into a speculative basis for the soul's recollection of eternal Forms known in a prior life.[17]

Plato inherited the Pythagoreans' slot in the intellectual field, but he was not alone in exploiting their patrimony. The Pythagoreans had already in the generation around 430–400 B.C.E. released their mathematics into public circulation; and their puzzles such as squaring the circle encouraged a takeoff of mathematical activity which had considerably overlapped the community of

Sophists (Heath, [1921] 1981: 1:220–231; Fowler, 1987: 294–308). Not only Plato but Eudoxus as well built on this milieu; Eudoxus' school at Cyzicus was famous above all as a school of mathematics and astronomy. But it was also a full-fledged philosophical school, propounding the doctrine of Ideas in much the same form as Plato (Reale, 1985: 63–64; *DSB*, 1981: 4:465–467), while diverging in ethics by holding a hedonistic doctrine that brought the school closer to the Cyrenaics. Eudoxus' school was the prime center of mathematical creativity in its day; Plato acquired some of the prestige of mathematics by drawing in individual mathematicians such as Theaetetus, Philip of Opus, and Heraclides Ponticus, and having Eudoxus himself visit the Academy with his followers to teach the more advanced subjects.

This source of rivalry soon collapsed; the Cyzicus school moved and then disappeared, enriching the next generation of the Academy with mathematicians. It is possible that there was a struggle at Cyzicus itself between two factions; we know of an early follower of Epicurus who had apparently converted from the Cyzicus mathematical school, and of Epicurean charges which circulated at that time implying at least one of the factions had attached its astronomy to Babylonian star worship (Rist, 1972: 7). At about this time, Plato's third-generation successor as head of the Academy (ca. 340–314 B.C.E.), Xenocrates, promoted star worship for a while, making astronomy a sacred practice attached to demonology (Dillon, 1977: 24–38; Cumont, [1912] 1960: 29–30). The general drift seems clear: the Cyzicus school and the Academy more or less divided the same turf for a generation, leaving Plato leeway to experiment with other intellectual strands. When the Cyzicus school collapsed, its doctrines became predominant at the Academy, and mathematics was exalted as the major form of knowledge. Speusippus, Plato's successor in 348 B.C.E., placed all emphasis on supra-sensible reality, and hence on numbers as the first principles of the world (Guthrie, 1961–1982, 5:459–461).

The mathematicians' takeover had the further consequence that Aristotle split off to establish his own school. Aristotle developed the doctrine that numbers are inessential, since mathematics contributes nothing to understanding movement and change. Since a mathematics of change eventually proved possible, one should say that Aristotle was not interested in encouraging a mathematics along these lines; his structural motivation was to break with the mathematical faction, representing the side of the Academy that held out for non-mathematical pursuits.[18] Aristotle seems to have taken the empirical researchers with him; first on his biological expeditions around the Aegean, and later into his rival foundation at Athens.

The Academy in its first generation appears to have been rather non-doctrinaire. Not only did Plato explore a diversity of positions, as indicated in the range of his own writings, but also the Academy included specialists not necessarily sympathetic to his philosophy (*DSB*, 1981: 11:22–23). We take it for granted that Plato was "Platonic," just as we take it as part of his essential qualities that he was Socrates' star pupil. But this view is the result of many generations of filtering. Let us try to reverse the angle of perspective in time. Instead of taking "Plato" as a reified thing whose attributes we already know, let us place ourselves in the crowded network, amid its streams of cultural capital and its eddies of emotional energies as they would have existed in the early 300s B.C.E.

What we see in Figure 3.4 that distinguishes him from his rivals among the fellow pupils of Socrates is Plato's wide-ranging network contacts. Plato was not the only one to build on the mathematical heritage of the Pythagoreans; and on the metaphysical side, the Elis school and in a different way the Megarians continued the elevated Being of Parmenides. We moderns think of Plato's eminence as above all his raising the level of epistemological reflection; but such epistemological acuteness was very high in the Megarian school, and indeed was carried on more in the next generations by Eubulides and Stilpo than by Plato's own successors. The fact that their texts do not survive, but Plato's have, is not merely a historical accident; rather it is the result of structural domination over a period of generations, which selected which texts were to be elevated above the others. In an important sense, Aristotle's split helped constitute "Plato" in the long run as we have come to think of him. The division of the school into Speusippus' line, which elevated mathematics as a transcendent ideal of all knowledge and being, and Aristotle's line, which reduced this ideal to a part in a larger synthesis, crystallized out "Platonism" as one pole in an opposition. In view of the history of the next eight generations—which turned over the Academy first to religions of star worship and mystical numerology, and then to a very un-Idealist skepticism—we may even say that Aristotle's school was crucial in carrying along the memory of the ideal-type Platonism as a foil during the time when it no longer had an active home base.

The key to Aristotle's success was his explicit focus on the problem posed by the diversity of schools of his day, and his reflective awareness of how this grew out of the prior history of philosophical schools. Rival schools were also aware of this development; Aristotle's contemporary Pyrrho took the disagreement of the schools as explicit warrant for relativism. Aristotle was anchored in conflict with the dialecticians, such as his disputes with Eubulides the Megarian. Aristotle's distinctiveness became the opposite intellectual strategy: to reduce disagreements by synthesis. The tools that he forged in this process are his long-enduring contribution to philosophy.

It is not surprising that Aristotle and his school produced the first historical treatments of philosophy. These not only occur as a specialized genre but also figure throughout Aristotle's arguments, where he sets up his own position as an answer to long-standing disputes. Part of Aristotle's masterly tone is the detachment with which he reviews contending positions, striving to pull out the best side of each doctrine as he sees it. There were of course broad-ranging intellectuals before Aristotle. Empedocles had taught (if not written) on nature, medicine, religion, practical politics, and magic; the Sophist and mathematician Hippias of Elis boasted of encyclopedic knowledge, which he mastered by his system of *mnemonics;* Heraclides Ponticus (for a time in Plato's entourage) was astronomer, rhetorician, and wonder worker (Reale, 1987: 179–180, 354; 1985: 65–66, 390–391; *DSB,* 1981: 6:405). More centered on purely intellectual matters, Democritus ranged over epistemology, physics, mathematics, geography, botany, agriculture, painting, and the other special sciences and arts. An admirer of Democritus and an appreciative critic of Empedocles, Aristotle constructed an encyclopedic system, as if he had deliberately set out to synthesize and mediate every rival school in existence.

Against Isocrates and the new schools of rhetoric, Aristotle provides a philosophically grounded theory of rhetoric and of literature; against the lifestyle schools and debaters over value, he provides a systematic analysis of ethical doctrine as well as his own deliberately middle-of-the-road defense of conventionality and moderation. He systematizes logic and metaphysics in consciousness of the achievements of all existing schools, and thereby goes beyond them in reflexive abstraction. Even the qualitative theory of music put forward by his follower Aristoxenus is aimed at undercutting the rival doctrine of the Pythagoreans based on numerical proportion (*DSB,* 1981: 1:281).

Aristotle's creativity lay in finding a device for synthesis, and thereby for reducing the surfeit of contending schools of his day. The most important result was his fourfold classification of causes as material, formal, efficient, and final, and his distinctions of potency and act, substance and accident. These classifications intermesh. The material cause (identified with substance) is potential; formal, efficient, and final causes are actual. With these tools Aristotle unraveled the conundrums of the Eleatics and Heracliteans, mediated between Platonic forms and the world of the senses, and rejected the relativists as propounders of category mistakes. These were still hot contemporary debates at a time, when the Megarians were pushing pre-Socratic paradoxes about the illogicality of change, and Cynics and Skeptics were denying the possibility of both knowledge and ethical judgment. Aristotle rescued both Being and change with his analytical distinctions; found a place for *nous,* thought, in the material universe by distinguishing potential and actual components of mind; and answered the debate over the natural or merely customary nature of virtue by distinguishing a natural potential for doing good from its actualization in socially acquired habits.

Aristotle seems to have been acutely aware of the growing presence of a purely grammatical approach in the newly popular schools of rhetoric. Whereas Isocrates and his followers taught language merely as technique, Aristotle was at pains to coordinate the basic categories of the newly emerging systematic grammar with his philosophical categories. The recently distinguished parts of speech, nouns and adjectives, and the syntactical relations of subject and predicate, are coordinated with his metaphysical distinctions: substance and accident, species and genus, and thus with potency and act, and with the universal metaphysics of causality. Aristotle's corpus is not only comprehensive but architectonic. It is an exemplar of the synthesizing mode at its most impressive.

His strategy paid off, in both the short and the long run. Most of the rival schools collapsed, leaving the Aristoteleans the field—but only part of it, owing to the law of small numbers. His conceptual armory, forged in the most intense period of intellectual maneuver that Western philosophy was to see for dozens of generations, was to prove potent in battles far removed from Aristotle's own time. But the very process of reducing the number of schools transformed the field on which the Peripatos stood, and shifted its own position away from Aristotle's hard-wrought synthesis.

The Hellenistic Realignment of Positions

Around 300 B.C.E. we note an abrupt shift in the entire field. As virtually all of the older schools and lineages died out, two new major organizations were founded out of their intellectual remains.[19] While the Epicureans and Stoics made their appearance, the two remaining older schools, the Academics and Peripetetics, shifted their own grounds in intellectual space: the Aristoteleans to materialism and empirical science, the Academics to skepticism.

Epicurus took the atomism of the Abdera school and the hedonism of the Cyrenaics to formulate a thoroughly materialist doctrine in theology, physics, psychology, epistemology, and ethics, explicitly paralleling Aristotle's in synthetic style while rejecting it in substance (Rist, 1972: ix). The Epicurean school simultaneously moved into the space left by the demise of the lifestyle movements. This organization resembled a religious community (although pointedly rejecting any connection with traditional deities), practicing a collective life supported by the goods of its members, and centered on quasi-religious ceremonies in honor of the founder (Frischer, 1982: 38–86). To take over the ideas and practices of an existing intellectual faction is to risk losing one's identity in theirs; but to take over their ideas after they are dead is both safe and profitable. Epicurus established his independent identity by attacking his Democritean teacher Nausiphanes and criticizing the Abderan tradition to the extent of denying that Leucippus even existed. His appropriation of their capital sealed their fate.

Zeno of Citium in founding the Stoics reached far back for a distinctive collection of intellectual forebears: Heraclitus for a cosmology of change (including such specific doctrines as the periodic extinction of the world by fire); Antisthenes' ethical exemplar Heracles as emblem of the conquest of pain; the *logos* doctrine of a transcendent world order. Initially the Stoics incorporated something of Cynic extremism, and aroused a good deal of scandal with their tolerance of incest and their doctrine of replacing the family with a community of men with women in common (Bryant, 1996: 439). This unconventionality gave way within another generation, and by the time of Chrysippus, the Stoics had taken the opposite space from the Epicureans (and their predecessors in this respect, the morally anti-conventional Cyrenaics and Cynics) with respect to externals of lifestyle. Doing one's ethical duty in social obligations was a doctrine that appealed to the religiously secularized upper class, and gave the Stoics a broad market base as a respectable form of education.

The Stoics captured the middle ground of public opinion about religion. They declared temples superfluous because man's intellect is a portion of the divine substance, and the true temple is the mind. Zeno and Chrysippus rejected the anthropomorphic gods but allowed them as symbolic (Dodds, 1951: 238–240). In a larger perspective, the Stoics and Epicureans were competing over the same rationalistic religious space; the Epicureans too allowed that the gods existed, but declared that they, like everything else, were composed of material atoms. This was in effect a defensive concession to popular religion, which placed legal penalties on outright atheism in places such as Athens during these centuries. But the two schools were at pains to differentiate themselves within this space, the Stoics taking a pantheist line, the Epicureans the view that the gods existed concretely, but that they had nothing to do with human affairs, living in remote places in the void. The rival schools also carried on the broad consensus of the preceding period that virtue resides in detachment, while disputing the nuances of *apatheia* (freedom from passion) and *ataraxeia* (tranquillity of spirit). Underlying this dispute was a real difference in lifestyle orientation: the Epicureans withdrawing socially to achieve harmony through contemplation, the Stoics interpreting the ideal condition as an inner equanimity with which the wise man carries out his worldly duties.

The shift to Hellenistic philosophy is usually attributed to changing external conditions. A long-standing interpretation calls it a failure of nerve, a loss of the acute intellectual edge of Plato and Aristotle's generations, and more generally the falling off into overripeness which in art history makes the very term "Hellenistic" a synonym for post-creative decadence. But in fact, periods of peak artistic creativity are not closely correlated with such periods in philosophy, as is clear from a generation-by-generation comparison in Greece, China, medieval through modern Europe, and elsewhere. The notion of an all-encompassing zeitgeist, whether golden or decadent, will not get us very far. A more explicitly sociological argument by Joseph Bryant (1996) attributes the new contents of Stoic and Epicurean philosophies to the Macedonian conquest of the 330s, which destroyed the city-state democracies and replaced their citizen armies with mercenaries. If philosophy flourished in Athens because public debate encouraged the skills of argument and focused on concepts of public law and civic virtue (an argument also of Lloyd, 1990), the destruction of those external conditions is responsible for the shift to privatized ethics, a withdrawal from the ideal of citizen participation.

What we miss here is the fact that the entire field of intellectual oppositions shifted at this time. Aristotelean science, and the technical argument of Academic skepticism (and Stoic logic as well), were equally part of the Hellenistic cultural field. The timing, too, is not quite right. Bryant's thesis works best not for the Stoic and Epicurean schools but for their predecessors in the lifestyle movements of the previous three generations, especially the Cynics and Cyrenaics. The content of their doctrines is that of non-citizens, freed of military, family, and civic obligations. That describes well these men without a city, some of them exiles (such as Diogenes, from far-off Sinope on the Black Sea), moving from place to place with little or no means of support. They survived by a display of contempt for the conventional virtues, an *épater le bourgeois* which appealed to a sufficient audience of onlookers. And the very existence of this audience depended on the fact that an intellectual community was now well established, carrying on a distinctive forum of debate whose contents changed across the generations.

Most of the shift in ideas that followed the Macedonian conquest was produced not by change in the political context but by the law of small numbers. It was a time of great strain within the intellectual community. The competition among too large a number of schools and factions meant that most of them could not survive in the long run; the successful schools were those which seized on the weak ones, to amalgamate their doctrines into a few workable mixes. Aristotle had originated this maneuver, bringing together many of the finest available materials and crowning them with his synthesizing creativity. Epicurus acquired what was probably the most powerful doctrine still left without a strong base, that of the atomists, who heretofore had no well-supported material organization in the Athenian metropolis. Plato's Academy had early drawn on a wide range of materials, and was the best positioned of the older schools, both materially and in intellectual turf, to survive in the time of rival syncretisms. The Stoics, last to appear, took an uneven grab bag of leftovers. Their stance was to compromise among all the important positions. This left them with inconsistencies, such as between their materialist physics and cosmology and their immaterialist religious strains, or between their original Cynic rigorism and their emphasis on conventional duties.[20]

Here organizational strength made a virtue out of intellectual weakness. A school stays alive by its controversies, and the Stoics attracted much attention and produced a series of creative thinkers through the next two centuries. Immediately after Zeno, the school almost broke apart in internal controversies, between the religious emphasis of Cleanthes (successor ca. 262–232 B.C.E.) and an extreme faction of logical rigorists led by Ariston of Chios (Reale, 1985: 216, 320, 417). The inconsistencies of Stoic doctrine were vigorously pointed out by rivals, the Academics in particular. The result was not the destruction of Stoicism but its vitality. Chrysippus, "the second founder," carried out an impressive systematization on all fronts (unfortunately all subsequently lost), deriving directly from his confrontation with the Academic Arcesilaus.

The opposing schools shifted their intellectual contents together, their ideas driven by underlying realignment of positions under the law of small numbers. The Academy repudiated the Idealism and mathematics-centeredness of the doctrine of Forms, and took over the stance of skepticism; the Peripatos abandoned Aristotle's carefully wrought compromise with Platonism and moved toward materialism and empirical science. The Aristoteleans under Theophrastus had already criticized the conception of an unmoved Mover outside the world; the third *scholarch,* Strato (ca. 287–268 B.C.E.), allowed only immanent forces of weight and motion, and excluded final causes (*DSB,* 1981: 13:91–95; Reale, 1985: 103–105). Even the soul, he said, has no transcendent or immortal qualities; mental activity is the movement of the breath *(pneuma).*

The Aristoteleans took this turn as a network connected with the outpouring of scientific activity at Alexandria. Through one of the ironic reversals characteristic of intellectual conflict, the Aristotelean-Alexandrian camp ended up with the leadership in mathematics as well, even though Aristotle himself had downplayed the role of mathematics as part of his struggle against that faction in the Academy. The Academy's shift to skepticism left mathematics adrift to be picked up by whoever wanted it. Epicurus, however, had polemicized against mathematics, even throwing out Democritus' considerable advances, probably to keep himself at the opposite pole from the idealist camp; and the Stoics had inherited the qualitative and teleological theme which had played a role in Aristotle's original formulations. The connection to mathematics and natural science at Alexandria proved an easy alliance for the Aristoteleans, especially in the case of astronomy. In this orbit were produced Euclid's systematization of geometry (ca. 300 B.C.E.), building on the Aristotelean and Stoic methodology of definitions, postulates, and common notions; the mathematics of Eratosthenes (who headed the Library ca. 234) and of Archimedes;[21] the heliocentric astronomy of Aristarchus of Samos (ca. 270); and the mechanics of Ctesibus and others. In addition, the Hippocratic medical schools of Cos and Cnidus migrated to Alexandria at this time, where connections were kept up in medical science with the Aristoteleans, especially through Erasistratus;[22] Herophilus the anatomist was directly connected with Strato's circle. This scientific tradition lasted down through Hipparchus' astronomy in the next century.

There was little in the external conditions of life of the Hellenistic period that turned thought in the direction of natural science. The explanation lies in competitive forces internal to the intellectual field. The Aristoteleans were moving in response to the popularity of the two new schools—the Epicureans' successful championing of materialism and the Stoics' eclectic mix—and to the Academics' shift on the other side. It was safe to poach on Epicurean grounds, for there was no danger of losing identity with them, and the Aristoteleans were already leaning in a materialist direction because of their conflict within the Academy. The Stoics probably tipped the balance toward a materialistic extreme, for they had already usurped a middle position combining a material world with a ruling spiritual form, the cosmic soul. The Aristoteleans' attack on the notion of an immortal soul, and their reduction of soul to material *pneuma*, which seems directed against the Stoics, propelled them into the materialist corner.

The Academy during this time underwent a paradigm shift amounting to revolution. Under Arcesilaus, a generation after Strato and a contemporary of Cleanthes at the Stoa, the Academics threw off their idealist metaphysics and epistemology and adopted skepticism. The way was prepared structurally by the disappearance of the Skeptic lineage after Timon (Arcesilaus himself is the last known tie; see Figure 3.4), and the collapse of the Megarian school. The Megarians, defending the Eleatic thesis and attacking all forms of pluralism, including the Platonic forms (Reale, 1985: 50–53), had been, so to speak, the "right wing" of the philosophical world, with the Platonists occupying a slightly more moderate position. The Epicureans represented the "far left" of materialism, with the Stoics in the compromise position at the center, and the various dropout positions (Cynics, Skeptics, later Cyrenaics) taking a deliberate tangent off from the center with a "plague on all houses" stance. In the realignment of schools, the anti-intellectual positions disappeared, though their moral force was appropriated by the Epicureans. The Aristoteleans switched from a moderate position, a little to the "left" of the Platonists, to the extreme materialist left—a move which I judge to have been in response to the competition from Stoics in the center.

Arcesilaus' skepticism appropriated a tool that had formerly been used on the far "right" and among the dropouts standing above all the schools. Now it was being used as a stance within the intellectual field itself rather than to uphold a lifestyle movement as Pyrrho and Timon had done. Its focus of attention was not to defend a positive doctrine, as in the case of the Megarians' Eleatic metaphysics, but to attack the technical doctrines of the Stoics. A purely intellectual skepticism of this sort is parasitical on a strong opponent. The revolution of the Academy, like that of the Peripatos, indicates just how dominating a presence the Stoa had become.

The pre-reformed Academy had staked out a religious claim that the Stoics directly challenged. Plato in his late work the *Laws* was advocating worship of heavenly bodies, with the sun as object of a compulsory state cult. Speusippus and Xenocrates formulated a philosophical religion which foreshadowed the Neoplatonism of five centuries later. Numbers were worshiped as a hierarchy of existence culminating in the One of pure Being (*DSB*, 1981: 14:535; Dillon, 1977: 11–38). The Academy wavered over the introduction of Babylonian star worship as an astronomical religion; other early *scholarchs*—including Xenocrates' successor Polemon, who was one of Zeno's early teachers—tried out ethical preaching, and attempted to mediate the ethical debates among the older Cynics and Cyrenaics and the new Epicureans and Stoics. Where Academic religion was esoteric, the Stoic school acquired a much more successful base in popular religion, with the doctrine of the divine world-soul and its worship in the temple of the mind, a doctrine which made room for participating simultaneously in public worship as an outward symbol. Zeno's successor Cleanthes, Arcesilaus' contemporary, was especially known for his piety and his hymns.

Whereas Xenocrates had eliminated the dialectical element in Plato in favor of the religious, the new skeptical Academy reversed the emphasis. This in effect signaled a decision not to contest the Stoics' conquest of their religious ground, but to attack them for purely intellectual adequacy. Arcesilaus ended the Academy's wavering with a forceful shift to negative skepticism, elaborated at a high level of technical sophistication. In religious questions its stance became a polemical agnosticism.

Although we have lost most direct record of these generations, the battle among rival Hellenistic schools was fruitful for a good deal of development in philosophy. Later generations of Academics and Stoics lived in symbiosis, posing challenges for each other. Chrysippus, who deserted his teacher Arcesilaus, reformed Stoic metaphysics and promoted an innovative logic. Building on the first school of logicians, the now defunct Megarians, Chrysippus broadened logic far beyond Aristotle's logic of syllogisms to a theory of conditional and other complex propositions, providing formal proofs adumbrating modern

European logic.[23] Chrysippus' monistic system, which appropriated for Stoicism elements of the now disused Platonic metaphysics, was a springboard for Carneades' sharpening of skepticism with a doctrine of probabilities; and this in turn spurred the reformulations of Stoic physics and epistemology by Panaetius and Posidonius. Pupils crossed over between the schools—Zeno, Arcesilaus, Chrysippus, and Carneades among them—honing the edge of debate across the generations.

The Roman Base and the Second Realignment

The material bases of the entire philosophical attention space drastically changed when geopolitical triumph made Roman patronage the arbiter of intellectual life. The balance of power among the kingdoms and military leagues that had divided Alexander's empire was gradually brought into the Roman protectorate; by 86 B.C.E., when Athens was sacked by a Roman army, conquest was complete. Additional proof that the doctrines of the opposing schools were keyed to one another is provided by the intellectual realignment which occurred when their organizations collapsed between 100 and 50 B.C.E. This is one of those places in history where the plate tectonics of social life slip, and the organizational bases of the older mentalities go down in the temblor. After 50 B.C.E. there are no more long-lasting philosophical schools, in the sense of propertied organizations belonging to the teachers of a particular doctrine. There remain individual teachers, sometimes constituting chains of leading figures. But such organizations as might have existed were very short-lived.[24]

In the transition to the Roman base comes an outburst of innovation, which then yields to a different way of intellectual life (see Figure 3.5). Stoicism receives a new system with Posidonius, Epicureanism its classic formulation in Lucretius. Aristoteleanism loses its independence from Platonic Idealism, while Platonism repudiates skepticism and goes back to an emanationist religious ontology, in syncretism with a revived neo-Pythagorean numerology. Skepticism, set adrift by the counterrevolution in the Platonic school, is picked up as the medical schools undergo their own doctrinal realignment, and receives its classic formulation at the hands of Aenesidemus.

In the generation when the Athenian schools disappeared, there was a flurry of innovation at the school of Stoicism at Rhodes, the last intellectual center outside Roman hegemony. Posidonius overthrew Chrysippus' monism, substituting a duality of matter and reason bridged by mathematical forms, and defending Stoic epistemology against Carneades' skeptical attacks on the uncertainty of sense perception by holding that reason is a criterion of truth independent of the senses (*EP*, 1967: 6:413–414). Posidonius followed the path

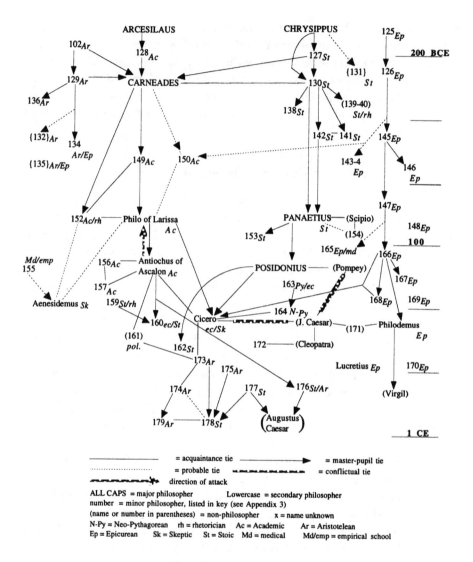

FIGURE 3.5. REALIGNMENT OF SCHOOLS IN THE ROMAN
CONQUEST, 200 B.C.E.–1 C.E.

of synthesis, as if picking up doctrines from the wreck of the other schools,
incorporating the mathematics, astronomy, and geography of Eratosthenes and
Hipparchus, and contributing scientific advances of his own (*DSB*, 1981:
11:103–105). The reformed Stoicism of Posidonius, although famous in his
day, did not survive much past his lifetime, nor did his school at Rhodes; the
later Roman Stoics went back to preaching a crude amalgam of doctrines—

Heraclitean fire, world-soul—that had been the object of so much refinement under Academic attack.

The other schools went through equally large doctrinal shifts. The Aristoteleans, who were already fading from intellectual prominence in the previous century, took the typical path of a weakening position and were becoming eclectic, wavering toward Epicureanism and Pythagoreanism. By the time Aristotelean doctrines came into Rome around 70 B.C.E., they were no longer carried by members of the Peripatetic school but by freelance scholars such as Tyrannio and Andronicus of Rhodes (*CHLG*, 1967: 112–115; Guthrie, 1961–1982: 6:60–61). The materialism of the intervening period was forgotten, and Aristotle's texts were now seen as a modification of the Platonic doctrine of Forms.

As the maneuvers of the past two centuries became unraveled, the Academy again went through a revolution. Philo of Larissa (ca. 110 B.C.E.) had already softened the skeptical stance to fallibilism, emphasizing the difficulty of knowing but upholding the goal of knowledge (Tarrant, 1985: 3, 54–57). This might be regarded as a concession to lay audiences, since a pure skepticism is intellectually respectable only within a well-buffered intellectual community, which was now collapsing. Philo was now dependent on the patronage of Romans, who had been shocked by Carneades' famous speeches while on an embassy in 155 B.C.E., when he defended justice one day and attacked it the next. Philo's pupil and successor Antiochus of Ascalon, who had high-ranking Roman sponsorship, went still further, to proclaim belief in the sage who reaches full truth with unerring certainty. Antiochus attacked not only all-out skepticism but also the moderated forms of probabilism and fallibilism upheld by his predecessors in the Academy. His religious turn evoked protest among the more traditional members of the skeptical Academy. The controversy appears to have been responsible for the major creative development of the Roman transition.

Skepticism has the peculiarity of acting as a meta-school above the clash of positions in intellectual space, and thus has a special appropriateness for times when intellectual lines are chaotic. As the factions of Roman philosophy settled down into syncretism, skepticism became their constant accompaniment. It also acquired a distinctive material base within the medical schools, which now took a heightened organizational significance as organized philosophical training lapsed.

Both realignments of the philosophical schools—the Hellenistic realignment around 300 and the Roman realignment after 100—coincided with a rearrangement of medical schools. Around 300–250—which is to say, at the time of the first great realignment in Hellenistic philosophy—the Empiricist physicians had appeared (Frede, 1987: 236–239, 243–260). Empiricists stressed the value of practical experience exclusively, against the philosophically oriented medical schools of the day, based variously on Empedocles, perhaps on other pre-Socratics, on Democritean atomism, and more recently on Peripatetic doctrines and associated anatomical researches. Empiricists adopted somewhat of a skeptical stance in taking a plague on all houses approach to divergent theories, but their main contention was not itself a thoroughly skeptical epistemology but rather the knowability of the observable and the unknowability of the unobservables posited by philosophical-medical theories. As the older philosophical factions died out, so did their medical branches, and they were replaced by current fashions in the philosophical field. Epicurean atomism made its first big impact at Rome with the popular medical lectures of Asclepiades of Bythynia (ca. 100 B.C.E.); and the Pneumatist school of medicine appeared about the same time as the result of Posidonius' innovations in Stoic philosophy.

As the Athenian philosophical schools collapsed in the next generation, the medical schools realigned. A new faction, the Methodists, challenged both the Rationalists (i.e., all the older philosophical and physical doctrines) and the Empiricists, proposing a middle position claiming that observations of dilation and constriction provide a basis for medical practice. This transformation of the medical turf seems to have been connected to the association, from this time forward, of the Empiricists with skepticism in philosophy. The Empiricist physician Heraclides of Tarentum (ca. 100 B.C.E.) was perhaps the teacher of Aenesidemus (Frede, 1987: 251–252). Aenesidemus went beyond the Academic Philo's fallibilism to systematize the famous tropes, and rejected as dogmatic even the claim to know nothing or to know probabilistically. Michael Frede (1987: 249; cf. 218–222) goes so far as to propose that "Pyrrhonian skepticism" was invented at this time and retrospectively attributed to a famous founder.[25] Aenesidemus' position became a minority voice within philosophy over the next two centuries; the Academy had given up any part of the skeptical stance, and no other faction picked it up, as syncretism of positive doctrines became the order of the day. Skepticism was to have one last flourish of attention with Sextus Empiricus, in the intense fractionation of positions that peaked around 150–200 C.E., just as the basis of intellectual life began to shift again.

One mystery remains. Every philosophical school had undergone repeated revolutions through these series of realignments, with one exception: the Epicureans. How did the Epicureans remain unchanging in doctrine despite all this competition and organizational shift? One might also wonder how intellectuals can keep up any eminence at all by merely repeating an inherited position. But Epicureans had a series of fairly well known spokesmen for two hundred years, who wrote numerous books (Reale, 1985: 183–184). Their intellectual activity was sustained by applying their doctrine to current topics in the special sciences, and by carrying on polemics against Stoics and Academics. These activities were remarkable for the steadiness of the battle lines, having little or no effect on either Epicurean doctrine or their opponents, nor contributing much to the development of the special sciences.

One answer is that the Epicureans were organizationally more insulated than the other schools as a lifestyle community principally concerned with ritual devotion by lay followers. Epicureans seem to have had little contact with the networks of the intellectual world, judging from the infrequency of ties or crossovers to other schools (see Figures 3.4 and 3.5). It was well known in antiquity that unlike in other schools, persons who joined the Epicureans never left, giving rise to the famous jibe that they were like eunuchs in this respect (D.L., 1925: 4:43).[26] But the lack of intellectual change remains a puzzle; their commitment to a lifestyle of withdrawal and non-intellectual contemplation is paralleled by other organizations elsewhere, such as Buddhism, which nevertheless developed an active intellectual sector which got swept up in the dynamics of doctrinal change.

The stagnation of Epicurean doctrine is attributable principally to the lineup of factions across the intellectual field. The Epicureans anchored the field as the most extreme doctrine, materialism. It was the positions nearer the center that rearranged their alliances in the maneuvers over intellectual turf. One might question why the opposite extreme on the idealist side did not remain firm; here the answer seems to be that the holders of that side—at one time the Megarians with their Eleatic principle, Eudoxus' school of mathematical Idealism, the early Platonists—were nevertheless flanked by religious positions in the popular culture, including astrology, star worship, the mystery cults. The transcendental-immaterialist side of the field was more crowded than the materialist end. The Epicureans early got hold of a coherent statement of extreme materialism and were subject to no competitive pressures to change it. Although their slot was never a highly popular one, it had a sufficiently steady clientele, and their lack of great size kept them from the danger of fragmenting with success which characterizes the law of small numbers.

Within this general stability, the Epicureans show some perturbation at just the time one might expect: the period of organizational transition, when the school of Athens became defunct and intellectual life moved into the orbit of Roman patronage. The upheaval in the organizational basis of intellectual life affected Epicureanism as well. Zeno of Sidon, perhaps the last Epicurean *scholarch* at Athens (166 in Figure 3.5), criticized the Stoic epistemology and went on to develop a philosophy of mathematics, based on the derivation of all knowledge from experience (*DSB*, 1981: 14:612). This was an innovation in Epicurean doctrine, since Epicurus had pointedly disdained mathematics.

Zeno of Sidon also criticized Euclid (who was associated with the Aristoteleans at Alexandria) and implied the possibility of a non-Euclidean geometry.

In the next generation, Zeno's pupil Philodemus was at Naples, where for a brief period Epicureanism received patronage from eminent Romans, including the circle of Julius Caesar. There was even something of a split in the Epicurean ranks at this time—the kind of thing one usually sees in a period of success, as opportunities open up—with Philodemus debating other Epicureans over theories of logic and mathematics (Rawson, 1985: 58–59, 295–296; Windelband, [1892] 1901: 195). There was even a move in the direction of a theory of induction, a significant break in the logic of antiquity. In this same period Lucretius set forth his—strictly orthodox—statement of classical Epicureanism, apparently in a different circle than Philodemus'.[27] The opening for Epicurean popularity was brief; by the time of Augustus, a political crackdown on religious unorthodoxy had driven the Epicureans out of Rome, and we see no more creativity from them through the end of antiquity.

Formal Support in the Roman Period

What stars there are in philosophical life are in the transition, when intellectual capital is readapted to the upheaval in its institutional base. Here we find Posidonius, Aenesidemus, Lucretius, Cicero who acted as the broker for introducing Greek ideas into Rome. For the next half-dozen generations, intellectual life settled into a routine. There were contending positions, to be sure, but the well-known names are not very original by the standards of what went before, reformulators of doctrines with a backwards-looking bent, typically syncretizing positions by taking off the sharp edge of critical acuteness. Beneath this popularistic syncretism lies a new kind of material base.

After the organized schools had broken up, unorganized movements reappeared. Many authors described themselves as "Pythagoreans"; but although there had been an effort to revive a political movement at Rome under that name (led by Cicero's friend Nigidius Figulus around 50 B.C.E.), it is likely that the connection was merely figurative. Some positions retained the familiar labels—Platonist, Aristotelean, Stoic—but their proponents were now freelancers rather than organizational members.[28] Correspondingly, they were less trammeled in adhering to a pure line of doctrine. The Cynic style reappears for several generations after 100 C.E., with an outpouring of wandering street preachers, often blending showmanship and magic; they made up part of the movement of commercial teachers of rhetoric, on the one hand, as well as occultist movements such as Gnosticism, on the other, characteristic of that age (EP, 1967: 2:284–285; Hadas, 1950: 274–278, 287–290). The eclecticism of the Roman period was due in part to the lack of solid organizational backbone for distinctive network lineages.

A type of formal position was later established, but these were positions which the philosophers themselves did not control, and which did not constitute schools in the organizational sense. In the period from 250 to 500 C.E., there were municipal chairs of philosophy at Athens, Alexandria, and (after 330) Constantinople. These were filled and paid for by the municipal authorities, occasionally by the emperor (*CHLG*, 1967: 274). Usually there was one chair, occasionally two, for a Platonist and an Aristotelean. The origins of this practice seem to go back to 176 C.E., when Marcus Aurelius established four chairs at Athens, for Platonic, Aristotelean, Stoic, and Epicurean philosophy, with an annual salary of 10,000 drachmas (Dillon, 1977: 233).[29] The variety of chairs dwindled down to the first two schools, and eventually only to Platonists; we know of no more living exponents of Epicureanism anywhere after about 200 C.E. or of Stoicism after 260 (*DSB*, 1981: 14:606).

For the most part, incumbents of these municipal chairs were undistinguished. Formal control by lay authorities was not conducive to intellectual innovation, a situation paralleling the performance of the official Preceptors of the Han dynasty. The number of positions was small and fixed. The Imperial Academy at Constantinople, enlarged by the emperor Theodosius II in 425, had some 31 chairs, all but one of them in grammar and rhetoric, and these were granted a monopoly on teaching in the city (Jones, [1964] 1986: 999; *CHLG*, 1967: 483–484). Private schools were allowed alongside the municipal ones; most positions, both official and private, were in grammar and rhetoric, not philosophy. Many of the philosophers of later antiquity, from Apuleius and Herodes Atticus (ca. 150) onwards, were rhetoricians by profession; this was particularly true of the Christian philosophers, especially before their conversions. Augustine, trained in the famous rhetoric school at Carthage (where Apuleius had studied two hundred years before) acquired the important position of municipal professor of rhetoric at Milan; since this was the capital city, his duties included delivering official panegyrics on the emperor and consuls each year (Brown, 1967: 69). This was also the weakness of such positions: florid verbal demonstrations in an archaizing style were valued over acuteness judged by an intellectual community.

The big stimulus to intellectual life in later antiquity was not these municipal lectureships but the autonomous organization of the growing Christian Church. This new kind of organization underlay the shift to sharper doctrinal stances in late antiquity, provoking greater definition on all sides of the oppositional space. The impetus was not the new religious movements per se. The Gnostic movements which spread at the same time as early Christianity overlapped the milieu of freelance intellectuals, and had much the same syncretizing style. By 200 C.E., the training of Christian priests became increasingly formalized, and Christian intellectuals appeared, marking out their distinctive stance amid the older philosophies. Formally organized pagan schools began to revive in opposition. Plotinus moved from Alexandria, where he had been part of a network including Christian philosophers, to teach at Rome under aristocratic patronage, and attempted unsuccessfully to establish a utopian community, called Platonopolis, in Campania (south of Rome) for his followers; his disciple Porphyry attempted to maintain the school, but was away from Rome (perhaps back in Egypt or Syria) a good deal in his later years (*CHLG*, 1967: 202, 284). The later Neoplatonists, from Iamblichus to Proclus, show every sign of attempting to organize their own religion as a pagan counterpoint to Christianity, primarily in Syria and Asia Minor (especially Pergamum).

When Christianity became the state religion, pagan philosophers made a concerted effort to revive at least one of the old schools. In the generations around 400 C.E., the Platonic school reappeared as an institution at Athens (Glucker, 1978: 153–158, 306–315). With this new Athenian base, Neoplatonism, which after the end of Plotinus' Roman school had been propagated largely as an occultist movement, once again developed as systematic philosophy, leading up to the major synthesis of Proclus, *scholarch* around 450. At Alexandria, too, Neoplatonism was introduced at about the same time (*CHLG*, 1967: 314–315). There were formal successions of *scholarchs* down through 529, when Justinian banned pagan philosophy in the empire. The Alexandrian philosophers converted to Christianity before the Athenians, who held out to the bitter end.

Syncretisms in Time of Organizational Weakness

Strong positions subdivide, weak positions combine: this is the inner dynamic of intellectual politics. For about 10 generations after the collapse of the Athenian schools, the organizational basis of intellectual life was in disarray. It would become firmly reshaped only with the consolidation of the Christian Church and its bid for power around 250, just at the time when a pagan united front emerged around the Neoplatonism of Plotinus. Let us briefly view the pattern of the intervening centuries.

The doctrines of all existing schools had undergone changes at the time of the organizational collapse, even (in their limited range) the Epicureans. Some version of all the major positions survived, but now without self-confidence; instead of polemical attacks and staunch defenses, the tendency was to syncretize (see Figure 3.6). There was a telltale sign already at the time of Philo of Larissa (ca. 110 B.C.E.), who started the shift away from the skeptical Academy and also began the migration of philosophers to Rome. Philo reconciled philosophy and rhetoric (Rawson, 1985: 146), a seemingly innocuous step, but one which ended a long-standing rivalry. Antagonism between the two learned professions went back to the opposition between the types of

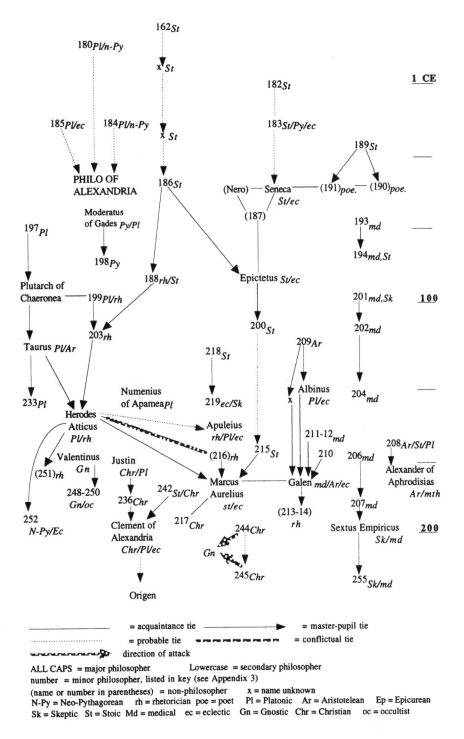

FIGURE 3.6. SYNCRETISMS AND SKEPTICISM, 1–200 C.E.

schools founded by Plato and Isocrates, and before that to the struggle of Socrates (or the image of Socrates projected by Plato) against the Sophists. Philosophers were seeking a new material base. The market for rhetoricians to train orators and lawyers would become the prime support of intellectual life during the Roman period.[30] This alliance of philosophy and rhetoric was to be a fateful one for subsequent thought, since it tended to make philosophical doctrines merely part of the rhetorician's bag of tricks. The resulting tendency toward eclecticism was especially prominent during the "Second Sophistic" of the 100s C.E., when public displays of flowery rhetoric were a prominent form of public entertainment.

On the philosophical side, the overwhelming tendency was toward syncretism. The philosophical schools in their own right were weak and lacking firm organizational bases, and they tended to huddle together for support. The Academy no longer existed as an organization; instead we find free-floating Platonists, whose main activity was to syncretize some version of the earlier doctrines (i.e., from Plato through Xenocrates) with the old rivals. Aristotelean doctrines were now up for grabs. The original texts had been recovered and publicized, with no organized school to impose an orthodoxy upon them or to sustain the materialist science of the later Peripatos. Several versions of Aristotle were current; one of these amalgamated Aristotle with Plato into a dualism of ideas (forms) plus matter, with mathematics (taken as equivalent to the psychic level of the soul) as an intermediary between them. Another form of syncretism combined Plato's dialogues with an ontological interpretation of Aristotle's logic; this was pursued especially by the Platonic teachers such as Apuleius at Athens and Albinus at Pergamum in the 100s C.E. (*CHLG,* 1967: 64, 70).

Yet another direction was to syncretize Plato with Stoicism. Antiochus of Ascalon had initiated this move from enmity to alliance, proclaiming Platonic knowledge the possession of a Stoic-like sage. Seneca taught a Platonizing Stoicism as part of his all-around syncretizing; he also frequently cited the Stoics' old foil Epicurus in support of Stoic ethical doctrines, and drew on popular Cynic moralizing. Marcus Aurelius presented Stoicism as a grab bag, with little care for the incompatibility of different metaphysical strands and an overwhelming emphasis on a moral stance. By the next century, Stoicism no longer had a distinctive identity and gradually disappeared.

The main intellectual action at this time consisted in positions pro and con syncretisms of various sorts. Numenius of Apamea (ca. 150 C.E.) claimed that Plato and Socrates were Pythagoreans, that the Stoics derived their philosophy from the Academy, and that Aristotle's philosophy had nothing to do with Plato's (*CHLG,* 1967: 90, 96). Other Platonists during the century were anti-Aristotelean but pro-Stoic, while yet others, such as Calvenus Taurus, were pro-Aristotle and anti-Stoic (Dillon, 1977: 265; *CHLG*, 1967: 73–83). Some of these syncretisms provoked opposition and led to restatement of the more pointed doctrines. The famous Herodes Atticus polemicized against the syncretism of Plato with other doctrines. Lucian of Samosata, a rhetor, philosopher, and popular writer who settled in Athens around 150, made fun of Platonists, Stoics, Cynics, and Skeptics alike, especially on the grounds of encouraging superstition, and stood up for the materialist position of the Epicureans (*EP*, 1967: 5:98–99).

The last notable Skeptic, Sextus Empiricus, appears in this context (ca. 200). Skepticism was a long-standing weapon in the dispute between medical theorists, and Sextus came from an empiric medical lineage in Asia Minor (and probably Alexandria), though he was known primarily at Rome. He thus moved in the same circles as his near-contemporary Galen (fl. 160–190), the last great constructive medical theorist. Whereas Galen was a synthesizer of doctrines, Sextus took up the rival stance of criticizing them all, and Galen's medical theories in particular. Both Galen and Sextus seem to have spoken primarily to lay audiences and ranged much more widely than medicine. Galen defended Aristotelean logic and interpreted the works of Chrysippus and Epicurus, while his synthesis reached out to reconcile Plato with the Hippocratic medical doctrine of the four humors (*DSB*, 1981: 5:227–237; Frede, 1987: 279–298). Galen was operating in the world of the Second Sophistic, where public lectures and debates in a popular style provided the material basis for intellectual careers, and even medical professionals got their patronage not primarily through practice but through their impressiveness in exposition. As if to show off his erudition, Sextus criticized all the arts and professions as well as all intellectual positions; his *Adversus Mathematicos* piles on a veritable overkill of skeptical arguments. As Figure 3.6 shows (see also unconnected persons listed in the key), the intellectual world around 150–200 C.E. was crowded with diverse positions, a situation which provided a slot for skepticism.

This situation changed rapidly in the next century. The battle lines became overwhelmingly aligned with religious positions, and both materialism and skepticism disappeared as a grand pagan coalition formed against Christianity.

The Stimulus of Religious Polarization

In late antiquity, religion triumphed over secular philosophy. Nevertheless, it included abstract philosophy of much greater long-term significance than anything in the Roman period between the collapse of the Greek schools around 100 B.C.E. and the eminence of Christianity after 250 C.E.: the work of Plotinus, Augustine, and a new level of rationalized theology including formal proofs of

God. Again, creativity was connected to the shift to a new organizational base. The organization of Christianity made it victorious amid the outpouring of new religious movements, for it was a centrally organized church, whereas the others were not. Its incipient rational-legal administration fostered abstract intellectual activity, and its challenge to the old philosophical networks produced the oppositions that fostered a burst of creativity on both sides of the divide.

Early Christianity formed around 30 C.E. in Palestine and spread rapidly in the Jewish diaspora communities of Syria, Asia Minor, and the eastern Mediterranean over the next two generations. It remained particularistic in its cosmology and its ethics of salvation. Other branches of the anti-Talmudic reform movements within Judaism, from which Christianity sprang, pushed Hebrew monotheism into syncretism with Greek philosophy. The most successful figure along this line was Philo of Alexandria (fl. ca. 25–50 C.E.), a contemporary of Jesus and Saint Paul, who seems to have known nothing of the Christian movement, and drew only on the Old Testament circulating in Greek within the diaspora communities. Philo assumed that the Greek philosophers were indebted to the Pentateuch, identified Yahweh with Zeus, and interpreted the cosmology of Genesis allegorically (*CHLG*, 1967: 137–157). Philo pushed a grand syncretism among Platonism, Pythagoreanism, and Stoicism, together with a religious monotheism largely shorn of its particularistic elements. Philo's work was extremely popular, although not among Christian apologists of the first few centuries. It was carried, it appears, by a continuing movement of proselytizers for a universalistic Judaism: that is to say, a rival movement to Christianity, which had begun by working the same market, but which had broken with its Jewish roots entirely at the time of Paul. This Jewish proselytization continued until after 200, when it was prohibited by the Roman Empire; the Christian preacher John Chrysostom at Antioch was still warning against it around 390 (*CHLG*, 1967: 156).

A three-sided struggle took place in and around Judaism during the first two centuries C.E. Two of the wings were Christianity as an anti-philosophical religious movement, and syncretism with Hellenistic philosophy such as Philo of Alexandria's. A third wing had a militantly anti-rabbinical tone; this comprised many of the Gnostic sects, which went so far as to incorporate Yahweh as one of the demons or as the evil demiurge responsible for the ensnaring material world (Jonas, 1963). For a long time Christianity was not very visible among these sects, at least from an intellectual's point of view. Celsus (ca. 160 C.E.) did not distinguish Christians from Gnostics (*CHLG*, 1967: 80).

It is characteristic of the occultist movements of this time that they were polemical and exclusive; they also proliferated across the landscape like a confident social movement expanding into widely available niches. This describes the various Gnostic sects and the secret societies that promulgated the many versions of pagan Hermeticism. Occultist secret societies and more open religious organizations were the expanding structures of this period, and they underwent the doctrinal splintering characteristic of their strength. Their doctrines were usually only marginally philosophical: they did not typically operate with very abstract concepts or conceptual and logical self-reflectiveness, but they asserted particularistic symbols—good and evil gods, demons—all with rather concrete characteristics and modes of ritual propitiation. Intellectual territory per se began where these concepts were rationalized, typically by association with some version of idealist philosophy.

The structure of the Gnostic and occultist groups may be inferred from the proliferation of anonymous and pseudonymous manuscripts claiming to represent the ancient wisdom of Hermes Trismegistus, of Pythagoras, of the Chaldeans (Babylonian priests) or Egyptians. The form and content of the texts imply a series of small secret groups, based on transmission from a revered master to initiates (Fowden, 1986: 156–160, 189–193). But secrecy was often broken, and the organizational chains were rarely sustained beyond the lifetime of particular charismatic leaders. Some of the Gnostic organizations did better, such as those of Valentinus or Mani, which widened out beyond little circles of the "elect" to build churches encompassing ordinary people (Fowden, 1986: 189). This gave them greater staying power, and also put them into direct competition with the Christian Church, which typically treated them as heretical rivals.

Whereas the Gnostic sects and other occultist movements were usually small-scale secret societies, the Christians concentrated on building an organizational hierarchy, with centralized procedures for appointing priests and a unified discipline and doctrine (Jones, [1964] 1986: 873–933; Chadwick, 1967: 54–66; Telfer, 1962). The fact that Christian texts are not anonymous but are attributed to persons whose names are tied to the church's hierarchical succession represents the routinization of charisma and the bureaucratic continuity which the Gnostics lacked. The crucial inheritance from Judaism was not merely monotheism but the fact that, in contrast to other monotheisms such as the cult of Mithras or a universal goddess such as Isis or Cybele, it was a *religion of the book*. The scripture itself was the focus of holy ritual, and the organization necessarily had a core of literate specialists, providing a base for its own intellectuals. Even if the contents of the original scriptures were particularistic histories and mythologies, the combination of the focus on a text plus the centralizing organization provided key elements of a rational-legal bureaucracy, and hence the basis for more abstract and universalistic interpretations of doctrine. Whereas the Gnostics and their pagan equivalents were ad hoc networks of part-time participants, the church had a material foundation which enabled it to support full-time priests, to send out missionaries, to publicize martyrs and support widows and orphans of those fallen in the faith.[31] It was this organization that eventually proved attractive to the Roman state administrators as an adjunct to their own organization; and it was an organization whose material basis was to prove more enduring than the state itself at the fall of the empire.

It took numerous struggles to consolidate such an organization, especially welding the sphere of control by bishops and metropolitans. The heresy disputes which wracked the church were a sign of emerging organizational strength, for only a centralized organization can enforce doctrinal orthodoxy. The most serious external rival were the Manichaeans, not because they based their doctrine on Gnostic themes, but because they formed a mass-recruitment church competing in the bastions of Christian strength—Carthage and Rome. All of the church's moves in the heresy disputes can be seen as a defense of its distinctive organizational structure. Any doctrine was opposed as heresy which destroyed the chain of command of the central church hierarchy, which disputed the right to appoint priests or to retain control over ascetic monks. It would be even more accurate to say that the faction within church politics which made these organizational choices emerged as the orthodoxy; whichever faction favored the most permanence-enhancing organizational structure was in fact the one to win out. Meditative monks living in the desert gave a great deal of trouble, and mysticism and occultism were rejected if they broke from the community of lay worshippers under the ritual leadership of centrally appointed priests. The Gnostics, as movements of part-time amateurs meeting around favorite personalities, were an organizational enemy. So was any great emphasis on magic, since it is decentralizing, with little call for a formal hierarchy. Also ruled out were purely intellectual modes of salvation, since these would exclude the mass of the population, especially the popular base which, among monotheistic religions, Christianity had made almost uniquely its own.

The result was that Christianity could not go to extremes of idealism, rejecting the value or the reality of the material world. Idealist intellectual doctrines could be admitted, but only as an activity of specialized theologians within the organizational hierarchy of the church. Such doctrines could not be allowed to have an effect on practice to the extent of devaluing ordinary work, money making, or politics, which were activities on which the church depended for its strength. For this reason, Christianity came to incorporate more and more of the surviving elements of materialist philosophy in late antiquity, especially as the pagan united front centered on mysticism and idealism.

The Showdown of Christianity versus the Pagan United Front

Consider the successive stances taken by Christianity and the pagan philosophies toward each other. The earliest Christian philosophers, writing in consciousness of their weakness, are apologetic. Justin (ca. 150 C.E.), who studied at Ephesus before his conversion, tries to justify his faith by showing its compatibility with Platonism and Stoicism (*CHLG*, 1967: 158–167). In the next generation, Clement of Alexandria, who was taught by an ex-Stoic and had likely been at Athens, echoes the same themes as the pagan syncretizers, as well as drawing on the Jewish syncretism of Philo of Alexandria two centuries before. As the church gathers strength in the following generation (the early 200s), Origen uses Philo's allegorical methods, but the emphasis now has left the abstract plane of metaphysical similarities with the pagan philosophies (*CHLG*, 1967: 189–192). Instead Origen stresses the particularistic elements, and strikes back at the pagan critic Celsus by claiming that the Old Testament provided the basis of Greek ethics and science. This is argument on the same plane as that of the Taoists who disparaged their Buddhist rivals in China by claiming that their doctrine had been taught to them originally by Lao Tzu on his travels to the West.

Until 200 C.E., the professional philosophers seem oblivious to the threat of Christianity. Sextus, though he attacked everything else, did not bother to attack the new religions, which must indicate that as yet they had little presence among intellectuals. The "pagan" philosophers of this period did not defend traditional polytheism, or even pay much attention to it; their interest in religions, if they had any, was in mystical doctrines which could be interpreted as universalistic metaphysics. The Gnostic and occultist sects were a separate enclave, full of particularistic doctrines and generally looked down upon by serious intellectuals.

Now a new organizational player became visible on the field, and the terms of play were transformed (see Figure 3.7). Around 250 C.E. the power of Christianity was becoming visible, with sympathizers in high political circles. In the series of political coups around the middle of the century, there were sharp reversals of religious policy. The reign of Alexander Severus (222–235) was sympathetic to Christianity, and Philip the Arab (r. 244–249) was rumored to be a believer; in between, Maximinus (235–238) was hostile. Decius (249–251) launched a crackdown by ordering everyone to participate in sacrifices to the gods, but the edict was withdrawn by Gallienus in 260. Aurelian in 274–275, seeking to replace the traditional cults, tried to establish the monotheism of the sun god (Chadwick, 1967: 119–122). The strength of Christian organization was beginning to tell. The first large-scale systematic persecutions of Christians, begun under Decius in 250, resumed under Diocletian in 304 as

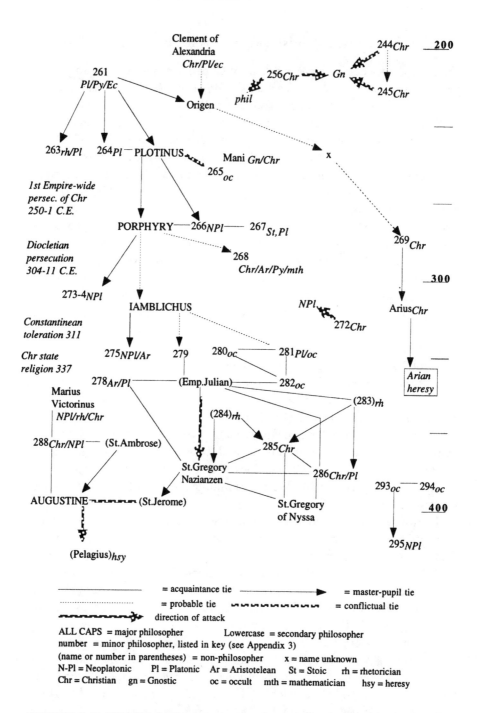

FIGURE 3.7. SHOWDOWN OF NEOPLATONISTS AND CHRISTIANS,
200–400

a death-grip struggle over power. When the persecutions were called off soon after Constantine's victory ending civil war in 311, it was only a short step to the adoption of Christianity as the official religion of the empire, which had transpired by the time of his death in 337.

The transition brought one more major burst of creativity. Plotinus put together an all-encompassing system based on Platonism, which served simultaneously as a religion. Plotinus had been educated in the circles in Alexandria which produced Origen, and he was in the entourage of the emperor Gordian in Mesopotamia when the latter was murdered in 243 by adherents of Philip, the emperor rumored to be a secret Christian (*CHLG*, 1967: 201).[32] The politics of this period were volatile, and it was not yet so clear that Christianity was to be the dominant religious force. But occultist movements were extremely prominent, and Plotinus threw his energies into capturing their essence for a rationalistic philosophy while purging their particularistic and "lower" forms. He attacked the blasphemous silliness of astrology, and he and his followers were especially hostile to Gnostic magic, which competed directly for the interest of his own circle (*CHLG*, 1967: 205–210).

The metaphysical elements of Plotinus' system were already long in existence. The hierarchy of ontological levels based on the Pythagorean doctrine of numbers goes back to Speusippus and Xenocrates, before the Academy turned Skeptic. Aristotle's analysis of levels of generality in logic provided another version of a hierarchy which could be bent to this purpose; and the syncretizing Middle Platonists and neo-Pythagoreans had elaborated various versions of the ontological scheme. In Plotinus' version there are three hypostases: the One, which is beyond number and name, and can be spoken of only metaphorically; the Intelligence *(nous)*, made up of Ideas in something like the Platonic sense, which are models of particular things but also their substance and true Being; and the Soul, the maker of the Cosmos, and which refracted through matter is Nature, the realm of sense and multiplicity, with lower and vegetative souls as well as individual human souls. The lower hypostases emanate from the higher, which also provide a path upward to the One as the goal of everything below.

Most of these elements can be found somewhere among Plotinus' predecessors, but the package is different. Many of the Middle Platonists placed emphasis on the intellect as the supreme principle of reality, whereas Plotinus stressed the distinctive level of transcendence beyond intellect and being. Plotinus was most original in arguing that the level of the intellect is not separate either from mind (after the fashion of the Platonic Ideas) or from particular objects. Instead the world, mind, being, and thought are unified; the acts and objects of thought are identical. Plotinus' system is a more thoroughgoing idealism than any other ancient philosophy.

Plotinus was vastly more famous and influential than these predecessors, in part because he was more systematic in his exposition, writing coherent treatises instead of commentaries and defenses of earlier philosophers. More important, the context and purpose of his writing had changed. Plotinus reflected above all on the nature of transcendence, on what can be conceived to be beyond the finiteness of every plane, whether material, mental, or formal. Earlier thinkers had approached their highest categories—God, the Pythagorean One, the Form of Forms, Goodness, the Unmoved Mover—from below, as logical extensions of a number philosophy or a physics or an examination of the formal level beyond particulars. Plato, who in the intellectual context of his day was most concerned to combat the schools of relativism and paradox, gave no consistent doctrine on the issue of the plurality of Forms and their source; for him, these were rough edges at the outer limits of his thinking. For Plotinus, transcendence was the starting point, which he set out to make philosophically respectable. This new emphasis can be attributed to the structural change that was occurring in the intellectual world around 250 C.E.

The Stoic and Epicurean schools had disappeared by about this time; so had the neo-Pythagoreans, the wandering Cynics, and the popular rhetors of the Second Sophistic; so too had the development of Aristotelean science. Plotinus forged a united front of all the surviving philosophies, together with the most intellectual elements from the non-particularistic religious or occult movements. For this purpose he appropriated elements of the schools which had now collapsed, purging them of their materialism. He used Aristotelean categories, and drew on Stoic elements such as the universal sympathy of nature. He took over what he could of natural science, interpreting cause-and-effect relations as reflections of higher forms, with light as a visible manifestation of divine goodness (*DSB*, 11:41–42). He rejected occultist practices such as spirit-calling because they reinforced the particularism and fragmentation of the inchoate religious movements. Plotinus sublimated them all into pure transcendence as a banner under which all could unite. The period of the loose syncretisms and debates among disorganized schools of thought which had characterized the previous two centuries gave way to a sense of showdown against an external enemy. Plotinus provided the tightly argued system that drew together what was now identified as pagan philosophy against the growing power of the church.

The next generations of Plotinus' followers intensified the battle. By 275 C.E., the time of Aurelian's official cult of the sun god, Porphyry had become the outspoken opponent of Christianity. Plotinus died in 270. His writings, which circulated only within the circle of disciples, were edited for publication by Porphyry around 305, as if deliberately to throw them into the death struggle against Christianity. Porphyry concentrated on technical argumentation, borrowing Stoic logic of propositions and terms, and augmenting Aristotelean categories to structure the metaphysical system (*CHLG,* 1967: 283–293). So far, philosophy prevailed over the religious elements in the synthesis.

In the next generation, Christianity triumphed politically. The Neoplatonist school became the center of political opposition to Christianity and campaigned for the restoration of traditional cults (*CHLG,* 1967: 279–280). Plotinus' pure intellectuality forged at the moment of transition could not be maintained; popular techniques of magic increasingly prevailed as the movement went underground. Iamblichus put theurgy—the process of becoming a god by magical procedures—above intellectual philosophy. From now on, Neoplatonists claimed powers such as clairvoyance, the ability to raise phantoms and to work magic spells. The coalition was widened into one last grand effort to oppose Christianity. Iamblichus brought in Gnosticism (anathema to Plotinus), the Egyptian mysteries, the anachronistic Chaldean Oracles (*CHLG,* 1967: 277–279, 295–301). The movement was not without political successes: a circle of Iamblichus' spirit-calling followers at Pergamum encouraged the young Julian in the direction that would lead to his brief overthrow of official Christianity during 361–363. (Chadwick, 1967: 157; *EP,* 1967: 5:175).

The last great thinker of pagan philosophy, Proclus, followed in the revived chain of Platonic *scholarchs* at Athens. Proclus was devoutly religious in anything non-Christian, observing all the holy days and rituals of the Egyptian and Greek calendars and all the mysteries from the Chaldean to the Orphic, practicing theurgy (which he learned from a daughter of Plutarch, the Athenian *scholarch*) and claiming to conjure luminous phantoms of the gods (*DSB,* 1981: 11:160; *CHLG,* 1967: 302–313). What makes Proclus intellectually significant is that his extreme syncretism now attempted to preserve all pagan learning. He commented on Euclid and Ptolemy, and arranged Aristotelean physics and astronomy into systematic form with propositions and proofs. Emulating Euclid, he even produced a systematic *Elements of Theology,* in which the elaborations of post-Iamblichian gradations of being are given in geometrical reasoning. For all its arbitrary contents, the last wave of the pagan united front put everything into a grand synthesis under the most rigorous method achieved by the entire historical community of Greek intellectuals.

While the pagans' creativity went into joining ranks, the victorious Christians were expanding laterally across intellectual turf. The great wave of heresies internal to Christianity took off as the church gathered strength; unlike the earlier argument against the Gnostics, who were non-organizational factions, these were battles over control of the church organization itself. The heresy disputes around the Monarchians, Arians, Monophysites, and Pelagians were on one plane power struggles within the church. But they were carried out with intellectual tools, on the level of philosophical abstractions, rather than merely by asserting the precedence of one's particularistic symbols over others' (such as the names of gods and demons, characteristic of the Gnostics).[33] Arius and his adherents, involved in a struggle in the 320s and 330s that tested the power of the bishop of Alexandria against the other great church metropoles, made use of Origen's transcendent monotheism, formulated with the development of Christian philosophy two generations before (*EP,* 1967: 1:162–164). By contrast, the "Cappadocian fathers," influential in court circles in the 370s and 380s, and thus victorious in the struggle to constitute orthodoxy, made use of Aristotelean and Middle Platonist doctrines in expounding theology (*CHLG,* 1967: 432–447; Chadwick, 1967: 148–152). (Figure 3.7 shows the connections of Saint Gregory of Nazianzen, Saint Gregory of Nyssa, and others with pagan philosophers at Athens, Constantinople, and Antioch.)

The Christians represent the victorious side of the law of small numbers, subdividing intellectually to fill the expanding space available to them. Like all strongly based intellectuals, they appropriated intellectual capital from movements which were collapsing: Middle Platonism at first, and later when its political strength was vitiated, Neoplatonism as well. Pagan concepts became the weapons for heresy disputes. The Christian doctrine of the Trinity, which emerged after 150 C.E., may well have been inspired by the propensity of the Middle Platonists and neo-Pythagoreans to expound triadic hypostases of the originating One.[34] Puzzles in reconciling identity and difference among parts of the Trinity were taken up as occasions for dispute around the time when Christianity came into political respectability and then power. Technical categories taken over from the amalgamation of Aristotelean logic with Platonism *ahomoousios* (of dissimilar essence) and *homoousios* (of identical essence), were the slogans of the Arians and their opponents, and the logic-chopping *homoiousios* (the likeness of an image to its archetype) became the heated subject of would-be compromise. The Council of Constantinople in 381 used the doctrine of *hypostases* to expound orthodoxy concerning the parts of the Trinity (Chadwick, 1967: 129–151). From another angle, one sees the pagan networks migrating into the center of action, which is now on Christian terrain. Saint Jerome was connected with the Middle Platonist faction; his doctrinal opponent Saint Augustine derived from a Neoplatonist lineage (Marius Victorinus, Simplicianus) which was now giving up the struggle and converting under pressure to Christianity (*CHLG,* 1967: 342–343; Brown, 1967: 271–275). These abstract heresy disputes are a sign of the intellectualization of Christianity as it took over the philosophical attention space.

The great Christian philosophers are those most centrally involved in intellectual networks connecting back to the accumulated sophistication of the pagan philosophers, as well as into the church power hierarchy at the time of the heresy disputes. It is not surprising that figures such as Augustine and

Ambrose should appear at this time.[35] The most talented and ambitious intellectuals, heretofore pursuing careers as rhetors and officials, went over to the church. It was now an institution of increasing power whose wealth and privileges were rapidly coming to exceed those of Roman officialdom (Jones, [1964] 1986: 904–910, 933–934).[36]

The most important philosophical result came from Augustine's effort to win over the remnants of his own intellectual class, the sophisticated Roman aristocracy, for whom Neoplatonism, and indeed the whole pagan philosophical tradition, was superior to the particularisms of Christian doctrine.[37] In the late 380s, just after Augustine's conversion, he produced his major contributions in pure philosophy. Mindful of the Ciceronian bias of rhetors like himself, he developed a refutation of skepticism (Weinberg, 1964: 30–43; Brown, 1967: 102). Augustine's argument was a version of the "cogito ergo sum" later used by Descartes to undergird a system much the opposite of Augustine's. The proof developed by Augustine moves from the certainty of self-knowledge, to an interior sense by which the exterior senses are judged, and to the implication that a standard exists by which reason operates—a standard which Augustine identifies with God. Augustine thus anticipates both Descartes and Anselm, and elaborates a more refined psychology around the capacities of memory, understanding, and will. In his subsequent career, Augustine was largely caught up in harsh polemics against religious rivals. He rose to a higher intellectual level when he wrote again for educated pagans, producing his *City of God* to show the drift of world history toward the triumph of Christianity rather than of the now crumbling Roman Empire (Brown, 1967: 299–307). Its success was due not just to his being on the victorious side, but to its encyclopedic display of pagan cultural capital in a Christian context.

There were intellectual consequences on the losing side as well. Theurgy disappeared from philosophy after the failure of the pagan united front. It had been an alliance of desperation in the heat of battle. Now the vulgar elements could be dropped, and the integrating structure of idealism was no longer necessary. Aristoteleanism and materialism made a comeback at Alexandria and Constantinople (see the tail end of Figure 3.8). Ammonius (304) son of Hermias, who held the Platonist chair at Alexandria in the late 400s, turned from Neoplatonism back to Aristotle (*CHLG*, 1967: 316). John Philoponus, a Christian and probably the last holder of a philosophy chair at Alexandria before it was abolished by the emperor Justinian in 529, rejected Proclus' hierarchy of spirits, and defended empirical science as more compatible with the Christian God, creator of a material world. Philoponus attacked the idealist elements of Aristotelean metaphysics, including the distinction between the celestial realm of perfect mathematical motion and the sublunar world of qualitative matter, and revived Stoic materialism and observational science

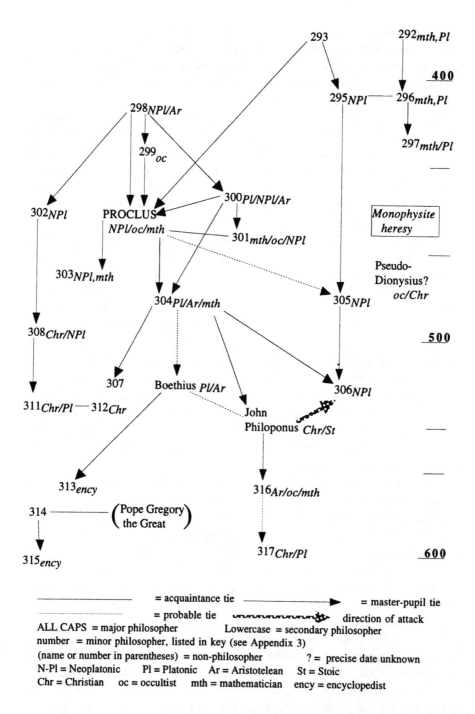

FIGURE 3.8. NEOPLATONISTS UNDER CHRISTIAN TRIUMPH,
400–600

(*CHLG*, 1967: 478–483; *DSB*, 1981: 7:134). From Philoponus and his response against Proclus' last round of pagan critique, too, came the development of new formal proofs of God, which would become the substance of later rational theology. The whole pagan syncretism had fallen apart with the triumph of Christianity; the elements which had been buried under the idealist united front now were released again into general circulation.

Two Kinds of Creativity

Creativity is forced by changes in the structure of intellectual communities, like fluid squeezed through the spaces as blocks shift their alignment. There are two polar types of creativity: the creativity of fractionation as thinkers maximize their distinctiveness, and the creativity of synthesis as intellectuals makes alliances among weakening positions or attempt to reduce a crippling overload as factions exceed the law of small numbers. The grand philosophical systems are the high points of the synthesizing dynamic. Here we find Aristotle forging new analytical tools to reconcile the quarrels among the outpouring of schools in the post-Socratic generation. Here is Plotinus blending the accumulated sophistication of the long-standing schools into a rationalized pagan religious philosophy to stand against the new menace of Christianity. The creativity of the fractionalizers is more polemical and extremist. At its most brilliant, it rises to the poetic visions of Heraclitus and Parmenides.

Synthesizers are necessarily dedicated to a vision of an overarching truth, and display a generosity of spirit toward at least wide swaths of the intellectual community. Each contributes partial views of reality, Aristotle emphasizes; so does Plotinus, and Proclus even more widely with the ecumenism of his bizarre coalition; even errors move us forward. Fractionalizers, with a contrasting spirit, are attached to their opponents only in a negative way. The earliest Greek philosophers, moving into an empty field, create one doctrine of cosmological elements after another. In much the same way the small Gnostic sects move into a new religious space, proliferating particularistic differences among themselves. Socrates too is a fractionalizer, blithely spinning off possibilities with the prodigality of a colonizer of empty spaces. A high degree of splitting in the field opens a slot for skepticism, attacking any standard of truth at all; when this emerges as a doctrine, it is a sign of overcrowding in the intellectual field.

One might suppose that fractionation and synthesizing would be symmetrical. When one organizational side of the field is growing stronger, its rivals should be weakening. Thus we find the pagans from Plotinus to Proclus in the synthesizing mode, while the aggrandizing Christians are busy with heresy disputes. We shall see this reciprocal pattern between Hindus and Buddhists in India, and again between weakening and expanding Buddhist lineages in China. But it is not necessary that there should always be a strong organizational position; this depends on external conditions, such as the political forces which determine the ups and downs of religions. There is also an internal dynamic which will produce splits, and if this goes on long enough, counter-moves toward synthesis to reduce the diminishing attention enforced by the law of small numbers. The fractionalizing mode prevailed alone in Greek philosophy for the first six or eight generations, and the synthesizing moves of Aristotle, Epicurus, and the Stoics occurred in response to the self-engendered weakness of this proliferation of schools. For the earliest period, there was no way at all to prevent splits; given the opening up of an empty field, it was structurally impossible that Greek philosophy could have reached consensus around a position like that of Thales or Pythagoras.

The pure forms of creativity, fractionalizing and synthesizing, are ideal types. They have real exemplars when appropriate conditions prevail, but much of intellectual history consists of mixed cases. There are both strong and weak forms of synthesis; the latter is better called syncretism. The lowest level of syncretism represents an effort to overcome factional differences by the intellectual equivalent of brute force, declaring that Buddha's doctrines were stolen from Lao Tzu, or that Plato and all the other schools had their ideas from Pythagoras or ancient Egypt. We see a more moderate but weak form of syncretism in the first two centuries of the Roman Empire, when there was a relatively stable array of philosophical positions, none of them enjoying very strong organizational bases. Here Platonists, Aristoteleans, Stoics, and rhetoricians wavered back and forth, asserting mixtures of one version with another. The period is characterized by no great analytical advances. The same is true later, when Iamblichus and his followers arbitrarily chop new rungs into the Neoplatonist hierarchies of ontological emanation to fit a panoply of deities and magical forces from their grand alliance of cults. A weak organizational base and correspondingly permeable boundaries between intellectuals and lay concerns produce the admixture of particularistic elements which is one of the conditions promoting syncretism rather than synthesis.

The grand systems of synthesis are those which take differences seriously rather than overriding them. Logically inconsistent elements are worked upon, and this results in a new framework or new analytic conceptions. Plotinus, much more than his Middle Platonist predecessors, is aware of the differences between Plato and Aristotle, and is willing to criticize the Stoics on the soul as a material substance at the same time that he adapts from them moral teachings to use against the Peripatetics (*CHLG*, 1967: 197–199, 226). It is this effort to shape existing elements selectively into a comprehensive picture that distinguishes strong synthesis from weak syncretism. The key condition is the moment of organizational transition. Since there is more analytical work to be done in reorganizing intellectual alliances, the creative advance is the more impressive. Plotinus' vision of the material universe floating in soul like a net in the ocean could be equally an expression of his predecessors' ideas in relation to his own harmonious system: "The cosmos is like a net thrown into the waters, immersed in life, unable to make that in which it is its own. Already the sea is spread out, and the net spreads with it as far as it can, for no one of its parts can be anywhere else than where it is. But because it has no size the Soul's nature is sufficiently ample to contain the whole cosmic body in one and the same grasp" (Plotinus, *Enneads* 4.3.27.9).

Can we conceive of all intellectual history as the working out of these two forms of creativity, with their varying degrees of strength and their mixed forms? In China, one can already feel the affinity of figures such as Mo Ti, Chuang Tzu, and the Ch'an Buddhists with the fractionalizing style, and the grand syntheses of Tung Chung-shu or Chu Hsi with organizational alignment. Let us see.

COMPARATIVE HISTORY OF
INTELLECTUAL COMMUNITIES

Part I: Asian Paths

CHAPTER 4

◭

Innovation by Opposition:
Ancient China

As we turn from Greece to China, it is tempting to indulge in visual insights about the "spirit of the place." Some have found the lucid rationality of the Greeks a mirror of the pure light and clear skies of the Mediterranean. Chinese philosophy has seemed filled with a spirit like the crooked shapes of tree branches looming through the mountain mist in the paintings of Ma Yüan or Shên Chou. This resonance with the landscape is our self-imposed illusion. The golden sunlight beat down on the blue Mediterranean in late antiquity as it did in the classic epoch; only philosophy had moved indoors to temple rooms filled with the smoke of idols delivering messages from demons and gods. The change convinced Spengler that the geometric space of the classic Greeks had given way to a Magian-Gnostic vision of the cosmos trapped inside a cavern. Yet it was Plotinus at Rome and Proclus at Athens who epitomized this interior atmosphere, while outdoors they still strolled the marble colonnades. What had arisen was an inability to see things any longer in the clear sunlight, just as it was the rise of Buddhist and Taoist movements that shaped the way Chinese painters came to present their environment.

Ancient China illustrates a principle of worldwide application. Intellectual creativity is driven by opposition. Philosophical positions develop by taking one another as foils. The attention space is shaped by arguments, not by resolutions. It is when the oppositions come to an end, when Chinese philosophy settles into a period of hegemonic consensus, that creativity freezes. This is not only an application of the formal sociological point that creative leaders appear simultaneously, dividing the field under the law of small numbers. The contents of philosophical ideas are also made up by the pattern of oppositions.

The Sequence of Oppositions in Ancient China

Chinese philosophy begins in dispersion and conflict. Confucius and his followers sprang up around 500 B.C.E. in conscious opposition to existing political and religious practices (see Figure 4.1). The Mohists emerged two generations later with doctrines explicitly contradicting many Confucian points. Both schools of moralistic activism were soon challenged by Yang Chu, with his anti-moralistic and anti-activist alternative of withdrawing from society into individual selfishness. Mencius in turn counterattacked the Yang Chu movement with an explicit defense of the goodness of human nature; this opened up yet another slot in intellectual space which Hsün Tzu filled with the opposing doctrine that human nature is evil and requires the imposition of social and ritual restraints. By the time of Mencius (ca. 300 B.C.E.), the intellectual network was beginning to take off into a self-conscious concern for its concepts and its methods of argument. Oppositions were renewed on a higher level of abstraction: idealism versus naturalism, sophistry versus transcendent standards, the rectification of names and standards versus the aconceptual Nameless of the *Tao Te Ching*.[1]

The oppositions which eventually became philosophy began in the external arena of military-political strife. Wars among the contending states made regimes unstable and put a premium on alliances, and hence on diplomats circulating in a cosmopolitan network along with reformers and political place-seekers. External politics gave birth to an intellectual attention space, rising to higher levels of abstraction and dividing along inner lines of fractionalization. The inner focus of attention which constitutes an intellectual community became autonomous as the community acquired a distinctive network structure: the intersection of multiple factions at a few key centers of debate.

It is conventional to explain Confucianism by the breakdown of political order in the Warring States. But the timing is not very close. Disintegration of the Chou dynasty into a large number of feudal states was already advanced when the Chou capital was sacked by an uprising in 771 B.C.E. Yet the first philosopher, Confucius, did not begin teaching until about 500. Around this time the intensity of warfare escalated, and chivalrous ideals of knightly combat gave way to ruthlessness and strategy. Armies expanded from relatively small numbers of knights to massive peasant infantries. States began to levy large masses of workers to build roads and canals, clear swamps, and construct defensive border walls. Along with this we find an upsurge of trade, the spread of metal coinage, and tax collection by state officials. A new level of organization came into being, superimposed on the earlier society of independent clans and fiefs. Religion had been a state cult, legitimating royal authority. Now the structure of clan society was subjected to new geopolitical relations, a cosmopolitan arena that simultaneously replaced old symbolic frameworks while offering opportunities to mobilize movements beyond and across local regimes.

The Confucians proposed to overcome both the warfare and the symbolic

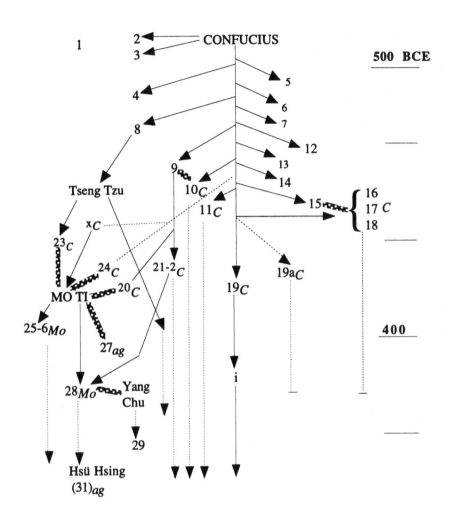

500 BCE

400

———————▶ = master-pupil tie

····················· = probable tie   ∿∿∿∿∿∿∿∿∿ = conflictual tie

ALL CAPS = major philosopher   Lowercase = secondary philosopher
number = minor philosopher, listed in key (see Appendix 3)
i = incidental person (not known independently of contact with known philosopher)
x = name unknown   C = Confucian   Mo = Mohist   ag = "agriculturalist" primitivist

FIGURE 4.1. EMERGENCE OF CHINESE NETWORK, 500–365 B.C.E.:
RIVAL CONFUCIAN LINEAGES, MOHISTS, PRIMITIVISTS

strangeness of the period with a backward-looking doctrine of religious correctness. Confucius was harshly critical of dukes and lower-ranking nobles who had too many dancers in their court ceremonies or too many carts in their funeral precessions (e.g., *Analects* 3.1.6). Not only were these usurpations of the ritual badges of rank, hence showing disrespect for the traditional authority of the dynasty, but also such ceremonies could not have their proper magical effect. The Confucians extolled the reified attitudes of traditional ritualism, but in doing so they stepped outside the cocoon of primal naïveté. Theirs was the beginning of a sophisticated defense of unsophisticated practice.

The anthropomorphic Lord on High was reinterpreted as an impersonal Heaven *(T'ien)* or Destiny *(T'ien-ming)*. The latter could also be interpreted as the "Mandate of Heaven," in this way turning supreme religious power into a principle of retribution. Incorrect rulers—those who neglected the appropriate sacrifices and other forms—would lose a favorable Mandate of Heaven, and eventually be overthrown by a ritually correct dynasty. This lesson was illustrated by accounts of the rise and fall of earlier dynasties (including some mythical ones) in the *Book of History (Shu Ching)*, which was compiled during the first generations of the Confucian school. The Confucians could not help supplementing ritual correctness with a new inner dimension of morality: rituals must be carried out with the proper attitude of respect, and this attitude should permeate other aspects of behavior as well. In the morality tales of the bad emperors, drunkenness and sexual carousing took their place as sins along with neglect of the rites.

Soon after the Confucians opened an intellectual space, the Mohists moved into it with an oppositional stance. The law of small numbers was already operating. Confucius' followers soon split into some half-dozen schools, differentiated apparently on how much strictness they applied to ritual formalism.[2] The Mohists created a more radical alternative, both doctrinally and organizationally. Ceremonies, funeral processions, music, and other public displays—the center of Confucian concerns—were condemned as expenses burdening the common people. Whereas the Confucians idealized the ritually correct founder of the Chou dynasty, the Mohists idealized the Hsia, a dynasty of primitive culture-heroes preceding the ancient Shang. For the Confucian ethical obligation to family and ruler, the Mohists substituted an ideal of universal altruism. In opposition to the impersonal cult of Heaven and Destiny, Mo Ti personalized Heaven as a god rewarding the righteous and punishing sinners. Whereas Confucius strove to keep the spirits at a distance, the Mohists emphasized the existence of ghosts as avengers of evils done to them during their lives. One of the Ten Theses of Mohism is a refutation of fatalism, which Mo Ti associates with some opposing factions. Mohism developed as one extreme just as the other extreme was emerging inside Confucianism in connection with the new religious conception of *T'ien-ming,* or Destiny. As the determinism which goes along with a formalistic ritualism was brought to light, Confucianism engendered its antithesis, a rejection of the whole ritualism complex, with its associated intellectual justification.

At this time what we call Confucians were not yet a cult around the person of their founder; their transformation into a new religion was to come later. The movement instead was simply called *ju,* "scholars." These were the first educated men, self-conscious specialists in compiling and interpreting the ancient documents which legitimated both political authority and their own claims for employment. Traditional Chinese religion had no special class of priests. Kings themselves had carried out the major ceremonies, later usurped by feudal lords in the manner of which Confucius was so critical. Adherents of the Confucian movement were something like the beginning of a specialized priesthood, offering themselves as advisers to the feudal lords on ceremonial matters. The Mohists found a rival niche, forming a military-religious order bound by commitments of loyalty to the death. Their organization is reminiscent of the orders of crusading knights in Christian Europe. The Mohist practical strategy was to counter the evils of the Warring States by purely defensive warfare, based on their expertise in fortification. This military organization probably did not last many generations, as the scale of warfare soon far outstripped the numbers of Mohist troops.[3] By the generation of Mencius and Chuang Tzu (ca. 320 B.C.E.), the Mohists survived only as an intellectual faction. The fate of the rival movements was parallel. Confucians too were unsuccessful in their political-religious reform. They became instead the archetype of the intellectual: custodians of the texts. In both camps the original policy doctrines became logically acute as an internal attention space took shape.

Other factions in the external arena of political policy contributed to the thickening web of argument, and thus to the emerging space of intellectual focus. Yang Chu debated with Mo Ti's major disciple. In these generations (ca. 400–335 B.C.E.) a variety of thinkers offered alternative policies: return to "primitivist" self-sufficiency, or the autarky of the "agriculturalists." On the opposite wing, others advocated an explicit concern for political solutions, including a "Diplomatist" school proposing a path to state security through negotiation and alliance.

Diplomacy was more than one factional alternative among others. It was becoming a distinct profession, and the common basis for the careers of many intellectuals of whatever stripe. The large number of feudal territories of the previous centuries had been reduced to a moderate number of contending states, from perhaps 1,000 down to 14 by 480 B.C.E. (Eberhard, 1977: 47). A balance of power emerged among the strongest states. The military-political plots and negotiations that linked them into a network of conflict was giving rise to an inner structure, which became the incipient intellectual community.[4]

The Intersection of Rival Centers and Multiple Factions

At the height of the Warring States period, military success or even mere safety depended on a web of alliances. A coalition of Chao, Wei, and Ch'in armies turned back the aggressions of Ch'i, the most powerful state, about 284 B.C.E., then went on to counterattack by invading Ch'i. In 257 an alliance of Wei, Chao, and Ch'u defeated a Ch'in attack; again in 247 Ch'in, which was fast becoming the biggest and most powerful state, was beaten back by the combined armies of five states. Courts had become places of discussion and debate among visiting diplomats carrying proposals for alliances, together with domestic officials and traveling scholars offering their services in either capacity; all of them circulated schemes for administrative reform, military strength, and/or religious blessings. Most of the reform schemes came to nothing. Despite the intellectuals' failures in long-term policy, their skill in argument was made important by the salience of diplomacy. Such a figure as Hui Shih, whom we think of mainly as a paradoxer or propounder of abstract logical

INTELLECTUAL CENTERS IN THE WARRING STATES, 350 B.C.E.
(Chi-hsia Academy is in Ch'i; P'ing-yuan court is in Chao)

distinctions, was given important political responsibilities. Other famous persons were known for their ability to argue convincingly on either side of a question; this was considered politically useful, although encouraging fears of alliance-switching and palace intrigues. The movement of intellectuals and diplomats from place to place, and in and out of various states' service, fostered cosmopolitanism; intellectual reputation became autonomous from services rendered.

The earlier movements—branches of Confucian *ju,* Mohists, Yang Chu-style primitivists, and advocates of rural self-sufficiency—consisted of wanderers with no fixed intellectual bases. As we see in Figure 4.2, the growth of philosophy in a more formal sense took place as intellectual life settled down, largely at four overlapping centers (Knoblock, 1988: 5–11, 20–34, 54–64).

The court at Wei, one of the powerful Warring States, in the center of existing China, began to patronize the Tzu-hsia school of Confucians about 380 B.C.E. This continued for three generations. In the latter part of the century, the king gathered a notable collection of scholars at his capital, Ta Liang. Hui Shih, the famous logician, served as prime minister and diplomat. Other personages included the famous debater Shunyü Kun (39 in Figure 4.2), Mencius, and perhaps Chuang Tzu, a friend of Hui Shih. With the accession of a new king (ca. 320), the group dispersed; Mencius and Shunyü Kun went to the Chi-hsia Academy. The Wei center reappeared several generations later (ca. 270–260), when Prince Mou, himself something of a traveling intellectual, supported Kung-sung Lung and his circle.

The powerful state of Ch'i, in the east, began to patronize scholars about 350 B.C.E., perhaps in emulation of Wei. At the high point, around 320–300, this Chi-hsia Academy had its own Scholars' Hall, supporting seventy-six scholars with honored titles and emoluments. Intellectual life was becoming autonomous; scholars were not asked to participate in government but were expected to deliberate and propound. Hundreds of additional scholars gathered to listen and take part. Because of the invasion of Ch'i in 284 the academy dispersed, but ten years later it was reconstituted; in this period its most eminent figure was Hsün Tzu, until around 265 Tsou Yen arrived and brought to dominance the Yin-Yang philosophy.

Yet another center was at the court at P'ing-yuan, under one of the princes of Chao, to the north. This prince was said to have patronized some 1,000 scholars and retainers around 270–250. These included Hsün Tzu, who had moved over from the Chi-hsia Academy when Tsou Yen arrived; Kung-sun Lung and other logicians; and Prime Minister Yü Ch'ing, who wrote a *Spring and Autumn Annals of Master Yü.* Tsou Yen arrived here as a visitor too, beating Kung-sun Lung in debate, whereupon the latter retired to the court of Wei. Hsün Tzu, too, eventually left P'ing-yuan to take a position as magistrate

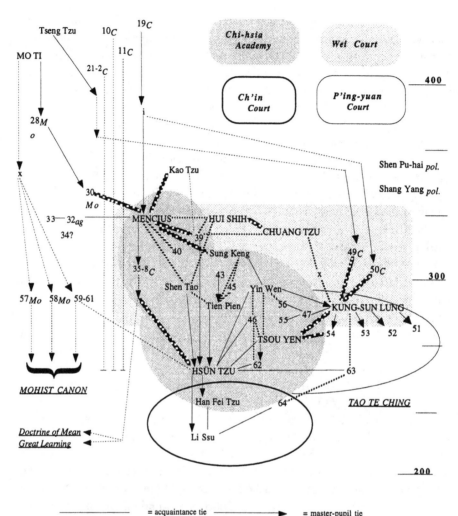

FIGURE 4.2. INTERSECTING CENTERS OF THE WARRING STATES,
365–200 B.C.E.

for the state of Ch'u. Ch'u was the large southern state, then on the frontiers of Chinese settlement, where Mohist logicians had for several generations enjoyed support. Hsün Tzu was posted to Lanling in southern Shantung (the eastern seaboard), where he set up his own school. Here he attracted pupils such as Han Fei and Li Ssu. The Lanling school and its network offshoots continued to be influential down to the beginning of the Han dynasty, when its scholars dominated the intellectual life of the new regime, producing high imperial officials as well as the scholars who fed the system of state Erudites (Knoblock, 1988: 38–39).

States came to find prestige in sponsoring intellectual centers and emulated one another. Wei, Ch'i, Chao, and apparently Ch'u (with less emphasis on an "all comers" approach) had their centers; the intellectual stars circulated among them as local conditions changed. Even the "barbarian" and ruthlessly practical state of Ch'in, on the western frontier, took as prime minister Fan Sui (271–265 B.C.E.), a famous debater and former diplomat in the service of Wei. In the next generation Lü Pu-wei, a rich merchant connected to the Chao court, maneuvered to become prime minister at Ch'in, and assembled at his own expense a group of some 3,000 scholars.[5] This group probably drew heavily away from the older centers at P'ing-yuan (in Chao), the Chi-hsia Academy, and Hsün Tzu's center at Lanling, from which was recruited the arch-Legalist Li Ssu. The Ch'in state, as it conquered the rest of China in the 220s, acquired a reputation as anti-intellectual, above all because of the burning of the books of rival factions engineered by Li Ssu in 213. Nevertheless, we ought to see this as an act of rivalry among intellectuals, one faction of whom had finally come to absolute power. It was the last act of a situation of intellectual emulation, which had promoted creativity for half a dozen generations until the structural independence which undergirded the competition was closed down to a single source.

It was in this period of "the hundred schools" that Chinese intellectual life was most similar to that of Greece. The debaters moving among the courts of the Warring States remind us of the Sophists, many of whom were diplomats too, as well as refugees or participants in colonization schemes of the Greek world. Greek philosophers were concerned not only with military alliances (the Persian wars, the Athenian and anti-Athenian coalitions, later the wars of the Macedonian and Hellenistic states), but also with internal factions of aristocrats against democrats. Greek tyrants, who played opportunistically on either side of this class conflict, were especially likely to act as patrons of philosophers, like some of the upstart ministers of Chinese states. In both China and Greece the external structure gave emphasis to public argument, and growing prestige to the intellectual community per se. In China this happened at the time of the Chi-hsia Academy and its rivals; the comparable center was Athens from the generation of the Sophists on. In both places cosmopolitan and competitive networks broke through into abstract self-reflection.

Originating Structures of Philosophy in China and Greece

The substantive contents of philosophy are different in China and Greece; the similarities are at the level of the network structure. In both the law of small numbers was operative early, as multiple factions emerged to fill the new intellectual attention space. In both cases the precipitating conditions involved political pluralism, the cosmopolitanism of commercial development and literacy, and a breakdown of traditional religious practices.

For the Greeks, cosmological doctrines first became the object of attention; the nature of the gods was considered, and the search was launched for the constitutive elements of the physical universe. For the Chinese, naturalistic or proto-metaphysical questions took a back seat initially to political and ethical questions. Even when the intellectual community became more self-reflective, Chinese philosophers built on the cultural capital already accumulated along these lines. The Chinese entry point to metaphysical abstraction was the question of human nature: whether it is selfish and asocial (as apparently in Yang Chu), naturally benevolent and therefore socially responsible (in Mencius), or naturally evil and in need of control by rites (Hsün Tzu) or coercion by laws (the Legalists). Even the development of a mystical cosmology in Chuang Tzu and the *Tao Te Ching* was largely connected to questions of whether to withdraw from civilized society; in the twist associated with "Lao Tzu" at the time of the Legalists, withdrawal was made the essence of social responsibility through the claim that the magical sage-king can order human society through perfect quiescence. The nearest parallel to the Greek cosmology of elements emerged late, with the Yin-Yang and Five Processes doctrines of Tsou Yen (270 B.C.E.), and these too were connected with political questions of the rise and fall of dynasties.

In Greece, philosophical contents went through almost the reverse development, issues of ethics coming to the fore only after the intellectual community acquired an internal density and hence a push to higher levels of abstract self-reflection. Although the *physis-nomos* debate among the Sophists is something like the issue raised by Yang Chu, the question of human nature was never the focus of debate in Greece as it was in China. There is a rough equivalence between the continua of positions in each place. But the conventional political participation extolled by Aristotle and the Stoics falls far short of the worship of ritual and tradition which anchored the conservative end of the spectrum in China. Toward the other end, the withdrawal into *ataraxeia* counseled by Epicureans and Skeptics did not take on the mystical and magical connections which we find in the tradition of Chuang Tzu and incipient Taoism; nor do we find Chinese debates over hedonistic suicide comparable to those of the Cyrenaic school. By contrast, ethical debates in Greek philosophy (at least until the time of the religious movements of late antiquity) covered a narrower territory; from the Cynics and Stoics onwards, the issue was the purity of the ideal of goodness and how much compromise there should be with worldly and sensual goods—a spectrum of argument that never greatly concerned the Chinese.

The underlying condition has to do with the different ways external political conditions shaped the starting points for the contents of philosophical discussion. In Greece the state cults under the leadership of priest-kings were undercut by the democratic revolutions between 700 and 500 B.C.E. The civic cults remained, though manned by citizens as part of their political duties, with little or no influence by a class of professional priests (Burkert, 1985; Bryant, 1996).[6] The volatility of military power among the numerous city-states prevented the dominance of any particular state cult over the others. The inability of the state to monopolize the focus of religious attention was furthered by the resulting influence of non-state cults; centers such as Delphi, Olympia, and elsewhere depended on an "international" market of clients and gave considerable attention to private religious concerns (Fontenrose, 1978). For intellectuals in the city-states, career possibilities depended increasingly on the attention of public audiences. The space of religious cosmologies became an arena in which secular intellectuals now competed for attention. G. E. R. Lloyd (1987: 56–70) points to the uniquely Greek combination of "innovations and egotism" resulting from this struggle for reputation. The pantheon of nature gods used as initial cultural capital was transmuted into philosophies of cosmological elements.

Lacking city-states and democratic revolutions in China, intellectuals were oriented toward the support of princely patrons. Drawing at first on traditional cultural capital, scholars made the initial issue restoration of the old state religious cult; the alternatives ranged from Mohist anti-ritualistic monotheism, to withdrawal from the state religion entirely, to infusions of peripheral magical cults as answers to political legitimacy. Since they were appealing directly to authoritarian regimes, Chinese intellectuals stressed the traditional legitimacy of the ancient religious cosmologies, and disguised whatever innovations they made by reading them into ancient texts, even inventing the texts if necessary. Hence there are no "Presocratic" nature philosophers in China. Explicit philosophical argument was confined to the realm of the newly forming state and the relation of the individual to it.

For the Greeks, religious legitimation of the state was never a grand issue to be pursued by abstract philosophy. Community rituals, although all-pervasive, went on largely as a matter of practical conformity; occasionally philosophers such as Anaxagoras and Socrates were attacked by political enemies on the excuse of offending against the cults, but the prevailing attitude of intellectuals down to the Roman Empire seems to have been that religious tradition was irrelevant to their concerns. For this reason, ethical issues in Greek philosophy hinge almost entirely on the actions of the individual; even the advocates of political participation saw this largely as an issue of how the individual should behave, not a question of what was best for the state.[7]

The similarities between Greek and Chinese philosophy are at the inner level of structural relationships within the intellectual community. The early generations in each place stand in structural parallel. Thales, Solon, and the other "sages" of the founding generation were politicians known for their pithy sayings and their lawgiving; they were leaders in the period of political reform brought about by the overthrow of the old aristocracy (and of the associated monopoly of the state cults by priest-kings). These Greeks are parallel to Confucius and his students, and to such early "Legalists" as Shen Pu-Hai and Shang Yang, whose overriding concern was political reform. The changes in Chinese political structure followed a different path than in Greece—crucially lacking the democratic revolution within the decentralized state system—but reflections on political disorder and religious change are common to both. Mo Ti's disciplined organization, which proposed to take political matters into its own hands, is parallel to the Pythagorean brotherhood, which won political power in some cities of the outlying colonies. Differences in the external setting, its politics-religion nexus, started off the Chinese and Greek intellectual worlds with different problems; these heritages of cultural capital were elaborated along divergent tracks even as the networks developed in structural parallel. Both external and internal social conditions affected the contents of Chinese and Greek ideas; the external setting the topics and the internal driving the turn toward logic, argumentative technique, and conceptual abstraction which would go on in both places in the next period.

In Greece the decentralized situation of warring states continued down to the final Roman conquest about 85 B.C.E. Even then Rome never monopolized intellectual life the way the centralized Chinese dynasties would from the Ch'in and Han onwards. The resemblance is most striking between China from about 335 to 235 B.C.E.—the three generations from Hui Shih and Mencius, down to the Mohist *Canons,* Hsün Tzu, and Han Fei Tzu—and the five or six generations in Greece between 500 and about 300 B.C.E. Intellectual life in both places hinged around the emergence of what we might call "sophists," or professional debaters. A network of argument gave rise within a couple of generations to logicians and epistemologists, making discoveries about the nature of inferences and ideas. Contemporaries experienced the initial phase in this discovery of the abstract as the emergence of paradoxes. Hui Shih's famous statements—"a brown horse and a dark ox make three"; "the wheel never touches the ground" (Chan, 1963: 234–235)—may constitute an argument for the unreality of distinctions in physical time and space; some of his paradoxes about motion are similar to those of Zeno of Elea. Hui Shih also seems to have introduced the challenge of deducing a hidden object from the definition of its name (Graham, 1978: 62). Kung-sun Lung a generation later argued more explicitly about names, forms, and substances, though he still made a splash with paradoxes such as "a white horse is not a horse." Kung-sun Lung appears to have been attempting to solve epistemological problems, distinguishing whiteness from stone and the seeing of the mind from the seeing of the eye (Chan, 1963: 242).[8]

A new intellectual space opened up, and in keeping with the law of small numbers it was soon filled with opposing positions. Tendencies toward sophistry and idealism were countered by defenses of empiricism and naturalism. The formulators of the Mohist *Canons* in the generation after 300 B.C.E. came close to a Western-style empiricism in natural science and to Euclidean methods in mathematics (Needham, 1956: 171–184). They made use of new concepts of "a priori knowable" (*hsien,* probably introduced by Hui Shih) and "necessary" *(pi),* and went on to derive principles of ethics and geometry from strings of definitions (Graham, 1978: 62–63). This constituted a certain parallel to Plato's school, with its use of mathematics as a standard for grounding a non-relativistic ethics. From the Confucian camp, Mencius reacted to the debaters, utilitarians, and anti-moralists by arguing for an objective ideal of human nature and morality. Although his object was merely to preserve the Confucian faith, he was forced to adopt the concepts of logical debate, and thus was pushed into defending the conception of properties shared by concrete objects (Schwartz, 1985: 258–265). Mencius' intellectual tools could then be turned to still other applications. His substantive stance became the foil for yet another Confucian wing, no longer touting the intrinsic merit of ritualism but making an explicit defense of naturalism in both ethics and logic, at the hands of Hsün Tzu. His pupil Han Fei took this naturalism into open revolt against the Confucian tradition.

In propounding the doctrines of legalism, Han Fei was not simply taking advantage of an opportunity in the external political situation for legitimating the centralizing policies of the rising power of Ch'in. Legalism also emerged from the inner dynamics of the intellectual world. Both Confucianism and the larger array of intellectuals were discovering the alternative poles of idealist and naturalist standards from which to argue. Growing conceptual sophistication also stimulated and transformed cosmologies. Han Fei could take the opposite tack from traditional Confucians, and from archaizing primitivists such as Chuang Tzu and the *Tao Te Ching* author, in criticizing the adulation of historical precedent; at the same time he borrowed from the newer metaphysics by turning the concept of *tao* into a naturalistic principle of order in the physical world.

Compared to the Greeks, Chinese intellectuals of this time placed little stress on the preeminence of metaphysical abstraction. Although there were several arguments driving toward idealist or transcendental conceptions, there was no move like that of Plato and his followers to identify levels of conceptual abstraction with degrees of metaphysical reality. The book later known as the *Tao Te Ching*, which appeared under an archaizing pseudonym late in this period, built upon the epistemological reflections of Kung-sun Lung and the "School of Names" for its conception of the Nameless. Here the greatest metaphysical reality is attributed to what one might call the last word (or the last non-word) in philosophical argument; and the Nameless is identified with a preexisting conception, the *tao* (way), as the inner principle of the natural and social worlds.

But this route toward an explicit metaphysics of abstractions does not go any farther. The stimulating effect of logic and epistemology on cosmology, characteristic of both the Greek classic period and the Chinese "hundred schools," breaks off. It is here that we find a crucial difference between the two intellectual communities. The Greek community carried on its "argumentative" period for 12 generations, most famously from 500 to 300 B.C.E., with another half-dozen generations of epistemological argument down through Carneades, the Stoic logicians, and Aenesidemus' skepticism. For the Chinese, the sequence was shorter: four or five generations at most, from Yang Chu down to Han Fei Tzu. Then external forces intervened to limit sharply the extent of debate within the intellectual world, with the unification of China by the Ch'in and its successor, the Han dynasty. The opportunity to pile on successive levels of reflection was cut short. The intellectual maneuvers that came next were much more constrained to appeal to non-intellectual audiences. Instead of pushing farther into epistemology and abstract metaphysics, Chinese philosophy moved back toward lay concerns. What became in retrospect the distinctively "Chinese" cast of philosophical ideas was formed in the Han period of centralized authority by the fusion of intellectually generated abstraction with externally conditioned political-religious ideology.

Overcrowded Attention Space and the Generation of Syntheses

Just as in Greece the outpouring of schools in the generation following Socrates resulted in overcrowding and instability of most lines of transmission, in China the upper limit of the law of small numbers was being severely strained by around 300 B.C.E. In both cases we see a period of confident fractionalizers, pouring into a newly opened space for abstract considerations, taking up extreme positions and disdaining compromise with rivals. This is noticeable among the Mohists of the time: the most tightly disciplined group of its day, it nevertheless had split into three factions (*Chuang Tzu,* chap. 33; Graham, 1978: 22–24). Their disputes included logical and conceptual problems ("difference and sameness," "the incompatibility of odd and even") which they took seriously enough to call one another heretics. In the generation around 250 B.C.E., the split had been mended by a new synthesis.[9] The great work of reforming their alliance, the Summa of the Mohist position, was the *Canons.* It has the conceptual acuteness, comprehensive scope, and systematization that are characteristic of creativity in the synthesizing mode. The notion that the "Chinese mind" is incapable of abstract logical argument is refuted by the existence of the *Canons.* This very ideology of interpreting Chinese history became possible only because realignment in the intellectual networks at the time of the Han dynasty eliminated the Mohist tradition.

The *Canons'* approximate contemporary, the *Tao Te Ching,* is a synthesis on the other side of the field. Playing on the same kind of oppositional appeal as Chuang Tzu, it is a much more unified composition than the compilation later put together under Chuang's name. It shows more sophisticated consciousness of its philosophical opponents, turning the tools of the School of Names into a device for transcending names, and the techniques of argumentative sophistry into substantively meaningful paradox. It is also a political-religious synthesis, weaving together the older primitivists and anti-ritualists with the newer themes of occultist direction of the state. But whereas Tsou Yen's Yin-Yang school proposed to intervene on the magical-concrete level of divination, the *Tao Te Ching* incorporated a more properly religious mysticism with its sage-ruler emanating cosmic powers, the *te* of meditative withdrawal.

It is a mark of its synthesizing success that the *Tao Te Ching* was to become a favorite of many subsequent factions; even the Legalists in the very next generation could find a use for it in legitimating the smoothly operating bureaucratic system of rewards and punishments that would allegedly make society operate as effortlessly as the *tao* in nature (Schwartz, 1985: 343–345). Part of the synthesizing success of the *Tao Te Ching* is its ability to be read in so many ways; as Holmes Welch (1965: Foreword) remarked, no translation can be satisfactory because no translation can be as ambiguous as the original. It would be inaccurate to say that the author took a preexisting mysticism and wove other doctrines into it, for it seems clear that there was no explicitly formulated—and thereby metaphysical—mysticism before this time. A philosophical mysticism, rather, was created by just this effort to forge a position uniting and transcending a host of philosophical and political schools.

The "hundred schools" were winnowing down. In addition to the Mohist and the *Tao Te* syntheses, two other important synthesizers were the naturalistic Confucianism of Hsün Tzu and the Yin-Yang/Five Agents doctrine of Tsou Yen. Hsün Tzu was another systematizer, in some ways reminiscent of the style of the Mohist summits, whom he probably contacted on his sojourns in Ch'u. His school at Lanling was the center of the networks at the end of the Warring States. With his multiple contacts throughout the factions of the intellectual world (see Figure 4.2), Hsün Tzu was in good position to be a synthesizer. He coordinated concepts and laid out the relation among fields of knowledge in a fashion parallel to that other synthesizer, Aristotle. Hsün Tzu occupied the middle of the field, maintaining naturalism but without the radicalism of the Mohists; his followers were above all *ju*, epitomizing the archetypal Confucian role of preserving the classical texts and defending the ancient rites.

The most successful faction in gathering external sponsorship was the Yin-Yang school. It too was a syncretism of the period around 265 B.C.E. Tsou Yen combined two different divination schemes, which apparently went back to the previous century: the ebb and flow of *yin* (dark, female, passive) and *yang* (light, masculine, active) with a cycle of five basic elements or processes (water, fire, wood, metal, earth). This seems reminiscent of pre-Socratic cosmologies, especially of Empedocles;[10] but in this case Tsou Yen was less oriented toward displaying a naturalistic cosmology, and more concerned to demonstrate an immediate appeal by using his device for political prediction. He produced an encyclopedic ordering of natural phenomena—rivers, mountains, plains, celestial bodies—progressing through the cycle of the elements. Human events were also cyclical, and hence the rise of fall of dynasties could be predicted. Tsou Yen made a great splash in the court debates, embarrassing Kung-sun Lung at P'ing-yuan, and motivating Hsün Tzu to leave Ch'i (Knoblock, 1988: 11, 63). In sheer longevity of his ideas, Tsou Yen is one of the most influential figures in Chinese history.

In the lineup of rival positions, the chief political philosophies up to this time were polarized between the Confucians, who claimed that traditionally correct ritual would restore social order; and the Mohists, who advocated a virtuous military activism based on universal altruism. The intellectual dilemma was that the Confucians were political ultra-conservatives advocating a long-lapsed dynasty, while their religious stance (anchored against the Mohists) was detached and instrumental. The Mohists in turn were politically utopian radicals, but religious conservatives with their belief in benevolent and avenging spirits. Tsou Yen reshuffled the ingredients with a religious doctrine justifying political change—indeed, precisely the opportunistic changes of power politics. At the same time, his occultist cosmology preserved the veneer of legitimation that the Legalists had stripped away with their blatant naturalism.

Centralization in the Han Dynasty: The Forming of Official Confucianism and Its Opposition

The crisis of overcrowding in the attention space had produced a wave of syntheses among the multiple factions of the late Warring States period. Synthesis was accelerated still further by external conditions when the Ch'in conquest state and the subsequent Han dynasty centralized intellectual life. The rival centers which had promoted creativity were now reduced to a single center under imperial patronage. Which intellectual faction would gain control of the new material base? In the Ch'in, the Legalists had imposed their hegemony. But the Han revolution had put them under a cloud. Tsou Yen's Yin-Yang school and other occult divination schemes remained popular. By the time centralized Han administration was firmly established around 130 B.C.E., Confucianism had made a dramatic comeback and was elevated to the sole official doctrine.

All subsequent Chinese history has been written in the light of Confucian-

HAN DYNASTY, 200 B.C.E.–200 C.E.

ism, but its continuous hegemony should not be taken for granted. In the late Warring States, Confucianism was one faction among many, and not the dominant one; nor was its position especially high through the first two generations of the Han. The Confucian *ju* maneuvered their way into power through a series of moves on both intellectual and organizational terrain.

The first move was to establish a tie to the divination practices which appealed so strongly to lay politicians. At the time of transition between the Ch'in and Han dynasties, when books of the philosophical schools were banned, divination texts were exempted. They became the turf on which intellectual schools scrambled for survival. One faction of Confucians adopted a relatively recent compilation of old divination records, and added commentaries, ascribed to Confucius himself, interpreting the hexagrams of broken or unbroken lines in terms of advice for the Confucian "superior man" (Graham, 1989: 358–359). Within a generation or two the book was regarded as one of the canonical ancient texts, now called the *Yi Ching*—"Classic of Changes." From this base in the divination camp, the Confucians next were able to absorb the Yin-Yang school into a dominant synthesis. All others of the old Warring States intellectual schools disappeared, leaving Confucian occultism in the center of the attention space.

The material base was built up, first by restoring the cult of Heaven in the sacrificial ritual of the court. Later Confucius himself was deified. A periodic ritual was established, offering homage to the emblem of their group identity, in effect putting Confucians in the position of ritual precedence. The doctrine was developed that Confucius himself had held the Mandate of Heaven as de facto earthly ruler, and furthermore that there was a series of such sages, periodically reappearing, leading one to expect further such Confucian rulers. On the mundane plane, this ideology corresponded to the change by which the Confucians were turning from *ju*, custodians of ancient texts, into bureaucratic officials claiming a monopoly on official positions in government. A state university was founded in 124 B.C.E. to train officials; by 5 C.E. it had grown to 3,000 students (*CHC*, 1986: 756).

Confucian claims for ideological and administrative monopoly were idealized; reality fell considerably short. Only a start was made at an administrative bureaucracy recruited as a meritocracy of educated officials. Clans and noble families still held sway in the provinces, and patrimonial politics remained influential at court. Admission to the state university was not by competitive examination but by patronage of notables. The effects on intellectual creativity occurred principally at the moment when the structure was first established. In the early Han, the court patronized official teaching by 70 Erudites, covering the range of texts and specialties which had come down from the Warring States. Under the new emperor Wu Ti (r. 141–86 B.C.E.), the Confucians struck:

first experts in the Legalist and Diplomatist texts were banned from government positions; then in 136 B.C.E. the Erudites were reduced to five lecturers on what henceforward became the paramount Confucian classics (Knoblock, 1988: 39–41).[11] A Confucian synthesis was put forward by one of the Erudites, promoting simultaneously a divination scheme, a philosophical system, and the new Confucian religion.

The individual whose fame arose through this intellectual coup is Tung Chung-shu, although he was not alone in these maneuvers (*CHC*, 1986: 709–710; Knoblock, 1988: 38–39). Pre-Ch'in Confucian secularism was submerged in Tung's all-encompassing system of correspondences. The Five Agents of the Yin-Yang school, not yet incorporated by the Confucian authors of the *Yi Ching* Appendices, now were moralized into a social hierarchy: "Earth serves Heaven with the utmost loyalty. Therefore the five agents are the actions of filial sons and loyal ministers" (Chan, 1963: 279). The cosmos was moralized and the human order described as a series of correspondences with natural phenomena. Building on the doctrines of Tsou Yen's school, Tung propounded how each dynasty had its reigning element, its predominant color and quality; government officials should have four ranks because there are four seasons. These correspondences sanctioned establishing a bureaucratic structure, and claimed for experts on natural portents a key place in government. All wrongdoing by human officials, according to this theory of correspondences, was connected to abnormalities in nature. Tung Chung-shu gave both a teleological and a mechanistic explanation of the weather and other natural phenomena, and incorporated many empirical observations along with references to mythical creatures. Confucian officials were to scan both human and natural worlds for signs of abnormalities and correct them by ritual and administrative measures.

The intellectual effect of this realignment was to bring philosophy down to a concrete and particularistic level. Divination systems bent philosophy to the service of political legitimation and oriented intellectuals toward alliances with political factions rather than toward the autonomy of intellectual issues. The first Ch'in emperor adopted Tsou Yen's system by taking water as the ruling element of his new regime, replacing fire, the element of the Warring States period. In the early Han, intellectual life was dominated by successive imperial counselors propounding cosmological views as to what element (fire or water) was the prevailing force of the new dynasty. The intellectual practice pioneered by Tsou Yen and the Yin-Yang school now became Confucian practice as well. To this drag on the intellectual world were added the liabilities of divination on the political side: since portents could be manipulated by all political factions, such as aspiring heirs or dissident branches of the nobility, they could provide alternative legitimations carrying magical and emotional overtones befitting an atmosphere of plots and coups. Divination schemes enjoyed a dangerous popularity in the Han and in subsequent dynasties. Tung Chung-shu, who surrounded himself with ritual pomp to the extent of lecturing from behind a screen out of the sight of mere mortals, was exiled to the provinces for his zealous advocacy of a divination scheme by which he attempted to manipulate government policy.[12]

The intellectual effects were not entirely destructive in the long run for the development of abstraction in Chinese philosophy. The synthesis of Confucian moralism with the divination schemes opened the way for a Confucian metaphysics. The crucial development was the third appendix to the *Yi Ching*, the so-called Great Treatise, which asserted ceaseless change as the fundamental reality of the universe. At the same time, the system of hexagrams composed of all permutations of strong *(yang)* and weak *(yin)* lines can be regarded as the structure out of which the empirical world is formed, analogous to Heraclitus' *logos* shaping the flux of experience.[13] The *Yi Ching* Great Appendix, along with several other extracts and commentaries from classic texts about this time—the *Doctrine of the Mean* and the *Great Learning,* both developed from the *Book of Rites*—became the textual capital on which the Neo-Confucians of the Sung dynasty were to develop a Confucian metaphysics.

The centralization of ideological production in the Han reorganized the material practice of intellectual life. The imperial library was founded, staffed by officials whose task it was to define the paramount reality through compiling official histories and putting in order the texts that would constitute tradition. Any rival to official definitions of reality would also take the form of an encyclopedia or bibliographic collection. Collections of books and their rubrics now crystallized identities, making up the "schools" into which all subsequent historians have organized Chinese intellectual life. Inclusion or exclusion from a bibliographical collection had fateful consequences. The canon of Confucian texts omitted the works of Mencius and Hsün Tzu, which constituted a Confucian underground, and Mencius was not brought back into prominence until the revolutionary upheaval promoted by the Neo-Confucians.

Even in periods of centralization, what innovation did take place came in the form of oppositions, the usual driving force of intellectual life. Opposing doctrines appeared simultaneously, contesting key points within similar materials. In the same generation when Tung Chung-shu was carrying out his Confucian synthesis, an anti-Confucian position was organized. It gradually acquired the label "Taoism," although the term is anachronistic if we expect it to carry particular metaphysical or religious connotations. There were two such oppositional developments. Tung Chung-shu's contemporary Ssu-ma T'an, the imperial historian, in organizing the official library classified the books into schools, coining the term "Tao-te chia" for a category of texts similar to the *Tao Te Ching.*

More sharply in opposition was a group in the provinces, gathered around the prince of Huai Nan (in the south below the Yangtze), in a collateral branch of the imperial family which resisted the move toward bureaucratic centralization. Prince Liu An patronized thousands of scholars and magicians, who produced an encyclopedic treatise, the *Huai-nan Tzu,* covering metaphysics, astronomy, government, the army, and every area of extant knowledge. Chuang Tzu's paradoxes and nature mysticism were turned into a cosmological sequence. Vacuity gave rise to *tao,* which gave rise to space and time, which in turn gave rise to material force, and then to the manifestations of the material universe. There was a time before *yin* and *yang,* Heaven and Earth (i.e., the received cosmological categories), and even before non-being—thus going back beyond the *Tao Te Ching* as well. This was not yet religious Taoism; the Huai Nan group attacked meditation and reinterpreted "non-action" as "no action contrary to nature." Earlier traditions of mystical quietism and political withdrawal were turned in the direction of political activism. When the prince of Huai Nan rose in rebellion in 122 B.C.E., it was put down by an army led by a disciple of Tung Chung-shu (Woo, 1932: 30–31).

The intellectual-religious identity of an anti-Confucian opposition persisted, even as Confucian hegemony at the centralized court was established. "Taoism" gradually crystallized as a distinctive collection of texts, outside the Confucian classics and their official commentaries. The *Chuang Tzu* was also compiled at this time, including its late syncretist chapters, perhaps at the Huai Nan court itself, perhaps in the oppositional group at the Han court around Ssu-ma T'an (Roth, 1991: 86–93; Graham, 1991: 280–283). The *Chuang Tzu* remained somewhat to the side, since its anti-political stance and its idiosyncratic attitude about death did not fit with either the activist stance of the *Huai-nan Tzu* or the religious cult of immortals which became the center of popular Taoist religion.

The most important identity was simply negative, an anti-Confucian opposition. Eventually "Taoism" became a bibliographic collection which took under its wing all the surviving bits of rival philosophies. By 300 C.E., Mo Tzu was listed as a minor Taoist immortal, and his book was included in the *Taoist Canon,* along with such disparate figures as the Legalist Han Fei Tzu and (in a late forgery) Kung-sun Lung (Graham, 1978: 65–66). This was syncretism of the most external sort, with no effort to assert intellectual similarities beyond the common property of being outside the official Confucian fold.

After the defeat of the Huai Nan rebellion, what intellectual action there was took the form of a split within Confucian ranks. In opposition to the Confucian religion, an Old Text school arose, initially a bibliographical movement critiquing the newer occultist commentaries (the so-called New Text school) and demanding a return to the original texts as they were before the burning of the books. The most prominent leader of the Old Text school was the imperial librarian Liu Hsin; his network of teachers descended from Liu An, the prince of Huai Nan himself (see Figure 4.3). Structurally the old anti-Confucian opposition continued in the new opposition within Confucianism. Liu Hsin was joined by contemporary Confucian dissidents Yang Hsiung and Huan T'an, anti-occultist skeptics with connections to the mathematical and other scientific work around this time.[14] Two generations later, the most radically secularist, anti-teleological Confucian appeared: Wang Ch'ung. This was a period of two-sided struggle rather than a swing in the zeitgeist away from occultism. It was in these same generations that the movement to deify Confucius was at its height.[15]

The struggle gave rise to little sustained creativity in Chinese philosophy. Figure 4.3 shows how sparse and broken were the networks of notable figures; little reflexive abstraction built up. On the level of political realities, both the New Text and Old Text schools were tied to external allies, whose dynastic political struggles they bolstered with rival prophecies from occult numerology and portents (Gernet, 1982: 163–165). Even the most extreme of the "rationalist" anti-occultists, such as Wang Ch'ung, did little more than to lay down a negative position, implicitly linked to the occultism which constitutes its topic.[16] Confucian religion and Confucian rationalism set the lines of long-standing internal opposition within Confucianism, in effect a division over the question of how much the scholars should mingle in the external politics of religious-political factionalism. It was an opposition on a low level of intellectual abstraction, anchored in the external world, promoting little autonomy for inner developments in intellectual space.

The Changing Landscape of External Supports

The Han dynasty, especially in its earlier period, aimed at a totally controlling bureaucratic state, attempting to regulate the entire economy, providing public works, monopolizing manufactures and their distribution. Armies consisted of conscripts armed and supplied by the state. The predominance of a civilian bureaucracy gave some basis for intellectual life, in the bureau of religious rites and the imperial library, and an educationally credentialed profession of higher administrators provided some positions for teachers. We have seen the limitations on intellectual life under these conditions. Most officials—there were 120,000 of them by 100 C.E. (CHC, 1986: 466)—were narrowly concerned with practicality or with political maneuvering; much of the innovativeness around the bureau of rites took the form of particularistic cults, including divinization of Confucius. The expansion of the state university, which reached 30,000 students by 125–144 (CHC, 1986: 756–757), was not associated with philosophical creativity. We see again in later dynasties, especially the T'ang

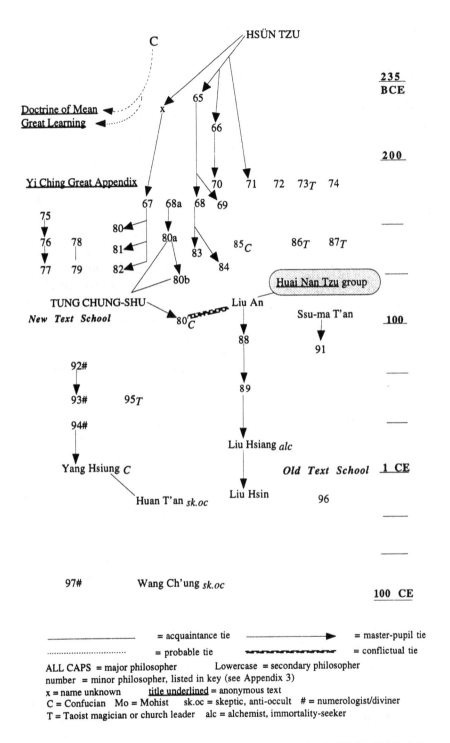

FIGURE 4.3. HAN DYNASTY TRANSITION AND FORMING OF
OFFICIAL CONFUCIANISM, 235 B.C.E.–100 C.E.

and the Ming, that the formal educational system can promote cultural traditionalism and rote learning rather than innovation.

In the later Han this effort at autocratic state control of the economy, never entirely successful, increasingly broke down. Peasant farmers generally became debtors and tenants of large private estates. State monopolies, which had been operated through the intermediaries of franchised merchants, were transferred to local administration and eventually into private hands. The centralized bureaucracy continued in existence, perhaps even expanded, but exerted less control. Power struggles went on among the patrimonial household staff, the court aristocracy, and the various factions of central and local administrators; something like an educated gentry stratum was forming as education expanded, but its effective control was small. After 100 C.E. government revenues fell, and the government became incapable of providing disaster relief in the countryside. Peasant uprisings were organized around religious movements, using the cultural capital of the anti-Confucian opposition, and giving shape to an incipient Taoist church. When the military resources of the large estates surpassed that of the central government, the state broke apart.

The "medieval" period of the next 400 years was one of political fragmentation. At first there were the warring Three Kingdoms, then a brief reunification under the Chin dynasty (265–316). The old Han capital at Loyang saw an upsurge of intellectual life at this time, somewhat misleadingly labeled "Neo-Taoist"; its carriers were the court nobility and what remained of a Confucian gentry or officialdom. The functions of the bureaucracy must have been nominal. The money economy largely disappeared; economic control was in the hands of the large estates, and the ruler's private estates near the capital provided most of his resources. The landed magnates collected their own armed retainers, including nomadic tribes recruited as mercenaries. When these military forces formed their own opportunistic alliances, the nominally centralized state was again destroyed. In this way armies of Huns took north China in 309–316, with considerable devastation and loss of population. Many Chinese fled to the south, where an independent state was maintained until China was reunified by the Sui dynasty in 589. South China underwent considerable economic development, but the military and administrative power of the central government was weak, and economic control was in the hands of large autarkic estates. There were uprisings and civil wars throughout the period, and five nominal changes of dynasty. North China, by contrast, was frequently divided among warring states built on tribal coalitions of Huns, Turks, Mongols, or Tibetans. There was one period of fairly considerable unification in the north, from about 440 to 530, when the Toba (Turkish) Empire subjugated most of the other northern states.

The overall process was not so much a conquest of China by ethnic aliens

SECOND PERIOD OF DIVISION, 250 C.E.

as a fragmentation of military power from within. In the north, the tribal armies usually became organized as allies in the power struggles of the large estate holders, and their victorious leaders soon became part of the indigenous structure. Their rulers inherited the problems of supplying and controlling troops and of taxing the population; their military supporters tended to become landed magnates in their own right. At times there were reactionary "nativist" movements among tribal groupings who remained at the borders, but these were rarely successful against the organized forces of the center. Typically the northern states attempted to emulate the Han tradition of autocratic direction of the economy, but with only partial success. Some bureaucracy was reestablished, and Confucianism regained a foothold; intrigues among the palace staff, royal relatives, and court aristocracy were overlaid by ethnic factionalism; the predominant trend toward cultural Sinification was complicated by a new religious pluralism with the growth of Taoist and Buddhist sects.

This was the period in which monasteries appeared, and eventually became a new base for intellectual production. In the south, Buddhist and Taoist sects underwent considerable growth, patronized by emperor and aristocracy. Especially in the northern states, monasteries received massive grants of land, serfs, and slaves; in effect, the rulers used monasteries as agents in controlling and reorganizing the population, resettling devastated areas, and colonizing the frontiers. Buddhist monasteries soon became the leading edge of economic growth; their wealth and privileges became objects of contention between landed magnates and court factions.

Religious factions converged on the center when government reunified. Military struggle eventually resulted in reunification under the Sui (581–618) and, after further civil war, the T'ang (618–900). There was a successful effort to rebuild the central administration and to regain civilian control over a conscript army. Revenue collection, public works, and state rituals were expanded in the Han tradition; professionalized Confucian administrators recruited by a formal examination system once again began to expand their influence. Their usual struggles with the palace servants and the court aristocracy were now complicated by patronage for Buddhists and Taoists. Battles over the imperial succession often took on overtones of religious factionalism. Taoism and Buddhism had brief episodes as state-imposed religions. More usually, the panoply of state rituals took precedence, administered by Confucians who were much more bureaucrats than priests. The structure had become one of religious pluralism under the umbrella of a state administration that typically sought ritual legitimation simultaneously from all religions and cults.

When Does Rivalry Produce Creativity and When Stagnation?

A conflict theory of intellectual life emphasizes opposition as the generator of creativity. But Chinese philosophy points up the pattern in which opposing factions exist, sometimes for dozens of generations, without much intellectual change. We see one such instance in the later Han, in the stagnant rivalry between the religious and scholarly wings of the Confucian school. After the disintegration of the Han dynasty, the prevailing pattern becomes a broad three-way competition among Confucian, Taoist, and Buddhist camps. But for long periods Confucianism shows almost no creativity; except for one generation around 800 C.E. (see Chapter 6, Figures 6.1 through 6.4), we find no notable Confucian philosophers until 1050, when the Neo-Confucian movement comes alive for half a dozen generations. Buddhist philosophers monopolize creativity for much of this period, especially from 400 to 900, then gradually tail off to around 1200, and produce nothing significant thereafter. Taoism shows intermittent religious changes during this time but with long phases of stagnation, especially on the level of abstract philosophy.

Yet there were plenty of confrontations among these major positions. There was a lively struggle for patronage; Taoists and Buddhists especially instigated intermittent purges, confiscations, and suppressions of each other. Intellectual challenges were not lacking; debates among Confucians, Taoists, and Buddhists took place at many courts during the period of fragmentation after the Han, during the centralized T'ang dynasty, and indeed down to the time of the Mongol regime. The material underpinnings of intellectual life expanded when an official examination system was established. In the T'ang and later dynasties, there were at times several such examination systems, for Buddhist and Taoist monks as well as for the state bureaucracy. All this one might expect would have stimulated a great deal of philosophical innovation. But we find surprisingly little outside of Buddhism.

This material provides an opportunity to sharpen our theory through comparison. On many occasions structural conflict fosters philosophical creativity. We have seen it in China in the Warring States period, with both the polarization of positions and the push toward higher levels of epistemological and metaphysical abstraction during the "hundred schools." We see again a brief creative antagonism in the Three Kingdoms period after the Han downfall between Taoist and Confucian tendencies transmuted into a higher philosophical plane. In Greece the same dynamic of innovative opposition and the sharpening of abstractions went on through 12 to 15 generations of debate; here too we found periods of relative stagnation, such as the loose and inconclusive syncretisms of Middle Platonism between 100 B.C.E. and 200 C.E., and we witnessed the long-term conservatism of the Epicureans.

Simmel's sociological theory fits one side of the problem: conflict increases solidarity and conformity within a group. Hence we would expect a time of heightened conflict to be one in which opposing sides stick dogmatically to their positions. The level of intellectual sophistication would decline as nuances are driven out and positions of compromise are forced to join battle on one side or the other. This is a pattern we find in intellectual life, as well as in political, military, and personal conflicts. It helps explain why philosophers can lose higher levels of abstraction achieved by earlier generations and revert to crude reifications, dogmatism, and name-calling rather than analytical advance. The lower rather than the higher level usually characterized the debates among Taoists, Buddhists, and Confucians.

Our theoretical problem is to integrate this sub-theory into the overall picture. We have abundant evidence that conflict is sometimes creative. The law of small numbers gives a structural shape to this struggle. The issue is to show what kinds of structural rivalry drive innovation by opposition, with associated shifts upward in the level of abstraction and critical self-reflection, and what kinds of conflict have the opposite effect on intellectual life, producing stagnation and particularism. Part of the resolution lies in distinguishing two kinds of innovation: that which takes place on the particularistic level, as in the formation of religious cults and of anthropomorphic or magical doctrines, and that which produces abstract metaphysical, epistemological, and ethical conceptions.

The underlying issue is the way in which intellectual life rests on material and social supports of the surrounding world. The abstract level of philosophy is determined by the dynamics of inner networks among intellectuals. Here we have a two-step causality: the external world is indirectly influential insofar as it supports those organizational structures which allow an intellectual network to face inward upon its own struggles. This structural autonomy for intellectuals does not always exist. We have seen it build up during the pre-Han Warring States; we will see it again during the heyday of Buddhist philosophical networks in the T'ang, and yet again in the neo-Confucian networks of the Sung. At other times network autonomy is greatly diminished, for example, to a considerable extent during the Han, and during much of the following period of political disintegration. During such times intellectual life does not necessarily come to a halt. But its inner dynamics are greatly weakened. The content of intellectual doctrines is now filled much more directly by the cultural interests of the social classes and external institutions which support intellectuals.[17]

There are, then, two sociological questions about the relationship between intellectuals and the external world. We can ask about the conditions under which the internal autonomy of the intellectual network is high, low, or at points in between. And we can ask about the patterns of intellectual production when autonomy is low. The latter is the question of the effect of class cultures on intellectuals, the traditional topic of the sociology of knowledge. I have argued that class determination is not a very useful theory for dealing with the highest levels of creativity, the sequences of abstractions produced within the core of the intellectual community; but class determination is applicable in periods when structural bases of autonomy are absent. These are typically periods of intellectual stagnation for an abstract discipline such as philosophy. What innovation occurs will be at a more concrete and particularistic level, such as the developments of anthropomorphic religions and magical doctrines.

Let us be clear: periods of low intellectual autonomy can also have moments of innovation; only they are not driven by the inner network structure of the field. Left to themselves, intellectuals produce their own factions and alliances. Their competition over intellectual attention space leaves behind a trail of abstractions which constitute the inner history of ideas. When intellectual autonomy is low, this self-propelling dynamic is absent. Instead, new ideas occur at the moments when the class structure changes, when there are new external bases for intellectual life—new political conditions fostering religious movements, new economic and administrative conditions raising or lowering the salience of court aristocrats, state bureaucrats, or propertied gentry, and other such shifts. These changes in external conditions are much more episodic. Intellectual changes, typically in the form of concrete religious doctrines or of lifestyle ideologies, come about when a new kind of structure is created. Once in place, they are likely to remain conservative as well as concrete, like the patterns of Taoist religion or gentry lifestyle. Once laid down, these are anchors of intergroup conflict rather than items of cultural capital to be parlayed by intellectuals into an ever-lengthening sequence of conceptual abstractions.

I have of course been speaking in ideal types. There is usually some overlay between autonomous intellectual networks and direct class influences. Even the most inwardly directed networks will incorporate some items of class culture, if only as starting points on which to play inner intellectual games. And direct class control of the intellectual world usually allows some degree of structuring by the law of small numbers. The relative degree of innovation or stagnation of intellectual life at the level of abstract philosophies depends on the degree of inner autonomy along this continuum.

The development of Taoism is a good place to explore the conditions of low intellectual autonomy from lay influences, and the ways different class cultures affect intellectual life in such circumstances.

From Anti-Confucian Opposition to Taoist Church

"Taoism" is perhaps the most controversial category of Chinese historiography. The concept *tao* was the common property of virtually all intellectual factions in the Warring States. In the *Analects* it is used to refer to the proper course of human conduct, which the Confucians identified with the "way of the ancients" (Graham, 1989: 13). At the opposite pole, the Legalists also made use of the concept in grounding their doctrines. As late as 1200 c.e., the movement that we call Neo-Confucianism and that gained official status as interpreter of the Confucian classics was known by its contemporaries as *tao-hsüeh,* the *tao* study or school. The writings of Chuang Tzu and the *Tao Te Ching* are mixtures of various elements from the philosophical field of their times and do not constitute a united front with the doctrines and practices of the contemporary magicians and shamans that might also be called "Taoist." According to this line of reasoning, Ssu-ma T'an's category "Tao-te chia"— "school of the Way and its Power"—which later became "Tao chia," is merely a bibliographical classification. As Strickmann and others (Strickmann, 1979: 166–167; Zürcher, 1959: 87; Sivin, 1978) have stressed, this kind of "philosophical Taoism" is so different from the religious Taoism which built up during the Han as to be incomparable. These scholars advocate reserving the term "Taoism" for the Taoist church from 150 c.e. onwards. In particular the so-called neo-Taoism of the "Seven Sages of the Bamboo Grove" and their compatriots around 250 C.E. is a misnomer, and should be replaced by the contemporary terms "Pure Conversation" *(ch'ing t'an)* and "Dark Learning" *(hsüan hsüeh).*

This definitional strategy buys clarity in some areas at the cost of obscurity elsewhere. What we miss is the oppositional stance which crystallized while Confucianism was becoming a state orthodoxy and a religion, and the fluctuating lines of syncretism which took place within this oppositional united front. One can agree that "Taoism" is an anachronism before the time of Tung Chung-shu, though not after. But the elements that became "Taoism" preexisted this time. Schematically, these included: (1) *wu* (sorcerers) and *fang shih* (shamans or spirit mediums), with their methods of curing the sick, prophesying, inducing trances and visions; (2) a practice of physical hygiene which sought longevity through breathing exercises and gymnastics; (3) experimenters with drugs and metals seeking an elixir of life; and (4) politically and philosophically oppositional hermits and primitivists, ranging from the followers of Yang Chu up through the author of the *Tao Te Ching* (Welch, 1965: 88–112).

These doctrines represent quite different social settings and historical periods. The magicians and shamans were members of surviving aboriginal tribes or practitioners among the lower classes. The philosophical primitivists, by contrast, were members of the educated classes. Where we hear of them putting their ideas into practice, such as Ch'en Chung of the ruling house of Ch'i, ca. 320 B.C.E. (Fung, 1952–53: 143), we find something like a utopian community or "hippie commune," quite different in spirit from the involuntary primitiveness of life among the peasantry. Some ideas and practices of the magicians percolated into court circles by the time of the Ch'in and early Han. Magicians vied for the patronage of superstitious and aging emperors; in response, court intellectuals propounded new methods of physical hygiene and concocted new elixirs, intellectualizing and extending the themes of tribal magic. In this evolving mix, the political and metaphysical themes of Chuang Tzu and the *Tao Te Ching* stand apart from the crude materialist goals of longevity and physical immortality for the individual.[18] Nevertheless, all these elements were thrown together in compilations such as the *Huai-nan Tzu* (130 B.C.E.) and the *Lieh Tzu* (ca. 300 C.E.). Such amalgamations gave pointed contrast to the officializing doctrines of public morality and political-religious responsibility that made up the core of the Confucian position. The earliest group identity as "Taoist" was a coalition formed of disparate elements, which began just as Confucianism was putting together its synthesis with the cosmologies of the divination schools.

The Taoist church began to form in the late Han as factional struggles at court against the official cult of the Confucians, sponsoring sacrifices to a multiplicity of gods and supernatural beings associated with immortality and other magic (Welch, 1965; Strickmann, 1979; Kaltenmark, 1969; Ofuchi, 1979; Stein, 1979). As the dynasty disintegrated, rebel movements in the provinces organized several kinds of Taoist churches, one of which ruled an independent Taoist state in Szechuan for four generations. In the chaos of fragmented states between 300 and 550, the several branches amalgamated into a formal Taoist religion. Its practices gradually shifted from magic and immortality-seeking through drugs and alchemy to ritual worship and interior meditation, as it built up a monastic organization and a set of disciplinary rules imitated from Buddhism. Old texts supporting a "Taoist" identity, along with alchemical lore and new spiritual revelations expounded by the organizers of monastic Taoism, were syncretized into a textual canon during the 400s. Thereafter the Taoist canon stayed fixed; the printed version of 1447 has the same rubrics it had a millennium earlier.

The Taoist religion exemplifies the external determinism that limits innovativeness on the intellectual plane. Taoist intellectual life consisted mainly in elaborating doctrines directly connected with practice. These shifted only at the moments when Taoist cultural capital was being adapted to appeal to a different external audience. Thus developed a succession of particularistic concepts: changing the lineup of the pantheon which claimed a place in Han court patronage; health magic for a peasant-based movement at the time of political disintegration; doctrines of immortality-producing elixirs and exercises for a withdrawn gentry elite; scriptural regularities and meditative exercises as a monastic organization developed. Doctrinal changes episodically followed changes in external conditions, but drove no philosophical development at a higher level of abstraction. Each succeeding version of Taoist religion stayed close to the class culture of its external audience.[19]

What was specific to Taoist religious organization that had this result? For Buddhism went a contrasting route. Although appealing successfully to lay audiences, Chinese Buddhism developed inward-looking intellectual networks which for many centuries drove just the kind of abstract intellectual creativity that was lacking in the Taoist church. Consider the range of organizational forms in Chinese religion: state-supported cults, carried out by government officials (i.e., typically "Confucian"); monasteries, which might be nearly self-sufficient estates, or might depend on outside patronage; temples providing religious ceremonies for the public in return for donations, and ranging from grand urban buildings to tiny village shrines; solo-practitioner priests or hermits, who usually made their living by dispensing medicinal or magical potions and charms. Some organizational forms can be compared to a "Catholic" structure in which religious personnel are autonomous from the people and supported by the government or massive property accumulation; others resemble a "Protestant" type in which priests are independent religious entrepreneurs living directly off public consumers. In the latter category we should add religious secret societies, whose members were preponderantly or entirely laypeople; these resemble in some respects the Christian lay brotherhoods of the late medieval period, differing in China in that their activities were particularly likely to include political rebellion.

Of all these organizational forms, the ones which were most often a basis for autonomous development of intellectual communities were the monasteries and the large urban temples. These "Catholic" types are the most characteristic Buddhist organizations. The Taoist church, in contrast, was predominantly based on the "Protestant" style of decentralized religious organizations; and these were the forms which brought the religion closest to the immediate concerns of lay culture. This helps explain why Buddhist organization favored abstract intellectual creativity so much more than Taoist organization did. It suggests, too, a reason why Buddhism lost its philosophical creativity at the end of the medieval period, when its great monasteries and temples lost their autonomy. Popular salvation-oriented Amidaist Buddhism was structurally much closer to a Taoist organizational form; when Buddhism became reduced to little more than Amidaism, abstract Buddhist philosophy died out as well. We shall see a similar pattern in Europe in the development of scholastic philosophy in medieval Catholicism, and the shift toward lay orientations in the Protestant Reformation.

The Gentry-Official Culture: The Pure Conversation Movement and the Dark Learning

For abstract philosophy, the most famous developments were not in religious Taoism but in an interconnected group of gentry and officials which flourished for two generations around 235–300 C.E. This was the last occasion in Chinese history when there was any creativity on the purely philosophical side that had a significant connection with Taoism. Later Neo-Confucianism would absorb philosophical Taoism so completely that there was nothing left but the religious side, with its particularistic practices. Although the earlier movement has usually been labeled "Neo-Taoist" or "philosophical Taoism," the question has arisen whether it is Taoist at all. It included the themes of individualistic withdrawal from the duties of conventional society, metaphysical mysticism, and non-action (wu-wei); and it explicitly developed its cultural capital from the *Tao Te Ching, Chuang Tzu,* and similar texts. All this fits our conventional picture of "Taoist"; indeed, it is the "Seven Sages of the Bamboo Grove" who best define our retrospective image of what a Taoist should be.

Yet this was very different from the religious Taoism forming at the same time, and antagonistic to it on key points. These philosophers and poets had no interest in the religious pantheon or the doctrine of immortals; though some were interested in alchemy, their cult of wine drinking and sexual carousing was directly contrary to the puritanical hygiene sects, with their efforts to control internal bodily processes. Moreover, these "philosophical Taoists" were precisely in the milieu of court Confucianism. They were educated gentry, whose culture was now taking on the pattern in which Confucianism controlled the official part of one's life, while a kind of aesthetic hedonism, legitimated by texts that were now called "Taoist," guided one's leisure and retirement.

The organizational basis of these movements confirms their connection with Confucianism. The term "Pure Conversation," or *ch'ing t'an,* implying philosophy for its own sake, came directly from the Old Text school, the Confucian rationalists who opposed both the Confucian and the Lao-Huang religions and occultism at the Han court. As the Han dynasty disintegrated, a thousand or more of these scholars congregated at Ching-Chou in Hupei under the sponsorship of the local governor (Demiéville, 1986: 826, 830; Rump and Chan, 1979: xx–xxi). In the next generation, the libraries of major Confucian scholars connected with the Ching-Chou group passed via family inheritance to the young aristocrat Wang Pi. Notable for erudition at an early age—rich in cultural capital when few others had access to such texts—Wang Pi formulated his own reinterpretation of the classics, beginning the so-called school of Dark Learning (see Figure 4.4).

The time was one of political decentralization. The money economy largely disappeared; salaries were paid in silk or grain, and trade took the form of barter. At first China had divided into three states. Then in 263 the northern state of Wei conquered the southwest state (in Szechuan) and in 280 the southeast state, bringing about a brief period of reunification (280–307). It was around the capital of the northern state of Wei (subsequently named the Western Chin dynasty), continuing at the old Han site of Loyang, that all the notable philosophical activity took place. The religious sects of Taoism were predominant in other regions: the Five Pecks of Grain cult formed in the west; the alchemical sects and later the development of Taoist monasticism and the church pantheon were in the south.

The northern state was politically unstable. Internally it was wracked by assassinations and coups among the leading families; externally it was subject to inroads of barbarian tribes from the north and west, who ultimately overran the dynasty in 309–316. The decay of the central bureaucracy at this time helps account for the decline of Confucianism, and hence its willingness to syncretize with other intellectual positions. Moreover, as the internal situation changed within the intellectual community, the interests of Confucian scholars turned in an entirely new direction. The skeptical rationalists of the Old Text school

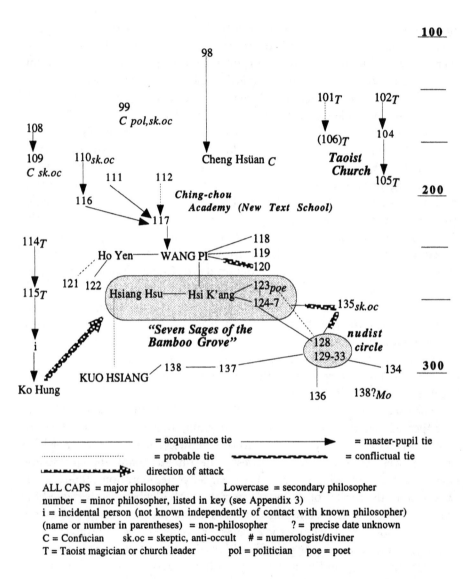

FIGURE 4.4. LATER HAN DYNASTY DISINTEGRATION AND THE
DARK LEARNING, 100–300 C.E.

lost their opposing anchors—the court religions—when the Han fell; now their
scholarship was turned loose in free space. It soon developed its internal
oppositions.

The "Pure Conversation school" turned toward an elitist, aesthetic hedonism, specializing in witty repartee, paradoxical sayings, wine drinking, sexual

affairs, and other behavior scandalous to Confucian mores. The notorious Liu Ling (ca. 221–300) used to go naked in his house. To a shocked Confucian visitor he retorted, "The world is my house, and these walls are my garments. What, then, are you doing standing in my pants?" (Fung, 1948: 235). Liu belonged to the group called the Seven Sages of the Bamboo Grove, members of the upper gentry who met to drink, write poetry, and appreciate the fleetingness of beauty on their country estates outside the capital, disdaining the conventional life of the court. In the next generation younger relatives of this group indulged in a nudist circle as well as in sensual extravagances and intellectual witticisms. One style-setter would practice *ch'ing t'an* (pure conversation) "while he held in his pale hands a feather-duster with a jade handle, with which to sweep away, symbolically, the dust of this vile world" (Balazs, 1964: 248–249). Yet these were members of the ruling aristocracy, including generals, officials, and relatives of the ruling houses.

In intellectual opposition to the Seven Sages was another group which also drew upon Taoist cultural capital, but made an explicit effort to combine it with Confucian orthodoxy. The school of Dark (or Mysterious) Learning *(hsüan hsüeh)* was a network of Wei state officials. Ho Yen (d. 249), a Wei minister, synthesized *yin-yang* cosmology and Taoist ontology, giving a rational explanation of the paradoxes of the *Tao Te Ching.* His protégé Wang Pi (226–249), another Wei minister, wrote influential commentaries on both the *Tao Te Ching* and the *Yi Ching,* bringing together the Taoist sacred text with the Han Confucians' divination classic. Wang Pi's philosophy might be regarded as a set of abstractions designed to unify these positions by removing both from the level of religious practice or particularistic portents onto an ontological plane in its own right. Wang was not so much a mystic as a practitioner of metaphysics. With Wang Pi the philosophical community built to a metaphysical level that had been seldom touched in China, and it was this which gave such work the reputation of being a "dark" or "mysterious" learning.

Wang Pi developed in an original fashion a metaphysical interpretation of Taoist non-being *(wu-wei).* One cannot put non-being on the same plane as being, even as its opposite. "The cessation of activity always means quiescence, but this quiescence is not something opposed to activity. The cessation of speech means silence, but this silence is not something opposed to speech" (quoted in Fung, 1952–53: 181). But this original non-being, *pen-wu,* is not an emptiness on which a meditator might focus. It is, rather, pure being in the sense of original substance. Commenting on the *Yi Ching* and its Confucian Appendices, Wang Pi argues that the hexagrams represent not concrete objects of predictions but principles of the multiple things; behind these in turn is a unity transcending multiplicity, which in a sense may be regarded as the referent of Taoist non-being. Yet it is a substance and is permeated by principle, *li*, which governs everything down through the multiplicity of things. Being is the functioning of the original substance; but regarded apart from its functioning, it is a purity that can be thought of as non-being. Wang Pi's philosophy, interspersed as commentaries on earlier texts, is not developed very systematically, but it shows unmistakably the push toward a consistent metaphysical interpretation to overcome the paradoxical tone of the Taoist classics.

The intellectual community at midcentury had become dense and competitive. One faction (Wang Pi, Wang Tao, Ouyang Chien, and others) maintained that ideas can be fully expressed in words, while an opposition led by Yin Jung defended wordlessness. Here we find an epistemological debate of the sort rarely reached in Chinese philosophy. Wang Pi seems to have made the most sophisticated formulation. He distinguishes ideas as a realm that can be grasped by means of symbols (such as the *Yi* hexagrams) and words; once the words and symbols have served their purpose, they can be dispensed with (Fung, 1952–53: 184–186). Wang seems to have recognized the nature of abstraction in its own right, beyond the symbols through which it is expressed. Having clarified this distinction, he holds that, contrary to Taoist mysticism, words and symbols are completely adequate to express ideas. In conjunction with other remarks in which both non-being and the original state of the universe are identified with the mind (Rump and Chan, 1979: 109; *Chou Yi* Commentary, quoted in Fung, 1952–53: 181), this suggests that Wang Pi seems to have been considering a position in the direction of a Platonic idealism.

There was a concerted effort to redevelop the cultural capital of the various pre-Han texts as consistent philosophical positions. At this time were produced the first major editions and commentaries on the *Chuang Tzu*, as well as the compilations of reconstructed (or forged) classics, the *Lieh Tzu* and the *Yang Chu*, representing the opponents of the older Confucian tradition. The arguments of Hui Shih and Kung-sung Lung and of the Mohist logicians were also revived, and played a part in philosophical debate; they were attacked by Wang Pi and defended a generation later by Kuo Hsiang. Independent rationalists and skeptics flourished, along with developments in mathematics and empirical science. What we find (visible in Figure 4.4 as the biggest network cluster in four hundred years) is a dense, competitive intellectual community, in which the major philosophers have direct connections with their opponents, and vertical chains across the generations go on from the Confucian rationalists of the late Han down to the early 300s. These exemplify the structural conditions for creativity on the level of abstract philosophy, in contrast to the philosophically static rivalries or at best particularistic religious developments in the surrounding centuries.

The metaphysicians of this period are much more than "Neo-Taoists," though they built on the philosophical texts that we may call the Taoist tendency within the late Warring States period. This was a community of textual scholars who revived much of the full range of texts as of about 250 B.C.E., and went on to develop them on an intellectual plane. It is as if these thinkers picked up where the intellectual community left off its internal discussions, before the Ch'in and Han states narrowed the issues down to religious and occultist themes appealing to lay politicians. The purest intellectuals of the Han, the Old Text school, had been able to do little more than keep up an ideal of scholarship and skepticism. Now, as an untrammeled intellectual community formed again, metaphysical and epistemological dimensions were explored in their own right as never before.

The "Taoist" philosophical classics became central for this group because they were a springboard for metaphysical discussion. There is some resonance between the older tradition of withdrawal and nature primitivism and the aesthetic hedonism of the Seven Sages type (although there is reason to suspect that they were not as anti-political as the ideology makes them out to be). The metaphysics of the "Dark Learning," by contrast, was largely formed in opposition to mysticism. Wang Pi, Hsiang Hsiu, and Kuo Hsiang all declared that Confucius was a greater sage than Lao Tzu and Chuang Tzu—because he never talked about non-being but manifested it in action (Fung, 1952–53: 170–173). Ho Yen and Wang Pi interpreted the Confucian classics in Taoist terminology, and Hsiang Hsiu and Kuo Hsiang interpreted the *Chuang Tzu* in a Confucian spirit. All these men were government officials, pursuing a synthesis of rationalistic Confucianism with the classic Taoist philosophers. Their work exemplifies the creativity of structural realignment, in which the effort to combine positions seriously defended in the intellectual world forced them to develop new levels of conception.

The last of the group, Kuo Hsiang (fl. 290–310), takes this the furthest.[20] For him the nature of the universe is change; hence it is foolish to worship the doctrines of the past, such as Confucian ceremonies which no longer meet the needs of the time. Kuo attacks religious beliefs in a creator, as well as the search for magical methods of prolonging life, and even the practice of meditation, declaring that the sage is not one who "folds his arms and sits in silence in the midst of some mountain forest" (Chan, 1963: 327). Kuo instead is a naturalist. *Tao* now gives way as a ruling principle to nature *(tzu-jan),* a spontaneously developing principle immanent within things themselves. Moreover, Kuo does not stand pat with the stance of the Dark Learning of the previous generation. Philosophical arguments were reaching a new level of acuteness: ontological claims were no longer merely asserted but were being scrutinized in terms of a newly developing standard of logical analysis.

Kuo attacks Wang Pi's doctrine that being comes from an original substance or condition because that argument leads to an infinite regress. In an argument similar to Parmenides', Kuo states that non-being can never become being, nor can being become non-being. This leads him to a general denial of ultimate causes, as nothing can (in an absolute sense) produce anything else. Kuo seems to have considered this from several angles. The whole universe is the condition for everything within it; and every item, no matter how insignificant in itself, is necessary for everything else to exist. Moreover, everything is imperceptibly changing. "Therefore the 'I' of the past is no longer the 'I' of today" (quoted in Fung, 1952–53: 213). At the same time, Kuo asserts that nothing can autonomously determine anything else: "Things are what they are spontaneously and not caused by something else" (Chan, 1963: 335). Kuo Hsiang combines metaphysical aspects that recall both Parmenides and Heraclitus in the same system. But instead of reconciling the inalterability of being with the omnipresence of change after the fashion of the Greek solutions, Kuo finds a different resolution. It is neither the atomists' substance with its combinations, a Platonic distinction among realms of ideal being and empirical becoming, nor an Aristotelean mixture of matter and form. Kuo Hsiang instead denies the absoluteness of being, letting reality reside in the phenomenal flow of the whole universe, incessant but necessary in its patterns. Paradoxes like those of Chuang Tzu and the Taoists arise from the partial viewpoint of a single actor in the universe; logical consistency lies only in grasping the whole.

Class Culture and the Freezing of Creativity in Indigenous Chinese Philosophy

In the generations connecting Wang Pi and Kuo Hsiang, Chinese philosophy opened up a realm of abstract philosophy encompassing epistemology and metaphysics at levels comparable to the most intense periods of the Greeks. The external conditions which supported this intellectual structure were ephemeral. The creativity of the Pure Conversation and Dark Learning came from a conflict between class cultures. Neither the leisure gentry culture nor the bureaucratic administrative culture by itself fostered creativity in the realm of abstract philosophy. Intellectual creativity moved forward only when these two structural bases were in a conflictual balance, with both components linked together in the same network, such as existed around Loyang from about 240 to 300. Here we find the typical creative structure of multiple bases intersecting at a geographical center. Typical, too, is the pattern of creativity by opposition. The Seven Sages of the Bamboo Grove and their followers developed an iconoclastic aestheticism against the Confucian proprieties of those holding office. The Dark Learning was developed among officeholders counterattacking the Taoist ideology that legitimated withdrawal. Kuo Hsiang, himself a high official and participant in political intrigues, held that the sage is one who governs by "non-action" only in the sense of spontaneity in one's social role. All social activities, including politics, are natural, and withdrawal from public life is itself an artificiality.

It is worth stressing that creativity here was not a clash of class cultures alone but a contest of real structural possibilities contained within the same interpersonal network. Hsiang Hsiu, whose ideas Kuo Hsiang carried on, was himself a member of the Seven Sages before withdrawing to take public office: here the multiple bases intersected in a key individual. Refusing office and withdrawing to one's estate was part of political bargaining over conditions of power. Hsiang Hsiu thus aroused considerable resentment within the group after he ended a long holdout against taking office, especially because of the switch in political loyalties involved (Demiéville, 1986: 834). Situated in this densely balanced network structure in which no single group exercised power, the conflict of class cultures gave impetus to a higher level of struggle over intellectual space; and this in turn resulted in epistemological and metaphysical explorations on a new plane.

Philosophical creativity came abruptly to an end when this structure was destroyed. It is not merely that Kuo Hsiang was (in all likelihood) killed in 312 in the Huns' conquest of north China. A good many other philosophers had been killed earlier: Ho Yen in a coup in 249, Wang Pi the same year at age 24, and three of the Seven Sages in dynastic violence around 265 (Demiéville, 1986: 830; Balazs, 1964: 234–236). Until the final conquest, all this external conflict was part of the conditions which made creativity possible, and new intellectual leaders took the place of those who died. The weakness of the government both gave autonomy to the gentry on their estates and weakened the bureaucratic niches of traditional Confucianism. The cult of Confucius as a state religion had no political strength in the absence of an extensive administrative class when central control of the economy, public works, and military logistics had disappeared. By the same token, the secular scholars lost their organizational base with the decay of state schools and examinations. In themselves, both religious Confucians and scholar-bureaucrats were conservatizing forces on the intellectual plane; only when they competed from a position of weakness against other cultural groups were they aroused into creativity.

This creative balance was wiped out with the downfall of the Western Chin dynasty. Military devastation was not the ultimate problem, for a number of states soon reestablished themselves. For the most part these were states with weak central administration, and power was in the hands of militarily autonomous landed estates. It was under these circumstances that the gentry culture became established. Poetry writing, calligraphy, and painting became popular entertainments, developing especially from about 300 C.E. onwards. The most famous calligraphers and the first great brush-stroke artists in Chinese history appeared in the 300s. A good deal of creativity took place in these realms, but it was a creativity that cut in an aesthetic direction antithetical to the development of formal and abstract philosophy. In this respect the situation resembled Muromachi Japan and Renaissance Italy, where the means of cultural production were under the decentralized control of lay-oriented aristocracies: great eras in the arts but antithetical to abstract philosophy. When China reunified under strong governments, this gentry culture remained a class basis for one version of intellectual life, and correspondingly an underpinning for conservatism in philosophy.

The metaphysical advances of the Dark Learning were a hybrid of Confucian scholarship with this emerging gentry culture. When Confucian administration was reestablished in the strong dynasties, this philosophy was not absorbed into orthodox Confucian scholarship. The scholars instead went back to the Han rationalism, leaving abstract philosophy to be carried along, if at all, as part of the opposition grouped under the rubric of "Taoism." But Taoism was now an organized church concerned primarily with scripture and practice, with hardly any philosophy at all. No doubt all the ingredients were present for indigenous Chinese intellectual traditions to regroup into a conflictual balance that might drive philosophy onward again.

But now there was a new player in the game: Buddhism. With its network of economically powerful monasteries and its internal hierarchy of trained specialists, Buddhism was organizationally much more powerful than indigenous Chinese institutions as a basis for intellectual life. And in the realm of ideas, it imported traditions of abstract philosophy built up over more than 20 generations of dense competitive networks in India. It is not surprising that Buddhism should hurtle into the forefront of philosophical activity in medieval China. In this new field of intellectual forces, Taoist priests, Confucian officials, and gentry alike were thrown on the defensive, reinforced in their conservative stance in the realm of abstract ideas. Opposition shapes intellectual life in two different ways: inside the dominant faction, by splits which drive innovation at higher levels of abstract reflexivity; and in the external relations between dominant and defensive camps, by forcing the latter into the siege mentality of name-calling and a focus on emblems of identity which keep ideas fixed and concrete.

CHAPTER 5

External and Internal Politics
of the Intellectual World: India

With India we round out the world's three great indigenous intellectual traditions. For all the differences in atmosphere, there is no need to transpose our theory into a different key than for Greece and China. In India the dynamics of conflict, both inside and outside the intellectual world, stand out with architectonic clarity. Social conflicts affected the fluctuating strengths of Vedic, Buddhist, Brahmanical, and devotional religions; inside the intellectual networks, conflicts among the subfactions of these religions shaped the pattern of philosophical creativity. India is a particularly good place to observe the two-step causality which governs intellectual life: external politics favors one or another organizational base within which intellectuals build their networks; inside the dominant base factions divide to take up the lion's share of the space available under the intellectual law of small numbers, while factions on the weakening side ally into syncretisms. The philosophical schools of India developed against one another, and the background for their struggles was set by the sociopolitical dynamics behind the rise and fall of religions.

An India driven by conflicts goes counter to the image prevalent not only among Westerners but among Indian thinkers themselves. We have been taught to think of India as essentially static, even "timeless," under a perennial otherworldly mysticism. The image had to be created. It came about through a series of events: the destruction of medieval Buddhism, which had anchored the first great round of debates; the tactic of archaizing one's own tradition to elevate its prestige over that of factional rivals; and the predominance, in the centuries since 1500, of popular devotional cults of an anti-intellectual bent at just the time when Hindu scholars were in a syncretizing and scholasticizing mode in defense against alien conquerors. The result has been that the acute and extremely varied intellectual developments of the Indian Middle Ages were obscured, along with the dynamics which produced them. Among Western scholars, Indian philosophy is one of the great undiscovered histories of ideas, as technically sophisticated as European philosophies through quite recent centuries. The cultural history of India is the history of struggle on multiple levels, which eventually brought about almost total denial of its pathway.

In what follows we move from the outside in. We look first at the outer layer of causality, the historical patterns of Indian state formation; then the rise and fall of religions tied in different ways to political and economic patronage; and finally the rise and fall of factional oppositions within the intellectual attention space which shaped the contents of philosophies.

Sociopolitical Bases of Religious Ascendancies

India historically is the land of weak states. India's complicated political history can be summarized as a series of cycles between expansion of dominant states and fragmentation into many small warring kingdoms. Most of the time the centralizing swings of the pendulum did not reach as far as a single hegemonic state, but only simplified to a balance of power among a few large regional kingdoms, which held sway for a while before disintegrating.[1] And even when states held military control over considerable territories, they were typically rather weak internally. Rulers had difficulty extracting revenue, and as time went on, they became even weaker as control over the legal system and property relations was lost to the Brahman caste.

Two underlying causes of this weakness are geographical dispersion and geopolitical vulnerability. Early India was a frontier land of migrant agriculturalists, moving down from the northwest into sparsely populated jungles. When the fertile plains of the Ganges were settled around 600 B.C.E., the buildup of population and economy allowed military conquest states to form. People again escaped the cage, spreading civilization to the south and east, where coastal and trading states grew up to counterbalance the peasant-based extractive economies of the north. Cycles were set in motion which reinforced the weakness of Indian states. To the northwest, a corridor to distant population zones allowed intrusion and conquest by military forces organized on the state patterns of the Mediterranean and Middle East, from the Macedonians in the 320s B.C.E. through the several waves of Muslim armies after 1000 C.E. Indian states had difficulty mustering resources to match the invaders because their control over property was weak. Increasingly the social-religious pattern which was becoming "Hinduism" undermined state control; and state weakness in turn enhanced the local power of the Brahmans.

The Rival Religions

The several phases and competing patterns of Indian religion are correlated with these changes of the state. The early Vedic religion was the ritual organi-

GANGES STATES, 500 B.C.E.
(From Davies, 1949, p. 7)

zation of the frontier-settling clans. The incipient growth of strong states promoted symbiosis with monastic religions, above all Buddhism, which accumulated landed property. Jainism, beginning in the same milieu as Buddhism, found its niche in the coastal trading states. Hinduism emerged as a religion of the second diaspora, centered on families of landholding priests. Settling in the peripheries among pre-agricultural tribes, the Brahmans and those who emulated them molded ritual around exclusionary lines of racial purity rather than political hierarchy. A later phase set in when monastic religion declined along with its strong state patrons; now Hinduism recolonized the northern homeland, transforming itself into quasi-monastic orders and mass religious movements of its own. In the last act, native religions were overlaid by Muslim conquerors. Let us examine each of these phases in a little greater detail.

VEDIC CULTS AND THEIR BREAKDOWN

In the old Vedic period, incipient state organization consisted of the frontier-settling kin group under a war leader, among whom some families acquired hereditary succession to the kingship. The Brahman priests ritually officiated at tribal ceremonies including the consecration of kings, making up a Brahman-political alliance. In the early Upanishadic period (from about 700 B.C.E. continuing perhaps down into the 300s or later in some places), this alliance broke down; the validity of the Vedic ideology was questioned by competing religious and philosophical practices, while kings dispensed with Brahman legitimation, patronized religious questioners, and sometimes claimed their own superiority in the spiritual field. States consolidated power by military conquest and political coup, and by ruthlessly breaking the bonds of family and clan loyalty, dispensing with religious legitimation.[2] The prestige of the Vedic priests declined as their political base disintegrated, spurring the formation of rival movements.

Among these movements emerged two well-organized religions: Jainism and Buddhism. Both were centered at first in Magadha and Kosala, which is to say the strongest of the consolidating states, where their founders had royal connections (Mizuno, 1980). From now on for the next thousand years, Buddhism was a strong contender for state patronage, scoring its most spectacular success in the first great conquest state, the Maurya Empire. What emerged as Hinduism—a renovated Brahmanism but with social bases which limited the power of rulers—came later and in opposition to Buddhism; its strength was above all on the frontiers, where states were weakest.

What does it mean to say that a given religion is "supported" by a political regime? In India there was virtually never a question of what we might call a state religion, along lines familiar in the Christian, Islamic, and Chinese orbits. Typical state support consisted of building monasteries and religious monu-

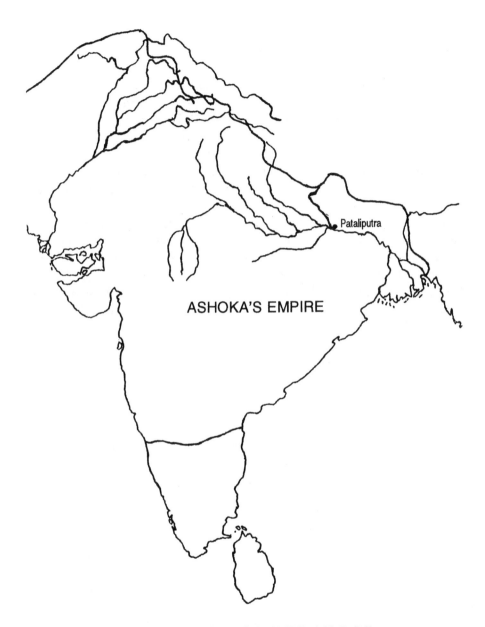

HEIGHT OF MAURYA EMPIRE, 250 B.C.E.
(From Davies, 1949, p. 13)

ments, donating property, such as the incomes of villages, for the support of monks, and protecting previous property donations by leaving them exempt from taxation. Religious donations were most often made by private persons, such as merchants or female relatives of the royal family; but this was especially common in periods when the state also gave its protection and support. Some states threw their material support heavily toward a particular religion, but many rather evenhandedly patronized all the important sects. A big difference in the support of Buddhism and Hinduism is that the former was much more institutionally organized, and hence patronage took the form of massive propertied foundations; whereas the Brahman priests were from landholding families and did not depend on donations for their survival.

The scale of political support for a religion was largely a matter of the extent of material patronage. At the extreme there was exclusion and persecution: confiscating property, prohibiting ceremonies, or killing monks and priests. But these actions only tipped the balance when the material base was weak; and that base depended not only on state patronage but also on the strength of religious carriers outside the state. By these criteria, let us consider how the various religions fared under different regimes.

BUDDHIST MONASTICISM

Buddhist patronage is easiest to document because it took the form of substantial material edifices. Most of the surviving works of art and architecture for India until after the fall of the Maurya dynasty are from Buddhist sites, and when Hindu temples expanded in the Gupta period and thereafter, they followed Buddhist models (Craven, 1975: 117–121; Dutt, 1962: 142–143, 204–205). During the Maurya Empire, Buddhism began to spread outside its Magadha homeland, encouraged in its missionary efforts by the wide reach of the Maurya regime. The emperor Ashoka became a lay Buddhist, and promulgated Buddhist principles in public edicts while prohibiting the sacrificial cults as contrary to Buddhist benevolence. This is the closest we get to all-out religious conflict; the successor regime, the Shungas, not only reinstituted the sacrifices but also persecuted Buddhism, though apparently without much success (Dutt, 1962: 81). The proliferation of Buddhism south of the Vindhya range, which cuts laterally across central India, dates from around 200 B.C.E. down to 100 C.E.; in the Andhra kingdom in the 200s C.E., magnificent monasteries were built on donations from commercial wealth and aristocratic families, while kings gave immunity from taxation (Dutt, 1962: 114–133, 158). The post-Maurya period also saw the beginning of state support in outlying kingdoms of the northwest, including the kings of Kashmir, whose patronage continued a last outpost of Buddhism down to 900–1100 C.E.

The Gupta Empire was a time of Hindu cultural efflorescence, but in the

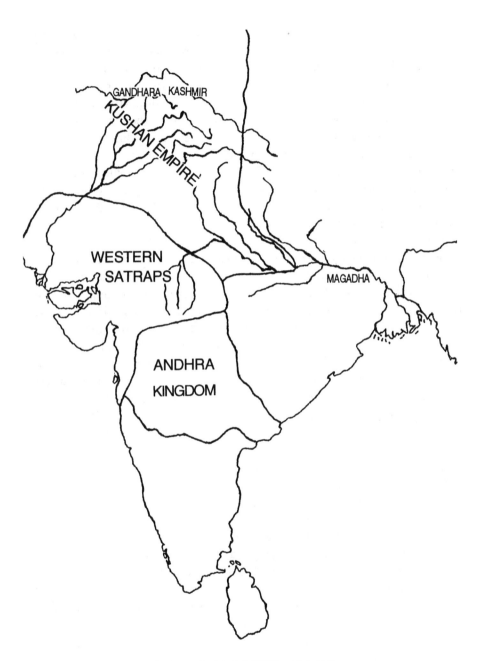

BALANCE OF POWER, 150 C.E.
(From Davies, 1949, p. 15)

Ganges plain Buddhism was supported by half the population, and its precepts were widely observed. Rulers and wealthy laity gave lavish material support to the great Buddhist monasteries.[3] The famous monastery-university at Nalanda near the capital received the income from over 200 villages, donated by a succession of kings. When the Guptas disintegrated, the kings of the trading corridor to the west (Gujarat), though they were themselves Shaivites, patronized Buddhist monasteries. Their great Buddhist center of learning at Valabhi from about 490 to 780 was supported by royal land grants and incomes from villages, designated for everything from buildings and victuals to incense and books; one senses a rivalry over the prestige of having a great monastic center to compete with Nalanda in Magadha. At its height, victors in the public disputations at Valabhi's "university" could expect government preferment.

Harsha's brief empire in the 600s included Buddhism in its eclectic patronage; later we find the monks embroiled in disputes over possession of these donated villages (Dutt, 1962: 313). By now Buddhism had disappeared from the Deccan and the south and was largely confined to its lower Ganges homeland. Chinese visitors describe deserted monasteries and neglected stupas (popular reliquaries of Buddhist saints) around the country, and even in Magadha much was in decline. Buddhism's last great supporters were the Pala kings of Bengal, who encroached on Magadha and founded several monastery-universities during the 700s and 800s (most notably Vikramashila, with the last foundation around 1100). These last Buddhist monasteries declined with the power of the Pala state, and were finally pillaged by Muslim invaders in the 1200s.

Buddhism flourished in the strongest states, except of course in the Islamic ones, where a state-religious alliance of an entirely different sort was imported. Buddhism was structurally more compatible than Hinduism with a centralized officialdom autonomously extracting economic resources and breaking down traditional rights. At the earliest period of centralized state formation, we see the kings competing for the prestige of having the new religious sages at their courts, while the Vedic priest guilds represented the old family and clan structure that was being displaced. In the same way, Buddhism later was welcomed by centralizing rulers of previously clan-organized areas throughout Asia; in Tibet, the struggle between court-sponsored Buddhism and Bon ritualists coincided with the vicissitudes of the early monarchy in subjugating the clans (Stein, 1972: 47–71).

Although Buddhist monasticism was deliberately remote from the state, it was useful for rulers: it preached a moral pacification of the populace and provided an institution for literate education. In Mongolia, China, and Japan we see Buddhist ritualists at court, providing ceremonial impressiveness, some-

GUPTA EMPIRE, 400 C.E.
(From Davies, 1949, p. 19)

times under the guise of magic, a pattern that existed for Buddhist tantrism in Bengal and perhaps elsewhere in India as well. Buddhist leaders such as the Theravadin Moggaliputta-tissa at Ashoka's court were sometimes friends of rulers, and in some cases were relatives of upper-class families. For kings of frontier areas or conquest regions, founding monasteries was a means of settlement or of removing property from rival lords (a pattern particularly noticeable in the Buddhist-supporting conquest states in northern China, and paralleled by royal support of Christian monasteries in early medieval Germany and eastern Europe). Monasteries, too, as the only forms of collective organization transcending the family, were preeminent at accumulating property; as early as the Kushan Empire (in the northwest around 100 C.E.), there were indications that laypersons were transferring property to monasteries and circumventing family inheritance, provoking legal counterattack by Brahman legists (Dutt, 1962: 201, 313). Donations to monasteries might come from far away, including incomes from grants of land and villages by distant kings or merchants, as well as expenditures of students and pilgrims; thus a great monastery or shrine in one's kingdom would be a center for trade and for amassing wealth.

In all these respects Buddhism contrasts with the Brahmanism which grew out of the old Vedic priest guilds. Brahmanism expanded the importance of kinship structures throughout society, through marital and ritual regulations which made up a greatly elaborated caste system. Learned pandits became formulators and custodians of legal codes which restricted the autonomy of the state while bolstering the economic and social powers of local elites. Brahmans not only tended to make themselves tax-exempt, but also limited the abilities of rulers to mobilize resources to expand the state. Hinduism flourished where rulers were weak; conversely, the social penetration of Hinduism perpetuated a pattern of weakly centralized, ephemeral states.

Indian Buddhism and Hinduism are two points along a continuum; neither is a state religion, although Buddhism has a closer symbiosis with strong states, Hinduism with weak ones. Buddhism, carried by monks as missionaries or refugees, was much more transportable across lines of civilizations than Hinduism. Buddhist monasticism could be incorporated into strong states with well-established literate civilizations, and could introduce state administration into preliterate tribal regions. Brahmanism was much less transportable. It could not take root merely by the migration of a few Brahman priests to a foreign court, such as took place at times in China, the Archipelago, and even Sri Lanka. Its successes came by permeating tribal areas, as it did during its spread from the Ganges to southern India, as well as into Nepal; from around 100 to 600 C.E., it spread into Burma and southeast Asia, but was largely displaced when Buddhism received patronage from consolidating states

(Davies, 1949: 30; *OHI,* 1981: 186). Hinduism was a full-scale social complex, in which Brahmans functioned not only as ritualists but also as upholders of a system of kinship and material stratification organized around caste.

The extent of state interference within Buddhism had important consequences for intellectual creativity. The state rarely became involved in disputes between sects within Indian Buddhism. In contrast is the pattern in states where Buddhism was especially closely connected with the royal house, notably Sri Lanka and Southeast Asia (Gombrich, 1988: 138–145, 158–166; Zürcher, 1962; Kalupahana, 1992: 206–208). The closer the identification of Buddhism with the state, the more closely sectarian fortunes within Buddhism were tied to politics; this in turn restricted the playing field on which intellectual activity took place. Although there were flourishing centers of studies in Malaya and great temple complexes at the Burmese capital, state enforcement of orthodoxy kept philosophy in these countries largely traditionalist and uncreative. We see the same pattern at the very end of Buddhist patronage in India. The Pala kings of Bengal not only founded a new set of monastic universities but also kept them under close royal control; all posts in an elaborate hierarchy of teachers and administrators were held on commission, and all degrees were awarded by the king (Dutt, 1962: 360–361). Intellectual creativity did not flourish under this tight control. This situation is comparable to the stagnation in Confucian philosophy after it became adopted by the Han bureaucracy, and again during the enforcement of state orthodoxy during the Ming; by contrast, the creative period of Confucianism during the Sung occurred when both religious orthodoxy and the state ideological apparatus were in flux. In India the greatest intellectual creativity in Buddhism took place when states eclectically patronized not just Buddhism but non-Buddhist religions as well, leaving a breathing space in which Buddhist factions could take maximal advantage of their organizational base for intellectual life.

JAINA ASCETICISM

The early spread of the Jainas is parallel to that of the Buddhists. Beginning in Magadha, their shrines reached Andhra in the southeast and Mathura in the upper Ganges in the post-Maurya period, and continued under the Guptas (Craven, 1975; Coomaraswamy, [1927] 1965; Dutt, 1962; Zimmer, 1951: 181–279; *OHI,* 1981: 98–102, 137–138). The Jainas had close royal ties during the early buildup of imperial power. Thereafter Jaina patronage was largely confined to the regional kings and coastal merchants of the west and south, leaving Buddhism in exclusive possession as the ascetic-monastic religion in the Ganges heartland and the north.

Jainism's strict practices confined its lay followers to urban pursuits; over time, it found a distinctive niche by shaping its doctrines so that urban merchants were attracted while agricultural pursuits were excluded. Its base was narrower than that of the popular Hindu cults or the Buddhists in their prime. In periods when coastal trade flourished, Jainas were capable of accumulating wealth on a scale unmatched by the Brahman-centered rural economy. Since this was the same resource base which made possible most of the stronger states in the south and on the western coast, Jainism became embroiled in violent state conflicts with overtones of religious war. Jainism was displaced from the south after 1130 as new Shaivite and Vaishnavite movements modified the caste system to allow Hindus access to commercial enterprise, in which they became predominant by Mogul times (Braudel, [1979] 1984: 484–520). Never as large a religion as Buddhism, Jainism survived longer. From its relatively weak base, it played a rather cautious role as a bystander in the unfolding of intellectual space.

HINDUISM

The ascendancy of Hinduism was not simply a result of the caste system. Caste was compatible with Buddhism, too, as far as the activities of the lay world were concerned; throughout its history in India, Buddhism often recruited from among the Brahmans, and transcendence of caste took place only among monks. We find kings using Brahmanical rituals even while they were giving Buddhism some of its richest patronage: Horse sacrifices were performed, one by the Andhran king to inaugurate his capital, at the very site where the great monastery complex at Nagarjunakonda was built a few years later, another by the Gupta emperor who founded the great monastery-university at Nalanda; even the extremely pro-Buddhist Sri Lankan and Southeast Asian kings used Brahmans for royal rituals for lack of a Buddhist form of coronation (Dutt, 1962: 126–128, 330; Gombrich, 1988: 145). Yet Hindu cults themselves sometimes transcended caste. This was true of the antinomian Shaiva ascetics, and of the popular bhakti cults (such as the followers of Krishna), which promised salvation to worshippers from any caste (Pandey, 1986; Eliot, 1988: 2:248–256). Caste became most explicitly an issue between Hindus and Buddhists relatively late—in the 600s and 700s C.E., when Mimamsakas and Naiyayikas defended the philosophical basis of caste, and Buddhists such as Kamalashila attacked it. But this was at the turning point of Hindu ascendancy over Buddhism, when militancy peaked on both sides.

Hinduism was not a primordial religious identity but a self-conscious united front that gradually built up in opposition to Buddhists and Jainas. At first there was only a series of separate strands coming down from the ancient theistic cults and the Sanskrit literature that accumulated upon the Vedas. Such movements did not necessarily have much unity; the Shaivas were at first scorned by the Brahmans as phallic worshippers, and most of their Vedic connection came from the *Atharvaveda,* the magic spells incorporated only late into the Vedas. The Vaishnavas, worshippers of Vishnu, formed their own collection of sacred texts around 100 B.C.E.–100 C.E. (alternatively, ca. 300–800 C.E.) as rival to the Brahmanical *samhita* (Pandey, 1986; Eliot, 1988: 2:136–205; Dasgupta, 1922–1955: 3:12–93; Raju, 1985: 439). Virtually all the most prominent Hindu religions in the Common Era were unorthodox from the point of view of traditionalist Brahmans.

The Hinduism which we can speak of as acquiring political power was rather a mixed bag. The old Vedic alliance between Brahman priests and the kings for whom they performed court rituals was gone. Replacing it were several divergent forms of religious organization. New theistic cults were celebrated at court. Many kings identified with Shiva in their official propaganda, perhaps because of his ferocious aspect as destroyer and creator of the universe; there was also much royal identification with deities who were not central to the Hindu literary pantheon, especially Surya the sun god (Craven, 1975: 55, 104, 177, 181; Eliot, 1988: 2:206). Such court ceremonial sometimes went along with performance of the great Vedic sacrifices under Brahman auspices, but could also replace them. Another variant consisted of the popular devotional cults of the late medieval period. Unlike the Vedic ceremonies, which had no temples and were carried out either in the house or at outdoor turf altars, these bhakti cults had a new material base—the permanent temple with its autonomous staff (Smith, 1989: 151; *OHI,* 1981:32–33). Here a second form of state-religious patronage was possible; some kings built temples to Hindu deities and endowed their priests with incomes from land. Such temple building generally came later and followed earlier patterns of Buddhist endowments, which had pioneered collective religious property in India. From the 800s onward, the ascendancy of the bhakti devotional cults displaced the Vedic gods and shifted the center of popular attention to the temples. Both these forms of Hinduism had a rather conventional alliance with the state. They posed some rivalry to patronage of the monastic religions but were not necessarily incompatible with it. There was nothing organizationally incongruous about a ruler's spreading largess simultaneously to several religions; ideologically the adjustment was made by each cult's recognizing some of the other's spiritual symbols while assigning it a lower place in one's own religious cosmology: the Buddha was eventually regarded as an incarnation of Vishnu, and Jainas in their late syncretizing period incorporated lay worship of Hindu gods as junior spirits subordinate to their own enlightened Tirthankaras.

The more radical challenge came from the version of Hinduism that emerged as the Brahmans reorganized their power position vis-à-vis the state. Indian states, following a tradition dating back to the entrepreneurial kings who cleared the forest frontiers, always claimed absolute ownership of the land, the produce of which constituted the main basis of state revenues. After the disintegration of the Maurya Empire, this capacity to control land revenues began to dissipate into a form of religious feudalism. Buddhism was the opening wedge, already receiving land grants to support its monasteries by Maurya times. Brahmans also began to receive land grants, especially as they carried agricultural development into virgin territories in the south. By 100 C.E., the kings were giving away cultivated lands and the rights to administer them without interference from royal officials. By the late Gupta period, rulers were dispensing grants including all revenues, labor dues, and powers of criminal justice. In the political chaos of the 500s following the Gupta collapse, the Brahman-centered localistic social structure seems to have become dominant. When Harsha reestablished an empire in the early 600s, it was administered through a lavish distribution of land grants. As in most subsequent states, the state apparatus consisted of little more than the military officials, and the ruler kept control only by incessant travel or campaign. After 1000, centralized powers collapsed virtually everywhere. Land grants fell into the hands of a flux of military lords, while the temples became major centers of accumulated wealth.[4]

During this development, Brahmans completed the transition from priests allied to the royal courts to arbiters of local social relations independent of the central state. Caste law, administered by the Brahmans, was built up to control all local economic production and much of its distribution. Buddhism, living in symbiosis with the centralized agrarian state, was threatened by the new Brahmanism capable of cutting off its flow of material resources. The displacement of Buddhism from India and the victory of Hinduism followed when these several lines of movement converged: on the one hand the creation of the Brahman-centered legal system and the institutionalization of the weak state; on the other the undercutting of Buddhist patronage and popular support by the emergence of rival Hindu temples and eventually Hindu monks. When the sociopolitical foundations shifted, the Hindu side mounted an ideological attack which delegitimated Buddhism.

Conflict between Hinduism and Buddhism took place over a long period and in both intense and diffuse forms. There were times of explicit battles at the royal courts, when court ceremonial was at issue, or when laws were promulgated enforcing Buddhist precepts among the population. Beneath this was a larger drift, first the spread of Buddhist monasteries and stupa cults, then their decline. Some points stand out: the advent of the Shunga kings, who took over the disintegrating Maurya Empire and reversed its ban on sacrifices (here we have the most extreme pro-Buddhist state followed by one of the most militantly anti-Buddhist); the widespread adherence to Buddhist rules in northern India during the early Guptas, followed by a growth of Hindu patronage in the Ganges valley to match Buddhism; the destruction by the Shaiva king of the Hunas of Buddhist stupas and monasteries in the northwest in the early 500s; the weak penetration of Buddhism in south India, and its disappearance around 500 or 600 amidst militantly Hinduizing states; the spread of Hinduism into Kashmir, balancing Buddhism and then displacing it in the 900s; and the battle of Buddhist and Hindu kings in the lower Ganges—a deliberately Hinduizing king in the late 700s, followed by the militantly pro-Buddhist Pala kings, then a reverse swing with the Hindu destruction of Buddhist temples in Bengal ca. 1050. By 1200 Buddhism had expired entirely, the coup de grâce administered by Muslim raiders (*OHI*, 1981: 171, 201; Dutt, 1962: 206–207, 376).

After Buddhism was gone, internecine political conflict within Hinduism escalated to take its place. During the time when Buddhism was fading out, Jaina-Hindu conflict was at its height, and the most violent persecutions centered in those places, especially in the south, where the Jainas were most closely identified with the rulers. Here too, in the centuries following Hindu victory over court Jainism (roughly 1100–1400), were kings who supported either Shaiva or Vaishnava cults and persecuted the other. Creativity peaked among the religious intellectuals located at the key transition points—both on the way up and on the way down.

The Long-Term Politics of Intellectual Splits and Alliances

Strong schools subdivide; weak schools ally. This is the general principle governing the long-term dynamics of intellectual factions. Hence the two-step causality whereby external sociopolitical changes strengthen or weaken the base for an intellectual-supporting organization, and motivate its members to fractionate or unify their philosophical positions.

Intellectual politics is further governed by a second principle. The intellectual law of small numbers holds that the attention space allows three to six distinctive positions; this constitutes the limit within which a politically dominant school can split. The law of small numbers can be violated, but with a penalty: beyond the upper limit of about a half-dozen positions, additional intellectual factions fail to propagate themselves across the generations. They fail to recruit successors, and their memory fades out, either because they are neglected or because they are lumped in with some more prominent position.

The long-term intellectual history of India nicely illustrates these principles. (1) When the sacrificial cult is dominant, the Vedic priests split into five factions; later they unite in opposition to the Buddhist ascendancy. (2) The Upanishadic pre-Buddhist period spawns a large number of individual philosophies, most of which are squeezed out by the law of small numbers. (3) Bud-

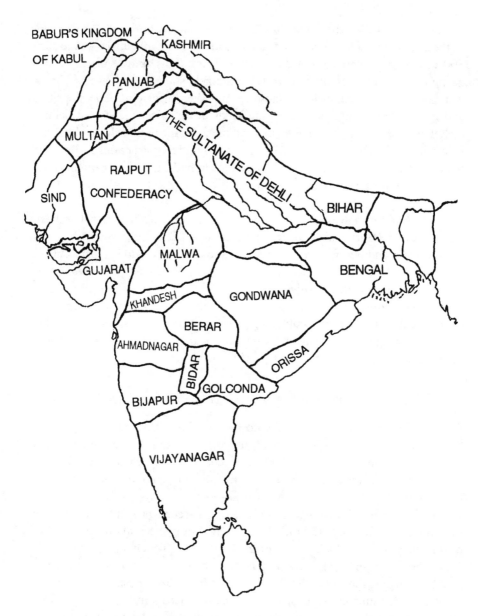

EVE OF MOGUL INVASION, 1525
(From Davies, 1949, p. 39)

dhism during its period of strong political patronage splits into numerous factions, from which are winnowed a moderate number of long-standing positions; when its bases in India shrink, Buddhist philosophies amalgamate. (4) Jainism keeps a modest, steady basis of support and a unitary philosophical position, aimed at mediating within the larger intellectual field. (5) When Hindu intellectuals take over the Buddhist organizational resources and displace them from the center of intellectual networks, Hindu philosophies crystallize into about a half-dozen well-defined positions.[5] (6) Advaita Vedanta is especially successful, building a new material foundation by organizing orders of Hindu monks; as Vedanta grows, it splits into subfactions which dominate the intellectual debate, while non-Vedantic schools tend to syncretize and are eventually absorbed into theistic Vedanta. (7) The Vaishnava theists, worshippers of Vishnu and his avatar Krishna, are the most successful movement, splitting into branches with their own technical philosophies. (8) Still later, under the pressure of Muslim and then European conquest, the Vedantic factions downplay their philosophical differences and amalgamate into a syncretic pan-Hindu front. The politics of intellectual subdivision and alliance-making runs through five broad repetitions: Vedic, Buddhist, Hindu, Vedantic, and Vaishnavite.[6]

Religious Bases of Philosophical Factions: Divisions and Recombination of Vedic Ritualists

The Vedas, a word which originally meant simply "knowledge," are not abstract philosophy but the earliest transmission of specialized intellectual productions. Let us see what they reveal about the organization of priestly politics.

The orthodox Hinduism of medieval India adulated "the four Vedas." One can discern a long-term pattern of splits and recombinations among organized intellectual groups before this end point was reached.[7] Sometime before 1000 B.C.E., a collection was formed out of liturgical materials, including hymns, prayers, incantations, and sacrificial formulas. This collection, known as the *Rigveda* ("knowledge of verses"), must have coincided with formation of a unified guild of priests. Subsequently two more Vedas were formed, both consisting of different arrangements of much the same materials as the *Rigveda*. The *Samaveda* is the knowledge of *samans,* sacred songs. The *Yagurveda* contained spells and formulas used in the rituals, plus meaningless-sounding words chanted as mantras *(yagus).*

The orthodox interpretation is that separate Vedas come from a division of labor in the ceremonies, each Veda constituting the liturgy of one of the priests. The original single priest was increased to 3 and then more; the number of priests required for sacrifice increased over time from 4 to 16 (Stutley, 1980: 80). But the distinct Veda texts did not simply correspond to the number of roles; more likely the divisions emerged as rival lineages spun off, concerned more with the proto-intellectual activities of memorizing and teaching a particular text than with the ritual itself. The old Rigvedic guild had split, and each sect propagandized for its own primacy (Krishna, 1991: 73, 93).

Further splits occurred. The *Yagurveda* had at least two versions, White and Black; the latter included prose discussions of the rituals, indicating that it belonged to the group which pioneered in creating the *Brahmanas*, shifting from a liturgical to a more intellectual orientation.[8] Yet another group became organized as proprietors of the *Atharvaveda*, a collection of magical rites and charms originating outside the Rigvedic camp. They seem to have been a coalition of magicians from the indigenous non-Aryan population, first coalescing into a rival guild; then they adopted Aryan gods and ritual forms and became players in the ritual politics and ideological fractionation of the mainstream. Orthodox Vedists looked askance at the *Atharvaveda* and did not accept it among the "four Vedas" until late, when the whole enterprise was in the syncretism of a weakening base.

The competing sects emulated one another over the generations. All of them added the same kinds of texts to their original *samhitas* (canonical collections): prose *Brahmanas,* discussing the practical and theological significance of the rites (before 800 B.C.E., perhaps continuing later); *Aranyakas,* comprising liturgies for individual Brahmans to carry out in retirement; and finally *Upanishads,* recording the discussions of reforming sages who emerged after about 700.[9] It is apparent that the priest guilds were no longer engaged mainly, or even primarily, in carrying out public rituals. The addition of lengthy texts to the *samhitas* implies that a great deal of time was now being spent in discussion and education. Something like an intellectual community was becoming a focus of attention in its own right. Socially, the Brahmans were becoming a landowning class, engaged in other occupations besides priestcraft. What they retained in common was the mark of having studied the Vedas, and the right to teach them. The Brahmans shifted from a priest class to an educational status group. The very nature of ritual activity shifted. The Vedas were no longer so much liturgies which priests used in great public ceremonies as texts which pious Brahmans recited daily in private.

After about 500 B.C.E.—the time when the old tribal kingdoms were rapidly consolidating under the geopolitical dominance of the Ganges states—the period of splits and rivalries among the Vedic schools ends. A reversal sets in, with all the sects eventually merging into a common front of Vedic education. In the Upanishads, students typically mention that they have learned all of the

Vedas. One is no longer learning a particular priest role in the ceremonies; all the Vedas are now regarded as essentially one body of knowledge, to be learned by everyone in the educated class. For a long time there is indecisiveness about whether the Atharvas belong in this sacred alliance. Many Upanishads refer to the "three Vedas"; sometimes they add "with the *Atharvana* as the fourth."[10] The term "four Vedas" becomes firmly established only with the formulation of a Hindu culture in opposition to the Buddhists'.

The long-term process conforms to the law of small numbers. In the early period, the Vedic priests have the entire attention space to themselves; they split into four factions (counting both Black and White *Yagurvedas*), while the oppositional faction, the Atharva magicians, pulls together as a single collection. Then comes the attack on the Brahmanical guilds by a proliferation of dissident sages, leading to the ascendancy of the Buddhists. Now the Brahmans, on the defensive, overcome their differences and syncretize into a united front. Strong positions divide, weak positions unite.

The Crowded Competition of the Sages

The breakdown of the Vedic cults is more obscured by retrospective ideology than any other period in Indian history. It is commonly assumed that the dominant philosophy now became an idealist monism, the identification of *atman* (self) and *Brahman* (Spirit), and that this mysticism was believed to provide a way to transcend rebirths on the wheel of karma. This is far from an accurate picture of what we read in the Upanishads. It has become traditional to view the Upanishads through the lens of Shankara's Advaita interpretation. This imposes the philosophical revolution of about 700 C.E. upon a very different situation 1,000 to 1,500 years earlier. Shankara picked out monist and idealist themes from a much wider philosophical lineup.[11] The doctrines of karma and escape from rebirth, too, are by no means dominant among the Upanishadic sages, but come to the forefront in the networks around the Buddha. It was the formation of Buddhism and Jainism which focused the basic themes of the religious-philosophical attention space; what we call Hinduism emerged as a reaction to these monastic movements.

The social characteristics of the intellectual community depicted in the Upanishads are much the same as we find in the early Buddhist and Jaina texts. There is a multitude of sages, teachers with competing doctrines, engaging in public debates. In the Upanishads these debates most often take place under the auspices of kings; in the monastic recollections they also occur in shelters and rainy season retreats for the wandering ascetics.[12] In both sources the Brahmans are under attack.

The Brahmans by now are no longer merely professional priests; they have become teachers and caretakers of traditional knowledge, like the Confucian *ju,* although much less political. According to the ideal, the student goes to live at the house of his teacher, acting as his servant (alternatively a student can be taught by his own father). Learning consists in memorizing and reciting a text; allegedly it takes 12 years to learn one Veda, although this can hardly be accurate, given that students were now learning three or four Vedas, plus a good deal of other knowledge such as grammar, etymology, numbers, astronomy, portents, demonology, and so on (e.g., *Chandogya Upanishad* 7.1.2). The Brahmans are now not so much performing religious rituals as engaging in a lengthy scholastic routine.

It is apparent that the educational business is booming. There is also a good deal of questioning traditional teaching methods and contents. The Upanishads take for granted that students attend various schools and learn many religious and non-religious specialties. Some stories tells of students who learn from cattle, or from gods who appear to them; the idiom expresses the fact that students are producing ideas from their own inspiration. Such individualists would likely include the ascetic sages depicted in the Buddhist and Jaina texts, a rival type of intellectual who makes a point of his independence from traditional teaching and its methods. These sages known as *shramanas,* make a sharp break with the economic and social base of the Brahmans, who are now wealthy householders and landowners; the dissidents are alms men, holy beggars who have given up householding to become lifelong ascetic recluses. Nevertheless, one gets a sense that the *shramanas* too are competing for student followers. The common greeting among wanderers was to ask one another about their teacher and doctrine; the lives of the Buddha and Mahavira describe conversions of followers from one teacher to another.

There is an upsurge now of cultural production and dissemination. In part this comes from the breakdown of the Vedic cults and the spread of education to a much wider group than the priests. It is also during this period (by the 500s B.C.E.; Thapar, 1966: 63) that writing appears. It does not have a very direct effect on the educational world, since most of what we see is oral recitation and debate. The use of writing most likely began with record keeping in the expanding governments of the time, and with merchant accounts; the religious intellectuals were the most conservative, centered as they were on the ritualized transmission of their knowledge. This is a pattern we find elsewhere, such as in the exclusively oral traditions of the Celtic Druid priests long after writing was available in the secular world. The availability of an alternative form of knowledge outside of priestly circles, however, must have contributed to the delegitimation of Brahmanical claims for cultural dominance.

The Upanishads contain many stories of students whose teachers do not know the new doctrines, of old-style priests who are embarrassed by ceremonies put on by others who know their secret meanings. There are kings who can pose questions that the Brahmans cannot answer, and kings who are teachers. None of this is surprising in view of the political realities of the expanding states. Many Upanishads have the theme that Brahmans should not be too proud to learn new doctrines, even in their old age, or from outsiders. Many sages are named in the Upanishads, but none who is uniformly depicted as dominant. Uddalaka Aruni is described several times, sometimes as ignorant, sometimes as wise.[13] Yajñavalkya wins debates in the *Brihadaranyaka Upanishad,* but so does the king of Banaras. No one founds a notable intergenerational school of followers.

The main questions discussed within Brahmanical circles are to explain the meaning of ceremonies and to name the gods who are behind them. This continues the main theme of the *Brahmanas* and *Aranyakas,* the explication of liturgies. But in the Upanishadic circles and among the *shramanas,* the gods begin to be downgraded or interpreted in an etymological sense, and the favorite question now shifts to a more abstract level: to list the elements out of which the world is composed or created. There are many different lists. In the Upanishads, the elements include sun or fire; the person in the right or the left eye; sight, smell, and other senses; earth; water; air/breath (treated either as one element or as two); ether/space; food; power; force; name or form; and so on. Such lists typically mix physical and psychological categories. Often, long lists of elements are all accepted; in other accounts there are creation stories which begin with one of these elements, or sometimes with "nothing" taken as an element, then going on to generate the rest of the list. Sometimes the cosmology is dualistic, sometimes extremely pluralistic.

Many Upanishadic texts compile contradictory positions. When specific debates are described, argument does not usually involve finding logical contradictions in opposing doctrines. The favorite style of debate is to pose a series of questions until the other cannot answer. "What is the origin of *that?*" "X." "What is the origin of X?" "Y." And so on. No one in the Upanishads sees this as an infinite regress. Generally the account ends with the interlocutor ceasing to question. Sometimes the questioner is told to stop "lest your head should fall off."[14] The argument that the ultimate is inexpressible is made only occasionally (primarily in the *Brihadaranyaka Upanishad,* e.g., 4.2.4; 6.1); the Advaita-style distinction-transcending mysticism later attributed to the Upanishads is far from dominant. Instead what we find are contests of rhetorical impressiveness, in which a debate is won by asserting one's primal element with the highest degree of confidence. Given the extreme variety of elements mentioned, it is apparent that the rhetoric triumphant on one occasion does not deter rivals elsewhere.

Some elements are named repeatedly. One complex is fire, sun, or light. A second is ether, space, or the void.[15] A third kind of favorite element is *prana*, or breath, which frequently figures in creation tales and in anecdotes about the five senses leaving the body. *Prana* is a favorite also because it is the key to speech, which in turn ties in with the line of argument that the names of things constitute their forms. Here we have something like a Platonist pluralism. Yet there are also primitive shamanistic themes, such as those expressed by the breath/wind magicians in the *Brihadaranyaka* (Chattopadhyaya, 1979: 149–154). A fourth theme is that there is a self within the body, or within the heart or the eye; some texts assert that this self is also in the sun or moon. A common argument is that the self is conscious even when asleep, as in dreaming; and sometimes it is argued that dreamlessness too is a self. Occasionally the secret doctrine mentions where the self goes at death, or in deep sleep. Some texts assert that the self is behind everything. Such passages in the *Chandogya* and *Brihadaranyaka* became retrospectively famous, but even in these Upanishads they are by no means the only cosmological doctrine.

The purposes of this new knowledge are several. (1) To upstage other priests with one's superior wisdom. Here emerges a genuine intellectual competition, which hits on a topic opening the disinterested search for knowledge, asking after the elements of which the world is composed. (2) New knowledge is also touted as a superior magic for worldly ends. Often this is tied to passages on rituals "that will grow leaves on a dead stick," or for ends such as acquiring cattle or achieving sexual pleasure or even revenge.[16] (3) Frequently the new knowledge is said to bring immortality in heaven. Knowledge is often claimed to be for the time of one's death, incorporated into death chants and rituals, or into the lore of the "forest-dwelling" stage of a Brahman's old age. Here emerges a genuinely new religious theme, since life after death is not important in the Vedas. Various heavens or after-death states are now posited: the realm of the Fathers, the realm of the gods and pleasures, with a few sparse reference to possible hells.

This religious doctrine is not what would later become the classic Hindu complex of karma, reincarnation, and liberation through insight or yoga. It often exalts material life prolonged into a rather worldly afterlife. Many Upanishads regard a long life as good.[17] Among earlier Upanishads, reincarnation is only sporadically mentioned; the doctrines are unsettled and distinctly non–classic "Hindu." Some assert that one's thought at the moment of death determines one's next life, which might be in heaven (*Prashna Upanishad* 3.10). Some assert that one has a choice between reincarnation and immortality; if the latter, one's good acts go to one's favorite kinsmen, while bad acts go to disliked ones (*Kaushitaki Upanishad* 1.2–4). Another account is that the soul after death goes to the moon and falls back to the earth as rain. There is no generally accepted sequence.

Through the main period of the Upanishadic sages, there is little or nothing on the karmic consequences of one's actions chaining one to a cycle of rebirths.[18] Nor do most Upanishadic sages seem to practice yoga or one-pointed concentration *(samadhi)*. The early sages, Uddalaka, Yajñavalkya, and their debating partners, are concerned with scoring philosophical points. Some Upanishads enjoin thoughtful contemplation during hymns and rituals *(Aitareya Upanishad* 2.1–3). A full-fledged description of Yoga method as a route to liberation does not come until the middle-period *Shvetashvatara Upanishad* (1–2), ca. 300–200 B.C.E., and again in the late *Maitrayani Upanishad* (6.18–29). It appears that most Brahmans spent their time either in rituals, in reciting their ever-lengthening texts, or sometimes in debates.

The Upanishads describe the period of debating sages from the point of view of the Brahmans. In heterodox descriptions we also find the *shramanas* formulating rival element cosmologies. The Buddha converts three brothers of a Brahman family and their followers, ascetics who carry out ceremonies near a volcano and apparently regard fire as the primary element (Mizuno, 1980: 61). Other famous contemporaries of the Buddha (25 and 26 in Figure 5.1) proposed that the world is made out of seven elements, or four. Some of the *shramanas* carry denunciation of Brahmanical orthodoxy to an extreme, asserting a purely naturalist position that the world consists of nothing but the working out of the elements. These are the Lokayata, or "materialists." What distinguishes the *shramanas* as a whole from the Brahmans is that the former have organized a new lifestyle, cut loose from householding and centered on the practice of austerities. It might seem peculiar that the Lokayata, preaching purely worldly existence, should also be ascetics. But this is the social milieu of the charismatic teachers; the Lokayata are a faction which emerges from the debates among the element philosophers in the sector competing over who has gone furthest in overturning the Brahmanical lifestyle.

It is in the *shramana* circles that the doctrines of karma and samsara (rebirth) become central topics of debate, and the issues on which top intellectual reputations are made. Both the Buddha and Mahavira founded movements claiming the overcoming of karma. For the Jainas, the karma doctrine was cast in the concepts of a materialist element philosophy; karma is the fruit of action, conceived as material particles which stick to the soul and keep it from its natural omniscience. The Buddha conceived karma in a more abstract fashion, as a chain of causality which leads to attachment to the forms of the material world and hence to rebirth. The third successful movement organized at this time, the Ajivikas of Makkhali Gosala, exalted the idea of karma into an inescapable fate; each person's life inevitably goes through its chain of consequences and rebirths until it reaches the end, like a ball of thread being unwound.

Other famous contemporary philosophers made their reputations by deny-ing karma. Pakudha Kaccayana, who espoused a cosmology of seven elements, was disputed by the Buddha over the denial of karma, which the Buddha excoriated as the denial of morality. Purana Kashyapa was famous for deny-ing karma and morality; he associated personally with both Mahavira and Makkhali Gosala (Basham, 1951: 138, 278; Hirakawa, 1990: 16–19).

The great creative generations (ca. 500 or 400 B.C.E.)[19] in which philoso-phies and religious movements crystallized is also the time in which the karma doctrine seems to have become the center of attention. What is crucial is that the intellectual community hit upon a problem in terms of which far-reaching consequences for lifestyle and for thought could be formulated. It would be false to assume that karma was a long-standing issue, that Indians suffered for centuries under a pessimistic belief that they were bound to a wheel of rebirths, in a suffering world and an oppressive caste system, until the Buddhists and Jainas seemed to show the way to liberation. The problem and its solution appeared more or less simultaneously. Karma is a vague concept in the Upan-ishads, where emerging beliefs about immortality were more likely to be focused on the afterlife in heaven than on return to the world. No doubt there were primitive tribal beliefs about reincarnation; but these differ from the Buddhist-Jaina problem insofar as nothing was assumed to be negative about life and hence about living again. In addition, the moral dynamics of reincar-nation, lacking in tribal beliefs, were made the center of causation, especially in the Buddhist view (Halbfass, 1991: 292–294, 321–325; Obeyesekere, 1980).

It was the Buddhists who formulated the pessimistic idea that life is fun-damentally suffering; at the same time, they expounded their solution, the path to overcome karma. The problem and its solution go together; it is their joint formulation that constitutes one of those long-standing successful moves in intellectual space—the discovery of what we may call a "deep trouble." A variant of this move is found in most great religious doctrines. In moralistic salvation religions, the concept of hell as a place of punishment is formulated (sometimes building on previous conceptions of the afterlife as a shadowy land of death) at the same time that the religion shows the path toward avoiding punishment; the one is an incentive for the other. The Buddha is the first great figure in Indian philosophy because he took the concepts emerging in the networks of his time and created a unifying complex of the key problem together with its solution.

Monastic Movements and the Ideal of Meditative Mysticism

That there is a crystallization point is apparent from the fact that Buddhism, Jainism, and the Ajivikas all emerged at the same time and from the same network (see Figure 5.1). Several factors were involved.

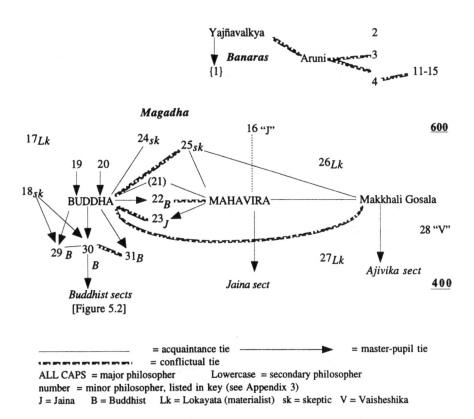

FIGURE 5.1. INDIAN NETWORK, 800–400 B.C.E.:
THE FOUNDING RIVALRIES

1. Inside the attention space of the competing sages, a high degree of overcrowding had been reached. The law of small numbers holds that beyond three to six distinctive positions, most intellectuals will be unable to acquire followers and keep their position going in the reputational space across the generations. This is what we see in the Upanishads: a very large number of positions, none shaped into a well-recognized doctrine, and a multitude of sages, virtually none of them receiving widespread reputation. At the time of the Buddha there were the famous "six non-conformist teachers," plus many other positions; one Buddhist sutra mentions 62 sects, while the Jaina canons refer to as many as 363 schools (Chakravarti, 1987: 35; Isayeva, 1993: 23). The focus of attention created by Buddhists and Jainas drasti-

cally simplifies intellectual space to well within the bounds of the law of small numbers.

Buddhism's content was shaped by the overcrowding of intellectual factions at its time of foundation. Across world history, periods in which the law of small numbers is violated tend to give rise, somewhere among the factions, to a position which declares that truth is impossible. Citing the plethora of opposing positions and the endless debates, one gains a certain meta-prominence in the field by espousing a philosophy of skepticism. In India the person who created such a position explicitly was Sañjaya (18 in Figure 5.1). He was close to the Buddha in the network, and some of his most prominent followers converted and became leading Buddhists. Early Buddhism appropriated a strong streak of skepticism. The Buddha cautions his followers to stay aloof from intellectual disputes, since they are fruitless and distract from the practices leading to enlightenment.

Yet it is impossible to avoid all intellectual activity once one enters the field. Gautama Shakyamuni became elevated as the Buddha by formulating a doctrine which negated the major claims of the rival positions while building upon them at a new philosophical and religious level. Using the skeptics, he asserted the non-existence of the ego, thereby combatting those Upanishadic sages who sought the ultimate self. Creating a new position by opposition, Shakyamuni held that attachment to a permanent self in this world of change is the cause of suffering and the main obstacle to liberation. The same skeptical weapons negate the existence of Brahma or any high god or spiritual reality, delegitimating both traditional and iconoclastic religious methods for reaching a transcendent reality.[20] Shakyamuni broke new ground by going on to explain the source of the apparent ego: it is merely the result of the aggregates (skandas) which make up experience. Here the Buddha was heir to the element philosophies, while eliminating mythological rhetoric and systematizing world components into five groups (corporeality, feeling, perception, mental dispositions, and consciousness).[21] By coordinating material components with psychological ones, it became possible to formulate (perhaps not by Shakyamuni himself but soon after) a model of how the entire world of experience is built up, a twelve-fold chain of causality beginning with ignorance and leading through volition, consciousness, material form, the senses, impressions, feeling, craving, attachment, and becoming, to birth, old age, and death. By understanding and reversing this chain in meditation, one is able to return to the origin and achieve liberation. Although the Buddha denies the transcendent world of the religious sages as yet another reification, he is able to incorporate a more subtle sense of transcending the world of name and form.

The conception that the world is governed by a chain of causation arose among Shakyamuni's immediate predecessors and rivals in the concepts of karma and fate. The Buddha developed this conception into a system-grounding category of dependent origination, drawing out the connection between universal causality and the transitoriness and ultimate unreality of a world composed of aggregations. The philosophical creativity of the Buddha is in raising these ingredients from his surrounding network into a rationalized position on a higher level of abstraction and coherence.

2. Organizationally, the new monastic movements were a sharp departure from the usual life of the *shramanas*. The Buddhists were the first organization with formal rules and a collective identity. They met in local communities and sometimes in pan-community councils, and subordinated individual members to the *sangha*, the body as a whole. (Chakravarti, 1987: 46–64; Hirakawa, 1990). Although the Buddha is a charismatic leader, he pushes his organization away from personal followership. Instead of naming a successor, he admonishes the monks to be "lamps unto themselves," focused on the teachings and collective practices. It is indicative that the first teachings which his followers collected were not the philosophical doctrines but the *Vinaya*, the disciplinary rules of the monks. The Jainas (and apparently the Ajivikas; see Basham, 1951) also formulated similar rules centered on monastic community government. In contrast, the other *shramanas* had consisted of personal followings of particular teachers; they were purely charismatic movements, unable to outlive their leaders.

This tendency toward an autonomous collective identity was reinforced as the Buddhists and Jainas acquired property. Property-holding was contrary to the basic stance of *shramana* lifestyle, the rejection of householding; nevertheless, there was already a custom of kings and pious laypeople providing groves or buildings for the wandering ascetics to use for their meetings and rainy season retreats. Wandering seekers often moved from one teacher to another, and the *shramana* stratum as a whole seems to have mingled rather promiscuously in such places. The Buddhists now pulled apart, acquiring retreats set aside for themselves alone, and formulated rules as to how the members of their communities were to comport themselves (Dutt, 1962: 53–57; Wijayaratna, 1990). Although the Buddhists stressed the renunciation of individual property, they also formed organized settlements, and from a very early period—the Buddha's own lifetime—acquired considerable collective property in the important kingdoms. The early Jainas were rivals of the Buddhists in the same locations, such as Nalanda in Magadha, and in Vesali, capital of a nearby rival kingdom to whose royal house Mahavira was related; and this institutional competition must have been part of the engine of growth in both movements.[22]

3. The Buddhists became the most successful movement because they were oriented toward acquiring the largest social base. Buddhism calls itself the

"Middle Path," explicitly avoiding the extremes of asceticism as well as the indulgence of ordinary life. Meditation was turned into a practice of inward concentration, regulated to facilitate insight based on doctrinal understanding. Buddhists turned away from the more typical *shramana* path, which followed traditions of *tapas*, extremes of self-denial and torture. Such austerities were perhaps shamanistic in origin, referred to occasionally as far back as the early Vedas. *Tapas* were believed to bring visions or magical powers; in the competition among the *shramanas*, they served as the most visible item of social identification. In the eyes of ordinary people, the ability to undergo wondrous self-inflicted hardships was the source of the *shramanas'* emotional appeal, and was a prime motivation for giving them alms. In rejecting *tapas*, the Buddhists risked undercutting their own social charisma. This was compensated in several ways.

The shift to a moderate meditation practice must have greatly widened the recruitment base by making life as a monk more appealing. The rejection of *tapas* also shifted the focus from magical or charismatic impressiveness toward the ethical purpose of the monastic life. On these points the Buddhists and Jainas divided the turf. The Jainas continued more closely the tradition of austerity, taking propertylessness to the extreme of going naked and contempt for life to starving oneself to death. But the Jainas also went beyond *tapas* for magical purposes, emphasizing the moral point of their practices: to burn away the accumulated karma of evil action.

The trump card of the Buddhists was their accommodation with the lay world. Although they were themselves withdrawn from the world into their monastic communities, at the same time they made a place for a continuing relationship with their lay supporters. This was not just a matter of living off the alms of laypeople, as did all *shramanas*. The Buddhists were the only movement which explicitly promoted missionary activities and made preaching to laypersons a central religious duty.[23] The Buddhists were concerned to allow a modus vivendi between lay supporters and the world-denying monks; their rules held that a monk could not join without parental permission, and required that at least one son should remain to care for the family. This also ensured that lay families would be available to give alms to the monks. In this same vein were the good relations that the Buddha, as well as Mahavira—themselves members of the aristocracy—kept up with kings and wealthy donors.

Most important, Buddhism formulated not only a practice and a philosophy for monks but also a simpler morality for laypeople. Killing, lying, stealing, and sexual improprieties were described as producing bad karma and a bad rebirth. Moral behavior, as well as giving alms to the monks, produced good karma and good rebirth. Buddhism elevated the karma doctrine into a prop for secular morality, as well as a motivation for monastic life. Buddhism became successful by filling the moral vacuum in the new social world of commerce and city life with a universalistic social morality which was lacking in both the Brahmanical and the *shramana* religions.

Buddhism laid down a basic cultural framework for lay society which eventually became Hinduism. Buddhism cannot be understood as a reaction against the caste system, any more than it is simply an effort to escape from karma. Just as karma and reincarnation were not considered a major problem before the Buddha, it is likely that the caste system was only very loosely adumbrated at the time (Eliot, 1988: 1:xxii). It is apparent from the Upanishads that the prestige of the Brahmans was breaking down and their distinctness from the political-military *kshatriya* caste was crumbling. Buddhism gave the caste system renewed significance by making it part of one's religious duties to carry out the activities proper to one's station in life (Chakravarti, 1987: 94–121, 180). Certainly, Buddhism was a challenge to the traditional Brahman practices, attacking its rituals and especially its sacrifices by the doctrine of *ahimsa,* non-harming. But Buddhism should be seen as more of a reform within the milieu of the educated religious people—who were mainly Brahmans— rather than a rival movement from outside. Thus, although the Buddha himself was a *kshatriya,* the largest number of monks in the early movement were of Brahman origin.[24] In principle, the *sangha* was open to any caste; and since it was outside the ordinary world, caste had no place in it. Nevertheless, virtually all monks were recruited from the two upper classes. The biggest source of lay support, however, the ordinary donors of alms, were the landowning farmers. Chakravarti (1987) points out that this *gahapati* group also constituted the main tax base for the emerging states of the period, whose kings were allied with the Buddha. For this group the Buddhists preached a secular morality, encouraging them to stay in the world, to respect their superiors, and, not incidentally, to provide the alms which the *sangha* needed to survive.

The early Buddhists' support of the caste system, like their dependence on the concepts of karma and reincarnation, was another example of tying a prominent new doctrine to its apparent opposite. Buddhism gives the appearance of being a protest against the caste system because it offers a solution from reincarnation in the world where one has no control over one's caste. But the solution and the problem are all part of the same intellectual situation. A successful philosophy—and a successful religion—formulates an entire problem space, not just a solution.

4. The turn toward meditation set Indian culture in the direction of Yoga techniques as a means of transcending the world. The Upanishadic sages did not draw their insights from meditation, nor apparently did they practice it much. The *tapas* ascetics sought a kind of magical charisma. The Buddhists

permeated meditation with an ethicized philosophy. Mysticism emerges now in the sense of a philosophy of those who practice meditation. It might seem that the mystical philosophy is derived from the experience of meditation: an aconceptual insight into what lies behind experience and which has a powerful motivating effect. The Buddhists refer to enlightenment, one of whose components is the experience of an inner light, and to the bliss of deep meditation. These might seem to be experiential inputs which shape the philosophy.

Nevertheless, meditation is shaped by the direction of philosophy more than the reverse. There are two sorts of reasons. Historical comparisons turn up a wide variety of techniques of meditation,[25] and an equally great variety of ways in which the experiences of meditation are interpreted.[26] Meditative experiences do not speak for themselves, nor do they even occur without an understanding of what one is seeking, an understanding shaped by the social group in which meditation takes place. Abstract or transcendental interpretations of meditation do not appear until a community of intellectual debaters has developed abstract philosophy.

A common interpretation holds that mysticism is a result of despair at worldly conditions. This would presumably apply only to the varieties of mysticism which aim at otherworldly transcendence. But in fact the historical correlation is not at all good. Buddhist mysticism originated in a time of economic growth and unprecedented prosperity in the Ganges civilization. In China, mysticism became important in the prosperous T'ang dynasty, and the spread of Ch'an monasteries was most pronounced during the late T'ang-Sung transition, when the rural commercial economy was taking off; the height of medieval Chinese proto-capitalism, the late Sung, was the period when meditation spread into the Neo-Confucian movement.

The more apt generalization is that otherworldly mysticism is especially likely to thrive in a social structure which favors monasticism. Periods when monasteries are expanding are high points of mysticism, and these are times when monasteries are agents of economic growth in the countryside. Lay-oriented movements of meditative practice, by contrast, have a strong organizational potential as a basis for political movements, especially in authoritarian societies which allow no other means of political mobilization outside the aristocratic families. It is here—as in the Taoist political movements in China, the Sufi political movements in the Islamic world, and the Kabbalist movements in medieval Judaism—that mysticism turns into political activism. Of another sort are the hedonistic-intellectualistic versions of mysticism, such as the "Sages of the Bamboo Grove" of the Three Kingdoms period in China, or the occultism of educated Europeans around 1900, revived in the psychedelic "counterculture" of 1960s hippies. These take place in prosperous, even pampered social classes; if such movements sometimes coincide with times of political upheaval, that is not so much because mysticism is a compensation as because state and religious regimentation have lost their grip, allowing exploration of what was previously heretical or disreputable.

Max Weber ([1922] 1968: 503–505) advanced a narrower interpretation of the rise of salvation-oriented mysticism: it is embraced by a declining aristocracy losing its political power to the centralizing state. Thus the Buddha, a prince of the Shakya tribe on the fringes of the expanding Ganges states, would have been motivated by declining political fortunes. Mahavira, founder of Jainism, came from a similar political background. But this argument does not hold up either as a generalization or in the particulars of the Indian case. A survey of declining aristocracies would hardly show that their general tendency is toward otherworldly mystical religion. The displacement of the aristocracy by the absolutist state in Europe during the 1600s and 1700s contributed no trend toward world-escaping mysticism. In Japan, the aristocracy supported Buddhist mysticism most strongly during the feudal period 1300–1600, when the political alliance between the rural monasteries and aristocratic power was at its height; during the displacement of Japanese aristocracy by the Tokugawa bureaucracy after 1600, Buddhism declined among the upper classes and was replaced by Confucianism. In India, the status of the *kshatriyas* was not declining preceding the rise of Buddhism, and in any case the main recruitment base of Buddhism was the Brahmans.

The biggest question left unanswered by these deprivation-compensation explanations of mysticism is why the mystics were so socially honored. It is conceivable that hard times might motivate a certain class of individuals to withdraw from social life; but why should the rest of the society honor them for doing so? The movement of *shramanas,* from which Buddhism and Jainism grew, consisted of holy alms men who could exist only because their social prestige was spreading, motivating a widening tendency to give alms. Here we see one connection between increased social *prosperity* and mysticism: the mystics' dropping out from society presupposes increased economic surplus to support them. The successful expansion of the Buddhist movement, with its surge of monasteries and monuments, depended on a growing economy, together with increased political organization capable of extracting and channeling surplus.[27]

There remains the question why *shramanas,* and subsequently monks, become the bearers of so much social charisma. This happened at a time when the means of emotional production were newly expanding, and the means of intellectual production as well; in both dimensions the center of these new media was the free-floating community of non-householders. The *shramanas* played on the emotional capital of techniques for violating the ordinary, especially in their grotesque displays of asceticism. This was facilitated by older traditions of magic, now enhanced by the scale of the mass movements of wanderers, whose concentration in great assemblies like those we find in the early Buddhist texts constituted a social technology of Durkheimian interaction rituals producing unprecedented amounts of emotional energy. The monks further expanded the reach of this charisma by the emotional appeals of moral preaching, filling a vacuum in the surrounding society of new commercial and political relations outside the traditional kinship structures. The Buddhist-Jaina version of mysticism now connoted the highest moral respectability, and lay-persons gained moral status by their homage to it, and by offering material support. By now an intellectual community had formed which interpreted the emotional highs of meditative experience as the highest point on all religious dimensions, a fusion of moral and ontological peaks.

It is because Buddhist mysticism, and its later Hindu counterpart, existed in the context of these social relationships that meditation had such a charismatic status. For this reason, movements in the modern West to transplant mysticism seem doomed to failure. The technique and the philosophy can be revived, but the practice is individual, or at best takes place in religious communities which are private and without honor from the surrounding community. Meditative mysticism in Europe or the Americas becomes little more than private occultism, lacking in social charisma. It is doubtful whether anyone in our own time—at least outside of south Asia—can become enlightened in the sense that ancient and medieval persons could have experienced.

Anti-monastic Opposition and the Forming of Hindu Lay Culture

The consolidation of monastic organization made Buddhism the center of religious and intellectual life. This in turn gave rise to a slowly developing movement of opposition. The main organizational base which remained consisted of the lay householders who served as teachers and ritualists, that is, the Brahmans. But now they acquired new intellectual contents to keep up with the monastic trendsetters. This took place in three ways.

First, the residue of the freelance sages, those who remained outside the monastic orders, collected under the auspices of Brahmanical education. This was the period when most of the Upanishads were formulated; that is, the stories of various sages were collected as texts appended to one or another of the Vedas. Although a few Upanishads (the *Brihadaranyaka* and *Chandogya*) precede Buddhism, and several others may be contemporary with its rise, the so-called Middle Upanishads were created ca. 350–200 B.C.E., and some date from around 200 C.E. or even later.[28] Together these constituted the set of Upanishads that came to be considered classic texts of Hinduism, but only after Shankara turned them into an orthodox canon around 700 C.E. There was in fact a good deal of selection to be made, since texts calling themselves

Upanishads continued to be written even later: for instance, Yoga-Upanishads were eventually appended to the *Yogasutra,* compiled around 500 C.E., and the Shaiva, Shakti, and Vaishnava sects all composed their own Upanishads, some as late as 1300 C.E. The prestige of Hindu orthodoxy became attached to having an Upanishad for one's particular doctrine, but only, it would seem, after around 200–400 C.E. The contents of the "classic" Upanishads, those collected during the phase when an anti-Buddhist syncretism was being built up, show no sense of orthodoxy at all, and in fact offer a rather pervasive criticism of traditional Brahmanism. Yet most custodians of the Vedic texts were impelled, no doubt by weakness, to ally with their critics; those Vedists who held out against the Upanishadic movement revived later, when Hinduism gathered strength, as Mimamsa. The Upanishads' contents suggest great diversity of opinions in the Brahman camp during this time, with nothing yet crystallizing into a doctrinal rallying point (see Figure 5.2).

The second process consisted in defining a distinctive Hindu social identity. The first clear indications are the law books of Manu and of Yajñavalkya, both attributed to ancient or mythical figures, but reaching their canonical forms around 200 C.E.[29] These books lay out caste duties and prohibitions and their penalties. This was essentially a new development. In ancient times, the four *varnas* were primarily a categorization scheme; the Vedas carried no prohibitions about commensualism or intermarriage. There were, however, a large number of *jatis,* originally probably tribal lineage groups; it was the latter which became organized, through the work of the Brahman legists, as castes and fitted into a Vedic ideology.

The caste system expanded into secular life as a regulative code of social and economic transactions. From now on new social relations were constructed by creating distinctions among subcastes; henceforward any occupational, kin-linked, or regional group had to compete for status by instituting its own purity and marriage rules in emulation of the Brahmans. A new relation developed between the Brahmans and the state: caste laws were to be enforced by political officials, but they had no autonomy to makes laws, instead relying on the learned Brahmans. Moreover, the center of gravity shifted toward the local arena as Brahmans became economically central to the village. Their rituals regulated every activity, while collecting fees for their performance; resistance was crushed by the threat of ritual exclusion from the division of labor. Caste laws now controlled everything from guilds and interest rates to criminal penalties. Domestic rituals become the vehicles of family property transfers and independence of householders (Smith, 1989: 148–149; Moore, 1966: 319–337). The transformation of the Brahman priests into their new role as linchpin of the caste system was simultaneously the transformation of the functioning property system.

Caste regulation grew over a long period as the states lost control of landed

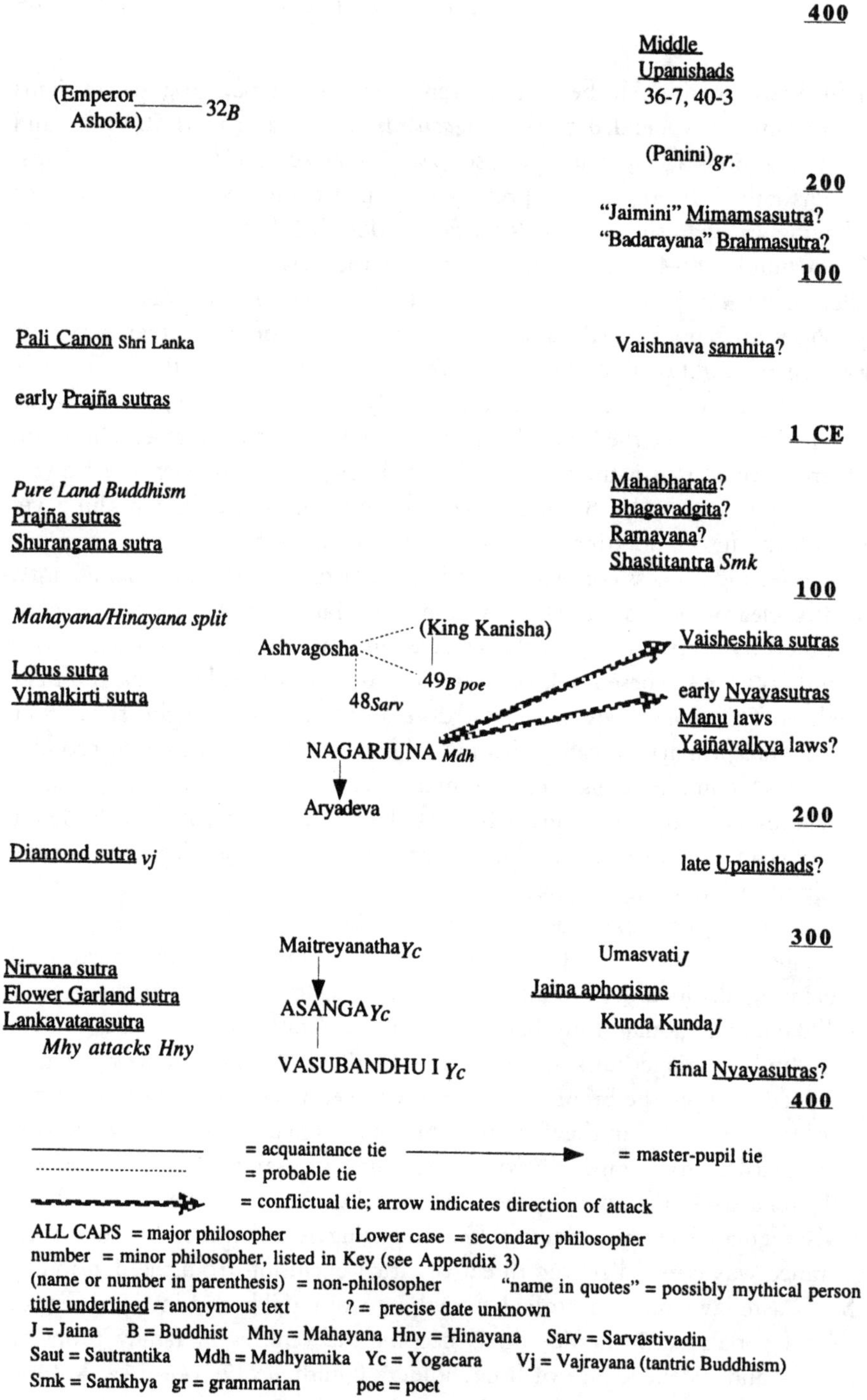

                                                                    400

                                                    Middle
                                                    Upanishads
                                                    36-7, 40-3
(Emperor_____ 32*B*
   Ashoka)
                                                        (Panini)*gr.*
                                                                    200
                                                    "Jaimini" Mimamsasutra?
                                                    "Badarayana" Brahmasutra?
                                                                    100

Pali Canon Shri Lanka   Vaishnava samhita?

early Prajña sutras

                                                                    1 CE

Pure Land Buddhism   Mahabharata?
Prajña sutras   Bhagavadgita?
Shurangama sutra   Ramayana?
                                                    Shastitantra *Smk*
                                                                    100
Mahayana/Hinayana split   Vaisheshika sutras

                        Ashvagosha⋯⋯(King Kanisha)
Lotus sutra   early Nyayasutras
Vimalkirti sutra   49*B poe*   Manu laws
                         48*Sarv*   Yajñavalkya laws?

                        NAGARJUNA *Mdh*
                                                                    200
                        Aryadeva

Diamond sutra *vj*   late Upanishads?

                                                                    300
                    Maitreyanatha*Yc*   Umasvati *J*
Nirvana sutra   Jaina aphorisms
Flower Garland sutra   ASANGA*Yc*   Kunda Kunda*J*
Lankavatarasutra
   Mhy attacks Hny   VASUBANDHU I *Yc*   final Nyayasutras?
                                                                    400

————————   = acquaintance tie ——————————▶ = master-pupil tie
······················· = probable tie
∿∿∿∿∿∿∿▸   = conflictual tie; arrow indicates direction of attack

ALL CAPS = major philosopher   Lower case = secondary philosopher
number = minor philosopher, listed in Key (see Appendix 3)
(name or number in parenthesis) = non-philosopher   "name in quotes" = possibly mythical person
title underlined = anonymous text   ? = precise date unknown
J = Jaina   B = Buddhist   Mhy = Mahayana Hny = Hinayana   Sarv = Sarvastivadin
Saut = Sautrantika   Mdh = Madhyamika   Yc = Yogacara   Vj = Vajrayana (tantric Buddhism)
Smk = Samkhya   gr = grammarian   poe = poet

FIGURE 5.2. INDIA, 400 B.C.E.–400 C.E.:
AGE OF ANONYMOUS TEXTS

revenue, with a key transition perhaps at the downfall of the Guptas and coming fully into place only around 1000–1200 (*OHI*, 1981: 63). The political ascendancy of Hinduism, and its displacement of Buddhism's political and social base, came about by this indirect route. The Brahmans' influence spread in the regions of weak or formative states; by controlling law, they became the more enduring element in Indian social organization, whose power was never challenged by the series of ephemeral states. Here Indian social structure took a fundamental turn onto a path contrasting with that of China or Rome, where the administration of law was dominated by government officials. This structural relation between Brahmans as hereditary monopolists of the law and the weak state was a basic cause of the pattern which Louis Dumont (1980) and Murray Milner, Jr. (1994), have seen as the autonomy of a pure hierarchic or status principle over economic and power stratification.

Hinduism acquired its definition by its opposition to the monastic movements. The law books mark the point when Buddhism and Jainism became systematically denounced as "heterodox" *(nastika)*. Reverence for the sacrifices enjoined in the Vedas became the criterion.[30] The Brahman intellectuals now allied around their traditional ritual practice, downplaying the criticism of Vedic sacrifices which pervades the Upanishads. The new emphasis was on finding a rallying point which would clearly separate the Brahmans from the ritual practice of their monastic rivals. But although ideological continuity was stressed, a revolution had taken place in the social practice of Vedic rituals. The old Vedas and *Brahmanas* had promulgated large public sacrifices, carried out by Brahman priests in attendance on the kings. A grand ritual like the horse sacrifice was a claim for political overlordship. Strong rulers such as Ashoka suppressed such rituals by rivals to their own power; yet as the Brahmans found a more valuable niche by controlling local social relationships, the expensive and ostentatious public sacrifices became unnecessary. In their place were put a new class of domestic rituals regulating the occasions of everyday life, cheaper but reaping a reward of consistent social control. The ideological work of transforming Brahman prestige from one activity to another came about by interpreting the smaller and inward sacrifices as emblems of the larger (Smith, 1989: 120, 143–145, 193–196).

In the third phase, a self-consciously "orthodox" Hinduism challenged Buddhism intellectually. Now occurred the formation of philosophical traditions, *darshanas,* engaging in debates with the Buddhists. This phase culminated around 700 in what might be called the "Advaita revolution." Hinduism appropriated the core of Buddhist philosophy, its anti-materialism and aconceptual mysticism, at just the time when Buddhism was institutionally on its last legs in India.

Whereas Buddhist monasticism flourished best in strong state-building re-

gions, Hinduism spread most successfully where there was a large-scale migration and cultural influx into a previously unorganized tribal area, setting off
emulative formation of subcastes along lines of ritual purity. In the latter
respect, Hinduism is similar to Judaism after the destruction of its temple began
its period of depoliticization and diaspora. The rabbi is something like the
Indian pandit: both were laymen and householders, with little or no organization around church property, salaries, and hierarchy. Religious leadership
merged with the lay status system, giving a special charisma to the possession
of education. Both diaspora Judaism and pandit-centered Hinduism emphasized ritual purity, thereby structuring group barriers through commensualism
and marriage. Hinduism is a more extreme version of the organizational forms
of diaspora Judaism. The Hindu diaspora over the multiethnic Indian subcontinent occurred in circumstances of weak and ephemeral states, where no rival
religion predominated, whereas Judaism survived under Roman, Persian, and
Islamic states in the niches for conquered peoples allowed by the state-allied
religions. Hinduism is what Judaism might have become if fragmented political
conditions had left all the other circum-Mediterranean ethnic groups to compete with and emulate Jewish ritual purity.

The great Hindu epics which crystallized the identity of Hinduism as a
popular culture began the reinterpretation of previous Indian traditions. These
texts, which arrived at canonical status around 400 or 500 C.E., are exercises
in anachronism (Van Buitenen, 1973: xxi–xxxix). The name *Mahabharata*
extols the territory of "great Bharata" (i.e., the Punjab, the ancestral Vedic
homeland in the northwest), while its action is set in the period of the original
Aryan migration into the lower Ganges. The *Ramayana* contains a mythical
version of the colonization of Sri Lanka, which had been carried out by settlers
escaping the cage of the centralized Ganges states around 500–200 B.C.E. Both
epics are a kind of anti-Buddhist propaganda, depicting Hindu conquest of
territories—Bihar and Sri Lanka—which at the time of writing were the main
Buddhist strongholds.[31] The period in which the bulk of these epics was
written, ca. 200 B.C.E.–200 C.E., coincides with the outpouring of Mahayana
sutras, as well as with a Buddhist epic by the poet Ashvaghosha, written as if
in rivalry with the new fame of the Hindu poems (ca. 80 C.E.; Nakamura,
1980: 133–35). Hindu and Buddhist texts now began to make extravagant
claims for the antiquity of their cultures, the Buddhists by inventing cosmic
incarnations of the Buddha who lived in prior eons; this feature was imitated
by the Jainas, who list a series of 24 Tirthankaras (exalted founders) prior to
Mahavira, some going back millions of years. Now sets in the contest of "more
ancient than thou," which displaced the prestige of doctrinal innovations found
among the Upanishadic sages and in early Buddhism, and which henceforward
distorted Indians' conceptions of their own history.

Partitioning the Intellectual Attention Space

Upon these slowly shifting social bases arose the long-term networks which constituted the intellectual community in India. Let us envision this network of intergenerational continuities and conflicting factions as the actor, and the names of individual philosophers, famous or otherwise, as surges of intellectual activity produced by the network. Why does creativity occur at particular times and in particular conceptual regions? We may trace this process through three major phases: (1) the early period of Buddhist domination, when Buddhism underwent a large number of sectarian splits; (2) the period of challenge to Buddhism by Hindu *darshanas*, an apex of creativity on both sides; and (3) the struggles within Hindu philosophy after the demise of Buddhism.

The Victorious Proliferation of Buddhist Sectarian Philosophies

Buddhism rapidly expanded for its first 10 or 15 generations, first in northern India, then throughout the subcontinent. During this time Buddhism underwent numerous divisions, somewhat over-schematically attributed to a succession of seven schisms. Within 6 generations or so after the Buddha's death, there were 18 recognized sects; overall, scholars have assembled the names of 34 factions, and suggested that there may have been as many as 200.[32] The pattern is in keeping with the principle that strong schools subdivide to fill intellectual space (see Figure 5.3).

How can we account for fractionation on this scale, far beyond the upper limits of the intellectual law of small numbers? Doctrinal differences among most of these "schools" were minor. Some are organizational lineages of monasteries; others are labels subsuming a variety of positions; some are variant names for the same school or for its different generations over time. Even allowing for this simplification, we are left with many more factions than the half dozen which the law of small numbers says is the maximal number of distinctively memorable positions which can sustain themselves across time. The answer is that the law of small numbers applies to intellectual positions rather than to the number of organizations per se. Organizations do not compete if they find separate geographical bases or resource niches. But intellectual factions, by their very nature, compete in the universal attention space; if they become specialized or localized, they simply do not receive any wide recognition, and are obscured behind those that do. That is what the intellectual law of small numbers means. Buddhist fractionation reflects both kinds of conditions. On one level were conditions external to intellectual life: issues of monastic discipline, geographical dispersion, disciples of particular leaders. On the second level intellectual differences emerge. It appears that organiza-

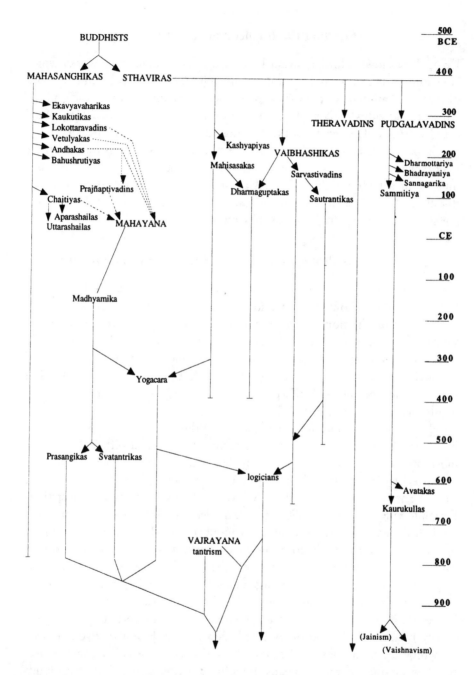

FIGURE 5.3. LINEAGES OF BUDDHIST SECTS, 400 B.C.E.–900 C.E.

tional splits were much the more numerous, and that divergence among intellectual positions is about what one would expect from the law of small numbers.

For the period down to the beginning of the Common Era, our ability to reconstruct a network is very imprecise. The names of significant individual thinkers are only occasionally known. Figure 5.3 shows the approximate structure of the organizational fractionation, subject to some disagreement over dates and genealogical connections and to spelling variants.

The first great schism occurred at the Second Council, about 100 years after the death of the Buddha. The issues were not at all philosophical or even theological, but matters of discipline. At issue was a crisis of institutionalization for a newly successful movement. The Mahasanghikas, or "majority of the council," favored loosening the ascetic rules and allowing monasteries to accumulate property. The Sthaviras, followers of the "way of the Elders," upheld the tradition of the wandering alms men. The Buddhist movement had no headquarters or hierocratic succession; councils were general meetings among the independent monasteries, without means of enforcing church unity. Both the Mahasanghikas and Sthaviras underwent a series of fractionations over the next 200 years. We may group the outcomes into four main camps which acquired distinctive intellectual lines.

1. The Pudgalavadins, branching off from the side of the Elders, held that there is a *pudgala,* or "person," over and above the bundle of aggregates which makes up human experience. This was a first-order heresy in Buddhism, since a basic tenet was the non-existence of a self. The Pudgalavadins, however, did provide an answer to a favorite early debating point: If there is no soul, what is it that is reincarnated from one life to another? The Pudgalavadins seem to have undergone a number of short-lived organizational sub-splits, or perhaps they are merely referred to by one well-known leader after another. Nevertheless, their main doctrine remained constant throughout the life of the sect. The Pudgalavada was one of the longest-lived Buddhist sects; it was still one of the four largest during the 600s C.E., and members remained down to the end of Indian Buddhism around 1200.

2. The root-lineage Sthaviras, under their Pali name Theravadins, also remained stable and conservative in doctrine. Originally the Theravadins were strong in western India (the home of the Pali dialect); they owed their survival, as well as their doctrinal conservatism, to the fact that they were the sect which had colonized Sri Lanka about 250 B.C.E., where they remained entrenched, despite various political vicissitudes, down to the 1900s (Gombrich, 1988). Their philosophical doctrine, the basis of which they shared with the Sarvastivadins, was an *Abhidharma* scholasticism.

3. Another large set of sects branches from the Sthaviras. The best known

are the Sarvastivadins, among the most philosophically oriented sects. Their name itself is philosophical, meaning "everything-exists theorists." Sharing lineage links with them, or possibly branching off from them, is a group called Vibhajyavadins, "those who make distinctions"; one of these groups survived as a numerically important sect down into the Gupta era. The doctrinal positions of most of these sects are not known, with the exception of the Sarvastivadins, and their fission, the Sautrantikas. What we are probably seeing here is a long-term effect of the law of small numbers: the philosophical differences among the sects were obscured over the centuries of competition for intellectual attention; only the most distinctive positions were remembered, and only their texts were propagated and developed.

Buddhist meditation involves taking experience apart into its elements until one realizes that there is among these elements no self to which one can be attached. The *Abhidharma,* held in common by most of the early sects, comprised lists of the elements of which experience is composed. These numbered lists, no doubt a mnemonic device from a time when transmission was oral, grew far beyond their practical relevance for achieving enlightenment. Scholastic pedantry grew over the generations, and various classifications were added—the 5 *skandas* ("aggregates"), 12 sense fields, 18 elements (6 sense organs, 6 sense objects, 6 sense consciousnesses)—together with sub- and cross-classifications; in some sects the total number of *dharmas* (elements) reached as many 75, 82, or 100 (in the late Yogacara), while types of causal relations among them numbered 24 (Nakamura, 1980: 125–126; Guenther, 1976; Conze, 1962: 178–179). Intellectual acuteness also grew; as definitions of the elements were refined, ontological and epistemological issues emerged.

Buddhist meditation takes its distinctiveness from the doctrine of dependent origination, the chain of causation which leads to reincarnation in the phenomenal world. This soteriology, when formalized by professional teachers, developed into a more abstract issue regarding the dependence that leads from one element of experience to another. The nature of causation was to be Buddhism's major contribution and challenge to the rest of Indian philosophy. Potter (1976) argues that most of the positions of Indian philosophy can be arrayed across the space of possible stances on this issue.

The Sarvastivadins, concerned to show how dependent origination operates among their long list of elements, took the position that "everything exists," including past and future. The so-called objects of everyday life are not real, for they are mere transitory aggregates, but the elements of which these aggregates are composed are real and permanent. The Sarvastivadins were realists about the world constituents; the one item they were at pains to show does not exist is the subjective self. The *dharmas* have their own self-natures or essences which exist eternally; indeed, all three time-periods are real substances. Even unmanifested karma is regarded as a type of matter. This omni-realism probably developed from epistemological argument. The Sarvastivad-ins held that no true cognition is possible without a real object; if past and future did not exist, nor any of the non-substantial *dharmas,* we could not cognize them (Conze, 1962: 137–141; Guenther, 1972: 43–47, 65).

Now there emerged lines of genuine philosophical disagreement among the Buddhists. The Sarvastivadins, centered in Kashmir, underwent a schism of their branch in Gandhara which become the Sautrantikas, those who reject the *Abhidharma* and claim to return to the sutras. The Sautrantikas rejected the doctrine of the intentionality of consciousness by which the Sarvastivadins defended their realism. Instead, they distinguished between the things of expe-rience, which exist but only as transitory point-instants of space-time; and non-concrete categories, which do not exist; the latter are permanent and real but only as abstractions. There is a non-referential aspect of mind whereby dharmas which are not existing substances can be objects of valid cognition. The Sautrantikas were phenomenalists about the world, nominalists about general categories. Whereas the Sarvastivadins held that dependent origination is an interlocking net of simultaneously existing causal elements, the Sautran-tikas were the first to emphasize that there is no causality except in temporal sequences. The world, although independently existing, is a flux of evanescent instantaneous beings (Guenther, 1972: 75–76).

Another variant, the Kashyapiyas, tried to pare down the scope of depend-ent origination. Taking another stance in the array opened up by the Sarvasti-vadins, they held that only that part of the past exists which continues to have an effect on the present, and only that part of the future exists which is inherent in the present. The Sarvastivada-Sautrantika split, sometimes referred to as the seventh Buddhist schism, came near the end of the period of division of the old Buddhist sects, around 100 B.C.E. These philosophical positions were to be the background from which emerged the critical philosophy of Nagarguna.

4. Meanwhile, the other major branch of Buddhist sectarianism, the Ma-hasanghika, was also subdividing. Some of the subsects were developing philo-sophical positions. The Vetulyakas (around the time of the third schism, ca. 300 B.C.E.) held that nothing has its own nature, but instead all the elements are void *(shunya).* This has the ring of a direct opposition to the Sarvastivadins, and also foreshadows Nagarjuna. The Uttarapathakas (in the fourth or fifth schism) interpreted each element not as void, but not as determinate either in the sense of the Sarvastivadin realism; instead each thing was said to have its own-nature *(tathata,* or "thusness"), an inexplicable indexicality which brings to the fore the radical particularity of existence. Around the same time, a branch known as the Andhakas took a more radical departure from Buddhist tradition by moving toward a form of idealism. The objects of mind were held

to be the same as mindfulness itself. Furthermore, meditation arrives at a steady consciousness which is not momentary, but shows an immutable nature beneath the phenomenal changes. The Andhakas were still operating in the *Abhidharma* mode of classification, but they added nirvana itself to the list of elements and gave it a controlling function; nirvana became a *skanda* pulling the human individual toward liberation. This doctrinal shift brought the Andhakas into debate both with the lineages of the Elders and with the other Mahasanghikas.

Other splits among the Mahasanghikas came from theological innovations.[33] The Lokottaravadins held that the body of the Buddha is supra-mundane *(lokottara)*; the historical Buddha who appeared in the world was only an appearance, as indeed is the mundane world in general (Conze, 1962: 163). The Chaitiyas, located in the southern kingdom of Andhra, were apparently stupa worshippers, in contrast to orthodox monastic meditators. The Mahasanghikas generally came to hold that the body of the Buddha pervades the universe, and that there is a plurality of Buddhas, including transmundane ones. One can see a number of trends in the direction of Mahayana, which appears to have arisen largely out of the Mahasanghika sects, and especially the Andhakas.

The Mahayana is not a sect in quite the same way as the others. It seems to have emerged both inside the monasteries and, perhaps more important, among lay orders. There is a connection between early Mahayana or proto-Mahayana and the stupas, mound-shaped reliquaries or monuments (Hirakawa, 1990: 256–274). These were established and kept up by lay donors as alternative centers of worship and teaching outside monastic routine. Doctrinally, the Mahayana innovations downplayed the monk seeking individual salvation, and extolled the Bodhisattva, who continues in the world to preach salvation to everyone. Such a doctrine would have exalted the status of the semi-professional staff of caretakers at the stupas and the lay orders which surrounded them. Original Buddhism had won its organizational advantage over its early rival meditative orders by forging stronger ties to lay donors and providing a morality for laypeople. Mahayana was a revival of and expansion toward this lay base.

Mahayana practice turned away from the prolonged meditative exercises of the monks. It elevated the ceremonial making of vows, which might also be taken by laypersons. The physical text itself became the focus of ritual worship; copying and reciting scriptures became major acts of religious merit.[34] Mahayana emerged as a set of scriptures alleging new revelations from the mouth of the Buddha; and it was by a copying campaign that these scriptures spread. Such newly appearing scriptures were of course scandalous to the learned monks (Nakamura, 1980: 151). They were justified by the doctrines of the supra-mundane and trans-historical Buddhas, so that new sutras were attributed not to the Shakyamuni Buddha of the Elders but to inspiration from some prior or current Buddha. The reincarnation doctrine must have been given a boost at this time by its added usefulness in legitimating Mahayana and its practitioners. Popular Mahayana gave rise to a variety of new religious paths: beliefs in rebirth in a Pure Land, a paradise presided over by one of the future Buddhas; worship of Vairocana Buddha, an all-pervasive cosmic God; prayers to merciful and world-intervening Bodhisattvas. These innovations added many alternatives to monastic meditation, especially lay rituals, as well as promoting rather naive theistic beliefs that undercut the philosophical path of detachment from a cosmos of illusory permanences.

There was no sharp or prolonged split between lay-oriented Buddhism and the monastic life. It appears that the phase of enthusiastic Mahayanist lay movements did not last long in India. Mahayana had no *vinaya* disciplinary rules of its own, and became not so much a development of separate monasteries as a movement within existing monasteries (Dutt, 1962: 176; Hirakawa, 1990: 308–311). The Bodhisattva path did not negate what came to be called the Pratyekabuddha ("private Buddha") path, but added another level of religious status beyond it. When Mahayana first crystallized, there was a phase of hostility to "Hinayana"; the *Lotus sutra* (compiled in the first two centuries of the Common Era) derided early Buddhism as the "lesser path" and its teachings as provisional expressions for an unsophisticated audience. About the same time the *Vimalkirti sutra* depicted a layman achieving an enlightenment superior to that of the monks. Nevertheless, in the centuries that followed, we find Mahayana monks in the same monasteries as Hinayana; this mixing was facilitated by the shift toward central monastic centers or "universities," the *mahavihara* ("great monastery") complexes where all the various sects resided and taught. Stupa worship decayed; Mahayana became a movement again largely consisting of monks.

Such sequences repeat many times in Indian religious history. Monastic organizations generate a new focus for social charisma, which becomes monopolized by full-time specialists, leading to emulation by lay movements. In turn the latter, when successful, develop a professionalized elite who become monastic specialists in their own right. We see this in the development of lay Mahayana from monastic Buddhism and its reabsorption into monasticism; in the borrowing of Buddhist and Jaina doctrines and meditation practices by lay Hindus, eventually culminating in the Advaita monks founded by Shankara; and again in the dialectic between Vaishnava orders and the popular bhakti movements which spin off from them. The continuous expansion of the market for religious charisma cycles through institutionalized and deinstitutionalized forms.

From the point of view of intellectual fractionation and the law of small numbers, we may regard the Mahayana-Hinayana split as a framework which brought intellectual life into focus around some four to six significant schools. The multiple splits within the Sthaviras dried up by around the time Mahayana appeared. But this regrouped "Hinayana" remained strong; from reports of Chinese visitors in the 400s and again in the 600s, their monks outnumbered the Mahayanists by about three to one (Hirakawa, 1990: 119–123). Hinayana now boiled down to the Sarvastivadins taking the intellectual lead, with some dissent from the Sautrantikas, who were however gradually reabsorbed into the Sarvastivadins, plus the Theravadins, and, off on the fringe, the Pudgalavadins, with their soul heresy. On the other side of the first schism, the Mahasanghikas, for all their proto-Mahayanist tendencies, remained a large independent sect into the 600s. Mahayana, though it had a number of theological variants (Pure Land, Vairocana, various quasi-theist cults), had only two main representatives in the philosophical attention space: Madhyamika, as developed by Nagarjuna, and Yogacara. The background of multiple organizational fractionation boiled down in the intellectual attention space to a manageable number of philosophies.

Philosophies on the New Mahayana Base

Within the philosophical world strictly speaking, Mahayana doctrine did not determine a particular stance. Theologies of Boddhisattvas, cosmic Buddhas, and Pure Lands did not entail a particular epistemology or even a metaphysics. Mahayana philosophers became distinctive by taking up the slots available for opposition within the lineup of existing Hinayana philosophies. Sarvastivadins held a realist and pluralist position, with the Sautrantikas taking a nominalist slant and stressing the momentariness of all phenomena; the Mahasanghikas, closer to Mahayana theology, were still pluralists, with their innumerable Buddhas, but the Andhakas had moved toward idealist monism. The most successful Mahayana philosophers carved out positions which outflanked their philosophical opponents'; no doubt they chose only a few of the many positions that could have been made compatible with Mahayana theology.

Ashvagosha, around 100 C.E., is identified as the first famous individual philosopher in Buddhism, although it is possible that a somewhat later philosophy was propagated under his name (Dutt, 1962: 277–278; Nakamura, 1980: 232; Raju, 1985: 157). Ashvagosha was the most famous of a Buddhist circle of court poets, and whose epics rivaled the contemporary *Ramayana,* suggesting the emergence at this time of a cosmopolitan attention space on which individuals were competing for intellectual reputation. Ashvagosha looks like a traditional *Abhidharma* philosopher of the Sarvastivadin type, accepting the empirical reality of the 5 aggregates, the 12 bases, and the 18 elements. But the nature of these items is indiscernible, an indexical "suchness." Ashvagosha raised this "suchness" to the ultimate reality of the universe and identified it with the "womb of Buddha," *tathagatagarbha;* it was a monist origin from which pluralism emanated through the traditional 12–link chain of causation. Ashvagosha's "suchness" provided an alternative path between Sarvastivada realism, Sautrantika nominalism, and the somewhat inconsistent mentalism of some of the Mahasanghikas.

A generation or two later, Nagarjuna eclipsed Ashvagosha while taking much the same space among the opposing philosophies. Whereas Ashvagosha seems an ambiguous precursor to Mahayana, Nagarjuna was the great Mahayana standard bearer, giving his theological movement a famous success in the most recondite philosophical arguments. For Nagarjuna, ultimate reality was not merely "thusness" but *shunyata,* emptiness. This was in keeping with the emphasis on emptiness in the Lotus sutra, the leading Mahayana scripture, finished during or shortly after Nagarjuna's lifetime. Nagarjuna, however, did not leave his position simply as a negation; not only did this sound like a pessimism which he did not wish to imply, but also negation would have been on the same level of analysis as the realism of the Sarvastivadins, which he combatted, and the constructs of other philosophical factions.

Nagarjuna rose to a meta-level. He defended a position which may be regarded as classically Buddhist; but he acquired his great personal reputation not merely as a conservative overturning the accretions of the *Abhidharma* scholastics, but by introducing an explicit concern for the standards of argument. All arguments hinge on a concept of identity, the nature of the items that are argued about. Nagarjuna undermined identity by using the classic Buddhist model of causality: all things are caused by dependent origination; therefore nothing has an essence of its own, standing outside the stream of causation; therefore everything is void. Identity turns out to be the same as *shunyata* (Nakamura, 1980: 247–249; Sprung, 1979: 4–11; Streng, 1967; Robinson, 1967). Nagarjuna's criterion of being is like Parmenides': the self-existent must not be dependent on anything else; but—unlike in Parmenides—no such thing exists. Nagarjuna used this argumentation to refute the realism of the Sarvastivadins. There is neither future nor past nor any motion; everything is substanceless. By Nagarjuna's strict criterion, no concepts are intelligible. Hence, Nagarjuna could assert these skeptical statements as a positive doctrine. His omni-negation applies to his own philosophy, holding itself to be a "theory of no-theory." Like some Greek Skeptics, Nagarjuna sought tranquillity through disengagement from intellectual positions; but, unlike the Greeks, he had an institutionalized religion to defend. One must operate with levels of two-fold truth: the truths of religious life within the world, and the ultimate truth of Mahayana, which is inexpressible.

Nagarjuna's doctrine is called "Madhyamika," the superlative of the middle; it steers between the previous camps of the philosophical world, realism and nihilism, or rather rises above them. In one respect its philosophical content is traditionalistic, with nothing of Mahayana avant-garde theology about it. One of its implications, however, is taken to justify the Mahayana stance. Since everything is void, nirvana is not different from samsara; the world of phenomena is itself the realm of enlightenment. One does not have to leave, to transcend in meditation, to do anything special to reach freedom from attachments. Madhyamika omni-negation revives the world of phenomena and allows them to be interpreted as part of the cosmic Buddha—who is after all void as well. This line of argument was emphasized by later Madhyamika thinkers. Chandrakirti (600s) explains that the negativity of *shunyata* is the negation of the "essential nature" or "thing-in-itself" of the Sarvastivadins, not the negation of life-as-lived. This brings Madhyamika into line with the theology of the Boddhisattvas remaining on earth to bring salvation to all sentient beings; in true recognition, they already have it.

An omni-skeptical position like Nagarjuna's Madhyamika was designed to end philosophical debate. Nevertheless, Nagarjuna was just the beginning of the great period of Buddhist philosophy. Far from fading, the Hinayana positions acquired their most famous representatives. Mahayana philosophers as well found additional slots in the attention space besides Nagarjuna's. The Yogacara school emerged in the 300s C.E., coinciding with the last big output of Mahayana sutras and their attacks on the Hinayana. There is a chain of famous thinkers: Maitreyanatha, the founder, who acquired such a reputation that he was later turned into a mythological figure, the Buddha Maitreya; his pupil Asanga; and the latter's half-brother Vasubandhu I.[35]

Yogacara built upon epistemological disputes in its sectarian lineage. The Sarvastivadins held that consciousness always implies an object because the knower cannot know itself but only something else (Guenther, 1972: 16, 66, 92). They had set out to formalize the Buddhist doctrine of taking apart ordinary objects into underlying elements; but their reductionism and anti-mentalism landed them in a similar problem as the logical positivists of the Vienna Circle: the difficulty of defining all meaningful expressions in restrictedly objective terms (Griffiths, 1986: 50–51). In both cases a bifurcation developed, in which logical realities were recognized alongside elementary substances; the Sautrantikas posited a level of logical abstractions, although allowing them only nominal existence. Yogacara extended further this non-referential consciousness by accepting pure mental experience. One cognizes patches of color and shapes of objects; cognitions do not disclose independently existing objects but only reveal object-like mental images. It is only the relation of externality, supplied by consciousness, which makes objects appear as if they exist. In a reversal of the Sarvastivadin position, there is in fact nothing but non-referential consciousness; the apparent world is merely "consciousness representing itself to itself" (Griffiths, 1986: 102).

Asanga approached the epistemological issue from the point of view of the Madhyamika doctrine of emptiness, which allowed him to assert the emptiness of the external world; at a deeper level consciousness too is void, although the voidness of the phenomenal levels are, so to speak, derivative of it. The early formulators of Yogacara may well have had no intention of going beyond Madhyamika. Nevertheless, Yogacara already was moving beyond Madhyamika's omni-skepticism and anti-metaphysical stance. Yogacara was a full-fledged scholasticism; it extended the *Abhidharma* texts which Madhyamika had repudiated.

Yogacara represents the penetration of Mahayana into the core of the traditional scholasticizing monasteries and the abandoning of its lay roots which took place around this time. Asanga was concerned mainly to provide a systematic guide to meditation techniques, and to describe how the world appears as ideas in meditative experience, rather than actually to deny the existence of objects (as distinct from asserting their voidness) or to stress the foundational role of consciousness (Nagao, 1991; Willis, 1979). As its name implies, Yogacara was the specialty of the professional meditators; and their technical tradition too had grown scholastic over the generations. Whereas the Theravadins and Sarvastivadins had recognized 3 *samadhis,* the *Prajña-paramita-sutras* recognized 152 trances or "doorways to nirvana"; the *Avatamsaka-sutra,* completed contemporaneously with Asanga around 350 C.E. (Nakamura, 1980: 194–195), listed 250. Trance states themselves were ranked and became criteria for levels of salvation, and thus for social ranking among the monks. The differentiation of meditative levels paralleled the inflation of ranks within the community; the Sthaviras had recognized 3 categories of enlightenment, whereas the later Abhidharmists categorized dozens of kinds of Arhats and Never-Returners, and Yogacarins such as Asanga described as many as 50 ranks at the Mahayana super-level of Boddhisattvas.[36] Ontology differentiated correspondingly; by the 700s, late Buddhist scholasticism was dividing ultimate nothingness into 16 types under 4 headings. Yogacara could not help becoming philosophically innovative as it sought to explain the differences among meditative ranks. Whereas Madhyamika emphasized salvation through a simplifying, skeptical wisdom, Yogacara made salvation dependent on a very complex training process of mastering many refinements of meditation simultaneously with their philosophical basis.

However loyal and traditionalist the originators of Yogacara may have been, their position was soon being interpreted as a distinctive school of full-fledged idealism, Vijñanavada, consciousness-theory. It acquired a prominent position in the attention space, as the opposite of Sarvastivadin realism, and provided Mahayana with a metaphysical position on scholastic turf to supplement Madhyamika skepticism. Whereas Asanga was ontologically ambiguous, and primarily concerned with meditation, Vasubandhu I shifted to philosophical concerns in defending the doctrine that there are no extra-mental entities (Willis, 1979: 33; Griffiths, 1986: 82–83). A positive doctrine emerged regarding the construction of world appearances. Asanga had described the process in meditation whereby one observes the rise and fall of thoughts; tracing them back to their origin, he referred to a store-consciousness. The metaphor of "seeds" from which experiences grow had been used before, by the Sautrantikas. With Vasubandhu I's dynamic idealism, the biological analogy came to represent the fecundity of consciousness, containing the infinite potentialities which constitute the world. What kept Vijñanavada from becoming an idealism of Absolute Mind in the style of Vedanta or of European Idealists was its Buddhist commitment; enlightenment comes not with the realization of mind but with its cessation (Wood, 1991).

Across the Buddhist attention space there were now a range of positions, from Sarvastivada element realism to Madhyamika dialectical emptiness and Yogacara idealism. These completed the period when Buddhist philosophy was created by its own internal fractionation.[37] Subsequent developments in Buddhist philosophy, from the 400s through the 700s, were driven by a widening intellectual struggle against the emerging Hindu philosophies. As the material base of Buddhism weakened, its final creativity was to come from a recombination of positions among Hinayana and Mahayana philosophers.

The Buddhist-Hindu Watershed

The greatest creative period of Indian philosophy occurred when Hinduism first challenged the Buddhist schools. In Figure 5.4, the generations from about 400 to 800 C.E. contain both the first great names of Hindu philosophy and the greatest outpouring of Buddhist philosophies. In this watershed period there is one interlocking network, not two; both sides of the intellectual attention space develop in symbiotic conflict.

The material basis for intellectual production is now at its height. Now exist the great intersectarian monasteries, of which Nalanda is the prototype; here not only are the various sects of Buddhism represented, but Hindu laymen as well. There is a good deal of crossing of the lines. Around 500 C.E. the Hindu philosopher Bhartrihari is said to have alternated between monastic discipline and lay life, and to have lived in the Nalanda monastery as a layman. Bhartrihari's teacher was the brother-in-law of one of Vasubandhu II's pupils (Dutt, 1962: 290; *EIP,* 1990: 121). In the 600s Gaudapada, Shankara's reputed grand-teacher, apparently switched among Mahayana, Samkhya, and Vedanta.

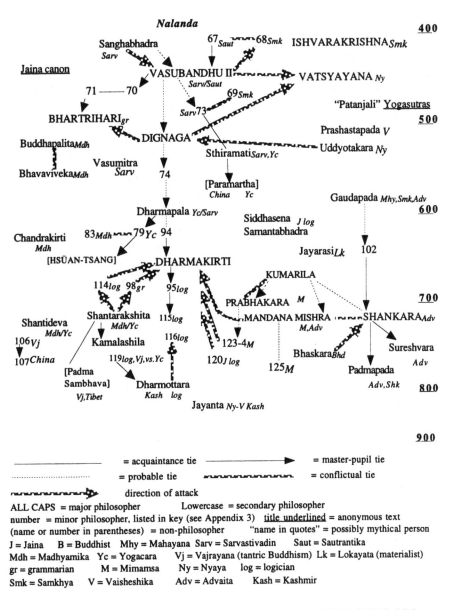

FIGURE 5.4. CONFLICT OF BUDDHIST AND HINDU SCHOOLS,
400–900 C.E.

Biographies from this period are full of stories of the philosophers traveling from center to center, debating and sometimes converting their rivals. The Buddhist logician Dignaga defeated a Brahman at Nalanda, and both the emperor Harsha and the regional kings held public disputations among philosophers of all religions (Stcherbatsky, 1962: 1:33; Dutt, 1962: 266). Hindu philosophies became prominent in the intellectual world, first by contacting the Buddhist networks, then by emulating their debates and eventually their organizational structure. Since so many of the Buddhist philosophers were also Brahmans, we must envision this transition as a shift in the strength of centers of attraction in intellectual space. Dignaga and Dharmakirti (and many others before them, such as Buddhaghosa and Nagarjuna) were Brahmans from the south, just as Asanga and Vasubandhu I were Brahmans from the northwest (Eliot, 2:86); when they traveled to the center, it was the great Buddhist philosophers they sought; and the factional space they opened up created new positions on the Buddhist side. Later, fewer and fewer of the Brahman educated class were making this choice; instead they opened up positions on the Hindu side of the turf. After Shankara, there were Shaiva monks with their own monastic headquarters. Eventually all the Hindu sects had their *maths*, or centers of learning.

The Buddhist monastic centers from about 400 to their last vestiges in the 1100s became universities in much the sense of the Christian universities of Europe in the 1200s. Philosophy had grown up from "theology." Conditions were optimal for creative conflict, a few centers of attention with connecting networks: Nalanda, above all, the "University of Paris" of its day, known for its "row of monasteries with towers licking the clouds"; an outlier at Valabhi in the west, made eminent by some of Vasubandhu II's disciples (Dutt, 1962: 225–231); on the Hindu side, Mithila,[38] very near Nalanda, which became the headquarters of Nyaya-Vaisheshika; and Varanasi (Banaras) 150 miles upriver, a holy city for both Hindus and Buddhists, a center of intellectual factions in Upanishadic times which became active again during the days of the great Mimansakas and Shankara.

Chinese visitors in the 600s described Nalanda as a marvel, with its carved walls and mosaic floors, brickwork brushed with vermilion paste and polished with oil to shine like mirrors, its balustrades and turrets and tile-covered roofs, its temples where Buddha images were surrounded by jewels and ornaments of lustrous gold. There were 100 professors and 3,000 students, both monks and laity, with crowds of servants and porters. When learned Nalanda monks went out, they were carried in sedan chairs surrounded by attendants. Water clocks kept time for the events of the day, which were announced by drum strokes and blasts on a conch shell. Books were locked up at mealtimes to prevent stealing. During lessons the monasteries "hummed with teaching and recitation." Nalanda was a center for advanced teaching, and by the 600s pupils had to pass an entrance examination, perhaps to keep down their numbers. After passing preliminary courses and tests in Mahayana philosophy, students took specialized schools of discussion. Debates before the assembly were the place where one acquired a reputation, and learned men came from around India to advance their careers. In all, there were five such *mahavihara* universities in Bihar and Bengal at the time; the second most famous was Vikramashila, with 1,000 students (Dutt, 1962: 204, 235, 313, 327, 331–348, 360).

Cosmopolitanism was also promoted by the appearance of libraries, such as the one at Nalanda which burned uncontrollably when sacked by the Muslims. We know that at Nalanda not only were the texts of the rival Buddhist philosophies studied, Hinayana as well as the Mahayana, but also secular topics such as logic, medicine, and grammar, and even the Hindu specialties, the Vedas, magic *(Atharvaveda),* and Samkhya (Dutt, 1962: 333). On the other side, it was from this time forward that Hindu philosophers wrote critiques of rival factions, both Hindu and Buddhist. Cultural capital was explicitly borrowed; an instance of repeated crossover between the camps is the work of Shankarasvamin (600s), a Nyaya logician whose commentary on Dignaga became the most famous introductory logic text in Buddhist China and Japan (Nakamura, 1980: 300).

This society was sophisticated and rather worldly. As we can tell from the classic Hindu dramas and poetry of the Gupta period (Kalidasa, Bhasa, the novelist Dandin) and from the lifestyle depicted in the erotic handbook the *Kamasutra,* religion was a taken-for-granted institution of the social world, not necessarily an otherworldly preoccupation, and monks could be spies and go-betweens for love affairs. The culminating Buddhist philosopher Dharmakirti, whose philosophy limits knowledge to the world of experience, had a rather secular reputation. It is not surprising that the Lokayata, the materialist "heresy" dating from the time of the Buddha, had its last living representatives in Jayarasi and Purandhara, contemporaries of Dharmakirti (Dasgupta, 1921–1955: 3:536). The changeover to Hindu intellectual dominance that followed resembles somewhat a "Protestant" Reformation against a Renaissance-like decadence of Buddhist "Catholicism."

In this period crystallized what later came to be regarded as the orthodox Hindu "six *darshanas.*" Retrospective ideology traces Samkhya, Yoga, Nyaya, Vaisheshika, Mimamsa, and Vedanta back to the early Upanishadic period or before. But it is reasonably clear that until around 200–300 C.E. or even later, there were no Hindu philosophical schools as such, holding distinctive territories in the intellectual attention space. There was a morass of positions and tendencies, none of which rose clearly above the others, and none defended by an intellectual champion who commanded the respect of followers and rivals. Hindu "philosophy" was in the shade of Buddhist philosophies in this period because its inchoate tendencies considerably exceeded the upper limits of the law of small numbers. A proto-Samkhya existed in the form of various concepts which were mixed with others in popular works such as the *Mahabharata*.[39] Mimamsa consisted in a number of very specific textual interpretations of the meanings of words in the Vedas, not as a coherent philosophy at an explicit higher level of abstraction. Badarayana's *Brahma-sutras* were just one commentary among others on the grab bag of traditional texts that constituted Brahmanical education. The Upanishads had not yet been reduced to a canonical set of 11 or so; in fact more than 100 Upanishads were recognized, and they continued to be written as late as 1500 C.E. (Nakamura, 1973: 77). And within the Upanishads, as we have seen, there were dozens of philosophies, none worked out in any depth. All this material so strained the law of small numbers that it made no very definite impact on the attention space. The creation of Hindu philosophies was a paring down to a small number of positions, and a sharpening into an explicit level of abstraction and systematization in the battle against Buddhist philosophies. From here date the higher levels of sophistication in Indian philosophy, comparable to the cumulative generations of European intellectual chains.

I will treat clumps of Hindu and Buddhist schools together as they mutually shaped one another.[40]

The Dialectic of Nyaya, Buddhist Logic, and Epistemology

The Intersectarian Theory of Argument. The *Nyaya-sutras* appeared around 100 C.E., and reached their mature form sometime around the lifetime of Nagarjuna or shortly after (*EIP*, 1977: 4). *Nyaya* is usually translated as "logic," but its contents are a good deal broader than the Aristotelean and Megarian logic which dominated in the West. Early Nyaya consisted in classifying modes of knowledge, including a description of the bodily senses, and of the components of a debate. Extensively treated are various kinds of invalid debating tactics such as sophistries, caviling, and quibbling, all of which gives the impression that the sutras arose as a kind of rule book for judges in awarding victory and defeat.

Included is a relatively brief treatment of what looks like a five-step syllogism: (1) to prove there is fire on the mountain; (2) because there is smoke; (3) for example, as in a kitchen; where there is no fire, as in a lake, there is no smoke; (4) the mountain has smoke; (5) therefore there is fire on the mountain. The work of argument is packed into steps (2) and (3), called the "reason" and the "example." The principles which are implicitly or explicitly invoked are sometimes a priori, but for the most part they are inductive; and in general the Nyayas emphasized sensory perception as the origin of knowledge. None of the Indian schools distinguished between formal and empirical validity. They always assumed that arguments should be substantively true, unlike the Greeks, with their concern for the validity of inference apart from its contents. Later logicians, led by the Buddhists, extensively classified the modes of syllogistic argument;[41] but Indian logic remained closely tied to arguments for particular epistemologies and ontologies. A concern for pure technical logic emerged only with the Neo-Nyaya school around 1350.

Emerging from the inchoate competition of the Upanishadic sages, Nyaya became the first real Hindu philosophical school, forming a meta-theory of argument, useful across the factions. Not surprisingly, this was the first school to make contact with the Buddhist side of the field. The Buddhist schools had habitually formulated their arguments as ontological assertions; epistemology seems to have remained implicit or at most uncritical assertion, and formal logic was unknown. At the time Nyaya emerged on the Hindu side, the Buddhists were entering a phase of intensified dispute, as Mahayana took the offensive and Nagarjuna set out to destroy all rival ontologies. Nagarjuna used no formal logic, but he was aware of the incipient Nyaya school logic, which he attacked (Nakamura, 1980: 238–239, 287). Some of the impetus for formulating the full *Nyaya-sutras* may have been in response to the Madhyamikas. Given that Nagarjuna, like many Buddhists, was a Brahman, it is possible that Nyaya and Madhyamika both emerged in the vague borderland of Buddhism and Hinduism, where a common pool of educated intelligentsia shared early training by Brahman teachers while often moving on to the better institutionalized and more advanced philosophy in the Buddhist networks. Perhaps for this reason, in discussing the objects of knowledge the *Nyaya-sutras* (1.1.18–22) sound much like the Buddhist discussion of the chain of causation from attachment, aversion and ignorance to worldly pain and transmigration, and finally to release.

Buddhist logic developed in symbiosis with the Nyaya school: first as imitation, then as debate. The first explicit Buddhist logical writings were manuals of debating tactics, including the five-member "syllogism," produced by the founders of Yogacara: Maitreyanatha, Asanga, and, with a little more originality, the first Vasubandhu (Nakamura, 1980: 294; Dutt, 1962: 265; Stcherbatsky, 1962: 1:28–29). Later on the Hinayana side Vasubandhu II would incorporate more elaborate logic into the *Abhidharma*. The first great individual name in Nyaya, Vatsyayana, was a contemporary of Vasubandhu II and a target of his attacks. In the network (Figure 5.4) we also see a connection between Vasubandhu II and Bhartrihari, whom Dignaga would in turn both criticize and develop. Dignaga became the great Buddhist logician by making a wholesale onslaught on the bases of the Nyaya system. From now on, Dignaga and his successor Dharmakirti were *the* representative Buddhists in the eyes of outsiders, targets of attacks by many notable Hindu philosophers, and defended by counterblasts which made up much of the activity of later Buddhist philosophy.

Bhartrihari's Language Philosophy. Bhartrihari (ca. 500) is emblematic of the new creative situation that arose with the confluence of Buddhist and Hindu networks. He weaves together common themes of Buddhism and the increasingly philosophical Hinduism, and sets off major new directions in both. Bhartrihari was a grammarian, an old technical specialty among the Brahman scholars which enjoyed considerable repute across religious camps. Bhartrihari made strong claims to raise the religious and metaphysical importance of his discipline. He is associated with the revival of an Upanishadic cult which held that chanting the sacred syllable *aum* brings contact with Brahman, the essence of reality. This was a broadening of the most conservative Vedic tradition that the correct pronunciation of the hymns is the key to their ritual power. As in so many other instances, a reactionary move set in motion a creative innovation. Bhartrihari participated in Buddhist circles at Nalanda, where one Mahayana faction was *mantra-yana,* or tantrism, which also focused on chanting magic syllables, among which *aum* was especially honored. Bhartrihari's cult of language may well have been an attempt to transcend the philosophical differences between Buddhism and Hinduism.[42]

For Bhartrihari, the world is constituted by language. Language itself is divine, the manifestation of Brahman. The world of multiplicity does not really exist; it merely comes from the way in which language is spoken. Bhartrihari uses the old grammatical distinction, going back to Patañjali (ca. 150 B.C.E.), between the meaning of a word and the actual sounds by which it is spoken; the latter vary among speakers, but the former is constant. Bhartrihari generalizes this to argue that the meaning of a word, which may be ambiguous when uttered alone, emerges from the context of the sentence as a whole, or from the larger passage in which it appears. Bhartrihari uses this theory of language to support philosophical holism. He goes so far as to argue that the parts of language do not really exist; to split a sentence into words, and these into roots, suffixes, and so forth, is useful only for analysis, or for teaching someone who does not yet know how to speak, and is superfluous for those who can (*EIP,* 1990: 10–11). Bhartrihari's argument is a counterpart to the Madhyamika analysis of the reification of aggregates. An action such as "cooking" takes place over time; the word *cooks* merely collects these events. Ultimately all the distinctions of language are unreal separations within a single whole. Bhartrihari's *sphota,* the trans-verbal unit of meaning, is something like a

Platonic universal; but ultimately meaning goes beyond language and distinction. Only Brahman exists, the distinctionless ultimate. The phenomenal world appears by making distinctions within Brahman; these are due to Brahman's primary manifestation, the power of time, which produces grammatical tenses in language and all the apparent differentiations of experience.

Bhartrihari is the hinge around which changes turn on both sides of the intellectual field.[43] On the side of Hindu orthodoxy, he repudiated Nyaya-Vaisheshika pluralism, as well as the Mimamsa language philosophy which gave primacy to individual syllables, and launched arguments for monism and the doctrine of world illusion that would culminate in the Advaita. On the Buddhist side, Bhartrihari's younger contemporary at Nalanda was Dignaga (ca. 480–540). Direct network contact was thus likely between the greatest star of medieval Buddhism and the most important early Hindu philosopher. Often quoting his predecessor, Dignaga adopted Bhartrihari's notion that experienced reality consists in verbal constructions which promote ultimately unreal distinctions, while giving the argument a traditionally Buddhist thrust toward negation.

Dignaga's Epistemology of Negation. In the debating schools, Dignaga made a stir by reducing the syllogism from five members to three. This looks like a simple elimination of redundancy, but it implies a shift to a higher level of abstraction, focusing on the logical core and away from the concern with procedures of debate which characterized the Nyaya. Simultaneously Dignaga eliminated the traditional discussion of quibbles and other tactical fallacies, and expanded the classification of syllogistic argument. The treatise on logic became a vehicle for developing philosophical positions, displacing the unwieldy *Abhidharma*-style compendium. The Buddhist "Nyaya-vadins" amounted to a good deal more than a technical reform in logic; they became the most famous school within later Indian Buddhism by their synthesis of Buddhist doctrines and their attack on the Hindu schools.

Dignaga attacked the common epistemology of Nyaya, Vaisheshika, and Mimamsa. All these held a realist position, taking raw sensory perception as a basis for valid knowledge. Indeed, the Mimamsakas described perception as the physical transmission of a beam from the eye to the object, grasping its form and carrying it back to the observer (Stcherbatsky, 1962: 1:23). Samkhya held that the senses actually become the objects perceived; seeing involves becoming the color seen (*EIP,* 1987: 99).

Dignaga reduced the sources of knowledge to two (the lists of the Hindu schools had included as many as six): sensory perception and inference which follows from it. Perception is always of particulars; and since experience consists only in particulars, it is inutterable, an indexical "thusness." All words are in the realm of post-sensory inference, and they are all universals. As in much traditional Buddhist doctrine, universals do not really exist; they are merely mental, illusory products of consciousness whose overcoming, like all illusions of permanences over and above momentary aggregates, constitutes enlightenment.

Dignaga's most famous theory is that names are negative. A 'cow' is merely a 'not–non-cow'. This might seem to beg the question, as some meaning of 'cow' is already assumed in the definition. But Dignaga stresses that any name whatsoever is a universal; it refers to all possible appearances of this thing (this is true even in the case of proper names, since their objects are a series of appearances in the flux of experience). To refer to something as 'white', one cannot show that one knows all possible instances of 'white'; all one can do is to demarcate this particular experience from 'non-white' (Stcherbatsky, 1962: 1:459–460). Pure sensation is all that exists, and that is always particular, and wordless. Verbal thought makes it definite by negation, differentiating concepts vis-à-vis one another.[44] Negation is the defining characteristic of thought; and since negation itself is not to be reified, thought is ultimately an illusion. It is valid only on the plane of ordinary human experience in samsara. On the higher plane, reached in the illumination of meditation, one perceives things as they really are, a world of evanescent particulars.[45]

Dignaga disposes of the Vaisheshika reified ontology, and of Hindu theories of language, both the Mimamsa with its verbal reports and eternal sounds, and Bhartrihari's primacy of the verbal sentence. Dignaga's philosophy emerges in dialectical opposition to these positions, but it also continues and builds on a main premise accepted throughout the Hindu schools of the time: the reality of sensory perception and the building of mental inference upon it. Dignaga radicalizes these concepts by interpreting them through the traditional Buddhist doctrines of momentariness and nominalism, upheld in his day by the Sautrantika school. The response of the Nyayas is equally dialectical. Nyaya-Vaisheshika seems to have become a united front at this time; under common attack by the Buddhists, Naiyayikas led by Uddyotakara (ca. 550–600) put forward a common defense. Their response to the Buddhist negativity and illusoriness of concepts was to become even more realist. The Buddhists, constructing the mundane world out of negation, denied that negation is a reality; the Naiyayikas added non-existence as a seventh category to the traditional Vaisheshika six (Stcherbatsky, 1962: 25, 1:48–49). The Naiyayikas multiplied the number of entities which they regarded as real: relations are real; relations among relations are real as well. These issues became the puzzle contents which would link Buddhist and Hindu philosophers for several centuries. The Naiyayikas urged that existence itself must exist; the Buddhists denied it, holding that existence is inexpressible reality itself.

In the 600s, readjustments in the Nyaya and Mimamsa schools were bringing about developments which would culminate in the turning point of Hindu philosophy, the Advaita revolution. But first we must retrace our steps to examine a second dimension of Hindu-Buddhist interaction, on the onto-logical side.

Rival Element Cosmologies

Let us go back to the centuries following the rise of Buddhism. The major Upanishads as late as 200 C.E. describe a tremendous diversity of positions among the Brahman intellectuals engaged in continuing debates. We see a great many individual sages, none of whose substantive position received sufficient focus to achieve lasting fame. The problem of intellectual success is to find a distinctive position vis-à-vis one's rivals; the Brahman philosophers of this period fail to stand out from the morass of crosscutting positions. The first movement to appropriate a clearly delineated slice of the turf was the Nyaya, with its textbook of debating tactics. But the Nyaya philosophers were simul-taneously participants in substantive debates about ontological issues; the Nyaya sutras had their own position on the elements which constitute the universe, and in this respect they overlapped with other philosophers, especially those of the Vaisheshika school, which was also solidifying out of the morass of Upanishadic positions. A third position which gradually crystallized an identity around this time was the Samkhya. These positions eventually became more distinctive, and more famous, as they carved up the field in opposition to one another, the pluralist realism of Nyaya and Vaisheshika against the Parmenidean tendencies which came to the fore in Samkhya.

All this took place on the Hindu side of the field, among the religiously orthodox Brahmans; the real intellectual dominants of the time were the Buddhists, and it was Buddhist ontology and soteriology which set the style for the emerging Hindu philosophies. There is a striking parallel between *Abhidharma* scholasticism developed ca. 300 B.C.E., and the regroupings of later Upanishadic philosophies in the Nyaya, Vaisheshika, and Samkhya. All these positions are element philosophies; they enumerate the contents of the cosmos, albeit with rival lists, and with increasingly distinctive and explicit ontological assumptions. And all these positions progressively lengthened and systematized their lists in what looks like imitation of one another. In some of the Upanishads, especially the earliest ones, there was a tendency to look for a single, ultimate constituent of the universe, but these monist strains were overtaken by the scholasticizing tendency, as if in competition over the most comprehensive list of all the things that various philosophers had mentioned as constituents of the world.

Vaisheshika Realism of Plural Substances. The *Vaisheshika-sutras* appeared sometime around 100 C.E.; their roots were earlier, but their "orthodox" interpretation as a coherent school occurred around 500 C.E. with Prashasta-pada. The emergence of a distinctive position has been reconstructed as traversing the following phases: (1) an enumerative philosophy of nature; (2) a theory of atoms in a mechanistic universe; (3) a more abstract doctrine of ontological categories, arising from the effort to combine and coordinate various lists of elements; (4) finally, the reorganization of the old philosophy of nature under six categories, perhaps by Prashastapada himself (Frauwallner, 1953–56; Halbfass, 1992: 75–78). In the older layer of the *Vaisheshika-sutra,* there seem to be only three categories: substances, qualities, and motions. To this physical depiction of the universe were later added three more categories: universals (or genus), particulars (species or universals of smaller scope), and the relation of inherence. Presumably these latter categories arose in debates over the nature of relationships among the earlier categories; inherence seems to have been added to explain the relation between substances and their attributes, or between substances and their universal genus. Under these categories are arranged further lists, such as 24 or so qualities, a style of arrangement bearing an unmistakable similarity to the Buddhist *Abhidharma.*

A field of intellectual attention is constituted by a topic and a style of argument. The field then divides into oppositions by substantive distinctions within that space. Early Vaisheshika reified the qualities, and provoked Buddhist and Jaina criticism as to how a substrate of bare, quality-less substances could be the locus for certain qualities or universals rather than any others (Halbfass, 1992: 94–99). Prashastapada attempted to evade the difficulties by redefining substance as per se a possessor of attributes. His move did not cut off subsequent critiques, but it opened new turf by separating the cosmological from the logical dimensions of concepts. Prashastapada's commentary overshadowed the original *Vaisheshika-sutras,* and became the main vehicle for later commentaries which made up the lineage of the school. Vaisheshika remained vulnerable to further attack, but by the same token it guaranteed its prominence in the intellectual field by staking out an ultra-realist position, and expanding it to meet a succession of opponents.

Samkhya Dualism. A rival category philosophy was elaborated as Samkhya, a name which means enumeration or categorization.[46] Samkhya as a philosophical position formed during the Upanishadic period as a grab bag of heterogeneous concepts, part abstractions, part mythological personifications. It gradually crystallized as a dualism of *Prakriti* and *Purusha,* the two world substances, roughly matter and spirit, reminiscent of the mythology of world production from the copulation of god and goddess.[47] Over many generations an identifiable intellectual faction emerged specializing in this kind of enumeration, apparently going through a number of rival versions. The Samkhya mentioned in the *Gita* and elsewhere in the *Mahabharata,* and that was known to Buddhists around 100 C.E., had not yet settled on a clear dualism. Emphasis was still placed on a single overriding peak principle. There were eight *Prakritis* instead of a monistic material substance; the list of categories which make up the world was not as elaborate as it was to become later (*EIP,* 1987: 121–122). This vague proto-Samkhya turned into a conscious philosophical system, perhaps at the hands of Pañchashikha ca. 200 C.E., and definitely with Varshaganya (early 300s) and Vindhyavasin, whom we find debating with the Buddhists in Vasubandhu's circle. Around 400 Ishvarakrishna produced a version of Samkhya which became canonical, sharpening up philosophical issues apparently in response to Buddhist and Vaisheshika criticism. By the next generation rival versions of Samkhya, such as Madhava's, are referred to as "heretical" and are lost in the subsequent attention space (*EIP,* 1987: 148).

The unique feature of the mature Samkhya philosophical system was that it rigidly separated the realm of *Purusha* from the material world; spirit merely looks on as a witness consciousness, illuminating without interfering in the differentiated realm at all. *Prakriti* was regarded as the source from which emanated the entire phenomenal world, including even the discriminating intellect, ego, and mind—thereby giving this part of the Samkhya system a rather materialist and reductionist slant.

As Samkhya took shape in the philosophical attention space, its metaphorical imagery became subject to critique. Buddhists ridiculed the tension between its monist and pluralist tendencies (Stcherbatsky, 1962: 1:18). *Purusha* is supposed to be a pure unchanging light of consciousness, witnessing the unfolding of *Prakriti* without interfering with it; but how can the connection between these two substances be explained? On the side of *Purusha,* how can one hold that it consists in an undifferentiated substance and yet is divided into a plurality of individual souls? On the side of *Prakriti,* how explain why matter starts evolving in the first place and why it eventually comes to rest? The problem is exacerbated because Samkhya builds on the ontological arguments of a Parmenidean immutability and self-containedness of being. Already in the *Gita* (2.16) the argument was advanced, "Of the non-existent there is no coming to be; of the existent there is no ceasing to be"; and the full-fledged Samkhya philosopher Varshaganya held, "There is no origination for what is not, nor destruction for what is" (Halbfass, 1992: 59). The inconsistency of this stance with a dynamic universe, and with relations among a plurality of substances and modes, provided a fertile field for critique. During these battles Samkhya rose to prominence in the attention space.

Samkhya became the core philosophy of popular Hinduism by rationalizing its mythological heritage. One of the ingredients it took over (found in contemporary Mahayana as well) was the periodic creation and destruction of the world through an endless round of *kalpas,* world epochs. In the rationalized version, Samkhya reconciled this with its Parmenidean substance stasis by elaborating the concepts of potentiality and latency. *Prakriti* is always the same; it merely emanates or withdraws the world of actuality like a tortoise protruding and retracting its legs (Halbfass, 1992: 56–61). Potentiality *(shakti)* now becomes the next philosophical battleground. Vaisheshika took the opposite stance from Samkhya, positing a pluralism of entities with maximal distinctiveness across time; there is no latency, but continuously new combinations which make up new realities, wholes which have existence over and above their parts. A later Vaisheshika philosopher, Udayana (ca. 1000), went so far as to argue that a tree that has a small part cut from it becomes a totally new tree (Halbfass, 1992: 94).

Potentiality and Ontological Pluralism. The Samkhya-Vaisheshika debate gave prominence to an issue that reverberated through monist-pluralist lineups of Indian philosophy for over a millennium. In the orthodox formulation by Ishvarakrishna, Samkhya held the position of *satkaryavada:* the effect preexists within its material cause. Vaisheshika upheld *asatkaryavada,* denying that distinctive entities could be so connected, since this would reduce one substance to another. Here again the Hindu philosophers were elaborating a conflict which had emerged among the Buddhists. Already in the early *Abhidharma* period, Buddhist factions had argued about the causality of dependent origination: Sarvastivadins held that past, present, and future all exist in their own right as momentary point-instants of space-time; the Kashyapiyas had argued for existences across time in the form of effects which are inherent in an earlier existent. Nearer the era of the Samkhya-Vaisheshika disputes, the Madhyamikas eliminated entirely the reality of time as well as of any substance in which causality could inhere; the opposite stance was taken by Yogacara, whose storehouse consciousness containing the seeds of all experience implies an unlimited scope for preexisting potentialities.

Samkhya and Vaisheshika reproduced a Buddhist problem space on the Hindu side of the board, but they maintained their distinctive non-Buddhist identities by making different combinations out of the common stock of philosophical ingredients. Samkhya shared the Buddhist dislike for reifying qualities, as well as the Buddhist sense of the illusoriness of manifested world appearance, but differed by positing an unchanging substance beneath it all—in fact, two of them. Vaisheshika resembled the Buddhist doctrine of ever-changing aggregates assembling and reassembling across time, but maintained its distinctiveness by accepting the reality of all manner of physical and metaphysical entities. Samkhya and Vaisheshika were almost reciprocal images of each other in their relations to Buddhist doctrines. On the other side, later Nyaya-Vaisheshikas (Shridhara ca. 900s, Udayana ca. 1000) took over the concept of potentiality (Halbfass, 1992: 57–58). By then Samkhya had faded and no longer counted as a rival, and the Vaisheshikas' concern was to give their position maximal opposition to Buddhist momentariness. In characteristic Vaisheshika fashion, they did so by reifying potentiality and adding it to the list of elements which constitute the universe. This comprised Nyaya-Vaisheshika turf: every dispute led to expanding the categories of their realist system.

Samkhya, like the Yoga which became textually associated with it, had greater influence in popular Hindu culture than among philosophical circles; its greatest appeal was the mythological residue in its concepts and metaphors.[48] On the technical side, Samkhya's ungainly and memory-taxing enumerative lists overlapped too much with similar classificatory systems of Nyaya-Vaisheshika and several Buddhist positions. Greater prominence in the intellectual field went to newer systems which pushed forward a few basic unifying principles on a higher level of abstraction. The Advaita revolution displaced Samkhya from the lineup of active positions, borrowing its arguments for *satkarya* and its terminology, while eliminating the embarrassment of its dualist inconsistencies and transferring its Parmenidean stance to a purer monism. Hereafter there are occasional Samkhya commentators, but they seem remote and uncertain about the original system. After ca. 600–700, Samkhya no longer responds to external critiques as a living philosophy; it has become an inert record (*EIP*, 1987: 16, 29–30, 45).

The Ontology of Evanescent Point-Instants. On the Buddhist side, the effects of the Samkhya challenge are seen in Vasubandhu II. Why did the greatest creativity of the Hinayana schools occur much later than the greatest Mahayana philosophies, the Madhyamika in the 100s C.E. and the Yogacara idealism in the 300s? Nagarjuna had explicitly critiqued both Sarvastivadin essence realism and Sautrantika nominalism; Madhyamika had good claim to express the detachment from philosophy and the attainment of nirvana that was the hallmark of original Buddhism. Nevertheless, Vasubandhu II (ca. 400–480) put together the ingredients for a powerful intellectual comeback on the Hinayana side. It was his network, more than that of the Madhyamikas or Yogacaras, which produced the greatest creativity; the ontology of evanescent point-instants expounded by the great logicians Dignaga and Dharmakirti was a development of Vasubandhu's Abhidharmist metaphysics.

I would reconstruct the dynamics of the situation as follows. The Hindus made their attack by moving into the central attention space occupied by the Buddhist schools. There, although the Mahayanists had been the creative movements in recent centuries, the conservative "Hinayana" sects were still institutionally most numerous. So when Hindu philosophers such as Vindhyavasin, Ishvarakrishna, Vatsyayana, and Bhartrihari made their moves, the schools they were most likely to encounter were the Sautrantikas and Sarvastivadins. Vasubandhu II, who was the Buddhist point of contact in the challenge of Nyaya and the grammarians, was also at the center of this additional line of network contact with Hindu philosophers. Vindhyavasin (68 in Figure 5.4), a leader in the mature formation of philosophical Samkhya, defeated a Sautrantika Buddhist (67) in debate, who turned out to be the teacher of Vasubandhu II; Vasubandhu is said later to have defeated Vindhyavasin in return (*EIP*, 1987: 11–12, 135). Sautrantika extreme nominalism had been shown up by the substance philosophy of Samkhya. Vasubandhu became a famous name by answering the provocation to his teacher.

Vasubandhu's answering move was to update the *Abhidharma* substance philosophy of the Sarvastivadins, with all its prestige as the long-standing philosophical "basket" of Buddhist scripture, by making many amendments in the direction of the Sautrantika school in which he was trained. Vasubandhu raised the level of abstraction, reinterpreting the older scholastic list of heterogeneous categories, all of which had been given reality as elements of the world construction. The melding between essentialism and nominalism was carried out by defining some elements as point-instants, others as conceptual. Substances were believed identical with flashes of causal energy in time; but now they were distinguished from "non-forceful" elements, which escape the chain of karmic causation by occupying an epistemological realm of knowledge rather than the ontological plane of being (Potter, 1976: 130–137; Nakamura, 1980; Dutt, 1962: 291). That this epistemologization was a countermove against the Hindus is suggested from critiques directed by Vasubandhu's Sarvastivadin pupil Gunamati (73 in Figure 5.4) against the Samkhyas, Vaisheshikas, and Jainas, some of them in personal debate. Henceforward Vasubandhu's *Abhidharmakosha* would become the classic statement of the already 800-year-old *Abhidharma* tradition.

Now we have a rearrangement on the Buddhist side of the field. The old rivals Sautrantika and Sarvastivada become a united front, though some of the sparks that fly from the merger are struck by efforts of more traditionalist Sarvastivadins (such as Sanghabhadra in Kashmir) to combat it. The Mahayana tide is checked; some of its members convert to Sarvastivada and attack Mahayana (e.g., Guñaprabha; Dutt, 1962: 292). Others use Vasubandhu's new ammunition to incorporate Yogacara. The old element realism and the pure idealism are brought together by later generational links such as Sthiramati. Dharmapala, in the main line of masters at Nalanda, tries on behalf of the

Mahayana camp to incorporate the prestige of Vasubandhu's *Abhidharmak-osha* by interpreting it through the lens of Yogacara idealism. It is this lineage which the Chinese pilgrim Hsuan-tsang encounters in the 630s, and brings back to China as the hyper-sophisticated Yogacara system called Fa-hsiang.

Dharmakirti's Synthesis. The greatest intellectual success from this flow of energy in the Buddhist camp where all the networks ran together at Nalanda was Dharmakirti (ca. 650). He met the challenges both against Buddhism and within it by purifying and synthesizing its major philosophical doctrines. Against the conservative Madhyamika attack on the new logic, Dharmakirti set out to extend and vindicate the logical innovations of Dignaga, while using them as a frame into which to pour his own substantive philosophy. That philosophy was essentially the old Sarvastivada-Sautrantika ontology of point-instants, stripped from its casing of memory-taxing classifications that makes *Abhidharma* scholasticism so tedious. Dharmakirti drove out the last vestiges of a realist tone, reducing every element to unreality. He ensured that Buddhist aggregation doctrine would stand at the extreme opposite from the realists of the Hindu camp, and in this respect Dharmakirti moved toward the Yoga-carins. His most creative stroke was to use Madhyamika tools to transcend both realism and idealism.

Everything hinges on the meaning of being, existence, or reality, which Dharmakirti treats as interchangeable terms. Reality is that which is causally efficacious. A real fire is that which burns: an action, not an entity. The real is that which causes something, and therefore that which is changing. There is nothing but the chain of dependent origination—the classic doctrine of the Buddha, which Nagarjuna had used in demonstrating that nothing has an essence of its own. This flow of change cannot be broken into ultimate elements, little static bits with change connecting them; there is nothing but causality itself (Stcherbatsky, 1962: 1:85–91; Halbfass, 1992: 165). Our conceptions of entities are not reality but mental constructs, differentiations imposed by the mind, according with Dignaga's doctrine of the negativity of distinctions.

Abhidharma scholasticism had included time and space as real elements of the universe; in fact Sarvastivada tended to identify empty space or ether with nirvana as the object of meditation (Conze, 1962: 164–165). Yogacara idealism, breaking with this heterogeneous omni-realism, had denied the reality of any external world, including space and time. Dharmakirti applied his criterion: since the real is that which is causal, time and space are unreal constructs, without efficacy apart from the "thusness" of immediate point-instants. Dharmakirti further subjected time and space to dialectical dissolution, something like Leibniz's criticism of "the labyrinth of the continuum"; one cannot say that there is an enduring, extended "thing" which comes in and out of existence, nor does it make causal hops between rests. Extension and duration, like all concepts, are merely distinctions imposed by the mind. Dharmakirti gave Buddhism an aspect of both idealism and realism. The world really exists, it is not merely mind; but the ordinary world of distinct and enduring objects is mentally constructed, not the inutterable "thus-ness" of reality. Because of Dharmakirti's skill as a synthesizer, subsequent commentators and historians of Buddhist philosophy classified him in many different camps.

Dharmakirti synthesized Buddhism in a form which maximally opposed the dominant positions in Hindu philosophy up to this time: the pre-Advaita period when Hindus held the realist side of the field.[49] Against Uddyotakara's Nyaya criticism as to whether causal efficacy is itself real, the Buddhist replies that reality is not a stable quality that is added on; to be real is only to be causally efficacious, and it is superfluous to add that causal efficacy is causally efficacious. In the same way, it is no conundrum to say that non-existence does not exist; it is only a name, "a flower in the sky" (Stcherbatsky, 1962: 1:90). There is no alternation between reals and moments of producing the next real; one cannot say momentariness has any duration in reality. This has meaning only in the realm of mental inference.

Dharmakirti's synthesis is the apex of Buddhist philosophy, at the moment when it was institutionally fading. Nalanda was still bustling, buoyed by cosmopolitan incursions of Brahmans and lay students, but the weeds were growing around the deserted stupas not just in the south but in northern India as well. Dharmakirti is the last flaming of the torch before it blows out, the owl of Minerva taking wing at dusk: the creativity of synthesis as a fading institutional base goes on the defensive. Dharmakirti himself was a lay Buddhist, not a devout monk, and his personal tone sounds like secular ambition rather than a quest for salvation. The closing stanza of his great work laments the dearth of capable intellectuals to follow his philosophy: "My work will find no one in this world who would easily grasp its deep sayings. It will be absorbed and perish in my own person, just as a river in the ocean." A Tibetan historian says that when he finished the work, his pupils showed no appreciation, and his enemies "tied up the leaves [of the palm-leaf manuscript] to the tail of a dog and let him run through the streets where the leaves became scattered" (Stcherbatsky, 1962: 1:35–36). In fact, Dharmakirti did end up dominating the leading philosophers of the last generations of Indian Buddhism. But his pessimism was prescient. Leaving Nalanda, he retired to his home in the south, where he founded a monastery. The next successful Brahman student from the south was to be Shankara, and when he came north, it would be to plunder the carcass of a dying Buddhism.

The Double Revolution in Hindu Philosophy:
Mimamsa Ultra-realism and Vedanta Non-dualism

At the turn of the 700s, Hindu philosophy moves into the center of intellectual space. Until this time the Buddhists have been dominant, and their innovations generate the responses of imitation and counterattack. Hereafter Hinduism acquires that space, and the dynamics of creativity become the splits and adjustments among Hindu schools. Two major new positions emerge on the Hindu side—Mimamsa realism and non-dualist Advaita Vedanta. These are genuinely new philosophies, though both claim ancient links; they emerge in the process of creating the Veda-centered ideology which is the defining mark of "Hinduism." They establish a new standard of sophistication in Hindu philosophy, upstaging Samkhya as amateurish, and pushing Nyaya-Vaisheshika to a new level of argument to regain its stature.

The emergence of philosophical Mimamsa and Advaita constitutes a rearrangement of networks. During its period of dominance, one of Buddhism's advantages had been that its organizations focused the center of intellectual attention, above all in the northern heartlands of the major empires. Hindu domination in the south had few intellectual consequences, insofar as these were the "provinces," away from the high-prestige cultural centers, too scattered to focus attention. The initial upsurge of Hinduism in abstract philosophy (not popular literature and religion, which developed centuries earlier) comes when leading Hindus make direct contact with the Buddhist networks.

In the generations around 700, the Hindu invasion of Buddhist territories is especially visible. Gaudapada, the supposed grand-teacher of Shankara, is in northern Bengal, a longtime Buddhist stronghold. Kumarila, who sets off the new Mimamsa with his rival Prabhakara, is located in the central Ganges, perhaps at Allahabad; his pupils supposedly include Mandana Mishra, who is reputedly delegated by his aged master to debate Shankara.[50] Into this network comes Shankara, a youth from south India, moving to the center to study at the holy city Varanasi and debate the Buddhists in their own monasteries; he leaves a lineage of famous pupils after him. Visible in the network for the first time are clusters of major Hindu philosophers matching those which Buddhism displayed for centuries, repeating the world pattern in which the most influential thinkers tend to appear in personally connected groups. From now on until the rise of Vaishnavism in the south about 1100, insofar as we can trace locations, much of the intellectual action of Hindu philosophies is in the older Buddhist strongholds. In the 800s and 900s, the great Nyaya-Vaisheshika philosophers are in Kashmir, the old Sarvastivadin territory; at the same time comes the upsurge of Kashmir Shaivism and Shaktism. Mithila, in Bihar, has become the center for Hindu philosophy, challenging nearby Nalanda. Mandana Mishra is there in the days of the Mimamsa-Advaita revolutions in the 700s; the great syncretizer Vacaspati Mishra is there in the 900s; and from the 900s down into the 1300s it is the base for most of the leading Nyaya-Vaisheshikas. Neo-Nyaya grows up there before migrating farther downriver into Bengal.

The founding generations of the new Mimamsakas and Advaitins interlock with the Buddhists. Gaudapada is reputedly a converted Mahayanist; by some indications he also wrote a Samkhya commentary before becoming an Advaita Vedantist (*EIP,* 1981: 104; *EIP,* 1987: 209–210). In other words, Gaudapada traversed both the leading old Hindu philosophy, Samkhya, and the wing of the Buddhist world which was being challenged by Vasubandhu's followers—Madhyamika anti-conceptualism. He (or a series of authors who assembled a text under this name) adumbrates a new space on the Hindu side, an anti-conceptualism which claims orthodox roots in the Upanishads.[51] Intellectual revolutions take place by simultaneously rearranging opposing sides of conceptual space, and the move to Advaita goes along with the development of the most extreme realism in Indian philosophy, by the Mimamsakas Kumarila and Prabhakara.

Shankara brings together both these chains. Picking, choosing, and rearranging, he splits Mimamsa from within. We thus have double revolutions in rapid succession: the "Mimamsa revolution," which rises above Vedic exegesis to a realism which multiplies ontological entities to an extreme degree; and a "revolution within the Mimamsa revolution," in which Advaita explicitly rejects realism. Once again it is creativity by negation, a movement in rapid succession to opposing extremes. For all its attacks on Buddhism, early Advaita is taking over Buddhist conceptual space. Prior to 600 or 700, the prominent Hindu philosophies (Samkhya, Vaisheshika, the various naive theisms) were on the pluralist and materialist side of the field; it was the Mahayana Buddhists who occupied the wing of the field comprising monism, idealism, and illusionism. We see here the result of a long-term shift in the philosophical center of gravity within Buddhism. During its centuries of institutional dominance, the classic Hinayana philosophies were on the realist side, led by the Sarvastivadin pluralism of evanescent world elements. A shift begins as *Abhidharma* realism is challenged, but not displaced, by Madhyamika and Yogacara. The turning point is when Buddhism starts to cede the turf of realist element cosmologies. Already in the early generations of Hindu attack, the Buddhists respond by distancing themselves from the realism represented by Samkhya and Nyaya-Vaisheshika. Vasubandhu II's revision of *Abhidharma,* and its anti-conceptual development by Dignaga and Dharmakirti, move the pluralist branch closer to the position which regards the ordinary world as illusory. The climax of Buddhist philosophy, as is so often the case, is the creativity of realignment during a grand intellectual retreat.

Gaudapada, Mandana, and Shankara now invade the monist side, and they do so with Buddhist conceptual tools, apparently acquired by direct contact with the Buddhist camp. Institutionally dying, Buddhism falls open for scavenging by its enemies. Both its sophisticated dialectic and its distinctive ontology provide the basis for its successors on the Hindu side of the field.

Mimamsa as Reactionary Radicalism. Let us consider first the Mimamsa revolution, then the Advaita hyper-revolution. Mimamsa began as a narrow technical specialty of exegesis of the old Vedas, discussing doubtful points *(mimamsante)* in the performance of sacrifices; it continued the activity of those who had composed the *Brahmanas,* and scorned the abstract discussions of the Upanishadic intellectuals (Chattopadhyaya, 1979: 1:157–161, 188). The Mimamsakas acquired a philosophical identity as their opposition to other Brahmanical schools became more acute. They held the most conservative side, claiming that the Brahman's role was purely that of professional ritualist. Nevertheless, as they were drawn into the intellectual discussion space, defense of their externally conservative stance drove Mimamsa into internally quite radical innovations. It is a common dialectic of intellectual history; we see it again in the socially reactionary but intellectually radical Neo-Confucians of Sung China, the innovative "Ancient Learning" and "National Learning" schools of Tokugawa Japan, and the anti-Enlightenment and anti-positivist philosophers of modern Europe. In the case of India, we have proof that a self-conscious ideology favoring innovation is not necessary for creativity; adulation of an allegedly eternal tradition can be creative, since tradition itself is always interpreted by the present. Constituted as part of a field of forces, as the oppositions change, conservatives cannot but change as well.

The early Mimamsakas developed the self-promoting ideology that the old Vedas were the final authority; to bolster it, they theorized that the sounds which make up the text are eternal. In reaction to theistic worship in non-sacrificial and non-Brahman cults, the Mimamsakas became strident atheists. Shabara, the first commentator on the Mimamsa sutras (ca. 200 c.e., contemporary with the crystallization of Hindu law and the other philosophical schools), argued that gods are mere names, mantra sounds made in rituals (Chattopadhyaya, 1979: 1:206). By the time of Kumarila, the argument was expanded to deny that God created the world, since the world is eternal, and a transcendent, undifferentiated God would have no motive for creating anything, let alone a world of imperfections and miseries; and to deny the value of salvation, since this could consist in nothing but a stone-like unconsciousness without enjoyment (Raju, 1985: 58–61). Furthermore, the purpose of religious sacrifices is to bring worldly wealth and pleasure; ethical behavior is no substitute for this way of accumulating a store of merits.

The early Mimamsaka "Jaimini" (possibly mythical, between 200 b.c.e.

and 200 C.E.), a conservative Brahman rejecting the new theisms, had held that rewards are not given by the gods but accrue from the acts of sacrifice themselves (Clooney, 1990). Such arguments raised the question of how the rituals could bring about future consequences, especially when opposing schools developed theories of causality. How can causality take place if there is a time interval between cause and result? The Mimamsakas, defending a primitive magic conception of rituals against the implicit idealism of symbolic or moral interpretations, were driven onto the philosophical field in a realist position. Implicitly they took up the stance of *asatkaryavada,* shared by Buddhists and Nyaya-Vaisheshika (in opposition to Samkhya), that effects are separate from, not inherent in, their causes.[52] Kumarila therefore postulated a soul substance onto which karmic potentialities accumulated as qualities.

Drawn into philosophical debates, the Mimamsakas developed an elaborate epistemology and ontology. Here again we see debates over substantive and ontological issues giving rise to a meta-level of epistemology; treated at first as a neutral, common property across the factions, in the next step it becomes a turf for further intellectual divisions in their own right. The early Nyaya commentator Vatsyayana (400s C.E.) gave as example of the syllogism a proof that a sound is not eternal, denying the central Mimamsa doctrine. In defense, the Mimamsakas of Prabhakara and Kumarila's generation adopted the Nyaya epistemology, while expanding it to provide tools for their own purposes. The Nyaya and the Samkhya had accepted three or four *pramanas,* valid methods of reasoning: perception, inference via the "syllogism," verbal testimony, and in the case of the Nyaya comparison. Kumarila added two more: negation and postulation. The latter meant postulating unseen entities to cover a gap in what was actually perceived; a prime example was the stored potency of karmic action which connects the sacrifice with its fruits.

Having embarked on the path of multiplying metaphysical entities, the Mimamsakas pushed pluralism to an extreme. The Mimamsa systematizers Prabhakara, Kumarila, and Mandana adopted their own versions of scholastic category lists, overlapping with many of the standard categories of their Samkhya and Nyaya-Vaisheshika counterparts. Kumarila's list has 13 substances, 14 qualities, 5 types of action, 2 kinds of universal (Raju, 1985: 59–60). Similarity is reified as a substance, since it is qualified by being greater or lesser.

Kumarila knew the Madhyamika and Yogacara texts well, and was playing here on Buddhist conceptual turf, especially the central role of negation in Dignaga and Dharmakirti's logic (Chattopadhyaya, 1979: 1:62). The major Mimamsa philosophers emerged in the generation just after Dharmakirti and appropriated this new intellectual resource for their own purposes. At the cosmopolitan Nalanda "university," Bhartrihari, Dignaga, and Dharmakirti had worked on the central ontological problem, the conceptual contradictions within monism and pluralism, and developed a refined theory of negation as the key to resolving them. Prabhakara and Kumarila shaped their systems in different directions over the question of how to incorporate this new material. Kumarila's most radical tendency was to build categories of negation, taken as real entities. Darkness, he said, is not the mere absence of light, but a substance with its own qualities of thickness and thinness. Negation not only is real but also comprises four of the eight fundamental categories of existence: prior negation (the absence of an object before it is born), posterior negation (the absence of an object after it is destroyed), absolute or infinite negation (the absence of an object in all times and places except where it happens to be), and mutual negation (the exclusion of two existing things from each other).

Prabhakara took the radically opposite stance from Kumarila: negation does not exist; reality is always positive, and the forms of negation are merely statements of inference. Here Prabhakara seems to be borrowing Dignaga's doctrine that negation is purely conceptual, while attempting to avoid Dignaga's corollary that the world is a positive existent without distinctions, which Prabhakara as a pluralist realist could not accept (Stcherbatsky, 1962: 1:480). He attempted to control the damage by arguing that there is no negation in general, no non-being as a negation of nothing in particular; all negation is of a definite and positive object, and being is all that exists. Kumarila, by contrast, implicitly responded to the Bhartrihari-Dignaga-Dharmakirti doctrine that if negation is purely nominal and illusory, then objective reality must be undifferentiated. For Kumarila, the pluralism of real entities must be defended, and that calls for the reality of negation—indeed, a whole array of negations to account for differences in time as well as among contemporaneous objects.

Debate over Knowledge and Illusion. Predictably, Prabhakara and Kumarila also split over epistemology (Raju, 1985: 50–56; Potter, 1976: 197–212). Both adopt a viewpoint that is close to the Buddhist: everything that is known, is known through one's consciousness. Since there is no criterion of the validity of knowledge outside of consciousness, Prabhakara draws the conclusion that knowledge is valid in itself. False judgments arise not because of conscious perception but because of the intrusion of other factors, such as physical interference with one's eyes, or memories and inferences superadded to the perception. When one mistakes a rope lying on the jungle path for a snake, the simple perceptual judgment is nevertheless true. The object exists and causes the perception. There is no way to falsify a simple judgment; if it is falsified by a second perception (looking more closely at the rope), this proves that the first judgment was not itself simple. Subsequent cognitions do not prove that a first cognition is true; they can only confirm that it was a simple cognition. The truthfulness of the cognition can be given only by itself.

Prabhakara defends an extreme realism against any Buddhist-like epistemology of world illusion. Kumarila, however, works via the path of negation: errors arise by the imposition of non-presences (memories) upon the present. Since Kumarila takes particular negations as real entities, there continues to be perception of the real, even in the case of error. These arguments rework Buddhist concepts in the interest of defending realism against Buddhist world illusion, and are part of the matrix from which Advaita emerged.[53] Prabhakara's emphasis on consciousness as the self-valid starting point of all knowledge is reminiscent of Yogacara, and it points the way to a foundational use of the cogito by Shankara and Mandana to establish the reality of the universal atman.

As a pluralist realist, Prabhakara derives knowledge of the "I" from the perception of objects. Three things are known simultaneously and inseparably in each cognition: the subject who knows the object, the object known, and the knowledge of the object. The "I," however, cannot be known as an object for itself, because a subject is never an object. Kumarila debates this point, arguing that the three entities are not revealed simultaneously, and that knowledge of the "I" emerges by inference. Shankara made these points of disagreement into a launching pad for his own radical turn from pluralist realism into transcendental non-dualism.[54]

As a powerful Advaita school emerged in the next generation, Mimamsa established its hyper-realism on the opposing front. But the contending versions of Mimamsa could not all survive in the available attention space. The slot went to the followers of Kumarila Bhatta, while Prabhakara's branch soon faded, his own texts were lost, and Mandana, the third contender, converted from Mimamsa to Advaita. Prabhakara's weakness was that he was both less extreme in his realism than Kumarila (especially on pluralism and negation), and in some respects too close to Buddhism. The decisive split may well have been over a matter which set the boundaries of Hindu orthodoxy against heterodox religions: the caste system (Halbfass, 1991: 367–378). Kumarila argued that castes are eternally fixed because they are real universals (something like 'natural kinds'). Performance of the sacrifices is the only way to accumulate merits, but only a Brahman male may perform them. Moreover, one cannot lose one's identity of being a Brahman, no matter what unethical acts one may perform—an explicit rejection of Buddhist criticism of the caste system and the Buddhist concept of merits as arising from ethical actions. On this issue Prabhakara was more liberal. He disagreed with Kumarila, holding that there is only the universal of humanness, shared by both Brahman and untouchable, men as well as women. Prabhakara's compromise left him vulnerable to subsequent neglect as Hinduism became definitively victorious over Buddhism, and Kumarila's followers captured the slot in the attention space anchored in their uncompromising extremism.

The outbreak of Advaita revolution inside the camp of Mimamsa radicalism is especially clear in the case of Mandana Mishra. Regarded as the third great systematizer of Mimamsa, Mandana was also known for his grammatical commentaries, in which he defended Bhartrihari's *sphota* theory. Bhartrihari had worked on traditional Mimamsa turf; his defense of the cult of the word-Brahman, the identity of God with the syllable *aum,* was another version of the old Mimamsa claim for the eternity of the Vedas as an eternity of sounds. Bhartrihari, however, had pushed the argument into an extreme monist direction, positing an undifferentiated transcendent unity which degenerates into the illusory pluralism of words within time. Buddhist interest in the *sphota* theory of eternal word-meanings, too, was no doubt one of the catalysts of Mimamsa creativity.

There are echoes of this debate in the discussions between Prabhakara and Kumarila. The former held, Bhartrihari-like, that the unit of meaning is the sentence, and that meanings do not exist apart from it, especially from the sentence verb, which shows the action which is the basis of the word-meaning. Prabhakara's tendency to pragmatism and holism brought him close to Buddhist no-substance doctrine, and earned him the accusation by Advaitins such as Shri Harsha (1100s) of being "a kinsman of Buddha" (Raju, 1985: 48). Kumarila replied to Prabhakara, with a characteristically radical pluralism and reification, that words have fixed meanings before and apart from their use. For Kumarila, as in the traditional Mimamsa, words are identical with the letters that make them up; in response to the criticism that words are pronounced differently by different speakers, he argued that the phonemes exist in their own right, while each utterance is merely their realization (*EIP,* 1990: 6; Halbfass, 1991: 372). Here, too, Bhartrihari's influence shows in Kumarila's conception of a universal not as a static entity but as a potentiality for realization in time. Mandana in turn critiqued Kumarila and defended the full force of the *sphota* doctrine. Mandana attempted to make this consistent with Mimamsa realism and its primacy of plural individuals by claiming that the *sphota*-meaning can be fully manifested in each phoneme (*EIP,* 1990: 181); in effect this opened the way for seeing the empirical world of individuals as manifesting a transcendental meaning at every point. One step beyond this would be to declare that meaning a unity, indeed Brahman itself; taking this step, Mandana became an Advaitin.

The Break from Mimamsa Pluralism to Advaita Non-dualism. Advaita came out of the Mimamsa network, and initially was identified as a branch of Mimamsa doctrine. Haribhadra, describing his "six *darshanas*" in the 700s, does not see a distinct Vedanta but only "Jaiminiya," followers of the old Mimamsa sutra writer. The split in Mimamsa at first went under the names of

Purva (earlier) Mimamsa (or Yajña-Mimamsa, the Mimamsa of sacrifice), and Uttara (later or higher) Mimamsa, concerned with the doctrine of Brahman (Chattopadhyaya, 1979: 3:173, 286; Eliot, 1988: 2:310). The latter referred to commentaries stemming from Badarayana's interpretation of the Upanishads in the *Brahma-sutra*. But Badarayana, a possibly mythical figure whose text may go back to the time of Jaimini's *Mimamsa sutras* (ca. 100s B.C.E.?), was not yet an Advaitin. Badarayana lacked not only the explicitly technical philosophical argument that Shankara took from his Mimamsa connections, but also such distinctive doctrines as the ultimate unreality of the empirical world (Chattopadhyaya, 1979: 3:282–283). It is Shankara who attacks the practice of treating Purva Mimamsa and Uttara Mimamsa as if they were one *shastra* ("science"), and he sharply rejects the doctrines of his Mimamsa seniors in the process of establishing his own school.

Shankara criticizes all the other schools, Buddhist and Hindu alike. He is especially hard on Kumarila's Mimamsa for its pluralism and ultra-realism, and on Samkhya for its plurality of selves and its material substance. In staking out the opposite position, Shankara has to walk a thin line in regard to calling the world an illusion, *maya*, since this brings him dangerously onto Buddhist turf; and indeed Shankara is appropriating arguments from Madhyamika and Yogacara.[55] Shankara's stroke is to posit a three-level world, rather than two levels comprising nirvana and samsara, transcendence and world-illusion. The three levels are (1) the Absolute or Brahman; (2) Appearance; and (3) phenomenal illusion. The second level is our world of ordinary experience; though it is not ultimately real, nevertheless one can operate in it by the normal principles of perception and inference. On this level, logical relations continue to hold, including the principle of non-contradiction, and illusions such as the rope/snake or logical impossibilities can be detected. Such relations are transcended only on the level of the Absolute, which lies beyond the subject-object distinction. Shankara rejects the Yogacara idealism in which the world is a manifestation of the perceiving subject; as long as one operates on the level of Appearance, the world is objective and not an aspect of the mind. The falsity of the world emerges only from the standpoint of the higher Absolute. Shankara defends not the bald assertion of transcendental monism but the more nuanced position of ultimate non-dualism.

Shankara's Cogito. Shankara no longer accepts Brahman on tradition but presents proofs. Shankara's method, sharpened by the debates of his Mimamsa predecessors, is essentially epistemological. To doubt something requires that there be a ground on which doubt arises; to call anything self-contradictory presupposes something non-contradictory (*Brahma-sutra-bhasya* 3.2.22). The argument is a version of the cogito, but instead of proving the existence of the empirical self, it focuses on an absolute standpoint which is reached through the self.[56] The highest standpoint, that which is ultimately and completely real, is that which is absolutely undoubtful; and this is Brahman, which admits no standpoint from which it might be doubted. The world, by this criterion, is relatively unreal, although it is relatively real when compared to the phenomenal illusions (e.g., rope/snakes) which it throws into doubt. The world should be called neither real nor unreal, but appearance.

Within the phenomenal world, however, the cogito leads to a world of plural objects. The experience of the phenomenal "I" always includes a sense of separation from objects standing outside oneself (*Brahma-sutra-bhasya* 2.2.28). It is this very plurality, and the possibility of subjecting objects to specific doubts, that makes this world inferior to the higher Absolute, which transcends doubts by transcending the subject-object distinction.

The problem then arises of accounting for how the Transcendent, about which no distinctions or qualifications can be made, gives rise to the world of apparent plurality, how Brahman produces *maya*. Shankara adopts the position of *satkaryavada*, the Parmenidean conception of being held by the Samkhya and opposed by the Nyaya-Vaisheshika and Mimamsa. The world cannot be produced by a relation of distinct cause and effect; for the relation between a cause and its effect adds a third reality, the relation itself, and thus leads to the necessity for further relations to fill in the intervening links, and these in turn to further relations, ad infinitum (*Brahma-sutra-bhasya* 2.1). It is an argument against the reality of distinctive causal moments, which reflects backwards to Nagarjuna and forwards to Bradley. The effect preexists in its cause, and indeed is ultimately non-different from it. How this could be so would provide a fertile ground for differentiation among subsequent Advaita philosophers.

Shankara became the most famous individual thinker in the history of Hindu philosophy by embodying almost every aspect of Hinduism's rise to institutional and intellectual dominance. He critiqued rival positions across the field, drawing from them a set of sophisticated technical arguments while discarding the rest. After Shankara, most other Hindu schools lost their capacity to generate further creativity; only Nyaya-Vaisheshika was able to rise to a new level of defense. Advaita laid down the basic position to which all other factions adapted, and out of which new lines of division emerged; it controlled not so much the solutions as the puzzle space of the new intellectual field. Shankara was not the only individual who made the move toward Advaita, with its combination of transcendental monism and world illusion. But Shankara was the great energy star, and his activities gave him several advantages in long-term reputation over predecessors such as Gaudapada and Bhartrihari, as well as his contemporary Mandana.

Shankara as Turning Point of the Networks. Shankara's creative energy came from his having grown up in close proximity to the surge of creativity of the Mimamsa revolution; he reaped the charged-up energy of the group, while his cosmopolitan travels put him in touch with the opportunities for filling the institutional gaps left by a declining Buddhist base. Shankara carried on the impetus of establishing the basis of Hindu orthodoxy, but he broadened the cultural turf beyond Kumarila's criterion of accepting the authority of the oldest Vedas (Smith, 1989: 18). Shankara's lifework succeeded almost as if it had been deliberately calculated to give Hinduism an institutional identity. He produced the first comprehensive set of commentaries on the Upanishads; the set of "major" Upanishads became those which Shankara selected.[57] By institutionalizing the enterprise of Upanishadic commentary, Shankara created a distinctive identity of "Vedanta," to which his predecessors were retrospectively assimilated. Similarly it was Shankara who moved the *Bhagavad Gita* from the heterodoxy of Vaishnava theism (i.e., the worship of Vishnu as paramount god) into a topic for orthodox Brahmanical commentary (Raju, 1985: 528).

Shankara gave this intellectual program a material base by organizing a Hindu order of celibate monks to take the place of the Buddhists, and establishing *maths* as centers of scholarship to replace Nalanda and the Buddhist *mahaviharas.*[58] Henceforward, the traditional Brahman householder-teacher role would be challenged by a new form of organization for religious intellectuals. At the same time, Shankara separated his Smarta order from wandering Hindu ascetics such as the antinomian Shaivas by prohibiting extreme practices such as branding one's body, as well as by establishing propertied settlements. Here too Shankara paralleled the original move which made Buddhist monasticism successful, staking out a moderate path between organizational extremes.

Fanning-out of Victorious Vedanta. Dominant intellectual positions split to fill the available slots in the attention space, and the successful Advaita revolution was followed by subsidiary branchings. The creativity of philosophy is a process of controversies, and four positions emerge among Shankara's contemporaries and followers. The main points at issue arise from the relation between Brahman and the world; the arguments hinge on older conceptions of substance, difference, and causality. The Vedantins were recirculating older cultural capital in a new framework.

Vedanta was not exclusively the development of Shankara, even in conjunction with predecessors such as Gaudapada and a few little-known earlier figures whose doctrines were less clearly formed (Isayeva, 1993: 39–41). A movement was forming around commentaries on the *Brahmasutra* and the strategy of formulating a Hindu orthodoxy extracted from the Upanishads. One such position was the theistic school of thought called Bhedabhedavada, whose leading figures were Bhartriprapañcha (104 in the key to Figure 5.4) and Bhaskara. Accusing Shankara of capitulating to Dharmakirti, Bhaskara countered that Brahman cannot be a consciousness devoid of attributes, nor can the world simply be *maya*, illusion, in the style of Buddhism. Brahman has the dual aspects of a transcendence beyond form while at the same time possessing real characteristics as the cause of the world, which is manifested as its effect (Isayeva, 1993: 14, 178, 243). In opposition to this more conventional theism, Advaita promoted as the central doctrine of the Vedantic tradition—and therefore of Hindu orthodoxy—the Upanishadic doctrine of the identity of the human soul with the Absolute. For the first time among the organized Hindu *darshanas*, the cosmos itself was to be interpreted as fundamentally and solely consciousness. The territory proved to be fruitful in ambiguities. Within Advaita itself three stances emerged.

Deep Troubles of Ontological Monism. The ex-Mimamsa philosopher Mandana Mishra produced a version of Advaita which eventually became known as Bhamati. To protect the purity of the higher Brahman, it gives a certain independence to individual souls as the location of the ignorance which constitutes the world of illusion. Using the tools of the logicians, Mandana points out there can be no relation between Brahman and nothing, since the relation would lack one of its terms; the world exists in some sense, but it is "that about which one cannot speak" (Potter, 1976: 163; Halbfass, 1992: 44; Isayeva, 1993: 66–67). This resembles Dharmakirti's inutterable "thusness" upon which distinctions are imposed by linguistic inference.

The second stance of Advaita was formulated by Shankara's pupil Padmapada and developed by Prakashatman (in the period 1100–1300) and the so-called Vivarana school. They chose the other horn of the dilemma: rather than diminish the powers of Brahman, Brahman is declared to be the source of illusion. Vivarana comes close to absolute idealism and solipsism; it holds that the plurality of the world depends on the knowing subject, and the plurality of selves is an illusion like the many moons reflected in rippling water (Potter, 1976: 168–181). But Brahman itself must contain two natures, described as essential and accidental: the pure witness consciousness, plus a primal ignorance which is the material and efficient cause of the world. The difference between Bhamati and Vivarana Advaita parallels the differences between Dharmakirti's radical empiricism and Yogacara idealism in the Buddhist camp (Potter, 1976: 232–233; Isayeva, 1993: 240–243).

This idealist strand in turn was criticized by a third Advaita branch, stemming from Shankara's pupil Sureshvara. The latter's follower, Sarvajñatman, pointed out the conundrum: if the plurality of selves is an illusion, how can one self become liberated without all the other selves being liberated at the same time? Sureshvara held that there is no solution to the dilemmas of transcendent unity versus the plurality of experience except to leap beyond concepts. This version of Advaita resembles Buddhist Madhyamika. Sarvajñatman argued in parallel to Nagarjuna, for whom samsara is the same as nirvana: after liberation the world does not disappear, but one has a flash of understanding beyond distinctions (Potter, 1976: 180). This stance is the opposite of Mandana's emphasis on logical argument; it eventually became dominant in Advaita. Shankara was retrospectively interpreted as the champion of what Karl Potter calls "leap-philosophy," while the position of Mandana, who seems to have been viewed by other schools as the leading Advaitin through about the 900s, eventually faded (*EIP*, 1981: 17). In this battle, Shankara's eventual fame rested on the organizational base of having founded an order of monks, while his opponents were overshadowed even as their arguments were picked up.

The Advaita revolution reinstated a parallel to the three main schools of late Buddhism on the Hindu side of the board: Bhamati, Vivarana, and Sureshvara's "leap-philosophy" parallel Dignaga-Dharmakirti negative logic, Yogacara, and Madhyamika. What is left out is *Abhidharma* pluralism and realism, but this slot was already taken on the Hindu side by Nyaya-Vaisheshika, the one rival Hindu school which prospered after the advent of Advaita. To be sure, Advaita philosophers resisted their opponents' charge that they were crypto-Buddhists, and stressed the difference between Buddhist momentariness and the illusory nature of the self and their own emphasis on a permanent self which is identical with Brahman. In Potter's view (1976) the Advaita revolution shifted attention in philosophical space from the "left" side of causal multiplicity to the "right" side of Parmenidean causal monism. But, given these shifts in the fundamental turf, the disappearance of Buddhism as an active player made available much of its cultural capital to be used in the new context. And in the next round, as the mystical, anti-conceptual version of Advaita (i.e., quasi-Madhyamika) gained dominance, the intellectual resources of its defeated rivals became available to fuel new rivals to Advaita within an expanding Vedanta camp.

Jainas and Other Side Eddies: Intellectual Stability in Minor Long-Term Niches

To complete our picture of intellectual dynamics, we must pause to consider several positions notable for their conservatism amid the realignments going on around them. Such schools exist for a very long time with little change or internal disagreement in their intellectual stance. They have relatively little effect on the creative realignments of other factions; one could introduce the discussion almost anywhere, since their positions rarely change, and anywhere they would tend to break the flow of the narrative. The difficulty of writing smoothly about them illustrates exactly what was their problem in the intellectual field: they were always a side issue, never able to get into the center of the argument. We see the pattern in three such schools.

The Pudgalavadins were a well-established sect virtually throughout the lifetime of Buddhism in India. Although they were attacked both early (e.g., by Moggaliputta-tissa, ca. 250 B.C.E.) and late (e.g., by Kamalashila, early 700s C.E.) for their doctrine of enduring personality, they appear to have undergone no important intellectual changes. Their extreme position within Buddhism, a heresy from the point of view of every other sect, helped to keep them doctrinally stable; their extremeness precluded alliances and the intellectual changes that come with them. One is reminded of a parallel in Greek philosophy. The Epicureans were famous for the unusual stability of their doctrine across the five hundred years of their existence, as well as for their social isolation from other philosophers; this too fits the pattern of an extreme school at a disreputable end of the philosophical spectrum.

Another such case is the Ajivikas, who originated in the same network as Mahavira and the Buddha, and survived down through 900 C.E. (Basham, 1951). Their distinctive doctrine was an extreme fatalism with regard to karma, whose effects cannot be overcome by any effort. They also appropriated the early atomism of Pakudha Kaccayana. This gave them a distinctive slice of intellectual turf among the movements of the time, whereas in social practice they were similar to the other charismatic ascetics, and especially close to the Jainas in their nakedness and extreme asceticism. Although the apparent inconsistency between their fatalism and their liberation-seeking practices was frequently pointed out by their opponents, as often happens, the inconsistency did not prevent them from surviving for many generations; external attacks on their emblematic doctrine may even have contributed to group solidarity.

Such schools are long-standing when they have a stable niche, if only a modest one, in the realm of material support as well as within intellectual space. The Jainas had a niche of this sort. The Jainas nicely illustrate the difference between organizational fragmentation and intellectual splits. Sometime between 300 B.C.E. and 100 C.E., the Jainas split into two branches, Digambaras ("space-clad") and Shvetambaras ("white-clad"); the former carried on the old tradition of asceticism to the point of nakedness, while the latter mitigated this strictness. This was a split over disciplinary practices and property, rather like the first Buddhist schism. The larger, more moderate white-clad branch went on to split further into some 84 sects, while the more extreme group maintained its unity (Raju, 1985: 105; Basham, 1989: 64; Chattopadhyaya, 1972: 132; Zimmer, 1951: 210–211; *OHI*, 1981: 80). Nevertheless, their differences were over minor matters of practice, and without consequences for intellectual life.

The first Jaina philosophers of individual fame appeared after the great schism: Umasvati, who compiled the Jaina sutras, and Kundakunda, the second great authority, both around 200–400 C.E. (Halbfass, 1992: 92). Although the Jaina oral traditions were not put into writing until about 450 C.E., and both naked and clothed Jainas were active in philosophy, both branches accepted essentially the same canon as well as the same leading philosophers and logicians. This holds true throughout the entire history of Jainism. The Jainas became active members of the intellectual field, generally following trends among the Buddhists and Hindus. The early Jaina sutras from the oral tradition give a sparse picture of the ascetic life of Mahavira, while the full-fledged scriptures resemble contemporary Mahayana sutras such as the *Lotus,* full of cosmic landscapes and huge expanses of time populated by predecessors to the founder, now elevated in rather sybaritic splendor above a pantheon of Hindu deities.

Early Jaina metaphysics resembles the Buddhist causal chain leading from wrong knowledge to bondage in the mundane world. But the Jainas staked out a key difference early: they accepted the existence of the atman, or self—in fact a plurality of selves—and argued against the single cosmic self defended by the Advaitins, just as they disputed later Nyaya proofs of a highest God. For the Jainas, the self is an extended substance, which varies in size to fit the body in which it is located. Each self is omniscient, knowing the past and future of the entire universe; but its knowledge becomes obscured by acquiring a covering of karma, which is conceived as yet another material substance, something like particles of defiling dust. Jaina ontology carries on a rather naive realism or reification, treating abstract conceptions on the same level as material objects.[59] The extreme practices of Jaina penitences were conceived as wearing away accumulated karma until final release.

Jaina philosophy became elaborated as something like an *Abhidharma* classification scheme, but one in which everything is treated as a substance, including motion, rest, space, and action. This classification of substances is reminiscent of the Nyaya and Vaisheshika ontologies developed in this period. The Jainas hit their most distinctive note as they began to criticize other schools for being one-sided. The Buddhist doctrine that all is suffering is true from one viewpoint, untrue from another. The same is said about the Sautrantika doctrine that everything is fleeting, or the Sarvastivadin claim that everything is substantial. The Jainas compromised among the various schools in their intellectual environment. Their epistemology emerged when Siddhasena and

Akalanka (600s–700s) joined the Buddhist-Hindu crossfire over logic. The Jainas added to the accepted logical categories another set of judgments, "indescribable" or "undecidable." Cross-classifying these with the judgments "true" or "not true," "exists" or "does not exist," they built up a complex scholastic logic uniquely their own.

Applying this logic to questions of ontology of the sort debated by the Madhyamikas and other Buddhist and Hindu schools, the Jainas held that every object has an infinity of modes or characteristics. All propositions are true from one point of view, false from another; every object is both identical with and different from every other.

The Jainas' defensiveness made them especially cosmopolitan, oriented toward their outside rivals, while at the same time keeping them intellectually unified within. The first general survey of Indian philosophy was by the Jaina Haribhadra, probably in the 700s, who formulated the rubric of "six *darshanas,*" and the scheme was promulgated by Jaina commentators throughout the 1300s and 1400s. The Jainas' became an unusually tolerant position within the heated disputes of Indian philosophy. This seems surprising from the point of view of Jaina practice, which was the most extreme of any long-lasting Indian religion. One would hardly expect that naked fanatics who carried asceticism to the extremes of covering their bodies with filth or starving themselves to death would care much about creating an abstract philosophy, much less one of harmony and compromise. Once again we see that it is the interaction of positions within the intellectual space that shapes intellectual development, much more than the external conditions of life which constitute each sect separately. The Jaina philosophy of seeing some valid aspect in every position gave them a kind of meta-position from which to survey the rest of the intellectual field, and which contributed to their intellectual survival as a unitary position. At the same time, this was a position that did not convince anyone else, and the Jainas were largely ignored by their rivals. The Jaina strategy was a reliable but somewhat timid one. Like other tolerant onlookers throughout intellectual history, it missed the creative energy that other intellectual factions got from their more aggressive moves in disputing the changing territories of intellectual space.

The Post-Buddhist Resettlement of Intellectual Territories

After the Vedanta revolution, readjustment under the law of small numbers was once more set in motion. On the victorious side, the Advaita network split into three factions, along with a fourth Vedantic faction. On the fading Buddhist side, and among the non-Advaita Hindu schools, the tendency was toward syncretism.

Syncretism in Dying Buddhism

The old Buddhist schools now drew together defensively. Shantarakshita and his pupil Kamalashila in the mid-700s synthesized the rival Mahayana schools of Madhyamika and Yogacara, folding in Dharmakirti's Sautrantika epistemology as well (Raju, 1985: 161; Nakamura, 1980: 283). Kamalashila warded off Hindu attacks on Dharmakirti's logic while counterattacking every school: Samkhya and Kumarila's Mimamsa soul reification, Nyaya-Vaisheshika universals, Yoga's God, and the Upanishadic Vedantist self. Everything was drawn into this culminating and futile battle. The Yogacara-Madhyamika-logician synthesis was the last prominent school in technical Buddhist philosophy, and Shantarakshita and Kamalashila were the last important philosophers at Nalanda; symptomatically, both ended up as missionaries in Tibet, along with Padma Sambhava, the proselytizer of tantric magic.[60]

More popular but less intellectual was the rise of Vajrayana ("diamond vehicle") tantrism. Here Buddhist transcendental salvation concerns were turned into this-worldly magic. Practices turned from *sunyata* meditation to visualizing inner god-forces and mandalas; chanting mantras whose syllables were supposed to resonate with the bodily *chakras* of occult physiology; and sexual-yogic intercourse. Since the community of family-less and property-less ascetic monks was the organizational basis of Buddhism, sexual tantrism involving male and female devotees suggests a shift in that base; and indeed, most of the Buddhist intellectuals whose names we know from Dharmakirti onward were lay followers rather than monks.[61] As the last outposts of Buddhism were winnowed down to Kashmir and the Pala kingdom of Bengal, even the monastic universities became dominated by tantrists. What scholars were still present were generally eclectics; some were reputed experts in all schools of Buddhism, but teaching Vajrayana seems to have been their biggest stock in trade.

Tantrism was an end of philosophy, bringing Buddhism down to a lower level of abstraction, as well as displacing most of its moral emphasis. It also acted as the last vehicle for syncretism. Even Nagarjuna's name is attached to the magic-alchemical texts which circulated from the 700s onward. Around 1040, when Buddhism was about to expire in Bengal, a last philosopher, Ratnakarashanti, classified all the Buddhist sects into a sequence of understanding leading up to Vajrayana. In these late centuries the number of students dwindled to a few hundred, and the monastic universities were kept going mainly by missionaries and foreign students (Dutt, 1962: 375). Already in the 700s, Buddhist missionaries such as Amoghavajra introduced tantric rites into the Chinese court, from whence they were further transmitted to Japan. The famous Tibetan adept Naropa began as admissions "gatekeeper" at Vikramashila university, and the chain of founders of the major Tibetan sects (Tilopa–Naropa–Marpa–Mila Repa) derived from this tantric tradition in Bengal.

It is tempting to regard Buddhist tantrism as a submerging into a larger pan-Indian movement. The deities of energy forces, the practice of symbol worship, occult physiology chants, and orgiastic rites were spreading in the medieval centuries, especially in the Shaiva movement, which came from outside orthodox Hinduism (see note 62). But the Buddhist and non-Buddhist tantra had different trajectories. On the Buddhist side, tantrism was a last gasp; intellectually it became an umbrella under which rallied what was left of Buddhist philosophy, fossilized and no longer undergoing creative development. Organizationally, it represented the decline of the monks and a shift of the last wavering center of support to the lay community—which is the underlying organizational reason why philosophical abstraction was lost. On the non-Buddhist side, tantrism was going in the other direction, becoming respectable in Hindu orthodoxy. Instead of losing intellectual acuteness, it was building it up, incorporating technical philosophy and moving from an inchoate movement of primitive ritualists into a recognized part of the world of educated pandits.

Nyaya Attack and Advaita Counterattack: The Sophistication of Indian Dialectics

From now on our concern is exclusively with the Hindu side of the field. With the Advaita factions holding the major slots in the attention space, the other *darshanas* readjusted. Their first move was toward syncretism among themselves. Nyaya and Vaisheshika, already drawing together in tentative (if not uncontested) alliance against Buddhism at the time of Uddyotakara in the 500s, fused completely in the 700s (Halbfass, 1992: 73). The non-Vedanta schools lost their edge as rivals within the Hindu camp and amalgamated with the dominant monism of the Advaitas. Vacaspati Mishra in the 900s was the syncretizer of the losers, writing commentaries on Nyaya, Samkhya, Yoga, Mimamsa, and Advaita, the last two following the versions of Mandana, whose school Vacaspati seems to have continued at Mithila; even the version of Advaita that he defended, Mandana's Bhamati school, was losing ground to the branches spawned by Shankara's pupils (see Figure 5.5).

The adjustment in Samkhya was especially large. Samkhya had been the archetypal Hindu philosophy for the centuries preceding the Mimamsa and Advaita revolutions. Now its materialism and dualism had been repudiated by the leaders; worse yet, the dominant Advaita had stolen the Samkhya theory of inherent causation and aspects of its cosmology, incorporating them into

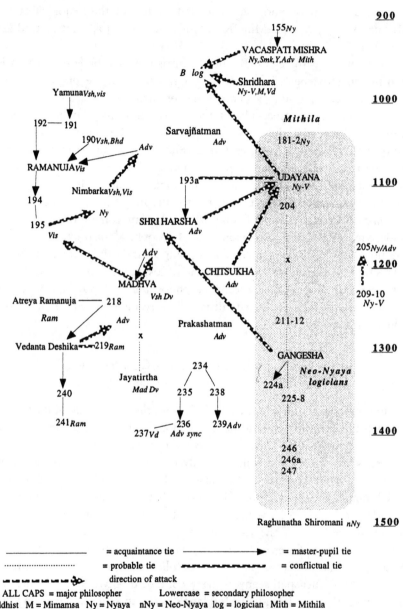

FIGURE 5.5. HINDU OPPOSITIONS, 900–1500: NYAYA REALISTS, ADVAITA IDEALISTS, VAISHNAVA DUALISTS

the intermediate levels of truth ascending to the undifferentiated Brahman (*EIP,* 1987: 29–32; *EIP,* 1977: 453). From now on, Samkhya was a passive tradition, surviving at the hands of commentators who stressed its compatibility with the dominant schools. Mimamsa, too, dried up as a creative school. First Prabhakara and Mandana's branches were driven out by Kumarila's Bhatta Mimamsa, but even the latter became static, no longer engendering any creativity in later generations. Mimamsa had occupied the ultra-realist niche in intellectual space. Its rival in that slot, Nyaya-Vaisheshika, was the only Hindu school which remained creative outside the Vedantic camp after the rise of Advaita; while the other *darshanas* were fading and syncretizing, Nyaya went on the offensive against the new philosophical dominants, and later, shedding Vaisheshika metaphysics, produced a massive technical reform in its own ranks in the form of Neo-Nyaya.

After 1000 came an upsurge of new conflicts in the Vedantist camp. The topics were theist and dualist challenges to Advaita monism, together with a sharpening of logical tools and their incorporation into the metaphysical-theological battles. A dress rehearsal for this set of conflicts had taken place several generations earlier in Kashmir, encapsulated largely in Shaiva sectarianism.[62] In both cases an initial impetus came from logicians. We see this in the network patterns and the battle lines of the debates, and also in the gradual permeation of logical techniques into the sectarian philosophies. The inner politics of Indian philosophy after the late 800s was in large part driven by the struggles and mutual adjustments of Nyaya and Vedanta.

Nyaya logicians were the most cosmopolitan of the philosophical schools, with close counterparts among the Buddhists and Jainas, and a good deal of exchange across the lines. This distinctive niche within the larger intellectual community kept Nyaya immune to the Vedantin dominance which destroyed the other Hindu schools, and gave it the élan to launch a counterattack. Nyaya had already been involved in a long debate with the Buddhists over ontological issues. In conflict with Buddhist nominalism and its doctrine of the unreality of aggregates, Nyaya and Vaisheshika formed a realist united front; across the generations, this realist position became increasingly extreme, defending the reality of substances, relations, and indeed all language categories as corresponding to real entities of the world. As philosophical discourse expanded the categories of argument, Nyaya-Vaisheshika assimilated them to the position that everything could be treated as on the same level as everyday objects perceptible by the senses; inherence, for instance, it treated as a kind of glue which exists eternally in the universe (Halbfass, 1992: 38; Stcherbatsky, 1962: 1:25). This ontology was the opposite of Advaita with its transcendental monism, anti-conceptualism, and doctrine of world illusion. As Advaita took over Buddhist turf and that religion faded, the Nyaya-Vaisheshika alliance automatically lined up against its successor.

Naiyayikas from Uddyotakara in the 500s down through Shridhara in the 990s combatted the Buddhist doctrine of momentariness—the basis for rejecting the reality of aggregates—by arguing that it destroys the distinction between being and non-being. If each moment annihilates the last, is not annihilation (or negation) another entity added to the thing annihilated? The issue was a hot one in the last generations of important Buddhist philosophers. Shantarakshita in the 700s countered that there is no combination of entities; "the momentary thing represents its own annihilation" (Halbfass, 1992: 151; Stcherbatsky, 1962: 1:95). The arguments transferred readily to a Nyaya-Advaita clash. Against the Nyaya-Vaisheshika inherence entity relating a part to its whole, Shankara used an infinite regress argument paralleling Nagarjuna's critique of substance philosophies and Shantarakshita's denial of relations. Shridhara in turn responded by declaring that inherence exists by its self-nature, not as the product of relationships. The issue was to become a long-standing puzzle space on which Nyaya could operate; later the Neo-Nyaya school investigated in depth the concept of "self-linking connectors" in an attempt to clarify reciprocal and non-reciprocal relations among identity, dependence, and inherence (Potter, 1976: 122–128). The debate parallels Western discussions around 1900 between Bradley and Russell about internal and external relations.

In Kashmir, links between Buddhist and Hindu intellectuals were particularly close. Here, during the last fading of the Buddhist outpost, we find the upsurge of the new aggressive Nyaya, at just the time when the Shaiva ontologies were being created. The most important Nyaya thinker since the 400s was Jayanta Bhatta, who founded a lineage in Kashmir in the late 800s. Jayanta attempted to show that everything knowable can be defined and thus is subject to formal argument. This was an explicit counter-move against Advaita, which had argued that ultimate reality is indefinable. Since Shankara had placed the path of knowledge higher than any other path, including faith and practice, Jayanta argued that Nyaya, rather than Advaita, should be the core of Hindu philosophy. This claim was made even more strongly by Udayana (mid-1000s), considered the greatest of the Nyaya-Vaisheshikas, from their lineage headquarters at Mithila. Udayana explicitly subordinated every other position to Nyaya; even Advaita was a preliminary stage for Nyaya, which he called the "ultimate Vedanta." (Halbfass, 1991: 56, 310; Dasgupta, 1922–1955: 2:51; *EIP*, 1977: 10). Udayana now produced formal proofs of the existence of God, as supernatural cause of the world, as standard of right knowledge and of authoritative commandments. Nyaya became the upholder of a positive theology against the non-conceptual reference point of the Advaita cogito.

About a generation after Udayana, Shri Harsha launched an Advaita counterattack.[63] He produced a detailed and comprehensive critique of empiricist ontology and epistemology. He subjected to scrutiny the concepts in the Nyaya armory, and in the Buddhist systems as well. 'Being', 'cause', 'relation', and 'class concept' were criticized as leading to inevitable contradictions. The notion of 'difference' or 'distinctness' had been at the heart of Dignaga and Dharmakirti's logic; the relative non-reality of objects was covered by defining them as the absence of an absence, a jar as the absence of non-jars. Shri Harsha refuted the very notion of 'difference', thereby setting up one of the stock topics of anti-Advaita debate. Shri Harsha attacked not only Nyaya but also the memory of the now departed Buddhists, concentrating on the non-Madhyamika schools most remote from Advaita.[64] Key Buddhist concepts such as 'non-being' and 'invariable concomitance' (the chain of dependent origination) were subjected to dialectical debasement. Advaita had built originally by appropriating Buddhist *shunyata,* Nagarjuna's aconceptualism, and the Madhyamika levels of relative truth. Shri Harsha seems to have been attempting to show that the advanced Advaita could burn down the Buddhist ladders by which it had arrived at its position. In this Shri Harsha was not entirely successful, for a stock claim of later Vaishnava opponents was to accuse Shankara, and even Shri Harsha himself, of being Buddhists in disguise (Raju, 1985: 384–388; Dasgupta, 1922–1955: 2:125–171; Eliot, 1988: 2:73).

Shri Harsha was the first of a series of distinguished Advaita dialecticians, who, not content with merely defending Advaita, took the offensive against any concept wielded by their opponents. Shri Harsha and Chitsukha mustered something like the arguments of Berkeley and Hume, Kant and Bradley. How can there be knowledge of an object apart from the act of knowing it? To assume an independent reality lands one in the contradiction of knowing the object before one knows it. No one ever perceives a substance, but only groups of qualities; and since qualities cannot act, how can there be action of objects upon one another? The relation of substance and quality is incoherent; how can a relation be related to its terms without infinite regress? The Advaita dialecticians maintained one distinctive twist of meditation-oriented Hinduism, that the "only reality is the self-luminous Brahman of pure consciousness" (Dasgupta, 1922–1955: 2:126). For "everything that is self-contradictory presupposes something that is not self-contradictory; it is self-contradictory with reference to something," the one point of ultimate if inexpressible reality (Raju, 1985: 388).

In the 1100s or 1200s, as the Vaishnava philosophers begin to carp at Advaita from a renewed pluralist position in the Vedanta, another Advaita star appeared. Chitsukha added to the list of concepts which Shri Harsha had demolished: time, space, numbers, and qualities are equally unreal and self-contradictory, as are Nyaya-Vaisheshika distinction and distinctive identity. Chitsukha does not shrink from solipsism: his negative dialectics destroys every item of metaphysics except the self; without plurality or differentiation, this can only be solipsism. Chitsukha is one of the few philosophers in world history frankly to embrace this conclusion.[65]

As Advaita went to the anti-conceptual extreme in its battle with Nyaya realism, it opened up room for philosophies in the Vedanta camp to occupy a more commonsensical pluralist position. The dance of position and counter-position went on. In the next round the space vacated by the Advaitins was exploited by Vaishnava sectarians, who developed a variety of positions which qualified monism in varying degrees. During these generations of debate, both Advaita and its Vaishnava critics absorbed Nyaya logic even as they rejected its ontological realism. This takeover of Nyaya turf led to one last surge of Nyaya independence, the movement of Neo-Nyaya formalism. With this, Indian philosophy reached a showdown of extremes.

Ontological Turf Wars in Vedanta Monotheism and the Climax of Indian Metaphysics

Later Hindu philosophy came in the guise of sectarian religious battles. As elsewhere in the world, theism emerged later in the philosophical networks than the development of impersonal cosmologics and ontologies. Proponents of rationalistic secularism tend to regard this as a backtracking or "failure of nerve," but theism is also a philosophical development from deep troubles within transcendent ontologies. Ramanuja in the 1000s to 1100s, Madhva in the 1200s, Nimbarka who launched the Krishna movement in the 1300s, Chaitanya and Vallabha with the bhakti devotionalism of the late 1400s or early 1500s: these are so many leaders of religious movements, their successors much like anointed "pontiffs" of their "churches." All these were Vaishnavas—followers of Vishnu, of whom Krishna was regarded as one name or manifestation—and much of intellectual as well as political life was taken up by their quarrels with the Shaivas. Particularly in south India, communities were divided and kings supported one faction while persecuting the other, sometimes destroying their temples and killing or mutilating their priests (Dasgupta, 1922–1955: 3:303, 113; 4:52–54). Nevertheless, under this surface of religious argument was developed the highest level of sophistication in metaphysical and epistemological argument in Indian history. Logical tools sharpened over the centuries became widespread in debate. Although the wider intellectual significance is obscured by the sectarian context, the climax of Hindu philosophy produced positions comparable to those of the Cartesians, Hume, and the logical positivists, as well as the more predictable parallels to Spinoza, Berkeley, and Kant.

Given the dominance of an idealism exalting a transcendent spiritual center, it might seem surprising that Hindu orthodoxy should have produced this variety of positions. This variety is the product of two conditions. One is the inevitable workings of the intellectual law of small numbers: a dominant position has a number of slots available in the attention space, and its thinkers find the lines of dispute which can fill them. Philosophical division provides intellectual ammunition for religious factionalism, which thrives on the material conditions of political decentralization and instability. The second condition is the nature of theism itself. Theistic cults are closer to the conceptions of everyday life, exalting an anthropomorphic god presiding over the world in which worshippers live. This sets up a tension with pure religious monism, which is the product of intellectuals who follow to its extreme implications the concept of an all-powerful entity and reduce everything else to nothingness. Both sides of this argument can locate religious contradictions in the other. Using the criterion of highest respect for God, the monists can accuse the theists of bringing God down to human categories and allowing the world to encroach on Its infinite capacity. Theists can accuse monists of disrespecting God by merging Him with mere humans, demeaning the higher by absorbing it in the experience of the lower. We see a parallel in the period of Christian ascendancy in the late Roman Empire, when the pure monism of Neoplatonism was countered by the emphasis given by Christian theism to the independent existence of the lower material world. The theist-monist debate is one of those puzzle spaces which can sustain interminable controversy, a fruitful territory on which intellectuals can generate both passion and attention.

Theological issues, departicularized, are issues of metaphysics. In the case of Hindu theologies after Shankara, the metaphysical field forms around the assumption of a single highest substance. The struggle for intellectual differentiation can then seize on the problems of explaining the experience of empirical plurality—indeed the very existence of the phenomenal world—from a monist viewpoint. In addition to the obvious poles of monism and dualism, there are a number of intermediating tacks: substance and attribute, stasis and process, mind and body. The Indian development differs from the philosophical theology of Christendom and Islam by a greater emphasis on sheer ontological issues and less concern for the moral dimension of free will, divine foreknowledge, and responsibility for evil. This difference comes in part from the more depersonalized theology of the Indian cosmology and its praxis of salvation through meditation or insight, as opposed to the Western insistence on God as an authoritative Person and the concomitant praxis of salvation through moral attitudes. Thus the European philosophy which most resembles the Vedantins' is that of the period of transition to secularism, the post-medieval ontologies worked out from Descartes through the German Idealists.

In India after 1100 we see once again one side of the intellectual field split into subfactions, while the other side remains relatively stable. In this case the splitters and innovators are the expanding movement of Vaishnavas. The followers of Vishnu had never been strictly orthodox in the eyes of Hindu pandits, since this meant a Brahmanical education guided by respect for the Vedas. The Vaishnavas claimed their own revealed scriptures and thus were regarded as something of a heretical challenge, although the popular appeal of the Vaishnava epic the *Mahabharata* enabled them to capture much of the central Hindu identity. The Shaivas had an even more shockingly unorthodox background; but while skull-carrying phallic image worshippers repelled the orthodox, there were also more socially conventional followers of Shiva among the core intellectuals: generally they had the sympathy of the Nyayas and Vaisheshikas, and Shankara himself was claimed by the Shaivas (perhaps inaccurately; *EIP,* 1981: 119; cf. Pandey, 1986; Eliot, 1988: 2:209–210). A tendency developed for Shaivism to be identified with Advaita monism, with a spiritual force which transcends the world through paradox into the unspeakable, whereas Vishnu acquired more of the normal qualities of theism, a creator-and-ruler God, and was thus philosophically compatible with pluralist positions such as Samkhya and Mimamsa.

Nevertheless, as Vaishnavism expanded and split, over the long run it appropriated a range of philosophical tools and acquired a variety of philosophical positions. The Vaishnava upsurge, from Ramanuja down to Nimbarka, was directed philosophically against the Advaitas. That is to say, the Vaishnavas took the opposite philosophical tack from the most prominent and respectable of the Shaivas, the well-established monastic movement founded by Shankara. By challenging Shankarites, Ramanuja (ca. 1100) was making a claim to bring Vaishnavas into an equal position of orthodoxy within Hinduism; he built an order of monks as a direct parallel and competition.[66] Shankara had explicitly rejected Vaishnava devotional theism as non-Vedic (Raju, 1985: 438). Ramanuja, originally trained in Advaita philosophy in a Shaivite *math,* launched a counterattack against the Shankara ontology of Maya, the world illusion which is mere appearance. Yamunacharya, Ramanuja's predecessor, had already criticized Shankara's fundamental argument, the cogito: the self cannot perceive itself unless it is split, and to perceive the second one in turn leads to an infinite regress of separate selves (Potter, 1976: 83). Ramanuja exploited the pluralist tensions within monism, creating a position known as Vishishtadvaita, qualified non-dualism. Brahman is the one reality, but the modes of its existence comprise both matter and souls and may be regarded as the body of God pervading the universe. Borrowing technical ammunition from the Nyaya, Ramanuja describes the relation of the world to the Absolute, Spinoza-like, as that of attributes to an underlying substance.

It follows that the visible world cannot be an illusion. Rejecting Shankara's distinction between appearance and ultimate reality brought Ramanuja onto epistemological grounds. Shankara had epistemologized ontology, changing the veil of illusion from world substance to insubstantial ignorance. Shankara argued that ultimate reality is unqualified and in the normal human sense unknowable. Ramanuja asserted instead that all knowledge is real and all arguments are qualified. Ramanuja used the principle of the self-validity of knowledge, which originated with Prabhakara Mimamsa, and had been appropriated from that declining school by the Advaita. But whereas the Advaitins recognized the existence of objects of knowledge, at least on the level of worldly appearance, Ramanuja held that knowledge is self-valid in a much more absolute sense. (Raju, 1985: 440; Isayeva, 1993: 245–246). Inner experiences, even dreams and illusions, are self-valid, insofar as they are pragmatically significant for the practical goals of life. And the practical goal is direct contact with Brahman, which is everywhere; there is no world of illusions distinct from the Absolute. This extreme epistemology became the hallmark of the Ramanuja school. To put it ontologically: consciousness is intentional, always carrying with it an object. Consciousness always thus involves plurality; and although such differentiating consciousness cannot be the Absolute substance but only an attribute of it, the differentiatedness of world experience is not to be denigrated as unreal. As the contemporary Advaita stars Shri Harsha and Chitsukha moved toward the dialectical dissolution of the empirical world, Ramanuja was moving in the opposite direction.

The conflict of Shaivas against Vaishnavas in south India was the outer framework within which these philosophical moves were set in motion. Ramanuja's creativity came from close-hand conflict with the sophisticated Advaita philosophy in which he was trained. The occasion for his split from this tradition was provided by his family network contact with a burgeoning Vaishnava movement at just the time when it was ready to become organizationally institutionalized. This in turn provided a base and a demand for philosophical rationalization to match Shankara's organization.

Advaita and Vishishtadvaita as yet had explored only a relatively small range of ontological positions possible for monotheism. The emergence of full-fledged dualism came next. Madhva (1197–1276?), leader of the second great Vaishnava movement, built his career through an even more extreme break from the Advaitas. Born near the southern headquarters of the Shankaras, at Shringeri in Mysore, Madhva was educated in Shankaraite *maths* but broke away into theism. Traveling through India, Madhva became a religious leader, working alleged miracles, meeting rival philosophers in the north, and stirring up waves of political battles, persecutions, and counter-persecutions in the south with the Shankarites. Madhva formulated a Calvinist-sounding theology of salvation by grace: God remains separate from the lowly worshipper, and the Advaita merging of man with God is treated as sacrilege (Dasgupta, 1922–1955: 4:52–54; Eliot, 1988: 2:237–240; Potter, 1976: 249).

On philosophical terrain, Madhva defended an explicitly pluralistic metaphysics. He repudiated not only Advaita but also the qualified non-dualism of Ramanuja. Seizing on prior traditions of logic, and occupying an intellectual space left vacant since Dharmakirti's Buddhist followers, Madhva argued that everything is a particular, including both eternal and transient things, even God. The Nyaya-Vaisheshika included particulars among their fundamental categories, but had reified them as entities different from the substances in which they inhere. Madhva radicalized the concept, making the particular the basic feature of beings; for it is "the power of everything to be itself" (Raju, 1985: 475). Madhva similarly radicalized the concept of universals, which Nyaya-Vaisheshika treated as eternal entities. Madhva held that the universals of non-transient entities are themselves transient, and he attacked anything like Platonist realism in favor of an omni-particularism that cut through every ontological level. Through the same move, he counteracted the anti-conceptual dialectics of Advaitins such as Shri Harsha. The pluralistic world is real exactly as it is—as particulars.

In these same centuries (ca. late 1000s to early 1400s), Nimbarka launched yet another Vaishnava sect. He and his followers continued the fight against Advaita, refuting Shankara on the illusory nature of the world but simultaneously separating themselves from the philosophical terrain of the Ramanujans. Duality, Nimbarka holds, cannot be an attribute of Non-duality because attributes distinguish a substance from other substances, but only one substance exists. Duality is a subordinate reality within the Non-duality, and is both different and non-different from it: different because a subordinate dependent existence; non-different because it has no independence existence. (Hence the name of the position, Dvaitadvaita.) Drawing on concepts from both Advaita and the energy-ontology of Shaktism, Nimbarka describes the single Substance as comprising a static self-identical aspect and a energetic and potentiating aspect (Chattopadhyaya, 1979: 1:267–270; Isayeva, 1993: 250). The result is something like Spinoza transposed into the Indian modalities of the aconceptual and the energizing rather than the mental and material.

Vaishnava splits continued, led by Chaitanya in the 1400s or early 1500s, and soon after him by Vallabha (Eliot, 1988: 2:248–256; Dasgupta, 1922–1955: 4:320–448). Splitting from the Madhva sect, Chaitanya turned to bhakti devotionalism. He repudiated his own youthful training in intellectual argument and dominated debates by pure emotionalism. His Krishna sect downplayed asceticism and allowed its monks to marry; in place of ceremony, worship took the form of repetition of divine names to the accompaniment of music and rhythmic bodily swaying. Chaitanya was known to dance until he bled from his pores, and to march obliviously into the ocean. Chaitanya left no writings, although some of his followers and successors in the bhakti camp came back to articulate philosophy. Vallabha turned bhakti in the direction of monism, breaking from the long-standing allegiance of the Vaishnava movements with some variety of dualism, holding that the Absolute comprises the world as a relation of whole and part. There were now so many factions on the Vaishnava side that they spread out imperially across ontological space. One faction among them, as the philosophical arguments of the schools had grown hyper-technical, even became part of the current of anti-intellectualism.

Neo-Nyaya Formalism: Technical Logic and the Clouding of Philosophical Attention Space

Along with the rise of Vaishnavism and its inner splits and its polemics with Advaita had come the spread of argument about epistemological validity into every intellectual camp. The emergence of Advaita had stirred up a response in Nyaya; in the next round, the Advaitins launched a deep refutation of Nyaya which pushed them even further into anti-substantialist terrain. This Advaita anti-conceptual monism left an opening into which moved the Ramanujans and Madhvas by reformulating anti-monist metaphysics; they also turned, sooner or later, to logical grounds for their polemics. Nyaya did not wither under attack; instead it produced another wave of even more refined logic, which too was eventually taken up as a weapon by the sectarian schools.

The most famous of the later Advaitins, Shri Harsha and Chitsukha, had thrown down the gauntlet to conceptual and empirical logic in general. The founder of Neo-Nyaya, Gangesha, around 1350 countered this Advaita anti-logicism by reforming logic so as to be immune to the dialectitians' attacks on positively expressed concepts. Shri Harsha had uncovered vicious regresses everywhere. How is an individual known to be an instance of a universal without invoking yet another cognition of this relation, and then a cognition of that cognition, and so on? Similarly, how are universals distinct from one another without qualities of distinctness which lead to yet another infinite regress? And without distinctness, everything falls into the undifferentiated monism of Advaita. Gangesha responded by raising the level of reflection on the role of primitive terms in philosophical argument (Phillips, 1995: 100–101, 122–132). Cognitions, he held, are divided into determinate verbal awareness and indeterminate awareness of primitives, which we recognize only upon analysis. Questions of truth or falsity apply only to determinate awareness; the items of indeterminate awareness simply are. Gangesha then defined the primitives of his argument such that regress does not arise.

By painstakingly classifying various types of absence or negation, Neo-

Nyaya rescued the crucial concept of distinctness, defining it as a particular type of mutual absence between entities. The hallmark of the school was to produce extremely complicated negative definitions for every part of the syllogism; 'smoke' is rendered "the counterpart of the absolute non-existence of the smoke" (Stcherbatsky, 1962: 1:482; 52). Neo-Nyaya appropriated the negative theme of the now-defunct Buddhist logic; once the rival of Nyaya realism, it was now pressed into service against monist inexpressibility in much the same way that Dignaga countered Nagarjuna.

The end result was to cut Neo-Nyaya loose from its longtime realist partner. It no longer carried the old alliance with Vaisheshika; instead it produced its own complex new theory of space and time. The last and most radical leader of Neo-Nyaya, Raghunatha Shiromani in the late 1400s, underscored the independence of the logic school from its old ally by critiquing Vaisheshika atomism. Raghunatha added new primitive terms to the Nyaya system of reals and reformulated the problem of ontological reduction. The traditional theory of universals, which Naiyayikas had treated as something like the "natural kinds" of Western philosophers in the mid-1900s, was no longer seen as the natural cutting point of the universe; Raghunatha's system became closer to nominalism.[67]

Neo-Nyaya became something like the European logical positivism of the early 1900s in its concern for extreme logical formalism and strict rigor. By the time Neo-Nyaya petered out in the 1600s, it had given up polemics with other schools and become preoccupied with technical minutiae.[68] Its trajectory toward ever-increasing formalism was more than a parochial development. Those schools of Indian philosophy which had not repudiated intellectual life for bhakti emotionalism were all becoming scholastic. The mainstream Advaita school, for all its doctrinal commitment to defending aconceptual reality, developed its own complicated logical formalism as early as the 1000s; this so-called *mahavidya* mode of syllogistic argument even influenced the practice of dialecticians such as Shri Harsha, and was an object of debate in the Nyaya school before it formulated its own roundabout methods in the form of Neo-Nyaya (*EIP*, 1977: 646–652; Dasgupta, 1922–1955: 2:119–125). The Madhva school, too, institutionalized in its own monastic order, and its *maths* adopted the successive reforms of logic for their own purposes; the Ramanuja school resisted for a while but eventually acquired its own logicians. By the 1300s, formalism had infected all the schools.

Scholasticism and Syncretism in the Decline of Hindu Philosophy

These centuries show a growing scholasticism throughout the field, rooted in the routinization of studies in the *maths,* which turned even the hot religious issues of the past into historical compilations. The energy of Indian philosophy was dying of its own success, in much the same way that the technical sophistication of the Nominalists in the Christian universities of Europe obscured the attention space in esoteric refinements. It is not merely that intellectual acuteness was lost as bhakti emotionalism gained popularity; the excitement of the intellectual networks was declining from within. Although long-term reputations, especially of hyper-technical fields such as Neo-Nyaya, make it hard for us to appreciate it, this drying up occurred at the climax of the most sophisticated philosophical activity in Indian history.[69] The creative networks lost their reputation and their impetus at a time of institutional success as well as cumulative development. The social pattern of such failures is revealed by comparative analysis, provided at the end of Chapter 9.

We see a tendency toward a "neutral" scholarly heritage in the growing acceptance of the "six *darshanas*" scheme. Originally this was the rubric used by Jaina historians, on the sidelines of the intellectual action, observing the scene around them in the 700s. In the 1300s Vidyaranya introduced the "six *darshanas*" scheme into Hinduism; by this time it was already archaic, since Yoga was hardly a live philosophical school, Vaisheshika was not independent, and virtually all the intellectual action would have to be categorized under the contending varieties of Vedanta. Old schools were now revived, but more as memories than as independent lineages defending their own positions; their sharp edges were rounded off, and all were made compatible with a currently orthodox theism. The most independent as an organizational base seems to have been Mimamsa, which still had its specialists in textual exegesis down into the 1800s and beyond. Its glory days as a realist epistemology and ontology had long since passed; abandoning its aggressive atheism, late Mimamsa turned theist.[70]

The last creative flurry of Hindu philosophies was in the 1500s, this time largely under the banner of syncretism. The last big name was Vijñanabhikshu, who put together a combination of scholastic doctrines—Mimamsa, Yoga, Nyaya, Samkhya, most of these long since fossilized and out of date—with contemporary Vedanta. If Vijñanabhikshu drew together Hindu scholasticism into a grand non-Advaita syncretism, Appaya Dikshita (ca. 1600) was the syncretist within the monist camp. Considering the violence of the conflict in previous centuries between Shaivas and Vaishnavas, this was a remarkable conciliation. The acute philosophical differences between Advaitins and pluralists, and the dialectics of conceptualist and aconceptualist epistemologies, were smoothed over, no longer a matter of living interest. This is not to say that no one was still creatively defending a distinctive position in the 1500s; two of the great dialecticians, Madhusudana of the Advaitins and Vyasa-tirtha of the Madhvas, still carried on the debate over knowledge and world illusion.

Nevertheless, Madhusudana harmonized the Hindu sects as different paths to the same goal, corresponding to different personal inclinations (Halbfass, 1991: 73; Dasgupta, 1922–1955: 4:204–320). A new note was struck by Prakashananda (1500s); whereas other Advaitins were realists, decentering the perceiver from the ultimate transcendent reality, Prakashananda turned Advaita into a pure Berkeleyesque subjectivism, in which objects come into existence when perceived and go out of existence when they are not perceived (Potter, 1976: 244–247).

But this was to be the last piece of significant original philosophy. Syncretism became more and more the mode. Indian philosophers from the 1600s on are minor figures, commentators on the old traditions. The Advaitins lost their sharp edges and syncretized with their theist enemies. The writers of the most famous manuals put together Nyaya with Advaita and Mimamsa (Annambhatta, 1500s), or Samkhya with Nyaya (Vamshidhara, 1700s). After about 1550, Neo-Nyaya recombined with the older Nyaya. In the 1800s and 1900s, Advaita became a kind of "official" philosophy of India, absorbing every school into what Karl Potter calls a "bhaktized Advaita leap-philosophy," that is to say, a faith that everything leads to the same spiritual conclusion although that conclusion is not in the end conceptually demonstrable.[71] The creative conflicts of Indian philosophical history became sublimated into a sentimentalized nativism.

These modern philosophers syncretized positions whose political underpinnings had been weakened. They pulled together a Hindu national philosophy in united front against European colonial domination after 1800, and contrasted it as sharply as possible with modern European secularism and materialism. Just at this time the concept of a unitary "Hindu" culture was formulated, first by British administrators, then embraced by Indian nationalists themselves (Inden, 1992). But why did the syncretism set in even earlier, in the 1500s? The reason is Islam. Although there had been prior inroads of Muslim conquerors in India, these had been relatively unstable conquest states largely confined to the northwest, until the Mogul Empire spread rapidly from Afghanistan beginning in the 1560s through the 1600s to cover virtually all of India. The great syncretizers Vijñanabhiksu and Appaya Dikshita lived during the late 1500s and early 1600s in the last major Hindu state in the south while this Muslim wave expanded; the later Hindu scholastics lived under Muslim rule or under the European colonials. In a much earlier wave of conquest, during the Islamic invasion of the Ganges around 1100, the Buddhists just before their fadeout were urging an alliance with Vaishnavas and Shaivas to repel the Islamic threat (Nakamura, 1980: 339). Dividing in strength, in weakness philosophies unite. Given that among the modes of syncretism there is the sloppy loss of conceptual sharpness, there is generally more creativity in their dividing than in their uniting.

Ironically, the anti-conceptual monism that modern Indians and Westerners alike tend to regard as the perennial philosophy of India came to dominate because of a recent turn in a long series of intellectual conflicts. The Muslim and European conquests, which put Hinduism into a philosophical united front for the first time in its long history, illustrate a deeper, more truly perennial process: the creative episodes of division and alliance inside intellectual space, each episode set off by the clashing of external political forces around its organizational base.

CHAPTER 6

Revolutions of the Organizational Base: Buddhist and Neo-Confucian China

Political and economic conditions affect ideas not directly but via the intermediate level of organizations supporting intellectual networks. In this chapter I focus on the middle level of causality. The example of medieval and early modern China allows us to see how creativity occurs under transitions both on the way up and on the way down, in times of organizational growth and organizational crisis and destruction.

Transplanted from India, Buddhism dominated the intellectual life of medieval China. This should be no surprise. At its core, Buddhism is an intellectuals' religion. Not that its doctrines are overtly favorable to intellectualism. On the contrary, the world of "name and form" is the obstacle to enlightenment, and intellectual attachments are just one of many to be rooted out. At the same time, the very structure of Buddhism as a hierarchy of meditators brings its practitioners to focus on these mental obstacles. As its hierarchies mounted higher and its historical traditions lengthened, the subtlety of its analyses mounted too. It is characteristic of Buddhist meditation to take apart the world on the path toward Emptiness, and this gives scope for metaphysical constructions of just how the world of illusion is produced. Once such philosophical systems were formulated, there was strong incentive within Buddhism to take them apart in turn. This anti-intellectual religion bred its own intellectuals of an especially probing sort.

In external respects, too, the organization of Buddhism provided fertile ground for intellectual life of an extreme purity. As practitioners of a monastic religion, devoted to withdrawing from the world, its monks were not preachers or administerers of sacraments to lay congregations. This ideal of Buddhist monasticism often slipped away into practices of making a livelihood from preaching, ritualism, or magical display. But the core form, the organization of world-withdrawing meditators, gave Buddhism its central identity. Detached from family life and practical concerns, focusing on the analysis of inner experience, viewing even the particularism of gods and the ritualism of religion as parts of the world of illusion to be transcended, the Buddhist monk might be regarded as living the life of philosophy at its extreme. Even religion in its conventional sense, with its categories of salvation, immortality, and the sacred, constitutes no more than another set of attachments to be understood for what they are and thereby transcended. Buddhist enlightenment might itself be seen as the pure emotional energy of creative consciousness, detached from all contents and transformed to the highest voltage by focusing on itself. Reflexive insight is raised to the status of a sacred act.

All this rested on supporting conditions in the material world. Monasteries had to have sources of revenue if monks were to devote themselves to meditation; Buddhist life at some level was always entwined with the mundane realities of economics, politics, and social status. The social causality cut both ways. Not only can we trace the outward-to-inward flow of material conditions on the formation of Buddhist intellectual networks; but also we find a profound transformation of Chinese society resulting from the spread of monasteries. Corporations recruiting universally and operating outside the family-based structures of patrimonial society, the monasteries became centers of economic accumulation and the cutting edge of structural change. If Europe with its bureaucratic and capitalist structures was built upon Christianity—first of all the monastic Christianity of the Middle Ages—China was no less shaped by an organizational revolution that was due in considerable part to medieval Buddhism. Both Europe and China, too, ended their period of medieval takeoff with downsizing reformations. As the secular economy overflowed the monastic sector and state administration built on the new resources, the monasteries were plundered and their rituals were displaced. Buddhist property was confiscated for lay ends; it was not lost, however, but turned into new channels, just as Buddhist intellectual sophistication was circulated in a new guise by the Neo-Confucians.

The middle level of causality has a dynamic of its own. Buddhist organizational growth not only affected the intellectuals within but also transformed the surrounding political and economic structure. This did not happen without a fight. Confucianism, and to some extent Taoism, grounded in the older structures, became bitter rivals of Buddhism. The political struggles that ensued shaped the contours of intellectual life. Because its organizational base provided more autonomy for abstract philosophy, Buddhists dominated the intellectual attention space for many generations. Political attacks from external enemies had indirect effects. When the organizational base of court Buddhism began to crumble, the Ch'an (Zen) movement broke out in the branch of Buddhism which moved to a safer base; still later, Neo-Confucianism represented the intellectual creativity of transition when the Confucian literati regained control of the means of intellectual production.

We examine first the organizational growth of Buddhism in China and its social effects. Moving from outside toward the inner intellectual field, we take up next the foreign relations of Buddhism with its rival religions. After this we come to the inner patterns of creativity within the networks of Buddhist philosophers, culminating in the grand visions of T'ien-t'ai and Hua-yen metaphysics, followed by the iconoclasm of Ch'an. Finally, as the material base of Buddhism crumbled under political attack, we arrive at the outburst of Neo-Confucianism bound up with Buddhism's fall and the rise of a new organizational base of intellectual life.

Buddhism and the Organizational Transformation of Medieval China

Buddhism entered China in the Han dynasty and underwent tremendous growth during the period of disunity that followed.[1] If the figures are even approximately accurate, around 550 C.E. as much as 4 to 6 percent of the Chinese population were practicing Buddhist monks, along with their novices and slaves (and even more in the northern states); around 830 C.E. the figure must have been about 2 percent, in the late Sung (ca. 1220) the numbers were still very large, but the overall population of China had grown, so that the Buddhist sector had declined to about 1 percent. During the T'ang, it is estimated that the annual money expenditure of the monks for subsistence alone was equal to one half of the state's total revenue, and this did not include building and investment expenditures by the Buddhists. For a time, Buddhist organizations were bigger than the state.

As the first universalistic mass religion, Buddhism brought a huge change in the structure of religious organization in China. Confucianism was a class-specific cult, the privilege and badge of the Chinese gentry. It might best be characterized as a meta-religion, an elite policy of patronizing and administering court rituals and traditional local cults; it was especially concerned to enforce the ancestral cult within families, using governmental punishments and rewards to ensure that the populace was continuously involved in the round of rituals which bound them to family hierarchies, and through them to local government (CHC, 1986: 552–553). Confucian officials deliberately regulated traditionalism and localism for purposes of central state control. The tendency to deify Confucius merely added one more cult observance to this predominantly particularistic structure.

Buddhism as a proselytizing religion of mass recruitment created a new kind of organization, breaking the ties of kinship and patrimonial household. Potentially such organizations could mobilize huge numbers of people. Whereas local cults kept the ongoing status order in place, mass religious movements could unleash waves of emotional enthusiasm for political upheaval or new self-discipline. The openness of mass recruitment meant that successful religious organizations shifted toward a bureaucratic form of administration. Inadvertently an organizational weapon was shaped which could become a state within the state, or an administrative adjunct allied to the secular ruler. The far-flung organizational network extracted economic resources from traditional routines and reinvested them in new circuits of capital. As Buddhism became rich, it transformed the economic base of Chinese society, just as it later would the economy of Japan. Buddhism was bound to clash with Confucianism, for it undermined the status order that Confucian ritualism upheld.

Buddhism came into conflict with Taoism for a different reason. The autonomous organization of religious specialists nevertheless had to gain a foothold by appealing to lay supporters. Especially in the early period of Buddhism in China, when it confronted a localistic structure of clans, tribal conquerors, and autarkic estates, Buddhists accommodated to the traditional idioms of concretized magic. Cosmopolitan monks, enveloped in religious charisma as the result of their own pursuit of transcendence, were treated as possessors of magic usable for fecundity in childbearing or fertility of crops, for rainmaking, luck-bringing, or fortune-telling. At higher social ranks, the court aristocracy adopted the most elaborate Buddhist rituals for political impressiveness and status display. At a later period tantrism, developed in India at the time when autonomy of Buddist organization from the laity was crumbling, became popular at the Chinese court for its rituals invoking an aura of magic power by means of pictures, music, and gestures. On a more modest scale, little emotional eddies of magic ritual with cheaper props went at a retail rate among the common people; in this market niche Taoists were already on the ground, and remained more successful than Buddhists.

Taoism and Buddhism began as market competitors which gradually settled into adjacent but overlapping niches. Taoism developed, not as an organization of specialized religious practitioners but as a combination of several forms of lay practice, including the leisure pursuits of Chinese gentry, the ideologies of political dissidents, and the ritual lore of low-status folk magic and medicine. Taoism first acquired a churchlike organization as a political movement. In the Five Pecks of Grain movement at the end of the Han, its political-military power was based on exchange of ritual magic guaranteeing health in return for payments to support a regional government. Taoism only gradually, and in imitation of Buddhism, developed the more autonomous structures of monasteries with rules of celibacy. Taoism had no strong central organization, and there was a large variety of sects, perhaps 80 or more, many composed of lay practitioners (Welch, 1965: 144).

Taoist religious ideology centered on the overlapping themes of health, longevity, and immortality. On the continuum of religious aims, Taoism took up a spot adjacent to the goal of pure salvation or enlightenment. Immortality was close to salvation, but Taoist immortality was an extension of physical well-being into a transcendent, unearthly plane, or sometimes within the material world itself. The contrasting ideal of Buddhism was to become enlightened out of the realm of bodily illusion entirely, although the Buddhist salvation cults which developed in China compromised this with the aim of rebirth in a future paradise.

The difference between the pure transcendent and worldlier goals was grounded in the different forms of organization; the similarity came from a shared technology of religious practice. Both Taoism and Buddhism practiced meditation; both surrounded this with ritual and liturgy. Similar techniques of controlling breathing, concentrating attention, and focusing on inner experience were given different interpretations: one might focus on the Taoist 36,000 interior gods in order to achieve what one believed was physical purification and health (Welch, 1965: 106–107, 130–131), or on a Buddhist Bodhisattva such as Maitraya to attain rebirth in the Western Paradise, or on Emptiness to attain enlightenment; later the Confucians would adopt similar techniques for the purpose of Sagehood. These are micro-sociological techniques for constructing interior realities. The ideas and experiences so constructed could range across the continuum from the worldly and particularistic up through the most rarified and metaphysical. The differences in these religions were differences in the ideological interpretations placed on their practices; and these came from the intellectual themes communicated through the larger organization. Buddhist monks, even when turned toward magical applications, were linked to an organization of intellectuals specializing in an inward focus on pure transcendence; Taoism was linked more exclusively to the laity, whether these were the gentry, political dissidents, or low-status audiences for popular magicians.

Buddhism and Taoism at times came quite close to each other. In its early centuries in China, Buddhism had lost most of its meditative practices and monastic discipline, and relied heavily on magical practices and ritual to impress political patrons. Buddhism recovered its distinctiveness in a series of reform movements, from 530 into the 800s, resulting in a variety of new sects, from elite movements such as T'ien-t'ai and Ch'an, to simplified salvation cults of the personified quasi-deities Maitreya and Amitabha among the common people. Taoism, battling Buddhism in the struggle for court patronage and imitating its organizational forms, moved closer to its doctrines as well; but it never caught up with Buddhism's organizational massiveness, and its primary niche remained the magically oriented sphere of health and immortality-seeking.

Buddhism's main organizational advantage was that it was always centered on full-time specialists cut loose from family ties, which is to say, monks. Taoist monasticism, which developed in imitation of the Buddhists, was never as thoroughgoing or as successful. In its initial growth during the period of dynastic division, the Taoist church was in the hands of families of southern aristocrats who used it to further their political interests; and later Taoism tended to center on small temples catering to the peasantry. Buddhist monasticism, by contrast, had achieved a spectacular success already in the period of post-Han disintegration. Its success was based on its material advantages in transforming a society in which most resources were locked up in patrimonial households. Because of their open recruitment and independence from family inheritance of property, the monasteries provided a new organizational flexibility for structuring the economy. This in turn fostered the transformation of China into an expanding market economy, the first real takeoff of proto-capitalism in world history.[2]

The Buddhist temples became great landowners, if not quite on the scale of the Christian monasteries and cathedrals, which held one third of the cultivated land in medieval Europe. Especially during the period of the ethnically alien northern dynasties, the monasteries were centers for cultivating conquered and devastated territories under the patronage of the kings; in much the same way early Christian monasteries and crusading orders were frontier outposts for royal power in northern and eastern Europe. When the Toba rulers of the Northern Wei conquered Shantung in 467 C.E., they enslaved part of the population and put them to work cultivating fields given to the Buddhist monasteries and doing manual labor on the monastery grounds. Local families were organized into Sangha Households responsible for collecting grain to be stored at the monastery for redistribution at times of famine (Ch'en, 1964: 154–157). Since land attached to the Sangha Households was free of taxation, other private families voluntarily attached themselves, and the institution spread widely. Monasteries fostered economic expansion, increasing agricultural production and opening up new agricultural lands. Monks used the storehouses of grain to make loans at interest, thus turning to systematic speculation and creating a financial marketplace.

In the absence of a money economy, or of a state machinery strong enough to collect taxes reliably, the monasteries with their stores of wealth and their system of trading were the banks and the long-distance commercial structure of China. Buddhist monasteries, like their Christian counterparts in Europe, provided the systematic cultivation, reinvestment of profits, and even the beginnings of industrial production which laid the foundations for growth in the secular economy in the later T'ang and the Sung. Monasteries established "Inexhaustible Treasuries," a kind of bank for goods donated by pious laypeople (Ch'en, 1964: 265–266, 299–300). The famous Hua-tu temple in Chang-an during the T'ang dynasty was fabulously wealthy; it made donations to the poor, but accepted so many donations that it was able to make large loans and investments, and lay administrators embezzled sums to make private fortunes. Monasteries were also important in trade. The Ching-tu monastery in Tun-huang on the Central Asian trade route (about 920 C.E.) received half its income from interest on loans, another third from revenue from temple lands and rents of its oil presses (Ch'en, 1964: 266–267). In the large monasteries, wealth not needed for consumption or charity was typically put in the hands of a monastic agent who was charged with organizing trade caravans or otherwise investing it and returning a profit. Monastic wealth was transformed into industrial production and technology (Needham, 1965: 400–403). Big monasteries acquired water mills, which they leased to private businesses or operated themselves. These mills were sources of large profits, and during the T'ang were often objects of conflict with the government over irrigation rights or exemption from taxation.

To this intensive growth of the big monastic property holders around the chief administrative cities was added the extensive growth of local market relations in the rural countryside. The vehicle for this market spread was a new wave of popular theistic Buddhism. Most prominent was the Pure Land sect of Amitabha (Amida). There had been earlier worshippers of popular Buddhist deities; but from 530 through about 680 there appeared a much larger movement of simplified Buddhism promising rebirth in the Western Paradise simply by reciting the holy name. Its appearance at this time coincided with the economic reorganization of society. Partly owing to the stimulus of the larger monasteries, rural production was beginning to break out of local isolation, estate autarky, and direct government appropriation of surplus, and to develop rural market networks. Small Buddhist temples sprang up in this newly dynamic environment, and contributed in turn to expanding networks of travel and trade as well as to the spread of cultural capital. The wildfire spread of a simplified Buddhism in this situation marked the first penetration of a universalistic religion into a truly mass market in China.

As the centralized state and secular economy took hold, Buddhist organizations lost their economic centrality but remained useful in economic maneuvering. The aristocracy would nominally give land to a temple in order to evade taxation, while retaining use of it through provisions of the gift. The great urban monasteries and those surrounding the capital became fabulously wealthy. At the other end of the scale, small village temples and rural monasteries were ill endowed, and staffed by poorly educated monks from the local peasantry.

During its height in the Northern and Southern dynasties and the T'ang, the wealth of the church made it a target for periodic persecutions and confiscations. This too had its European parallels: the suppression and confiscation of the Templars by the French king in 1307, and the secular takeover of monastic properties in the Protestant Reformation. Until the end of the T'ang, Buddhism had considerable resilience. The successive persecutions hit hardest at the gentry Buddhists at the top of the church, leaving the popular base intact; and the economic usefulness of its organization usually allowed the elite superstructure to rebuild when political winds again blew more favorably. The wealth and power of Buddhism fed the antagonism of Taoists and Confucians. Confucians as state officials attacked Buddhism for withdrawing resources from the taxable control of the state. Taoists were vulnerable to the same charge, but their poorer monastic organization made them a less tempting target. At the same time, their emulation of Buddhism put the Taoists in a direct competition over status, which made them the prime instigators of the persecutions of Buddhism. On occasion, pro-Buddhist reactions resulted in counter-suppressions of Taoists, though without much long-term effect. By the early Sung, the Chinese market economy had far outgrown the Buddhist sector, and neither government nor aristocracy depended much on its material organization. The centrality of Buddhism within China came to an end; and with its decline, so too declined its Taoist imitation.

Intellectual Foreign Relations of Buddhism, Taoism, and Confucianism

During periods of weakness in their external fortunes, the "foreign policy" of these religions downplayed philosophical differences with their rivals. Conversely, strongly based religions became aggressive, scorning syncretism and attacking their enemies. From 165 to 400 C.E., when Buddhism was cautiously making its way into China, it tended to syncretize, especially with Taoism. A leading Buddhist monk maintained contact with the Taoist-oriented "Pure Conversation" circle in south China, translating Buddhist terms with Taoist terminology. Copyists borrowed almost word for word from the *Tao Te Ching* in translating Buddhist texts: "Emptiness [*sunya*] that can be made empty is not true emptiness" (Zürcher, 1959; Demiéville, 1986: 839–840, 866–867).

The process helped to mold what became the "Taoist" classics increasingly toward the mystical side and away from their political or magical interpretations. Chinese intellectuals with an interest in mysticism were at first inclined to favor Buddhism as an intellectual ally. Taoism was just becoming organized, and had as yet no clear intellectual identity. Nor was Taoism politically powerful. The Taoist churches which organized political rebellions among the peasantry with millennial appeals merely added another military faction to an unstable struggle; so did families of Taoist aristocrats, who fomented palace coups by occult prophecies and revelations. Buddhist organization was more stable. Its monasteries, holding independent property and united by lineages owing allegiance to written scriptures, were able to shelter from political winds while their material base grew. Governments often found economic and administrative advantages in an alliance with monasteries.

Taoists came to seek the advantage of this organizational base. By the 420s in the Toba Empire of north China, the ruler set up a Taoist "pope" in his capital, with authority over the entire Taoist church. The "pope" had Buddhist masters and network contacts, even with the famous Kumarajiva (Mather, 1979: 112, 120–121). The code for Taoist monks was a direct imitation of the Buddhist *vinaya* rules. In the early 500s in the south, a canon of Taoist scriptures was formulated, an imitation of Buddhist sutras which came close to plagiarism (Ofuchi, 1979: 267). Rivals for the same organizational niche became doctrinal enemies. Taoism now went on the offensive in doctrinal disputes and instigated political persecutions of Buddhists. In the Toba state, Taoism was proclaimed the official faith in 444, and in 446 the Buddhists were persecuted and their vast properties confiscated. A change in political fortunes after a failed coup allowed the Buddhists to return in 454. In 520 and again in 555, court debates between Taoists and Buddhists ended with the Taoists banished and ordered to convert to Buddhism. In the south, a pro-Buddhist emperor in 517 abolished Taoist temples and defrocked their priests. In one of the northern states Confucians were declared the victor in a debate in 573, and Confucianism was declared the state religion; both Taoism and Buddhism were suppressed, and their property was confiscated.

For many centuries none of these religions was successful in eliminating its rivals. Confucians held a distinctive niche as officials, reviving their fortunes whenever a centralized state expanded bureaucratic control. Beyond this Confucians were ill suited to go. In the early T'ang, on the rebound from a strongly pro-Buddhist emperor in the preceding Sui dynasty, Confucianism became institutionalized as a religion: every city had its state-supported Confucian or "literary" temple, including a school; Confucius and his seventy-two disciples were represented by images and received sacrifices. But these Confucian temples had no priests, and were guarded by local scholars and officials who never competed seriously with Buddhism for popular support. Conversely, occasional Taoist and Buddhist intrusions into government administration came to nothing. Buddhist theocracy under the empress Wu and her successor flourished briefly between 690 and 710; the next emperor, reversing course, built Taoist temples in all cities, and required all nobles families to have a copy of the *Tao Te Ching*. In 741 Taoist works were made official classics, an alternate basis of civil service examinations alongside the Confucian texts; but this policy lapsed with the crisis of the empire in 755 (Needham, 1956: 31–32; Welch, 1965: 153; Cleary, 1986: xii; *CHC,* 1979: 411–412).

None of these attempts to usurp the power of rival religions lasted long enough to be effective through the shifts of political faction and dynastic change. The intermittent pattern of Buddhist persecution is reminiscent of the growth of Christianity in the Roman Empire. Occasional massive persecutions broke out when the insurgent organization was becoming threateningly large. The north China persecution of 574–577, just before the unifying Sui dynasty (589–618) shifted favor to Buddhism, is reminiscent of the great persecution of Christianity in 303–311, just before Constantine shifted imperial favor to Christianity in 313. Revived Buddhist growth preceded the great persecution of 845. The large-scale confiscations of property were virtually a matter of taxation policy, allowing the monasteries breathing space to recover before being put once again under material contribution. Hard-pressed rulers often were motivated less by ideological fervor than by fiscal demands for the gold and jeweled statues of the temples which represented much of the movable wealth of the realm.

Conflict is the driving force of intellectual change, but in these cases nothing was created on the level of abstract philosophy. Argument between Taoists and Buddhists remained at a very low level: Taoists claimed that Lao Tzu had gone to the West (i.e., to India) in his old age and converted the barbarians, who misinterpreted his doctrine as Buddhism; Buddhists in turn replied that Lao Tzu was only a disciple of the Buddha (Demiéville, 1986: 862–864; Welch, 1965: 151–155). Confucianism took no intellectual stimulation from its conflicts with Buddhism and Taoism: Confucians merely accused their rivals of neglecting family and state duties by their monastic behavior, or ridiculed meditation as "sitting like a blockhead." Until the Neo-Confucian movement emerged in the Sung dynasty, medieval Confucianism took the side of rationalism and secularism by its opposition to religious opponents. The debates which took place among the three religions occurred in the external arena, typically at court before a public of politicians weighing power shifts and economic interests, not intellectual matters. Lacking insulation for the autonomy of pure intellectual struggle, the interreligious conflicts remained on the particularistic level.

Creative Philosophies in Chinese Buddhism

This inner autonomy emerged only within the Buddhist camp. Abstract philosophy developed in the big Buddhist monasteries, typically those at the

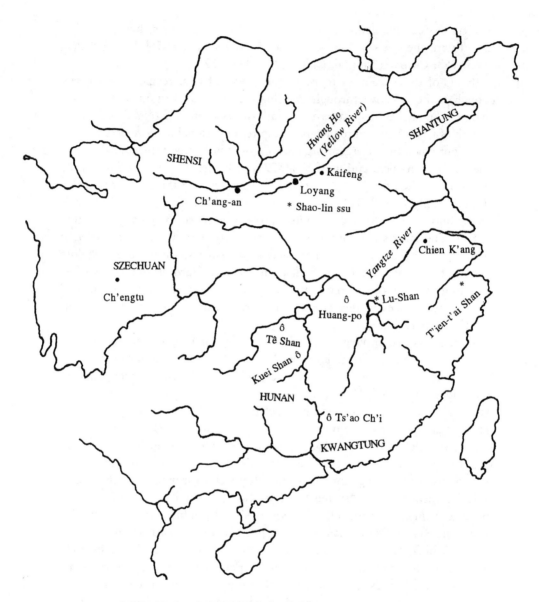

PRINCIPAL CHINESE BUDDHIST MONASTERIES
* = Buddhist monastery
ô = Ch'an (Zen) monastery

capital under court patronage, but also in a few large, well-endowed mountain centers. For centuries the core of the Buddhist community supported networks of intellectuals with considerable autonomy for their internal maneuvers. Decentralized bases allowed rival sects and distinctive identities. What transmuted this rivalry into intellectual creativity in the realm of philosophical abstraction was the unifying focus of a few organizational centers where the networks of leading monks crossed. The great translation centers at Loyang in the Toba dynasty and again during the T'ang at Ch'ang-an along with its Hua-yen temple; the famous monasteries at Lu-shan and Mount T'ien-t'ai in the south, and Shao-lin ssu in the north near Loyang: open to all comers, these places focused intellectual capital and generated debate. Multiple factions intersected at a few centers of attention.[3]

By around 500 C.E., the lineages of Buddhist philosophers in China were about six generations deep. They had already split into a number of factions: the Madhyamika–Three Treatise school, several Pure Land sects, the Sautrantika school, apparently also a lineage specializing in meditation (Ch'an, but without the antinomian qualities that later became the "Zen-like" trademark of this school). In the 500s came several new waves of popular Buddhism, including Amidaism. Buddhism was fanning out to fill a broad doctrinal and intellectual space. These positions had all been imported from India or modified from Indian doctrines. So far there was no Chinese philosophical creativity in its own right, as imports filled all the niches of intellectual space. The great translator Kumarajiva indiscriminately imported rival positions, both Nagarjuna's dialectical negation and the Sautrantika philosophy of world elements. Even so, the network structure that we see in Figure 6.1 for these generations has the familiar shape: chains from one outstanding leader to another, and the simultaneous appearance of opposing positions. For all his lack of originality, Kumarajiva served structurally as an energy node; his translation school at Ch'ang-an became a center of attraction, and out of it proceeded the founders of a variety of important positions and new monastic centers.

Under the law of small numbers, the intellectual field was now becoming crowded. By 600 appeared creative developments driven by the internal structure of Chinese philosophy. The first great development of Chinese Buddhist philosophy, T'ien-t'ai, was a synthesis bringing order into the array of Buddhist schools. Imports were no longer substituting for indigenous creativity. When Hsüan-tsang returned from India in 645 he received popular honor, but his imported Yogacara doctrine did not dominate the attention space; instead, within his own circle of translators an opposing doctrine was stimulated in response to the challenge of Indian sophistication, Hua-yen metaphysics. A few generations later came what I will call the Ch'an (or Zen) revolution, in response to a crisis in the material basis of the intellectual field.

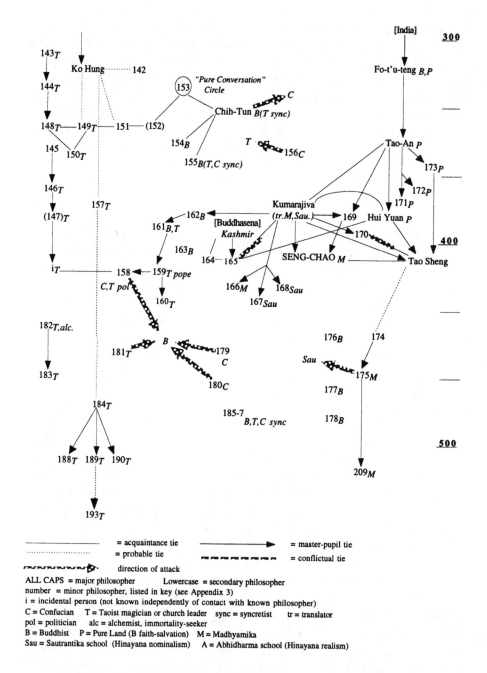

= acquaintance tie   ———————▶ = master-pupil tie

········· = probable tie   ▬ ▬ ▬ ▬ ▬ = conflictual tie

🔺🔺🔺▶ direction of attack

ALL CAPS = major philosopher   Lowercase = secondary philosopher

number = minor philosopher, listed in key (see Appendix 3)

i = incidental person (not known independently of contact with known philosopher)

C = Confucian   T = Taoist magician or church leader   sync = syncretist   tr = translator

pol = politician   alc = alchemist, immortality-seeker

B = Buddhist   P = Pure Land (B faith-salvation)   M = Madhyamika

Sau = Sautrantika school (Hinayana nominalism)   A = Abhidharma school (Hinayana realism)

FIGURE 6.1. TAOIST CHURCH AND IMPORTED BUDDHIST
SCHOOLS, 300–500

The T'ien-t'ai Hierarchy

The official organizer of T'ien-t'ai was Chih-I (538–597), who established the great Mount T'ien-t'ai monastery in Chekiang in 577, using revenues from an entire district given him by the southern emperor (Takakusu, [1956] 1973: 126–141; Ch'en, 1964: 303–313; Fung, 1952–53: 360–383). Much of the philosophical basis of the doctrine derived from his lineage of teachers, Hui-wen (ca. 550) and Hui-ssu (515–577), who had attacked the worldliness and corruption of the monks in the northern capital and striven to raise the intellectual and meditative traditions of Buddhism above magical, lay-oriented doctrines. Chih-I's synthesis introduced an order into the proliferation of Buddhist texts, classifying them into levels of partial truths appropriate for teaching persons at successive stages of intellectual and spiritual development. All existing schools, Hinayana and Mahayana alike, were interpreted as a series of preliminary studies leading up to the crowning T'ien-t'ai doctrine. Possibly the sequence was actually followed as a curriculum of education in the T'ien-t'ai sect. From this time on, the great T'ien-t'ai monastery became a center for intellectuals of all Buddhist factions; it was from here above all that Buddhist philosophy was exported to Japan.

The T'ien-t'ai worldview built on Indian doctrines, such as the Nirvana sutra school, which had reified the symbolism of the scriptures (dharma) as Buddha's earthly body into a cosmology in which the universe is literally the cosmic body of the Buddha. The Nirvana school justified this turn toward the phenomenal world by using the paradoxes of the Madhyamika school (i.e., Nagarjuna's Indian texts), which emphasized transcending all distinctions. The T'ien-t'ai masters interpreted this to mean that the transcendental level of mystical experience is identical with the phenomenal world of causality and with the realm of name. There is no noumenal world apart from phenomena; all things are void, but at the same time all exist temporarily, and these conditions interpenetrate each other.

Applying this scheme, T'ien-t'ai took the concrete categories of popular Buddhist religion, from the various kinds of Buddhas down through the gods, humans, demons, and hell; arguing (on the basis of the interpenetration of all things) that each of these categories, 10 in all, is immanent in all the others, T'ien-t'ai enumerated 100 realms. These in turn were cross-classified by 10 metaphysical categories (form, nature, substance, force, action, cause, circumstance, effect, remuneration, and the ultimate state), and again by further distinctions, yielding an architectonic system of 3,000 worlds. T'ien-t'ai managed to bring together into the same system the concrete mythology of Buddhist religion along with a set of metaphysical abstractions. It took as its explicit topic the current problem of Chinese Buddhism, the disparity between popularistic concrete and abstract philosophical doctrines. The whole took an idealist turn with the assertion that all 3,000 worlds are found everywhere: "In every particle of dust, in every moment of thought, the whole universe is contained" (Ch'en, 1964: 310). All phenomena of possible experience were revealed as categories of an absolute mind embracing the universe.

Hua-yen Metaphysics of Reflexivity

After 600 C.E. the intellectual field reorganized. T'ien-t'ai absorbed most of the earlier schools, with the exception of the Pure Land sects, which were just then undergoing their great expansion in the rural hinterlands; after this time we hear of no more developments in the Three Treatise school, Sautrantika, or independent specialists in the Nirvana sutra or the Lotus sutra. At the time of renewed struggles between Buddhism and Taoism over support of the new T'ang emperor in the 620s, the monk Hsüan-tsang secretly left China against imperial orders to make a pilgrimage to India. The situation of intellectual realignment no doubt made it seem a propitious time to import new intellectual capital. Hsüan-tsang spent 16 years (629–645) studying at the great Buddhist center at Nalanda, where he learned the sophisticated Yogacara idealism directly from the lineage of Vasubandhu and Dignaga, as well as the systematic Hinayana realism of the *Abhidharmakosha*. Like other famous importers of foreign ideas (Kumarajiva, Cicero, the medieval Arab and Christian translators), Hsüan-tsang seems to have been more concerned with the sheer quantity of materials than the tensions among them, for he brought both of these complex systems into China, setting up a bureau at the capital Ch'ang-an to translate the Indian texts.

The philosophical efforts of Hsüan-tsang and his disciple K'uei-chi (632–682) concentrated principally on the idealist side, formulating the Fa-hsiang, or "Consciousness-Only," school. Based on the work of the great Indian logicians, it was the most sophisticated level of philosophy yet seen in China, making many distinctions and arriving at high levels of abstraction. Despite Hsüan-tsang's fame, the Consciousness-Only tradition was not carried beyond his immediate followers. It has been suggested that technical philosophy of this sort was too abstract for the Chinese mind, but this begs the question why the Chinese philosophical mentality did not develop further in this direction.[4]

The weakness of the school was structural. Hsüan-tsang publicized not one but two philosophies (Consciousness-Only and Abhidharma), and antithetical ones at that, muddying rather than clarifying the intellectual field. Hsüan-tsang's philosophies were upstaged by a proliferation of new developments, and two of Hsüan-tsang's own pupils split off to create their own sects. If we defocus from the individual to the network, we see a network in transformation. Figure 6.2 shows Hsüan-tsang and his group in the midst of lateral con-

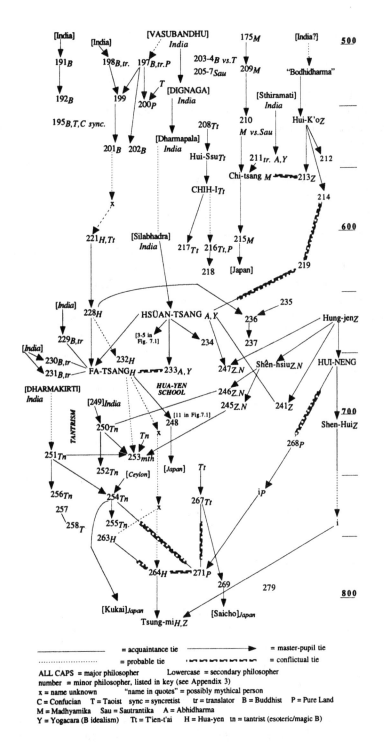

FIGURE 6.2. T'IEN-T'AI, YOGACARA, HUA-YEN, 500–800

nections with the other main developments of the mid-600s: on one side debating with and training monks from the meditation school, on the other side both propagating and debating with the emerging Hua-yen school. Hsüan-tsang's reputation is the popular fame of the central node at the moment of transition.[5]

Of greater intellectual importance was Fa-tsang (643–712), associated with Hsüan-tsang's translation bureau in his youth, who opposed the Consciousness-Only doctrine with a new system, the Hua-yen school. Fa-tsang brought together the strands of several lineages. He had intellectual ancestors from both the Pure Land and T'ien-t'ai traditions, as well as contact with several translators direct from India. As in the case of most Buddhist philosophies, Hua-yen philosophy had predecessors in the Indian scriptures, in this case the *Avatamsaka sutra,* which had received a commentary from Vasubandhu (Takakusu, [1956] 1973: 109–113). The flowery rhetoric of the sutra, praising the Buddha in extravagant metaphor, was transformed into a technical philosophy of great subtlety by a chain of Chinese masters: Fa-shun (557–640; 221 in the key to Figure 6.2), Chih-yen (600–668, 228 in the key), and above all at the systematizing hands of Fa-tsang.

The Consciousness-Only school described reality as a continually changing flow of ideas from the storehouse consciousness at the bottom of every individual mind. In contrast to this absolute idealism, the mature Hua-yen view is closer to an objectivist realism, but with a distinctive Buddhist twist. It distinguishes things as they appear from things as they really are. At the first wave of analysis, all aspects of apparent things disappear into emptiness. Things of the world exist only relative to one another, and thus do not exist independently. Things which change have no absolute existence (a parallel here to Parmenides, as well as to Kuo Hsiang's version of Dark Learning). And ideas exist only in the mind, not in reality. "Data are not themselves objects—they must depend on the mind; mind is not of itself mind—it must depend on an object" (Cleary, 1983: 24). Fa-tsang followed the path of undercutting the reality of the empirical world as if he were leading to a Platonic idealism, but then pushed the argument to undercut ideas as well.

There followed another wave of reflexivity. Transcendence is not to be made an object. Emptiness itself, the ultimate reality, interpenetrates the world of appearance; indeed it *is* nothing more than appearance, impermanence, and change. Each level mutually implies and requires the other. Phenomena could not exist if they were absolute; only their lack of inherent identity makes it possible for them to be relative and changing. In the other direction, relativity and emptiness could not exist either if there were no phenomena as medium; transience cannot exist without time. Fa-tsang solved the Parmenidean paradox not by a transcendent substance but by the lack of substance. The interdependence of metaphysical levels is the ultimate reality. Fa-tsang described this in a number of famous metaphors. Reality is a hall of mirrors endlessly reflecting one another; a circle of views through multiple gates, each in turn becoming the center; a web of jewels, each of which reflects not only the other jewels but also the reflections in each other jewel, an infinity of infinities. This last image, the famous "Indra's net," is reminiscent of Leibniz's universe of windowless but interconnected monads. Whereas Leibniz posits a "horizontal" mutual constitution of phenomenal attributes among substances of the world, the Hua-yen stresses the "vertical" mutuality of transcendence and appearance, and the ultimate reality of change.

On the phenomenal level, too, everything interpenetrates. But this comes about because the nature of everything is identically empty. The transience of any particular thing is the same as the transience of anything else. In this way the tip of a Buddha's hair (or anything else) "contains the whole universe." Hua-yen has something in common with a philosophy of continuous flux, a Heraclitean vision in which the *logos* itself is downgraded into one more item in the metaphysical net. Hua-yen is far more metaphysical than the indigenous Chinese flux philosophies, such as the *Yi Ching* Great Appendix, since Hua-yen undercuts any constituent elements other than the whole structure itself. Fa-tsang criticizes any notion of emanation. The world does not originate or flow from vacuity or nothingness, but is continuously interdependent with it. There is no emanation of the "many" from the "one"; one and many, totality and part, mutually imply each other, and cannot exist apart from each other (Cleary, 1983: 35). The cosmologies of the Sung Taoists and early Neo-Confucians, with their *T'ai chi* ("Great Ultimate") giving rise to *yin* and *yang,* and thence onward through the hexagrams and their combinations, are thin and concrete in comparison to the subtle metaphysics of Hua-yen.

Unlike Consciousness-Only, Hua-yen philosophy was extremely successful. It enjoyed precedence at court, and was strong enough to have an internal split (between 263 and 264 in Figure 6.2) in the mid-to-late 700s, spreading over the attention space at a time when most other Buddhist schools were disappearing.

The last important Hua-yen master, Tsung-mi, came five generations after Fa-tsang. By this time, the early 800s, the crumbling of T'ang government and the increasingly precarious position of court Buddhism had left only the decentralized schools, Ch'an and Pure Land, as organizationally viable. The textually oriented schools could no longer support their grand philosophical visions alone and went looking for allies. Fa-tsang had classified the Buddhist philosophies into a hierarchy, in effect a metaphysicalization of the hierarchy of positions in T'ien-t'ai classification a century earlier; indeed, Fa-tsang incorporated T'ien-t'ai as a stage, now no longer at the top, but followed by Consciousness-Only, Ch'an, and finally Hua-yen itself as the highest stage of enlightenment. Tsung-mi, broadening the synthesis even to external religious allies, added Confucianism as the first step on the philosophical-religious path. Tsung-mi's is the creativity of amalgamation in time of weakness. Having studied with Confucians, a Ch'an lineage as well as Hua-yen, he combined all the positions, downplaying Ch'an antinomianism. The Ch'an school, now becoming increasingly institutionalized, was transforming its initially anti-intellectual and anti-scriptural attitude into an intellectualism of its own; Tsung-mi's doctrines were widely adopted in the Ch'an school, and survived there after his death, when the Hua-yen succession was broken and its major texts lost.[6]

The paradox of Ch'an anti-intellectualism combining with Hua-yen intellectuality is not so great as it might seem. Both in their own ways were at the tip of a hierarchy. Hua-yen crowned the networks of philosophical lineages which had been building up in China. Its vision of the interpenetration of every level of reality was a synthesis at the highest level of reflexive awareness on the interpenetration of Buddhist doctrines. Ch'an, for all its surface anti-intellectualism, arose from a high level of intellectual reflexivity as well. The two reflexivities merged without difficulty because the level of vision was much the same.

The Ch'an (Zen) Revolution

Ch'an originally meant "meditation" (Sanskrit *dhyana*, "concentration"), which was, after all, the original basis of Buddhism. The fact that there was a specific meditation school in China, unlike in Indian Buddhism, indicates the extent to which the practice had become marginalized in the early centuries. The popular and politically influential schools, especially in the north, emphasized magic and liturgy; in the gentry-intellectual circles of the south, clever conversation largely displaced meditation (Zürcher, 1959: 33, 114, 127, 146, 180). The development of the intellectual schools, from Three Treatise to Consciousness-Only, made salvation a matter of insight, although the T'ien-t'ai and Hua-yen schools did incorporate considerable emphasis on meditation. What was distinctive about the Ch'an school in its full flowering was its emphasis on meditation as a form of life—rather than as deep trance—together with its hostility to all other forms of Buddhist practice.

This anti-intellectual and anti-ritual theme appeared only after meditation specialists had maintained a Chinese lineage for five or six generations. The Ch'an lineage is traced retrospectively back to Bodhidharma (ca. 500 C.E., possibly mythical), and a number of successors are listed. It appears that there may be a break between the alleged "third patriarch" and the fourth (213 and

220 in Figures 6.2 and 6.3); the notable lineages start only after this time (Dumoulin, 1988: 98; McRae, 1986: 30). Several things are noticeable: none of the early Ch'an masters had any of the idiosyncrasies that we have come to associate with "Zen"; and there was a tremendous proliferation of Ch'an lineages starting around 700, at the point when the school began to create its iconoclastic style.

The nature of the "Zen revolution" is best understood against the backdrop of the political situation facing Buddhism at this time. As in medieval Europe, secular stratification penetrated the church. The official temples were supported by the state and performed ceremonies connected with the imperial cult, and their leaders had de facto or even legal rank as court officials. The wealthy urban monasteries and temples were dominated by monks from the higher gentry, and the great abbots enjoyed lavish lifestyles. Especially in the leading establishments of the capital, high Buddhist figures held considerable political influence in a friendly regime. During 672–705, patronage of Buddhism reached its apex. A former concubine of the emperor T'ai Tsung, who had been for a while a Buddhist nun, became Empress Wu and then de facto ruler around 680. From 690 to 701 she ruled openly, even establishing a new dynasty. Although she was deposed and the T'ang dynasty reestablished, in 705–712 another empress and vehement supporter of Buddhism was elevated to nearly the same power. Empress Wu attempted to supplant Confucianism and make Buddhism a state religion, with herself as Caesaro-papist ruler.

With the overthrow of female rule came anti-Buddhist reaction. The new emperor Hsüan Tsung (r. 712–756) had 30,000 monks defrocked and made Taoism a near-official religion. Yet popular support was too great for Buddhism to be hurt badly; the Amidaist temples among the people and the Ch'an mountain monasteries flourished, and there were still some prominent Hua-yen preachers in the capital. After 755, the central government was too weak to enforce religious orthodoxy of any sort. A later Hua-yen master, Ch'eng-kuan, had a position of court influence from about 780 to 820, when the government was again very pro-Buddhist; Ch'eng-kuan was made National Preceptor and official supervisor of the monks of all sects in China. In the 840s, the emperor Wu Tsung wavered from Buddhism to Taoism; under the influence of a circle of Taoist alchemists, he issued a series of anti-Buddhist decrees, culminating in the great persecution of 845 confiscating virtually all Buddhist property and defrocking all monks and nuns. But the next year a new emperor called off the persecution and had the head Taoist executed.

After the failure of Empress Wu's theocracy in the 690s, Buddhism was made subject to increasing government regulation. In 747, people wishing to become monks were required to get an ordination certificate from the Bureau of National Sacrifices. In 755, during the crisis of the An Lu-shan rebellion, the practice began of selling these certificates to raise revenue. Ordination carried economic advantages such as exemption from taxation and corvée labor. The system gradually became very corrupt. Local officials began to sell ordination certificates for their own benefit; many ordinations were purely nominal (Weinstein, 1987: 59–61). During the period of disintegration after the collapse of the T'ang (900–960), entry examinations for monasteries were administered not by monks but by government officials. These exams were similar to the Confucian ones; they called for composing an essay and a commentary, plus reciting a sutra and practicing meditation. Only Ch'an escaped from these restrictions, partly because its monasteries were remote and self-sufficient, partly because Ch'an monks avoided taking full ordination except under special circumstances.

The self-identification of Ch'an as a distinctive kind of Buddhism began with a controversy over legitimate lineage succession. In the year 734 the monk Shen-hui (670–762) created a furor in the capital by declaring that the sixth head of the Ch'an lineage was not Shen-hsiu (600–706)—a popular preacher who had resided at Loyang as a favorite of the empress Wu—but Hui-neng (638–713), hitherto a relatively obscure southern monk. The attack was based on the story that the fifth patriarch Hung-jen (602–675), had secretly given the succession to Hui-neng on the basis of his having won a contest of poems. This incident, which had allegedly taken place 60 years before, was not mentioned in any other document. The controversy among the Ch'an monks of the capital raged for 20 years. In 753 Shen-hui was arrested and banished to the remote south; but two years later the government collapsed after military defeat followed by rebellion and civil war. In 757 Shen-hui was back in the capital as a popular religious leader, and was even delegated to lead a money-raising campaign for the bankrupt government by selling monastic ordination certificates.

On the surface, this looks like a quarrel over political favors at court. The "Northern school" patriarch Shen-hsiu had been intimately connected with Empress Wu's Buddhist theocracy, which had been violently deposed, and other court supporters of the Ch'an lineage at the capital fell from power in the 730s and 740s (McRae, 1986: 242); the creation of an alternative lineage was perhaps an attempt to dissociate Ch'an from unpopular political memories. More deeply, it was only the most dramatic manifestation of structural and doctrinal movements that had already been in motion for two generations.[7]

In Shen-hui's polemic, the bone of contention between the "Northern school" of Shen-hsiu and the "Southern school" of Hui-neng was the latter's defense of sudden as against gradual enlightenment. This seems to have been an exaggeration. Neither of these was an organized school until after Shen-hui's attack, and both branches shared a broad set of ideas and practices (McRae,

1986: 245). Moreover, the issue of sudden enlightenment was a long-standing one; when it was raised by Tao Sheng 300 years before, it had brought controversy but no new movement within Buddhism. The principal weakness of the "Northern school" was its location at court, where it was exposed to political vicissitudes, and diluted its meditation practice with intellectual concessions to the court literati. Neither the "Northern" nor the "Southern" faction continued long after this controversy; in Figure 6.3 we see that their connections were confined to the intellectual circles of the capital. The controversy of "Northern" and "Southern" schools was elevated retrospectively into a symbol for the larger social movement. The real "Zen revolution" was taking place among those lineages which cut themselves off from the basis of court patronage as sharply as possible.

For these radicals, the doctrine of sudden enlightenment was pushed to an extreme and given a deep organizational significance. The conventional Mahayana path to enlightenment was through a series of (usually 10) ranks of spiritual achievement, which implied considerable social stratification within the monastic community. "Enlightenment" was the test by which a monk was promoted to be head of the lineage, or to the rank of an abbot capable of heading his own monastery. To attack the doctrine of the gradual stages of enlightenment was to increase drastically the possibilities for mobility of religious status within the meditation school. This took place within a context in which the openness or restrictedness of religious status was a matter of open conflict.[8]

The radical Ch'an masters opened up elite religious mobility not with philosophical argument but in practice. They eliminated liturgy and intellectual studies, and even attacked the practice of prolonged meditation, substituting tests of dramatic and paradoxical insight. The "Zen revolution" made possible a rapid organizational growth, and at the same time legitimated decentralization of self-supporting new monasteries and lineages. Some of the famous Ch'an masters had as many as 100 enlightened disciples. The creativity associated with this process was an outburst of emotional energy flowing into an explosion of organization-building.

From the mid- and late 700s on appear the flamboyant characteristics associated with Zen. Ma-tsu (709–788) began to teach by means of paradoxical sayings, out of which came the famous contests of repartee for which the Zen quest for enlightenment came to be known. One of Ma-tsu's pupils, Huai-hai (720–814), began the practice of requiring monks to engage in manual labor. This was a sharp break with the old Buddhist custom of begging for alms, and with the prevalent Chinese Buddhist practice of living, often rather opulently, off gifts of land, serfs, and slaves from emperor or nobility. In place of the wealthy urban monasteries and lavish court circles in which

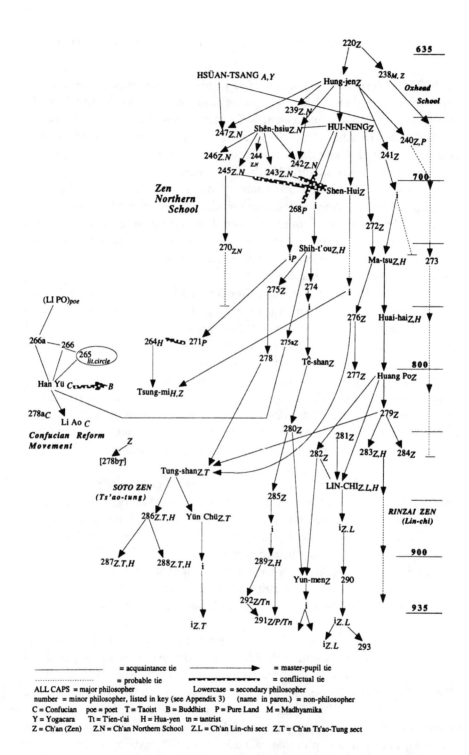

FIGURE 6.3. CASCADE OF CH'AN (ZEN) SCHOOLS, 635–935

most of the leading monks (especially the famous intellectuals) lived, radical Ch'an moved into self-supporting monasteries, usually in remote mountains (see map, page 282). This had the effect of making Ch'an monasteries relatively safe from political purges and economic confiscations, and hence contributed to the survival of Ch'an Buddhism at a time when most other Buddhist sects were failing. Ch'an was not entirely original in requiring monks to work; some rural monasteries in the pre-T'ang southern dynasties had used this method of self-support as a temporary expedient during political troubles. Within Ch'an, the obligation to work was connected to the doctrine of sudden enlightenment: ordinary physical actions—chopping wood, carrying water—could be a path to the ultimate religious status. In this respect Ch'an is something like a Protestant ethic; and its opposition to deep trance-inducing meditation reinforced its tendency to reduce barriers between the religious and secular realms. But enlightenment, sudden or not, was apparently not easy to come by; and the abbots seem to have extracted a great deal of labor out of the lower-ranking and novice monks by this incentive. The Ch'an monasteries prospered materially at the same time that their reputation grew.

In the 800s and 900s, Ch'an monasteries proliferated throughout China. This was the period of the famous masters whose doings were later to provide the study texts for Zen monks in China and Japan: Tê-shan (781–867), famous for shocking his pupils into enlightenment by hitting them with his staff; Lin-chi (d. 867), known for his sudden shouts; and a host of other witty paradoxers. This full-blown Zen was vehemently anti-intellectual and anti-liturgical; study of the scriptures was generally abjured, and a fortiori the philosophers; even the Buddhas and Boddhisattvas were regarded as obstacles to immediate enlightenment: "If you meet the Buddha, kill the Buddha!" Nevertheless, one would have to call this an intellectual's anti-intellectualism, for only on the basis of subtle understandings and the ability to express them delicately and poetically was one honored for this kind of stamping on sacred icons. Ch'an is philosophical reflexivity turned to a high level of self-consciousness. The creative conflicts which energize the intellectual attention space were here transformed into the repartee of words pointing beyond words, of gestures stripped to their capacity for pure contentless communication.

Ch'an from 650 through 900 was in the factional mode of the intellectual field. In Figures 6.2 and 6.3, we see the Ch'an lineages splitting and subsplitting, while the other Buddhist lineages are dropping out. The urban-based intellectual schools fell away. T'ien-t'ai and Hua-yen, which had absorbed all the earlier intellectual schools, managed to hang on only by syncretizing with the Ch'an or Amidaist monasteries. Amidaism too was flourishing materially, but is not represented on the network chart among significant intellectuals. A few more exotic materials were still being imported from India, but without long-lasting effects. In the early and mid-700s, tantric Buddhist masters made a showing at court with their elaborate magical and erotic ceremonies, from whence their doctrine was exported to Japan as Shingon; but tantric Buddhism never achieved either a popular or an intellectual following and disappeared with the changing tides at court around midcentury.

Ch'an had the Buddhist side of the intellectual attention space to itself for six or eight generations; indeed, in the absence of important activity from Taoists or Confucians, it dominated philosophical creativity across the board. Under the law of small numbers, the internal dynamics of Ch'an itself now produced its own contending positions to fill the attention space. There were the famous "five schools of Ch'an" during the 700s and 800s, a number which is only approximate since some successions died out, while the surviving sects split to fill their space. Some of the weaker sects at the end of their lines followed the characteristic route of syncretism: the last important figure (291 in Figure 6.3) of the weak Fa-yen sect of Ch'an attempted to syncretize Ch'an with T'ien-t'ai and Amidaism; T'ien-t'ai Te-shao (292 in Figure 6.3) syncretized the Ch'an Ts'ao-Tung sect with T'ien-t'ai. After 950, while most of the other Ch'an sects were dying out or syncretizing, the Lin-chi lineage proliferated, building new monasteries across China and in the process splitting into sub-sects, as the Ts'ao-Tung sect had done in its heyday in the 800s. It is a wonderfully symmetrical case of simultaneous growth and contraction of different parts of the field under the law of small numbers.[9]

It is sometimes argued that the distinctiveness of Ch'an comes from the influence of Taoism on Chinese Buddhism. Vaguely similar paradoxical stories center on the early "Taoist" figure Chuang Tzu, and the *Tao Te Ching* extols mystical transcendence of words. But at the time of the "Zen revolution," contemporary Taoism was a highly liturgical church, with just those elements of theistic hierarchies, magic, and immortality-seeking that were antithetical to the Ch'an style. Taoist influence is structurally unlikely as well: the expanding, materially prospering Ch'an Buddhists were making themselves as distinctive as possible, while syncretisms occurred in times of organizational weakness. There is some resemblance between the "light conversation" of the "Seven Sages of the Bamboo Grove" and the poetic repartee of the Ch'an masters. But "light conversation" displays little that is comparable to the round of ongoing spiritual jousts that took place as the Ch'an masters traveled among the monasteries, testing one another and leaving a trail of iconoclastic moves at successive levels of reflexivity. Organizationally, the "Seven Sages" lacked the monastic lineages which were so important in the growth of Ch'an. Insofar as Ch'an is similar to the "Taoism" of the gentry, it is because they share some similar social conditions. Ch'an is Buddhism adapting to a niche away from court settings and temple liturgies, based on the self-sufficiency of country estates. The difference is that the Taoist gentry owned their own property; the Ch'an monks owned theirs collectively, and hence had to pay more attention to organizational hierarchy in the legitimation of lineage masters.

After 1000, the organizational bases of Buddhism within Chinese society were undermined once again. This time the threat was not confiscation of property or political purges. Buddhist monasteries and temples in the country-side and remote mountains were no longer threats to the increasingly powerful central bureaucracy; instead, Buddhism was strangled slowly by government regulation, instituted for the most part as fiscal measures. Sale of ordination certifications was revived under the Sung dynasty in 1067. This soon gave rise to market manipulations as individuals bought certificates not for their own use but for resale, speculating on future rises in price (Ch'en, 1964: 241–244, 391–393). The long-term result was an inflationary spiral reducing the value of the certificates. The Sung government also began to raise money by selling the higher monastic ranks, and in the 1100s added a series of monastic titles to spur further purchases. The church prospered physically under this system; there were 460,000 monks and nuns in 1221, still a substantial number, if a proportional drop from the previous high of 700,000 around 830, when the population was half as large. No doubt the market for ordination certificates had an expansionary effect at the lower levels. But Buddhism died intellectually as governmental regulation set in. Only Ch'an was creative for a while, a direct consequence of its efforts to move to remote areas where it could escape government regulation.

Eventually even Ch'an creativity weakened and dried up. Externally, the religious economy of the monasteries, once so important in opening up the agrarian state–coercive structure of China, was now surpassed by a burgeoning market economy in the secular society of the Sung. The status appeal of Buddhist culture for the upper classes faded. Once members of the educated gentry or court nobility might have frequented the more intellectual or colorful Buddhist circles, or even pursued careers as abbots of the wealthier monaster-ies. Now there was a massive new pull on the cultivated classes from the expansion of a government examination system and of Confucian schools connected with it. Under declining resources, Ch'an lineages dwindled and narrowed across the intellectual space.

Even this last organizational transition had its own form of creativity. Stories of the classic paradoxes and repartees of the great Ch'an masters were now collected: *The Record of the Transmission of the Light* in 1004, *The Blue Cliff Record* in 1128, the *Wu-men Kuan* in 1229. Lineage factionalism was no longer important; old rivals assembled into a grand retrospective coalition of this movement in decline. The later Ch'an masters added successive layers of poetic commentaries and meta-commentaries. In place of the live experiences they depicted, these stories of six or eight generations past were now used as cases (Japanese: *koan*) on which students were tested. Intellectual eminence now passed to the editors, who added layers of cryptical remarks and poetic lines to koan collections. The meta-comments themselves are repetitions of the koan style, showing mastery by adding further twists, yet another panel in the hall of mirrors.

In the following excerpt, the case is the koan, an incident from one of the T'ang masters, Pai Chang (720–814); the notes are by the Sung dynasty master Hsueh Tou Ch'ung Hsien (980–1052), who originally compiled the cases *(kung an)*; the commentary is by Yüan Wu K'o Ch'in (1063–1135), who published the whole as the *Blue Cliff Record* in 1128.

Case
A monk asked Pai Chang, "What's the extraordinary affair?"[1]
Chang said: "Sitting alone on Ta Hsiung Mountain."[2]
The monk bowed;[3] Chang thereupon hit him.[4]

Notes
1. There's an echo in the words. He demonstrates his ability in a phrase. He flabbergasts people. Though this monk has eyes, he's never seen.
2. His awesome majestic air extends over the whole country. The one standing and the one sitting are both defeated.
3. A clever patchrobed monk! There still is such a man who wants to see such things.
4. Chang is a competent teacher of our school: why does he not speak much? The imperative is not carried out vainly.

Commentary
. . . This monk's bowing was not the same as ordinary bowing: he had to have eyes before he could do this. He didn't spill all his guts to others. Though they knew each other, they acted like they didn't. (*Blue Cliff Record,* 1977: 172)

The great Ch'an anti-intellectuals, advocates of extreme spontaneity, were now subjects of quasi-scholastic routine. The final burst of creative controversy within Ch'an revolved around whether to accept this final stage of intellectual practice. Ta-hui (ca. 1140) of the Lin-chi line, defending "koan-gazing Zen," fought off the polemics of Hung-chih (352 in Figure 6.4) of the Ts'ao-Tung line, who upheld "silent-illumination Zen" (Dumoulin, 1988: 256–260; Kodera, 1980: 85–101). But in the very next generation, Chu Hsi was already on the scene, and Ta-hui's disciples were most notable for their friendly discussions with Neo-Confucians—the syncretizing sign of a declining intellectual base.

Ch'an creativity disappeared into the dominance of Neo-Confucianism, and with it ended fresh intellectual developments in Chinese Buddhism.

The Neo-Confucian Revival

The wave of philosophical creativity that made up Neo-Confucianism fits the classic pattern of reciprocal expansion and decline under the law of small numbers. In the network of Figure 6.4, we see Buddhist philosophy declining and syncretizing, while the Confucians expand and subdivide into contending factions. The apex is Chu Hsi's grand synthesis, bringing together the factions into a dominant Neo-Confucianism, in counterpoint with a new metaphysical idealism. Neo-Confucianism was known to its contemporaries as "Tao-hsüeh," the Tao-learning, implying that it was appropriating (or reappropriating) concepts circulating in the Taoist world, and which had been out of style in orthodox Confucianism. Neo-Confucianism was in part a religious movement, which took over cultural capital both from Taoism and from Ch'an Buddhism.

Religious territories were realigning as part of an organizational transformation in the basis of intellectual life. This is what underlies the historical moment of philosophical creativity. Neo-Confucianism broke out at just the time of major political upheaval. The Sung dynasty drastically expanded the size and intensity of government bureaucracy and the examination system for selecting officials. Rudiments of the examination system had existed before, but the Sung was the first to be truly a scholars' government. It was also a period of massive economic growth, the takeoff of a market economy freed from government control. The resulting situation of population displacement, financial inflation, and government fiscal crisis led to the emergence of party politics and ideologies. The height of the party struggle, the famous Wang An-shih reforms, coincided with the generation that crystallized a Neo-Confucian philosophy. Moreover, this period was a high point of the natural sciences in Chinese history, as well as a time of creativity in poetry.

The Neo-Confucian movement was directly connected to all these networks, generally in opposition: to the expanding examination system, to the Wang An-shih reforms, and to the poets. Neo-Confucianism was in large measure a reactionary movement; its creative energy in philosophy came from its oppositional stance in the political conflicts of the time. In some respects the Neo-Confucians were radical innovators: in overturning the traditional Confucian stance on religion, as well as in their participation in the scientific empiricism of the time. The creativity of Neo-Confucian philosophy was a process of maneuvering in the cultural space opened up through the multi-sided institutional transformations of Sung society. Let us examine its components in turn.

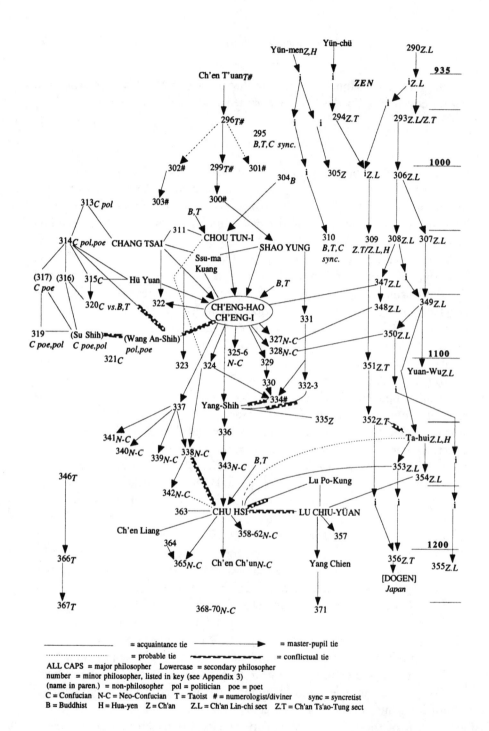

FIGURE 6.4. NEO-CONFUCIAN MOVEMENT AND THE
WINNOWING OF ZEN, 935–1265

Political Struggle and the Wang An-shih Economic Reforms

The Sung dynasty was experiencing a takeoff of economic growth, making it the most productive economy thus far in the history of the world. Along with this prosperity came financial and military strains. Sung government income peaked in 1021, then declined into chronic revenue crisis; inflation and polarization of wealth produced a sense of upheaval that had become acute by the 1060s. Wang An-shih (1021–1086) proposed radical reforms, including price controls, new taxes aimed at the large landlords, and low-cost credit for small farmers. His reforms were supported by the young emperor Shen Tsung during his reign (1068–1085); Wang served as prime minister from 1069 to 1076, during which time he reformed the exam system to include engineering and science subjects instead of the literary classics. But there was considerable opposition even under Emperor Shen Tsung, and in 1086 Ssu-ma Kuang became prime minister in a new regime that undid the reforms.

The Neo-Confucian movement as a whole constituted one of three interconnected groups whose struggles made up the politics of the mid-Sung dynasty. Despite doctrinal disagreements among themselves, the Ch'eng brothers and their friends and teachers Chou Tun-I, Shao Yung, and Chang Tsai were united in opposition to the economic reform movement. Ssu-ma Kuang (1019–1086), himself a major scholar and historian, was the friend of both Shao Yung and Chang Tsai and patron of the Ch'eng brothers; he was the most important political leader of the anti-reform group.

In a second camp were followers of the reformer Wang An-shih. His political and economic movement also had an intellectual side—not surprising in a period when the examination system administered by scholars had become the most important route to high office. Wang An-shih, himself a poet and scholar, led a group of scholars in revising the Confucian classics to justify state controls.

A third group comprised orthodox Confucians who defended literary and textual scholarship against Neo-Confucian religiousness as well as against the economic reformers. This orthodox faction also had its significant network: in Figure 6.4 we see the chains around the notable scholars Fan Chung-yen (313) and Ouyang Hsiu (314), as well as Hü Yuan (the orthodox teacher of the Ch'eng brothers) and Sun Fu (315). In the earlier years of the century, they had been the reforming faction within Sung politics (Liu, 1967). Wang An-shih, a protégé of Ouyang Hsiu, carried the reform movement in a more radical direction at a time when the older generation were pulling back, exalting literary cultivation as a standard of gentility which they expected to provide social leadership. Toward the latter part of the century, the leadership of the conservative clique was taken over by a family of noted poets, headed by Su

Hsun (317) and his son Su Shih (1036–1101), one of the most famous of all Chinese poets—and, despite political enmity, a literary friend of Wang An-shih.

The Neo-Confucians carried out a two-pronged fight against both wings. Ch'eng I was an uncompromising moralist and struck out against literary Confucianism. Chou Tun-I too had declared, "Those who engage in purely literary expressions are vulgar people" (Chan, 1963: 478). To carry out an anti-literary reform of the examination system was to strike at the status culture of the mainline Confucians; opposition from the orthodox side dogged the Neo-Confucians for generations, down to the time of Chu Hsi.

The careers of the core Neo-Confucians were tied up with the struggle against Wang An-shih. Ch'eng Hao was demoted in 1070 for opposing the new reforms, and again 10 years later after he had made his way back into favor; Ch'eng I held himself remote from official position during the Wang An-shih period. Chang Tsai and Chou Tun-I resigned from the government at the beginning of the reforms, and advocated counter-reforms such as a return to the archaic land tenure arrangements of the ancient texts. In contrast to Wang An-shih's utilitarian policies, the Neo-Confucians declared that reform must be moral and ceremonial. "To hope for perfect government without restoring ancient and changing modern music is to be far off the mark" (Chan, 1963: 473): this was a characteristic utterance of Chou Tun-I.

The Wang An-shih reformers held power only briefly, but the struggle of factions went on for some time. Ch'eng I became director of education (1087) in the regime following the reforming emperor's death, but was twice dismissed from office, banished, and had his teaching prohibited, as well as being twice pardoned and returned to office before his death in 1106. The Wang An-shih group briefly recaptured power at the turn of the century, while the orthodox Confucians around Su Shih fought for their version of hegemony. Still other changes in direction were instituted after 1100 by Hui-tsung, an artist-emperor who was hostile to the moralistic and anti-literary Neo-Confucians as well as to the economic reformers. None of these maneuverings improved the financial weakness of the government; crumbling militarily, the Sung was forced to move south in 1127 when north China was overrun by the tribal Jürchen kingdom.

The Examination System and the Growth of Schooling

The Sung emperors were committed to a policy of civilian control, and built up the formal examination system as a device to keep government free of military dominance. As the gentry class competed over educational qualifications, the size and elaborateness of the examination system developed enormously. In the T'ang there was one examination, open to candidates recommended by prefectural officials or to students at the schools in the capital for relatives of officials (Chaffee, 1985: 15–23). These and other preferential paths for families already in the elite remained and even expanded in the Sung; but a sequence of more openly competitive examinations developed alongside them. The most important route went from local prefectural examinations (conferring the degree of *chü-jen*) to the metropolitan examinations, from whose graduates *(chin-shih)* officials were selected.

Competitiveness also accelerated drastically, with the first big crunch coinciding with the Neo-Confucian movement. The system had begun to expand early in the Sung. Between 977 and 992, the number of candidates for the metropolitan examination grew from 5,000 to 17,000. At the prefectural qualifying examinations, there were between 20,000 and 30,000 candidates in the early decades after 1000 C.E., and 80,000 around 1100, burgeoning to 400,000 near the end of the dynasty around 1250 (Chaffee, 1985: 35–36, 50–53). At the end of the funnel, however, the numbers of *chin-shih* who were recruited in each round of examinations averaged fewer than 200 (Chaffee, 1985: 16). Quotas were set for the lower examination as well, and these became increasingly restrictive. In the years between 1005 and 1026, 40 to 50 percent of candidates were awarded the *chü-jen* degree; but this figure began to drop sharply in the 1030s and 1040s, falling to 10 percent in 1066. This was the period when the early Neo-Confucian movement was forming, as well as the time of various reform movements, leading right up to the Wang An-shih reforms in 1069. Reforms increased competitiveness still further; by the Southern Sung, ratios had fallen another quantum leap, to 1 in 100 in 1156 and 1 in 200 in 1275. This enormous competitiveness was to continue in the Ming and Ch'ing dynasties, making preparation for repeated examinations virtually a lifetime pursuit of the gentry class.

Gentry politics and social organization came to center increasingly on issues of access to education or alternate routes to office. There were struggles over the content of the examinations; various factions of "reformers" pushed for emphasis on the Confucian classics, poetic style, relevance to governmental policy, or specialized subjects such as technical and scientific fields. Within this struggle, the Neo-Confucians tended to take an extreme position: they were opposed to the examination system per se as a method of selecting officials, since its formal, anonymous procedures and its emphasis on written scholarship ruled out the selection of men on the basis of their demonstrated moral qualities such as loyalty and filial piety. Chang Tsai advocated instead recruitment from the kin of illustrious families as a method of applying Confucian values. The Neo-Confucians represent a split in the Confucian ranks, dividing those who emphasized their qualifications as literati from those stressing the moral content of their familistic ideology.

Nevertheless, all these factions depended on the changes in the organization of intellectual life brought about by the expansion of examinations. For the most part, gentry prepared for the competitions by private study. With growing competitiveness, large numbers of scholars who had not passed the final examination or who were out of office because of politics were becoming available as private teachers. There was a large increase in the number of schools, including those established in local Confucian temples, as well as Buddhist schools and the private academies of well-known scholars. Famous scholar-officials continued to teach personal disciples while in their official posts. Some schools were official, notably the Imperial University and other schools in the capital such as the Directory of Education; initially for sons of officials, they began to be opened to others in the 1040s (Chaffee, 1985: 30, 73–80). Local government schools were also promoted, with the height of school-building during 1020–1060—again, the early takeoff point for the Neo-Confucian movement.

During 1100–1120 yet another twist of factional reforms brought a radical effort to replace the examination system with a hierarchy of government schools. These comprised primary, county, and prefectural schools, each divided into three grades; promotion from rung to rung in this ladder was based on internal examinations, leading finally to selection for the Imperial University and thence to the *chin-shih* degree for officials. This system attempted to combine the supervision of moral character with academic testing. Its policy was a compromise among the different factional positions. But it was administered in a spirit of hostility to most of them, especially to the Neo-Confucians; "unorthodox" books and ideas were banned and private schools prohibited. These government schools enrolled 200,000 students. The expense of supplying them with room and board brought the system to an end in 1121. Subsequently, private and locally controlled education was again dominant.

The Neo-Confucians, as well as most of the various "reform" factions, were typically based on careers in one or another portion of these educational organizations. Chang Tsai and Shao Yung had their own schools, which were carried on after their deaths by disciples. Ch'eng I, despite his qualification for office, nevertheless spent most of his life as a private teacher. In the Southern Sung, Chu Hsi had his famous White Deer Hollow Academy in the middle Yangtze valley; his rival Lu Chiu-Yüan was a professor at the national university, but visited the private academies for debates. Neo-Confucians declared that education should occur not merely for the utilitarian purpose of passing the examinations but for moral development. But though they often preached holding oneself aloof from examinations, most of the Neo-Confucian leaders had passed the *chin-shih* degree; they were recruited from the elite of the educational competition, not from its failures. Their theme arose by opposition to prevailing conditions in the literati class. Materially the very existence of their schools depended on the intensified demand. Organizational expansion of the means of intellectual production created the conditions under which autonomous intellectual networks could take off.

Doubtless these same conditions were involved in the upsurge of many other forms of cultural innovation during these centuries. The Sung dynasty experienced a sudden outpouring of work in science, archaeology, and mathematics (Needham, 1956: 493–495; 1959: 38–51). Beginning around 1030 and continuing into the 1300s, there was a stream of scientists producing research and reasoned compilations in biology, astronomy, fossil records, medicine, agriculture, and mathematics, as well as critical historical scholars who attacked apocryphal books and established careful editions of old records. All the contending factions of Sung political-intellectual life seem to have been involved in this scientific and rational-scholarly movement. Although Neo-Confucian politics was archaizing, and the movement's religious wings bordered on the mystical, nevertheless many of its leaders supported empirical science. Ssu-ma Kuang, the minister who undid the Wang An-shih reforms which had put science into the examinations, was himself a historical scholar, he agreed with the slogan of Ch'eng I that knowledge derives from the investigation of things: "Every blade of grass possesses principle and should be examined." This ambiguous statement might be taken as advocacy of scientific induction, or as a doctrine of knowledge as a flash of insight resulting from Buddhist-like meditation. Chu Hsi, who promoted both empirical science (especially geology) and spiritual exercises, shows a similar combination.

The Neo-Confucian movement drew on diverse cultural capitals; its long-term success came from working out a synthesis that appealed to various intellectual and career interests within the gentry class. Its opposition to the examination system was not to last, and eventually its own works took over the curriculum. But the initial opposition was crucial for shaping its innovations. At a time when the examination system was in flux and contending factions disputed its content, Neo-Confucianism outflanked the narrower positions by uniting key elements of the scholarly world with some of the main appeals of the non-Confucian religions.

The Decline of Elite Buddhism and Taoism

To understand why the Neo-Confucians were philosophically creative and not merely reactionary, we must see them as appropriating a religious space that became open at this time. Colonization of this niche distinguished them from other movements among the gentry on both the reform and conservative sides. They remained Confucians by adhering to their core strategy, the claim by literati on government positions; within this stance, the Neo-Confucians reshaped the content of literati culture. The traditional ritualism and particularistic deities whose worship the Confucians supported as forms but not as beliefs had fallen into low repute among the Sung gentry (Gernet, 1962). Ch'an Buddhism, which once had considerable prestige in this social class, was declining institutionally. The elite monasteries had suffered from confiscation and government regulation; the Buddhism that survived was primarily a popular religion supported by the lower classes.

Reverting to the policy of weakness, some of the last Buddhists of any intellectual note developed syncretisms with Taoism and Confucianism (see, in Figure 6.4, 295 and notably 310, the last representative of a failing Ch'an lineage). On their side Taoism moved closer to Buddhism. No longer were they instigating persecution and confiscation against Buddhist rivals. During the Sung, popular Taoism underwent several reform movements; one sect claimed to be a synthesis of "the three doctrines," although it was most similar to Buddhism in its stress on ascetic control over desires and especially sexuality, to ensure rebirth in heaven among the Immortals (Gernet, 1962: 214–215; Welch, 1965: 145–148). Another Taoist reform sect allowed priests to marry and to live without monasteries. Taoist priesthood became a hereditary status, carried along by practitioners of ordinary petty occupations, supplemented by making and selling talismans and performing magic.

After Neo-Confucianism emerged, Taoism was abandoned by the upper class. Its popular divinities overlapped increasingly with those of the Buddhists; eventually Taoist monks were welcomed in Buddhist monasteries and vice versa (Welch, 1965: 146, 156–157). This was a syncretism of weakness at a time when the political fortunes of both religions had sunk. By the Ming, the once contentious Buddhist sects had amalgamated into a common set of doctrines and practices, combining a version of Ch'an meditation with the *nembutsu* invocations of the Amidaists (Dumoulin, 1988: 286). As sophisticated intellectuals comparable to the educated gentry disappeared among the Buddhists and Taoists, the dominant Neo-Confucians were scornful of popular religion.

The collapse of elite Buddhism and Taoism left their intellectual capital up for grabs. Those conservative Confucians who moved into this open space became the "Neo-Confucian" movement. Their successful tactic was to borrow elements of occultism and spiritual cultivation from Taoists and Buddhists while tying it to the core gentry concern for official careers. The official was redefined as the sage, and sagehood as the Confucian equivalent of Buddhist enlightenment.

The Struggle for a Neo-Confucian Religion

Sung Neo-Confucianism was created by men who connected personally with Taoist and Buddhist philosophers while criticizing and modifying their doctrines. Shao Yung developed his cosmology from a chain of Taoist numerologists, interpreters of diagrams based on the *Yi Ching,* going back to the Taoist Ch'en T'uan around 950. Chou Tun-I had studied with various Buddhists and Taoists, including five Ch'an masters, although none of these were significant enough to appear in our lineage charts (Dumoulin, 1988: 268). The Ch'eng brothers were students of both Shao Yung and Chou Tun-I, and Ch'eng Hao followed up by seeking out Buddhist and Taoist teachers for a number of years before he and his brother formulated their own position. The doctrinal connection to Taoism was so close that the works of Shao Yung, Chou Tun-I, and Liu Mu (303 in Figure 6.4, another offshoot of the Ch'en Tu'an lineage which led up to Chou Tun-I) ended up being included in later centuries in the Taoist collection (Graham, 1958: 159). Later generations of neo-Confucians continued their religious contacts. Ch'eng I carried on an interchange with a member of the Lin-Chi Ch'an lineage, as did several of his immediate disciples (see 347, 348, 327, and 328 in Figure 6.4; also in the next generation the connection of 335 to the leading disciple of the Ch'eng brothers, Yang Shih). Still later Chu Hsi studied with Buddhists and Taoists, and in his maturity contacted important Ch'an masters, including their last famous figure, Ta-hui, while Chu Hsi's rival Lu Chiu-Yüan also had contacts in the same Ch'an lineage (354).

How to relate to this Buddhist and Taoist material was the point of contention which generated the creativity within Neo-Confucianism. Shao Yung attacked the heaven cult of orthodox Confucian religion. His cosmology was a form of occult divination, based on a new interpretation of the *Yi Ching* hexagrams, rearranging them into an evolutionary sequence. He laid the groundwork for a new cosmology, declaring that mind, tranquil and enlightened, is the Great Ultimate at the basis of the physical universe (Chan, 1963: 493); on the material level, the cosmos is governed by numerical progressions and goes through great cycles of creation and destruction, rather like Buddhist *kalpas.* Shao Yung's reputation was primarily as a prophet, and his followers constituted a school separate from the emerging main line of Neo-Confucians. Polemical battles were fought between these camps at the time of Yang Shih (the early 1100s).

Another faction contending for religious reform, though less well organized as a lineage, was that of Chou Tun-I, who advocated as instruments of government divinations by the *Yi Ching* hexagrams and by evocation of spirits. His technical philosophy took the form of a Taoist-like diagram describing cosmic evolution as a series of emanations from the Supreme Ultimate *(T'ai Chi),* through *yin* and *yang,* to the Five Agents, the hexagrams of the *Yi Ching,* and finally to man as a spiritual being. Chou Tun-I's position is a syncretism of all the various divination schools. He was retrospectively elevated among the five great founders, but his works were little known in the 1000s. The Ch'eng brothers, who had studied with him before going on to Buddhist and

Taoist masters, rarely referred to him substantively, and called him disparagingly (and somewhat inaccurately) "poor Zen brother." Chou Tun-I's branch of occultist cosmology, centered on the Supreme Ultimate, was quite different from the more rationalist position of the Ch'eng brothers, based on *li* (principle) and lacking the diagrams which were so central to Chou Tun-I (Graham, 1958: 160–166; Chang, 1957–1962).

In addition to the two occultist wings represented by Shao Yung and Chou Tun-I, there was a third lineage of Chang Tsai and his followers. He too developed a cosmology based on the *Yi Ching* appendices. But Chang Tsai moved farther away from occultism, rejecting spirits of the dead and giving a more naturalistic interpretation of the universe. He identified the Supreme Ultimate with *ch'i*, (matter/energy), which produces all things by different states of dispersion and condensation. This enabled him to dismiss Buddhist void and Taoist non-being as a mistaken view of *ch'i* in a state of extreme dispersion. Chang Tsai's own religious theme came in the form of pantheism: since *ch'i* is everywhere, it makes up one's own mind and body, which are akin to the rest of the universe. He extended Confucian universal love from humanity to the entire universe, and implied that human sincerity upholds the natural as well as the social order. At the same time, since *ch'i* is everywhere, one is mistaken in trying to escape from the world, as the Buddhists do; the sage simply lives a normal life, attuned to the universe. Chang Tsai carved out a stance combining religious sensitivity with a rationalist philosophy; he attacked both the occultists and the archaizing of the orthodox Confucians. It was probably Chang Tsai who began the Neo-Confucian practice of meditation aimed at the goal of attaining "sagehood," which the Neo-Confucians carefully distinguished from Buddhism and Taoism by interpreting the result not as a state of self-absorption or immortality-seeking but as an ethical condition.

The Ch'eng brothers were personally connected with all three of these intellectual factions, and they made the most abstract philosophical advances and had the most successful lineage of followers. They were quite selective in which predecessors they endorsed. They avoided mentioning the ideas of Chou Tun-I, though he was their neighbor and friend, and never referred to the Supreme Ultimate; conversely, Chou Tun-I never used the Ch'engs' favorite concept, *li,* or principle (Graham, 1958: 158). The Ch'engs also militantly criticized all Confucians since Mencius, rejecting alike Tung Chung-shu's occultism, Yang Hsiung's naturalism, and even Han Yü's effort to create a Confucian sage religion during the late T'ang. The Ch'engs alone claimed to be restoring the ancient sage wisdom. They rejected contemporary occultism as well, and especially disliked the *Yi Ching* and its appendices as mystical speculation (Graham, 1958: 143, 162). Among their contemporaries the only ones they praised as not "deluded by false doctrines" were Shao Yung, their uncle Chang Tsai, and the scientist-statesman Ssu-ma Kuang. The Ch'eng brothers' contacts, even with the positions they rejected, shaped their creativity by opposition. It was because of their central position amidst the antagonisms and opportunities of the field that they came to forge the most successful philosophy.

Ch'eng Hao gave an especially moralistic emphasis to his philosophy, tending to anthropomorphize nature as having a mind, and animated by the basic Confucian virtue of *jen,* humanity. His main philosophical contribution was to add another level of abstraction besides *ch'i,* the basic substance: there is also *li,* principle, which underlies both natural and moral phenomena. Ch'eng I, the most original thinker of the group, developed a cosmological model in which new *ch'i* is continuously created as old *ch'i* is burned up: "The universe is a vast furnace." Physical and mental are aspects of the same thing, while abstract principle *(li)* governs the whole. "A thing is an event. If the principles underlying the event are investigated to the utmost, then all principles will be understood." "Principle is one but its manifestations are many."

Graham (1958: xix) calls Ch'eng I "the greatest Confucian thinker of the last two thousand years." If we are concerned with the higher levels of abstract philosophy, we could extend this judgment all the way back to the beginning. The Chinese themselves made a cult of the pre-Han thinkers, and cast themselves in the role of mere commentators. Modern historians have been willing to see later Confucians as nothing but footnotes to a fixed body of ideas. In reality, Confucius, Mencius, and Chuang Tzu are not in the same league with the later philosophers at constructing sophisticated arguments for clearly recognized metaphysical conceptions. Long cumulation across intellectual generations opens new realms of creativity which are beyond the purview of early generations.

Test Case: An Abortive Confucian Sage Religion in the Late T'ang

If the sociological explanation of Sung Neo-Confucianism is correct, similar conditions should have been involved in an episode in the late T'ang in which a similar doctrine appeared. Sung Neo-Confucianism developed among the factions contending for political control in a government dominated by scholars. The expanding examination system provided the material basis for intellectual movements as burgeoning numbers of students opened up careers for teachers and led to the founding of numerous private schools. Competition became severe for the small number of government positions at the end of the educational sequence, building up dissatisfaction and fostering proposals for curricular reform. Educational factions split over revising, reinterpreting, or replacing the classics on which the examinations were based, and over the issue of utilitarian versus literary cultivation. The lines of these scholarly networks that became Neo-Confucianism consisted of those rebelling against the status quo in the name of traditional Confucian appeals to the moral superiority of the classic past. This could be given a novel philosophical content by appropriating from the Buddhists the religious ideal of the enlightened sage, an option that was structurally available because the social base of Buddhism was crumbling.

The same conditions—political struggle rooted in reformers of the examination system, together with Confucian traditionalists appropriating Buddhist religious space—had appeared in the late T'ang but with different intensities. Han Yü and Li Ao, both T'ang officials and professors at the national university, around 800–820 had ineffectually attacked government support of Buddhism, especially its ritual displays of magic. At the same time they borrowed elements of Buddhist philosophy, claiming that Confucianism gave a transcendent cosmological vision as well as rules of social conduct. In imitation of the Buddhist lineages, Han Yü and Li Ao invented a transmission of an inner Confucian truth from the mythical sages Yao and Shun through the duke of Chou, Confucius, and Mencius. Thereafter, they claimed, the transmission was interrupted by the mundane Confucianism of Hsün Tzu and Yang Hsiung, until Han Yü himself restored the lineage.[10] Li Ao claimed that he had personally recovered the key insight, apparently a Buddhist-style meditative experience revealing the nature of the universe. This stance of opposing Buddhism while borrowing from it in order to set up a rival Confucian cosmology and mysticism is structurally parallel to the Neo-Confucian movement seven or eight generations later.

There are a number of similarities in background conditions. The later T'ang was undergoing a period of political and economic reconstruction after the severe disruptions of the An Lu-shan rebellion and civil war during 755–762. In addition to the usual power struggles of military governors and palace eunuchs, scholar-officials were active in proposing ideologically oriented reforms (Pulleyblank, 1960). There was an archaizing faction attempting to bring back the arrangements of the ancient Chou dynasty, and a reform party which wished to dispense with tradition and streamline administration of the economy and tax system. The former resembles the archaizing pronouncements of the Sung Neo-Confucians, while the latter is a forerunner of the Wang An-shih reformers. The political movements were connected to intellectual groupings among the scholars. Most notable among these were the *ku-wen* movement in literary style, which rejected current formalisms and returned to the simpler prose of classical times, and a critical movement which demystified the classical texts by putting them in their historical context and rejected them as guides to current policy.

These scholarly movements were rooted in the increasing focus on formal civil service examinations. From beginnings early in the dynasty, these had first become important around 700; although the size of the examination system was small compared to the Sung, by the late 700s it had become an important route for recruiting high-ranking officials, and there were large numbers of unsuccessful degree candidates (Pulleybank, 1960: 104; *CHC*, 1979: 179, 213–215, 274–277, 329–330). There were similar criticisms and struggles as in the Sung: some wanted expansion of the system to ease the competitiveness; others criticized the inflexibility of examination-based recruitment and the remoteness of its cultural content from current reality.

Han Yü was in the midst of the networks linking all of these factions. His ideological predecessors were the *ku-wen* literary reformers, whose classical emphasis Han Yü expressed as a Confucian ideal of moral regeneration through the return to tradition. Some of his colleagues in the *ku-wen* movement had already expressed the idea of an esoteric Confucian lineage of sages, and Han Yü may be the only figure who reaped public fame from the ideas of the group (Pulleybank, 1960: 97, 112). Han Yü's special advantage was his wide connections to the most creative poets and writers of the time. His father was allied with one of the most famous poets in Chinese history, Li Po (699–762); his older brother was connected to the founders of the *ku-wen* movement. Han Yü himself became a notable poet, participating in a network of other important poets, and acquired the stature of one of the classic prose stylists.

The various reform movements came to a head around the turn of the century. The literary reformers were allied for a time with the political and economic reformers, an oppositional group centered on the Crown Prince from about 785 until it briefly acceded to power in 805. Here again there is an apt parallel to Wang An-shih's movement in the Sung, with its roots in the poets and classical scholars of the previous generation. In the T'ang case, everything aborted; not only were the economic reformers thrown out of power by factions of palace eunuchs and the military, but also the proto–Neo-Confucianism of Han Yü and the *ku-wen* movement soon petered out. The struggles among the intellectual factions did not line up the same way in both instances. The Sung Neo-Confucians were strongly opposed to the poets, while in the T'ang both were united in pressing for reform of the examination content.[11] And the split between cultural conservatives and institutional modernizers, although latent in the T'ang groupings, never came to the sharp break that characterized the Sung controversies.

The main line of opposition was between the most extreme claims of the Confucian movement and the Buddhists, but this became acute only when Han Yü began his famous polemics around 805–820. The Confucian sage religion was appropriating cultural capital from the Buddhists, and this was shaped in the preceding years by personal links. In the T'ang, both the literary reformers and the Crown Prince's practical reformers were linked to Buddhist intellectuals, in this case from the T'ien-t'ai sect rather than, as in the Sung, from the Ch'an. Buddhist dominance in philosophy, although wavering with the political winds, was still based on strong material supports. Against a history of successive persecutions of Buddhism during the past century, Han Yü must have felt some grounds for confidence in attacking the magical tantrism popular at the court. But although court Buddhism was on its last legs, Buddhism as a whole was still in its last wave of creativity. Ch'an Buddhism was expanding and victoriously fractionating in the rural monasteries. Only after this base too was reduced would the Confucian sage religion successfully appropriate the Buddhist space. The T'ang flurry of proto–Neo-Confucianism arose from conditions approximating the first generation of the Sung movement, religious and philosophical innovations comparable to those of Chang Tsai or Chou Tun-I. Neither examination system expansion nor Buddhist collapse was extensive enough yet to allow the movement to go on to constructive second and subsequent generations comparable to the Ch'eng brothers and their followers.

The Emergence of Neo-Confucian Metaphysical Systems

The Sung Neo-Confucian movement, in keeping with the law of small numbers, expanded into an open intellectual space not as a single position but as a set of rivals. For the first two or three generations there were four main contenders: the occultism of Shao Yung and of Chou Tun-I, the naturalist school of Chang Tsai, and the followers of the Ch'eng brothers. Controversies and alliances among these groups provided the intellectual activity after the death of the founders. The numerologists of the Shao school in particular were strong rivals of the Ch'eng disciples down to around 1150, while another faction, the Hu school (337 to 342 in Figure 6.4) kept up a branch independent of the main Ch'eng lineage which centered on Yang Shih.[12]

All these lines came together around 1170–1200 with Chu Hsi, who produced an encyclopedic commentary on and synthesis of his predecessors. Chu Hsi's system combines the most disparate branches by identifying Chou Tun-I's Supreme Ultimate with *li,* or principle. Chu Hsi brought out clearly the dualism between principle *(li)* and matter/energy, *(ch'i)* and explored the implications of his metaphysical synthesis. Chu Hsi continued much of the Neo-Confucian religious emphasis, including the practice of sitting in meditation to achieve sagehood. By seeing the *li* in things, one achieves "sudden enlightenment"—a term borrowed from Ch'an Buddhism. But Chu Hsi was predominantly naturalistic. He criticized divination and disbelieved in life after death and visitations of ghosts and spirits, reiterating the secularist side of

Confucianism, which had been in existence among critical scholars since the later Han. Chu Hsi incorporated much contemporary natural science and historical scholarship into his system, including his own theory of the evolution of the universe from vortices, and giving a paleontologically correct explanation of fossils. At the same time, he incorporated a good deal of alchemy and the hexagram system of the *Yi Ching,* which had been repudiated by Ch'eng I. In his systematic arrangement and philosophical comprehensiveness, Chu Hsi resembles Thomas Aquinas, while his contents are more like those of Albertus Magnus. More than his predecessors, Chu Hsi gives an explicit metaphysical emphasis, recognizing the difference between logical and factual priority in his discussion of *li* and *ch'i,* principle and energy/matter. In this respect, Chu Hsi reaches a degree of reflexive awareness about abstractions comparable to Plato and Aristotle.

Chu Hsi split this new attention space with a rival. Lu Chiu-Yüan put forward the doctrine that *li* as well as time and space are entirely within the experiencing mind. This radical idealism was a new departure for Confucianism; hitherto its idealist tendencies had gone only to the extent of emphasizing the moral unity of humanity with the universe, or positing a metaphorical emanation of the hexagrams from an ultimate mind. Lu was a popular teacher in his day, and debated personally with Chu Hsi over whether mind is itself principle (Lu's position), or whether human nature more restrictedly is the principle which gives rise to mind (Chu's position). For Chu, the Supreme Ultimate is above physical form and yin-yang is within physical form, whereas Lu refused the distinction. The two most abstract metaphysical systems to date in Chinese philosophy (outside of Buddhism) emerged together, mutually constituting each other by opposition.

The synthetic branch of Neo-Confucianism combining the Ch'eng brothers with Chu Hsi (called Ch'eng-Chu Neo-Confucianism) eventually won official dominance, becoming adopted as the required curriculum for the examination system. Thereafter Neo-Confucianism became just the kind of scholasticism it had begun by criticizing. Neo-Confucianism dominated because it brought together all the main social interests of the literati: the investment of Confucian cultural capital in the examinations, but also frustration with the bureaucratic examination competition; the status appeal of spiritual cultivation, but also of scholarly and scientific exploration; and a generally conservative stance on economic changes which might challenge gentry dominance. As the radical economic reformers faded out, the Neo-Confucians usurped the central position from the narrower Confucian traditionalists.

Like Confucians generally throughout Chinese history, the Neo-Confucians were creative only when they were in opposition; even then they always stood at the door of official power, drawing creative energy from the prospects of victory which lay within their reach. The pattern of opposition was repeated three times. Typically opposition starts off when a partisan political struggle becomes entwined with an intellectual issue. The first round of creativity crystallized against the Wang An-shih economic reforms and their aftermath. The resolution of the political conflict eventually de-energized the intellectual creativity. The ban on the Ch'eng brothers' writings, imposed intermittently early in the 1100s, was lifted in 1155 as the Southern Sung government abandoned efforts at structural reform.

The second wave of Neo-Confucian creativity was connected to a new partisan issue, military policy toward the Jürchen state in the north. Chu Hsi and his father (an important government official) were in a faction that favored military reconquest of the north against dominant government policy that was pacifist out of fear of losing civilian control. Chu Hsi several times rose to high position, including vice minister of the army, but was repeatedly demoted and dismissed for his attacks on other officials. Chu Hsi's teachings were banned in 1196 because of his political subversiveness. By 1237 the issue of northern reconquest was moot, for the Mongols had taken the north and were pressing the attack on the south. Neo-Confucianism was adopted as official state doctrine; henceforth examinations were based on Chu Hsi's editions of and commentaries on the classics. The downfall of the Southern Sung to the Mongols in 1279 temporarily eliminated this privileged position; but when the examination system was reinstituted in 1313, Neo-Confucianism of the Ch'eng-Chu school again became official. The Ch'eng brothers, Chou Tun-I, Chang Tsai, and other Sung Neo-Confucians were awarded state sacrifices in Confucian temples (Chan, 1970: 43); the religious radicalism borrowed from the Buddhists had been absorbed back into the official cult. Thereafter the Neo-Confucians remained ritually and intellectually dominant for almost 20 generations, down to the abolition of the Confucian examinations in 1905. After Chu Hsi's death, there were no notable philosophers for 300 years.

The third wave of creativity again follows the pattern: political factionalism connected with a movement of intellectuals dissatisfied with the pressures of the examination system; the philosophical doctrine taking the form of a religious syncretism put forward as a new cultural standard for choosing officials. The last great philosopher, Wang Yang-ming (Wang Shou-jen, 1472–1529), represents a split in what had now become the Neo-Confucian orthodoxy of the Ch'eng-Chu school (see Figure 6.5). Politically, Wang Yang-ming was involved in factional disputes, taking the rather typical stance of a Confucian official against the power of court eunuchs, and also advocating decentralization of military commands, thereby raising fears at court over losing civilian control (Tu, 1976). His career fluctuated between political and military tri-

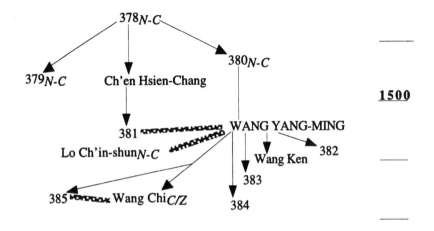

————————▶ = master-pupil tie ◆◆◆◆◆◆◆◆◆◆◆◆ = conflictual tie
ALL CAPS = major philosopher   Lowercase = secondary philosopher
number = minor philosopher, listed in key (see Appendix 3)
N-C = Neo-Confucian   Z = Ch'an

FIGURE 6.5. NEO-CONFUCIAN ORTHODOXY AND THE IDEALIST
MOVEMENT, 1435–1565

umphs and denunciation and punishment. During a period of banishment, he experienced "enlightenment" while meditating on the nature of bamboo; again this is a syncretism with Buddhism and Taoism, although subordinating meditation and immortality-seeking to an intellectual insight with political overtones. Reinterpreting Chu Hsi's "investigation of things" as an inner rather than an outward process, Wang held that the world is produced by the thought of a world spirit, identical with the thoughts of all people collectively. Wang's idealism supported the conclusion that everyone has the same innate moral intuitions, and everyone could potentially become a sage by uncovering the original mind from the obstacles of selfish desires: "The streets are full of sages."

Wang Yang-ming's doctrine constituted an egalitarian attack on the ladder of examinations, which had grown even longer and more formalized in the Ming than in the Sung. The earlier two-level system of local and metropolitan examinations was complicated still further into three levels with the addition of a provincial examination and subdivision of the first, prefectural examination into three consecutive steps (Chaffee, 1985: 23, 183). Competition had become enormous, in part because alternative routes to office were closed, as a huge number of candidates struggled for a tiny set of positions. Like previous waves of oppositional Neo-Confucians, Wang and his followers attacked the standard of literary compositions and rote memorization. Wang drew the inference from his philosophy that knowledge is identical with action; this was turned into an attack on scholasticism: "Learning before they can act, they never get to the end of it" (Chan, 1963: 678). Yet although Wang held that the grind of examination study was incompatible with sagehood, he regarded it as a necessary step for an official career, which would allow one to put one's ideals into action (Tu, 1976: 131). Wang's idealism constitutes not so much a cosmology as a pragmatism identifying moral ideals with the process of putting them into effect. His philosophy glorifies intellectual activity outside the examination life, since truly experiencing moral ideas is already a form of action; it also exalts action, thereby legitimating politics. Again opposition shapes the line along which creativity emerges. Since the official philosophy tended toward a secular and materialist rationalism, Wang Yang-ming turned toward subjectivity and intuition.

Wang Yang-ming's disciples became a quasi-religious movement, making his philosophy the most popular in China during the next century. While the Ch'eng-Chu rationalist Neo-Confucians remained dominant in the official examination system, Wang Yang-ming's idealist pragmatism was supported by an underground, including secret societies gathered for political as well as spiritual purposes. During the generation of Wang Yang-ming's immediate followers, there continued to be philosophical developments, following the familiar path of splits into rival schools after his death. As the movement became absorbed into politics, lay concerns again prevailed, and intellectual creativity along this line came to an end. We will not follow the further developments of Chinese philosophy, including the repudiation of Neo-Confucian metaphysics in the late 1600s and 1700s, which shifted intellectual activity toward materialism and historical scholarship in a purely secular vein.

The Weak Continuity of Chinese Metaphysics

The idealism formulated by Lu Chiu-Yüan and Wang Yang-ming is an unusual development within Chinese philosophy; the only truly comparable instance is the Consciousness-Only doctrine of the mid-T'ang, a Buddhist philosophy insulated from non-Buddhist thought. This absence of idealism is connected more with the halting continuity of philosophical abstraction than with a deep-rooted cultural trait. Idealism is never an early form but a sophisticated philosophical construction. A halfway house between revealed religion and rationalistic philosophy, idealism is couched at a level of abstraction which can be attained only through a long cumulative development of an intellectual network refining its concepts. The heyday of idealist philosophies in the Greek world was in late antiquity;[13] in India, Buddhist Yogacara and Hindu Advaita Vendanta arose well into the medieval period; in Europe the great idealist systems spanned the 1780s to the 1920s, building on the technical tools of earlier generations. This idealist halfway house can be approached from several directions. The bases of European idealism were religious universities on the path to secularization; in Greece the idealists were generally moving in the other direction. The Sung and Ming idealisms emerged in competition with metaphysical systems dividing the intellectual field, sharing out the ingredients of rationalistic philosophy and of religious transcendence that were available.

Idealism is of course not the only form of metaphysical abstraction. We can draw the lesson more generally. It is often asserted that the Chinese mentality is concrete and practical, with no taste for metaphysics. Yet metaphysical abstractions were periodically created in China. It is true that early positions are only ambiguously metaphysical. The *Tao Te Ching* and the *Chuang Tzu* are skewed toward ethics, in the sense of how one should behave and not behave rather than indicating what exists at higher levels of reflection. The *Tao Te Ching* is skeptical rather than constructive; yet its skepticism about what is nameable is the tool by which it develops its metaphysical implications. And this is characteristic of metaphysics in general. Higher levels of abstract reflection are reached by applying epistemological considerations to conceptual problems. At least this is one route toward metaphysics, prominent in Greek, Indian, and European philosophy. The issue in China is less the absence of metaphysics than the rarity of sustained epistemological consideration.

Epistemology becomes a focus when an intellectual community is balanced in debate, with sufficient continuity across the generations to give rise to specialization in the techniques of argument. Sophistical debate is a typical first step toward consideration of epistemology in its own right. Density of the network structure in the time of the ancient Chi-hsia Academy and rival centers produced a sophistical epistemology countered by positive assertions about the conditions of knowledge, themes similar to what emerged in Greece under comparable conditions. In both cases a variety of positions divided the intellectual field. Metaphysical and epistemological strands in Mencius and Hui Shih were the setting in which Chuang Tzu created his oppositional stance. Over the next generations, the opposing epistemologies of the Mohist *Canons* and of Kung-sun Lung became the backdrop against which the *Tao Te Ching* could proclaim its negative metaphysics. When the destruction of intellectual networks interrupted further development on the abstract level, philosophical doctrines during the Han were carried on at a level closer to lay concerns. When structural conditions were again favorable to skeptical and sophistical debate, in the brief generations of the Pure Conversation circles of the Three Kingdoms, abstract philosophy emerged again. The earlier cultural capital was not only revived but, at the hands of Wang Pi, Kuo Hsiang, and others, pushed in the direction of both epistemology and metaphysics.

Epistemological debate is not the only route to metaphysics. We have seen in India how a religion based on world-fleeing ascetic meditation anchored a skeptical stance toward the reality of the ordinary world. This encouraged intellectual networks to push to higher levels of metaphysical abstraction: in part because independence of the core elite of meditators from lay-oriented rituals and ethical preaching led to a focus on pure insight as the mark of religious standing; in part because tension within the sacred concepts of the transcendental and the aconceptual provided just the kind of deep troubles that motivate layers of reflexive refinement. Transplanted to China, these conditions fostered further philosophical creativity, reaching its metaphysical high point with the Hua-yen synthesis of all the Buddhist schools. Here metaphysical construction literally packed abstraction back into abstraction, taking pains to incorporate all viewpoints of the intellectual-religious field into a unified system. To do so, the Hua-yen philosophers had to push through the particularities of religious sacred objects and discover the mutual constitution not only of different abstractions by one another, but also the interdependence of different levels of abstraction. In demonstrating the interpenetration of change and emptiness, concepts and phenomenal objects, Hua-yen may well be the most significant Chinese contributor to world philosophy.

In this light, the most important institutional fact shaping the medieval and subsequent development of Chinese philosophy was the insulation between the Buddhist scholastics and the Confucian gentry. During the period when the great constructive Buddhist systems were prominent, Confucianism was far too much on the defensive religiously, organizationally, and intellectually to profit from them even at the level of creative opposition. When Buddhist and Confucian network contacts and intellectual syntheses finally became significant, the material base of intellectual Buddhism had long since collapsed. The Buddhist contacts of the Sung Neo-Confucians were confined to the Ch'an masters. But Ch'an was, on the surface, a predominantly anti-intellectual movement, and what the Neo-Confucians took from it was a meditation-oriented technique that they could transmute into their own Sage religion, but little in the way of refined metaphysical concepts.[14]

Neo-Confucian metaphysics started over again from a relatively lower level of philosophical abstraction than the Buddhists had attained. The early generation of Sung Neo-Confucians picked up the cultural capital of the old divination schools; and this had been transmitted largely on a concrete level through lay-oriented practitioners. There is a temptation to regard this emphasis on a system of continuous worldly change as the archetypal Chinese worldview; certainly it is an attractively realistic vision, if regarded on a sufficient level of generality. But it is hardly an aboriginal or eternal item of Chinese culture. Its classic statement, the appendices to the *Yi Ching* added during the Ch'in or early Han, was produced at the very end of ancient Chinese philosophy. This remained a set of particularistic portents, and was raised only ephemerally to the level of a general assertion of a universe of change, in the short-lived movement of philosophers at the time of the Dark Learning. Thereafter, once again the metaphysics was slighted until the classic texts became materials for the Neo-Confucian networks.

From here quite different intellectual paths were possible. By abstracting from their use as a magical practice, the *Yi Ching* hexagrams could be turned into a proto-science. In this direction, the emphasis was no longer on the reality of change but on the underlying elements which in combination generate the empirical world. It became something like a chemistry, equivalent to the element theories of the Presocratic Greeks which led in the direction of atomism. And indeed Sung Neo-Confucianism developed in connection with an upsurge in physical science. When the hexagram sequences were asserted as governing empirical events, they became the content of an empirical science, but a scientific theory whose elements are fixed without the refinements of observation and experiment. The Neo-Confucian thinkers were often better scientists than this; Chu Hsi in particular includes a level of concrete investigation which involves some accumulation of empirical information.

Yet as *philosophy* this kind of proto-science is a bringdown from the path of metaphysical creativity. To be sure, science and metaphysics are not mutually exclusive; the Sung experience fits with abundant evidence from Greece, Islam, and Europe that creativity can take place on both fronts in the same generations, and sometimes by the same individuals. Ch'eng I's vision of the universe as a vast furnace, continuously burning up matter/energy while creating it anew, is more appealing as an abstract cosmology than as a scientific theory. In Chu Hsi, the metaphysical payoff seems comparatively banal; the realm of principle existing within things gives us a doctrine supportive of scientific investigation, but not much of a exploration of constructive metaphysics.

The episodes of idealism with Lu Chiu-Yüan and Wang Yang-ming show that there was more to be poured from that pot. But the creative networks were broken off, leaving no sustained intellectual argument to carry philosophy onward in its own right. With Sung Neo-Confucianism, Chinese philosophy had traversed, in bursts interspersed with long periods of lay-oriented ideologies, a range of abstract philosophical development equivalent to that of the Greeks from the early Presocratics up through approximately the generation of Plato or a little later, the predominant Chinese position resembling Stoicism without its technical logic. Why were there such long periods of stagnation, even retrogression, on the plane of abstract philosophy? It was not simply a matter of declining material supports for intellectual life; the fall of the great dynasties with their material wealth is correlated not with philosophical mediocrity but often with the opposite. The Han, T'ang, and Ming were periods when the stagnation of abstract philosophy, at least outside of Buddhism, was at its worst.

Here we see the importance not of material supports for intellectual life in general, but of the particular kinds of structural underpinnings which support or stifle creativity. The deadening touch in all these stagnant dynasties was precisely the way Chinese intellectuals were controlled by material incentives linked to the selection of officials for the state. The Han Confucians worked successfully to build the core of a Confucian bureaucracy, in the process bringing philosophy down to the level of rituals and portents, or at best a scholasticism of state librarians. The T'ang was the period when the formal examination system took off; the Ming was the dynasty during which the state became permeated by exam-selected officials and the gentry spent virtually their entire lives studying to pass through those narrow hoops. Once the examination system took hold, the principal episodes of creativity among the Confucian gentry occurred when movements were mobilized to struggle against the artificialities of the examination life.

We may state the lesson more generally. The stifling effect on philosophical creativity of the government examination system was paralleled by the deadening effects of requiring certificates of ordination for Buddhist and Taoist monks. The policy of taxing and regulating these religions by government certification, set in place during the later T'ang, was directly connected to their decline in intellectual creativity from that point on. Ch'an Buddhism escaped for a while by evading regulation, but it too eventually succumbed. Again, it was not a question of eliminating material foundations. The Buddhist and Taoist churches survived and even prospered in the Sung dynasty and later, but only as religions of the lower classes; their upper layer of educated intellectuals almost entirely disappeared. Within Ch'an itself, the period of its own creative masters, with their paradoxical encounters and dramatic enlightenment experiences, was dried up in their own formal scholasticism. By the period of Ch'an decadence in the Sung, tales of the Ch'an masters of the T'ang were formalized into koan collections treated as texts for a series of exercises to be passed on the way to higher monastic rank. The examination system of the Confucians became paralleled by a similar set of formalities within Ch'an.

We encounter here a major theme of the formal organization of education. Schooling, which we associate with the life of culture, often operates as a deadening of culture, preserving the ideas of the past at the expense of creativity within the present. The long-standing Athenian and Alexandrian schools, once past their founding generations, show a similar pattern of stagnation. In medieval Europe, too, the universities are a two-edged sword: centers of creativity during their early periods, associated with a stagnant scholasticism after 1350.

On the theoretical level, what we see in China is the causal dynamics of material base and inner intellectual networks. Creativity occurs when lineages recombine intellectual capital in their struggle to divide the attention space; such recombinations are set in motion at those times when the underlying base shifts. Hence there is creativity at both the moment of expansion and of contraction. Ch'an Buddhism was the last wave of Chinese Buddhist creativity, occurring when the institutional base of government-supported monastic properties was collapsing under political pressure. Ch'an temporarily found a new base, the self-supporting monastery in the countryside. The distinctive Ch'an sensibility was a militant anti-intellectualism, in keeping with its work-oriented surroundings and in reaction against the textual studies and philosophizing of court Buddhism. The initial burgeoning of the Ch'an movement was nevertheless philosophically creative because it fostered competition among an expanding wave of masters, displaying their enlightenment while traveling among the newly founded monasteries. Ch'an became an intellectual's anti-intellectualism—indeed, epitomizing this stance forever after—because its several generations of status competition built hyper-sophisticated layers of reflexiveness expressing each new master's detached superiority to the already sophisticated symbolic gestures of preceding masters.

Ch'an was a movement of the institutional decline of Chinese Buddhism. When Ch'an too faded into routinization and its material base decayed, it lost its threat in the eyes of the Confucian literati. The Neo-Confucians intellectually cannibalized their fading rival, just as in India the Advaita movement under Shankara took over Buddhist omni-denial of substance when that religion was dying. The creative edge of Neo-Confucianism rode on the growth of its new organizational base, the rapid expansion of the government examination system; this is an obverse case to the initial wave of Ch'an creativity under organizational crisis. There is some irony in the fact that Sung Neo-Confucianism began in the oppositional circles of elite degree holders who objected to the vulgarization and routinization of the new educational ethos; but Neo-Confucianism eventually became adopted as the content of the examination system itself once its creativity had faded to rote. For the sociology of institutions, this irony is merely that of the dynamism of structures over time. Creativity comes from the moment of rearrangement; old creativity becomes new routine when the underlying bases stop moving. Later, in Japan, these same late Ch'an monastic routines and Neo-Confucian academies would give off yet further waves of innovation, as they became once again energized by new changes of the organizational base.

CHAPTER 7

☗

Innovation through
Conservatism: Japan

Religions generally look backwards to the sacredness of past tradition. But religions cannot avoid changing in changed social circumstances, and the tension of religious elites declines by accommodation with lay society. New religious initiatives often take such accommodation as a foil, putting themselves forward as a revival, a conservative return to original purity. Yet what is revived is constructed out of contemporary ingredients, and turns out to be innovation in conservative guise, no less than religious movements which announce a new revelation.

Philosophies embedded in religions undergo the same dynamics; so do secular philosophies cutting free from a religious base. This is most forcefully illustrated in the case of Japan. Innovation in the conservative mode, however, is not merely Asian traditionalism. Intellectual life is driven by oppositions, filling attention space under the law of small numbers; intellectual fame goes to those who carve out maximally distinctive positions. Conservative innovation is a mode of all intellectual life.

Japanese society in many respects is a continuation of China's. More to the point, Japan gives an approximation of what China would have become if it had continued the trajectory of the T'ang and Sung dynasties. It was during those periods that Japan acquired organized structures of state and religion beyond the level of clans; literate culture, art, and architecture all developed by importing Chinese models. Japan broke free from the direct influx of Chinese culture at just the time when China was turning, institutionally and intellectually, in a different direction. It was medieval China, Buddhist-dominated China, that Japan continued; the stifling bureaucratic centralization of Ming and Ch'ing, after the independence of Buddhist high culture had been crushed, occurred while Japan was becoming autonomous. In tracing modern Japanese development, we have a laboratory for what a society built on Buddhist organizational structures would produce, economically and intellectually.

322

Japanese philosophy in the centuries up through about 1300 directly continued Chinese networks; all the major Chinese Buddhist schools were imported, with a bias toward those dating from the end of the creative period of Chinese Buddhism. Hence the predominance in Japan of Zen, since the most intense flow of Japanese sojourners and Chinese missionaries coincided with the late Sung and early Yuan, when active Buddhism had winnowed down to the Lin-chi (Rinzai) and Ts'ao-Tung (Soto) lineages. These dynasties too were the time of the Neo-Confucian movement, and the moment when it was keeping up contacts with the Ch'an lineages; thus the most philosophically abstract of Confucian metaphysics was carried into Japan and taught in the Zen-based education which proliferated from the Muromachi period onward.

In several respects the Japanese were Chinese-style intellectuals. Lay concerns penetrated the intellectual sphere, keeping thought more concrete and at a lower level of philosophical abstraction. During the phase when the monasteries dominated culture production, Buddhist leaders were political monks, consorting with political-military factions and intervening weightily in their struggles with monastic armies. Zen set itself off as the most conservative wing of Buddhism, in opposition to the radicalism of the Pure Land movements among the commoners. But Zen too underwent its own accommodation with the upper strata, resulting in the style-conscious gentry Buddhism developed in the most elite Zen monasteries, where religious practice turned into a refined aesthetics which became the mark of highest secular prestige. The backlash against monastic political power, when the era of feudalism was finally overcome by the absolutist Tokugawa state, was a secularizing reformation. Now the politicization of the intellectuals shifted in a new direction. Beneath the veneer of Confucian and Shinto revivalism, Tokugawa intellectuals resembled their contemporaries, the anti-clerical activists of the French Enlightenment. Burgeoning market competition both in education and in mass culture produced intellectuals oriented toward secular topics of history, philology, and economics, while despising metaphysical speculation. Despite the reactionary and authoritarian tone which made up the surface ideology of Tokugawa discourse, Japanese intellectuals became modernists on their own path; both their secularist wing and their neo-traditionalist opponents sound like quarreling European intellectuals after the downfall of the state church and religious control over education.

The organizational bases of intellectual production became similar in Japan and Europe, insofar as both went through a long transition to religious secularization and the corresponding loss of religious control over the educational system. It is no coincidence that Japanese Buddhism became the more "Protestant," breaking with monasticism to allow married priests, and encouraging lay participation within the remaining celibate orders. Both places went through a "Renaissance" period when the wealthy clerical elite secularized from within, turning most of its attention to artistic production. There came a further phase of religious decline under state regulation, building up to full-fledged outbreaks of anti-clericalism. And both places experienced counter-waves of religious neoconservatism within the secularizing tide. Structurally, Tokugawa Japan and the most secularizing and capitalist-dominated parts of Europe underwent a rapid expansion of the educational and printing markets, with the resulting proliferation of mass popular culture. This too left its mark on the tone of intellectual production; "Enlightenment"-style "philosophes" and popular authors appeared virtually contemporarily in both places.

We should remind ourselves again that intellectual creativity is no mere reflex of economics and politics. There are three layers of causality: (1) economic-political structures, which in turn shape (2) the organizations which support intellectual life; and these in turn allow the buildup of (3) networks among participants in centers of attention on intellectual controversies, which constitute the idea-substance of intellectual life. Economic-political conditions determine ideas not directly but by way of shaping, and above all by changing, the intermediate level, the organizational base of intellectual production.

We see this pattern by a very general overview of the networks of Japanese intellectuals in the five figures in this chapter. In those figures are all the philosophers and religious-intellectual leaders who commanded much attention across the generations.[1] The networks show four periods of creativity, each of which coincides with one of the major shifts in the political and economic structure of Japan.

Around 800 (and apparently within a year of each other), the first two major Japanese Buddhists, Saicho and Kukai, found the schools of Tendai and Shingon, which would dominate for 400 years thereafter. This happens at just the time of the founding of the capital city at Kyoto, beginning the Heian period of ceremonial court rule (794–1185).

In the generation 1165–1200 there begins a network of notable Buddhists, which extends densely down to 1335–1365, followed by isolated figures of secondary eminence in the next two generations. Here we see a burst of tightly connected creative figures, with the usual splits and simultaneous rival lineages, continuing for six generations, with a decline in network continuity and creative eminence for two generations thereafter. This marks the foundation of the Zen lineages, and includes virtually all of their famous members (leaving aside a last flourish of Zen in the Tokugawa); typically in each generation there is at least one memorable Rinzai master, plus an equally distinguished rival (usually in Soto). In addition, in the early generations, where the most important Zen masters appear, the main versions of Japanese Pure Land popular Buddhism are created in another tight network. The beginning of this period of creativity coincides with the major institutional break, the transition from the Heian court rule to Kamakura feudalism.

After five generations empty of major or secondary philosophers (and sparse even in minor ones), another dense, competitive network of creative thinkers appears in the generation 1600–1635. This network continues to turn up significant rival thinkers down to 1800 and, more loosely connected, to 1835. The underlying transition is the Tokugawa unification; again we see a thinning out of its networks of creativity after six generations.

After an interval of minor figures during two or three generations in the 1800s, there is a burst of major and secondary creativity, linked in a tight network, during 1900–1935. This is the Kyoto school, which suddenly revives Buddhist philosophy in a blend with Western (mainly German) metaphysics. The underlying shift is not precisely the Meiji restoration, which is followed by a single generation in which philosophy is dominated by imitative imports of European ideas. What has shifted by the 1890s is a new organizational base for intellectual production: the autonomous university, which becomes the home of the Kyoto school and its rivals and offshoots.

In general, then, we find four major networks of creativity, corresponding to the onset of four major institutional transitions in the outermost political-structural base. Looking more closely, we can see that the immediate means of intellectual production also changed at each period, opening up new opportunities for intellectual life and stimulating the formulation of new positions. In two of these instances (1165–1365 and 1600–1800), the network lasts for half a dozen generations before petering out. In one case (800–835) there is only a single creative generation (in the case of 1900–1935 it appears that the network continues, but I do not trace this further). What keeps the networks going for such six-generation periods is not the transition per se, but the ongoing dynamics of the intellectual competition.

There is an almost perfect correlation between the onset of new political-economic structures and the onset of intellectual creative networks, with one negative case: the transition from Kamakura to Muromachi. This marks the shift between the rule of clan feudalism by the Kamakura shoguns (1185–1330) and the much more decentralized (and commercialized) feudalism which set in with the weak Ashikaga shogunate (1338–1573). The latter (especially the Sengoku or "Country at War" period after 1467, when Japan was a patchwork of rival military domains, self-governing cities, and monastic states) was the major economic growth period, the time of Buddhist penetration into the countryside, and of the fusion of the hierarchy of Zen monasteries with the feudal aristocracy. But although it was a time of cultural flourishing, in arts which have come to characterize the Japanese aesthetic (tea ceremony, brush painting, garden architecture), it was a vacuum for noteworthy philosophers, religious or otherwise. In what follows I shall be concerned to show why surrounding conditions did not stir up another wave of intellectual creativity at that time; or, more precisely, why creative energy built up in gentry aesthetics but not in abstract philosophy.

Japan as Transformer of Chinese Buddhism

The Japanese state arose around 600 C.E. as an imitation of T'ang dynasty centralized administration.[2] But no status group of Confucian literati appeared. Government became controlled by a web of marriage politics manipulated by regents who married their daughters to emperors, who were themselves stifled by ceremony and encouraged to abdicate in favor of child figureheads. Shadow rule dispersed authority as sexual politics multiplied claimants to the throne. Further layers of shadow rule emerged; ex-emperors, sometimes retired to Buddhist monasteries, exercised "cloistered rule" of behind-the-scenes manipulation. Court factions allied with provincial warrior clans whose fighting brought the Heian rule to an end after 1165. In the following period of feudal usurpation, families of regents as well as ex-shoguns and ex-emperors manipulated layers of front-stage officeholders from behind the ceremonial screen.

The Buddhist monasteries became military powers, whose lower-ranking temple workers became shock troops, intervening in succession and property disputes, at first between rival monasteries, then from 1100 on in the political disputes of the capital. The centralized tax system was undermined, beginning as early as the 800s, as private estates were withdrawn from state land-ownership. At first favored monasteries, along with self-interested court families, acquired the privilege of private property and fiscal immunity; when these advantages eventually were acquired by the provincial aristocracy, centralized government collapsed into feudalism.

One consequence of shadow rule was to preserve Shinto, despite its archaic character as a plurality of animistic cults lacking central organizational structure. Originally the most important of the Shinto deities symbolized the leading clans; clan chiefs had been simultaneously (even primarily) priests in charge of the ritual. After the emergence of Chinese-style central government and of the wealthy and literate Buddhist monasteries, one might have expected Shinto to fade to the level of local folk religion; Shinto managed to preserve itself on the national scene down to the 1300s only by being taken under the organizational and ideological auspices of Buddhism. Shinto remained politically alive because shadow rule focused attention on the imperial line almost exclusively in its ceremonial and symbolic character. Without the substance of power, the emperors were defined by their religious ancestry; the old clan chief–priest role was brought again to the fore. Given the parcelization of power, the imperial cult could be used as a weapon whenever a major challenge to de facto authority was mounted. The upsurges of Shinto ideology correspond to the three main periods of struggle against the shogunate: Go-Daigo's brief restoration of imperial power in the 1330s, the cult of National Learning in the mid-Tokugawa, and the Meiji restoration. It is a glib rhetoric which characterizes Japanese cultural tradition as a harmonious syncretism of Shinto, Buddhism, and Confucianism. The relative strengths of the three religions varied considerably under different historical conditions; periods of intense conflict among them were among the main dynamics of Japanese intellectual creativity.

Buddhist monasteries became the basis of intellectual life. By the mid-700s, six philosophical schools had been introduced from China, some even by direct pupils of the famous Hsüan-tsang (see 3–5 in Figure 7.1). But there was nothing intellectually original in these first half-dozen generations. The prestige of imports filled up the attention space. This is typical enough of idea importers, as we see in Rome, Islamic Iraq, Spain, and Christian Europe (see Chapter 8, Coda). Philosophical content was subordinated to sectarian identification; the great temples at Nara came close to direct theocratic rule. The first great names of Japanese Buddhism, Saicho and Kukai, appeared as a pair in the same circle of court officials. The setting was the power vacuum that occurred when government moved to Heian-kyo (Kyoto) in 794 to escape monastic power at Nara. Saicho and Kukai went to China, where they acquired lineage connections as yet lacking in Japan, receiving ordination directly from Buddhist masters superior in prestige to the Nara schools.[3] Saicho's new monastery, on Mount Hiei overlooking Kyoto, became the primary ordination hall for Japanese monks. His new sect, Tendai (T'ien-t'ai), thereby became the organizational center of Japanese Buddhism; for the following 15 generations, down to 1300, virtually every notable Buddhist, including the leaders of the Pure Land and Zen sects, would be a pupil at Mount Hiei. Kukai made a different selection from the network of Chinese masters, most impressively by securing ordination from the tantric lineage.[4] He returned to Japan to found the Shingon school, with its great monastery on Mount Koya, beyond Nara. Thereafter Shingon and Tendai between them become effectively the national religions.[5]

Both schools incorporated shamanastic orders. Magical Buddhism became the card to trump Shinto; the indigenous gods *(kami)* became interpreted as manifestations of the Buddha. Tendai developed its own esoteric branches, like Shingon giving prominence to magic and ritual over meditation and philosophy. Buddhist monasteries of the Heian period became so powerful in mundane affairs that they fused with the outermost economic and political layer of society. In the sociological three-level causal model, the inner organizational level providing a base for intellectual specialists was largely eliminated, and

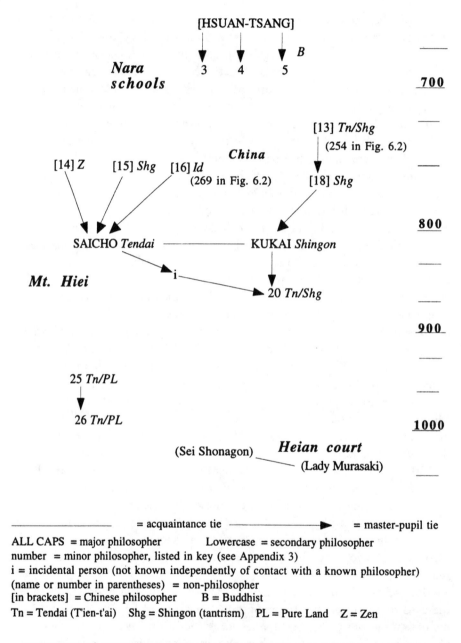

FIGURE 7.1. NETWORK OF JAPANESE PHILOSOPHERS, 600–1100:
FOUNDING OF TENDAI AND SHINGON

there was no longer much autonomy left for internal networks of intellectual argument and creativity. The content of Buddhism became largely identical with lay concerns for the fortunes of daily life; Heian society was permeated with taboos and pollutions manifesting this fusion of religion and society.

The creative eminence of Saicho and Kukai is a blip amid the surrounding generations, where virtually nothing of intellectual note occurred among the religious leaders. The only important creativity in these centuries was not in philosophy or religion at all, but in the most secularized sector: the sophisticated observations on marriage politics and shadow rule in Lady Murasaki's *Tale of Genji* and Sei Shonagon's *Pillowbook*. In Figure 7.1 there are no other names of any sort in that generation (1000–1035), when the court women's literary world reigned alone.

When philosophical creativity suddenly came alive, it did so simultaneously in several branches each of Pure Land and Zen. This was not an emergence of new religious doctrine. Zen and Amidaism had both existed for many centuries in China. In Japan, Zen had been part of the Tendai synthesis since at least the time of Saicho. The Amida salvation cult, with its characteristic ritual of *Nembutsu* (chanting the savior's name), was similarly long-standing. It too had come in during the early days of Tendai; around the mid-900s Mount Hiei leaders had traveled among the common people, popularizing communal recitation, founding lay groups, singing and dancing to the accompaniment of drumming on begging bowls. What was new about the Pure Land orders which burst on the scene between the time of Honen (who founded the Pure Land sect, Jodo, in 1175) and Nichiren (who founded the Lotus sect, Hokke, in 1253) was not so much doctrinal as organizational. These new orders, emerging within the older centers, broke with their lineages, often with unprecedented exclusiveness and militancy, and reshaped the social form of Japanese Buddhism. The same is true of Zen, with a different social base and a different method of reforming contemporary magical-ritual practice. The rapid upheaval of Buddhist organization on so many fronts, after centuries of stagnation, accompanied a deep shift in the surrounding political and economic structure. The doctrinal ingredients had long been in existence; they were merely put in a new and purified form, to create distinctive ideologies supporting the new organizational paths which had now become available.

Population had grown and spread widely beyond the home provinces of central Honshu; an economic base developed in considerable part through the organizing activities of Buddhist evangelists, which could support Buddhist temples beyond the court-centered monasteries near the old capital cities. Politically, the great monasteries and their troops were tied to the factions of regents and ex-emperors who struggled over control of Kyoto. Central control disintegrated as local administrators built up their own forces, and fragments

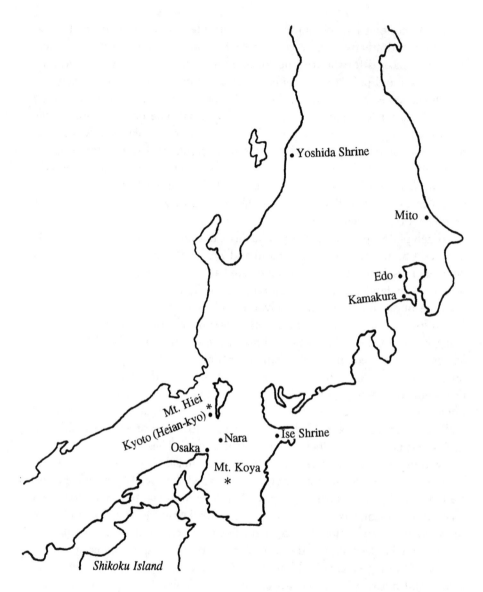

INTELLECTUAL AND RELIGIOUS CENTERS OF JAPAN

of the ever-dividing imperial kin eventually mobilized them for battles over the center. In 1180–1185 full-scale civil war resulted in the new shadow government of the military shogun, moving the de facto center of government eastward to Kamakura. In 1221 the ex-emperor Go-Toba renewed the struggle, using warrior-priests from the old religious-court alliances of the home provinces, especially the Tendai establishment at Mount Hiei. These forces proved insufficient against professional warriors. The old lines of religious-political power were disrupted; their provision of ritual as well as military resources to the old factions of the center was now outmoded.

The warriors of the provinces marshaled under the great military clans now far outweighed both the old court forces and the thinly armed and unruly mobs of monastic armies. A new counterbalance was arising. The Pure Land organizations were creating a new economic resource that could be mobilized into truly significant military strength. Popular Buddhism, spreading throughout the countryside, led to the development of trade links, amassing and reinvesting capital. Missionaries and traveling evangelists, and the pilgrim routes left in their wake, built up links of popular communication and material flow.

The crisis of religious-political legitimation comes across most clearly in Nichiren. Why had the imperial forces lost in 1221 despite the incantations and prayers of Tendai and Shingon? Nichiren saw the occasion as a crisis of faith. What path for salvation could take the place of these disproven methods? The old orders belonged to the corruption of the times. The ecclesiastical lineage for transmission of office, the center of previous struggles over ordination halls and masters' certificates, was radically abrogated by a purely charismatic, spiritual succession. Reveling in newfound social resources, Nichiren declared that the throne should be subservient to religion.

Nichiren's was only the most militant of the movements oriented toward proselytizing the new popular base at this time of breakdown of the old religious-political alliances. Honen, too, had been stripped of his clerical status in 1207, and his Pure Land sect banned from the capital, for declaring the *Nembutsu* the favored path to rebirth in paradise. His pupil Shinran—like all the other Pure Land reformers a former Mount Hiei monk—made the sharpest organizational break of all. His True Pure Land sect (known as Ikko, single-minded), founded in 1224, broke down the fundamental structure of Buddhist monasticism. Monks could be married; religion became a practice of lay congregations rather than world-rejecting virtuosi. In this respect Shinran is the Martin Luther of Buddhism. In the breakdown of religious authority during the overthrow of the Kyoto government, Honen was radical enough to be pushed out of the monastic establishment. In his circle of declericalized followers Shinran took the further step of declaring that a non-institutionalized religion, apart from the monasteries, the court, and their rituals, was the true religious path. The magical Buddhism of ceremonies and chants, aimed at cleansing pollutions and achieving worldly success, was replaced by an inner sense of sinfulness, from which only faith could provide salvation. Shinran's version of popular Pure Land became a purely ethical form of Buddhism. In subsequent generations, Shinran's followers became a network linking the countryside and the commercialized towns into a church so powerful that its wealth and its armies made it the equal of any feudal domain.

Zen as Conservative Innovation

The outburst of Zen lineages occurred in the same generations as the radical Pure Land movements, and took the opposite side of the field from them. Instead of proclaiming social and religious transformation, Zen was conservative; it reasserted the traditional Buddhist stance in its purest form, meditative detachment from the world. Nevertheless, conservatives in a situation of structural opposition are forced into their own path of innovation.

The leaders of the Zen orders began, like the Pure Land founders, as offshoots of the Tendai establishment, the great Mount Hiei center from which all the action emanated. Whereas Pure Land quickly shifted to popular recruitment in the provinces, Zen retained its upper-class connections; soon it was taking ex-emperors into its ranks, and several of its famous leaders were sons and grandsons of emperors. Zen became known as the religion of the warrior class, but it never broke its links with the court aristocracy. Throughout the civil wars, including the effort of the ex-emperor Go-Daigo to restore direct rule in the 1330s, leading Zen masters such as Muso Soseki maintained close ties with the emperor, while making the transition to patronage by the victorious Ashikaga shoguns. Although Zen has the reputation of having provided a religious ideology for the samurai, this was largely a matter of social connections. The truth is that Zen monasteries were far more peaceful than either the Pure Land orders or the traditional power centers such as Mount Hiei; abjuring political involvement, they rarely became involved in the internecine combat among monasteries or in secular warfare.

Zen was structurally more cosmopolitan than the Pure Land orders and pursued an intellectual trajectory at a higher level of reflexivity. Only the Zen networks made contact with China. The reason for this connection should not be taken for granted. Chinese Buddhism at this time was far from flourishing. Ch'an was on its last legs. The great creative period was far in the past, and the major activity of recent Ch'an leaders was the historical compilation of their legendary doings into the koan collections. As Figures 6.3 and 6.4 display, the fanning out of rival Ch'an lineages during the centuries from 700 to 900, typical of the filling of dominant attention space under the law of small numbers, had given way to the winnowing out and amalgamation of lineages. Virtually all other Buddhist sects had disappeared except Ch'an and Amidaism; in the defensive mode, Ch'an had become doctrinally syncretist, reversing its anti-scriptural path of pure and direct enlightenment which had prevailed in the heyday of its organizational expansion. Hua-yen (Japanese Kegon) and T'ien-tai (Tendai) survived only by being carried along inside Ch'an houses.[6] Heinrich Doumoulin (1988: 284, 287) traces no lineages after 1300, and refers to the period after the Sung as a time of "syncretistic tendencies and decline," without creative figures. Within Rinzai, one line absorbed all other schools, and by the Ming dynasty, Soto as well. In the Ming all Chinese Buddhist sects fused around a combination of Zen practice and the simplified *nembutsu* chanting of the Pure Land movements. Here too the organizational base had shifted; Zen's elite base declined, and organizationally everything was carried by popular Amidaism.

This does not seem much of a magnet for a movement of independent Japanese Zen, breaking away to revive the pure meditation practice at just the time when Amidaism was claiming exclusive possession of religious turf. What the Zen leaders were seeking was not inspiration but organizational legitimation. The earliest figures of the Zen independence movement were explicitly concerned to establish their own lineages, and they did so by means of connections with China. As usual, this happened simultaneously among rival innovators (see Figure 7.2). Dainichi Nonin (fl. 1189) achieved enlightenment on his own and founded a monastery; but he was not recognized as a Zen master until he had sent pupils to China to bring back a certificate of enlightenment, making him a dharma heir, fifty-first in the line from Shakyamuni Buddha.[7] Nonin's better-known rival Eisai studied in China in 1187–1191 to acquire a certificate of enlightenment and Zen lineage credentials. The movement seemed to be feeling its way gradually toward Zen radicalism. Eisai's reputation as Zen founder was created largely in retrospect, as the lineage that came after him pushed toward a radically purified Zen which set it in sharp contrast to all other schools.[8]

This is a particularly clear instance where we see that the network is more important than the individual. Reputations are built up over a period of generations. Especially where innovative ideas and practices come from a long-term change in the organizational base, the full ideological ramifications of what has transpired do not emerge for many decades; after that, the change is likely to be attributed disproportionately to some early names, who become emblems for what the entire lineage has accomplished. We have seen the same thing in China, where the Ch'an movement made sacred emblems out of Bodhidharma, and secondarily out of the patriarch of the southern school, Hui-neng, associated with the famous break; whereas the true innovativeness of the Zen style was the work of Shih-t'ou, Ma-tsu, and others in the following generations. In Japan, the transformation of the entire religious attention space by the 1220s, above all with the spectacular breakaway of the Pure Land sects, drove home the reality that a new organizational path was available. Japanese Zen was the conservative branch of innovation, a movement of radical purifiers and ultra-traditionalists, sucked into radicalism by unfolding circumstances.

The new slot in the attention space was quickly exploited by several lineages of contenders. Eisai's pupils and grandpupils, taking up the prestige of the

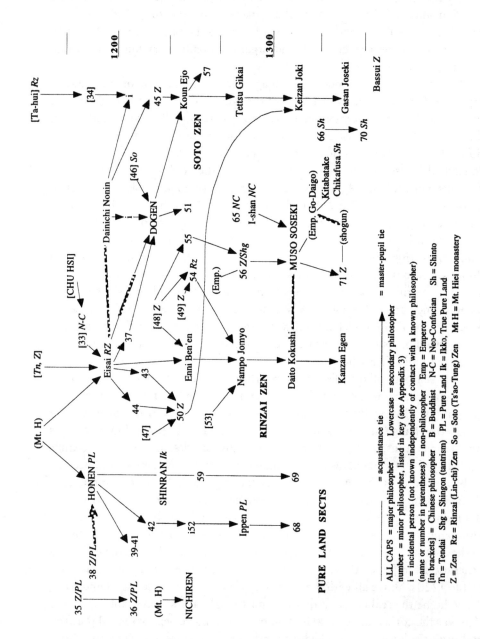

FIGURE 7.2. EXPANSION OF PURE LAND AND ZEN, 1100–1400

ALL CAPS = major philosopher   = acquaintance tie   Lowercase = secondary philosopher
number = minor philosopher, listed in key (see Appendix 3)
                                      = master-pupil tie
i = incidental person (not known independently of contact with a known philosopher)
(name or number in parentheses) = non-philosopher   Emp = Emperor
[in brackets] = Chinese philosopher   B = Buddhist   N-C = Neo-Confucian   Sh = Shinto
Tn = Tendai   Shg = Shingon (tantrism)   PL = Pure Land   Ik = Ikko, True Pure Land
Z = Zen   Rz = Rinzai (Lin-chi) Zen   So = Soto (Ts'ao-Tung) Zen   Mt H = Mt. Hiei monastery

Chinese Lin-chi (Rinzai) line, soon produced a number of figures of at least secondary fame. Among them, Enni Ben'en was instrumental in giving precedence to Zen meditation as the one practice that carries the mind of Buddha throughout the centuries; though he still allowed the practice of rituals and scripture readings, Enni downgraded miraculous powers to insignificance, thereby breaking with the prevalent themes of Tendai and Shingon. Enni's great-grandpupil Kanzan Egen in the mid-1300s brought a full revival of classical Lin-chi rigor, handing out enlightenment with shouts and blows of the staff.

Parallel with the line of famous Rinzai masters in these generations, there emerged a line of Soto masters. Soto was officially imported from China by Dogen. Japanese networks reorganized to fill the attention space with rival schools. Dogen began as a grandpupil of Eisai, but he already had a trajectory toward independence since he and his principal follower, Koun Ejo (who played a similar organizational role in Soto as Enni in Rinzai), were also trained by the lineage of Dainichi Nonin. The Soto-Rinzai rivalry continued the conflict which already existed in the generation of the proto-founders of Japanese Zen. Other lineages too were founded at this time, typically by a combination of splitting off by pupils of the earlier Japanese masters, plus travel to China to pick up direct credentials—a practice which was at its height throughout the 1200s, despite the upheavals of the Mongol conquest and the atmosphere of Japanese chauvinism during the Mongol invasion threat from the 1260s through 1300.[9]

Soto and Rinzai: Rival Niches

The moment of transition during the organizational break which first opened up the Zen movement promoted a rare peak of philosophical creativity. The outstanding figure here was not in the Rinzai movement but from its opponent. Dogen built on two conflicts. In China he studied under the master T'ien-tung Ju-ching (356 in Figure 6.4), notable primarily for attacking the famous Ta-hui for syncretizing Ch'an with Confucianism and Taoism (Kodera, 1980: 102–103)—a doctrinal retreat characteristic of schools in organizational decline. Upon returning to Japan, Dogen developed his independent position by extending the controversy. He criticized Ta-hui for emphasizing the doctrine of emptying and quieting, instead of the original Buddha nature; more generally, Dogen accused Chinese Ch'an of slandering the sutras and reducing Buddhism to a few sayings of Lin-chi (Dumoulin, 1990: 57–62). In effect this was an attack on the central Lin-chi/Rinzai practice of koan meditation. Since Ta-hui was a famous ancestor of the Rinzai line, Dogen's criticism put him in immediate confrontation with his Japanese contemporaries. Perhaps this was Dogen's intention. Dogen's position in the 1230s had been moderate and even included some koan teaching; but after Enni returned from China in 1241 and received massive patronage for building the Tofuku-ji, Dogen began to polemicize against the lack of true succession in Japanese Rinzai. The correct practice was not solving koan but "sitting straight" without effort at enlightenment. Soto became the unembellished practice of *zazen,* without paradoxes or deep trance. Enlightenment itself is not to be overstressed as a goal; post-enlightenment practice was especially important. The creativity of Japanese Soto was a negation of the previous Zen innovation. If the Zen movement generally was a conservative throwback against Pure Land innovation, Dogen was the innovator who found the ultraconservative path. Against his intention, this moved him dialectically onward.

Dogen's philosophical writings articulate Zen without the paradoxes. In place of the paradoxical koan style, he explains the identity of conventional oppositions: existence and nirvana, time and mind and the Buddha. Truth is fluid, daily experience: "The very impermanency of grass and tree, thicket and forest, is the Buddha nature. The very impermanency of men and things, body and mind, is the Buddha nature. Nature and lands, mountains and rivers, are impermanent because they are Buddha nature. Supreme and complete enlightenment, because it is the Buddha nature, is impermanent. Great Nirvana, because it is impermanent, is the Buddha nature" (quoted in Dumoulin, 1990: 85). Enlightenment is the grasping of this identity.

Part of Dogen's motivation was to downplay the deliberate seeking of enlightenment experience in conventional Zen practice. This led to Dogen's most original thinking, on the nature of time. Buddhahood does not reveal itself to us on some occasion, as the culmination of Zen practice. Instead, Buddhahood is itself time. "He who wants to know Buddhahood may know it by knowing *time* as it is revealed to us. And as *time* is something in which we are already immersed, Buddhahood also is not something that is to be sought in the future but something that is realized where we are" (quoted in Kitagawa, 1987: 301). One's self is time. Dogen criticizes the view that time flows from past through present into future, as if "while the time and mountain may still exist I have now passed them by and I, at the present time, reside in a fine vermilion palace. To [a person who believes thus], the mountain and river and I are as far distant as heaven from earth." But past and future are really all one time, only one moment, "the absolute presence, in which all that is present or absent is as such present" (quoted in Dumoulin, 1990: 88). Fully grasping one moment is to touch all of reality.

Dogen's philosophy was not followed up by any notable intellectual descendants; eventually it was rediscovered in the 1920s, when it became ammunition for the Kyoto school of modern academic philosophy. Organizationally and ideologically, however, Dogen launched a successful new trajectory for Zen. He consummated the shift from Zen syncretism to the doctrine of pure meditation. His monasteries were the first to build a detached monks' hall solely for meditation. In part he was moved by fortuitous political pressures; in the 1230s, as he raised his claim to the truest Buddhist path, his Kyoto center was attacked by Mount Hiei troops, leading Dogen to establish his head monastery in then-remote Echizen Province (some 100 miles north of the capital). In fact he was following the population flow, which had spread from the home provinces to the north. Dogen's disowning of paradoxical koan fitted well with a movement away from the sophisticated elite; and his emphasis on the identity of enlightenment with everyday life was an incentive for ordinary work. Soto's practices emerged at the same time that the Pure Land movements were spreading to much the same audiences. Dogen had originally studied with Pure Land teachers, and his Soto was in effect a Zen competitor to Pure Land.

In the generations after Dogen, Soto spread very widely, away from the capital cities where Rinzai flourished. Soto monks worked in the fields alongside the people; lay associations were formed around the temples, through which the laity, including women, could join in meditation (Dumoulin, 1990: 138–143, 208–210, 213–214). Organizational success watered down Soto's distinctiveness. The third-generation disciple Keizan Jokin inherited a great Shingon temple as well as a Soto lineage; from this base Keizan initiated the nationwide Soto movement, at the cost of mixing Zen with Shingon rituals, burial services, incantations, and prayers for worldly well-being. Dogen's original polemic notwithstanding, koan were reintroduced as an aid against distraction during meditation. Keizan's pupil Gasan Joseki, in the mid-1300s, eliminated the unorthodoxy by replacing koan with a five-stanza formula which pithily summarized the essence of the Hua-yen (Kegon) metaphysics, taken over from the Kegon school, now largely defunct in Japan. The formulas now took precedence over the study of Dogen's philosophy; an extensive scholarly literature became developed in commentaries on this so-called doctrine of the Five Ranks. Soto took on the character of an educational institution, paralleling Rinzai, but at a different social level: whereas the Rinzai monasteries of the Five Mountains became cultivated academies of the elite, Soto monasteries became schools for the rural populace. Thereafter Rinzai and Soto carried on in their independent niches. In both branches the routinization and scholasticism of organizational success was setting in.

The Rinzai Establishment and Secularization by Aesthetic Elite

Rinzai Zen lost little time in becoming accepted into the highest level of the new political establishment, while keeping on excellent terms with the old court aristocracy. Rinzai's organizational basis became the provision of aesthetic high culture which linked all the rival elites into a unified status group. In 1246 under Enni, Zen acquired its first grand temple, the Tofuku-ji at Kyoto, designed to compete with the splendor of the cathedrals of the traditional Nara schools. Its sponsor was a retired official from the once-dominant Fujiwara family. Around the same time the Kamakura shoguns built a similar string of great Rinzai temples, beginning with the Kenchoji (1251) and the Engakuji (1282), with their imposing architecture and spectacular hillside settings. Their heads were the most prestigeful monks who could be found, including Lan-hsi (an immigrant disciple from one of the main Chinese masters), and Koho Kennichi, a son of the ex-emperor. From this lineage, in the early 1300s, came Muso Soseki, himself an imperial relative, who gathered further connections with the highly prestigious Chinese lines. Muso went on to found several more great Zen monasteries at Kyoto, including one in a palace donated by the new shogun.

Under the Ashikaga shoguns, the great temples of Kyoto and Kamakura became recognized as the "Five Mountains" (in fact, five in each city), which presided over a hierarchy of secondary and provincial temples. The Ashikagas made Rinzai the de facto state religion. Zen temples were built in every province throughout the country; their revenues were property of the Rinzai hierarchy, under a civil official who supervised all Zen and Vinaya monasteries. In actuality, this state minister was drawn from the Zen masters, and in 1379 the office was handed over to monastic administration. Materially, the Rinzai elite were the apex of Japanese society. The Zen culture that emerged set the high-status standards of aesthetized lifestyle which have prevailed in Japan ever since. Muso Soseki designed temples and gardens as symbols of the cosmos, including the first of the famous Kyoto rock and moss gardens. Flower gardens, which had been conventional to that time, were displaced by a purified aesthetic permeated with the abstract consciousness honed by Zen meditation. Tea, which began to be cultivated in Japan on temple grounds after seeds were brought from China by Eisai, was expanded into a cult ceremonial, carried out in special pavilions in idyllic garden settings. The Noh play was invented in the context of the increasingly secularized mixture of Zen aesthetics and aristocratic entertainment. Zen monks established the vogue of painting with simplified and spontaneous ink strokes; the most famous lineage of painters— Josetsu, Shubun, and Sesshu—were all priest-artists in the 1400s connected with one of the Kyoto Five Mountains.[10]

In the period from 1300 to 1600, the Rinzai monasteries, with their libraries and art collections, were the material centers of cultural production and display. In retrospect, we tend to take for granted that this is simply what "Japanese culture" *is*. In fact, the cultural style emerged at this time as a sharp transition within Buddhism. Previously, in the Kamakura period, Buddhism had not produced significant works in painting, sculpture, or literature; these arose with the organizational transition in the Muromachi (Yamamura, 1990: 582). The artistic productivity that appeared after 1400 shifted decisively in a secular direction. Paintings broke free from traditional religious themes to take up worldly subjects, as well as non-Buddhist "classical mythology" from Confucianism and Taoism.[11]

This secularization of the means of cultural production took place in the transitional generations as priests became mixed with a new semi-laity. In the process, religion lost its tension with lay practices; the essentials of religion became redefined as aesthetic. In Kyoto during the 1300s, taking the tonsure was a means of freeing oneself from court rankings; such *tonseisha* priests had no formal ties with temples and continued a secular lifestyle (Varley, 1977: 186–189). These individuals promoted the secularizing aesthetics of the artistic golden age of the 1400s; by decreasing the gap between laity and clergy, they helped delegitimate Buddhism in much the same way that the Humanists of the European Renaissance began a wave of neo-paganism culminating in the cultural displacement of medieval Catholicism.

The breach in the clergy-lay border opened the gates for the extreme social fluidity of the Muromachi period. Rinzai schools became open to lay pupils as well as monks. This is the path toward the secular university, which we have seen in India at great training centers such as Nalanda, and which we will follow in the Christian universities of Europe. From the outset Rinzai sojourners in China had brought back Neo-Confucianism; it was propagated in Japan not as a separate school but as part of the general literary education at the Rinzai temples. In the late 1300s the Ashikaga shoguns supported an academy with thousands of students, many of them laity, taught by a staff of Zen monks (Kitagawa, 1990: 126). Central to the curriculum were the Chinese classics, taught in much the same spirit as Latin and Greek within Christian Europe, as purely cultural accomplishments apart from religious orthodoxy. In this mode of secularism and scholarly eclecticism, the Neo-Confucian commentaries were kept alive in Japan under Buddhist auspices.

Why then did this proto-"university" structure fail to produce the takeoff into abstract philosophy that characteristically went along with it elsewhere? No philosophical creativity came out of these studies; the classics were simply memorized and used as materials for historical allusions (Dumoulin, 1990: 176). No competitive network emerged among rival centers in philosophy; a single center dominated, without opposing schools of thought. And focus of attention was not on an inward orientation to argument among intellectual specialists but on the aesthetics shared with a leisured upper-class laity. Such outward orientation of a religious elite toward social standing in a decentral-

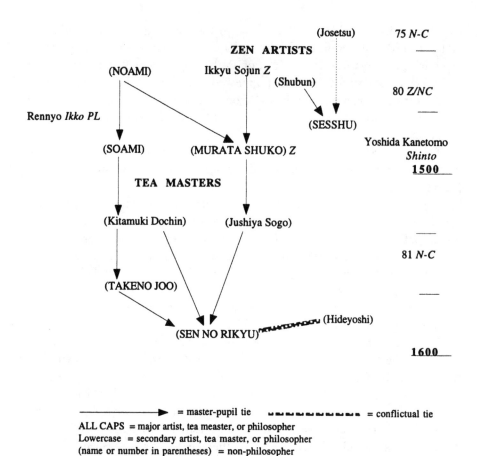

FIGURE 7.3. ZEN ARTISTS AND TEA MASTERS, 1400–1600

ized aristocracy produces the culture of lifestyle aestheticism. The respective "Renaissance" periods of Europe and Japan share another similarity besides concentration on artistic creativity: they are also troughs in first-rate philosophical creativity, as we can see by comparing the 1400s and 1500s in Figures 9.6 and 9.7 and the virtually coinciding period (1365–1600) in Figures 7.2 and 7.3. In both cases the philosophical intellectuals were taken up with imports of "antiquarian" culture, ancient Greek and Latin and Neo-Confucianism, respectively. Imports and revivals were filling up the attention space, substituting for the formation of new lines of intellectual fractionalization. It would take a break with the entire Buddhist base and the rise of a new mode of intellectual production in the Tokugawa educational marketplace to jolt a new intellectual restructuring in the direction of abstract thought.

The Inflation of Zen Enlightenment and the Scholasticization of Koan

The material expansion of the Zen lineages brought problems of organizational control and status legitimation. Enlightenment was not only a personal religious experience; it was also a socially recognized rite of passage. When accompanied by a certificate of enlightenment from an authenticated master, it entitled one to become head of one's own monastery, even founder of a lineage. Organizational expansion thus went along with the increasing commonness of enlightenment, and sowed the seeds of organizational fragmentation.

Soto managed the expansion more smoothly, downplaying enlightenment, and instituting from the early 1300s a periodic rotation of abbots in office. Each master would appoint five main disciples, who shared in authority, allowing for expansion while linking new foundations to the center (Dumoulin, 1990: 197, 206–210). In Rinzai, the elite Five Mountains at Kyoto and Kamakura, with their huge properties, kept a semblance of ranking at the top; but a proliferation of masters in outlying areas became known as the Zen "forest" *(rinka)*, repudiating authority and giving out enlightenment certificates without requiring the recipient to renounce affiliation to his current lineage. By the late 1400s, an inflation of enlightenment certificates set in; pupils traveled from master to master collecting as many as possible. One reaction was iconoclasm. The most famous Zen figure of that generation, Ikkyu Sojun, allegedly burned his enlightenment certificate (Dumoulin, 1990: 194).[12] Ikkyu, an illegitimate son of the emperor, was very much part of the aesthetic elite. For him, Zen meant a spontaneous, wandering life, devoted to artistic pursuits which made him the most famous calligrapher of the Muromachi period, and a founder of the ink-stroke painting style.

The underlying problem of maintaining religious tradition was that Buddhism had set off an economic transformation of Japanese society. Buddhist organizations from 1200 through the 1500s proliferated physically and structurally throughout Japan. The dynamic market economy dates from these centuries; the monasteries and the popular Buddhist movements unleashed the commodity and financial networks which made Japan by the outset of the Tokugawa unification a society of large population and economic prosperity on a level at least with any other part of the world. Zen, as a conservative elite, was less involved in entrepreneurial activities than the Pure Land movements, but it too benefited materially from the expansion of wealth in which monasteries acted as the leading edge of economic growth. As the temples became rich, a superordinate market arose in sale of offices; by the 1380s abbots and senior monks (especially of the far-flung Rinzai Five Mountains organizations) were paying fees for their appointments. Since they often held office for less than a year, and dispersed gifts and held lavish ceremonies at their accession, it is apparent that a great deal of wealth was being extracted from the monastic economy by these officials. The shogun began to rake off fees from certificates of appointment, and in the 1400s was inflating the turnover to maximize income from the monastic sector.[13] The business atmosphere of these monasteries was so intense that the iconoclastic Zen master Ikkyu described the monks as more like merchants than Buddhist priests.

The material success of Japanese Buddhism and its "corruption" were part of the same process. Spiritual careers blended with careerism in the pursuit of power and status, and of the material wealth which concentrated in the great monasteries to a greater extent than in lay society. Even the monks who were most inwardly oriented toward pure religious experience were caught up in an organizational dynamic which required them to compete for widening rewards in terms of inflationary criteria of advancement. Enlightenment was becoming structured by an expanding marketplace.

Soto, whose niche was the small-scale rural monastery catering to the needs of the common people, abjured koan and emphasized the purity of meditation, although rigorous practice faded into ritual and scholasticism. Rinzai in contrast made koan the very center of practice. In its elite monasteries, where lay aesthetes merged with religious virtuosi, koan practice in effect became a literary practice, based on the texts of the koan collections which became prominent in Japan in the mid-1200s and 1300s (Dumoulin, 1988: 248–251; 1990: 30–31, 47). The koan and their commentaries, written in elegant and paradoxical form so as to constitute meta-koan in their own right, were very close to poetry (if differing in the formal rules governing number of syllables and the like). By the generation of Gido Shushin, a pupil of Muso Soseki and adviser to the Ashikaga shoguns, the koan form was being assimilated to the composition of secular poetry.

Conflict over the place of koan went along with the changing external fortunes of Zen. During the Sengoku period (1467–1580), the "Country at War" when central political authority had collapsed, the abbots of Buddhist monasteries were literally independent feudal lords, and the armies and huge financial resources of the greatest Pure Land orders held the military balance of power. The worldly power of Buddhism tended to delegitimate it spiritually; and the military lords who finally reimposed secular control by a quasi-centralized state, from Oda Nobunaga to the Tokugawas, took steps to crush the monasteries' power and confiscate their economic base. Zen, which as a conservative elite had stayed remote from the Pure Land radicals, remained in relatively good graces politically; but it too was subjected to increasing government regulation. It was reduced in effect to an administrative branch of the state church, used for enrolling the populace under approved religious practices. The fluidity of monastic careers which had once allowed creative crossovers among lineage masters was gone; movement within career hierarchies was restricted to bureaucratized channels. The choking off of Buddhism was one reason why the most ambitious intellectuals had shifted by the second generation of the Tokugawa regime into the Confucian schools and become expressly anti-Buddhist.

For those whose remained within Buddhism, eminence went to dissident masters such as Bankei Yotaku who repudiated the koan because of their artificiality. Written in Chinese, with their subtleties packed into the nuances of a classical language, the koan cut off Zen students from the masses. Bankei became a Rinzai evangelist, preaching to mass audiences and proselytizing the common people to realize the unborn Buddha mind (Dumoulin, 1990: 321–323). Recapitulating the Soto style, Bankei downplayed the distinctiveness of enlightenment.[14]

Tokugawa Zen underwent a crisis of bureaucratization, arising through the sheer size of the Buddhist establishment, and enforced by the government. The Tokugawas thoroughly recentralized the Buddhist orders after their period of feudal proliferation; every temple was made a branch subordinate to its headquarters, and that in turn to government oversight. In 1614 Buddhism was made the official state religion; every household was required to register as members of one of the recognized Buddhist sects.[15] Along with responsibility for vast numbers of purely nominal adherents, this presented Buddhism with the problem of control by an efficient and increasingly unsympathetic secular administration. In 1627 controversy arose over a new regulation that abbots of the elite Rinzai temples should have mastered the entire corpus of 1,700 koan. The leading Zen master of that generation, Takuan Soho, protested that such mastery was impossible and would vitiate the spirit of Zen enlightenment. On the other side, Takuan's condemnation was called for by Suden, governmental supervisor of all Zen establishments (who was the original drafter of the 1614 religious regulations), and by Hayashi Razan, a former Zen monk who had gone over to neo-Confucianism and was in the process of establishing an official Confucian college under the shogun (Dumoulin, 1990: 275; Sansom, 1961: 70–74). The regulation was upheld; Takuan was sent into exile.

High religious status—and along with it an honorable career position ending as abbot in one's own right—involved the increasingly competitive seeking of certificates of formal legitimation. It was this credential inflation and the accompanying jostling for organizational position which motivated many of the bureaucratic reforms and restrictions of the Tokugawa period. The requirement of learning 1,700 koan for the highest abbotships was part of this atmosphere. So too were reform efforts within Soto in the late 1600s, when collecting multiple enlightenment certificates was prohibited, so that a disciple could be dharma heir to only one master. In 1703 central authority in Soto was confirmed by the shogunal administration, and its rules of succession were enforced by law (Dumoulin, 1990: 336).

Koan practice became increasingly bureaucratized not only at the top but for the rank and file as well. Hakuin, the last famous Rinzai master, sought to reinvigorate Zen in the early 1700s. Proselytizing among the common people, he opposed intellectualism as too elitist for these audiences. This intellectualism he identified not with koan but with the practice of silent enlightenment and its doctrine of no-mind; this practice, he declared, along with the *nembutsu* syncretism that had crept into popular Zen, was responsible for the current decline of Zen in Japan (Dumoulin, 1990: 383–386). Fighting for his sect's identity, Hakuin stressed what was organizationally most distinctive about Rinzai. Koan practice was something to be carried on everywhere, continuously occupying one's consciousness. To this end, Hakuin systematized koan into sequences. Pursuit of freshness nevertheless led to another layer of routinization. Among his successors, the result was a scholasticism which categorized koan by form and content, making them into an educational curriculum that could be pursued throughout one's career. The issue of koan versus silent enlightenment recapitulated a conflict which had taken place in Chinese Zen during the 1100s, at just the time when Ch'an was fading from social prominence (Dumoulin, 1990: 383). These were long-standing structural alternatives for the meditation specialists: the elitist-intellectual path and the path of assimilation to everyday life, including common work. In the Tokugawa a third path emerged mixing the two: koan practice as an educational routine.

The conception of enlightenment changed in correspondence with these external changes in monastic careers. The old, undifferentiated conception of enlightenment was increasingly refined. Distinctions were made between "little" and "great" enlightenment (Dumoulin, 1990: 139, 373). Masters imposed increasingly stringent requirements. Hakuin, in the early 1700s, had a classic ecstatic experience. Following normal procedure, he formed his enlightenment verses for presentation, but several masters refused to confirm his experience; finally he submitted to a master who put him through eight months of koan meditation, together with laughs, insults, and blows, before allowing him to collect his own disciples.[16] Merely solving one koan was no longer enough, as in the tales of the original Ch'an masters; a series of koan must be passed. Other forms of practice escalated as well. In the early 1700s we hear of monks undertaking well-measured ascetic feats, such as a strict 1,000–day retreat, which secured one's reputation and resulted in invitations to head important temples (Dumoulin, 1990: 338).

Hakuin eventually became famous, both as an organizational leader in the last phase of Zen proselytization and as the creator of a new form of Zen exposition. His writings are meta-reflections on the process of solving koan. Hakuin writes about his personal experience, about the efforts and strains of going through the koan training. He takes the reader into his confidence, leading one by sympathy into the path of following a similar training. Hakuin adopts the stance of the teacher encouraging a non-elite audience. Although his medium is still the koan, the interaction of teacher and audience has shifted drastically from the parrying of wits which made up the original materials for the Chinese koan, and away from the witticisms by which the old commentators had set themselves as equals to the old masters whose doings they recounted.

Historically, numerous procedures have led to enlightenment experiences. Dogen in 1225, soon after arriving in China, experienced enlightenment and received the dharma seal after a few weeks of intense meditation; the precipitating moment came when his master admonished a monk for falling asleep during a midnight session: "In Zen, body and mind are cast off. Why do you sleep?" (Dumoulin, 1990: 56). Dogen had his enlightenment experience very quickly, while on his visit to China with the intention of receiving a lineage transmission to take back to Japan. Many Japanese sojourners in China at this time similarly progressed rapidly to enlightenment, in contrast to the many years of training typical of enlightened masters during earlier, intensely competitive generations in Chinese Ch'an, or again during later periods in Japanese history. My point is not that the enlightenment experiences were not genuine, but rather that the contrasts are evidence that they were socially constructed.

Muso Soseki (in 1305), walking under a moonless sky, was enlightened when he tried to lean against a wall where there was none, fell down, and felt the "wall of darkness" disintegrate; a few months later he received the seal of enlightenment upon presenting his verses commemorating this event. Another master, Shuho Myocho (in 1304), attained his enlightenment upon solving a koan, which left him covered in sweat and feeling that a barrier had been smashed through. Ikkyu attained his while working on a koan when he was suddenly startled by the cawing of a crow. Still another was enlightened when his dying master, asked for a last word, gave him a slap on the face. Another was said to have experienced his first enlightenment at age 15 by falling down stairs. These paths include verbal realizations, with and without koan paradoxes, and in some cases a state of tension and preparation in intense meditation, precipitated by a physical shock. Some monks put themselves through grueling discipline, lengthy periods without sleep or food, sometimes sitting on pointed rocks, making themselves sick in order to abrogate normal consciousness.[17] It was also possible to reach enlightenment simply by the practice of tranquil meditation.[18] The tranquil paths to enlightenment appear to have displaced the more spectacular ones as Zen became routinized and flamboyant *rishi*-like masters no longer commanded much social charisma.

Such processes on the organizational plane do not exclude the reality of the religious experience of persons such as Muso or Hakuin. Historical and sociological writing inevitably becomes the external history of ideas and events. This is so even when written by sympathetic religious participants (such as Dumoulin), not to speak of secular sociologists. It is the same for every religion. The Christians martyred for their faith in the early Tokugawa were, true enough, actors and pawns in the political struggles of national unification; but on an inner level many of them must have experienced the gospel of love and salvation, whose worth cannot be judged outside itself. Our histories lose the religious dimension of such experience. The language of religious evocation and the language of scholarship tend to be mutually exclusive, separated by a gestalt switch that defocuses the content of one from the other.

Writers of history and sociology can take heart from the fact that this process is not merely imposed from outside by secular scholars; it has happened within the historical development of every religion. Leaders of the faith have been periodically aware of the undermining tendency of scholarship, even as it derives from one's own sacred books. Islam, Christianity, Buddhism alike all went through early struggles against intellectualism, and all gave rise to academic traditions. Without such displacements there would be little history of philosophy. The conflict cuts both ways. After the creation of a literate tradition, a permanent possibility in the space of religious positions is a movement of anti-intellectualism, whether in the direction of fideist return to commonsensical readings of the scriptures, or toward the mysticism of wordlessness. The dialectic does not stop here. The scholastic path is a permanent possibility as well. Scholasticism provides organizational continuity and transmits legitimation and prestige; these advantages ensure that religious intellectualism will be resumed again after every counter-movement.

The "history of Zen" is a contradiction in terms. Zen is the sophisticated level of awareness that arises from recognizing the gestalt switch between words and the ultimate reality they try to describe. Nevertheless, enlightenment experiences do not arise of themselves. Falling down steps, receiving a slap on the face, a sudden release from tense concentration are not religious experiences until they are interpreted. That is why there is a network of Zen masters, passing along the sensibilities which shape future possibilities of experience. Zen enlightenment is stepping beyond words, but the Zen masters transform it into poems and imagery, thereby making a transient inner experience into a publicly accessible object. This is the path toward scholasticism, with its future chains of verbal commentaries; but it is also the path along which other persons can find their own transient ineffable experiences.[19]

A similar quality is found in the debates observed by Kenneth Liberman (1992) in Tibetan monastic practice. Here the contents are much more overtly intellectual than in Zen, consisting in problems descending from the *Abhidharma* and Madhyamika philosophies brought to Tibet from medieval India. As in Zen, what Tibetan debate encourages in practice is not intellectual innovation (in fact, the same arguments have been used for a thousand years) but instead fluid engagement in the exchange. There is a premium on making quick replies, on laying traps for one's opponent through a series of questions, on springing triumphantly into the breach (also with shouts, gestures, and musical percussion) when one's opponent hesitates or breaks down. The coordinated rhythms and emotional intensity make us aware that Tibetan debate is a ritual in the Durkheimian sense; specifically it is a ritual of membership in the spiritual community of transverbal detachment, conferring marks of spiritual progress.

There is no religion without sacred objects, without symbols representing the focus of attention and the distinctive sense of membership in the group; it is these symbols that set apart the experiences which are transcendent from those which are profane. And even when one's purpose is to transcend thought, that trajectory can only be set in thought, and through the medium of symbols which represent the group and its history. Symbols are the residue and the continuity of experiences over time. They flow through individual brains, shaping their attention and emotions, setting up the possibility of transcendent private experience, and then bringing those experiences back into the network of social relations which give them meaning, and which re-create the possibility of other persons' acquiring their own private experience.

From the level of material organization, through the interpersonal networks, the flow of symbols and the building up of emotional energies, peak experiences are fashioned. These same conditions undermine pure religious experience, bringing attention down to the mundanities of organizational power, the blandishments of material property, the displacements into scholasticism and intellectual discourse. Social reality is at once creating and bringing down religious experience. The one flows into the other in waves, and peak and trough share aspects of each other. The same can be said in religious language: samsara is nirvana.

Tokugawa as a Modernizing Society

The Tokugawa regime was a time of spectacular economic growth, taking off from the market relations established in the Buddhist economy of the previous period, and turning its confiscated wealth into secular channels. The government of the shogun was reestablished at Edo (Tokyo) at a symbolically significant distance from the old site at Kamakura, where the Five Mountains temples of the Zen hierarchy had formerly held sway. The shogun's administration *(bakufu)* remained feudal in form, but became in substance an absolutist bureaucracy with a high degree of success in pacifying the aristocracy in a web of legalistic and status formalities. Military forces remained under the lords of the feudal domains; but loyalty was ensured by requiring the lords' frequent attendance at the court at Edo, while fragmentation at the lower levels was cut off by withdrawing all samurai from living on the land and concentrating them in the castle towns of the domains. Three great cities under the *bakufu*'s direct control became the nodes of economic and cultural life: Edo, which by 1700 had burgeoned into the world's largest metropolis at 1 million inhabitants; Kyoto, where most lords kept up an alternate establishment, paying pseudo-court to the ceremonial regime, and where the schools proliferated; and Osaka, the former monastery-citadel of the wealthiest Pure Land movement, now the commercial hub of the Tokugawa economy.

The Educational Marketplace and the Intellectual Desertion of Buddhism

Buddhist intellectual and cultural domination was on its way out, but it shaped events once more at the time of transition. By 1600, Zen had transformed Japanese culture by establishing an educational system. The system was two-tiered. Popular elementary education was provided around the countryside by Soto temples, and the elite Rinzai monasteries offered advanced training (Dumoulin, 1990: 261–262, 333–334). The latter diverged into various branches or tendencies. In some places pure training in koan continued. At the leading Kyoto temples, aesthetic cultivation over the centuries had blended with secular training, nurturing painters, garden designers, tea masters, and even actors. Pupils, masters, and other inhabitants of the monasteries might or might not be in clerical orders. Another branch of Rinzai education was more strictly textual and academic. It too had become essentially secular in content.

In the early Tokugawa, the Neo-Confucian contents of academic Zen were mobilized as a vehicle for revolt. Although some ideological strands of this movement give the appearance of a shift from one religion to another, from Buddhism to Confucianism and then to Shinto, such a formulation would be misleading. There was no shift in official religious ideology; on the contrary, in 1614 (and more forcefully in 1638) Buddhism was made compulsory for all households, a regulation not dropped until Meiji times. Confucian ceremonies were introduced here and there but, outside of a few centers of Confucian militancy such as the Mito feudal domain, never became widespread. Neo-Confucianism gradually became the favored educational doctrine of the *bakufu*, but was not officially required until the 1790s (and then only in the *bakufu*'s own schools, a small portion of the whole), by which time it had long since gone out of style with the leading intellectuals. The only thing that can be called a genuine religious reformation was the promulgation of State Shinto during 1868–1882; but after an initial struggle to confiscate Buddhist property and return monks to secular life, religious tolerance was quickly adopted (Kitagawa, 1990: 164, 201–214; Collcutt, 1986). State Shinto turned out to be a minimalist version of the Shinto cult, and coincided with the full-scale secularization and de-clericalization of the school system. What we see is a series of attempts by the government to prop up religious orthodoxy, but inconsistently, and with enforcement only at a pro forma level, while both the means of intellectual production and the ideas receiving attention in most intellectual circles drifted continuously away from organized religion.

The key should be seen as the gradual secularization of the educational base. The earlier phases embody the same kind of process in which university-trained intellectuals during the European Renaissance, with the aid of new sources of political patronage, broke free from the clergy-dominated base and established their own secular schools. By the 1700s, leading Japanese intellectuals were promoting the independence of worldly secular studies in a fashion paralleling that of the *philosophes* of the European Enlightenment; still later, when the Meiji government took full control of public education, there was a phase of full-scale anti-clericalism when priests were displaced from the lower reaches of teaching.

When creativity came alive in Japanese philosophy after centuries of stagnation, it happened as a breakout from within Zen. That is to say, there was a revolt within the religiously dominated educational establishment, and therefore a critique of the dominant religious ideology. The leading thinkers of these early generations—Fujiwara Seika, Hayashi Razan, and Yamazaki Ansai—all began their careers as monks, and the anti-Buddhist militancy of the latter two was that of apostates breaking free. Seika was still a transitional figure, a Rinzai monk who shifted emphasis to the Neo-Confucian part of the curriculum, but without disparaging rival emphases. Seika laid down the basis for the new network trajectory when he became adviser to Tokugawa Ieyasu; his pupil Hayashi after 1608 performed Ieyasu's secretarial work, along with chief Buddhist officials including the Tendai abbot Tenkai, and Suden, the supervisor of the Zen hierarchy. So far this was the traditional ministry of religious affairs, pressed into bureaucratic service for the now powerful shogunate; and it was this secretariat, under Suden, which drafted the 1614 order for all households to register under a branch of Buddhism. Hayashi broke only gradually, establishing his independent Neo-Confucian school at Edo in 1630, three years after his fight with Takuan over the regulation of koan teaching.

Even so, Razan taught in clerical robes and tonsure, indicating how closely clerical status remained identified with the teaching profession. Ansai did not leave the monkhood until 1647, and opened his successful Confucian school at Kyoto in 1655. Hayashi's school, headed in a hereditary line by his descendants, was elevated to an official "university" only in 1691, with an annual income as a state-sponsored shrine. The new philosophy was not simply a matter of the new Tokugawa regime shifting from Buddhism to Confucianism in search of a new political legitimation, nor a revenge against Buddhism because of the military battles of the unification wars. Zen in any case had stayed out of the fighting of the previous period. It was above all the popular Ikko sect which had been the military threat, yet even Ikko received concessions under Hideyoshi.[20]

Zen still exerted some attraction during the first generations of the Tokugawa. The samurai class did not immediately desert for the new ideologies. Contemporary with Hayashi Razan are Zen stars from samurai families such as Takuan Soho.[21] Another such is Suzuki Shosan, who abandoned the military life after the great battles of 1615 to become a monk. He promoted an innovative direction in Zen, denying the significance of ritual, declaring that "working the land is Buddha practice," and formulating an ethics for merchants which stressed the performance of work duties without greed. Suzuki's doctrines have been pointed to as a Buddhist version of the "spirit of capitalism."[22] In the generation 1665–1700 there appeared a major Zen figure, Bankei, who came from a family of *ronin* (masterless samurai) and converted from Confucianism; his contemporary Basho was similarly from the ranks of the lower samurai, and though not a monk, he infused his haiku poetry with Zen sensibilities. Still later, Hakuin was also from a samurai family.

What we have is a conflict breaking out within the status group of Zen-educated intellectuals. As usual, conflict fuels creativity simultaneously on all sides. In the long-term network (compare Figures 7.3 and 7.4), the period 1600–1735 is much more populated by Buddhists of major and secondary rank than the five preceding generations; it includes, in the mid-1600s, the first founding of a new Zen sect (the Obaku sect, brought by Chinese émigrés) since the 1200s. The generations which lead up to Hakuin are a typical buildup of eminence within a creative network; and if Hakuin is the last gasp of Zen in its time of troubles, the pattern is in keeping with the principle that creativity results from shifts in the underlying organizational base, both on the way up and on the way down.

Fueling the revolt within the ranks of Zen was a conflict between its aesthetic and academic branches. The elite level of Rinzai was largely secularized already. Appointments to top posts of the Five Mountains were in imperial hands, reserved for members of the highest aristocratic families (Dumoulin,

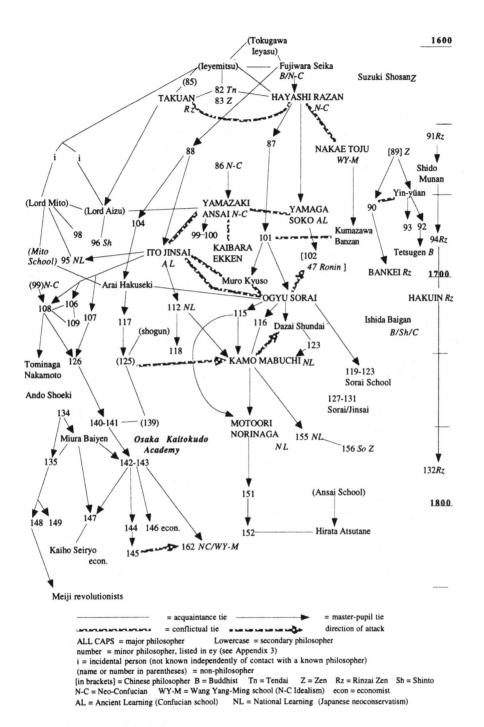

FIGURE 7.4. TOKUGAWA CONFUCIAN AND NATIONAL LEARNING
SCHOOLS, 1600–1835

1990: 270). The worldliness of the Zen establishment undermined its religious legitimacy; some of the criticism, both by wandering monks and by the advocates of neo-Confucian ethics, took the form of purification movements within the ranks. The Zen hierarchy had already been splintering in the 1400s and 1500s, giving off separate lineages specializing in teaching purely aesthetic arts. A hierarchy of specialized tea masters arose alongside conventional enlightened meditation masters, eventually claiming precedence over religious and even political ranks (See Figure 7.3).[23] The spread of aestheticism was muddying the status hierarchies; in the tea cult in particular, wealthy merchants from port towns such as Sakai were mingling with, and even taking precedence over, prelates and warriors. The Neo-Confucians of the early Tokugawa were in part reasserting the ranking of samurai over aesthetic challengers, in part restoring morality as the central criterion of religious life. The most important of these early Confucian schools, that of Yamazaki Ansai, had a militantly puritanical tone, forbidding the composition of poetry, and condemning any emphasis on calligraphic style as a frivolous distraction from the moral seriousness of the texts.

The underlying dynamic of Tokugawa intellectual life was the expansion of educational markets. Zen education by no means disappeared after the great monastic properties were confiscated; the Soto elementary schools in particular flourished. Buddhist temples in total proliferated from some 13,000 to over 460,000 (in the 1720s) in connection with the requirement that every family hold a temple certificate; every sect expanded its academies for training priests (Kitagawa, 1990: 164; Dumoulin, 1990: 333; McMullin, 1984: 246). But the temples were now tiny; cosmopolitan connections and competition over positions disappeared as temples were made hereditary family properties. There was no longer any centralized elite, no apex of the status hierarchy such as had been constituted by the Five Mountains at the time of the Muromachi shoguns. Many different cultural providers could find an audience. Among them, Ansai's attack on aestheticism acquired many disciples, but it could not definitively prohibit or displace some other branch of the market from offering aesthetic products. Indeed, one of the popular areas of specialization that opened up soon thereafter was the academic study of literature, first Chinese, then native Japanese poetry. On these academic bases rode the philosophical innovations challenging Neo-Confucianism.

Several different types of education developed.[24] First in importance were the private proprietary schools *(shijuku),* catering to the samurai class, though gradually amalgamating with wealthier commoners. Such schools were small-scale, consisting of lectures in an individual teacher's home for pupils who became his personal disciples. This was the predominant form of schooling until the mid-1700s, and it continued to hold its own despite the challenge of rival forms of schooling thereafter. Virtually all notable intellectuals were teachers of proprietary schools.

Official state schools, by contrast, grew very slowly. Before 1690 there were only a handful of such schools, under auspices of the feudal domains or of the Edo government. Thereafter came a modest growth (to a few dozen) until 1770, followed by a considerable expansion to virtually every domain in Japan. Such schools had relatively little intellectual impact. Designed to occupy and control the samurai class of each domain, they combined elementary and advanced curricula in a prolonged drilling in literacy, the Confucian classics, etiquette, and stylized military arts. In the full development of the system, lower samurai might be required to attend until age 24, higher-ranking nobles until age 30 or even 36. Education here was an adjunct to hereditary rank, an extension of the elaborate etiquette which filled the lives of officials and headed off potential military conflict. Education did not determine access to official careers, since higher positions were filled largely by hereditary rank and connections; failing grades were never issued, and school progress was reported in a rhetoric of superlatives upon superlatives. The ritualism of schooling meshed with the administrative routine of formal requests and reports, by which documents were accepted only if they followed precise stylistic conventions. To tighten the system, in 1792 the *bakufu* made an effort to establish Chinese-style examinations for appointments, but without much effect on the usual status criteria for officeholding.

At the other extreme were elementary schools for commoners. Their origin was in the Buddhist religious schools. In the early 1600s half of the teachers at such *terakoya* were priests, and in the mid-1800s the proportion was still around 25 percent. The big takeoff took place in urban areas in the 1750s, resulting in widespread literacy and numeracy; by the 1840s a massive elementary school system had been developed at local initiative.

With the exception of the proprietary schools, most of this expansion of education had little direct effect on intellectual creativity. The outburst of new philosophy was concentrated in the generations from the mid-1600s to the mid-1700s, when there was still only a small number of schools. In the early creative period there may have been no more than a few dozen. But these made up an intensely focused competitive network, structurally reminiscent of the formative period of the old Chinese philosophical centers in the Warring States. Kyoto around 1665 was acquiring the classic creative structure of a center of intersecting circles of rival movements; in the next generation it was supplemented by network branches at Edo. The huge educational expansion of the late Tokugawa would not be expected to do much positively for intellectual innovation; its organizational base went far beyond the limits of the law of small numbers, and it suffered from the stifling effects of bureaucratization, just as in the comparable expansion of Chinese schooling after the Sung. The official Neo-Confucian orthodoxy decreed by the *bakufu* in 1790 (just before its attempt at a formalized examination system) was hard to put into effect among independent intellectuals; but it was indicative of the mood of the times, when the entire structure was formalizing under its own massive weight.

For the early period when education was just taking off, we should add schools of the specialized arts: the private teachers and academies of swordsmanship, painting, poetry, flower arranging, and the like which proliferated in the 1600s. Strictly speaking, these were not part of general schooling but were more of a continuation of the aesthetic high culture of the pre-Tokugawa period, expanding forms such as the lineages of famous tea masters. In the late 1600s, at the time of Basho, there were some 700 haiku teachers in Kyoto, divided into rival styles and lineages (Moriya, 1990: 119; Maruyama, 1974: 115). Such schools did not promote the kind of abstract thinking which is the territory of philosophy, but their expansion reveals something of the underlying structure of cultural production. Many of the teachers were samurai, displaced from their feudal lords or blocked for promotion into higher officialdom by hereditary families. Teaching was one of the few careers which did not forfeit the status honor of the samurai rank (as entering commerce would have); and the audience for such teachers was not only other samurai but also the burgeoning population of the commercial towns.

A domain school might hire several rival instructors to teach swordsmanship to its samurai, each preserving his own ritual closure through oaths of secrecy. Despite the demilitarization of society—indeed, because of the shift to purely ritualized peaceful status competition among the samurai—such schools proliferated in the Tokugawa. Schools of swordsmanship were organized around lineages of masters, awarding certificates of proficiency to their pupils, modeled on the Buddhist notion of secret transmission of supreme understanding to highly selected disciples. The fusion of Zen with samurai culture which took place at this time was part of the increasing formalization and scholasticizing of status rankings in both sphere.[25] The eliteness of these emblems of transmission was breaking down as certificates proliferated in a veritable inflation of credentials. The proprietary schools went further, breaking with samurai exclusiveness and offering open lectures to the public, without oaths of loyalty or secrecy (Nosco, 1990: 31). These schools thereby provided the competitive public attention space within which intellectual creativity could emerge.

The status culture of the higher ranks was now offered in a competitive market, raising the standing of the wealthier urban classes. In the artistic schools, and in the proprietary schools of Chinese philosophy as well, commoners and samurai blended into a new cultural ranking. In connection with this cultural marketplace came an outburst of the publishing business: again starting off in Kyoto, and expanding in the 1700s to Edo and Osaka, there were hundreds of publishers turning out over 100,000 volumes per year. (Moriya, 1990: 115–117). Most of their content was not philosophy but popular literature and religious tracts. Along with this came the mass market for entertainment in the theater and the mass production of art prints. The first great flowering of this popular culture industry was the Genroku era (1688–1704), and it was approximately at this time that the creativity of the philosophical schools also peaked.[26]

The Network of Creative Oppositions

Consider now the network pattern of philosophical innovation during the Tokugawa.[27] First came the Zen apostates. Institutionally, breakaway Neo-Confucianism became crystallized with the founding of the Hayashi school in 1630. Over the next two generations, the Confucian network split into four factions, expanding to fill its now dominant attention space.

The first of these was the Hayashi school itself. Increasingly defined in the eyes of the shogunate as the orthodox lineage, it maintained an important presence in the network down through the early 1700s. But its stance shifted to the defensive against splitting movements which had made it the favorite target. Its last notable figure was Muro Kyuso, who spent his time counterattacking against a sea of troubles: Buddhism, Shinto, Yamaga Soko's Bushido, Ito Jinsai, Sorai. In Muro's generation, the Chu Hsi school had official support from the shogun, but little else to uphold it.

Second appeared the Wang Yang-ming (Yomei) school of Neo-Confucianism, represented by Nakae Toju on the heels of Hayashi Razan, and by Toju's pupil Kumazawa Banzan through the following generation. This was an easy and natural path to diversifying Neo-Confucian offerings, insofar as the Wang Yang-ming school was already available as a Chinese rival of Ch'eng-Chu orthodoxy. Against the orthodox dualism of *li* (principle) and *ch'i* (material force), Toju promoted metaphysical monism, which he expressed as the unity of mind with external nature. In good Neo-Confucian fashion, Toju supported ethical and social conclusions from his metaphysics: there is innate knowledge in the human conscience, and self-cultivation is equivalent to social action. Toju attacked Razan as merely parroting Neo-Confucian texts, without absorbing the spirit of ethical practice. Banzan in turn became the first notable heretic attacked by the Hayashi family. As usual, a creative period was ushered in by its conflicts.

Kumazawa Banzan used the slogan "unity of knowledge and action" to shift the emphasis of Confucianism to social and economic policy. He sharpened the split between worldly Confucianism and the sage religion of Ansai, rejecting both puritanism and otherworldliness.[28] The Yomei school became a favorite ideology of administrative reformers—a case of metaphysical idealism being used for practical activism, outflanking the dualist-materialist doctrines of the conservatives. Yet this is not so much an anomaly when we compare the similar use of idealist justification in Fichte's reform policies.

The significance of these new schools was also organizational. Hayashi Razan, and a fellow student of Fujiwara Seika, Matsunaga Sekigo, had both sought official sponsorship for their schools. Razan's support at Edo was rather meager and offhand at first (Ooms, 1985); Sekigo did better at Kyoto, under the patronage of both the *bakufu* representative and the emperor. Nakae Toju was the first to establish a school of higher studies without official support. It was not particularly successful, in part because it was located away from the cultural centers of the main cities. The model was soon picked up at Kyoto, where fully independent schools were established by Yamazaki Ansai and Ito Jinsai. Banzan promoted his position in the burgeoning market for education, organizing a clan school for a *daimyo* (feudal lord) and attempting a Kyoto school in the formative period of the 1650s.

The competitive educational market hit full stride with the generation of 1665. Two more splits in the Confucian camp quickly appeared. Yamazaki Ansai's school at Kyoto became the greatest success of all, attracting 6,000 disciples. Ansai attacked the Hayashi scholars as mere drudges, failing to practice what they preached. Ansai claimed to offer the pure Chu Hsi tradition, shorn of compromises and accretions. In this direction Ansai was primarily a textual scholar, editing the Confucian classics with their approved commentaries and limiting his pupils to a narrow set of works stressing morality and decorum. Ansai's forcefulness made Chu Hsi Neo-Confucianism into a full-fledged religious movement. He revived and stressed the "sage religion," which the original Sung Neo-Confucians had borrowed from Ch'an; the move was a natural one for Ansai as a former Zen monk.[29]

Ansai's stance becomes clearer when we note his relations within the network (Figure 7.4). Unlike most of the other Confucian branches of these generations, he did not derive from the Seika-Hayashi line. Instead he had an independent Confucian lineage, in the somewhat out-of-the-way Shikoku school of Tani Jichu.[30] Ansai crossed this line with his Zen heritage; in addition, he collaborated with the domain school of the Lord of Aizu, Hoshino Masayuki, an active promoter of scholarship at Edo. Masayuki represents the emergence of yet another institutional form of intellectual promotion, something like an academy of noble patronage; in addition to Ansai, he collected under his wing Yoshikawa Koretaru, the first important reformer of Shinto ideology along modern metaphysical lines, and also sponsored the Hayashi school to produce a chronology of the imperial family.

Masayuki's patronage academy is paralleled by another sponsored by his cousin, the Lord of Mito, Tokugawa Mitsukune.[31] At Mito, Mitsukune collected a group of scholars for another massive historical project, in this case to write the history of Japan from its legendary origins to the present, a work which went on for generations after Mitsukune's death. In the Mito circle we find a number of notable scholars, including the Ming refugee Chu Shun-sui and the Buddhist monk Keichu, who became the ancestor of the National Learning movement. There was, in short, an upsurge of intellectual status emulation among the great lords. It became fashionable to promote new religious ideologies; the Mito domain was among the most militant in attempting to suppress Buddhism, while Lord Aizu meddled in the factional politics of Shinto. The overall effect was to encourage the flow of scholarship in autonomous paths.

Ansai took maximal advantage of the new prestige of scholarship, which he turned into a religion in its own right. He energetically explored two different religious niches: reviving the Sung sage cult and then going on to formulate his own version of Shinto. Stimulated by his contact with Koretaru in the Aizu circle, Ansai extolled reverence as the principle which Shinto and Neo-Confucianism have in common, and equated the cosmogonic myths of the *Nihon-shoki* with Chinese cosmology. His followers venerated Ansai as a living *kami* (god) and fitted out his school with initiation rites of an amalgamated Confucian-Shinto cult.

The fourth major school was created by Yamaga Soko, a former student of Hayashi Razan. In the new educational system he represents a different niche, having spent his early career as a military instructor in a domain school. In 1666 Soko formulated Bushido, the Way *(do)* of the Warrior. Samurai codes were not new; versions had existed since the 1100s, stressing loyalty to superiors unto death. Soko, however, was living in peacetime conditions, and he raised the question of what was the function of the samurai, since they did not work. The answer was drawn from Confucianism: the samurai role was to punish people who transgressed moral principles.[32]

Soko broke with both the Chu Hsi and Wang Yang-ming schools, on grounds that their doctrines had brought not peace to the Sung but foreign conquest. Striking a new political note, he stated that since China had repeatedly been conquered but Japan never (and had in addition twice conquered Korea), Japan was superior and had right to the title of Middle Kingdom. The adulation of Chinese culture, which had shaped Japan from Buddhist times through the Neo-Confucians, now began to be thrown off. It would be an error of tautology to attribute this to an incipient nationalism in the society at large. The dynamic can be found within the new structure of Tokugawa intellectual competition. Soko carved out his position in opposition to the surrounding schools of his time, above all to the Neo-Confucians, arch-adulators of China. Most sharply, Soko was a direct counter to Ansai's sage religion, rejecting meditation and seriousness as the basic moral principle.[33]

Soko's new position called forth a new metaphysic. Soko gave primacy to materialist monism and eliminated Neo-Confucian quiescence, holding that it is merely the motions of nature that produce good and evil. Soko wielded as his main resource an increasing depth of scholarship. He undercut Neo-Confucian claims of antiquity by noting that "the teaching of the sages consists only in rites and music." Soko did not, however, dispense entirely with his Confucian cultural capital; he found a new space within Confucianism by separating the classics from their Sung accretions. From Soko came the Edo school of *kogaku*, Ancient Learning. This represented simultaneously a move toward traditionalism and antiquity, and a shift toward naturalism.

By the end of the century, Neo-Confucianism was becoming old hat. The older networks continued, but their new offshoots were twisting the lineage of cultural capital into new channels. Ansai's acquaintance Kaibara Ekken pushed the naturalist aspects of Chu Hsi virtually into empiricist materialism. Matter/energy *(ch'i)* was seen as fundamental, principle *(li)* merely derivative; the important thing was the accumulation of knowledge through research, which Kaibara carried out in the realm of medical botany. With Kaibara we meet a new phenomenon, a Japanese intellectual who is detached from any school, merely an outstanding individual with a unique position. The marketplace now was offering recognition for such individuals; rivals such as Dazai called him the most learned man in Japan (Sansom, 1963: 87).

The more influential, however, succeeded by establishing proprietary schools. Of these the new leader was the Kyoto school, the Kogido, founded around 1662 by Ito Jinsai.[34] Adopting the stance of Ancient Learning, Ito took a crucial step: he separated values from cosmological principles. In Chu Hsi, *li* is simultaneously moral law and physical law. Although they are identical, the former aspect takes priority; the universe is regulated by sincerity. There is nothing like this in Western idealism; it would be equivalent to holding that Christianity's "God is love" provides a way of ordering and controlling the physical cosmos by religious action. Chu Hsi's cosmic anthropomorphism was grounded in the practice of the sage religion. Impurities and turbidity of the *ch'i* are the source of human desire and hence of evil on the lower plane; this is repaired by meditation on *li*, whereby the sage restores human and cosmic purity. The Sung Neo-Confucians had adopted the technique and part of the doctrine from Zen by identifying *li* with the Buddhist Original Nature; the chief difference was that instead of ultimate emptiness, the Supreme Ultimate is the world-logos, and this in turn is equated with moral sincerity.

Ito Jinsai now broke the link. He attacked the practice of sitting in quiescence (meditation) on the principle *(li)* underlying all things: "In things, there are the principles of things. But a single primal material force is the basis, and principle is posterior to material force, *ch'i*" (quoted in Maruyama, 1974: 446). There is no single principle, but only the multiple principles of natural phenomena. The way is opened to develop cosmological or metaphysical principles independently of human nature. By the same token, ethics is freed up as a separate realm of discussion. Ansai's moral rigorism now appears as merely inhumane. Ito Jinsai's school became the linchpin of subsequent developments, organizationally and in network structure. The Kogido was imitated by other innovators, who founded proprietary schools that broke free from the Neo-Confucian pattern. Among Jinsai's pupils were Keichu and Kada no Azumamano, who were instrumental in National Learning, as well as the leaders of the Kaitokudo merchant academy. Jinsai's doctrines were systematized in the next generation by his son Ito Togai; the school remained prominent in subsequent scholarship until 1871, when all Confucian schools were abolished in favor of Western education.

The 1665–1700 generation was the most creative in many centuries; altogether it included five major philosophers (Ansai, Yamaga Soko, Kaibara Ekken, and Ito Jinsai, as well as Bankei on the Buddhist side), plus two secondary figures (Kumazawa Banzan and the Buddhist scholar Tetsugen).[35] The momentum of innovation continued in the following generation.

The conservative path to innovation carried on. Jinsai had freed Confucianism from religion by shifting emphasis to the original texts, promoting naturalism in the name of tradition. This opening was exploited most forcefully by Ogyu Sorai. Sorai was in the center of power at Edo. Formerly a pupil of the Hayashi school, he had advanced to chamberlain of the fifth shogun, Yoshimune. Advance guard to Sorai's position was his colleague in the court bureaucracy, Arai Hakaseki, trained in the same lineage as Ito Jinsai, and in contact with the Mito scholars. Arai is an all-round Confucian scholar, but chiefly engaged with purely secular concerns of history, and above all practical problems of the fiscal condition of the government. Arai played down ideology in favor of pragmatics. Holding Christian doctrine to be nonsense posing no danger to the state, he saw less need for seclusion from foreign commerce. Ansai's approach to history downplayed the omens of traditional Confucian annals in favor of a rational interpretation of events.

Upon retiring from office in 1714, Sorai established his Edo school, where Ch'eng-Chu orthodoxy was definitely repudiated in favor of Ito's *kogaku* (Ancient Learning). This move of rebellious philosophy into the seat of power had its risks, insofar as the Hayashi school had recently been elevated to a state shrine; but Sorai's excellent government connections shielded him, and his school soon became the center of intellectual attention.

Sorai proceeded to take the distinction between Neo-Confucianism and the ancient texts as legitimation for radical revision of accepted principles. "The Way" consists in human norms only, not in laws governing the natural world. Although valid norms are taught by sages, there have been no sages since ancient times (a direct slap at Ansai's Neo-Confucianism, in which every gentleman meditates to become a sage). This being the case, ethical beliefs are a purely private matter. The only norms that can be generalized are those of social ethics, which boil down to propriety and obedience to government. From this Sorai drew radical consequences for current social policy. He suggested eliminating social ranks, the fourfold order of samurai, farmer, artisan, and merchant which had been justified as corresponding to the Confucian social order. Instead, he said, "All the people of the world are officials who assist the ruling prince, who is the parent of the people" (quoted in Maruyama, 1974: 92).

The military samurai appeared to Sorai an outmoded group, whose troubles were to be understood in terms of the mundane realities of modern economics. The samurai were becoming an impoverished class because they did not work, but lived on fixed stipends in the midst of a market economy.[36] More generally, demand for goods was unlimited but supply was limited. The result was increasing prices, while the circulation of gold and silver pieces diminished because of heavy debts. Sorai thought like an analytical economist, recognizing that long-run adjustments were necessary. His proposal was to give samurai fiefs and make them live on the land, while fixing supply and demand by regulation and restoring frugality through sumptuary legislation. The entire economy was to be put into stasis; people's movements were to be controlled by a registration system. Sorai's view of economics led him to profoundly conservative, even reactionary policies. But it was in keeping with his analytical style that society should be regarded under the aspect of naturalistic order, with explicit recognition that the market, if allowed to operate, has principles of its own. Solutions must be economically feasible ones, not merely edicts of moral exhortation or threats of military coercion. In Sorai's own school his chief disciple, Dazai Shundai, a year after Sorai's death (1728) reversed his master's position to favor an economy based on trade rather than agriculture. With Dazai, the acceptance of an inevitable social order broke through into the instrumental consideration of policy options. Although it was mercantilism rather than free trade which he favored, the intellectual basis was an analytically independent economics.

Sorai and his school raised philological scholarship to a value in its own right. The break came under cover of ideological continuities from the past. Confucian legitimation continued to be claimed. The pathway was already opened by previous scholars who had maneuvered their own positions into an orthodox light by selective attention to their favorite classics. For Chu Hsi these had been the *Doctrine of the Mean* and the *Great Learning,* hitherto obscure ancillaries to the old *Book of Rites;* for Jinsai the favorite vehicle was the *Analects;* for Sorai it was the Six Classics made canonical by Confucius. In the hands of older scholars, mere verbal similarity and the obscurity of meaning in ancient texts were used to justify the desired new readings. By the early 1700s, three generations of Japanese schools had built up a critical standard of textual scholarship, motivated by open competition among classical and Sung Confucian factions. Sorai simultaneously invoked respect for the sages while distancing them from modern conditions. Since the world and languages had changed, the only way to recover the ancient Way was to master ancient language and adhere to the old rites and music. China had obviously changed, and therefore deteriorated, over time. But one cannot simply imitate the past; what is recorded in texts is to be treated as history.[37] Wielding this weapon, Sorai recognized that Sung Confucian teachings stemmed from Buddhism. Similarly, the Shinto put forward by its modern advocates did not exist historically, as shown in ancient texts. Sorai declared that Shintoism had been invented by Yoshida Kanetomo in the 1480s. Sorai drew a policy consequence favorable to his *bakufu* connections, rejecting even nominal sovereignty of the emperor. Dazai was even more dismissive: "Shinto is no more than the Way of the sorcerers. It is not a matter to be studied by a gentleman" (Maruyama, 1974: 154).

In their utilitarian emphasis on worldly practicality and rejection of metaphysical speculation about heaven's law, Sorai and his school resemble European intellectuals of the Enlightenment. Sorai is often compared to Machiavelli or Hobbes; one might also say that he is something like a mixture of Voltaire, with his anti-clericalism and his appeals to the rational absolutist despot, and Rousseau, with his reasoned rejection of the evils of market civilization. This is so not because the European and Japanese thinkers are interchangeable as individuals, but because their respective situations contained similar sets of ingredients. Defining what these were must be deferred until we have further pieces of the puzzle in hand.

The Divergence of Secularist Naturalism and Neoconservatism

Sorai's success signaled a near-revolutionary collapse in the popularity of Neo-Confucianism. The Hayashi school was almost deserted until the period of enforced orthodoxy at the end of the century. Ansai's sage religion fell to a minor conservative sect. In the 1730s and 1740s, Sorai's disciples dominated discourse. The price of becoming a scholarly hegemon was paid; creativity dropped, and scholarly specialization and routine set in. After 1750 the Sorai school became embroiled in minor disputes with the Ito school; many thinkers adopted an eclectic path amidst the issues, further muddying the sharp edges of doctrine which had once characterized the systems in their creative periods.

In these two generations the naturalistic line of thought inspired more radical innovations. The most extreme of these, isolated in the network of Figure 7.4, did not rise to more than secondary eminence in the attention space. Ando Shoeki, a medical scholar living in the isolation of northern Honshu, pushed the Neo-Confucian *kigaku* (doctrine of material force, *ch'i*) to virtual materialism. He was the only Tokugawa scholar to criticize explicitly the feudal order; his stance was a Rousseau-like condemnation of samurai, priests, and merchants alike as socially useless. At the other end of Japan, Miura Baiyen at Nagasaki promoted a dialectical logic of things, advocating experimental methods and investigating economics.

Closer to the center, naturalism invaded the Kaitokudo, the Osaka academy established in the 1720s for merchant families, explicitly breaking the samurai monopoly on officially sanctioned education. Its founders were pupils of both Ito Jinsai and the Ansai lineage of neo-Confucianism, and the Kaitokudo in its early years was timidly eclectic (Najita, 1987; Najita and Scheiner, 1978: 23–43; Ketelaar, 1990: 19). In the next generation a pupil, Tominaga Nakamoto (son of one of the wealthy merchant patrons of the academy), rebelled against this eclecticism, criticizing Confucianism along with all other religions in favor of a "religion of the facts." He was expelled, but by midcentury the naturalist attitude had become dominant at the Kaitokudo. The chief teacher, Goi Ranju (a grandpupil of Ito Jinsai), launched an empiricist attack on Buddhist doctrines, using knowledge of science and astronomy against the cosmology of the world-centering Mount Sumeru and the layers of hells and paradises. The next leader of the Kaitokudo, Nakai Chikuzan, combined attack on Buddhist irrationality with the study of economics and advocacy of the virtue of the merchants' profession. Here we see the European Enlightenment-style intellectual movement in full force, attacking religion as outmoded. That the merchant academy chose Buddhism to attack, one hundred years after the Confucian scholars had already dispensed with it, probably had to do with the differences in social milieux. Confucian schools were above all identified with the samurai, while Buddhism still remained the belief of the common people; and it was also no doubt safer to attack popular Buddhism than to take on Confucian sage religion.

A connection was now established with Miura Baien, who sent his pupils to study at the Kaitokudo; several became teachers there, shifting the emphasis to empirical science, especially astronomy. The outstanding pupil produced by the Baien-Kaitokudo connections was Yamagata Banto; in 1804 he propounded heliocentric astronomy as a touchstone, an epistemological image of objective science decentered from merely human biases. Yamagata's division of all knowledge into pre- and post-astronomy was not accepted by the Kaitokudo, but his empiricist secularism found new bases. Yamagata became head of a branch house of a big Osaka merchant, where mathematical and financial specialists were becoming in-house intellectuals. One of these, Kaiho Seiryo, built an empirical science upon the accounts of the great Osaka merchant houses and his travels to witness their operations. Kaiho was a veritable Adam Smith.[38] He equated *li* (principle) with the balance point of an exchange, recognizing a natural law governing buying and selling which is accessible by rational calculation. Everything is a commodity and has its exchange value. In the style of the radicals of the European Enlightenment, Kaiho rejected metaphysics in favor a materialist monism, critiquing as well Confucian traditionalism and the simplistic ethical maxims of the samurai class. Stratification is the result of historical conditions, he said, as can be seen by the fact that there are no classes among the Ainu of Hokkaido. Workers are best motivated by incentives rather than punishment. With Kaiho, we have class-conscious advocacy combined with analytical secularism.

By the generation of the early 1800s, the Kaitokudo had become upstaged by even more militant offshoots. A former pupil, Oshio Heihachiro, led his own small school of some 20 pupils in setting fire to Osaka in 1837 in an effort to provoke a general uprising against the *bakufu*. Another descendant of the Baien-Yamagata lineage, Ogata Koan, founded the Tekijuku in 1838 close by the Kaitokudo, as a school of Dutch Learning devoted to Western medical science. From this school came many of the militants and intellectual leaders of the Meiji restoration, including Fukazawa Yukichi, who introduced Western liberalism and positivism in the 1860s.

Until the mid-1800s, these Osaka lineages were out of the mainstream of attention, which remained focused at Kyoto and Edo. The more spectacular success in the attention space broke off from the Ito Jinsai and Sorai networks. In the familiar dialectic of creative innovation, this move now took a contrary direction. The pseudo-conservatives of the Japanese Enlightenment were calling forth an opposition of genuinely reactionary conservatism. To set the stage, we must consider the fact that Sorai separated public and private spheres: that is to say, public issues of law were to be treated by different standards than private matters of ethical belief. Thus, in the famous law case of 1702, when 47 *ronin* (masterless samurai) avenged the death of their former lord by killing one of the shogun's officials, Sorai held that their adherence to the samurai code of ethics was irrelevant, and they should be punished for breaking the public law.[39] Sorai's differentiation of intellectual realms went along with a corresponding shift in the structure of education as well. The teaching of non-orthodox religious doctrines was condoned, so long as it took place in private schools. In his own school, specialization emerged between those concerned with public matters (primarily economics and governmental policy) and those devoted to the scholarship as a cultural realm in its own right. Instead of religion and ethics, however, the focus of the latter was literature and philology. This continued the main textual concerns of Confucian literati; it also held potential for evoking disputes between Japanese and Chinese literature, as well as the long-standing line of cleavage between aesthetic and moral-religious values.

From literary disputes developed the ideological movement of National Learning. Catching the center of attention was Kamo Mabuchi. He derived from network connections which brought together the literary and philological side of the Sorai lineage with the growing militancy of Shinto priests. Among his teachers there was already a critical stance toward Confucian philosophy. Hori Keizan was explicitly hostile to the concept of *li,* precisely because it was an abstraction and therefore applicable in a meaningless fashion that did not explain anything concrete.[40] The philosophical defense of particularism was building up. Mabuchi was spurred to bring out its larger significance on the occasion of a dispute in the early 1740s over the teaching of poetry at the court of the shogun's son. The public affairs wing of the Sorai school, as well as the neo-Confucian line descending from Arai Hakuseki, attacked poetry as useless. The Shinto priest Kada no Azumamaro, a former pupil of Ito Jinsai, had lectured on poetry to the Edo court; since Mabuchi was also his pupil, the pro-poetry faction at court asked Mabuchi to prepare a defense of poetry, and rewarded him with an official stipend to teach Japanese poetry.

Mabuchi promoted national poetry as the linchpin of a new intellectual alliance. Confucian interpretations, he said, must be removed from obscuring the pure development of Japanese literature; scholarship must approach its materials through the Japanese language. It was much the same break as took place in Europe when the Romanticist movement repudiated Latin as the language of scholarship and replaced it with the study of national languages. Mabuchi connected this claim for the scholarly autonomy of his specialty with the study of the ancient Shinto chronicles and mythologies. In part this is to be seen as a move in the growing mobilization of Shinto priests; but it also had roots in the expansion and accumulation of textual scholarship through the previous three generations. The individual retrospectively named progenitor of National Learning, Keichu, was a Shingon monk in the 1665 generation, hired by the Mito school to work up a scholarly commentary on the *Man'yoshu* (the ancient poems in the *waka* style), which had first been collected in the late 700s. Such texts had been written in archaic Sino-Japanese from the period when writing was not yet standardized, and hence were long since unintelligible; explicating them became a new specialty, which Mabuchi continued (Nosco, 1990: 9, 57–58).

Here it is worthwhile to pause and survey the development of Shinto consciousness. Although very ancient, Shinto was always a sidelight to the main intellectual action, and never was able to sustain any independent development in the networks until it was finally adopted by a branch of the Tokugawa intellectuals. The reason for this was fundamentally organizational. Shinto was not one church but a rubric covering thousands of local shrines with their particularistic deities. Its material endowments were simple; there were no distinctive cult objects, no representations which could sustain an artistic network, no body of textual doctrines on which an educational system could be built in the fashion of the Buddhists. Shinto priests descended from particular clans, and each local shrine was inherited within a family; hence there was no wide network of recruitment or universalistic system of training as in the Buddhist monasteries. Shinto was carried through the centuries largely by the favorable policies of Buddhists, at first because Buddhists penetrating the countryside made use of indigenous shrines as material bases and local legitimation, then more generally by the policy of maintaining favorable connections with the imperial court, which owed its ceremonial position above all to its connection with a few of the most famous Shinto shrines. Buddhism helped give the Shinto *kami* (indigenous gods) a wider intellectual significance, at first by interpreting them as allies or manifestations of the Buddhas and Bodhisattvas. At periods of political upheaval affecting the religious establishment, Shinto downplayed its particularism and portrayed its doctrine as having larger moral and metaphysical significance.[41] As a generalized doctrine, Shinto was parasitical upon Buddhism. Such organizational dependence promotes doctrinal syncretism or at best thinly disguised borrowings.

In the early Tokugawa, the anti-Christian regulation requiring every family to register with a Buddhist sect was applied to Shinto priests as well. Although this wounded the status claims of the Shintoists, it also vastly improved their organizational connections. Shinto shrines were put under the same regulatory office as Buddhism, and brought into contact with the maneuverings of shogunal administration as well as realignments of the intellectual networks. When Buddhism suffered a drop in its upper-class patronage as a result of the Neo-Confucian revolt, Shinto suddenly had an opportunity to claim its place. The Watarai family of Ise now began to criticize Buddhism as a worse evil than Christianity, and proposed instead a Shinto-Confucian alliance. A more policy-oriented nationalist Shinto began in the Mito school, the most militant antagonist of Buddhism. Lord Mito's cousin and rival, Lord Aizu, promoted his protégé Yoshikawa Koretaru to be the *bakufu* official in charge of Shinto, and attempted to elevate the latter's Yoshida branch of Shinto into a national orthodoxy within Shinto. Shinto-Buddhist philosophical syncretism was rejected.[42] In its place Koretaru interpreted the *kami* as Neo-Confucian *li*, personalized manifestations of the universal metaphysical principle (Kitagawa, 1987: 164). Formerly dispersed and localized, Shinto was now becoming centrally organized for a fight. Sensing the opportunity, in this generation too Ansai proposed his own version of Shinto from the Neo-Confucian side.

The situation did not remain static. The Neo-Confucian school came under attack from the secularists, and its influence collapsed. Now Sorai's contemporary Kada no Azumamaro removed Shinto from under the wing of Confucianism, and his pupil Mabuchi legitimated the separation intellectually with a full-scale ideology of the superiority of Japanese studies.[43] In the next generation, National Learning (kokugaku) was elevated by Motoori Norinaga (another pupil, along with Kamo Mabuchi, of Hori Keizan) into a doctrine claiming to replace Confucianism of every variety. Norinaga's school happened to be near the Ise shrine; in this way he met Mabuchi on his pious travels, enrolled as his pupil, and sustained correspondence with him. Since Ise was becoming the center for pilgrimages organized by a national network, Norinaga acquired a large number of pupils at his private school.

Norinaga turned National Learning into a philosophically sophisticated defense of particularism. He rejected all metaphysics as foreign intrusions. Buddhist and Confucian doctrines alike, he declared, are full of logical contradictions; because they are formulated as universalistic philosophies, they are open to refutation. By the same token, the syncretism of Shinto with Neo-Confucian categories is unwarranted.[44] Nor is Confucianism morally superior; its doctrines, in Norinaga's eyes, reduce to Machiavellian amoralism and are inferior to Japanese practices. Norinaga elevated the historical viewpoint into a criterion by which all rationalisms, both neo-Confucian and post-Confucian, can be rejected. His own textual specialty was the Kojiki (Records of Ancient Matters, compiled from ancient annals and myths in 712), shifting from the literary texts of Mabuchi and his predecessors to a religious text which Norinaga now endowed with scriptural authority. There is no way to rationalize the age of the gods; one can only start with revelation as a miraculous intrusion into the mundane world. Heaven, nature, and human affairs are all due to the kami; but these are particularistic and ineffable, not principles accessible to reason.

Norinaga's position is a combination of positivist historical scholarship and theism. The kami can only be defined as "anything which was outside the ordinary, which possessed superior power or which was awe-inspiring" (Kitagawa, 1987: 165). Here we have an explicit parallel to Rudolf Otto's definition of the holy. Norinaga is like the Christian neo-orthodox theologians at the turn of the 1900s, in the fashion of Schweitzer and Barth, using careful textual scholarship to show that the original faith was not the ethical principles and Idealist metaphysics beloved of liberal Protestants. There is no naturalistic halfway house between secularism and religion. In a fully secular intellectual ethos, religion can indeed be defended, but only by showing forth religious tradition in its full particularism and non-rationality.

In the early 1800s, a contact of the later generation of Norinaga's lineage, Hirata Atsutane, elevated the militancy of the Neo-Shintoist movement still further. Shinto organization itself, he declared, must be purged of the tinges of syncretism, in both Ansai's *Suika Shinto* with its Chinese influences, and *Yoshida Shinto* with its Buddhism. Hirata was the last significant thinker in the direct lineage of the Ansai school, which had been intellectually dormant for generations. He took most of his inspiration from Norinaga, while downplaying the poetic-historical scholarship in favor of political-religious propaganda. Later in the century the Hirata school became known as nationalist extremists fulminating against Westernization. Hirata helped prepare the way for this escalation of intellectual experimentation. He had already rationalized Shinto by introducing a monotheist "heavenly center lord" above Amaterasu, the sun goddess, and incorporating notions of creation and eschatology taken from Christian sources filtering in with Dutch Learning. Despite his claims, Hirata was no deep-rooted reactionary but was a modern neoconservative. His Christian counterparts may be found in France and England in the same generation.

Conservatism and Intellectual Creativity

Throughout the history of Japanese intellectual networks we witness a conservative path to innovation. The ideological trajectory of Tokugawa thought pointed backwards in time. The Neo-Confucian revolt against Zen was legitimated by a nationalist note; Hayashi Razan pointed out that the Shinto shrines historically predated the import of Buddhism, although he twisted this into a support for Chu Hsi by equating *li* with the *do* (way) of the *kami*. Ansai claimed to purify Japanese Neo-Confucianism of the compromises left by the Hayashi school. Yamaga Soko's Bushido school and Ito Jinsai's Ancient Learning leaped over Sung Neo-Confucianism by appealing to earlier Confucian texts. This was not simple traditionalism. The progression was initiated by continual sharpening in the standards of scholarship, and energized by contemporary conflicts among rival intellectuals. These conflicts built up an accumulation of technical tools and conceptual innovations. Jinsai and Sorai, who justified their work as purified Confucianism, differentiated cosmology from ethics, public affairs from private sensibilities; their network fellows recognized and critiqued abstraction as distinct from concrete principles. The ensuing wave of criticism arising against the naturalism of the Sorai style further sharpened philosophical acuteness; the limits of rationalism were explicitly recognized along with the claims of particularism. By the time of Kamo Mabuchi and Motoori Norinaga, historical criticism itself was asserted as an independent and in some sense overriding ground for knowledge.

It is not simply that Neo-Shintoism had to be raised from inchoate roots into a formal doctrine in the intellectual attention space. Its intellectual substance was created in the process of scholarly accumulation over the generations of sustained argument. And it rested more specifically on the differentiation of scholarly specialists, first in received Chinese texts, then going on to explore classical and then national antiquity in a fashion that parallels the European sequence of medieval Neoplatonists and Aristoteleans, Renaissance Humanists, and eventually the Romanticist-nationalist scholars of the 1700s. The fact that the Göttingen school of philologists, along with Winckelmann and the brothers Grimm, were contemporaries of the secularists of the French Enlightenment should not surprise us; we see the same pattern in Japan, where secularist-naturalist and antiquarian-nationalist movements were contemporaries, and even network cousins. This is not a matter of intellectual life proceeding in cyclical reactions; rather, creative periods are always structured by contemporary oppositions. There is a common denominator on the level of underlying organizational bases: in both Japan and Europe these movements rest on the expansion of a cultural marketplace, combining literary publication and formal schooling. Modern conservatism everywhere arises from the secularization of society—in the sense of the declining institutional weight of religion—and the emergence of an autonomous educational system.[45]

Japanese neoconservatism is a phenomenon of modernity. To be sure, the political weight that it acquired in the overall balance of factions is almost unique and must be accounted for by conditions specific to Japan. But modern European history is not without its neoconservative and past-extolling ideologies, constructed precisely with the intellectual tools of modern sophistication. There is a more general lesson. Conservatism as an ideology is always a deception. There is no such thing as an appeal to the unreconstructed past. The very concepts of tradition and of particularistic faith echo the antitheses by which they were shaped. Conservatism, like everything else in the intellectual world, is born out of conflict. And even when the combination of religious-political alliance with an authoritarian regime would seem to make any innovation in the realm of ideas illegitimate, innovation is not choked off.

As soon as organizational conditions are assembled for sizable bodies of literate specialists to communicate about their affairs, the inherent fractionation of the intellectual attention space generates differences in emphasis. These are constructed out of whatever accumulated textual material is available. It matters not that the texts themselves may be ancient and particularistic, or that their overt content may adamantly assert immutability and oppose innovation. Innovation is easily cloaked in the guise of tradition—all the more so when it occurs by opening levels of abstraction and lines of questioning that are not included in the classical categories or antitheses, and hence pass unnoticed until they become deeply rooted.

In world perspective, the drive toward secularization of education often comes not from a strong anti-clerical or secularist party, but from the fact that rival religious conservatives fight to block one another's control. Thus in England during 1830–1870, pressure built up to remove the universities from church control in a struggle among rival factions within the established Church of England (see Chapter 12).[46] In the Tokugawa, de facto secularization of the educational market was promoted because the rival Confucian proto-religions, as well as state-mandated Buddhism, were so widely at odds. In the Meiji, the imposition of State Shinto was in effect a compromise, window dressing for nearly total secularization of education and the effective separation of state and church. It elevated the flimsiest and least organized of Japanese religions into a cult devoted solely to the emperor (who continued to be a figurehead without influence on the political elite), while cutting off the Confucian schools of the intellectuals, and the Buddhism of the masses, from influence over state cultural policy. Here again traditionalist conservatism did not prevent massive structural innovation, and even provided ideological cover.

The Myth of the Opening of Japan

The Meiji restoration and the opening of Japan to the West is by no means the turning point of Japanese history. Japan was not so very secluded from outside resources; its elites were merely in a position to be very selective about what they included. In fact, émigrés continued to bring in cultural imports. In this way in the 1650s there arrived the Obaku sect of Zen, as well as the Chinese dynastic historian (98 in Figure 7.4) who was invited to join the Mito school. Western learning was available through Chinese contacts, as well as through the channel of Dutch Learning, which in Eurocentric retrospect has received more attention than it deserves. If these materials had only minor impacts on Tokugawa intellectual life, it was because the creativity of indigenous networks was already quite high enough to fill the attention space.

Secularization of the Means of Intellectual Production

The major institutional structures of modern Japanese society were already laid down in crucial respects by the eve of the Tokugawa. Market capitalism was accelerated by the Meiji opening, not created by it. The same may be said for secularization. As sociologists of religion know from the perspective of the late 1900s, secularization is not an all-or-nothing shift in the realm of belief; it does not require that a majority of the populace reject the supernatural. What is more important is that an institutional watershed is crossed when the means of cultural production become preponderantly independent of the church. Once this institutional shift takes place, intellectuals—of all people those most directly concerned with the conditions of authority inside the sphere of cultural production—defend the autonomy of their own ideas. This does not require that many (or indeed any) intellectuals become militant atheists; rather they open a sphere of activity which they recognize as autonomous from ultimate religious commitments, and attack intrusions in this sphere as illegitimate, just as Ito Jinsai and Sorai did in the period around 1700.

Several forces press in the direction of secularization in this institutional sense. (1) An independently staffed governmental administration develops, no longer dependent on clergy for literate skills. This divide had been crossed by around the second generation of the Tokugawa. (2) A mass publishing market arises. It can of course sell religious tracts. When it is not controlled by church producers, their wares enter into competition with all manner of other mass entertainment.[47] Such a market was very much in evidence by 1665–1700. (3) Schooling becomes independent of the church. This mass educational market, which started up with the proprietary schools of the mid-1600s, had burst out into a mass system for all social class levels by 1735 or 1765. That is not to say that church schooling did not exist, especially in the rural areas, or that some of the proprietary schools did not attempt to make themselves into religious cults. The distinctiveness of the expansion of Japanese secular education was that it happened primarily through the private marketplace; government schools were a rather small and late part of the expansion.

What the Meiji regime did in the realm of secularization was to implement mass public education under government control. Japanese society now underwent a phase of de-clericalization in the strong sense of the term. There was a period of active defrocking of Buddhist monks, the suppression of Confucian schools, and the creation of a mass school system under governmental control (Ketelaar, 1990; Collcutt, 1986). These actions of the various parties in the de-clericalization struggle were well within the range of conflicts over the staffing of public education and the tax privileges of the church which occupied Bismarck's *Kulturkampf,* the French Third Republic, or Italy following its unification. Again the coincidence of dates with Japan is striking.

The ethos of intellectual life established in the Tokugawa educational marketplace flowed without much of a hitch into the new conditions of mass public education. The proprietary schools had become secularized and politicized; their orientation toward public policy, ranging from economics to the utilitarian engineering of social arrangements, carried over directly into the period of explicit reform. Such had been the prime interests of Japanese intellectuals in the preceding two generations of Tokugawa, from 1800 onward.

The one truly significant structural change of the Meiji, as far as intellectual life was concerned, was the importation of the European (which is to say German) university. Why should this be important? I have noted the similarity of Tokugawa intellectuals to European *philosophes* of the 1700s: their orientation toward practical affairs or to literature and their disparagement of metaphysics and abstract philosophy. The Enlightenment intellectual style was that of non-academic intellectual networks, antagonistic to the philosophical discourse that had grown up in connection with theology in the church-dominated universities. Abstract philosophy reemerged in Europe only with the German university reform in the generations of Kant and Fichte. Tokugawa intellectuals resemble those of Enlightenment Europe before the penetration of German university reform.

School teaching provided a more central base for philosophical creativity in Japan than was the case in Europe, but this differed from the university structure in two crucial respects. Japanese schooling was largely undifferentiated beyond the elementary level. The reformed European university, in contrast, instituted a hierarchy of topics and levels of training, between secondary/preparatory studies and advanced training; at the highest levels, scholars were trained to become advanced teachers in their own right, and to display their competence by the publication of independent research. It was this hierarchic structure which provided insulation for university specialists from the practical or literary concerns of the lay world, and thus encouraged the development of philosophical abstraction. The second unique aspect of the European university enhanced the tendencies of the first: it is that the universities were organized as a collegial group. The university professor was not an individual teacher but a member of a teachers' guild, which claimed monopoly rights to certify new members. This guild structure, which in Europe had its roots in the medieval guilds as applied to the academic vocation, supported collegial autonomy (Huff, 1993); indeed, its rites of passage in the form of the dissertation or *Habilitationsschrift* emphasized the membership-defining significance of specialized and esoteric intellectual production. In Europe, with the long development of struggles among the branches of the university faculty, the self-conscious identity of philosophy was connected with its independence of theology, its appropriation of a distinctive metaphysical and epistemological turf.

It was these academic structures which Japanese education largely lacked. Japanese schools were organized around individual teachers, without a collective guild organization. The predominant form in the Tokugawa, the Neo-Confucian academy, had begun with the fusion of philosophy and theology in the sage religion. The institutional revolution carried out by Jinsai and Sorai broke with religious concerns; the result was the Japanese version of the Enlightenment intellectual, not the equivalent of Kant or Hegel. The lack of autonomous university guild structures reinforced the propensity of Japanese intellectuals toward a politicized stance. Given the differences in content, the late Tokugawa is full of equivalents of the non-academic European intellectuals of that period. The predominant style is the parallel to Rousseau, Marx, and Mill, the non-academicized branch of intellectuals in the West. Political and social activism on the part of intellectuals is not distinctive to the West; its uniqueness is to add the intellectual stance of the university.

As if in experimental proof of this thesis, the introduction of the university into Meiji Japan resulted in an outburst of abstract philosophy. This was not merely a matter of importing European ideas along with the university structure. The philosophical effects of the introduction of the university into Japan took two generations.[48] In the first generation, 1865–1900, Japanese intellectual life was overwhelmed by European idea imports. In Figure 7.5 this generation has no thinkers of outstanding originality. The predominant lines of thought were materialism and evolutionism. Nishi Amane, the pioneer of Western philosophy in Japan, introduced an eclectic mixture of British utilitarianism, Mill, and Kant. Others brought in Comte, Haeckel, Spencer, and Lotze. Weaker at first, but growing in influence by the end of the century, were importers of Idealism, variously in the version of T. H. Green (Onishi Hajime) or a combination of Hegel with Amida Buddhism (Kiyozawa Manshi). The imitativeness and unoriginality of this generation are typical of idea importers. When we compare other periods of world history when the ideas from a deep intellectual lineage are imported into another region, the striking feature of Meiji Japan is how brief was the period of subservience to foreign imports. Such periods (early medieval China under Indian Buddhist imports, Renaissance Europe under the revival of classical antiquity) typically take some four to six generations before indigenous creativity takes off.[49] In Japan, however, major new thinking broke out as early as the second generation, with the Kyoto school of philosophy.

As usual, creativity takes off in the networks which have achieved the greatest degree of prominence in the previous generation. It was a combination of European teachers—some visited at their home bases by sojourning Japanese, others who taught in Japan—and local Japanese intellectual leaders that flowed together to produce the creativity of the Kyoto school. Nishida Kitaro was the great star of this school, but it will be convenient first to examine the network around him.

Inoue Tetsujiro was the first Japanese to hold a philosophy chair at Tokyo.

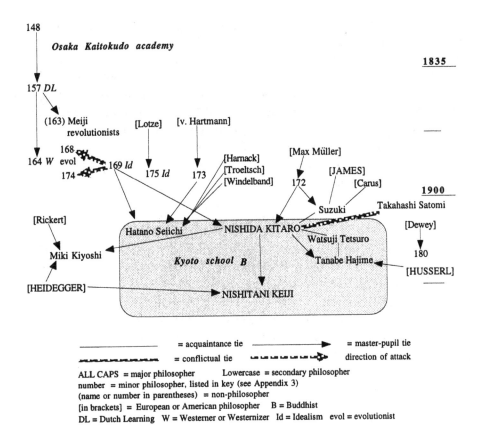

148

Osaka Kaitokudo academy

1835

157 *DL*

(163) Meiji
    revolutionists

[Lotze]   [v. Hartmann]

168
164 *W evol*   169 *Id*   175 *Id*   173
174

[Harnack]
[Troeltsch]
[Windelband]

[Max Müller]

[JAMES]
172   [Carus]

1900

Suzuki   Takahashi Satomi

[Dewey]

[Rickert]

Hatano Seiichi   NISHIDA KITARO

Watsuji Tetsuro

180

Miki Kiyoshi

Kyoto school B

Tanabe Hajime

[HUSSERL]

[HEIDEGGER]   NISHITANI KEIJI

——————— = acquaintance tie   ————▶ = master-pupil tie

·—·—·—·—·— = conflictual tie   ▭▭▭▭▭▷ direction of attack

ALL CAPS = major philosopher   Lowercase = secondary philosopher
number = minor philosopher, listed in key (see Appendix 3)
(name or number in parentheses) = non-philosopher
[in brackets] = European or American philosopher   B = Buddhist
DL = Dutch Learning   W = Westerner or Westernizer   Id = Idealism   evol = evolutionist

FIGURE 7.5. MEIJI WESTERNIZERS AND THE KYOTO SCHOOL,
1835–1935

As a mark of independence, he launched the counterattack against European thinking. His 1891 "Conflict between Religion and Education" rejected Christianity for placing Christ above emperor, and for its injunction of universal love as incompatible with national loyalty and filial piety. He also attacked the materialist evolutionism popularized by Kato Hiroyuki. Inoue represents the upsurge of Shinto conservatism and nationalism against the generation of the European importers; but as we have seen, Japanese conservatism was by no means an anti-intellectual movement, but a long-standing trajectory of innovation within indigenous Japanese networks.[50] Among Inoue's pupils at Tokyo were Hatano Seiichi and Nishida Kitaro.

Hatano, who became one of the secondary leaders of the Kyoto school, combined several network lineages: at Tokyo he studied under Inoue and also with a pupil of Eduard von Hartmann; sojourning at Berlin and Heidelberg, he studied with Harnack, Windelband, and Troeltsch. So far we have an eclectic mixture of Western vitalism, historicist theology, and Neo-Kantianism. Like Nishida, Hatano began as a historian of Western philosophy, suspended among its various positions before going on to develop his independent stance. More important, it was not just the content of European philosophy that was coming through but the creative energy of the European networks. The Kyoto school was not merely linked with figures such as Windelband, but transformed those links in just the way that contemporary networks in European philosophy were transforming.

The Stimulus of Exporting Ideas to the West: The Kyoto School

The distinctiveness of Japanese philosophy in the newly autonomous university structure also involves a key indigenous element. After generations of Confucian dominance, Buddhism suddenly made a comeback. This can have had nothing to do with events in the surrounding society; the Kyoto school followed close on the time when Buddhism was being attacked, sometimes violently, and the school system (which at its elementary levels had been heavily staffed with Buddhist priests) was being secularized. The key is rather in the intellectual network. We see here an instance of a phenomenon which we find in the history of Islamic and Byzantine philosophy as well: the exporting of ideas to a receptive foreign audience stimulates further production of just those ideas. In this case, the receptive foreign audience consisted of the European scholars exploring the history of Asian religions. In the network surrounding Nishida and the Kyoto school were links to just those European scholars who were most interested in what the Japanese had to offer in the realm of Buddhism. Nishida's teacher Nanjo Bunyu was a monk who had been sent by the Pure Land sect to Oxford to study Sanskrit with Max Müller; returning in 1885, Nanjo began teaching Indian philosophy at Tokyo. In turn, Nanjo's pupil D. T. Suzuki came to Chicago for the World's Parliament of religions in 1893, organized by Paul Carus. Suzuki stayed as Carus' assistant during 1897–1908, meeting William James (just then in his phase of exploring religious experience), and translating Sanskrit and Japanese Buddhist texts. Suzuki eventually became famous by promoting Zen in the West through his books of 1927–1938 (Kitagawa, 1987: 320–323).

The revitalization of philosophical Buddhism and more specifically of Zen took place as these networks crystallized in the autonomous Japanese university. This is hardly what one would have expected from the flow of ideas or the continuation of past intellectual trajectories. Zen had not had an important thinker since Hakuin in the early 1700s. Confucianism after eight generations of dominance had been disowned by the reform of the school system, but it was not Buddhism but Shinto that was on the rise in the Meiji public sphere. The Kyoto school threw out the materialist positivism of the early wave of reformers; drawing selectively on Christian, Idealist, and Neo-Kantian imports, it transformed them creatively into a new position. Nishida Kitaro was the star who emerged from the intersection of these networks. As a pupil of Nanjo Bunyu, he was a grandpupil of Max Müller; he was trained under Inoue Tetsujiro, whose search for a national intellectual identity Nishida contined; and he was a friend of Hatano, and a close friend of D. T. Suzuki since their secondary school days.[51]

As in all creativity, Nishida transformed the ingredients transmitted through these networks, sometimes by direct opposition. In 1911 he created an "oriental logic" as an explicit basis for oriental culture, to parallel the Western cultural foundation provided by Greek logic. Nishida's "logic of field" or "logic of place" combined German Neo-Kantian logic with the Mahayana nothingness of Nagarjuna. Nishida found his creative slot by working out the similarities and contrasts of Zen metaphysics with the logics of Aristotle, Leibniz, Kant, and Hegel; Nishida's later works distinguish his "place of nothingness" from the noumena of Leibniz and Kant. Against the popularity of neo-Kantianism at Kyoto and Tokyo universities, Nishida rejected the distinctions of value and being, meaning and fact; unity is derived from the self-consciousness exemplified in Zen meditation, as the internal union of meaning and reflection, the self-generation of concrete experience.[52] Nishida was the first in the world to produce a high-level confrontation of sophisticated ideas from Asian and Greek-European traditions. By contrast, his European counterparts—Deussen, Müller, Carus—acted only as translators and importers, not creative synthesizers of these lineages.

Nishida's pupils and followers found their creative space by following similar network combinations. A number of them sought out the leading German philosophers—both the Neo-Kantians and their network successors, the phenomenologists. Tanabe Hajime studied at Berlin, and at Freiburg with Husserl; his work proceeded from a philosophy of mathematics along the lines of Neo-Kantianism to a synthesis of Hegel, Husserl, and Heidegger into a religious philosophy combining Buddhism with the Christian doctrine of love. Tanabe bridged Nishida's "oriental logic" to both nationalist particularism and universalism, propounding a "logic of species" (i.e., the nation) mediating between individual and mankind. Watsuji Tetsuro, a friend of Tanabe, brought into play the primary contribution within Japanese intellectual history, in 1926 reviving philosophical interest in Dogen after centuries of neglect. Like others of the Kyoto school, Watsuji focused on the relations among Nietzsche, Kierkegaard, and Buddhism. In retrospect we may be inclined to take this as old hat, a Japanese importation of existentialism. In fact the European existentialist vogue did not really get going until the 1930s and especially the 1940s; the Kyoto school philosophers were much closer to the source of this movement, and not solely because of their network contacts with the phenomenologists in the early 1920s.

The most renowned Japanese philosopher of the following generation, Nishitani Keiji, was a Nishida pupil who spent three years studying with Heidegger in the 1930s. Nishitani perpetuated Nishida's central technique: juxtaposing Europe and Asia, and relying heavily on Dogen, he set forth Buddhist thought patterns as a solution to present-day cultural crisis. Nishitani criticized Western theism for its cleavage between God and creation, subject and object, out of which grows the twin evils of rootless science and technology and the egocentric nihilism of the existentialists. Against this Nishitani upheld Buddhist *sunyata* (emptiness) and conditioned co-production. Nishida and Nishitani had an ecumenical as well as a nationalist side. Nishitani drew links to the Western mystics (Plotinus, Eriugena, Eckhart, Boehme, Cusanus), but argued that there is a better grounding in "oriental logic."

Here we should be aware of a preemptive move by the Kyoto school vis-à-vis all other Japanese (and indeed Chinese and Indian) philosophical schools: it was Buddhist metaphysics, and specifically that of the Hua-yen–Zen tradition (rooted in the classical formulation of Nagarjuna), that was elevated to the title of "the Eastern Way of Thought." Schools like Sorai's worldly pragmatism were swept from the attention space.[53] Zen philosophers allied with nationalist self-assertion to take control of the newly imported university base. European philosophers were enlisted either as allies or foils, serving to shift the focus of attention to a Zen-centered agenda.

The Kyoto school coincided with the nationalist repudiation of Western ideas and institutions in Japanese political movements more broadly in the 1920s and 1930s. Nationalist and indeed fascist political ideologues and activists, such as Tachibana Kosaburo, formulated positions which paralleled Nishida's (*CHJ*, 1988: 711–761). In 1932 Tachibana too rejected the formalistic logic of the West as inapplicable to Asia; materialist domination of nature is alien to the spirit manifested in Buddhism, Confucianism, and Hinduism, emphasizing the non-self over the self. For Okawa Shumei in 1939, the independence of Asia from the West was historically awakened by the victory of Japan in the Russo-Japanese War of 1905. These ideas paralleled Nishida's and extended them into political activism, manifested in, among other things, bombings and assassinations of parliamentary leaders. On their side, the younger members of the Kyoto school (Nishitani, Koyama Iwao, Kosaka Masaaki, Suzuki Shigetaka) interpreted Nishida's ontological "space" as the "world stage" where Japan would takes its place in action. Kosaka and

Koyama went so far as to extol war as the test of moral hegemony in the world and advocated state enforcement of discipline in intellectual as well as social matters. Outside the militant ranks of the Kyoto school per se (while teaching in the same university), Watsuji expounded Nietzschean denunciation of rationalism and sought a parallel to Nietzsche's return to primordial Greek attitudes in a return to the spirit of ancient Japan. In 1942, just as the Pacific war was at its height, Nishitani took part in a major intellectual gathering at Kyoto on the theme of "overcoming modernity."

Despite the nationalist and particularist emphases of these movements, they cannot be considered merely a continuation of the previous tradition of National Learning or of Meiji-era Shinto. Those had arisen in a critical dialectic with Confucianism and were principally anti-Chinese (and secondarily anti-Buddhist). Both the Kyoto school and nationalist ideologues such as Tachibana and Okawa, however, tended to draw heavily on Buddhism as the common denominator of Asian culture as a whole; for Watsuji, Buddhist nothingness is the counterweight to Western alienation between self and nature. One may see this as an ideological stretch to legitimate Japanese imperial conquests on the Asian mainland. But although there was convergence between the philosophical trajectory of the Kyoto school and the ideologies of Japanese fascism, the inner community of intellectuals here did not simply resonate external political moods. In general, the intellectual world never reduces to external politics pure and simple; although the two spheres sometimes mesh, they have their own dynamics. Buddhism, revived by the inner dynamics of the Japanese university philosophers as they made their entry into the cosmopolitan networks of world philosophy, provided the key ontological concepts for the repudiation of Western rationalism. Although this provided materials for fascist propaganda as well, it would be absurd to consider Buddhism per se fascist or militaristic.

The Kyoto school, for all its nationalist affinities, depended on cosmopolitan networks and themes. Its repudiation of the West is itself a theme within contemporary Western philosophy. The struggle over rationality and science was a central issue in their network contacts—the Neo-Kantians, phenomenologists, and Heidegger. Any vigorous intellectual community derives its energy from oppositions. These same ingredients were combined by various members of the Japanese network to produce contending positions. Thus, among Nishida's pupils were the Marxist Tosaku Jun, and most famously Miki Kiyoshi, who studied also with Rickert and Heidegger. Miki too took up Nishida's ontology of "place," which he analyzed in terms of the expansion of world capitalism into Asia; the counter-stroke of the Japanese invasion of China in 1937 he interpreted as the movement toward Asian unification around a new era of cooperativism. Here the theme of Marxist socialism was blended with Shinran's Pure Land Buddhism. Miki envisioned an "Asian humanism" based on Buddhist compassion for all sentient beings. Despite his naive or opportunistic dallying with militaristic sentiments, the blend was not a politically acceptable one, and Miki died in prison. Others of the Kyoto school, especially the luminaries Watsuji and Nishitani, emerged onto the world philosophical scene after the war with reputations abstracted from politics, welcomed by the modern tradition of self-questioning which had become such a focus of attention in the West during these same generations.

Again we see in Japan broad parallels with Western intellectual development. The era of secularism which set in with the displacement of religion (Buddhism in one place, Christianity in the other) from monopoly over the means of intellectual production; the rise of the marketplace for education and for popular culture; the expansion of literacy and higher training that went along with capitalism and the bureaucratization of society: all these were indigenous developments in Japan, under way since the pre-Tokugawa era. By the 1700s, Japan had more than just its "Enlightenment" rationalists and its neoconservative traditionalists. Japanese political and intellectual movements of the 1800s were those of a society with cosmopolitan networks holding refined means of mobilization, facing a state whose problems were those of a relatively autonomous capitalist economy and a modern situation of religious and cultural action. It should not be surprising that in the early 1900s Japanese intellectuals were fully in the swing of the complex, even tortured combinations of intellectual lineages that are characteristic of its counterparts in the West.

For this reason it has not been only Eurocentric Westerners who harp on "the opening of Japan." Since the early 1900s, Japanese intellectuals and ideologists themselves have generally adopted the view of their society as a traditional one, suddenly beset by the pressures of the modern world imposed from without. It has been a convenient excuse. Since the Kyoto school of philosophers, it has been customary to attribute to the West the dislocating effects of the rationalized worldview, the deadly inhumanity of market relations, and the pressures of production. By adopting the myth that Japanese modernization was Westernization, Japanese intellectuals and politicians evaded the problems inherent in a dynamic that was substantially the same in every part of the world.

Conclusions to Part I:
The Ingredients of Intellectual Life

For a long time the West has regarded Asia as exotic. Even today in an ethos of tolerant multiculturalism, the stress is on non-Western cultures as unique sensibilities running on distinctive inner logics. What we see in examining the dynamics of Asian intellectual networks is quite the contrary.

We did not have to wait for the chapters on modern Western philosophy to meet the basic structures of intellectual life. The most important principles come out in full clarity in Asian histories, once we remove the lenses tinted with static primordiality that have kept most of us, Westerners and Asians alike, from seeing just how full of conflict and change these histories have been. Asian history shows us the basic ingredients of all of world history. A summary of the sociology of Asian intellectual life is a convenient summary of the central theory of this book.

First: Intellectual creativity is concentrated in chains of personal contacts, passing emotional energy and cultural capital from generation to generation. This structure underwrites all manner of contents: we see it in the chains of popular evangelists in Pure Land Buddhism, as among the masters of Zen, among Indian logicians and Japanese Neo-Confucians.

Second: Creativity moves by oppositions. Comparably important philosophers appear contemporaneously, their rivalry underpinning one another's fame. Chains of oppositions create the inner content of philosophies; new ideas unfold by negating the major points of rival positions on a shared topic of argument and a common level of abstraction. The dance of counterpoint is played over again as levels of abstraction shift, whether toward greater reflexivity or toward greater concreteness and reification. Not zeitgeist but structured rivalries constitute the successive moments of intellectual history.

Third: The emotional energy of creativity is concentrated at the center of networks, in circles of persons encountering one another face to face. The hot periods of intellectual life, those tumultuous golden ages of simultaneous innovations, occur when several rival circles intersect at a few metropoles of intellectual attention and debate. The ancient Chinese philosophers circulating among the four great centers of court patronage in the late Warring States; or the *mahavihara* at Nalanda where all the Buddhist sects debated and Hindu thinkers joined in cosmopolitan shifts from camp to camp: these are archetypes for Athens and Alexandria, Baghdad and Basra, Paris and Oxford, Weimar and Berlin, Trinity College Cambridge and Cambridge Massachusetts.

Fourth: The law of small numbers sets upper and lower limits to these oppositions. The number of contemporaneous creative schools successfully propagating their ideas across the generations is between three and six, a recurrent pattern for focal nodes in intellectual attention space.

Several corollaries follow. When external conditions enforce a single orthodoxy (as in the heavy hand of official bureaucracy in the Han dynasty, or again in the Ming examination system), creativity dries up; the stasis of Hindu philosophy was constructed after Mogul and British conquests drove Hindu thinkers into a monolithic defensive coalition. At the upper end of the scale, when the law of small numbers is violated by too many rival positions, as in the period of Upanishadic and heterodox sages at the time of the Buddha, skeptics attempt to reduce the cacophony by a stance of epistemological plague on all houses, and synthesizers emerge who reduce the number of contenders by constructing systems.

Fifth: The law of small numbers structures dynamics over time, connecting the outer conditions of social conflict with the inner shifts in the networks which produce ideas. Causality is two-step. First, political and economic changes bring ascendancy or decline of the material institutions which support intellectuals; religions, monasteries, schools, publishing markets rise and fall with these external forces. Intellectuals then readjust to fill the space available to them under the law of small numbers. Expanding positions split into rival philosophies because they have more slots in the attention space. On the losing side, weakening schools amalgamate into defensive alliances, even among former enemies. Winners and losers are reciprocals of each other. In the history of India, there are the successive splits and recombinations of Vedic, Buddhist, Hindu, Advaita Vedanta, and Vaishnava ascendancies and declines. In China, splits and recombinations take place among pre-Han philosophies, the Buddhist schools imported from India, the Zen schools, and the Neo-Confucians, like the opening and closing of a fan.

Two further corollaries follow. Creativity does not happen only during the happy times of material prosperity; there is creativity in the moments of closing down, sometimes the most memorable creativity, because it takes the form of crowning syntheses at a high level of reflexive awareness. And even organizational structures which later turn out to be stagnant, such as the Han bureaucracy, foster creativity at the moment of transition when the networks recombine cultural capital.

On the personal level, the stars of intellectual life tend to be those who are directly involved in the organizational transformations, or are close in the networks to the center of action. Such are the Neo-Confucians, emerging at the moment of struggle over the contents of the Sung examination system; or the Kyoto school, arising when Japanese professors gain control of the newly imported university system. We shall see it again in the circle of German Idealists who fought to construct the modern university.

Sixth: Because intellectual life is structured by oppositions, leading innovators are often conservatives. In their own eyes they oppose the intellectual and institutional changes of their time. Instance the ultra-reactionary Mimamsas, setting off the wave of higher epistemological argument in India; the Sung Neo-Confucians, arising to oppose the Wang An-shih reforms; or the waves of Ancient Learning and National Learning in the Tokugawa, which bring about a secularizing Japanese "Enlightenment." Such intellectual movements are nodes in a larger field of forces. In Europe we will see the creativity of anti-modernists from Rousseau to Heidegger. Conservative opposition under new conditions of heightened abstraction and reflexivity results in innovations under a veneer of pseudo-conservatism.

Historical specificity is the result of combining general principles of social causality; it is too little appreciated that specificity and generality are not mutually incompatible, and that combinations of a fairly small set of causal principles can generate a huge variety of historical realizations. When we add the successive recombinations that can take place over time, the total number of distinct historical paths becomes infinite. Sociological analysis is our x-ray vision, allowing us to see the combinations which make up the specific configurations of history as the arrangement of universal ingredients.

Using the sociological ingredients just set forth, we could go on to review how combinations of social conditions have constructed the historical uniqueness of Indian, Chinese, Japanese—and indeed European—philosophies. To pursue this argument would take us to background conditions of geopolitics and political economy, the place of monasticism and the strength of government bureaucracy, conditions which varied widely among the parts of the world. Even on this level the histories of social structures are not so divergent as Western-centered narratives—including Max Weber's—have supposed. Viewed in the perspective of the long run, China and Japan worked out the variants on a set of institutional ingredients; the combination of Buddhist monasticism with a balance between centralized bureaucracy and decentralizing feudalism eventually led to the takeoff of the capitalist market, and to religious secularization—a China-Japan sequence which parallels on separate tracks the Christian dynamic culminating in modern secular capitalist Europe.

Indian history combines the ingredients in a rather different way, although the intellectual results are more similar to European philosophy than the Chinese are. Structural analysis enables us to pick out some turning points. It is likely that without the Mogul conquest in the 1500s and the timing of its disintegration, which left the way open to European intrusion, Indian intellectual life would have continued along the pathways of highly technical abstraction already reached by its networks.

Before moving on to the second part of this book, we already have the theoretical tools in hand for understanding the social dynamics of Western intellectuals. That is not to say that there is nothing analytically new to address in the West. Islam and European Christendom are second-order civilizations, in the sense that their intellectual networks started out with cultural capital imported from an ancient civilization, Greece. Once they threw off the subservience that comes with being an idea importer, they were able to launch themselves on a level of abstraction and reflexivity already built up in the previous networks. But this pattern is not unique to the West; China had a period of dependence on idea imports from India, and Japan was similarly dependent on China. After about 1765, however, European networks added levels of reflexive self-analysis on the nature of conceptual knowledge which are distinctive in world philosophy. This is connected with two innovations in intellectual life.

One is that an offshoot emerged from philosophical networks in the 1600s, resulting in a version of intellectual life that escaped from the law of small numbers. This was not the birth of natural science, which had existed in many places around the world, but a distinctive form of social organization which I shall call rapid-discovery science. Not that scientists' networks now displaced philosophers' networks; rather, they added another network alongside the older intellectual genealogy—indeed, two such networks, one of scientific and mathematical researchers, and in symbiosis with it a second network comprising genealogies of machines and techniques which generated an ongoing stream of new phenomena for scientific research. Rapid-discovery science became a kind of cyborg network that challenged European philosophers, who remained locked in the oppositional dynamics of the law of small numbers. The result was not the disappearance of philosophy into science, but a new problem in philosophical space which spurred reconceptualization on a higher level of reflexivity.

The second structural innovation of the West was the research university, an organizational revolution in the expanding educational system which put philosophers, for the first time in history, in control of their own material base.

The differentiation of disciplines, and the routinization of the impetus to innovate, have shaped the reflexively modern world we have inhabited ever since. Yet even here we are not entirely without Asian parallels. The scholasticization of large-scale bureaucratic education was pioneered in China, and has some parallel in the technicalities fostered by the *maths* of late medieval India. And the same inflation of formalized cultural credentials in the shape of the degree-seeking which erodes contemporary American academic life is visible in the inflation of grades of Buddhist enlightenment at periods in India and Japan. Many of the ingredients have existed before; the modern West has taken them to unpredecented levels.

Common ills imply a common makeup. In the 1980s it became fashionable, indeed considered morally proper, to defend cultural uniqueness. But culture is no deeper than skin color, though we have convinced ourselves it is more respectable. To exult in the uniqueness and endurance of one's own cultural configuration is conservative ethnocentrism. To praise the same kind of enduring essence in others is regarded as laudable humility; but as to the other it remains ethnocentrism, merely at second order and projected into the distance. The individual personalities that we take pride in as our own egos, and the collective personalities we reify as cultures are fluid products of sociological principles that are the same for all of us. We share a common humanity under the skin because we are constructed of the same ingredients.

COMPARATIVE HISTORY OF INTELLECTUAL COMMUNITIES

Part II: Western Paths

CHAPTER 8

⚜

Tensions of Indigenous and Imported Ideas: Islam, Judaism, Christendom

Philosophy in the medieval societies of the West built on earlier cultural capital. In the long historical view, we are tempted to skip over that which is derivative and to concentrate on that which is originating. Our deprecating image is an unsophisticated society overwhelmed by imports from a previous civilization and unable to get its own creativity off the ground. The image is doubly misleading.

Importing ideas has its own intellectual rhythm: passive at first, it is capable of turning into the normal creative process within a few generations. We see this in the Buddhist philosophies of medieval China, where the receiving environment already had a well-established tradition of literate culture—no peripheral region here overwhelmed by sophisticated imports. In the regions of Islam and European Christendom, the imports came into tribal societies newly organized into state and church. What made their philosophies distinctive in quality was not so much their initial dependence on imports—which in the case of Christendom was repetitively dependent, repetitively importing ideas from other civilizations, including Islam—as that the receiving context was dominated by a politically powerful religion. Idea imports are tagged for their relevance or opposition to religious orthodoxy.

Such a situation is ready-made for a Whiggish interpretation of intellectual history, in which defenders of tradition battle against openness to new ideas. But openness to new ideas initially takes the form of adulation of old ideas, hardly creative in its own right. Our received tradition of a Greeks-to-Arabs-to-Christians sequence imposes a second kind of blindness. We miss the opportunity to peer into the cauldron where indigenous intellectuals develop their own disputes. Starting from religious-political disputes, the Muslims drove up the level of abstraction and revealed the ontological and epistemological issues which are distinctive to monotheism. Imports are rarely passive; indigenously developed factions have their own motivations for seeking out imports and reacting to what comes in. Our aim must be to look at the creative and uncreative aspects of idea imports, in the usual context of multi-sided intellectual conflict which drives creativity everywhere. The viewpoint will give us an unexpected bonus: we will see that not only importing but also exporting ideas to an eager recipient can stimulate its own form of creativity.

Philosophy within a Religious Context

What difference does it make when intellectual communities arise as offshoots of religious organization? One might suppose that this circumstance affects only arbitrary aspects of the context of thought. Once an intellectual network becomes organized, it generates its own problems and standards. Intellectuals competitively appropriate whatever cultural capital exists, and will produce contrasting positions by the dynamics of creation through opposition. The Qur'an, the Bible, the Vedic hymns, the sayings of the Buddha are so many starting points which become increasingly overlaid by the accumulated debates of generations of intellectuals. Abstract issues of metaphysics and logic emerge and become autonomous questions in their own right: religion spawns philosophy.

Religious doctrines are put forward as charismatic revelation or as inalterable tradition; they are to be learned, recited, and put into practice as guides for ritual or for living. They are not, on the face of it, subjects for discussion and intellectual development. There is a limited exception in the period when a religion first assembles its written canon, for example, the period ca. 150–200 C.E. (Aland and Aland, 1987) when the Christian Gospels, letters of Saint Paul, and a few other texts of the founding generations were accepted as holy scripture while other candidate texts were excluded, along with rival organizations (such as the Gnostic circles) which carried them. Similarly in Islam, the generations after the death of Muhammad were devoted to the redaction of Muhammad's revelations (the Qur'an, ca. 632–656) and to compiling (which went on into the mid-800s) *hadith,* the recollections of the Prophet's companions used as alternate sources of legal tradition (Watt, 1985: 57; Lapidus, 1988: 103–104). Beyond this point the canon is closed, and the activities of the scholars should now be reduced to a simple transmission of the received word.

The extent to which this closure happens is a sociological phenomenon in its own right. Quasi-canonical literature may continue to grow, if the religion lacks an authority which monopolizes the definition of the holy texts. Buddhist sutras claiming the status of charismatic revelations and bolstered by allegations of antiquity continued to appear for many centuries, from 400 B.C.E. down to 300 C.E. and later (Conze, 1962: 200). The Hindu world was extremely decentralized after the breakdown of the old Vedic priest guilds; scriptural status could be claimed not only for later commentaries and supercommentaries on the Vedic hymns, but also for new mythological collections (the *Puranas* down through 1500 A.D.) and poetic epics (the *Mahabharata* ca. 300 B.C.E.–300 C.E., and the *Ramayana* ca. 200 B.C.E.–200 C.E.; O'Flaherty, 1975: 17–18). Judaism, after the destruction of the Jerusalem temple in 70 C.E. and the dispersion of Jewish communities, developed an accretion of religious law and interpretation, the Mishnah, which was collected and codified in several editions between 200 and 500 C.E. (Segal, 1986: 16, 133–136). The Talmudic literature of the famous teachers continued to grow; the systematizing efforts of Maimonides and his successors around 1200 attempted again to reduce this material to a simpler conception of orthodoxy, but there was no agency to enforce it.

Christianity and Islam stand out because the organizational conditions were present relatively early to close their holy canons.[1] It was here that the relations between religion and philosophy became explicitly an issue. In these circumstances a crucial topic of philosophy must be the relationship between "faith" and "reason." This in turn gave impetus to questions of epistemology. When religion is armed with coercive political power, the range of answers is limited; the prudent thinker is forced to claim either that reason and faith harmonize, or if they do not, that faith is superior. Bold advocates of the independence of philosophy, if protected by enough organizational insulation, or if they find chinks in the system of political enforcement, might push the border.

The philosophical path which starts here may continue farther. A crucial push is given when such epistemological issues are taken up by theological conservatives. Once elaborate metaphysical constructions are produced across several generations of philosophers, the intellectuals who are closest to the space of conservative dogmatism can turn philosophical sophistication against itself by raising the epistemological level, and can question the validity of arguments within the realm of reason itself. We find this in Islam with al-Ghazali and Ibn Taymiyah, and in Christendom with the conservative condemnations of 1277 leading to the refined positions of Scotus and Ockham. If the philosophical community continues under religious challenge, further positions are generated, and the field is propelled into a full-fledged epistemology. This is much more apparent in Christendom than in Islam, where the fundamentalist attacks increasingly constricted the philosophers, and the sophisticated conservatives themselves lacked technically oriented followers; the significance of the issue disappeared with their opponents. The result was reinforced because of the tendency of later Islamic intellectuals to take refuge in a secret doctrine accessible to the initiates of reason, while scripture was taken as metaphoric expression for the crude masses. This removed the creative tension of argument with the orthodox; the esotericism of later Islam turned to a poetic mysticism, and away from the analytical issues of epistemology.

This devious path from enforced doctrinal orthodoxy to critical epistemology is not found unless religion is state-enforced. This route toward epistemological issues did not exist in China, where the state usually supported all manner of ritualistic exercises, in a kind of pluralistic tolerance. There was no sacred scripture to be officially enforced; the nearest thing to it was the Confucian texts, but these were held to be products of human reason, and thus on the side of philosophy. Taoist religion by the late 400s C.E. claimed its texts to be charismatically revealed, but political weakness prevented Taoists from elevating them to uniquely enforced scriptural truth. It follows that if the Taoist church had acquired long-term political power, its relations with non-dogmatic intellectuals would also have given rise to epistemological issues. The same should have happened if Buddhism had continued as the state religion beyond its short episodes of imperial favor in the T'ang.[2]

The initial effect of religion on philosophy is not to produce epistemological controversy; that tends to come later as philosophers build up their own positions. Initially the religion sets forth a content on which intellectuals may work. The Western religions begin with a pre-reflective anthropomorphism. God is a person, possessing human attributes such as knowledge, power, goodness, and will, raised of course to a superlative degree. God creates the physical world, and will bring it to an end, much as any human could manufacture an object and then destroy it. Islam includes other supernaturally endowed persons: the Prophet and various angels, with their missions and announcements. Christianity in some ways redoubles the anthropomorphic elements, focusing not only on God but also on Christ, who is both a man and Son of God; on the miraculous elements of his virgin birth (which thereby elevate the person of his miraculous mother) and his crucifixion and resurrection; the doctrine of human sin and redemption, the Day of Judgment, and the resurrection of human bodies to eternal life in heaven or hell. Human events are given cosmic significance; conversely, the cosmos is tied to a personal scale.

Such doctrines give rise to problems if the church, as a social organization carrying out rituals and justifying them by faith in holy scripture, declares that the texts are to be taken in a literal, commonsensical way. Originally it is not laypersons who question the literal meaning of these doctrines; it is, after all, the miraculous aspect of this picture that makes it so impressive for ordinary people. It is the specialists within the church entrusted with the care and teaching of the holy documents, who feel a need to reduce the anthropomorphic elements because of their sophisticated conception of religious impressiveness. If God is superlative in every respect, how can he have merely physical qualities? The Qur'an speaks of God sitting on his throne; the early theologians argued that this is only a metaphor for his grandeur. In response the conservative legalist Malik thundered: "The sitting is given, its modality is unknown.

Belief in it is an obligation and raising questions regarding it is a heresy" (Fakhry, 1983: xvii). But Malik, against his own intentions, was thereby staking out one of the corners of philosophical turf. The Muslim intellectual community went on for generations after this, taking various sides on the issues which arose directly out of the anthropomorphic scripture: the responsibility of humans as against the providence and power of God, and then to more metaphysical issues surfacing in these discussions.

Various philosophical issues are provoked by anthropomorphic religion which are not shared by more cosmologically oriented religions such as Confucianism, Taoism, or Indian mysticism. The philosophical confrontation with anthropomorphism focused attention on the nature of transcendence and infinite perfection and their relations to limitation and contingency. The issue of free will arose distinctively in the West, not in India or China, and with it the nature of causality and determinism. It is the character of the oppositions generated by religious doctrine, as much as the slant of that doctrine itself, that is fateful for the trajectory of philosophical problems.

It is distinctive of the Western religions, not the Eastern, that philosophers devoted much effort to proofs of the existence of God. Such proofs from a religious viewpoint are superfluous; the philosophers were not free in any case to consider whether God does not really exist. The justification was sometimes offered that proofs were needed in order to convince unbelievers or convert members of other faiths, but this seems a patent rationalization: Christians, Muslims, and Jews could not convert one another by proving the existence of God, since all three faiths admitted this, and the differentiating items of faith were not proved in this fashion;[3] and atheist unbelievers were an imaginary foil under these authoritarian regimes. The philosophers' construction of proofs for items of faith was a matter of creating a turf for pure intellectual activity within the institutional space of the religious schools. These proofs became grounds on which metaphysical and epistemological doctrines could be worked out. With a sufficiently complex network of philosophers, such as arose in Christendom by the late 1200s, it was no longer a foregone conclusion that one would have to succeed in proving the existence of God or the immortal soul. By the time of Ockham and his followers, it was acceptable to conclude that these items could not be conclusively proved by reason; this was taken as demonstrating the superior power of faith, and also of demarcating the territory of distinctively philosophical techniques.

The religious communities did not set out to have philosophies. Virtually all of them began with the notion that intellectual life is superfluous, indeed an obstacle to religious devotion. But the very structure of having specialists in sacred texts created an intellectual community with its own dynamics. Greater abstraction and self-reflectiveness about one's own tools was one of the weapons which the intellectual community forged in order to carry out its struggles over the turf of theology. By a further twist of organizational development, the more abstract topics could become a focus in themselves. This was not without dangers from the political arm of the church. Philosophical insiders pursuing the logic of debate on questions such as free will or the attributes of God could find themselves entangled in heresy disputes with theologians. Such accusations and condemnations ring right through medieval Christian and Muslim philosophy. From one angle they certainly represent the chilling hand of power upon intellectual autonomy. But condemnations in themselves do not distinguish between periods of creativity or stagnation; creative philosophers were just as likely to accuse their own opponents of heresy. The distinctive philosophies of the West are those which were wrung out through these channels of conflict; the danger was a cost of the creativity.

The Muslim World: An Intellectual Community Anchored by a Politicized Religion

Islam begins as a theocracy. Here theological factions are always in the first instance political factions; to claim theological orthodoxy is the same as claiming political rulership of the Islamic state. After Arabian military conquests swept the Middle East in the generation after Muhammad (taking Syria, Egypt, Iraq, and Persia between 634 and 654), Islamic warriors fractionated along lines of charismatic succession to the rulership. The line divided supporters of the winners and of the losers in the civil wars of the succession: roughly, the position eventually known as Sunnites, who accepted the political status quo and the victorious lineage, and the Shi'ites, intransigents who held out loyally for the family line of the losing faction. On each side in turn there was further fractionation. The victorious majority developed a pragmatic group who offered compromise with the losers, in effect declaring its willingness not to pursue the old issues of legitimacy and illegitimacy of various claims. On the Shi'ite side, the more vehement rebels were eventually displaced by a faction which held that the Imam, the true successor to the Prophet was in hiding. This gave a somewhat otherworldly tone to the expectation that in some future generation the correct theocratic lineage would reappear, and it allowed Imamites to operate as a spiritual sect within the Islamic state without necessarily rebelling against it politically. Other Shi'ite factions remained more militant, sometimes winning political power in particular states.

Islamic factions became a reflex of geopolitics and revolutionary success. The initial wave of conquests, uniting the tribes of Arabia, swept into the power vacuum created by the stalemate between the Byzantine and Sassanian Persian empires. The 'Abbasid caliphate consolidated power after three civil

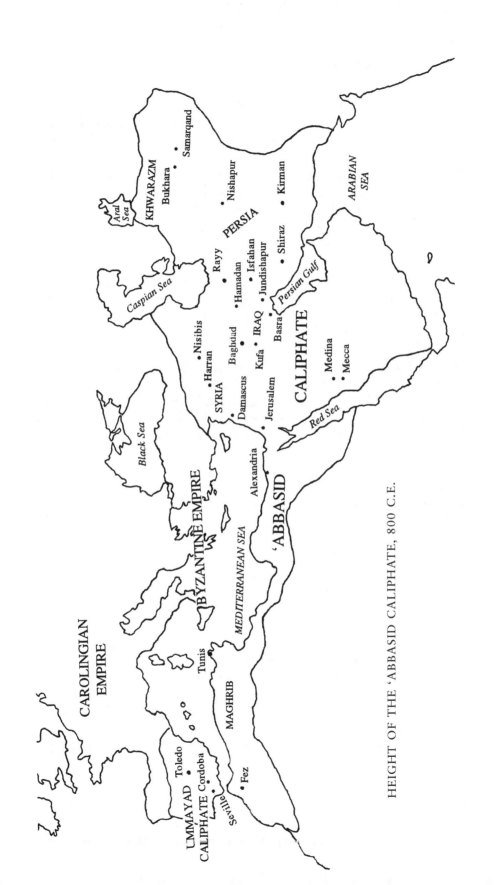

HEIGHT OF THE 'ABBASID CALIPHATE, 800 C.E.

wars, and from 750 administered an empire centralized at Baghdad.[4] After 830 the caliphate began to lose de facto power to regional administrators, and full-fledged independent states divided the region between 950 and 1200. These in turn became subject to waves of imperial conquest; the most successful were the Seljuk Turks around 1040–1100; the Mongol conquerors 1220–1260, who soon converted to Islam and split into smaller states; and the Ottomans, who expanded from Asia Minor from the 1360s. Some of the Shi'ite factions acquired state power, notably the Isma'ili activists in Egypt, 970–1170. Winners and losers, orthodox and anti-orthodox traded places on a geopolitical checkerboard.

The principal consequence for intellectual life was that Islamic religion never acquired a centralized church organization. According to theocratic tradition accepted by all factions, the caliph was successor to the Prophet and leader of the faithful; but his legitimacy was questioned by important factions ever since the early generations of Islam, and was further broken up with the dispersion of political power. De facto religious authority devolved into the hands of the 'ulama, or religious scholars. As befits a theocracy, the law was the religious law, and the religious schools in effect monopolized the activities of law courts as well. Orthodox religious scholars were quasi-independent of the state, without forming an organized church comparable to the Christian papacy. Only the 'Abbasid caliphate at its height had enough power to attempt uniform control of religious life; the powerful caliph al-Ma'mun (r. 813–833) and his successors attempted to impose doctrinal orthodoxy on all Muslim scholars. But this inquisition on behalf of caliphal power was resisted, and finally abandoned in 848 as the caliphate began to disintegrate; thereafter the 'ulama dominated religious law and doctrine without challenge.

Insofar as the schools of the 'ulama were centers of intellectual life, they were anchored in the particularistic concerns of daily ritual, holy texts, and practical law. Although more abstract consideration of theology did emerge from this base, it was continually open to attack. More detached intellectual life was supported by patronage of the political rivals of the 'ulama, especially the courtly circles around a political ruler. Precisely because the ruler at Baghdad or Córdoba was a theocrat manqué whose religious claims were always overshadowed by the truly devout of the religious schools, court circles could tend toward the opposite pole of speculation or occasionally downright secularism. This kept intellectual life in a precarious situation, at the mercy of geopolitical events that might overthrow a particular regime. The high point of the non-religious philosophers was under the patronage of the 'Abbasids at Baghdad, and faded with the loss of protection after 950. One mitigating factor was the existence of secret societies. Although these were predominantly political and religious in their concerns, the secret societies were always in opposition to at least some part of the status quo around the Islamic world; and they sometimes looked for allies among unorthodox factions on the intellectual front. Thus one could find unholy alliances between Isma'ili or Imamite conspirators and hard-pressed rationalist theologians and philosophers.

Four Factions

Fractionation of the intellectual field moved slowly at first, then picked up speed in the generations after 800. Four main groups of intellectuals gradually formed, three of them religious, one secular. First came the practitioners of rational theology, *kalam,* of which the most important group was the Mu'tazilites; in opposition emerged the scriptural literalists. In addition there were the Sufi mystics, and on the secular side, the translators and practitioners of Greek and other foreign science and philosophy, *falsafa.*[5]

Indigenous Theological Philosophers

The prevailing attitude of intellectual historians is that only the Greek *falasifa* (philosophers) are worth paying attention to, since it was they who transmitted the main line of European philosophy. These blinders prevent us from seeing what is more significant: the dynamics by which Islamic theologians broke into philosophical terrain of their own accord. Indigenous theological disputes, like any other sustained intellectual conflict, spontaneously drive up the level of abstraction and uncover issues of metaphysics and epistemology. We have a laboratory for how philosophy emerges nearer to us than the obscure beginnings of the Chinese, Indians, and Greeks, as well as a picture of the independent path by which were created positions paralleling those of later European developments at the time of Descartes, Locke, and Malebranche.

The first notable intellectuals appeared in the early 700s (see Figure 8.1). At first there was an undifferentiated style of scriptural scholar, such as Hasan al-Basri, who was famous for his pronouncements in law as well as theology, and was claimed as a predecessor to the Sufis for his asceticism. In the next two generations the field began to crystallize into factions. The early center of theological discussion was at Basra, founded by the Arab conquerors in the Mesopotamian river delta. When Baghdad was founded in the 760s as the capital for the new 'Abbasid caliphate, these two cities about 250 miles apart became the twin centers of intellectual life, displaying the familiar pattern of intersecting networks circulating at rival centers.

The earliest issues emerged out of religious politics. On one front there was a dispute between predestination and free will, on the other flank the question of the unity of God as against dualism or anthropomorphism. Predestination

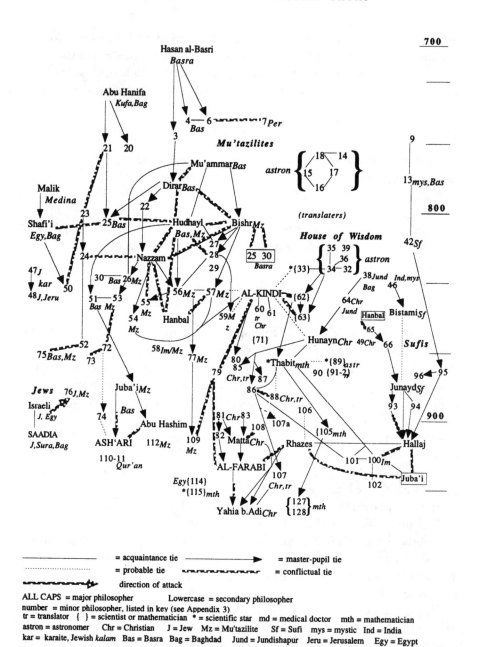

FIGURE 8.1. ISLAMIC AND JEWISH PHILOSOPHERS AND
SCIENTISTS, 700–935: BASRA AND BAGHDAD SCHOOLS
(all at Baghdad unless marked)

had become an issue because of an early political dispute over the legitimacy of the caliphate. The succession had been won by violence and treachery, and some Islamic factions held that sins such as these make one cease to be a Muslim and render a ruler subject to overthrow. Those willing to accept the status quo tended to accept as well the argument that the caliph's acts were predestined. Free will was accordingly condemned as an incitement to rebellion. As late as 743 some advocates of free will were executed by the caliph. This political connection was ephemeral. Within a few generations the political implications had been reversed; for a period in the 800s the Mu'tazilite advocacy of free will was put forward as orthodoxy by the caliphate.

A faction was formed at the mosque at Basra out of those who took an intermediate position on the debate over sinners—the issue implying how much loyalty one must give to a sinful caliph. A further split reacted against the theological moderation of Hasan al-Basri; this faction stressed the predestination of human acts and the omnipotence of God so strongly as to hold that actions can be imputed to humans only figuratively. Intellectual debate was now driving positions to extremes. The next step was the Mu'tazilite defense of free will, the typical pattern of intellectual development through escalating conflict between opposite sides of the field. The defenders of free will were forced to elaborate their position, declaring that God does no evil. This led to a recognition that the standards of good and evil are not conventional or arbitrary. To reconcile this stance with the power of God, these theologians concluded that God has a rational nature, and that moral laws are part of this unchangeable essence of reason.

This was one route which led from literal scriptural piety into a philosophical metaphysics. Joining it was another stream of argument over the unity and attributes of God. The Mu'tazilite faction forming at Basra and Baghdad entered into a multi-fronted war against rival theologies, attacking the Zoroastrian and Manichaean dualists (the former the traditional religion of Persia, now under Islamic conquest; the latter a Christian heresy centered in Mesopotamia) as well as the Trinity of the Christians (widespread in the Islamic domains of Iraq, Syria, and Egypt). This controversy led to proofs that there is only one God, undivided and without plurality. The Mu'tazilites became famous for their proofs, not only of the unity of God but also of the createdness of the world, and thus of the existence of the Creator as well. Theology became rationally defended and set on the path to where reason itself could be exalted above scripture and revelation. The Mu'tazilite proofs were adopted wholesale by contemporary Jewish thinkers who became the first notable Jewish philosophers of the Middle Ages.

Both Muslim and Jewish practitioners of *kalam*, or rational theology, argued for the harmonization of rational proofs with their scriptural doctrines.

The Mu'tazilites met opposition from the faction of Islamic scriptural literalists crystallizing at the same time, and were goaded into a more uncompromising stand (Hodgson, 1974: 1:386–389). The *hadith* scholars were fighting for their own brand of scripturalism, attempting to formulate alongside the Qur'an a canon of the recollections of Muhammad's companions; their stance exalted the status of scriptures over everything else. They attacked the application of personal judgment in legal cases; the doctrine of free will, as limiting the powers of God; and the unity of God because it contradicts the personal and even physical attributes of God, which are mentioned in scripture. The rational theologians, who had been arguing for the metaphorical nature of these passages, were driven onto more extreme grounds. Adopting Aristotelean language, they held that God is a substance of absolute unity and simplicity, and that there are no attributes apart from his essence.

Defenders of *kalam* now took the offensive against the *hadith* scholars. Marshaling their arguments for the unity of God, they held that the Qur'an is a created object, not an eternal truth; to elevate scripture to a holy object, co-eternal with God, is to fall into dualism, even idolatry. This stance undercut the status claims of the *hadith* scholars as keepers of the primary cult object of Islam. Charges and counter-charges of either anthropomorphism or blasphemy eventually led to a political showdown between the two camps.

A clearly identified Mu'tazilite school emerged out of the disputes among kalamite factions in the two generations from Dirar and his contemporary Mu'ammar ibn 'Abbad in the late 700s, to Abu-'l-Hudhayl, Bishr ibn al-Mu'tamir, and al-Nazzam shortly after 800. They are connected in a network of masters, pupils, and rivals, and split into the schools of Basra and Baghdad. Abu-'l-Hudhayl became the great systematizer, laying out the main points of Mu'tazilite orthodoxy, stressing the unity and justice of God, and as its corollary free will. To this other Mu'tazilites added the createdness of the Qur'an, and the doctrine that everything exists only as attributes of atoms in time, and must be continually re-created.

Why did the Arab theologians develop time-atomism? The influence of Greek philosophical texts at this moment is hardly a sufficient explanation.[6] Why should the Arab thinkers have adopted a doctrine which was opposed by all the Greek authorities then being introduced? Moreover, time-atomism was by no means an ontological support for their major theological doctrine, the defense of free will, since perishing atoms require God's continuous intervention. Neither of these external influences, Greek imports or theological politics, explains the line of intellectual development. What seems to have happened is this. The attempt to support free will led to refinements in the theory of causality, ways in which God could be kept clear of direct responsibility for what happens in the world. The other theological question, the unity of God (and the related issue of the createdness of the Qur'an), led to consideration of substance and attributes. The combination of these two issues generated a new intellectual space. Muslim philosophers began to compete for attention by innovating over their own problems. By taking apart the notions first of attributes, then of substance, they arrived at the doctrine of atomism. At this point a true intellectual competition existed. Islamic philosophy swung free from being a mere reflex of political positions and onto an autonomous path.

Fueled at first by theological energies, the philosophical arguments became more subtle. The Aristotelean concepts of substance and accident were subjected to scrutiny in the generation just before 800. At Basra, Dirar ibn 'Amr rejected the notion of substance; he held that a body is a collection of accidents, arranged in a hierarchy; once constituted, an accident may become the substratum of other accidents (Fakhry, 1983: 53; Watt, 1973: 194–195). Perhaps Dirar's contemporary Hisham ibn al-Hakam (22 in the key to Figure 8.1) had driven him to this position; Hisham held that there is no distinction of substance and accident, since every substance is divisible ad infinitum. Hisham was an avowed anthropomorphist, defending the literal descriptions of God in the Qur'an; since attributes (or accidents) were at issue, he was willing to reduce everything to an attribute. Some of the Mu'tazilites (e.g., 30 in Figure 8.1) adopted the same position. Substance was dissolving; out of this came the distinctive Mu'tazilite metaphysics, time-atomism.

Dirar was also struggling for a way to defend free will; he held that God controls what happens in the outer world, but man, not God, acquires the moral responsibility by inward assent or dissent (Fakhry, 1983: 48–49). Dirar's solution was apparently controversial among his contemporaries, for he was attacked as a determinist. He held that there is no bodily substance but only accidents, and these cannot exist for two successive moments; this implied that they are continuously re-created by God. This is the first mention of time-atoms, as yet applied only to attributes rather than substances.

A rival stance was taken by another Basra theologian, Mu'ammar. Far from eliminating substance, Mu'ammar held that God brought about the original existence of bodies by creating the atoms they are composed of (Wolfson, 1976: 158, 560–576; Peters, 1968: 144). Accidents are caused in turn by the aggregation of bodily atoms. God thus causes accidents only indirectly, and is not responsible for their good or evil qualities. For Mu'ammar, man is an immaterial, knowledgeable substance connected to the body. Free will exists only inwardly; the body is part of the external world, subject to the necessity of nature. It is a dualism not unlike Descartes's.

So far, Dirar has no atomic substance but only attributes which are temporal atoms. Mu'ammar has atomic substances, although they are not time-atoms, but are permanent once created by God. The next generation appears to have developed a thoroughgoing atomism. Abu-'l-Hudhayl, who success-fully systematized the Mu'tazilite theological position, produced an influential compromise among the ontological positions. He declared that some, but not all, accidents exist for only a moment in time; if they are to appear again for a second moment, they must be created afresh by God (Watt, 1985: 53; Wolfson, 1976: 531–532). This applies above all to the accidents of will and motion, that is, those qualities which are involved in action in the world, and hence are implicated in the question of moral responsibility. By contrast, Abu'l-Hudhayl, along with many other Mu'tazilites, reserved certain features of the physical and spiritual world for the category of durable accidents, including color, life, and knowledge (Fakhry, 1983: 54); presumably this was in order to preserve a responsible human entity across moments of time. God causes both the duration and the destruction of accidents; this in turn raised the question whether duration and destruction are themselves accidents which exist in a spatial substratum. Secondary metaphysical problems were emerging, and the ontological status of existence and change became a topic of debate.

In this same generation a rival Mu'tazilite school formed at Baghdad, led by Mu'ammar's pupil Bishr al-Mu'tamir. Bishr gave a more realist ontological slant to time-atomism. Even though God continuously intervenes in creating and destroying attributes, every creation of existence involves a real duration, and every destruction is a real action too (Wolfson, 1976: 522–543). God creates these time-atoms out of nothing. But (according to later commentators) this Mu'tazilite school held that "nothing" is also a substantive "something"; this implies that God creates things out of a pre-existent matter.

The atomist position was not yet settled. The most radical of the Mu'taz-ilites, al-Nazzam, kept up Dirar's attack on substance. Al-Nazzam argued that substance does not exist, since it can be infinitely divided. The more moderate Mu'tazilites had taken this argument only to a point; they were willing to reduce attributes to instants in time, without duration, and to reduce substance to atoms (though disputing whether they were with or without size). Al-Naz-zam pushed onward, into an extreme time-phenomenalism: there exists nothing but accidents, and none of these are durable. All other accidents reduce to the accident of motion, which is inherently transitory (Fakhry, 1983: 49–51, 215–6; Wolfson, 1976: 514–517). Al-Nazzam's Heraclitus-like position led to difficulties of the sort raised by the Eleatics. Since a distance consists of an infinite number of points, how is it possible to traverse all of them and arrive anywhere? Al-Nazzam attempted to overcome this Zeno-like paradox by pro-posing a process of "leaps" from one atomic point to another over the inter-vening points. His doctrine of perpetual motion also had difficulties in explain-ing the apparent rest of bodies in one place; al-Nazzam countered this by arguing that rest consists in bodies moving into the same place twice in succession.

Al-Nazzam was among the most creative of these philosophers, and also the most extreme; on the issue of the createdness of the Qur'an, he held that it cannot even resemble the transcendent word of God (Wolfson, 1976: 274–275). He died just before the great crisis affecting the Mu'tazilites, which threw them from political favor into unorthodoxy. Al-Nazzam was attacked by orthodox Mu'tazilites and scripturalists alike. His doctrines do not appear to have had any immediate followers, and the Mu'tazilites gathered together in defense of their more moderate atomism. Some versions of time-atomism also held that the atoms are bearers of accidents which exist Platonically, apart from the realm of time (Fakhry, 1983: 216). Later doctrines were to dispute whether any accidents are exempt from existing as time-atoms continually recreated by God. It is not clear whether Abu'l-Hudhayl held that substances as well as accidents are atomic time-instants; but by the early 900s, the Baghdad Mu'tazilite al-Ka'bi (109 in Figure 8.1) was holding that every substance and accident must be created afresh every moment by God (Watt, 1973: 301–302). This emphasis on God's direct causality put increasing strain on the doctrine of free will. At this moment, the Ash'arite camp broke away and produced a more politically respectable version of Mu'tazilite time-atomism.

Scriptural Anti-rationalists

Islamic thought was by no means primordially scriptural and conservative. Literal defenders of holy scripture emerged gradually, in increasing polarity with the rational theologians. There were hundreds of schools of scriptural specialists across the Islamic Empire, dispensing religious law for local concerns (Makdisi, 1981: 9). Their practical orientation kept their work relatively concrete and unintellectual; abstract theological issues were not their main interest, except insofar as these were points of political significance. The rational theologians who emerged at the mosque at Basra and then at Baghdad were initially part of this same undifferentiated occupation of learned 'ulama. Some of them became caught up in a network of argument which pushed the politically significant issues onto abstract grounds, and thence into philosophical constructions which took on attention in their own right; others, including many followers of Hasan al-Basri himself, joined the *hadith* specialists. The emerging argument among these factions gradually brought several of the schools of Qur'anic legal scholarship to prominence above the others because of their stands on larger questions of Islamic orthodoxy. The dispersed local schools began to shape into something like political parties among the Sunni loyalists of the regime, and the number of positions winnowed down around the most successful legal schools.

Their initial position was not necessarily hard-line scripturalist. The first prominent school, organized at Baghdad in the middle generation of the 700s, was the Hanifites, followers of Abu Hanifa, who took a relatively soft position of political compromise on questions of legitimate succession to the caliphate and a moderate line on predestination. The emerging Mu'tazilites tended to be allied with this legal school. In the next generation came a reaction led by Malik ibn Anas (at Muhammad's city, Medina), founder of the Malikites, who took a vehemently literalist position against the rationalist theologians. But Malik's own pupil al-Shafi'i founded a more moderate lineage (the Shafi'ites); they softened the emphasis on Qur'anic literalism by sanctioning the use not only of the Qur'an but also of *hadith*, recollections of the Prophet's companions, which could be used as a basis for interpretation. No doubt energized by this controversy, major work was done in al-Shafi'i's generation to establish a canonical collection of *hadith* (see 68 and 69 in Figure 8.1). In counterpoint came the fourth of the main legal schools, the Hanbalis (followers of Ibn Hanbal), who used *hadith* to reinforce traditionalist views, and who vehemently attacked the rational theologians.

Liberal and conservative impulses tended to alternate during these generations, with the conservatives coming later and in reaction to the liberal side. The turning point came with a showdown over the political power of the liberals. The 'Abbasid caliphate had taken power by military force, and its legitimacy (like that of the preceding Umayyad caliphate) was disputed by various factions. The caliphs were casting about for religious legitimacy in various ways, at times offering alliance with the Shi'ites, and bringing them into their administration, at times supporting Sunni scripturalists, at other times patronizing the practitioners of *kalam* (Lapidus, 1988: 123–125; Massignon, 1982: 250–254). In the early 800s, the 'Abbasids were at the height of their economic prosperity and military power. Turning away from the Qur'anic conservatives supported by his predecessor Harun al-Rashid, the powerful caliph al-Ma'mun moved to establish theocratic control by championing the doctrines of the Mu'tazilites. Among the central points was the doctrine that the Qur'an is created and not an eternal aspect of the divine essence. To enforce this policy would be to reduce the independence of the scriptural caretakers of the Qur'an and justify the intervention of the caliph in interpreting religious law.

Islamic historians refer to this episode as the "Inquisition." The pejorative term results from the eventual failure and disgrace of this effort. Under caliph al-Rashid (r. 786–809) there had been a persecution from the other direction, on behalf of the emerging school of *hadith* and against *kalam*, during which the head of the Baghdad Mu'tazilites, Bishr al-Mu'tamir, had been imprisoned (Watt, 1985: 53; Hodgson, 1974: 1:388–389). In 827 caliph al-Ma'mun attempted to force religious scholars to accept the doctrine of the created Qur'an; al-Ma'mun died in 833, and his successors continued the policy intermittently for 20 years. Most of the *'ulama* gave in under political pressure from the caliphs; but opposition was tenaciously led by Ibn Hanbal, the most prominent *hadith* scholar, situated in the capital Baghdad itself. Ibn Hanbal became a hero of the conservatives by enduring imprisonment and threats of execution. Eventually in 847 caliph al-Mutawakkil capitulated to the political opposition and abandoned the effort to impose the Mu'tazilite theology. The triumphant Hanbalis in turn attempted to impose their own position. In future generations the Hanbalis became one of the leading legal schools, and the conservative anchor of the intellectual field, taking the leadership in attacking theological moderates as well as practitioners of philosophy.[7]

The defeat of the "Inquisition" was a turning point in the structure of Islamic religion and intellectual life generally. If the caliph had won, Islam would have been moved toward a more centralized and bureaucratic church, less centered on the local *'ulama*. Rational theology could have become institutionalized rather than marginalized. Intellectual structures would have more nearly parallelled those of the Christian Church, centered on rational theology rather than scripturalism and breeding its philosophical adjunct. Indigenous theologically based Islamic philosophy displayed its own creative dynamic through these early generations, developing atomic occasionalism, theories of free will and of causality, proofs of the existence and nature of God, theories of time and motion, distinctions among primary and secondary qualities. The period flashes with themes we associate with Zeno and Heraclitus, and again with the successors of Descartes. That is to say, Islamic philosophy at this point parallels developments in Greece and Europe prior to the dominance of Plato and Aristotle, and again after their overthrow. Creativity was not yet over, for it is fueled by conflict, and the shifting of external supports brought about a realignment of positions over the next few generations, and thus the innovative reorganization of intellectual space. But the center of gravity was pushed increasingly toward the conservative side. The Mu'tazilites did not disappear for several centuries,[8] but they were frozen into a defensive posture from which creative energy had drained. Their decline opened a space in the intellectual field; and it was this vacuum that imports of Greek ideas now proceeded to fill. Importing is less creative than indigenous construction. What Eurocentric history regards as the only worthwhile topic constituted in its time a decline in the creativity of Islamic networks.

Importers of Foreign Philosophy

Just at the time when the Mu'tazilites were going into their political showdown and crisis, a concerted effort was made to import the "ancient learning" of Greek science and philosophy into the Islamic world. It was at this point—the middle generation of the 800s—that a network of translators and commentators sprang up in Baghdad. Sporadic translations of Greek texts had appeared before this point; and there were long-standing schools of Christian and other non-Islamic scholars in various outlying places. But their work had produced neither novelty nor attention. In 830 Caliph al-Ma'mun—the same who attempted to impose an Inquisition on behalf of Muʿtazilite theology—established a "House of Wisdom" at the capital, a bureau of translation supporting many scholars.[9] For the next three generations this network was active in translating Greek science, mathematics, logic, and philosophy.

It should be stressed that this group was tangential to Islamic intellectual life. Most of its members were non-Muslims: they were Nestorian Christians (an excommunicated sect which had left the Byzantine Empire for Persia around 430 C.E.); a few were Jacobites (a wing of the Monophysite heresy in Syria of the mid-500s), Sabians of the old Babylonian star worshippers, occasionally Zoroastrians.[10] They did not take part in the controversies of the ʿulama over theological-philosophical issues. Their niche at first was as carriers of practical skills, as court physicians, astrologers, and astronomers. Since teaching in these professions took place by personal apprenticeship, this group had some concern with the transmission of ideas and texts. Once a critical mass of such experts was assembled at Baghdad, it began the usual intellectual struggle for attention, in this case concentrated on their distinctive cultural capital, their access to textual traditions. Their claim to fame was not originality but possession of more texts, and eventually better translations.

The science, medicine, and mathematics thus introduced were religiously neutral. But they did establish an occupational base for intellectuals outside the career of Muslim religious scholar, primarily as court physician or court astrologer. Later we find that many of the prominent Muslim exponents of *falsafa*, from Rhazes and Ibn Sina down to Ibn Rushd (Averroës) and Abu'l-Barakat, were doctors. Philosophical creativity within these roles did not come about until the translation movement was over. During the early generations, idea imports were a substitute for creativity.

The main area in which this did not hold was in mathematics and astronomy. In the first generation of the House of Wisdom appeared al-Khwarizmi, from a Zoroastrian family. He coined the term *al-jabr*, translated by the Europeans as "algebra," while "algorithm" was taken from his name; he laid out basic principles for solving equations of the first and second degree. A generation later the Sabian Thabit ibn Qurra developed versions of integral calculus, spherical trigonometry, and analytic and non-Euclidean geometry, and reformed Ptolemaic astronomy (*DSB*, 1981: 7:358–365; 13:288–292). Translations were made of Greek mathematics, from Euclid and Archimedes to Plutarch and Diophantus, along with the science of Aristotle and Galen. It is striking that the areas in which creativity occurred are not simply those in which prestigious Greek texts were introduced but rather areas in which there was a cross-connection of imports from India—apparently in the form not of textual translations but of practical knowledge. Thus, Thabit ibn Qurra began as a money changer in Harran (*DSB*, 1981: 13:288), and al-Khwarizmi, an Iranian from the Oxus delta, appears to have introduced the decimal system of Indian numerals (i.e., what Europeans call Arabic numerals). A single line of imports tends to stifle creativity; this is circumvented by multiple and heterogeneous sources of imports, which reinstate the creative competition and recombination of ideas.

This scientific creativity remained largely insulated from philosophy. But Greek cultural capital was now spilling over into the sphere of Arab intellectuals. The first to take advantage of it was al-Kindi, who happened to be closest to the scene, in his position as court overseer of the translators at Baghdad. The result of his labors was not very original; he popularized Greek learning in Arabic, writing an encyclopedic range of treatises across all the sciences, not omitting logic and philosophy. He had contacts with the Baghdad school of Mu'tazilites—then at the height of their political dominance—and he made an effort to accommodate Greek philosophy to Muslim theological issues. Titles of his books indicate he wrote on such Mu'tazilite themes as atoms, the essences of bodies, and the unity of God (Watt, 1973: 207–208). Al-Kindi's own position was largely Neoplatonic, but modified to defend theologican doctrines of the creation of the world ex nihilo, the possibility of miracles and prophecy, and God's eventual destruction of the world. Al-Kindi's position was essentially eclectic, and was adopted neither by the theologians nor by the Greek-oriented *falasifa*. As the latter position came into its own after 900, it took a stronger stand, in opposition to theological particularism, in the form of Neoplatonism championed by al-Farabi. By this time al-Kindi's importance had faded, and the period of translating Greek texts was largely over.

The Sufi Cult of Religious Experience

What became known as the Sufis (after *suf,* the wool cloak worn by wandering ascetics) began to appear in the 700s and 800s as an outcropping of ecstatic religious persons apart from the teachers at the official mosques. Some were wandering preachers; some were ultra-ritualists, making pilgrimages to holy places and saying prayers every step of the way; some were visionaries, who claimed a personal flash of divine contact or inspiration. There was at this time no emphasis on the practice of meditation or systematic methods for inducing visions. A frequent theme was asceticism, giving away one's goods and wandering in poverty, along with practicing sexual celibacy; yet the Sufis did not usually become organized into a monastic life, although there were later a few approaches to it, such as the spiritual community which al-Ghazali formed in Persia. In the early period, asceticism was widely displayed as a badge of religious commitment by members of various positions, including some of the famous Mu'tazilites. Later, when Sufism spread as a mass movement, it generally was organized as lay brotherhoods of persons who practiced ordinary trades but who met periodically for religious initiations and activities.

Sufism never broke organizationally from the conventional structures of Islamic society and religion; it provided supplementary communities in which men from all walks of life (and in rare instances women) could participate. The common theme of this rather inchoate Sufi movement was an emphasis on personal religious experience, away from the collective public rituals such as the five-times-daily prayers at the mosques and other public observances. The more radical Sufis carried this to an anti-ritualistic, anti-conventional extreme: the externals of the pilgrimage to Mecca were nothing, and one might break even the most sacred rules to demonstrate one's inner commitment to a spiritual level transcending anything visible.

This tendency in Sufism took up the opposite side of the field from the scripturalists of the juridical schools and especially the collectors of *hadith*. It is not surprising to find the archconservative Ibn Hanbal polemicizing against al-Muhasibi (65 in Figure 8.1), who helped to crystallize Sufism from pious asceticism into full-blown mysticism. In the same generation (the mid-800s), we find at Baghdad the even more radical Sufi al-Bistami; influenced by an Indian teacher, he declared his identity with the Divine with the words: "Glory to me, how great is my glory!" Such radical expressions could be gotten away with, if just barely, during the period of upheaval in the struggle between Mu'tazilites and their opponents, with the defeat of the Inquisition. Even with such outrageousness, Sufism was becoming organized. As we see in Figure 8.1, the major Sufis were connected in lineages and centered on the main places of intellectual action, Basra and Baghdad; they were part of the division of the intellectual attention space. The leading figure at the end of the 800s, al-Junayd, drew on both Bistami and Muhasibi, and unified Sufism with an analytically argued theosophy. His pupil in turn was the famous al-Hallaj, who studied with all the Sufi networks, debated with the Mu'tazilites, and had personal contacts with Rhazes, the heretical philosopher.

Radical Sufis, as enemies of scripturalists, were capable of making alliances with all sorts of intellectual positions. Both a Neoplatonist like Ibn Sina and an antagonist of philosophy like al-Ghazali could have Sufi teachers and contacts; and we find Ibn Massara (1 in Figure 8.4), the first Muslim philosopher in Spain, setting up a school for both Mu'tazilite theology and Sufism. The fact is that Sufism had no hard kernel of doctrine one way or the other;

it was simply an organized flux of religious energy sweeping around Islamic society on the loose organizational pathways of popular respect for religious piety, plus a politically generated distrust of the official expressions of religious ritual. How this vague religious experience was interpreted depended on the structures that divided the intellectual world at any particular time. Mystical experience, trans-intellectual though it may be, is always interpreted in terms of ideas, and these are produced by the historical networks of the intellectual community.

The radical al-Hallaj epitomizes a particular interpretation of Sufi mysticism (Massignon, 1982). It is a philosophical vision of the world capped by a divine reality beyond words and concepts; compared to this the world itself is unreal, and the individual experiencing this vision loses all sense of duality and becomes absorbed into the divine light and power. In 922 the outraged authorities responded to al-Hallaj's claims with ritual vehemence, mutilating, torturing, crucifying, and burning his body, while from his cross al-Hallaj ecstatically called to the Baghdad crowd: "I am the truth!" For all the monstrousness of this drama, it is a product of the social structure of the intellectual field. Al-Hallaj did not depart from Islamic society into the periphery, experiencing his mystic union in remote solitude; he challenged Islamic religious power in its capital. His was not an inspired idiosyncrasy; he was a direct pupil of the lineages of the most important Sufis. In Figure 8.1 we see the Sufi networks, which had been building up for five generations, brought together in al-Hallaj. And he was an intellectual cosmopolitan, with connections to all the important factions of his day. Even his doctrine of extreme person-centered pantheism was itself a version of Neoplatonism, just then emerging as the dominant position among the *falasifa*. Al-Hallaj's extraordinary self-confidence, deliberately provoking martyrdom, was a boiling-over of emotional energy at a time when the intellectual community of Islam was maximally focused.

Realignment of Factions in the 900s

The early 900s were a time when all the structural tendencies of intellectual life came to a head. In Figures 8.1 and 8.2 we notice in this generation the first two really dominant figures in Islamic philosophy: al-Farabi and al-Ash'ari; Saadia, the first major Jewish philosopher;[11] plus a concentration of notable secondary figures, including Abu Bakhr al-Razi (Rhazes),[12] the most important secular and anti-religious philosopher; the Sufi extremist al-Hallaj; plus notable logicians (Matta), developers of rational theology (al-Maturidi), and the last creative Mu'tazilite (Abu Hashim). This was also the generation in which occurred a crucial event for Islamic theological politics: the long-standing Imamite pretenders to the caliphate withdrew from active political opposition by formulating the doctrine of the hidden Imam, with its implication that an inner faith would substitute, during the indefinite future, for political activism. If we separate the Jewish positions (since they would have been ignored by the Muslims, and in any case paralleled Muslim factions), we still find seven or eight distinctive stances struggling for attention in the intellectual field (see Figure 8.2). This strains the limits of the law of small numbers, and it is not surprising that only a few of these positions were successfully propagated to succeeding generations.

Most of these thinkers were at Baghdad. Basra had had its last gasp of activity; by the end of the century, its lineages had shifted to Nishapur, far to the east in Persia. Baghdad hung on for a few more generations, but hereafter its philosophers became increasingly embattled by anti-intellectual forces. Already by the end of the 900s, Persian cities such as Rayy (near modern Tehran) were becoming rival centers, and henceforth creativity was much more scattered, not only in Persia but also in central Asian Khwarazm and Afghanistan, as well as back to the Mediterranean coast, where Cairo, Damascus, and Aleppo acquired intermittent prominence. With this geographical dispersion, in later centuries the philosophical networks became less concentrated, their creativity more sparse.

Greek philosophy, *falsafa,* had by the early 900s largely passed the era of translations. The philosophers and logicians up to now had been almost entirely non-Muslim—Christians, together with some Sabians (Babylonian star worshippers) among the astronomer-mathematicians. Since translation ceased to be patronized by the court, the main social support of *falsafa* was the practice of medicine. In the Greek medicine of antiquity, the doctor was not merely a dispenser of cures but a public figure; arguing and lecturing was a major part of legitimating medicine at a time when its practice was not very effective. This style carried over into the Islamic context. Isaac Israeli, the first notable cosmopolitan Jewish philosopher, was a court physician at Tunis. His medical books, translated from Arabic into Hebrew and Latin, were more famous than his philosophy, and served as the medium by which his name as a philosopher became known. The same would happen to another doctor, Ibn Sina.

Galen's and Aristotle's logic was part of the medical apprenticeship and provided the terrain on which took place much of the innovations of the *falasifa.* Logic was treated broadly, as a means of classifying the disciplines of knowledge and expounding the modes of reality as well as of argument.[13] The doctor Abu Bishr Matta, and his pupil al-Farabi, and in turn his pupil Yahia ibn 'Adi (another doctor), led the logical developments of the "Baghdad school"; two generations later, Ibn Sina would construct the most comprehensive treatment of logic to date.

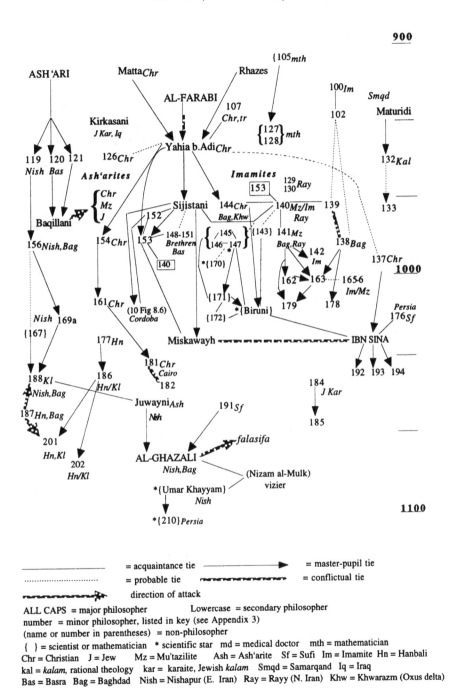

FIGURE 8.2. ASH'ARITES, GREEK *FALASIFA*, AND THE SYNTHESES
OF IBN SINA AND AL-GHAZALI, 935–1100

Al-Farabi was one of the few Muslims in this group, and he made his mark by transmuting its cultural capital into Islamic terms. An independently wealthy individual living quietly without court patronage, he dedicated himself to gathering everything he could from the cosmopolitan network, seeking out the leading teachers and traveling as far as Byzantium. Al-Farabi represents the culmination of idea importing into Islam. He surveyed all the available Greek works and enumerated all the natural sciences, the main concern of the Baghdad translators, systematizing everything into a Neoplatonic hierarchy of emanations. Al-Farabi was most original in adapting Plato's *Republic* to Islamic conditions: the Prophet, as head of Islam, is the true philosopher-king; just as the universe emanates from the absolute One, the successive ranks of political hierarchy emanate from the political head. Al-Farabi implies that after the Prophet, the headship is delegated to a being of secondary grade, whose qualities and powers are lessened. The vagueness of al-Farabi's formulation is perhaps a deliberate appeal to cover all factions; the "second head" could be equally the caliph, the *ulama,* or even the Shi'ite Imam. Al-Farabi's hallmark is political caution and the avoidance of theological disputes. His Neoplatonism is a religion of reason, combining the naturalism of the sciences with the most abstract and general form of Islam that he could safely espouse.

Why would this religion of reason now rise to dominance in the network of philosophers? External political forces helped move the network in this direction. Islam, originally a religion of the Arabs, was pressuring its subject peoples to convert. Zoroastrians had already been persecuted and largely eliminated in the 800s. In 932–934, the caliph launched a persecution of Sabians, and the last of them in the scientific network (notably 105 and 127 in the key to Figure 8.2) converted to Islam. Christians came under increasing pressure, although we find them in the network of Yahia ibn 'Adi's successors down into the next century. The Muslim intellectuals who inhabited these circles had no reason to defend Christianity or any other religion; their structural location motivated them to take a studied neutrality. The freethinker Ibn al-Rawandi took the most dangerous stance, claiming the autonomy of science, superior to religion. Al-Farabi's contemporary Rhazes even more explicitly rejected the clashing religious sects; he held that prophecy is superfluous to the light of reason, and indeed the cause of violence among religious rivals (Fakhry, 1983: 105). Rhazes, one of the first Muslims among the elite medical doctors, drew widely on the cosmopolitan communities intersecting at Baghdad, from India as well as Greece. Rhazes postulated a system of co-eternal principles, including atoms moving continually in the void, souls undergoing a cycle of rebirths, and a creator-God who sets in motion these preexistent materials. Rhazes's eclectic synthesis was condemned on all sides; in his grandpupils' generation it would be picked up by another heretical group, the secret Brethren of Purity.

Al-Farabi's philosophy was an attempt to be politically safe, avoiding the dynastic partisanship inherent in the various Sunni and Shi'ite theologies. In this respect he moved onto Mu'tazilite turf, an earlier attempt at a religion of reason and a neutral stance on dynastic issues. Increasingly powerful enemies were now accusing the Mu'tazilites of heterodoxy. This was the final generation in which anything creative would come from them in philosophy. Other practitioners of *kalam,* notably al-Ash'ari and his followers, were retreating toward a more conservative position. The Neoplatonism of al-Farabi is the kind of structure-driven creativity which emerges to fill an emptying slot in the intellectual field as external political forces destroy their social bases. Al-Farabi, like al-Kindi before him, attracted no notice from his contemporaries in the networks of Muslim theology. This gave him a certain amount of safety; on occasion he fled Baghdad to avoid political troubles. As the Christians disappeared and Mu'tazilites faded out in the next few generations, al-Farabi's philosophy was the one that survived and prospered. Later *falasifa,* as well as their critics, came to regard al-Farabi as preeminent.

The Crystallization of Rational Theology in a Conservative Direction

For Muslim intellectuals, the big news of the early 900s would have been the split which took place in the Mu'tazilite camp. Al-Ash'ari, pupil of the head of the Basra school, al-Juba'i, denounced the Mu'tazilites in 912 and announced his reconciliation with the *hadith* scripturalists. Al-Ash'ari now admitted that the Qur'an is not created; using the distinction of essence and existence, he met objections by showing that any particular copy of the Qur'an is created, whereas its essence is eternal. There was some personal rivalry in this move, as the Basra headship was passed at just this time to al-Juba'i's son, the acute metaphysician Abu Hashim. But the break was not merely personal, as we can see by the fact that Mu'tazilite creativity more or less dried up at this point, while the Ash'arite lineage prospered; its future generations would include the important thinkers al-Baqillani, al-Juwayni, al-Ghazali, and al-Sharastani (as we see in Figure 8.2). Moreover, among al-Ash'ari's contemporaries was al-Maturidi, in far-off Samarqand, who founded another lineage of theological moderates, somewhat closer to the Mu'tazilites on the issue of free will (Watt, 1973: 312–316). The theological factions were being revamped at this time across the board, on both the Sunni and Shi'ite sides.

If the Ash'arites were the most prominent lineage philosophically, it was because they had accumulated the intellectual capital of the Mu'tazilite debates.[14] The Ash'arites firmly adopted time-atomism as their metaphysics. As we have seen, this doctrine emerged only gradually and with many disagreements in the Mu'tazilite camp; and in fact the strongest statement of time-atomism by a Mu'tazilite came from al-Ka'bi (109 in Figure 8.1), a contemporary of al-Ash'ari. By the time of al-Baqillani, the Ash'arites were laying out time-atomism systematically as their own doctrine. The impression widespread in the West that Muslim theology is fatalistic, holding that an all-controlling God determines everything that happens in the world, is the result of the orthodox stamp which the Ash'arites put on this Mu'tazilite doctrine.

The Mu'tazilite-Ash'arite network, for all the concessions the latter made to scripturalism, took indigenous Muslim philosophy toward issues comparable at many points to positions later argued by the famous philosophers of medieval Christendom and early modern Europe. Let us note the following:

1. Al-Ash'ari rejected the Mu'tazilites' extreme emphasis on the unity of God in order to agree with the traditionalists' view that God has positive attributes (power, knowledge, life, and so on as described in the Qur'an). These cannot be considered identical with God's essence; but they are eternal, and subsist in God's essence (Fakhry, 1983: 53, 58–59, 204–205, 214–215). This line of argument had already become acute with Ash'ari's Mu'tazilite teacher al-Juba'i, and his son Abu Hashim. The latter worked out subtle distinctions of state and attribute, moving along a path similar to that of Duns Scotus in the Christian network four centuries later. Abu Hashim took the discussion of bodies and their accidents to its most extreme step, holding that a body can be stripped of all accidents except being. Other Mu'tazilites had argued about which attributes were most primordial; al-Ka'bi, the strongest advocate of time-atomism, held that bodies can be divested of all attributes except color, while the Ash'arites distinguished between primary and secondary accidents, the former of which necessarily accompany substance, and include motion, rest, and location. The argument looks something like Locke's primary and secondary qualities, although the Ash'arites went on to include among primary accidents features such as taste and smell, dampness and dryness, heat and cold. The primary-secondary distinction was not worked out with the radicalness of Locke because the level of abstraction upheld by the intellectual network did not remain very high.

2. The Ash'arites held that God's decrees are fiat, independent of and superior to any rational or moral conditions. Al-Baqillani argued that if God desired, he could have created an entirely different world, or refrained from creating the world at all. Here we have a position like that which was taken by Duns Scotus and the Ockhamists, emphasizing the unlimited and miraculous power of God's will. The condemnation of Averroist determinism by the Paris authorities in 1277, which led to this conception of the unlimited power of God, is structurally paralleled by the political condemnation of the Mu'tazilites' rational restrictions on God as following from his unity and justice. In both cases a philosophy is constructed which extends the implications of the opposite position.

3. The mature Mu'tazilite and Ash'arite time-atomism foreshadows the occasionalist system of Malebranche. In the latter's system there is a psycho-physical parallelism in which bodies are moved not by the human will but by God. Malebranche, a priest arguing against the mechanistic worldviews of the 1600s, was doubtless not imitating the Muslims; it is simply that in both cases, the type of argument serves to make God omnipresent even within a world which philosophical argument has concluded consists of material substances.

4. By the late 900s, the Ash'arites denied that there are unchanging essences and eternal laws (Wolfson, 1976: 543–544; Fakhry, 1983: 210–212). Moving to the opposite pole from the Neoplatonists, now on the scene among the *falasifa,* they held that facts are concrete and particular. Al-Baqillani's version of atomic instants held that every particular event is produced by the will of God; God may make a sequence of repetitive events, but there are no natural laws, no necessity of repetition. Here the argument foreshadows Hume's denial of causality, and paves the way for al-Ghazali's anti-causal argument in the Ash'arite lineage three generations later. Al-Baqillani also held that bodies in themselves can have any sort of qualities; that they have one particular form rather than another requires a determinant, which implies the existence of God. This also makes explicit the notion of contingency, which was to be stressed by Ibn Sina and by al-Juwayni.

5. The Mu'tazilites and Ash'arites worked out a series of proofs of theo-logical positions: for the existence of God; for God's unity; for the creation of the world ex nihilo; against the Aristotelean preexistence of matter and eternity of the world. Abu-'l-Hudhayl, in the early 800s generation, produced an argument for the creation of the world that was to be characteristic of *kalam:* all accidents are generated; all bodies have accidents (including the accident of being composite); hence the world as a body must be generated (Davidson, 1987: 134–136). About the same time al-Nazzam held that an infinite cannot be traversed, and that one infinite cannot be greater than another infinite; these points imply the finiteness of the world in time (Wolfson, 1976: 416–417). Saadia summarized related Mu'tazilite arguments for creation, such as the argument that if past time were infinite, then the original cause of existence could never reach me; since I exist, there must be a temporal beginning (Hyman and Walsh, 1983: 348). The procedure of *kalam* was to prove the creation first, then use this as basis for the proof of a creator. The Jewish academies came alive in this period through factional arguments between Karaites and Rabbanites, paralleling *kalam* and *hadith;* they were similarly concerned with reasoned critique or defense of anthropomorphic images in holy scripture. Such proofs became one of the staples of Jewish philosophy leading up to Mai-monides.[15]

These issues, more than anything else, propelled Islamic philosophy in the direction of explicit proofs and conceptual analysis. More subtle arguments were added in the next centuries, especially in the Ash'arite lineage (al-Baqillani, al-Juwayni, al-Ghazali); for instance, the proof that if an object (the world) has particular characteristics but could have had others, there must be something (God) which caused it to be particularized (Davidson, 1987: 174–178). This line of argument, foreshadowing Leibniz's principle of sufficient reason, was developed by al-Juwayni in the mid-1000s. Further subtleties arose as the creationists debated Aristoteleans over the eternity of the world. Al-Farabi, Ibn Sina, and later Ibn Rushd (Averroës) responded to *kalam* by distinguishing among different types of infinities and infinite regresses (Davidson, 1987: 127–143). Ibn Sina broke ground beyond these cosmological proofs by arguing on the basis of analysis of the concepts of necessary and possible being.[16] By the time of al-Ghazali (al-Juwayni's pupil), it had become possible to point out that even a proof of the existence of a creator or first cause does not prove its unity or incorporeality, and that philosophy comes up against epistemological limits beyond which it must cede to religious authority.

6. The payoff of this accumulation of arguments is not only in the philosophies of Ibn Sina and al-Ghazali; it is also already found in al-Baqillani, the first systematizer of the Ash'arite position. In order to undergird his time-atomism and his proofs of God and creation, al-Baqillani set forth a theory of knowledge. He divided knowledge into God's eternal knowledge and creatures' knowledge, and the latter into what is known through the senses, through discourse, or authoritatively through history or revelation. Among necessary knowledge he included knowledge of one's own existence; here we have the "cogito ergo sum," but al-Baqillani did not separate its indubitability from that of other sensory knowledge. Al-Baqillani's epistemology is uncritical and not very sophisticated. But the emergence of epistemology is itself a breakthrough. Further Ash'arite systematizers in this lineage, such as al-Baghdadi (167 in Figure 8.2) and al-Juwayni, also now based their expositions on an epistemology. The major conceptual ingredients for more abstract and critical philosophy were in place, on which was built the creativity of Ibn Sina and al-Ghazali.

The Shi'ite Alliance and the United Front of Heterodoxies

The 900s mark a turning point in the intellectual and political history of Islam and in their connecting link, religious politics. Religious factions lined up for a power showdown. The large number of Sunni legal schools had winnowed down to a few main schools of law; the earlier struggle between *hadith* and Qur'an as scriptural basis was now resolved by inclusion. On the Shi'ite side, the old factional opposition, once fragmented among many contenders, became unified as well. The Shi'ites posed a danger not only of military uprisings on the periphery but also in the core of the empire; in Baghdad itself, the Shi'ites made up 30 percent of the population (Massignon, 1982: 240, 252). In the early 800s, Caliph al-Ma'mun had attempted to negotiate a settlement by offering the succession to the current Shi'ite pretender; the failure of this move led to the ill-fated Inquisition, an attempt to assert caliphal autonomy from theological factions (Lapidus, 1988: 124). Now, in the early 900s, the caliph's regime was full of Shi'ite administrators, especially in finances and tax collection, though reserving the executive branch for Sunnites; his personal staff was drawn from Mu'tazilites. There was constant concern for Shi'ite rebellions in the provinces and conspiracies at court. In this context, al-Nawbakhti (100 in Figure 8.1), a wealthy Baghdad businessman involved in court finances, formulated the doctrine of the Hidden Imam. The Imam was the alleged successor to the Prophet, on the side which lost the earliest civil war. Al-Nawbakhti now held that the twelfth Imam was in hiding, and would reappear at some time in the future to establish the reign of justice. This also meant giving up concrete claim to the succession and transforming the Imam into a transcendental symbol, depicted as a luminous divine substance transmitted to a human intermediary in each generation. A colleague of al-Nawbakhti (102 in Figure 8.2) put the Shi'ites on a comparable basis with the Sunnites by formulating their own canonical Imamite law and *hadith*.

For a time the Shi'ite front won political support. The caliphate, which had been gradually losing de facto power in the provinces since the mid-800s, was subordinated in 945 by a Buwayid sultan. The Buwayids encouraged Imamism, as the doctrine no longer threatened rebellion in favor of an heir to the line of Ali, while it delegitimated the caliphate and was indifferent to secular rule. The chief remaining Shi'ite faction, the Isma'ilis, established a rival caliphate in Tunisia in the early 900s, and conquered Egypt and Syria from the crumbling Baghdad caliphate in 970. No Shi'ite orthodoxy could be imposed, however. The empire continued to disintegrate, and the Sunnites shifted to other power bases outside the crumbling capital—new conquering states from the east, as well as the Sufi missionary movements spreading from within.

Along with geopolitical disintegration and shifting religious fortunes came intellectual realignment. On the Sunnite side were the bulk of the scriptural scholars in the law schools, along with the Ash'arite theologians and the Sufis. The eventual synthesizer of this entire alliance would be al-Ghazali. On the Shi'ite side, appeared a coalition combining a new theology with themes of the entire non-orthodox philosophical and scientific community. Here the synthesis came in two phases: first with the Brethren of Purity, then in more sophisticated form with Ibn Sina.

Intellectual history is driven by conflict, and therefore is full of ironic reversals. From the short-run perspective of the late 1900s, we are used to seeing the Shi'ites as archconservatives. In medieval Islam they were the radicals and the intellectual cosmopolitans. In Figure 8.1, at the time of al-Nawbakhti we see the network of Baghdad Imamites casting around for allies, including both Mu'tazilites and the famous mathematician Thabit ibn Qurra, a Sabian star worshipper. In the late 900s, as the empire disintegrated, the vizier (140 in Figure 8.2) of the provincial court at Rayy (near modern Tehran) patronized both Mu'tazilites and Imamites, as well as a collection of scientists and logicians. In this generation are clusters at Rayy, Baghdad, and Basra: an interconnection of all the heterodox non-Sunni groups. The most famous among them was al-Sijistani, a logician at the center of a literary discussion circle at Baghdad; he was a pupil of Yahia ibn 'Adi, and in the midst of the Christian logicians. His protégé al-Tawhidi (153 in Figure 8.2) was an eclectic popularizer of heterodox positions, who acquired a reputation as the "archheretic of Islam." Al-Sijistani was the reputed leader of a mysterious underground group at Basra, the "Brethren of Purity."

The Brethren's position was an eclectic synthesis of non-Sunni heterodoxy. It asserted an allegorical interpretation of the Qur'an, combined with Neoplatonist emanation of souls and forms from God, and the Hermetic astrology of the Sabians (the line of Thabit ibn Qurra, friend of the earlier Imamites). They held that the series of emanations reascends through minerals, plants, animals, and humans, the description of which gave the Brethren opportunity to show off their scientific knowledge. All worldly things are ruled by particular numbers, according to the system of Neo-Pythagorean numerology which describes occult correspondences among the levels. Astrology is given great significance; the planets not only foretell the future but also determine when each Imam passes from concealment to open rule, and when comes the periodic destruction of the world at the end of a cycle of 7,000 years. Human souls are arranged in a hierarchy of ignorance, and are reincarnated Hindu-fashion, except for those who are enlightened, who permanently ascend to the higher level of the Intellect. The Imam is the highest human, the point of contact with the Divine. He rules a hierarchy of initiates, divided into four levels, according to their knowledge of the sciences.

Organizationally, the Brethren's secret society appears to have had some real success in the underground of Shi'ite missionaries and conspirators; numerous copies of their encyclopedic "Epistles" are found across many centuries. Their doctrine is eclectic and inconsistent among its various strands, and its appeal seems to have been more to the general populace than to intellectuals. It represents the last gasp of the old Basra-Baghdad cosmopolitans, huddled together in a defensive coalition while shifting to new social-religious bases of support.

The Culmination of the Philosophical Networks:
Ibn Sina and al-Ghazali

If the Brethren of Purity were an unsophisticated and popularistic synthesis, Ibn Sina in the next generation was a sophisticated one, the height of philosophy in the Islamic East. One can see in Figure 8.2 how networks of significant intellectuals simplified in his time, and even more so in the generation of al-Ghazali: the Baghdad base began to be deserted; the Basra intellectuals were no more. In the background, geopolitical and political shifts were pressing on the bases of intellectual life. The Buwayhid sultans could not hold the remaining empire together. On the periphery in inner Asia and Afghanistan, conquering states expanded, the Ghaznavid Turks expanded from Transoxiana (south of the Aral Sea) into Persia; by 1055 they would conquer Baghdad and impose a puritanical Sunnism against the Shi'ites. The Mu'tazilites were already being persecuted in Iraq; their survivors spread east into Persia, and the more moderate Ash'arites also shifted their main base to Nishapur in eastern Persia. The Ghaznavids caught doctrinal deviants in the other arm of a vise, burning books and killing the Isma'ilis and other rebellious Shi'ite sects and the Mu'tazilites (Afnan, 1958: 73–74). Strict Sunni orthodoxy, starting from Baghdad, had spread east by 1000.

Christianity and Judaism too were being squeezed out, along with the Zoroastrians. The Sufis, now spreading among the people rather than among the intellectuals, acted as missionaries in Persia and inner Asia. There was a reversal of the earlier Muslim tolerance of the other religions of the "peoples of the book." Previously, Islam was regarded as a privilege of the Arabs. This elitism declined as warfare and the destruction of the older conquering clans rearranged the class structure; we find now a combination of status-striving on the part of non-Arabs, forced conversion by Muslim militants, and missionary zeal. By 1000, Islam had become a majority religion in Iran and Iraq, eliminating most rival religionists. The network of *falasifa*, once primarily Christian and Sabian, had been turned over to Muslim followers such as al-Sijistani, Ibn Miskawayh, and al-Biruni.

Ibn Sina appeared in the generation when the Christians were disappearing and the intellectuals were migrating away from Baghdad. He was the son of a provincial official at the very edge of the Muslim world, in the region of the Aral Sea. Largely self-educated because of lack of accomplished teachers, he acquired his comprehensive knowledge through access to the library of the sultan of Bukhara. How could someone like this become the greatest Muslim philosopher? In part because the old networks were now migrating for patronage toward the new geopolitical powers on the periphery. Although Ibn Sina was connected to none of the significant philosophers, he did encounter a

Christian teacher of medicine (137 in Figure 8.2) from Baghdad (who thus probably constituted a network connection to Yahya ibn-ʿAdi), who introduced him to the issues debated at the center, and especially its logic. Medicine was the main social base for cosmopolitan intellectuals, and Ibn Sina made his greatest reputation through his encyclopedic synthesis of Greek and Arabic medical texts. In addition, Ismaʿili missionaries who visited his father no doubt brought him into contact with the "Epistles" of the Brethren of Purity.

Most important, at the Khwarazm court the young Ibn Sina encountered al-Biruni, one of the scientific stars of Islam (Afnan, 1958: 62–71; *DSB*, 1981: 2:147–156). Al-Biruni was a great astronomer and a famous geographer, the first Muslim expert on India; a cosmopolitan both of thought and of travel, he connects back into the scientific network at Baghdad in its last generation of greatness, including the important mathematician and astronomer Abuʾ-l-Wafa al-Buzjani (147 in Figure 8.2), as well as to Christian logicians from the lineage of Yahya ibn ʿAdi. In the network we can see that the generations just before and after 1000 are nearly the last to be full of scientific stars: besides those just mentioned, there is Ibn Yunus (159) at Cairo, one of the greatest astronomers; Ibn al-Haitham (known to the Latins as Alhazen), famous for his optics; and Al-Karaji (170) at Baghdad, who developed the arithmeticization of algebra and the calculation of polynomials. Alhazen, contemporary of al-Biruni and Ibn Sina, also migrated away from Iraq to new sources of patronage in Cairo. One can surmise that Ibn Sina first acquired creative energy from these contacts early in his career; his first field of endeavor was scientific, primarily medicine, and he also compiled new astronomical tables.

When al-Biruni and the other stars of the Khwarazm court were called by the conqueror to Ghazna, Ibn Sina fled in the other direction. He moved into western Persia, becoming court physician, sometimes vizier, and sometimes living under private patronage at Rayy, Hamadan, and Isfahan, embattled states between the crumbling Baghdad empire and the expanding Ghaznavids. It appears that he was fleeing the religious intolerance of the conqueror; his travels are reminiscent of those of Descartes, who moved between Catholic and Protestant battle lines during the European religious wars; both sought a safe spot in the middle where they could take advantage of the opportunities for intellectual synthesis opened up by the rearrangement of cultural connections.

Ibn Sina turned from his *Canon* of medicine to composing an encyclopedia of philosophy. He took over the Neoplatonic cosmology of al-Farabi and the Aristotelean logic developed by the Baghdad school of Christian logicians, but he formulated metaphysical issues in their own right and with a thoroughness and depth that went beyond anything in his predecessors. His originality is seen above all in the prologue which he adds to the Neoplatonic system. Before plunging into describing the levels of emanation that make up the cosmos, he builds a foundation of systematic definitions and proofs. In other words, he integrates Neoplatonism around the problems bequeathed by *kalam:* the nature of substance and attributes, proofs of God and the creation of the world.

To begin at the beginning, Ibn Sina holds, is to study being, the most fundamental of all concepts. He proves this with an argument that foreshadows Descartes's cogito but is used for a different purpose. Imagine a man flying in a dark and completely empty space; though he would know nothing of sensory qualities or material bodies, he would unquestionably know that he exists.[17] When the senses are restored, these would show only further modifications of being.

Although there is no other notion prior to being, it admits distinctions. The mind can think of what something is—its essence or "whatness" (as the Christian scholastics would say, its *quiddity*)—without its actually existing, and even without its possibly ever existing. Existence is thus superadded to essence, making up the two fundamental aspects of being. This distinction was an old one, found in Aristotelean logic. But Ibn Sina does not merely leave his distinctions within a logical treatise; in his *al-Shifa* he elevates them to metaphysical principles as the foundation of an ontological system (Afnan, 1958: 115–130; Davidson, 1987: 281–310; Hyman and Walsh, 1983: 241–255). Within existence, Ibn Sina adds the further distinction between necessary being—that of which to assume its non-existence would lead to an impossibility—and non-necessary being. Ibn Sina criticizes the theologians and logicians for failing to make adequate distinctions; they define "necessary" and "possible" in a circle, in terms of each other. Ibn Sina argues that there is a further category, the contingent: that which is neither necessary nor impossible. Thus we can conceive of (1) being which is necessary of itself, and (2) being which is merely possible in itself but necessary as the result of some external cause.

If a being were necessary purely of itself alone, it could contain no internal distinctions; it would have to be unified, simple, and incorporeal: in short, it would be God. Does such a being exist? Ibn Sina notes that since we know something does exist, it must be of either type (1) or type (2). If it is the former, the proof is complete. If it is the latter, it must depend on a separate being to maintain it in existence; and that can only be (1). A being with all the characteristics of God must accordingly exist; and the rest of the world can be logically derived from it.

If Ibn Sina reaches a high level of abstraction, it is because he builds on the whole preceding Islamic intellectual community. The central problems that he sets for himself—to delineate the attributes of God; to show how the world was created; to demonstrate the different components of what we call causality—were those around which Muslim rational theologians had traded accusations of heresy. Ibn Sina was in a position to stand back and survey the whole development, and then systematically set forth the fundamental metaphysical terms in which these issues could be resolved. To de-particularize this development, one should say that the Muslim intellectual community after eight generations of debate had pushed these problems to successively higher levels of abstraction; Ibn Sina was the individual in whom the process reached an explicit metaphysics, detached from theology, and systematized into a comprehensive chain of proofs. Proofs of the existence of God go back to the Mu'tazilite theologians; chains of logical argument were developed as technical skills by the Baghdad specialists in this art; the Neoplatonic cosmology of emanations had been Islamicized by al-Farabi and popularized by the Brethren of Purity. Ibn Sina was heir to all these developments. His work is a grand synthesis, carried out with a logical thoroughness that goes far beyond mere eclecticism. Structurally, his scholasticism represents the drawing together of the entire corpus of rational thought in Islam, at a time when the social space on this side of the field was closing down and the anti-rationalists were palpably growing in strength.

Ibn Sina, like other very great intellectuals, was an energy star. He wrote encyclopedically and fundamentally on numerous subjects. This outpouring of energy was what carried his work to later generations, despite the fact that his personal network broke off with a few minor local disciples. His philosophy was criticized and rejected by the Hanbali and Ash'arite theologians who now dominated. Ibn Sina's reputation was kept alive by his eminence in the world of medicine; and it was along with his *Canon* that his philosophy eventually spread, via Spanish doctors and translators, into the Latin world under the name of Avicenna.

Creative networks had become even thinner by the time of al-Ghazali. Figure 8.2 shows no rival philosopher in his generation of even secondary importance. He does, however, have significant network ties backwards and forwards in time: he was a pupil in the main line of Ash'arite theologians; he was in the main intellectual centers of the time, Nishapur and Baghdad; and his lineage led on to the relatively more important figures of subsequent generations. The fact remains that al-Ghazali's generation had the thinnest network of significant thinkers in the history of Islamic philosophy up to this time; it was the turning point between the dense competition among rival chains that characterized the heyday of the Basra and Baghdad networks, and the later period of thinner and rather routinized networks of Sufis and *madrasa* theologians. The content of al-Ghazali's thought incorporates this change; his is the creativity of structural crisis.

Al-Ghazali was connected with all the main trends of his time. Toleration for philosophy was disappearing. In Baghdad, violent outbreaks took place during al-Ghazali's youth. Al-Qushayri (188 in Figure 8.2), a Nishapur theologian from al-Ghazali's own Ash'arite lineage, had been violently attacked by mobs stirred up by the Hanbalis in 1072. Ibn 'Aqil (201) was also violently attacked and forced to recant his use of *kalam,* rational methods. The Hanbalis were now so dominant that their own ranks had an internal split; Ibn 'Aqil was a Hanbali moderate, and we see in Figure 8.2 that he came from a branch of the Baghdad Hanbalis (177, 186, 202) that had been combining *hadith* with *kalam.* The last of this lineage (202) had to move to Damascus, a safer environment away from this persecution. Al-Ghazali too would go from Nishapur to teach at Baghdad, then flee the city as politics heated up again in the 1090s.

Not surprisingly, in this atmosphere philosophy declined. Ibn 'Aqil lamented that in his time there were no more serious thinkers (Watt, 1985: 102). Al-Ghazali's one important contemporary was 'Umar Khayyam; a famous poet, he was even more eminent as a mathematician, developing techniques for extracting cube and square roots of algebraic equations. He and his pupil al-Khazini (210 in Figure 8.2) were the last two great scientific stars of the Islamic East for a century (*DSB,* 1981: 7:323–325, 335–351). 'Umar Khayyam overlaps with al-Ghazali's networks: Khayyam was about 10 years older and had studied at Nishapur before him. Khayyam and al-Ghazali had the same patron, the Seljuk vizier Nizam al-Mulk, who appointed Khayyam head of the court astronomical observatory at Isfahan, and al-Ghazali to teach at the great *madrasa* which Nizam al-Mulk founded at Baghdad. Khayyam himself wrote philosophical treatises late in his life; his poems, contemporary with the writings of al-Ghazali, make disillusioned reference to his own contacts with the "two-and-seventy jarring sects" and to his student days at Nishapur:

> Myself when young did eagerly frequent
> Doctor and saint, and heard great argument
> About it and about: but evermore
> Came out by the same door where in I went.

Khayyam's advice is the same as al-Ghazali's:

> Waste not your hour, nor in vain pursuit
> Of This and That endeavour and dispute.

Al-Ghazali's philosophy is an anti-philosophy. He was the great agent of the traditionalist reaction, but he was great precisely because he was a defector from the core network, turning the weapons of philosophy against itself. Like Ibn Sina, whom he attacked, al-Ghazali had a commanding overview of the cultural capital of the Islamic intellectuals. He scrupulously set forth their views before refuting them; and he carried out the refutation not by fulmination but by using the highest techniques of argumentation. In *The Incoherence of Philosophy* he examines the proofs of the major propositions given by his opponents and finds them wanting by stricter logical standards. His major weapon is to attack the notion of necessary causality, using arguments like those later made famous in Europe by Hume. For al-Ghazali, necessity is limited to logical relations; possibility excludes necessity, and hence the things of the world can become actual only through the action of a voluntary cause, God's will.

In this al-Ghazali justifies the traditional position of the Ash'arites: exalting God's omnipotence so that God alone is the cause of everything that happens in the world. There are no spheres of emanation, no realm of secondary causes which diminish God. But *kalam* is not very important; it is useless for the religiously healthy person unafflicted by doubt, while its ability to settle doubts is far from perfect, as we can see by holding it up to the logical standards of *falsafa*. Here epistemological acuteness was raised by religious traditionalists seeking to puncture the claims of rational argument. But al-Ghazali faced further problems on the religious front, especially the challenge of the Isma'ilis, then in open revolt against al-Ghazali's Seljuk patrons (Hodgson, 1974: 2:180–192). By what criterion could one tell if the Isma'ili Imam were to be accepted or rejected against Sunni religious claims? Reason cannot decide, since it leads only to recognizing the need for an authority beyond itself on ultimate matters. But there is a faculty capable of recognizing valid spiritual authority, and that is the insight given by Sufi mystical experience. We have come a long way from the condemnation of al-Hallaj; Sufism of this sort is no longer a heresy, but is brought close to the orthodox center.

Al-Ghazali himself, after lecturing on conventional Ash'arite theology at Baghdad, underwent a personal crisis that caused him to withdraw from teaching (al-Ghazali, 1951; Hyman and Walsh, 1983: 277). He recalls that he vacillated between giving up philosophy and continuing to teach (after all, he held the preeminent chair in the Islamic world), until finally his tongue dried up in his mouth, whereupon he slipped away from the city to make a long pilgrimage in search of mystical experience. Al-Ghazali responded to the increasing prestige of the Sufi ideal replacing the decline of philosophy and *kalam*, for as he himself laments, the mystical experiences did not come; he was motivated by a theoretical ideal. There were also political reasons for his leaving Baghdad in 1095. It had been only 20 years since his Ash'arite predecessors had been mobbed by the Hanbalis, and in 1092 his protector Nizam al-Mulk (who had reversed the policy of persecuting Ash'arites) was assassinated by the Isma'ilis. After al-Ghazali's period of wandering in unsuccessful search of mystical enlightenment, he returned to Nishapur and organized a contemplative community. His brother (211 in Figure 8.3) became a famous Sufi, and their lineage established an Ash'arite version of Sufism.

Al-Ghazali is the focus point at which all the trends of the time gathered. We see the disappearing basis for philosophy and the pressure on *kalam;* we see the expansion of Sufism into respectability and its integration into the scholastic curriculum. For al-Ghazali also rides on a decisive change in the organizational basis of intellectual production. Schools of law and theology were ceasing to be lineages of private teachers assembling in the mosques. Now there were *madrasas,* formal foundations of properties supported by donors or by the government. Al-Ghazali's sponsor Nizam al-Mulk as vizier established *madrasas* in every major city, shifting the basis of education and Islamic thought from ad hoc groups of teachers at the mosques into foundations under government support. Nizam al-Mulk was no doubt following a trend already in motion; his theological politics gave vigorous support to Sunnis against Shi'ites, and we find that competition between the sects was producing a proliferation of *madrasa* foundations on both sides (Nakosteen, 1964: 42–44).

It is fitting that al-Ghazali should have produced the great conservative synthesis, for he was teaching in the founding generation at the most important *madrasa* in the Islamic world. Al-Ghazali's most enduring legacy for Islamic thought was not his acute philosophical skepticism, which was largely forgotten (Watt, 1985: 76), but the fact that he made logical methods respectable among conservative theologians as a neutral tool that could be used for any correct form of thinking. Of all the heritage of the *falasifa,* logic was rescued from destruction by al-Ghazali and his followers and incorporated into the curriculum of the *madrasas.* It soon became part of a rather droning scholastic routine.[18]

Routinization of Sufis and Scholastics

After 1100, philosophical creativity became rather thin, at least in the Islamic east; a brilliant episode was taking place in Spain, but encapsulated in the far west. In the heartland of Islam, there was no longer the innovative struggle between multiple lineages densely intermeshing at great intellectual centers. Simplified networks of the relatively notable figures still existed; even the Sufi poets, rejectors of systematic thinking, tended to be offshoots of these networks. Thinner networks of theologians also continued, linking together the more significant names (see Figure 8.3).

This was the great era of institutional Sufism. Already in the late 900s, the Sufis were making alliances of respectability with the conservatives, and we find Sufi Hanbalites proclaiming Sufism as a branch of the *'ulama* legalists (134 and 135 in Figure 8.2). In the 1000s, Nishapur theologians (169, 188, and 190) were drawing up registers of Sufis, collecting their biographies, explaining mystical terms in a scholastic manner. Contemporary with al-Ghazali there began a long series of foundings of Sufi orders. At least 12 Sufi orders arose

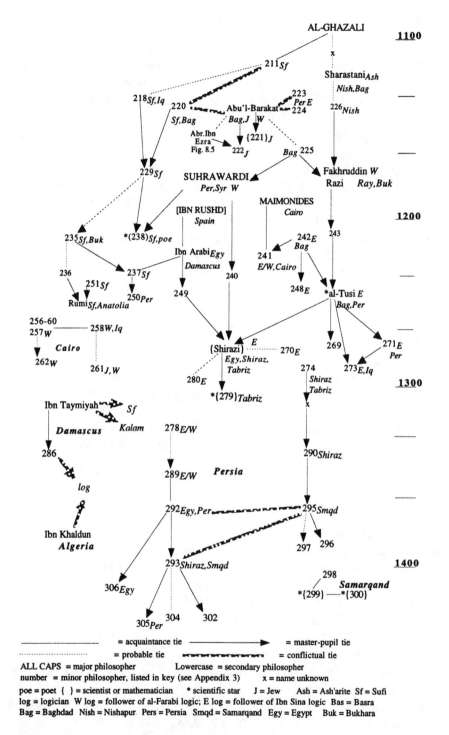

FIGURE 8.3. MYSTICS, SCIENTISTS, AND LOGICIANS, 1100–1400

in the 10 generations from 1065 to 1400, founded at a nearly regular beat one generation after another.[19] These orders were spread out geographically from one end of the Islamic world to the other, from India to the Maghrib (western North Africa). In central Asia and the eastern frontiers these orders were part of the missionary process that was spreading Islam. There was a spate of orders in Anatolia as the Byzantine Empire collapsed in the 1100s and 1200s and Islam moved into the religious vacuum with the conquering Turks. Most of these frontier orders were not very significant intellectually, and their leaders were unconnected to the philosophical networks. Their appeal was to layper-sons rather than to those with full-time religious vocations. They developed their distinctive varieties of rituals, dancing, chanting, music, meditation; they varied from politically activist to quietist. Most of the orders were geographi-cally localized and did not intersect with one another around significant figures to form a network; the Sufi orders do not seem to have competed with one another, which is one reason why their structures generated traditionalism rather than philosophical innovation.

Sufism also was spreading in the intellectual core of Islam. In the generation after al-Ghazali's death, a leading figure at Baghdad was 'Abdulqadir Gilani (220), who became one of the most famous Sufi saints. He was a Hanbali in theology but also a visionary; the order that was later founded in his name around the worship of his tomb stressed techniques for inducing ecstatic spiritual states. Gilani himself was rather unmetaphysical, and he attacked even the moderate and pro-Sufi *kalam* of the Ghazali brothers. Gilani's pupil Abu-Hafs al-Suhrawardi (229) was appointed by the caliph as head of all Sufi establishments in Baghdad; Sufism was getting government recognition and, where the government was powerful enough, regulation. Abu-Hafs in turn was one of the teachers of the great Sufi poet Sa'di; another pupil, Najmuddin Kubra, founded a famous Sufi order which turned from pious asceticism toward visionary speculation. As the networks became denser, even among the Sufis, intellectual constructions were created. Kubra's pupils in turn were connected to the philosophical mystic Ibn 'Arabi, as well as producing a generation later the most famous Sufi poet. This was Rumi, active at the time of the Mongol conquests, which destroyed Baghdad in 1258 and temporarily left Islam without a center of doctrinal enforcement. Perhaps this was why Rumi could get away with a radical pantheism without being accused of heresy: "I am the mote in the sunbeam," he declared; "I die a stone and become a plant."

The period from the mid-1100s to the mid-1200s was the apex of creativity on the mystical side. Here are concentrated virtually all of the famous Sufi poets: foreshadowed by Sana'i (227) in Afghanistan, where the Sufi orders were first forming; in the early 1200s, the great stars Sa'di at Baghdad and Shiraz,

'Attar at Nishapur; and in the next generation (and another part of the same network) Rumi. Their poetic style is at the opposite pole from the arguments and proofs of the philosophers; it is filled with anecdotes, especially stories of the spiritual impressiveness and sometimes the magic powers of the Sufi heroes, along with their cryptic sayings. The message is typically esoteric, delivered through allegory and metaphor.

In the same period, the intellectual networks are centered on two figures whose fame came from combining philosophy with mysticism to produce theosophy: Shihabuddin Yahya Suhrawardi (not to be confused with Abu-Hafs Suhrawardi in the same generation), and a generation later Ibn 'Arabi. Although their intellectual positions radically shifted from those of the philosophers and rational theologians, nevertheless their network connections are typical of major intellectuals. Suhrawardi had studied widely with the masters of the time; his network sibling, so to speak, is Fakhruddin Razi, the leading Ash'arite and logician of the time, who shared with Suhrawardi the same teacher (225). Ibn 'Arabi was a youthful acquaintance (Corbin, 1969: 41–43) of Ibn Rushd (Averroës), in the culminating generation of creativity in the Islamic west, who migrated east after Ibn Rushd's funeral and the collapse of the Spanish networks. And the intellectual networks that remained after their days largely consisted of the descendants of Suhrawardi, Ibn 'Arabi, and Fakhruddin Razi.

Suhrawardi drew on the cultural capital of Neoplatonism, which was still being handed down in medical circles along with the medical writings of Ibn Sina. His own Baghdad teacher (225) could well have been in the orbit of Abu'l-Barakat, a Jewish physician and Muslim convert, who criticized and combined elements from Ibn Sina and from *kalam* (Sirat, 1985: 133). Suhrawardi colored the Neoplatonic hierarchy with a different spiritual tone—more pantheistic and dramatically visionary. Reviving Zoroastrian religious images, Suhrawardi set forth a metaphysics of Light and Darkness. The essence of material bodies is night, death, in themselves nothing more than corpses; light and life come from above, through a hierarchy of angels. Angels vary in intensity of luminescence, and these in turn produce the different species which populate the world. The Aristotelean logical universal is only the dead body of an angel. Suhrawardi expressed an emotional antipathy to the logical and conceptual abstractions of the philosophers; he drew upon them to overturn them for a more palpable vision. Perhaps inspired by the conflict between "eastern" and "western" logic that went on among the specialists (notably beginning in the previous generation with Abu'l-Barakat and his opponents), Suhrawardi proposed to build an alternative logic (Afnan, 1958: 105). In this Suhrawardi had no notable success, but the project reveals how much his greatness came from his combination of ingredients.

For Suhrawardi, the intermediary levels between the world and the divine are not abstraction or ideals; light is not a metaphor but the visible spectrum of brightness and color which literally produces the world below. The "Orient," the home of light, is both the dawning place of knowledge and the rising sun, whose rays can illuminate the soul. There are temples of light in the intermediate cosmos, with archangels of purple and mystic green. The human ideal is to become the "perfect man," the sage who combines philosophical knowledge with mystical experience; he becomes the "Pole" of "the invisible mystical hierarchy without which the universe could not continue to subsist" (Corbin, 1969: 22).

Ibn ʿArabi produced a similar position, somewhat more coordinated with Muslim scriptures and less tied to the Zoroastrian religion of light. For him the "universal man" contains the Platonic essences, which are the archetypes simultaneously of the macrocosm which is the universe and of the human microcosm; these essences provide the ideal model toward which the person should strive. The "universal man" rationalizes the powers of the scriptural prophets; he has a magical ability for seeing the esoteric significance in visible physical objects, like the ability of Moses to see God in the burning bush. Here the position of Ibn ʿArabi and of Suhrawardi has turned away from the scientific causality incorporated into the lower regions of the world hierarchy by Neoplatonists like Ibn Sina or Aristoteleans like Averroës. Ibn ʿArabi's philosophy is a deliberate repudiation of the dying Spanish rationalist tradition from which he came. The cosmos was being reenchanted by the philosophers. We can see how far the intellectual atmosphere had changed from the time of al-Ghazali, with his moderate use of *kalam* and his skepticism about metaphysical constructions. Al-Ghazali had attacked the esotericism of the Ismaʿilis and Imamites; now Suhrawardi and Ibn ʿArabi gave a philosophical basis for Shiʿite belief that the Imam is the terrestrial pole of the cosmic Intelligences, or an angel hidden between heaven and earth (Corbin, 1969: 80–81, 86). By the mid-1300s, Shiʿite leaders (such as 291 in the key to Figure 8.3) were identifying Sufism with Shiʿism. At the same time, orthodox Sunni theologians had incorporated Sufism into the curriculum of the *madrasas*. Sufism was both systematized and reconciled with *kalam*.

By this time there was not much intellectual life left. There continued to be networks (see Figure 8.3) connecting the more important teachers and pupils all the way into the 1400s. But for the most part they were academics in the worst sense: unoriginal compilers of handbooks and summarizers of predecessors' texts (Rescher, 1964: 68–69, 76). The most innovative were scientists: in the mid-1200s Nasir al-Din al-Tusi, one of the greatest astronomers of Islam, eliminated some of the Ptolemaic planetary eccentrics and foreshadowed the Copernican system (*DSB*, 1981: 13:508); his pupils and grandpupils carried on the creative pulse. But scientific topics had grown marginal to Islamic intellectual life and faded from the attention space.

The last important outbursts of philosophical creativity came from critics of this syncretizing establishment. Ibn Taymiyah at Damascus in the early 1300s was a Hanbali fundamentalist of the old style. He attacked rational argument and denied that a Muslim could be a philosopher or practice logic. This seems anachronistic, since by now there had been little prominent Islamic philosophy for generations. But Ibn Taymiyah was especially attacking the speculative Sufism which was becoming the respectable orthodoxy of the schools, especially the illuminationism of Ibn 'Arabi and Quth al-Din al-Shirazi. Why his position should have emerged at Damascus and in this generation becomes visible in the key to Figure 8.3: Syria along with Egypt had become a center for what remained of logic and science since the disintegration of the Seljuk Empire in the 1100s, especially with the Mongol sack of Iraq in the mid-1200s. The tide of foundations of Sufi orders was at its height, with three founded in Taymiyah's lifetime. Pressures for religious uniformity were growing. The last Crusader states had been conquered in 1291, and the long-standing Christian population under Islamic rule in Syria was finally converted.

Taymiyah was a voice of traditionalism and intolerance. But he also was part of the dynamics of the intellectual field, structurally motivated to punch holes in the accepted intellectual dogmas of the schools. He produced an acute criticism of every component of syllogistic logic (Fakhry, 1983: 316–318). Definitions give no knowledge of what they define; self-evident propositions leave their own basis hanging in air; the syllogism is based in universals, but it is useless because all being is particular. Taymiyah's doctrines resemble those of William of Ockham, but they had none of Ockham's revolutionary effect on his intellectual community. Whereas in Christendom the networks at this point of debate were at their point of maximal density, Taymiyah was isolated, and the creative impulse of his conservative opposition resulted in nothing. Two generations later, in the late 1300s, there was one more upsurge of critical thought. Ibn Khaldun is best known for his universal history, a harbinger of sociology, a secularism which kept its distance from theology and metaphysics. In the preface to his great work, Ibn Khaldun criticizes the rote learning of logic in the *madrasas*. Here we find again arguments like Ibn Taymiyah's (and Ockham's) rejecting the syllogistic arguments of the schools, excluding philosophy as useless, and advocating induction from empirical reality. But Ibn Khaldun worked in Algeria, remote from the intellectual centers;[20] indeed, the central networks no longer existed. Without significant structural ties of his own, Ibn Khaldun's critique was without consequences for Islamic philosophy.

Spain as the Hinge of Medieval Philosophy

It has been possible to bracket the golden age of Spanish philosophy—the five generations bounded by Ibn Gabirol after 1035 to Maimonides and Averroës just before 1200—from the rest of Islamic philosophy. Influences flowed from the east to this western end of the Islamic world, but little flowed back again. The later descendants of both the Muslim and Jewish intellectuals of Spain are found to the north, across the religious frontier in Christendom. Although subsequent Islamic philosophy continued in the east, a channel had diverged which drained into another sea; once emptied, it disappeared, leaving the two great realms of medieval philosophy, heirs of the Greek and eastern Mediterranean culture, to their separate fates. The complex intellectual life at the time of the Baghdad, Basra, and Nishapur centers was running out just as the Spanish episode began. The last great eastern thinker, al-Ghazali, in the generation just before 1100, is most famous for his conservative attack, *The Incoherence of Philosophy*. In Spain just the opposite was taking place, as speculative philosophy flowered, and its greatest representative, Ibn Rushd (Averroës), delivered his rejoinder to al-Ghazali, *The Incoherence of the Incoherence*.

Spain was a high point not only for Islamic philosophy but also for the Jews; virtually all the innovative Jewish philosophers of the Middle Ages were from Spain, or closely tied to its networks. In addition to this double upsurge of creativity, there is another structural anomaly about Spain: as we examine the network charts, we find here the only connection between important Jewish and Muslim philosophers. And by way of the translators at Toledo, there is a connection to the network of Christian philosophers based in northern France: from Gundisallinus to Adelard of Bath and Gerard of Cremona of the schools of Chartres and Laon. This is the only place where we find an explicit link between the networks of Figures 8.1 through 8.5 and Figures 9.1 through 9.6, and the Jews center the chain. The period of greatest creativity in Spain was also the most cosmopolitan.

It was here that the scientific and mathematical texts of the Greeks and the Hindu-Arab algebra and number system were transmitted north; it was here too that Aristotle was revived, with such revolutionary effect on Christian philosophy after 1200. We should resist the habit, however, of seeing this period as nothing more than a transmission belt for ancient knowledge. There is a sociology of what is translated and how it is understood; intellectual history in such times cannot be reduced to a slow-moving empiricism whereby texts rather than things are the objects which are gradually perceived.

The Social Construction of Aristotle in Medieval Spain

The social process of importing ideas constructs the meaning of what is being conveyed; and not only importing but exporting ideas can stimulate such construction. The strongest instance of this is the so-called rediscovery of Aristotle. But Aristotle's texts were not lost. In the earlier Middle Ages, Aristotle was seen through the lens of Neoplatonism. In Christian Europe he had been known since the time of Boethius (530 C.E.) mainly for his logic, in Latin translation and through the introduction by Porphyry. As Plotinus' follower, Porphyry elaborated Aristotle's classification of the levels of abstraction from genera and species down to individuals as exemplifying Plotinus' metaphysical hierarchy of emanations. This was a reversal of ontological emphasis. For Aristotle the greatest reality is at the level of the concrete individual, whereas for Porphyry and the Neoplatonists the true reality is the transcendent One, with each descending level more and more shadowy until the concrete individual is almost an illusion. This identification of Aristotle with Neoplatonism was so firmly accepted that one of the most widely known texts circulating under his name was the so-called "Theology of Aristotle," which actually consisted of portions of Plotinus' *Enneads*.

For centuries Aristotle was regarded as part of the prevailing Neoplatonic worldview, merely adding some logical classifications and providing a vocabulary in which to discuss additional complexities regarding substance and form, potency and act. But although this is understandable for Christian Europe, where few Aristotelean texts were known before 1150, it does not explain the fact that the Arab philosophers interpreted Aristotle the same way. For translators at Baghdad had made available virtually all of Aristotle's original texts by around 850–900 (Fakhry, 1983: 14–19). Yet al-Kindi and al-Farabi, who were in the same networks as the translators, assimilated Aristotle to their dominant Neoplatonism.[21] Ibn Sina, three generations later, self-educated in the provinces, had access to all of Aristotle's texts in the library of the local prince. He claims that the one text he could not understand was Aristotle's *Metaphysics,* which he read 40 times. Small wonder! He was trying to see it as Neoplatonic. It was only when Ibn Sina read al-Farabi that he saw how Aristotle might be pressed into the dominant framework. There was no challenge to this distortion until the Spain of Averroës, in the generation 1165–1200. Averroës sharply attacked the interpretations of al-Farabi and Ibn Sina, and produced a massive commentary on Aristotle's whole corpus, setting it free from the framework of Neoplatonism. It was this commentary which was soon translated and had such powerful repercussions in Christian philosophy in the 1200s and 1300s.[22]

Why then did it take 300 years—nine generations of intellectuals—to break through a gross distortion of perhaps the most famous of the classic philosophical texts of the time? There are two sociological questions here: What determined the prevailing interpretation of Aristotle against the grain of the existing texts? And what made it possible suddenly to reinterpret the texts?

The distortion was made possible in part because elements in Aristotle are compatible with Platonic and Neoplatonic views. Although Aristotle had criticized Plato's doctrine of self-subsistent Forms, his own work is a critical synthesis incorporating Form as one of four causes, along with material, efficient, and final. In order to see the world as emanating downward from Forms, one would have to ignore Aristotle's stress that Forms never exist apart from matter. Similarly, although Aristotle did not regard the world as created by or flowing down from God—nor did he see God as something transcending the universe—his cosmology is hierarchic in a more concrete way. His astronomy depicts the earth surrounded by concentric crystalline spheres which carry the moon, sun, and planets around in shells inside the sphere of the fixed stars. There is an idealist element in this, insofar as Aristotle needed something to move each sphere; and just as the human body is moved by its soul, regarded as the Form of the body, each astronomical sphere is moved by its own soul/Form. God has a place in this physical system as the unmoved mover of the outermost heaven. Aristotle's God does not move anything by efficient or formal causes, but exists only as the final cause toward which other things are attracted. The Neoplatonists, especially under religious impulses in Islam and in Christianity, could reinterpret this physical world-picture as if it were a series of metaphysical emanations. God was transformed from final cause into a source of Being and of Forms; each astronomical sphere could be identified with a level of abstraction; angels could be inserted to move the spheres, or to represent various levels of metaphysical reality above the spheres.

For this reason, an interest in empirical science could reinforce rather than undermine this Plotinian view of the world and its identification as Aristotle's. The Baghdad translators also imported Ptolemy, Euclid, and Galen, and the surrounding network of philosophers showed considerable interest in the empirical sciences. The sciences were treated as filling in details of the overarching hierarchic worldview. The same happened when Aristotle's corpus first became known in Europe. Albert the Great, who even used Averroës's commentaries, still saw the whole thing through Neoplatonic eyes. For Albert, the symmetry of the whole system provided a convenient framework into which new information on gems, minerals, and plants could find its place as a grand compendium of the sciences, and he saw no reason to break out of the Neoplatonic metaphysical hierarchy to stress the materialist elements in Aristotle's ontology. One can even say that there is a scientific core to the aspects of Aristotle that are closest to Neoplatonist hierarchy. Aristotle's logical classification of genus, species, and individuals was suggested by his biological researches; it was Aristotle's attempt at a classificatory theory of his data that seemed to show the existence of "higher" and "lower" levels. Scientific empiricism was no challenge to hierarchical idealism, so long as it stuck to description and classification of natural phenomena.

Let us attempt to departicularize the historical context of the acceptance of the Neoplatonic Aristotle. It was not only the Muslims until 1150, and the Christians prior to the upsurge of Averroism at Paris around 1260, who forced Aristotle into idealist garb. One can ask how Aristotle got into this mode in the first place. This question has nothing to do with the transmission of texts. These were continuously available in the eastern Greek world from 50 B.C.E. on. We have seen in Chapter 3 how Aristoteleanism was gradually submerged before the dominance of the Middle Platonist schools, and the materialist side of the field had been preempted by the Epicureans. Aristoteleanism became part of an eclectic middle ground of pagan religious politics. With the growing power of Christianity, it became fused into the Neoplatonic pagan coalition that huddled together for strength against its external enemies. After the fall of the Roman Empire, none of the subsequent regimes was very favorable to philosophy as an alternative to scriptural theology. In Islam the balance of power was strongly on the side of the theologians. Under the law of small numbers, this implies that the theological thinkers had more space to develop oppositional schools than the secular philosophers, who had to maintain a coalition of defense; hence the continuation of the Neoplatonic fortress mentality. Possibly something like this also applies to philosophy in Byzantium, where little innovation is evident, and the more assertive philosophers such as Michael Psellos and Eustratios (in the generations just before and after 1100) were condemned by the authorities for intruding on theology (*EP*, 1967: 1:436–439). What is to the point is that, although Islamic scholars at the time of the Baghdad House of Wisdom (including Hunayn, Qusta ibn Luqa, and later al-Farabi; *DSB*, 1981: 4:523, 11:244, 15:230) visited Constantinople in search of texts, as did European Christian scholars in the mid-1100s (*DSB*, 1981: 1:270), none of them got anything which challenged the prevailing view of Aristotle.

The Neoplatonist Aristotle was already a fait accompli when Aristotle was transmitted into the Arab world. The acceptance of this interpretation was no foregone conclusion, given the availability of all the important original texts and the dynamism of the Islamic intellectual community. The law of small numbers suggests that the idea-importing faction in Islam had to maintain its unity, a coalition of the weak against the attacks of the nativist theologians. If this is correct, we should expect the basis of the entire intellectual field to look different in Spain at the time when Averroës broke up the Neoplatonist coalition.

The Hinge of the Hinge: Realignment in Jewish Philosophy

The Jews formed the hinge of intellectual development in Spain, and they underwent a crucial shift in their relationship to their host communities at just the time of the Spanish creativeness in philosophy.[23]

Judaism, Christianity, and Islam are the three great monotheistic religions. Each has a universalistic core, mixed with particularistic loyalties and symbols. Each is capable of veering to one or the other side. The question is: What determines when the stress will be on the universalistic side, and when it will be on community distinctiveness and the arbitrary aspects of its tradition? Building on the same cultural capital, one might regard the three as rival universalizers of the Middle Eastern monotheism that emerged when the Hebrew cult of Yahweh temporarily unified the tribes of Palestine around 1000 B.C.E. Christianity developed in the Hellenistic orbit at the time when the last hopes of restoring an autonomous Jewish state (and state religion) were being crushed. Jesus, who died in the political crackdown on Jewish revolutionaries, is of the same generation as Philo, who reconciled Judaism with Platonic philosophy through an allegorical reading of the Pentateuch—the core of the Mosaic Old Testament, already translated into Greek by the Hellenizing faction within Judaism, the Sadducees. The growth of Christianity happened in the same centuries as the rabbinical movement, which cast Judaism into what became its standard form (Segal, 1986: 45–46, 52–54, 116–141). In the communities cut off from the temple-oriented state cult at Jerusalem, religious leadership was taken over by lay teachers, or rabbis. These developed a body of interpretations of scripture expanded for application to conditions of life in exile. This oral lore was organized into a vast literature, beginning with the Mishnah around 200 C.E.

Without political sovereignty or a cult center, Jewish religion emphasized private piety and ethical standards. Early Christianity was a rival movement within the same social group—disenfranchised Jews of the Roman Empire. Both movements involved an interplay of universalism and particularism. The rabbinical movement elaborated purity rules, especially the kosher laws, which had the effect of separating out a particularistic community oriented around food rituals. But monotheism and ethical emphasis encouraged a wide membership, and Judaism attracted many converts. It was in this community of converts in the cities of the Roman Empire that Christianity grew. Even after this point Judaism continued to proselytize, until its Christian rivals became hostile and the Christian emperors made conversion to Judaism a crime (Segal, 1986: 101–102, 177). After Christianity's political triumph in the Roman Empire, the center of Judaism shifted to Babylon, where Jews were a tolerated minority under the rule of the Zoroastrians of the Sassanid Persian Empire. The first centuries of Islam continued this pluralistic religious tolerance.

In Spain, the early Jewish population was persecuted by Christian rulers, especially the Visigothic successors to Roman rule. The Jews welcomed the Islamic conquerors of 711 as liberators, and for several centuries were closely allied with the Muslim state (Pelaez del Rosal, 1985: 14–33). Eminent Jews were court advisers, sometimes viziers and military officials, active in diplomacy and warfare against the Christian states of the north.

Two patterns are important among the philosophers of Spain. First, in the east, Jewish philosophers were unoriginal, imitators of the prevailing schools in Islamic philosophy and theology; only in Spain did Jewish intellectuals become creative. The second point is that this was the time when Jews began to move predominantly into the Christian world; by the end of the period (ca. 1200), Jewish intellectuals had shifted over to living within Christendom, while relations with Islam had deteriorated into hostility. Jewish philosophical creativity took place at the time of this uneasy reversal of religious alliances, and this catalyzed philosophical creativity among the Spanish Muslims as well.

Earlier Jewish philosophy in the east consisted of parallels or even branches of Islamic thought. The Karaites produced a Jewish version of *kalam;* the Rabbanites resembled the *hadith* scholars. In the 800s and early 900s, just at the time when these Muslim schools were arguing over the canonical status of their own oral tradition, the Jewish academies came alive in a similar round of argument. The Karaites rejected the oral tradition of the Talmud and Midrash interpretation, the province of the rabbinical scholars, to base themselves solely upon scripture. What began as particularistic argument over texts became increasingly rationalistic. The Karaites attacked anthropomorphism and elaborated metaphysics. Saadia defended the Rabbanites with alternative metaphysics and compiled proofs of God. Isaac Israeli, in the cosmopolitan circle of medical doctors, was a Neoplatonist drawing upon al-Kindi; his network contact and rival Saadia, who took over the Jewish academy at the center of action in Baghdad, adopted the arguments of the Mu'tazilites. The first round of medieval Jewish philosophical creativity, as the attention space split into three factions, represents a competitive appropriation of rival lines of philosophy established by the Muslims.

Linguistically too the Jewish intellectuals merged themselves with the Muslim culture. Virtually all the Jewish intellectuals of this period wrote in Arabic, in philosophy as well as science and medicine.[24] Saadia even translated the Talmudic Bible into Arabic. Saadia also produced a Hebrew grammar, paralleling another Arab preoccupation; the difficult Arabic grammar had been elaborated by Arabic grammarians and made a mark of elite culture. When Hebrew grammars were written among the Jewish circle at Córdoba and the nearby Jewish academy at Lucena, they were written in Arabic. Hebrew poetry, which enjoyed a creative burst in Spain in the same circles as the grammarians (940–1020), was written by adaptation of Arabic metric forms. A key figure in this development was Dunash ben Labrat, a disciple of Saadia who migrated to Córdoba under patronage of a prominent Jewish official of the Muslim court. Arabic was the common spoken language of Spanish Jews.

In Spain, in contrast to the Jewish communities of the east, the situation

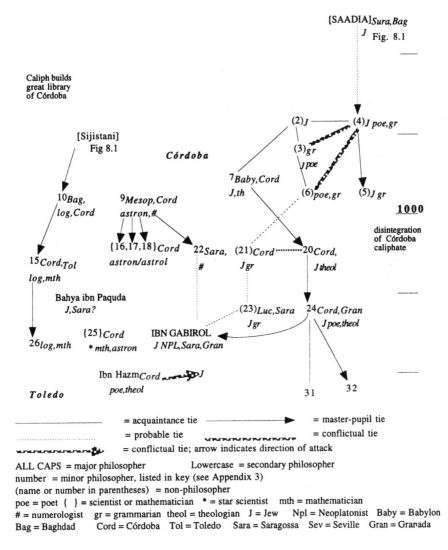

FIGURE 8.4. ISLAMIC AND JEWISH PHILOSOPHERS
IN SPAIN, 900–1065

began to move along its own lines (see Figure 8.4). At first the Rabbanites alone were active in Spain. The Jewish philosophers then split. There appeared more extreme universalistic positions, Neoplatonist and others, which pushed toward a religion of all intellectuals and cut loose from particularistic roots; and in reaction there were explicit defenses of Jewish tradition and a denial of rationalistic philosophy. The first wave of these Jewish philosophers in Spain appeared in the same generation—around 1035–1065—as the first memorable

Muslim philosophers. Neoplatonism, aside from Isaac Israeli never prominent among the Jews of the east, now came to the fore as a kind of trans-sectarian faith. Ibn Gabirol set out a modified Neoplatonism in which every level of emanation from the One consists of matter; matter is no longer taken as a privation or evil at the bottom of the hierarchy (as in Plotinus), but is itself the one created substance underlying all levels of the world hierarchy, the spiritual and intelligible down through the lowest spatially extended corpore-ality. This spiritual matter gives the basis for occult influences and correspon-dences throughout the universe (Husik, 1969: 79). Ibn Gabirol's *Fountain of Life* contains no scriptural references, and the Latins were unable to tell whether "Avicebrol" was Muslim, Christian, or Jew.

About the same time, Bahya ibn Paquda produced a popular manual of piety reminiscent of the Sufis, downplaying ritual and scripture in favor of the attitudes of the heart; he mixed in kalamite theological arguments while expounding a Neoplatonic journey of the soul, aided by reason, toward union with the Divine Light. On the other flank from these universalists there was Ibn Hazm, an anti-metaphysical theologian and poet in Córdoba, who struck a new note in attacking not only the rationalistic theologians of Islam (both Mu'tazilite and others) but also the Christians and Jews (Hodgson, 1974: 2:31–32).

In the generations after 1100 this polarization in Spain erupted with full force: at one extreme an ecumenical community of intellectuals cut loose from particularistic elements, and at the other end an upsurge of nationalist particu-larism on both Muslim and Jewish sides. These positions were themselves subdivided: the universalistic intellectuals pursued various themes, which is to say they show the contending structures which are characteristic of all creative life. Among the Jews, Ibn Zaddik at Córdoba expounded a Neopla-tonic doctrine of man as physical and spiritual microcosm of the world hier-archy, and combined this with kalamite proofs of the existence and unity of God, modified to preserve some traditional anthropomorphic features. Various minor figures (Moses ibn Ezra, Abraham bar Hiyya) compiled and translated an eclectic mixture of Neoplatonism, Aristotle, astronomy, astrology, and mathematics.

In the same generation appeared Judah Halevi at Toledo and Córdoba, mounting a nationalistic attack on the philosophers and rational theologians. He was particularly concerned to refute the Rabbanite rivals, the Karaites, with their adoption of Muslim *kalam,* their rejection of the Talmudic traditions, and their allegorical interpretation of holy scripture. Halevi set out the superiority of Judaism over philosophy, Christianity, and Islam alike; their endless disputes show that reason can never settle anything. The only proof of God, Halevi asserts in *Kuzari,* is the special revelation made to the Jews in the Hebrew language, which is accepted by both Christians and Muslims as the basis of their own religions (Sirat, 1985: 86–87, 97–131; Husik, 1969: 114–196).

This split between the philosophical positions and this fideist critique predictably gave rise to an intermediate position. Ibn Daud, who migrated from Lucena to Toledo in the Almohad invasion, was a cosmopolitan with reservations (Pelaez de Rosal, 1985: 137). He aided Christian translators and wrote a history of Latin Christendom in Hebrew, as if in an explicit effort to open a wider world for his coreligionists (*EP*, 1967: 4:267). At the same time, Ibn Daud was concerned to reconcile philosophy and faith, and attacked Ibn Gabirol's stance as heterodox to the Jewish faith and as bad philosophy (Husik, 1969: 198). Responsive to the new situation of Jewish nationalism and the rejection of the older cosmopolitan position, Ibn Daud promoted a purified version of Aristotle against the Neoplatonists. Ibn Daud's strategy of using Aristoteleanism to support a middle position combining both particularistic faith and universalistic philosophy was the same one Moses Maimonides would pursue at the end of the century, thereby making himself the dominant Jewish philosopher of the Middle Ages. This was the stance that became Averroism.

The Cosmopolitan Network

We should visualize a single community of philosophers and scientists comprising Muslims, Jews, and Christian translators, gradually coming together in Spain.

These were the centuries of the Reconquista (see Figure 8.5). The Christians had held the corner of Spain around Barcelona and the mountainous northern regions of Léon and Navarre since the 800s. After 1010, the caliphate of Córdoba disintegrated into petty principalities, and these began to be eaten up by feudal Christian lords driving down from the north. The geopolitics is patchy and episodic. Toledo, the major city in central Spain, was captured in 1085. By 1120, the Christians were nibbling at the principality of Saragossa in the east, near Barcelona. Around 1170, they had taken all of the northern half of Spain and were beginning to push into the Muslim heartlands of the south. There were two waves of counter-conquest on the Islamic side: the Almoravids in the 1090s, who swept northward into the power vacuum from Morocco and temporarily reestablished the caliphate; and again the Almohads, who did the same a generation later from the 1140s through the 1160s.

The religious atmosphere across these decades alternated between fanaticism and tolerance. On the Muslim side, rulers wavered between militant orthodoxy and patronage of the cosmopolitan philosophers. The war policy instituted by the fanatical Almohads who took Córdoba in 1149 was conversion or death

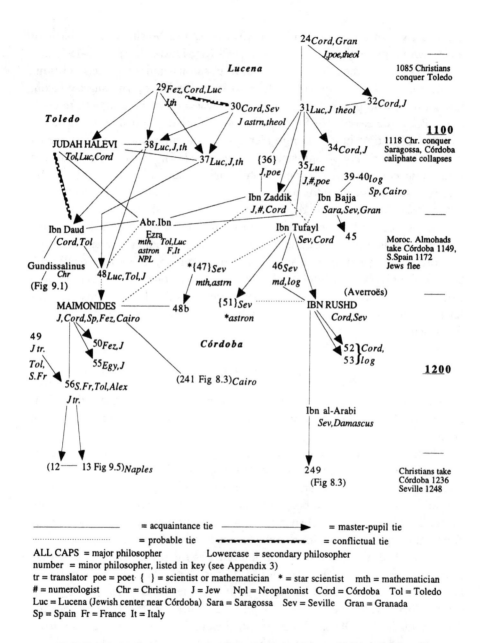

FIGURE 8.5. SPAIN, 1065–1235: THE HINGE OF THE HINGE

to unbelievers. But only a few years before, the nationalistic Jewish philosopher Judah Halevi had been a court physician at Córdoba; and again in 1169 the caliph himself, when Ibn Rushd was introduced by his companion and physician Ibn Tufayl, raised metaphysical questions and invited Ibn Rushd to produce a definitive commentary on Aristotle. The pendulum could swing back just as easily; Ibn Bajja was reputedly poisoned by his enemies at the Morrocan court at Fez, and Ibn Rushd was exiled in 1195, then called back into favor.

On the Christian side, the Crusader mentality of the warriors gave way surprisingly easily to the movement within the church to learn from the Arabs. Toledo, recaptured in 1085, continued to have a largely Arab-speaking population, including a large community of Jews. The bishop of Toledo established his school for translation around 1125–1150; among other things, it produced a Latin translation of the Qur'an. And in the period of political chaos, with "party kingdoms" on both sides, there were even occasional diplomatic alliances between Christian and Muslim states against their local enemies (Pelaez de Rosal, 1985: 69–72). Jews frequently acted as diplomatic intermediaries.

The Muslim intellectual community at first was much less cosmopolitan. In fact, the Malikite jurists who dominated in the Islamic west were hostile to *kalam* and Sufism, let alone *falasifa* and non-Muslims. For this very reason, the factional lineup was different than in the Muslim east. Both Mu'tazilites and Ash'arite theologians of any significance are missing from the Spanish networks, and neither Sufi innovators nor rank-and-file Sufi movements nor the Shi'ite sects have much prominence there. This leaves more room, under the law of small numbers, for divergences within the remaining positions. Significant intellectual development began among the Spanish Muslims in the late 900s in the religiously neutral topics of science, primarily in medicine and pharmacy, as well as astronomy and mathematics. The material base of this development was created by the patronage of caliph 'Abd-ar-Rahman III and his successor al-Mansur, who built a great library at Córdoba around 960 in a bid to overshadow the prestige of the rival 'Abbasid caliphate, now declining in the east. Paralleling developments at the House of Wisdom in Baghdad two centuries before, the accumulation of texts and work in science began first, before autonomous philosophical creativity would emerge five generations later. It was at 'Abd-ar-Rahman's court that the great Jewish patron of intellectuals, the medical doctor Hasdai Ibn Shaprut, became an important official (Pelaez de Rosal, 1986: 62–76). The Jewish intellectuals were at the core of the Spanish world from the beginning.[25]

With the fall of Toledo and the development of intellectual networks in northern France during the early 1100s, Christian translators appeared in Spain looking for scientific texts of the Greeks, Arabs, and Jews alike. Now we find both Jewish and Muslim philosophers connected to the scientists; indeed, virtually all the important philosophical names here were also scientists to some degree. It was the activity of the scientific network which stimulated broader creativity as Muslim philosophy suddenly took off in Spain. Judah Halevi, Ibn Bajja, Ibn Tufayl, Ibn Rushd, Maimonides: all were medical doctors. Important scientific work in mathematics and astronomy was carried out by the Jewish philosophers Abraham bar Hiyya (41 in the key to Figure 8.5) at Barcelona in the early 1100s,[26] and again in the next generation by Abraham Ibn Ezra of Toledo, whose Neoplatonism is permeated with astronomy and astrology. It is worth noting that Ibn Tufayl, Ibn Rushd, Ibn Daud, and Maimonides were all active astronomers as well as philosophers (*DSB*, 1981: 4:504; 7:37–38; 12:1–2; 14:637; 15:33; Husik, 1969: 198). Ibn Rushd is directly connected to Ibn Zuhr (Avenzoar), a famous physician at Seville (46); and Ibn Tufayl was the master not only of Ibn Rushd but also of the outstanding astronomer al-Bitruji, the Latins' Alpetragius (51), who developed an alternative to Ptolemaic astronomy, dispensing with eccentrics and epicycles. The scientific stars emerged in Spain at the same time as the most notable philosophers; another was the developer of spherical trigonometry, Jabir ibn Aflah (47), Geber for the Latins, who was in Seville apparently with Ibn Tufayl, and whose astronomy was explicated by Maimonides.[27] The cosmopolitan community was organized above all on the universalistic medium of natural science.

The intermeshing of intellectual networks, within and across religions, became densest at just this time. Gundissalinus, a converted Jew, was apparently helped in his Avicenna translations by Ibn Daud, another Jew in Toledo, a refugee from the networks at Córdoba and Lucena.[28] Both Gundissalinus and Ibn Daud had some reputation among Christian philosophers in northern France. Halevi lived in Toledo around this time, and was in Córdoba in his old age.[29] Halevi, as court physician in Córdoba, must have been in the same circles as Ibn Tufayl and Ibn Rushd, both court physicians in their own right. Ibn Bajja, in the earlier generation, moved from the Muslim court at Saragossa[30] to court circles at Seville, Granada, and Fez. There are Jewish philosophers in these same places: Moses ibn Ezra (35) from Granada; Abraham ibn Ezra from Toledo, a world traveler in both Christian Europe and the Muslim Mediterranean, who connects not only with all the other Jewish philosophers in Spain but also (directly or indirectly via his son) with Abu-l-Barakat in Baghdad (see Figure 8.3). Ibn Zaddik was the chief Jewish judge in Córdoba between 1138 and 1149; it is unlikely that he would not have encountered court officials such as Ibn Tufayl and possibly the young Ibn Rushd.

The most striking coincidence is that Ibn Rushd (1126–1198) and Moses Maimonides (1135–1204) grew up in Córdoba at virtually the same time, and went on to become the most important philosophers of their respective religions. It is unlikely, however, that they ever met. Maimonides left Córdoba with his family in 1148, fleeing the Almohad conquest; he would have been 13 years old, Ibn Rushd 22. Nevertheless, the parallels between their intellectual trajectories are strong, and this is explicable by their common context. During the next 17 years, Maimonides moved from place to place in Spain, ending with a short stay in Fez before moving to Egypt in 1165, where he eventually became court physician. At a minimum he must have been in the network of the most eminent teachers of medicine, which he would have had in common with Ibn Tufayl and Ibn Rushd—especially Ibn Zuhr (46) at Seville. It seems inconceivable that in accumulating intellectual capital during his travels he would not have been in the Jewish communities at Toledo, Seville, or Granada—and thereby in the cosmopolitan networks of those places as well.[31] As the Muslim centers came under increasing political pressure from reactionary regimes, the Jewish centers became ever more important for cosmopolitans of all faiths. They become the nodes where the several chains cross, the structural key to creativity.

The Religion of Reason

As Jewish philosophy reached its peak after 1100, Muslim philosophy in Spain simultaneously burst into high creativity. There is an intergenerational chain of important philosophers: Ibn Bajja at Saragossa, Seville, and Granada; his admirer Ibn Tufayl at Seville, Córdoba, and Fez; and in turn his protégé Ibn Rushd at Córdoba, Fez, and Seville, who became famous as the great Averroës. All of them were concerned with the reconciliation of philosophy and faith, which for them was also a political problem owing to the intermittent dangers of persecution from the Malikite literalist jurists so often dominant in the Muslim states. In this respect the Jews had more freedom, since they lacked state power and hence the means of coercing the non-orthodox; the Jews (especially Ibn Gabirol and Ibn Zaddiq) appear to have led the way toward universalization. Ibn Bajja, Ibn Tufayl, and Ibn Rushd were, moreover, state officials—viziers, judges, or court physicians—and were intimately aware of the vagaries of power.

Ibn Tufayl's philosophical novel sets out their typical strategy. In a setting foreshadowing Robinson Crusoe (and which might have inspired Defoe, through a Latin translation in 1671; see Windelband, [1892] 1901: 317), Ibn Tufayl depicts a boy growing up in solitude on an uninhabited island, who by sheer reason arrives at a philosophical conception of the universe. This consists largely of the Neoplatonic hierarchy: the Forms of things, the soul, the world spirit, finally culminating in an ecstatic vision of God beyond words and concepts. Later he meets a Muslim from an inhabited island, and they discover that the truths of faith and of reason are the same. But—and this is characteristic of the political consciousness of the Spanish philosophers—when the two friends travel to the inhabited island and try to explain their discovery, they are attacked by the literalist theologians. Sadly the young man withdraws again into solitude, having learned that his truth is only for the enlightened, and not for the superstitious masses.

This position was shared by Ibn Bajja, Ibn Rushd, and Jewish contemporaries such as Ibn Zaddiq and to some degree Ibn Daud and even Maimonides; later it would become the hallmark of the Averroists of the Christian and Jewish world. Their doctrine is an insider's position: truth has a double aspect, crude and literal for ordinary believers, which can be reinterpreted at a higher level, in keeping with the philosophy of the elite. The elitism is reinforced by the doctrine that salvation happens only through the intellect. Bar Hiyyah had distinguished classes of souls up through the wise and just who are reabsorbed into pure Form; Ibn Zaddiq held that science is a necessary part of the worship of God, and that only philosophers reach the perfection of the prophets (Sirat, 1985: 86–87, 98).[32] In Ibn Rushd's version, heaven and hell are crude allegories, and there is no material resurrection of the body; the only immortal part of the human individual is the intellectual soul, and indeed only that part of it which is filled with universal truths from the transcendent world soul, the Active Intellect (similarly Maimonides' *Guide* 3.51, 54; see Maimonides, 1956). Ibn Rushd was above all a fanatical admirer of Aristotelean logic: since salvation is achieved through the intellect, without knowing logic one cannot even be saved. This means that crude literalists have no real religious status; their religion as they take it is a delusion and brings them nothing. Ibn Rushd, however, somewhat cynically declares that ordinary people should be required to adhere to the literal religion for the good of the state; heretics should be given no voice, but must be executed (Fakhry, 1983: 277–283; de Boer, 1903: 189).

So far this stance of an insiders' and outsiders' truth could be compatible with several different philosophies; Neoplatonism or Neo-Pythagoreanism would work just as well as a secret doctrine as Aristoteleanism. Ibn Bajja and Ibn Tufayl were still Neoplatonists; so were the Spanish Jews such as Ibn Gabirol, Ibn Zaddik, Abraham ibn Ezra, and many minor figures. How does it happen that Ibn Daud, Ibn Rushd, and Maimonides deliberately broke with Neoplatonism and brought about the rediscovery of Aristotle?

Creativity at the Point of Political Breakdown

Why is it that the generations of the mid- and late 1100s had such fateful intellectual impact? One important reason is that, whereas earlier Neoplatonism was the acceptable cosmopolitan position, defended by declaring that the religious masses could never understand it, these militant Aristoteleans now also tried to take over some of the territory of the scriptural faith. In both the Jewish and Muslim camps there had been an upsurge of religious nationalism against the older philosophical rationalisms. The philosophical innovators now carved out a new position between the older camps, claiming to incorporate the best of both. Ibn Tufayl, rather typical of the cosmopolitans, was also ecumenical about religion. His ideal religious practice incorporates vegetarianism, cleanliness, asceticism, and a respect for plants and animals, seemingly taking over items from Persian and Hindu religion (de Boer, 1903: 186). Ibn Daud and Maimonides, in contrast, want to defend the specific truths of the Jewish scriptures, and Ibn Rushd does the same for the Qur'an.

Ibn Rushd proceeded by working on theology as well as on philosophy. He defined the core theological beliefs[33] in such a way that his rational philosophy would coincide with them. This was the same strategy pursued by the Jewish philosophers closest to Aristotle. Ibn Daud, a generation earlier than both Ibn Rushd and Maimonides, inaugurated the strategy, for instance, reading the categories of Aristotle into Bible passages such as the Psalm 139th, or interpreting angels as secondary causes between God and the lower material spheres (Husik, 1969: 198, 205, 221, 239). Ibn Daud's main book was published in 1161, Ibn Rushd began his Aristotle commentary in 1169, and 1180 he used the method of harmonizing religion with philosophy by finding the latter in the Qur'an. Maimonides first acquired his reputation, perhaps before leaving Spain (*DSB*, 1981: 9:28), by his masterly commentary on the rambling rabbinical literature constituting the Mishnah; and he wrote a rabbinical code which culled from this huge mass of precedents the items of faith as 13 in number. Since medieval Judaism had no central authority or monopolistic ecclesiastical organization, Maimonides owes his eminence to having provided a famous, if controversial, systematization of the central items of faith. This in turn gave him a base which he could harmonize with abstract philosophy. This was the task of his later life, his *Guide for the Perplexed,* appearing in 1190.

Maimonides and Ibn Rushd are like most dominant intellectual figures in that they stand out for the scope and depth of their work. They are energy stars, filled with ambition to take on major tasks and the cultural capital and emotional force to carry them through. Although following the path pioneered by Ibn Daud, Maimonides overshadows him by the depth of his scriptural studies and his philosophical thoroughness. Maimonides systematically expounds and refutes rival viewpoints, and he sets out his own arguments with an abundance of proofs, along with scriptural references and etymological interpretations to overcome literalism. Ibn Rushd has a similar fund of emotional energy. He puts it into his massive commentaries on the whole corpus of Aristotle, into an attack on the Muslim Neoplatonists from al-Farabi and Ibn Sina right down to Ibn Bajja (exempting only his own patron, Ibn Tufayl), and into a counterattack against al-Ghazali's attempt to destroy philosophy.

Ibn Rushd is no mere transmitter of Aristotle, he elaborates Aristotle into his own system. He depicts Aristotle's world as eternally in a process of becoming: Forms are not so much classifications or levels of reality as the dynamic side of matter, moving everything in the world from potentiality to actuality and back again endlessly. Since Ibn Rushd is also committed to making this a religious vision, he cannot avoid certain aspects of Neoplatonism, such as the hierarchy of Forms on up to the divine eternal Mover. But his emphasis is as far as possible from the Neoplatonic stress on a transcendental flow upward, still less an emanation of reality downward. Everything on every level is eternal, and the whole makes up a vast interacting system. There is even an eternal place in it for the Philosopher, who perceives the reality of all the levels and thus participates in a special kind of intellectual Eternity.

Ibn Rushd and Maimonides represent different branches of this culmination of Spanish philosophy. In Maimonides we find much more a compromise of evenhanded reasoning with scriptural particularism; he is willing to give reason its due, demonstrate its limits, and show how it can peacefully coexist with dogma. Maimonides directs his criticisms largely against the Mu'tazilite atomists, by now the traditional school within Jewish rational theology (represented by Saadia and by the Karaites, the same enemy Halevi a generation back had singled out for attack). Ibn Daud is more concerned to attack Ibn Gabirol's version of Neoplatonism (which was popular among current Jewish thinkers such as Moses ibn Ezra and Ibn Zaddik); he declares Gabirol full of bad arguments, as well as contrary to Jewish faith.[34] Ibn Rushd is an extremist of philosophical reason capable of producing a complete religion in itself, with which scriptural religion must coincide. Ibn Rushd is much more the pure philosopher. He takes to its extreme the structural opportunities of the intellectual field: not only to reject *kalam* but also to overthrow Neoplatonism as the reigning religion of reason and replace it with his vision of Aristoteleanism.

His stance becomes clearer when we consider his rejoinder to al-Ghazali, who had turned the weapons of philosophy against itself in favor of Sufi mysticism. Ibn Rushd's counterattack declares that al-Ghazali did no more than destroy the Neoplatonism of al-Farabi and Ibn Sina, not the purer philosophy of Aristotle. Ibn Rushd even offers an alliance to the most conservative jurists, for he declares that the rational theologians occupy a ridiculous and even subversive position, and their attempt to use philosophy to interpret the scriptures only confuses the masses without enlightening anyone to the true philosophy. Ibn Rushd makes a bold effort to overturn the whole Islamic intellectual field; he would drive out all the rationalized positions except his own, and leave the rest to the dogmatists.

Such ambitions are always overreaching, but Ibn Rushd's nevertheless had a certain basis in contemporary realities. The cosmopolitan world of the Islamic Neoplatonists was indeed collapsing, and the rational theologians had had their day; Ibn Rushd himself was virtually the last significant constructive Muslim philosopher. And yet there was a basis for his vast emotional energy, a region in which he could tacitly feel the prospects of success. This was not to be in the Muslim world, where Ibn Rushd had no disciples, and where indeed the originals of most of his texts were lost.[35] It was the cosmopolitan community of Spain that made possible his philosophy. It is not Ibn Rushd who is known as a great philosopher but Averroës. He could not, of course, have known that his works would be translated into Latin 30 years after his death and produce a shock wave in Christendom a generation after that. Perhaps he was aware that he was being read by the Jews in the late 1100s, and was admired by Maimonides and his circle (Fakhry, 1983: 274–275).[36] Among Jewish philosophers he was even more influential than Maimonides; whereas Maimonides was most famous among the ordinary Jewish religious public, the intellectuals tended to use Averroës as a vantage point from which to understand *The Guide for the Perplexed* (*EP*, 1967: 4:269).

The structural field which produced Ibn Rushd's creative energy and transformed him into the renowned Averroës was an unusually wide one. The field of forces which centered on Toledo at the time of the translators, with tentacles as far north as Chartres and Paris, charged up a current whose outcomes were Averroës's vision and the reemergence of Aristotle beside the long-dominant philosophical Neoplatonism.[37]

After Ibn Rushd's death in 1198 and the departure of Maimonides, Spanish intellectual life rapidly fell apart. The Christians came down through the passes to defeat the Moorish army on the southern plain at Los Navos de Tolosa in 1212. By 1236 Córdoba had fallen, followed by Seville in 1248. The Muslims survived until 1492 cooped up in the mountain enclave of Granada. There were no more networks of Muslim philosophers or scientists in Spain, nor in the states surviving in the Maghrib. It is emblematic that the young Ibn 'Arabi attended Ibn Rushd's funeral before departing for the east; already this last representative of the Spanish intellectual lineage was abandoning rational philosophy in favor of a theosophical reconciliation with revealed religion.

The Jews too were leaving, this time disappearing from the Islamic intellectual world for good. Maimonides's translators and disciples, especially the several generations of the Tibbon family (49 and 56 in Figure 8.5, 12, 15, and 24 in Figure 9.5), had moved north into southern France. The Jewish community now saw battles between Maimonidists (who were often also Averroists) against rabbinical traditionalists, and more generally a split between universalistic philosophy and nationalist particularism. The most famous philosopher to emerge from this orbit was Levi ben Gerson, in contact with the papal court at Avignon, who is now known primarily in the world of Latin scholasticism (hence his fame as Gersonides), following up the problems raised by Averroës as well as in astronomy. Against this tendency there was a nationalist reaction represented by Hasdai Crescas and Joseph Albo, living in now-Christian Spain in the late 1300s and early 1400s. Here too emerged the Jewish Kabbalah, propagated especially by Abraham Abulafia (in the old Neo-Pythagorean center, Saragossa) and Moses de Léon, as a kind of secret code for the Jewish faith under the growing persecution in Christian Spain. The Jews, who centuries before had welcomed Islamic rule as more favorable than Christian hostility, left the lands of Islam again in the late 1100s as Muslim religious tolerance disappeared. For better or worse, Islamic-Jewish intellectual interaction was a thing of the past.[38]

Averroës and Maimonides, in their respective communities, are among the clearest examples of the owl of Minerva flying at dusk. For the Jews, the Almohad invasion sent most intellectuals fleeing Muslim Spain for Christendom; Maimonides fled east to the court of another caliph, but his followers were all in Christian Europe. Could he have known that after his time there would be no more Jewish philosophers in Islam? Did Ibn Rushd know that he was the last of his breed, and that the cosmopolitan intellectual community was disappearing in the east as well as in Spain? Could he have known that 14 years after his death the Muslim power in Andalusia would be crushed? Geopolitical events are rooted in shifting resources and alliances, and no doubt cast their shadows before them; by the mid-1100s, Spanish intellectuals must have felt the ground slipping underneath. It is such shifts in the underpinnings of intellectual communities that set the opportunity to rearrange the contents of the intellectual field, which we know as these episodes of creativity.

Coda: Are Idea Imports a Substitute for Creativity?

Translating philosophical texts from a foreign culture inhibits creative philosophy among the receivers. When the eminent figures in the philosophical community are the translators or expositors of alien philosophies, their imported capital becomes a substitute for creating their own. This does not violate the structural principles of the intellectual field but follows from them. Under the law of small numbers, there is room for three to six positions to command public attention; it does not matter whether these are filled up by new creations or come from abroad. Presenting a foreign philosophy can preempt one of these slots. Where there is little competition from others, the chief idea importers become energy stars, pseudo-creators in their own right.

Consider the reputation of Cicero, in the generation when Greek philosophy made its first impact on the Roman intellectual world. Not himself a translator of texts (that was a low-status activity of slaves), he was patron of the slave-curators and editors of Greek manuscripts, and reaped the fame of the Greek philosophers by expounding several of them with literary polish for his Roman audience. Varro did much the same for Greek science. Lucretius was the competitive counterweight to Cicero in his generation, giving literary expression to Epicurean philosophy, the one major Greek position Cicero did not appropriate. Rounding out the range of oppositions of the Roman intellectual community were their first Stoics. There were no indigenous creators, as the entire field was divided up among the idea importers.

We see similar negative effects on indigenous creativity in each case where imports dominate the attention space. In China during the early centuries of the Buddhist period, local schools of thought were merely imports of Indian schools. Similarly, for the first half-dozen generations in Japan, the notable names were merely those who imported one of the Buddhist schools from China. In Muslim Spain it was not a question of translating texts from a foreign language, but nevertheless texts had to be imported from the east; there was a lag of three generations between the founding of the Córdoba library, providing a material base for intellectual life, and the emergence of creative philosophers. In Carolingian Europe, virtually all the well-known scholars were textual importers, from the founder of the Jarrow monastery in England, who journeyed repeatedly to Rome for books, through Bede and the York scholars, to Alcuin, who transplanted this learning to the Continent at the Carolingian court (Gilson, 1944: 187–227). The usual lineage of masters and pupils dominated intellectual life, only in this case their ideas were imported rather than created. Innovation finally broke out in the fifth generation, when Alcuin's followers split into rival centers. The most notable name is John Scotus Eriugena, though he is known mainly for reworking the philosophy of pseudo-Dionysus, which he had translated from the Greek; Eriugena's reputation is, so to speak, another pseudo-reputation. In high medieval Christendom the generations of most intense importing from the Arab world form a trough in indigenous philosophy, the break in the networks in the late 1100s and early 1200s that we see in Figures 9.3 and 9.4. There is another trough at the end of the period, during the breakdown of the medieval university base, when the Humanists again focused attention on ancient texts.

These are cases of imports swamping the entire attention space. A phenomenon peculiar to these periods is that the biggest stars are typically eclectics, importing several mutually incompatible philosophies. In early Buddhist China the famous figure is the translator Kumarajiva, who has a central position in the vertical and horizontal networks and oppositions just like any other notable creator, although his own work is unoriginal. Kumarajiva is like Cicero in that he imported not just one but two main factions of alien philosophy—both Madhyamika negative dialectics and Sautrantika pheno-menalism—even though Nagarjuna formulated the Madhyamika doctrine in opposition to the Sautrantikas and other Hinayana schools. Seven genera-tions later Hsüan-tsang traveled to India and brought back texts which made him one of the most famous figures in the history of Chinese philosophy. He too sponsored two incompatible Indian schools, Yogacara idealism and *Ab-hidharma* realism. Boethius became the last memorable Roman philosopher through his eclecticism, attempting to translate all of Plato and Aristotle into Latin in the early 500s, when knowledge of Greek was being lost under barbarian rule, and also incorporating Stoicism into his *Consolation of Phi-losophy* (*DSB,* 1981: 1:228–229). Ibn Massara (1 in Figure 8.4), the first importer of philosophy into Muslim Spain, brought in Mu'tazilite, Sufi, Neo-platonist, and Neo-Pythagorean schools alike. Among the Christians at the Toledo translation school, the most eminent figure (ranked as a secondary philosopher in Figure 9.3) is Dominic Gundissalinus (Gonzalez), a converted Jew, who translated Avicenna (Ibn Sina) and Avicebrol (Ibn Gabirol), the most important Muslim and Jewish philosophers to date, then wrote his own trea-tises based on both (Knowles, 1962: 204). Once again we see the eclectic stance of a translators who makes a double-barreled impact, expounding two rival positions. It is a sign that the contents are not taken as seriously as the prestige of importing per se.

In some cases dependence on imports is brief, or imports do not swamp the field at all but only become one faction among others engaged in indigenous creation. In the Islamic world the first three generations of Greek translators were themselves uncreative, but they never took over the attention space; as *falsafa* became established, it became one faction entering into alliances and oppositions with the ongoing arguments of the Muslim schools. In T'ang China, Hsüan-tsang was unoriginal, but his translation bureau enriched the contending networks and gave rise, through a former assistant, Fa-tsang, to one of the great intellectual innovations in China, the Hua-yen totalist philoso-phy. By this time the Chinese Buddhist schools had institutionalized their own lines of argument; the continuing rounds of imports added pressures to reor-ganize the attention space, resulting in simultaneous innovations, including the Ch'an revolution taking place in the meditation school. In Japan the first round of imports from China were sterile, but the second round, from the late 1100s through 1300, coincided with indigenous outbreaks of Buddhist innovation, starting with the Pure Land movements; the Japanese Zen schools which took off at this time had Chinese links but diverged in their own pathways. And in medieval Christendom, the striking thing is that dependence on translations and imports was relatively short-lived; indeed, translation was a continuous interest from the early 1100s through the early 1300s, but indigenous factional lineages kept up their own creative arguments during most of this time. The impact of translation on creativity depends more on the structure of the surrounding factions than on the carriers of foreign ideas themselves, who tend to be traditionalists within their own camps. Idea imports stimulate innovation only to the extent that indigenous factions have strong enough bases and the energies of ongoing disputes, so that the imports enter into a conflictual realignment of the attention space.

If importing ideas stifles creativity, in the reciprocal part of the world network exporting ideas can have stimulating effects. In the case of Muslim Spain in the mid-1100s, contact with a network of Christian importers at Toledo fostered the upsurge of cosmopolitan philosophy among the Jews who bridged the Arab side, stimulating Averroës and Maimonides to break free from dominant Neoplatonism and formulate an aggressive Aristoteleanism.

The stimulating effects of exporting to an eager audience are seen most strikingly in places where intellectual life was flat before exports began. The pattern is found in the Renaissance, not on the side of the Italian importers but among the Byzantines. Gemistus Pletho was the leading actor (261 in Figure 9.6), a cosmopolitan diplomat in both Turkey and Italy in the 1430s, and an inspirer of the Medici circle at Florence which fostered Ficino and Pico. In the early 1400s he broke with Christian Neoplatonism and reintroduced elements of paganism, indeed reviving the old Platonist religion. It was his position which was so influential in Italy, and which Ficino followed; other neo-pagans of this network, such as Bessarion, included even a cardinal of the church. A receptive market on the importing side makes bolder the exporters, even as it makes the importers more dependent.

Pletho's position is equivalent to the religion of reason which emerged among the Muslim cosmopolites in Spain of the late 1100s. There are parallels too in the surrounding circumstances: the disintegration of the Córdoba caliphate, heading toward its climax in the years after Averroës's death; and the final decline of the Byzantine Empire, reduced by Ottoman conquests in the 1300s to a tiny survival, which was finally extirpated in 1453. The episode is conventionally explained as a contingent event, the fortuitous flow of Byzantine exiles to the west, which brought in "new" Greek texts and helped set off the Renaissance. But in fact Byzantine philosophy became creative only in the very process of migration, and previously had been stagnant for many centuries.[39] The geopolitical crisis in the background was important only because, as in Spain, it introduced cosmopolitan connections and rearranged the networks.

A third case is post-Meiji Japan. When the European university system was introduced, the period of dependence on Western intellectual imports was remarkably brief, only one generation. Buddhist philosophy, long since stagnant, suddenly revived, and captured the new institutional base through an innovative philosophical network centered on Kyoto University. What had happened was that Japanese Buddhist sojourners in the West had discovered that they had something to offer European and American sophisticates. The leader of the Kyoto school, Nishida, was a childhood friend of the most popular Zen exporter, D. T. Suzuki. In the particulars of these histories we can see another variant on the central pattern of intellectual life. In all these cases the exporters became creative because they were actively drawn into a new network, in this case a long-distance one, full of migrations and upheavals on the exporting side as much as or more than among the receptors. The bases of intellectual productivity were rearranged, opening the possibility of new alliances and conflicts within the networks. A foreign audience can help build up an attention space as much as a domestic one, above all when the most important networks on both sides come into contact face to face. Then the intensified interaction rituals of intellectual life occur which raise emotional energy for new combinations in the realm of symbols. Who best reaps the excitement of these periods depends on whose indigenous networks are already most familiar with the ingredients; for the newcomers, the excitement of introducing old ideas blots out the fact that, outside of their local attention space, the ideas are not original.[40]

CHAPTER 9

✦

Academic Expansion as a Two-Edged Sword: Medieval Christendom

Medieval Christian philosophy builds on the same ingredients as Muslim philosophy: the politicized, socially activist monotheism of Judaism, together with imports of sophisticated abstractions accumulated across many generations in the intellectual community of the Greeks. The intellectual fields of Christendom and of Islam go through much the same structural conflicts. The important differences between medieval Islam and Christianity are quantitative, not qualitative, matters of weight and timing rather than intellectual substance. Islam and Christianity do not exemplify the divergence of East and West; both are equally West, as we can see by comparing the truly divergent intellectual orbit demarcated on the east by Buddhism and Brahmanism. The long-term trajectory of Islam is, so to speak, the bad dream of the West; it is what Christendom would look like in recent centuries if theological conservatives had become entrenched, along with a routinized scholasticism challenged only by poetic mystics.

Consider the factional history of Islamic intellectual life across its first 18 or 20 generations. As the spaces of the intellectual field are first filled in (the period 800–900 in Figure 8.1), there emerge four main factions: (1) rational theology, *kalam;* (2) scriptural traditionalists, *hadith,* the special province of lawyers; (3) importers of Greek (and to some extent Hindu and Babylonian) science, logic, and philosophy; and (4) Sufis: ascetic religious virtuosi at first, later developing an anti-ritualistic mysticism (see Figure 9.1).

Then comes a round of realignments and consolidations: The Ash'arites compromise between *kalam* and *hadith* (1 + 2). The Shi'ite faction of political theology develops its own doctrine, the hidden Imam (this might be considered 1a, a rival version of rational theology); and this amalgamates in turn with the imported science and Neoplatonist–Neo-Pythagorean hierarchical cosmology in the doctrine of the Brethren of Purity (1a + 3). The philosophical high point comes with further amalgamations in the next generations: Ibn Sina combines the now-declining tradition of *kalam* with the Neoplatonism and logic of Greek

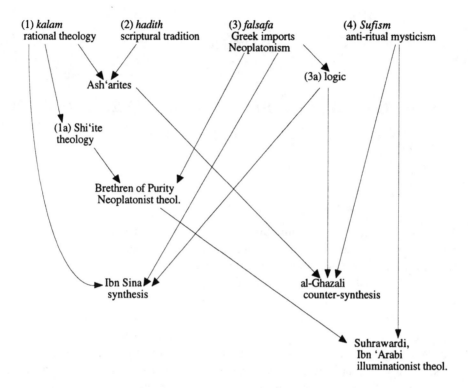

FIGURE 9.1. ISLAMIC FACTIONS AND COMBINATIONS

philosophy (1 + 3). This *falsafa* is attacked by al-Ghazali, who combines the Ash'arite lineage of conservative *kalam* with Sufism on the one hand, while extracting from the Greek imports the tool of formal logic on the other (call this 3a).

Al-Ghazali's grand coalition ([1 + 2], + [3a + 4]) now becomes the orthodox culture of Islam. *Falsafa* (except for scholastic logic, i.e., 3 − 3a) disappears. The remaining rivals are largely branches of Sufism (4): on the one hand the illuminationist hierarchical theology represented by Suhrawardi on the heterodox side, and by Ibn 'Arabi among the Sunnis, a combination of Sufi mysticism with the politicized emanationism of the Pure Brethren (4 + 1a + 3); on the other hand a poetic mysticism which holds itself aloof from intellectual alliances. After 1200 the prestige of Sufism is so high that its followers can go their own way while virtually all other intellectual factions try to make coalition with it. The one exception comprises the surviving *hadith* legalists, such as Ibn Taimiyah and the Malikite judge Ibn Khaldun, who produce isolated outbursts of philosophical criticism against the now-predominant mysticism-cum-logic of the *madrasas*.

We may trace the same development at the level of the material institutions of intellectual life. Originally *kalam* theologians and the *hadith* lawyers represent splits within the same base: they are all teachers at the mosques, where new factions can form when a leader withdraws from a circle with his followers to another pillar. The Sufis are distinctive at first because they base themselves not in the mosque but outside: they are street preachers or religious exemplars; later when their orders devoted to *tariqah,* the way of mystical life, become routinized (in the Weberian sense), they acquire their own specialized meeting-houses. The imports of philosophy and science are treated as secular, which means that they are never allowed into the mosque; they depend on patronage of the courts and the wealthy, and on secular careers of doctors and astronomers or astrologers.

The height of the battles between *kalam* and *hadith* takes place between 900 and 1100 over what kinds of teachings are to be allowed in the mosques. This conflict is resolved toward the latter date with the founding of *madrasas,* specialized schools with their own buildings and endowments. Al-Ghazali, who appears in the founding generation of the *madrasas* (and at the most famous *madrasa* of the capital), puts together the orthodoxy which becomes the curriculum of these schools. In other words, Sufism eventually is brought into the intellectual coalition in the *madrasas,* although it keeps expanding its independent external bases too. Philosophy, however, is excluded; its decline must be largely due to the fact that it can no longer compete for intellectual attention, based on scattered and episodic lay supports, once an organized school system exists. Only logic, split off from philosophy, is allowed into the *madrasas'* curriculum; but on its own it survives only as a stagnant scholasticism.

Again I have left the Spanish episode of 935–1200 to one side, encapsulated as it was from the history of Islamic life in eastern Islam. Here the structures are more like the early period in the east: *madrasas* do not exist; the Sufi orders are weak; *hadith* is dominated by the most conservative school, the Malikites, and rational theology (whether Mu'tazilite or Ash'arite) has no important representatives. Instead the cosmopolitan community is especially strong. The Jews are in close contact with both Muslim and Christian intellectuals, and all share a cosmopolitan interest in science. Among the Jews, the Neoplatonism of the Greek philosophical importers becomes expanded into a universalistic religion of reason, and this acquires followers among the Muslims as well; this is a synthesis of (1) rational theology in its Jewish branch and (3) Greek imports. Jewish scriptural conservatives—the rabbinical equivalent of (2) *hadith*—respond by a nationalist attack on cosmopolitanism. This sets the stage for a sophisticated compromise by Ibn Daud and above all Maimonides, who repudiate the Neoplatonic religion of reason and elevate instead a purified Aristoteleanism which they harmonize with religion. Averroës on the Muslim side follows the same path: combining the cosmopolitanism of the scientific networks with the conservatism of his lineage of Malikite jurists, he too excludes traditional *kalam* and replaces philosophical Neoplatonism with a new cosmopolitanism of Aristotle. Structurally, one might say that in Spain the cosmopolitan Greek import sector (3) has the field so much to itself that it splits into factions that never existed in the more beleaguered intellectual space to the east.

Compare now the factional skeleton of Christendom. The initial ingredients are the same as in Islam: (1) rational theology, (2) pious scripturalists, (3) Greek imports, and (4) mystics of direct religious experience. Many of the same tendencies and conflicts are acted out. The Sufi virtuosi, prostrating themselves at every step on the pilgrimage to Mecca or sitting on their rooftops for hours staring at the sun, have their exact counterpart among Christian ultra-ritualists and ascetics. Saint Peter Damiani, who called pagan philosophy the work of the devil, and Saint Bernard of Clairvaux, who attacked Abelard and the other rationalists in the name of faith and spiritual discipline, are structurally similar to the Hanbalite theologians who incited mobs to attack the kalamites in the streets of Baghdad and Damascus. Ibn Sina piles up arguments and distinctions in a fashion foreshadowing Christian scholasticism at its most assiduous, and the *madrasas* exhibit the disputations and the routinized curricula that would characterize the universities.

What differs is not the conflicts but their long-term outcomes. Controversies of heresy and church councils condemning philosophers' doctrines become almost a routine part of Christian intellectual life. But although texts are burned and doctrines prohibited, the overall pattern does not give any special weight to the conservative scripturalists. The standpoint from which heresy is judged slips further and further into the terrain of technical philosophy for six or eight generations. It is as if Christendom were full of Ibn Sinas and al-Ghazalis repeatedly pushed to make use of the conceptual weapons of their opponents, each time driving the controversy to a new level of sophistication.

If the outcomes are different, it is because the factional alliances take a different pattern. Within Christendom, (1) *kalam,* or rational theology, and (3) Greek imports are not initially split, institutionally and intellectually. Indeed, they begin as the same faction. The combination had already been made by the Patristic writers of the 300s C.E., especially Saint Augustine, whose works were taken as the major source of theological orthodoxy. Islamic *kalam,* by contrast, had its own institutional base (the mosques) and several generations of building its own networks and ideas before Greek *falsafa* was imported in strength; and the imports were admitted only fractionally into its base. To be sure, in later Christendom too the successive waves of Greek imports tended to come loose from the existing theological orthodoxy, and to some extent they were supported by secular intellectual bases in the aristocratic courts, outside the institutions of the church; but this separation was never as extreme as in Islam. It is above all with the Humanists of the Renaissance that this institutional split approached that found in Islam. This constitutes a striking difference in chronology: the Muslims experience the separation of secularist imports versus orthodox theological philosophy early in the life of their networks, whereas Christendom experiences it late.

The other major difference in factional alignments is that the Christian version of (2) *hadith*—scriptural loyalists—has a different kind of structural base than in Islam. The *hadith* specialists are teachers and practitioners of law; the legal world is the most scripturally traditionalist part of the Muslim educated classes. In Christendom, by contrast, law and scriptural traditionalism are split very early. The strength of the law schools is found in different places from the institutional strongholds of theology (northern Italy versus northern France and England); the lawyers are even more connected to secular, pre-Christian traditions (in this case Roman rather than Greek). So there arises a faction not prominent in Islam, which might be called *rational law*. Hereafter the scholastic tools and methods of the law schools become some of the ingredients that penetrate the practice of Christian rational theology and philosophy. Lacking a tie with law, scriptural traditionalists in Christendom have a much weaker base than in Islam, and are much less able to control the terms of the struggle with other intellectual factions.

If Islam and Christendom diverge intellectually, it is not so much because of different ingredients as by divergent outcomes of their conflicts. Moving the relative point of balance within the same kind of structure brings about quite different long-term products. We look first at the external conditions of intellectual life that channeled the European network on its path.

The Organizational Bases of Christian Thought

The crucial institutions of medieval Christendom are three: the monasteries, the papacy, and the universities.

Northern Europe began as a thinly populated frontier, in which civilized settlement was introduced largely by rural monasteries.[1] The church developed in alliance with the local aristocracy; monks were recruited among their sons and relatives, endowed with buildings, landed property, and serfs to work it. Monasteries were devoted to ritual in honor of their founders, masses for their sins and their memory, providing emotional mobilization and cultural legitimation as the military rulers set themselves apart from the ruled. Around 1050–1100 there began a second wave of monastic expansion and reform. The original Benedictine monasteries began to decline in numbers of monks and in revenues; their scattered properties were becoming inadequate to support the lifestyle of grand consumption and ceremony as a market economy began to compete with their fixed sources of income. The new wave of monasteries was more ascetic and economically rationalized than the first.

The Augustinian canons arose in towns, where they lived on donations of tithes and small rental properties; their base of support had shifted to the minor gentry and the middle class, which now had enough property to invest in religious status on a modest scale. The Cistercians continued to recruit from the aristocracy, but now they militantly pursued organizational independence. They were rigidly ascetic. Illicit marriages were cut off, emphasizing the separation of their order from the family ties which had previously been their principal support. They abjured ostentatious ritual and refused to carry out funerals and masses for the laity. Instead, as a source of income they took donations of property without strings attached; to work their land they recruited a subordinate rank of lay brothers as religious serfs, who were rewarded for their discipline by a minor share in the status of religious life. Like a number of other new orders, the Cistercians were involved in military Crusades, but above all they expanded the agricultural cultivation of Europe into the frontiers (Spain, Scotland, eastern Europe) and onto wastelands and mountains. Their emphasis on action rather than ritual made them economically productive, while their asceticism prevented them from investing in consumption and display and motivated them to plow back their gains into further expansion. The Cistercians are a case of the Weberian Protestant ethic in Catholic and corporate guise. Their monasteries became large landowners, buying up intervening parcels and consolidating properties. Their rationalized agriculture spilled over into wool production, mining, mills, and ironworks. The Cistercians were the most spectacular organizational expansion of the period (see Figure 9.2), but monastic growth was shared by other new orders. Taking advantage of a new market economy, they become a major impetus in economic expansion (Gimpel, 1976).

The papacy expanded organizationally on the growth of the monasteries. In the early Middle Ages, the church was part of the feudal dispersion of power. Bishops acted as territorial princes, and were closely entwined with the politics of local aristocracies (Morrison, 1969: 266, 354, 387–388). The papacy's main power was as local ruler in central Italy; its controversies with the emperor over supreme authority did not extend much beyond doctrinal claims over each other's domain, and neither side effectively controlled the clerical aristocracy. The seat of the pope at Rome was little more than an honorific center containing the relics of Saint Peter, which constituted a physical symbol of the transmission of charismatic authority; but it had no far-reaching organizational apparatus, and its ties to most of Christendom were primarily as a focal point

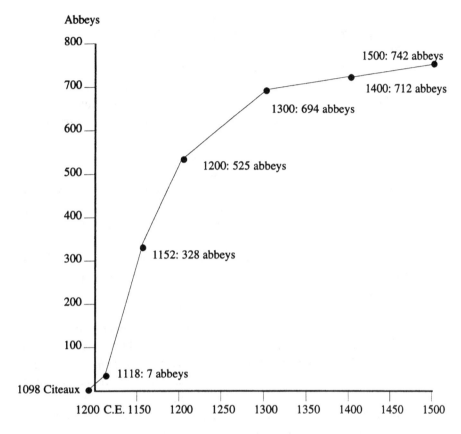

FIGURE 9.2. PROLIFERATION OF CISTERCIAN MONASTERIES, 1098–1500 (Source: Southern, 1970: 254)

for pilgrimages (Southern, 1970: 94–100). In these respects it was like Mecca, which never did develop any "papal" authority.

Between 1050 and 1130 Rome began to experience a rapid growth in litigation coming from the monasteries, asking for autonomy vis-à-vis local bishops, confirmation of their property rights, and special insignia of religious rank. R. W. Southern (1970: 113) calls it "a scramble for honours, dignities and exemptions." The growth of the new monastic orders was riding on a competitively expanding market for symbolic goods. Around 1130–1150 this monastic litigation was joined by other ecclesiastical as well as secular claimants. The pope was asked to settle disputes over property appointments among rival jurisdictions, and to confer exemptions and benefits. By the early 1300s, the volume of papal correspondence had grown a hundredfold since 1130 (Southern, 1970: 109). Rome became full of lawyers, and the papacy grew wealthy off the fees of litigation and the spoils of the lawsuits. A large administrative staff sprang up at the papal court, the first bureaucracy to appear in medieval Europe.

The papacy now had a patronage network extending all over Europe, outshining that of any secular ruler. The pope began to exert control over the regional bishops, disputing the appointment power of secular rulers; by the 1300s, the papacy was claiming control over lower clerical appointments as well. Central authority was enforced by sending papal legates to oversee matters on the spot. Local episcopal bureaucracies expanded in turn. With its heavy hand in property holdings and legal transactions, the church became indispensable to the growing commercial economy. Trained clerics became the mainstay of secular governments because of their monopoly over literate administration. The church also moved to take control over armed force. Militant evangelists as well as popes preached Crusades against infidels on the Muslim and pagan frontiers, and against heretics within. Combined with the efforts of the church to enforce domestic peace by ending the fighting among feudal lords (Bloch, 1961: 412–421), these developments now fostered the concept of Christendom as an armed state in which the military aristocracy followed the chain of command from the church. Riding the momentum of its successful drive for organizational independence from the kings, the papacy at its height in the mid-1200s went on to claim supremacy in temporal power.[2]

The universities resulted from the combined expansion of monasteries and the papacy (Rashdall, 1936; Cobban, 1975, 1988; Ferruolo, 1985; Stone, 1974a). As competition among the monastic schools increased, the network of teachers detached itself into specialized organizations in their own right. The thickest part of the network formed into universities, specializing in theology and in the subjects that led up to it. The papacy and the universities fed off each other. As church administration turned bureaucratic, its ranks became filled by university-trained theologians and canon lawyers. Conversely, the growing centralization of the church put at its disposal benefices and offices which were used as patronage for students and graduates of the universities. There were other roots of university schooling; guilds of the teachers of secular law and of medicine were also forming, but these soon attached themselves to the church-sanctioned university structure in order to gain the legal right to monopolize teaching and grant official degrees.

The universities became the center of intellectual life. The greatest creativity in abstract ideas took place in subjects preparatory to the advanced degrees, that is, in logic, philosophy, and natural science, which made up the "undergraduate" part of the curriculum. As the university elaborated its internal structure, the autonomous dynamic of the intellectual community was set free in the sector which was most insulated from outside concerns. Theology stayed closer to external conditions; it too experienced plenty of controversies and developments, but these were in the realm of more anthropomorphic and particularistic conceptions, such as the cult of the Virgin Mary, or tied to political struggles over the wealth and secular power of the church. The field of law was creative in its own sphere, especially in the areas of corporations and property, subjects which had great long-term significance for the European economy and for the political trajectory of self-government (Berman, 1983). But law was largely separate from philosophical developments, and their creativity was specialized into different universities (Radding, 1985, 1988). Philosophy was strong in the universities specializing in theology, above all Paris and Oxford; law was creative especially in the universities of northern Italy, headed by Bologna. This was the region where the church-state conflict was most intense, the battleground of territorial struggles between the papacy and the Holy Roman Emperor. Law was stimulated as an instrument of this struggle.

Institutional Divergence with Islam

Islam and Christendom have many external conditions in common. Both are regions organized by universalistic religions on the periphery of old bureaucratic empires, Rome and/or Persia; both were built on tribal coalitions newly developed into states; both have doctrines of anthropomorphic monotheism, modeling their God on an omnipotent political ruler who demands both obedience and action on his behalf. Both religions, along with their progenitor, Judaism, symbolically exalt a ruling personality and thus give an emphasis to moral relationships and to political and social activism.

But Islam's variants on the central Christian institutions are significantly different. Monasticism is virtually absent in Islam. There are ascetics and devotees of religious exercises, but they do not form property-owning corporations. Sufi asceticism was not especially concerned with celibacy. This is important because a celibate organization necessarily breaks its ties with families; thus it can become an independent force acting apart from the interests of kinship groups. The Sufi brotherhoods, in contrast with Christian monastic orders, were much more embedded in the politics and status concerns of lay society. In addition, the monasteries had a much greater capacity for amassing wealth and organizational resources. There was a modest equivalent in Islam in the form of religious endowments *(waqf)* such as schools, hospitals, and charities (Hodgson, 1974: 2:51, 136; Makdisi, 1981: 35–74). These could hold property, and were used by wealthy patrons as a device to evade inheritance laws and restrictions on investment (Garcin, 1988: 121–123). But such religious corporations lacked autonomy from lay interests and control. What is missing is the dynamic role of the monasteries of Christian Europe, both in amassing wealth and power for an autonomous church sector, and in providing a base for intellectual networks.

The papacy had some parallel in the caliphate, but the trajectory was different. The leader of Islam was simultaneously a military and a political ruler. Islam emerged as a successful military conquest, whereas Christianity in northern Europe made its way by conversion and cooperation with the tribal rulers, who eventually became a feudal aristocracy. Islam initially was a theocracy such that the strongest popes of the 1200s dreamed of becoming. Even when the caliphate after 900 crumbled into de facto independent secular states, Muslim religious movements aimed at the reconquest of political power. Islamic religious organization was less autonomous, more tied to the families of the ruling aristocracy; the various Shi'ite movements all aimed to restore the purity of dynastic succession. This gave a particularistic emphasis to Islamic theology and made a social basis for the long-standing opposition to rational theology, which shifted to more universalistic grounds.

Because of its political connection, Islamic religion never became a bureaucratically organized church, and there was no specialized (and celibate) priesthood. Rulers were expected to uphold Islamic law, to appoint religious judges, and to provide for the material upkeep of mosques; the church itself had no property. Pious laymen could take the initiative in learning and expounding Islamic texts and traditions; the learned *ulama*, something like the Jewish rabbis (teachers, not priests), were simultaneously religious, legal, and political leaders of the community. They provided a quasi-democratic (or at least decentralizing) counterbalance against the rulers, and in times of government weakness became de facto political dominants. They formed the basis of a religious intellectual life, but one which was closely attached to the politics and the indigenous symbolic life of the community. As a structural base for ideas, they supported particularism and traditionalism more than did the autonomous Christian Church.

Universities in a strict sense did not exist in Islam. One can speak loosely of the Baghdad House of Wisdom or the Córdoba library in this way, but these were not centers of instruction with bodies of teachers and students, much less universities which granted degrees and monopolistic licenses over the higher professions. In the period of the strong caliphate, the centers of higher education were in the mosques, where circles of pupils gathered around particular teachers. The rational theologians emerged in this way in the mosque at Basra and developed circles elsewhere; the most common type of teaching circle, however, consisted of those that formed around teachers of law. After 1050 more formally organized schools became widespread. The *madrasas* were *waqf* endowed colleges, providing salaries for teachers and dormitories and stipends for students. The *madrasas* resembled universities in some aspects, though with crucial differences (Makdisi, 1981; Huff, 1993).

Whereas the European university was a self-governing corporation which acquired privileges and immunities from local control, the *madrasa* was under the control of the lay *waqf* donor. Most of the universities were guilds of teachers, who pushed their internal autonomy to set sequences of degrees. Teachers' guilds existed in Islam to some extent, but these were separate from any particular school and did not act as a corporate body in the actual administration of school affairs. In effect the university was a combination of guild and *waqf* in one corporate institution, whereas in Islamic education the two components were separate. The Islamic teachers gave formal degrees in the shape of certificates denoting that a pupil had learned a particular book, and these eventually became licenses to teach and to issue legal opinions. The Christian universities developed formal degrees more extensively: the sequences of Master of Arts, Bachelor and Doctor of Laws, of Medicine, and of Divinity. These were issued by the corporation rather than the individual teacher, and validated by the charter of the pope or ruler. The university degrees elaborated into a system of credentials, used both internally within the teaching world and as a claim to positions within the church hierarchy. Whereas in Christendom the bureaucratic papacy developed arm in arm with the expansion of the monopolistic system of university credentials, in Islam the lack of a church hierarchy, and eventually of any central religious authority at all, turned the educational structure in a different direction.

The most fateful difference for intellectual matters was the much greater differentiation of theology from law in the Christian universities, and the resulting opening for philosophy. In Islam, both law and theology were based on the same texts, the holy scriptures and traditions. Islam made no distinction between civil and canon law, faculties which were separate in the Christian universities. In the period before 900, Islamic law and rational theology were differentiating, but the separation never became institutionalized and legitimated. Since the teachers of law were also practicing judges, law was more practical than theoretical; and since law was closely tied to scripture, lawyers and theologians were rivals over the same turf. This difference in organizational bases is one reason why there was more conflict between literal scripturalism and rational theology in Islam than in Christendom. The rise of the *madrasas* was simultaneously the victory of law in monopolizing formal teaching institutions. There was no independent faculty of theology, nor along with it a place where philosophical issues could become a specialty. Secular philosophy from Greek and non-Islamic sources was officially excluded from the *madrasas* as an enemy of orthodoxy.

Nevertheless, logic and dialectic found their way into the curriculum as auxiliary studies. Formal argument was studied as a preparation for legal practice, and disputations in the *madrasas* resembled the disputations which undergirded the scholastic method of textual argument in the universities. The *madrasas* never became creative centers either in logic or in philosophy more broadly. They lacked the internal structure of the universities, where the separation of the preliminary arts from theology and law allowed networks of innovating intellectuals to build up in the most insulated areas of the organization. As elsewhere in Islam, there were institutional elements which were similar to Christianity, but they were combined in different proportions; the balance was different, the outcome intellectually more conservative and traditional.

The Sequence of External Changes in the Bases of Intellectual Life

Recall our sociological conception of intellectual change. There is a two-step flow of causality. External conditions change the material bases in which intellectuals work; their networks then adjust to the new competitive space, rearranging the cultural capital they have carried over from the previous period. Creativity is especially prominent at each institutional turning point. Schematically, then, we expect the following in medieval Christendom:

1. The takeoff of the reformed monasteries. This is a period of intense competition over religious status and expansion of religious participation throughout the society. It is the period of the wandering dialecticians, culminating in the creativity of Anselm and Abelard.

2. The growth of the bureaucratic papacy, shifting the center of intellectual life to the universities. This is the time of high scholasticism, the building of formal systems, the search for additional cultural capital by imports from the old Mediterranean sources. Philosophical creativity results from the synthesis of these materials. Another institutional factor emerges in this period. The monastic sector, which is now taking a back seat to the new church organizations, puts forth another set of movements. These are the friars, orders of monks outside the monasteries, active in doctrinal disputes and in the life of the cities. The Franciscans and Dominicans move to where the intellectual action is, and soon their rivalry dominates theology and philosophy at the universities.

3. The last phase of medieval intellectual life, following from the crisis of the papacy which sets in around 1300. The bid for theocratic power crests and fails. The very organizational resources that were built up by the church are turned against it. The dynamic monasteries had built a wealthy economy, which now spills over into the non-church sector. Kingdoms consolidate, especially in England and France; the city-states of northern Italy prosper under rival patronage of emperor and pope. There are now positions for lawyers and

administrators outside the church. The loyalty of the clergy is split. National blocs appear within the church; secular power over clerical appointments reasserts itself. The election of the pope itself becomes a target for secular factions. During the Avignon period, the papacy becomes increasingly dependent on the French, its old ally in struggle against the German-based emperor. Instead of becoming a theocracy of Christendom extending across Europe, the papacy concentrates its temporal power in its own feudal possessions in central Italy. By 1400, the pope is largely embroiled in Italian warfare and is reduced to acting much like another local prince.

4. The declining international orientation of the papacy and the shift of administrative patronage to secular courts, constituting the surrounding conditions for late medieval thinkers. Universities still exist, indeed proliferate with the rivalry of national and city patrons. But they become bases of factions rather than points of creative intersection. The scholasticism and philosophical theology of the university synthesis is put on the defensive by intellectuals who are now based outside, constituting the lay-oriented movements of mystics and Humanists.

5. The breakup of its organizational base, which puts late medieval Christianity in a decentralized condition somewhat like that of the later period of Islam. Both religious regions end up with a number of features in common: the loss of a network center, the decline in creativity, the attack on abstract ideas, the predominance of mysticism. But the cultural capital each has accumulated is different. One source of the difference is that the Christian intellectual networks develop later, and part of their cultural capital consists in importing the most sophisticated abstractions accumulated during the thickest period of the Islamic networks. Christian thinkers are able to use Ibn Sina and Averroës, late products of the Arab networks that were closing down in their region of origin. But these could be imported so eagerly—indeed, were deliberately sought out—because an initial similarity between the institutions of the two regions guaranteed that Christendom could import the kinds of ideas with which it was already familiar. Added to the more "leftward" balance of factional disputes within Christendom, these imports made for a richer accretion of philosophy by the time their own creative period was over.

The Inner Autonomy of the University

First Thickening of the Networks

Christian philosophy became creative in a movement of wandering dialecticians that rapidly grew up in northern France after 1000.[3] Figure 9.3 shows the familiar pattern of linkage among the most important intellectual creators,

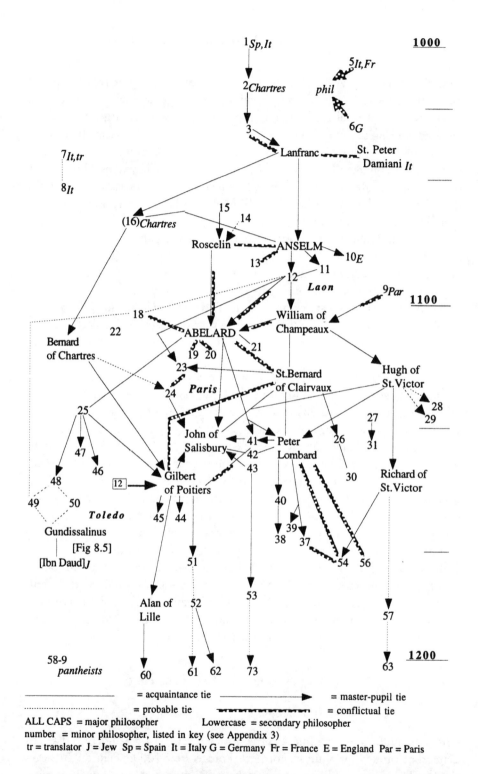

FIGURE 9.3. CHRISTIAN PHILOSOPHERS, 1000–1200: FORMING
THE ARGUMENTATIVE NETWORK

not only in chains of significant masters and pupils but also in rivalries. The network center shows where the action is: around Abelard, who not only studied with everyone but also debated with everyone; and in the extraordinary complication of the network of important thinkers four to six generations later, where the lightning bolts of controversy surround Thomas Aquinas, Henry of Ghent, Duns Scotus, William of Ockham, and several others (see Figure 9.4). The network builds up charges of creative energy and discharges them at its points of maximal tension, like an electric field giving off current.

From the beginning, the networks are organized in chains of leading masters and pupils interwoven by conflicts. Anselm's teacher, the most eminent of the time, was Lanfranc, who disputed with Berengar of Tours over the existence of universals; in the next generation Anselm disputed with Abelard's teacher Roscelin. There was a third party to these disputes, comprising scripturalists such as Peter Damiani, Otloh of St. Emmeran, and Manegold of Lautenbach, who attacked the whole business of dialectic as un-Christian. There was no doubt provocation in Berengar's application of dialectic to deny the transubstantiation of the Host, or Roscelin's application of nominalism to the Trinity with the conclusion that it must consist of three individuals. The intensity of creative energy was being driven upward by this Christian version of the dispute between *kalam* and *hadith*. It was this context which fostered Anselm's creation of one of the most famous of all metaphysical arguments, his ontological proof for the existence of God.

Scripturalists such as Damiani had taken the line against the dialecticians that God is superior to logic, indeed that God's will can change the laws of logic. Anselm, educated in the secular schools of Italy, and teaching at the Norman monastery at Bec, where recruitment and even income depended on its fame as a center of learning, was primed to rise to the challenge. For him, reason is the very basis of scripture. If Christ had never existed, it would still be possible to show the logical necessity of human salvation, the Incarnation, the Trinity, even details such as the virgin birth (*Monologium,* esp. Preface; *Cur Deus Homo*)—points which more moderate philosophers such as Thomas Aquinas later regarded as mysteries understandable only by faith. The oppositions of the intellectual field threw Anselm's energy into the extreme rationalist corner. Against nominalist philosophers such as Roscelin, he held out for the primacy of general ideas, prior to and untouched by experience. From this arose Anselm's dissatisfaction: Could he find a single sufficient proof of the most important reality of all, the existence of God, which did not depend on chains of argument that included empirical premises? After much struggle the answer came to him: the highest of all concepts must be that which includes its own existence; for if it did not exist, it would be less perfect than another conception which did exist. Anselm builds his proof using the sole rational criterion of avoiding contradiction.

Anselm's proof is one of the monuments of Western philosophy, provoking controversy immediately and at intervals ever since. Its fertility comes from the way it succinctly poses boundary issues of the field: the nature of rational criteria, of self-reference and contradiction, of the border between the transcendental and the humanly accessible. How was this metaphysical peak reached so early in the medieval Christian network? This was no situation of conceptual naiveté; the networks were relatively new but built on the accumulated concepts of Greek philosophy. The reality of universals was an issue transmitted from late antiquity by the attempt of Boethius to synthesize Plato and Aristotle.[4] The relatively shallow networks at the time of renewed intellectual life after 1000 set up fairly simple, intense lines of conflict, as a result of which the anti-rationalists within theology allowed the rationalist position to come out in full purity.

The chain of followers of Lanfranc, Anselm, and Roscelin, as well as the anti-philosophical conservatives, soon produced a more complex lineup of conflicts. This thickening of the network shifted the focus toward the nature of concepts and of argument itself. The self-consciousness of the network manifests itself in the person who is most thoroughly connected among its factions. Peter Abelard, a knight-errant of dialectic, wandered from group to group challenging the masters. Abelard is linked with Anselm at second remove, and directly with at least three secondary figures and a host of minor figures of his time. In this vortex Abelard rejected both realism and nominalism, innovating an epistemology focusing on the process of abstraction itself, breaking new ground in logic and theory of meaning. The sharpening of logical concepts was the second great monument of medieval creativity.

Abelard's most powerful opponent, Saint Bernard of Clairvaux, was the greatest of the anti-philosophers, building in opposition to the dialecticians a mysticism of devotion. The two men were rival organizers of the social structures taking shape at this time. Abelard was the foremost of the new breed, the professional teachers now proliferating in northern France; his technical interests were those of a group which was gradually becoming self-conscious as an occupational guild that would soon form the university. Bernard was the charismatic leader of monastic reform, whose Cistercian order was exploding with hundreds of new foundations (Figure 9.2). Bernard's energy came from the possibilities of power within burgeoning social organizations and movements. He preached the Crusade as the church became the vehicle for the military coordination of Christendom; at home he attempted to stamp out divisions within the church, persecuting Abelard and his like for heresy. Nothing epitomizes the situation better than Bernard descending on Paris in 1139 to preach the danger of mere learning and to bring back converts from the schools to the Cistercian citadels on the frontiers (Ferruolo, 1985: 47).

For all the success of Bernard's monasteries, the pull of the intellectual marketplace was even stronger. Although Abelard in his old age was condemned to imprisonment in a monastery, the network of teachers continued to thicken, and the schools became more concentrated and permanent. Saint Bernard's mysticism, not so much contemplative as a program of spiritual exercises and virtues, was developed by other members of his austere order of Cistercian monks. By the next generation, their anti-intellectualism was already fading into philosophical interpretations of mysticism. A comprehensive academic mysticism was taught at the Abbey of St. Victor in Paris, where Hugh of St. Victor included all the secular arts as a basis of contemplation, leading up through a hierarchical classification as allegorical signs of God in the world.

As the Parisian schools became institutionalized, a rival node of the network gathered prestige at Chartres. Bernard of Chartres and his pupils defended classical learning and a theological Platonism, staking their claim for attention on their stock of ancient culture. It is not surprising to find the Chartres network taking the lead in seeking translations from the Arab world, sending emissaries to Toledo and to Sicily in search of texts to bolster its position.

Around 1200 the older chains gradually ran out (see Figures 9.3 and 9.4). The older mysticism, in both anti-intellectual and systematic forms, had faded; so had nominalism and even Abelard's sophisticated technical logic. Although Abelard had many important pupils, the most famous of them exemplified the skepticism and eclecticism that emerged after two or three generations of a crowded intellectual field. John of Salisbury was a network sophisticate, pupil not only of Abelard but also of Gilbert of Poitiers, acquaintance of Hugh of St. Victor and even of Saint Bernard. John regarded the controversies of his time with mild skepticism, and espoused a doctrine that knowledge can be only probable at best. For him the problem of universals had existed since ancient times and was no doubt insoluble.

From this time dates the development of the sheer technical aspect of intellectual life—not in the subtleties of Abelard's logic, which were forgotten, but in what became the scholastic method. Abelard's most successful pupil was Peter Lombard, not an original thinker but the compiler of *Sentences,* a book of opinions on disputed questions. It became the most popular textbook of medieval times; the predominant mode of composition came to be the practice of writing a commentary on Lombard's *Sentences.* The success of his compilation against others which were appearing at the same time was primarily due to the place of his chain at Paris, where Lombard was master of the cathedral school at Notre Dame from 1140 to 1159, and then bishop of Paris. For the cathedral school was then turning into the nucleus of the University of Paris, and Peter Lombard's faithful pupil Peter of Poitiers became its first chancellor.

The vivid battles of Abelard's day contrast strangely with the unoriginal and pedantic fruits of his intellectual children and grandchildren. But the genealogy is palpable nevertheless. Abelard and his fellow combatants had made Paris the focus of intellectual attention, a central meeting place that became institutionalized in famous schools. And Abelard himself laid down the first great example of a textbook, his *Sic et Non,* early in the century, in which he set forth contradictory passages from the Church Fathers arranged around abstract philosophical issues. The method had emerged a generation earlier in the hands of canon lawyers; shortly after Abelard, the concordance of conflicting legal texts was made a systematic compilation by the great Gratian at Bologna (Grabmann, 1909–1911; Kantorowicz, 1938). The legal and theological faculties were forming simultaneously and in mutual influence. Abelard's *Sic et Non* gave the intellectual community one of its great pieces of cultural capital, a set of puzzles over which to work. The scholastic method was to flourish in a kind of architectural splendor; later commentators from Bonaventure down to Ockham would marshal authorities first on one side of a question, then on the other, systematically refuting and approving and weighing in the balance. As intellectual life heated up again in the next century, these texts became monuments to the thoroughness and subtlety of an intellectual community taking seriously its history and its conflicts, the two structural ingredients of creativity.

Universities and Encyclopedic Science

The intellectual life that took off again in the generations after 1200 was shaped by several factors. The free-standing schools were amalgamating and formalizing into universities. With this came a move to extend the branches of knowledge and to present them in encyclopedic compendia. The Arab philosophies were imported, in two waves represented by Avicenna's Neoplatonism and Averroës's Aristoteleanism, followed by the Greek texts themselves. The gap in the chains of important names at the end of the 1100s coincides with the time when texts were pouring in from the Arab world. The temporary downturn in indigenous creativity is typical of what happens during a generation of importers. The narrower base of Neoplatonist and late Roman texts on which the first wave of Christendom had built its philosophy was now swamped by the wider range of rediscovered Greek philosophy. The nominalism which Christian philosophers had constructed was forgotten in the prestige of ancient texts; nominalism would not be heard again until Ockham four generations later. In world perspective, what is striking is how quickly Christian philosophers recovered from their dependence on imported ideas. Impetus was given by their new organizational base.

The first philosophical reputations among those congregating at Paris (and to a lesser degree at Oxford) arose from the struggle to assimilate or refute the Arab ideas (see Figure 9.4). William of Auxerre produced a Christianized version of Avicenna; he was appointed by the pope in 1228 to a commission to correct the dangerous newest import, the Averroist texts of Aristotle. William of Auvergne, theology master and then bishop of Paris from 1228 to 1249, systematized a doctrine in reaction against the Arab Aristoteleanism, drawing on Saint Augustine but bolstered by pieces of Avicenna. Alexander of Hales produced a scholastic *Summa* that compiled conservative Augustinian and Victorine ideas while dealing with problems posed by Aristotle.

At the same time, specialized branches of knowledge were expanding and pulling free of theology, finding niches in the differentiating organization of university studies. Scientific texts were being translated from Arabic, comprising ancient Greek works in astronomy, mathematics, medicine, and other sciences, together with Arab advances. Those individuals who were closest to this inflow were able to carve out a distinctive niche in the field. Albert of Bollstadt, a German nobleman who as a young man studied near the Italian centers of translation, became filled with the ambition of compiling and completing the scientific works of the Greeks. He became Albert the Great out of the sheer energy with which he pursued this goal, ranging through all the fields of knowledge from theology to botany, and from plants and gems to occultism and magic.

Albert's encyclopedic works are impressive mainly for their scope. Albert regarded himself as following Aristotle, which he did in the arrangement of the sciences, and in holding that knowledge is based on the senses, and that there is no certainty regarding insensibles. Yet Albert's ontology is much closer to Neoplatonism. For him the soul is an intellectual substance, not the form of the body (as it was for Aristotle and for Aquinas). Universals are divine Ideas situated in God; the human soul has knowledge of universals by divine illumination, much along the lines of Augustine's doctrine of the inner light. Albert and several generations of followers remained more Neoplatonist than Aristotelean. Here the Europeans repeated the stance of the Muslims before Averroës; although Aristotle was available in his own words, he was interpreted conservatively, as close to an idealist religious metaphysics as possible. An independent Aristoteleanism awaited the radical Averroists and Albert's own independent pupil, Thomas Aquinas.

Natural scientists and encyclopedists are concentrated in these two generations, 1200–1265.[5] The most famous are those who combined these secular imports with theology. In England, Robert Grosseteste, ahead of other scholars of his day in acquiring Greek, synthesized what he had learned from geometry texts with the older Augustinian doctrine of divine illumination (on

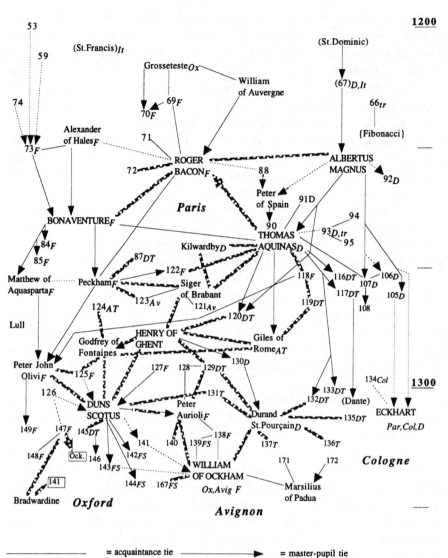

FIGURE 9.4. FRANCISCAN AND DOMINICAN RIVALRIES,
1200–1335 (All Paris unless marked)

Grosseteste, see Southern, 1992). For Augustine this had been a psychological and epistemological doctrine; for Grosseteste it became expanded into a cosmology. His speculative system declares that the world is formed of light. God created a point of light, Grosseteste posits, which spread out as a sphere, rarefying until it reached a limit; this constituted the outermost celestial sphere recognized by contemporary astronomy and cosmology. From this sphere light bounced back by reflection to the lower spheres of the planets, eventually forming the earth at the center. Grosseteste worked out the geometric theory of angles and lines of reflection, drawing on the Arab science of optics. This splendid visual image of the universe of spheres, rays, and golden light had a powerful appeal throughout the century; three generations later Dante used it, though associating it erroneously with Averroës.

Out of Grosseteste's circle of scholars promoting Greek learning came Roger Bacon, who became the most famous by taking the most radical line. Like a number of others of his day interested in science, Bacon had considerable independent wealth to put into his researches (he reports spending the huge sum of £2,000 on experiments; *DSB,* 1981: 1:377). Structurally he was a competitor of his contemporary Albert, whom he violently attacked, along with Alexander of Hales, Thomas Aquinas, and most others; even where Bacon grudgingly respects Albert, he accuses him of teaching before he has learned. Bacon is nevertheless dependent on Arabic doctrines. He uses an Averroist vocabulary, but his cosmology is the familiar light universe. Bacon's main originality is in advocating and promoting experimental science; his own researches led to nothing concrete, and his encyclopedic efforts ranging into fields such as astrology and alchemy yielded little advance. Even his epistemology is rather naive; though resolutely overthrowing Platonic realism and illuminationist doctrines, he expects that experience and experiments will produce complete certitude.

Bacon was in fact a propagandist, publicizing his position by violent attacks on contemporary rivals, holding that they were living in a time of barbaric superstition and awe of authorities. This historical condition he explains, after the fashion of a moralistic preacher, as the result of human sins which have caused us to lose the ancient wisdom. Here Bacon gives away the source of his own energy: he was the most aggressive importer of pagan cultural capital at the time when the market was just opening. In a maneuver strangely foreshadowing Newton's maniacal private studies 400 years later, Bacon wrote a synthesis of pagan myths and biblical history. Atlas, Prometheus, Apollo, Zoroaster, and others down to the time of King Solomon are held to have known the true science of nature; because this was subsequently lost, we must now work empirically to regain it.

Bacon paid the price for his contentious stance. Having joined the Franciscans about 1257, he was accused of indiscipline and confined under arrest in their house in Paris for perhaps as long as twenty years. But to see this as the story of a lonely rebel against authority is to miss the structure which constituted Bacon's originality and his fame. He was far from isolated, and indeed put himself at the center of the major networks at a time when the realigning blocs were opening up possibilities of creativity in many directions. Bacon's friendship with the scholar Guy Foulques, who became Pope Clement IV in 1265–1268, provided both the immediate instigation of his major writings and their dissemination. Bacon achieved nothing substantive in his program. His creativity was to push his network relationships as antagonistically as possible and to formulate a doctrine from this opposition.

The Friars' Movement: Monks outside the Monastery

Another structural feature of this period was a new line of organizational rivalry superimposed on the rest. Grosseteste and William of Auvergne were virtually the last important philosophers for a century who were ordinary clergy; most of the rest were either Franciscans or Dominicans. There was a flood of enthusiasm for these movements which brought even the most hardcore academics and intellectuals into their ranks. We have seen the trouble his membership made for Bacon, but his act of joining was not idiosyncratic. Alexander of Hales, well established as a theologian in Paris, joined the Franciscans late in life, and was rewarded with their theology chair at the university in 1231. Albert of Bollstadt was recruited by the head of the Dominicans himself, an associate of Saint Dominic, while at the schools in Italy.

The structural rivalry between Franciscans and Dominicans existed from the outset. Saint Francis and Saint Dominic were contemporaries, and their orders were given papal sanction around 1220, within a few years of each other (Brooke, 1959; Mandonnet, 1937; Bennett, 1971). On the surface there is a sharp contrast: the gentle Francis preaching to the birds and humbly visiting the poor; Saint Dominic combating heresy amid the Albigensian Crusade in Languedoc. Together they constitute the second great wave of the expanding monasticism, following the first wave of economically successful monasteries epitomized by Saint Bernard's Cistercians a century before. Christendom was acquiring a unifying organizational core. The papacy was becoming a state above the feudal states, and the universities were growing with the spread of church bureaucracy. The new monastic movements, oriented toward activism in the world, were part of a growing mood of victorious Christianization of the social order. The status order was changing, and a sense of enthusiasm spread among the population, which now had the possibility of appropriating these status-giving religious activities for themselves. The rival movements of friars—*frères,* brotherhoods of religious participation—were organizationally similar because they were halfway between laymen and monks: living under monastic vows and commitments, giving up family life and private property, but residing in the public world, where they exemplified the religious life of good works.

Within less than a generation the friars had arrived at the universities, and were soon bidding to dominate them. This was not at all their original intention. The Dominicans were on an ideological campaign to stamp out unbelievers within a doctrinally unified Christendom; the Franciscans were on a mission of charity among the poor. But their rapid organizational growth, their success in sheer numbers, brought a rapid rationalization in the Weberian sense. The Franciscans were particularly successful, mushrooming to some 28,000 by 1300, against the Dominicans' 12,000.[6] The new universities, awarding recognized degrees, were laying out formal credentials that rapidly permeated church bureaucracy, legal practice, and the monopoly over teaching. The Dominicans, whose explicit mission was to preach orthodoxy, easily gravitated toward formally organized teaching. At first they organized their own training schools, but these quickly became residential adjuncts to universities or (as at Cologne) the nucleus of future universities. In the 1230s established and aspiring university teachers themselves joined the orders in droves, thereby bringing the center of gravity of the friars' own training into the university world.

There was a material advantage favoring the friars over the secular students. Most students had to struggle for patronage to support their studies, spending a good deal of time applying for prebends, and usually interrupting their studies between their M.A. (taken around age 25) and their doctorate in theology or law (taken around 40) to serve their patron in ecclesiastical or governmental administration (Southern, 1970: 292–295). The friars' houses underwrote the expense of student life; for their teachers, the orders provided endowed positions. The orders separated studies from the political scramble for preferment, thus clearing a space in which intellectual life could be pursued uninterruptedly and on its own terms.[7]

For the preaching-oriented Dominicans, the move into the universities was less of an ideological contradiction than for the Franciscans, with their emphasis on poverty, charity, and the mission to the poor. Nevertheless, organizational rivalry pulled them along the same path, where their very success made entanglements permanent. The connection of the orders with the papacy at the time when it was bidding for theocratic power within Europe brought them into the inner corridors of church politics. Friars were pressed into service as bishops and even archbishops and cardinals. The success of the Franciscans pulled them all the more rapidly into the establishment.

Once inside the university realm, the friars found that their ideologies were rapidly replaced by the normal abstract concerns of academic intellectuals. Lines of struggle over the focus of attention within intellectual networks became superimposed on their identities as Franciscans and Dominicans. Within a generation the Franciscan John Peckham could declare that his order and the Dominicans were so separate in philosophy that they had nothing in common but the fundamentals of Christian doctrine (Gilson, 1944: 540). At the same time, there were struggles within each order over its philosophical position.

Much of the intellectual history of the next three generations was taken up with the Franciscans' internal factions, dominated by Bonaventure, Duns Scotus, and Ockham. The Dominicans also embraced two related positions: that of Albert's Neoplatonic Aristoteleanism, originally a framework for an encyclopedia of natural science, later modified in a mystical direction by his follower Meister Eckhart; and that of Thomas Aquinas's Aristoteleanism, which eventually became the official doctrine. For a short period there was also an anti-Thomist conservatism within the order, represented by Robert Kilwardby. To complete the picture of the university field, there was a third party based outside the two orders: the secular priests and clerics, often jealous of the friars, sometimes opposing them over university privileges. It is among this group that one finds a struggle for a third party intellectual position, most conventionally with Henry of Ghent, but with greatest effect—not to say consternation—by the perceived advocacy of extreme "Averroism" by the young secular arts masters of the 1260s and 1270s.

Let us take first the Franciscans in the generation of the mid-1200s. Bacon we have already met, the house radical. The house master was Saint Bonaventure, in the center of the network at Paris. Bonaventure attempted to uphold the conservative Augustinian vision as best he could in the new conditions of intellectual struggle. Nevertheless, he was a scholastic, marshaling arguments pro and con with the best of them. His metaphysical vision is a variant of the doctrine of spheres of light, but carried through with more metaphysical skill than in Grosseteste. The world is not an imitation or God or even a resemblance, since God is entirely different; yet the hierarchy of the world consists of expressions, signs of God to be read by humans, both externally through the senses and internally in their own soul. Bonaventure incorporated Anselm's ontological proof into his system, adding the characteristic Augustinian doctrine that it is God's illumination within the soul that allows one to grasp the concept of God which implies its own existence. It is not for nothing that Bonaventure acquired the soubriquet Seraphic Doctor; he offers the closest thing possible to Saint Francis's bird sermons turned into a technical philosophy.

At the fairly young age of 36, Bonaventure was elected general of the Franciscan order, responsible for its politics and its internal discipline even more than its intellectual life. The silencing of Bacon must have taken place with his support, if not his initiative. This was doubtless a sideshow to more serious conflicts. Already the Franciscans were being rent by a struggle between purist "spirituals," who defended Francis's original aim of a life of poverty and charity, against those wielding power in the church and the universities. But the struggle was necessarily fought out in the realm of politics, where the advocates of poverty were repeatedly condemned as their faith carried them into currents of doctrinal heresy. To survive, the spirituals had to enter the terrain of academic subtleties. On the intellectual front, things would not stand still long enough for Bonaventure's system to take hold. His main pupils, John Peckham and Matthew of Aquasparta, found themselves fighting rear-guard actions against the Averroists and against Aquinas. Before the dust of that struggle could settle, the battle lines had moved. The great Franciscans from the 1270s into the next century went far beyond Bonaventure: Peter John Olivi, Duns Scotus, Peter Aureoli, and William of Ockham.

Revolt of the Arts Faculty

The emergence of the Averroists at Paris was a direct consequence of importing the great commentaries on Aristotle from the Arab world. The transmission of cultural capital was more than an accidental intrusion; factions of Christian intellectuals had been seeking out new texts to fill the knowledge space opened by the growth of education. Can we say that they were seeking just this sort of text? The translators and the schools which sent them sought the prestige of ancient wisdom, that is to say, knowledge beyond the horizon of the existing Christian culture. Natural science was an appropriately neutral ground on which to expand in this way. And if the situation of intercultural contact in Spain had motivated Averroës to produce a new Aristotle and a new "religion of reason," there was also a structural slot in the Christian intellectual world two generations later which was prepared to exploit this product.

The newly formalized universities had four higher faculties—civil law, canon law, theology, and medicine—though not every university had all of these, and most universities were eminent in only one. Preparatory to these was the arts faculty, in which were taught the preliminary "undergraduate" studies—dialectic, mathematics, and metaphysics. These were the slots into which natural science expanded most readily. The universities where philosophy was most developed were those in which theology dominated the higher faculties, giving an especially abstract emphasis to its preparatory courses.[8]

As the university became increasingly regulated, the theology masters jealously guarded their turf against the arts masters, repeatedly legislating against mere philosophers teaching subjects belonging to theology. The prohibition did not easily hold. God could also be taken as a subject of philosophy (for instance, as the Unmoved Mover of Aristotle's system of astronomical spheres). On the other side, rational theology easily turned into abstract issues of philosophy, and most of the great philosophers, on into the 1300s, did at least part of their work while teaching theology.

The struggle which broke into the open in the 1270s is obscured in hindsight by the polemics which have survived, primarily those expressing the official position of the conservatives. The young radicals in the lower faculty are much less well known from the published record. At first, the very term "Averroist" was likely a hostile one imposed by their persecutors. The radicals, those who made the most extreme use of Aristotle and of "the Commentator," as Averroës was honorifically known, were the arts masters, above all at the preeminent university, Paris. Averroës's version of Aristotle, formulated in a Muslim world when theology was much more estranged from philosophical circles, was a kind of religion of the intellectuals. It held that scripture is a gross kind of metaphorical truth, sufficient only for the masses; and that pure philosophy is not just intellectually higher but itself the path to salvation. This was supported metaphysically by the doctrine of the Agent (or Active) Intellect, a sphere of Ideas which shapes the sublunar world, and in which the human intellect participates when it knows truth. For Averroës (and perhaps for some of his Parisian admirers) there is no individual immortality of the soul; each human soul is immortal only to the extent that it is filled with philosophical truth and directly participates in the larger Agent Intellect of the world. When in 1270, and more forcefully in 1277, Averroism was condemned by the church authorities, probably the touchstone among the long list of prohibited propositions was the one which maintained the unity of the Agent Intellect—the single world-soul in which all human souls participate.

Also condemned was the proposition that the highest happiness humans can know is philosophy, which is to say, rather than the Christian happiness of salvation. One of the few radicals who is known by name, Boethius of Dacia, wrote a prayer to the First Principle, discovered and contemplated by reason, the highest delectation of the soul. The religion of reason came into confrontation with Christian religion. Most famous, perhaps because the relative moderateness of his claims made him especially appealing, was Siger of Brabant, who would have been about 25 years old at the time when the controversy started in the 1260s. Siger was the public figurehead of the movement and the personal target of philosophical attacks.

The condemnation of 1277 was a concerted effort by conservatives of all camps. The most important secular theologian of the period, Henry of Ghent, was on the panel of Bishop Tempier of Paris which issued the condemnation of 219 theses. The Dominican Kilwardby, in his capacity as archbishop of Canterbury, issued much the same condemnation 11 days later, making the prohibition effective for Oxford as well. The Franciscan Peckham carried on the battle in the spirit of his master Bonaventure. The so-called "Averroism" of the 1260s and 1270s may well have been rather mild; nothing very radical made its way into the surviving texts. The condemnation made it into a symbol of opposition to conservative dogmatism, an emblem for the self-styled progressive faction. This faction continued to have an underground existence at Paris, and even more openly at other universities, especially in Italy over the next 200 years. Opposition outside the university became even more pointed. Intellectual life was becoming more cosmopolitan. Contact with the Muslim world was fading, but the rationalistic wing of the Jewish network had moved north, driven out of Spain in the atmosphere of increasing intolerance after the success of the reconquest in the early 1200s. Maimonidist Aristoteleans and Averroists found their niche primarily as translators in the Latin world. Jewish cosmopolitans (15, 16, 23, and 26 in Figure 9.5) active in southern France and in Italy may well have been the leaders in spreading a purer Averroism in the generations after the condemnation of Siger of Brabant.

As a philosophical doctrine within Christendom, Averroism was not particularly creative. It advocated a finished system of truth, already perfected in Aristotle (or, more precisely, in Averroës's interpretation of him). The Averroists became the structural equivalent of the Epicureans in the Greek networks, anchored in an extreme, and thus immune to new idea combinations emerging in the conflicts which made up the creativity of the network center.

The significance of the struggles at Paris lay not so much in the doctrine of the "Averroists," although they served as the catalyst, as in the rearrangement brought about in other intellectual factions. At first the counterattacks of the conservatives were too weak to do more than goad the conflict. The condemnation in 1270 of 15 propositions was evaded. The conservatives were infuriated, and charged the radicals with using transparent dodges, declaring that the Averroist themes were false opinions set forth for purposes of debate or by the doctrine of a double truth—that what is true in philosophy is not necessarily true in theology. The charges may well have been exaggerated, but the resistance was real.

By the time of the more sweeping condemnation of 1277, the circles of conflict had widened on all sides. Kilwardby and Peckham attacked Aquinas along with Siger, despite the fact that Aquinas himself had led the critique of the doctrine of double truth. For Kilwardby, the conflict was part of an internal struggle within the Dominicans; for the Franciscan Peckham, it was an opportunity to attack the rival Dominican order itself. Some of Aquinas's doctrines were themselves included in the 1277 condemnation, but within a few years

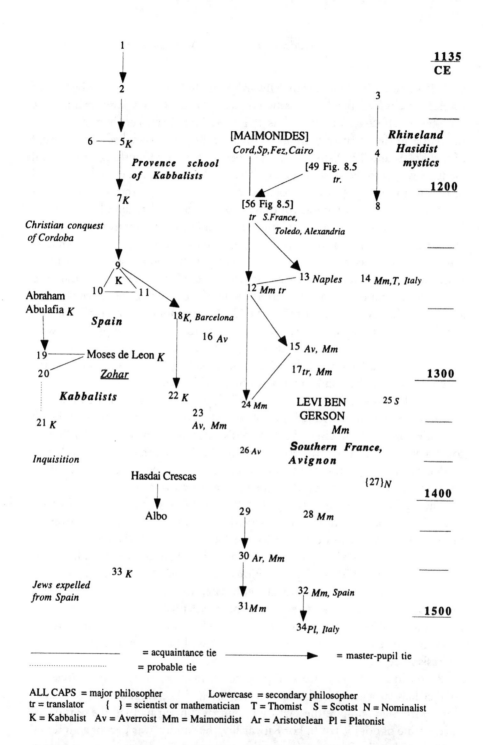

FIGURE 9.5. JEWISH PHILOSOPHERS WITHIN CHRISTENDOM,
1135–1535: MAIMONIDISTS, AVERROISTS, AND KABBALISTS

these had become obligatory doctrine for the Dominicans, prohibited texts for study among the Franciscans. After Aquinas's relatively early death in the midst of the struggle (indeed in the stress of his journey to Lyons, where he faced condemnation), his pupil Giles of Rome defended his doctrine in famous debates with Henry of Ghent.

The time was the beginning of reversal in the fortune of the papacy, and of its allies in church politics.[9] Not only were the Franciscans by far the biggest order, but by the end of the century, they had achieved virtually a lock on papal influence with a majority on the Roman Curia. But the papacy itself was overreaching in its claims of secular power over the kings, and the political tides were turning. The condemnation of 1277, going far beyond the Averroists to attack the other philosophical enemies of the dominant Franciscans, must have looked like an arrogant abuse of power by a faction no longer strong enough to carry it off. The precipitate of these realignments was the greatest round of medieval philosophy.[10]

Aquinas's Compromise

The greatness of Thomas Aquinas is as an intellectual politician. He was a man of moderation, going as far as possible with the new intellectual capital of the time, but sharply distinguishing himself from the radicals. It is not surprising that the church in centuries long past his time would lean increasingly upon him for its official doctrine in a world of secularism and science. Aquinas strikes the balance between science and theology, and he does it far on the side of reason and, as much as possible, of empiricism. Aquinas holds that each level of being has its mode of knowledge. Since humans are not angels (which are simultaneously pure forms, logical species, and Intelligences), we cannot directly apprehend the intelligible world of universals, as the "Averroists" claimed; instead humans must proceed by means of particulars. It is emblematic of Aquinas that he places man in the very middle of the metaphysical cosmos: highest of the material order, the human soul is just below the angels, which are the immaterial Ideas leading up to God.

Aquinas is the great systematizer of philosophical and theological doctrine. If there is a core to his doctrine, it concerns the nature of the human soul. This is, so to speak, not only the midpoint of the universe but also a key point of contention between Averroists and Augustinian traditionalists. Furthermore, Aquinas's conceptual strategy now ramifies into his arguments about the nature of God and into the rest of his system. For a traditionalist such as Bonaventure, matter is not corporeal only; incorporeals like angels are also individuals in matter, although they are also universal forms, following the classic Neoplatonic hierarchy. This doctrine makes it easy to prove that the human soul is immortal *as an individual*: it has a matter, quite apart from the intellect which cognizes universals, and also apart from the form of the human body. Thus there is no danger of falling into the Averroist position that only the intellectual part of the soul is immortal by absorption into the world-soul Agent Intellect; nor is there danger of implying that the soul dies with the body, as a form of that body.

Aquinas, however, directly courts these difficulties. For him, the soul is the form of the body—a traditional Aristotelean position. In hot debate against the Franciscan Peckham in 1270, he held that the sole principle of life and of intellect in man is the soul, thus making the body an integral part of human nature, not an inferior dross to be shed by the spiritual part. How then to avoid falling into the Averroist or materialist side? Aquinas's creative stroke is to attack a more fundamental metaphysical point: he overturns the accepted argument, which Bonaventure had taken from Avicenna, that *essence,* what a thing is, is a higher reality than *existence,* as if the fact of something's existing were merely an accident tacked onto its essence. This was a Platonic way of looking at the world, in which eternal essences come down from the spheres below God into the realm of mere temporal existence.

Aquinas reverses the situation: essence is merely potentiality, which becomes actual only by the act of existing. But here he goes against traditional Aristotelean views as well, since Aristotle had held that matter is potentiality, given actuality by form. Aquinas presses onward, rearranging these concepts: composite substances of the ordinary world are made up not only of matter and form, but of essence and existence as well. The essence of the human body, for instance, is a combination of matter and form; and both of these are actualized, drawn from the realm of mere potentiality, when they come into existence.

This became the rallying point of the Thomists, the doctrine of the unity of form in the composite. A composite essence is made up out of all the forms that are applicable (e.g., a man shares in the forms of human, rational, animal, etc.). This doctrine allows for full participation in the reality of the material world, and for sensory knowledge, while holding on to Christian doctrine of individual immortality and bodily resurrection. The cost, however, was to overthrow prevailing Platonist and Augustinian metaphysics and epistemology. Applied to God, Aquinas's concepts meant that God is a composite of Form and Act, not a Form of all forms, as in the Neoplatonic tradition carried on by Aquinas's own teacher, Albert. Nor is God preeminently the locus of Ideas, as in the Augustinian version defended by Bonaventure. Nor is God a mystical One beyond being, since Aquinas argues that One is only a division of being.

Aquinas's compromise, together with the weight of Aristotelean thinking in both heretical and nonheretical guises, completely reconstructed the premises of philosophical argument. The Franciscans were particularly badly hit, since Bonaventure's grand system was now unacceptable and in need of replacement. Something was needed to fill the gap: this turned out to be the ultra-system of Duns Scotus.

Duns Scotus and the Franciscan Counterattack

Consider the overall condition of the intellectual field in the generations around 1300. There was a remarkable richness of positions. The basic cultural capital of the field was being broken apart once again; sizable new pieces were added to the pool by contentious reflection, and there were great opportunities for creative recombination. Conservatives as well as explicit reformers shared in the riches. Henry of Ghent reacted against Aquinas and his followers by rejecting the primacy of existence and stressing that God possesses Ideas—essences—before Creation. In order not to reduce God to the level of Ideas, Henry described God as yet a further level of essence, the *esse essential*. To avoid individuation by matter, Henry analyzed individuation as double negation: the negation of all differences within itself, and the negation of identity with all others. Henry even incorporated the Muslims into his position, declaring that Augustine's concept of the divine illumination of the soul is the same as Avicenna's Agent Intellect (Gilson, 1944: 430). But this creative defense of traditionalism merely provided a tempting target for Duns Scotus's attack.

There is little doubt that Duns Scotus was groomed by the Franciscans to be their champion in restoring the philosophical eminence of their order. Though born in remote Scotland, he was picked up by the organization from an early age and given plenty of attention and encouragement; when he showed growing intellectual powers, he was sent to the centers of controversy and set the major intellectual tasks of the day.[11] Much as Thomas Aquinas had been ordered to the trouble spots of intellectual life as spokesman for the Dominicans 30 years earlier, Duns was delegated to do battle for the Franciscans: restoring their prestige at Paris (Oxford remaining by and large a Franciscan stronghold), and even invading the Dominicans' own stronghold at Cologne.

Given the sociological principle that creativity takes place along lines of maximal opposition within the current level of abstraction in the intellectual field, what might we predict that the champion of the Franciscans would do? The battlefield is no longer the same as that on which Aquinas maneuvered between Averroists and Augustinians; the nature of the soul and its immortality is no longer a key point. Instead the highest prestige must be on the terrain of the new metaphysical doctrines Aquinas had introduced as weapons for his struggle. The impressive thing, however, is not to turn back the clock, rejecting Aquinas's concepts in the name of reasserting Augustine and Bonaventure;

Henry of Ghent, outside Franciscan ranks, already took that tack. Duns Scotus instead now attacks both sides. He seeks for doctrines giving maximal points of distinctness, and overturns not only old Neoplatonism and Augustinianism, but new Aristoteleanism as well. When Duns Scotus is through, the terrain of the intellectual field has been revolutionized as never before.

In epistemology, Aquinas and the Aristoteleans gave primacy to sensory knowledge of particulars: the human intellect most easily knows the essences of material things. For Henry of Ghent, following the Augustinian tradition, the prime object of the intellect is God, who gives knowledge by illumination of the divine Forms. Duns attacks both doctrines. What the human intellect knows most immediately and certainly is *being,* the absolutely unqualified, fundamental concept without which one could not think at all. Furthermore, being is univocal; it is behind all distinctions among modes of being. Duns cleverly establishes this with an argument about doubt: we can conceive of being even if we are doubtful whether it is being in itself or being in another thing (i.e., whether it is existential assertion or predication, the logical copula). Duns undercuts here the Avicennean distinction between existence and essence, which had become conventional among Christian scholastics.

Since being is the most primitive concept, he maintains, it is from being that we must start if we wish to prove the existence of God, or even to speak about him. Moreover, a science cannot prove its basic principles but rather begins with them; hence it is because the highest object of metaphysics is not God but being that we can prove the existence of God through metaphysics. Being is an absolutely transcendent concept, common to both the infinite and the finite, to God and to creatures, to substance and accidents, matter and form. Duns reorganizes the entire scholastic tradition, which had awarded primacy to one or the other wing of these dichotomies.

Starting from being, Duns is able to state a proof of God which avoids depending on the empirical existence of contingent facts, that is, the kind of proof that Aquinas had used in starting from causality, movement, or order in the sensory world. Duns instead adopts a version of Anselm's strategy. Let us suppose that an ultimate or highest cause of the world does not exist; what could cause it not to exist? This would be self-contradictory, since the ultimate cause by definition has no cause; hence it is impossible that the uncaused cause should not exist. It is also impossible to infer the existence of contingent beings—of the ordinary world—from the existence of God. There is, in other words, no necessity why God should have created the world. The route of Neoplatonic emanation is thus cut off, and so is any route which posits eternal Forms in God. Although God is necessary, the world is logically unfounded. The world must be a miracle, to be seen with much the same awe as in naive holy scripture.

Having overturned both the Platonic-Augustinian epistemologies and their links to theology, Duns presses his attack on the principles of individuation. This had been one of the main areas of controversy and innovation in the previous generation. Aquinas, overturning Platonic Forms and Bonaventure's spiritual matter, had given matter as the principle of individuation. Henry of Ghent—for whom universal Forms are the higher reality—had held that individuation is nothing in itself but consists in a web of negations. Duns again attacks them both. Matter, he holds, is neither Aristotelean potentiality nor merely part of a composite of forms, as Thomas had held; rather matter has its own actuality and could exist without any form at all. That is to say, it is not logically contradictory that God could create matter without form. Matter is real; therefore it cannot be merely the principle of individuation of forms.

Duns arrives at a similar conclusion against Henry, for whom universal Forms are the true realities and individuation merely negation. But the essence of a thing is neither a universal nor a particular; all horses have a common nature, which we can call "horseness," but distinctions of universal and particular do not arise in "horseness" in itself. Parallel to what Duns says about being, essence is univocal with respect to universality and particularity. The universal is the way the common nature of a class of things is apprehended in the mind; ideas are part of the realm of the intellect, and are founded in the common nature of things, but they are not things, nor even the constituting principle of things. Duns here is drastically repudiating the Platonic heritage of Forms. For "horseness" in general to be the "horseness" of *this* particular horse, there must be another metaphysical condition. Duns calls it *haecceitas,* "this-ness" (Latin: *haec,* "this").

It is, so to speak, the principle of individuation. But to call it a principle does not capture the force of Duns's conception. It is the opposite of Henry of Ghent's claim that particularity is a mere aspect of negation in a world composed of universals. *This* is immediately real, and that, and *that.* The world is radically particular in a sense far beyond Aquinas's world of forms individuated by matter. It is this vision of Duns Scotus that made him admired by modern existentialists such as Martin Heidegger: *haecceitas* is like *Dasein,* radical contingency of existence in the here-and-now, the being which is never captured by abstractions. Propelled by opposition to the surrounding intellectual field, Duns arrived at a radical break with the entire Greek tradition; we find its nearest counterpart in distant traditions, above all in Buddhist mysticism. The Madhyamika Buddists (particularly Nagarjuna) had much the same term, *tathata,* "thus-ness" (Sanskrit: *tat,* "that"), the reality that the meditator seeks when overturning attachment to name-and-form. The paradoxes of the Ch'an meditators, attacking the inadequacy of words, were directed toward this experience.

Duns is not a mystic. He did not arrive at *haecceitas* as the result of meditation or the attempt to explain what the meditation experience might be about. His train of argument comes from contentions within the highly rationalistic intellectual community of his time. In Duns's *haecceitas,* this community argues itself beyond its own deepest premises. From now on it has two possible frontiers of transcendence, God and immediate reality: possible frontiers, because the struggles of the intellectual field did not immediately push upon both of them.

Duns overturns the hierarchical conception of the cosmos which had prevailed for centuries. The Neoplatonic hierarchy of concepts and realities, as well as Aristotelean levels of generality, are ordered according to their degrees of universality. But Duns declares that universals are merely a way that humans think because of the imperfection of their cognitions. If one could know the *haecceitas* of all things, one would have all possible knowledge of reality—although this is impossible for a merely human intellect in its present condition, and presumably only God can know everything in this way. This position is the extreme opposite from that of the Muslim philosophers, for instance Avicenna, who held that God knows only through universals, not stooping to particulars in their contingency (Leaman, 1985: 112).

The world is not only radically particular; it is much more a realm of will than of intellect. Thomas Aquinas had made the human intellect relatively passive, guided by reason. He cleverly saved the doctrine of free will by arguing that although one always acts toward what one conceives to be good, one does not necessarily judge things very clearly, and hence one exercises freedom of choice. Duns is more radical. The *haecceitas* of a person is, so to speak, centered on that person's will; what ideas one has is also fundamentally a matter of one's volition. Duns does not push this doctrine into a glorification of irrationalism; God acts consistently and not illogically. But God did not have to create the world out of any necessity or reason. Duns's universe seems rather existentialist. God is logically remote, separated by a gulf from the world; the fundamental reality, both high and low, is volition and *haecceitas,* the contingent particular force of the way things happen to be.

Duns Scotus indeed provided the Franciscans with a champion. But although his doctrine gave rise to a movement of dedicated Scotists, counterposing the spread of the Thomists both within the Dominican order and beyond, the intellectual outcome was unstable. Duns had again radically rearranged the cultural capital of the field; among the Franciscans themselves as well as outside their ranks, the more radical implications were soon taken much further. It appears that many thinkers jumped at the opportunity, though the credit and the designation of leadership were given to William of Ockham. At the same time came a reaction in the other direction, salvaging the most extreme elements of Neoplatonism, in the form of a purified mysticism. On this front the fame went to the Dominican Eckhart.

The Breakup of Theological Philosophy

William of Ockham personifies the field of Christian philosophy-cum-theology coming apart. Although he came from within the Franciscans,[12] Ockham lumped Duns Scotus with his predecessors and antagonists—Aquinas, Bonaventure, and all the rest—into what became known as the "via antiqua." Ockham by contrast exemplifies the "via moderna." The Franciscans, the biggest and strongest order, could afford the most internal diversity.

There were numerous other creative positions at the turn of the century, working out the metaphysics of essence and existence, act and form, composite and unity: Thomas Sutton, Giles of Rome, Godfrey of Fontaines, Giles of Orleans, Hervé Nedellec, Dietrich of Freiberg, Peter John Olivi, Richard of Middleton, and Raymond Lull before the turn of the century; Durand of St. Pourçain, Peter Aureoli, Henry Harclay, Walter Chatton, and Eckhart shortly after. Most fall into the shadows beside Scotus and Ockham. There were too many creative positions for all of them to become recognized, and they squeezed one another out of the possibilities for propagating their ideas. They all worked on the same intellectual space; all had grand visions of God, Ideas, angels, forms, souls, material things, the nature of knowledge and the modes of being. They resemble the generation of 400–365 B.C.E. in Greece, with its superabundant energy forming new schools, most of which were fated not to survive. At Paris, little attention was given to the weird character Raymond Lull, a kind of wandering showman with his "Great Art," a grid of boxes generated by combining items from a list of fundamental elements of the universe. In its combinations all things of heaven and earth are contained. This was both a universal metaphysics and a grand mnemonic device for dealing with intellectual chaos. A self-educated nobleman from Majorca on the fringes of the action in Muslim Spain, Lull came from too far away at the periphery to have more than an outsider's sense of the intellectual world, and his device was ignored, though later revived in the Renaissance. In relation to the overcrowding of the medieval attention space, Lull's "Art" is emblematic of the actual social condition.

Ockham, the most successful of the critics, worked a strategic synthesis between the anti-religious critics of theology and the extremists of the opposite end, the anti-philosophical fideist theologians. He almost explicitly aimed, by eliminating superfluous metaphysical entities, to simplify what had become an extremely complicated intellectual field. Ockham's so-called "razor" was not original to him. In the previous generation a fellow Franciscan, Peter John

Olivi, in the fray against the Aristoteleans had declared that "entities are not unnecessarily multiplied," and argued that from the multiplicity of concepts one cannot deduce the multiplicity of beings (*EP*, 1967: 5:536–537). And Ockham's Franciscan contemporary Peter Aureoli, in the thick of debate with Thomists and ambivalent toward Duns Scotus, also argued that the constitutive elements of things are to be limited. Aureoli's epistemology held that universal concepts have psychological reality but no objective grounds; knowledge of individuals is preferable because of its clarity. Ockham represents a movement in formation, reaping the fame and putting the others in his shadow—the usual consequence of the law of small numbers. If Ockham was especially radical, it was because he used the "razor" most ruthlessly to get rid of metaphysical essences as well as other abstractions that had proliferated within the dense networks of the field.

Ockham's strategic stroke is to carry out this destruction while creating a new turf on which intellectuals can work. By classifying acts of language, Ockham points the way to a new field of logic. He breaks out of the old Porphyrian-Aristotelean hierarchy of forms and classification of syllogisms, opening up considerations of the logic of possibilities, conditionals, and other innovative topics. This constitutes a structural break in the organization of intellectual life. For these topics in logic can now be pursued as specialties, whereas the Porphyrian logical hierarchy was part of an overarching metaphysical system.

Ockham lays down that propositions are composed of terms, and these have meaning only when they signify, that is, when there is an object for which they substitute within the proposition. Words carry three main types of representation: other words, concepts, and things. Ockham concentrates his attack on universal concepts. No one ever observes an essence; what they think they observe always coincides with a particular thing. Ockham asserts that a concept is only a confused, indistinct way of referring to individuals, as a near-sighted person looks at objects far away blurs them together; universal concepts are merely terms which we use when we cannot pick out the actual thing we are talking about. Accordingly God, who has perfect perception, has no ideas but can see everything in its particularity. One can find here an echo of Duns's God, who can perceive every *haecceitas*.

In many ways Ockham is a radicalization of Duns, but ruthlessly pruned of metaphysical abstraction. Like Duns, Ockham stresses primacy of the will but takes it to more radical conclusions. Since there are no universal essences, nothing impedes God from making the world in any fashion at all, and nothing impedes him from changing it by a miracle or destroying it at any moment. The moral good is good solely because it is God's will; God could make stealing or adultery right if he willed it. Other thinkers such as Mirecourt were to press this line of argument into what seemed almost blasphemous examples: God did not have to become incarnated as a man, Jesus Christ; he could just have well chosen to be incarnated as an ass, or a stone.

Ockham lets loose conservative anti-rationalism and mysticism on one side, radical empiricism on the other, and a technical logic in yet another direction. He goes along with the conservative demand to keep theology safe from the invasions of the philosophers. The realm of theology is miraculous; Ockham also concludes that the order of nature must always be investigated in concrete cases, since a priori reason conveys nothing, and any general principles could be overturned by God's miraculous intervention. In effect, Ockham has turned back the clock to the struggle between Abelard's sophisticated nominalist logic and Saint Bernard's anti-rational faith. Since the intervening generations had built up an enormous middle ground of metaphysical realism, Ockham's revolution consists in combining the old enemies into a single position.

The Arts Faculty and the Nominalist Movement

It is tempting to portray a "nominalist movement" springing up in rebellion against the metaphysical establishment, progressive thinkers unified around empiricism and taking many steps toward the eventual dominance of natural science. But William of Ockham himself has few personal pupils of significance, and his network soon peters out. Although there were henceforward many "nominalists" and even "Ockhamists," these labels are loosely applied to a rather decentralized and intellectually diverse set of thinkers. Often these are terms of abuse, bestowing unity only through the ill will of opponents.

This at least gives us a clue to the structural situation. After 1300 intellectual life was rapidly moving toward factional orthodoxy. The Dominicans had made Aquinas their compulsory theology in 1309; the Augustinians and the Cistercians about this time also joined the Thomist camp, the latter through the teachings of Giles of Rome (Geyer, 1928: 549). The Franciscans in response prohibited the reading of Aquinas in their order. Thomas Aquinas was sainted in 1323 with the support of several orders. The Franciscans were unable to have Duns Scotus canonized despite repeated efforts, in part because of internal splits, but a self-conscious Scotist movement grew up in rivalry to the Thomists and zealously defended its turf in the universities (de Wulf, 1934–1947: 3:214–215).

What constituted a "nominalist" opposition was the residual category outside these rival orthodoxies, where free-floating innovation still went on. This category included, first of all, true "nominalists," specialists in developing Ockhamist logic. Also lumped in were a second faction, the Averroists. In the form of a "religion of reason" Averroism was not in itself forward-looking and innovative, and its Aristoteleanism was on the other side of the divide from the radical metaphysics of the Ockhamists or even the Scotists. Nevertheless, Averroism flourished in a broader oppositional front, especially in the anti-papal territories of northern Italy under protection of the emperor, where they penetrated the university faculties of law and of medicine (see 172, 178, 179, 216, 264–266 in Figures 9.4 through 9.6).[13] Third, we may mention a critical tendency in general, especially oriented toward overturning Aristoteleanism in philosophy and natural science. The most extreme of the critical philosophers were Mirecourt and Autrecourt, who overlapped with the Paris network around Buridan specializing in natural science. A counterpart groups existed at Oxford, centered on the Merton College "calculators." Here the "nominalist" label is stretched beyond the breaking point, for these critical innovators included anti-nominalists such as Bradwardine and Burley.

What the so-called nominalist opposition had in common was a feature of internal university structure. We may take as emblematic the fact that William of Ockham never acquired a higher degree as Doctor of Theology; his radical work done as a Master of Arts was already enough to have him called to answer heresy charges at Avignon, cutting off his university career. William fled to protection at the court of the emperor in Bavaria, where he turned to writing defenses of the secular state against the church. His companions in exile and fellow ideologists of anti-papal secularism, Jean of Jandun and Marsilius of Padua, were also arts masters, both former rectors at Paris, elected by the masters of the arts faculty. Thomists and Scotists represented the university power structure oriented externally to papal politics, for which philosophy was subordinate to a reasoned theology. The oppositional front consisted of those who specialized in the subjects of the arts: logic, mathematics, natural philosophy. Although Ockham himself wrote on theology as well, he was asserting the primacy of his logical methods over the procedures of the chair-holding theologians. Most subsequent nominalists pursued their own specialties; this is true too of the Italian Averroists, the Parisian and Mertonian scientists, and the rest of the "opposition." What they have in common is that their intellectual orientation was toward the arts faculty and its topics. Buridan, for example, apparently remained a Master of Arts his entire career (*DSB*, 1981: 2:603). The struggle between theologians and philosophers, once so creative, now was ending in divorce.

The emphasis on logic and natural science was not original to nominalism. Science, or natural philosophy, had been the common ground of virtually all philosophical positions for generations. Most of the major philosophers had written in this area: Grosseteste, Albert, Bacon, but also Bonaventure, Aquinas, Henry of Ghent, Duns Scotus, even conservatives such as Peckham (*DSB*, 1981: 10:473–476). After 1252 the Paris arts faculty added to the trivium and

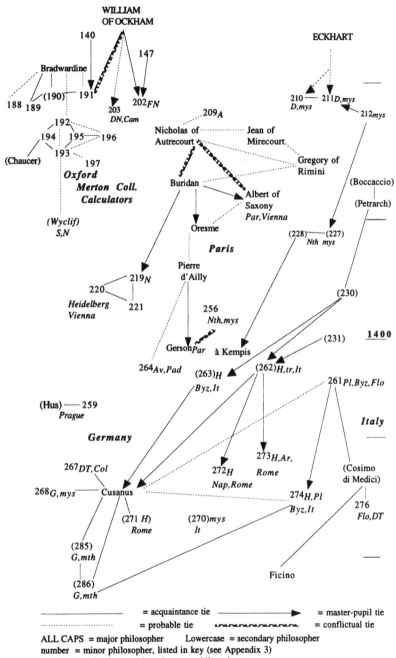

FIGURE 9.6. SCHOLASTICS, MYSTICS, HUMANISTS, 1335–1465

quadrivium three more required sciences, based on Aristotle's texts in natural philosophy, metaphysics, and moral philosophy (*CHLMP,* 1982: 521–523). Logic and natural philosophy, above all Aristotle's *Physics,* became the core of the arts studies, the major subject of lectures and disputations among the younger students and masters, and also a magnet of attention for the theologians.

This wide concern with natural science continued after Duns's death in 1308. The nominalists of course were involved, but so were anti-nominalists such as Burley and Bradwardine, and Scotists such as Francis of Meyronnes (*DSB,* 1981: 5:115–116). What had shifted was that such topics were much closer to monopolizing the focus of philosophy, as its theological border was being willfully depopulated. Intellectuals now were concentrating on the most autonomous areas of the arts curriculum.

It has been stressed (Grant, in *CHLMP,* 1982; Blumenberg, 1985) that the condemnation of 1277 had paved the way for nominalism, and for the independence of natural science from theology, by mandating that no restrictions be placed on the omnipotence of God. In effect, this meant the end of rational theology, and of theologized philosophy, leaving the two segments to go their own ways. Nevertheless, the events of 1277 were no arbitrary turning point. The conservatives who engineered the condemnations faded away; and indeed the positions they condemned, including both Averroism and Aquinas's measured Aristoteleanism, remained as examples of unified rational theology-cum-metaphysics. It is, rather, that the balance point of the conflicts shifted, so that now Aquinas became the "right wing," the bedrock of the conservative position. Although there was a widespread Thomist faction in the 1300s, it was confined to minor figures (see key to Figures 9.4 and 9.5) with none of the innovative prestige of the Scotists and especially the nominalist critics. The extremes of the intellectual spectrum—Thomist orthodoxy at one end, Averroist heresy and anti-papalism at the other—became its static anchors; dynamism shifted to the realigning camps of the organizationally uncommitted. It was these contentions which carried some implications of the 1277 condemnations to highly unorthodox results. The arbitrariness of theology vis-à-vis the world was now used to break apart the unified hierarchical cosmology that had been shared by both old Neoplatonists and Aristoteleans. The attack on Aristotle's physics and metaphysics, itself permeated by astronomy, became the turf on which intellectual contests were now fought.

The Paris Network and the Oxford Calculators

Church authorities in Paris by 1340 were condemning unnamed groups of students and young masters who were gathering privately to read banned texts such as Ockham and Marsilius of Padua. Marsilius and Jean of Jandun had been Paris masters from the 1310s through their exile in the mid-1320s, and in the same decade Nicolas of Autrecourt and Gregory of Rimini were students. Ockham's Oxford opponent Walter of Burley was also present as theology master. Undoubtedly there was overlap among these circles, keeping up a continuity of controversies that burst out into the extreme radicalism of Autrecourt and Mirecourt.

Jean of Mirecourt, a Cistercian monk (and thus outside the main factions of Franciscans and Dominicans) specialized in drawing out shocking consequences of the critical movement. God could make it that the world had never existed. God could cause a man to hate Him, and could even have misled Christ. There is no certainty except that which is based on the principle of resisting self-contradiction. All other evidence is from experience, and only experience of one's own existence is certain; to doubt it is to recognize the existence of the doubter, thereby passing the contradiction test. Mirecourt's argument echoes Augustine and foreshadows Descartes's cogito, but he has none of Descartes's system-founding purpose. Mirecourt instead reduces knowledge to a minimum. He would go on to conclude that between the self and external things, there is no ground for intermediaries; substance and accident are alike fictions.

Autrecourt used a similar criterion of evidence, foreshadowing Hume, arguing that there is no line which unites cause and effect. Since substance, whether material or intellectual, involves a specific kind of causal inference used to explain the properties of events, substances do not exist. Autrecourt expressly overthrew Aristotelean physics as well as metaphysics. Here we see the anti-Aristotelean front at its most militant. Ockham in his 1317–18 Oxford lectures had already criticized Aristotle's physics, using his razor to dispose of motion as an existent over and above the moving body (*CHLMP,* 1982: 530). Ockham had debated with Burley's refined realist theory that motion is a succession of distinct forms. Autrecourt pressed this very point. Since movement and change are not the succession of different forms in the same substance, they must be a rearrangement of atoms. Nor was this atomism entirely original, as it had been proposed in the previous generation by Henry of Harclay (141 in Figure 9.4), Ockham's close predecessor; by Gerard of Odo, the Franciscan General (148), and by Walter Chatton (147)—that is, in the heart of the Paris-Oxford-Avignon network (*EP,* 1967: 5:497–502; *DSB,* 2:394). Autrecourt took the argument to shocking extremes, going on to speculate that since the human soul is liberated when the atoms of the body disintegrate, the soul leaves and becomes reunited with another body. Autrecourt thus managed to be both a radical skeptic and a believer in reincarnation.

Not surprisingly, Autrecourt was condemned and forced to burn his books in front of the University of Paris in 1347. In the same year Mirecourt's theses also were condemned. The conflictual situation generated further creativity, provoking more moderate efforts to fill the disputed space of Aristotelean physics. Jean Buridan, rector twice during this period, was among the university officials who approved the condemnations. He argued against Autrecourt's skepticism of causality, preserving a space for the validity of scientific generalizations. Explicitly using Ockham's logic of terms, Buridan distinguished between concepts of concepts and concepts of the first degree: the latter apply to individuals and are the subject of science. Having licensed a moderated empiricism, liberated from Aristotelean substance and teleology, Buridan and his pupils went on to re-create the principles of physics, developing a theory of the impetus of moving objects. Nicolas Oresme recognized the phenomenon of uniformly accelerated movement, and appears to have anticipated Descartes's mathematical representation of motion by rectangular coordinates. Albert of Saxony expounded the theory that gravity is an attraction from the center of earth's mass rather than a natural propensity of objects, and applied the impetus theory to celestial motion. These theories overturned the Aristotelean physics and cosmology, eliminating the motors attached to celestial spheres, and anticipated Copernican astronomy by holding the movement of the earth to be possible.

These philosophers were respectable; Buridan was honored and became rich accumulating benefices. Their theses were not condemned. But neither were they followed. Buridan's network stopped in the second generation and dispersed. Some moved to the new universities at Vienna and Heidelberg, but the creativity of these lineages went no further. The moment of conflict between the extremes of nominalist criticism and the now-canonical Aristoteleanism passed, and with it the creativity of the intermediate position was forgotten.

Paralleling these generations in France was the network of creative controversy at Oxford from which Scotus and Ockham had emerged. It had cosmopolitan contacts across the channel, primarily at Paris, later at Avignon and in the south: Harclay, Chatton, Burley (191 in Figure 9.6), and Bradwardine moved in the normal academic circles and also sometimes were emissaries or courtiers of the English king, then involved in a series of French wars. Burley defended the realism of universals against Ockham, and disputed the logical status of time-instants in the physics of motion. Harclay and Chatton, on the "nominalist" side, put forward atomism—the position which Autrecourt was to take to such radical extremes in Paris. Bradwardine was goaded into action by his English compatriots to defend Aristotle's physical continuum, showing that it cannot be composed of indivisibles; Bradwardine used a Euclid-like axiomatic method to show the contradictions between non-extended points (i.e., atoms) and geometric theorems. Under pressure from the radicals, Aristotle was now being creatively used by the conservative camp.

A group centered on Balliol and Merton colleges carried these ingredients to more refined conclusions: William of Heytesbury (192 in Figure 9.6), Richard Swineshead (193), Richard Billingham (195), Richard Kilvington (189), John Dumbleton (196), and others. Many of them were nominalists in the strict sense, working out technical advances based on Ockham's logic; they also generalized Bradwardine's mathematical functions for uniformly accelerated motion and expanded his physics. More specialized than the generation of Bradwardine, Burley, and Ockham, they stayed away from the controversies of theology. Bradwardine in his later years did the opposite, perhaps because of his visits to Paris with the king, where he would have encountered the radicalism of Autrecourt's circle. Bradwardine attacked the Ockhamists as "Pelagians" for their emphasis on free will, while he himself fell back on realist doctrines of cause to assert God's deterministic qualities. Oxford was no closed school of nominalists but a network in creative tension.[14] The Merton calculators were friends of "new thinkers" in other realms as well, such as the poet Chaucer. The most famous product of the Balliol-Merton axis, at the end of the 1300s as the calculators had faded, was the theologian Wyclif, a Scotist and extreme realist, theological follower of Bradwardine, and inspiration for the proto-Protestant heresy of John Hus.

The Balliol-Merton calculators exemplify the concentration on the topics of the arts curriculum which was the key to the creativity of this period. At the same time, this was one of the limitations on their influence. Much of their work was meant for disputations of advanced undergraduates, rather than for the purpose of making discoveries in natural philosophy (Sylla, in *CHLMP*, 1982: 540–563). They did not make theoretical physics independent of academic logic or philosophy, but emphasized imaginary cases as aids in preparing for scholastic arguments. If there was no connection to empirical research, neither was the connection to mathematics taken very far. Burley and Kilvington rarely calculated; Bradwardine and Heytesbury typically surveyed mathematical possibilities but gave only a general indication of results. This work culminated in Swineshead's *Liber Calculationum* (ca. 1350), which treats physics problems through verbal reasoning about relationships among variables but contains little actual numerical analysis (*DSB*, 1981: 13:184–213). (Similarly among the Parisian group, Oresme's "Cartesian coordinates" were described but apparently not actually used for mathematical constructions.) This work was later admired by mathematicians such as Cardano and Leibniz for its achievements beyond the level of the Greeks; yet the Humanists of the next century saw in it nothing but involuted reasoning on scholastic exercises and dismissed it as barbaric. The Oxford calculators could be recognized retrospectively once a more broadly organized science had been created; we find in them a calculating approach to theory, but without organized research or a mathematical technique, and without the social supports that later upheld these. The "calculators" had a narrower base—the interest in currently fashionable disputes around the nominalist movement. As the intensity of this argument faded, their creativity rather abruptly came to an end.

Growth of Independent Mysticism

At this time when the specialized philosophy of the arts subjects was separating from theology, there was a corresponding tendency for theology to break free of philosophy into mysticism. We must be careful to distinguish this mysticism from fideism, as well as from transcendentally oriented metaphysics in general. It is not helpful to refer to every assertion that faith is superior to reasoning as "mysticism," or to make the term equivalent to "mysteries." A religion does not necessarily call for mysticism as a direct experience by individuals. The path to what is considered "salvation" could consist entirely of scripturally prescribed rituals; even when these are carried out not just collectively but individually in the form of personal prayer, the internal experience does not necessarily have to be interpreted as a direct vision of God; it could just as well be "soul-searching" to examine one's faith and moral commitments. Mystical experience cuts in a different direction, an immediate experience of the divine in which one loses self and the ordinary world, including scripture and ritual. Mysticism tends to come in conflict with the church hierarchy and with a ritually oriented community. For this reason, mysticism creates discipline problems for a centralized church, manifested on the doctrinal front in heresy disputes. Mysticism flourishes best where religion is organized by independent entrepreneurs, whether these are individuals, ad hoc movements like the Sufis, or independent monasteries of the sort found in Ch'an Buddhism.

All religious rituals and symbols, however, tend to give glimpses of this kind of direct experience, which the church organization can acknowledge and call on for legitimation. Medieval Christianity always included some aspects of mysticism in this sense. The emphasis on direct religious experience was strengthened when there was opposition to rational philosophy and academic life. Thus Saint Bernard was sometimes regarded as a mystic, although his emphasis on religious experience is tightly connected to moral attitudes and exercises; similarly Saint Francis remained doctrinally orthodox, and his movement—like Bernard's, oriented toward activism more than contemplation—remained part of the conventional church. From here it was not much of a step to integrate the idea of mystical experience into a fully academic philosophy. Hugh and his followers at St. Victor in the generations following Bernard added this as a supreme stage in a progression of knowledge, and Bonaventure built a metaphysical system around it. Neoplatonic philosophy, from Eriugena to Albertus Magnus, was essentially a hierarchical metaphysics with mystical experience as the category from which all other levels emanate. Thus mystical elements could be integrated into either conventional scripture and ritual or a purely intellectual system; in neither case was there any necessary emphasis on the practice of direct personal experience, on rejecting official doctrines, or on moving outside the conventional organization of the church.

After 1300, mysticism emerged in a stronger sense, becoming anti-philosophical as well as organizationally independent. Such mysticism tends to take itself out of the orbit of philosophy. We notice it here because there was a creative high point just when the transition occurred, for it is by the tools of philosophy that philosophy effaces itself. Meister Eckhart, from the lineage of Albert the Great and his pupil Dietrich of Freiberg, was active at Paris and Cologne at the time of Scotus. Eckhart took the opposite line from Duns: existence does not apply to God as to creatures; rather God is pure essence, virtually above being. Just as Aristotle had said that the faculty of vision is without color in order that it may see all colors, Eckhart put it that God has no Being, in order to cause all being (Gilson, 1944: 696). This highest essence, like the Platonic idea of the One, must be pure unity, which Eckhart regards as the pure *intelligere*, Intellect. This is far above immaterial things or Forms, since these are multiple rather than one, and above material things, since they are composites of matter and form. But there is an inner connection from the creature to God. God is so high, so transcendent, that one can say nothing about his divine unity; a creature is so low that it is also nothing, so to speak, nothing in itself. Thus the citadel of the soul contains a divine "spark," whereby the human being is no longer distinguished from God. From this spark there is a Plotinus-like flow backwards from the creature to God, a return into the One.

Eckhart does not seem to have been a meditative mystic, but he argued himself into a mystical position by the logic of oppositions within the intellectual field. As we have seen in the origins of Buddhism, meditative experience in itself is susceptible to interpretation in all sorts of ways; the specifically mystical interpretation always depends on a heritage of philosophical ideas. Thus it is not surprising that the real meditative mystics of the later Middle Ages began directly from this network. Tauler and Suso, although they were preachers and not professors, were pupils (certain or likely) of Eckhart and of the other followers of Albert at Cologne (210 and 211 in Figure 9.6). But the mysticism now established as a tradition broke free from the universities. These were not academic theologians, and indeed they tended to come into conflict with official theology because of their independence. Structurally as well as doctrinally the mystics become the negative counterpart of the nominalists based in the most insulated academic faculty of the universities.

The most influential mystics established their own lines of organization. Jan van Ruysbroeck, a preacher without formal training in theology, and of imperfect Latin, was influenced by Eckhart's writings and established a devotional community in Holland in 1343. His colleague Gerard Groote later in the century organized the Brethren of the Common Life. Although its raison d'être was devotions, it became a house of studies turning out some famous pupils: Thomas à Kempis, whose *Imitation of Christ,* circulated from 1422 by the copyists of the Brethren, was the most popular devotional book of the period; then in successive generations a series of notable scholars, including Cusanus, the nominalist systematizer Biel (300 in the key to Figure 9.7), and Erasmus. The period was also rich in practicing mystics of a non-intellectual type (e.g., 168, 184a, 269, 270, 288); some of these became saints through their devotions, from Saint Catherine of Siena (229), down through the ascetic reformer Saint Teresa of Avila and her circle in the late 1500s.

Notice a parallel in Islamic intellectual life. After the creative philosophical networks disintegrated (after al-Ghazali in the east, Ibn Rushd in Spain), activity was increasingly dominated by Sufi mystics. Ibn 'Arabi, who emerged directly from Ibn Rushd's orbit, was the most systematic combination of mysticism and philosophy, a parallel to Eckhart at the point of transition. There is an organizational reason for this parallel development: mysticism thrives on decentralization. Jewish philosophy provides a confirming instance.

The networks of Jewish rationalistic philosophy in Spain had peaked during their overlap with Islamic and Christian networks. In the late 1100s this cosmopolitan network broke up as the political situation polarized between the fundamentalist Almohad invasion from North Africa, then the Christian reconquest. Religious particularism and intolerance intensified. Jewish cosmopolitans migrated north and were absorbed into the movements of their Christian counterparts. Within the Talmudic academies, Maimonides's Aristotelianism was repudiated in favor of defending the distinctness of Judaism against Christianity. Doctrines were revived from the period of Jewish Gnosticism, interpreting traditional texts as esoteric symbols of cosmic correspondences and prophecies (Scholem, 1946, 1990). In Provence and Catalonia, spanning the Pyrenees, regions of the Catharist movement and Christian heresy-hunting, a network of rabbinical scholars in the late 1100s began to produce Kabbalist texts. These were successors to the network propagated most widely in Spain, a region of growing religious persecution. The Neoplatonism of the cosmopolitan trans-religious period gave way to an esoteric defense of Judaism. In the late 1200s the most popular texts of the Kabbalah appeared, interpreting prophecy as a mystical union with God, and teaching breathing techniques to induce the experience (Scholem, 1946: 139, 203). The *Zohar* was written to combat the rationalism of educated Jews; its watchword is "back to the Torah," interpreted as a secret code; meditative ecstasy for the elect is broadened into a theosophy for the Jewish masses (see Figure 9.5).

In the context of increasing ghettoization and persecution of the Jews, mysticism shifted from personal experience toward political and sometimes apocalyptic prophecy. In this respect Jewish mysticism was closer to Islamic mystical orders, which frequently took on a political motivation, whereas the greater organizational strength of the Christian Church kept its mysticism centered on private devotions, watchfully guarded against heretical implications. After 1400, as the strength of the papacy eroded and then was openly challenged by the Reformation, Christian mystics too became increasingly politicized. The Kabbalism which had become widespread among ordinary Jews was now used as a cultural resource by cosmopolitan Christian intellectuals in mobilizing their projects for a new political-religious order.

Intellectuals as Courtiers: The Humanists

The prominence of mysticism in the later Middle Ages was one of several directions of intellectual dispersion. There also appeared a new brand of intellectuals. Some were laymen rather than clergy, or remained in the ambivalent standing of the minor grades without consecration as priests. They wrote in the vernacular tongues and in a Latin which they took from the manuscripts of Roman times, and which they held superior to the "barbarisms" of the university scholastics. These "Humanists" had a different cultural capital and a different organizational base; they were court nobility or administrators, in the service of the secular rulers. In Italy, as the papacy disintegrated into a minor feudal power, its patronage style came to match that of the local aristocrats. In the 1400s there were humanist cardinals and even popes taking part in a common round of status display with this non-scholastic culture. Courtiers had existed before, but they had never been able to compete with the university teachers and the church theologians as the center of intellectual life.

From now on scholastic and humanist styles were typically rooted in different careers. Thomists, Scotists, and nominalists continued to be university professors, especially in the old strongholds of theology and in the universities which emulated them in Germany and Spain. The Italian universities had previously stood apart from the theological philosophy of the scholastics; now they became home to two other factions of professors: the Averroists (e.g., Paul of Venice, Vernias, Achillini, and Nifo at Padua and Bologna; see 264 in Figure 9.6 and 306, 307, 326 in Figure 9.7) and the Aristoteleans (Pomponazzi, Bar-

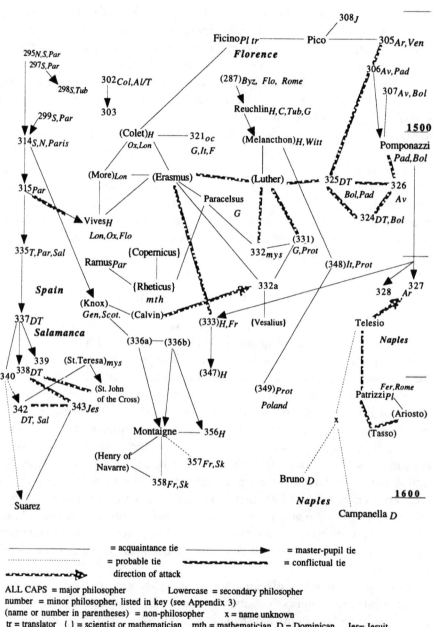

FIGURE 9.7. REFORMERS, METAPHYSICIANS, SKEPTICS, 1465–1600

baro, 305, Zabarella, 352), who base themselves on original Greek texts and ancient commentators such as Alexander of Aphrodisias. (Hence the name "Alexandrians" for opponents of the Averroist interpretation of Aristotle.)

The Humanists, by contrast, usually had careers as courtiers or church politicians. Some of them were Greeks, fleeing the collapsing Byzantine Empire: Chrysoloras, Pletho, Bessarion, Trebizond, Argyropoulos (231, 261, 274, 273, 287). After them came their pupils and followers: Valla, Piccolomini, Cusanus, Ficino, Pico della Mirandola, Reuchlin. There were a few professional academics among them, notably Vittorino da Feltre and Guarino di Verona (263, 262), but outside the older philosophy-theology positions. They acquired new chairs in Greek or the classics at the northern Italian universities, or established new schools: Da Feltre created a private school for children; Ficino was made head of the Platonic Academy at Florence by Cosimo di Medici. In the next century Peter Ramus was given a chair for his anti-scholastic logic at the new Collège Royale at Paris; his method spread not so much in the universities as in the secondary schools springing up as a form of alternative education. The most famous humanists often had mixed careers—part courtier, part teacher of classics. They were above all textual scholars, editors, and translators. Their links to court circles gave an emphasis to literature and history from the Greek and Roman classics, items of lay culture rather than abstract philosophy. By around 1500, when the Humanist program was established in the northern universities, it was centered on the arts course aimed at producing "the graduate destined for a civic or legal career (the articulate civil servant)" (Jardine, 1983: 253). When philosophy was brought in, it tended to involve a lay appeal through occultism (pushed by Reuchlin, Agrippa of Nettesheim, Paracelsus, Bruno, all of whom had mixed careers in and out of academic circles), or through claims that ancient texts are the higher basis of religion, as in the ambiguous Platonism—part paganism, part esoteric Christianity—of Pletho and Ficino.

The humanists were most fruitful for philosophy where their networks combined with the leading intellectual factions of the church. Nicolas Cusanus owed his eminence to contacts which put together most of the sources of cultural capital of the early and mid-1400s. He studied at the leading center of mysticism, the school of the Brethren of Common Life while Thomas à Kempis was active; then philosophy in the nominalist stronghold, Heidelberg; canon law at Padua, where he also heard lectures of the preeminent Humanists and made his Humanist reputation by recovering Latin literary texts. His connections brought him into the center of church politics. He was active at the Council of Basel in 1431 on the side favoring shared rule of the church. When the conciliar faction proved unable to organize itself, Cusanus switched sides. Diplomatic service with the papacy took him to Constantinople and further contacts with the cosmopolitan importers of Greek texts. Cusanus knew everybody: the north German mystic Denis the Carthusian (268 in Figure 9.6); the humanist Piccolomini, a key patron as papal secretary and then pope; Pletho, the paganizing Byzantine scholar who influenced Cosimo di Medici to found the Platonic Academy in Florence; the anti-scholastic philologist Lorenzo Valla. Later Cusanus corresponded with the young German scholars Peurbach and Regiomontanus, subsequently the leading mathematicians of the century.

Cusanus's great work, *On Learned Ignorance* (1440), was the precipitate of these contacts. Here he defends the reality of universal Forms, freeing Platonism from its connection to the Aristotelean cosmology of nested spheres. Developing the mathematical notion of infinity, Cusanus arrives at the coincidence of opposites: all geometrical shapes merge when enlarged to an infinite scale; applied to cosmology, this means that the universe is a sphere whose periphery is nowhere and its center, accordingly, is everywhere. The universe is no longer hierarchical but decentered. In part this is a philosophical expression of the mystical vision, but also of the implications of nominalism; all ultimates are paradoxical, and man at best can only become aware of his own limits, which is his own transcendent nothingness. Cusanus was the only outstandingly creative philosopher during several generations. The scholastics were stalled in their factionalism; the mystics had largely abandoned abstract discourse; the Humanists were engrossed in reviving the classic texts of antiquity. Cusanus was the individual in whom these opposing negations intersected; in him the coincidence of opposites flared up briefly into a vivid and idiosyncratic vision.

The bases of intellectual life continued to decentralize still further. Universities, once centered in France and England, now proliferated, especially in Germany. The most sustained network of successful Humanists were the religious politicians who constituted the intellectual core of the Reformation. Martin Luther was a biblical professor at Wittenberg, a newly founded university on the eastern frontier of Germany; his colleague and collaborator Philipp Melancthon was a protégé of Reuchlin. Humanist skill with classic texts was turned to the politically explosive issues of biblical scholarship and to throwing off medieval accretions of scholastic theology and canon law. Colet, Erasmus, Agrippa, Vives, and Paracelsus are linked in another network, based in typical Humanist careers: partly courtiers under political patronage, partly university professors of theology, Greek, and even Kabbalism.[15] But the Reformation was radically decentralizing and these networks, marginally philosophical at best, lead no further in abstract philosophy.

In the chaos of lay-oriented positions at the end of the 1500s, two characteristic styles are represented by Bruno and Montaigne. Like the occultists and Protestant sect leaders before him, Bruno was a feverish entrepreneur in an unsettled religious and intellectual situation. He abandoned the Dominican convent in Naples and wandered from court to court—from Geneva to Paris, from London to Germany to Venice—denouncing the university scholars and seeking patrons for his scheme to replace the warring sects of disunited Christendom. For him, religion and philosophy had metamorphosed into an eclectic mix of pagan hermeticism, Jewish Kabbalah, magical symbolism, and new science. Bruno was full of the boldness of new combinations, but insulation from politics was lacking, and he was burned for heresy.

The aristocrat Montaigne took a more cautious path. Montaigne's interest in allaying doctrinal conflicts was stimulated by the diverse religious ties of his family and political connections. Through his mother he was related to Portuguese Jews, forced converts to Catholicism, who had settled in Bordeaux; his distant cousin Francisco Sanchez, from this same mixed religious background, attended the same college in Bordeaux, and developed an anti-scholastic skepticism about the same time as Montaigne. In the 1570s, just when he was writing his *Apologie de Raymond Sebond* and beginning his *Essais,* Montaigne was active in mediating between the Catholic Royalists and the French Protestant leader, Henry of Navarre, whose conversion to Catholicism and ascension to the French throne Montaigne finally negotiated in 1588.[16] Montaigne's creative energy was no doubt multiplied by the successful trajectory of his political connections; it also helps explain why he became far more famous than Sanchez. Montaigne sought to mediate religious strife by a classically tinged skepticism, expressed with a literary touch. His philosophy makes light of doctrinal conflicts as well as the claims of Copernicus and Paracelsus to have produced a new science. Montaigne's "plague on all houses" represents the culminating skepticism in an age when the bases of intellectual life were fragmented and in flux.

Medieval Christendom was built on the monasteries, the papacy, and the universities. By now the first two had crumbled, and the third had become unfocused and scattered.

The Question of Intellectual Stagnation

Studies of intellectual life have preferred to focus on periods of creativity. Yet we recognize what is creative only by contrast. Comparison of the dark side against the light, and against the gray in between, is necessary for seeing the structural conditions associated with all of the varieties of intellectual life. A second reason to study stagnation is perhaps of greater immediate significance. There is no guarantee that we ourselves—denizens of the late twentieth century—inhabit a period of creativity. There is some likelihood that future intellectual historians looking back will concentrate on the great ideas of the first third of the century, and regard the rest as a falling off into mediocrity.

Almost all subsequent periods regarded late medieval philosophy as a period of stagnation. The Renaissance, especially the Italian intellectuals of the late 1400s and 1500s, viewed the preceding period as barbaric and pointed to the universities of their own times as exemplars of its most decadent phase. By the late 1300s, scholastic thinkers themselves felt that their own intellectual culture was dead. In 1402 Jean Gerson, the last important philosopher at the University of Paris for over 100 years, condemned the rationalist philosophy of his predecessors (Gilson, 1944: 716). Echoing both nominalist and fideist themes, he declared that intellectuals engage in arbitrary and absurd speculation; they follow pagan philosophy instead of penitence, humility, and faith; their overestimation of reason is the source of heresies, like those which proceeded from the realist Bradwardine to Wyclif and Hus. Gerson's contemporary Peter of Candia, who became pope in 1409, observed the factional wars of his time as ones which no one expected to have any resolution (Gilson, 1944: 615). He considered various opinions, not citing them as authorities for arguments in the manner of the scholastics, but with detachment like that of an intellectual of our own time who falls back from participation into historiography. This sounds not unlike the "end of philosophy" themes and the disparagement of "foundationalism" of present-day intellectuals. We thus find another reason to be interested in the social causes of stagnation: the suspicion that we might be in a similar situation today.

Stagnation is not a simple condition; there are at least three kinds.

Stagnation (A): Loss of cultural capital. Ideas may simply be forgotten as later intellectuals are unable to do what earlier ones could. Aristotle's doctrine was lost for several centuries after his death; the achievements of Stoic logic were forgotten by late antiquity, Megarian logic even sooner. In India after the 1600s, the acute metaphysics of the previous periods was swallowed up in a simplified Advaita Vedanta. In China the sophisticated positions of the late Warring States period, especially Mohist logic and its rivals, were largely eclipsed by the religious Confucianism of the Han dynasty. In the late T'ang, the metaphysical subtleties of the Consciousness-Only philosophy, as well as most other schools, were lost among the Buddhists. And to leave philosophy for an area in which technical criteria of puzzle-solving are especially clear, the breakthrough into generalized and explicit algebraic methods achieved during the Sung and Yuan dynasties (ca. 1050–1300) was lost in the Ming (1366–1644), so that later mathematicians could no longer understand the earlier texts (Qian, 1985: 69–70; Ho, 1985: 106; Needham, 1959: 38–145; Mikami, 1913: 110). The loss of ideas makes us think of a Dark Age, brought about by destruction of material conditions of civilization, such as the decline of Rome in the West. But these examples show that idea loss can also happen during prosperous periods of high civilizations; indeed, the loss of Greek culture had started in Rome long before the barbarian conquests.

Stagnation (B): Dominance of the classics. An opposite form of stagnation occurs when the ideas of the greatest thinkers overshadow those of their successors. There is no new creativity, which necessarily would displace the old. Such a period should not be called a low level of culture; one might say that it stays at the peak: the ideas that are taught and circulated are the best yet achieved. It is an irony of the intellectual world that we are not satisfied with this. We admire creativity, but when great creativity gets its rewards, we soon regard it as stagnation. There are two sides to creativity: the energy of creation and the visions it produces. In the long run each undermines the other. Since creativity is driven by chains of eminence, some earlier figures are bound to be overshadowed by their successors. The greatest rewards tend to go to those who are last in a dense and competitively balanced chain. This is why Hegel could say, "The owl of Minerva spreads its wings only with the falling of dusk." Stagnation as well as creativity is at the heart of the network structure of intellectual life.

Historical comparisons show that there is nothing automatic about this enshrinement of the classics. In India, where the ideology strongly favored immutable wisdom from the past, there were long periods of change in both Buddhist and Hindu camps. Greek philosophy, too, tended to forget earlier doctrines rather than to repeat them; when it thought it was reiterating Pythagoras or Plato, it often was grafting new doctrines onto them. In China the enshrinement of Confucius, Lao Tzu, and the ancient divination texts nevertheless went along with periods when there was considerable innovation disguised as commentaries on these texts. There is a tradeoff between Stagnation (A) and Stagnation (B). More precisely, at least one way in which old cultural capital is lost is through creative reinterpretation of it (although there are more extreme forms of forgetting, and other versions of creativity). A civilization may have episodes of either kind of stagnation. In China, after Chu Hsi had formulated his grand synthesis around 1200, Ch'eng-Chu Neo-Confucianism acquired a stranglehold on Chinese intellectual life for over 300 years; to put the matter in a different light, Chinese intellectuals could rest serenely in enjoying the great philosophy that already existed.

Late Christendom exemplifies Stagnation (B) more than Stagnation (A). The achievements of Thomas Aquinas and Duns Scotus towered over constructive philosophy, just as Ockham did on the critical side. The late medieval scholastics enshrined an extremely high level of creativity; yet its very solidity eventually provoked an attack from advocates of intellectual movement. The textbooks of the 1500s and 1600s, especially those of the Spanish and French universities of the Counterreformation, came to represent sterility in the eyes of Francis Bacon and Descartes. One could also say that the Renaissance, which coincided with this stagnant period of medieval philosophy, provides only a rival stagnation of the same type in its adulation of the ancient classics.

Stagnation (C): Technical refinement. A third type of stagnation may indeed be not stagnation at all but only the appearance of such. Intellectual life does not stop in its tracks, but its very progress breeds not respect but alienation. A common claim about late medieval philosophy has been that the field had gotten too technical, overrefined, spinning angels dancing in conceptual air. Duns Scotus was aptly called "Doctor Subtilis," the Subtle Doctor. The Renaissance Humanists were particularly put out by Duns's style, both his neologisms in metaphysics (certainly not known in the days of Cicero!) and the long tortuous sentences with clause after clause of careful qualification. This is more than emblematic of the time. The writing of a centrally located philosopher is a precipitate of the energies and concepts built up by the intellectual community. Duns's abstractions and distinctions, his complicated and rarefied worldview, and his patient tenacious threads of argument are the embodiment of the conflicting factions of philosophers who had been realigning for three intense generations, and driving up the level of abstraction and subtlety at every step.

The Scotists did not stop in their tracks after the death of the master; they continued to defend and elaborate, now attempting alliances with nominalists, sometimes making anti-nominalist coalition by playing down their differences with the Thomists. But the excitement of new synthesis did not appear. The nominalists, loosely designated, were often very creative, by the standards of modern analytical philosophy.[17] But they were now specialized in logic or other technical subjects. Their work provided no strong focus for the intellectual field, no vortices of emotional energy. The technical innovations did not propagate very widely; they were no challenge to the image of the overpowering masters, no visible alternative to Stagnation (B). And in time, because such creativity does not attract followers, it cannot reproduce itself; it dries up, and the situation begins indeed to approach Stagnation (A).[18] By the time of the Renaissance, beginning in the 1400s in circles far outside the university world which had sustained medieval intellectual life, there was genuine loss of ideas, ignorance of what medieval philosophy was about. Duns Scotus, the Subtle Doctor, was on his way to being caricatured as the "Dunce," the stupid pupil forced to sit in the corner wearing a "dunce cap."

Reversal of the External Conditions

How does stagnation happen? In principle, the conditions should be the obverse of those for creativity. If intellectuals are allowed to form a community, they automatically tend to develop issues and divide the attention space among factions. Creativity is the energy that builds up as this process continues over several generations of personal contacts within the network. External conditions determine when such a network structure comes into existence and how long it will last. The crucial conditions for creativity are those which sustain multiple bases of intellectual conflict across a primary focus of attention. Creativity depends on a center, crisscrossed by material resources that can uphold opposing factions; a small number of centers linked by intermobility of their participants can provide this necessary intermeshing of focus and conflict.

As long as this structural shape continues to exist, external conditions may intervene by destroying, prohibiting, or promoting a particular faction. This in itself does not damage the creativity of the whole network, as it may rearrange intellectual space and set the occasion for new internal alignments. Upheavals in the external bases of factions, destructive as they may be to the people within them, are not a bad thing for intellectual life as a whole, provided that the overall structure still contains multiple factions and a common focus of attention. Surrounding social conflict, organization-building, and destruction—the rise and fall of schools and states, of religious factions and orders of monks, of the papacy or the caliphate—will in fact promote creativity by causing the realignment of factions. Creativity comes to an end when external conditions either end the bases for multiple factions or eliminate the common center.

Let us briefly survey the overall structure of the intellectual world in the creative and non-creative periods of philosophy.

Greece. In the pre-Socratic period, creativity was centered at first in a network of cities on the Ionian coast, with Miletos at the core. Then the network migrated to a number of colonies in southern Italy and Sicily, where the main institutional continuity was provided by the Pythagorean brotherhood; another branch dispersed around the Aegean, to Abdera in the north as well as the medical schools at Cos and Cnidus in the southeast. It is possible that creativity would have dissipated, but geopolitical events now provided a center. The Persian conquest of Ionia and the Greek coalition and counterattack fostered migration, as did the democratic revolutions and the upsurge of tyrants; refugees and ambassadors formed the milieu for a cosmopolitan intellectual network which came to center on the imperialist power at Athens. The metropolis was just that: a center of intellectual attraction, filled almost entirely with foreigners. Socrates and Plato were virtually the only Athenians among the important intellectuals of their city for hundreds of years; Aristotle, Diogenes, Epicurus, Zeno, and others came from the remote provinces. The situation is similar to that of medieval Paris during its great generations of the 1200s, when there was scarcely a Frenchman among the leading masters.

For a couple of generations, Athens was flanked by peripheral nodes at Megara, Elis, Cyrene, Cyzicus, and elsewhere. These were specialized homes of particular schools, and almost all connected to the networks of the center. Originally independent schools such as those of Abdera, Lampsacus, and Mytilene achieved their fortune when they finally established their school in Athens, like that which made the Epicureans famous. The center provided a focus of attention and the opportunity for the meshing of networks. Creativity is sustained when there are multiple bases for contending factions. Athens at its height was cross-cut by a variety of schools, anchored in external differences in political support, religious orientation, and lifestyle radicalism. Shifts in these external bases provided the ultimate forces that drove internal realignments in carving up intellectual space.

In the Hellenistic period, the external bases narrowed. Most of the peripheral nodes dropped out (see Figure 3.3); the rival schools by and large were now based only in Athens, displacing those with an independent center of support. There was one other center of intersecting circles: Alexandria absorbed the medical schools from Cos and Cnidus, as well as Peripatetics and Stoics from Athens. For a century there was a balanced situation of creativity between the rivals, down to the generation of Chrysippus or Carneades. With the growing hegemony of Rome and the political collapse of Athens, by around 100 B.C.E. the material bases provided by the Athenian schools had disappeared. Intellectual centers migrated away, to Pergamum, Rhodes, Naples; but each of these fostered a single school, not a cosmopolitan center, and none survived more than a generation or two. Alexandria still functioned institutionally, but too much alone to sustain much creativity. Philosophy became largely absorbed by the practice of rhetoric, an occupation of municipal lawyers and wandering speech makers, a base which provided neither centralization nor insulation for intellectuals to pursue autonomous concerns.

The coming of Christianity and other popular religious movements further decentralized the intellectual world. The Gnostic sects were small and organizationally dispersed; the Christian church was more hierarchical, but its bases were geographically far-flung and dependent on regional political fortunes. The most creative period was marked by the balance of rivalry when Christians entered the philosophical schools at Alexandria, provoking the great pagan synthesis of Plotinus and his followers. But both Christian philosophers and Plotinine pagans migrated away to the centers of political patronage, respectively to Syria and to Rome, from whence the networks soon further dispersed. By late antiquity, Athens and Alexandria had become not centers of intersecting factions but local strongholds of a particular faction. Elsewhere religious intellectuals were active at Constantinople, Pergamum, Antioch, Milan, Carthage. Centralization was lost first, leading to the defocusing of intellectual life, the general loss of abstraction, and the predominance of particularistic theology and magic. Later the material bases for multiple factions were drastically curtailed with the general material decline of the empire; accumulated cultural capital was then largely forgotten.

China. In the early creative period of the Warring States, intellectuals circulated among the Chi-hsia Academy and the courts at Wei, P'ing-yuan, and Ch'in. The greatest of these were centers of intersecting circles. Political and prestige rivalry between the major courts was overlaid by the autonomous organizational movements of Confucians and Mohists; these conditions fostered a third party of unaffiliated intellectuals who carved out a variety of positions across the turf provided by a focus on the life of debate. Again in the great period of Buddhist creativity, there was competition among several organized factions intersecting physically at a few places: the capital of the pro-Buddhist dynasties, especially the T'ang, with its court and great monasteries, counterbalanced by the great intersectarian monasteries at T'ien-tai, Lu-shan, and Shao-lin ssu. A later period of creativity in the Sung was based on intellectual exchange among factions centered on the two northern capitals, Loyang (the old capital and cultural center for out-of-office officials) and Ch'ang-an, where the ups and downs of Wang An-Shih's reform movement were taking place. Here was a multiple meshing among political-literary factions of the gentry, reforming and traditionalist officials of the examination system, and the quasi-religious schools of the Neo-Confucians and occultists. In the Southern Sung there were again interconnected rival centers: Chu Hsi's academy, which was the most successful of the private schools living off and simultaneously opposing the examination system; and the professors of the national university such as Liu Chiu-Yuan.

The stagnant periods of Chinese intellectual life were either dominated by a single center or drastically dispersed. The huge but uncreative national university of the Han, reaching 30,000 students at its height, exemplifies the former. We see the dispersion and loss of focus in the later period of Ch'an Buddhism, when its monasteries proliferated in rural China but interconnections among its lineages faded away; it was then that Ch'an creativity gave way to its own version of scholasticism, making koans out of the exploits of its earlier leaders. The huge development of the material conditions of education in the Ming shows dispersion without creative focus. There were hundreds of thousands of students in small scattered schools, supporting an industry of printed books (Chaffee, 1985). The national university and the mass gatherings for the provincial and metropolitan examinations did not stimulate the debate of philosophical factions, but only encouraged the individual pursuit of scholastic forms.

India. The creative periods in philosophy occurred when the networks were geographically most concentrated. The Upanishadic sages were in the middle Ganges, notably at Banares. In this region the rival consolidating states, Magadha and Kosala, were the locations where the rival networks of debating ascetics built up, culminating in the organizations of Buddhists, Jainas, and Ajivikas. The literary creativity of the Hindu "renaissance," by contrast, came in dispersion, the epics assembled by pioneers migrating away from the Ganges heartland. The apex of abstract philosophy occurred in the generations when Hindu and Buddhist networks meshed and debated, above all at Nalanda, the headquarters monastery in old Magadha which became an intersectarian center, cosmopolitan and virtually secularized as a modern university. Flanking this Buddhist center were a few others monastery-universities, in wealthy Gujarat in the west, and downriver in Bengal. On the Hindu side, Banares became an intellectual center again at the time of Shankara, drawing Hindu students from the south.

As Buddhism disappeared from India, Hindu monastic orders took its place, expanding and splitting into rival movements. Educational organizations *(maths)*, were created teaching the doctrine of each sect. For a time abstract philosophy continued to develop; this was concentrated at the moments when splits occurred, leaders of new factions such as Ramanuja and Madhva branching off from the older networks and developing new philosophical standpoints to go along with the particulars of their theology and the independence of their organization. Some creativity flared up where the older schools of the established *darshanas* intersected the new religious movements, as in Kashmir during 800–1000, where the tail end of a longstanding Buddhist lineage amalgamated with the Nyaya logicians and entered debate with Shaiva sectarians, resulting in a unique brand of Shaivaite energy ontology. Another center was in the old central region of the middle Ganges, where the Nyaya school—the last holdout from the pre-sectarian schools of Hinduism—maintained a headquarters at Mithila (very near Nalanda), and where the technicalities of Neo-Nyaya were created, a last gasp of innovation from 1350 to about 1500. The *maths* became increasingly sectarian after about 1300, immersed in articulating their own position; formal education proliferated around India, but there were no great central places where debates were focused. Indian philosophy dissipated in scholastic handbooks and eclectic syncretisms, flanked by popular devotional cults outside the ranks of the professional scholars. The material bases of schooling were more abundant than ever at just the time when philosophy dried up.

Japan. During the Buddhist period, virtually all of the important new developments spun off from the great monastery complex at Mount Hiei overlooking Kyoto; the several Zen movements were an intersection between Mount Hiei and Chinese lineages contacted by Japanese sojourners. The creative moments happened when former Mount Hiei pupils established their new bases during the initial process of splitting from the center. As Zen and Pure Land temples proliferated and dispersed, the focus of intellectual life was lost. The elite Zen temples of Kyoto became centers for new movements in the arts; but aesthetics replaced religious doctrine and its associated philosophies. In this situation the expansion of formal education did not help. A single "university" under the Ashikaga shoguns had thousands of students, but the curriculum, Neo-Confucian philosophy and other classic texts imported from China, stagnated. The Soto temples spread elementary schooling in the countryside. Although their founder, Dogen, was the greatest of the Zen philosophers, after his death advanced studies turned into formalistic summaries and commentaries. The Rinzai temples maintained the tradition of Chinese koan collections. These too turned to scholasticism, most elaborately in the early Tokugawa, when the temples were absorbed under government bureaucratic regulation; solving a lengthy sequence of koan became the requirement for gaining enlightenment certificates, a pursuit of credentials entitling their holders to office as abbots.

Buddhist intellectual and spiritual life was demoralized through its own careerism and material success. Under the Tokugawa regime, philosophy took off again in new culture-producing institutions: the private proprietary schools for samurai, most of them at Kyoto, with a few at Edo. The division of cultural life between the old and the new de facto capitals fostered a salutary competition, while the number of schools remained relatively low. Helping focus the competition of intersecting circles were the two great patronage centers sponsored by the shogun's relatives, the lords of Mito and Aizu. Cross-breeding of networks led to a series of vigorous new schools, including a merchant academy at Osaka, which went on to produce the most radical secularists and naturalists. Creativity was limited to the non-official marketplace of private schools; the training schools established by the *daimyo* for the higher officials in their feudal domains were no more than a formalistic drill. From the late 1700s onward many new schools were founded at all levels; but the growth of mass education went along with intellectual stagnation. The attempt in the 1790s to establish a Chinese-style examination system did little more than add to the formalization of rote learning.

In general, it was those types of schools which were newest, and still confined to a small number of places, which were intellectually creative. The movement of National Learning in the mid- and late 1700s, and the Osaka merchant academy with its few spin-offs into schools of Dutch Learning, were a limited set of institutions but with much more intellectual action than the

Neo-Confucian samurai schools, Buddhist schools, and *daimyo* schools which became so widely available around 1800. When the European university was imported, the pattern repeats: the early generations, when there are only a few key centers, is the time of greatest creativity in philosophy.

Stagnation and Loss of a Center in Islam

In Islam and Christendom, philosophy follows a similar pattern: conditions for rising creativity are followed by those of stagnation. As we have noted, the differences between the two regions were matters of degree, although they would accumulate into differences in substance.

In the earliest period of the Islamic Empire, the principal centers of philosophy were dispersed: Jundishapur in southwestern Persia, where the pagan school of Athens had moved after being closed down in 529; Antioch, inheritor of the Alexandrian school after 718, before it moved on around 850 to Harran in northern Syria, where a school of Sabian star worshippers also existed; and the Nestorian school at Nisibis in Syria (Nakosteen, 1964: 16–19; Watt, 1985: 37–39; see map in Chapter 8). These preserved the ancient cultural capital but were not known for innovation. It was only when their scholars became gathered in Baghdad, at the caliph's translation project and under other patrons, that the creative network density was achieved. During the great creative period of Islamic life from 800 to 1000, virtually all the intellectuals were at Baghdad and at the port city Basra 300 miles down the Euphrates. It was a close network, with much movement between the two places.

Baghdad and Basra provided the creative combination of a central focus of attention together with multiple bases of intellectual factions. These bases included the court as well as other aristocratic patrons supporting groups engaged in collecting libraries, translating foreign texts, and maintaining charitable hospitals where medicine was taught together with related Greek learning. On the side of the "ancient learning," there were rival groups of translators: the Jundishapur lineage exemplified by Hunayn, now at the House of Wisdom, as well as star worshippers from Harran, such as the family of Thabit ibn Qurra. Nestorian Christians, Sabians, Zoroastrians, and Hindus crossed at this center under Muslim sponsorship; the first great Muslim philosophers, al-Kindi and al-Farabi, were at the center of these networks at Baghdad. Basra was the initial center of philosophical creativity on the side of the "Islamic sciences"; its mosque was where the rational theologians, including the Muʿtazilites and Ashʿarites, were formed, and Basra was the home base of the secret society of the Pure Brethren. These networks also had branches in Baghdad, in the orbit of Greek *falsafa*. The early Sufis, too, though they were a dispersed collection of wanderers, made their greatest impact at Baghdad; this was the site of their most famous early representatives, al-Bistami, al-Junayd, and al-Hallaj.

The other important ingredient in the intellectual scene is the lineages of the teachers of jurisprudence (legal "schools" in a metaphorical but not institutional sense). Initially these were regionally based: Malik and his followers at Medina; al-Shafi'i in Egypt; Abu Hanifa at Kufa and Baghdad; yet other styles of interpretation in Syria, Persia, and elsewhere (Lapidus, 1988: 164–165). There was a huge proliferation of such legal sects; it is estimated that by around 800 c.e. there were some 500 of them (Makdisi, 1981: 9). By around 900 to 1000, some four or five schools took the lead; by the 1100s, acceptance of one of four schools had become the criterion of orthodoxy as a Muslim. The law schools were by and large a decentralizing agent, even when they had been winnowed to a few lineages. In the creative period of philosophy, it was the Hanbalis who were most active as a scriptural, anti-rationalist opposition. This traditionalist lineage was centered originally at Baghdad, in most immediate contact with the rational theologians.

A nucleus for these competing factions existed at Baghdad with an outlier at Basra. The sometimes violent conflicts among these groups did not threaten the overall structure as long as the general conditions remained intact. But as the Baghdad caliphate lost its political power, its importance as a patron of intellectual life declined, and the central focus where networks might confront one another began to disappear. For a time Nishapur, in eastern Persia far beyond the Caspian Sea (two months' journey from Baghdad), became important, but mainly in theological studies; it was the chief Ash'arite center from 900 until about 1100. For a while some network connection was maintained between it and Baghdad; al-Ghazali, as well as some of his teachers, was active in both places. Intellectual life was now dispersing; after 1100 even Nishapur no longer maintained any central focus for the theologians, who were found now in Isfahan, Kirman, Damascus, Jerusalem, and elsewhere (Watt, 1985: 92).

The *madrasas* which proliferated in every city after 1050 added to this dispersion. The factional competition between Sunnite and Shi'ite motivated many of these endowments. But the factions did not intersect institutionally; *madrasas* specialized in one sect or the other. In addition, they remained small, typically around 10 to 20 endowed students with a single professor, although some of the large colleges reached as many as 75 students (Nakosteen, 1964: 42–44, 49–50; Makdisi, 1981: 31). At most, *madrasas* of the four legal schools might amalgamate physically into a single architectural complex. Large and internally differentiated faculties did not come into being. The expansion of Sufi orders in this period also enhanced dispersion; particular orders dominated in outlying regions such as Anatolia, Transoxiana, North Africa, and India, as well as in Persia and the Middle East (see Figure 8.3 and its key.) Again there were few institutional points of intersection among rival groups. The Sufi orders were largely based on lay members and thus compatible with other pursuits. The *madrasas* tended to become permeated with Sufism, which took the edge off the mysticism and subordinated it to traditionalism and law. The *madrasas* ended by producing a type not unlike the Confucian gentry, oriented to government and propriety but preserving a tinge of Taoist mysticism for their private lives.

The Spanish episode, which was a temporary break in the later Muslim stagnation, recapitulates the early creative structure. Córdoba and Toledo provided the focus for interconnected networks. Cordoba as the center of the western caliphate contained the legal, theological, and secular court networks characteristic of Baghdad of an earlier period. The balance existed for a relatively short time. As early as 950, the caliph had imported a huge library from the east, competing with the eastern caliphate for prestige as a center of learning, and patronized Jewish scholars as a cosmopolitan counterweight to Muslim religious factions. The conservative side was also strong; law was monopolized by the Malikites, the most literalist and anti-innovative of the law schools, being opposed even to *waqf* foundations, which in the east had been used to endow *madrasas* (Makdisi, 1981: 238). Politics swung between pro- and anti-secular learning. For a few generations after 1050, the balance of networks broke into creativity. Network density was enhanced while Toledo was a base where Christian translators, Jewish religious intellectuals, and Arab scientists intermeshed. The Christian reconquest, which took this great city from the Arabs in 1085, at first added pluralism to the networks rather than destroying them. We find intellectuals of all three faiths moving about, stimulating one another around the twin hubs, Toledo and Córdoba. Other cities and their schools fed into these networks: Almería, Seville, Granada, Lucena, all close to Córdoba in the south. After 1200, the structure was lost. Córdoba fell to the Christians in 1236; the Jewish-Arab networks were no longer linked; the translators moved on to Italy. Its structural bases gone, the Spanish golden age was over.

Which type of stagnation characterizes the later age of Islam? In some respects there was a loss of cultural capital (Stagnation A). Ibn Rushd's great achievement in freeing Aristotle from Neoplatonism, as well as his own constructive philosophy, were largely unknown in the east (Fakhry, 1983: 275). Mu'tazili rational theology was driven out as well. Insofar as there was adulation of the classics (Stagnation B), it was in the realm of the religious texts of Islam, and in a narrow aspect of philosophy, the studies of logic which became incorporated as adjuncts to legal argument in the *madrasas*. Even here there was some movement, as commentaries and supercommentaries were added onto the texts to be mastered by students. The consensus of most historians is that these commentaries are unoriginal and pedantic. But it is possible, as Marshall Hodgson argues, that they merely have not received attention from Western scholars, and that technical advances are buried within. Around 1450, in Shiraz (Persia), al-Dawwani included in his supercommentaries on school logic a solution to the liar's paradox which anticipates Russell's theory of types (Hodgson, 1974: 2:472), and there may be more advances of this sort. But surely this was at least Stagnation (C), technicalities too refined to come to wider notice. Al-Dawwani's reputation was largely as a religious moralist, while his technical creativeness had little following. In the social organization of the intellectual world, flashes of brilliance had no reflection; the illusory stagnation of technical refinement led to the real stagnation of classicism and loss of past achievements.

Center and Disintegration in Christendom

In European Christendom we can follow the steps by which the central focus of intellectual life built up. There is nothing inherent about the initial attraction of Paris. In the Carolingian period, the network centers were farther east: at Fulda and the Palatine court of the emperor, as well as the court at Laon. The schools of Italy were active by 1000, though their most famous members moved north. An early dialectician, Anselm of Besate, wandered from Parma to Mayence, and Lanfranc from Bologna to Bec. Rosecelin taught at Compiège, Loches, Tours on the lower Loire, Besançon near the Alps (Gilson, 1944: 233–234). Abelard was famous for his travels around 1100–1140, but now the net was confined to northern France, and he spent increasing time in Paris. Chartres was a rival center for several generations in the 1100s, but its network flowed away into Paris by the end of the century. The advantage of Paris was that it provided in close compass multiple bases for intellectual life. It included rival jurisdictions of the cathedral, the religious abbeys, the patronage of the monarchy and eventually the pope (Ferruolo, 1985: 16–17). Italy, despite its lead both in possessing classical learning and later as a place for Arabic translations, became a periphery to the network centered on Paris. The teachers from Bec, Laon, Chartres, and Tours found maximal attention by congregating in Paris. By 1200, their intersection had promoted the organization of the university.

The height of creativity, from 1230 to about 1360, was a time of optimal background conditions. Paris provided the focus, but it was balanced and fed by other universities and schools linked by migrating teachers and students. There was an especially important exchange of masters between Paris and Oxford, both of which had the rare privilege of faculties of theology, owing

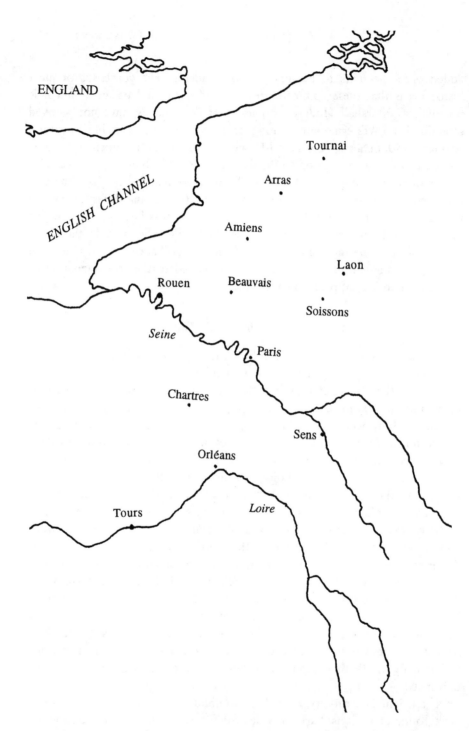

CATHEDRAL SCHOOLS OF NORTHERN FRANCE, 1100 C.E.
(From Southern, 1995, p. xix)

to the political importance of the French and English kings to the papacy. Cologne with its Dominican house of studies was a third outlier, with strong network ties to Paris. For a generation in the early 1300s, the papal court at Avignon became a fourth center, but full of scholars with Paris and Oxford connections. The highly creative philosophers (as we see in Figures 9.3 through 9.6) are those in geographical overlaps, belonging to several major centers; Grosseteste, Bacon, Albertus, Aquinas, Ockham, Eckhart were at two centers, Scotus at three. These figures incorporate in their own persons the intellectual representations of the intersecting centers.

At the same time, the centers contained multiple grounds of factionalism. There were the rival orders of Franciscans and Dominicans; there were internal organizational conflicts within the most powerful order; there was the jealousy of secular theologians against the privileges of the orders at the universities; there was a struggle for control and autonomy between theological and arts faculties. Conflicts took place across multiple dimensions. The two great orders, emerging in the 1220s, by 1231 had laid claim to two theology chairs at Paris. In 1255 the secular theology masters tried to have the mendicant orders forbidden from lecturing at Paris; it was only with the intervention of the pope that in 1257 Bonaventure and Aquinas were confirmed in their chairs—the latter surrounded by an armed bodyguard to protect him from the seculars (Gilson, 1944: 438; Hyman and Walsh, 1983: 505). This was the setting in which the secular theologian Henry of Ghent attacked Aquinas at Paris in the 1270s, and Aquinas had attacked the claims of the arts masters to independence from theological orthodoxy. Around 1315 the chancellor, Henry of Harclay, attacked the Dominicans for attempting to teach at Oxford without receiving a local M.A. (Gilson, 1944: 632); soon after, Harclay's (probable) student William of Ockham attacked the Realism of the theological philosophy, which was now official doctrine of the orders. Such external bases of factional struggle within the university provided part of the energy of intellectual creation.

The inner differentiation of the university and its autonomous field of intellectual combat were two important ingredients of creativity. But they were effective only when combined with the centralization which brought all the networks together. For the life of philosophy, the university structured around the higher faculty of theology was the key. Paris was not the only place where a university corporation was formed. Law teachers and students were forming guilds at Bologna by around 1100. Parallel with Paris in the late 1100s, universities were also growing up at Oxford, Montpellier, and Salerno, the latter two predominantly medical. With the exception of Oxford, which became a network satellite of the Paris metropolis, these other universities had almost no impact in the world of philosophy of this period. The same was true in the 1200s, when universities were formed at Naples and Padua (along with smaller ones) in Italy; at Salamanca and Valladolid (again with smaller ones) in Spain; Cambridge in England; and Toulouse, Angers, and Orléans in France itself. Many of the smaller schools specializing in law did not even have arts faculties (Cobban, 1988: 3). As far as philosophy is concerned, the other universities acted at best as feeders for higher studies at Paris.

After 1300, the situation began to change. In Figures 9.5 and 9.6 we see the dispersion of intellectual life to many places, both inside and outside the universities. Especially in the late 1300s and the 1400s, we find independent mystics in Germany and the Netherlands, Humanists in Italy, Jews in southern France and Italy, and Averroists in the medical and legal faculties in Italy, where philosophy had previously shown little penetration; nominalists were prominent in the universities in Germany. After 1350 Oxford no longer stood out, and the Paris networks were fading.

The decline of abstract philosophy was not due to the decline of the university itself. On the contrary, this was a period of accelerating growth of the university system as a whole (see Table 9.1). By the end of the 1200s, there were 18 universities, 12 of them major in size and importance. By 1400 there were 34 universities, 18 of them major; by 1500 there were 56. Even more universities were founded, but many of them failed. The failure rate went up during these centuries; between 1300 and 1500, about half of all university foundations were failures.[19] The market for educational credentials was expanding explosively, but at the same time flooding the market, raising the risk of failure and of losing former prestige.

More universities existed, but they were becoming smaller. Paris at its height around 1280–1300 had some 6,000 to 7,000 students; the number began falling in the 1300s and dropped below 3,000 by 1450. Bologna rivaled Paris's size in the early 1200s but fell behind thereafter. Oxford may have had a maximum of 3,000 students in the 1200s; there were an estimated 1,500 in 1315 and fewer than 1,000 in 1438; by 1500–1510 the yearly average was down to 124. Toulouse may have had 2,000 students at its height; this fell to 1,380 teachers and students in 1387 and below 1,000 in the 1400s. Avignon (founded in 1303) and Orléans had 800 to 1,000 students, mainly in law, in the 1390s; these numbers fell off drastically in the following century. The smaller French and Italian universities never had more than a few hundred students at their height, and they often closed for lack of students.

The proliferation of universities was especially rapid in Italy and Spain, and here the failure rates were highest. Italy had an overwhelming 80 percent failure rate in the 1300s and 1400s. France too experienced a considerable number of foundings; it reached a failure rate of at least 78 percent in the 1400s. Expansion in Germany and in central and far northern Europe was more suc-

TABLE 9.1. UNIVERSITY FOUNDATIONS AND FAILURES, 1000–1600

Total	Italy	France	Britain	German Empire, Scandinavia, Low Countries	Iberia
1000s					
F = 1	F = 1				
f = 0					
T = 1M					
1100s					
F = 6	F = 3	F = 2	F = 1		
f = 17%	f = 1				
T = 5M	T = 2M	T = 2M	T = 1M		
1m	1m				
1200s					
F = 19	F = 8	F = 5	F = 1		F = 5
f = 37%	f = 3	f = 2			f = 2
T = 12M	T = 4M	T = 4M	T = 2M		T = 2M
6m	4m	1m			1m
1300s					
F = 34	F = 15	F = 5	F = 1	F = 10	F = 3
f = 47%	f = 12	f = 1	f = 1	f = 2	
T = 18M	T = 4M	T = 5M	T = 2M	T = 6M	T = 2M
14m	7m	4m		2m	3m
1400s					
F = 41	F = 5	F = 9	F = 3	F = 15	F = 9
f[a] = 48%	f = 4	f = 7		f = 4	f = 5
T = 22M	T = 5M	T = 5M	T = 2M	T = 8M	T = 2M
34m	7m	6m	3m	11m	7m
1500s					
F = 54	F = 5	F = 4	F = 2	F = 18	F = 25
f = 31%	f = 2	f = 1		f = 2	f = 12
T = 23M	T = 4M	T = 4M	T = 3M	T = 9M	T = 3M
70m	11m	9m	4m	26m	20m
Totals 1000–1600					
F = 155	F = 37	F = 25	F = 8	F = 43	F = 42
f = 39%	f = 60%	f = 44%	f = 13%	f = 19%	f = 45%

Source: Collins, 1981, p. 517. From Rashdall, 1936; Shepherd, 1964: No. 100; *The Cambridge Modern History Atlas* 1912, Map 9; Kagan (in Stone, 1974:355–405).

Notes: F = foundations; f = failures; T = total in existence at end of century; M = major universities; m = minor universities.

a. Includes "paper universities" given legal charters, but which did not actually come into existence. Rashdall (1936, Vol. II:325–331) lists 10 of these, mostly in the 1300s, and notes that his list is probably very incomplete for the 1400s. Hence this failure rate is probably 10–15% too low.

cessful.[20] Here there was less initial competition over students. The first university in the region was founded at Prague in 1347, which carried on successfully with some 1,500 students until the early 1400s. Vienna, Cologne, and Leipzig succeeded to the leadership, with as many as 1,000 students at various times in the 1400s. The smaller German universities varied from 80 to 400 students, hitting their peak around 1450–1480 and declining thereafter.

One might expect this institutional growth to be associated with intellectual creativity, but the opposite happened. Significant networks were not maintained; a central focus was lost. None of the new universities acquired anything like the drawing power that Paris once commanded. Instead of a structure in which multiple bases of factionalism intersect at a center, factionalism itself became geographically localized. Intellectual borders hardened; conflict no longer produced creative realignments but merely resulted in a habitual reiteration of dividing lines. Partly responsible was a decline in the internationalism of the old high medieval centers, set in motion by external political forces. Already in 1303 the French king was putting pressure on the Paris theologians to support him in conflict with the pope; foreign scholars who refused, including Duns Scotus, temporarily left Paris (Gilson, 1944: 710–711). There was a growing tendency for scholars to stay at home. Now the French and English wars restricted Englishmen from studying or teaching in France, and vice versa. This nationalism was a new development, since earlier wars had not disturbed the unity of Christendom. It was the new efforts of the rulers to control the now highly developed church bureaucracy that was removing the institutions of religious learning as a neutral meeting place. The papacy, responding to slights in one place, licensed universities elsewhere; for instance, in 1316 the pope licensed Toulouse to teach theology, overturning the monopoly of Paris theologians in France. In 1359 a theological faculty was granted to a new university at Florence, although it failed quickly for lack of students. In 1364 the preeminent legal university, Bologna, finally was granted a theological faculty (Cobban, 1988: 144). The schism in the papacy, in which rival popes arose almost every year from 1378 to 1449, fostered yet further foundations and rivalries.

Nationalism and local factionalism made a self-reinforcing spiral. Previously the Paris masters had the right, granted by the pope, to teach in all universities without reexamination; now this was contested by Oxford and Montpellier. Universities now tended to break apart along intellectual lines (de Wulf, 1937–1947: 3:50–196). Strong nominalist universities included Vienna (founded in 1365), where the curriculum required only nominalist texts, Heidelberg (founded in 1386), Erfurt (1392), Cracow (1397), and Leipzig (1409). Cologne, where the old Dominican school was displaced by a degree-granting university in 1388, was a stronghold of Thomism. At Louvain, founded about 1425, the statutes prohibited the teaching of "nominalists," including Ockham and Buridan. The nominalists were periodically forced out, leaving Paris in 1407 and returning in 1437 after Paris was recaptured by the English; in 1474 Louis XI banned nominalism, though rescinding the edict in 1481. Oxford, by contrast, became strongly nominalist. The orders, once centers of creativity, now were frozen in their official doctrines. The Dominicans, who had made Thomism compulsory in 1309, were increasingly barred from England by the strength of the Franciscans. Life for the Dominicans on the Continent became uneasy as well: they left Paris in 1387, then returned in 1403 as the result of changing fortunes in the Hundred Years' War. The stronghold of Thomism became primarily the universities of Spain, where the Counterreformation eventually added its weight to make Thomism virtually the criterion of faith against heretics; by the same token, it became anathema to Protestants.

The universities now were intellectual fortresses. Change came no longer by internally generated creativity, but when a school was taken by storm when external politics changed. The very labels "nominalist," "realist," "Scotist" had now hardened from the inchoate movements of the earlier period into names hurled in battle.

The Humanists, who treated all the "schoolmen" as an object of satire, added no relief but only one more faction. Humanism was a symptom of the crisis of decentralization and fragmentation of the attention space. The Humanists did not begin the critique of scholasticism; it had already started from within. Nor was Humanism and the inflow of texts from the east a historical deus ex machina which just happened to restart intellectual life in a new direction after the fall of Byzantium. There had been plenty of contacts with Byzantium since the period of the Crusades; but there was no intellectual life there, and European Christian thinkers had no need to rely on imported texts while they were creating philosophies of their own. There was a structural reason why intellectuals began looking for new imports once the universities had lost their focus, and why those who did the most energetic searching were those who had acquired a rival base as courtier-intellectuals. And once the field starts relying on imports rather than indigenous creativity, philosophy enters the usual trough. The shift from the dense creative networks of the High Middle Ages to the sparse and broken ones of the Renaissance period is typical of generations of importers; the motive to import came from the crisis of success in the expansion of universities.

Academicization as a Two-Edged Sword

We face a disturbing paradox. Schools provide the material base and the insulation from lay conceptions which allow intellectuals to pursue their own ideas. But schools are also places of routine and pedantry. Formalism develops for its own sake; texts are memorized and covered with commentaries; refinements become narrow and trivial. We see this in the Christian universities after 1300. Even the surge of new foundations in this period did not breathe fresh life into learning. The Islamic *madrasas* were scholastic from the outset; their expansion brought activity only in the form of piling up supercommentaries upon traditional texts. The *maths* of the rival Hindu orders were for the most part similarly scholarly, sectarian, and dogmatic. In Greco-Roman antiquity, too, the level of support for formal education does not correlate with the times of creativity; the municipal schools of 250–500 C.E., with their high salaries and their representation of the rival philosophies, repeated the traditional positions in set rhetorical forms. Most of these educational systems centered on dialectic and debate, but without promoting innovation. The contest itself became a static form of training and display.

Neither *madrasas* nor Greek schools were universities in the European sense. Academic institutions in China came closer to this structure. The imperial university of the Han, and especially its expansion in the T'ang and subsequent dynasties, had a differentiated faculty and trained for a series of academic degrees. It was involved in much the same credentialing dynamics for bureaucratic careers found in medieval Christendom when the universities prepared students for careers in papal administration. But the prosperous periods of the university tended to be intellectually the most stagnant. The height of student population in the Han was the time when Confucianism was formalized into textual orthodoxy; the huge examination system of the Ming enforced Neo-Confucianism as an endless set of standard exercises. Similarly, Buddhist intellectual life was stifled after the late T'ang, when the government required formal examinations for certificates to become a monk.

The tendency of schools, with their formal curricula and examinations, is conservative. Yet sometimes the schools are the center of creativity. We see this when formal schooling was first institutionalized in Athens and in Alexandria, and there were later moments of upsurge especially at the latter. In China, the creative period of Neo-Confucianism was connected to the development of private schools and the movement to reform the university and the official examinations. In Japan, the first three generations of the Neo-Confucian schools were the height of innovation in philosophy, falling off as the number of schools multiplied in the later Tokugawa. The forming of the European schools in the 1100s was the milieu of creativity; in the next century the process of formalization in the university, the piling up of authorities and proofs known as "scholasticism," was the vehicle for the higher development of philosophy. Only in the Islamic *madrasas* was a creative phase missing; and even here one can point to al-Ghazali's sophisticated destruction of philosophy, formulated at the great government-sponsored *madrasa* in Baghdad within the first generation of its foundation.

Academicization is a two-edged sword. The material base that schools provide for intellectual life can be positive or negative in supporting creativity. The tendencies toward rote learning, narrow technique, and a routine of exercises and exams are always present. When they are overlaid by the energies of building new career paths and reorganizing intellectual space, the result is creative breakthroughs in the realm of higher abstractions. It is only when a fine balance holds among intersecting factions at a focus of attention that creativity exists. Disturbing the balance or removing the focus, one may be left with the material institutions and large numbers of intellectuals, but settled into scholastic routine. With this comes the stagnation of classics and technicalities, and eventually an atmosphere in which the more creative high points may even be forgotten. Stagnation in all its forms is a danger of academic success.

Coda: The Intellectual Demoralization of the Late Twentieth Century

De te fabula narratur. What we see around ourselves in recent decades has been an enormous expansion of cultural production. There are over 1 million publications annually in the natural sciences, over 100,000 in the social sciences, and comparable numbers in the humanities (Price, 1986: 266). To perceive the world as a text is not too inaccurate a description, perhaps not of the world itself, but of the life position of intellectuals: we are almost literally buried in papers. As the raw size of intellectual production goes up, the reward to the average individual goes down—at least the pure intellectual rewards of being recognized for one's ideas and of seeing their impact on others. The pessimism and self-doubt of the intellectual community under these circumstances is not surprising.

Which of the three types of stagnation do we exemplify? Loss of cultural capital (Stagnation A), certainly, marked by the inability of today's intellectuals to build constructively on the achievements of their predecessors. Simultaneously there exists a cult of the classics (Stagnation B): the historicism and footnote scholarship of our times, in which *doing* intellectual history becomes superior to *creating* it. And also we have the stagnation (C) of technical refinement: to take just a few instances, the acute refinements and formalisms of logical and linguistic philosophy have proceeded apace in little specialized niches; in the same way among all factions of the intellectual world today we find the prevalence of esoterica, of subtleties, and of impenetrable in-group vocabularies. As with the nominalists and other scholastics of the 1300s and 1400s, today's intellectual technicalities sometimes offer a high level of insight in their own spheres, but they are overrefined to travel well outside.

In our own day, as at the end of medieval Christendom, all three types of stagnation exist and interact. The underlying cause rests not with any individual failure, nor with the quality of our ideas, but with the structure of intellectual communities and their material foundations. Dark Ages of the mind are not necessarily ushered in by material collapse, but can occur in times of material abundance; a major cause is overabundance and dispersion of the material means of intellectual production.

An enormous expansion and decentralization of the academic world has taken place since 1950. The United States, which began this process somewhat earlier than other wealthy societies, has more than 3,000 colleges and universities, and scores of them are in the running to claim intellectual attention. Similar expansion took place in the decades after 1950 in France, Germany, Britain, Italy, Japan, and subsequently throughout the world, with similar decentralizing effects. Education has become a currency controlling opportunities for employment; it now expands autonomously through the interplay between credential inflation, driven by the competition for more schooling, and the resulting rise in the credential requirements of jobs. As each level of education becomes saturated and deflated in value, superordinate markets for cultural credentials are added beyond them. The relations between the supply of and demand for education are circular and self-reinforcing; the spiral is pointed upward with no end in sight (Collins, 1979; Ramirez and Boli-Bennett, 1982; Bourdieu, 1988).

The production of academic intellectuals rides on this wave of credential inflation. As demand expands for educational certificates, there comes an increase in the numbers of higher degree holders to train those of the next rank down, an explosion of Ph.D.'s. And since these scholars struggle for positions by means of their publishing reputations, the output of scholarship follows the same inflationary path as the competition for lower academic degrees, a meta-market driven upward upon the expansion of higher education.

Analogous processes take place in the commercial markets of popular culture. In this atmosphere of superordinate arenas of cultural production pyramiding upon one another, the content of modern culture has become self-reflex and ironic. We see this both in the pop culture, with its themes of privatized alienation and showy nihilism, and in the successive waves of ironicization among intellectuals, of which postmodernism is only the latest. The content of the postmodern message is an ideology of cultural producers in a highly pyramided market structure, where nothing in sight seems to touch solid earth.

Our structural condition as intellectuals can be summarized in the phrase: loss of a center of intersecting conflicts, loss of the small circle of circles at which our arguments can be focused. It is not a center of agreement that is lacking; creative intellectual periods never had that. What is lost is a nexus where disagreements are held in tension, the limited attention space which historically has been the generator of creative fame.

CHAPTER 10

♈

Cross-Breeding Networks and
Rapid-Discovery Science

In comparison to what went before, modern European philosophy comes on with a bang. Creativity revives in many directions, beginning around 1600, and is sustained for generations. Not least is the core of abstract philosophy itself. There is a takeoff in epistemology, which becomes much more thorough and central than in any previous philosophical community. Metaphysics too has a surprising rebirth, often spurred by the new epistemology. Value theory flourishes along aggressive new paths in aesthetics, ethics, and political philosophy. All this happened with an explicitly innovative consciousness that contrasts with the surreptitious character of creativity in most earlier epochs.

In addition, and most spectacularly, there is the scientific revolution of the same period. This overlaps with the networks of philosophers, especially in its formative generations. Henceforward science becomes a key reference point, whether positive or negative, for philosophers. Science rearranges the rest of intellectual space.

Why all this innovation? Our general theory holds that creativity results when intellectual networks reorganize, and this happens in opposing factions simultaneously. We expect not a uniform zeitgeist but a changing array of oppositions. In the two-step flow of causality, network reorganization is driven by institutional changes in the material bases of intellectual life. In this revolutionary period, there are two major structural changes:

1. Specialized branches of the intellectual networks concerned with naturalistic knowledge suddenly attract wide attention, then gradually separate off into a distinctive form of intellectual organization, leaving behind a sparer but more clearly delineated activity of philosophy. This is conventionally called the scientific revolution, but it will need considerable unpacking. There is a double revolution, a takeoff in mathematics as well as in science, with the mathematics revolution building up several generations earlier. In what does this double revolution consist as a social reorganization of intellectual practice? It is not simply a new focus on knowledge of nature, nor a heightened intensity of em-

piricism, nor even experimentation per se, as historical comparisons will show. The social change in the intellectual world consists in focusing attention on a rapidly moving research front; and this in turn comes from technologizing the research front. The key here is not so much the material research equipment as, more broadly, the invention of technique, first in mathematics, then in empirical research. The new technique consists in procedures which can be manipulated to produce new discoveries at the same time that it makes results repeatable and hence exportable in standardized forms to other locations. It is a machinery for making discoveries, a machinery that breeds and cross-breeds into new techniques which further accelerate the speed of innovation. A network of techniques and machines now comes into symbiosis with the intergenerational network of human intellectuals. Here is a genuine revolution in the inner organization of the intellectual world, overthrowing the law of small numbers which keeps the philosophical community fractionated. There now appears an alternative organization focused on rapid discovery which leaves a trail of consensus behind.

2. There is another, very different structural change in the bases of intellectual life: displacement of the church from control of the central means of intellectual production. Secularization is long-term and goes through many twists and turns. It is by no means reducible to the Protestant Reformation; it had already begun with the courtiers and lay officials of the late Middle Ages. Through the mid-1600s its intellectual center of gravity was the politics of the Catholic Church under the Spanish and French monarchies, the matrix for a surge of Catholic religious movements—Jesuits, Jansenists, Oratorians—whose intersection undergirds the new networks. Political maneuver among rival Catholic states, and the convoluted diplomacy of the religious wars, opens up a new space for Jews and religious cosmopolitans, for Deists, and for outright cynics and secularizers. The Protestants are more theologically particularistic; their philosophical developments hinge on contact with the cosmopolitan network to the Catholic side. The most significant philosophies in the Protestant lands come later, with the stalemate of religious mobilization and the emergence of toleration. Still later is yet another wave of institutional secularization. In Chapter 11 I examine the struggle to secularize the educational system inherited from the medieval church. This is the university revolution, set off in Germany around 1800 and gradually adopted in all the other leading school systems. There are many stages of intellectual reorganization in response to these changes in the religious-secular base; the alliances, halfway houses, militancies, reactions, and recombinations of positions drive much of the philosophical creativity from 1600 through the early 1900s.

These two structural changes—the revolution in math and science and secularization—are analytically distinct. Secularization represents a long-term shift in the organizational power of the church, and is not fundamentally caused by science or any other novel rationality. Nor is science the ideology of the Reformation, or indeed of the secularizers. We must beware of adopting Protestant propaganda, or of projecting the alignment of secularizers and scientizers which would predominate in the 1800s back into the intellectual politics of earlier generations. The connection between the two great changes is structural: the organizational breakdown of the church led theological intellectuals on all sides to seek new alliances, energizing conflicts in astronomy and mathematics and endowing them with general significance. For a time, competition over technical innovation became a main focus of intellectual attention. As techniques of rapid discovery built up, the newly prestigeful mathematics and science became resources taken up by virtually all the factions struggling over the shifting power base of the church.

One consequence of secularizing the means of intellectual production is that philosophy entered the political arena as an independent actor. Courts had been a source of intellectual patronage, alongside the church, throughout much of history. What was new is that intellectuals were no longer merely praising their patrons but shaping a new intellectual and political turf. One result was that the intellectual network became the base of political factions in its own right; we have here not merely political ideologies but intellectualized ideologies. Another result happened within the inward focus of the intellectual networks: the topics of political concern became new pieces of the intellectual attention space and were turned into specialized disciplines. Thus arose the social sciences, further subdividing the old philosophical networks.

It is conventional to begin this history with Hobbes and Locke, but the pattern first becomes visible in the Catholic sphere, with Vitoria, Suarez, and the Spanish liberals who created international law. Modern political philosophy emerged from the power relations of Church and state. Before it became secularized, the turf was carved out on issues such as the reunification of the church and the pacification of Europe, the subject of schemes ranging from Bruno and Campanella to Leibniz. As the church became institutionally displaced, political philosophies turned secular; every philosophical turn, including Idealism and Utilitarianism, was pressed into duty. The lineage passes directly from the German universities training theologians for the Prussian state church, to the state-conquering movement of Marxian socialists. At the same time, the structure of intellectual space is freed up for new disciplines. As we see in Figures 10.1 through 14.2, the retroactive founders of virtually every social science, from Hobbes and Smith to Comte and Wundt, Freud and Durkheim, branch off from the main philosophical networks.

All three institutional patterns—science, secularization, social sciences—give some grounds for interpreting philosophy as dying. For almost 400 years, one or another faction in the intellectual wars has declared philosophy to be nothing more than embryonic science, whether natural or social, perhaps with a residue of outworn religious beliefs. What needs emphasis is that philosophy since 1600 has been as creative on its own turf as at any time during world history. The conditions which produced the ideology of the death of philosophy have given philosophy new materials with which to re-create itself. The generations from 1600 to 1665 believed that their new philosophy, which consisted of natural science, would completely replace the old; yet the last generation of the 1600s saw the greatest outburst of metaphysical system-building in centuries, culminating shortly after 1700 in one of the most extreme idealisms in history, Berkeley's. The Enlightenment Encyclopedists recapitulated the attack in the more secularizing mode, to be immediately upstaged by the German Idealists.

Science and secularization rearranged but did not replace a core philosophical network that had carried down its own concepts and problems from earlier periods. Metaphysics is not exhausted by theology, nor does it fold without overlap into scientific cosmology. Nor even, despite the claims of political intellectuals from Marx's time to our own, does it disappear into politics. Philosophy is an analytical region which is revealed all the more sharply when religious dogmas as well as models of nature are stripped off into specialized sectors of the intellectual world; and this is so whether philosophers think they are doing metaphysics or science. Epistemology is not part of the core activity of scientists; it is part of philosophers' turf to argue over the bases of knowledge, however knowledge may be exemplified in a particular period. Thus we find philosophers of science, such as Bacon and Descartes, who want nothing better than to destroy philosophical argument and promote science, but whose effect is to make epistemology a creative center for the philosophical field. Splitting off secularized political ideologies and specialized social sciences goes along with sharpening the focus on value theory inside philosophy, giving it more autonomous content than it had in the days when it was circumscribed by theological orthodoxy and authoritarian rule. Hence the militancy of various kinds of modern value theory, from Hegelians, Marxists, and Utilitarians down to existentialists and postmodernists.

The differentiation of specialties from the philosophical networks lays bare the inner terrain of abstract reflexivity which makes up the intellectual field. Philosophy, re-creating its own space in the midst of the others, increasingly builds what is distinctively its own.

A Cascade of Creative Circles

The skeletal structure of creativity is its network lineages, and the history of modern philosophy can be traced through a surprisingly small number of social circles (see Figure 10.1 and its continuation in Figures 11.1, 12.1 and 12.2,

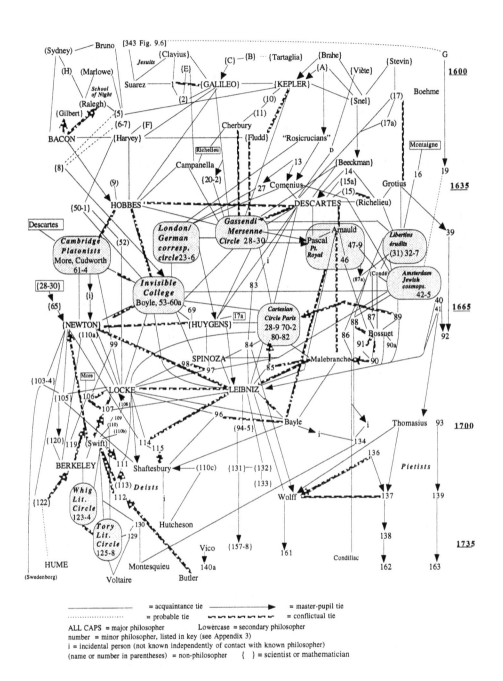

FIGURE 10.1. EUROPEAN NETWORK: THE CASCADE OF CIRCLES,
1600–1735

13.1 and 13.2, and 13.8, and 14.1). These are circles in a strong sense: groups which regularly meet, in which everyone knows everyone else. In the network figures they are designated by an enclosed border within the network. They are self-conscious; typically they have a name, as well as allies and often enemies on the outside; usually they have a program and issue their manifesto. They are the material core of intellectual movements; in the terminology of modern social movement theory, they are SMOs, social movement organizations. They are the nodes at the center of networks, recruiting and publicizing and thereby building waves of creative energy in intellectual attention space.

For the time when intellectual life moved outside the church and the universities, circles provided the indispensable stage and the backstage machinery of theater. In our two-step model, rearranging the material bases of intellectual production makes possible new networks and sets off intellectual realignment. The key circles of modern Europe are those which reorganized the means of communication; they set up networks of correspondence and created the first intellectual periodicals. The intellectual networks of the 1600s were full of diplomats, refugees, and commercial travelers; in the absence of a postal system, they controlled the key resource for organizing a truly cosmopolitan network, making possible the meta-circle of circles which emerged in this period. Later in the century the dominant circles arose where they could find new bases of collective material support: academies which did not depend on individual patronage relations. Still later such circles captured university positions or formed out of student groups, although the shift back into the university base usually replaced circles with academic lineages. Groups arise where they control a special niche in the means of intellectual production. Each new phase in the development of the publications business tends to have associated with it a famous intellectual circle. In tracing these circles we are tracing the major episodes in reorganizing the bases of intellectual production.[1]

In 1623 from his monastic cell in Paris, Mersenne formed a circle of correspondence, working closely with Gassendi and connecting to Kepler, Galileo, Campanella, Descartes, Hobbes, Torricelli, Fermat, and other mathematicians and scientific researchers of the time. Mersenne was the organizational leader; Descartes emerged as the intellectual leader whose works became the movement's emblem and program statement. Mersenne's circle lasted until 1648; in 1657 its survivors began regular meetings at the houses of wealthy patrons, Montmor and the Cartesian leader Rohault. This circle too served as a clearing house of letters announcing scientific and mathematical discoveries, and it made available Descartes's unpublished manuscripts to Malebranche and Leibniz.[2] Another temporary visitor was Leibniz himself, who went on to organize the first scientific journal in Germany, *Acta Eruditorum,* in 1682, and the academies at Berlin and St. Petersburg; together these provided the base for much of mathematics in the next century.

Other circles around Paris contemporary with the Mersenne-Cartesian group became prominent for the history of philosophy: first the so-called Libertins Érudits in the 1630s through the 1650s, connected to the court. Immediately after this came the Port-Royal circle of Pascal and Arnauld, from 1655 through the early 1660s, during the height of the struggle between Jansenists and Jesuits.

A parallel and to some extent derivative structure emerged in England; a scientific correspondence circle formed in the 1630s around German Protestant travelers settling at London. This gave rise to the famous Invisible College at Oxford in the 1640s during the Commonwealth, from which came Boyle's famous scientific experiments in the early 1660s. In 1662 its members formed the Royal Society in London, whose *Transactions* became the first scientific periodical. Meanwhile at Cambridge from 1633 to 1660 was an oppositional Platonist circle of Whichcote, Henry More, and Cudworth; Newton was intellectually initiated by its members early in his life, and Locke connects to it too, as well as to the other major circles of his generation.

Counting the successor circles across the generations as one, we see six circles in the great revolutionary period of the mid-1600s: the Platonists and the cosmopolitan scientific movement in England; a similar scientific-philosophical movement in Paris, with more extreme tendencies presented by the Port-Royal group and the Libertins Érudits. Completing the lineup is the Amsterdam community of religious cosmopolitans (1640–1680s), largely crypto-Jews in exile from Portugal; they connect not only to Spinoza but also to French religious and anti-religious factions and to cosmopolitan travelers such as Locke. Bayle publicized their views by founding *Nouvelles de la République des Lettres* in 1684.

In the early 1700s the only notable circles were in London, organized around the emerging publishing business: the Whig literary circle of Addison and Steele and, more important, the Tory literary circle of Pope, Bolingbroke, and Chesterfield. Through Swift the latter circle connected with Berkeley; and its members hosted and inspired the young French visitors Montesquieu and Voltaire in the 1720s.

In the mid-1700s Paris had another major circle: the Encyclopedists (1745–1772), whose core was a new kind of publishing enterprise; contact with it inspired Rousseau and the wealthy Helvétius. During the 1770s and 1780s, the group re-formed at Auteuil at the estate of Mme. Helvétius, recruiting Condorcet, Cabanis, and Destutt de Tracy as well as scientific stars such as Lavoisier and Laplace. It was especially active after 1792 as a refuge from the Revolutionary period of the Terror. In the late 1790s and early 1800s, many of the group were in the Chamber of Deputies or the Senate, forming a moderate monarchist–anti-religious faction called the Idéologues. Its protégés included Comte and Maine de Biran.

The English counterpart in the late 1700s was a prominent scientific circle, the Birmingham Lunar Society, in contact with the French circles. More important for philosophy were the Philosophical Radicals at London (1810–1830), followers of Bentham including James Mill and Ricardo. Institutionally they controlled the *Encyclopedia Brittanica* and founded the *Westminster Review* and the University of London, the first break for centuries in the Oxford-Cambridge monopoly. At Oxford from 1833 to 1841 there was a counterbalancing movement of the religious conservatives: the Tractarians, led by Newman. London struck back in the next generation with a group of evolutionists led by Huxley and Spencer and encouraged by John Stuart Mill, flourishing in the 1850s to 1870s. Their institutional bases were the new political-intellectual journals: *The Economist, The Leader,* and *Fortnightly Review,* along with the Utilitarian *Westminster Review;* Spencer found a publishing niche for his work in the form of a personal encyclopedia. Now Cambridge philosophy revived, while its most notable thinkers connected through the Society for Psychical Research, founded in 1882. Meanwhile at Oxford there was the Idealist movement led by Green. Finally we come to the student society known as the "Apostles" at Cambridge, in a burst of glory (1890–1915) with McTaggart, Whitehead, Russell, Moore, Keynes, Lytton Strachey, Leonard Woolf, and Wittgenstein; many of them overlapped with the Bloomsbury literary circle around Virginia Woolf and her husband's publishing house.

The history of German philosophy is likewise a chain of circles. In the mid-1700s the Berlin Academy under the patronage of Frederick the Great sponsored Euler's mathematics and offered asylum to Voltaire; it recombined the older French network with Leibniz's lineage. The Berlin network catalyzed German intellectual life. From this base Maupertuis interfered in the religious disputes of the German universities. A Berlin intellectual circle built up around the bookseller Nicolai; contact with this circle spread the action to Königsberg with Kant, Hamann, and Herder. What followed went along with the explosion of a literary marketplace in Germany. From 1775 through the 1820s, Goethe assembled a literary group at Weimar, which in the 1780s sponsored Kantians at the nearby university of Jena; Fichte, Schelling, and Hegel were there in the period 1794–1806, while during 1795–1800 the Romantic circle formed at Weimar around the Schlegel brothers, moving in the early 1800s to Berlin, where it connected to Schleiermacher. These two clumps of circles, Berlin-Königsberg and Weimar-Jena, disappeared after the founding of the University of Berlin in 1810. About 1837–1842 at Berlin appeared a coffeehouse circle calling themselves first the Doctors' Club, subsequently "Die Freien": these were the left-Hegelians following Feuerbach, led by Bauer and Ruge, including Stirner, Bakunin, and the young Engels and Marx. Their house organ was the

Hallesche Jahrbücher, succeeded by the *Deutsch-Französiche Jahrbücher* co-edited by Marx.

German philosophy was established within academic chains thereafter, and there were no more important circles until 1925–1936, when Schlick, Neurath, and Carnap led the Vienna Circle of logical positivists, with its manifestos and its journal, *Erkenntnis.* In the late 1930s to 1940s in Paris appeared the counterpoise: the existentialist circle of Sartre, Camus, Merleau-Ponty, de Beauvoir, and the young Lacan, importers of German cultural capital from the phenomenologists and Freudians. Once again the circle has a distinctive base of publicity: the Gallimard publishing house, with its pioneering mass-distributed but intellectually elite paperbacks, the avant-garde theater, and politically militant publications, especially *Les Temps Moderne.*

Philosophy in the United States came alive with three circles: in the 1830s and 1840s the Transcendentalists around Boston, led by Emerson and Thoreau; the St. Louis Hegelians of the 1860s and 1870s, who eventually migrated to New England; and in 1871–1875 the Cambridge Metaphysical Club, whose members later to be famous included the young Peirce, William James, and Oliver Wendell Holmes. Out of this group came the renowned Harvard philosophy department of 1885–1920.

In the 11 generations from 1600 to 1965, European thought has been organized by some 15 circles: half a dozen circles in the mid-1600s (two of them predominantly scientific); the Whig and Tory literary circles of the early 1700s; then the three great intergenerational successions: the Encyclopedists-Auteuil-Idéologues in France; in Germany the overlapping circles of Berlin-Königsberg from the 1750s to the 1780s and Weimar-Jena-Romanticists in the 1780s to 1810, revolving back to Berlin at the end of the period with the Young Hegelians in the 1830s as the last of this chain. There were a few anti-modernist religious circles in the anglophone world: the Oxford Tractarians of the 1830s, the New England Transcendentalists in the 1830s and 1840s, the Green-Jowett circle of Idealists at Balliol College, Oxford, the St. Louis Hegelians in the 1860s and 1870s, and the Society for Psychical Research in the 1880s. On the scientific side during the 1800s were the Philosophical Radicals and Evolutionists in London, and an offshoot, the Cambridge (Massachusetts) Metaphysical Society, in the 1870s. Finally there were the three great centers of the early 1900s: the Cambridge Apostles, the Vienna Circle, and the Paris existentialists.

The major and secondary philosophers did not all belong to one or another of these circles, but a large proportion did; if not members, virtually all of the important philosophers were at least connected to one or more circles.[3] The circles energized the creativity; like Hobbes and Rousseau, most successful individuals made contact with the group first, then were sparked into the intellectual action for which they became famous. This is not to say that the most famous philosophers were typically the organizers of these groups. Studies of similar intellectual groups in recent fields show that there is usually a division between an organizational leader who builds the material underpinnings and an intellectual leader who makes its doctrine famous (Mullins, 1973; Griffith and Mullins, 1972). This is a division of labor which describes the relation between Mersenne and Descartes, or between Bauer and Marx. Some of the greatest philosophers are connected to multiple circles, members of none; especially in the late 1600s, we see in such network positions Spinoza, Leibniz, Locke, and Bayle, along with the great freelancing scientists Newton and Huygens. The greatest creativity consists in making new conceptual combinations, playing off the oppositions of existing groups, and laying down new alliances that become institutionalized in the groups of the immediate future. Circles are the accumulators of attention and the resonators of emotional energy; the sparks which fly between them are the thoughts of persons situated at the nodes where the networks intersect.[4]

The question lingers: Why these circles rather than others? There were many more salons and discussion groups than these eminent 15; academies existed in every provincial town in pre-Revolutionary France, just as in the following century students and lecturers gathered for talking as well as drinking in every Germany university town and in many a British college. Most of these groups were patterned on earlier and more famous ones, the pioneers who located a new intellectual base. Even where the circles were all on the same footing materially, there was advantage in being the first or nearly first on the scene; where several early networks began to form, the first to acquire a reputation for its arguments could build an accelerating lead, attracting recruits and pulling away from the others. Whether composed of circles or of individuals, the intellectual world is constructed on a limited focus of attention, a space that allows only a small number to be successful.

Philosophical Connections of the Scientific Revolution

The Emergence of Rapid-Discovery Science

Why are philosophical networks implicated in scientific creativity? To solve this problem, we need to answer two related questions. First, what is the difference between the social organization of science before and after the scientific revolution? And second, what is the sociological difference between science and philosophy?

The scientific revolution was not the emergence of science. Observational and calculational knowledge existed in all of the major world regions before

Europe of the 1600s; that is why it is possible, as we will shortly see, to consider the overlap or non-overlap between philosophical networks and those of astronomers, mathematicians, or medical scientists in Greece, China, and India.[5] What did the scientific revolution do to change science as a form of social organization? The question need not hinge on asserting the greater validity of modern scientific knowledge. Some portions of Chinese or Greek mathematics, biology, or planetary astronomy may be considered sufficiently valid even from a modern European point of view, so here validity is not a distinguishing characteristic. Leaving aside these issues about the contents of science, there are two major social differences.

First, European science moved much more rapidly. It focused on a fast-moving research front, making and discussing new discoveries for a few years and then moving on to something else. European intellectuals became highly conscious of this movement of rapid discovery. We find it in the explicit scientific ideologies of Francis Bacon, Descartes, and Boyle: the notion that a method of making discoveries had been found, and that future problems would be rapidly solved. This was not only an ideology; the accumulation of scientific research literature did indeed accelerate continuously from this point onward.[6] We might thus designate science before and after the scientific revolution as "traditional science" and "rapid-discovery science," respectively.

Second, European science acquired a higher degree of consensus. This is not to say that there were no controversies, but rather scientific controversies became socially resolved over a period of years, and the community of scientists came to treat old issues as settled while concentrating on new ones. Again, European intellectuals were highly conscious of this characteristic; after 1600 they tended to elevate science and mathematics as exemplars of the highest level of consensus possible. In general, non-European science had much less of this consensus, and little or none of the reputation as exemplar of secure knowledge.

This is not to say that there was never social consensus over particular aspects of non-European science. The elementary portions of Greek geometry after Euclid, for example, were widely accepted among mathematicians. But the more sophisticated work of Archimedes, Eratosthenes, and Apollonius was only sporadically represented in later textbooks; in the Roman period, Nicomachus was generally followed but Diophantus was often ignored, and late texts such as Boethius' omitted the proofs that constituted the main Greek achievement in abstract mathematics. Greek mathematical practitioners as a whole achieved only a "lazy consensus" largely by neglecting more complex developments. This was even more pronounced in Chinese mathematics; in many instances sophisticated results and methods were subsequently lost.[7] There were also widespread and long-standing areas of dissensus in traditional science. In Greek astronomy the homocentric planetary spheres of Eudoxus (ca. 370 B.C.E.) became prominent; Aristarchus' heliocentric model (ca. 270 B.C.E.) was not generally accepted. After 300 B.C.E. Babylonian astronomy and astrology were imported, which added two more systems for solar and lunar predictions, plus a large variety of planetary theories. After 150 C.E. Ptolemy's mathematically sophisticated comprehensive model eventually became the textbook standard, although other models survived for centuries (*DSB,* 1981: 11:188, 202; Neugebauer, 1957: 115; Jones, 1991). In harmonics there were rival theories dating from the Pythagoreans and from Aristotle's protégé Aristoxenus; Ptolemy proposed an improved model, but the rival systems continued, and several were included by Boethius around 530 C.E. (*DSB,* 1981: 11:203). Outside Greece, dissensus in the technical fields of science was common.[8]

The emergence of European rapid-discovery science sharpened the difference between science and philosophy. Here the crucial difference was the heightened degree of consensus in science. Philosophical controversies tend to remain unresolved, and old positions are typically subject to revival. Rapid-discovery science, however, arrives at agreement, and the older work is either incorporated as a partial contribution or regarded as outdated. The contrast between philosophy and science first became an explicit item of attention after 1600. Descartes and the other ideologists of the new "mechanical philosophy" intended to replace one mode of intellectual life with the other. The fact that philosophy survived as a distinctive activity, and indeed that rivalry among philosophical positions continued in Descartes's own day, underscores the point that these are two different ways of organizing intellectual communities.

Nevertheless, there is similarity and even overlap among scientific and philosophical networks. In both kinds of networks, creativity clusters in groups and builds up in intergenerational chains. Consider now the sociological implications of scientific consensus for the structural organization of the community. Does this consensus mean that science escapes from the rivalries which drive intellectual fields, while philosophy remains stuck in the fractionation of three to six active positions which makes up the law of small numbers?

In fact science shows both patterns at different phases of the research process. Science is based on rivalries and controversies while a topic is on the research forefront. Eventually these controversies are resolved, and the losing positions are abandoned. At this point the winning position is taken as secure knowledge, while the field goes on to controversy over something else. These are Bruno Latour's (1987) two faces of science: science-in-the-making operates like philosophy; science-already- made is science after the research front, when consensus and cumulation prevail. Science on the research front follows the law of small numbers, as scientists struggle by dividing along rival structurings of the attention space.[9] But this is given up in time, primarily because scientists are more eager to move on to a new research front than they are to stay and defend losing positions. Thus, in the two ways in which science differs from philosophy—eventual consensus and a fast-moving research front—the latter is what makes the difference for the former. Science arrives at social consensus because the research front is still moving, and it is easier to make a reputation there than by clinging to old controversies.

What then are the social conditions which brought about this combination of rapid research front plus consensus on older results? One possibility is empiricism. Many kinds of organized empiricism had developed in Europe by the 1600s. Dissections at the Padua medical faculty led to Vesalius's new anatomy in 1543; Tycho Brahe's observatories in Denmark and Prague produced detailed astronomical data from 1576 to 1600; by the late 1600s there was a veritable enthusiasm of private naturalistic collections. But the difference between European rapid-discovery science and traditional science is not a matter of empiricism. Traditional science is essentially empirical. We see the limits of sheer empirical accumulation in the official Chinese astronomical bureaus, which brought neither rapid discovery nor consensus despite many centuries of observation; similarly, Albert the Great's naturalist collection set off no research front. The collections fashionable among the gentry of the 1600s tended toward curious anomalies and did little to develop explanatory theory (Impey and McGregor, 1985; Girouard, 1978: 163–80). One may conclude that empiricism by itself does not reach very high levels of intellectual abstraction and systematization, and does so only when naturalistic empiricists are brought into contact with the competitive intellectual community of philosophers. Philosophy-plus-empiricism does not yield research-front science, but philosophical networks are one of the necessary ingredients.

What else is needed? Two other possibilities are *research technology* and *mathematics*. Both of these went into accelerated development at the time of the scientific revolution. In some respects they are alternatives; some of the scientific takeoff, such as that of Galileo or Boyle, was associated with research technologies; other parts of the takeoff, such as the astronomy of Copernicus and Kepler, were essentially mathematical. At a deeper level, we shall see that both research technology and mathematics acquired a similar social organization at this time.

TECHNOLOGIZING THE RESEARCH FRONT

Rapid-discovery science is not just a network of persons or of ideas; it is the connection between the human network and a genealogy of research technologies. The research front consists of the most recent edge of those technologies. The scientific revolution coincided with the setting in motion of this technological front of laboratory equipment and tools of observation and measurement.

The chief dynamism of scientific discovery, as Derek Price (1986: 237–253) suggests, is driven by laboratory technology rather than by theories. The scientific takeoff of the 1600s is exemplified by Galileo's use of the telescope to discover new phenomena in astronomy. Galileo adopted or invented technologies: a pendulum for measuring time, lenses for telescope and microscope. His followers invented barometers and thermometers and vacuum pumps. There followed a wave of imitation of Galileo's *method:* using new instruments to make discoveries. Modifications of the telescope led to the microscope, hence to discoveries in other arenas far removed from Galileo in mechanics and astronomy. The general notion of trying out new apparatus for experiments led to Galileo's own work on mechanics using ramps; application of existing pumps led to new instruments and discoveries regarding pressure and temperature.

Technologies evolve by tinkering. Earlier machines are modified, adapted to new circumstances, combined with other lineages of technology. Hence they may be conceived of as networks—indeed as genealogies—in their own right; there is a crucial connection *from machine to machine,* and not merely from person to person.[10] Technology usually exists in a historical stream of its own before it is picked up by an intellectual network; thus lenses go back to eyeglasses in the 1200s before being adapted to scientific purposes by Galileo's generation, and Boyle and Guericke adopted pumps from mining to scientific experiment. In the non-intellectual world of practical activity, a technology is not usually a subject of experimentation and change. When the intellectual network organizes itself around research equipment, however, it begins to tinker with the technology in order to generate phenomena which its members can use in their arguments, their struggle for attention. Research technology is not an embodied theory but is embodied accumulated practices; the lab equipment on the research forefront is an embodiment of the generations of past tinkering. Scientific theories are the ideologies—the socially negotiated interpretations—which legitimate this genealogy of tinkering.

Why should this change philosophy into science? That is, why should research technology create a fast-moving research front, with agreement behind the edge of the front? Technology is not necessarily fast-changing when left to the non-intellectual world;[11] it is intellectual competition which speeds it up. How then does research equipment result in resolving intellectual rivalries, overcoming the law of small numbers which prevails in philosophy?

Research equipment is easy to monopolize, especially if it is constantly changing on a fast-moving forefront. Discoveries can be made rather predictably by tinkering with equipment used in previous discoveries. "Normal science" consists in making small modifications in existing equipment and observing the empirical results, or in applying equipment to untouched areas of observation. More revolutionary developments can be produced by inventing new kinds of equipment, usually by analogy, recombination, or reapplication of older equipment, deliberately cross-breeding equipment genealogies. The telescope and microscope opened up new realms in which discoveries were more or less guaranteed; the invention of the electrical battery in the late 1700s and its application to electrolysis of fluids resulted in the discovery of dozens of chemical elements, just as successive generations of particle accelerators were responsible for producing the next round; the shift from optical to radio astronomy widened the range of stellar phenomena, as did the combination of spectroscopic analysis with optical photography (Price, 1986: 237–253). When tinkering with the prior generation of research-front equipment becomes normal procedure, scientists come to expect new discoveries as a matter of routine.

The greatest attention goes to whoever is on the research forefront using the latest equipment. New discoveries upstage older ones. The result is a social consensus once a field stops being an area of hot research news. Scientists give up competing over older theoretical rivalries so that they can move on to the forefront of the newest, most successful equipment; they abandon old controversies so they can get into new controversies. Of course not everyone abandons old positions. Thomas Kuhn argued that proponents of defeated paradigms never give up but only die out. It is likely that when the research front is moving quite rapidly, adherents of older theories just as rapidly lose attention, and stubbornness does them little good. Thus the law of small numbers may prevail on the forefront itself as it gives way to domination of one position behind it, precisely because the lure of working on the forefront is much greater than expounding an already known position.

There is another way in which research technology produces consensus. When a new technology is tried out, the practical activity of scientific research consists in tinkering with it to produce new phenomena, and then further tinkering until those phenomena can be reliably repeated. This is not an easy or automatic process. It took about 15 years for Boyle's generation of air pumps to produce consistent results; and today controversies swirl when cold fusion or gravitational waves cannot be routinely evoked (Shapin and Schaffer, 1985: 274–276; more generally see Galison, 1987). The equipment—and the theory—are perfected simultaneously when these effects are routinized, that is to say, when the machinery embodies enough past practices of tinkering so that one can follow explicit procedures and get expected results. This technical repeatability is what makes science seem certain and hence objective.

Science is socially constructed, but I would stress that it is constructed not so much by the imposition of ideas upon the world *(idealist constructivism)* as by the dominance of physical practices, embodied in material equipment (one might call this *materialist constructivism*). It is possible that a different line of research equipment or a different line of tinkering could produce repeatable results as well; and this might be combined with a different lineage of idea interpretations from the intellectual community. Because research discoveries are driven by recombining equipment genealogies, a fan-shaped pattern of discovery paths is hypothetically possible, although some of these are not followed up because of the social focus of attention. Different sciences might be historically constructed from the same point in time. It is the social process of seizing on the lineage of equipment that advances most quickly on the research front which cuts off some of these directions and exalts one of them.

Our formula for high-consensus science becomes: competitive philosophical networks plus empiricism carried out with a fast-moving genealogy of research technologies.

MATHEMATICS BECOMES A DISCOVERY-MAKING MACHINE

There is an alternative route to rapid-discovery science. Another key to the scientific revolution was not laboratory equipment but mathematics. Copernicus overthrew geocentric astronomy not with new observations but by mathematically simplifying old data. The two routes may coincide; many aspects of the scientific revolution of the 1600s and 1700s were carried out not only by experiment but also by formulating quantitative principles for the results. But the two routes were not identical. A mathematical revolution preceded the takeoff of scientific research by two or three generations; the upsurge in the number of noteworthy mathematicians in Europe started in the 1490s,[12] and the first big advances began around 1520–1550 with Ferro, Cardan, and Tartaglia in the general solution of higher-order algebraic equations, leading to the expansion of new mathematical fields with Viète.

According to a familiar line of argument, mathematization of the worldview produced modern science. The difficulty is that traditional mathematical science, such as astronomy among the Greeks, Chinese, or Indians, does not have the characteristics of consensus and rapid discovery which are central to modern science. Mathematics in general is not sufficient to bring about consensus-making, fast-moving science; only a particular kind of mathematics provides the key.

What kind of mathematics can this be? The mathematical revolution unfolds when mathematics itself becomes a research technology. That is to say, technology is a set of embodied practices which bring about reliable, repeatable results. Such techniques, although not consisting in a complex physical apparatus, nevertheless are material: they consist in methods for writing equations on wax or paper, or placing sticks on a counting board, following procedures for moving emblems from one place to another until certain kinds of results are obtained. Platonic ideologies to the contrary, mathematics does not exist purely in the mind; it is a set of practices, developed by generations of tinkering, and an integral part of these practices is the physical "equipment" with which they are connected. This is not so distant from our implicit definition of a machine as a material entity, for every machine consists in the combination of the physical object with skills for manipulating it. Sets of mathematical symbols on paper, lined up in equations and rearranged according to rules, represent a practical activity rather than simply a set of abstract ideas.

Turning mathematics into a problem-solving machine was not simply a matter of new notation, although the emergence of symbolism did take place at the time of the mathematical revolution. There had been episodes of syncopated, or abbreviated, algebra before (Diophantus ca. 250 C.E., Brahmagupta ca. 630 C.E.), but these had not been consistently followed up, and most of Chinese, Greek, and Muslim mathematics was argued out in words, with the assistance of geometrical diagrams. In medieval Christendom, Fibonacci's math (ca. 1200) was rhetorical; so were the difficult and involved proofs of Swineshead "the Calculator," as well as the generalizing efforts of Regiomontanus in the mid-1400s. Syncopated forms arose in the early 1500s in arithmetic and algebra, especially with the "reckoning masters" of the commercial German cities, and the symbolic apparatus moved rapidly forward with Viète, reaching what became more or less the standard modern form with Descartes.

There are several reasons why we should not take notation per se as the key to the mathematical takeoff. Much of the development of notation took place not among mathematicians producing creative new results, but in the textbooks explaining commercial arithmetic which proliferated from the 1480s onward.[13] Still less should we regard the spread of Hindu-Arabic numerals, with place notation and the zero sign, as the key. These were not associated with higher mathematics in their place of origin; they provoked no creativity at all when they became available in Byzantium, and they were known in medieval Europe centuries before the mathematical takeoff of the 1500s (Kazhdan and Epstein, 1985: 145; Smith, 1951). On the side of the intellectuals, the mathematical "machinery" which began to automate the solution of equations was often formulated without benefit of the more concise notation. Cardan's exposition was rhetorical, but he gave general rules for solving equations by manipulating and substituting terms so as to turn unknown expressions into the form of solvable ones. Viète was more syncopated than symbolic, still using some verbal argument; but he clearly recognized the generality of the unknowns, distinguishing assumed unknowns from assumed givens. Even with this unwieldy apparatus, he developed the machinery of problem-solving procedure by creating new equations to substitute into old ones. Pascal, as late as the 1650s, gave his theorems rhetorically; nevertheless he was in the swing of the new abstract procedures, and he gave the first clear explanation of the method of mathematical induction (Boyer, 1985: 335, 397).

More significant for mathematical discovery was the drive to find devices for improving scientific calculations. First came the expansion of trigonometric tables as a tool for improving the precision and speed of astronomical calculations. In the 1460s, Regiomontanus compiled a text of trigonometry from Greek and Arab sources, based primarily on sine functions. Two generations later Copernicus produced new trigonometric tables, and his assistant Rheticus worked out a trigonometry of all six functions with elaborate tables for each. Such tables may be regarded as a rather low-level empirical extension of existing mathematical methods into adjacent areas, but the effort spilled over into shortcuts in calculation. Formulae for substituting the addition of cosines for their multiplication were a great improvement in the clumsy arithmetic of the time; these algorithms of trigonometric algebra were developed in the 1580s by Viète and others. This labor-saving device was quickly picked up by astronomers such as Tycho Brahe. From there a visitor brought it to Napier in Scotland, who generalized the idea into logarithms in the early 1600s. The concern for a technology of calculation led to mechanical devices as well as conceptual ones. Galileo in 1597 constructed and marketed computational compasses, a device analogous to a slide rule for quick computations. The focus of concern at this time is shown by the fact that Galileo was competing against a similar device invented by Burgi, a rival of Napier in the discovery of logarithms. Still later, in 1642 we find Pascal at the very beginning of his career building and selling a mechanical calculating machine (Boyer, 1985: 338–340, 351, 396).

The revolution in algebra followed the same path in a more abstract way. Algebra initially consisted of shortcuts in arithmetic, principles which cover whole classes of calculations. Algebra advanced to new terrain when it formulated such methods in the form of meta-rules about how to solve abstract equations. The very substance of algebra, and of abstract mathematics generally, comprises the methods for solving lower-order problems. Pure mathematics becomes an independent activity when intellectuals concentrate on developing algorithms apart from their application. The takeoff of abstract mathematics in the early 1500s came as just such a research forefront was emerging, with the discovery of general methods for solving the cubic and quartic equations by the mathematicians around Tartaglia and Cardan. By the time of Viète, techniques were being developed for problems of much higher degree. In the process, other areas of mathematics such as trigonometry and geometry were being brought in as tools, resulting in cross-fertilization among these fields. The genealogies of mathematical techniques were beginning to propagate.

The onset of the mathematical revolution was marked by a surge of interest in improving the efficiency of problem solving all across the board. We see the same impulse in many areas. The development of abbreviated notation in commercial arithmetic was one version; the expansion of trigonometric tools for astronomy was another; the search for general algebraic methods of solution was yet another. Only the third of these explicitly led to an arena of pure mathematics, but the competition soon pulled the other branches into ongoing contact.

These were the leading areas of activity in mathematics, but not the only kind. Traditional Greek mathematics, which consisted largely of geometry, was revived, extended, and combined with the newer branches. Among Humanist scholars there was an increased interest in Greek mathematical texts (Rose, 1975). The fact that most of these had already been available in medieval Christendom suggests that the concern for new translations was the result of the upsurge of mathematical creativity rather than vice versa. In the late 1500s and into the 1600s, interest peaked in a Humanistic brand of mathematical puzzle: restoring the lost portions of texts such as Apollonius (Boyer, 1985: 330, 351, 380). Since the mathematical revolution was already launched, it appears that the most advanced Greek work was sought out and extended because the Europeans under their own impulse now were working at this level. Transmission of old texts, in other words, was not the cause but to a considerable extent the effect of the crescendo of new mathematics.

Greek geometry was recruited to the new mathematics but was certainly not its leading edge. Geometry was the most conservative area of mathematics from the point of view of problem-solving technology, attached as it was to concrete representations without general notation or higher-order rules for solution. Descartes, who put the final touches on the mathematical revolution, introduced his reform of geometry by explaining that his aim was to free geometry from the figures that fatigue the mind; like Fermat, who simultaneously developed a version of coordinate geometry, Descartes was concerned to break out of the clumsy geometric methods of the Greeks (*Discourse on Method* 2.17, in Descartes, 1985: 119; see also Mahoney, 1980). Descartes was a militant advocate of the modern algebraic approach, freeing the last remaining area of mathematics from the Humanistic revival of the classics and turning it into a rapid problem-solving technique.

Even in classical geometry, new methods were formulated as the mathematical revolution got under way. The initial concern came from painters interested in the theory of perspective; the first new curve since ancient times was constructed by Durer around 1525, about the same time that Copernicus produced a new curve by compounding two circular motions (Boyer, 1985: 320, 326). The work of Kepler in the early 1600s on planetary orbits and of Galileo in the 1630s on projectiles fitted these motions to conic sections known since the Greeks. The upheaval in mathematical method incorporated these classical curves into the central achievements of the new mathematical science. Kepler generalized Archimedean methods to various solids of revolution, and showed that the familiar conic sections were transformations of one another; Galileo reinterpreted conic sections as products of the combination of two motions (Boyer, 1985: 356–358). These discoveries were results of the new algebraic vision applied to geometry.

Sustained discovery in mathematics was well along by the time of Viète in the 1580s. With Viète the combination of different mathematical fields became a discovery-making technique: the new higher algebra was combined with geometric methods of solution, the new trigonometry turned into algebraic functions. The new algebraic geometry developed by Viète, Descartes, and Fermat went beyond traditional plane and solid figures into a more abstract space, in which lines, squares, cubes, and higher powers were all treated as quantities in the same equation. Descartes's *Geometry* closes with an explicit overview of the theory of equations. By the mid-1600s, whole regions of higher mathematics were emerging through recombining subspecialties. New methods were developed for the algebraic solution of problems relating to curves, especially where the new curves raised issues of motion and of infinitesimal changes and their summation. Out of these problems arose a crude calculus in the hands of Galileo, Roberval, Cavalieri, and Torricelli, perfected in the next generation by Newton and Leibniz.

Between the time of Viète and Descartes, mathematics was transformed into a machinery for manipulating equations. In part this marked a change from verbal arguments to abbreviations to the invention of symbols for givens, unknowns, and operations. The decisive step was to set up systems of equations with explicit rules for how to substitute and recombine them; by following these rules of manipulation, one could gain the same advantages that resulted from introducing a forefront of research equipment into science. Tinkering with the mathematical machinery could open up new areas of application and generate new results, turning mathematics into a moving forefront of research. And perfecting the procedures for manipulating equations—the equivalent of tinkering with the machinery until it is reliable—yields absolute certainty of results, because results are absolutely repeatable.

This procedure is not exclusively modern; the history of mathematics consists in building up just such a technology for manipulating classes of expressions so that results are highly repeatable. One might say that this is what defines mathematics: it is the cumulated practices of tinkering with the operations of counting and measuring, proceeding on to higher-order gener- alizations about classes of such operations. These skills have always been embodied in a technology, though usually tacit and not sufficiently portable to have the kind of widespread repeatability that is the social basis of certainty. It was this takeoff in manipulating the machinery of mathematics that constituted the European mathematical revolution.

Overlaps among the Networks: World Comparison

How then did this revolution come about? Why did a genealogy of research technologies build up, promoting rapid discovery, first in mathematics, then in natural science? For a sociological answer, let us look at the networks.

The scientific-mathematical and philosophical networks overlap to a high degree in the 1600s, so much so that they appear to be one revolution rather than two. Of 6 major philosophers in that century, 5 are active scientists; 2 of them—Descartes and Leibniz—are mathematicians of the first rank. If we go to the secondary philosophers of the 1600s, 3 of 14 are scientists, but these 3 include another scientific star—Pascal—and two others, Gassendi and Mersenne, who are at the center of the network of correspondence which organizes the self-conscious movement that becomes in the next generation the Royal Society and the Académie des Sciences.[14]

European philosophy in the 1700s and 1800s continues to be linked to science, although not to the same degree as in the Golden Century.[15] Major philosophers in the West seem to have acquired some of their special creativity from close connection to science, as the connection was much stronger than among secondaries. Even philosophers known for their critiques of science—such as Berkeley, Hume, and Rousseau—were in close contact with scientific networks.

Although this connection reached its peak during the scientific revolution, a connection between the networks of science and philosophy was long-standing in the West. In ancient Greece, the mathematical network was interwoven with the philosophical one throughout their classical periods of creativity.[16] Of the three earliest lineages of philosophers, all began with a reputed mathematician: Thales, Pythagoras, and Leucippus. Not only the Pythagorean but the Sophist network as well was full of mathematicians. It was in the milieu of the latter that the first "mathematical revolution" took place; by the late 400s B.C.E., the classic puzzles were being posed (trisecting an angle, squaring a circle, tripling the volume of a cube), axiomatic proofs were afoot, geometric results were collecting. Plato established his Academy by surrounding himself with former Pythagoreans and other mathematical innovators.

Throughout the 300s B.C.E., the network of mathematicians and astronomers in Figure 10.2 broadly overlaps with the philosophical network comprising the interconnected schools of Plato, Eudoxus, and Aristotle; there is also some scientific competition from the lineages of Democritus and of the Stoics.

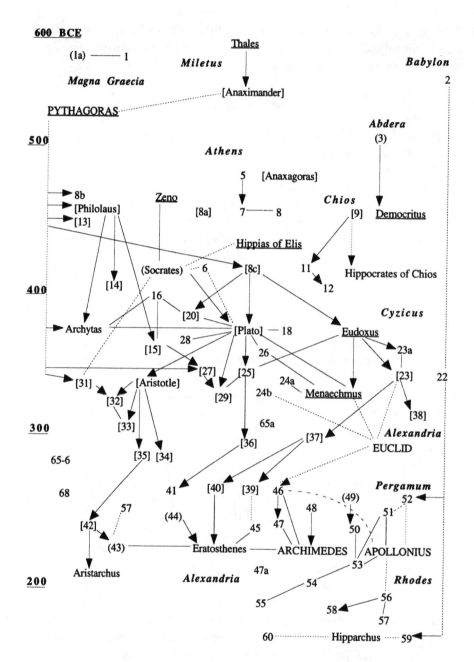

FIGURE 10.2. NETWORK OVERLAP OF GREEK MATHEMATICIANS
AND PHILOSOPHERS, 600 B.C.E.–600 C.E.

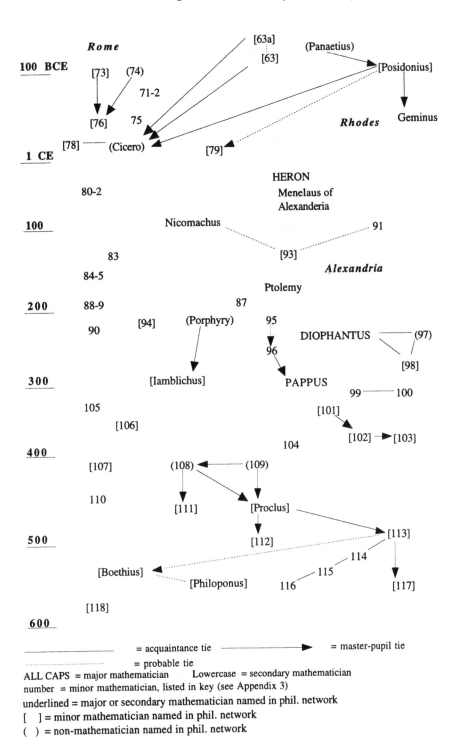

= acquaintance tie   ⟶ = master-pupil tie

.... = probable tie

ALL CAPS = major mathematician   Lowercase = secondary mathematician
number = minor mathematician, listed in key (see Appendix 3)
underlined = major or secondary mathematician named in phil. network
[ ] = minor mathematician named in phil. network
( ) = non-mathematician named in phil. network

Every head of the Academy from Plato through Arcesilaus (excepting only Polemon) is known as a mathematician (albeit a minor one); the same is true of Aristotle's school through Strato, whose pupil was the great heliocentric astronomer Aristarchus. Aristotle, though critical of the mathematical philosophy of the Platonic Forms, nevertheless is important for having laid out explicitly the formal procedures of mathematical proof. When the scientific center at the Alexandria Museum was founded about 300 B.C.E., it was staffed largely by the later generations of these networks. After 200 B.C.E. we find that the creativity of both the philosophical network and the mathematical thins out; thenceforward, what important activity there was tended to take place in separation from the other. Yet again in late antiquity, when the Academy was formally reestablished around 400 C.E., mathematics revived there, although without much creativity.

Whatever is distinctive about Greek philosophy and creative about its mathematics in its classical period seems to have come from their association with each other. Ancient medical science also flourished in much the same network milieu as the Athenian and Alexandrian mathematical scientists; and its scientific innovativeness tended to fade too at about the same time, by 200 B.C.E. In later centuries the best-known physicians were those connected with philosophy, from the Skeptics and Methodists down to the generation of Sextus Empiricus and Galen.[17]

Medieval Islam not only acquired Greek cultural capital but also has an even more extreme network connection of philosophy with mathematics and science. Virtually all of the major Islamic and Jewish philosophers (9 of 11) are within two steps of the scientific network, and 5 of 11 are themselves scientists (al-Kindi, al-Farabi, Ibn Sina, Averroës, Maimonides). Among secondary philosophers, 18 of 41 are close to the scientific network, and 8 of them overlap. As with the Greeks, the first-rate scientific stars are usually not the most important philosophers (only Ibn Sina in medicine fits that description), but 2 of them are secondary philosophers (the mathematician-logician Thabit ibn Qurra and the astronomer al-Tusi). In Spain the connection between the networks is especially complete: all 4 of the major Islamic and Jewish philosophers and 5 of 7 secondaries are no more than one tie away.

Most of the Islamic scientists in Figures 8.1 through 8.5 constitute a single network, which began in Baghdad with the translators at the House of Wisdom, and was later transplanted to Iran, Cairo, and Spain.[18] This network had two bases: court support for astronomers and astrologers; and medical doctors, with their independent base in endowed hospitals. The astronomers' and the doctors' networks intertwined at Baghdad, brought into rivalry and contact with the indigenous network of Islamic theologians; the result was to create the hybrid role of the Greek-oriented *falasifa* (the "Arab philosophers" most famous in Europe), as well as the theosophical hybrids with Shi'ite and other sects. The indigenous Muslim intellectuals had distinctive and ultimately more powerful bases: the theologians at the mosques, the Sufi movements in the general populace. Eventually the *madrasas* combined into their curriculum the content of most of these networks, though excluding most of the Greek tradition of science. But the most famous thinkers from these theologically oriented networks also tend to be only a few links away from the scientists. The anti-philosopher al-Ghazali is two links away from the mathematician 'Umar Khayyam; the leading theosophists and mystics are only a link or two from the cosmopolitan philosopher-scientists.

Why should contact with the scientific network be so important for philosophers? It was not transmitting a specific cultural capital, for the philosophies of al-Farabi, Ibn Sina, Averroës, and the others owed nothing to the algebraic breakthroughs of the mathematicians; at best they incorporated an astronomical vision into their hierarchical cosmologies. Al-Ghazali and the mystics al-Hallaj and Suhrawardi were even less concerned with scientific content. There is, however, a sociological pattern: in the Islamic networks, as elsewhere, the major philosophers are closer to the scientific networks than the secondary philosophers. A larger proportion of the major philosophers were themselves active in science, although usually with only minor success.

The leading philosophers were interested in science because of a coincidence among cosmopolitan orientations. Mathematics, astronomy, and other sciences are cosmopolitan topics, detached from the particulars of theology and value theory. The network of scholars assembling scientific texts at Baghdad, then migrating from home to home for almost 20 generations, began as an intersectarian network of Christians, Babylonian star worshippers, Zoroastrians, and Muslim travelers to India and Byzantium. In the later period, after the suppression of most of the non-Muslim religions, the core network was mediated by cosmopolitans among the Jews. Correspondingly, the major philosopher was the one whose ideas had the most general scope; and this came from bringing together links from the most diverse networks. Contact with the cosmopolitan scientific network became the intellectual base for all the more universalistic Islamic philosophers. And since creativity occurs by negation as well as by synthesis, even the anti-scientists and anti-cosmopolitans had their greatest originality when they were shaped by conflict with cosmopolitan scientists or the networks connecting to them; this is so even if the result was to promote a mystical or particularistic alternative, as among many prominent Muslim and Jewish conservatives. Conversely, the energy of focused network conflicts among philosophers, and the drive toward philosophical abstraction, helped promote creativity on the scientific side.

By itself, philosophers' interest in science does not guarantee that science will be very creative. We see this by comparison to medieval Christendom (Figures 9.3 through 9.5). This was not a very notable period for scientific innovation, but there is a remarkable overlap between scientific interests and the main philosophical networks. In the 1200s Grosseteste and his lineage (Adam Marsh, Roger Bacon) made science the center of their philosophies; so did Bacon's great contemporary and rival Albertus Magnus. Aquinas, though only marginally dabbling in science, was close to the network of scientific translators and researchers. Bonaventure's student John Peckham (who was Bacon's student too) is best known as the antagonist of Siger and the Averroists, but he was also a scientist in his own right, contributing to optics and cosmology. Medieval Christian philosophy has as much network connection with science as we see anywhere in the Western tradition—indeed more, if we count the at least minimal interest that a large majority of the most important philosophers showed in science.[19]

But there were no scientific stars in medieval Christendom.[20] In what way, then, can a connection with the core philosophers promote science in such a period? A clue is given by an abortive episode. The mid-1300s generation of philosophers at Balliol and Merton represent the high point of creative developments in medieval mathematics, kinematics, and mechanics; at the same time, the Paris circle around Buridan and his pupils overthrew Aristotelean impetus theory, proposed coordinate geometry, and considered the movement of the earth. These were not detached networks of scientists or textual translators; both the Oxford and Paris groups were offshoots of the main networks, engaged in theological disputes (Bradwardine, Wyclif), and in avant-garde questions of metaphysics and epistemology (Autrecourt, Mirecourt, Buridan; see Figure 9.6). The dynamics of the philosophical network, the nominalist movement, and the shift toward the arts curriculum turned attention toward topics of science; the combative energy and the drive toward abstraction in philosophy for a brief period now spilled over into scientific innovation. What lives by the philosophical network dies by the network. As the entire intellectual arena of the late 1300s went into crisis, technical developments in philosophy and in science alike became buried in factionalism and loss of focus in the attention space. The accomplishments of Swineshead, Buridan, and Oresme and their circles were lost from view as the attention space lost focus in the chaos of decentralization, whose sources were examined in Chapter 9.

A similar analysis may be performed for the late Muslim scientific stars, including al-Tusi (mid-1200s), whose astronomy was mathematically equivalent to that of Copernicus. Nevertheless, the Islamic network surrounding al-Tusi is marked by neither rapid discovery nor consensus (Huff, 1993). Here too the scientists are in the mainstream of the philosophical network; al-Tusi and al-Shirazi are notable for synthesizing Ibn Sina's Neoplatonism with the

Sufi illuminationism prominent at the time (*DSB*, 1981: 11:249). Their science became buried by the scholasticism of the *madrasas* which dominated later Islamic intellectual life. In both cases of abortive scientific advance, Christian and Islamic, loss of focus by the entire philosophical network dissolved the possibility of cumulatively building on high points of scientific creativity, or even remembering it.

Consider now a case in which scientific and philosophical networks sustained interaction, indeed bootstrapped themselves cumulatively to levels long remembered by the generations which followed. In Greece from the very beginning of philosophical activity, from 600 down to about 200 B.C.E., the network of mathematicians is virtually identical with a major segment of the philosophical network. What difference did this make for mathematics? As an ordinary practical activity of reckoning or measurement, mathematics generally shows little tendency toward formulating abstract theorems or rapidly innovating. It was the intellectual networks that seized on mathematics, interpreting it as a clue to a cosmology rivaling other cosmologies (Pythagoras), or turning it into a challenge to solve paradoxical problems (the Sophists). It was the philosophical network which made Greek mathematics competitive and innovation-oriented as well as generalized and abstract. As results accumulated, the philosophical schools most interested in orderly synthesis promoted the axiomatic method of formal derivation; these networks, deriving from Democritus, the Platonists, and Aristoteleans alike, led to Euclid, Eratosthenes, and Archimedes. Astronomers, and in another branch medical practitioners, became part of the central network and were spurred to generalize abstract systems on the terrain of philosophical cosmologies. Greek science set the model for generalized science because it no longer represented a range of practical activities pursued in private by low-status occupations, but rather signaled a competition in the philosophical attention space.

AN EAST-WEST DIVERGENCE IN SCIENTISTS' AND PHILOSOPHERS' NETWORKS

Compare a crucial episode in the network history of China. Chinese mathematics differed from the Greek puzzle-solving contests, with their impetus toward proofs and axiomatic systems of abstract principles. For the most part, Chinese math was practical calculation related to surveying and astronomy; abstract developments were little valued and often forgotten by the official textbooks. The cause of this difference may be seen in the relationship among the networks. In China the practical mathematicians and astronomers were largely separate from the philosophers.[21] Initial development could have gone a different way; during the late Warring States, philosophers such as Hui Shih and Kung-sun Lung produced quasi-mathematical paradoxes reminiscent of the Eleatics and Sophists, and the Mohists responded with formal geometrical definitions. Here Chinese intellectuals seem to have been on a similar path as the Greeks. But this development of mathematics from the philosophical side was not followed up after the Mohist chain disappeared.

When bureaucracy consolidated in the Han dynasty, mathematicians, astronomers, and philosophers alike compiled canonical texts. The mathematics textbook *Chou Pei* was apparently assembled by the Confucian school and endorsed the *kaitian* astronomical system; the *Nine Sections* textbook favored the rival *huntian* cosmology. Later the leading skeptical and anti-occultist Confucians of the Old Text school overlapped extensively with the astronomers of the *huntian* system. The upsurge of mathematics and astronomy at this time seems to have been connected to the struggle between rival branches of Confucianism. The scholasticism of this period did not encourage abstract philosophical treatment, however, as Confucians absorbed the divination texts into their synthesis and emphasized numerological correspondences for magical prognostication. The tail end of the Han intellectual network did produce one last flurry of abstract mathematics in the governmental disintegration of the late 200s C.E. The greatest of the early Chinese mathematicians, Liu Hui, was apparently a scholar-official who recombined surveying techniques from a low-status bureau with those of astronomical calculation used in a higher-status bureau, treating higher-degree equations and introducing the first explicit proofs (Swetz, 1992). This combination of specialties happened at the time of (and in some network links with) the philosophers of the "Dark Learning" movement, which similarly reorganized official and oppositional networks, revising their classic texts and thereby raising Chinese philosophy to its high point of abstract metaphysics.

Thereafter the networks of mathematicians and philosophers were almost totally separate. In subsequent dynasties the mathematicians were almost all government officials, cut off from the administrative and historical bureaus and literary circles in which the Confucian philosophers worked. The Buddhists who dominated philosophy down to 900 C.E. were generally entirely outside the realm of government administration and cut off from official mathematics.[22]

There was one more round of innovation in Chinese mathematics, the generalized "celestial element method" for solving higher algebraic equations in several unknowns, produced in the Sung dynasty. It is tempting to connect this to the Neo-Confucian movement in philosophy, but there were very few network connections between that movement and mathematics. Neo-Confucianism began with a branch concerned with occult numerology, but its most successful lineage was opposed both to numerology and to reformers who wanted to elevate mathematics in the official examination system. Nor do the peak generations coincide; the outburst of Neo-Confucianism came in the years 1030–1100, and the culminating systems of Chu Hsi and Lu Chiu-yüan were produced 1170–1200. The celestial element algebra, however, began to develop after 1100 away from the court circles of the Neo-Confucians, and the star mathematicians were active in the period 1240–1300.

If there is a connection, it is a conflictual one, based on struggles over the external base. The early Neo-Confucians were the conservative faction in a period of administrative crisis when rival reforms of the examination system were alternatively implemented and reversed. Then came full-scale state break-down; during the disruption of official bureaucracy, the celestial element algebra was created by private teachers and out-of-office officials during the alien Jürchen monarchy of north China after 1126, culminating during the Mongol conquest (1220–1280). The efflorescence of mathematical schools at this time had overtones of a popular religious movement; the mathematics itself was more abstract than practical; conditions of life during the military conquests were violent and unsettled; and the terminology and titles of the books imply miraculously new and secret methods. The movement is obscure and in need of greater study. The breakdown of the segregated governmental bureaus for practical mathematics seems to be a key; when they were reestablished, the new algebra died. In 1313 Neo-Confucianism became the official basis for the examination system; soon after, the ability to understand the celestial element method died out in China.[23]

In India the separation between science and philosophy was even more complete. Chronologies for India are weak and biographical data meager. For what it is worth, there are no recorded contacts between philosophical and mathematical networks, and no individuals overlap both activities (*DSB,* 1981; Smith, 1951; Pingree, 1981). Indian science and mathematics were especially fragmentary, full of disagreeing systems. Mathematics and astronomy imported from China and Greece and contact with the Arabs combined with bits of indigenous science in a jumble of texts which the Arab traveler al-Biruni (ca. 1030) in his *India* described as "a mixture of pearl shells and sour dates . . . both kinds of things are equal in their eyes." Organizationally, the mathematicians, astronomers, and medical doctors were based in private familistic lineages and guilds, never part of the sustained argument provided by philosophical networks. Public networks of argument did exist in India; its philosophical lineages reached high levels of abstract development. Only mathematics and science were not carried along with it.

WHY DO PHILOSOPHICAL NETWORKS PROMOTE SCIENCE?

The philosophical networks represent the central attention space of the community of intellectuals, where arguments of widest consequence are carried out. Philosophy drives up the level of abstraction and reflexivity, promotes periodic movements of synthesis, consciously argues over methods, and thereby lays down epistemological principles. Transferred to the topics of naturalistic observation and mathematics, the philosophical networks turn empirical compilations into theories, lay methods of commercial arithmetic or practical geometry into puzzle-solving contests carried out under increasingly stringent rules. The philosophical networks import not only consciousness of abstraction but also a social impetus to innovation. This appears to have happened in early period of ancient Greece, for a time in the Islamic networks, and again in Europe after 1500. But the inherent tendency of abstract philosophers to concern themselves with cosmopolitan topics on the terrain of science does not in itself lead to sustained scientific innovation, or indeed to consensus. There were periods of relatively accelerated discovery in Greece and Islam, but the research front as a whole did not become "technologized" with explicit concern for tinkering with methods for producing new results. The rather widespread concern of the philosophical stars of medieval Christendom with topics of science was not sufficient to create much science.

The lesson of abortive episodes such as the Mohists, the Oxford-Paris nominalists, and al-Birtruji's and al-Tusi's astronomy is that philosophical networks by themselves can provide a temporary impetus to scientific innovation. But the philosophical network itself is subject to the law of small numbers, inherently anti-consensual in its creative periods, while the imposition of a forced consensus in an official doctrine or the deadening effect of a scholastic curriculum results in losing innovation entirely. Scientific takeoff is promoted by overlap between practical mathematicians or other empirical and observational professions and the philosophical networks; but sustained development in mathematics and science depends on growing genealogies of technologies for rapid discovery, allowing scientists to outstrip the factionalism of the philosophers. The impetus of philosophical competition and abstraction which promoted Greek and Hellenistic science was lost as astronomy became transformed into astrological religion, number theory into numerology, and both into Neoplatonist cosmology. The dynamics of philosophical networks can launch episodes of scientific discovery but can also undermine them.

The development of scientific networks is a special application of the general process governing all intellectual change. External conditions rearrange material bases for intellectual occupations, and these in turn lead to restructuring networks, generating new alliances and oppositions in the attention space. We have seen clues in China, where the usual segregation of mathematicians and astronomers into specialized and low-status segments of the imperial bureaucracy was broken down precisely during the episodes of creativity in abstract mathematics.

For the takeoff of rapid-discovery science in Europe, there are two major candidates for external conditions: early capitalism and the Reformation. Capitalism gives an impetus to commercial mathematics.[24] But low-status practitioners do not usually attract the attention of the core intellectual network; and by itself, the contents of commercial arithmetic does not automatically lead to the abstract puzzles of higher mathematics. Capitalism also gives some impetus to new technology, and we have seen that some of this equipment—most famously, mining pumps—was brought into the network of "mechanical philosophers" and made into a technology of discovery. We must beware of crude technological determinism, and of projecting backwards the relationship between technology, capitalism, and science, which became characteristic only after the "second industrial revolution" following the 1880s. As Weber ([1923] 1961: 129–136; Collins, 1986: 19–44) pointed out, the rationalized capitalism which generates self-sustaining growth depends on a mixture of social ingredients. Background conditions must free up all the factors of production (land, labor, capital) so that they can move on the market, under the control of entrepreneurs, and protected by a legal system guaranteeing private property and facilitating its transactions through organized financial instruments. Sustained technological innovation typically occurs late in this process; conversely, the first few centuries of the capitalist takeoff involved rationalized procedures in agriculture typically without any new machinery at all.[25] Capitalism in Europe during the 1500s and 1600s made available some fragmentary developments of machinery that could be pressed into intellectual service by the philosophical networks; but the impetus to speed up their evolution as pieces of research equipment came from the side of the philosophical network with its dynamics of competition over the attention space.

Capitalism by itself did little to rearrange the intellectual networks. Of greater importance as an external condition was the Reformation, or more precisely, the struggle over church politics culminating in the Reformation and Counterreformation. Let us avoid any reflection argument. Science does not reflect the spirit of Protestantism, nor indeed of Catholicism or wearied secularism either. The familiar arguments of Weber and Merton rely too heavily on an episode rather late in the rearrangement of networks, the coincidence of the British Invisible College with the Puritan Revolution; the Catholic side of the network was older, and in many respects more central. Most important, the late medieval church had been breaking apart for centuries. The papal bid for theocratic power over Christian Europe had crested in the mid-1200s; thereafter the consolidating national states, most prominently France and Spain, had struggled to make the papacy the instrument of their national power; other states, in response, withdrew into increasingly nationally organized churches. The conciliar movement of the early 1400s, in which Cusanus was so prominent, was one of many organizational schemes to decentralize and democratize the church. The Reformation is just one spectacular episode in a long series of conflicts and reorganizations of political and religious power.

The Catholic side was by no means the lineup of reactionaries that Protestant propaganda made it out to be; movements for reform which antedated the Reformation continued to proliferate. Some, like the Jesuits, Jansenists, and Oratorians who figure largely in our narrative of networks, were concerned to revitalize the unitary Catholic Church from inside. Other prominent individuals, such as Bruno, were freelancers between Protestant and Catholic camps, promoting schemes for ending religious strife and reuniting Christendom by still more radical doctrinal reform; often they appealed to a liberal pope as more promising and less fanatical than militant Protestant princes. Occasional Protestants were picked out by the cosmopolitans as the center for religious reunification, as in the Rosicrucian movement of the early 1600s, and the hopes pinned on the Elector Palatine (Yates, 1972).

Here we have an external basis for network reorganization of grand proportions. Between the church and the rival courts were encompassed all the bases of intellectual life: the old universities as training centers of the church; the new Protestant universities; rival educational schemes put forward as Protestant academies or Jesuit schools; papacy, church politicians, and secular courts alike as patrons for Humanists and freelance intellectuals. The so-called "stagnation" of philosophy in the late Middle Ages was, sociologically speaking, a chaotic fragmentation of networks in this multi-sided attention space. The increasing polarization of Reformation and Counterreformation provided simplification, focusing attention on a few key lines of controversy at the same time that it greatly increased the level of emotional energy. That is why we now see the intersection between theology and a scientific topic such as astronomy. It is not that astronomy reflected theological positions, for it was not just Protestants who looked for innovation of the kind exemplified by Copernicus and Kepler; there are mixtures of traditionalists and innovators on both sides. The church politics of the Reformation period had again elevated theologians in the attention space. Theological intellectuals now hit on the slow-moving developments which were taking place in the cosmopolitan arena of science. Attention gradually built up, as innovations such as Copernicus's were translated from the narrow sphere of technical specialists into the largest arena, where they became emblems for questions of tradition or change. Astronomy, and by their preexisting connections mathematics, now became the focus of attention for the entire intellectual community. Tremendous emotional energy was generated; competitiveness rose; educated persons everywhere were pulled into the magnet of recruitment. Technical contests in mathematics, and the rush for discoveries in science, became public; their stakes became the acclaim of large audiences. The takeoff of rapid discovery in mathematics and science was the result.

HOW DO SCIENTIFIC NETWORKS AFFECT PHILOSOPHY?

Our main concern for the moment is the effects of the network overlap on the scientific revolution. Let us briefly consider the effects in the opposite direction, implied by our world comparisons. What is distinctive about the Western orbit is that the mathematical-astronomical networks are often very closely integrated with the main philosophical networks: this is so in the key formative period for philosophy as well as for mathematics in Greece; it is one of the key lines of development in Islam, and a foil for the important indigenous lines. Their joint overlap was central for the community of Muslims, Jews, and Christians which formulated a cosmopolitan "religion of reason" in Spain, and it continued to shape the interests of Christian philosophers. What does this mathematized, astronomized, philosophical tradition of the West have that is distinctive on the philosophical side? The simultaneous creation of abstract mathematics and self-consciously abstract philosophy in Greece made mathematics into an ideal of transcendent reality. The order of the numbers was taken as the frame of the universe, on both the lower level of cosmology and the higher level of theology and ultimately of ontology. One consequence in the West, lacking in Asia, was an emphasis on a graded hierarchy of being, from one ontological level down to the next. This hierarchical conception of the universe made astronomy philosophically much more important in the West than in the East; the planetary spheres could be identified with gradations of ontological perfection. Physical science was easy to carry along in a Western philosopher's baggage; even if parts of it concerned rather degraded levels of metaphysical reality, it had a place in the system.

In metaphysics, Western mathematized philosophy was constantly reminded of levels of abstraction. Its bias was toward the realism of universals (just the opposite of the Buddhist bias toward nominalism and world illusion); this became fruitful for philosophical exploration whenever the energy of controversy started up, since the concepts of universals and particulars were a ready-made arena in which one might initiate a dispute. And since the concept of a hierarchy of abstraction was coordinated with the more concrete cosmology of observational science, disputes over nominalism and radical particularism (as in Duns Scotus) could stir up revisions of scientific theory, just as universals also implied scientific laws. These interconnections explain why so many of the most innovative medieval Christian philosophers often touched on scientific topics, if only from the conceptual side. In epistemology, wherever the mathematical-hierarchic view was dominant, the effect was to identify universals with reality and truth with that exemplified by apparently non-sensuous, a prori mathematical proof. The issues of epistemology, whether and how truth can exist, were settled by fiat, built into the conceptual frame itself. That is one reason why, whenever Neoplatonic ontology is challenged (by Ibn Taymiyah and Ibn Khaldun among the Muslims, by the Christian nominalists, again in the breakdown of the entire medieval-cum-ancient-Greek apparatus in the 1600s), epistemology comes again to the fore.

We see here additional reasons why European philosophers, at the time of the crisis of church politics, would be motivated to seek out the developments among technical specialists in astronomy and mathematics. It is not that medieval philosophy was anti-science; quite the contrary: a particular version of science was built into its conceptual framework. Upheaval in the philosophical networks could not avoid overturning the framework of traditional science as well.

Three Revolutions and Their Networks

What is commonly called the *scientific revolution* was actually three overlapping restructurings of the intellectual field. The math and science revolutions consisted of transformation into rapidly moving research fronts, in effect the discovery of discovery-making techniques. To speak of "revolution" here is a bit metaphorical, since the acceleration of discovery making built up over four to six generations; it was only toward the end of this development—in the mid-1600s generation of Descartes, Mersenne, and Boyle—that the intellectual world became decisively convinced that a new basis of knowledge making existed. It was this recognition that set off what we can call the *philosophical revolution,* the putting of philosophy to new uses, which gave Descartes the reputation as founder of modern philosophy.

The takeoff of philosophical creativity that began at this time was not a revolution in the same sense as the math and science revolutions; philosophy remained philosophy, which is to say it continued to be structured by irreconcilable rivalries and did not acquire a rapidly moving research front distinguishing it from previous philosophy. But the philosophical networks are crucial in the math and science revolutions nevertheless. Not only did the philosophical revolution put the seal of approval on the previous revolutions, giving them general significance for the world. But also from the outset all three networks were entwined; without their interconnection, the accelerated discovery that made up the mathematics and science revolutions could not have come about.

The Mathematicians

The mathematical revolution built up first. Part of the increasing interest in mathematics came from practical interests, and one can date the gradual outpouring of commercial math textbooks from the late 1400s. But practical math was not the source of the innovation in problem-solving techniques which constituted the core of the new mathematics. The more abstract realms of mathematics were created as mathematicians made discoveries about general procedures. Puzzle-solving techniques, such as algorithms for solving higher-order equations, became topics of discovery in their own right. The takeoff of math occurred when it became an intellectual game as well as a matter of practical application. Contact with the network of philosophers turned the activity of low-status reckoning masters into the high-prestige competition of the intellectuals who made the claims to matters of greatest importance.

Innovative mathematicians emerged in the philosophical networks. Regiomontanus came from the network around Cusanus and was patronized by the Humanist leader Bessarion. Cusanus was not a skilled mathematician in a technical sense, but his philosophy was permeated with mathematical conceptions, and we see here a general intellectual concern raising mathematics into its orbit. Copernicus came from these same networks in central Europe; he studied first with a pupil of Regiomontanus at Cracow, and later lived near Königsberg (from which Regiomontanus originated and received his Latin name). During 1496–1505 Copernicus studied in Italy, making contact with the humanistic network, as Cusanus and Regiomontanus had previously; Copernicus met Ficino's Platonist followers and overlapped at Padua with the Aristotelean Pomponazzi and at Bologna with the mathematician Scipione del Ferro. Not that Copernicus necessarily borrowed his mathematical or astronomical ideas from these contacts; more important is the pattern that creativity is stimulated by contact with the central focus of intellectual attention.

To the extent that Copernicus's work was propagated, it was through the more general intellectual network; his publisher Osiander was a theology professor at Königsberg, and his assistant Rheticus was visited by Ramus, the Parisian reformer of school logic.[26] His heliocentric astronomy did not make much impact for two generations; when it was picked up again in the 1590s it was by Kepler, a theology student at Tübingen under the theologian Maestlin (*EP*, 1967: 4:329–333). What is worth stressing here is that astronomy in this period was most significant as a vehicle for innovations in mathematics. Copernicus is as much a part of the initial wave of the mathematical revolution as he is of the scientific revolution per se;[27] by the time of Kepler, the discovery-making revolution was expanding from the one realm to the other. Astronomy was a fertile ground for innovations in calculation, such as trigonometry and logarithms, as well as in geometry. And astronomy attracted ambitious and innovative intellectuals because it was a focus of concern for a dominant field such as theology, just now in the midst of controversies because of the crisis in church politics (cf. Westman, 1980).

Careers of other early mathematicians show the practical and commercial math coming together with the status-centered activities of the intellectuals. Pacioli, a pupil in the atelier of the painter Piero della Francesca, published in 1494 the first important mathematics textbook; Pacioli stressed the practice of bookkeeping, but incorporated geometry from the works of Piero, and his figures were drawn by Leonardo da Vinci.[28] None of this constituted a new discovery in math, but the painters added public attention to the subject, and soon the network gave rise to the first great breakthrough in modern algebra. Cardano's father was a friend of Leonardo; Cardano himself moved through the same universities where Copernicus had studied 20 years before, picking up a secret formula for solving particular types of equations of the third degree from a pupil of Ferro, a probable acquaintance of Copernicus at Bologna. Tartaglia, a teacher of commercial mathematics at Venice, engaged in public problem-solving contests with several men in this network; by the 1530s and 1540s, this set of contestants had come up with general solutions for both cubic and quartic equations.

Mathematics was becoming a matter of public prestige. Cardano and his assistant defended a mathematical challenge from Tartaglia in the cathedral of Milan in 1548 with the governor acting as judge. Cardano somewhat unscrupulously took secret formulae from his acquaintances and published them, but this in itself shows that he was playing to a different arena than local mathematics teachers advertising their skills by winning public contests by means of secret techniques. Cardano was a medical professor at the major Italian universities who wrote widely on philosophy and theology as well as science and mathematics. The great upsurge in the innovativeness of mathematics came just at the time when it was shifting from a humble commercial activity to an attention-getting contest among high-status intellectuals. These contests were pushing activity into the realm of pure discovery making, far beyond issues of practicality. By the turn of the century Galileo, taught by a pupil of Tartaglia, was in the core intellectual networks only a few links from leading philosophers such as Suarez.

With Descartes, the leading edge of creativity in mathematics and in philosophy merged. The prestige of one became the basis of the elevated prestige of the other. In mathematics Descartes was not the progenitor of the revolution, but he was its first culmination. The symbolic notation had first been developed in commercial arithmetic books; Descartes raised its level of generality and made it the standard for pure mathematics as well. Descartes trumpeted the news that mathematics has an infallible discovery-making method. Not surprisingly, the network around him pushed rapidly into still further advances in mathematics. Along with this spread the belief that science would follow the same path.

The Scientific Revolution

If by scientific revolution we mean the invention of the techniques of rapid discovery making, the scientific revolution came later than the mathematical revolution. From the early to mid-1500s we can speak of a quickening pace of innovation. In astronomy, Copernicus drafted his heliocentric system in 1514, finished it in 1530, and gradually publicized it over the next 13 years. But it was another 50 years before Brahe's intensive observations, and his assistant Kepler formulated the laws of planetary motion only in 1609. There was no consensus in astronomy in the 1500s, nor was there a rapid and sustained movement of the research front. As an astronomer, Copernicus was not unlike other medieval thinkers. Oresme in the 1350s, as well as other medievals, had raised the possibility of the earth moving in space; so did Cusanus. Regiomontanus foreshadowed Copernicus's work in many respects, elaborating trigonometry and proposing before his early death to reform astronomy, possibly with a heliocentric model (Boyer, 1985: 304). As an account of the observables, Copernicus's model was not superior to Ptolemy's geocentric system; many professional astronomers were unconvinced on technical grounds. Without the takeoff of sustained developments in the next century, Copernicus might well have been a forgotten late medieval figure in the same category as Oresme or, in the Islamic world, al-Tusi.

Although we cannot speak of scientific revolution during the 1500s in the strong sense, there were several parallel strands of activity building up. In addition to astronomy, there were innovations in medical physiology. Servetus, at the Paris medical faculty in the 1540s, put forward a new theory of the circulation of the blood; his colleague Vesalius, moving on to the medical faculty at Padua, published empirical support in 1543 and 1555. A network of Padua professors carried on the doctrine, although empirical work was broken off until around 1600, when Fabricus discovered valves in the veins; his pupil William Harvey in turn performed dissections of many species of animals and experiments with tourniquets, and between 1616 and 1628 formulated a mechanical theory of circulation in which the heart acted as pump. Again we have an intermittent buildup culminating in the early 1600s; in this case the method was largely empirical rather than mathematical.

A third front comprises work in chemistry, including the "occult philosophy" of Agrippa von Nettesheim around 1515–1530 and the alchemical and medical theories of Paracelsus in the 1530s. In common with the developments in astronomy and in physiology, there was an explicit willingness to innovate and to challenge received theories of the Greeks. But although Paracelsus and other alchemists did some experimental work, there was nothing that could be called a sustained development of discoveries nor heightened consensus.

I have already noted a fourth chain that I have called the mathematical revolution. By the 1580s to the early 1600s, with the work of Galileo, this flow of mathematical discovery making spilled over into experimental work in physics. Around the same time, Stevin in Holland, who contributed to mathematical calculation by introducing decimal fractions, developed mechanics and hydrostatics. Stevin's associate Snel worked on astronomy and refraction of light (ca. 1618–1621); Snel's protégé Beeckman conducted experiments (1626) with pumps on hydrodynamics and combustion using equipment from his father's factory for candles and water conduits.[29]

The four chains all use different methods: the mixture of math and observation in astronomy; dissection and eventually some experiment in physiology; alchemical purifications in chemistry; the focus on simplifying calculations which leads to the takeoff of mathematical discovery making, eventually spilling over into giving mathematical descriptions of mechanical experiments in physics. Is there a common impulse in these developments during the 1500s? The most important social feature is that each chain gets its start when particular fields of investigation become entwined with the core intellectual networks. We have seen this already with the mathematicians from Cusanus on through Galileo and Descartes. In astronomy, I have suggested that its intellectual energy comes from its ability to attract the interest of theologians; dangerous as it might be, the energy of controversy at the centers of attention introduces innovative dynamics into specialized technical fields.

In physiology, the creative chain starts off with Servetus, a Spanish liberal during the heady days of the early Reformation. Servetus deliberately moved in the leading circles. From the court of the Emperor Charles V, he traveled to Basel and Strasbourg to meet Erasmus, Bucer, and Schwenckfeld; at Paris he met the young John Calvin—just then launching his own radical reforms—and put forward his reform both of Galen and of the Trinity. Servetus is characteristic of an era when cosmological-scientific speculation and theological novelties could all be created together. There is the same mixture of scientific occultism and theological reform among the "chemists"; Agrippa was a friend of the English reformer Colet, while Paracelsus associated with Erasmus and Franck as well as with Copernicus's disciple Rheticus.

The impulse to innovate in scientific topics appears on the fringes of the network of major intellectual controversy in the 1500s. Since the center of attention was the rearrangement of theological doctrine which followed the organizational breakup of the church, it is not surprising here that theology fuels science. This helps explain the upsurge of innovation; but the latter is not itself a scientific revolution. Sustained discovery need not follow, as we see in chemistry. Still less does the atmosphere of theological controversy tend toward scientific consensus. We have already noted, in the conclusion of Chapter 9, that European intellectual life from the late 1300s onward became dispersed and fragmented; the landscape was populated by various scholastic factions, Humanists, mystics, and occultists without a focal point for their controversies. At first the Reformation made the situation worse. It multiplied religious sects and systems of occultism; Copernicus, Paracelsus, and Servetus added to the cacophony of oppositions. That is why a characteristic voice of the late 1500s is Montaigne, proposing skeptical detachment from all intellectual positions; for him, Copernicus was just another absurdity of this ideological chaos.

We seem as far as possible from the consensus on a body of knowledge, and from the discovery-making techniques which would become the hallmarks of modern science. Nevertheless, a new focus was beginning to crystallize in the attention space. The Counterreformation was organizing and polarizing opinion, above all with the burgeoning Jesuit educational movement providing a new intellectual base. The mathematicians had launched their revolution of discovery-making technique; and their network overlapped significantly with astronomers and with general philosophical intellectuals. The medical physiologists, too, were about to be pulled into the center of intellectual attention.

Soon after 1600 most of the chains, with the exception of the chemists, came together. Astronomers, mathematicians, and physicists first formed a self-conscious front. Descartes met Beeckman in 1618 and acquired an interest in science. Stevin and Descartes both served in the army of Prince Maurice of Orange; in the same alliance was the Huygens family, who acted as frequent host to Descartes, and whose son Christian Huygens was encouraged in a scientific career by their distinguished visitor. In Figure 10.1 we see this Dutch circle of physicists and mathematicians connecting with the astronomical lineage of Brahe, Maestlin, and Kepler; Kepler in turn is in contact with Galileo and with the court circle in England. Galileo connects with the mathematical lineage of Tartaglia, and also with the Jesuit thinkers in Rome. By the 1620s, Mersenne had formed his circle of correspondence, linking together virtually all the scientific actors and inspiring a new generation in mathematics, science, and philosophy.

Somewhat apart from this math–physical science complex had been the lineage of medical physiologists. The link was forged by Harvey, whose experimental method was probably influenced by contact with Galileo at Padua, where the latter was professor of mathematics. When Harvey returned to

England as royal physician, science acquired another center of public fame. In 1616, the very year Harvey announced his mechanical theory of circulation of the blood, his fellow physician Fludd launched a campaign for Cabalistic science that brought him into controversy with Kepler and soon after with Mersenne and Gassendi. Scientific links between England and the Continental group were now multiplying. The intellectuals of the English court circle had been predominantly literary; but Raleigh's protégé Harriot was a mathematician, a correspondent of Kepler; and in 1620 the poet John Donne paid a visit on Kepler. The creative energy focused at the English court was now flowing into attention to science. The opportunistic politician Bacon was promoting it with all his literary skill; his protégé Hobbes—the friend of Harvey and of Ben Jonson—was traveling to meet Galileo, and eventually to a rendezvous with the Mersenne circle and Descartes.

With this we are in the mid-1600s, and into the self-conscious social organization of modern science. The discovery-making network had taken over the mainstream of the intellectual community, the center where the most attention was focused. Contact with the philosophical networks had been important all along, since 1500 or even earlier, in imparting to scientists and mathematicians the competitive dynamics of innovation over matters of high generality. Now, for a period, the networks were virtually fused. At this moment the world became aware of the scientific revolution.

The Philosophical Revolution: Bacon and Descartes

The philosophical revolution began as the announcement of the supremacy of science as the one true path to knowledge. Appropriate hedges were expressed to avoid infringing on the status of religion, but the thrust was clear enough. The names that became famous for expressing this were Bacon and Descartes; they represent the networks on the observational and mathematical sides of the scientific revolution, respectively. But why should fame for this move have gone to philosophers, instead of to the statements of the scientists themselves? And indeed, why should philosophy have continued to exist at all after this point, since the avowed ideology was to replace the old philosophy with new science?[30]

There was in fact no dearth of general arguments by the leading scientists on behalf of their methods. Nevertheless, there was a difference in the attention space commanded by the scientists and the philosophers. What constitutes philosophy is the most general claim to attention, the arguments of widest note which frame all the others. The scientists' and mathematicians' specialized techniques of discovery making were turning the social organization of their fields into a tighter structure than existed on the philosophers' turf. Whether they knew it or not (and in fact they did not), philosophers continued to operate by a dialectic of disagreement under the law of small numbers; even as philosophers took the sureness of scientific knowledge as their topic, they were bound to create diverging constructions upon this realm. Of course it is possible for the same person to operate in several attention spaces, as a practicing scientist or mathematician, and also as philosopher. Descartes was famous in all three, while Bacon attempted to lead as a naturalist, though success came only for his general philosophy.

We want to know, then, why the ideology of the scientific revolution came through in these distinctive forms. By around 1600, many intellectuals were aware that a revolution was afoot. Bacon's and Descartes's versions of the announcement came to dominate the philosophical attention space; the others either were too narrowly encapsulated within particular scientific specialties, or attached themselves to a part of the philosophical field which remained traditional and non-revolutionary. Galileo, a famous and eloquent expositor of the new science, embedded his arguments for the new method in the discussion of specific discoveries in kinematics, which in any case represented only one style of scientific advance. Kepler expressed an acute understanding of the methodological points which separated the new astronomy from the old; but these arguments made little impression at the time (McMullin, 1990: 65, 86). Kepler's and Galileo's fame came from the substance of their science; as philosophers of scientific methodology they were upstaged.

Explicit philosophical claims failed to capture the forefront because they were not revolutionary enough. Kepler was well known as the follower of a Neoplatonic cosmology. Servetus had incorporated his argument for the circulation of the blood in a Christocentric pantheism, merging Neoplatonism with a Cabalistic interpretation of the Bible. Cardano, for all his boastful innovation in mathematics, regarded Aristotle's texts as the criterion of truth in other matters (*De Vita Propria;* Cardan, [1575] 1962: 46–47). Even Gassendi, with his championing of Epicurean atomism, was a weak rival to Descartes. What proved a weakness in capturing the philosophical attention space was the lack of a clean break with the past. Whereas Bacon and Descartes radically simplified down to what they claimed was a new starting place, prior philosopher-scientists had continued the muddy and unfocused condition of the late medieval philosophical space, touting one or another selection from the old array of contending positions.[31] This is not to say that the leaders carried over no philosophical capital from the past; Descartes drew quite heavily on scholastic philosophy, but he was at pains to disguise his sources, and presented his method as a technique for disposing of all accepted knowledge and building anew.

There is another characteristic of the philosophical break engineered by

Bacon and Descartes. Instead of mingling their science with theological positions, they presented it in as pure and unentangled a form as possible. This was in sharp contrast to previous self-announced radicals. Bruno, a defender on occasion of Copernican astronomy and other scientific innovations, proclaimed Christ a magus and hermeticism and magic as the bases for universal religious reform. Campanella, less heretical, limited the appeal of his philosophy by attaching it to the religious politics of church reunification under the pope. The strategy of Bacon and Descartes went entirely the other way. Both were conventionally respectful to religion; both assiduously avoided theological specifics and any taint of heresy. Their philosophy was designed not to rise or fall with the fortunes of religious reform. It was a philosophical revolution precisely because it successfully claimed an autonomous attention space.

Bacon was a busy lawyer, politician, and litterateur; in science he was a dabbler, but this was his advantage over specialized scientists writing on method, since he could take an overview of the broadest ideological basis for every field of investigation. Bacon wove science into a classification of all the branches of knowledge, comprising poesy (knowledge of the imagination), history (knowledge of memory), and philosophy (knowledge of reason) (*De Dignitate* 2.1). Bacon's most striking claim is that "the art of discovery" itself may advance, and that with its use "the discovery of all causes and sciences would be but the work of a few years" (*New Organon*, 130, 112). Bacon captures most explicitly the underlying social characteristic of the scientific revolution, the emergence of rapid-discovery science.

That is not to say that Bacon's method formulated what the scientists had actually been doing, nor did it provide any real guidance to the work that was to come. Bacon was more of a philosophical outrider to the scientific revolution than its leader. His inductive program was to collect information and classify and compare it in "Tables of Difference," from which principles of successively higher generality might be derived. It was not the method of Copernicus and Kepler in astronomy, nor of Galileo's physics, nor even of Vesalius and the anatomists. Although Bacon touches on subtle points regarding unobservables and experimentation and occasionally mentions mathematics, his emphasis is on the overall effect of his rhetoric rather than penetration or even consistency in the details. His description of Salomon's House is of a royal endowment indiscriminately collecting marvels and reports from travels and from old books, with only a minor part from new observation and experiment; it reads like a Baconian set piece from his *Essays* depicting the perfect garden adorned with every flower and fruit. The *New Atlantis* is one of Bacon's more popularistic works, but the propagandistic touch is characteristic. Bacon's vision served later to give some legitimation to the Royal Society but did not foreshadow its activities very closely. The active scientists no doubt welcomed

Bacon's support but deprecated his advice; Harvey said, "He philosophizes like a Lord Chancellor" (*CMH*, 1902–1911: 5:724).

Bacon's creativity was grounded in the intellectual networks around the English court, where scientific interests were best represented by men Bacon considered his rivals. The royal physician Gilbert published his famous compendium of information on the magnet in 1600, five years before Bacon set out his program with *The Advancement of Learning*. Bacon frequently cites Gilbert as exemplar of an obstacle to the true method, overgeneralizing from "the narrowness and darkness of a few experiments" (*New Organon* 64.347; also Bacon, 1965: 349, 233). Another rival was Raleigh, who introduced potatoes and tobacco in the 1590s from his explorations of the Americas, did chemical experiments, and wrote a *History of the World* in 1614 while imprisoned in the Tower. Bacon, who had switched to the winning side in the same court intrigue which ruined Raleigh, prosecuted him officially and brought about his beheading in 1618. Bacon's scientific efforts were in the same vein as his rivals'; he carried out a few scrappy collections on "The Natural History of Winds," on "Life and Death," and planned vast compendia, never finished, on topics such as "The History of Sympathy and Antipathy of Things" (Bacon, 1965: 9–10). The only sciences that Bacon knew much about were the naturalist observations, and these were the areas where interest had been building but no techniques of discovery had emerged such as those in the mathematical or mechanical fields.

Bacon's method reflects these connections. The method of collection and comparison was most appropriate for the naturalist. We find a parallel version of "Baconian" inductivism formulated independently in Hamburg, in the 1630s, in a work of logic by Jungius, otherwise known for his classification of plants and chemicals.[32] Bacon sharpens his arguments against the looseness of Gilbert's experimental inferences, whom he lumps with the alchemists. Experiment, as represented by the alchemical practice of repeated heatings and refinings, is not enough to establish a broad basis of knowledge; wide comparisons of similarities and differences should take one further. He observes too that narrowly seeking immediate practical results does not pay off, and deprecates "idle magical ceremonies" of just the sort that Raleigh and his assistant Harriot were reputed to carry out in their notorious "School of Night" (*New Organon* 52.392, 349; Gatti, 1989). Bacon too was an offshoot of the network of empiricists and occultists which gathered around the court; but he was an offshoot of opposition, critically assessing the others' shortcomings, and building his critique into a general method.

The real distinction of the Elizabethan court was not scientific but literary. Sidney, Marlowe, Spenser, and Shakespeare were already famous in the 1580s and 1590s. The literary and philosophical-scientific networks are connected, as we see in Figure 10.1; Bacon's rival Raleigh in particular was close to the avant-garde poets and was a successful poet himself. And it was back through this network, in the early 1580s, that Bruno made contact with Sidney and his circle while propagating his astral magic at London and Oxford. Bacon too was first inducted into intellectual life through the Sidney circle around the political patronage of the earl of Leicester (Martin, 1992: 24–38). Bacon's creative energy was set off by the literary scene; his first and greatest fame came with his *Essays* in 1597, and he expanded them throughout his career, though incorporating in them hardly a mention of his scientific project.

Bacon personifies the situation at the court, pursuing opportunities in literature, science, politics, switching courses as the occasion arises. His distinctive impact derives from the blends he makes of these elements. His literary prose has the rich pungency of poetry and the aphoristic bite of a political realist. He writes on a unified empire of knowledge like a consummate courtier offering intellectual conquests to the throne; he visualizes a centralized directory of research as if patenting a government monopoly to be delegated to himself. His intellectual ambition knows no bounds; he expects that his Tables of Difference will produce the axioms not only of nature but also of politics and ethics, of logic and mind. Rising above the special sciences, he visualizes a *Philosophia Prima* of principles holding good across fields as diverse as physics and morals (*New Organon* 127.371; *De Dignitate* 412–414). After many machinations, his political career peaked with the chancellorship, then quickly and inevitably fell. His empire of knowledge too remained more grandiose than can be realized. But Bacon's ideology, like his prose style, makes one of the great conquests in the realm of intellectual reputation, attaching his name to the structural transformation of his age.

Descartes is a structural parallel to Bacon in a number of respects. Both acquired first-rate reputations in disparate fields, Bacon in philosophy and literature, Descartes in philosophy, mathematics, and for about a century in science; he too established the criterion of style in his vernacular language, the famous "Cartesian clarity" of French prose. Multiple participation across intellectual fields is not unusual throughout world history, but multiple leadership of this sort is very rare; where networks overlap, it is usually because the stars in one are minor contributors to the other. Here is a another sign that intellectual networks were realigning on a large scale. The setting of a vernacular prose style as well implies a crucial moment of transition in the means of intellectual production.[33]

The content of Descartes's thought varies as his network position differs from Bacon's. He was much less of a politician (although he received patronage from Richelieu), and less surrounded by glamorous literary circles. He was also much more closely connected with current religious movements; he was both encouraged on the Catholic side and sought after by the Protestant standard-bearers from the House of Palatine, and was visited by reformers such as Comenius. Descartes was inducted into science through the Dutch network of mathematicians and experimenters, Stevin, Snel, and Beeckman. Of crucial importance, Descartes was sponsored by Mersenne's circle, the center of organized scientific correspondence; Mersenne arranged debates to publicize Descartes's philosophy and treated him as the intellectual leader of the new movement.

Descartes played this role not because of preordained genius, but because by the accidents of geography he fell into the maximally effective combination of network connections. His beginnings were undistinguished, a boy from the minor provincial nobility in a small town in Poitou; but he was sent to the college newly founded nearby at La Flèche, the spearhead of Jesuit educational expansion in France, where he was a fellow pupil with Mersenne. Then came various travels as a military freelancer, which happened to bring him into contact with the Dutch scientists. This may have struck a chord because of Descartes's background connection with Viète, the greatest French mathematician of the previous generation.[34] Soon after, in 1619, Descartes had his famous dreams in which he envisioned a great system of mathematical philosophy.

In mathematics, Descartes plays the role of synthesizer of prior achievements. He builds on Viète's work, but pushes it to explicit statement on a higher level of abstraction.[35] The work of Cardano and Viète in the theory of equations is turned into a machinery; the use of geometric methods for algebra, and vice versa, becomes formulated as a normal technique. As he does in prose style, Descartes sets the standard for mathematical notation. His originality is in his synthesis; most of the techniques of equational notation were scattered in commercial textbooks, while many of the advanced problem-solving techniques were still expressed verbally by leading mathematicians. Descartes brings it all together and transmutes it into an essentially new thing, a philosophical mathematics.

Descartes's contribution to the scientific revolution is also a matter of synthesis. Like Bacon, he was a propagandist for the future development of science; he believed that he could show the method by which all scientific problems could eventually be solved. Descartes proposed to do this by deriving science from the techniques of mathematics. The result was that he downplayed the empirical side of science. This was not through lack of familiarity, the counterpart to Bacon's unfamiliarity with forefront mathematics, but because Descartes's principal network resource was his mathematics, which he wished to use to build a philosophy of complete certainty. His method, beginning with clear and distinct ideas and proceeding through regular deductive steps to in-

568 · INTELLECTUAL COMMUNITIES: WESTERN PATHS

controvertible conclusions, was a generalization of mathematical argument. In using it to build a science of the materially extended world, Descartes missed the significance of empirical measurement and inductive mathematical princi-ples in physics; he went so far as to dismiss Galileo's law of gravity because it was merely empirical.[36] Descartes's methodological pronouncements missed the actual procedures of the scientific revolution as badly as Bacon's. Nevertheless, Descartes's deductive system became for a generation or more the leading emblem of the "mechanical philosophy"; his *Principles of Philosophy* in 1644 was the most comprehensive statement across the range of science, incorpo-rating everything from physics, chemistry, and physiology to celestial mechan-ics into a single materialist system. Especially on the Continent, Descartes's science became the rallying point of the core scientific network, even as its discoveries moved beyond him.

Descartes had no intention of retaining philosophy as a discipline distinct from science; metaphysics was merely to contain the fundamental axioms from which the scientific conclusions were to be deduced (Descartes, [1644] 1983: xxiv). What makes Descartes dominant for the intellectual network is not his originality but his clear arrangement of his materials. The pieces of his argu-ment were lying about in contemporary discourse. The skepticism which Descartes used as his famous starting point had been prominent both in the previous generation and in his own. Montaigne had made it famous; this was a typical appearance of skepticism in a period when the intellectual field was overcrowded and no position was able to command much following. In an-other direction, we find the fideist use of skepticism; Descartes's teacher at La Flèche, the Jesuit Veron, used it in famous polemics against the Protestants. But Descartes turned the weapon to an entirely different strategy, to eliminate his predecessors on the intellectual field and clear the grounds for the indubi-table axioms from which secure knowledge could be built. Even this strategy was not unique; Mersenne's friend Gassendi had begun his career around 1621 by wielding skepticism against the Aristoteleans and occultists (Popkin, 1979: 100). Closer still to Descartes's approach, Campanella had previously argued in 1591 that philosophy begins in universal doubt, which is resolved by the certainty of self-consciousness (*EP*, 1967: 2:11–12). But Campanella had not exploited this opening with the single-mindedness of Descartes; Campanella had gone on to argue for empirical knowledge on the claim that the knower becomes transformed into the object known through intuition, whereas Des-cartes invoked a mathematical standard and hence the prestige and resources of the mathematical revolution.

Another crucial resource of Descartes was the scholastic philosophy that he claimed to supersede. His procedures of universal doubt and self-evident certainty enabled him to dispense with textual references, though his use of

Anselm's ontological proof of God is obvious, and it is not improbable that Descartes knew of Augustine's prior use of the cogito against skepticism. What was important for Descartes was that he could proceed through a chain of demonstration which led to the knowledge of substance, and thence of attribute, bodily extension, and the properties of material objects, which made up the contents of his science. (This is developed most explicitly in *Principles* 1.51–76.) Not only did this procedure draw on some of the leading conceptions of scholasticism; but also Descartes made his move at just the time when scholastic philosophy was being modernized in its home camp. Suarez, the most famous of the Jesuit thinkers, had recently formulated metaphysics as an independent field rather than a commentary on Aristotle. The term *ontology* first appears in 1636 in scholastic circles—almost simultaneously with Descartes's epoch-symbolizing *Discours de la Méthode*—reflecting Suarez's position that being as such is the first philosophy, before theology and before the categories and contingent contents of experience. Not only is this approach implicit in Descartes's starting point; Descartes also carried Suarez's *Disputationes Metaphysicae* (1597) on his travels, although he virtually never cited Suarez or any other scholastic (*EP*, 1967: 5:542; 8: 30–32).

If we defocus from Descartes personally, we can see that the "philosophical revolution" which set off modern philosophy was a transformation, not an abolition, of the medieval field. Descartes's ideology of a new beginning hides the revival of a long-standing metaphysical problem space. Spinoza, Leibniz, Wolff, Kant—the whole tradition of "rationalism" is not merely Cartesian; all draw heavily on a purified scholasticism. The new era of philosophical creativity builds upon the capital of the older era, even as the energy of creation comes from a new set of tensions structuring the intellectual community. The space which constitutes philosophy does not disappear when the techniques of rapid-discovery science give the latter heightened noticeability and prestige. From now on philosophers are concerned to negotiate and define their boundaries with science, much as they were previously concerned with their boundaries with theology. Both borders now become the external sources of action in modern philosophy.

CHAPTER 11

✣

Secularization and Philosophical
Meta-territoriality

The shifting power of the church was bound to change intellectual life. This was the material base on which most intellectual networks had centered, and these networks would necessarily respond to the closing of some opportunities and the opening of others. The intellectual revolutions were not simply a matter of breaking down the alliance of church and state which had imposed authoritarian control over the limits of thought. In the narrow sense, the liberalization of thinking had less effect on creativity than one might suppose. Many episodes of creativity had gone on within the authoritarian church, and when liberalization came, the most extreme freethinkers were not generally the most innovative, in either philosophy or science. Often their products were narrow and banal, while greater subtlety in constructing philosophy came from the conservatives defending religion, or in cautious halfway houses. Freedom of thought is a wonderful thing; but it is realistic to recognize that it is not the main engine of creativity.

Nor can we attribute the major changes to Protestantism. For one thing the timing is wrong. Luther nailed up his theses on the Wittenberg church door in 1517; by 1560 the major Protestant sects and the lines of the national churches had been established. But the thought of the 1500s still moved largely in well-worn paths: Humanists, Aristoteleans, scholastics, Cabalists, mystics. The big reorganization of philosophy did not come until the mid-1600s. Of course there were Protestant thinkers; but they were mainly concerned with theological issues and biblical texts. Erasmus, Luther, Melancthon, Calvin, Schwenckfeld, and Franck do not constitute a revolution in philosophy. The Reformation increased the particularistic emphasis in thought, not the abstract level where philosophical and scientific creativity takes place.

The Protestant-centered line of argument rests on two false premises: that religious control is inherently antithetical to intellectual innovation, and that Protestantism is more liberal or less authoritarian than Catholicism. The second was certainly not true at any time before 1700. The notion that it was so became part of Protestant propaganda after the condemnation of Galileo in 1632. But Servetus had been burned at Geneva in 1553; Grotius was condemned to life imprisonment by the orthodox Calvinists in Holland in 1618, and escaped to Catholic France; Bayle was dismissed from his chair at the Protestant academy in Rotterdam in 1693 under theological attack. Because intellectual history written in English or German has been under the sway of the Protestant viewpoint, we are not prepared for the idea that Spain at the end of the 1500s was more of a creative center in philosophy than England or Germany (see Figure 9.7). We miss the blunt fact that Galileo and his scientific faction in Italy were based in Jesuit and papal networks, and that Catholic France was the center of gravity of the leading philosophical networks from the generation of Montaigne to that of Malebranche. It was by contact with this network that most outsiders, from Hobbes to Leibniz, had their creativity sparked. Catholic monks and priests ranged from Bruno and Campanella to Arnauld (a Sorbonne theologian), Malebranche, and Bossuet.

In science the picture is more mixed across Catholic-Protestant lines. Copernicus was a Catholic church official, Gassendi and Mersenne were priests, Clavius and Cavalieri Jesuits, Torricelli and Viviani Jesuit pupils, Pascal a Jansenist convert. The men who made the mathematical revolution—Cardan, Tartaglia, Viète, Descartes, Fermat—were all Catholics. On the Protestant side we can muster Brahe, Kepler, Napier, Gilbert, Stevin, and Snel; Harvey was a Protestant who studied at the Catholic university of Padua. When we come to the generation of the Invisible College, there is a more consciously Protestant identity, not surprising during the English Commonwealth; but this group generally consists of moderates and opponents of the Puritan extreme, who structurally were closely linked to their Catholic counterparts on the Continent. Our long-term comparisons ought to have prepared us for the idea that science is theologically neutral. Among the Muslims it had practitioners in virtually all theological factions. In medieval Christendom we find science incorporated in the worldviews of Victorines and Albertists, Thomists, Scotists, and nominalists, among both Averroists and their persecutor Peckham; indeed it is hard to find a significant university philosopher who did not make room for science. Among the Greeks, science was compatible with Sophists, Platonists, and Neoplatonists, Aristoteleans, Epicureans, Stoics, and even some branches of medical Skeptics. Science is not necessarily theologically controversial, and many different philosophical camps can incorporate it.

Of course the Catholic Church was capable of being authoritarian; we see this in the torture of Jews by the Inquisition in Spain, the prohibition of della Porta's writings by the Inquisition in 1592, the burning of Bruno in 1600 and of the Averroist Vanini in 1619, the restrictions on Galileo in 1613–1616 and his condemnation in 1632. There are episodes throughout the century: Jesuits hounding Gassendi and Arnauld, Bossuet persecuting the Oratorian Richard Simon in the 1680s and the mysticism of Fénelon and Mme. Guyon in the 1690s. But intellectual creativity is driven by conflict, and much of the innovativeness within the Catholic world was due to the existence of a steady balance of internal conflicts. Thus della Porta, no outsider but a Jesuit lay brother, was taken off the Index in 1598 and subsequently went on to participate in the scientific Accademia della Lincei established at Rome under the eyes of the pope in the early 1600s. Campanella had been imprisoned by the Spanish at Naples from 1599 to 1626; when he fled it was to the pope, who in turn sent him to royal protection in France. Galileo was alternatively feted and warned in Rome; his sentence was soon commuted into house arrest, amounting to an aristocratic patronage arrangement which allowed him to continue his researches. What we see here are the twists and turns of contending forces within Catholicism. The church had a rich lineup of competing bases, each sufficiently elaborated so that there was room for intellectual maneuver.

By contrast, the Protestant world often gave less autonomous space for intellectuals. Especially where the Reformation found a strong local power base, the church was prone to be dogmatic. The Calvinists, with their fusion of church and political community, represented an extreme authoritarian milieu. Local self-rule here meant that the means of controlling opinion were especially direct and immediate. Perhaps now we can see the logic in the fact that the leading edge of the philosophical revolution was not only Catholic but from the sector that was most explicitly anti-Calvinist. If the Descartes-Mersenne circle is the network core, notice where it derived its impetus and sponsorship: the most famous teacher at La Flèche when Descartes and Mersenne were studying there was Francois Veron, who became the king's official anti-Calvinist debater (Popkin, 1979: 70). Descartes's philosophical career was launched in 1628, when he was encouraged by Cardinal Bérulle, the French anti-Calvinist leader, to develop his system. Descartes's weapon, the use of skeptical arguments to clear the ground for certainty, was a piece of cultural capital inherited from the previous generation of French thinkers; and here we find Pierre Charron, Montaigne's friend, who was not only a skeptical fideist but also a militant anti-Calvinist. In the crucial period of the philosophical revolution, it is closer to the mark to see Catholic intellectuals playing the liberators against the image of the Calvinists as anti-intellectual authoritarians.

The Protestant Reformation was another act in the long-term struggle over church organization which had been going on since 1300, a struggle full of schisms, anti-popes, heresies, and reformers. In some respects the Reformation was a backward movement against secularization, for the Catholic Church was an international organization in tension with the consolidating national states, while the successful Protestant movements represented a downsizing of the church to the state (sometimes the city-state) level, and hence a fresh fusion of religion with political power. In a larger organizational frame, the Protestant-Catholic struggle added another dimension of conflict to the underpinnings of intellectual life; for several generations it was Catholic intellectuals who were best positioned to take advantage of this.

Secularization of the Intellectual Base

Secularization is more structural than doctrinal. Secularization does not mean that no one is concerned with religion any longer. Religious movements may still flourish, but now they become private movements. Secularization means removing control of intellectual production from the authority of the church. That authority had been backed up by the coercive power of the state; church and aristocratic rule were organizationally intertwined. The same families made careers in both; church property was a portion of aristocratic property; in daily life the church provided the means of ritual production, enacting the ceremonial impressiveness of the political classes. Accordingly, secularization began as a type of political revolution; as with all revolutions, its structural key was breakdown at the top, caused by internal struggle among the elites, and brought to a crisis by costly escalations and exhaustion of resources.[1]

Secularization was the result of stalemate. The papacy itself first underwent an insidious secularization during the Renaissance period, for it was a center of worldly wealth but also uncontrollable worldly debts (above all from its untenable geopolitical position); its far-flung networks and its riches made it the center of factional strife and the target for plundering by adventurers. The Reformation translated the strife and plunder to a new level—wholesale confiscation and religious war. In each phase the structural pattern is the same: conflict among church-state elites, politicized churchmen and politicians with religious slogans on their tongues, whose protracted struggles eventually exhaust the power of the church, materially and emotionally. Ritual impressiveness and the capacity for legitimation are lost as the struggle winds down in political maneuver and compromise. In sociological conflict theory, the process of exhaustion and de-escalation of conflict is as important as the original mobilization and polarization.

On the macro-level, the structural situation of church politics was a balanced conflict of cross-cutting powers, a gridlock of political alliances and religious factions. That was the formula for political stalemate, and, because of the exhaustion of resources as conflict escalated in this unwinnable situation, for eventual breakdown of the old church-state. But with one added ingredient: it was also the formula for intellectual creativity which we have seen in so many parts of the world, the intersection of rival circles at a center of attention.

The Catholic world was the intellectual center during this period of church breakdown and exhaustion because it remained the cosmopolitan center. That was its structural advantage over the parochial national churches of the Protestants; that is why English and German intellectuals made their key network ties to the Paris of Richelieu and Mazarin.

Balance of power among cross-cutting networks had effects at three different levels. The exhaustion of politicized church conflict led to secularization, the gradual neutralization and downgrading of the role of the church in the state, and the loss of church control over the means of intellectual production. For intellectuals, cross-cutting networks were the formula for a period of creativity. The stars, such as Descartes and Leibniz, are the persons situated at the nodes among the inner circle of circles. The character of ideas was also affected: the cosmopolitan networks, especially during the time of political compromise when particularistic doctrines were tainted with the failure of fanaticism, drove up the level of abstraction which constituted the terrain of philosophical discovery. Religion turned universalistic; once again, as in the Spain of Averroës and Maimonides, philosophers provided a religion of reason beyond sectarian strife. But this too was doomed by the structural shifts of secularization; no religious doctrine, even the most universalistic, could recover the dominance once held by the old state-enforced faith. Depoliticization of the church opened an inner space for intellectuals to pursue their own puzzles. Philosophy recovered from its eclipse, launching a new era in the higher regions of metaphysics and epistemology.

Geopolitics and Cleavages within Catholicism

Spain was an early center of intellectual ferment because it was the first great state power and the dominant force in the Catholic world. The creation of the modern state structure was largely a matter of geopolitics and military organization and of the internal fiscal structures to support it. Spain was the first to carry out the military revolution, shifting to a disciplined and centrally armed infantry; along with this went intensified struggle with the landed nobility over the increased fiscal requirements of the state. Religious organizations were entwined with both sides; the Inquisition, the monasteries, the universities, the church lands, which made up almost 50 percent of Spain (Wuthnow, 1989: 34), were simultaneously places where aristocrats made their careers and resources the government grasped for its own power. This tug-of-war was taking place not between haves and have-nots, but between rival ways of organizing at the top; this meant that there would be factions rich in resources in the heart of the church itself, a major ingredient for intellectual action.

Spain of the 1500s was becoming the first great European empire, expanding simultaneously with the unification of the Iberian kingdoms, the conquest of the Americas, and dynastic marriages and alliances which brought it the Netherlands, Austria, and a string of territories up the eastern border of France. Not least was its expansion into Italy, building on its possessions in Sicily; this was driven by rivalry with the French, the other great consolidating post-feudal state. Spanish and French armies marched back and forth from Milan to Naples from the 1490s to 1530, liberating and sacking Rome on the way. The pope was reduced to maneuvering for allies, perhaps the main reason why central religious authority was broken at last during these years by the Lutheran Reformation. From 1530 down to 1700, large parts of Italy were directly annexed to Spain, and the rest, including the Papal States along with Tuscany and Venice, were uneasy regions of mixed resistance and acquiescence. Here was a major cleavage within the Catholic power, and one reason why Naples suddenly became a center of intellectual action—Telesio, Bruno, Campanella, della Porta—embroiled in movements against the Spanish occupation with intermittent support from the pope.

France and Spain remained locked together in the north by their geopolitical conflict. The Spanish Habsburgs hemmed in France on every border. The Low Countries, "the cockpit of Europe," became the equivalent of a buffer zone of shifting political fragments, and this made it more vulnerable to religious decentralization in its most extreme, Calvinist form. This is ironic only if we think that a military power ought to be able to impose its religious orthodoxy; in fact the huge resources of the French and Spanish states allowed each to check the other, including their efforts to dictate religious policy. As Spain eventually became the standard-bearer of the Counterreformation, France was driven into the surreptitious policy of supporting Protestants. Geopolitics refers not merely to dominance by the strongest state but to the pattern of relations between rivals' resources. As Spain became the Catholic authoritarian state, France became the center of Catholic liberalism. And the Netherlands, for all its tendencies toward Calvinist authoritarianism, by the 1600s had become the center of religious war-weariness and the home of cosmopolitan movements transcending religious factions.

The Spanish Intellectual Efflorescence

Although Spain eventually settled into a hard-line effort to enforce Catholic traditionalism, this did not happen before several generations of internal struggles, which brought intellectual creativity as a result. Spain was not automatically anti-Reformation, especially since it had its own military and political problems with the pope over its Italian policy. Robert Wuthnow (1989: 26–35, 102–113) has shown that the landed aristocracy derived its strongest legitima-

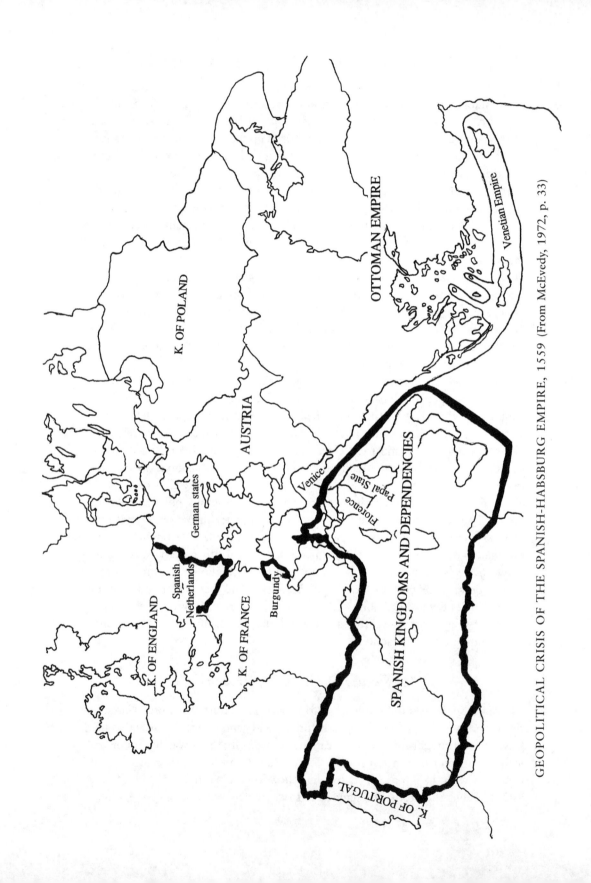

GEOPOLITICAL CRISIS OF THE SPANISH-HABSBURG EMPIRE, 1559 (From McEvedy, 1972, p. 33)

tion from participation in the old Catholic ritualism, and this faction was strong enough in Spain to defeat the new state-centered actors and choke off movement toward all-out Reformation. Nevertheless, organizational resources were shifting, especially during the great expansion of empire in the 1500s, and the people closest to these organizational changes became open to new ways of combining intellectual capital and new forms of generating emotional energy. That these changes continued to be defined as "Catholic" meant that there was no overt break from the papacy and no radical decentralization of church authority. In most other spheres of content and practice, innovations went far.

The Jesuits were the vehicle of much of this innovation. The movement was organized by the nobleman Ignatius Loyala (López), invalided from the Spanish army, who turned in 1522 to the traditional religious practices: pilgrimage, conversion of infidels, zeal in caring for the sick, personal austerity. As his reputation grew, Loyola began to transform the monastic life, abolishing choir, prayers, seclusion, and distinctive uniforms. The Jesuits criticized magic, legends, and the worship of saints. Their initial purpose was to become missionaries in the world-system just then expanding under Iberian lead. But universities were undergoing a sudden boom in Spain, and Loyola followed the flow of current excitement in seeking his recruits. Adopting the ideal that missionaries should be the best trained of the church, he studied at the elite Spanish universities of Alcalá and Salamanca, and then at Paris, where in 1534 he organized the Society of Jesus with a few companions. By Loyola's death in 1556, it had 1,000 members; in the next century it had over 600 colleges and academies and was the largest educational institution in Europe (Heer, [1953] 1968: 26–27; O'Malley, 1993: 200–242).

The timing of the Jesuit movement strikingly parallels the Reformation. Loyola's conversion was almost contemporary with Luther's rebellion; the launching of the Jesuits in Paris in the 1530s happened at the center of controversy over the new doctrines, and overlapped the presence there of Jean Caulvin (Calvin), who fled to Basel in 1536 to publish his *Institutes of Christian Religion,* and established his theocracy in Geneva in 1541, the year after the pope approved Loyola's order. In practice, these were both anti-monastic, anti-ritualistic reforms, although they found different political and organizational niches in their relations to papal authority.

The Jesuits' growth was largely shaped by exploiting a niche resulting from reorganization of the medieval educational system. The medieval universities had been guilds of teachers, licensing the higher professions of law, medicine, and theology, and giving a formal degree structure to the arts course which prepared for them. It was a two-tiered system with universities as the top rung, while elementary literacy and grammar was provided in local schools attached to churches and monasteries. We have already seen (in Chapter 9) the crisis of the universities which set in after 1300, as universities proliferated, enrollments dropped, institutions failed, and the licensing monopolies over the professions tended to break down. Especially in England and France, the core of the old system, the universities, now shifted toward becoming collections of colleges, that is to say, boarding schools for undergraduate students, taking away instruction from the arts faculty. In the 1500s these university colleges began to expand downward to incorporate the elementary Latin curriculum as well, that is, taking over the territory of the lower grammar schools. Medieval schools never had any strict age grading, and the colleges now had an age range from 8 to 20. Most students were day students, who attended for only a few years. The only remaining link to the old university structure was that if a student did persevere all the way to the end of the course, he could take the old M.A. degree; but the value of this credential was now disappearing. The medieval two-tiered system was now divided along a different line: instead of grammar schools and universities with teenagers and young adults in the latter, there were now colleges and professional faculties, with the former extending down to children (Ariès, 1962: 195–237; Simon, 1966; Grendler, 1989).

As many towns began to set up colleges independently of the universities, the status advantage of university education disappeared. The Jesuits made their success by pushing this tendency to an extreme. Their colleges were free and open to all social classes; in the 1600s, 50 to 60 percent of students were sons of artisans and the lower-middle class. Emphasis was still on Latin, the old high-status language of the educated. Within this frame, the Jesuits made a point of incorporating the newer culture offering science, literature, and the latest modes of philosophy and of theological argumentation. We see another significant overlap with Loyola's presence at Paris in the 1530s: Ramus took his M.A. there in 1536 and began teaching a reformed, non-Aristotelean logic, mixing in Humanistic cultural capital by combining logic with rhetoric into a single art of discourse. This became the model for textbooks in secondary schools, spreading widely in the new Calvinist middle schools that grew up, especially in Germany and England, as an alternative to the traditional universities. The Jesuit colleges too adopted a version of the Ramus textbooks, such as the one Descartes studied at La Flèche (*EP,* 1967: 7:66–67). Here again we find the Jesuits paralleling on the Catholic side the organizational reforms that opened up with the collapse of the medieval system of religious education.

Educational reform provided the organizational basis for intellectual innovation. The Jesuit college in Rome became a center for high-level scientists and theologians from the 1560s through 1620, including Clavius, Suarez, and Bellarmine, and connecting to Galileo (Wallace, 1984). Perhaps most strikingly, the Jesuits were at the high point of the intellectual creativity which broke out in the Spanish universities. Christian Spain had never been an intellectual center, except when Toledo in the mid-1100s had been the translation center with the Muslims; after the fall of the Córdoba caliphate in 1236, the only activity of philosophical significance comprised the Jewish Maimonidists, Averroists, and Kabbalists, typically in an underground against the authoritarianism of Christian orthodoxy. There were two large medieval universities, at Salamanca and Valladolid, but these were never important in philosophy. So it is rather abruptly in the early and mid-1500s that we find Spanish thinkers of world importance—Las Casas, Vitoria, and Soto—developing the theory of natural rights and international law.

In network structure the Spanish intellectuals were a spinoff from the main scholastic lineage at Paris.[2] An early Spanish Humanist, Juan Luis Vives, like Loyola went to Paris but did not return. By the mid-1500s, the leading Dominican Thomists were in Spain, and some of the northerners, such as the Latin stylist Buchanan, even sojourned there. The typical structural pattern of creativity emerges: lines of conflict among interlinked factions. The famous Carmelite reformers, the mystics Saint Teresa of Avila and John of the Cross, were attacked by the Dominican Melchior Cano; a proponent of scientific method, he saw these mystics as anti-intellectual reactionaries. Teresa was supported by her confessor, Bañez, a Salamanca metaphysician and another Dominican Thomist. In the heart of these conflicting networks emerged the most important Jesuit philosophers, Molina and Suarez.

Molina formulated the distinctive Jesuit philosophy, the sophisticated calculation bordering on cynicism which would characterize much of the leading secular thought of the following generations. In 1588 Molina published a philosophical path out of the dilemmas of predestination, the trademark theological issue of the Calvinists. He proposed a *scientia media,* a middle kind of knowledge between Aquinas's two kinds, God's vision of concrete existences and God's knowledge of possibilities. The traditional Thomist position, that man is physically predetermined by God to act freely, Molina charged, is only a disguised form of determinism. Molina argued for God's knowledge of conditional future contingent events, and hence the cooperation of free will with divine grace, bringing down on himself the attack of Cano and Bañez. The theological dispute had a wider significance, affecting the concept of knowledge and hence of the emerging epistemological space within philosophy. Three generations later Leibniz was to draw on Molina's *scientia media* to overcome the rigidities of Cartesianism (Brown, 1984: 26). Molina created a theology and ethics of probabilism: cognitions are less true the more general they are; concrete activity in the world always entails choices involving mixtures of greater or lesser evil consequences. Molina launched the famous Jesuit emphasis on casuistry and situational ethics, a version of relativism. For the Jesuits at this time, it was a liberal position against the authoritarians and absolutists of both the Protestant and Counterreformation hard-liners. Crusades and holy wars could not be justified, since no convictions could be certain enough to support no-holds-barred conflict; this led naturally into a criticism of the divine right of kings and of the absolute authority of the state. In this Molina was followed by other Jesuits, including Bellarmine (Galileo's critic) and Suarez.

Culminating three generations of creativity in Spain, Suarez was the last great scholastic philosopher; in subsequent Catholic circles his reputation was second only to that of Aquinas. He produced a massive synthesis of Scotist and Thomist metaphysics. The two high points of medieval philosophy, rival lineages for 300 years, were brought together just when the medieval structure was in its final collapse. Here we find another case of creativity driven by the rearrangement of the attention space, the creativity of intellectual alliances which we have seen exemplified in the grand pagan synthesis at the end of the ancient Greek world. Suarez formulated metaphysics as the science of being qua being; it comprises acts of existing, but also real essences, characterized by non-contradiction. Breaking with Scotus, Suarez held that being is not univocal but is a concept derived by analogy from the various kinds of being.[3] Suarez shaped the heritage of philosophy that was to be passed along to the modernists, who believed they were breaking with medieval thought.

Suarez's philosophy became the center of the curriculum in Catholic and many Protestant universities (especially in Germany) for 200 years; and this tradition kept resurfacing whenever philosophy became consciously metaphysical. Wolff's masterwork *Philosophia Prima Sive Ontologica* (1729) builds explicitly on Suarez (*EP*, 1967: 8:340–341). Wolff takes ontology as purely self-contained argument over first principles, governed by the principle of non-contradiction. From thence he deduces the principle of sufficient reason which governs physical, non-logical necessity: that in every case there must be a reason why something exists rather than not. This is a touchstone of Leibniz's philosophy as well, and it is implicit in Kant's problematic of pure reason, the justification of the synthetic a priori. When Schopenhauer at the beginning of his career proposed to overthrow constructive idealism and return to Kant, his first statement was *The Four-fold Root of the Principle of Sufficient Reason*, with its explicit admiration of Suarez. Still later, Heidegger—the product of a Catholic seminary education—revived the ontological question, returning explicitly to Scotus and overturning the Principle of Sufficient Reason by declaring the logical unfoundedness of existence. This was one more move on the turf delineated by Suarez.

Figure 10.1 shows Suarez contemporaneous with Bacon, Campanella, and the scientific predecessors of Descartes. This is no anomaly. Once again creativity breaks out simultaneously on rival sides of the field. The modernists of the scientific revolution scorned the old university metaphysics; the Spanish university networks revived and carried forward the sophisticated abstractions of the scholastic tradition. When the later generation of the revolutionists' network got over their anti-metaphysical ideology, it was Suarez's line of cultural capital that they continued.

Expansion and Crisis of the Spanish Universities

Why then did the Spanish intellectual world disappear again from view in the 1600s? The easy answer would be the dominance of reactionary Catholicism; but this begs the question of cause and effect. Authoritarianism was not always dominant, and the Inquisition itself was not uniformly reactionary in intellectual matters; the first wave of liberalism at the beginning of the 1500s was led by the Grand Inquisitor, Cardinal Cisneros, who supported the Erasmian reformers (Heer, [1953] 1968: 8–9, 13, 29–31). Cisneros founded the new university of Alcalá, near Madrid, in 1509, with chairs for the ancient languages and Bible study in the original texts; this Humanist move was balanced by founding chairs for Thomist, Scotist, and nominalist philosophy against the late medieval tendency toward sectarianism and exclusiveness. Salamanca responded by founding its own rival chairs, and from here the material base of the Spanish intellectual takeoff was established.

That material base went through a boom and bust which coincided with the rise and fall of Spanish philosophical creativity. Spanish universities of the Middle Ages had been modest in number and size. In the 1400s the rate of new foundations picked up, reaching a deluge in the 1500s and early 1600s (see Table 9.1 and sources cited there). Of the 32 Spanish universities of this period, three were overwhelmingly dominant. Salamanca alone had some 6,000 students most years between 1550 and 1620—a figure matched by no previous university except Paris in the 1200s, and by none subsequently until the late 1800s in Germany. Alcalá at its height had 2,500 to 3,500 students, Valladolid 2,000. Three or four other universities had as many as 600 students, while the others were small, reaching 60 to 70 students at most. At the height in the late 1500s, approximately 3 percent of young Spanish males were attending universities, and perhaps half of them took degrees. The immensity of this educational movement in a relatively small population needs to be appreciated. The United States, the modern pioneer of mass higher education, did not pass this ratio until 1900, modern England until 1950.[4]

The underlying dynamic was a market for educational credentials. By the late 1500s, the lower arts faculty had largely dropped out, displaced by the mushrooming Jesuit colleges. The universities now consisted almost entirely of theology and law students, seeking places in church and state; Spain was the first society in history to be swamped by doctorates. This was a case of genuine credential inflation; the arts degrees were displaced by advanced degrees after 1550, with increasing emphasis on legal degrees as a ticket to administrative positions in the government. The big three universities monopolized the market, with increasing inbreeding by particular colleges within them (Kagan, 1974: 369; Elliot, 1970: 317). Graduates of Salamanca, Alcalá, and Valladolid held a majority of top clerical and secular positions in the Habsburg administration, and a complete monopoly in royal councils and provincial courts of justice. Poorer provincial nobility flocked to the universities, causing enormous expansion and an escalation of degree requirements, but without breaking the monopoly of the wealthy aristocrats holding favored connections. The result was a large floating population of penurious petitioners, living on hopes of patronage. The king even prohibited graduates of the non-major universities from coming to Madrid, but with little success. It is this atmosphere that is described in the outburst of Spanish novels at this time, from *Lazarillo de Tormes* (1554) to Quevedo and Cervantes in the early 1600s; and it was this "intellectual proletariat" which underlay the literary production.

After 1620 the system went into decline. By 1660 student numbers had fallen by half, with decline continuing into the early 1800s. The great outburst of foundations came to an end, and no new universities were founded after 1620 until 1830. Of the 25 or more founded in the 1500s, half failed and many of the others limped into the 1700s with 30 students or fewer. The major universities fell in size along with the others. The expansionary phase had carried the intellectual life of Spain from the time of Cisneros and Las Casas down to Suarez. With the downturn of the intellectual base, creativity dried up as well. Spain's conservative authoritarianism was not congenital; it triumphed when organizational expansion ended.

The Intersection of Movements in France

The Jesuits epitomize what could be constructed on this situation. There were new material bases supporting multiple competing intellectual circles. Creativity is the making of new combinations by moving opportunistically through such a structure, transcending narrowly polarized loyalties and borrowing from enemies for new purposes. The Jesuit order sprang from Spain, but its intellectual base was far wider. Its schools now dominated education in the Catholic world. Their grand college at La Flèche was founded in 1607 in a château given by King Henri IV, along with sumptuous endowment, to celebrate the return of the Jesuits to France after their expulsion in 1595 (Chauvin,

1991). The intellectual and organizational leaders of the new philosophy, Descartes and Mersenne, came from among the students of the first cohort at the Jesuit center. The list of former pupils of Jesuit schools is impressive, including Molière, Bossuet, Huet, Simon, and Bayle, down to Voltaire, Diderot, and Condorcet. Obviously the pupils are united more by their creative energy than by adherence to a theological line. The Jesuits are nothing if not activists, intellectual and political; they play realpolitik with their eyes open, perhaps the main reason why they have a long history of expulsion from so many states. Descartes, who spent his life moving between the battle lines of the religious wars and carefully choosing opportunities to publish new ideas, represents an extension of the Jesuit strategy into the heart of the intellectual turf.

The Oratorians, founded in 1611 by Cardinal Bérulle, were opponents and rivals of the Jesuits (Heer, [1953] 1968: 189). They were ordinary secular priests, a group whose status had always suffered in contrast to the monks, the friars, and now these new missionary and educational orders. Bérulle gave them the dignity of their own order, with an emphasis on avant-garde education. Originally anti-Calvinist, they soon found their niche in intellectual space. Bérulle, a minister of state under Richelieu, gave Descartes protection and encouragement to develop his philosophy, whereas the Jesuits eventually abandoned him despite his efforts to get their support.[5] The Oratorians and their college at Juilly, near Paris, produced its own list of famous members and pupils over the succeeding generations: La Peyrère, Simon, Malebranche, Boulainvilliers, Montesquieu, virtually a lineup of avant-garde thought in France for over a century.

France was now the center of Catholic cosmopolitanism and the cross-cutting pressures for secularization. Paris became the center at which the movements intersected. The Jesuits and Oratorians were there; anti-Jesuit movements such as the Jansenists sprang up, contesting the leaders of the attention space.

Mersenne's circle became eminent by connecting all the movements. He put together the scientific network; he publicized Descartes and made Hobbes and Arnauld known for the first time when he solicited their comments to be published with Descartes's *Meditations on the First Philosophy* in 1641; he initiated the youthful Pascal by giving him mathematics lessons. Gassendi, who was driven from his position at the University of Aix in 1623 by the Jesuits, was recruited by Mersenne as collaborator on the strength of his recent skeptical attack on metaphysicians and occultists. Mersenne's unifying strategy was to use science as a weapon against the Protestants and the dissolution of church authority. Mersenne launched his correspondence circle in 1623; in the same year he made his first move on the intellectual scene by attacking atheists, Deists, Cabalists, and astrologers, denouncing the English theosophist Fludd as an evil magician. Mersenne and Gassendi used skepticism against what they saw as the prime enemy of established religion, the Neoplatonist occultism which claimed to know the essences of the universe. Mersenne held up Galileo's science as an appropriately modest form of knowledge; eschewing essences, it settled for a mathematical description of the pattern of sensory appearances. Mersenne held that mathematics provided a way to detect the principles out of which God had fashioned the universe, and that science, more than theology, was an effective basis for sermons (Schuster, 1980; Popkin, 1979; Joy, 1987; Dear, 1988).

Gassendi used many of the same ingredients as Descartes: clearing the decks with epistemological skepticism, proposing a system of physics, working in mathematics, for which he acquired the chair at the Collège de France in 1645. But he occupied the attention space too close to Descartes to keep up an independent identity, and became famous mainly as the reviver of the old Epicurean atomism. He criticized his rival Descartes with the skeptical argument that the criterion of clear and distinct truth needs a further criterion of what is clear and distinct, but he was unable to stop the juggernaut of Cartesian rationalism, even its revival of the philosophy of essences. Gassendi's reputation became assimilated to the growing camp of corporeal philosophy; the doctrine of Descartes, who kept his distance on the periphery of the Mersenne circle, was propagated as its emblem.

Raison d'État *and Secularization by Opportunism*

The intersection of clashing movements is a wonderful transmuter of fervors and hostilities. Out of polarization, held together long enough in a balance, comes political realism and opportunism that borders on cynical secularism. Emblematic of the period is Richelieu, who figures prominently in the networks as patron and protector of Grotius, Comenius, and Campanella, of Descartes and the circle of the Libertins Érudits. A cardinal of the church, he destroyed the French Huguenots in 1628 but subsidized the Protestants in the Thirty Years' War against Spain. Like his protégé and successor Cardinal Mazarin, Richelieu was backstage ruler of France, manipulating a weak king while fighting off the plots and intrigues of the nobility. This subordination of religious fanaticism to political opportunism has a long history. Henri IV, the patron whose coat of arms is on the Jesuit college at La Flèche, was the Huguenot king who converted to Catholicism with the words "Paris is worth a mass." After Richelieu's death in 1642, the premier patron of intellectuals was the duke of Condé. He was the military commander of the French armies against Spain in the 1640s, but eventually went over to the Fronde, the domestic uprising of aristocrats against Mazarin's centralizing hand; defeated in 1653, he became a general in the Spanish army until he was defeated by the

French in 1659—with the help of Cromwell's troops practicing a Protestant version of realpolitik. Nevertheless, Condé made his peace with the king, had his estates restored, and went on to lead the French army again against both Catholic Spain and Protestant Holland. The recipients of Condé's patronage are an amazing assortment—the pre-Adamite heretic La Peyrère, who served as his librarian; the Libertins Érudits; Molière, Racine, and the court literary world—while later in his life Condé switched from scoffing to hosting conservative defenders of devoutness such as Bossuet and La Bruyère.

This side-switching is a structural key to the cosmopolitanism and the creativity of the time. French alliances with England and Sweden at the height of the religious wars made France the nexus of religious politics; there was no domestic tolerance for Protestant true believers, but an extension of traditional Catholic rationalism was acceptable. Dangerous connections were open to those who were willing to seek them out. Once again Descartes carried off the prize. He began as a professional soldier, enlisting in 1617 on the side of Prince Maurice of Nassau, champion of the Dutch Calvinists; in 1619–20 he was in Tilly's army of the Catholic League and was present at the destruction of the Protestant stronghold at Prague. It was on these travels that Descartes made his first contacts with Dutch scientists and had his famous dream—while bivouacking with the Catholic army on the Danube—about mathematics as the key to knowledge. This would be the pattern of the rest of his career, as he moved back and forth between Paris and Holland, seeking cosmopolitan allies and evading dogmatists on all sides of the religious strife.

The mental detachment resulting from this atmosphere permeates the period. The priest Gassendi wanted to defend religion but associated with the group around the aristocrat La Mothe Le Vayer, reputed a secret atheist; others of these Libertins Érudits include Patin, rector of the medical faculty of the Sorbonne, bastion of theological orthodoxy; Naudé, librarian to the cynical Richelieu and Mazarin; and the freethinking satirist Cyrano de Bergerac. Moliere, a former pupil of Gassendi, was another member of the circle, and reflected a satirical tone in his plays. The most forthright expression of this outlook is the *Maximes* (1665–1678) of La Rochefoucauld. This high-ranking nobleman had intrigued against Richelieu in the 1630s, joined the Fronde over a slight from Mazarin, negotiated the release of Condé from prison, rebelled again, made his peace, and recovered his estates. He retired into amusing his aristocratic correspondents by exchanging cryptic *sentences*, distillations of cynical wisdom on the self-interest and moral self-deception of mankind. Yet his collaborator, Mme. de Sablé, was a Jansenist sympathizer, a resident at Port-Royal in the 1650s, and La Rochefoucauld himself became an intimate of the religious authoritarian Bossuet. The cynical outlook was rationalized as compatible with religion by showing the sinfulness of the world.[6]

The Jansenist movement began as fervent rather than cynical, but its theological struggles had as their most famous result the secular philosophies associated with their retreat at Port-Royal. Jansen died in 1638 as a Louvain theologian, just as he finished his treatise on Augustine. Casting the Jesuits, as followers of Molina, in the role of the Pelagians, Jansen repudiated the role of free will and stressed man's intrinsic sinfulness and the irresistibility of interior grace. This was treading on dangerous ground, close to Calvinist predestination, which was the flash point for so many conflicts; it also provided a rallying point for Catholic opposition to the power of the Jesuits (Heer, [1953] 1968: 133–134, 194–195). Jansen's work was immediately banned by the Inquisition and the pope but acquired a following in France. Antoine Arnauld became famous in 1643 for his Jansenist arguments. Arnauld accused the Jesuits of excessive worldliness; they in turn had him expelled from the Sorbonne in 1655.

Arnauld withdrew to Port-Royal in the Parisian countryside, a convent which had been under the control of Arnauld's family for 50 years; his older sister Angelique had been appointed abbess there in 1602, at the age of 11. His father, too, was a long-term enemy of the Jesuits; as attorney general of France he had led the legal defense of the University of Paris against them in 1594, a trial culminating in the temporary expulsion of the Jesuits from France. The lovely estate at Port-Royal now became a retreat for Paris intellectuals. Pascal went there in 1655, repudiating his worldly life and turning from mathematics to the defense of religion. Nevertheless, the ties with secular intellectual life were not broken; Arnauld and Nicole wrote their *Port-Royal Logic* in this period, following Cartesian methods. Like the rivals to the Jesuits that they were, the Port-Royal intellectuals adapted religious institutions to secular opportunities. The visiting "Solitaires" opened a school outside the walls of the abbey, which soon propagated its intellectual energy; one of the pupils whose career it launched was Racine, whose worldliness as a dramatist in the 1660s and 1670s offended the puritanism of his former teachers.

The philosophical contributions of Pascal were a precipitate of these conditions. For several years he was a roué and a gambler, the latter providing the materials on which he invented the mathematics of probability. This period came to an end with an emotional conversion in 1654, whereupon he joined his family members at Port-Royal. His famous defenses of religion are investments of a worldly cultural capital. "The eternal silence of these infinite spaces frightens me": this is the human dimension of the new scientist's worldview, looking outward toward its boundaries (*Pensées* 206). And Pascal's famous wager over the existence of God—a minimax solution of the costs of nonbelief together with the possible benefits of belief—is scandalously secular in tone.

There is much human pathos in the attacks and retreats, the weariness and the side-switching of this time. We associate enthusiasm with creativity and respect the courage of one's convictions among the highest of human qualities. But in association with power, fervent ideals mean polarizing conflicts, leading to destructiveness and, in the eyes of an increasing number, cruelty and injustice. In this context opportunism starts to become a virtue. Whether we see it as cynicism or as tolerance, these are alternative gestalts for the same configuration. Whether we think Pascal and Descartes are calculating or sincere, they became great because they embodied the historical moment when such questions could now be raised.

Reemergence of the Metaphysical Field

The Cartesian circle at Paris in the last third of the century was something of a bringdown from the excitement of the previous generation. Its very routinization indicates a crucial feature of the reconstituted intellectual world. Philosophy had survived; it had not been replaced by science, nor faded away as a mere residue of religion. Descartes's grand ambition failed, but left a set of problems and concepts distinctively defining philosophical turf. In fact, Descartes was not as philosophically radical as he pretended, drawing heavily on scholastic cultural capital; and the Jesuit scholasticism of Molina and Suarez was prominent in many universities. But now metaphysics was practiced openly among the modernists who were in the center of the intellectual attention space. Creativity proceeds by dividing that space according to the law of small numbers. The Cartesians party was so victorious in setting the focus of attention for the avant-garde network that its majority began to split into factions, even disputing with Descartes himself.

Descartes's chief followers suffered the fate of epigones, being insufficiently distinctive to have major reputations of their own. Rohault deduced the existence of the self from eight self-evident axioms. Régis as systematically extended the consequences of the cogito, deriving from it 14 further irrefutable principles. The major religious conservatives also made their reputations on Cartesian capital. The extreme fideist Huet used skeptical arguments against the cogito: since it consists of statements uttered in time, there is no guarantee that the "ergo sum" is still true when it is uttered in a following moment. "I think therefore I am" means no more than "I thought therefore perhaps I was" (Popkin, 1979: 200). Foucher revived the skeptical Platonic Academy's criticism of sense perception, eliminating Cartesian extended substance. These efforts to tighten up Descartes's arguments, or to repudiate them entirely, attracted less attention than the more radical moves to divide up the revitalized territory of metaphysics.

The Cartesian loyalists occupied the center of attention which everyone attacked; their dualism of mental and material substance was the puzzle on which everyone focused. Around this were arrayed the occasionalists (Malebranche and others), giving primacy to the spiritual side; at the other extreme the sensualists, giving primacy to material extension, most notably in Locke's version; a third major alternative was Spinoza's monism; a fourth was Leibniz's monadology, which combines mind and matter in each of an infinity of distinct substances. A fifth position, aloof from this array of positive systems, comprised the skeptics, rejecting all. If we add to this the Cartesian loyalists, we have six positions, more or less the upper limit under the law of small numbers, the set of positions that can acquire attention at the same time. In fact there were even more philosophies grappling for attention, and some were bound to be squeezed out of the memory of subsequent generations. The 36 years from 1674 to 1710 contained one of the biggest and most colorful outbursts of metaphysical systems since the early 1300s; the only other burst like it is the variety of German Idealisms produced between 1780 and 1820. Berkeley was part of the same generation of structural creativity (his chronological age is irrelevant, and his youthful creativity is explained by the network links affording him the opportunity to take advantage of the structural transformation of the intellectual field). Berkeley's idealism is thus a seventh position on the continuum, outflanking Malebranche on the spiritual side. It is probably for this reason that Berkeley ended up occupying the reputational slot on that side of the field, becoming one of the classic philosophers while Malebranche's reputation faded.[7]

Malebranche accepted dualism but shifted the primacy back toward the religious side. This was a natural enough combination of ingredients for a young priest out of the Sorbonne. As a member of the liberal Oratorians, around 1668–1674 he frequented the Cartesians, who lent him Descartes's unpublished manuscripts. He seized on the major point of controversy, the difficulty of a causal connection between mind and body, and in 1674 proposed an occasionalist solution. Evidently the link does exist. Malebranche took this as evidence for the continuous intervention of God in the world; when a human spirit wills, it is God who moves his or her body; going in the other direction, perception depends on God's transmitting the motion of matter into the ideas humans experience. Malebranche defended the relevance of God in a time when secular intellectual life was spinning free. Malebranche was not the only religious thinker who hit on the occasionalist route out of Descartes. Geulincx, who studied at Louvain with a Cartesian professor before converting to Calvinism, developed an occasionalist account of causality, denying the substantiality of created particulars; this was published only posthumously in 1688, after Malebranche had reaped the fame. Others in the Parisian network of religious thinkers found this slot as well; Cordemoy (who was associated with Bossuet as reader to the Dauphin) and La Forge also gave an occasionalist solution to the mind-body problem.

Malebranche came to represent this position in the public eye as he was caught up in a swirl of controversies with his most famous opponents: in 1683 Arnauld polemicized with him over the implication that humans have no ideas of their own if they see all things in God; later Leibniz criticized Malebranche for obscuring the scientific status of the laws of motion. On the other side he was attacked by Fénelon and Bossuet. To make God the sole cause in the universe appears to eliminate free will, and Malebranche's theological unorthodoxy landed him on the Index in 1690. This was hardly fatal to one's intellectual reputation; but there was a deeper problem in reconciling the party of religious orthodoxy with Cartesianism while solving the philosophical puzzle of how to relate two dissimilar substances. The intermediation of God in effect provides a third substance. If one wishes to emphasize the spiritual side, Berkeley's idealism is a cleaner route to that goal. If one is impressed with Mallebranche's conceptual tools, Leibniz provides a superseding version. Malebranche sharpened the problem not just of mind-body interaction but of how anything can act causally on anything. If we stick to observables, we find only a succession, never a causal force; Malebranche gives the very image of billiard balls moving on a table that one later associates with Hume (quoted in Brown, 1984: 84; also Lévi-Bruhl, 1899: 63–64). In the same way, it is unintelligible how a spirit can communicate with another spirit, except, Malebranche says, via God; and God's intervention is necessary also to uphold the order of the physical world. Malebranche left a heritage of puzzles that would be exploited by others.

The monistic path out of Descartes's two-substance problem was taken by Spinoza, then given a distinctive twist by Leibniz. Both men encountered the Cartesian network and its puzzles, each with ties to the international scientific community, and each with strong motivations to transcend religious disputes.

Jewish Millennialism and Spinoza's Religion of Reason

Spinoza was formed in the midst of controversies at Amsterdam, when the opportunism of religious politics in Europe was at its height. The Jews had become an important element in the larger intellectual scene. This was a role they had played in Muslim Spain during the 1100s, but never before in Christian Europe. Now the actors were mostly Portuguese Jews newly arrived in exile, fleeing persecution by the Spanish Inquisition, which had been extended to Portugal when that kingdom was incorporated into Spain in 1580. But Spanish Jews had been under pressure to convert or flee ever since the reconquest; the philosophical results had been particularistic Kabbalah, not universalistic doctrine. In the mid-1600s there was an additional factor from the Christian side: a growing interest in a universal religion pruned of dogmatic elements. Judaism was attractive on this score; leaving aside dietary and other ritual, the theology itself is a simpler monotheism than Christianity. Some claimed that Judaism was the universal religion arrived at by reason.

Amsterdam Jewish circles divided among secularizing religion, synthesis with Christianity, and defense of Jewish orthodoxy.[8] In 1643 a Portuguese refugee, Isaac La Peyrère (la Peireira), launched a sensational thesis: the Messianic age was soon to begin, since it was heralded by the conversion of the Jews. La Peyrère was an experienced side-switcher, a convert to Calvinism, living at the time in Paris under Condé's patronage and in contact with the Libertins Érudits; when he traveled to Amsterdam, the safest haven in which to publish his works, they were picked up by the Jews. In 1650 Rabbi Menasseh ben Israel, an Amsterdam printer from a Portuguese refugee family, predicted the imminent coming of the Messiah when the Jews were spread over the world. This must have seemed borne out by contemporary events, in this time of forced conversions and a new diaspora; it blended, too, with scientific speculation over new geographical discoveries, including the idea that the tribes found in the Americas were the lost tribes of Israel. The fervor of contemporary religious politics in the Protestant camp contributed to the atmosphere in which Jewish millennialism appeared. In 1655 Cromwell, who believed that the Commonwealth was re-creating ancient Jewish theocracy, invited Menasseh to England.

Meanwhile La Peyrère announced a more scandalous thesis: in 1655 he proposed that non-biblical peoples had existed before Adam, and the Bible is the historical record of only one of the world's people, the Jews. This pre-Adamite thesis was published in Amsterdam, where it was debated in an interdenominational circle around Menasseh. Boreil, in touch with Cromwell and with the Invisible College of scientists forming in England, hosted the group and followed the millennial line that the conversion of the Jews was penultimate to the coming of the Messiah. The young Spinoza attended the Menasseh circle and was expelled from the Amsterdam synagogue at the height of these controversies in 1656 along with Ribera, who expounded the pre-Adamite thesis of La Peyrère.

Spinoza took a third line between Jewish orthodoxy and millennial hopes, the stance of toleration and transcending partisan furor. Spinoza's distinctive brand of cosmopolitanism came from his additional network connection, the Cartesian scientists. He expounded Descartes's physics in geometric argument in his first publication (1663), hoping to arrive at a self-evident demonstration of rational philosophy as a basis for a universally acceptable theology. But Descartes had brought no universal agreement, and Spinoza found the flaw in the inconsistency of having two substances.[9] One attraction of monism is that proof of a single substance simultaneously unifies theology with mathematical science. This is a bolder path than Descartes followed; he was willing to leave conventional Catholic theology in place so long as he could reorganize philosophy along scientific lines. Spinoza took over the space vacated at Descartes's death; for Spinoza in Holland was still at the crossroads of the international scientific networks. But now it was a Holland becoming weary of religious conflict and de-ideologized with the settling of the Spanish war. The defeat of Protestant millennialism with the fall of the English Commonwealth in 1660 must have given a heady moment to hopes like those of Spinoza for a rational overcoming of religious differences. In this he was politically naive, and his position, the most thorough of all rational theologies, became synonymous with the new brand of heresy as religious orthodoxies were reestablished in power, above all in France.

Spinoza's main accomplishment was inside the core of the intellectual network. Spinoza was the last and most extreme of those who hoped to deduce scientific laws axiomatically; at the very same time, Huygens and the empirical scientists were giving up this criterion of certainty. Spinoza's eminence in the attention space came from his setting a new standard for ambition and boldness in metaphysics. Untrammeled by religious orthodoxy, he was willing to follow deterministic premises to their conclusions. Not only in his geometric method of argument but also in the breadth and consistency of his unification of ontology, epistemology, and ethics, Spinoza demonstrates in extreme form what it is to have a philosophical system.

Leibniz's Mathematical Metaphysics

Leibniz took a more cautious approach on religion, but he was equally ecumenical. Coming on the scene at the end of the religious wars which ravaged Germany, he planned at first to reunify the Protestant and Catholic Churches around a common theology. To this end, he developed a universal combinatorial logic and a calculating machine, which he hoped might be used by missionaries and which he dreamt would overcome religious disagreement (Brown, 1984: 56–57). Leibniz was an ambitious seizer of opportunities, and he worked the international networks more energetically than anyone else. Born into two families of professors at Leipzig, the best of the medieval Germany universities, he tried the Rosicrucians, made the rounds of service to various German princes, and got himself a diplomatic posting to Paris and London in the 1670s. Coming from Germany helped him break through the loyalties now becoming set among the second-generation Cartesians; and the German universities still retained the traditional scholasticism which provides a key ingredient for new combinations. Leibniz's religious plans and his calculating machine were not well received, but he soon found other grounds of activity. He met all the important circles of scientists and philosophers, picked up on the latest ideas, and quickly developed them into his own. He learned mathematics from Huygens and from access to Pascal's unpublished work; from hints of Newton's calculus (and despite Newton's guarded suspicion), he developed his own version (Hall, 1980; Hofmann, 1972; *DSB*, 1981: 8:149–168, 10:330). Overlapping international networks open opportunities and generate high emotional energy in the individual who takes the lead in this niche, the subjective feeling of momentum that comes from exploiting the first-mover advantage.

Leibniz was so full of network opportunities that he hadn't enough time for all his projects, and many of them were left in fragments. Law, history, diplomacy claimed his most immediate attention. He took service with the duke of Brunswick and produced genealogical research that aided his patron in acquiring the Duchy of Hanover, from whence the family eventually (in 1714) inherited the throne of England. When his employer's daughter became queen of Prussia in a dynastic marriage, he used the connection to establish an Academy of Science in Berlin. More organizationally astute than Newton, Leibniz founded his own journal and found patronage for new scientific academies, through which his followers—the Bernouillis, l'Hospital, and Euler—made his mathematics dominant.

Leibniz developed his philosophy in the course of his network's concerns. His early training at Leipzig was scholastic, and reflections on Molina and Suarez become his distinctive intellectual ammunition.[10] In Paris, Leibniz's philosophical connections were mainly with the anti-Cartesians, especially Huet and Foucher. He also traveled to seek out Spinoza in 1676 and spent several weeks reading his manuscripts. Leibniz became intimate with Malebranche at the time when the latter's famous work appeared. Soon after the battle broke out between Malebranche and Arnauld, Leibniz developed his own philosophy and broached it in correspondence with Arnauld, modifying it as the result of Arnauld's criticisms (Brown, 1984: 123; Broad, 1975).

The point of entry was that Malebranche's occasionalism had eliminated human free will as well as human ideas. Leibniz intervened with points from Molina and from the scholastic tradition. Discussions in late Thomist logic suggested the principle "in every true proposition the notion of the predicate is included in that of the subject" (quoted in Brown, 1984: 74; Funkenstein, 1986: 98–99). All true statements about an individual person, Leibniz continues, are contained in the essence of that person, including everything he has done and will do in the future. The individual essence is thus its own causality. But this also means that no essence can affect another; all are causally independent. This raises an extreme form of the problem of non-connectedness among unlike substances, the central puzzle of the post-Cartesian field. Turning the problem around, Leibniz notes that many true statements about an individual appear to describe his relations with other individuals; yet each is causally independent. This means that each individual essence reflects others from its own perspective; extending links onward, each reflects the whole universe.

Leibniz is conservatively reinstating the doctrine of essences which Galileo and his movement had overthrown in physics in favor of mathematical description of matter in motion. But contemporary science is part of Leibniz's armament as well. His calculus alerted him to another dimension beyond the conventional representations of matter in motion. When he says that each substance contains traces of all its past and future states, he can visualize a point moving along mathematical coordinates. Geometrically a moving body is indistinguishable from one at rest; hence there must be an additional quality, "living force"—later called "kinetic energy" (Broad, 1975: 65)—which implies its past and future. A similar line of thought connects his calculus to the controversy over atoms and infinite divisibility. Descartes's extended substance was being criticized by Foucher as infinitely divisible, and hence not really a substance at all, while atoms were rejected as incapable of making up a continuum (Brown, 1984: 42). These problems were reinforced by recent discoveries by microscope of microorganisms, which led Leibniz and others to suppose that there are infinite arrays of infinitesimals within each order of size. Leibniz's calculus made it familiar for him to invoke a transcendent order of reality, rather than the physical dichotomy of atoms versus infinitesimality. Leibniz reformulated all mathematical and metaphysical distinctions as qualities of a continuum. Rest may be conceptualized as infinitely slow motion, equality as infinitely small differences.[11]

Borrowing from Spinoza and Malebranche, Leibniz proposed a coherent explanatory system. The world is composed of an infinity of substances; each is unique, each having an essence which contains logically and causally all that it ever is. Leibniz accommodates atomism and microscopic biology by supposing that visible bodies are made up of many such monads; he accommodates living organisms and the human soul by supposing that they too are monads on their own scale. He accepts Spinoza's solution to the mind-body problem by positing that each substance is simultaneously mind and matter. But these ultimate entities are not bare atoms, interchangeable except for their positions in time and space; each has its individual essence, the equivalent of Duns Scotus's *haecceitas,* the principle of individuation. They cannot be interchangeable in time and space, because time and space are not independently existing containers but are internal characteristics of the monads themselves, their modes of relating to one another.[12] The relations among these self-subsistent monads seem paradoxical, a mark of Leibniz's inability to force through a complete synthesis of his disparate materials. Nevertheless, the underlying thrust of his argument may be interpreted as holding that the essence of each—its logical definition—contains attributes which make conjunctions with the attributes of others at the same time that it is particularly, indexically, itself. Leibniz expresses this in theological language, reminiscent of Malebranche, as a pre-established harmony set by God.

But the system does not rest on the theology; it rests on Leibniz's conception of a universal logic of all propositions. In his hands the concept of God becomes a way of referring to a world order of intelligible reasons. Omniscience is the equivalent of an infinitely perfected science; omnipotence is subordinated to the order of reasons. Leibniz's system is the embodiment of all the network ties that he brings together. Its central ingredients are the sophistication of mathematical science at the cutting edge of the new dynamics and infinitesimal calculus, plus the accumulated scholastic metaphysics which had gone underground before the ideology of the modernists, only to reappear when its cultural capital became a key resource in the philosophical attention space.

Rival Philosophies upon the Space of Religious Toleration

In the last generation of the 1600s, the Protestant world was becoming the leading edge of secularization in intellectual life. Earlier conditions were now reversed. The Protestant styles of organizing religion were both more centered on the national state and more decentralized to local congregations than Catholicism. This meant that Protestant movements easily fused with dogmatic enthusiasm and political coercion. Nevertheless, the trajectory of political conflicts laid the grounds for a trend toward secularization. The greater dispersion of organizational resources for religious mobilization into politics shifted the balance of power and eventually led to stalemate in the state's ability to coerce religious uniformity. This did not happen in every state, but inevitably within an array of religious conflicts across Europe, some regions would come out at a balance of forces around the point of mutual exhaustion. Toleration and secularization occurred not because any of the strong factions desired it, but because these forces exhausted themselves through their conflict. Secularization set in as a process of de-escalation when the struggle for domination no longer had the means to continue.

This exhaustion of religious conflict occurred both between states and within some of them. The culmination of alliance-building was the Thirty Years' War between the Protestant Union and the Catholic League; its ending in 1648 left Germany devastated and Spain more deeply bankrupt than ever. At the same time, Spain had to give up its costly crusade against the Dutch Republic. One result was that France was no longer a captive of its anti-Spanish policy, and it could turn to defending Catholic orthodoxy; we find this in the greater dogmatism of the French national church under Bossuet. If France thereby became less of a world intellectual center from about 1680 to 1740, religious politics in Britain now made it a creative substitute.

England was the site of some of the most vehement and multi-sided religious conflicts. It had a centralizing monarchy which used the nationalization of church property as a means of patronage; an old-line Catholic aristocracy whose status was tied to traditional church ritualism; and urban, mercantile, and artisan populations whose non-traditional community structures provided a fertile base for the decentralized Protestant congregations. Alongside these had emerged a newer gentry and aristocracy, based on new opportunities thrown out by the patronage of the crown dispensing honors and commercial monopolies (Wuthnow, 1989; Hochberg, 1984; Stone, 1967). This last group was structurally opportunistic, capable of serving royalty in the cynical manner of Francis Bacon, or turning against it to lead a rebellious coalition in the manner of Oliver Cromwell. The important point is that Britain (now including not only England but also Scotland and newly conquered Ireland) contained well-entrenched resources for several factions, and these eventually fought one another to exhaustion. Britain became the philosophical center between the time of Locke and Hume largely because religious and political stalemate was reached there first.

Secularization is not a zeitgeist but a process of conflict. Philosophical creativity occurs in the range of stances that emerge as intellectuals take up their new positions on various sides of the shifting balance of power. To establish this, let us go back to the period of the Civil War, when compromise was most definitely *not* the condition of British life. There is the typical opposition of intellectual extremes: at one end Hobbes and his thorough-going materialism; at the other end the Cambridge Platonists.

Hobbes's position branched off from the Mersenne circle in Paris, which he encountered as a traveling tutor on the Continent during 1634–1637, and which he frequented while in exile in the 1640s. This connection set off his creativity, for although he had been associated with Bacon in the 1620s, Hobbes had produced little. Soon after meeting Gassendi and Galileo in the 1630s, Hobbes developed a grand scheme to derive everything from the motion of bodies, including a system of government designed to overcome the turbulence of the times. He first emerged in the public intellectual arena when Mersenne invited him to critique Descartes.[13] Soon after Hobbes was writing in geometric argumentation; like Descartes, he too attempted an optics but found more original grounds when he applied Galileo's physics of motion to psychology. Hobbes gained his fame in just the territory that Descartes avoided in his caution to stay away from political entanglements and keep from antagonizing the religious establishment. Here political connections were determining; Hobbes was in the Royalist faction at a time when the religious activists overthrew the crown. Drawing on the resources of his intellectual network, Hobbes radicalized the "mechanical philosophy" and constructed a scientific materialism as a support for government authority and for the supremacy of the state over faith. In this mood of political showdown, he had no desire to compromise with a soul substance; simultaneously he carved out a distinctive intellectual space for himself against Descartes and against the religiously oriented scientists then forming the Invisible College.

Hobbes's connections with the king after the Restoration gave him protection, but his position was too offensive to religious policies to be accepted (Shapin and Schaffer, 1985: 133, 293–296). Hobbes's creativity reflected the period of exile in the somewhat cynical atmosphere of Richelieu and Mazarin's Paris. But it was English politics that anchored him, as we can see by comparison with La Rochefoucauld's *Maximes,* which were germinated around the same time, in the late 1650s. La Rochefoucauld had much the same viewpoint on self-interest as the springs of action; but he made no effort to develop his argument into a system, and he ignored its consequences for politics. The French version is a literary amusement, politely accepting the religious status quo; the English version makes claims for an intellectual and political reorganization.

In counterpoint to this materialism was the upsurge of mystical Neoplatonism at Cambridge. This circle was organized in 1633, as relations between Parliament and king broke down and hysteria grew over the possible reestablishment of Catholicism. The Platonists, like Cambridge University generally, were strongly identified with Puritans and the Commonwealth. Their intellectual distinction was that they were a moderate offshoot of the Calvinists, inclined to Latitudinarianism and tolerance, downplaying doctrinal questions in favor of morality and Plotinine contemplation of divine reality. Neoplatonism did not make for very orthodox theology, since it undercut the particularistic elements of dogma; and its previous appearance in Italy with Ficino had a decidedly cosmopolitan slant. Under current conditions, though, the Platonists came to occupy a defensive stance against secular intellectual currents.

The philosophical creativity of the group did not appear until after the Restoration, in the 1660s and 1670s. An impetus was the growing fame of Hobbes's materialism. Ralph Cudworth, in *The True Intellectual System of the Universe* (1678), took the offensive against Hobbes and Gassendi, declaring that materialism reduces to sensationalism, and that the senses are too deceptive, as Plato showed, to be the basis of knowledge. Our true ideas are of things imperceptible to the senses, including the idea of a perfect Being. Earlier, Cudworth and More had been relatively favorable to the Cartesians, with whom they had had friendly correspondence; but now they turned against

Descartes as the enemy of religious faith. Cudworth rejected Descartes's dichotomy between spiritual and material worlds, in favor of a "ladder of perfections in the universe" through which things are produced by a descent from higher to lower (quoted in Copleston, 1950–1977: 5:60). Henry More, who wrote in the form of poetic allegories, described the world as animated by a world-soul, God's instrument. This was not a rejection of scientific explanations but a rival to the mechanistic philosophy then coming to the fore; the world-soul offered a non-materialist explanation of magnetism and gravity. More argued in 1671 that Descartes's geometric interpretation of nature implies the existence of an absolute space; and this cannot be an attribute of things but is an intelligible reality in itself, a shadow counterpart of the Divine. Contrary to Descartes's definitions, More asserts that not only matter but also spirits are extended (Copleston, 1950–1977: 5:64; Funkenstein, 1986: 77–80).

The Cambridge Platonists are structurally one of the pivot points of British intellectual life. From them we can trace the network in Figure 10.1 in several directions: on one side, Locke's sensualist empiricism as well as Shaftesbury's revival of innate moral ideas; on the other, the series of reconceptualizations of religious turf represented by Newton and Berkeley. These trains of development should not be too surprising, for the Platonists formulated most of the issues which Locke and Newton would develop, if with the significant reversals of emphasis which are characteristic of chains of intellectual creativity. Cudworth pointedly raised the issue of sensualism; and he explicitly denied, using the very image that Locke was to make famous, that the mind is merely a "white sheet of paper that hath nothing at all in it, but what was scribbled upon it by the objects of sense" (quoted in Copleston, 1950–1977: 5:61). Ideas are not abstracted from objects but are merely awakened by them; nor does sensation give the essence of things or of scientific laws. Locke was to agree with the last point but in a moderated form, giving up essences in favor of the probabilistic knowledge yielded by the senses; for the other points, Locke could have found many of his formulations by reversing Cudworth's position.[14] Creativity is structured by opposition.

Locke was personally connected to the Platonist circle. Its leader, Whichcote (61 in Figure 10.1), was Locke's favorite preacher in London. His friends during exile in Holland were their friends. In his later years Locke lived with Cudworth's daughter, Lady Masham (Fraser, [1894] 1959: xxxiii–xxxv). Like them, Locke strongly favored religious moderation and toleration and opposed doctrinal strife. This political stance shaped Locke's entire career. Locke was associated with the innovative milieu of Boyle and the Invisible College at Oxford in the 1650s, but these early scientific contacts did not arouse his energy, and his academic career was undistinguished; he left in 1667 to become personal physician to the first earl of Shaftesbury, a position he held until

Shaftesbury's death in 1683. Shaftesbury reminds us of an English version of the duc de Condé, the practitioner of timely alliance-switching. Shaftesbury changed sides twice during the Commonwealth, and negotiated for the return of King Charles II under a program of toleration and amnesty to all sides. With the revival of the party of Catholic legitimacy under the Stuarts, he led the parliamentary opposition and fled to Holland in 1682 under a charge of treason, shortly followed by Locke.

Shaftesbury played the power game of religious animosities and factions during the Restoration, but his machinations flowed with the structural drift of the time. Opportunism and intermittent toleration was the most practical policy for ending religious strife and its accompanying political turmoil. Locke raised the lesson to the level of a principle. Social peace is possible only through a reasoned disengagement from religious fanaticism; and this means secularization. Locke announced his philosophy at just the moment when his political allies were making their triumphant return from Holland with the House of Orange. Locke, as advanced in age as Hobbes was when he first began publishing his major works, was stirred to complete his first creative fruits: *Essay on Human Understanding* in 1688–89 (age 56–57), *Letter on Toleration* in 1689, and *Treatise on Government* in 1690 (age 58).

We cannot attribute Locke's position simply to the cause of toleration. That position was widely shared among cosmopolitan intellectuals. The philosophical creativity of the 1670s through the 1690s consisted to a considerable extent in working out different varieties of a nonsectarian religious stance: Spinoza's monism was a religion of reason, while the Cambridge Platonists revived an older religious universalism. In Holland, the experienced side-switcher Pierre Bayle, who had gone from the Jesuits to the Calvinists, was now calling for disengagement from both sides; in the 1690s his *Dictionary* ridiculed the inconsistencies of dogmatic religion and favored a secularist skepticism. Philosophical creativity now appears as a dividing up of the territory of religious liberalism. Again we see the pattern: as external political conditions shift the space within which topics can be discussed, intellectuals respond to the opportunity by filling the space with a small number of contending positions.

How then did Locke happen to find his distinctive piece of the turf, and why did his position prove so fruitful? Consider the trajectory of Locke's career. He began his *Essay on Understanding* in 1671, in a circle of intellectuals around Shaftesbury, as a way of clearing up debates over revealed religion. His notion was that doctrinal speculation could be avoided by limiting the understanding to what can be derived from sensation and putting aside further attempts to "penetrate into the hidden causes of things" (Fraser, [1894] 1959: xvii, xxiv–xxvi). This position is not unlike that of scientists such as Boyle—an intimate friend of Locke—who chartered the Royal Society on the premise that science should stay apart from religious disputes. The propagandist for the Royal Society, Glanvill (who was at Oxford in the 1650s with Locke), was a liberal rationalist Anglican; under Henry More's influence, he delivered in 1661 a skeptical criticism of causality against the deceptiveness of the senses, defending empiricism on moderate probabilistic grounds. Glanvill's ingredients, as well as the upshot of his position, are similar to Locke's. How did Locke arrive at a position which is far more famous, which turns the emphasis onto a critique of innate ideas and principles? It was not a matter of defending science by a moderate empiricism, since this needed no defense. Locke instead crafted a position over the years which critiqued the foundations of all the rival philosophies.

What distinguishes Locke from Glanvill and others of that milieu are his travels and his resulting wide network contacts. Locke developed his philosophy while in France during 1675–1679, where he encountered the Cartesians and possibly Malebranche, and again during 1681–1689 when he was in Holland, in contact with the Portuguese Jewish Spinozaists and with Bayle.[15] The 1670s were the time when the Cartesian system was under intense debate. The loyalists Rohault and Régis were expanding the array of self-evident axioms to bolster the deduction of the cogito and its consequences, and Spinoza (1677) had taken the geometric method to a further extreme. On the other side, Huet supported religious fideism, using skeptical arguments against the cogito, and Malebranche (1674) was shifting the emphasis to the perception of all ideas in God. Empirical scientists backed away from the extreme claims of Cartesian rationalism. Its axiomatic method of obtaining certainty was modified by Leibniz into a criterion of plausible rather than absolute arguments (Brown, 1984).

Locke joined the movement rejecting the Cartesian position, but he did this in a distinctive way. He turned probabilism and empiricism into a weapon against all philosophies of substance—materialist, rationalist, and idealist alike. At a time when metaphysical positions were returning to the field, Locke staked out an anti-metaphysical position which nevertheless held metaphysical implications. His empiricism moved ideas into the focus of attention, in opposition to any substance that lay behind them. Locke opened a path beyond the disputes between the Platonists and Hobbes, as well as between Cartesians and fideists or Malebranchian spiritualists. In Locke's mature position, all that can be known derives from simple ideas, received passively through the senses, and their recombination into complex ideas by the mind. This is all there is to abstractions and generalizations; there are no essences of things but only names, and these in turn are only ideas bundled together for convenience in discourse. All the Cartesian traits of the world of extension are reduced to ideas. There is no certainty from "clear and distinct ideas" in Descartes's sense of the term, for these are not simple ideas at all. But there is no need to worry about skepticism as applied to the external world; simple ideas are neither true nor false, since truth and falsity can apply only to propositions, not to ideas (*Essay* 1.52; see Locke, [1690] 1959).

Locke rejects not only innate ideas but innate principles as well. These include the axioms which were proliferated by the Cartesians of the 1670s, and also the moral axioms laid down by the Cambridge Platonists. Cudworth, in arguing against the mechanistic philosophy, had pushed the position that the human mind depends upon God's mind, which includes the eternal *rationes* of all things. In 1668 Henry More, against Hobbes's moral conventionalism, argued for the existence of moral principles whose truth is immediate and evident (Copleston, 1950–1977: 5:62–63). Locke's creativity was patterned by opposition not only to his Platonist acquaintances but also in the larger restructuring of the intellectual field. At the same time that Locke was finishing his *Essay*, Leibniz was formulating his doctrine of self-causative and non-communicating substances, which implies that all our ideas are innate. The strongest modern derivation of innate ideas and their strongest critique appeared at the same time, and unknown to each other.[16] Leibniz's and Locke's opposing positions found their slots in the intellectual field and their external bases of support. Leibniz's position was supported in the Protestant universities of Germany, where it represented religious liberalism in scholastic terminology. In England, Locke became the hero of the victorious Whigs; his rejection of the philosophy of essences with its theological overtones went along with his championship of secularization as the route to social peace.

Deism and the Independence of Value Theory

The framework of religious-political compromise after 1700 does not mean that partisan conflict ceased. On the contrary, vicious struggles continued, both in the factional and dynastic intrigues of parliamentary politics and on the religious and intellectual front. English Catholics labored under legal disabilities and public suspicion, although like other Dissenters they were allowed private worship. Anglican dogma was enforced in the universities, but these faded from the focus of intellectual life. The new balance of power proved stable, and toleration and moderation were imposed by the circumstance that no one was strong enough to overturn them. Religious toleration now shifted the central issues of intellectual conflict. The generation following Locke was the heyday of Deism; on the other side emerged the first explicitly reactionary defense of religion.

Deist tendencies had existed earlier, but they became the center of controversy in the wake of Locke. Many of the popular Deists are found close to

Locke in the network.[17] The most famous Deist work is the *Christianity not Mysterious* (1696) of Toland, who was attacked from all sides. Nevertheless, Toland (107 in the key to Figure 10.1) had excellent connections; he was recommended to Locke by William Molyneux (in the Newton-Berkeley network); although Locke repudiated Toland after the controversy erupted, the latter was patronized by Shaftesbury as well as by the government minister Lord Harley and received diplomatic appointments. Another Deist close to Locke's circle of patrons was Blount (109), a nobleman who followed the materialism of Hobbes; he too avoided persecution under the blasphemy laws through his high connections. Anthony Collins (111), a rural justice of the peace, carried on witty controversies against the religiously orthodox, including Jonathan Swift; Collins was an admirer and friend of Locke, and became the trustee of Locke's estate.

By the 1720s, Deism was close to winning its battle for respectability. The last gasp of religious coercion occurred in 1729–1731, when the Cambridge fellow Woolston was jailed for blasphemy for writing pamphlets on the allegorical interpretation of the scriptures. The Oxford ecclesiastical pensioner Tindal in 1730 produced "the Deist's bible," *Christianity as Old as the Creation,* and declared that no state authority can compel conformity. By now Deism was successful enough to split into Christian and non-Christian wings. The dissenting minister Morgan in 1737 defended a Christian Deism against its rivals; Butler harmonized *Religion Natural and Revealed* in 1736, and was rewarded with a series of bishoprics and the friendship of King George II. Again we see the significance of stalemate in religious politics and the influence of career opportunism. Church livings were now the explicit spoils of party politics, and there were strong incentives to cross over religious lines. Now we find religious side-switchers who become Deists, in effect rationalizing their careers by advocating the religious common denominator. Tindal, who began as an orthodox Anglican at Oxford in the 1670s, converted to Catholicism—at just the time when Catholic restoration was the policy of the Stuart monarchy—and then recanted in 1688 when the Stuarts were overthrown. Butler, who came from a Presbyterian family, prospered by becoming an Anglican priest (*EP,* 1967: 8:139).

This opportunism was not confined to the Deist side; the religious traditionalist Swift changed his loyalties from Whig to Tory in 1710 with the shift in his prospects for patronage. Political opportunism was the condition of intellectual life in this period; the emergence of the party system simultaneously marked the emergence of a new kind of structural competitiveness among intellectuals. Literary creativity was underpinned by a publishing market which depended heavily on the subsidy of aristocratic subscribers. Writers were no longer household dependents of their patrons, but to make a decent living they needed the support of a political faction. Poets and dramatists such as Dryden, Pope, and Addison could make large fortunes, not so much from the sale of their works on the open market as in the form of sinecures and subscriptions raised by their political supporters.[18]

Political opportunism and mobility were central to the growth of universalism. Religious doctrines were no longer so cleanly lined up with political factions. The Whigs, who carried out the Glorious Revolution, were the party of religious moderation and toleration; and here we find the Deist sympathies and connections of the Shaftesbury family and of Locke. Once in office, the Whigs soon fell into intrigues; their leader, Lord Harley, switched to become head of a Tory government. Tory conservatives, too, defenders of the old aristocracy and tending toward the old Stuart dynasty, become caught up in the wheeling and dealing of parliamentary and dynastic politics. The atmosphere of sophisticated manipulation carried over into intellectual matters. Lord Bolingbroke, who led Tory ministries in 1704–1708 and 1710–1714, frequented a literary circle which included Pope, Gay, Congreve, and Swift.[19] Bolingbroke was a conservative; after the fall of his second ministry, he was accused of plotting to bring back the old Catholic dynasty, and fled to France. Pardoned, he returned in 1723; never regaining political office during the long years of Whig ministries, he turned increasingly to literary activities. By the late 1720s, he was filling Tory periodicals with Deist philosophy, emphasizing natural religion and the superiority of the state of nature over civil society. One of his young friends, Lord Chesterfield, originally a Whig, broke with Walpole in 1730 and went over to the opposition, becoming the Tory secretary of state in the 1740s; hanging around with the Tory literary crowd, he made his lasting reputation with backstage advice on worldly success in his *Letters to his (illegitimate) Son.*

Philosophically the most significant of the Deists was the third earl of Shaftesbury, grandson of Locke's patron, personally educated under Locke's tutorship. Shaftesbury's works appeared soon after Locke's, in 1699 and in 1708–1711, and built dialectically upon them. Locke's dismissal of innate ideas went too far, Shaftesbury held, in implying that there is no intrinsic human nature and intrinsic morality. To remedy this, he postulated an innate moral sense, analogous to the sense of harmony or proportion in music and art. The life of aesthetic appreciation and literary style is Shaftesbury's ideal; he even regards God as a good-natured being who can be understood only by those who have a sense of humor. Religion is taken almost lightheartedly as a subject for tolerant discussion; religion is secondary to morality, since the latter is presupposed in concepts such as the wrath and justice of God. Shaftesbury occupies a space similar to that held by Lord Herbert of Cherbury, whose epistemology Locke had criticized while supporting Cherbury's Deism.

Shaftesbury's position opened up a terrain which was to comprise much of philosophy throughout the century in Protestant societies, Britain and Germany, where gradual secularization was taking place. Value theory became the topic of conflicts and developments. Aesthetics, which had rarely been central to philosophical interests before, now came into its own (Eagleton, 1990). Aesthetics became metaphysics by other means, in the anti-metaphysical atmosphere of the Lockean movement. The Deist position was now so dominant in the British intellectual world that attention shifted to controversies within it. The Cherbury-Shaftesbury line of innate propensities became more and more explicitly contrasted with the Lockean line of construction out of experience. In 1749 Hartley developed Locke's empiricism into an explicit associationism in which ideas—including aesthetic ones—are selected for their intellectual pleasures and pains. Adam Smith's *Theory of Moral Sentiments* (1759) converted Shaftesbury's innate moral faculty into an associationist psychology of pleasures and pains through the device of imagining oneself in the place of other persons. In Shaftesbury's generation the innate faculties of morality and beauty had been a halfway house for the naturalistic basis of religion. By the middle generation of the 1700s, both religion and its bases were being derived from experience, paving the way for the radical Utilitarianism of Bentham at the end of the century.

The Reversal of Alliances

In England, Deist universalism was a doctrine for transcending religious strife. In France, when Deism emerged, it was part of a militant anti-religious movement; and this in turn led to a new opposition, the first explicitly reactionary anti-modernism. Why did the exhausting stalemate of religious warfare, and the political side-switching which engineered the settlement, result in toleration and Deism in England but militant atheism in France? Here we must look to the outermost layer of social causality, the political lineups which structured the networks of intellectual life.

In places where the centralizing monarchy became more powerful, the independent aristocracy went into intellectual and religious as well as political opposition. Wuthnow's (1989) theory of the Enlightenment concerns essentially this anti-religious front. His comparisons across European societies show that Enlightenment intellectuals appeared where there was a combination of conditions. First, expansion of state bureaucracy produced a patronage base among civil servants, lawyers, and salons vying for prestige in the government centers, who in turn became both a recruitment base for intellectuals and a literate audience reading and publicizing their work. Second, divided authority among independent judiciaries and representative parliaments fostered competition among political factions over the spoils available at the center. Wuthnow's model is a version of the structural pattern of creative networks summarized at the end of Chapter 9: the intersection of multiple bases for intellectuals at a central focus of attention. My analysis of the French Enlightenment differs from Wuthnow's on one point: not only was there creativity among intellectuals dependent on the patronage network of civil servants (Voltaire, the Encyclopedists), but also creativity broke out among the feudal lords who opposed the centralizing state (Boulainvilliers, Montesquieu). In England after the Glorious Revolution, the government Establishment was the aristocracy; its principled moderation on the religious question was a key element of its control through an institutionalized balance of power. In France, the bases of political power remained deeply divided between the officialdom of the absolutist state and the aristocracy, now politically marginalized but still socially privileged. These bases for political factions gave rise to a new division in intellectual space.

The French Deists, unlike the English, were not merely arguing for a reasonable toleration and an end to religious strife, but were becoming outright opponents of the church. The comte de Boulainvilliers extolled feudalism against the centralizing monarchy. His *Three Imposters* (1719) holds that revealed religion is created by the false legislators, Moses, Christ, and Muhammad; the true religion he builds on the philosophies of Descartes and Spinoza. Boulainvilliers's freethinking circle included disciples of Fontenelle and Bayle, and copied clandestine manuscripts that eventually became the ammunition of the Voltaire circle.[20]

The same combination of feudalism and natural religion made its biggest splash with Montesquieu. He came from the provincial *noblesse de robe*, graduated from the Oratorian College in 1705, and was initiated into intellectual life by Boulainvilliers's circle. His first literary success came with his cosmopolitan juxtaposition of different manners and religions in his *Persian Letters* (1721), not least because of its titillating scenes of sexual life in a Muslim harem. Visiting England during 1729–31, he befriended the Tory intellectuals around Bolingbroke, especially the young Chesterfield; when he returned to France, he spent the next 17 years writing his *Esprit des lois* (Collins, 1908). In it aristocracy is raised to a general doctrine of the separation of powers and the defense of liberties against the crushing, oriental-style central state, harems and all. Montesquieu's work, published anonymously in Geneva in 1748, was attacked by the Jesuits and placed on the Index; the attention of controversy reinforced its success.

Rival positions sprang up to fill the anti-religious side of the field. Voltaire, who shared Montesquieu's Deism, nevertheless attacked his *Esprit des lois* as a reactionary defense of aristocratic privilege. Voltaire pinned his hopes on the enlightened absolute ruler. Voltaire and Montesquieu had different bases of material support; Montesquieu had hereditary property, while Voltaire depended on intermittent patronage of the French court, aristocratic salons, and, during the 1750s, a post as philosopher-poet in Berlin to Frederick the Great. These external bases underwrote the difference between Montesquieu and Voltaire; their commonalities came from their belonging to the same intellectual networks, including the one which crystallized into the *Encyclopedia*. Earlier both had been formed in the same London milieu; Voltaire in his first exile in 1726–1729 had also frequented the Tory literary circle around Bolingbroke and Pope. Prior to this network contact Voltaire had been a rather conventional epic poet and playwright, but he found his niche when he returned to France and published his *Lettres philosophiques sur l'Anglais* (1734). It contains the essentials which Voltaire was to embellish throughout his life, in the form of oriental tales (emulating Montesquieu's early specialty), allegories, satires, and histories. Voltaire presents Newton and the English as having found an enlightened, tolerant world based on reason and moderation.

Voltaire claimed to occupy the middle ground between the intellectual factions of his day; his Deism combatted not only the cruelties and superstitions of dogmatic religion but also the materialism of the atheists. Scientific discoveries he now took as the central argument for a reasonable religion: God is proven only by the argument from design, the watch proving the existence of the watchmaker, scientific laws proving the existence of the Lawgiver. The emphasis is on the laws, not on a material substance or on a mind-substance; Voltaire uses Newton to reject materialism as well as metaphysics. Voltaire represented the emerging attitude of militant scientism: science alone is enough; no other philosophy of any type is desirable. Cartesianism, once the pretender to constitute rational science, was now swept away as a mere philosophy. Voltaire rejected the Deisms of both the Spinozaist and the Platonic lineages in favor of an anti-metaphysical Deism.

This turn away from metaphysics was characteristic of the French and English intellectual worlds of the time in contrast to the German networks; there was no French equivalent of Wolff, Baumgarten, or Kant. The French universities, with their connection to traditional training of clergy, were of no significance even as centers of creative reaction; since 1600 their enrollments had collapsed, and they lost control over the degrees monopolizing practice in the professions.[21] The weak position of the universities and the more comfortable base of secular intellectuals among the salons and the government officialdom allowed Voltaire to be a militant Deist. He defended the true religion of humanity, while he attacked the church as the defender of corrupt privileges using the weapons of mystifying ritual and dogma. Metaphysics is the soil on which transcendental superstitions grow. Voltaire's philosophy was an ideology for secular intellectuals feeling their victory over the old church bases of intellectual life. The *philosophes* lost the abstractness of traditional philosophical topics; their creative energy came from opening up secular topics. The older role of philosopher concerned with first principles was now differentiated into the specialized sciences and disciplines.

Coinciding with the Jesuits' expulsion from France in 1764, Voltaire became a crusader for the victims of religious persecution and published his strongest attacks on religion. Voltaire is a militant from a Deist stance, however, and his intellectual quarrels were increasingly against the group of *philosophes,* who were now turning toward materialism and atheism. The baron d'Holbach, whose Paris salon hosted the Encyclopedists and their descendants from 1749 to 1789, began to produce secret anti-Christian writings in the 1760s; in 1770 his materialist *Système de la nature* set off the debate between atheism and Deism. Voltaire and his patron Frederick the Great upheld the side of Deism. Diderot, who had begun his career in 1745 by translating Shaftesbury's deism into French, now supported d'Holbach and atheism. The most extreme members of the group were those with the most personal security. Voltaire stayed within the range of his patrons' religious tolerance; d'Holbach was freer as a wealthy German expatriate in Paris; and the first really radical naturalism was expressed in 1758 by Helvetius, a retired sinecure holder who had made a fortune in tax farming for the French crown.

The central network of this period was the Encyclopedists (see Figure 11.1). They built on the new material base provided by a market for publications. It was the same structure which had appeared a generation earlier in England, supporting the Tory and Whig literary circles; and it would appear a generation later in Germany, with the literary outburst at Berlin, Göttingen, and Weimar. Diderot and d'Alembert derived their chief income and occupation from the *Encyclopedia* from 1746 to 1772, and most of the famous intellectual careers of this period were begun by contact with this enterprise. The Encyclopedists flourished as a group. D'Alembert was the only significantly creative one, with his mathematical *Traité dynamique* in 1743, before the group formed in 1745. Its wealthy supporter d'Holbach (26 years old when he joined the Paris group in 1749) gradually moved from scientific articles to his own materialist philosophy in the 1760s. Condillac, a young theology student at the Sorbonne in the 1740s who happened to be d'Alembert's cousin, was pulled in and produced his metaphysical *Traité des sensations* in 1754.[22] The young Turgot, studying at the Sorbonne in 1749–1751, was introduced to the group and immediately produced his *Tableau philosophique des progrès successifs de*

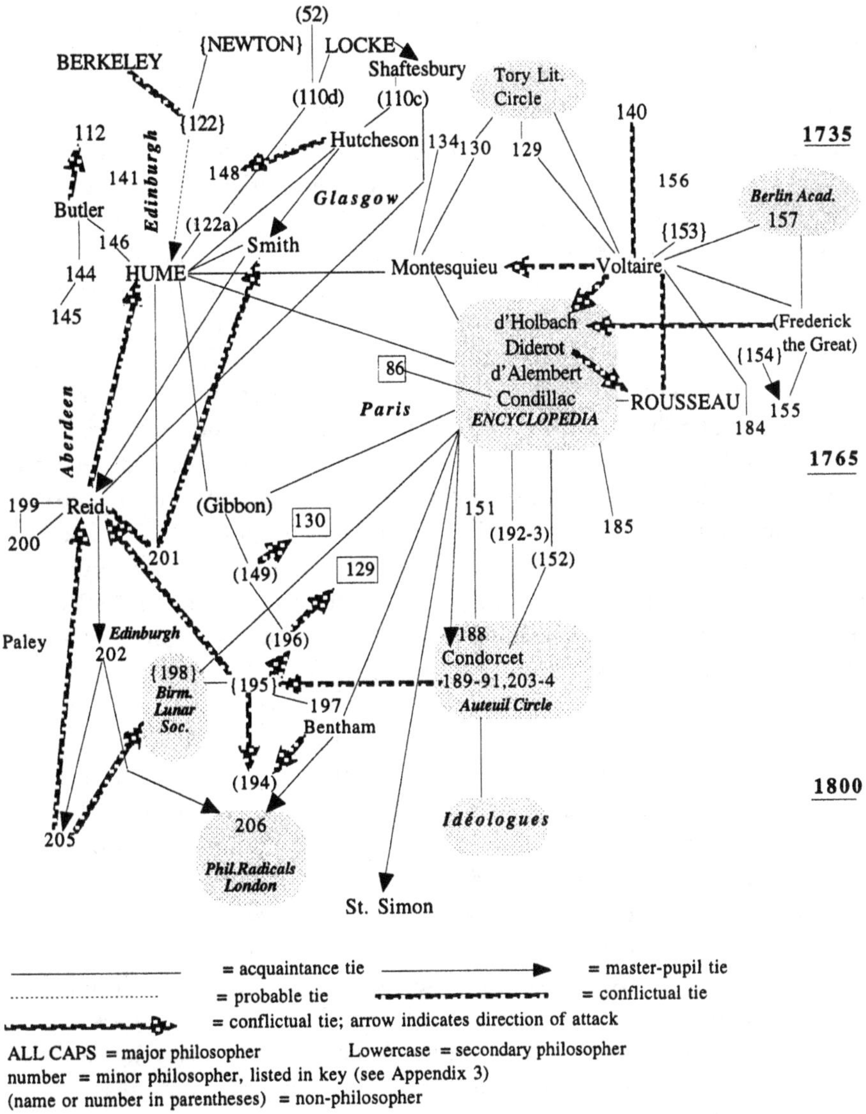

FIGURE 11.1. FRENCH AND BRITISH NETWORK DURING THE
ENLIGHTENMENT, 1735–1800

l'esprit humain (1750), with its historical evolutionism. Another wealthy patron, Helvetius, began to host the group in 1751, and came out with the radical
anti-religious naturalism of *De l'Esprit* in 1758. The group was a center of
creative energy that suffused those who came in contact with it.

Rousseau became the most famous of the *Encyclopedia* network by breaking
with it—which is to say, by finding a new axis of opposition. His wide-ranging
creativity corresponded to the range of his material bases of support. He sought
traditional sources of personal patronage in the homes of the nobility, as well
as literary reputation in the salons, the newly established prize competitions
of the academies, while also joining in the new publishing ventures. The young
Rousseau reminds one of Leibniz; an ambitious young man from the provinces
(in fact a former servant and music master who had risen by love affairs with
his mistresses), he showed up in Paris proposing a new musical notation. This
line of innovation met no response, but he cast about in all directions until
something did. In 1745 (now at the age of 33) he met the *Encyclopedia* group;
in 1750 he won a prize by his critique of human progress, in 1755 another
with his discourse on the origins of inequality and had an opera performed
before Louis XV. Rousseau now quarreled with the reigning star, in 1758, and
the rivalry energized a peak creative burst. On the heels of Voltaire's philosophical novels, including his masterpiece, *Candide* (1759), Rousseau topped
everything in 1761–62 with his three most famous works, the *Social Contract*
and his own ventures in the genre of the novel, *La Nouvelle Héloise* and *Émile*.

Rousseau managed to be a political radical at a time when the institutions
of the old regime were fading, but he did it with a slant that made him
distinctive from his comrades. His earliest fame came from his *Discours sur
les sciences et les arts,* which declared that human inventions do not contribute
to human happiness—this at a time when the *Encyclopedia* was booming with
its promise to take an overview of all the arts and inventions that had contributed to progress. Rousseau extended the Deist themes of a natural religion
transcending the arbitrary conventions of human histories; but he took it into
a distinctively anti-modern space, extolling the state of nature against the
chains of civilization. At the same time, the implied political radicalism in his
critique made him famous with the coming generation of revolutionaries. In
breaking with science, Rousseau also broke with Deism and with scientific
atheism of the kind propagated by Helvetius and d'Holbach. In the mid-1760s,
just as Voltaire and Diderot were becoming more openly critical of religion,
Rousseau took the opposite side of the field, putting forward a sentimental
basis for religion.

The Encyclopedists, more radically than their predecessor Voltaire, had
formulated the modern alliance of science with the politics of progress and
justice, together with a critique of dogmatic religion. They crystallized what

was to become the liberal, progressive, leftward beliefs of modernity. Rousseau stepped in at virtually the founding moment of this intellectual synthesis, selected the negative strands, and wove them into a position that was equally viable under modern intellectual conditions. Rousseau was not a reactionary, and he used none of the older resources of the established church, the university metaphysics, or the legal privileges of the aristocracy. He was instead the anti-modernist modernist, and the turf he discovered proved to be fruitful for a major faction of modern times—indeed, down to its postmodernist incarnation. Once again we see that as the underlying conditions of intellectual productivity change, creativity bursts out simultaneously on rival fronts.

Anti-modernist Modernism and the Anti-scientific Opposition

We are now in the midst of the great reversal of intellectual alliances between religious positions and science. Most creative intellectuals from Kepler through Leibniz and Newton argued for the compatibility of science and religion. Religious intellectuals such as Gassendi and Mersenne appropriated science for their own theological purposes; on the other side, most scientists liked to claim religious legitimation for their activities. The English scientists around Boyle were particularly concerned to show the religious orthodoxy of their science, and Boyle funded public lectures for the confutation of atheism by means of the evidence of science. With Locke, however, science went over to the side of secularization; henceforward, scientists and their philosophical advocates would become increasingly associated with a minimalist religion such as Deism, and eventually with outright atheism. At the same time, religion began to turn against science; this trend emerged in the British milieu during Locke's lifetime, with Berkeley and Swift. In short, we are now arriving at the "modern" lineup in which a "liberal" in religious matters tends to claim the support of science, while religious "conservatives" turn against science.[23]

We have been tracing the growth of the philosophical "left"; for its polarizing counterpart on the "right," let us return to the English networks of the late 1600s and trace the connections which flowed from the Cambridge Platonists. Their first important offspring was Newton. Newton in turn had a network of scientific followers whose own network descendants were philosophers: Berkeley, Hume, and Swedenborg. It seems surprising that the arch-representative of the successful scientific revolution should have a train of followers which led up to turning away from science, or even to an attack upon it. What we are seeing is a division within the camp of science itself. With the isolated exception of Hobbes, the older mechanical philosophy, in both its British and French branches, had been in solidarity with religion. Now the religious politics of science were changing. Locke's followers used scientific philosophy as grounds for Deism; on the other side, a religious opposition emerged which increasingly repudiated science. Since intellectual fame is made by engaging in current controversies with current weapons, the most successful of the new spiritualists came from the most active scientific networks and turned the tools of the scientific philosophy against itself.

Newton was a key link in this process. Eventually the most famous of all scientists, he nevertheless was something of an outsider. The Invisible College had formed at Oxford in the 1650s, then moved to London; but Newton was at Cambridge, where the leading intellectual circle was the Platonists, critics of the mechanical philosophy. Newton got his intellectual start from contact with the Platonist side. He was born near Grantham, Henry More's home; he was first taught mathematics by a pupil of More, and More was his country neighbor as well as his university colleague. Newton's philosophical position was close to More's metaphysics.[24] When Newton published his first paper in 1672, its theory of light was criticized by Hooke and Huygens as inferior to their own theories. Newton largely withdrew from scientific work and spent much of the next decades on anti-Trinitarian theology and research on biblical prophecies, and in searching for a primordial philosophy which he believed was held in common by the ancient Pythagoreans and Chaldeans and expressed in a secret language used by the alchemists. Until 1684, when the astronomer Halley encouraged Newton to develop and publish his mathematical science, Newton was active largely as a philosopher in the occultist tradition mixed with the theology of the Cambridge Platonists. His conflict with the mainstream of materialist scientists continued the oppositions that we saw earlier in Figure 10.1 between Fludd and Mersenne, or More and Cudworth against Gassendi and Hobbes. Even after the triumph of Newton's astronomy (1687) and his optics (1704), there is an echo of Cudworth versus Descartes in the debate between Newtonians against the French Cartesians over Newton's action-at-a-distance in the framework of empty space, where the materialists visualized a world of continuous matter.

Although Newton became the icon of the scientific modernists, he originated outside the core of the mechanical philosophers, and his own network of followers soon exploited the anti-modernist and even anti-science side of the field. Among Newton's followers was William Molyneux (105 in the key to Figure 10.1), who founded the Dublin Philosophical Society in 1683 as an affiliate of the Royal Society. Molyneux worked in astronomy and optics, concerned especially with the principles of telescopes, and corresponded in the 1690s with Locke, raising issues in the sensory theory of ideas by considering a hypothetical blind man who later acquired sight. His son Samuel Molyneux (120) continued this work on optics at Trinity College, Dublin; he was Berkeley's friend during the period (1705–1709) when Berkeley was writing his mathematical notebooks and his *New Theory of Vision* (1709), the very topic on which Newton had published his most popular book, *Opticks*, in 1704.[25]

With Berkeley, the scientific philosophy turned into an attack on science. Empiricism was pushed to an extreme and used as a weapon against materialism. Berkeley criticized the current doctrines of optical science, extending Locke's empiricism and frequently using Molyneux's hypothetical blind man. The mathematical explanations of how distance and magnitude are perceived depend on calculating angles of light rays at the eye. Berkeley appeals to experience that we have no such consciousness of rays and calculations. Geometry itself is unreal when it goes beyond experience to points without dimension and lights without breadth. And since there is always a minimum visible object, microscopes are not really an improvement on normal sight; they show us a different world, one that no longer has any connection with the objects we know by touch. Every different sense gives its own experiences and ideas. Our conception that there is an object uniting all the senses is only a prejudice, resulting from language which applies a common word to experiences which have usually gone together. Berkeley's extreme phenomenalism takes the world of experience apart into separate streams; he accepts Locke's method but demands it remain consistent and admit no further entities.

That Berkeley was counterattacking science in the name of religion is apparent from the publications which followed hard on the *New Theory of Vision*. His *Principles of Human Knowledge* (1710) declares in its subtitle that it examines "the grounds of skepticism, atheism and irreligion," and he announces the same thing in the title of his *Three Dialogues between Hylas and Philonous, in Opposition to Sceptics and Atheists* (1713). Berkeley was a clergyman, holding a succession of clerical posts and ending as a bishop. The great plan of his life was to found a missionary college in Bermuda from which to evangelize the Americas for the Anglican Church. He attacked Locke and his followers as leading to Deism, now polemically equated with atheism. Berkeley took apart the scientific doctrine of primary and secondary qualities, a guidepost of materialist research since Galileo. For him the primary qualities of pure extension do not exist; experience shows us sensations which always have color and other "secondary" qualities. There is no material world of primary qualities behind those we experience; this conception arises only from an error based on false use of words—Locke's critique of false names, but pushed far beyond Locke's purposes. Berkeley then turns his pure phenomenalism into an argument for God: if experience shows consistency, it is because God is always there presenting human minds with coherent experiences.

This anti-scientific turn within the intellectual network which had hitherto been dominated by scientists was not an isolated incident. Berkeley's principal supporter at the time he formulated his critique was Swift, then in Dublin as chaplain to the Lord Justice of Ireland; Swift introduced Berkeley to the Dublin court, and soon after into the Whig literary circle at London. Swift was busy just then fighting Deists, publishing his satirical *Argument against Abolishing Christianity* in 1711, and carrying on controversy with Collins in 1713 (Luce, 1968). Swift too followed a clerical career; like Berkeley, he had studied at Kilkenny College ("the Irish Eton") and at Trinity, Dublin, sought government preferment, and acquired a church living in Ireland. Swift's early network connections, however, were not with the scientists but with a literary circle. Swift was Dryden's cousin, and in the 1690s happened to be chaplain to the diplomat Sir William Temple, who had imported into England the quarrel of the ancients versus the moderns. This had originated as a literary dispute over the merits of classical versus modern poetry and drama; when Fontenelle had revived the debate in France in 1688, he had marshaled science on the side of the moderns. Swift's first publication (1704) joined the side of his employer, attacking modern scientists and philosophers in *Battle of the Books*. It was a slot Swift never left. The same vehement satire is found in 1726 in *Gulliver's Travels*. One section recapitulates the battle of ancients and moderns: (*Voyage to Laputa,* Chapter 9); Gassendi's and Descartes's systems are described as exploded, and Newton's as a fashion which will go the same way. Bacon's house of learning is satirized as a collection of impractical fools engaged in odoriferous experiments such as returning human excrement into its original food. One scientist is a blind man who attempts to mix colors by feel and smell, a joke straight out of Berkeley and Molyneux.

Less scatological than Swift, Berkeley shows a similar concern to cut down science. Numbers are never found in experience but are only an imputation added by the mind (Berkeley, [1709] 1925: 119); the immediate objects of sight are fleeting and mutable, and "to compute their magnitudes," even if possible, "must yet be a very trifling and insignificant labour" (Berkeley, [1709] 1925: 84). Berkeley criticizes Newton's fluxions and the differential calculus; infinitesimals cannot exist, since they are not matters of experience (Robles Garcia, 1991).

Berkeley's idealist move was there to be made in the existing structure of the intellectual field. We can see this through several other British clergymen nearby in the network, who followed a similar path but whose fame was preempted by Berkeley. John Norris (106) was a former Oxford fellow and village rector, a correspondent of Henry More and of Locke, and a religious poet of the "metaphysical" style. Norris quarreled with Locke, who considered the former reactionary, and criticized the Deist Toland. In 1701 Norris produced his own philosophy, a version of Malebranche's occasionalism—God is always present, upholding the causality of the world. Norris's neighbor, Arthur

Collier (119), another Oxford graduate and rural clergyman, published his *Clavis Universalis* in 1713, almost coinciding with Berkeley (and apparently without knowledge of him). Collier declared that perception gives no direct evidence that the external world exists; indeed, the concept of an external world is self-contradictory, as is the notion of infinite divisibility.

A more popular version of the attack on materialism also sprang from the English scientific network. Swedenborg, the son of a Swedish bishop, visited England during these same years (1710–1713) and met with the Newtonian astronomers (103–104). Returning to Sweden, he became a mining assessor and worked in geological and other sciences. Later (during 1734–1756) Swedenborg transmuted science into theosophy, creating a metaphysics out of metallurgy and a cosmology of three heavens and three hells with correspondences among the levels. The realm of creation, he said, is dead; life is only apparent, the investing of matter by an omnipresent God who alone is alive. Swedenborg combined the same strands of cultural capital as Berkeley—Lockean empiricism together with the superiority of Christianity—and both came out with a new idealism. Swedenborg became a constructive dogmatist, aiming at a popular following and producing a theology for a new sect.

Berkeley explicitly addressed himself to the cognoscenti, whose intellectual errors he wished to combat (see Preface to *Principles of Human Knowledge*). Compared to his rivals in this intellectual niche, Berkeley was much more in the center of intellectual networks, and he stuck to an austere argument using the dominant philosophical techniques to undermine themselves. Norris and Collier were upstaged; Malebranche's influence, largely limited to France, died with his generation; Swedenborg left the realm of tightly argued philosophical abstraction for a popular reception. Berkeley became famous in the long-term philosophical community by exemplifying the distinctiveness of its turf. The struggle over science moved epistemology into the central region of philosophy in its own right. Berkeley's idealist position anchored one extreme in the array of philosophical arguments and opened a heritage of problems to which successors keep returning.

The Triumph of Epistemology

Berkeley and Hume formed two prongs of the movement by which the empiricist movement inadvertently renewed abstract philosophy. Berkeley's wing turned scientific analysis against itself, thereby exposing the terrain of more highly reflexive epistemological and metaphysical argument. Hume crystallized the opposite wing, loyalists of the new secularism and empiricism, which nevertheless found its own methodological issues returning to abstract philosophical terrain. Hume had strongly secular ambitions, to use a thoroughgoing empiricism to build the human sciences, where he expected the rewards to be even greater than in the natural sciences (Mossner, 1954; Passmore, 1980; Greig 1932). Book 1 of his *Treatise of Human Nature* (1739), containing Hume's philosophically fateful criticism of causality and of the identity of the self, is merely preliminary, laying the foundations of a science of human understanding; the payoff comes in the later books, comprising a psychology of human motivation, a science of morality (1739–40) followed by a science of aesthetic taste and of human societies. The last two never appeared as such, but Hume did go on to write his theory of economics (1752) and his *History of Great Britain* (1754–1762), which contained the essence of his political theories and established his contemporary fame.

Hume inadvertently occupies philosophical turf in formulating a programmatic statement as the basis for the moral sciences. He begins with the *principle of empiricism*—"all of our ideas are copied from our impressions"—(*Treatise* 76) and argues deductively for its consequences. Hume purifies the empiricist tendency of his predecessors, allowing no other source of logic or of ideas than our experience of sensory impressions. He critiques all previous metaphysical positions. He allows neither material substances behind the phenomenal flux nor any immaterial substance; Cartesian dualism, Spinoza's monism, Malebranche's occasionalism, Newtonian space, abstract ideas, and primary qualities distinct from secondary qualities all go down under the critique. So do the certainty of mathematics, the necessity of causes, the identity of the self, and implicitly the nature of the soul and any argument for the existence of the Deity. Hume's main positive doctrine, the principle of the association of impressions by which the human mind builds up its habitual ideas, is itself a philosophical argument rather than a result of empirical investigations. His program makes his moral science superior to the natural sciences; indeed it becomes their basis, for it is the psychological law of association which is "the cement of the universe" (*Abstract* 32; see Passmore, 1980: 105) rather than an externally existing causality or a freestanding mathematics.

Why should it be someone like Hume who took this step? Hume was part of an intellectual movement, the Scottish Enlightenment, which ran through Adam Smith to Ferguson, Millar, and Stewart. The other Scots shared Hume's program for building the human sciences, and laid the basis for fields such as economics, sociology, and archaeology. For the most part they occupied specialized empirical turfs, and had neither Hume's creativity in philosophical issues nor his radical skepticism; nor were they generally as extreme as Hume in making the natural sciences subservient to moral science. One significant difference is that Hume came at the very beginning of this movement, writing his *Treatise* during 1734–1737, and it was the earliest part of his writings that formulated his philosophy and his metaphysical critique. Hume had the first glimpse of a new intellectual field opening up, the autonomous moral sciences, and rushed in to ground it and justify it: activities which took place on the territory of general philosophical argument.

In the intellectual network in Figure 11.1, Hume is connected early in life with the Deists. His relative Henry Home (Lord Kames) had been working on principles of natural religion, and Hume hoped to get from him an introduction to Butler, who had just published his famous *Religion Natural and Revealed* (1736). In addition, Hume is in the network of Newton's scientific followers, his teachers at Edinburgh; in this respect he is in a similar network position with Berkeley, which suggests why there are parallels between their positions. Creativity is not simply discipleship. Hume broke with his predecessors in important respects; his radical empiricism and skepticism destroyed Deism, and he critiqued Newtonian concepts and reduced natural science to an off-shoot of the laws of the mind which were for Hume the true equivalent to Newton's laws of motion. The young Hume apparently knew that there was a fundamental philosophical transformation at stake. He went for three years to study and write at La Flèche, site of Descartes's old college, where he deliberately informed himself about the Cartesians, Malebranche, Spinoza, and Bayle—in short, all the prominent positions on the Continent. These too he critiqued in his effort to clear the ground of all philosophical rivals to his empiricism.[26]

Consider now the dynamics of the intellectual world which underlay the various strands of Hume's position. The intellectuals of the Scottish Enlightenment were religious moderates, who pushed increasingly in the direction of naturalism.[27] The religious situation was propitious for this stance. Scottish politics had been a scene of strife between extreme factions: Catholic Loyalists and royal legitimists in the Highlands, where feudal relationships remained strong, and Calvinists in the commercial Lowland cities, who had obtained control of the state church. It had been the Scottish dynasty, the Stuarts, who had attempted to bring back Catholicism in England and precipitated the Revolution in 1688; and Scotland was the main center of Jacobite plots to put them back on the throne—plots which boiled over into rebellion in 1708 and 1715–16. There were riots in Edinburgh in 1736–37, leading up to the attempted invasion of England in 1745–46. Jacobitism attracted those who were dissatisfied with the conditions of the Union with England, which had been established in 1707: opponents of English tax and customs policies and those who were excluded from patronage for church and government positions dispensed from London. In this situation the Episcopalian Church—the official Church of England—was one of the dissatisfied outsiders; under the political compromise which formed the Union, the church was merely tolerated under the official establishment of the Presbyterians. Thus Scottish Episcopalians too were suspect as Jacobite sympathizers and activists.

The faction to which Hume, Kames, Adam Smith, and the other intellectuals of the Scottish Enlightenment belonged stood against the fanaticism of all these religious parties. These were the Scots who were closest to English political power. They were administrators of Scottish government under the Union: Hume's grandfather was Lord Chief Justice; Kames succeeded to the high court; Adam Smith had strong connections in London; Hume intermittently held English military and diplomatic posts in the 1740s and again in the 1760s and ended as undersecretary of state. The ruling political faction in Scotland had structural reasons to take a secular outlook, since every church faction, including the Episcopalians, was their opponent. The situation resembles that of Hobbes, promoting a militant materialism in Royalist circles during a religious-led rebellion; but it was more successful, since Hobbes became disreputable when the Episcopalian Church was reestablished after the Restoration, whereas in Scotland the government was essentially secular and bent on keeping control over religious factions, all of which were potentially subversive.

Once again illustrating the pathway from religious stalemate to an ideology of moderation, the Scottish intellectuals in these ruling circles became Deists, tending to go even further toward secularism. The opening up of the social sciences followed from the concomitant rearrangement of the means of intellectual production. Issues of value theory had been traditionally contained within church doctrine; analysis of the social world was usually circumscribed by the religious legitimation of political authority, or left without sustaining networks because such analysis did not come into the province of church-controlled university education. In Scotland the universities were bones of contention in politico-religious strife. As the secularizing government gained the upper hand, by the 1740s the crown was making the majority of the faculty appointments, at least at the Lowland universities of Edinburgh and Glasgow. The center of gravity was wrested from traditional theological subjects and shifted toward law, history, and natural philosophy. Innovators such as Smith and Ferguson turned chairs of moral philosophy into bases for economics, political theory, and sociology. By the 1740s, Scottish graduates were shifting from the clergy to careers in the civil service (Wuthnow, 1989: 254–260). At a time when the universities in England and France, still under clerical control, were moribund, the Scottish universities were flourishing with these new career paths and the intellectual opportunities that opened up for the teachers of these new subjects. The number of Edinburgh and Glasgow students almost tripled between 1700 and 1770; Edinburgh alone in the latter year, with 1,100 students, was three times the size of Oxford and Cambridge combined during this same period (Wuthnow, 1989: 252; Stone, 1974b: 91–92).

Hume was the first to see the intellectual space that was opening up.[28] His detachment from religion fit the trend of university politics, but it was only one ingredient in Hume's stance. He pushed into the new territory as aggressively as he could, aiming to reap fame for constructing the new moral sciences. Hume's skepticism was a by-product of his empiricist principle, a piece of cultural capital which he could now exploit without concessions to religiously based concepts; the demolition of causality and of the self were inadvertent consequences, which seem to have dismayed Hume himself. What was more valuable for him was his empiricist logic, his rules for induction, his principles of habit and custom which govern the human mind; and in his later writings, once the social sciences had taken off, he downplayed the critical extremes of his early writings. Hume's skepticism was not in any of the previous traditions: not an ancient Pyrrhonism aiming at *ataraxeia,* the tranquillity of withholding judgment on everything; certainly not a fideist destruction of rationality; nor again Bayle's tolerant skepticism striking a balance among competing fanaticisms. Hume was being an empiricist when he declared that no one ever sincerely follows skepticism, and that reasoning is not so much "cognitive" as "sensitive." (Hume, [1739–40] 1969: 179). Hume was not a skeptic but a psychological imperialist.

With Hume's empiricism one might expect the age of philosophical creativity to come to an end. His contemporaries, the Encyclopedists, banished not just metaphysics but the asking of any questions regarded as futile and insoluble. In place of these traditional activities of philosophers were now disciplines with limited empirical focus: the natural sciences, history, politics, economics, psychology. Nevertheless, the pure problem space which constitutes philosophy had been expanded, and Hume's new puzzle attracted several further stances. In the provincial Scottish universities, especially centers of Presbyterian traditionalism such as Aberdeen, Reid, Beattie and Campbell responded with a philosophy of common sense which confirmed both ordinary experience and the traditional objects of religion. Working with a richer mixture of ingredients from the German networks, Kant took up Hume's challenge as if the natural sciences had been undermined and needed to be propped up against the skeptical destruction of causality. Not only epistemology but metaphysics too was renewed.

Five generations before, the emergence of the rapid-discovery sciences had transformed intellectual space. Descartes and his contemporaries, attempting to replace philosophy with the new science, nevertheless made their programmatic arguments on philosophical terrain. The secularizers, hoping to end religious strife, banished metaphysics as a residue of theology but wove another mesh of abstract questions. The pattern repeats; again an effort to kill philosophy creates a higher ground upon which philosophy expands.

CHAPTER 12

Intellectuals Take Control of Their Base:
The German University Revolution

The period from 1765 to the present is institutionally all of a piece. The continuity may not be apparent at first glance; Kant and the German Idealists seem epochs away from the themes of our own century. But Idealism was the intellectual counterpart of the academic revolution, the creation of the modern university centered on the graduate faculty of research professors, and that material base has expanded to dominate intellectual life ever since. Kant straddled two worlds: the patronage networks of the previous period, and the modern research university, which came into being, in part through Kant's own agitation, with the generation of Kant's successors. The time of the Romantics and Idealists was a transition to our contemporary situation. University-based intellectual networks had existed before, but never with such autonomy for researchers to define their own paths and such power to take over every sphere of intellectual life. The philosophical issues of the last 200 years have been those generated by the expansionary dynamic of that system.

There have been two large consequences of the academic revolution, one internal to philosophy, the other structural.

The contents of modern philosophy have been built up in a sequence of struggles. The battle first fought in Germany recurred as the old religious schools were reformed in one country after another along the lines founded at the University of Berlin in 1810. Variants of Idealism appeared several generations later in Britain, the United States, Italy, Sweden, and elsewhere, when the German academic model was imported. Idealism was the battle doctrine of the first generations of secularizers, a halfway house for wresting theology into secular hands; as the tide turned, Idealism became adopted as a defensive doctrine by religious thinkers. In each case, the new generation went beyond the halfway house of their predecessors into rebellious movements such as materialism, positivism, and analytical and semantic philosophies. There occurred the usual splits to fill the new attention space under the intellectual law of small numbers; prominent movements acquired rivals, some settling in the gaps with hybrid doctrines such as vitalism and neo-realism. Later generations rebelled against their teachers, braiding the themes of their grandteachers into their work in revival movements such as Neo-Kantianism, neo-Marxism, and in our own day what amounts to neo-existentialism and neo-Idealism.

Underneath this cascade of rivalries, the space once held by the religious philosophers has anchored the array of positions; this remains so even in the present day, when secularizers have so fully won the battle that the old religious-philosophical positions have become reoccupied by secular thinkers. Religion did not retreat before the secularizers without a fight, and the sophistication generated by opponents of militant rationalism and materialism set the problems and tools of thought which have continued to shape the field even after the religious conservatives were driven from their chairs.

Structurally, the academic revolution divided the old all-purpose intellectual role of the philosopher into a multitude of academic specialties. The process of specialization, not yet ended today, has affected the contents of intellectual life in several ways. Most obvious is the crystallization of the subject matters of the new disciplines, ranging from psychology, sociology, and the other social sciences, to the natural sciences, humanities, and literature, now incorporated as academic subjects. Academic specialization affects philosophical topics, both early and late. At the moment when a field splits off to control its own academic appointments, its separate meetings and specialized publication outlets, there is usually an ideology which expresses on general grounds the rationale for the split. The vehement materialism which broke out in Germany in the generation that freed itself from the *Naturphilosophie* of the Idealists is an example of such an ideology of disciplinary independence. Often such moves are accompanied by a claim that philosophy has been outlived and superseded by its offspring.

Nevertheless, the general-purpose intellectual role continues to exert an attraction, and finds new subject matters in the very topic of the disciplinary challenge. One such reactive movement was Neo-Kantianism, playing off the historicist methodologies laid down by the academic historians; the emergence of pragmatism in the midst of the movement which formed experimental psychology was another; yet others were the development of both phenomenology and logical positivism out of reflection on the battle over the foundations of mathematics. In each such case the existence of rival disciplinary homes has meant that individuals could migrate back and forth between bases (the career of William James is an elaborate example), borrowing and combining themes from each. Far from emptying out the contents of philosophy, the rise of the disciplines created a new mode of generating intellectual innovations on the most general (i.e., philosophical) turf itself. This is one reason why, despite so many pronouncements to the contrary, modern philosophy has not faded away but prospered.

I will not carry the detailed analysis of the intellectual world down to our own times; I take it only to three generations ago, the philosophers of approximately 1900–1935. As throughout, my guiding thread through the labyrinth of philosophical positions is the inner network of personal relations, rivalries, and master-student chains among the most influential philosophers. New problems emerge for this network analysis as we come closer to the present. Previously, the methodological problem was too little information about the lives and personal contacts of the philosophers. From the 1700s onward documentation becomes ever more abundant, and this creates an opposite kind of procedural problem. The networks on which my analysis is based consist in ties not among just any persons at all, but among those who are influential enough to be remembered by generations in the future. The difference between a minor and a major figure is indexed by just that feature. We have seen that minor philosophers (for instance, in T'ang China or Hellenistic Greece) are often famous in their own day, but later fade away into the recollection of a name and a brief label for their doctrine.

As we near the present, we lose the ability to discern who will have this kind of lasting influence. There is little doubt that Kant is of long-term importance. But can we say the same of Bergson, or Russell, or Sartre? Is Nietzsche or Whitehead a figure of enduring significance? There are empirical reasons why I expect many of the great names in our own memories to fade out for subsequent centuries. In Chapter 2 we found that over the 36 generations of Greece and the 63 generations of China, there was an average of 0.4 to 0.8 major and 1.0 to 1.9 secondary philosophers per generation. Even in peak periods of creativity, the maximal numbers are about 2 major philosophers and 3 to 5 secondary philosophers per generation. Similar levels are found in Europe in the medieval period and up through the 1700s and even the mid-1800s. For the early 1900s, though, using the same criterion of space devoted to them in standard histories, I find some 8 candidates for the rank of major philosopher.[1]

We lack even this much perspective on the period 1935–1965, the generation just before our own. Consider the judgments of the historians writing around 1890–1910, including philosophers active in their own right such as Windelband or Royce, on the thinkers of their own midcentury background. The towering figure for many of them (e.g., for Merz, 1904–1912) is Lotze, who by current criteria seems secondary at best. Royce writes of "The *Spirit of Modern Philosophy*" (1892) as if Idealism still rules the roost, of course a partisan judgment by an active participant. Others who greatly impressed their contemporaries were James Martineau (Merz, [1904–1912] 1965: 4:376), Clifford, and Sir William Hamilton, as well as iconoclasts such as D. F. Strauss, Büchner, and Buckle. Of course, given the seesaw rivalry between adjacent generations, it is not surprising that thinkers who are very influential in the long run go through a reputational trough a generation or two after their death. Hegel's reputation was at its nadir in the 1850s, before the wave of neo-Hegelian revivals. Even Kant, whose fame was never seriously eclipsed once established in the late 1780s, was regarded as outmoded by his immediate successors.[2] Aristotle's reputation, like Mencius', declined markedly in a few generations and rose to towering heights only in the very long run. Scientists are not immune; Darwin was rather on the outs of his profession around 1910 and only recovered his preeminence in the 1930s (Degler, 1991).

This is not to say that everyone whose reputation dips after his or her death will be revived still later; the law of small numbers makes it certain that most of the big names of the early twentieth century will fade into minor ones in the twenty-first century and thereafter. It is important to discipline ourselves not to make this a game of "which heroic individual will survive." The theme of my sociological argument is that creativity is not a one-shot event, but a process stretching around the persons in whom it manifests itself, backwards, sideways, and forwards from the individuals whose names are the totemic emblems thrown up by their networks. It is intergenerational networks dividing up attention space that make intellectual history in every sense. The creativity of the thinkers of our own century is literally not fully created yet.

It would be safer to bring my analysis to a close around 1865. But I continue it nevertheless two generations forward, even as the haze of living partisanship closes in. The period of the 1930s (with a slightly later continuation of the same cast of characters) is just now coming into a calmer sight. The Vienna Circle and the existentialists, shrouded in polemic both in their own day and in the decades immediately following, are becoming subjects of historical study; the sediments are settling as the stream passes on. The sociological structures of early 1900s intellectuals are familiar enough: philosophers continue to group into rival circles, to divide up the attention space under the law of small numbers; there is the same clustering of the eminent with one another that we saw in China and Greece; the intergenerational chains of teachers and pupils run right down through Frege and Russell to Wittgenstein, and from the Vienna Circle to Quine (who also descends from Royce through C. I. Lewis), or from Husserl to Heidegger to Marcuse. Whatever the future historical significance of these last named, the chains at the center of the attention space are still there. And so my concluding chapter will run out in the mist of the near-present, even as the network now becoming visible in the middle distance begins to take on familiar contours.

The German Idealist Movement

In retrospect, everything is familiar. German Idealism does not surprise us because we know it happened. But from the perspective of 1765, what followed could only be a huge surprise. The themes of the Enlightenment were the death of philosophy and its replacement by empirical science, above all the death of metaphysical speculation and anything in it that smacked of supernatural religion. Yet the following generation was to make one of the most intense outpourings of philosophical creativity in world history, moreover taking the form of the strongest claims of Idealism ever seen. To be sure, Kant, who opened the door to this outburst, was not totally unprecedented, insofar as he continued the pro-science and anti-theological themes of the Enlightenment; yet his radical means were soon taken up by a movement that, far from destroying speculative philosophy, drastically widened its claims.

How can we account for this reversal in the self-perceived trend of the times? To label it a Romantic reaction is question-begging hindsight. The Idealist revolution provides a particularly clear example of the three layers of causal grounding for the social production of ideas. We consider first, in our usual way, the clustering of ideas and the social networks among those who produced them; second, the changing material bases of intellectual production which undergirded the Idealist movement; and third, the surrounding political-economic context which generated these organizational changes. From inward to outward, we will examine the outpouring of Idealist philosophies by a dense network of creative thinkers, from Königsberg to Jena-Weimar to Berlin; surrounding these, the crisis and reform of the German university system; and at the outmost layer, the French Revolution and the Napoleonic wars, which cracked the religious and political authority of the north German states and unleashed the period of reform.

One layer does not reduce to another; least of all do the contents of the philosophies reduce to the outermost material and political conditions. Intellectuals maneuver within their own attention space, reshaping the tools at hand from past and current controversies internal to their own sphere, while energized by the structural opportunities opening up in the material and political world surrounding them. Like pegs through the stack of concentric rings, Kant and Fichte are intellectual revolutionaries as well as network stars; again, prime movers in the struggle to reform the universities to the advantage of the philosophical faculty; still again, shapers of the German ideological response to the French Revolution. Idea ingredients flow inward from each surrounding layer, but the core which transmutes them into philosophy is the ongoing struggle in intellectual space.

The Network and Its Conflicts

German Idealism began with Kant's *Critique of Pure Reason* in 1781, and by the end of the decade it had erupted into a far-flung movement lasting down into the 1820s. To understand why it should have emerged in this way, we must start further back, with the pre-Idealist network from which Kant appeared. Creative networks beget further creativity, and the intersection of such networks drives up the level. Why should such a network have come into existence at Königsberg on the Baltic 300 miles east of Berlin? In part because Königsberg was the traditional university in the original east Prussian territory (although conquest had acquired Halle, in central Germany); Königsberg enjoyed a special connection with the new capital, remaining the site where Prussian kings were crowned. And again, why then should creative networks be fostered by Berlin, as late as 1800 an unattractive garrison town on the eastern plains with sand blowing in the streets? (Safranski, 1989: 121). Because under Frederick the Great, Prussia was the expanding geopolitical power of northern Europe. In emulation of the cultural greatness of his French enemies, Frederick had imported academicians from Paris, along with dissident (and therefore patronage-needy) stars such as Voltaire and La Mettrie. Combine this with Frederick's anti-clericalism, part of the drive to build a strong state by subordinating the church, and one can see a cultureless marchland conqueror quickly becoming a magnet for Enlightenment intellectuals. In sociological theory, at the outermost causal layer, the geopolitical and economic rise or fall of states shifts the location of resources, expanding the material bases for some intellectual networks at the expense of others. Networks realign; new philosophical positions appear.

Kant and his contemporaries grew up in a situation where opportunities for careers as culture producers were expanding, if spartan and competitive. In connection with the Prussian innovation of a conscript standing army came the first compulsory public elementary schooling, spurring further educational expansion at all levels. The growth of an educated and anti-clerical bureaucracy fostered a publishing industry; by the 1760s Berlin had its own intellectual circle outside the Academy of Sciences centered on publishers and writers such as C. F. Nicolai and Moses Mendelssohn (see Figure 12.1). What was happening in Prussia was emulated by many of the *Kleinstaaterei*. The geopolitical fragmentation of central and western Germany made competition in the new cultural marketplace of literary publication a substitute for military glory on the part of the smaller states. The structure made possible not only Berlin and

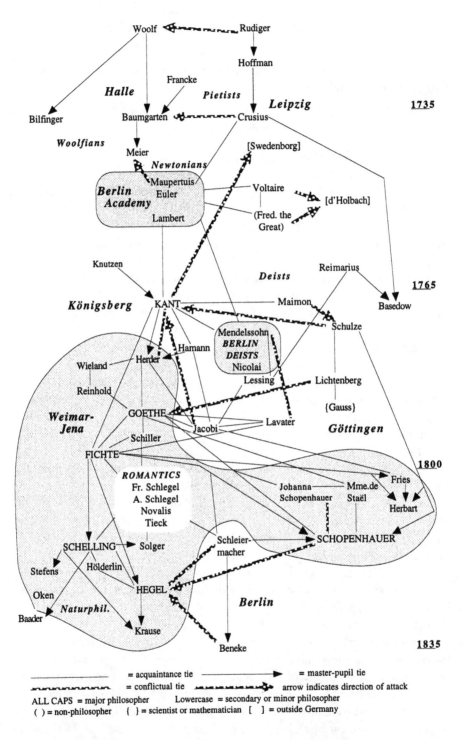

Woolf ◄╌╌╌╌╌╌ Rudiger

Hoffman

Halle   Francke   **Pietists**   **Leipzig**   <u>1735</u>

Bilfinger   Baumgarten ╌╌╌╌╌╌╌ Crusius

Woolfians

Meier   [Swedenborg]

Newtonians

Berlin   Maupertuis   Voltaire   [d'Holbach]
Academy   Euler

Lambert   (Fred. the
Great)

Knutzen   Reimarius   <u>1765</u>

Deists

Königsberg   KANT   Maimon   Basedow

Schulze

Mendelssohn
**BERLIN
DEISTS**   Hamann
Nicolai
Wieland   Herder   Lessing   Lichtenberg

Reinhold   {Gauss}

**Weimar-
Jena**   GOETHE   Jacobi   Lavater   **Göttingen**

Schiller

FICHTE   <u>1800</u>

Fries
ROMANTICS   Johanna   Mme.de
Fr. Schlegel   Schopenhauer   Staël   Herbart
A. Schlegel
Novalis
Tieck   Schleier-   SCHOPENHAUER
macher

SCHELLING   Solger

Stefens   Hölderlin

Oken   HEGEL

Baader   **Naturphil.**   **Berlin**

Krause

Beneke   <u>1835</u>

─────────── = acquaintance tie   ──────────► = master-pupil tie

╌╌╌╌╌╌╌╌╌ = conflictual tie   ╌╌╌╌╌╌► arrow indicates direction of attack

ALL CAPS = major philosopher   Lowercase = secondary or minor philosopher
( ) = non-philosopher   { } = scientist or mathematician   [ ] = outside Germany

FIGURE 12.1. GERMAN NETWORK, 1735–1835:
BERLIN–KÖNIGSBERG AND JENA–WEIMAR

Königsberg but Weimar as well. If there were also centers of religious reaction, like Bavaria (and for short periods Prussia itself), and counter-movements of Pietist anti-Enlightenment throughout the north German population, the competition of multiple centers conjoined to such conflicts provided energy and excitement for intellectual issues rather than choking them off by the imposition of orthodoxy.

In the 1760s and 1770s, German thinking was a branch of French themes; Enlightenment Deism forged ahead against religious traditionalism, and the focus of attention swung toward a newer conflict, Enlightenment versus sentimentalism. The latter was again a pattern from the French attention center, first exploited by Rousseau. Since the intellectual world lives on oppositions and by dividing up the dominant attention space, rationalists opened up a slot for anti-rationalists, and the opponents lived symbiotically by the attention they drew to one another. If Rousseau was warmly received in Germany, this cannot be explained tautologically by his "influence" or his "genius"; rather his sentimentalism fitted a situation that fostered just this opposition. Most of the north German states had gone much further in de-clericalizing than in France, reducing clergy to agents of secular government; this freed religious impulses in the populace for a private marketplace of emotional and moral symbols. If one of the hallmarks of modernity is the privatization of religion, and concomitantly the secular control of the school system, northern Germany was moving through the transition to cultural modernity earlier than virtually any other society. Not surprisingly, we find in Germany the first notable expression of the anti-modern intellectual stance, the *Sturm und Drang* movement of the 1770s.

How, then, did the network of Enlightenment academicians, Deists, and popular sentimentalists build up to the point where it could give birth to German Idealism? In the 1750s Kant was a middle-aged product of Königsberg University, submitting scientific memoirs to the prize contests of the Berlin Academy and corresponding with mathematicians such as Lambert. A far more famous Königsberger was Hamann, known as "the wizard of the north" for his 1760 book, *Die Magie aus Morgenlande* (The Magi of the East), explaining the symbolic meanings of astronomical observations. There was a structural rivalry here, for Kant had made his first small mark a little earlier with his scientific theory of the heavens (1755); in 1766 Kant struck back with an attack on Swedenborgian mysticism, *Dreams of a Spirit-Seer.* Just at this time, the early 1760s, Herder got his start as pupil and acquaintance of both Kant and Hamann—yet another instance of the pattern of network connections forged between intellectuals prior to the creativity that would bring them fame. In 1767, turning a favorite aesthetic concern in a new direction, Herder argued that the truest poetry is that of the people; in 1772 he won the Berlin Academy prize with his theory of the origins of language. Herder made his mark before his own teacher, and prepared the way for the movement that would make Kant its greatest name.

Now the Königsberg network begins to flow into the central network of German intellectual life. In 1769 Herder met the 20-year-old Goethe on his travels, both of them a few years prior to their fame. When Goethe went to Weimar in 1775 as a court official, his first move toward building a literary circle was to find a position for Herder. Goethe became the great energy star of German literature, and as with all such figures his reputation casts a glare that makes it difficult to see how he became that way. Goethe's life well fits the model that networks are the primary movers, and that individuals become filled with creative energies to the extent of their centrality when the networks reorganize around them.

Goethe from early on was a gregarious seeker of other intellectuals, both the bright young aspirants and the established names. A few years after meeting Herder, Goethe launched the *Sturm und Drang* movement with his drama *Goetz von Berlichingen* about a rebel medieval knight; he quickly followed this up in 1774 with a novel, *Sorrows of Young Werther,* which inspired a cult of romantic suicide protesting unrequited love and social convention. Goethe became a wonder of creative longevity and far-flung virtuosity because his creations mirrored the modes of those around him in every phase of a proliferating movement. Schiller's 1781 drama *The Robbers* glorifying revolution was a scandalous success. After he joined the Weimar circle in 1788, Goethe and Schiller became friends and collaborators in journal publishing, spurring each other on. Schiller produced his quasi-Shakespearean history plays, while Goethe produced his own tragedies and historical dramas and worked up the main part of *Faust,* incorporating themes of Spinozaist pantheism from one wing of the Idealist movement. When the Romantic circle popularized translations of Shakespeare, Cervantes, and other foreign classics and produced its own historical novels, Goethe turned his hand to the bildungsroman, producing *Wilhelm Meister.* In 1810, at the height of the *Naturphilosophie* movement, Goethe published his *Theory of Colors,* an attempt to overcome mechanistic-mathematical Newtonian optics by means of a qualitative, even animistic theory of "the actions and sufferings of light" (Safranski, 1989: 178–184). Goethe of course was no mere imitator; he created by conflict and opposition within the turbulent attention space, energized by contemporary enthusiasms while transmuting their materials into his own.

Goethe was a center for network contacts that brought him all the cultural capital at its point of emergence. To a large extent this was because he was a prime mover in assembling creative intellectual circles. Typically such groups contain both an intellectual leader whose work publicizes the group and an organizational leader who assembles the material conditions for members to work (Mullins, 1973). Goethe combined both roles. The ducal court at Weimar, with its nearby university at Jena, became a magnet in the attention space to which Goethe's creative energy attracted others; for many of them Goethe found a material base (Herder received a sinecure as state director of clergy, Schiller a position as history professor). These in turn sent out further resonances, generating creativity far beyond Goethe's own interests, and sometimes even opposed to them. Wieland, an old student friend of Goethe who began the wave of German Shakespeare translations, moved to Weimar and published there his popular literary magazine, *Teutscher Mercur;* through this magazine Kant's work first became famous as the result of articles in 1786–87 by the Jena professor Reinhold. Others introduced the teaching of Kantian philosophy into Jena and founded a journal to publicize the Kantian viewpoint. By the 1790s, Jena-Weimar had become a hotbed of rival groups, each with its own journal: Goethe and Schiller's *Die Horen,* the Romantic circle's *Athenaeum,* a little later Schelling and Hegel's *Kritisches Journal der Philosophie.*

Jena-Weimar, of course, was not the only location where salons and magazines existed in Germany. It became the center by a process which is quite general in the network theory of creativity. The highest level of creativity is determined by an intense focus of attention. One part of the network, initially quite dispersed, catches fire from a particular creative development, often a famous controversy. The first-mover advantage magnifies small beginnings; a circle grows ahead of others as it attracts attention and recruits, building up emotional energy locally and deference elsewhere. The first-mover advantage passes the point of critical mass; what was once one local circle among others now is bathed in fame that blots out the rest.[3] From a great distance we see only Kant, Goethe, Fichte, Schelling, and Hegel. Viewed from closer up, the networks shouldering one another aside for position in the attention space are crowded and rather breathless.

The Idealist movement crystallized from networks all over Germany. Two of Goethe's early connections were at the flashpoints of the controversies which brought on the storm. The first incident was precipitated by Lavater, a Zurich pastor. In 1769 Lavater challenged Moses Mendelssohn to demonstrate the falsity of Christian religious belief or to convert; Mendelssohn made a sensation with his reply that Judaism itself is the religion of reason. Here we see Lavater, still rather early in his own career (his fame built up between 1768 and 1778 for publications propagating enthusiastic mysticism as well as the new science of physiognomy and fortune-telling), jumping into the public eye by picking a controversy with the already famous; for Mendelssohn had been the leader of the popular essayists at Berlin since the 1750s, a winner of prizes from the Berlin Academy and defender of toleration and the separation of church and state. The 1769 incident made an attention center out of the cleavage between rationalist Deists and sentimentalists. Soon afterwards Goethe gave impetus to the latter by launching *Sturm und Drang*.[4]

The literary network, far more than the philosophical one centered on the universities, was the cosmopolitan path for making rapid contacts, spreading enthusiasm, and acquiring fame. The takeoff of Kantian philosophy came when it was adopted by the core literary network; and the first big waves of philosophical attention went not to Kant but to Jacobi, who used the literary network to publicize Spinoza.

The Spinozastreit, *or Pantheism Controversy of 1785*

The second flashpoint is around Jacobi. He belongs to the same network: an acquaintance of Lavater, a friend of Goethe on the basis of previous family connections since both were young poets in the 1770s, Jacobi made his entrée into the intellectual world on Goethe's coattails. Jacobi pursued a career not too different from Goethe's bread and butter as a lawyer-official at Düsseldorf on the lower Rhine. He was no literary success, but he kept aggressively cultivating the network, on the Deist side as well as that of its opponents.

Jacobi got himself into the confidence of Lessing, famous from the 1760s for his aesthetic criticism and his dramas extolling the rational basis of all religions, underlying Judaism and Christianity alike. After Lessing's death in 1781, Jacobi created a furor by publishing Lessing's letters to Moses Mendelssohn and declaring that he had been a Spinozaist. The year was 1785, four years after Kant's *Critique* but before Kant became famous. The ensuing quarrel in letters, pamphlets, and the major literary journals drew in not only Mendelssohn and the Berlin Deists but also Goethe, Herder, and Hamann, a gathering of the contemporary famous.

Jacobi did not openly endorse Spinoza, but declared the latter's monistic determinism the only rationally consistent philosophical position, while rejecting it as incompatible with Christian faith. Jacobi thereby shared in the publicity of the intellectual focus of attention without attaching to himself the onus of unconventionality. Earlier, in the 1770s, Jacobi had used his knowledge of Spinoza to impress the newly famous Goethe, who looked on Jacobi as a guide in his quest for a sympathetic philosophy of nature and spirit. As late as 1784, just before Jacobi's attack on Spinoza, he was conferring with Goethe and Herder at Weimar on Spinoza's significance. And as Jacobi became the storm center of attack on the new philosophy and maneuvered to draw the non-polemical Kant into combat, he kept up an unctuous correspondence with the very pro-Spinozaist Goethe; eventually, by cultivating Hamann, Jacobi engineered a friendly contact with Kant himself (Zammito, 1992: 230–237).

Jacobi leaves a strong impression of a man wanting above all to be in the center of intellectual action, at whatever cost to personal consistency.

Spinoza's fame as a philosopher dates from this moment. He had been an underground figure throughout the century, known through the caricature in Bayle's *Dictionary,* and increasingly as a heretical name bandied about in the quarrel between Deists and orthodox Christians. After Jacobi's intervention, Spinoza's became the main rival doctrine on Idealist terrain, used by many Idealists as the dogmatic foil for their doctrine of freedom. Spinoza and Kant, the "dogmatic" determinist metaphysical system versus the "critical" subjectivism, became the two poles of German philosophy. Formerly regarded as an atheist, Spinoza was resurrected in the liberal religious context of the 1780s as a possible compromise between rationalist materialism and religion. By this stroke Jacobi became Kant's major rival for the attention of the philosophical public.

Jacobi's move also upped the ante in the philosophical contest. He was simultaneously making Spinoza intellectually respectable, no mere fringe figure but the epitome of systematic rational metaphysics, while using Spinoza's heretical reputation to discredit the entire project of mainstream philosophy. Jacobi's was a heavy counterstroke against Kant's new philosophy. Since intellectual conflicts create attention, by connecting Kant's philosophy to the popular religious-antireligious issue of the day, he also helped to make Kant famous. The controversy guaranteed that Kant's critical position, limiting philosophy to the negative task of destroying the pretensions of metaphysics, would not remain stable. Spinoza was now the counter-position that Kant's followers would have to deal with, ambiguously appealing to political interests in liberation from religious dogmatism while simultaneously satisfying the desire for a romantic merging with nature.[5]

If Kant is one hinge of the emergence of Idealism, Jacobi is the counterhinge. Opposition to the Kantians and Idealists unfolds simultaneously with them, as an integral part of the field of conflictual forces. Jacobi produced the first anti-Kantian critique in 1787, almost simultaneously with its first widespread recognition. Using as his vehicle *David Hume on Belief,* Jacobi now extolled Hume's critique of causality and declared that Kant had failed to show how causality could apply to the thing-in-itself. Hume was by no means regarded as a famous philosopher until this time, but now both Kant and his self-styled rival were declaring that all philosophy must answer Hume's puzzle. One sees here a reason why Jacobi ultimately failed in his battle with Kant. Jacobi's tactic was to revive old, underutilized philosophical ammunition. He was responsible for creating the reputations of two intellectual giants, Spinoza and Hume, by moving them into the center of intellectual oppositions. The price Jacobi paid was his own independent reputation, while he played the part of animator of other figures upon the stage. Jacobi's own solution to the thing-in-itself was merely to declare it an item of miraculous faith, on a par with other items of religion. As key opponent, Jacobi was as central as Kant. It was around these two energy poles that the networks of the older generation were transformed into new intellectual tensions.

Proliferation of the Idealist Network

Kant's *Critique of Pure Reason* attracted little attention when it first appeared in 1781, leading him to restate the doctrine several times (1783, 1785) in more popular form. Once the rivalries broke out, Kant's reputation was assured. Kant became a magnet for critical opposition, which, far from destroying his popularity, focused attention on it. Jacobi and Herder in the 1780s were followed by a flood of Kantian expositions, commentaries, and critiques.[6] Kant was energized by the attention; now in his 60s and 70s, he published critiques of ethics, aesthetics, and teleology in 1788 and 1790 and a dozen books in the 1790s, cashing in on fame to express his position on religion, world peace, educational reform, and other political questions.

Königsberg became a center for pilgrimages by admiring followers. Among them was Fichte. He had been an undistinguished Jena theology student in the early 1780s, then (like many others) a household tutor. He first made contact with the central network in 1788, when in Zurich he met Lavater—the old instigator of intellectual action in the early days of the Deist-sentimentalist controversy.[7] In 1791 Fichte made his long trek on foot to Königsberg to meet Kant. Rebuffed at first contact, to gain Kant's favorable attention Fichte wrote, in Kantian fashion, his *Critique of Revelation*. It was a shrewd judgment about filling the slot in public attention, for Kant's own writings on religion were expected—at the very time when the French Revolution was abolishing Christianity[8]—and Kant's similar work appeared the following year as *Religion within the Bounds of Mere Reason*. Kant recommended Fichte's work to his own publisher; when it appeared in 1792, the printer omitted the author's name, no doubt in order to promote sales, and it was initially mistaken for a work of Kant's. Swept up by the enthusiasm of expectant audiences and entrepreneurial anticipations into identification with the most avant-garde tendencies of the Kantian movement, Fichte became famous. When Reinhold, the academic champion of Kantianism, resigned his professorship at Jena, Fichte was appointed to succeed him in 1794. Flushed by his success, in that year Fichte in his *Science of Knowledge* stepped beyond Kant's critical restriction of thought to the categories of the understanding, eliminated the thing-in-itself, and dialectically reconstructed metaphysics out of the process of criticism. On this turf there now proliferated a full-scale Idealist movement.

Controversial attention recruited new waves to the movement. In the late 1780s the Tübingen theological *Stift,* the main center of orthodox theology, officially protested to Berlin the subversiveness of Kant's work (Zammito, 1992: 242). Negative counter-moves are as important as positive initiatives in building the emotional energy of intellectual action. The local controversy attracted the attention of the rebellious young liberals Schelling, Hegel, and Hölderlin, roommates there in the early 1790s, converts to Kantianism. Fichte visited Schelling in 1795, attracted by the prospects of publishing in a journal connected with the famous theological center. Quick to seize the new intellectual opportunities, the 20-year-old Schelling expounded his own version of Fichtean Idealism. Via a chain of sponsorship, this youthful Idealist movement soon made its center at the literary and Kantian stronghold at Jena-Weimar. Schelling and Hegel found positions, after tutoring jobs, respectively as *Extraordinarius* (associate professor) and *Privatdozent* (lecturer) in 1798 and 1801.

Excitement breeds more excitement during those few years which constitute the upward path of a movement. Soon everyone of sympathetic belief or hungry for fame was flocking to Weimar and Jena. The so-called Romantic circle sprang up, a Bohemian colony practicing sexual libertarianism, centered on the brothers Schlegel, who lived during 1795–1799 in Weimar and held academic posts at Jena. The Romanticists by and large continued the themes of the earlier literary movement. The elder brother, August Schlegel, provided the major success of the movement with his translations of Shakespeare (1797–1810). Friedrich Schlegel was the firebrand of the movement, whose 1799 novel *Lucinde* popularized Fichte's Idealism and advocated the sexual rights of women. The young novelists Tieck, Wackenroder, and Novalis published at the height of this period, 1797–1800, extolling religious faith in an idealized Middle Ages. The Werther-like reputation of the group was enhanced when Novalis died in 1801 at age 29 after an unhappy love affair with a 13-year-old girl, motifs soon to be popularized by Byron's sister incest. In this circle the austere technicalities of philosophy were superseded by aesthetic and religious sentiment. Schelling, with his cherubic good looks and his wunderkind intellectual eagerness, became an intimate of the circle and precipitated one of its scandals when August Schlegel's wife, Caroline, divorced him in 1803 to marry Schelling, 12 years her junior.

The radicalism of these movements provoked opponents; but local controversies only encouraged migration to new centers. In 1799 Fichte was accused of advocating atheism, and left Jena. The Romantic circle moved to Dresden and then Berlin, where it burned itself out by 1801, but not before it was joined by Fichte and Schleiermacher, a prominent preacher at the Prussian court. Jena was gradually displaced by Berlin as the prime center. Fichte remained there most of the time, delivering his famous *Addresses to the German Nation* in 1807 at the Berlin Academy of Sciences to an audience which included Wilhelm von Humboldt. In 1809 von Humboldt, as minister in the Prussian reform government, founded the University of Berlin, naming Fichte professor of philosophy and its first rector in 1810. Schleiermacher simultaneously became professor of theology, and later succeeded Fichte as rector after the latter's death in 1814. Fichte's chair was filled (after war-related delays) in 1818 by Hegel. By the 1820s, the Idealist center at Berlin was in the routinized phase of normal science, and it was here in the 1830s that the Hegel school would undergo its splits.

As the network and its centers burgeoned and broke apart, intellectual positions were splitting and realigning as well. As in any successful intellectual movement, control of the dominant attention space was subject to the law of small numbers. The victorious side had room for sub-splits upon which rival careers could be made. The earliest manifestation was the rupture between the Kantians and Fichte's Idealism. By 1799 Kant had repudiated Fichte's doctrines. Idealism now was the crest of the surging wave, the center of attention and emotional enthusiasm, and the older anti-Kantian opposition began to rally behind Kant himself as a more modest defense against Idealist extremes. The main Idealist opposition now interpreted Kantian categories as facts of human psychology rather than as transcendental. Following this path, Bouterwek (1799, 1806) produced a psychologistic compromise between the out-and-out Idealists and scientific materialists. Fries (1803) tied Kantian doctrine to the exact sciences; Herbart, the most important later opponent of the Idealists, pioneered empirical research in psychology.

This opposition acquired its own centers. Göttingen had been the leading center of academic scholarship since the 1770s, especially historical philology and mathematics. Now it housed anti-Idealists: Lichtenberg, a mathematics professor who satirized *Sturm und Drang* sentimentalism, as well as Schulze, Bouterwek, and Herbart. The pre-Jena center became anti-Jena and later anti-Berlin. The most eminent in exploiting the anti-Idealist space was Herbart, a former Jena student of the early 1790s, who found a distinctive space from 1802 on in refusing to go along with the Idealist tide. As the Idealists split from the Kantians, Königsberg became another oppositional center.

The old battle lines of rationalists versus sentimentalists were now almost completely eclipsed. The Idealists, led by Fichte, had become religious radicals. Whereas Kant reduced religion to ethical practice, Fichte, whose philosophy made the entire world into a phenomenon of spirit, verged on promoting an entirely new religion, blending humanitarian political reform with universal spiritual enlightenment. This position was assailed by orthodox Christians, while the middle ground was seized by the theologian Schleiermacher, whose

On Religion: Speeches to Its Cultured Despisers (1799) used Romanticist enthusiasm to combat Enlightenment rationalism. The Berlin Deist circle did not fade away without a battle: Mendelssohn tried to refute Kant's arguments against a rational proof of God; Nicolai, a veteran who had mounted satirical attacks on Goethe, Hamann, Lavater, Herder, and Jacobi, in the 1790s accused Kant and Fichte of being crypto-Catholics (Beiser, 1987: 105–108). But Deism fell from fashion, squeezed out of the attention space by the new lines of conflict. In the end, Mendelssohn's daughter married Friedrich Schlegel, carrying a connection with the prestige and creative energy of the *Aufklärer* into the camp of their Romantic opponents.

The Idealists, now proliferating even faster than the Kantians, soon underwent their own sub-splits. Schelling, originally one of Fichte's disciples, in 1797–1800 turned philosophy to encompass the forefront of research in natural science. Magnetism and electricity had been hot areas of scientific discovery from Galvani in the 1780s through Volta's electric cell in 1799. For Schelling, what appears as the objects of nature are dynamic processes based on attraction and repulsion, paralleling Fichte's dialectic of consciousness positing and resolving oppositions. Chemistry was theorized around the polarity of acids and bases, mechanics as quantitative oppositions of forces, biological life as the unrestricted struggle of these forces. The universe is a world Soul, a unity of mutually conflicting forces. In astronomy the cosmos was theorized as the periodic expansion and contraction of the *Urmaterie,* primary matter. Schelling's *Naturphilosophie* attracted many followers among German scientists from the early 1800s through the 1820s, affecting biological studies even among scientists who later returned to the materialist fold.[9]

Ever sensitive to the unfolding of network opportunities, Schelling moved on to other positions. Among the Weimar stars was Schiller, who capped his reputation as a liberal dramatist by moving onto philosophical turf in 1793–1795 and expounding a Kantian interpretation of art and poetry. Following Schiller's lead, in 1800, at the emotional peak of the Romantic circle, Schelling converted to aesthetic Idealism. He now elevated the aesthetic faculty as unifying all the other faculties of mind (rational, moral, intuitive); ultimate metaphysical reality could be directly perceived through the eyes of the artist, and the aesthetic perception of nature became emblematic of the highest philosophical insight. It was in this version that Idealism became popular abroad: spread by Coleridge (who visited Germany in 1798–99 with Wordsworth), it was adopted by the Romantic poets Shelley and Keats in England, and later by the New England Transcendentalists. In 1801–1803 Schelling rapidly added a religious dimension to what he now called Absolute Idealism, giving a theological interpretation to his doctrines of nature and of aesthetic intuition.

Then Schelling's 15-year flareup of creativity in the center of public attention abruptly ended. After breaking with the Idealist network, Schelling ceased publication after 1809. He continued to lecture on the history of mythology as a poetic unfolding of the nature of God and hence of the cosmos. Schelling's religious phase, too, found disciples, notably von Baader (another mining engineer) in the 1820s. Schelling left a trail of network disciples behind him; after 1810, these movements based on his older positions were carrying along on their own, overshadowing Schelling's own later position in the attention space.

The Crisis of the Law of Small Numbers

By the first decade of the 1800s, there was altogether a considerable lineup of positions: Kant's critical philosophy; the psychological–scientific realist version of Kant developed by Herbart and others; Fichte's dialectical Idealism; *Naturphilosophie;* aesthetic Idealism; Schleiermacher's Idealist Christianity; and generally outside the fold of all these philosophical movements an increasingly self-consciously orthodox religiosity, which founded itself on fideism and traditionalism alone. These total seven positions, pushing the upper limits of the law of small numbers. How then do we account for the emergence of two more major thinkers, Hegel and Schopenhauer? The comparison between the success of one and the longtime failure of the other is instructive.

Hegel entered the scene relatively late.[10] His first important work (1801) pointed out the difference between Fichte's and Schelling's systems, precipitating a break between them. The topic shows that Hegel was well attuned to the shifting niches in the core of the intellectual field. As Schelling's old roommate and closest friend, Hegel had very good network connections, but he was effectively blocked from taking an independent position as long as he remained in Schelling's camp. By 1806, the lineup was changing. Schelling, so to speak, was a niche hog; he had already gobbled up two of the available slots out of the six allowed by the law of small numbers, and in 1803 was upstaging even himself by proposing a third position, Absolute Idealism. This also moved him closer to the orthodox religious camp, along with the rest of the Romantics.

Now Hegel sensed the opening of a slot: it was Fichte's dialectical Idealism, no longer being creatively developed by anyone. Since his great *Wissenschaftslehre* of 1794, Fichte had continued to publish prolifically, but largely on topics of popular controversy: the French Revolution and later the national revolt against Napoleon's conquest of Germany, religious crisis, political and educational reform. Fichte was devoting himself to being the organizational leader rather than the intellectual leader of the movement, politicking for a new material base, which would soon become the reformed university at Berlin.

In 1807 Hegel published his *Phenomenology of Spirit,* which develops Fichte's dialectics as applied to the historical unfolding of the world spirit, especially in social forms. Now Hegel had found his groove: the *Logic* (1812–1816) and *Encyclopedia of Philosophical Science* (1817) spelled out his system in scholastic detail, and in 1821 his last published work applied the system to law and the state in *The Philosophy of Right.*

The intellectual reorganization is paralleled by a split in the networks. The Jena circle had been breaking up, and Schelling was palpably moving into a different set of connections: the network of religious and political conservatives who had been the enemies of Kant and Fichte. Fichte had already departed in 1799, followed soon by the Romantics. In 1803 Schelling went as full professor to Würzburg in the conservative state of Bavaria, then in 1809 left the universities entirely to join the Bavarian Academy of Science. Jacobi had already moved to Munich in the 1790s, becoming president of the Academy of Sciences, 1804–1812. When Schelling joined him in Munich, the tentative split from the other Idealists crystallized into an opposition center to the Jena-Berlin mainline. Other fragments of the old Jena-Weimar camp also moved sharply to the right in politics and religion; in 1809 Friedrich Schlegel converted to Catholicism and became secretary to the arch-conservative Metternich in Vienna.

The old wunderkind Schelling had removed himself from the world of Idealist philosophy, with its rationalism and its system-building tools. He had removed himself too from Idealist politics, which was a rational reformism, extending to an anti-traditional reform of religion. On every point now Schelling was in the opposition. When Hegel arrived at Berlin, it was as the proponent of the rational constitutional state as consolidator of the accomplishments of the age of revolution. When Schelling finally made it back into the Berlin mainstream in his old age, in 1841–1846, it was as the chosen agent of political and religious reaction. In this too Hegel carried on Fichte's slot: for both of them the dialectical tools and the system constructing were turned most naturally to progressive political reform. A generation later, when the Idealist hegemony was over and its capital was being redistributed once again among the factions, Marx and Engels became prominent by reviving the Fichte-Hegel slot, with all its social and political resonances.

So much for Hegel over Schelling; what of Hegel over Schopenhauer? The key is the tremendous crowding of intellectual competition during this period, in a situation which raised extraordinary hopes of intellectual leaps from rags to riches. Hegel began with polemics against a host of rivals; it seemed almost everyone had his own system. Under the constraints of the law of small numbers, most were bound to be disappointed. Characteristic of many was Krause, a Dresden neighbor of Schopenhauer in 1815–1817. His system of

Idealism was ignored in Germany, but managed to attract attention among liberal reformers in Spain. Doubtless because of the crush of competition, at this time the popular image emerged associating genius with mental illness. (In general the evidence shows no such association: creativity deteriorates with mental illness; Herbert, 1959). The Jena-Weimar creative circle was one of the largest on record; the notable names, when we count the Romantic circle, the Kantian publicists, their connections in Königsberg, Berlin, Göttingen, and elsewhere, as well as the anti-Idealist critics, add up to 30 or more in the running for attention. The competition was mitigated to some extent by specialization, through less than usual because literary and philosophical concerns and channels of publication overlapped to a considerable extent. Intellectual competition in this period was as intense as at any time in history, and many creative thinkers were squeezed out of attention. That is why this generation accounts for so many of the famous cases of neurotic breakdowns and misanthropic withdrawals.

Hölderlin started out with the same trajectory as Schelling and Hegel. Beginning in the Tübingen group, turned on by contact with Fichte, he was sponsored by Schiller to a position at Jena, where he tried to lecture in philosophy. But he failed to be accepted in the Weimar circle and left in 1795. In addition to his poems (for which he eventually became known), he wrote a philosophical novel (like so many of the others) but was ignored by his contemporaries.[11] After moving about as a tutor, by 1804 he had gone insane and never wrote again. Compare Novalis, who was more successful in gaining the friendship of Goethe, Schiller, and the Schlegels; as the Romantic circle was breaking up in 1801, he died of consumption. Yet another example is the playwright and poet Kleist, who left the army to devote himself to intellectual life in 1799, and shot himself in 1811 at the age of 41. Up against the law of small numbers, many individuals cracked under the strain; early deaths too can be interpreted as results of the structural crunch.

The most famous of its victims was Schopenhauer. He is often regarded as another such neurotic genius, with his misogyny, his avoidance of company, and his violent outbursts. But these are traits of Schopenhauer while he was experiencing the "structural crunch" of intellectual competition, not of his early life, full of cultivating good network ties and feeling the hopeful surge of creativity.[12] Conversely, one might question how Schopenhauer managed to produce first-rate creativity at all, given that the slots were closing down for him. The answer lies in the networks. Schopenhauer had very good resources and network connections, with both the Idealists and their opponents, but he came onto them very late. He was born in 1788; by the time he was educated, the available attention slots were already filled. When he arrived at Weimar in 1807, the old circle was still a lively memory. His heiress mother had recently moved to Weimar and hosted the literary circles there, and through her

Schopenhauer was exposed to Goethe.[13] The young Schopenhauer made a favorable impression on the aging Wieland, whose journal had launched the Kantian movement 25 years before. His ambition buoyed by his sponsorship, Schopenhauer visited all the famous centers; he studied at Göttingen in 1809–10 under the old oppositional critic Schulze and the psychologistic Kantian Bouterwek, then in 1811 heard Fichte lecture in Berlin; he presented his dissertation for a degree at Jena in 1813, as if to identify himself with the old movement.

The slot which Schopenhauer spied, now that the psychologists had pre-empted the Kantian heritage, was a return to Kant. But he was too ambitious merely to repeat Kant. He transformed the dualism of categories plus the thing-in-itself into the dualism of representation plus will. Kant had always been a proponent of natural science; this naturalism was reinforced by Schopenhauer's exposure to Goethe at a time when the Great Man had felt in need of support on his neglected theory of colors. Just before working out his own system, in 1816 Schopenhauer had collaborated with Goethe and produced a defense of the latter's color theory. Schopenhauer's much more original contribution, that the thing-in-itself is the will, came from philosophizing his own sexual experience.[14] This blend of the personal with the philosophical, plus the iconoclasm of speaking openly about sexuality, was a heritage of the Romantic literary movement, which was still echoing at Weimar when the young Schopenhauer arrived there. Schopenhauer's creativity was in providing a philosophical slot in which this became crucial material.[15]

Just as Schopenhauer was beginning to publicize his position, he found himself in a contest for attention with Hegel. He is famous for having attempted to lecture at the same time as Hegel, making an abortive attempt to establish himself as a *Privatdozent* at Berlin in 1820 and intermittently during the rest of Hegel's life. Usually there were no listeners at all, sometimes one or two, while Hegel had a hundred or more. The attempt was not as arrogant as it seems in retrospect, for after Fichte's death in 1814, there seemed a vacuum in the Idealist leadership. *Naturphilosophie* was regarded by many as too extreme, Schelling's current mythologizing was disreputable, and in the contest for the Berlin appointment the Kantian Fries was for a while the favorite over the relatively unknown Hegel.[16] Although Hegel initially in 1818 attracted only modest numbers of pupils, his fame grew overwhelming in the 1820s. The Fichtean slot which he preserved and expanded had far more resonances and sources of alliance in the intellectual world than Schopenhauer's iconoclasm and religious pessimism. To the extent that he was known, Schopenhauer was misperceived as a version of Fichte's or Schelling's will philosophy (Safranski, 1989: 260). Supernumeraries outside the law of small numbers are penalized by being seen through the categories of the dominant schools.

By the time of his death in 1831, Hegel's pupils dominated the Berlin center;

along with Schleiermacher's and Schelling's students, they were to fill up most of the creative activity for the following generation. (See the networks in Figures 13.1 and 14.2.) As this reality became apparent, Schopenhauer gave up the contest and retired to Frankfurt to live off his personal fortune, never to lecture again. His fame would come only in his old age, when the collapse of Hegelianism and *Naturphilosophie* opened up the reputational space again.

Philosophy Captures the University

I have not yet explained why the Kantian movement should have appeared at the time it did, nor indeed why it should have appeared at all. We see the older networks transforming and taking on a new content; for a time this content stirred enormous enthusiasm and generated a panoply of opportunities for creativity. To understand this, we must move to the underlying material base which supports the networks. During the time of the Idealists, this base was expanding and transforming in Germany in a change that was laying down the conditions for the modern intellectual.

Before the academic revolution, the most important and best-known philosophers had for several centuries been non-academics. The chief material base for intellectual creativity was patronage. One might include in this self-patronage of individuals such as Descartes or Bacon, wealthy enough to support their own writing, or Spinoza, a frugal middle-class version of the same. Most typical was personal dependence on the aristocracy: Hobbes, household tutor in a Royalist family, and Locke, personal physician to the opposition leader Lord Shaftesbury, are structurally in the same position. After 1690 or 1700, there was some shift toward collective forms of patronage. Leibniz, an intellectual and organizational entrepreneur par excellence, spread the organizational form called the academy through central Europe, by which a prince established a material endowment for a group of intellectuals, thereby giving a measure of autonomy and permanence to their activities. Another such form of patronage was the custom of rewarding intellectuals with posts at the disposal of the government. This was particularly prominent in Britain as the political spoils system set in with parliamentary dominance. Berkeley and Hume both did a good deal of chasing patronage appointments, the former in the church, the latter most successfully in diplomatic service. In Germany of the *Kleinstaaterei*, apart from the Academy at Berlin, prominent intellectuals found positions as government officials under sympathetic princes (e.g., Lessing as a court librarian, Herder as superintendent of Lutheran clergy, Goethe as court counselor).

This is not to say that academic positions did not exist. But they were low-paying, low-prestige, and generally trammeled by pressures for religious orthodoxy. In Scotland, where the universities were an exception to the low condition elsewhere, intellectual life was more flourishing, but even there what took place in the chairs of philosophy tended to be pulled toward the magnet of the secular subjects found outside in the political world, while the more religiously orthodox (Reid, Beattie, Campbell, all connected to the clerical stronghold at Aberdeen) fought back philosophical innovations in the name of traditional religion and common sense. In the German universities, followers of Leibniz such as Wolff and Baumgarten wriggled between medieval scholasticism and the attacks of Pietists; their career troubles underlined the motivation of younger German intellectuals to seek their fortunes in modern bases of support outside the universities. In France, the Sorbonne was the bastion of theological orthodoxy, while provincial universities were mere shells with few students, places to purchase quick degrees on the cheap (Ariès, 1962: 201; Verger, 1986).

If there was an alternative to the patronage system during the 1700s, it would have appeared to contemporaries as the market for books and magazines. There was a rapid expansion of the publishing market in Germany during the 1770s, and the *Sturm und Drang* period of literature constituted a sensationalized advertising that went along with the outbreak of this middle-class market. By 1770, titles in German came to number twice those in Latin, reversing the situation of the previous century; secular literature for the first time outstripped religious publications. In France, the greatest publishing enterprise up to its time was the *Encyclopedia* (1745–1772); multiple volumes employed a staff of hundreds, and the circle of writers gathered around it was the catalyst of creativity for virtually everyone of importance in Rousseau's generation. It took some time for the patronage and the publishing systems to become distinct. Early in the century, the main intellectual circles in England were grouped around the Whigs and the Tories. These groups published periodicals and sponsored books. Political connections remained crucial because advance subscriptions from the wealthy were a key to a writer's fortune, and a political appointment would usually reward a writer who did honor, and ideological service, to his political faction.[17]

The publishing market did not encourage intellectuals to pursue autonomous concerns on a high level of abstraction; the attraction was toward partisan polemic, literary style, and topical public issues. The anti-metaphysical and in general anti-philosophical tone which characterized the writings from these secular bases of intellectual production was a result. Antagonism to traditional philosophy was enhanced by the struggle over religion. Secular intellectuals, having found bases free from dependence on the church, criticized the theologians and biblical scholars of the old religious establishment, and tarred metaphysics with the same brush. Abstract philosophy became emblematic of the old church-dominated intellectual base and ideological target of attack from the new intellectual base. Secular bases, close to lay audiences or lay patrons, brought about a de-differentiation of the intellectual role; the philosopher (or specialist in abstract ideas) now tended also to become the writer of literary entertainments and the political partisan. In contrast, the specialized role of philosopher within the medieval university had been to take charge of a technical portion of the curriculum. Because of the institutional change toward the popular literary market in combination with lay patronage, during this period one finds the predominance of the literary intellectual.[18]

Revolt of the Philosophical Faculty

The academic revolution pioneered in Germany marked a revival and reform of the medieval organization of higher education. The medieval university was a stronghold of the church, training priests and theologians; it also combined, in lesser or greater degree in various places, with guilds monopolizing the teaching of law and medicine, under the legitimation and control of the church. Given that after 1700 the church had lost its monopoly on the production of culture, what significance was there in reviving the university? To understand the question, it is desirable for us as modern intellectuals, and hence products of universities, to divest ourselves of hindsight which makes us take for granted the inevitability of this institution.

In the 1700s the university was nearly abolished. The ideological tone, especially among self-consciously progressive intellectuals, was to regard universities as outdated and intellectually retrograde.[19] Leibniz in 1700 had proposed that universities be replaced by government-regulated professional schools, with academies taking over the preservation and extension of science and high culture. The same proposal was made by the Prussian reform minister von Massow in 1806. This is in fact what the French had done in 1793, replacing universities with a system of academies together with government *écoles* for engineers, teachers, and other specialists.

To abolish the university would not have meant abolishing education. What significance, if any, could there have been to preserving the organization whose main distinction was that it was traditionally under church control? The 1700s were a period of expansion in secondary schools: in Germany, *Gymnasia* for classical subjects, *Ritterakademie* for aristocratic manners; in France, the Jesuit colleges which spread widely to serve the middle classes or even lower; in England, the elite Public Schools. Here again we must guard against anachronism. Today we take it for granted that there is a sequence, that one attends secondary school in order to prepare for the university. Before the German university reform, however, these two types of schooling were alternatives or rivals (and in fact the age range of the students tended to be similar in each; Ariès, 1962: 219–229). The "secondary" schools taught a largely secularized curriculum, appealing to the cultural aspirations of its clientele. This made them much more popular than the universities, whose curricula and credentialing sequence had been built up during the Middle Ages in connection with theology and careers in the church.

In Germany, the growing sense of crisis in the late 1700s was based on a career problem for university graduates. The church, deprived of its property in the Reformation, was no longer a lucrative career. Parsons had low status and pay, and served as minor functionaries of the state, keeping local records and reading decrees from the pulpit. Theology and its preparatory subject, philosophy, attracted mainly sons of peasants, petty shopkeepers, and clergy. The upper part of the middle class, the sons of urban patricians, the wealthier merchants, and the civil servants, studied law, a much more costly course of study. Although the number of nobles in the legal faculties was quite low, the group as a whole adopted a belligerently knightly style of behavior, emphasizing drinking and carousing, centered on dueling fraternities, which offended both the moralists and the modernists in the larger population.

At the same time, there was a structural attraction based on the new involvement of the bureaucratic state in education (Rosenberg, 1958; Mueller, 1983). Enrollments in the leading universities rose after 1740, fueled by prospects of government employment at several levels. The bureaucratic administration of the numerous absolutist states of Germany, both large and small, was expanding; in the late 1700s the proportion of officials to population was twice as high as it would be 100 years later. Educational requirements became increasingly important for these posts; in Hanover (where Göttingen was located), the proportion of government appointees who had some university education rose from 33 percent to 75 percent during the 1700s. At a lower level, new employment possibilities were held out by the establishment of compulsory state-supported elementary schools, first by a Prussian decree of 1717, which was largely unenforced, then by a stronger decree in 1763, which specified schools teaching in the German language rather than the old medieval Latin schools run by the church.

The numbers of university students increased sharply by the 1770s but unevenly, provoking equally rapid declines in some places. Competition in the expanding educational market produced both winners and losers. A population of the educated underemployed accumulated, building a sense of alienation and status hunger which resonated with *Sturm und Drang*. The venerable University of Cologne, one of the biggest in the early 1700s, had lost half its students by the late 1770s; Jena dropped from 1,500 to 400. With the political crisis of the 1790s, the university crisis came to a head. Numbers fell to tiny levels: Königsberg in 1791 (the height of Kant's fame) had only 47 students; Erfurt in 1800 had only 43; Kiel in one year had 8. Jena, despite its intellectual eminence, was closed for a time after the nearby battle in 1806. During the crisis period of the Napoleonic wars and their aftermath (1792–1818), 22 of the 42 German universities were abolished. The traditionalistic Catholic universities, about one third of the total, were hit particularly hard; only one survived. In the early 1700s there had been about 9,000 students in the 28 universities then existing; in the 1790s, with more universities competing, the total was down to 6,000 (Schelsky, 1963: 22–23; McClelland, 1980: 28, 63–64). Among "progressive" officials and thinkers, the opinion was widespread that the entire system should be abolished.

It would have been feasible, as well as culturally fashionable, to abolish the old religious universities entirely and replace then with a new system of "high schools" for general cultural status, together with professional schools for more specialized training. This did not occur, because an intellectual movement, led by the status-squeezed aspirants of the philosophical faculty, revived the prestige of the university as the center of creative thought; and that movement, in turn, succeeded because it played on a structural trend under way in the organization of the German educational system. Prussia had already pioneered in state-mandated elementary schooling; bureaucratic centralization also was moving toward formalizing credential requirements and hierarchizing the competing segments of the older educational system. In 1770 an examination was established for employment in the Prussian bureaucracy, placing a premium on university legal training. Nobles, however, were exempted at first, and university degrees were not absolutely essential. In 1804 this regulation was strengthened to require three years of study at a Prussian university for all higher offices. With the foundation of the University of Berlin in 1810 and an accompanying series of official examinations, university legal study became a rigorous requirement for government employment. Prussia thus became the first society in the West to establish anything like the Chinese imperial examination system.

Together with another Prussian reform initiated in 1788, and strengthened by 1810–1812, these regulations linked the entire educational system into a credentialing sequence (Mueller, 1987: 18, 24–26). In an effort to limit the number of university students, the government established the *Abitur* examination for admission to the universities. This put a premium on study at a classical *Gymnasium*, prior to this point more of an alternative to university education than a preparation for it. For instance, in 1800 the director of the Berlin *Gymnasium* had proposed that the universities be abolished in favor of his institution. Now it became part of the state-controlled sequence, but at a preliminary level; conversely, after 1812–1820, to teach in a secondary school which prepared students for the university one needed a university degree. The result of this formalization was simultaneously to cut the numbers of applicants, especially the unemployed intellectuals, while improving the prospects for wealthier students. The university became locked into the apex of the credentialing sequence that, since the worldwide spread of the German model, we have come to take for granted.

Is it not arbitrary which organizational form won out? If no university reform had taken place, there would still have been general cultural education, professional training, plus places where specialized scientists and scholars would pursue their work. What contribution if any does the preservation of the medieval university structure make to the role of modern intellectuals and to the content of their work? The key is that the medieval university had acquired a good deal of autonomy from lay society to create its own topics and methods of argument. It was the medieval university as a self-governing corporation which created the scholastic hierarchies and competitions manifested in the style and content of the academic disciplines. The medieval university was responsible for the field of philosophy as an abstract discipline, conscious of the methods and contents which make up the various regions of the intellectual field. It was the university structure, shaped by generations of turf battles over the space for intellectual debate in the preliminaries to theology and law, that crystallized the self-conscious enterprises of logic, metaphysics, and epistemology. Without the university structure, the role of the general-purpose intellectual—that is, the philosopher—de-differentiates back into the lay conception of culture. The level of abstraction and of self-reflection is lost; instead one has the literary or political intellectual, engaging sometimes in a rapid play of ideas, but deterred by the lay audience from exploring anything in depth. The development of philosophy in a technical sense depended on the survival of the university.

The university reform revived another strength of the medieval system at its height: its structural impetus to creativity. The German university revolution created the modern research university, where professors were expected not only to teach the best knowledge of the past but also to create new knowledge. This impetus toward innovation came from the structure of competition institutionalized within the medieval university: the public disputation; the dissertation and its defense, which made one a full-fledged academic professional; the competition with other professors and other universities to attract students.

It was these competitive, innovation-provoking structures which the university's Enlightenment rivals lacked. The eighteenth-century college or *Gymnasium* taught a finished culture to students who were not expected to go on to become autonomous producers in their own right; in the same way the professional school was in the business of transmitting a finished body of information to lay audiences who would then apply it. Only the academies of scientists or artists were expected to create new works. But in fact the centralized structure of collective patronage did not stimulate creativity very well; particularly in France, the great academies tended to be places for display of honors, for ceremonialism and rather traditionalistic standards as to contents (Heilbron, 1994). The centralized patronage system, lacking the internal autonomy and ongoing competitiveness of the university faculties, tended to degenerate into awards for the socially eminent and bastions of the intellectually conservative.

The key battle, fought out in Germany from the 1780s to the early 1800s, was to reform the position of the philosophical faculty within the university. Traditionally it had constituted the preliminary or undergraduate training for the higher faculties of theology, law, and medicine, and its teachers occupied a correspondingly lower level of pay and prestige. The reform made the philosophical faculty into a full-fledged higher faculty, claiming to teach the most advanced subjects, and with autonomy from the restrictions formerly imposed by the theologians.[20] This meant that the exercise of reason by its own lights was to be free of the guidance of doctrine and orthodoxy. A similar battle had been fought out in the medieval universities, and a good deal of creative energy went into maneuvering between the rival claims of reason and faith. The edict of 1277, which had enforced the superiority of theology and legislated against the encroachments of the philosophers, had beaten back a revolt of the philosophy teachers (i.e., the arts faculty) which was heading in the direction later consummated by the German university revolution. A little more than 500 years later, the arts faculty triumphed.

With the success of the university revolution, the university gradually asserted its superiority over the alternative bases of research and innovation. Scientific research, carried out by wealthy amateurs or under the support of patrons, was upstaged as soon as universities underwent sufficient internal differentiation to provide bases for the scientific specialties.[21] In philosophy, which is our central concern here, the university-based competitive structures quickly established a level of sophisticated conceptualization that dominated the attention space over the cruder argumentation of lay-oriented intellectuals. Since the German academic revolution, virtually all notable philosophers have been professors. The generalization is a loose one; a more precise way to say it is that within each national culture, as soon as it underwent a German-style university revolution, the academic philosophers took over the center of attention from philosophers outside the university.[22]

In England, the universities did not undergo the reform until 1872. Prior to that time dons had to be clerics, and higher research topics were subordinated to an undergraduate-oriented instruction in the classics. Independently creative philosophers in England thus preserved something like the Enlightenment style much longer than in Germany. The Utilitarians (at their height from 1810 to 1830) were amateurs, connected to law practice or business. Their successors at midcentury, mediated by John Stuart Mill (a typical amateur polymath, based at the East India Company), were the evolutionist circle around Huxley and Spencer. These two interconnected circles controlled the main centers of the now greatly expanded publishing industry; they edited the new political-literary journals such as *Westminster Review* and *The Economist* as well as the *Encyclopedia Britannica*. Spencer made a fortune by publishing in effect an encyclopedia of his own. Others of the period were the wealthy amateur Buckle, famous for his materialist determinism, and Carlyle, successful as a flamboyant and sentimentalist popular writer. We see here a continuation of the anti-metaphysical, militantly secularist themes of the lay thinkers of the previous century.

In the United States, the university reform was begun in the late 1870s and 1880s by sojourners importing the model from Germany. Prior to this, notable philosophy was amateur: the New England Transcendentalists in the 1830s and 1840s and a Hegelian circle at St. Louis in the 1860s and 1870s. In this case philosophy was not anti-religious, and in its content it even constituted an offshoot of the German philosophies, but it had the mark of amateur thinkers nevertheless. The major Transcendentalists were literary-philosophical hybrids, poet-essayists like Emerson and Thoreau; their methods were far from the critical and dialectical techniques of the Germans, instead extolling a popularized aesthetic nature-religiosity.[23]

If amateur philosophy remained intellectually non-differentiated and non-technical, wherever the university revolution occurred there was an upsurge of technical, metaphysically oriented philosophy. After the initial wave, usually in Idealist form, there were further developments; but now philosophy was distinctively academic, technically rigorous, and remote from the popularistic appeals of the lay-based philosophers whom it displaced.

The terrain of philosophy is that of the all-purpose intellectual, concerned with questions of widest interest; thus the role of "philosopher" will exist whether there is an academic position by this name or not. The non-academic philosopher, however, does not construe the realm of foundational issues as a distinctive ontological field, but tends to concretize it; metaphysics is replaced by the substantive contents of some other discipline—science, literature, social theory, reasoned political ideology. Marx, moving from his youthful academic career to political journalism and agitation, took a predictable path in transforming Hegelian philosophy into political economy. When Marx felt that he was turning Hegel's system from its head to its feet, he was passing through the reversal of perspectives typical of the division between the autonomy of academic philosophy and the lay orientation of non-academic intellectuals. The same thing had happened a century earlier, when Adam Smith wrote on moral sentiments while he held the chair of moral philosophy at Glasgow, but switched to popular concerns of economics when he moved into Continental circles as companion to a duke.[24]

Academicization promotes technical philosophy; but why should it come about by way of Idealism, against the grain of virtually every progressive intellectual for generations? German Idealism was one of the greatest efflorescences of Idealist thinking in all of world history. Moreover, in contrast to the Idealisms of India or of Greek Neoplatonism, or even the reactionary Idealism of Berkeley, which tends to treat the material world as an illusion, German Idealism claimed to be able to derive the laws governing the empirical world, scientific and historical alike, from the principles revealed in the Absolute. This Idealism was not world-escaping but world-dominating; it made as ambitious a claim to intellectual power as anything ever proposed.

The key to the puzzle is that Idealism was the ideology of the university revolution. In support of this premise are four kinds of evidence: (1) the major German Idealists were among the prime movers of university reform; (2) the contents of the Idealist philosophies justified the reform, and the succession of major Idealist positions closely corresponded to contemporary prospects of the reform movement; (3) the French Revolution, as surrounding context, produced an Idealist ideology of spiritual freedom only in Germany, where it meshed with the interests of the university reformers, whereas by contrast in England and France the chief ideologies of the revolutionary period were neither Idealist nor university-oriented; and (4) whenever the German university reform was adopted elsewhere, a generation of Idealist philosophers appeared, often in indigenous form.

Idealists as University Reformers

The creators of German Idealism were the leaders in the movement to reform the university. Kant would have preferred for science to become the dominant subject, but the university structure forced upon him an indirect path of reform. The low-status philosophical faculty had the largest number of positions; and within this faculty the most available chairs were in philosophy proper, the fewest in natural science. Leipzig, the biggest university of the time, had 12 chairs in the philosophical faculty (as opposed to 4 in theology, 8 in law, and 6 in medicine), of which 5 were in branches of philosophy and only 1 in a science (mathematics); the remaining 6 were in humanistic subjects (Helbig, 1961: 62). Kant's path was to upgrade philosophy as leader of the sciences while simultaneously capturing the territory now occupied by theology. In proposing a Copernican revolution in philosophy, he explicitly identified philosophy with the methods of the sciences, whose advance Kant argued took place through intensified, systematic investigation rather than random observation, through theory rather than raw empiricism. Metaphysics was to be restored to its "royal place among all the sciences" (Kant [1781] 1966: A.vii), for it alone could answer Hume's skepticism and demonstrate how scientific knowledge is possible. At the same time, religion—and even law—could survive in this secular age only with the support of philosophical reason.[25] In 1798, in his last published work, *Der Streit der Fakultäten,* Kant would go to on argue that philosophy has the task of establishing the limits and character of knowledge in all other disciplines; it should judge the claims of theology, and not vice versa.[26] For good measure, he threw in the claim of philosophy over the scope of law and medicine as well.

Fichte, who widened the claims of Idealism beyond Kant's critical method, was similarly aggressive in agitating for university reform. Simultaneously with the announcement of his metaphysical system, in 1794 Fichte's *Lectures on the Scholar's Vocation* argued for the negation of selfish and material interests and called on pure intellectuals as the saviors of the country. At Jena, Fichte created a storm by attempting to abolish the student dueling fraternities, emblems of the aristocracy-emulating, carousing style of the old universities, dominated by the legal faculty. Other Idealists joined in; Schelling (in his 1802–3 *Lectures on the Method of University Study*) and Schleiermacher wrote and agitated for intellectual freedom and university reform. Hegel, concerned with educational reform since the 1790s, put his plans into action during his Berlin period (Dickey, 1993: 306, 337; Harris, 1972: 1–47).

In 1807 Fichte proposed a plan for reorganizing the universities. They would contain no vocational, professional training—exactly the opposite of the Enlightenment model of educational reform—but would offer general education through philosophy, which would awaken understanding of the interrelatedness of knowledge. Fichte himself would hold a seminar for professors to tell them how to teach. Philosophy was to be a free inquiry and a critique of all other forms of knowledge (echoing Kant's critiques). Fichte's new university would educate the elite of the entire nation. In his 1808 *Addresses to the German Nation,* delivered at patriotic meetings in Berlin under French occupation, Fichte proposed that Germany would reattain greatness not through military but through spiritual might. He proposed to overcome disadvantages of poverty by setting up a system of public schools, operated as economic cooperative communities, enrolling youths of all social classes. At the university the needy would be supported at state expense. Germany would become like Plato's Republic, built around educational leadership. The university degree would give its holders claim to the most important positions in the state, replacing the old hereditary aristocracy.

It was Fichte's program, stripped of its utopian politics, that Wilhelm von

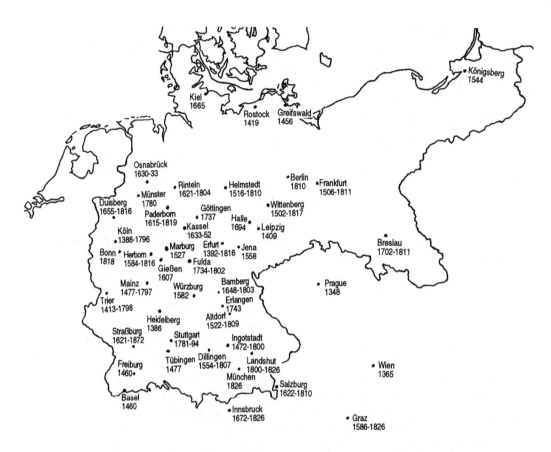

GERMAN UNIVERSITIES, 1348–1900
(Boundaries are those of German Empire in 1872;
dates are university foundations and closings)

Humboldt, one of Fichte's audience in 1808, put into effect. The University of Berlin was made a privileged corporation with self-government; professors were given the right to choose their own subjects, without restrictions of a standard syllabus. The philosophical faculty received full equality in status and pay with the other faculties, and could now award advanced degrees. Fichte was appointed first rector. After Fichte's death, the leading Idealist theologian, Schleiermacher, took over as rector, and Hegel was brought to Berlin as Fichte's successor in philosophy.

This is not to say that the University of Berlin bore the brunt of reform alone. Göttingen, founded in 1737, had already pioneered in the reorientation toward creative research. Both Wilhelm and Alexander von Humboldt were graduates of Göttingen (as were the Schlegel brothers), and it was in part the Göttingen ideal that was expanded at Berlin and subsequently emulated by the other universities of the German states (Turner, 1974; Leventhal, 1986). Nevertheless, there was a special connection between the Idealists and the sweeping university reform. Göttingen replaced the Latin and Greek classics of the medieval curriculum with lectures in German, and downplayed the theological faculty in favor of modern literature; Göttingen was known especially for its pioneering research in philology. The Idealists, in contrast, resuscitated the core medieval tradition of philosophy, and developed all the rational sciences (including rational theology) within its orbit. Göttingen was too close to the Enlightenment culture to produce this kind of revival; it was a center for literary criticism and popular literary publications, oriented more toward a lay audience than toward the academic world (Turner, 1974). Göttingen, as a sole model, would likely have furthered the Enlightenment trend toward the disappearance of academic culture and its absorption into the lay world.[27]

The point is not that Idealism alone brought about the university reform, but rather that the strains of the old university system—above all the plight of young aspirants in theology and hence in its traditional feeder discipline, philosophy—motivated Idealism. Jena and Königsberg, where the Idealist movement began, were not particularly distinguished universities. By the same token, they were traditionalist places (as of course was the Tübingen theological *Stift,* so central in the Idealist recruitment), where an effort to expand career opportunities for philosophy students was eagerly awaited. Kant, Herder, Fichte, Schelling, Hegel, and Hölderlin were mostly men from modest social backgrounds, who owed their chances to the expanding public school system.[28] They all had in common the career experience of starting as a tutor in a private household—Kant for nine years, Fichte for ten, Hegel for seven—while waiting for an academic post to open up. Kant waited until age 46 before getting a professorship, and so did Hegel, while Hölderlin never did find an academic post.[29] Such individuals were often attracted to the popular Enlightenment topics such as science or aesthetics; but such posts in the academic world were less available than the established positions in philosophy, and those in turn paid less than the high faculties of theology, law, and medicine. Kant was archetypal in finding that he could not afford a career in science, and thus gravitating toward the soft spot of philosophy on the theology track.

The path of men such as Kant and Fichte, although arduous, was nevertheless a hopeful one, for it followed a track of educational expansion and reform that had been in place since the 1730s. It was these very reforms which had widened the recruitment base and brought about a surplus of aspirants for positions. If this generated a hunger for further reform, it was connected to an expectation that the situation could improve if previous governmental policies were extended or more fully implemented. When Kant proposed to make the philosophical faculty arbiter of the other disciplines, he was carrying out a line which made academic careers in themselves superior to careers within the church; it simultaneously raised the power and prestige of those who practiced academic science, and elevated their salaries to equal those of the other higher faculties. When Fichte envisioned university philosophers as a new species of philosopher-king, he was putting in the most flamboyant form the tendency for academic degree holders to monopolize entry into government administration. The basis for these arguments had to be worked out in the concepts of philosophical discourse; but the motivation for creating these concepts came from the realistic assessment that the structure was moving in a direction favorable to a self-governing academic elite. When other German states emulated the Prussian model after 1810, there were no more university failures, and enrollments rose fairly steadily.[30] The entire system went into a period of controlled expansion that lasted into the 1900s.

Idealism as Ideology of the University Revolution

The contents of Idealism supported the claim of intellectual autonomy and dominance by the philosophical faculty. The initial phase of Kant's critical philosophy destroyed the claims of theology to know ultimate reality. It is impossible to know the thing-in-itself, and any such claims lead to inescapable antinomies. There is no justification for religion except that which is provided by transcendental critique demonstrating the necessity of moral and teleological categories of thinking. Kant's critical philosophy also demonstrates that no field can know the validity and limits of its own claims of knowledge until they have been examined by the transcendental methods of philosophy. Kant's revolution simultaneously downgraded theology and raised philosophy to arbiter of all knowledge. Kant did not cut off the validity of any phenomenal field of inquiry so long as its practitioners stuck to their delimited sphere. He encouraged empirical research as well as philosophical investigations to reveal how laws of specific fields are related to the transcendental categories.

Kant's argumentation was a precipitate of conflicts within the networks surrounding his career. Prominent was a three-way conflict among Pietists, Wolffians, and the Berlin Academy. Since the beginning of the century, Wolffian rationalists had made Leibniz's position the dominant philosophy in German universities. The splits typical of intellectual life followed. A lineage of Pietists and Thomasians, rival academics from the same Leipzig connections which had produced Leibniz, accused the Wolffians of determinism and atheism. Wolff and his follower Bilfinger were expelled from Halle in 1723 under the attack of Budde, Rudiger, and Francke. In 1740, with the accession of Frederick the Great, the Wolffians were allowed to return; this led to a second round of attacks, especially by Crusius, theology professor at Leipzig, the most prominent German university, and safely outside Prussian jurisdiction. Wolffian philosophy also came under pressure on a second front. The Berlin Academy, though originally founded by Leibniz, gradually fell under the influence of Newtonians, especially Maupertuis (at Berlin, 1744–1756) and Lambert (1764–1777). The scientific prestige of the academy rose to world class with the presence of Euler (1741–1765), the leading mathematician of his time, and Lambert, who introduced hyperbolic functions into geometry and proved that pi is an irrational number. This put a good deal of pressure on the Wolffians, who generally taught university mathematics along with natural and moral philosophy, to remain scientifically up-to-date.

Kant was at the intersection of all three factions. His upbringing was Pietist, and he continued that sect's antagonism to metaphysics and preference for moralistic rather than theological religion. His academic contacts and sympathies were Wolffian; his teacher at Königsberg, Knutzen, was a Wolffian in a Pietist university, an *Extraordinarius* for 23 years who was never made an *Ordinarius*. Throughout his career Kant taught from the Wolffian textbook of Baumgarten, which provided much of the formal framework of the *Critique of Pure Reason*. For Kant, Wolffian rationalism was a bulwark against Pietist nature philosophy, which the followers of Thomasius propagated as a world full of occult spiritual forces, unamenable to mathematics. One might have thought that Kant would take the purely scientific route, made prestigeful by the Berlin Academy; and indeed Kant in his early years was a Newtonian, and an eager participant in Berlin prize contests. His 1755 cosmogenic theory is based on Newtonian principles of gravitational attraction, in a vein similar to the work of Lambert. Kant's career opportunities in the university were constrained by the necessity to be an all-around teacher of the subjects within the philosophical faculty, of which mathematics and natural science were less significant than philosophy, and the best-rewarded route was into theology. Kant taught all these subjects, and as his prospects for a chair grew, he concentrated increasingly on putting them into the framework of philosophy.

The ingredients of Kant's critical philosophy existed in these networks before Kant pulled them into a distinctive combination. Leibniz had already held that space and time are ideal rather than externally existent, mere aspects of the order of monads (as indeed an abstract mathematician might see it). The issue remained salient in the debate with the Newtonians, who held the absolute existence of space. By 1770 Kant was expressing the Leibniz-Wolff doctrine in the version that space and time are a priori categories of sensibility.[31] Kant was not yet ready to say the same thing about causality, which was central both to Leibnizian philosophy (the principle of sufficient reason) and to empirical science. Nevertheless, the discussions of Bilfinger, Baumgarten, and on the other side the Newtonians and Pietists raised the issue of just how causality might operate. For the Wolffians, the monads are windowless, causally unable to affect one another; the observed laws of the physical universe must be due to preestablished harmony. This view was disliked by the Newtonians; but their doctrine of a direct external influence, especially the action-at-a-distance of gravitational force, appeared philosophically naive. A third solution, Malebranchean occasionalism—the mediation of God—was too close to the Pietist occultism that threatened university scientists on their home turf. These disputes convinced Kant that there are limits to understanding causal connections among objects themselves. This material became the basis for the antinomies of reason in the first *Critique*.

The first turning point for Kant took place around 1765. The issue had been provoked by the Berlin Academy, which had proposed the prize question whether the principles of metaphysics and theology may be demonstrated with the certainty of geometry. This was in effect Newtonian mathematical science thumbing its nose at both Wolffians and Pietists, and the prize contest attracted the major thinkers in Germany. Mendelssohn won with an anti-metaphysical, anti-religious argument, Kant taking second place. Kant was suddenly overwhelmed with skepticism. In his 1766 *Dreams of a Spirit-Seer* he rejected not only Pietist occultism but rational metaphysics as well, on the grounds that there is no knowledge beyond sensory experience. Crusius in the 1750s had already made this claim in order to deny the validity of Wolffian metaphysics. Empiricist skepticism was further bolstered by Hume, whose arguments had been introduced to Kant already in 1759 by Hamann (Beiser, 1992: 54), no doubt in support of the same debate of sentimentalists against mere reason. Now Kant turned Crusius's arguments back against the Pietists.

A second turning point came soon after Kant finally won his philosophy chair in 1770. Still struggling to save some power of reason to give knowledge of the causal interaction of things-in-themselves, in his inaugural dissertation Kant posited two faculties of knowledge, sensibility and reason, with substance and causality inhering in the latter, beyond the sensory screen of space and time. Again the Berlin connection raised difficulties. Lambert, Kant's correspondent since both had participated in the prize contest of 1764, pointed out that if there are two such distinct faculties as sensibility and reason, how can they ever cooperate? This raised in epistemological form the classic deep trouble of how distinct substances could interact—in this case subjective mind and external object. Since Kant rejected preestablished harmony, Platonic intuition of essences, and other access to occult qualities, he was forced to find a new path.

In 1770–1772 Kant put the final ingredient in place: the distinction between synthetic and analytic a priori. Here too was a background, including Leibniz's alignment of physical relationships among monads with logical relations of subject and predicate, and more recently the questions of the nature of mathematical knowledge stirred up by the 1764 Berlin prize question. Lambert's entry had discussed what analysis meant in mathematics and attempted a reform of Wolffian logic. Kant now took a new tack. Since Euclid, mathematics had been regarded as an a priori science, independent of experience, and the prototype of certainty. In the view of Lambert and others, a priori necessity is manifested only in the analytical method, which investigates the implications contained in its definitions and axioms (Coffa, 1991: 9–16). Such knowledge is tautological. This was unacceptable to Kant, a practicing scientist rather than a pure mathematician, who wanted mathematical laws to express real relations discovered by empirical research. Kant decided that mathematics must be synthetic rather than analytical, that is, providing knowledge which is non-tautological, ampliative judgements (*Erweiterungsurteile,* in contrast to analytical judgments, which are merely clarificatory, *Erläuterungsurteile*). Judgments which are synthetic a priori are both certain and informative, going beyond mere knowledge of concepts. Since mathematical knowledge exists, there are no doubt such things as synthetic a priori judgments; by extension, this should prove the secure foundation for scientific laws.

Kant regarded his discovery of the synthetic a priori as "the first step" in his critical philosophy (Coffa, 1991: 15). In 1772 Kant announced to friends that he was on the path to a new philosophy, although it took another nine years to work out a final draft. The ultimate step was to move causality and substance into the sphere of the a priori, along with space and time. This could be done if all were now regarded as categories of the understanding, imposed on experience, and through which all experience is filtered. But if the categories of causality and of time-space relationships, measurable by mathematics and describable in geometry, are a priori necessary in all experience, their a prioriness does not prevent them from revealing knowledge which goes beyond mere subjectivity, and beyond the tautological implications of concepts.

Kant now had a critical tool capable of cutting off theological and spiritualist speculation. At the same time, he believed that it validated not only science but also the rightful activity of philosophy as the perfection of scientific research from the theoretical side. Early in his career Kant had proposed the nebular hypothesis of the origins of the planetary orbits by deduction from Newtonian laws. Later, in the midst of his great *Critiques,* Kant went back to attempting to ground all scientific principles in the categories of time and space by way of intermediary concepts such as impenetrability and weight.[32] Philosophy meets empirical science halfway; the principles discovered by science, although not dictated by philosophy, were to be progressively generalized and mathematized until they meshed with instantiations of the highest philosophical categories. In the end, Kant found a way to continue the project of rationalist philosophers begun by Descartes and extended by Spinoza, Leibniz, and Woolf: to derive the principles of science from pure reason, at the same time guaranteeing their autonomous empirical reality. What was different was that Kant required this rationalism to pass under the authority of a new master discipline, critical epistemology.

Reinhold's *Letters* in 1786–87 made Kant famous by portraying the critical philosophy as a middle ground between theology and reason, that is to say, between Jacobi's fideism on one side and Mendelssohn's Deism or Spinoza's pantheism on the other (Di Giovanni, 1992: 427–429). Again the academic theologians were looking for help. Reinhold was a former Catholic teacher who had converted to Protestantism after the Jesuits were suppressed in 1773; he now saw alliance with the new philosophy as offering ammunition for theologians against both Deists and Pietists. The new opening, uniting philosophical and theological turf, quickly appealed to theology students such as Fichte, Schelling, and Hegel. Fichte was the first to see that Jacobi could be used as a stepping stone, and his writings often expressed admiration for Jacobi for pointing the way.

Schultze's *Anesidemus* of 1792, pressing the Humean skepticism pioneered by Jacobi, had charged Kant with being unable to show why the unknowable thing-in-itself exists, nor why there should be a sensory manifold at all. Even the categories of the understanding are not deduced but arbitrarily given. Like all creative thinkers, Fichte seized on unsolved puzzles as a valuable possession, a territory on which to make his own mark. Kant had given the tools, which Fichte now explicitly flourished: the transcendental method of searching for necessary presuppositions, and the synthetic a priori.[33]

The search for presuppositional grounding Fichte ([1794–1997] 1982: 95–96) illustrated as follows: Take any true judgment, such as the undeniable principle of identity, A = A. To say that it is true implies that it is permanently true; and this requires that there be a permanent subject or self for whom it is true. Fichte's Cartesian starting point is logic, not the self, but it demonstrates immediately the existence of the self, and in a far stronger version than Descartes's existent ego.

Let us posit also what seems undeniable, the existence of a difference. Not-A implies that A is also posited. Not-A = not-A implies an A opposed to not-A (Fichte, [1794–1997] 1982: 103–104). And by the previous argument, the grounding of oppositions must be the self. Any not-self implies also the self.

Now Fichte brings in Kant's other tool. The synthetic a priori guarantees that such deductions not merely are logical tautologies but have ontological consequences as well. Kant had noted that concepts linked together by the synthetic a priori, since they are not contained merely conceptually in one another, must be recognizable by a form of pure intuition or non-empirical perception (Coffa, 1991: 17–19). Fichte widens the implications of pure intuition into a full-fledged Idealism. He works both synthetic and analytical a priori into a combined system. For Kant, analytical judgments are based on the principle of contradiction, which, as Fichte notes, means that something cannot be A and not-A at the same time (Fichte, [1794–1997] 1982: 121, 111–112). Fichte widens the analytical method: it consists in seeking aspects in which things are opposed, which he now labels *antithesis,* making analysis more dialectical than it was in Kant. *Synthesis* is the discovery in opposites of the aspect in which they are alike. Thus both analysis (antithesis) and synthesis, or analytical and synthetic a priori, imply each other. Fichte emphasizes the radical consequences. There are no purely analytic judgments (a point echoed five generations later by Quine in a logical positivist context which had completely disowned Idealism). Bringing this line of argument together with Fichte's points just outlined, we find that all valid synthesis is based on or contained in the synthesis of self and not-self.

Here we have the formula thesis-antithesis-synthesis later used as a scholastic formula by Hegel's followers. For Fichte, it is purely a set of mutual implications, not a sequence which develops in time. (Obviously for a Kantian, time is merely a category of sensory understanding.) Fichte draws out the implications of Kant's synthetic a priori. Where Kant argues that $7 + 5 = 12$ is not analytic, that the concept 12 is not contained in the concept 7, Fichte recognizes that the truths of arithmetic are tied together as parts of a larger conceptual scheme. Fichte goes beyond Kant in showing how profoundly relational the world is. It is this method, rather than any mechanical dialectic, that Fichte makes available to other philosophers, the weapon by which so much territory was suddenly opened for conquest.

Fichte does not reject ordinary logic; the principle of contradiction is one of the devices by which he develops his own system.[34] Fichte solves contradictions by progressively redefining terms which turn out to be contradictory. The systematic interrelation of concepts, and their contradictory nature when seen from a one-sided viewpoint, is a discovery along the pathway laid out by the Kantian search for necessary presuppositions of one's initial judgments.

The process leads to an underlying, necessarily presupposed ground. Fichte declares that he has met Jacobi's challenge, demonstrating that there is something beyond reason, unconditioned by anything else, at the starting point. This identification with the ultimate in Jacobi's fideism enables Fichte to capture religion as having been deduced from philosophy. The move makes Idealism not merely a limiter of the claims of religion, as it had been for Kant, but a potential conqueror of religious turf.

Fichte's absolute self cannot be said to exist in the ordinary sense, for it is the grounding of existence. Only by rhetoric can it be called a self. It is discoverable through one's limitable, empirical self; but it is more like the Advaita self-luminous consciousness within which everything is manifested. Nevertheless, Fichte tended increasingly to humanize this self because it coincided with a key human quality: freedom.[35]

Fichte, Schelling, Hegel, and their philosophical compatriots were in the midst of the university revolution, successfully expanding the turf of philosophers' careers; they were, for the first time in history, intellectuals taking control of their own base. What they were celebrating above all was their intellectual freedom. With the characteristic enthusiasm of academics conflating their intellectual conquests with the topics that they are studying, they made this spirit of freedom into the ground for the universe.

Fichte's *Wissenschaftslehre* is one of the most astounding performances in the world history of philosophy. Neither previous Idealism nor any other position had attempted to deduce why the world exists. Religious idealists had vacillated between describing the material world as an illusion (as in Shankara or Berkeley), thereby making its existence a pseudo-problem, or arbitrarily positing (in the fashion of Plotinus and Ramanuja) that the Highest emanates the lower out of its own fullness or play. Nagarjuna's dialectic had come close to Fichte in denying any ultimate difference between nirvana and samsara; but the Buddhists had made no effort to try to derive the world from basic principles. Fichte's uniqueness was not to denigrate the natural world but to build it up from philosophical primaries. Fichte is no anti-scientist; he sounds like his contemporary Laplace when he argues that since every part of the universe is bound up with the whole, it should be possible "by means of thought alone, to discover all possible conditions of the universe, both past and future" (Fichte, [1800] 1965: 7).

In a more limited sense, Kant had envisioned philosophy as a scientific discipline, complementing the empirical sciences by deductions from the theoretical side. Fichte and his followers sensed a larger vacuum in intellectual space, which was simultaneously an opening in the organizational space of the university. Fichte soon became too busy with his proselytizing role, while others marked out the fields for conquest: for Schelling, *Naturphilosophie,* aesthetics, comparative mythology, and religion; for Hegel, history, law, and the social.

Just as Fichte made an explicit tool of Kant's transcendental methods, Hegel did the same with the dialectic. Fichte and Schelling had proceeded by demonstrating contradictions within any given determination and within its opposite, then overcoming both by a third determination (Forster, 1993: 159). As Hegel found his place in the intellectual attention space around 1806, he made the triadic method central to his own work and laid it out for pedagogic purposes in his *Logic,* the textbook written 1812–1816 during his years as a secondary school teacher. Whereas Fichte's dialectic kept going backwards, digging more deeply into presuppositions, Hegel's dialectic goes forward, generating history.

The dialectical method can be regarded as a self-conscious crystallization among intellectuals of debates which made up their own history. Traditional concepts and opposing positions had been subjected to ever more intense scrutiny; rather than destroying a given position, through these debates philosophy had dug more deeply. Distinctions had been made in concepts previously taken as unitary (as Kant had divided the a priori into synthetic and analytic), and on these grounds in turn whole new realms had been discovered. By the 1790s, the reflexive edge of the philosophical community had become aware of the changeableness and multi-sidedness of concepts—not only as an empirical generalization but as a permanent possibility. The dialectic could be used as a method. Philosophy could take control of its own history, deliberately creating its next stage.

Hegel was the individual in whom this recognition came to consciousness. Located at the center of action in a crowded and highly competitive space, he got virtually the last attention slot available under the law of small numbers. He found the slot by focusing on history, both of the intellectual community itself and of its links to the surrounding social world in general. Hegel was the first creative philosopher since ancient times who had an explicit sense of building on the entire chain of predecessors. He came to philosophy from an earlier interest in classical Greek history, which he extended to the less fashionable Hellenistic and medieval periods.[36] Historical studies were the first wave of the new academic research disciplines, pioneered by classical archeologists such as Winckelmann, a hero of the 1760s, and institutionalized by the Göttingen philologists. Hegel joined a historiographical movement well under way. That movement had already found its ideologist in Herder. But whereas Herder legitimized the particularism of nationalities, Hegel fused history and philosophy on the level of general principles. He gave history a theory, and thereby opened a wide terrain for the intellectuals of the philosophical faculty to exploit. Not surprisingly, Hegel's philosophy was routinized in the 1830s and thereafter by a lineage of pupils who became the great scholarly historians of philosophy.

Hegel grounded his most systematic pronouncements on the terrain of intellectual history. He first announced his originality in the section on Self-Consciousness near the beginning of his *Phenomenology of Spirit*. He unfolds the stages of consciousness emerging through social oppositions, first by the dialectic of master and slave, invoking classical antiquity, then through the stages represented in late antiquity by Stoicism, Skepticism, and finally Christianity. The last, which Hegel speaks about in an oblique and guarded way as the "Unhappy Consciousness," is critiqued in what amounts to a review of the main religious confessions and their respective practices of devotionalism, pietistic moral action, and monastic self-mortification. At the end of the *Phenomenology,* the Absolute Knowledge which rises above the state, religion, and art is "Philosophical Science as the self-comprehension of Spirit" (Hegel, [1807] 1967: xiii; cf. 805–808). At Berlin, Hegel's most elaborate and frequently repeated lectures were those on the history of philosophy.

For Hegel, metaphysics is historical, and is identical with epistemology. When he first summarizes his system, the terms he uses comment equally well on the history of philosophy: "Consciousness first finds in self-consciousness . . . its turning-point, where it leaves the parti-coloured show of the sensuous immediate, passes from the dark void of the transcendent and remote supersensuous, and steps into the spiritual daylight of the present" (Hegel, [1807] 1967: 227). This could be a résumé of the world of primitive nature, passing through medieval religion, emerging into modernity; it expresses equally a compressed intellectual history from the Enlightenment materialists to the Idealists (with an oblique reference to Schelling, from under whose wing Hegel was just breaking), and finally to Hegel's system itself.

Hegel sets out by demonstrating that dialectic dissolves the sensory world of commonsense impressions. Any ordinary object is made up of qualities which distinguish it from other things. But each quality is what it is only in relation to other qualities that it is not; an apple is what it is by virtue of not being an orange. In a rather explicitly Fichtean formula, Hegel comments that the identity of A (A = A) depends on the fact that A is opposed to not-A. The object dissolves in a sea of relations, not unlike Indra's net in Hua-yen Buddhism. With the characteristic touch of Idealism, Hegel formulates the qualities of objects not as being-for-itself *(Ansichsein)* but as being-for-another *(Andersein).*

Hegel's Cartesian starting point, leaving the self to be developed later, is the Here and Now of sensory immediacy. Here and Now negate all other moments and elsewheres of being. Although objects and relationships change, Here and Now are constant, universal throughout; the radically particular implies something universal. What is preserved through the flux of time stands over against every other thing that it has been, as things continuously perish into something else, as being-for-itself. Being is not univocal, but comes in modalities: a fundamental distinction is between being something, a determinate being *(Seiendes),* and being-as-such, the undetermined *(Sein).* Being is the predicate of every thing, but being as such is not a thing, it is nothing, "pure indeterminateness and vacuity" (Hegel, [1812–1816] 1929: 1:149). This is the position later revised in existentialist form by Sartre. Hegel uses it to generate the dynamism not only of human beings but of the universe as well. Every object in the world is negative, in a state of privation which drives it into activity.

The dialectic is a frame within which Hegel can theorize every field of research, and thereby implicitly legitimize all of them as food for the philosophical faculty. The longest section of Hegel's *Phenomenology,* taking up about 75 percent of the text, is an application of the method to "Free Concrete Mind," which comprises all the fields of natural science, as well as psychology, human social institutions, politics, law, religion, and art. Hegel's system encompasses empirical research; observation is a function of Reason, and moreover Laws which are uncovered in scientific investigation are really existing forces within nature. This is Kant's theoretical completion of empirical research in a much more assertive form. Hegel finds particularly apt the study of organic existence. The unfolding of the plant from seed to bud to blossom can be described as a progression of negations and sublations, flowing from a pregnant potentiality. He is harsh against downward reductions; Lavater's physiognomy is critiqued along with the current scientific fad of phrenology as tying the inner spirit down to its sensory appearances.

One field Hegel eschews: mathematics. Quantity is only an external characteristic of being, whose real essence defies formalization.[37] In part this shows a dislike of the mathematical method of proceeding by formally circumscribed axioms and operations, which ignore the larger interrelation of all concepts and the process of dialectical reconceptualization by which insight grows. Quantity, Hegel argues, is ultimately qualitative; the law is that quantity eventually reaches points where it passes into qualitative change, as water at a certain temperature turns into ice. Hegel is breaking here not only with Kant, for whom mathematical laws are the essential form of science, but also with virtually the entire philosophical tradition up to this time, and especially the modernists: Descartes, Spinoza, and Leibniz.

This was not just an idiosyncrasy of Hegel. Since his day philosophers have divided into those who assimilate philosophy to mathematical logic (the lineage from Bolzano and Frege through Russell), and those (in what twentieth-century anglophone philosophers somewhat inaccurately call the Continental tradition) who reject mathematics. No doubt Hegel had immediate motivations, especially his rivalry with Fries, a neo-Kantian who criticized the qualitative *Naturphilosophie* while proposing a rival speculative natural history with fanciful mathematical laws.[38] To depersonalize the rivalry, Hegel had a good sense for the moods of academic disciplines, and he might have felt the embarrassment that pseudo-mathematics like that of Fries was creating in the eyes of professional mathematicians. The technical frontiers of mathematics were moving far beyond the competence of non-specialists. And indeed, although Hegel never gave up his claim that philosophy covers the qualitative fields of *Natur-philosophie,* this was never a prime interest, for he had uncovered a terrain far more exploitable by historical-dialectical methods, in the human sciences, which Hegel calls the realm of the Spirit.[39]

Here the dialectic provides theoretical guidance for new realms of observation. The method of showing the one-sidedness of concepts and their dependence on others, when applied to the ideals of morality and politics, leads to the recognition that such ideals are always social. The freestanding individual and the moral absolutes of Kant are illusions arising when the viewpoints of particular historical phases take themselves for absolutes. In Hegel's eyes, Fichte's touting of freedom was superficial sloganeering. Although Hegel himself was an enthusiast of the French Revolution, he could express within his system how the attempt to set up an absolute of freedom can lead to despotism and Reign of Terror. Hegel opened up the social sciences as disciplines, and made dialectical philosophy available as an instrument of social criticism. Already in his Jena period he was arguing that the individual is free only in the context of property relations; the production of commodities for the market can lead to a higher unity only under the regulation of the collectivity embodied in the constitutional state. Reflecting on the relation between nature and humanity, Hegel broached themes to be taken up by Marx and Engels: the externalization of the self through labor, thereby overcoming man's estrangement from the natural world. Hegel kept himself informed about the progress of industrialization and parliamentary reform in England; the English factory inspectors, agents of the rational state, constituted his image of what social progress should look like.[40] Economics as an academic discipline in the German universities was to follow in Hegel's footsteps: statist, reform-oriented, anti-mathematical.

Hegel reconnoitered the terrain of virtually all the social sciences. His inaugural work for the Berlin chair, his *Philosophy of Right* (1820), was especially successful at the time, striking a balance between liberals and conservatives and making good on Kant's claim that philosophers should exercise influence in the legal faculty as well as every other. His lectures during the 1820s, as the academic system settled into place, were devoted to the philosophical (i.e., theoretical) interpretation of the history of the arts, to world history, and to the history of his own discipline.

Hegel is like a bright child who has broken into a toy store, enjoying himself playing in all the fields of knowledge opened up by the academic revolution. Although he calls it philosophy, it is really the theoretical impulse of the academic intellectual in a new research field. Once the specialized disciplines were institutionalized, they would throw off philosophical direction from above. Hegel's philosophy became outdated by the conditions of its own success.

Political Crisis as the Outer Layer of Causality

From the stance of the traditional sociology of knowledge, it is tempting to attribute German Idealism to the effects of the French Revolution and Napoleonic wars. If we except Kant's writings of the 1780s as not yet Idealist, the period 1789–1815 coincides nicely with the Idealist efflorescence from Fichte's optimistic *Critique of Revelation* in 1792 to Schopenhauer's resigned *World as Will and Representation* in 1819. The abolition of Christianity in France in 1794 contributed to a heady, even apocalyptic atmosphere among the Idealists, who boldly put forth philosophies which earlier would have been punishable as heretical substitutes for religion.

The flaw in this explanation is that it fails to explain philosophy in France itself. Far from supporting Idealism, the intellectual positions that flourished during the Revolution were the opposite of Idealist, religious, and voluntaristic ones. Materialism, which had been popular among the radical pre-Revolutionary philosophes, received its most extreme expression from Cabanis in 1802; the first statement of biological evolution, by Lamarck in 1809, saw the light during the days of freedom from religious dogma; Laplace could declare publicly that his model of the universe was completely deterministic and that he had no need for "that hypothesis" of God; and the sardonically atheistic writings of de Sade were published during 1791–1811.

One could try the causality the other way and see Idealism as a German nationalist reaction against the materialism of the French. But this does not work for the major German philosophers, most of whom were enthusiasts of the French Revolution, at least during the creative upsurge of the 1790s. After Napoleon's conquest of Germany in 1805–1807, Fichte turned nationalist, and indeed lost his life in volunteer hospital service during the liberation wars of 1812–1814. Schelling too turned conservative, and old Romantics like Friedrich Schlegel by 1808 had joined the Catholic Church; Schlegel eventually became a state publicist in Metternich's Austria. But the conservative turn happened at just the time these thinkers ceased to be creative. Hegel in contrast continued to be a fervent supporter of Napoleon all the way to Waterloo and beyond.

Nor did the intellectuals of other states at war with France generally take an Idealist stance. In England, the period saw the dominance of Utilitarian ideas (especially Bentham's publications in the 1790s) that bear no resemblance to German Idealism. The Romantic poets, Coleridge and later Shelley and Keats, picked up Schelling's aesthetic nature idealism; these poets tended to be political radicals, not anti-French anglo-patriots. There is no correlation between either proximity or hostility to the French Revolution and Idealist philosophy.

The effects of the Revolution on the content of philosophy were not so much ideological as structural. It coincided with quite different intellectual activity in various nations because the material means of intellectual organization were different in these places. We return to our three-level model of causality: the maneuvering for position within the internal network of German intellectuals, which explains the variety of positions taken by individual philosophers; the university reform, which accounts for the common content of the Idealist philosophies; and the surrounding political context, which helps explain the timing of the philosophical movement. The French Revolution, the German defeats in the Napoleonic wars, and the resulting phase of political reform within Germany consummated indigenous pressures for university reform, thereby catalyzing the inner networks affecting intellectual creativity.

Each level added something to the emotional energies and the contents of the ideas put forward by the intellectuals within their network. The French Revolution, Napoleonic conquests, and the wave of domestic reforms which followed in Prussia—the suppression of the ecclesiastical principalities among the German *Kleinstaaterei,* the abolition of serfdom, the establishment of legal equality by abolition of the Estates, the elimination of the aristocratic caste system in the army and state, even plans (discussed but not put into effect in Germany during 1807–1812) for democratic self-government—all contributed to the themes of freedom and historical movement among the Idealists.[41] The way in which these themes were apportioned among the various philosophers was determined by the network struggle for attention and the slots available under the law of small numbers. We can see why Fichte and Hegel were a succession, the latter coming to prominence only after the death of the former, both sharing the slot which combined university reform with political liberalism. It is in keeping with the pattern of dominant intellectual movements controlling an abundance of attention slots that Hegel's heritage would split, Right Hegelians taking the purely academic route as historical philosophers, while Left Hegelians continued the ideology of religious and political revolution.

The meshing of outer and inner layers helps explain too why Schopenhauer's pessimism and political conservatism, though mixed with genuinely Idealist ingredients, lost out in competition with Hegel. Schopenhauer was seeking a turf to distinguish himself from the Fichteans. Since Hegel had appropriated the dialectic, Schopenhauer downplayed any dialectic of contradictions and progress toward a higher unity. Although Schopenhauer declared that he was returning to the Kantian dichotomous universe, he too was post-Fichtean in claiming access to the thing-in-itself, recognizable within one's own self. Fichte had opened the path by identifying the self with will. Schopenhauer depicted the will as a blind striving, not freedom but a trap. Schopenhauer exposed his teacher's central concept in a new light, recombining cultural capital in order to oppose the Fichteans while maintaining his membership in the intellectual movement. History is an endless round of battles going nowhere; the Kantian sphere of ideas is a higher ground, not for scientifically comprehending the empirical world, but for transcending its change. Against the moral religion of Kant, the activism of Fichte, and the constitutional legalism of Hegel, Schopenhauer propounded a religion of escape. This position coincided with the social and political biases of Schopenhauer's network; his earliest contacts were with conservative French émigré circles, and his origin was in the salon society of the wealthy rather than the Idealist milieu of pastors and tutors struggling to shape academic career paths. But Schopenhauer was no typical representative of the conservatives, and his position was creative in precisely the way it used the concepts of the intellectual core.

These outer ideological resonances add something to the explanation of the movement of ideas; but they are carried by vehicles whose technical core is inside the structures of the intellectual community itself. The university revolution was the overwhelming impetus because it was a conscious struggle to take control of the immediate conditions of intellectual life.

The Spread of the University Revolution

Comparisons confirm that it was the university revolution, and concomitantly the changing position of orthodox theology within the educational system, that produced Idealism, rather than political revolution per se. For there were several upsurges of Idealist philosophy outside of Germany which did not coincide with similar political upheavals. These Idealist movements were hardly matters of keeping up with international philosophical fashion, since Idealism had long since fallen into neglect and disrepute in Germany. What they did coincide with was the reform of the English and American universities along German lines: the adoption of the reform carried out in Berlin in 1810, the transformation of the old medieval college (in America, the center of denominational piety rather than the state church) into the research-oriented graduate school, and the upgrading of philosophy into an upper-level subject based on intellectual innovation. British and American academics flocked to Germany for advanced training; what they brought back was not Idealist philosophy but a version of university structure that had the effect on philosophy of encouraging the re-creation of Idealism. Modern Idealism was an intellectual response to internal reforms in the structure of their university base.

Idealist Generations in England

The structure of the English universities was very different from that of the German universities before their reform. The medieval higher faculties had long since decayed; training in law had been monopolized for centuries by the Inns of Court in London, in medicine by independent medical colleges and teaching hospitals. Oxford and Cambridge were dominated by the residential colleges, some of which held extensive property endowments, and whose fellowships were valuable sinecures. University professorships existed, but in many cases their pay was minimal, and there was little demand for their teaching; often their incumbents did not lecture at all, but held them as absentee prebends. Even theology, the only vocational subject for those students for whom the university was more than an upper-class social club, was generally taught in a perfunctory manner. Intellectual standards were low; after 1800 a few colleges gradually instituted honors examinations, but these were optional and confined to a few classical subjects.[42]

Pressure for reform was bound up with external political movements for widening the franchise and attacking aristocratic privilege. The universities were criticized by the advocates of modern science, of Utilitarian practicality, and of the superior scholarship of the German university model. The issue which brought concrete reforms, however, was not intellectual, it was the restriction of university matriculation and of teaching positions to members of the Anglican Church, excluding both Protestant Dissenters and Catholics. The turning point came as the Anglicans broke ranks internally, in heated controversy during 1830–1860 among warring factions of puritanical Evangelicals, Broad Church liberals, and ritualistic High Church tendencies. The first round of intellectual fireworks in university philosophy was the result.

In 1833, in response to concessions made by the reforming Whig government to the Catholic majority in Ireland by redistributing church properties, a movement of Oxford dons arose to defend the autonomous rights of the Anglican Church (Chadwick, 1966; Green, 1969: 59). These so-called Tractarian discussions of the propertied-cum-spiritual superiority of the church soon took on a life of their own. In 1841 John Henry Newman, a defender of church ritualism as an expression of higher spiritual realities within the material world, went so far as to provide his own solution to the issue of Anglican exclusivity by interpreting Anglican tenets as congruent with those of Roman Catholicism. In the ensuing furor Newman was deprived of his fellowship, and in 1845 joined the Catholic Church. The Tractarians were the first lively evidence of intellectual creativity at Oxford in many generations, presaging the Idealism that was to emerge in the 1870s. In both cases struggle over church property—above all the prebends which materially supported church intellectuals—generated intellectual energy.

Although the Tractarians (including those who remained within the Anglican Church) were bitter enemies of university reform, they were members of the Oxford college—Oriel—which had gone furthest in throwing open its fellowships to competitive examination, and were themselves notable scholars. Newman was a religiously conservative innovator in philosophy. Arguing against both rationalism and sensory empiricism, he held that the modes of concrete individual being are subject only to judgments of probability rather than logical certainty; one must depend upon an "illative sense" for personally giving assent to beliefs, equivalent to the pragmatics of action in a world of concrete existents (the chief of which, for Newman, is a personal God). Newman represents the first of several cases where pragmatist philosophy emerged as a sophisticated response by religious conservatives to secularizing challenges.

Compromise on the issue of religious tests at the universities eventually led to secularization, not for lack of strong religious commitments, but because none of the theological factions was willing to see the others' doctrines enshrined in a formal criterion. Unlike Germany or France, where secularization was carried by an anti-clerical state bureaucracy, in England the stalemate among plural religious factions led to a de facto secularization that none had desired.

A series of reform bills passed by liberal parliaments in 1854–1856 and 1872 gradually eliminated religious tests, first for students, then for holders of fellowships and professorships. Faculties of law, theology, and arts and sciences were established in the German style. New professorships were founded and plans made for libraries and scientific laboratories, although funds remained largely in the hands of the colleges, and efforts to enforce their contribution to the support of university-level positions were slow to take effect. Although the German model of research-oriented professorships was not precisely duplicated, the English universities opened up an equivalent research base: the college fellowships themselves. The large number of colleges offset the existence of only two major universities and paralleled something of the competitive structure of the two dozen German universities. With the elimination of religious tests and other restrictions (such as appointments by extra-university patrons), fellowships became awards for the highest achievers in the honors exams. In those areas where there were many college positions, especially philosophy, classics, and history, Oxbridge scholarship quickly blossomed.

Alternative university bases began to be established as well. The civic universities, most founded after the Oxbridge reforms, were at first generally poorly funded and had difficulties in attracting students and first-rate faculty. The most prominent of the pre-reform rivals to Oxbridge were University College (1827) and King's College (1831), brought under the degree-granting umbrella of the University of London (1836); the former of these was dominated by Utilitarian emphasis on practicality and reform, and an explicit imitation of German secularism. But its initial funds were quickly exhausted, student numbers fell, and professors' pay plummeted (Green, 1969: 108–109). Even in the 1860s, the main base of the secular thinkers, Utilitarians and scientific materialists, remained the journalistic marketplace. After the Oxbridge reforms, the attraction of the rival civic universities fell even lower for a time; later they became branches of the career networks of Oxbridge scholars.

Although reform was enunciated largely in the name of Utilitarian and scientific ideas, the triumph of university secularization was followed by an outburst of Idealism (Richter, 1969; Nicholson, 1990). At the network center was Balliol College, where Jowett as Greek tutor had been outspoken for university as well as civil service reform and simultaneously for the liberalization of theology. A turning point was Jowett's trial and acquittal on heresy charges at Oxford in 1855. Jowett was a Plato scholar, more concerned with upgrading teaching standards in the classics than with encouraging German-style philosophy; nevertheless, his pupil T. H. Green (who arrived the year of the heresy trial) became chief tutor at Balliol when Jowett became master in 1870, and Idealism was promoted by a series of Green's students and associates: Bosanquet, Caird, Wallace (translator of Hegel), Bradley (a longtime fellow at Merton College), and many minor followers.

The Idealists were strongly attached to educational reform and anti-clericalism, at the same time treating philosophy as a reasoned substitute for religion. Their attitude resembles that of Hegel, who declared in the 1820s that religion henceforward could survive between the extremes of secularism and dogmatism only by taking refuge in philosophy (Dickey, 1993). Green was the first Balliol tutor not in religious orders; his friend Sidgwick had resigned his Cambridge fellowship during the height of the controversy on grounds of conscience as a nonbeliever, and resumed it only under the reformed regulations.[43] Idealism as a halfway house to secularization had connections both ways; Green and his compatriots upheld the independence of philosophical judgments from all other considerations (political as well as religious), at the same time claiming for philosophy the prestige of the highest moral activity. Green, Bosanquet, Toynbee, and others of the group were crusaders for social work, temperance, and popular education, carrying over the moral impulse of the Evangelicals (whose agitation had been principally for strict Sabbath observance) into liberal causes. But the Idealists were not intrinsically a political movement; they included political conservatives such as Bradley (who played something like the part of Schopenhauer or the older Schelling to Green's Fichte).

The leading Idealists were all sons of Evangelical clergymen (Richter, 1969); but we cannot explain their positions simply as a psychological reaction, insofar as it is quite as common for sons to follow their fathers' doctrines as to reject them. The determining situation was structural. Evangelicals were on the opposite fringe from Newman and the Oxford High Church movement; together their mobilization had broken up Anglican domination and led to the secularization of church-controlled education. These second-generation Evangelicals inherited leadership as the reform wing within the establishment; taking advantage of the new intellectual situation after the university reforms, they produced not an anti-religion in the manner of the Utilitarians, but a quasi-secularized version of religion.

The intellectual opening for the Idealists was initially in disputing the Utilitarian principles brought to the center of attention in the agitation over liberal reform. Green attacked the materialist doctrine of sense data on the grounds that impressions are never isolated; relations among them can appear only for a conscious mind. The world must be made by mind, and the apparent externality of sensory material reality rests on God. Redefining the ideological impetus, Green grounded the ethics of social reform in participation in "higher purposes," and argued that the spiritual self-realization of human beings must be made in cooperative, altruistic action.

Green's central argument made use of Hume's critique of causal order in the associations of sense impressions. Green's first major scholarly work (1874) was an edition of Hume; the result was to make Hume a canonical figure in modern academic British philosophy. Once again we see that the most valuable possessions for creative intellectuals are puzzles which can be used to bring out oppositions to currently dominant positions. Green parallels Kant in the use that both make of Hume, and Hume's reputation as a philosopher is largely owed to these later developments. It is not simply that philosophers' positions in intellectual history depend on the accidents of whether they are studied later. The significance of any individual thinker is not created by that person alone. The emergence of certain ideas in the mind and from the pen of an individual, as we have repeatedly seen, is the precipitate of prior and contemporary networks and conflicts in the intellectual community. Nor does the social causality stop there, for the processes that make a particular individual's statements of major or minor significance are above all the roles that these ideas play in future generations of intellectual alliance and opposition. Since Idealist movements in Germany, England, and elsewhere represent the academization of philosophy, it is not surprising they should be central in formulating the canonical sequences of philosophical history. And of course Idealism is the philosophy which above all others recognizes the embedding of the individual in larger contexts, and in the historical movement of ideas.

Bradley too began by taking Utilitarianism as his foil. His *Ethical Studies* (1876) held that good cannot be a calculus of pleasures and pains, but involves duties and ideals; these are social in character, historically changing, and interpretable only in concrete circumstances rather than in the abstract. Bradley's

Logic (1883) criticized John Stuart Mill's inductivism for glossing over the universals hidden in its "resemblances" among sensations, and argued that isolated propositions always rest on unstated assumptions.[44] Syllogistic and other formal logics are too narrow; the true subject of logic is always reality as a whole, and our thought at any moment is always an abstraction, incomplete and one-sided. In 1893 these ingredients were built into a full-scale metaphysical system in *Appearance and Reality*. Any relation between items is unintelligible without further relations which attach the relation to its relata, and these in turn give rise to an infinite regress of intermediating links. Both copula and identity are relations, and their downfall has far-reaching consequences. Causality is an infinite web of conditions, never complete, unintelligible in its relation to its effects, simultaneously continuous and discontinuous. Substances and their qualities are condemned by this critique; so too space and time, motion and change, selves and things. All these must be appearances only, not reality.

Yet error is never total; it too is part of the larger Reality (now capitalized, and referred to as the Absolute). Bradley wields the techniques of skepticism to clear the ground for something positive. There is an ultimate criterion for Reality, the non-contradictoriness invoked in Bradley's previous arguments; and this points the direction in which the Absolute reconciles our difficulties, even if we cannot know just how this is done. Our contradiction-riddled thought is not reality, but our inevitably relational form of thinking implies a completion beyond itself. Bradley resonates a religious sense of human finitude and dependence on a larger harmony. The latter part of his system takes on increasingly the shape of a philosophical if rather heretical religion. Evil is one-sidedness which somehow finds its place in the Absolute; so too must appearances of bodies and souls. Personal immortality, however, is improbable, and Bradley would rather be free of degrading superstition (Bradley, 1893: 448–452). Bradley's style is beautifully attuned to his message. Its concise formulations set up crisp paradoxes; its elegant puncturing of opponents and its polite self-deprecation are enfolded in the clarity and symmetry of its architecture; the whole moves to a stately rhythm which assures us ultimately that all is well. It is a perfect expression of the Oxford intellectual aristocracy at its height, the philosophical counterpart of the aesthetics of Walter Pater and Oscar Wilde.

Bradley illustrates the width of the turf which Idealism had located. He proceeds via the criterion of non-contradiction, reversing the emphasis on dialectic as used by Hegel and his followers (as in the evolutionary developmentalism of Caird, who was, not surprisingly, a critic of Bradley). Relations which Green had taken as evidence of mind in constructing the universe Bradley holds to be incoherent. Like all intellectual movements, Idealism prospered by finding sources of internal disputes for generating new variants, together with fresh amalgams of ingredients from other positions.

New trends in scholarship were pressed into support of religion; on the one hand, the techniques of the new experimental psychology; on the other hand, the opening to Asian philology and history, such as the translation of Hindu texts (beginning in 1875) by the Oxford professor Max Müller, an import from German philology seminars. This was the heyday of seances and spirit-callings, of Madame Blavatsky (who founded the Theosophical Society in 1875) and Annie Besant (the Theosophical leader in the 1890s). In 1882 Sidgwick and F. W. H. Meyers, a psychologist and fellow Trinity man, founded the Society for Psychical Research, seeking scientific evidence of the survival of bodily death.[45] Laboratory psychologists also promulgated Idealist metaphysics, including Stout's *Mind and Matter* as late as 1931 and his posthumous *God and Nature* (1952).

Sub-disputes proliferated as Idealists divided to fill their now-reigning attention space. The prominence of Bradley's impersonal Absolute left a space for the defense of theistic or personal Idealism, by James Ward among others. Against the personalists Bradley's follower Bosanquet defended Absolute Idealism by blending it with the aesthetics and the moralistic do-gooding of the liberal intellectuals; art, science, and religion, he held, are the higher aspects of Reality which we may touch through our own activities. On the other side, Ward's Trinity pupil McTaggart reconstructed a Christianity without Christ or redemption, and without a creative or controlling God; the world consists in a community of personal souls, connected by feelings of love. All this takes place on the level of Absolute Reality, which is beyond time. One consequence is that souls exist eternally, reappearing through successive births and deaths.

McTaggart nevertheless derived his system in a highly technical way, connecting it to the investigations of his colleague Bertrand Russell into the logical foundations of mathematics and physics. The key to McTaggart's system was formulated in a 1908 paper on the unreality of time. Time consists in two series: past-present-future and earlier-later. Only the former involves change and hence must be the essence of time. But past, present, and future are relational properties which change and hence must be related to something outside the time series. Equally fatally, the three temporal characteristics of events are incompatible, and cannot be made compatible via a concept of successiveness without begging the question. Time-bound events are appearances only, perhaps reflections of a non-temporal ordering.[46] Everything culminates, Bradley-like, in a "final" stage which is not temporal, but which absorbs all pleasure and pain and gives infinite value to the universe.

McTaggart speculates as to the relative maxima, limits, and bounds of various kinds of goods and evils in the series beyond time, in a fashion that reminds us of the tools which G. E. Moore had used in his anti-Utilitarian *Principia Ethica* (1903), and of Russell's innovations in mathematical logic (notably in *Principles of Mathematics,* 1903). And indeed McTaggart, Moore, and Russell were all intimates, members of the elite discussion society, the Apostles, at Trinity, Cambridge. Although Moore and Russell set off a movement of revolt against Idealism, their techniques did not in themselves destroy Idealism, but provided new means by which determined Idealists could open up still further reaches of their own terrain. We see once again that creativity proceeds via simultaneous oppositions, and that the institutional conditions which sustain an intellectual attention space are impervious to argument. Not until the fading of the generation brought up in the aftermath of the clerical stronghold in the universities was a religious halfway house no longer a major focus of attention.

Creativity comes from the energy and focus of the networks irrespective of their contents. Moore, Russell, and their followers were offshoots of Idealist connections, in this case of Ward, Stout, and McTaggart; they made their reputations by repudiating their own youthful Idealism. This anti-Idealist rebellion did not automatically displace the older lineage of cultural capital. Others in these networks continued down through the 1920s to construct systems which owe much to Idealism. Samuel Alexander, whose ties derived from Green and Bradley and from the experimental psychologists Munsterberg and Stout, repudiated Idealism in the sense of mind as the central constituent of reality. Nevertheless, his system has a quasi-religious quality.[47] Alexander developed a Spinoza-like two-aspect monism; in place of matter and mind, he substituted Space (extension) and Time. Drawing on his research in physiological psychology, Alexander (1927: 2:38) argues that mind is an emergent aspect of the spatial ordering of matter: "Time is the mind of Space" (i.e., time is the emergent aspect of extension, the generator of qualities). Such "emergence" of course is on a conceptual level, not itself in time. Further emergents are mind, in the more limited human sense, and at a conceptually "higher" level, Deity. Alexander preserves a place for God, but as derivative of more fundamental aspects of the universe; philosophy and science are the primary disciplines, but in their dominance they reserve a place for theology.

Whitehead's system, like Alexander's, resembles Bradley's religion of the Absolute, transposed into the terms of naturalism. What for Bradley are paradoxes, marks of the realm of Appearance and goads to move onward to the Absolute, Whitehead takes as evidence that the underlying concepts are defective. The result is not to transcend appearance but to derive it from a new conceptual scheme, in which the misleading traditions of language are replaced by conceptions inspired by relativity physics, and by the logical reformulations designed since Dedekind and Cantor to overcome paradoxes in the infinitesimal calculus and mathematical set theory. Whitehead had come from collaborating with Russell on the monumental *Principia Mathematica* (1910–1913); not surprisingly, his move back into metaphysics was regarded by Russell as apostasy.[48] The very concepts which Bradley had critiqued—substance and attribute, subject and predicate, particular and universal—Whitehead (1929: 76–80) declared the source of confusion. He replaced them with a scheme resembling Platonic eternal Ideas and Leibnizian monads, but which Whitehead calls the philosophy of organism. There are no atomic elements or particulars; the world is a plurality of "Actual Entities," analogous to biological cell complexes, whose components are inseparable. These are related not through causality or other familiar relationships but through "prehension," an analogue to emotional feelings and appetites on the human level. The connectedness of the universe as a whole has an anthropomorphic character of mutual appetition and satisfaction, which Whitehead refers to as "social"; it is manifested in a sort of vitalistic self-causation of creative process. Prehensions are conceptual as well as physical; there is an ultimate feeling-connection in logical propositions as in the physical universe. God is a derivative notion in this scheme, but Whitehead finds a place for the traditional religious values and for a species of immortality. Whitehead regards it as the task of philosophy to convey how science, morality, and religion all pervade one another; his system resembles the other products of British Idealism in doing just this.

Idealism was creative in England for two generations: the first generation of reform into the research university, and the next generation, when Idealism was challenged by anti-Idealist philosophies. In both cases the form of creativity came from mixtures and oppositions. Just as in the first generation Idealism built upon criticism of the Utilitarian reform ideology, in the following generation the leading systems would take the new cultural capital of psychology, mathematics, and physics to continue the Idealist trajectory of rationalized religion. Idea ingredients can always be combined in various ways; it is the surrounding institutional context that motivates which selections will dominate.

Idealism in the United States

In the United States, university reform dominated the period 1870–1900 (Vesey, 1965; Jencks and Riesman, 1968; Collins, 1979; Geiger, 1993). Hundreds of undergraduate colleges had sprung up in earlier decades, products of sectarian religious competition and decentralized political jurisdictions. Most colleges lacked higher faculties, since during the post-Revolutionary period of democratization professional training had been de-credentialed into apprenticeship with practitioners. There was a lively market for entrepreneurs purveying cultural currency in various forms: the Chatauquas and popular lectures for non-academic audiences without examinations, degrees, or advanced courses; the colleges; as well as a movement for compulsory state-supported elementary schools (since the 1830s) and secondary schools (largely between 1870 and 1890). There was a good deal of rivalry among these forms, and as yet no clear sequence which led from one to another. Emerson, the leader of the Transcendentalists, disliked schools; his famous call for "self-reliance" was no Nietzschean anti-moralism, but reflected his preference for going his own way as a writer and popular lecturer. The Transcendentalists were products of declining religious orthodoxy; when the Unitarians took control of Harvard divinity teaching and of the once-establishment Congregationalist Church in New England in the 1820s, some of the more flamboyant preachers such as Emerson split off on their own and successfully purveyed a more emotional religion than was provided by rationalistic Unitarianism.

On the western frontier, the high proportion of un-churched population provided opportunities for new sects of all kinds,[49] religious and educational alike. The St. Louis Hegelian Society, which flourished in the 1860s and 1870s, was one of many culture-seeking adult societies in the fast-growing frontier cities (see Figure 12.2). Its eminence above the others was due to its establishing a wider institutional base (founding the first American philosophical journal, *Journal of Speculative Philosophy*, which survived from 1867 to 1893), and the leadership of its members in educational reform. William Torrey Harris, founder of the St. Louis Hegelians, was a school administrator and became U.S. Commissioner of Education, 1886–1906, using Hegel as a scheme for planning the topics of the curriculum (Pochmann, 1948: 68–72, 113; Kuklick, 1977: 157). Here Idealism was limited to rote schemata, oriented toward popular audiences and secondary schooling.

More original Idealist philosophy was created where the German-style secular disciplines and graduate research faculties were introduced into the colleges. The main loci were the universities which led the reform: Harvard, with its new graduate department in 1872; even more trend-setting, Johns Hopkins (founded 1874) and Chicago (1892) stressed original research and set off a wave of competition to hire eminent professors. In the late 1870s Harvard considered appointing one of the St. Louis Hegelians, Harris or Howison, but the position fell to Royce, a protégé of the founding president of Johns Hopkins.[50]

Royce's *Religious Aspect of Philosophy* (1885) built systematically from a consideration of error and doubt. Again an Idealism was constructed on the moves of Descartes and Hume, seen through the lens of Kantian uncovering of presuppositions. The intentionality of picking out objects implies that one possesses pre-cognitive knowledge of them. Even doubting something implies

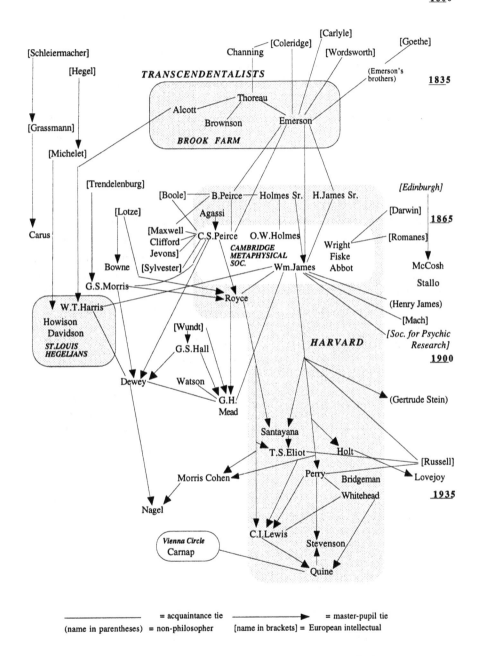

1800

[Schleiermacher]

[Coleridge]   [Carlyle]

Channing   [Wordsworth]   [Goethe]

[Hegel]

TRANSCENDENTALISTS   (Emerson's brothers)   **1835**

Thoreau

Alcott

Brownson   Emerson

BROOK FARM

[Grassmann]

[Michelet]

[Edinburgh]

[Trendelenburg]   [Boole]   B.Peirce — Holmes Sr.   H.James Sr.

[Lotze]   Agassi   [Darwin]   **1865**

[Maxwell Clifford Jevons]   C.S.Peirce   O.W.Holmes   [Romanes]

Carus   *CAMBRIDGE METAPHYSICAL SOC.*   Wright Fiske Abbot   McCosh

Bowne   [Sylvester]   Wm.James   Stallo

G.S.Morris   (Henry James)

Royce   [Mach]

W.T.Harris   [Soc. for Psychic Research]

Howison   [Wundt]   **1900**

Davidson

ST.LOUIS HEGELIANS   G.S.Hall   *HARVARD*

Watson   (Gertrude Stein)

Dewey

G.H. Mead

Santayana

T.S.Eliot — Holt

Morris Cohen   [Russell]

Perry   Lovejoy

Bridgeman   **1935**

Nagel   Whitehead

C.I.Lewis

Stevenson

Vienna Circle

Carnap   Quine

——————————— = acquaintance tie ————————▶ = master-pupil tie

(name in parentheses) = non-philosopher   [name in brackets] = European intellectual

FIGURE 12.2. NETWORK OF AMERICAN PHILOSOPHERS,
1800–1935: GERMAN IMPORTS, IDEALISTS, PRAGMATISTS

an apprehension of it in some measure. If one doubts one's power to transcend the moment, one has already transcended the moment; indeed, "this moment" has meaning only in opposition to other moments, and implies a universal within which one is enmeshed. This pre-cognitive apprehension can be achieved only by a self; for error to exist, there must be a disjunction between this deeper self and our momentary consciousness. So far, then, there must be a plurality of selves which make up the universe. But if there are many, there must be relations among them, and these relations in turn can be objects for true or false thoughts; and these again point to an all-inclusive Self which constitutes their meaning.

Once the university reform had produced Idealism as a halfway house between religion and secularism, further mixtures with surrounding intellectual movements became possible. As in Germany and England, it was these mixtures that made the next generation a creative one as well. Royce's Idealism influenced his Harvard colleagues for several decades. Chief among them was William James. In 1870, at the beginning of his career as a medical scientist, James had a personal breakdown, connected to the strains between his religious faith—his father, Henry James, Sr., was a prominent Swedenborgian spiritualist—and the enthusiasm for Darwinian naturalism among his young scientific friends. The conjunction of spiritual and scientific issues led him from physiological to psychological research in 1875, and thence to a junior position housed in the philosophy department. Soon thereafter James encountered Royce, whose Idealism came as a resolution to his own religious difficulties. It particularly meshed with James's activist psychology in the doctrine that judgments are intentional, picking out and actively meaning their objects (Kuklick, 1972: 37–40). James became a Roycean pantheist until the 1890s; when Royce stressed the Absolute aspect of his philosophy, James began to criticize what he called the "block universe" philosophies.

To make a place for free will, James developed his pragmatist doctrine: truth, lacking any objective referent, can only mean the consequences of beliefs as forms of action. The truth he wished to defend, as he made clear in *The Will to Believe* (1897), was that of religion, which is justified by its socially beneficial consequences. This was followed up in 1902 by *Varieties of Religious Experience,* which musters empirical evidence on mysticism, bolstering the reality of religion from yet another angle. These were James's first major publications outside of experimental psychology (where he had made his reputation with his synthesizing *Principles of Psychology* in 1890). Now that James had his own epistemology, he switched his chair back from psychology to philosophy,[51] and met Royce on his own turf with *Pragmatism* in 1907. Royce and James developed their positions in friendly controversy over the years, Royce moving closer to Christian theism, partially incorporating James's pragmatism but also limiting it so as not to jeopardize the objective truth guaranteed by the Absolute. On his side, James found his way to pragmatism via Royce.

Pragmatism was the product of interaction between religious Idealism and the research sciences fostered by American university reform. Peirce emerged from the same circle as James at Cambridge in the 1860s and early 1870s. Both were early graduates of the Lawrence Scientific School just established at Harvard; both grew up surrounded by the Transcendentalist elite of the earlier generation and by the militant Darwinists of the new one. James's family connections were more on the religious side, Peirce's on the side of science and mathematics. His father, Benjamin Peirce, was the leading American astronomer and mathematician of midcentury, and a prime mover in introducing science into the Harvard curriculum (Brent, 1993: 31). Charles Peirce's positions were primarily in research institutions, the Harvard Observatory, and (during 1861–1891) the U.S. Coast and Geodetic Survey, which his father had headed. His only academic post was in the mathematics department at Johns Hopkins (1879–1884); this was cut short by the animosity of respectably religious academics, who also blackballed Peirce from positions at Harvard and Chicago.

Charles Peirce must have personified every danger the academic establishment feared from reform. He was a scientist, arrogant and disrespectful of traditional propriety. To make matters worse, Peirce was a spoiled child of the New England elite trying to keep up with the status claims of the Gilded Age. He lived beyond his means and was irresponsible with research funds; he cut a figure as a dandy in Paris and New York, divorcing his Boston wife and living with a fashionable Frenchwoman. His later life deteriorated into a series of unsuccessful moneymaking schemes and mounting debts, which reduced him to poverty. Why should such a man have entered philosophy at all? This was the core discipline of the barely reformed religious colleges, where prejudices against Peirce would have been at their highest. He entered the lions' den as the protégé of his father, a mathematical Platonist at home in the older religious-academic milieu. Peirce found in Idealism the turf on which to develop his unique contribution, his theory of signs, situated at the overlap of mathematics and the logic of the philosophical curriculum.

Both Peirces were much more pathbreaking in mathematics than in research science. The older Peirce was known for solid but essentially derivative accomplishments in astronomy, following up others' discoveries in the 1840s and 1850s of the planet Neptune and of Saturn's rings. Charles Peirce's years of laboratory work made him a respected but minor scientist, best known for improvements in instrumentation for the measurement of gravity. In pure mathematics both Peirces were more original but still could not crack the first level of international leadership. Their work generally lost out in priority to De Morgan, Cantor, Dedekind and others. Charles's mathematics was sometimes erroneous, and not well received by cutting-edge algebraists such as Sylvester, his Hopkins department chief (*EP,* 1967: 6:76; *DSB,* 1981: 10:483–486). Peirce settled on logic as his preferred path to success because this was where his early resources best panned out. On European trips in 1870 and 1875, armed with introductions from his father, he met Boole, Jevons, and Clifford, and impressed them with his developments of mathematical logic, a new field in which his work was most clearly original.

Peirce's semiotic originated in the intersection of Idealism and mathematics (Murphey, 1961; Eisele, 1979; Brent, 1993). Peirce began in the 1860s as a Kantian and Platonic Idealist, a mixture typical of the Transcendentalists who frequented his father's house. He began with a triad of ontological categories: (a) abstract Ideas in (b) the mind of God, plus (c) the sensory world which appears as matter. What was original was that Peirce reformulated ontology through the lens of the logical propositions: matter, mind, and Ideas are equivalent to subjects, predicates, plus the intervening connection via an "interpretant" mind. Put another way, the copula is a sign relation, and the mind is nothing more than the user of signs. Peirce absorbed metaphysics into logic, producing his own semiotic Idealism.

Like the other Idealists, Peirce attacked the empiricist philosophy which derives knowledge from the association of ideas with sensory objects. Whereas Green argued that the mind provides relations not given in sensation, Peirce pointed to the missing ingredient as the *sign* intervening between object and mind (or "interpretant"). Signs are never isolated atoms, but part of infinite series of signs flowing off in several dimensions; the interpretant is itself a sign, and so is every part of a subject-predicate expression. The connectedness of meanings with one another had been a stock-in-trade of the Idealists since Hegel, and Idealist arguments through the turn of the century pointed to the cultural realms of art and science as evidence of a spiritual reality transcending the individual. Peirce, who had worked in Agassiz's laboratory classifying biological specimens, taxonomized his newly discovered array of semiotic forms into a vast Linnaean project that he expected would give rise to a science of all the sciences.

A Kant-like architectonic of categories appealed to Peirce because he recognized this as territory on which new discoveries could be made. Contemporary mathematics pointed the direction. In 1843 William Rowan Hamilton (not to be confused with the philosopher Sir William Hamilton) had created quaternions, an alternative algebra without the commutative law of multiplication. In the 1860s Benjamin Peirce had moved into this area; at the urging of his son, he developed a linear associative algebra which generalizes the method of quaternions to inventing multiple algebras and investigating their properties. Modern higher mathematics was just becoming conscious that symbol systems need not be taken for granted as neutral tools of the trade; results of this awareness included not only quaternions but also the non-Euclidean geometries discovered in the 1820s and systematized by Riemann in 1854. New symbol systems could be posited and new realms of discovery opened up by examining their consequences.[52] Young Peirce had an even grander vision: mathematics is the key to all symbol systems and therefore all knowledge; the method of positing symbols and exploring their consequences is the very stuff of the universe.

In the 1880s Peirce developed his combination of higher mathematics and Idealism into an evolutionary cosmology. Because he identified the working of logic in the mind with reality itself, Peirce anthropomorphized the universe. Borrowing a concept from the new experimental psychology, he argued that the unconscious habits from one sign to another, which constitute inference, exist throughout reality. Nature is an endless string of signs, each pointing beyond itself: "Even plants make their living . . . by uttering signs." There is nothing beyond signs: "Reals *are* signs. To try to peel off signs and get down to the real thing is like trying to peel an onion and get down to [the] onion itself." Peirce called his position "synechism," the doctrine that the external referent of any true proposition is a real continuum in the mathematical sense, "something whose possibilities of determination no multitude of individuals can exhaust." The same holds in epistemology and in ontology: "Our knowledge is never absolute but always swims, as it were, in a continuum of uncertainty and of indeterminacy. Now the doctrine of continuity is that *all things* swim in continua."[53] The technical basis comes from Cantor's work on higher orders of infinite sets, which Peirce followed up during his years in the Hopkins mathematics department. Pushing mathematics onto the terrain of philosophy, Peirce posited a collection beyond all trans-finite sets, an ultimate ground of reality in which there is nothing discrete and everything is welded into a continuum. There are no isolated sense impressions nor any logical particulars; only universals are real.

By the 1890s, as Peirce's career was cut adrift from scientific institutions, his philosophy increasingly took the form of a scientific-religious system from which he planned to make a fortune in mass-marketed promotions. These business ventures came to nothing, but Peirce sketched out his principles of popularized Idealism in the guise of evolution as a principle of self-sacrificing love, manifested in periodic laws of history analogous to those of chemistry. Alternatively, scientific laws themselves are the result of evolution. Matter is "effete mind." The universe is evolving from "a chaos of unpersonalized feeling," in which chance plays a decreasingly lesser part as habits emerge "until the world becomes an absolutely perfect, rational and symmetrical system, in which mind is at last crystallized in the infinitely distant future."[54] Peirce's evolutionist cosmology had a good deal in common with others of the time, especially Spencer's, which Peirce criticized for its materialism and lack of logical sophistication. Royce recognized the affinity between Peirce's system and his own, and was one of the few motivated to master Peirce's semiotic, which he incorporated into his late system, *The Problem of Christianity* (1913).

Peirce's blend of higher mathematics with Idealism and his totally new semiotics made his position extremely difficult for his contemporaries to grasp. His technical logic was obscured by popular philosophy, his semiotics by psychology, cutting him off from recognition by the practitioners of the specialized disciplines who alone were capable of following him. Peirce's recognition came late in life, in connection not with his Idealist system but with pragmatism. James had announced the doctrine in 1898, and by 1907 it had taken on the proportions of a popular movement (Myers, 1986: 299; Brent, 1993: 297). Peirce's generous supporter during these days of poverty, James made a point of giving Peirce credit for originating the doctrine. In 1905 Peirce entered the public eye by writing explicitly about his own version, which he now called pragmaticism.

Peirce's papers of 1877–78 had described the meaning of a concept as its observable consequences under various conditions of experiment. Truth is that which the larger community of scientists settles on in the long run, those items of belief which work so well that they become habitually fixed in the chain of signs. But Peirce had not used any term like "pragmatism," nor placed much emphasis on this as an epistemology; indeed, he was aware that his argument did not guarantee that the scientific community would always converge. Peirce's pragmatism was a retrospective construct, a strand selected from the tangled skein of his earlier projects. When James made pragmatism famous in the late 1890s, it was as a defense of religious belief. Peirce, who was always a deep-rooted Idealist, needed no pragmatism for this purpose. What James was doing was an entirely different project; he was pulling himself free from his Idealist allies such as Royce, and developing an alternative philosophy which could make Christianity compatible with science without embracing an Idealist system. If Idealism was a halfway house between secularism and religion, pragmatism was a halfway house to the halfway house.[55]

The context in which Peirce developed his own pragmatist strands was entirely different. His main tool was importing cutting-edge mathematical methods into logic. Following De Morgan's logic of relations, Peirce was developing the view that an object is defined not by its qualities but by its relations with other objects—its "behavior," so to speak, under various experimentally or mathematically defined conditions. Another strand in Peirce's thinking was a staple of academic philosophy in American religious colleges at midcentury: the critique of Humean doubt by the Scottish "common-sense" philosophy (Reid, Stewart), which had argued for the validity of ordinary faith in both the order of sensible nature and the existence of God. With his mathematical tools, Peirce was able to mount a more penetrating critique, both of sensationist induction and of rationalistic doubt.[56] Peirce in his later years called his position "critical common-sensism," as if to imply a blend of Kant and the Scottish philosophy. Peirce held that "all uncriticizable beliefs are vague, and cannot be rendered precise without evoking doubt" (Brent, 1993: 300). There is no such thing as a first sensation, for an object takes shape only after it has been subjected to interpretations via the chain of signs. By the same token, there is no final cognition because the reinterpretations can go on endlessly as further sign connections are made and the object thus evoked is seen in its further ramifications. And since the "object" itself is only a postulate, a sign hypothesized in order that its consequences might be investigated, there is neither clear-cut doubt nor clear-cut elements of reality. Vagueness is an inherent property of the universe, out of which definite concepts and laws can only evolve.

Pragmatism in the hands of Peirce was just the sort of Idealist block-universe that James had created his own pragmatism to replace. Peirce allowed himself to be attached retrospectively to the pragmatist movement, grasping at a few straws of fame amid his general failure. But even in his embattled old age, Peirce touted his own "pragmaticism [as] closely allied with Hegelian absolute idealism," and claimed that dialectic is a special case of his own triadic metaphysics (Brent, 1993: 299). Peirce's socially oriented pragmatism of the community of researchers resonates with the naturalistic philosophy and sociology of science that developed two generations after his death, but only because the Idealism that was Peirce's own intellectual milieu was dead and forgotten. The naturalistic side of Peirce was developed only in the mid- and late-twentieth century, after the social and semiotic sciences had expanded; he is a major philosopher retrospectively because the social conditions which determined his discoveries were long-term ones, ultimately giving rise to these independent disciplines. In his day Peirce struggled for recognition, and was overshadowed by much more clear-cut Idealists such as Royce, and on the other side by pragmatists such as James and Dewey. The chaos of Peirce's career is paralleled by the chaotic nature of his writings: a mass of scattered papers and voluminous disorderly drafts for a system which was never published. Our retrospective Peirce the semiotician is a cleaned-up version for modern tastes.

The moment when the American university system was differentiating created an opening for the combination of mathematics, philosophy, and religion, which were the ingredients of Peirce's system; he was a figure of the transition, who guessed wrong as to the future base for omni-comprehensive systems of his sort. Nor is it just a matter of Peirce's having come too soon. He was intrinsically a thinker of the late Idealist generation, and he would have been disappointed by the merely naturalistic specialty of semiotics in which his work finally found a niche. The trajectory of academic change explains Peirce's failure in his own lifetime, and the wavering and unfocused quality of his intellectual energies.[57]

Even in Europe mathematical logic existed precariously at the margins of recognized disciplines; in America, where the bases for scientific research and teaching were just being created, Peirce's best work went largely unperceived by his colleagues. Peirce was arrogant because he saw himself as a genius (a role for which his father had groomed him); he could see the ramifications of his new science of signs early on, but the whole project was invisible to most others. In light of his modest achievements in conventional fields, his claims sounded like those of a pretender and a charlatan. Peirce's neuralgia and personal irresponsibility may have multiplied his structural disadvantages, but a soberer and healthier person probably would still have failed to achieve recognition. The examples of Frege and, in an earlier generation, Bolzano show that the path to institutionalizing the field of mathematical logic was extremely rocky; both of these trailblazers were honored only retrospectively by a later generation of philosophers. Georg Cantor, who was Peirce's closest counterpart in developing (from 1874) the extreme implications of transfinite set theory, and who also argued that the continuum justifies the existence of God, was the object of controversy and even contempt in the German mathematical community. The strain caused Cantor a series of breakdowns from 1884 until his death in a mental hospital in 1918 (Dauben, 1979; Collins and Restivo, 1983). We will consider the social development of mathematical logic in Chapter 13.

Experimental Psychology and the Pragmatist Movement

A cleaner transition from religious Idealism to pragmatism is exemplified in the career of Dewey. Unlike the scientist-hybrids James and Peirce, Dewey was an offshoot of theological connections and the core curriculum of the old religious colleges. He began with the intention of becoming a Congregationalist minister, and taught Bible classes until well into his 30s (Kuklick, 1985: 230–241). His teachers, liberal theologians from Andover and Union seminaries, were receptive to popular Hegelianism as a way of reconciling religion with Darwinian evolutionism. At Johns Hopkins in the early 1880s, Morris introduced Dewey to the technical philosophy of T. H. Green.[58] From the point of view of liberal theology, Green's flaw was his static dichotomy of the spiritual world between individual selves and the absolute Self, precluding the evolution of the former into the latter. At Hopkins, Dewey encountered an ingredient for overcoming this problem, the experimental psychology introduced by G. Stanley Hall. The theological issue could be approached by scientific research; and this, Dewey concluded, showed the human mind to be a teleological activity of the living organism, whose trajectory points to the divine.

So far Dewey was just another theological liberal with an affinity for Hegelianized evolutionism. He found a more distinctive slot in legitimating the burgeoning research disciplines of the reformed university. Philosophy departments were establishing psychology laboratories, in which a branch of the old metaphysical terrain was made into an empirical study. Dewey propagandized for the significance of experimental psychology; it was an Ur-science (Kuklick, 1985: 239), foundational to other disciplines, since psychology is the point at which the absolute manifests itself in the world. From an Idealist viewpoint, the connection of psychology with the physiological organism was a gateway for attaching spirituality to the physical and biological sciences as well.[59]

At Michigan (1884–1894), Chicago (1894–1904), and Columbia (1905–1952), Dewey encouraged what would become some of the leading psychology labs. Under Angell at Chicago and Thorndike at Columbia, researchers were moving away from introspective-mentalistic studies in the style of Wundt and toward behavioral research. Recruitment to psychology was burgeoning, and tension was growing between the new-style researchers and traditional philosophers. By 1912, psychologists had an independent professional association and separate psychology departments in a dozen universities.[60] Militant behaviorism, which Watson announced in 1913, became the ideology for maximally separating psychology from philosophical content. Dewey himself never made the break, but during these years the experimental method displaced Idealism as his principal philosophical commitment. In the 1890s, Dewey called psychological research "experimental Idealism" (Kuklick, 1985: 239); by the early 1900s he was regarding it as the basis of "instrumentalism."

Having disposed of formal logic, and of the gaps between finite and infinite, between the human and natural worlds and the Absolute, Dewey no longer needed Idealism. Science exemplified the biological propensity of the organism to adjust to circumstances in order to survive. The scientific method of repeated ongoing experiments, with new goals and values emerging from every step, became the method applicable to all his concerns. Dewey grew less religious, more oriented toward good works in the movement for settlement houses, labor rights, and public education. The Idealist worldview of spiritual community was naturalized as the democratic cooperation of human society, and democracy was made the equivalent of the religious ideal; both were equated with scientific experimentation evolving toward solving problems. Dewey's reputation faded in the long run; in his day he was the most publicly prominent American philosopher, above all by legitimating scientific research and education through connecting it with the core political ideology.

The pragmatism of George Herbert Mead came from a background close to Dewey's (Miller, 1973; Joas, 1985). Mead's milieu was that of Protestant missionaries; his father was a theology professor, his mother a pious college president. Mead was inducted into intellectual networks as a tutor in James's family, as a student of Royce, and, while sojourning in Germany, of Wundt. Finally, he was a loyal protégé of Dewey, who brought him to Chicago in 1894, where they participated together in the Social Gospel movement. Like other Americans of his generation seeking to mitigate parental religious strictness, he became attracted to experimental psychology as the amalgam of science and spirituality. But psychology was secularizing, and Mead was exposed to its militant side by his friendship with the behaviorist John B. Watson (a graduate student at Chicago, 1900–1903). Against this tide, Mead preserved Idealist themes of the sociality and connectedness of mind by transforming them into a naturalistic social psychology.

In Mead's system, mind emerges from the social interaction of human animals. Words are verbal gestures whose significance is the intended action they convey to their hearers; understanding a language is made possible by taking the role of the other person. Universals do not exist in the world, but are produced by symbols, by virtue of meaning the same thing for everyone. It is the Generalized Other—the open-ended capacity of humans to take the point of view of anyone at all—which constitutes a world of permanent objects for the individual mind. Thinking is internalized conversation, the human animal's interchange of gestures carried out by splitting oneself into speaker and hearer. The upshot of Mead's philosophy is that mind is no longer mysterious; it is an empirical process whose variations are explainable by the methods of sociological research.

Mead's theory of mind was little recognized among philosophers. It was in the 1930s, after his death, that sociologists at Chicago made Mead famous in their own discipline as the founder of what they called symbolic interactionism. Mead resembles Peirce in leaving scattered unfinished manuscripts (notably Mead, 1938) but publishing little major work in his lifetime; his blockage of creative confidence is related to his ambivalent position in the intellectual field. Mead himself was never wholeheartedly a naturalistic sociologist; he retained a commitment to Idealism to the end. In lectures given in 1930 he describes time as a construct of human projects, and past history as constantly reshaped by the emergent concerns of the present. Objects are constituted as discrete units and definite forms only as these become the focus of action upon them;

the solidity of physical objects exists for us because we project ourselves into them—we take the role of the physical object—and imagine ourselves pushing back (Mead, 1938: 426–432). Lest this make the world too human-centric, Mead suggests that perspectives exist objectively in the sociality of nature, as planets, molecules, and the like constitute one another by their interaction (Mead, 1932: 47–66, 162–174). It is as if Mead had solved the Berkeleyan problem of "esse est percipi" by attributing the qualities of a mind to everything in nature, and identifying mind with the sharing of perspectives in social action.

Even in their heyday, the pragmatists did not dominate American philosophy. By the 1920s, Dewey was famous, but largely in connection with progressive education, his application of pragmatism to the reform of the secondary school curriculum, overturning the classical subjects in favor of life adjustment. His bastion was not the philosophy departments but the university departments of teacher training, which had grown up to coordinate the university revolution with the burgeoning public high school system. In philosophy itself, Idealism remained the dominant position down to the 1930s. Pragmatism was regarded by professional philosophers as epistemologically unserious in its relativism and human-centrism and inferior to the objectivity of Idealism (Schneider, 1963: 509–510). Personal Idealists continued to defend the individuality of souls and the personhood of God. In the 1910s, James's students, led by Santayana and Perry, abandoned pragmatism for New Realism, which fitted comfortably into naturalistic secularism but also reduced the leverage and prestige of a distinctively philosophical vantage point. The next big wave in philosophy, the analytical-logicist style introduced in the 1930s, was to sweep all this away with uncompromising militancy. As in England, Idealism and its hybrids dominated American philosophy during the two generations of the introduction of the German-style research university. When full-scale religious secularization of higher education was complete, Idealism was rejected.

Idealism in Italy, Scandinavia, and Japan

In Italy too Idealism arose in connection with the struggle for secularizing educational reform. The papacy had opposed national unification as a threat to its territorial possessions and privileges in the conservative states. From the period of political unification (1859–1870), nationalists were anti-clericals, fighting to wrest education from the church by constructing a centralized school system, modeled on the German educational laws (Barbagli, 1982). Italy had a large number of independent universities, the result of long-standing political divisions and of the spate of foundings throughout the Middle Ages. Before national unification, the universities still taught scholasticism. After unification, universities were incorporated into the centralized state system, and the German model of higher research faculties was imposed on them. In the secularized regions of the north, the universities quickly became integrated into international networks of science; positivism was strong, and the leading philosophers were hybrid mathematician-logicians such as Peano and his pupil Vailati.

Since priests had been a large proportion of schoolteachers, staffing the secularized system, especially in the south, was a long struggle over the degree of accommodation necessary with the church. The philosophers of Italian Idealism were a network in the south. Standing between the camps, the movement promoted education as a new spirituality shorn of otherworldly transcendence, while opposing as well the positivism and materialism of the northern liberals. The founder was Spaventa, an old Naples revolutionist, who returned from exile in the 1860s and formulated a pan-Italian intellectual alliance using Hegelian Idealism as a vehicle. The famous Idealists were Spaventa's pupils and grandpupils: Labriola, Gentile, and Croce (who was also Spaventa's nephew).

The Idealist group came together in the 1890s, discussing Marxism in a journal funded by Croce. The Italian labor movement was becoming organized; Labriola made contact with the leftist network by corresponding with Friedrich Engels and Georges Sorel. Labriola's Marxism downplayed the laws of historical sequence as inapplicable to the peculiar political circumstances of Italy, instead making a place for national consciousness. Italian Idealism emerged as Marxism shorn of its materialism, oriented toward social struggle and disavowing transcendence of historical process—in short, Marxism turned back to its Hegelian roots. Croce, who had begun as an antiquarian researcher, now declared history the master discipline. Neither religion nor science can transcend history; all thought is contained in particular historical circumstances. And history is action and strife; judgments are only pauses to assess obstacles to action. If one withdrew from action, there would be no thought. History is no positivist science of fact gathering; since the past is dead, all that can be recovered is its spirit. Gentile's Actual Idealism, promulgated in 1916, takes to an extreme the identification of reality with action and the denial of any transcendent values. Mind is the only reality; there is no separation of thought from an external world nor separation of thought from practice. "The true is what is in the making" (Gentile, [1916] 1922: 10); there is no outside criterion by which to judge.

Labriola had sought a compromise in educational reform: independence of schools from the church, but with respect for the inner spirit of religious sentiment (Kolakowski, 1978: 2:185). Gentile polemicized against modernists over the curriculum, and favored religious instruction in elementary schools.

Croce became minister of education in 1920–21, and Gentile succeeded him in 1922–1924 under Mussolini. In Italy the halfway house of Idealism corresponded all too well with a Fascist regime imposing an authoritarian synthesis between clerical conservatives and the secularizing left. As external circumstances stagnated, Idealism too hung on longer in Italy than elsewhere.

In Scandinavian philosophy, the timing of Idealism was earlier because the reforms were carried through earlier. In the Swedish universities, Idealism accompanied reforms paralleling the German reforms: under the constitutional monarchy of 1809, government offices formerly monopolized by the higher nobility were opened to "qualified" applicants through university examinations. The prestige of theology chairs, once the apex of academic careers, now declined, replaced by philosophical studies, which became high-status *Bildung*. Kantianism became prominent in the early 1800s, Hegelianism from the 1830s and 1840s, along with Boström's indigenous Swedish version of spiritualist Idealism (*EP*, 1967: 7:295–301; Liedman, 1993). In 1852 the Humboldtian elevation of research above teaching was officially decreed. The end of Idealist domination came with another wave of reform in 1902; the required general curriculum in philosophy was downgraded to the secondary school level and replaced by professional specializations. This reform was rapidly followed in philosophy by a movement, beginning in 1910 and continuing into the 1930s, militantly rejecting subjectivism and spiritualism. The Uppsala philosophy of Hägerstrom and Phalén reduced moral sentences to empirical statements plus emotions and commands, in a fashion anticipating the logical positivists. Similarly in Finland, after a century of Idealism, philosophy turned to logical positivism. These cases add to the list of anti-metaphysical movements in university systems after Idealist domination ended.

The Japanese sequence paralleled the European secularization struggles. The contents of traditional religion and the political ideologies of the modernizers are peculiar to Japan, but the institutional and intellectual dynamics are much the same. The Japanese universities set up in the 1870s through the 1890s were directly modeled on the German—as indeed was the case with the English, American, Italian, and Scandinavian reforms. The early Meiji generation of Westernizing pioneers emulated Utilitarianism and materialist science; but as soon as the universities achieved autonomy under Japanese teachers, philosophy quickly turned to an indigenous version of Idealism led by the Kyoto school. The halfway house in this case was of course not between secularism and Christianity, but between the militants of the newly secularized school system and Buddhism. In the early period of reform, Buddhists were subjected to atrocities just like Catholics at the hands of European anti-clericals. The Buddhist religion could not be so easily displaced, just as in Italy the Catholic teachers could not be so rapidly dispensed with. In the already widespread private education of the Tokugawa period, a considerable proportion of teachers in the lower schools were Buddhist priests. Anti-clericalism soon passed as the modernizing regime made de facto accommodation with Buddhist education.

The Shinto cult promoted at the national level was too particularistic and too artificial a construction to serve as a rationalized philosophy; on the other side, Neo-Confucianism, dominant in the elite schools during the Tokugawa, was already substantially secularized. Buddhist philosophy made an unexpected comeback because it could most easily take the form of a religion of reason. Nishida and the Kyoto school paid respect to tradition but relied not on dogma and faith but on articulate argument. Precisely because the institutional reformers had tested the imports available from world philosophy, the network of leading Japanese intellectuals soon recognized that in Buddhist materials they had available a rationalized religious philosophy that could hold its own with any in the cosmopolitan world. Even this pattern is not so distinctive to Japan; for each of the reforming educational systems—in America, Italy, and England—was also an international import. The intellectuals in each of these networks too were cosmopolitans reaching out from within their own school system in an attempt to loosen the hold of particularistic religious doctrine. Idealism is cosmopolitanism in religion; it is religious thought argued out independently of dogma and tradition, yet keeping a place in its system for a reasoned loyalty to transcendence and tradition. That is why Idealism everywhere is the favored philosophy in the transitional generation of secularizing reformers.

The Secularist Repudiation of Idealism

There was a revolt against Idealism in virtually every national academic system in the generation after university reform was complete. Secularization almost everywhere eventually won a complete victory within the academic world. Where this happened, the claims of religious specialists were reduced to those of one specialty on a par with any other. After the older generation died out, even a sentimental respect for religious tradition no longer had much influence. The younger generation of intellectuals, unconcerned about the sensibilities of their academic grandparents, took as their topic the weaknesses presented by the Idealist halfway house. The Germans, who first underwent the Idealist revolution, were the first to repudiate it. After Hegel's death came Feuerbach and Marx, Helmholtz and Büchner. In England, Bradley and Bosanquet became targets for Moore and Russell. In America, Royce and the religious-pragmatist James were superseded by C. I. Lewis, Stevenson, and Quine.

Nevertheless, philosophy everywhere flows in channels initially cut by the Idealist revolution. Although flamboyant Idealism has been repudiated, philosophy has not gone back to the style of thinking of the lay figures of the Enlightenment or of the Utilitarians. Academic philosophers are now irreparably technical; and even in internecine polemics, when they deride "philosophy" and call for its death, they continue to hold the turf colonized by the initial German Idealists.

Virtually all academic philosophers in the reformed systems since about 1800 have been post-Kantians. They all do "critical" philosophy, taking for granted that ontological claims must pass through an epistemological filter; all search for what there is in the mind, or seek to depersonalize it further, in the semiotic process, which shapes the nature of what is taken to be knowledge. Kant taught philosophers to use the technique of asking what it is that must necessarily be presumed for an argument to be made at all. Virtually all subsequent philosophy might be described as "transcendental" in the strict sense, however much later philosophers might despise the terminology.

It is no surprise that after the downfall of ambitious Idealist metaphysics there should occur the revival movement of Neo-Kantianism. The philosophical tools forged in the original academic revolution still mark out the turf of academic philosophy. The effort to delimit and then to take over the territory of theology has been outdated. What remains are the techniques initially used for that battle. Philosophers learned that the most widely applicable weapons in argument are those which probe the ground beneath the argumentative weapons of all other specialists. Philosophy claims the most general right of the autonomous intellectual community to carry on its arguments, and to judge the validity of everything else. This makes the same claim in intellectual terms that the academic revolution did organizationally: the autonomy of intellectuals to run their own affairs, and to bring all the world under the scope of their judgment.

CHAPTER 13

The Post-revolutionary Condition: Boundaries as Philosophical Puzzles

The upsurge of Idealist philosophies is the creativity of transition one expects when an organizational base changes. But what of the generations after the transition? The German universities, the first to undergo the revolution, were also the first to repudiate Idealism and settle down into academic routine. Nevertheless, German philosophy continued to be creative, even underwent new rounds of intellectual upheaval: materialist, positivist, logicist, phenomenological, existentialist, and others. We are used to seeing the German university system as a trendsetter, from the time of Feuerbach to the time of Carnap and Heidegger. This familiarity hides a theoretical problem.

Previously in world history we have seen academicization produce not creativity but stagnation: a tendency toward rote learning, the scholasticization of minute commentaries on old texts, intellectual conservatism rather than innovation. The pattern exists for the examination system and its preparatory schools in China, for Greco-Roman municipal lecturers, Islamic *madrasas*, and late Hindu sectarian schools. At best, there is a creative burst in the first generations, as when the ancient Greek schools were first established in the time of Socrates' pupils, and again in the founding period of the medieval Christian university, before the scholastic rigidification of the 1300s. How then can we account for the creative surge of the European universities, extending four or five generations into the 1930s and possibly beyond?

One difference is that creativity in the modern university rides on the ongoing process of disciplinary specialization. Chinese, Greek, Islamic, Hindu, and late medieval Christian schools stagnated in scholasticism; in each case their curricula became stuck in a set number of fields. The European university pattern, in contrast, has generated an ongoing stream of new specializations. It is the process of breaking off, and the resulting opportunities for new combinations of ideas, that drives creativity within the academic system.

Here we encounter a second problem. Perhaps the university as a whole prospers under this pattern; but does it not mean that philosophy is sucked dry of its contents by the growth of autonomous specialties? The death of philosophy has often been proclaimed on just these grounds. The anti-Hegelians of the 1840s declared philosophy to be failed science, just as the logical positivists of the 1920s were willing to replace it with a branch of mathematics, and the ordinary language philosophers of the 1950s would replace it with a science of language use. Nevertheless, philosophy has prospered in the world of the disciplines. It has been able to create new meta-positions by taking the stance of looking down on the disciplinary strife from above. And disciplines have provided a social mechanism for creativity within philosophy: the migration of individuals from one field to another, often between tight and soft spots within the academic labor market.

Since Germany underwent the university revolution two generations before the other university systems, German philosophy experienced the disciplinary breaks and repercussions that much sooner. The first wave, the 1820s through the 1840s, centered on theology; out of this came the split of Left and Right, Old and Young Hegelians, who churned up first religious reform and then political radicalism (see Figure 13.1). On the heels of this wave came another, the battle between Idealist *Naturphilosophie* and the differentiating scientific research disciplines. Philosophers in Hegel's generation were still teaching courses in astronomy and mathematics; and although the medical faculty provided an independent base for some researchers, it was not until the 1860s that a separate faculty for natural science split off from the philosophical faculty. As the height of the struggle for independence in the 1850s, anti-Idealism was rife among the leaders of the new laboratory researchers; the most extreme of their public spokesmen, Moleschott and Büchner, trumpeted reductionist materialism as a liberation from philosophical religion. Several other struggles splashed their waves in this basin: history versus philosophy—the oldest and most prestigeful of the social sciences against the Hegelian Idealism which claimed history for its own turf—and psychology versus philosophy, the first major disciplinary split inside the traditional philosophical terrain.

Neo-Kantianism was the omnibus movement of philosophy in Germany from the 1860s onward because it adjudicated such border disputes: theology, natural science, history, psychology, and more to come. Neo-Kantianism made every disciplinary question into an opportunity for creating a corresponding philosophy. Attacks on philosophy were converted from death threats into growth industries.

Neo-Kantianism repudiated Idealism, with its ontological claims as a religion of reason, so offensive to old guard theologians, and its a priori scientific theories, offensive to empirical researchers. "Back to Kant" became the slogan following the death of the Idealist systems, precisely because Kant epitomized the reflexive tools of epistemology: the study of what is presupposed in any

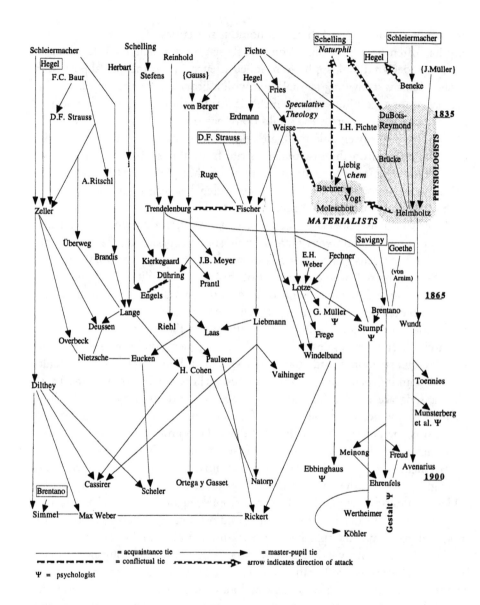

FIGURE 13.1. GERMAN NETWORK, 1835–1900: NEO-KANTIANS,
HISTORICISTS, POSITIVISTS, PSYCHOLOGISTS

statement of knowledge. Neo-Kantians now took as their turf the task of classifying various kinds of fields of knowledge by examining their conceptual presuppositions.

Already at the height of controversy between Idealism and materialism in the 1850s, Lotze, a medical researcher who had migrated into a chair of philosophy, became the most famous German philosopher of his day by proposing to adjust the disciplinary spheres. Rejecting Hegel's superiority of concepts over empirical findings, Lotze found the properly metaphysical territory not in ontology but in the distinction between a realm of value and the value-indifferent: the task of philosophy is to confer meaning on the meaningless material world. Another border adjustment was proposed by Helmholtz, a star researcher and laboratory-founding entrepreneur with network connections in the Idealist establishment. Helmholtz declared that philosophy and science are harmonized because Kant's a priori categories have been found built into the human nervous system. Where Lotze had adjudicated philosophy's turf as that of values, another strategy was to make it the terrain of epistemology. Zeller in 1862 promulgated the catchword *Erkenntnistheorie* (theory of knowledge), endorsing the position that Kantian categories are vindicated by the physiology of perception. Full-scale launching of the Neo-Kantian movement followed in 1866, when F. A. Lange published his *Geschichte des Materialismus,* declaring that Idealism and materialism alike are metaphysics of the thing-in-itself prohibited by the Kantian critique (Willey, 1978; Köhnke, 1991).

When psychology emerged as a research science, philosophy once again adjusted its meta-position. Kant had made clear that his categories are prior to all experience, but in the absence of a research science investigating consciousness, it was easy to fall back onto a glib defense of the categories as empirically justified. The border between epistemology and psychology sharpened when Wundt founded his psychological laboratory at Leipzig in 1875. Wundt was a former assistant of Helmholtz whose career in physiology was blocked because the chairs were all filled by the previous cohort. Migrating onto the more abundant job market in philosophy, Wundt proposed to turn this archaic discipline into the empirical field of psychology, the scientific study of consciousness (Ben-David and Collins, 1966). In the 1880s and 1890s Wundt's pupils, along with parallel chains emanating from Lotze's students Stumpf and G. E. Muller, and from Brentano, spread the experimental psychology approach throughout the German-speaking universities; growth was promoted especially successfully by foreign students who carried the method to America.

The Neo-Kantian philosophers took the opposite tack. Cognitive constructs per se are not to be confused with psychological operations; the latter exist on an empirical level and are subject to investigation by empirical methods, while the former have meaning, structure, or validity in their own sphere. Hermann Cohen, founder of the Marburg school, resurrected Kant's distinction of transcendental foundations and subsequent empirical investigation. When in 1875 Cohen repudiated the physiological interpretation of Kant, he was rejecting the intrusion of Helmholtz's medical science into philosophical terrain. At the same time that Helmholtz's former assistant, Wundt, was going full blast with his imperialist naturalism, the Marburg school launched a program of investigating the constitutive logic of the disciplines, from mathematics to jurisprudence.

Philosophy was not reduced to psychological research, but remained alive on its own terrain. Zeller's pupil Dilthey formulated a "critique of historical reason." Dilthey's distinction of *Geisteswissenschaften* from *Naturwissenschaften* proclaimed new lines of alliance, putting history and philosophy, along with the newer cultural and social sciences, on the side of spirit, where they are investigated with the methods of hermeneutic interpretation, against the sciences of dead matter and their methods of causality. Windelband, leader of the so-called Baden school of Neo-Kantianism, in turn pointed out that the distinction between nature and spirit did not fit the actual procedures of the existing disciplines, especially the new psychology, which applied experimental methods to the spirit. Windelband instead distinguished the disciplines according to the aspect under which they investigate reality: *nomothetic* search for general principles or *idiographic* description of particularities. His protégé Rickert in turn proposed that when we take an idiographic interest, our knowledge depends not on objects themselves but on their value-relevance, which guides concept formation. Culture is the mode in which we see the world as a totality of value-relevances; nature is the mode in which we see it in relation to laws.

Almost everything in Germany at turn of the century was touched by Neo-Kantianism. Simmel (a pupil of Dilthey and Brentano and friend of the Baden school) introduced the philosophy of forms and the tones of hermeneutic empathy into sociology. Max Weber, another of Dilthey's pupils, and a friend of Rickert, explicitly advocated Neo-Kantian methods in carving out a territory for the new discipline around the time Weber helped found the German Sociological Association in 1908. Cohen's pupil Cassirer rejected the separation of natural science from the domain inhabited by the humanistic disciplines; Windelband's ideographic-nomothetic distinction does not hold, he said, since a judgment always unites both universality and particularity. Cassirer gave license for philosophers to range widely in the general investigation of symbolic forms, which he proceeded to do with studies ranging from relativity physics to seeking the universal and perennial across the history of philosophy and the arts.

A third party in German philosophy between the movement of experimental psychologists and the Neo-Kantians was led by Brentano. He too had his strategy for re-elevating philosophy amidst the disciplines. Philosophy, he held, can become a progressive science because its topic is the study of empirical consciousness; psychology is on firmer grounds than any of the physical sciences because it alone rests on the certainty of inner perception. So far psychology is the master discipline, but the sensory and associative laws of the Wundtian laboratories and the British empiricists alike are wrongheaded because they miss the central point: consciousness consists not in content but in acts. The chief domain of mental acts is the "intentional," whereby the mind intends an object, giving it mental existence whether it exists externally or in imagination; as against Neo-Kantianism, the mind always reaches out to objects rather than passively screening objects through categories. Brentano was the most influential academic lecturer at the end of the century. At Vienna during 1874–1895, he taught Husserl, Meinong, Stumpf, Scheler, Simmel, and Twardowski, who began the Polish school of logicians, as well as Buber and Freud. Psychoanalysis and phenomenology were products of Brentano's pupils; the founders of Gestalt psychology were his grandpupils.

After the turn of the century, Brentano's position dissolved in a new array of schools, and psychology crystallized out as a separate discipline. Neo-Kantianism too broke down, coming under attack both from the philosophically oriented physicists in the Vienna Circle and from Heidegger's theologically oriented phenomenology. This was a reversal of alliances. Neo-Kantianism was generally close to positivism in its earlier phases: both shared the view that there is no thing-in-itself, and that science is a formal representation of the surface of phenomenological experience. Rather than undermining other disciplines, Neo-Kantianism gave them a supporting rationale. In another direction, Dilthey and Rickert reserved a realm for spiritual culture that protected theology against the reductionism of scientific militants and secularists. Nevertheless, in a fashion typical of intellectual change, the revolution took place within the very networks of the establishment. The Vienna Circle began as a revolt against Neo-Kantianism, but it was also a revolt within Neo-Kantianism. The networks tell a different story from the familiar ideological surface: most of the leaders of the generation of 1900–1935—Schlick, Carnap, but also Husserl, Scheler, and Heidegger—came from the breakup of Neo-Kantianism.

Against these German trends, English academic life for most of the century seemed archaic. England's academic revolution did not occur until 1860–1870. Before that time, philosophy remained within the mold of the Enlightenment lay intellectual. At the same time, England's industrialization and democratization put it in the lead in forming public political movements and thus in the creation of the activist social sciences. The result was a very different pattern from contemporary Germany: instead of the struggles of post-Idealism amidst the new academic disciplines, we see the formation of Utilitarian economics and political thought, along with movements of non-university natural scientists who united under the secularizing banner of evolutionism. After 1870 academicization set in with the familiar upsurge of Idealism; it also produced some distinctively British philosophical combinations when the academic Idealists settled affairs with non-academic Utilitarians, and then when a younger generation settled affairs with *them*. Before 1870 British universities had remained old-fashioned, but one discipline that was well established within them was mathematics, albeit a rather traditionalistic version. This too had philosophical consequences. As British mathematicians struggled to update their field, they found themselves in the midst of what looked to the traditional eye like paradoxes in the elementary parts of algebra. Another border became intensely scrutinized, resulting in a lineage of British mathematician-philosophers which burst into full bloom in the generation of Russell and Whitehead.

Border struggles are often nasty, as they involve challenges to old identities. Shucking off old skins is painful, and all the more so when it is a militant newcomer who is pulling the skin off someone else. We can never take these disputes at face value. The boundary issues which instigate so much of modern philosophy may begin in particular disciplines, but philosophy transmutes everything into its own key. What starts in one ideological tune often ends up in an entirely different one by the time counter-movements and philosophical reflexivity have done their work.

Meta-territories upon the Science-Philosophy Border

Disciplinary differentiation stimulates philosophy in several phases. First there is the struggle for separation, promoting accompanying ideologies of independence such as the materialism of the 1850s. Next, when the new disciplines are safely institutionalized, philosophy makes its peace with them; it is in this niche that Neo-Kantianism flourished, presiding over the conceptual map of disciplinary spaces. Third, once a variety of disciplines exist in the university, there arises the possibility of disciplinary imperialism, bringing new mixtures of ideas and new networks of personnel into play. Such flows often intrude on philosophical turf, in part because any issue pursued at a sufficiently high level of abstraction has an affinity for philosophical argument, and in part because philosophy was the largest and softest labor market. Migration of medical physiologists into philosophy produced experimental psychology; an influx of mathematicians promoted both logical positivism and phenomenology. Through the dynamics of social conflict, in response to such border-crossing comes a fourth kind of philosophical creativity: counter-movements to keep challengers out.

Modern philosophies are heavily influenced by the expansion of science within the universities, but not, as contemporary ideologies often had it, by becoming a mere branch or ancillary of science. The dynamics of intellectual networks, including the way they adjust to changes in the organizational base, remain fundamentally the same throughout world history. If modern European intellectuals differ from their predecessors, it is by adding onto the basic mechanisms they share with Asian and with ancient and medieval Western philosophers two further developments: rapid-discovery science and the autonomous research university with its proliferation of specialized disciplines. Modern academic philosophy, as the most abstract and reflexive of disciplines, takes as its problem space the results of these two revolutions. That is why mathematics became the instigator of so much of modern philosophy, even on the rebound and in fields far removed from logic and philosophy of science.

Methodological disputes built up within mathematics when the discipline became academicized. From the foundational crisis of mathematics at the turn of the century flowed the logical positivism of the 1920s, coming into full bloom in the Vienna Circle by meshing with methodological disputes in physics and with Neo-Kantianism. Another branch of the same networks produced phenomenology, which gradually sharpened its rivalry with and rejection of the mathematicians by giving birth to existentialism. The intrusion of logical formalism into philosophy energized in reaction a third large movement of twentieth-century philosophy, ordinary language. Both directly and through the dynamics of intellectual conflict, the major schools of modern philosophy all resulted from interdisciplinary pressures originating in mathematical science.

There is a deeper sociological reason why this would be so: by the generation of 1835–1865, mathematics had become the intellectual network which had achieved the highest degree of self-consciousness on its structures of argument; indeed, to a large extent this focus on its own operations constitutes the subject matter of higher mathematics. The next round of philosophy was taken over by the concepts and controversies arising from this new pitch of intellectual reflexivity.

Disciplinary border-crossings flow both ways at various times. First, modern rapid-discovery science proclaimed its independence, even its supersession of philosophy; not long after, scientists were creating issues at a high level of abstraction that eventually bid to capture the center of the philosophical attention space. The movement of formal logic was created largely by mathematicians migrating onto philosophical turf. Frege, Boole, and Peano were mathematicians their entire professional lives; Bolzano was primarily a mathematician, and Peirce's only academic appointment was in a mathematics department; Russell, Whitehead, and Husserl all began as mathematicians before finding positions in philosophy; Carnap and Wittgenstein studied mathematical science before entering the philosophical network.

The pioneers of formal logic received scant attention in their own times. Mathematical logic was a tangential interest among mathematicians as among philosophers, and it is a good question how this obscure area became the defining identity of a large movement of twentieth-century philosophers. Within philosophy, formal logic was regarded as a stagnant area where little of importance had been developed for centuries. Midcentury tendencies toward an inductive logic (such as those of Whewell and Mill) further denigrated the traditional syllogistic forms, leading away from a logical calculus and toward empiricism. Nevertheless, within the German philosophical attention space, deductive logic was slowly rising as a topic of controversy. On one side, Cohen and the Neo-Kantians identified philosophy with the investigation of the logics guaranteeing the validity of each intellectual discipline; on the other side, the movements of Wundt and Brentano proposed to derive logic from empirical psychology. This empiricist tendency acquired increasing fame in the 1880s and 1890s as the physicist Mach joined forces with the new laboratory psychologists, grounding his phenomenalist positivism on the propensity of the nervous system toward economy of thought.

The self-conscious takeoff of the formal logic movement came with Russell and his network in the early 1900s. It then became an ideology within philosophy, expanding beyond the specialized enterprise of building a logic system for the foundations of mathematics into a program to reconstruct all of philosophy and purge everything which could not be reconstructed. The logical formalists claimed to be putting first mathematics, then science in general, on a secure foundation. In fact these issues had arisen over and above the actual practice of scientists and mathematicians, and doubtless their fields would have continued much the same without the activity of the logicians. This is why the mathematicians who discovered the new logical tools tended to migrate onto philosophical turf, where they could get a better hearing.

Typically an intellectual movement in philosophy is fruitful when it opens a vein of troubles. Counterintuitively, the largest philosophical attention-getter is not a method which solves all its problems as promised; this would dry up the life flow of the field, leaving nothing for later generations to work on. A successful movement hits on a method which seems to promise a great deal, while in fact encountering unanticipated difficulties. These problems give rise to new efforts at solution, and to rival tendencies within the movement; the result is intellectual conflicts which publicize and energize, provoking further creativity and sometimes ending up far from the starting place. The original thrust of Frege's method was fruitful in all these senses. The takeoff came at just the time when Russell was promoting his famous paradox about higher-order sets. Now the movement had not merely the straightforward path of carrying out the formalist program in mathematics, but also a branch concerned with the underlying problems of set theory. Frege's Platonism, initially an innocuous position within mathematics, opened all sorts of controversies when it was expanded into militant claims about truth and meaningfulness. And the assumption that logic is the foundational language of mathematics, when widened into a program for all of language, turned into an almost polar opposite by the end of Wittgenstein's tortuous career. The logical formalists provide one of the strongest proofs that a philosophical movement lives not on its solutions but on its problems.

The Social Invention of Higher Mathematics

Mathematics by the time of Frege had become very different from that familiar to Kant. In the 1700s the field consisted mostly of analysis, exploring the branches of Leibnizian calculus and their applications in physical science. By around 1780, the belief had become widespread among leading mathematicians that mathematics had exhausted itself, that there was little left to discover.[1] Unexpectedly, the following century was the most flamboyant in the history of the field, proliferating new areas and opening the realms of abstract higher mathematics.

The sudden expansion of creativity arose from shifts in the social bases of mathematics. Competition for recognition increased with a large expansion in the numbers of mathematicians. The older bases for full-time professional mathematicians had consisted of the official academies of science, notably Paris, along with Berlin, St. Petersburg, and a few others. The foundation of the École Polytechnique in 1794 introduced continuity of training for a highly selected group of students while providing teaching positions for the most creative. In Germany, the new public school system widened the selection net to pick up penurious students of potential talent (such as Gauss, a mathematical parallel to Fichte in this respect). The university reform extended to mathematics the emphasis on innovative research, as well as giving a distinctive slant toward pure knowledge apart from practical application. The process of disciplinary differentiation split math from physics and astronomy, encouraging the tendency to abstraction.

Along with these organizational changes came journals devoted largely or wholly to mathematics, beginning with the journal of the École Polytechnique in 1794, and the private journals of Crelle in Germany in 1826 and Liouville in France in 1836. Competition among journal editors for notable pieces, and the rush of mathematicians to anticipate opponents in publication, must have heightened emotional energy, while the specialized journals focused attention inward on the mathematical community in its own right (Boyer, 1985: 561; Collins and Restivo, 1983). Cauchy, who controlled the official publication of the Académie, was famous for rushing into print, and for unsavory tactics to anticipate or block his competitors. Mathematicians from peripheral countries or low-status positions, such as the Norwegian Abel and the École Normale Supérieure student Galois, were scandalously treated when they attempted to get their work published in Paris during 1826–1832. Nevertheless, their work came to light through the support of the editors of the new journals, who no doubt were looking for material to launch their enterprises with a splash.[2]

Two results of these conditions were a movement toward rigor and the takeoff into pure abstraction. The mathematicians of the previous century in exploring analysis had left behind the deductive proofs of the Euclidean method; they argued by induction from particular examples, from intuition or physical cases. General theorems were often guessed at and left without proof. Without any inquiring into their validity, new concepts were used such as the convergence of series and integrals, differentials of higher order, infinitesimal increments, and procedures which amounted to discarding terms and dividing by zero (Kline, 1972: 392–394, 616–618, 1024; Kitcher, 1984: 235). Rigor was disregarded in part because mathematics was interpreted physically; as long as empirically useful results were obtained in the sciences, proofs were considered needless subtleties. Socially this attitude was a product of the lack of differentiation between the activity of the mathematician and the physicist or even the engineer. D'Alembert and others held that the traditional field of mathematics had now turned into mechanics, and the attitude of disregarding rigor continued among applied mathematicians such as Fourier and Poisson into the 1820s and 1830s. Even those mathematicians who, like Euler, were caught up in the game of inventing algorithms had confidence in the manipulation of symbols without inquiring deeply into their meaning; the "machinery" of mathematics was socially convincing because it gave repeatable results.

The shift to rigor was driven by the hyper-competitiveness exemplified by Cauchy, and by the academicization of mathematics brought about by the Polytechnique and the German universities. Unlike the virtuoso math of the academies, that taught in the schools was more systematic; scholasticism and pedantry contributed to a more careful statement of fundamentals (Grabiner, 1986). Even though the Polytechnique was intended for the training of engineers, it underwent a goal displacement typical of academic organization and began to treat the standards of mathematics as ends in themselves. Rigor is the form which bureaucratization takes inside the community of mathematicians as formal rules become treated as significant in their own right. In the German universities, independence from applied work broke the link with physical interpretations and eliminated a source of justification for intuitive concepts. Rigor was not a sudden realization of old faults but a social shift in relationships within the mathematical community.

In the previous century the lack of rigor had been criticized mainly from outside the ranks of mathematicians, by enemies of the scientific worldview such as Berkeley. Mathematicians could see the problem but did not consider it important.[3] From their point of view they were right. The rigor of the following generations did not invalidate any of the theorems of previous arithmetic, algebra, or Euclidean geometry but only put them on a new basis; even in analysis the old glaring expressions were remedied by more careful statement, but the results continued to be what mathematicians had previously known (Kline, 1972: 1026). It was not a practical matter of improving the utility of mathematics which gave rise to rigor but an internal development in the social game mathematicians were playing with one another. With Cauchy in the 1820s came the recognition that rigor was a way of beating one's opponents and simultaneously opening up a new field on which mathematicians could play. The increase in the numbers of mathematicians, their material bases, and the means of rival publications all amplified the drive toward new areas of innovation. The older belief that math was becoming stagnant and exhausted gave way to a feeling of unlimited vistas.

Rigor and abstract mathematics fed each other. Rigor was promoted by axiomatization, the return to systematic exposition and proof in the manner of Euclid, which had constituted the pedantic mathematics of the schools two centuries before.[4] Once the system of axioms was displayed, it became possible to vary the set, negating or eliminating some axioms and exploring the mathematical realm thereby opened up. In this way non-commutative algebras such as quaternions were developed in the 1840s. The most famous of these developments were the non-Euclidean geometries which became widely known in the 1860s (although formulated in the 1820s and adumbrated as far back as the 1760s), because they forced the recognition that mathematics had taken leave of physical interpretations.[5] In the new game of higher mathematics, entities were deliberately constructed whose properties are paradoxical from the point of view of common sense: continuous functions without derivatives at any point over an interval (Bolzano 1834; Weierstrass 1861, 1872); curves without length or curves which completely filled a space (Peano 1890); geometries in n-dimensional space (Cayley 1843, Grassmann 1844; see Boyer, 1985: 565, 604, 645; Kline, 1972: 1025, 1029–30). Paradoxes gave even more impetus to the movement for rigorization; distrusting spatial intuition and becoming aware of the naiveté of accepting traditional assumptions as self-evident, mathematicians began to split into rival movements for shoring up foundations.

By the 1860s, above all in Germany, recognition had dawned that a large part of mathematics consists in investigating arbitrary and abstract concepts without physical referents or even conventional geometric representation on paper. The result was a movement toward rebuilding the various branches of mathematics on numbers, arithmetizing analysis and geometry. Numbers, too, the last bastion of realist interpretation, came under scrutiny in the 1870s and 1880s by Weierstrass, Dedekind, Cantor, and Frege. When Cantor in 1879–1884 demonstrated the existence of transfinite numbers—successive orders of infinity—the movement of rigorization broke into open scandal. Kronecker, the powerful journal editor in Berlin, opposed publication of papers which created unnatural monstrosities, which he attributed to the methodological fallacy of using derivations going beyond finite series of steps. For Kronecker, only the natural numbers really exist; in defending a conservative position in this respect, he was provoked into formulating a radical program to reconstruct all of mathematics, which after 1900 became the intuitionist program. Cantor, who foreshadowed the formalists, was clearly aware of the power struggle taking place over the nature and organization of mathematics. In 1883 he argued that the distinctiveness of mathematics as a field is its freedom to create its own concepts without regard for reality (Kline, 1972: 1031). To back up his position, he pushed for the separation of German mathematicians from the Gesellschaft Deutscher Naturforscher und Ärzte, and became the founding president of the Deutsche Mathematiker-Vereinigung in 1891, and organizer of the first International Congress of Mathematicians in 1897, a stronghold of the formalist movement (Dauben, 1979; Collins and Restivo, 1983). The formalists represent the tendency of autonomous specialization in mathematics at its most extreme.

Frege's Anti-psychologistic Logic

It was in this context that Frege developed his project to found arithmetic on logic. In the process he had to create a usable logic. It was hardly a matter of supporting one discipline on a more prestigeful one; mathematics was much more advanced, and the prestige of logic dates largely from the adoption of Frege's system.

Logic was in the air, but the strongest winds were blowing from another direction. Just at this time the Neo-Kantians were intruding as usual into other specialties. Cohen and the Marburg school (starting in 1874) made a program out of investigating the logics of the various disciplines; the regulatory logic of jurisprudence, for instance, is ethics; other fields—mathematics, education, social justice, physics—each has its underlying logic. Psychologists too spotted logic as an old and stagnant field ripe for reform by new scientific methods. Brentano launched his *Psychology from an Empirical Standpoint* in 1874, which transforms all propositions into acts of judgment in empirical conscious-ness.[6] Brentano attempted to eliminate deductive, a priori logic and replace it with purely empirical judgments about objects. In the next year Wundt estab-lished the first psychological research laboratory, and touted psychology as an experimental science which would become the basis of all the human sciences and of philosophy as well. Logic was to be founded on scientifically discovered structures of the human psyche. Another branch of inductivist logic made inroads in Germany by import. A militant scientific movement in England had led the intellectual opposition to the unreformed religious universities; in the person of J. S. Mill, it took on the scholastic logic and proposed to replace it with a logic of empirical induction.

Frege's creativity was sparked by opposition to these movements. In his writings his principal foil is Mill and the latter's German followers; as psy-chologism flourished in the 1880s and 1890s, Frege's anti-psychologism grew more pointed. Frege saw a very different logic opening up from the mathe-matical controversies now coming to a head, owing to his position in the mathematical network as well as the philosophical one. As a student Frege had heard Lotze and had studied mathematics at Göttingen, the great center of German mathematics, where Riemann produced his generalizing work on non-Euclidean geometry in the 1850s. Frege became a friend of Cantor, nearby at Halle, already embattled in his struggle against the conservative mathema-ticians; it was Cantor's tools that Frege developed.

In 1879 Frege formulated in his *Begriffsschrift* (conceptual notation) the first comprehensive or general logic (Kneale and Kneale, 1984: 510–511; Coffa, 1991: 69–71). Traditional logic descending from Aristotle (what would now be called primary logic) was restricted to classifying various kinds of propositions. To some extent Stoic and medieval scholastic logic had gone on to formulate general principles underlying valid propositional inference; in the more general arena, Leibniz and later Boole had developed the aspects of logic concerned with attributes or classes. Frege parted company with logic in the form of subjects and predicates, of "all A's are B's." Ordinary language hides the crucial distinctions and elevates merely grammatical differences obscuring the underlying content. The lineage of ancient Greek logic, institutionalized in late antiquity in alliance with the profession of grammarians and continued in the curriculum of the medieval universities, was now displaced by the imperi-alism of mathematical methods. Modern mathematics arose around 1600 by breaking with verbally formulated geometry, and developing instead the new technical format of variables and functions in one area after another. The higher mathematics of the 1800s had proceeded by exploring successively more abstract levels of the function. Frege's stroke was to recognize that the central tool of modern mathematics could be extended to logic.

Frege starts not with concepts and what is predicated about them but with judgments. His key idea is that the step from a judgment or assertion to a concept is analogous to the mathematical relationship between a function and its variables. Instead of assuming that we already know the concept, Frege begins with it as an empty frame to be filled.[7] From this perspective singular and general representations are entirely different kinds of things, arrived at by very different procedures: the singular ("this horse") is a proper name given independently of judgment, while the general ("horse," "horses") arises only after a judgment has been made.

In Frege's vision, talking about the world does not consist in making connections, so to speak, horizontally on a plane; it is a hierarchy of levels. Making use of the technical tool by which the machinery of modern mathematics was created, Frege introduces a formal symbolism to force automatic recognition of new conceptual distinctions: using different print fonts to separate clearly use and mention; a symbol indicating that something is asserted, distinguished from what is asserted; strokes which replace "not," "and," "or," "if then"; and the universal quantifier "for every value of x," which renders the distinctions among the "all," "some," and "none" of ordinary language. Confusions in the older rhetoric now come into view. To speak of a "quality" had confused the unasserted content with the fact of its being asserted (Coffa, 1991: 63). The copula is not something separate which links a subject and its qualities, but an aspect of the functional statement; for this reason, Frege ([1883] 1980: 65) comments, the ontological proof of the existence of God breaks down, since existence is not a quality.[8]

Frege came upon the issue by way of clarifying the concept of number. Ordinarily "one" and "unit" are taken as synonymous. If we count three objects ($1 + 1 + 1 = 3$), how is it possible that objects which are different can all be treated as identical?[9] The number 3 is not an agglomeration of objects collected together, since they retain their properties which made them distinct; but if we are counting identicals, we never reach a plurality (Frege [1883] 1980: 50). The mathematical plus symbol ($+$) cannot be interpreted as the "and" of ordinary language. The solution is to recognize number as a self-subsistent object. Frege considers it the extension of a concept, that is, the set of all instances which fall under that concept. Frege's numbers are Platonic; they are not derived from counting or sequences, nor are they properties abstracted from things in the sense that colors are. This shifts our attention to the procedure by which we make assertions about numbers, to the judgment that the number of the wineglasses on the table is four—a statement of identity as to which number that is.

The procedure for establishing numerical identity is independent of counting; it is to establish a one-to-one correlation between the objects in each set, just as a waiter need not count all the silverware but only lay one fork alongside every knife (Kneale and Kneale, 1984: 461). Frege goes on to build the entire number system by purely logical definitions. Zero he defines as the set of all objects which are not identical with themselves; this is a logical impossibility, so nothing falls under it (a fateful move in view of Russell's later paradox). The category zero is absolutely simple in Frege's assumption, so now he can define "1" as the set of all sets which are identical with the zero set (not with the contents of the zero set). Further numbers are built up as sets which contain all of the preceding number sets (2 is [zero, 1]; 3 is [zero, 1, 2]; etc.). Paradoxes about infinite numbers, just then giving rise to scandal because of Cantor's unending series of transfinite numbers, are taken care of in Frege's nested levels. The number belonging to the concept "finite number" is an infinite number; it is not a number following in the series of natural numbers. Frege allied himself with Cantor, who had begun his theory of sets only a few years earlier in 1874.[10] This was an alliance of the radicals against the establishment controlled from Berlin by Kronecker, the rigorist enemy of paradox-generating abstract methods in mathematics.

In 1892 Frege introduced a distinction between sense and reference. The problem arises in interpreting the equal sign (=) in a mathematical equation. If this is strictly a sign of identity, then $1 + 3 = 4$ can be replaced with $4 = 4$, an uninformative statement. The equation is telling us something, but not about the referent of either side of the equation; that referent is the number-object 4 in either case. Each side has a sense as well as a reference; the sense of $1 + 3$ is different from the sense of $2 + 2$. The same can be said of verbal expressions: "the morning star is the same as the evening star" is uninformative insofar as both parts refer to the planet Venus; but each expression arises in a different semantic context and has a different sense. A referent is an object (which for Frege is not just something perceptible, but can include numbers, times, and so on). The sense is on a different plane, the semantic means by which referents are singled out for attention (Kneale and Kneale, 1984: 496; Wedberg, 1984: 113–122). Propositions as well as names and expressions have referents; for Frege, the referent of a proposition is its truth value. Thus all true propositions have the same referent, the True, just as all false propositions refer to the False.[11] Frege's sense-reference distinction was not picked up until the 1920s, when Carnap began to use it in a strongly reductive program, counting propositions as scientific only if every name in them has not only sense but also reference. Frege's Platonism, when broadened into an epistemology, gave rise to the imperious claims of logical positivism.

At the same time Frege opened the path for Wittgenstein and the recognition that a language or symbol system contains multiple levels. He forces us to see that all our intellectual activity takes place in a language, and exposes confusions between various levels within the language and what the language is talking about. One offshoot was the belief that philosophical problems are merely mistakes of this sort, which could be cleared away by careful analysis. Both the positivist and the analytical movements eventually discovered that matters could not be disposed of so easily. That too was foreshadowed in Frege. The world is more complex than is apparent in subjects and predicates, or in the distinction between the factual-empirical realm and the logical-conceptual. Frege points out that making definitions is not an arbitrary act of subjective creation; definitions show their worth by their fruitfulness in the chain of argument. Definitions have consequences that cannot be known in advance. "The mathematician cannot create things at will, any more than the geographer can; he too can only discover what is there and give it a name." Yet "observation itself already includes within it a logical activity" (Frege [1883] 1980: 99, 108). Recasting the refinements of abstract mathematical argument into tools for philosophy, Frege opened a puzzle space containing room for many positions.

In the eyes of the twentieth-century formalist school, the greatest figure of the previous century was Frege. He is depicted as the turning point in all modern histories of logic (Wedberg, 1984; Kneale and Kneale, 1984; Dummett, 1981; Coffa, 1991). In his time Frege was a minor figure, a mathematician in a not particularly eminent department (Jena, much declined from its glory days), unrecognized by his profession and never promoted to *Ordinarius*. He became known primarily because Russell drew on him as both ally and foil in a more prominent network of controversies.[12] Frege was not entirely isolated in the networks, but he was treated as supernumerary among the more central debates of the German attention space. Eventually the creative splits of the mathematical network came into contact around him. In the late 1890s Frege corresponded with the formalist radicals Peano, and Hilbert, the future leader of one wing of the mathematical foundations controversy. A few years before his encounter with Russell in 1902, Frege entered into correspondence with Husserl, another ex-mathematician working on the broader implications of the foundations of mathematics. Creativity occurs by structural opposition and recombination of networks. In Husserl, two antagonistic networks come together. When Frege critiqued Husserl's book in 1894, he made contact with a pupil of Brentano, the most famous representative of the empiricist logic which Frege was combatting. Frege is a central node in the formative period of both great movements of the early 1900s, movements that would grow up into the divide between logical positivism and phenomenology.

Advantages of Provinciality: The British Route from Algebra to Philosophy

Modern logical philosophy comes from the convergence of two lines, German and British. Russell, who brought them together, was the product of a British network going back several generations. As in Germany, British logic was produced largely by mathematicians. It is not obvious why British mathematics should have become creative in the 1830s, for it had been stagnant since the death of Newton. The social conditions which supported the advance of mathematics on the Continent were lacking: Britain had neither the educational reforms of the German universities or the École Polytechnique nor the virtuoso mathematics of the academies. British mathematics had been largely in the hands of the universities on the old unreformed model, where the Newtonian calculus of fluxions had become a scholastic tradition to be upheld against the Leibnizian rival.

When British mathematics came alive, it was in connection with the movement for university modernization on Continental lines. The Cambridge Analytical Society was founded in 1813 at Trinity College to introduce Continental developments in analysis; its youthful members, later to become famous in various fields, included Herschel (the future astronomer), Babbage, Whewell, and Peacock. In 1817 Peacock substituted differential for Newtonian fluxional notation in the mathematics tripos; he remained active lifelong in the movement for university reform. The network of reformers flowing from this group carried on a long struggle, to a considerable extent by exodus and detour from the traditional universities. Peacock's student De Morgan refused a university position because of the religious test, going instead to the reforming University College at London; for similar reasons Cayley (another Trinity pupil) and Sylvester (De Morgan's pupil, debarred as a Jew) spent long years in private life, at minor technicals schools, or in America, until positions opened for them at Cambridge and Oxford after the university reforms. Jevons, another of De Morgan's pupils, got his position at Owens College, the reform-oriented predecessor of Manchester University.

British mathematics owes its distinctive orientation to the advantages of comparative backwardness. Whereas Continental mathematics was concerned with the complexities of higher analysis, geometry, number theory, and the solvability of equations, British mathematics dug into the relatively elementary features of algebra (Richards, 1988; Kline, 1972: 773–776, 797, 805; Boyer, 1985: 621–626; Enros, 1981; Cannon, 1978: chap. 3). Ever since Berkeley in

1734 had attacked Newton's infinitesimals, British mathematicians had been on the defensive. Around 1830 there was a wave of controversy over the use of imaginary numbers in algebraic practice, despite their lack of a physical interpretation. Conservatives grew more aggressive during the escalating conflict against Continentally oriented reformers. Not only imaginary numbers but negative numbers as well cannot be said to exist; how then could any valid mathematics be built upon them? It was not the first time a conservative attack has provoked fundamental innovation.

In 1830 Peacock attempted to put algebra on axiomatic foundations similar to Euclidean geometry, which is to say on the model of the school classic and favorite of academic conservatives. Peacock thereby brought into the open the basic principles of arithmetic operations, the associative, commutative, and distributive laws; by abstraction from real numbers, he attempted to justify (but actually asserted only by fiat) that similar rules hold good for operations with any magnitudes, including complex numbers. In the same year De Morgan began to publish on double algebra (i.e., the algebra of complex numbers, combining a real number with an imaginary). The intentions of Peacock and De Morgan were traditional, in that they denied any other forms of algebra were possible than those following the laws governing positive integers; their model was empirical science, and they gave no truth value to an abstract mathematics in its own right (Richards, 1980). This attempt to incorporate higher mathematics into the conservative framework of non-specialist liberal education still prevailing in the English universities led to revolutionary combinations.

Peacock's and De Morgan's work provoked efforts to extend the method of representing complex numbers graphically as vectors on a plane. The Irish physicist W. R. Hamilton in the 1830s gave a quasi-physical interpretation of operations on complex numbers as rotations in a plane; for a number of years he attempted to extend this method to rotations in three dimensions, and in 1843 realized that the method would work only if one dropped the commutative law of multiplication. The resulting new form of algebra, quaternions, became famous because of the shock it gave traditional belief that the laws of arithmetic are natural. In fact the discovery came directly out of efforts to find a physical justification for imaginary numbers. Hamilton's methods attempted to rescue them by a spatial analogy, but at the cost of giving up traditional operations.[13]

In logic the conservative situation of British education again set the direction of innovation. Just as Euclidean geometry dominated the mathematics curriculum of the schools, logic—a field which had been abolished in the French curriculum and transformed in Germany into metaphysics—still loomed large in the philosophy course. The movement for modernization and scientific reform thus included attempts to replace Aristotelean syllogistic logic with a new logic of empirical inquiry. This was the subject of Whewell's work at Trinity, Cambridge, in the 1830s and of John Stuart Mill's first book, the source of his early fame, his *Logic* in 1843. On the side of the algebraists, De Morgan in the 1840s extended his axiomatization into logic. This brought him into a public dispute over priority with Sir William Hamilton (not to be confused with the physicist W. R. Hamilton) in 1847. Conflicts typically lead to widening the network of allies; in the same year Boole's first book, *The Mathematical Analysis of Logic,* was prompted by Boole's intervening in the dispute on De Morgan's side.

De Morgan and Boole were reformers, mathematical imperialists on the turf of logic. Sir William Hamilton was a philosophical conservative. An Edinburgh law professor, Hamilton had acquired the chair of logic and metaphysics in 1836 for his defense of traditional religion after the manner of the Scottish common-sense philosophy. Reid and Stewart had rebutted Humean skepticism by a classification of innate human faculties, including a faculty of common sense. In 1829—just the time when Carlyle was popularizing German philosophy at Edinburgh—Hamilton updated the position against the growing influence of Kant. Hamilton denied Kant's antinomies; by the law of contradiction, either space is infinite or it is not, although we cannot know which. There is direct knowledge through the senses of the existence of objects, although *what* they are must be inferred through logic. In conflicts conservatism cannot stay static; Hamilton too overthrows syllogistic logic as making inadequate distinctions. His doctrine holds that the quantities "all," "some," and "none" apply to the predicate as well as the subject. "All men are mortal" is ambiguous; it could mean "all men are all mortals" (i.e., only men are mortal) or "all men are some (of the) mortals." Hamilton's quantification of the predicate was buried in his better-known philosophical system and became known only in the 1840s, when Hamilton raised a priority dispute with De Morgan.[14] Since Hamilton by now was the most famous British philosopher of his day, he made an excellent sounding board for De Morgan's logic.[15]

Boole's *Laws of Thought* (1854) generalized this controversy over the most elementary parts of arithmetic. Boole was an autodidact, a mathematics teacher at an elementary school, seemingly an unlikely person to contribute to the frontiers of mathematics. But Boole looks less like an anomaly when we see that individuals with limited formal education dominated the philosophy network in the British midcentury generation, unlike at most other times: Spencer, Huxley, Lewes, George Eliot, Buckle all are similar to Boole in this respect. Non-academic creativity in philosophy peaked in the 1840s through the 1860s. This was the period when the traditional university system was most under criticism and alternative bases for intellectual networks were expanding—principally the middle-class journals of opinion on which the circle of London evolutionists supported themselves. Mathematics, however, was more closely attached to academic bases; Boole made his first connection here in the early 1840s by publishing, in the *Cambridge Mathematical Journal,* some elementary but pioneering work in the computation of algebraic invariants—one of the alternative algebras which Cayley was to develop (Kline, 1972: 927). Personal correspondence with De Morgan at the time of the Hamilton controversy brought Boole recognition and an academic position in Ireland.

Boole takes Peacock and De Morgan a step further. Mathematics is no longer to be seen as the science of magnitudes, but as a general method for operations with symbols of whatever content. Boolean algebra redefines arithmetical operations as unions and intersections of sets. Subsequently Boole's ideas were applied in Jevons's "logical piano" (1869)—a combination of logic machine and mechanical calculator—and in Venn's diagrams of 1881 (Kneale and Kneale, 1984: 420–421; Boyer, 1985: 672).

Most of the action in British algebra-cum-logic took place within the overlapping branches of a network (see Figure 13.2). One node is Trinity College, Cambridge, beginning with the mathematical and logical reformers Peacock, Herschel, Babbage, and Whewell, who produced a chain of pupils including De Morgan, Cayley, Sylvester, and Jevons, with Boole as an offshoot. Another lineage descends from the Utilitarian circle of philosophical radicals around Bentham and James Mill. By midcentury this group had spawned two successor groups: one at London, the Huxley–Spencer–George Eliot circle of anti-religious evolutionists; the other branch played back into Trinity College, where a circle formed in the 1850s around John Grote, younger brother of George Grote, who had belonged to the original Utilitarians. Among Grote's protégés were Venn and Sidgwick; the latter, who wrote the great work of ethics on modified Utilitarian principles, was the teacher of McTaggart and G. E. Moore. Together with Cayley, professor of mathematics at Cambridge from the 1860s down to his death in 1895, this constituted an intergenerational network leading directly to Whitehead and Russell.

The network was about to become fateful in philosophy. It also stimulated the creativity of another characteristic British field. British economics was created by much the same network we have been reviewing in philosophy: Locke, Hume, and Smith in the core philosophical networks of their time; Ricardo (1817) and J. S. Mill (1848) in the Utilitarian circles. The earlier ingredients were a non-academic social movement, combined with the analytical principles generated by an intellectual network. When the British universities reformed in the 1860s, economics now became academic, meshing with the nearest adjacent disciplines, thus intersecting with both philosophy and mathematics. Jevons, who developed the marginal utility theory in 1871 to displace the dominant labor theory of value, was part of the network of mathematician-logicians preceding Russell. The shift in organizational base of these networks in the 1870s was responsible for the revolution in economic method. Economics had long existed as a practical discipline in connection with political doctrines and movements. Jevons promoted a paradigm revolution as the field became academicized and de-politicized; economics found its slot in the universities as a broadening of the contents of moral philosophy, hybridized with mathematics. Jevons got his chair at Manchester (1866) in logic and political economy a few years before his development of marginal utility; as a pupil of the mathematical networks, he colonized the field for mathematical methods. Sidgwick, too, like most other Utilitarians, also wrote on economics. His lineage would extend into the following generation with both G. E. Moore and Keynes.

The Logicism of Russell and Wittgenstein

At Cambridge after the university reform, there occurred a confluence of all the major trends of British intellectual life: the algebraist-logicians; the Utilitarians; but also the Idealists, under whose auspices the newly reformed universities passed from religious to secular control. Russell epitomizes the resulting transformation, for he was involved in every aspect of these networks. His teachers (Ward, Stout) and early friends (McTaggart, Moore) were Idealists, but there were also Utilitarian connections.[16] On the algebra–mathematical-logical side, Russell not only inherited the Cambridge tradition but was also an aggressive internationalist, attending the new mathematical congresses led by Cantor and Hilbert and importing the latest techniques. These he promoted as solutions to long-standing puzzles that Idealists had used for mystifying science. Here Russell continued the tradition of British reformers who had been touting German advances ever since the Humboldtian revolution. Russell was a central figure in a group which carried off several revolutions at once. We take up first the mathematical-logical strand and its conjuncture with the anti-Idealist break; later we will return to the post-Utilitarian movement and ordinary language philosophy, which emerged out of this same network matrix and indeed in the same circle of friends.

In the late 1890s Cayley's pupil Whitehead extended the British algebraic tradition into a generalized treatment of logic.[17] His pupil Russell, in turn, writing in 1897 on the foundations of geometry, classified the various non-standard geometries around their axiomatic properties. In 1903 Russell's *Principles of Mathematics* took on the even more ambitious task of founding all of mathematics and physics upon a small number of concepts of symbolic logic. It brought together the logic of classes, Dedekind's and Cantor's theories of

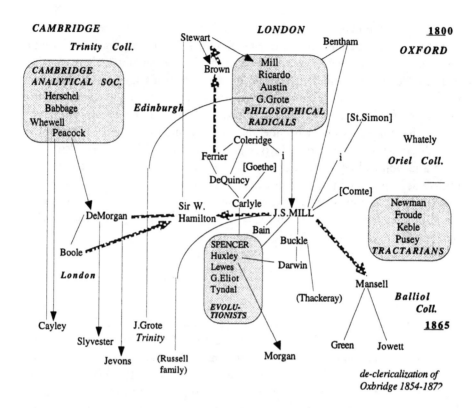

CAMBRIDGE   LONDON   1800

Trinity Coll.   Stewart   Bentham   OXFORD

CAMBRIDGE ANALYTICAL SOC.
Herschel
Babbage
Whewell
Peacock

Brown

Mill
Ricardo
Austin
G.Grote
PHILOSOPHICAL RADICALS

Edinburgh

[St.Simon]

Whately

Oriel Coll.

Coleridge

Ferrier

[Goethe]

DeQuincy

i

i

[Comte]

Carlyle

DeMorgan   Sir W. Hamilton   J.S.MILL

Bain

Newman
Froude
Keble
Pusey
TRACTARIANS

Boole

Buckle

SPENCER
Huxley
Lewes
G.Eliot
Tyndal
EVOLU-
TIONISTS

Darwin

London

Cayley

Mansell

(Thackeray)

Balliol
Coll.

1865

Slyvester   J.Grote
Trinity

Jevons   (Russell
family)   Morgan   Green   Jowett

de-clericalization of
Oxbridge 1854-187?

FIGURE 13.2. BRITISH PHILOSOPHERS AND MATHEMATICIANS,
1800–1935: UNIVERSITY REFORM, IDEALIST MOVEMENT,
TRINITY-BLOOMSBURY CIRCLE

numbers, the infinitesimal calculus, and the branches of geometry. Russell was importing a German mathematical movement to Britain; his work followed up Felix Klein's Erlangen program to unify geometry, and Hilbert's still broader program of axiomatic unification. In the process, Russell independently created much the same logic of sets as Frege. This is no surprise; both of them were in the same faction in the mathematical foundations conflict, allied with Cantor. The two branches of the movement toward axiomatization—the route through rigorization of analysis and geometry on the Continent and the route through elementary algebra in Britain—now converged.

Just as W. R. Hamilton had gotten credit for quaternions while Grassman was relatively ignored in Germany, Russell reaped the initial fame while Frege languished. This happened because algebra and elementary arithmetic were much more central in British mathematical interests than they were on the Continent, where the main action was in the more elaborately developed "advanced" fields. Peirce, who paralleled Frege during the 1870s in developing

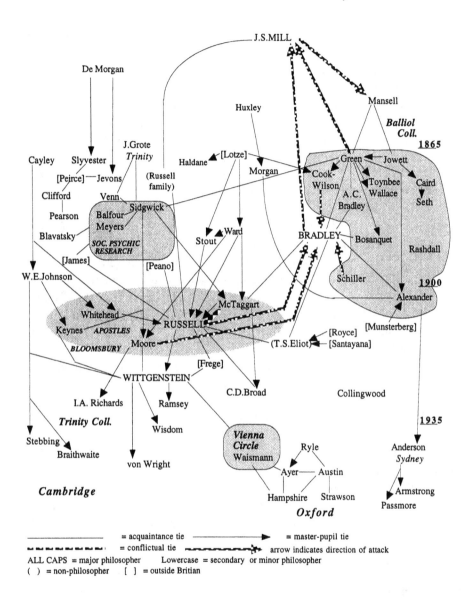

a new, highly generalized logic, branched off from the British mathematical tradition of investigating alternative algebras; Peirce too attracted little attention at the time. The coincidence of three efforts in basic logic—Frege's, Peirce's, and Russell's—indicates that the move was available to be made by extending current lines. Only after 1900, when the mathematical foundations controversy attracted general attention in philosophy, did interest in a new logic crystallize in the attention space.

Why should a highly technical area of mathematics spill over into philosophy? We find it happening across the board in the generation of 1900: Husserl, Russell, later the Vienna Circle. Mathematical logic was a meta-territory arising from the confluence of axiomatic programs in algebra, in geometry, and in the arithmetization of analysis. Having been formulated on an appropriately general level, it rose above mathematics like a balloon slipping its moorings and floating away. Although it arose out of disputes over the techniques of mathematical construction and proof, the axiomatic programs become unnecessary for mathematicians' ordinary work of discovering and proving algorithms; it became a goal displacement of the sort familiar in the sociology of organizations, an end in itself pursued by its own specialized community. Soon disputes and factions among meta-mathematicians were generating their own dynamics, no longer dependent on stimulation from ordinary mathematical work. Meta-mathematics now converged with philosophical turf, and thus with the community of philosophers. For philosophy is precisely the attention space of most generalized issues; the episode of meta-mathematics recapitulates the way philosophies have emerged throughout history, as the disputes of substantive areas (nature cosmologies of the early Greeks, salvation techniques in India, theological training for Christians) take on an attention focus of their own.

In this case logic got a tremendous boost in attention when it shifted from a technical concern within mathematics to an activity of philosophers. For philosophers occupy the space where claims are made about knowledge in general, and thus about the general-purpose role of all intellectuals; major controversies on this turf are hard to ignore. It was for this reason that mathematicians hostile to philosophy, such as Russell and Wittgenstein, ended up as philosophers, that is, in the attention space where they were most successful and where they could avoid the fate of Frege and the early Peirce.

The explicit emergence of meta-mathematics and of the logicist movement within philosophy occurred in a few years at the turn of the century. Russell was the shock center from which emanated the second wave of the mathematical foundations crisis, stimulating the competing programs of Hilbert's formalism (1904) and Brouwer's intuitionism (1907). Already in exchanges starting in 1897 and continuing through 1906 (Coffa, 1991: 129–133), the mathematician Poincaré had taken issue with Russell's approach, raising objections in the direction that would become intuitionism. Russell soon managed to escalate the crisis. In an appendix to *Principles of Mathematics* (1903), Russell draws attention to Frege's logic and points out a contradiction in the notion of sets which are not members of themselves. (Is this set a member of itself? If yes, no; if no, yes.) Since Frege's extensional logic depends on translating all predicates (i.e., concepts or intentions) into sets, and thus on forming sets of elements of any kind whatever, Russell's paradox was a blow at the heart of the entire system. This was no isolated incident; within a year, Zermelo made a sensation with his proof of a more generalized paradox.[18] Zermelo's axiom of choice set off much criticism by mathematicians, especially helping to provoke the formation of the opposing intuitionists, including once again the anti-logicist Poincaré.

Paradoxes and controversy do not derail logicism but launch it. Although Frege, emotionally exhausted by lack of support, declared the bankruptcy of his set theory approach, Russell forged ahead immediately to re-ground the program on a theory of types. There is an ontological hierarchy of individuals, sets, sets of sets, and so on; statements about membership in sets are meaningful only between adjacent levels (Wedberg, 1984: 134–135). Far from abjuring *The Principles of Mathematics*, Russell developed its sketch into a fully formalized system. He enlisted his old mathematics teacher, and by 1910 he and Whitehead in *Principia Mathematica* had derived in detail a portion of elementary arithmetic going considerably further than Frege. Logicians were more interested in the *Principia* than were mathematicians. A full-scale movement of logicist philosophers was springing up; and their favorite topics, in a well-worn pattern of intellectual life, were connected not with extending Russell's method along the path he had marked, but with re-digging the foundations at just the points where he indicated there was trouble. The logicist program claimed to build mathematics from the simplest possible starting point, reducing assumptions to the most unassailable and obvious premises. But the theory of types, like Zermelo's axiom of choice, was neither obvious nor simple. Replacing such devices became the central puzzle around which both meta-mathematics and logical formalist philosophies grew.

As Russell came into his own wielding the weapons of logicism, his stance toward philosophy was that it is a history of conceptual mistakes. Hazy metaphysical systems can be cleared away by using the tools which had worked so well in mathematics, just as Dedekind had cleared up Zeno's paradoxes of motion and modern rigor had given the final answer to Berkeley's objections to the calculus. Unlike the German mathematicians, who generally had no animus against philosophy, Russell took this militant stance because he was simultaneously engaged in two battles: for set theory in mathematics and against Idealism in philosophy. Idealism, as we have seen, was everywhere the philosophy of the transition from the old religious university to secularism. In Germany the transition was two generations past, but in England it had taken place in the generation of Russell's teachers. Russell himself along with his friends was an Idealist into the 1890s. Russell's break with Idealism was especially pointed because Idealists too tended to take logic as their turf. Bear in mind that logic, before the revolution worked by Frege and Russell, was widely considered an ancient and stagnant field, a soft territory tempting invasion by new philosophical methods. Thus Hegel could couch his dialectical metaphysics in the form of a logic; and in Russell's generation, Bosanquet (1888) and McTaggart (1910) continued to produce systems of Idealist logic.

The most famous logic was that of Bradley (1883), in which he used a critique of Mill's inductivism as stepping-stone to his Idealist system of 1893. Bradley's key argument (as we saw in Chapter 12) held that relations are illegitimate abstractions from an inexpressible Reality, as revealed by an infinite regress of relations which attach relations to their terms. Russell counterattacked accordingly. Bradley had assumed that relations are internal, constitutive of the objects that are related. The absurd consequences of this doctrine (including the mind-dependence of all objects) can be avoided by recognizing that relations are external; items that are related exist in their own right, unaffected by their relations with anything else. Russell's logical atomism directly opposed Bradley's Idealism.

Russell proposed a logically perfect language to overcome the mystifications of surface grammar in the subject-predicate form. All descriptive terms are to be replaced by logically proper names which simply designate. To use an un-Russellian example: "the son of God" is merely a circumlocution which can be replaced by "Jesus." For Bradley, who recognized no brute particular facts, it was the opposite: "Jesus" is above all "the son of God" and not vice versa. In Russell's reductionist program, all indirect, descriptive statements can be translated into statements about logically proper names, referring to things that one knows by acquaintance. Truth or falsity can be read off directly.[19]

As the controversy over meta-mathematics moved increasingly toward philosophical turf, Russell's own attention shifted to the larger consequences of his logical atomism. The basis of his influence was not so much the series of systems which Russell tried out during his lifetime as the direction he gave to subsequent philosophy. In fact the publication of *Principia Mathematica* posed a personal crisis for Russell; for all the investment of effort in three detailed volumes of formal derivations, the greatest attention was attracted to the ground-level flaws of the theory of types. At just this point Wittgenstein appeared at Cambridge and was adopted by Russell as the disciple to carry on his method and remedy its flaws (Monk, 1990: 36–65). Wittgenstein was undoubtedly an individual of high intelligence and powers of concentration; what alone was unique, however, and what fitted him for the role of iconoclastic genius, were the opportunities presented as he was welcomed into the core of the intellectual network at this challenging moment.

Wittgenstein saw that the method of a logically perfect language could be cut loose from mathematics—where Russell's trajectory had encountered a dead end—and generalized to all of philosophy. During 1912–1916, Wittgenstein reworked and radicalized Russell's ingredients. Wittgenstein postulates simple elements or objects—in effect, those designated by Russell's logically proper names—as the ultimate constituents of the world. Facts are combinations of objects into states of affairs; all meaningful statements allegedly can be translated into propositions about these, and the totality of elementary sentences would give complete knowledge of the world. Objects have purely internal properties; they are unaffected by one another, and contain all possibilities of entering into combinations. This logical atomism continues Russell's trajectory against Bradley's holism. Each state of affairs is independent of all others, and no inferences are possible from one to another. Wittgenstein gives no examples of simple things in the *Tractatus;* in his notebooks of 1914–1916, he wonders whether they might be like points of light or the particles of atomic physics (Wedberg, 1984: 166)—much in the same way that Russell vacillated as to the nature of his reals. In effect they are Wittgenstein's effort to postulate what the world is like before or "below" the making of propositions about it. The simples are not merely the ground level of an empirical reduction; they are possibilities in logical space out of which all combinations can be generated, beyond the changing configurations of mere experience.

Although Wittgenstein's system has the flavor of reductionism, it is an ontological hierarchy. The place of logic in the system is empty but nevertheless central. The new Fregean method of logic is the key ingredient which Wittgenstein had inherited, and it cuts in a different direction than the program of reduction to ultimate simples. Wittgenstein expresses this conflict by displaying logic as deriving from tautologies (in the case of logical truths) and contradictions (in the case of falsities). True logical propositions are known without our knowing the truth of their components; "it is raining or it is not raining" is true, regardless of the facts. Wittgenstein's technical contribution in logic was to work out a method of truth tables, based on the work of Russell's friend Sheffer at Harvard, to show which combinations of propositions are tautologies, contradictions, or contingent statements about facts.

Wittgenstein's most famous move occurs at the place where he criticizes Russell's tradition, and where he locates the deepest troubles for future philosophers to work on. This is the distinction between what is sayable and what can only be shown. One meaning of the unsayable is that the ultimate ontology is arbitrary, a brute reality that cannot be further explained. Unsayability is found on several levels. Absolutely simple objects, the ultimate constituents of the world, cannot be described, a claim already implicit in Russell's knowledge by acquaintance. Wittgenstein expands knowledge by acquaintance to every level of his ontology. At the level of propositions, what is displayed is the logical form of reality, a picture corresponding in the arrangement of its parts to the arrangement of states of affairs in the world. Wittgenstein asserts something like an overarching Platonic realm of logical form, that which propositions "must have in common with reality in order to be able to represent it." This form is shown but it is not said in the proposition; in order to do so "we should have to be able to station ourselves with propositions somewhere outside logic, that is to say outside the world" (*Tractatus* 4.12).

Similarly, in discussing Frege's technique of functions and their contents, the fundamental break from the subject-predicate logic, Wittgenstein points to a category of formal concepts beyond those discerned by Frege. These are not represented or said by the function but are *shown* by the kind of sign being used: name signifiers for objects, number signs for numbers, operation signs for operations, and so on (*Tractatus* 4.126–4.1272). In effect this is a generalization of Frege's founding of the number system on cardinal numbers, Platonic essences of numbers which are beyond the ordinal numbers of empirical counting. The most innovative part of Wittgenstein's version is that Platonic forms are no longer taken as the highest species of the rationally intelligible; quite the opposite, they are what is unsayable. With the weapon of the unsayable/showable, Wittgenstein is able to defend still further realms, the higher reality of ethics and mystical religion, unaffectable by anything that can be said on the merely verbal level.

Wittgenstein's distinction between saying and showing crystallizes from several aspects of Frege and Russell's work: Platonism, knowledge by acquaintance, and the difficulties of the theory of types. Saying/showing is supposed to obviate the theory of types. Actually it grows out of it, a reformulation and extension of the basic thrust of Frege and Russell in exploring the relations among hierarchical levels in propositions. Wittgenstein declares that the theory of types is unnecessary to avoid paradox because the different kinds of symbols used in a logical language directly show that various kinds of realms are to be treated differently and cannot be mixed. Implicitly, one knows that the kind of thing symbolized by "a" or "b" plays a different role from those symbolized by "x," "y," "z." The source of Wittgenstein's discovery of the saying/showing distinction is his explicit investigation of the way symbols do their work (Monk, 1990: 92; *Tractatus* 4.0312–4.0411). He resists the habit of seeing symbols as purely conventional, which had blinded previous logicians from seeing how symbols are chosen through their success or failure in expressing various things.[20]

Frege and Russell had developed logic symbols in the course of developing their programs; now Wittgenstein turned the technique of meta-attention, which he had learned from his predecessors, on what they were doing. Wittgenstein's move was like breaking a gestalt frame, since it is virtually impossible to see the structures of symbol use while we are wielding them for some purpose. This is why Wittgenstein had such an intense and painful struggle to realize what could be done next, and to express in words an insight about what can and cannot be said in preexisting language.[21] Wittgenstein had his own blind spot. He did not prevent subsequent philosophers from investigating the new meta-levels he had opened; by pointing to them, he opened the possibility of creating new language for this terrain. Wittgenstein did not see this because he was involved in a polemic, launched already by Russell in the campaign against Idealism. The distinction between the sayable and the unsayable/showable not only indicates the hierarchy of statements but legislates what is legitimate and illegitimate at each level.[22] The sayable/unsayable distinction carries on the polemical utility of the theory of types. And indeed the latter did not fade away; even if he regarded it as overly complicated for the fundamentals of mathematics, Carnap found it a powerful weapon to wield against metaphysics, which could now be eliminated as resting on category mistakes.

In the *Tractatus,* Wittgenstein supplemented his Russellian heritage with reflections in a very different tone on the meaning of life and the paramount importance of religious mysticism, coupled into his system via the doctrine of unsayables. This portion was added during the stress of combat in World War I, when Wittgenstein underwent a religious conversion to Tolstoyan Christianity (Monk, 1990: 115–123, 134–146). This segment was not generated by the core philosophical network; not surprisingly, it had little influence and received virtually no recognition when Wittgenstein later gravitated back into the philosophical network, especially in the Vienna Circle, which was interested only in the Russellian logicist line. Rereading the *Tractatus* in a religious-mystical light came only after Wittgenstein's death, after he had become the star of the ordinary language movement, above all during the post-positivism of the 1970s.

The Vienna Circle as a Nexus of Struggles

The period between 1910 and 1940 witnesses a massive realignment. The entire lineup of the preceding generations fades out: Idealists, Neo-Kantians, Brentano's act psychology (so-called Austrian realism), as well as vitalists, evolutionists, Utilitarians, and materialists. Representatives of some of these schools continue to publish, but they are in their last gasps, regarded as outdated and receiving declining attention. In their place come new schools: logical positivists, ordinary language philosophers, and phenomenologist-existentialists. These constitute new lines of antagonism, rising to new heights of militancy.

Not that there is a break in the intergenerational networks: many of the old lineages continue, but the latest pupils move in new directions (see Figure 13.3). In England, the old Idealist and Utilitarian networks give rise to Russell

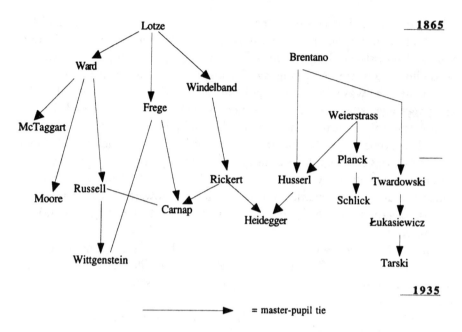

FIGURE 13.3. REALIGNMENT OF THE NETWORKS IN THE
GENERATION OF 1900

and Moore. In Germany, Brentano is upstaged by Husserl, and he in turn by
Heidegger; another branch of Brentano's succession, through Twardowski and
his pupils in the Warsaw-Lvov school, leads on to Tarski. The Neo-Kantians
too are breaking apart; Husserl had been a student at Marburg as well as
Vienna; Rickert was the teacher of both Carnap and Heidegger, the latter two
fratricidal network brothers; and it is a shock to see that, via Husserl, Heidegger's grandteacher was the mathematician Weierstrass. As usual, intellectual
energy is propagated down the wires of interpersonal contacts, while the
content of ideas is rearranged by horizontal strains of opposition reconfiguring
the attention space.

Realignment happened more or less simultaneously in each country. In
England and the United States, this period was the end of Idealism. The last
systems—those of McTaggart, Stout, Whitehead, Peirce, Royce—lingered into
the 1910s and 1920s but had an end-of-the-line quality. Pragmatism, too, as
a transition away from Idealism, flourished at the turn of the century, then
faded away by the 1930s before the logical positivists and ordinary language
philosophers. This pattern suggests that an underlying cause of realignment
was the completion of religious secularization in the universities. But this does
not explain why there was a simultaneous realignment in Germany, where

secularization had long since taken place. France, whose academic organization differed most from the German model adopted elsewhere, was least coordinated with the contents of realigning movements in other countries. Neither a logical positivist nor an ordinary language movement developed in France; when realignment came in the late 1920s and the 1930s, spiritualism and vitalism were replaced by phenomenology and existentialism imported from Germany.

At the cost of some chronological backtracking, we will trace each of the three main movements: first the logical positivists, whose flagship was the Vienna Circle; then the ordinary language movement, which originated in British networks simultaneously with Russell's logicist movement and claimed Wittgenstein as apostate from one movement to the other. Finally we return to the German side to pick up the parallel development originating in the networks of mathematicians and of Neo-Kantians that became phenomenology and eventually existentialism. The two big German movements, starting from much the same roots, reorganized the intellectual field around new conflicts and grew steadily more opposed. In the process the older Neo-Kantianism which dominated philosophy during the period of disciplinary differentiation, was displaced from the center of the attention space.

The Vienna Circle is an amalgam of three ancestral networks: Neo-Kantians, physicist-positivists, and mathematician-logicians of the foundations struggle.[23] In the personal intersection of these networks and the super-concentration of the oppositions going on both within and among each group, we find the source of the creative energy of the Vienna Circle (see Figure 13.4).

When logical positivists superseded Neo-Kantians, they broke up a modus vivendi among scientists and philosophers going back to Helmholtz in the 1850s. The laws of mathematical science had long been defended by Cohen's Marburg school. The interpretation by Cohen's pupil Cassirer of the new phenomenalistic physics was widely regarded as preserving objectivity better than Mach's extremism, and as providing the best philosophical interpretation of Einsteinian relativity theory. Cassirer in 1910 held influentially that matter, substance, and force have no ontological reality; the subject of science is mere phenomenological description, structured by theoretical statements of functional connections. At virtually the same time, Vaihinger became famous for his *Philosophy of As-If* (1911), stating that we operate on the basis of necessary fictions taken as if they were true.[24] Schlick and Reichenbach, too, were avowed Kantians up to the early 1920s, as were Carnap and Popper still later.

Neo-Kantianism was changing, but creative developments normally serve to keep a school alive. Why then did this one die? Cassirer read the lesson of relativity physics as showing that the particularities of Euclidean geometry could not be taken as a priori; there was a development of the categories that

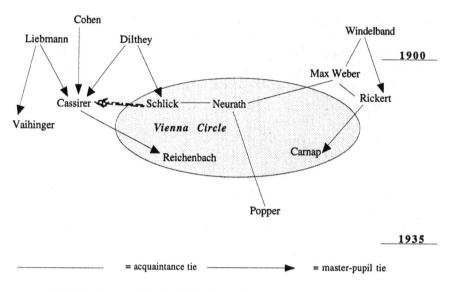

FIGURE 13.4. NEO-KANTIANS AND THE VIENNA CIRCLE

filter experience. Suddenly the atmosphere turned unsympathetic. Instead of allowing Neo-Kantians to broaden their stance, Schlick began to invoke a more rigorous standard. The narrower interpretation of the Kantian categories had been proved wrong, while Cassirer's wider interpretation could not be allowed because Neo-Kantianism's adaptability showed it to be a slippery, unscientific philosophy, unfalsifiable by experience. New rules of the game were imposed: previously it would not have been expected that a philosophy, especially one concerned with the grounds of experience, should be testable in the same way as a research science.[25]

Historical comparisons show that a school can find intellectual resources to defend itself indefinitely against criticism; it is never external criticism alone that kills a position.[26] Neo-Kantianism ceased being a vital contender for the center of attention; even those who owed much to it now turned against it. There are other signs of the loss of identification among the Neo-Kantians themselves: Natorp after 1910 abandoned the logical foundations of exact science for a metaphysics approaching Platonic religious mysticism; Cohen's student Nicolai Hartmann in the 1920s reversed the Neo-Kantian priority of epistemology over ontology; others became existentialists. The same thing happened with Brentano's school: despite the attention Meinong got around 1904, later pupils preferred to style themselves phenomenologists or logicians.

The law of small numbers was operating: as new movements discovered resources to wield in the attention space, there was an accelerating rush to take up the most energizing issues; older positions were squeezed out, not because they were no longer viable but because there was not room to maintain the half dozen older factions along with three or four new ones. Neo-Kantianism was especially vulnerable because, as the dominant German school of the past two generations, it had crowded the attention space with a variety of sub-positions. The Neo-Kantians had decentralized themselves in presiding over disciplinary differentiation, creating meta-topics out of questions of boundary adjudication. In an opposite spirit were Carnap's and Neurath's reductionist programs for the unification of science. Their physics-centered imperialism was transitory, but the gesture indicated a deeper thrust of the movement: toward a radical simplification of the attention space.

The Spillover of Physicists' Methodological Disputes

The impulse to criticize philosophy is not inherent in physics. The main previous episode of scientists' attack had been directed against the interference of *Naturphilosophie,* and had subsided when academic autonomy was obtained; the militant materialists of Büchner's generation had acquired no prestige among philosophers, much less provoking a reform of philosophy from within such as characterized the twentieth-century analytical schools. On the contrary, Neo-Kantian philosophers quickly seized on the contradiction that anti-metaphysical materialists were themselves promoting an uncritical metaphysics of matter, a critique in which they were joined within science by Machian phenomenalism. Positivism and Neo-Kantianism were fairly close, especially in the 1870s and 1880s, in their rejection of materialism; Cassirer's philosophy of physics in 1910 was close to Mach's. And until 1920 Schlick was arguing for the compatibility of Neo-Kantianism with the phenomenalism of Mach and Avenarius. How then did smaller points of difference over post-materialist physics grow into a gulf?

What would become the modern positivist movement started as an internal development among physicists, laying down methodological rules for their own discipline rather than legislating generally as to the scope of knowledge or the practice of philosophy. From the 1870s onward, experimenters in electromagnetism, light, and radiation formulated mathematical models which dispensed with depicting the mechanics of physical bodies. A radical movement of physicists led by Kirchhoff and Mach began to argue that concepts such as "mass," "force," and "atom" are merely convenient fictions for simplifying observations. Mach dismissed theoretical constructs as needless multiplication of metaphysical entities, even rejecting the existence of natural laws. Ostwald's vitalist "energetics" joined forces with the positivists, holding that atoms and matter can be ruled out by the principle of the economy of thought. On the other side, theoretical physicists worked to preserve the centrality of mechanical laws of bodies, a paradigm which had led to so many past advances into new research areas by introducing strategic modifications. The most successful of these was Planck, whose quantum theory in 1900 abandoned classical dynamics in postulating abrupt changes in energy levels; on this basis Einstein's special relativity in 1905 explained anomalous features of light, and Bohr in 1913 developed a theory of atomic structure.

Heated debates took place between the camps (Lindenfeld, 1980: 80–86, 105–110; Johnston, 1972: 181–8; *EP*, 1967: 7:15). Planck and Boltzmann, whose statistical mechanics provided the basis for Planck's defense of atomism, disputed repeatedly with Ostwald and Mach during 1895–1905. Neo-Kantians joined the battle, pointing out that Mach's extreme inductivism was unable to account for the theoretical aspects of science, its ability to predict the future, and its mathematical laws. Mach in turn rejected the a priori character of number, holding that the integers arose from the practical needs of calculation. Mach acquired a reputation as a naturalistic extremist by arguing that the simplest unification of the science occurs under the auspices of physiology: sensations in the nervous system are the only reality, and economy of thought is itself an adaptation of the organism to its environment. This reduction to physiological psychology raised echoes of the Neo-Kantian debates of the 1860s and 1870s over the physiological interpretation of the a priori categories, and gave energy to the renewed rejection of psychologism and the defense of objectivity in mathematics by Frege and Husserl. Planck from 1908 through the 1920s defended a version of Kantianism against Mach's reduction of reality to a flow of sensations; like Cassirer and the Neo-Kantians, Planck regarded Mach's position as relativistic subjectivism. These debates were a dress rehearsal for the Vienna Circle's campaign to drive metaphysics off the stage. So far it was a struggle over what is legitimate within physics; later it became a question of what is legitimate in any field of reason.

That movement began to crystallize during the uproar of public fame about Einsteinian relativity theory, following Eddington's astronomical evidence of the bending of light in 1919. In this vein was the publicity which surrounded Bohr's Copenhagen school and Heisenberg's quantum mechanics with its indeterminacy principle, announced in 1925. Philosophy was not simply responding to new discoveries in physics, however; similar problems had existed since Einstein's special theory of relativity in 1905, and even earlier, without upsetting the dominance of Neo-Kantian interpretations over Machian phenomenalism. Although verification was exemplified for both Schlick and Popper by the relativity verification, it was not the only interpretation. Eddington himself, the experimental verifier, hardly took it as grounds for rejecting metaphysics or for demarcating true science from pseudo-science, and even

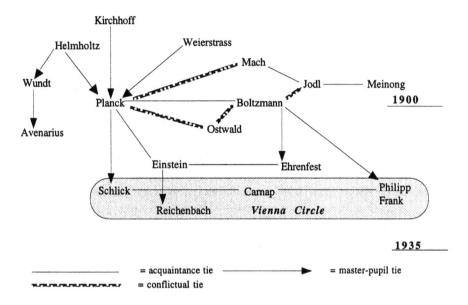

FIGURE 13.5. PHYSICISTS' METHODOLOGICAL CONTROVERSIES

adopted a Neo-Kantian stance (Passmore, 1968: 333). The popular pronounce-ments of relativity physicists such as Eddington and Jeans in the 1920s and 1930s, like those of Einstein, continued a tradition of reconciling physics with religion. The physics of the 1920s did not create the themes of the Vienna Circle, although by giving greater attention to the philosophy of science, it helped make them famous.

The Vienna Circle grew directly from the network of the leading German physicists (see Figure 13.5). Kirchhoff, Helmholtz, Planck, Boltzmann, and Einstein were their teachers or grandteachers. Institutionally too these physi-cists created the arena in which the struggle would be carried on. The chair of History and Theory of Inductive Sciences, crossing over from physics to philosophy, was established in 1895 to lure Mach to Vienna. The second incumbent was Boltzmann (1902–1906), who used the chair to sponsor public debates against the Machians; the third was Schlick, who arrived in Vienna in 1922 in the wake of his attack on Cassirer. It is the focus of arguments that counts, not the inheritance of positions; Schlick began as Planck's student, even though he eventually switched to the Machian side. The allied group at Berlin formed around Reichenbach, an Einstein protégé working on the mathematical philosophy of space-time relativity (*EP*, 1967: 11:355–356). Additional net-work ingredients besides physics resulted in the distinctiveness of the Vienna Circle. The Machians were not concerned with the foundations of mathematics or the reform of logic; it was Carnap and Wittgenstein who brought these into the center of attention at Vienna. The central members of the Vienna Circle were network hybrids of physicists and mathematicians who also had had Neo-Kantian teachers.

Physicists were emboldened that they had something attention-getting to say in the central territory of philosophy. Soon they launched into an attack on the dominant school, neo-Kantianism itself. In the process they found it convenient to wave the banner of Mach. When the Vienna Circle formalized in 1928, it called itself the Ernst Mach Society. This was to a certain extent rhetorical. The methods of the Vienna Circle, especially their logical tools, were not those of Mach and his psychological reductionism; and the physicalism of the 1930s was far from Mach's neutral monism. Phenomenalism was one theme among many explored by the circle. It was above all Mach's militancy that they invoked, now widened to exclude metaphysics not only from physics but from everywhere.

The first vehicle of this militancy was verification, a concept already launched by Schlick in pre-Circle days, in 1918, before he became a positivist. As Carnap, Wittgenstein, and others joined in, more resources were brought to bear on how scientific knowledge is constituted and how it differs from the forms of non-knowledge that are to be excluded. This proved to be a fruitful vein of puzzles, as each solution gave rise to new difficulties. Empirical verification foundered on questions about the nature of ultimate verifiers and the status of the principle of verifiability itself. Russellian logicism provided a criterion for rejecting some forms of expression as not merely false but meaningless; Schlick and Waismann shifted to meaningfulness as the demarcation between science and non-science. This in turn raised the question of the meaningfulness of the language in which the criterion itself was formulated. Popper eventually carried this internal conflict into a rejection of the verification program while continuing the demarcationist spirit that was the core of the Vienna Circle.

Rival Networks of Mathematical
Foundations and the Genesis of Gödel's Proof

The 1920s were also the height of conflict over mathematical foundations, the most active period for pronouncements by Brouwer, Hilbert, and their supporters. Alongside them remained a third (and indeed the oldest) faction, the Russell-Frege logicists, whose stronghold in the 1920s had become the Vienna Circle. Their conflicts became superimposed on those of the physicist-philosophers who first constituted the Circle, building to a grand intensity of creative struggle in the years around 1930.

The Frege-Russell line was represented by Carnap, who came to Vienna in 1926, and Wittgenstein, who began discussions with the Circle soon after (see Figure 13.6). Both had had formative contact with Frege early in their careers: Carnap had been a pupil at Jena during 1910–1914, and Wittgenstein visited Frege for early advice on his intellectual path in 1911 and again in 1912; thereafter Frege steadily encouraged Wittgenstein by correspondence while he was writing the *Tractatus* during the First World War (Monk, 1990: 36, 70, 115–157). Frege, who had gone without significant professional offspring all his life, suddenly acquired two. Both were strongly affected by Russell. Wittgenstein was Russell's personal disciple, anointed to carry out the logicist program. Carnap was galvanized into action in 1921 upon reading Russell's programmatic appeal for a movement of philosophers trained in science and resistant to misleading literary methods, which Carnap took—naturally enough as a Frege protégé—as directed at him personally (Coffa, 1991: 208). He entered into correspondence with Russell, and began to build the foundations of knowledge on a Russell-like perfect language hierarchized through the theory of types. Although Wittgenstein had already gone beyond the theory of types with devices of his own, there remained enough sense of commonality that in the late 1920s, Wittgenstein suspected Carnap of stealing his ideas and excluded him from his own personal meetings with the Vienna Circle (Coffa, 1991: 405). They are network stepbrothers, working out of the same patrimony, and thus rivals in the attention space.

The Hilbert lineage is represented in the Vienna Circle network by several former pupils, including the mathematics professor Hans Hahn, who had originally brought Schlick to Vienna and was a main organizer of the Circle (*DSB*, 1981: 14:88–92, 281–285; Wang, 1987: 52–57, 76–88). Gödel was Hahn's protégé; Hahn also taught Popper, who entered the periphery of the Circle in the same year that Gödel announced his famous proof. In the 1920s the Hilbert school made strenuous efforts to prove the consistency of arithmetic; among the most active was Reichenbach's colleague at Berlin during 1927–1929, von Neumann, who worked on a new axiomatization soon picked up by Gödel. The opposite camp, the Brouwer intuitionists headquartered at Amsterdam, also became entwined with the Vienna network and its issues. Hermann Weyl, who, like Reichenbach, had studied with Hilbert at Göttingen, had in the 1920s shifted to the Brouwer camp, mixing intuitionist and formalist methods in the attempt to reconstruct mathematics from the intuitionist side. These same mathematicians were intensely active at this time in the foundations of the new physics of relativity and quantum mechanics, overlapping with the central preoccupations of the physicists in the Vienna Circle. Further overlap occurred when Karl Menger, one of Hahn's favorite pupils, went to study with Brouwer in 1925–1927 before returning to Vienna, where he joined the circle

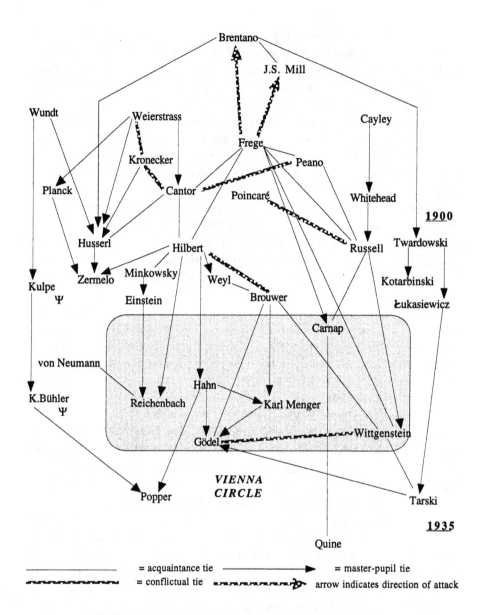

FIGURE 13.6. NETWORK OF MATHEMATICAL
LOGIC AND FOUNDATIONS

and was especially close to Gödel. It was with some sense of showdown that Brouwer was invited to lecture at Vienna in March 1928. Wittgenstein suddenly ended his long intellectual withdrawal and began talking about philosophy again immediately after hearing Brouwer's lectures, although he at first had to be coaxed by his Vienna Circle acquaintances to attend (Wang, 1987: 81; Monk, 1990: 249). That summer Hilbert, in a celebrated address to the International Congress of Mathematicians, challenged the field to solve four basic problems of the consistency and completeness of analysis, number theory, and logic. Gödel immediately chose these problems for his dissertation; by 1930 he had solved them all.

The conflicting philosophical schools also became tied to the mathematical foundations battle. Husserl was invoked by the intuitionists, especially as he moved in the 1920s to emphasize the pre-formalized life-world, within which geometry was seen to originate (Heyting, 1983; Coffa, 1991: 253–255). The growing sense of antagonism between phenomenologists and logical positivists became overlaid upon the rivalry between the mathematical camps. Tarski, who like Husserl was descended from the Brentano school, adopted from Husserl a hierarchy of semantic categories, which played the same role as Russell's theory of types but in a more guarded fashion by generalizing from logic to languages. Tarski visited the Vienna mathematics department during February 1930, with a galvanizing effect on Carnap.

Even more of a Trojan horse was Wittgenstein. Originally the heir apparent to the Frege-Russell program, by 1930 he was explicitly turning away in a direction that increasingly resembled that of the mathematical intuitionists. His strong personal influence led to a growing split within the Circle. In 1930 Gödel was challenging Wittgenstein in the Circle on philosophical issues: How does one distinguish the allowably meaningless statements which constitute Wittgenstein's own higher-order clarifications from the meaninglessness of metaphysics, which it is our business to destroy (Coffa, 1991: 272)? Soon everything clicked in new directions for philosophers and mathematicians alike. In the summer of 1930 Gödel, not yet 25 years old, conveyed to the Circle his proof that any logical system capable of generating arithmetic contains propositions undecidable within the system.

The creativity of Gödel and of the later Wittgenstein spun off from much the same point, and from their mutual disagreements. This was a clash between two highly sponsored group favorites, an older and a younger. Gödel was sponsored by his mathematical mentors in the Vienna Circle as the bright young student capable of solving the most central problems; through them, his results were immediately and widely publicized.

More fireworks exploded at this moment when the Circle's conflicts became most intense. Within the next year Popper, a peripheral member of the Vienna

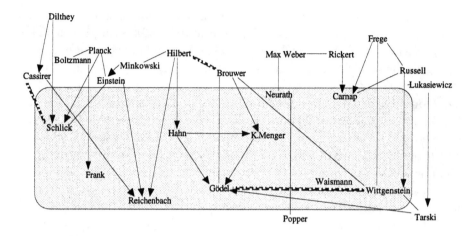

FIGURE 13.7. VIENNA CIRCLE: COMPOSITE NETWORK

Circle network, proclaimed the end of the verification criterion and its replacement by falsification.[27] The moment when Popper made his debut was the time when Gödel demolished the hopes of Russell-Carnap logicism for providing an unassailable foundation and hence as a possible demarcation criterion. Popper's ideas no doubt received an immediate and friendly welcome from some factions of the Circle because he stepped into a gap. Soon Carnap, Neurath, and Wittgenstein were announcing the abandonment of earlier programs for major new directions.

It is characteristic of creative circles that one innovation spawns another; and major creations must go in different directions, even in oppositions (see Figure 13.7). Gödel's undecidability proof was a fundamental defeat for the Frege-Russell logicist program; and it was formulated in the heart of the group where, of all the world, that program was most actively being pursued. Gödel's work was the result of the network mixture which constituted the Vienna Circle, a case of creativity by superimposed oppositions. In the field of fundamental issues which is philosophical turf, creativity is tightly focused conflict boring in on problems until deep faults are found; around these reconceptualization takes place. In this sense Popper accurately recognized in falsification something central to intellectual life—perhaps not in the actual histories of scientific discovery, but in the world of the philosophers that surrounded him.

The Stimulation of Insoluble Puzzles

Encapsulating the conflicts which had built up in the Vienna Circle, Gödel's meta-mathematics catalyzed a new round of creativity. Russell's paradox had been not the end of the logicist movement but the beginning of its fame; Gödel's proof did not destroy but added heat to the fire. It was from this point that Wittgenstein, whatever private misgivings he had held previously about the consistency of his own approach in the *Tractatus,* moved increasingly into public opposition to his old school—probably not least because his major rival in the Circle, Carnap, was sticking to the logicist road.

Gödel's proof did not derail latter-day logicists, but gave them new directions in which to work. Unlike Neo-Kantianism, Carnap's program was not a movement losing its position in attention space but an energetically expanding one. New and fundamental obstacles could not defeat it, but became grist for its mill.

Carnap's 1928 *Der Logische Aufbau der Welt* constructed all meaningful (i.e., empirically verifiable) statements out of a Russellian hierarchy: signs for individuals, classes, classes of classes, supplemented by a sign for empirical elements. Methodologically the system was solipsistic; it is *my* individual experiences which are the foundation. By 1934, under the stimulus of Tarski and Gödel, Carnap had shifted to the impersonal syntax of a universally valid language; the basic elements were now the natural numbers (integers), from which are successively constructed the real numbers and a four-dimensional space-time, which is a set of all points with numbered coordinates. In this language all statements of empirical science can be translated into something like "red appears at point (x, y, z, t)." This translation game did not actually go beyond sketching the form of descriptive statements, and took for granted that mathematical laws existed or would be forthcoming which would explain recurrent patterns in space-time; in short, it was a philosophical program sailing under the rhetoric of the unification of science. In the 1940s Carnap responded to criticisms by loosening the system still further, reintroducing higher-order concepts which he had previously rejected as meaninglessly metaphysical. By now he was dividing the language of science into an empirical observational language plus a theoretical language or formal calculus for deducing connections (Wedberg, 1984: 207–229). This formalism in turn provided the target for radical revisions by Quine and others.

Carnap's shift to the language of physics broke away from the older phenomenalism supported by Schlick, toward Neurath's rival camp. The Vienna Circle was splitting in not just two but three main directions: Schlick's old program, now reduced to following the lead of Wittgenstein—what Neurath called the "right wing"—plus Carnap's continuing development of logicism, and a "left wing" led by Neurath. Wittgenstein moved increasingly toward becoming a rallying-point for outright opposition to logical positivism; abandoning his older logicism to Carnap, he shifted abruptly toward Gödel's position and even surpassed him in extending the radicalness of its implications for philosophy. The action which kept the loyalists of the Vienna

Circle alive shifted to points at issue between the programs of Carnap and Neurath.

For Neurath, science can be sufficiently demarcated from meaningless philosophies by the program of the unification of science, with Carnap-like protocol sentences at the core and the laws of physics as connections. Undisturbed by the critiques of Popper and Gödel, Neurath jettisoned the search for a verification principle; science does not start from absolute foundations but rebuilds constantly, like a ship being repaired while sailing on the open sea. Even observational sentences are revisable, and all beliefs are fallible (Coffa, 1991: 363). After Neurath died in 1945, Quine inherited Neurath's slot within the array of oppositions of the late Vienna Circle. Quine was Carnap's longtime correspondent, but reputations are made by disagreement, and Quine made his by pushing onward to surprising consequences for the formalist program: the endless adjustability of languages to avoid falsification on particular empirical points, the indeterminacy of exact translation among languages, and even denial of the distinction between empirical and logical-analytic propositions. The first two of these points were paralleled a generation later by Kuhn's theory of conservative scientific paradigms and their incommensurability.

Yet a further legacy of the Vienna Circle to the post-positivist philosophy of the next generation was to come. Neurath had always been the organizational mover of the Vienna Circle; in the 1930s, as the group began to emigrate under the Nazi threat, Neurath transferred most of their publication efforts from *Erkenntnis* into the *Encyclopedia of Unified Science.* Eventually he transplanted this to the United States, where he joined forces with Charles Morris, and thus with the pragmatist lineage of Peirce and Mead. The last notable act of the *Encyclopedia,* and hence of the Vienna Circle's organizational core, was to commission Thomas Kuhn, a physicist turned historian, to write *The Structure of Scientific Revolutions.*[28]

The aftermath shows the fruitfulness of the Vienna Circle's vein of puzzles even in the failure of almost every item in its program. The radical consequences which Neurath and Quine turned up could be seized on by anti-formalists and anti-positivists, just as Kuhn was to become the darling of student Marxists and deconstructionists. But the underlying thrust of the movement was in the methods of philosophy rather than its contents. An array of formal logics was created to explore the rich vein of problems; analytical techniques became dominant, above all at American universities, in the midcentury generation. What made the logical positivist movement so effective in capturing philosophical attention space was not its solutions but the puzzles turned up by its formal methods. The real discovery of the Vienna Circle was the location of deep problems, and the conundrums of logical formalism were just what gave them the materials on which to continue their work.

The Ordinary Language Reaction against Logical Formalism

The ordinary language school became popular as a reaction against the logical formalists. In this respect it too was part of the realignment of positions; locally in England, the scene was the collapse of interest in Idealism, and new positions expanded to fill the vacant attention space. Originally, Russell's mathematical logicism was only a technical specialty on the periphery of British philosophy. The development of Idealist systems remained a primary interest down to the 1920s. Bradley (whose *Appearance and Reality* appeared in 1893) was reputed the greatest living philosopher. At Cambridge the leader was McTaggart, who produced amplifications of Hegel in 1896, 1901, and 1910, down through his great posthumous system (1927), and along with two other Idealists, Ward and Stout, dominated teaching for the philosophy honors examinations.

The opposition consisted in various versions of naturalism. Outside the academic world, Spencer went on enlarging his evolutionist system down through 1899 and sold widely for another decade; inside the universities, experimental psychology was becoming a battleground between naturalistic and spiritualistic approaches. Utilitarianism continued, most famously at the hands of Sidgwick at Cambridge, until his death in 1900. But now there was considerable crossing over among the schools, a sign of the realignment to come. Sidgwick had founded the Society for Psychic Research; among its members was Arthur Balfour, another Trinity student and Sidgwick's brother-in-law. Balfour adopted Humean skepticism to undermine anti-religious rationalism, and held (1895) that all beliefs including those regarding nature rest on a climate of traditional opinion. The Utilitarians, once considered outrageous political radicals, had given ground intellectually while gaining connections of high social respectability; Balfour was conservative leader of the House of Commons in the 1890s and prime minister 1902–1906. On the whole, prestige was on the side of Idealism as the sophisticated and up-to-date accommodation with religion.

The first major break in this structure of the attention space came in 1903 with G. E. Moore's *Principia Ethica.* Moore simultaneously criticized all the prominent schools, at least within the restricted grounds of ethical theory. Spencer's evolutionist ethics and the Utilitarianism of Bentham, Mill, and Sidgwick, all fall afoul of the naturalistic fallacy; Idealist systems, too, commit a version of the fallacy by identifying the good with an aspect of super-sensible reality. The good is an indefinable predicate because it is absolutely simple; here Moore approaches the position taken by Russell in his logic built up from ultimate simples, in opposition to the holistic logic of Idealism.[29] Moore further criticizes all other ethical systems by the argument that good cannot be identified with any one object, such as pleasure or (on the Idealist side) moral duty;

there is a plurality of good objects which need have nothing in common. On the practical side of ethics, Moore retains a Utilitarian theme in that the goodness of particular actions is to be judged by their consequences. Here too Moore turns Utilitarian arguments against their prior tradition, emphasizing the extreme difficulty of knowing the consequences of actions except in the very short run. Moore's practical conclusions go against the grain of all the previous ethicists, favoring neither religious ends, nor moral righteousness, nor the political activism of the greatest good for the greatest number. Instead he endorses personal aestheticism, suggesting that the highest goods are the immediate experiences of passionate friendship and the contemplation of the beautiful.

Most of Moore's ingredients were available from his own teachers and compatriots. Already in 1874 Sidgwick had modified Utilitarian ethics, recognizing that moral principles cannot be deduced from descriptive statements. While continuing to adhere to universal benevolence as a path to maximizing happiness, Sidgwick concluded that motivation so to act is greatly affected by moral intuitions and by beliefs in supernatural sanctions. Bradley had already stressed the imprecision of the Utilitarian calculus; and of course in his system the good, like everything else, is indefinable. Moore in effect uses Sidgwick and Bradley against each other, playing up the portions of each that he wants to reject: Sidgwick's continuing focus on political and economic calculation, Bradley's moralism and his subsumption of ethics in the Idealist Absolute. Nor are Moore's practical conclusions novel; he merely defends with a more formal argument the aestheticism promulgated by Pater and Wilde in the 1880s and 1890s, adding a somewhat more explicit endorsement of the cult of homosexual affairs which had become popular at the time of Lytton Strachey. If *Principia Ethica* made an immediate sensation, it was less because of its originality than because it symbolized a shift in the old lineup of intellectual oppositions.

Most of the creative developments in British philosophy, in all its branches, were concentrated in this period within a single network, centered at Trinity and King's colleges, Cambridge (see Figure 13.2 above). The group structure of creativity is familiar from other periods; in this case we have a wealth of information which enables us to study how such a group was formed and the dynamics of emotional energy that drove it.

Leading intellectuals are more elaborately connected by family linkages in the generations from 1840 to 1920 than at virtually any other time in history: there is an intermarrying network that links Russell, Moore, Keynes, Virginia Woolf, and the Bloomsbury circle to the Thackerays, Macaulays, Darwins, Maitlands, Trevelyans, Balfours, and many others. They are genuine cousins, in-laws, and nephews, not merely the metaphorical kinfolk produced by master-pupil lineages.[30]

The Victorian-Edwardian intellectual kinship network was based on the mobilization of political and religious reform movements in a segment of the upper-middle and upper classes, at a time when the state church was just being disestablished and the universities wrested from clerical control. In a highly class-stratified society, this set of intellectual dissidents from their class constituted a relatively small group which was drawn together socially and sexually by intermarriage. The components of this group were of three main kinds: wealthy Quakers (Moore's family background, Russell's by marriage); Evangelicals (prominent in the Idealist movement); plus the reform wing of the aristocracy (of which the Russells were the most famous family). For many of these families it became traditional to send their sons to Cambridge, especially to Trinity and King's, where further intermarriages were promoted by sisters' visits. Once numbers had gone beyond a critical mass, the inner group's culture began to drift in its own direction, away from the moral earnestness of its members' political origins. An elite organized within this elite in the form of a highly selective discussion society known as the Apostles. The smartest prospects were tapped with the help of former members who gave the prize examinations or taught at the famous secondary schools. The group met frequently to vie in producing wittily iconoclastic papers, surrounded by ritual which made it self-conscious of its intellectual superiority and the achievements of its predecessors (Levy, 1981). In this atmosphere young undergraduates such as Russell (inducted 1892) and Moore (1894) were encouraged to emulate the lineage going back to Tennyson and including their most famous teachers up through Sidgwick and McTaggart.

Upon publication of *Principia Ethica,* Moore became idolized by the younger Apostles. It was their later success that established his wider reputation, since they included Lytton Strachey, John Maynard Keynes, Leonard Woolf—in short, the male members of the Bloomsbury literary circle which formed soon thereafter. It is difficult otherwise to understand the adulation in which Moore was held throughout the rest of his life. His work on ethics was not strikingly original, and his later philosophy was mainly a negative reaction against subsequent innovations. Moore became a Durkheimian sacred object, symbolizing the ideal intellectual. He was structurally well situated for the role: in the early 1900s he was the longest-active member of the Apostles, famous for his frail, youthful good looks and his debating style, combining passion and wit and even sexual tease (Levy, 1981: 213). This image of Moore continued even into paunchy middle age; once he was separated from the Apostles, his passionate tone and his aura of avant-garde brilliance faded, but he remained a symbol, the group's preferred self-image.

In the 1920s and 1930s Moore turned to the defense of common sense. Statements such as that my body was born sometime in the past, or that this is a hand held up before my face should be taken as true; whatever the sophisticated philosophical alternatives that might be raised against such statements, none of their reasons are conclusive, and on the whole they are less certain than the judgments of commonsense language. The substantive position defended by Moore is banal; it makes a claim in philosophical attention space only because it was crafted in opposition to other positions. It gives a rationale for dismissing Idealism, now on its last legs, but also the ontologies of Russell and Carnap's mathematical set theory, Wittgenstein's *Tractatus,* and Husserlian phenomenology. Against the effort to create a logically perfect language, Moore responds with ordinary language. Nevertheless, it turned out that this was not the suicide of philosophy, for it had a continuity, if of a negative sort, with preceding technical developments. Russell had shown the deep problems in formal systems, and Moore's argument against non-commonsensical propositions raised to a principle Russell's frequently expressed admission that logical arguments that appear certain are typically subject to further revision.[31]

Ordinary language turned out to contain a vein of problems to be explored in its own right. The militancy of the Vienna Circle prodded these developments. Its debates over the nature of meaninglessness led to considerations of the multiple dimensions of meaning. When Ayer, arriving home from Vienna, declared in 1936 that all statements not filling the verifiability criterion have the same standing as the expression "ouch!" his condemnation of the language of ethics led to outrage and a search for ways to make such statements meaningful.[32] The strongest impetus was given by Wittgenstein, who now repudiated his earlier program for the logically perfect language and launched the exploration of the inexpressible ways in which language does not "say" but "shows." It transpired that what was inexpressible at one point in the self-consciousness of philosophers could indeed give rise to a new realm of language; and although Wittgenstein played on resonances between his later linguistic philosophy and his earlier concerns with religious mysticism, a more straightforward brand of academic investigation in this realm was soon operating under the label of Austin's speech acts and illocutionary forces.[33]

Wittgenstein's Tortured Path

It is tempting, in parallel to the case of Moore, to attribute these turns of events to the unique force of Wittgenstein's personality. The mystique and adulation surrounding Wittgenstein, which had begun already at Vienna in the 1920s and ballooned after his return to Cambridge in the 1930s, is more revealing when viewed sociologically, as a case study of the interplay of creativity, personality, and reputation. Creativity is driven by the struggle over the limited slots of attention space, and Wittgenstein's life was a movement between two of the core networks of his time. In each place he came in contact with the current attention leader: Russell in 1912–1914, Schlick in 1927–1932, Moore at Cambridge in the 1910s and again from 1929 until his death in 1951. Each time Wittgenstein became the darling of his sponsor, while quickly radicalizing the existing position in a fashion that transferred greater attention to himself. Another way of saying this is that Wittgenstein battened on the reputation already achieved—by Russell, by the Vienna Circle, by the ordinary language movement. He was so to speak an emotional energy vampire, sucking sustenance out of his sponsors and transferring it to his own position.

There are numerous examples (Monk, 1990; Levy, 1981). Russell's elation at finding Wittgenstein for a disciple turned to anger and depression as he felt superseded, overwhelmed with demands, and periodically rejected by Wittgenstein's fits of temper. Wittgenstein had the same effect on Moore, treating him alternately as confidant, enemy, and errand boy. Wittgenstein's famous moodiness made sense as part of the social dynamics of a small, intensely focused group, constantly reminding its members of their elite status; the rivalries and jealousies both over preeminence and over closeness to the favorite resemble the popularity contests and love affairs of an adolescent social club. In fact this is a fairly apt description of the Apostles, especially in their phase of homosexual affairs (for the most part rather platonic).

Wittgenstein's relationship with the self-conscious preciosity of the society was emblematic of both their stance and his. Reputations were made in the Apostles, after initial selection for intellectual brilliance, on the basis of iconoclastic performances. McTaggart had assumed the leadership in the late 1880s with a paper "Violets or Orange Blossom?" defending homosexual love; Moore ascended to new heights of candor in 1894 with "Shall we take delight in crushing our roses?" in which he endorsed heterosexual prudery together with masturbation. In 1902 Strachey took over leadership by outshocking everyone with a paper on defecation as the ultimate artistic act because an expression of oneness with Nature (Levy, 1981: 103, 144, 231–233). When Wittgenstein was invited in 1912, in the midst of a round of accusations of jealousy (against Russell for keeping Wittgenstein for himself, and more generally over homosexual ties within the group), he delivered the ultimate shock by promptly resigning after his first meeting. Wittgenstein had already had similar experience of the hothouse atmosphere of artistic reputations in Vienna, only there it was suicide which established one's reputation for passionate commitment; there was a rash of suicides around the turn of the century, including two of Wittgenstein's brothers (Johnston, 1972: 174–179). Wittgenstein's brooding over suicide during the first few decades of his life, whatever its subjective component, was also a claim for status membership in this elite; the obsession stopped after he established his independent intellectual reputation. Throughout his life Wittgenstein succeeded in finding groups of this sort and making whatever iconoclastic move would bring him into the center of attention.

Back in Vienna, Wittgenstein soon was playing his favorites, coyly making himself available to those who paid sufficient deference while blackballing others from his presence (Coffa, 1991: 241, 404–405). The split in the Vienna Circle dates from Wittgenstein's meetings with it. Structurally, the Vienna Circle was responsible for Wittgenstein's later philosophical position. As Carnap, Wittgenstein's major local rival for attention, explored the problem space of formalist semantic systems, Wittgenstein now threw himself into showing the impossibility of any such system.

The Wittgenstein personality cult is the structural counterpart to the way his reputation was formed, and to his style of expression. His whole published output during his lifetime consisted in the *Tractatus* (together with a 1929 paper which he soon repudiated); all other knowledge of his work came from word of mouth, a mode of transmission which made those who had privileged access to him into charisma-bearing disciples. His style of delivery is unconstrained by the canons of academic publishing: peremptorily assertive, typically without supporting arguments, but with an aphoristic flair and a literary polish that make his manuscripts the philosophical equivalent of poetry. Wittgenstein played his advantages into an unsurpassed level of intellectual independence. Independently wealthy (like Russell and Moore) and socially well connected, from a family which belonged to the cultivated elite within the Viennese upper class, he moved where he wanted and did whatever he was interested in; he was easily accepted among his counterparts in England, and just as easily could throw them off to seek escape in the mountains of Norway or a monastery in the Alps.[34] His cultural and social credentials gained him rapid entrée, while his tone of passionate dedication—giving himself over to the emotional energy of making maximal impact on the attention space—lent his arrogance and bad manners the recognizable excuse of being interpreted as unique genius. Wittgenstein's personality *was* his network position. He was the one individual who had been in all the analytical camps; and his creative shifts to new philosophies, which came at the moments when he changed physical location, came across as his extreme individualism. He was not merely personally idiosyncratic and egocentric; he had found the slot available for the boundary breaker, for the rearranger of factions, and there is room for only one such person to be successful in the attention space.

Wittgenstein became great because the network cores on which he fed were structurally deep and in the midst of realignment. Several generations of debates within the mathematical network had raised the reflexive recognition of meta-levels and the creative role of formal symbolism. When these issues became sufficiently generalized, some mathematicians flowed into philosophy, meshing with philosophical disputes and initiating the several prongs of twentieth-century philosophy. Ordinary language philosophy was a reaction of traditional philosophers against this invasion of their base. It remained sophisticated rather than banal because the formalists were implicitly present as a foil; the tension between the two became the "analytical" problem space.

From Mathematical Foundations Crisis to Husserl's Phenomenology

Realignment in the early 1900s happened on all sides. As we return to pick up the growth of the phenomenological movement, it is well to keep in mind that its origins in the networks and issues of the turn of the century are much the same as those of the logical positivists. The older network as a whole was transforming itself, and the sharp conflict between the two sides did not emerge until fairly late, as the attention space became organized around new lines of opposition. Both movements grew from amalgamations between the leading mathematicians of the foundational crisis and the Neo-Kantian lineage. Where the ingredients differ is that the positivists added a third strand, the physicists' methodological dispute centered around Mach, whereas the phenomenologists were tied instead to the movement of new experimental psychology in Brentano's branch. This is not to say that the intellectual ingredients remained untransformed by these new combinations. Phenomenology began as a sharp confrontation of psychological and anti-psychological positions, finding a compromise which shifted increasingly toward the anti-psychological side. Similarly, phenomenology's roots in mathematics became obliterated as the movement later turned into intense opposition to the entire scientific worldview at just the time when the logical positivists were making their most imperialist claims. The paths of phenomenology and of positivism in the larger philosophical space are those of a growing polarization between extremes.

Husserl's phenomenology popped up like a cork buffeted from all sides of the mathematical-philosophical controversies of turn-of-the-century Germany. He began at the heart of the mathematical establishment in Berlin, as a pupil of Kronecker and assistant to Weierstrass. Husserl's dissertation and first book (1889) combined his teachers' positions: Kronecker tried to reduce all of mathematics to a foundation of the natural numbers, while Weierstrass led the arithmetization of analysis. Husserl's *Philosophy of Arithmetic* generalizes the issue and treats it with the psychological approach of Brentano, another of Husserl's teachers during his *Wanderjahre* through the German universities. Frege had just published his masterwork (1884) eliminating psychologism from logic; in a review Frege criticized Husserl's work, resulting in correspondence between them and the conversion of Husserl to Frege's anti-psychological position. When Husserl moved to Halle as a *Dozent,* his colleague Cantor introduced him to Bolzano's logic and made him sympathetic to the program of transfinite numbers and set theory (Tragesser, 1984: 6; Mohanty, 1982).

Husserl came onto the scene in the midst of the foundational controversy in mathematics and was personally connected to most of the dramatis personae. Weierstrass had been the leading rigorist since the 1860s; Kronecker was the leading critic of apparent absurdities arising from the new axiomatic and set-theoretical methods; he was a bitter enemy of Cantor, who felt that Kronecker's persecution was destroying his career, and an opponent of Weierstrass, as chief promulgator of insidious methods. Cross-pressured by his conflicting contacts, Husserl established his own position in the early 1900s, contemporaneous with the rival foundational programs in mathematics: Russell's derivation of mathematics from logic in 1903–1910, Hilbert's formalism announced in 1904, and Brouwer's intuitionism in 1907. Husserl was Hilbert's colleague at Göttingen during 1901–1916 when the issue surfaced.[35] His own views moved away from Hilbert's radical conventionalism in a direction that got them taken seriously by the intuitionists in their concern to justify intuitions of mathematical practice which are deeper than artificial rules of logic.

Husserl's *Logical Investigations* (1900), growing out of the logicist camp, broadens beyond mathematics the search for secure foundations. His ambition was to provide foundations for all science and philosophy, to make philosophy itself a "rigorous science," in the title of his 1911 paper. Husserl was a hybrid between the mathematical lineages and Brentano's school. His added ingredient was Brentano's doctrine of the intentionality of consciousness, but interpreted in an anti-psychological fashion, moving away from the naturalism which Brentano had championed in opposition to Neo-Kantian Idealism. Brentano had ridden to fame with the movement to establish an empirical research discipline in psychology. His version of psychological imperialism had proposed to induce the laws of logic. Now this ran head-on into the movement of mathematical foundationalists, for whom logic was no longer an archaic discipline, a soft spot in the philosophical curriculum, but an arena of vigorous exploration in its own right. The split between psychological and anti-psychological approaches, manifested in Husserl's personal network—Brentano never forgave him for converting to the enemy's position—became explicit as ontological levels in Husserl's philosophy: on one side the natural attitude of the empirical ego; on the other the realm of essences, revealed by bracketing questions of the existence of objects. Husserl creates a new philosophical position by incorporating the defining ideas of his immediate networks into the contents of his own philosophy, turning conflicting doctrines into a hierarchy of levels of analysis—a Durkheimian reflection of social structure in the contents of ideas.

Husserl's *epochê* is not Descartes's skeptical doubt, clearing the decks of everything given; it retains the surface of phenomenal appearance as the starting point for a deep ontology. The essence of consciousness is to be intentional; objects are first and foremost things that are intended, whether or not they exist in sensory experience. Husserl twists this characteristic doctrine of Brentano into congruity with that of his mathematical logicist friends. As in Frege, for Husserl "to be" adds nothing to the object predicated, but operates only on the pragmatic, naturalistic level; as in Cantor, the realm of logical objects is eternal and transcends ordinary sensory experience. Geometry is the exemplar of phenomenology as the science of pure essence, studying ideal objects superior to lines scratched on a chalkboard (Roberts, 1972: 192, 195).

Husserl's work coincided with a general breaking up of the Brentano camp (see Figure 13.8). Meinong was Husserl's network sibling, as a pupil of Brentano, and the two were rivals for prime attention in the decade of the early 1900s, working out problems within the same cultural capital. In Meinong's case, the distinctive ingredient came not from hybridization with the mathematical lineages but by moving closer to the new movement of psychologists. Meinong regarded philosophy as a natural science and promoted empirical psychology in his own laboratory; his exploration of the constituents of consciousness was expressly modeled on chemistry (Lindenfeld, 1980: 115–123, 148–157). Between 1899 and 1904 Meinong elaborated a series of distinctions in answer to problems which had arisen within Brentano's doctrine of intentionality and in the new empirical psychology. What is the ontological status of perceptual gestalts, configurations over and above the particular qualities which receive their significance within them? What is the ontological status of negative ideas (e.g., hole, infinity, non-smoker)? For these too are intended by the mind and arouse feelings perhaps even stronger than positively existing objects. In what sense can consciousness intend a *relation* as an object (e.g., the similarity between a copy and its original; or indeed the higher-order relations among relations, which Bradley had recently cited as an infinite regress to prove the incoherence of relations)? And in what sense can one intend imaginary objects, insofar as they are not merely existences in the mind? For it is possible to distinguish between Hamlet and someone's thought of Hamlet. Meinong solves these problems by distinguishing three kinds of being: existence of objects; subsistence *(Bestehung)* of relations and imaginary objects, even contradictory ones like a round square; and so-being *(Sosein)*, the characteristics of objects independent of particular existence in time and space, known a priori and with certainty.

Meinong proposes a new science, *Gegenstandstheorie* (theory of objects), more general than metaphysics, which deals only with being, whereas subsistence and so-being are "indifferent to being." Mathematics is the science of

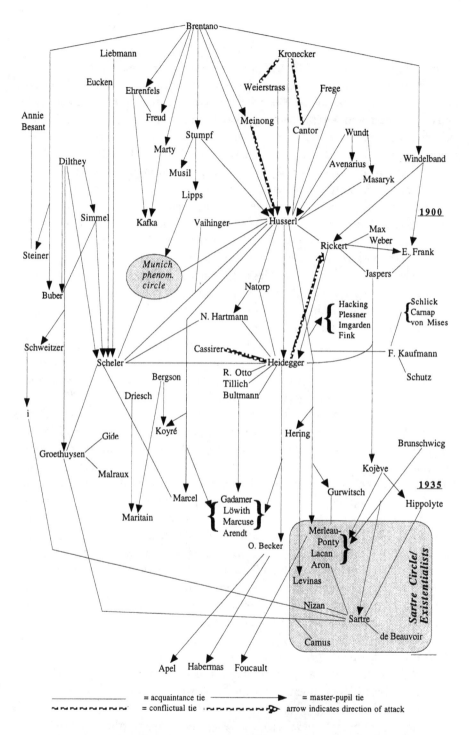

FIGURE 13.8. NETWORK OF PHENOMENOLOGISTS AND
EXISTENTIALISTS, 1865–1965

so-being, but it needs to be further generalized, since there are further realms of so-being which are not quantifiable. Meinong parallels Husserl's exploration of realms beyond naturalistic objects, and in several respects he too formulates something like Husserl's phenomenology and a generalization of mathematics. It is not surprising that these two philosophers, originating close together in the network, should have regarded each other's ideas with rivalry and distrust (Lindenfeld, 1980: 244–246). But each combined his own blend of ingredients. Meinong had links to empirical psychology and to naturalism, from which Husserl expressly distanced himself. Where Meinong grants logical paradoxes (the square circle) the quasi-ontological status of subsisting objects, Husserl, as an ex-mathematician seeking deductive essential truth, finds it absurd to do so. On the territory of logic, Meinong remained the loyalist of the Brentano lineage, willing to give priority to the empirical propensities of the mind to think in terms of noun slots, even if what we put into those slots is not coherent. Husserl moved in tandem with the mathematical logicists, scuttling the psychological level as the realm of superficial mistakes. For a few years Meinong was the more famous of the two; after 1910 Meinong's solutions were upstaged while Husserl's phenomenological movement took off.

As the Frege camp from which Husserl started developed toward the logical positivism of the Vienna Circle, and as Meinong expanded the realm of objects, Husserl shifted his alliances and moved toward a non-religious Idealism. The question arises of the status of the ego in the process of *epoché:* If consciousness is purely intentional, how can it intend itself, which is not an object but only an empty unifier or frame? Husserl uncovers successive levels of reduction: the empirical ego of psychology, the ego of the *epoché,* and finally an impersonal transcendental ego, which is the ultimate ground of the very possibility of consciousness. This position, developed around 1913 in *Ideas,* brought Husserl closer to the Neo-Kantians; at this time he became friendly with Rickert, with whom Husserl in 1910 had founded the journal *Logos,* and who recommended Husserl as his own successor to the professorship at Freiburg (Roberts, 1972: 159).

A phenomenological movement now grew up. At first it comprised two circles (Spiegelberg, 1982). One surrounded Husserl at Göttingen during 1907–1916; its object-centered phenomenology remained relatively close to Meinong. Among its members were Heinrich Rickert, Jr., son of the Neo-Kantian leader; Koyré, a former pupil of Bergson from Paris; Roman Imgarden; Helmuth Plessner, who later developed philosophical anthropology and was influential in German sociology; William Ernest Hocking, a Harvard protégé of Royce; and Jean Hering, an Alsatian who became the leader of a Strasbourg school of Protestant theologians, influential in introducing phenomenology into France after that region was ceded from Germany at the end of the First World

War. Another circle formed at Munich around 1905, initially among the students of Theodor Lipps;[36] its members maintained contact with Göttingen and fed recruits to Husserl as pupils, finally breaking up at the end of the war.

The most flamboyant new star to come out of these networks was Max Scheler. Of a slightly earlier generation, Scheler had already met Husserl in 1901 through their mutual connection with the Neo-Kantian Vaihinger, but his major creativity did not come until 1912, soon after he fell in with the circle of Husserl's followers at Munich, while simultaneously maintaining a bridge to Göttingen. Like the still bigger star-to-be Heidegger, Scheler was a renegade pupil of a Neo-Kantian teacher (in this case Liebmann, the originator of the "back to Kant" movement); both revolted against the subjective screen of Neo-Kantian categories, taking phenomenology as a mode of access to objective essences in themselves. Scheler dramatically widened the application of phenomenology to an emotional *epochê* and the intentionality of emotional acts. Scheler's phenomenology consists to a large extent in imputing underlying motives: for instance, he claims that modern ethical subjectivity, taking values as moral attitudes of the individual mind, is the result of *ressentiment,* a quasi-Nietzschean revolt of the weak against the objective values they cannot fulfill. This, together with the hierarchy of values culminating in the church, earned Scheler a reputation as "the Catholic Nietzsche." There is in fact a network contact: Scheler's teacher was Eucken, a former colleague of the young Nietzsche, who had become famous in the early 1900s for his vitalist spiritualism. All three of this lineage—Nietzsche, Eucken, Scheler—stood out by combining academic with popular audiences (Schnädelbach, 1984: 186–188; Gadamer, 1985: 29–33; Staude, 1967). Scheler quickly eclipsed Husserl's fame, especially for wider audiences; it was Scheler, less technical in his analysis, who spread the fame of the movement by the 1920s. He was the first to visit France and make contact with French philosophers, and the first to be translated into French.

As with many philosophers, Husserl's position was transformed by an implicit struggle over his own movement when he acquired followers. His most aggressive convert, Scheler, had taken command of the naturalistic level of phenomenological analysis; at just this time Husserl, dancing past him in the opposite direction, moved closer to the Neo-Kantian stance. As his own movement of technical phenomenologists became known in the 1920s, Husserl distanced himself once again.[37] He gave priority now to the life-world and to the historical unfolding of time, downplaying eternal essences. In his early work Husserl had characterized existence—the merely empirical, material realm—as what is here and now, in time and space. Space is recoverable for the ideal realm (via geometry), but time is not; time is the locus of individuation and matter (Roberts, 1972: 175). This lesser realm is promoted in Husserl's later work. The spatiotemporal frame is what unites the infinity of things. Eventually he would see it as the setting or "horizon" within which life can emerge, a realm of transcendence in the midst of experience. The concepts of a transcendent horizon of personal existence and of the primordiality of time became key points for the existentialism of Jaspers and Heidegger.

Heidegger: Catholic Anti-modernism Intersects the Phenomenological Movement

Now at the height of its drawing power, the phenomenological network underwent a public split. A rival center of creative energy crystallized around Heidegger, whose *Sein und Zeit* (1927) branched off from Husserl's middle period. As with all creative work, Heidegger's resulted from a confluence of networks. To recapitulate these in biographical form inevitably results in reconstructing the story in a Heidegger-centric way, since we have selected his life for study only in retrospect of his fame. It takes a gestalt switch to move into the foreground what we glimpse through the keyhole of Heidegger's life, and to see just those milieux as producing the intellectual transformation that receives greatest attention in Heidegger's work.

Heidegger begins as a bright young student of Catholic peasant background, no doubt one of many educated on church scholarships. After briefly attempting a Jesuit novitiate, Heidegger in 1909 enters the local university, Freiburg, one of the few in Germany which has an exclusively Catholic theological faculty (Guignon, 1993; Ringer, 1969: 253; Kisiel, 1993). It is the period of intense struggle against modernism within the church, culminating a conflict going back to the 1860s. The unification of Germany in 1871 was followed by the *Kulturkampf* as the Humboldtian revolution of secularized education, long since settled in the Prussian north, was forcibly extended to the Catholic states of the south. In these same decades the unification of Italy against the resistance of the papal state and struggles over secularized education in the French Third Republic had provoked the papacy into militant defense of tradition against science and secular culture. Some Catholic intellectuals resisted, among them Brentano, who left the priesthood in protest in 1873. Against recurring modernist tendencies within Catholic schools and universities, the pope in 1907–1910 wielded the charge of heresy and demanded fidelity to doctrines of miracles and other items of faith (Caputo, 1993: 271; Sheehan, 1993: 73–75). Heidegger enters the intellectual space as a manifestation of the anti-modernist movement, whose doctrine he upheld in Catholic house organs in his first publications.

Freiburg brings him into the orbit of other intellectual movements. The mathematical foundations crisis attracts him, through his Neo-Kantian teachers. But his career plan is to acquire the chair in Catholic theology, and in return for support by a church grant, he gives up a *Habilitationsschrift* on the logical essence of number—which would have made him a parallel to Carnap studying in these same years under Frege (1910–1914), or even to Wittgenstein, beginning work with Russell. Heidegger shifts instead to a topic from the Scotists of the late 1300s, whose technical acumen enables him in safe anti-modernist guise to engage the issues of the early 1900s. This medieval cultural capital fits the modern context, for it comes from the apex of reflexive argument that culminated the old academic networks. Scholasticism had long since become ignored in the attention space, reviled alike by Humanists, scientists, Protestants, and liberals. Now it reappears as a hidden treasure, at the time when modern university recruitment had expanded to take in even its enemies from the Catholic backwaters. The network of the 1300s could hold its own with the technicalities of 1900. Heidegger has no need to set aside his concern for the mathematical foundations crisis, and he depicts his task in *Sein und Zeit* ([1927] 1953: 9–10) as dealing with a foundational issue cross-cutting sciences as widely as the mathematics of formalists and intuitionists, as well as relativity physics, biology, and theology.

Brentano, the most famous and controversial of modern German Catholics, would inevitably become part of a young Catholic intellectual's reading; for an anti-modernist, Brentano's later psychology would be suspect, but Brentano's early work *On the Several Senses of Being in Aristotle* (1862) was safe, and the text had been given to Heidegger in his school days. In this work Brentano had put the cultural capital of medieval scholasticism back into play in the context of contemporary debate started by his own teacher Trendelenburg with late Hegelian historians and Kantians. Aquinas and Duns Scotus had raised the issue of the univocality of being, and Brentano had worked out this issue, using the tools of modern textual scholarship. Aristotle had taken being in various senses: as accident (copula), as being true, as potential versus actual being, and in the being of the categories (quality, quantity, relation, and so on). Brentano ([1862] 1975: 66–68) had held that the categories, as the most general predicates of first substance, are the highest genera of being. Heidegger is critical of Brentano's solution, but the question lingers and eventually is resurrected when Heidegger formulates his own philosophical project. The problem of the meaning of being, in the full sense raised by Duns Scotus and, according to Heidegger, forgotten since then, is to characterize the being which underlies God as well as creation. For Heidegger, the question raises again the wonder of being among the pre-Socratics, and subsumes the most profound modern questions: the reality of higher mathematical abstractions and of Meinong's impossible Golden Mountain or square circle which find a place in the intentionality of consciousness and which troubled Russell in the early 1900s.[38]

No doubt other Catholic students on the periphery of German philosophy had Brentano and Scotus available as cultural capital, without any real chance of moving them to the center of attention. Heidegger's own work remains unexceptional until after 1916, when two things happen: he is passed over for the chair in Catholic theology, and he meets Husserl, newly arrived at Freiburg. Heidegger undergoes a conversion, away from Catholicism and into the new movements of Protestant theology. Husserl, from an ethnic Jewish background and now calling himself a "free Christian," is suspicious of Catholic dogmatists and receives him only after assurances of Heidegger's conversion. Heidegger becomes his assistant and favorite disciple. Heidegger had known Husserl's early writings but only as relevant to his abandoned interest in logic and mathematics; it is personal contact in the network that jolts his emotional energy and sets him to work using Husserl's tools. By the early 1920s, without publishing anything new, Heidegger is acquiring an underground reputation as the most passionate and original thinker in Husserl's stable (Gadamer, 1985: 15, 46–48; Dostal, 1993: 150–151). For now the phenomenological movement is followed in some quarters with a fanaticism paralleling the followers of Marxism or Stefan George. Husserl programmatically divided philosophy into regional ontologies (material nature, animate life, persons) to be worked out by the phenomenological method. Heidegger is assigned the regional ontology of the historical sciences. This was to be *Sein und Zeit,* eventually published in Husserl's yearbook, established (in 1920) to bring together the results of these phenomenological researches.

Heidegger's social location made him more than a phenomenological disciple. His unique trajectory as lapsed Catholic theologian was reinforced when he moved to Marburg as *Extraordinarius* (1923–1928). Marburg was the great Neo-Kantian center, and its last head, Natorp, was treated by Heidegger with great respect. Rickert, his own Neo-Kantian teacher at Freiburg, he regarded with disdain; the epistemological and value concepts of Neo-Kantianism were just the kind of bloodless philosophy which Heidegger regarded as forgetfulness of the ontology of being. The aging Natorp, though, had turned away from the liberal ethicization of religion which had prevailed with Cohen and the earlier Marburg school, and was grappling with the question of the individuality of God and of concrete worldly being. Neo-Kantianism was dying as the spotlight shifted elsewhere. Nicolai Hartmann, the last star of the Neo-Kantian lineage, was Heidegger's rival on the young Marburg faculty, and he too was deviating in the direction of subordinating epistemology to ontology; even the Kantian critique presupposes a metaphysics, and the thing-in-itself can be approached by using tools borrowed from Husserl's phenomenology. Hartmann recombined intellectual ingredients which overlapped with those of Heidegger; but Hartmann remained more of a traditional Neo-Kantian, and the result of their similarity was that Heidegger's greater originality ended up putting Hartmann in the shade (Gadamer, 1985: 23–26; Schnädelbach, 1984: 209–216).

Scheler, who occasionally visited Marburg in the 1920s from his chair in Cologne, mixed cultural capitals in a fashion similar to Heidegger but with an opposite trajectory; having become a follower of Husserlian phenomenology around 1910, at the end of the war he converted to Catholicism. Scheler arrived in 1919 at his religious turn by claiming to uncover an objective hierarchy of values: at lowest, the utilitarian plane of pleasures; next, vital values promoting health and social well-being; still higher, spiritual values of justice, beauty, and truth; at the apex, the spiritual values embodied in religion. In action, the lower values are to be sacrificed to higher ones. After 1924 Scheler converted again, giving up the Catholic personal God for a kind of vitalist pantheism. Heidegger, who remained sympathetic to Scheler's restless searches until his death in 1928, was moving in a similar path of recasting theology in a depersonalized form. We find the same again in Jaspers: technical borrowing from phenomenology around 1913, in this case for the psychiatric description of pathological states;[39] teaching in a Neo-Kantian stronghold (Heidelberg), in the 1920s moving toward what later became called existentialism (in Germany, *Existenzphilosophie*). Jaspers's major works, emerging in 1931–1932 on the heels of Heidegger's fame, preserve traditional Christian themes of God, freedom, and immortality, not as demonstrable truths but as existential questions and choices beyond the limits of scientific reason.

Marburg at this time was a center of controversies in Protestant theology. Traditionally it had been a leader of the liberal historical school; out of this camp had come Bultmann, theology professor at Marburg from 1921 onward, who became Heidegger's close friend.[40] Also visiting at Marburg in 1924 was Paul Tillich, a leader of the Christian-socialist movement in the postwar revolts, just beginning to move into existentialism. The major stimulus in Protestant theology was Karl Barth, professor at Göttingen since 1921; Barth had just launched neo-orthodoxy in 1919, overthrowing the liberal theology of his youth, as a series of false steps in the direction of secularism. Schleiermacher had subjectivized the path to God into seeking within oneself. From Kant onward God had been narrowed into ethical and social concerns. Historical and textual scholarship was another false path: it is not man that seeks God but God that seeks man; true religiousness consists in making oneself open to revelation. Bultmann, as a leading New Testament exegete, entered into correspondence and controversy with Barth, seeking a way to reconcile textual scholarship and Christian revitalization. In the face of scientific criticism, the historical reports of Jesus' life and resurrection cannot be accepted; the message, however, is to be not merely ethicized but taken as the expression of universal religious experience, the sensations of awe and dread, of being a stranger in the world and open to something beyond it.

Heidegger was moving along the same path; reacting against his starting point in Catholic scholasticism, he overturned the secure ontologies of a God as highest and original Being, transforming his theological capital instead into a series of questions. Using phenomenological language, Heidegger produced a universal ontology of human existence underlying both Greek and Christian thought: the central realities are not immortality but being-toward-death; not salvation but angst, care, and decision; not sin but the sheer arbitrary fact of being thrown into existing in the world in a particular time and place. The themes emerged in common with Bultmann, Jaspers, Tillich, and others; after Heidegger gave them articulation in most general form in *Sein und Zeit,* they became all the more explicitly defended in a self-consciously existentialist theology which reached its height in the 1950s.

Why did this movement emerge, across a broad front, at the time when it did? To speak of the disillusionment of bourgeois culture after the First World War is not quite accurate, for there was neither disillusionment in every aspect of cultural life (certainly not in the popular culture of the cinema and of jazz, which appeared at this time), nor in many branches of philosophy, such as logical positivism. It is specifically a disillusionment with liberal theology that is at issue here. Nor was it a product of the war, since its manifestations go back to the first decade of the century, among other things, the height of vitalist philosophies in Germany and France. During 1910–1914 were published in Germany the first translations of Kierkegaard and Dostoyevsky—bringing about their first widespread fame—and the complete edition of Nietzsche's posthumous *Will to Power.* The theological responses of a Danish anti-Idealist of the 1840s and of a Russian anti-modernist Slavophile of the 1860s and 1870s were quickly incorporated into the conceptual armory of the new generation of philosophers and theologians of 1920. This could only have happened if motives existed for their reception. It was a movement against accommodation to secularism in religion, against turning religion into merely universal ethics or a social gospel, against rationalizing the mysteriously personal God into an abstract Spirit. In general it was a movement reasserting the emotionally committed faith of particularistic religious traditions in the face of the tolerant universalizing which reaches across confessional borders by reducing religious content to the blandest common denominator.

Seen in this perspective, the conservative or neo-traditionalist movements in theology beginning around 1910 are one turn of a very widespread cycle of religious accommodation and revival. It is not to be explained, with teleological pathos, as the forebear of Nazism, nor as a once-and-for-all downfall of liberal secularism. Sociologists of religion discern this cycle quite generally, in the United States as much as in European churches, and have uncovered a number of its mechanisms (Stark and Bainbridge, 1987). Movements for secularization, tolerance, and liberty of belief generate enthusiasm as rebellions against dominant established churches, especially ones which rule with the aid of state monopoly. But as secularization succeeds and religion becomes privatized, the liberal churches and their rationalizing intellectuals lose their distinctively religious offering. To fill the unmet demand for religious emotions, on one side spring up new religions and pseudo-religious cults. The Stefan George circle, Steiner's Anthroposophy, occultism, and many other movements of late Wilhelmine and Weimar Germany are analogues to the cult movements of any period of a volatile religious market, such as in the United States both in the 1920s and in the 1960s–1970s. On the other side, some intellectuals of the older churches, recognizing the decline of their organizations' appeal, sought to revitalize from within by a neo-conservative movement. Such religious movements can make allies with external, more purely political movements of conservatism, but it is a mistake to see their dynamic as merely a political one. The Protestantism of Barth, Bultmann, and Tillich, and the allied existentialism of Heidegger and Jaspers, are by no means simply a side-eddy of fascism, although there are some places of overlap. Much more generally the religious movement preserved its own standpoint against the encroachment of political totalitarianism.[41]

Division of the Phenomenological Movement

Sein und Zeit was the reputation-making work for Heidegger, and the great work of German existential phenomenology, because it synthesizes in abstract and general form the key intellectual resources of these several networks. Even as it proposes the destruction of the history of Western philosophy, it reconstructs that history around a central question, calling attention to the most general metaphysical issue that can be raised. The search for the univocal ontology of being resonates with the religious concept of God, but it is a properly philosophical question in its own sphere; it is precisely because Heidegger carries through his philosophical construction that theology receives a new resource. Scotism is not revived but transformed. Phenomenology is carried so far afield that it acquires not an extension but a rival. Neo-Kantianism dies serving as foil for a position which rejects epistemological issues centered on a subject over against a mind-filtered world, putting in its place a being, *Dasein,* whose primordial nature is existing-in-a-world. The question shifts elsewhere. It is no longer a question of whether and how there are facts, but of the ontology of dealing with the brute factuality of existence as presence. *Dasein* has access to being, but the meaning of being, especially the issue of a univocal being underlying all its modes, now comes to the fore. Philosophy, which lives on its problems, is set on a new course.

Technically, Heidegger was continuing Husserl's project. Husserl had long been concerned with the phenomenology of time, although in his earlier work it remained a subsidiary issue. In the 1920s, in parallel to Heidegger, Husserl increasingly focused on time as central to the being of entities in general. Husserl's phenomenological "now" has "retentive" and "protentive" aspects, not merely on the naturalistic psychological level of memory and anticipation, but at a deeper ontological level. In Heidegger's version, being in general is historical, constituted in its past and its project into the future. Husserl struggled inconclusively to work out the relations among time in general, the natural time of the spatial world, and the historical time of human consciousness.[42] Heidegger seized on the conjecture that human *Dasein*, which is manifestly temporal, is the key to the understanding of being in general as temporal. In the end, Heidegger too foundered on the difficulty in leaping from the human sphere to the more general one.

Several key points differ between the two philosophers. For Husserl, subjectivity remains the privileged reference point. But Heidegger wishes to break with any trace of the Idealist tradition; to assert the priority of the spiritual subject waters down religious tension and makes salvation virtually automatic. The Neo-orthodox theologians had already revolted against this easy form of religion, and Heidegger sharpens the distinction on ontological grounds. *Dasein* is being-in-the-world, and mortality rather than immortality is central to it; there is anguish as to whether spiritual transcendence can exist at all. Heidegger therefore jettisons the phenomenological *epochê*, which by bracketing the reality of the world had left out the fundamental trait of *Dasein*.[43] Husserl was moving in the 1920s toward depicting temporality as central to phenomenology; Heidegger greatly outpaced his teacher in dramatizing the significance of the move by stressing that *Dasein's* relation to temporality may be authentic or inauthentic, cutting itself off from its deepest reality by evading its own future, its death. A good deal of Heidegger's phenomenological analysis of the social world resembles that of other Husserl followers; both Heidegger and Schutz see the ordinary world as constituted by taken-for-granted routines. In Schutz's *Phenomenology of the Social World* (1932), this is merely a technical analysis completing Max Weber's social *verstehen* as the foundations of economic action. For Heidegger it is a target for preaching, like the medieval friar recalling worldly humans to meditate on their mortality.[44]

Heidegger's ontological project ended a failure. He never did demonstrate the univocality of being. In 1962 he declared that it had foundered on the problem of connecting *Dasein* and the extantness of the spatial world (Dostal, 1993: 160). Part II of *Sein und Zeit*, which was to reconstruct the historical path by which Western ontology had gone wrong, was left unfinished because of his inability to finish the last section of Part I, which was to move from the temporality of *Dasein* to the temporality of being in general. Heidegger's later work turns away from *Dasein,* and in mood of increasing hostility to Christianity, looks directly for a way in which Being "speaks to us." His search for the meaning of being in history takes on the appearance of seeking a new eschatology, of the possibility of God appearing again in the world.[45] Even in its failure, Heidegger's ontological project gave a new attention center and set of problems for the intellectual world. His *Dasein* analysis, designed merely as entry point to the general question of being, became a defining point for the burgeoning movement of existentialist theology and psychology. Late in the century his historicizing, shorn of its ontology and its eschatological overtones, became a favorite text for postmodernists. Heidegger also provided the way for one more grand attempt on the core territory of ontology; in the hands of Sartre, the inability to found being in general is turned into the central point of a system in which being is characterized by its negativity, its lack of foundation.

Husserl's phenomenology, like any successful movement, divides into opposing tendencies. Somewhat like Kant in his later years, Husserl was in part swept up in the movement he had spawned, in part appalled by the directions in which it was going. Husserl saw his own earlier formalism, his own search for rigorously scientific foundations, as typical of the pathological consciousness emerging within modern history. He declared that phenomenology must proceed by the "suspension of the presupposition of objectivity" (Roberts, 1972: 209); he was now an enemy of the scientism which he saw as the hallmark of the age, and which was becoming famous in the manifestos of the Vienna Circle. He took on an apocalyptic tone; the topic of his last work, *The Crisis of the European Sciences,* is equated in a 1935 lecture with "The Crisis of European Man." Crisis had been Husserl's stock-in-trade all his life. Now the foundational crisis of mathematics since the 1880s had been replaced in Husserl's perception by a crisis arising from the impersonality of scientism—the triumph of the natural attitude over the realm of eternal truths. At the same time, Husserl attacked in the other direction, against irrationalism—all too obvious in the ideology of the victorious Nazis—and against his protégé Heidegger: "The downfall of Europe is its estrangement from its own rational sense of life, its fall into hostility toward the spirit and into barbarity" (quoted in Natanson, 1973: 145).

But the Nazis were not primarily an intellectual movement at all, and their rise to power was based on geopolitical and economic crises that had nothing to do with philosophy. This did not prevent virtually every intellectual movement of the 1930s and for several decades thereafter from blaming their intellectual rivals for Nazism, as the alleged result of failing to adopt the proper premises, whether those of Marxism, logical positivism, ordinary language, Popper's fallibilism, existentialism, or phenomenology. The *intellectual* crisis

which by the 1930s Husserl was perceiving as the downfall of the entire
Western cultural tradition was the usual condition of intellectual life: its
creative bursts which come through exploiting the deep troubles of previous
movements, forming new movements which undergo splits and clashes of their
own. With Husserl, the explicit invocation of crisis became a key intellectual
resource. This was not the least of the cultural capital which was appropriated
by his followers.

The Ideology of the Continental-Anglo Split

The realignment of philosophical parties produced a double dose of intellectual
conflict. There was the expectable polemic of the new versus the old, as well
as new lines of dispute taking over the center of attention. All this is normal.
At the same time, each of the several post-realignment movements of the early
twentieth century became unprecedentedly vehement in their condemnation of
any other mode of doing philosophy. This partisanship outlasted virtually every
other substantive feature of their programs.

Although verification, physicalism, unified science, and logical foundationalism were gradually given up, the central characteristic of the Vienna Circle
became defining for a large wing of philosophy. Its hallmark was militant
rejection of all philosophies that could be styled metaphysical. The position
had its blind spot, insofar as the militants themselves usually had their ontological preferences, and in fact there was an outburst of systems that reduced
large areas of reality to fundamentals: atomic states of affairs in Wittgenstein's
Tractatus, Platonic reals and then sense-experiences in Russell's successive
systems, the entities of physics in Carnap and Neurath. These militant reduc-
tionists and demarcationists jolted everyone into awareness of a deep-seated
change in the bases of intellectual production: the old identity of the general-
purpose intellectual had given way to that of one specialist among others,
speaking a language and dealing with problems that are no more accessible to
outsiders than the technicalities of mathematics or chemistry. This would be
true, too, of the opponents of the logicists; phenomenologists, existentialists,
and later in the century poststructuralists would also speak in the technical
jargon of insiders. The militant ideology of the formalizers, even though it was
unable to make good on its substantive claims, sent a shock wave throughout
the intellectual world because it presented in exaggerated form what was
becoming inescapable in the ordinary conditions of academic work.

The lineup of enemies differed in the various national arenas. In Germany,
first it was Neo-Kantianism to be disposed of; with the popularity of Husserl's
phenomenology by the 1920s, that too became a target (for instance, in
Popper's attack on "essentialism"). When Heidegger's *Sein und Zeit* came on

the scene in 1927, his emphasis on negation was singled out by Carnap in the second issue of *Erkenntnis* (1931) as the epitome of meaningless statements arising by misuse of language. In England and the United States, the initial enemy of the logicist movement was the Idealism of the previous generation, during which the university had secularized; the attack had begun with Russell early in the century, and continued down through the 1960s in the tendency to brand all metaphysical philosophy an outmoded relic of religion. When existentialism came into vogue in France in the 1940s and in Germany and in U.S. literary circles in the 1950s, it replaced Idealism as the prime target for condemnation.

In this midcentury generation the scheme became widely accepted in the English-speaking world of a long-standing division between "Continental" and "Anglo" philosophical traditions. For the purposes of this polemic, the rivalry between logical positivists and ordinary language was downplayed into a grand coalition of "analytic" philosophy characterizing the "Anglo" camp. One side in the overriding dispute was styled as metaphysical (and, depending on one's loyalties, either meaningless pseudo-problems or the major questions of philosophy), the other as empiricist, scientific, and commonsensical (and hence either sound rationality or else banalities and narrow technicalities). This crude and inconsistent division was the partisan ideology of midcentury factions, projected backwards onto history. Its plausibility requires that we overlook the philosophers who happen to be in the wrong camp (most glaringly Berkeley, Green, Bradley, Royce, Peirce, and McTaggart in the Anglo sphere; Condillac, Comte, Feuerbach, Büchner, Taine, Frege, Mach, and of course the Vienna Circle on the Continent), or go through gyrations of selective reinterpretation (such as those applied to aspects of Leibniz, Berkeley, and Peirce).[46] In reality, the interpenetration of science and philosophy had been a common characteristic of all European philosophy, and the networks of significant philosophers had more often crossed the English Channel than they had been divided by it. The dichotomy was hardly one that would have come naturally to philosophers of Russell's generation or any previously. Lockean empiricism was the rage among Parisian philosophes; after the university revolution, first German Idealism, then German materialism and mathematics were the beacon stars for British modernizers.

What made this Continental-Anglo dichotomy dominant was the combination of the Nazis, World War II, and the emigration of the Vienna Circle. In the United States, where most of the logical positivists ended up, the influx coincided with the expansion of the universities under secular auspices and the final dying out of the Idealist generation. It also was the period of expansion for university research science and social science departments, for which Vienna Circle offshoots such as Hempel made careers writing methodological canons.[47] Anti-Nazi feeling coincided with the positivist ideology—most vehemently expressed in Popper's book *The Open Society and Its Enemies*—that metaphysics is not only nonsensical but dangerous. The fact that Husserlian phenomenologists too had gone into exile, and that French existentialists were active as Resistance fighters, should have neutralized some of this political animus; but the anticommunism of the cold war broadened the doctrine to count all extremisms as pernicious.

At its core, the anti-metaphysical movement was an internal battle in the disciplinary politics of philosophers; that the analytical camp was able to gain external allies on political grounds gave extra heat to the conflict. The political name-calling imported at midcentury into internal struggles among philosophical factions became a generalized technique, used in turn by the self-styled "post-positivist" movements from the 1960s onward, when political tides shifted and analytical hegemony weakened in its former strongholds. But even here, the hostility of phenomenologist-existentialist-deconstructionist lineages to their analytical rivals is not merely or even primarily an expression of external political hostilities. For at the same time that logical positivism and ordinary language were originally condemning the meaninglessness of metaphysics, the camp of phenomenology, religious neo-orthodoxy, and their allies were developing their own condemnations of naturalism and scientism. The deeper factional divisions which still exist at the turn of the twenty-first century are the same as those which emerged with the realignment at the turn of the twentieth; there has been no subsequent realignment, although some edges have blurred and factional names have changed.

In reality, the two allegedly antithetical traditions are network cousins, full of common ancestors two and three generations back. All sides of the realigning factions of the twentieth century emerged from the struggles over the foundations of mathematics at the turn of the century. Working from much the same heritage of problems, the several branches have tended to move in parallel in their basic conceptual shifts. In the development of act psychology and phenomenology from Brentano to Husserl to Heidegger, we see a parallel to the exploration of logical hierarchies: the sequence from Frege's use versus mention, through Russell's theory of types, to Wittgenstein's saying versus showing resembles the successive uncovering of levels of *epochê* and the existentialist repudiation of traditional ontological language, like a melody played in a different key.[48]

CHAPTER 14

Writers' Markets and Academic Networks: The French Connection

If academic disciplines have been the main driving force of modern philosophy, a rival if subsidiary base has also existed. This is the popular market for writing. Both are products of organizational revolutions: the reforms which removed the university from church domination and made it the center of autonomous research specialties, and the shift from patronage as the chief material support of writers' careers. In Germany the two revolutions occurred at about the same time; for this reason, Germany has been the archetypal modern culture in the intellectual sphere, the center from which leading ideas have been exported elsewhere. In England and France, the shift to the open market for writers began a little earlier, while the academic revolution lagged several generations behind, giving a special skew to their intellectual cultures. Indeed in France, the German-style university structure combining research and teaching was never adopted, and the French organizational base for intellectual life has remained distinctive to the present time.

Philosophy is the discipline which explores the most abstract portion of intellectual space; therefore the autonomous and inwardly oriented networks of the university, wherever they have existed, have usually dominated the philosophical attention space over the products of the commercial marketplace. Nevertheless, the writers' market has created some unique niches for intellectual production, and these in turn have made possible various interplays and blends with academic philosophy. During the patronage era which preceded the writers' market, both literary and nonfiction writing was generally set apart from abstract philosophy. In the networks we have examined throughout this work, abstract philosophy was usually produced by professional teachers, monks and priests, in organizational structures turned inward and away from the ordinary world. In contrast, writers' networks are more closely connected to, even embedded in, the status order of society, and their cultural content is much closer to lay concerns of class-appropriate entertainment, topical morality, and politics (Heilbron, 1994). In a patronage structure, writers reflect the concerns of their sponsors; in this I include self-patronage of the gentry literati, such as the Chinese gentlemen circulating poems as a form of leisure amusement and cultivated status display. With the shift to a writers' marketplace comes more room to maneuver, but the power of the audience results in a division between writers oriented toward the mass market and an inwardly oriented elite of writers pursuing their own standards of technical perfection. The latter group sets up a possible rapprochement with academic carriers of culture, but the meeting is laden with tension.

The bases and products of philosophy and of literature have usually been distinct. The networks of these two kinds of intellectuals have touched on occasion; a very small number of individuals have overlapped both networks and produced memorable work in both genres. Most have been successful in only one attention space or the other; nevertheless, something is transmitted structurally, for where the networks of philosophers and literary practitioners have connected, the result has been to energize outbursts of creativity in either field.

One of the most notable of these literary-philosophical overlaps occurred in Germany, in the founding generation of Idealism. Kant and Fichte were not literary figures, but their creativity cannot be explained without taking note of the rising level of controversy and enthusiasm in the literary networks. Several transformations in the material base happened in close sequence. This was the time when the publishing market burst out in Germany. As yet its careers were ill paid, and writers still relied on old-fashioned patronage where they could, which in the German *Kleinstaaterei* included government appointments and university positions. The Idealists carried off the university revolution, which opened up autonomously controlled careers within the academic world; a generation later, philosophers no longer needed the patronage or the literary connections. At the moment of victory, however, a branch of the Idealist philosophies expressed the attitude of hybrid academic-literary intellectuals. This was aesthetic Idealism, formulated first by Schiller and then by Schelling: the artist directly intuits the axioms of philosophy and synthesizes the opposites of Nature and the Ideal; aesthetics gives privileged access to the thing-in-itself.

Aesthetic Idealism was adopted as a vehicle for self-exaltation of European writers at the moment when the market opened. It conveyed the feeling of freedom from personal deference to patrons, trumpeting the status of the artist above any lay consumer, no matter how wealthy or powerful. Shelley's "poets are the unacknowledged legislators of the world" expresses the extreme claim. Ironically, this moment of self-glorification was made possible by the fact that enough of the patronage system still existed so that the writer need not feel pinched by the demands of the mass market: Schiller and Goethe adroitly played both bases. For the same reason, the moment of extreme artistic self-glorification was transitory. Within the next generations, intellectuals in the writers' market would take on an alienated tone whenever they attempted to work to higher and more esoteric standards than their audience would buy.

In Germany the intellectual world became academicized before anywhere else, and this made the fate of aesthetic Idealism different than in England and the United States. In the latter places it was a relatively ephemeral movement of literary Romanticism, later submerged beneath the outbursts of full-fledged technical Idealist philosophy when those university systems were finally secularized. In Germany the professional scholars in their autonomous university base had already seized control of the intellectual attention space; aesthetic Idealism became a rear-guard action, carried by anti-modernist protesters who were also outsiders relying on a popular writers' market against the dominance of the university. That is why so many of the thematic clashes of modernist sensibility first occurred in the German orbit.

The network lineage of the aesthetic Idealists consists of the predecessors of what later became existentialism, the modern movement of literary-academic hybrids par excellence. This was the highbrow end of the writers' market. There were other philosophical hybrids. In countries where the university revolution was delayed, philosophy continued to be produced by general-purpose intellectuals who made a living on the popular writing market. One such result was to give philosophy a slant toward political activism, comprising forms such as Utilitarianism or even, as in Russia, revolutionary radicalism. An even larger market niche, during the era of de-clericalization and disestablishment of the state religions, was for writings at the interface between religion and science. Religious tracts had always been the biggest seller since the inception of print media. Now countries with the appropriate brand of religious politics went through a period in which the popular best-selling philosophies were forms of vitalism.

After the academic revolution was completed and universities had expanded, the careers of virtually all intellectuals gravitated to some degree into academic channels. Philosophies oriented toward popular writing markets now came into conflict with those oriented toward academic specialists. In most places the academics unequivocally won. But in a few instances the two structures of intellectual production have held on in tandem, without one eclipsing the other. The result has been a distinctive mix of academic technicalities with ideologies resonating with the situation of intellectuals on the writers' market. The classic case is France, where the literary-academic hybrid underlies philosophical movements down through existentialism and postmodernism.

The Secularization Struggle and French Popular Philosophy

In France there have been two major episodes of vitalist science-religion: first during the Napoleonic era, the second at the end of that century. Institutionally, both were associated with reforms of the French university system and with the violent swings between state religion and secularization which characterized the bases of French cultural life.

Before the Revolution, education in France was largely in the hands of Catholic clergy or nuns, and all other teachers were under clerical supervision, with the exception of government technical schools for military and civil engineers.[1] The Revolution abolished the universities along with the privileges of the church. The new educational system constructed during the Napoleonic period left primary schooling to local authorities, and in 1808, after state rapprochement with the church, to Catholic teaching orders. Secondary schools and higher education were centralized under the Imperial University, which monopolized teaching for its degree holders, made all appointments, controlled salaries and curricula, and formed a regular career hierarchy of teachers, inspectors, and governors. The head of this bureaucracy was appointed by the state; under Napoleon this became a bishop, who restored Catholic orthodoxy in education. Unlike at the German universities, the professors at the highest schools were not expected to do independent research; this was reserved for members of the Institut de France, which in effect reconstituted the old Academies of Science, Inscriptions and Belles-Lettres, and Fine Arts. A section of the institute for moral and political science existed from 1795 to 1803 but was suppressed by Napoleon on account of the opposition to himself by its members, the freethinking Idéologues circle of Cabanis. The old university faculty of philosophy was eliminated, replaced by faculties of science and literature. Under this system innovative research continued in the mathematical sciences, where the École Polytechnique supported many leading scientists but languished in other fields. Philosophy was embarked on a century-long pattern in which creativity was carried largely by the popular writers' market.

The Restoration intensified clerical control, making all primary and secondary teachers subject to the bishops, multiplying ecclesiastical schools at the expense of those under secular auspices, and in 1822 dismissing religious moderates such as Cousin from university posts. Struggle between the Ultramontane papal faction and national Royalists blocked the more extreme claims of the former, however, and conservative secularists including Cousin were recalled in 1828. Rigid state control of the church pushed the Catholic conservatives into opposition to the government, playing a part in the agitation for liberal rights and electoral principles which led to the constitutional monarchies of 1830–1848 and the late 1860s and the revolution of 1848. Under the dictatorship of Napoleon III, degrees in history and philosophy were eliminated in 1854, and the medieval *trivium* and *quadrivium* were reinstituted in the university curriculum. In primary education, the trend toward secular schools in the 1840s was reversed again by the 1860s, when the majority of schools were again religious. Catholic militancy in turn stiffened the secularizers in the government defending the supremacy of their own administration. The struggle broke out in full force under the Third Republic in the 1870s. Secularists won the upper hand with the reforms of 1881, which excluded clergy from the university and from the right to confer degrees and established a centralized system of public and compulsory primary schools. Final separation of church and state did not occur until 1905, in the wake of the Dreyfus affair and in the face of popular counter-demonstrations, taking elementary teaching from the religious congregations and removing education entirely from the hands of the church.

Upsurges of quasi-vitalist philosophy occurred in conjunction with those moments when the secularizing movements had just peaked and receded. Heilbron (1994) points out that the salons of the ancien regime, which had promoted an anti-technical and literary style in intellectual life, collapsed with the dispossession of the aristocracy; simultaneously, the abolition of the ancient theology-dominated universities and the founding of governmental scientific bodies created a new orientation toward specialized disciplines. There was a reversal of intellectual hierarchies; instead of allying with aristocratic literature, philosophers now sought connections with the new elite, the natural scientists.

The first approach to French vitalism was the will-philosophy of Maine de Biran. Maine began in the circle of Idéologues around Cabanis and the comte Destutt de Tracy, a direct offshoot of the main circles of French intellectual life since the Encyclopedists and the Auteuil circle of Condorcet and Mme. Helvétius (see Figure 14.1). The Idéologues continued the main themes of the secularizing movement, associationism radicalized by the politics of the 1790s. Cabanis (1796–1802) held that Lavoisier's chemical analysis can be applied to ideas; Destutt (1798–1815) coined the term *Idéologie* for the zoological science which analyzes ideas into sensory elements. Since Destutt regarded his method as a means of undermining belief in religion, he and his supporters opposed Napoleon when the latter brought about the return of state religion. In this period virtually all the notable philosophers were political activists, and philosophy was taken explicitly as a weapon of politics.[2] It was as a member of the Chamber of Deputies and subsequently of the Institute that Maine de Biran, a moderate Royalist and opponent of Napoleon, became connected with the Idéologues.

Maine began in 1802 with a treatise on the influence of habit on thinking. By 1812 he had broken with the banned Idéologues, reversing their themes in

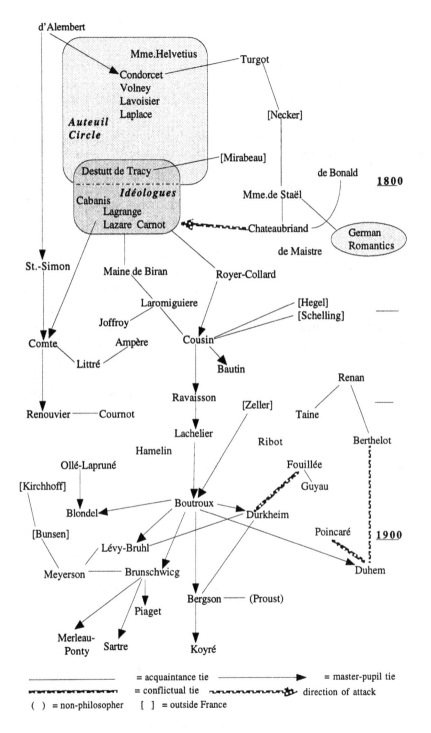

FIGURE 14.1. NETWORK OF FRENCH PHILOSOPHERS, 1765–1935

his *Essay on the Foundations of Psychology.* Neither sensation nor thought, but will, the internal sensation of bodily effort, is the primary experience; "I will, therefore I am," is the starting point of all knowledge. It is willed attention and movement which makes external sensations vivid; outward impressions fall prey to Hume's critique insofar as they reveal no necessary connections, but the inner experience of the will gives immediate certainty of causality. Maine's philosophy is a manifesto against associationism and mechanism; at the same time, it avoids the sentimentalism and emotionalism of Chateaubriand and the religious conservatives. Maine de Biran enjoyed a reputation among his contemporaries as the master philosopher, and his will-psychology, along with Royer-Collard's religious defense, briefly became the official doctrine of the university, before Cousin's scholastic eclecticism set in (*CMH*, 1902–1911: 9.133). After the Restoration, Maine worked inconclusively on his system until his death in 1824. The opening in which religious and disciplinary innovations seemed possible in the aftermath of the Revolution had shut down again as official religion reasserted control over education. Maine-like ideas remained in the air in non-academic literary circles. In the liberalization of the 1830s, Balzac's *Peau de Chagrin* describes ambitious young men during the episode of relatively uncensored Parisian journalism striving to make their fortunes by writing the definitive treatise on the will. Maine's will-philosophy has the flavor of a new religion compounded from the ingredients of modern science, which was something of a free-floating vogue in the era of Balzac and Stendahl.

Maine's work resonates with the founding of new scientific disciplines which went along with the reorganization of French intellectual production at the time of the suppression of the old university and the establishment of the Institute and the École Polytechnique. Maine's structural parallel is Comte, whose lineage connects similarly with the scientific establishment (Comte was a pupil at the Polytechnique, 1814–1816, suspended for political troubles, who hung on as an examiner in mathematics), and with 1790s politicians (Comte got his first ideas during 1817–1824 when serving as secretary to Saint-Simon, promulgator of socialist doctrines). Comte came to attention in the 1830s as classifier of the sciences and theorist of the sequence in which they appeared; he was among the first to recognize biology as a distinct science, and he initially attracted the support of mainstream research scientists, including Fourier. Comte's crowning science, sociology, superseded the Idéologues' favorite, psychology. Here too Comte was a territorial rival to Maine de Biran, all the more so since Comte declared the era of metaphysics past, while Maine built the psychology of the will into a metaphysics, claiming position as the core of academic philosophy in place of Descartes's cogito. Seemingly Maine should have the reputation of a classic figure of the French philosophical tradition, between the Cartesian cogito and the anti-rationalism of Bergson and Sartre; instead he is submerged by his affinities with the conservative spiritualism that dominated the generations which followed him.

At midcentury none of the leading French intellectuals was an academic philosopher. From the time of Napoleon until the reforms of the 1880s, university professors were essentially examiners of secondary school leavers and certifiers of teachers; classes for regular bodies of university students did not exist until the 1880s. Even thereafter, the education system promoted scholastic preservation of the classics rather than innovation. For decades educational administrators struggled over the extent to which modern languages and natural sciences were to be introduced in the secondary schools (Ringer, 1992: 40–46; Ringer, 1987: 26–29). The structure did not alter until well into the Third Republic; Sartre was still struggling with it in the 1930s. An academic philosopher holding the sole chair per university was expected to cover the whole field in an eclectic manner. Philosophy was further conservatized by being taught in the *lycées,* the elite secondary schools, where it consisted of a survey of philosophical classics in the last year of instruction (Fabiani, 1988). Philosophy's rationale was to serve as the crown of the curriculum, the synthesizer which overcame the fragmentation of the disciplines by bringing together the wisdom of everything pupils had learned. Most philosophers were trained at the elite school of education, the École Normale Supérieure (ENS) in Paris, and passed through a number of years teaching in provincial *lycées,* after which one might become a school inspector in the government bureaucracy, an administrator of centralized examinations, or a member of juries granting higher degrees. Success in such careers meant adhering to a conservative intellectual canon, concentrating one's scholarly activity on producing manuals or translations and editions of the classics; it was acceptable to publish little or nothing.

What innovation there was took place in the interstices of the system or outside the academic world entirely. Lacking an institutional position, Comte turned increasingly to a popularistic cult of social and religious reform; his followers were a non-academic sect. The biggest reputations came by default of philosophies claiming general importance. Renan, professor of Hebrew at the Collège de France and introducer of biblical higher criticism, and Taine, at the École des Beaux Arts, became notable as militants for secularization, which they supported by a doctrine of factuality modeled on natural science. Their inspiration was the autonomous German universities; but their avenue of publicity was popular writings on literature and religious history. On more strictly philosophical turf, Renouvier, a former Polytechnique mathematics student and attendee of Comte's private lectures, banned to private life for his Republican views, found an attention slot which reconciled liberalism and religion. In effect, Renouvier took the Cousinian eclectic curriculum and drew from it a moralizing lesson. His neo-criticism of the 1850s and 1860s expounds the history of philosophy, not as a progressive sequence in the manner of Comte, but as the irreducible opposition of one-sided positions. Human knowledge is relativistic, consisting only in the apprehension of oppositions; that one can choose among the sides is an expression of individual personality and an indicator of human freedom.

Educational reform under the Third Republic did not fundamentally change the career hierarchy of academic jobs. Under the slogan of catching up with the German system, promoted by Renan and Taine since the 1860s, there were some moves in the direction of decentralization and autonomy among regional universities. Policy toward the independent Catholic faculties went through a series of reversals, complicated by the contradiction between liberal reformers' desire for decentralization and their drive for state-imposed secularism. Throughout these shifts, state examinations still controlled the content of the curriculum, and the best careers flowed from the Paris training schools through a tour of the provinces and back to one of the elite showcases in Paris (Fabiani, 1988; Weisz, 1983). During the period of Catholic control of education, the natural sciences had been excluded, and the *lycée* was largely humanistic, stressing classical languages, history, and literature. Pressure to reform the curriculum, and to displace the humanities from their privileged position in the sequence of requirements, threatened the legitimating image of philosophy as the integrator of specialized knowledge, which could be maintained only so long as philosophy was the required subject at the end of the secondary curriculum.

Philosophers generally allied with conservatives in defense of their discipline; a majority joined the spiritualist camp, upholding subjective and ideal values against science. Typical was Lachelier, a *normalien,* educational administrator and inspector general, who led the neo-spiritualist movement, upholding skepticism against sensory phenomena and the world external to thought. His pupil Boutroux, fortified by a year with the Neo-Kantian Zeller at Heidelberg, became especially influential after he returned to teach at the ENS in the 1880s, arguing for the contingency of the laws of nature. At the same time, the battle for university reform in the 1870s and 1880s raised ambitions on the part of philosophy students willing to break from the conservative path. Ribot, Binet, Janet, Durkheim, and Lévy-Bruhl carved out new scientific disciplines on the turf of philosophy, giving rise to specialized social sciences, the anti-metaphysical disciplines of psychology, sociology, and anthropology (Fabiani, 1988).

It was in the context of this conflict that vitalism became prominent. Bergson reaped the greatest fame, but the movement could be discerned among a number of less notable individuals. Lequier, as a former *polytechnicien* a scientist rather than a trained philosopher, produced a book in 1865 anticipating themes of Boutroux, Bergson, James, Peirce, and Whitehead. Hamelin, in the neo-critical camp, developed Renouvier's criticism of Kant into a deduction of the categories from the category of relationship and proposed a dialectical evolution of reality from complementary opposites (1907). Fouillée, a *lycée* and ENS teacher of the 1860s and 1870s who because of health retired early, brought out a series of books from the 1870s through 1911 expounding an idea-force intermediate between private consciousness and objective things. Fouillée's stepson Guyau in 1885 used the *idées-forces* as the basis for a anti-formalist morality: not principles but feelings of obligation are the common denominator of all varied actions which people throughout the world have held to be moral (*EP*, 1967: 3:397–398; Copleston, 1950–1977: 9:174–177). The source is not a spiritual or rational realm imposed from above but vital moral impulses founded in biology. Life is action, and reflection merely inhibits spontaneity. Guyau shared the anti-clerical mood of the times; he condemned celibacy as the antithesis of life-morality, and proposed a religion of dependence on the universe, with man as his own savior.

Guyau died young after a life of illness; his work, containing much of the flamboyance of Nietzsche and Bergson, was overshadowed by that of his contemporaries. Here again we see that a rich combination of cultural capitals tends to be exploited simultaneously by various thinkers (we could add here Meyerson and Driesch in the movement of scientists against positivism); the narrow focus of attention enforced by the law of small numbers guaranteed that most of these names would be reduced to obscurity by the fame of the others. Guyau was on the periphery, a dropout from an academic career, after a short period of teaching at the elite Lycée Condorcet, where Bergson was a pupil, and Sartre later was to teach. Like his stepfather Fouillée, Guyau wrote as a freelancer; he had just enough connections to the intellectual center to carry on its themes, but worked in an isolation that fed his radicalism.

Bergson eclipsed everyone else in the vitalist slot, wielding many of the same ingredients but presented with superior literary skill which opened them to the widest popular audience. His career began in the organizational center of French academia; he studied at the ENS under Boutroux, in the same cohort as Durkheim and Jaurès, subsequently the socialist leader. Bergson spent 16 years teaching at *lycées* in the provinces and in Paris before being elected to the Collège de France in 1900; in his later career he lectured from an honorific position to the general public. Bergson was a skilled technical philosopher, open to the themes of the new disciplines; his works during the *lycée* phase drew on research in psychology, but harnessed to traditional philosophical issues of free will, matter, and time. Bergson's stance was to use empirical evidence to criticize positivism, lending support to the spiritualist battle carried on by his more traditionalist contemporaries while using the weapons of the newest sciences. After he found a public pulpit at the Collège de France, Bergson became a full-scale vitalist; his *Creative Evolution* (1907) and *Durée et Simultanéité* (1910) were first delivered to popular audiences who eagerly received them as a vindication of religion in the age of science.

The same career pattern reappears in the next generation with Jean-Paul Sartre. He went from the ENS (1924–1928) to teaching at provincial *lycées* (1931–1936), then to Paris *lycées* (1937–1944), finally moving into the Parisian world of literary publishing, theater and political journalism. The existentialists inherited some of the popular appeal of the vitalists in their concern to put something in the place of religion at a time when secularism had flattened into banal mundanity. But now the French had been transformed by connection with German academic networks and the new techniques of phenomenology. French philosophers from Maine de Biran onward were certainly not lacking in creativity, especially in exploring ontological forces which the dominant streams in Germany, positivism and Neo-Kantian epistemology, had pushed into abeyance. But the paths opened up by Maine's "I will, therefore I am," and the deepening of neo-criticism into the dialectical derivation of dynamic reality, never established a clear and overriding focus in the attention space. In the eyes of the secularists who dominated public attention, the technical advances of French philosophy were submerged by their popular implications for the defense of religion in a scientific age.

Existentialists as Literary-Academic Hybrids

Existentialism as a self-conscious movement appeared in the 1940s in a Parisian circle. It became famous in the fall of 1945, when the mass media turned their spotlight on Jean-Paul Sartre simultaneously as philosopher, literary success, and political activist. The existentialist movement retrospectively identified itself with a much larger body of writings: above all Heidegger (who rejected the existentialist label), but also theologians, philosophers, novelists, dramatists, and poets going back to the 1840s. The sociological intuition underlying this retrospective relabeling was not inaccurate. What was identified was a tradition of literary-philosophical hybrids. Sartre and Camus were key formulators of the canon, and themselves archetypes of the career overlap between academic networks and the writers' market. The phenomenon of existentialism in the 1940s and 1950s added another layer to this overlap. Sartre was the first philosopher in history to be heavily publicized by the popular mass media.[3] And existentialism was a new kind of movement in the publishing industry at just the time when cheap paperback editions were first being marketed. Its retrospective canon was the subject of an outburst of anthologies and reprints, popularizing many figures such as the neo-conservative theologians previously known only to specialists.

The retrospective existentialist canon has two main branches: dissidents who branched off the tail end of the network of German Idealists, and literary writers of heavily philosophical content, exemplified by Dostoyevsky and Kafka. On closer examination, this latter group turns out to comprise network offshoots of the mainstream German philosophical lineage as well.

The End of the Idealist Network: Kierkegaard and Nietzsche

The most famous of the retrospective early "existentialists" were Kierkegaard and Nietzsche. In Camus's version of the canon, *The Rebel* (1951), Stirner was also rediscovered and elevated to star quality. In the network (Figures 13.1 and 14.2) they all branch off from the Berlin Hegelians of the 1840s. Stirner was in the central circle of *Die Freien*. Kierkegaard was one of the auditors at Schelling's lectures, and his own creativity began immediately after this contact (see Figure 14.2).

A hallmark of the proto-existentialist style is to accentuate the personal choice points of life, and Kierkegaard's works are permeated with autobiography (Lowrie, 1942). His father was a self-made success as a merchant in Copenhagen, who brought up his children very strictly, with emphasis on sin and fear of God. Kierkegaard was a rebellious younger son; he spent 10 years at the university, studying theology but largely carousing, "in revolt against God" as well as his father. It seems the incentives of a wealthy inheritance then weighed in, along with pressures of guilt: in 1838, at age 25, he underwent a religious conversion and reconciled with his dying father, whereupon Kierkegaard became independently wealthy. For two years he applied himself to his studies, and finally got his degree in theology. Following the conventional pattern, he thereupon proposed marriage to an upper-class woman. Soon after he broke off the engagement; he may have felt guilty about his previous whoring, and perhaps also saw himself settling down to a conventional marriage resembling his father's lifestyle, giving up all that he had revolted against in the first place. It was at this point that Kierkegaard left for Berlin, where he heard Schelling lecture. This seems to have been a choice point for him: a conventional marriage and career as a pastor versus an intellectual career in the stance of a theological rebel. Kierkegaard started publishing prodigiously upon his return, some 3,000 pages during the years 1843–1848, sustained by a series of four trips to Berlin.

Kierkegaard proceeded to devote his wealth to publishing his own books; financial independence enabled him to write whatever he wanted, without con-

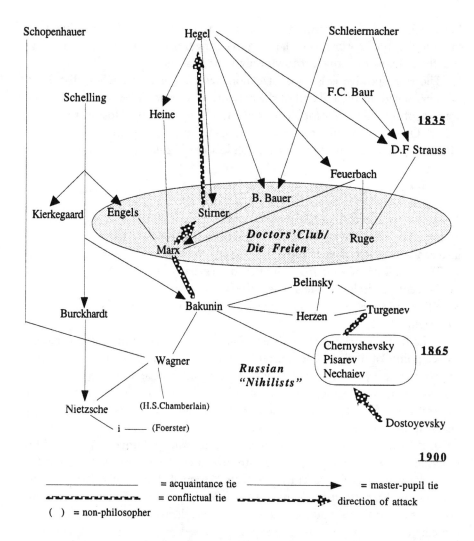

FIGURE 14.2. YOUNG HEGELIANS AND RELIGIOUS/POLITICAL
RADICALS, 1835–1900: *DIE FREIEN* AND THE NIHILISTS

cern for orthodoxy. This is shown by the fact that in 1848 he began to run
out of money, and published no more books. He now held back some of his
latest writings, since their attacks on establishment Christianity were jeopard-
izing his chances of getting a position as a theology professor, for which he
now was aiming. But he was already acquiring notoriety in his opposition and
did not get the chair. After six years of circumspect maneuvering, he launched
an all-out pamphlet attack on the Danish state church. Strains accumulated;

in 1856, in the midst of the controversy, he collapsed on the street while bringing home from the bank the very last of his inheritance and died shortly thereafter.

Kierkegaard's writings are a blend of literature and philosophy. His first breakthrough into creativity, *Either/Or* (1843), explicitly sets up a dialectic between aesthetic Idealism and Christian moralism. Most of the literary punch comes from the aesthetes he depicts in component works such as the novella "Diary of the Seducer," with its confessional tones echoing Goethe's *Young Werther* and anticipating Dostoyevsky's *Notes from Underground;* critical reflections in "The Immediate Stages of the Erotic or the Musical Erotic," which uses philosophical categories to extol Mozart and especially the Don Juan theme; as well as a Hegelian satire developing the principle "all men are bores." The sexuality is not the least of Kierkegaard's appeal, providing literary shock value while at the same time it epitomizes themes of Idealism as well as of bourgeois morality. In parallel with Schopenhauer (unknown at the time), who describes the will as simultaneously sexual drive and the spirit of music, Kierkegaard too ([1843] 1959: 41, 63) speaks of sounds as the key to what is hidden by appearances. Where Kierkegaard breaks new ground is by criticizing aesthetic Idealism as pseudo-salvation lacking in moral sensibility. Simultaneously he uses the categories of aesthetic criticism against rationalized and passionless theology. Value is in criticism and tension; systematic philosophy is impossible, and its topics can be approached only through the application of literary analogies. Theology must be apprehended under the mode of comedy; the truths of religion are paradoxical, even absurd, never demonstrable by logic. The Hegelian dialectic, which Kierkegaard rejects, is nevertheless employed in his *Concluding Unscientific Postscript* (1846), redeemed by being left perpetually open-ended. It was from Hegel, more than Schelling, that Kierkegaard acquired the weapons which he now wielded against all positions.

Kierkegaard's demand for a Byronic Christianity was put forward at just the time when the theologians of the Danish church were liberalizing and accepting the rationalized Hegelian theology. Denmark, which had long been an absolute monarchy allied to traditional landholding, by the 1840s was caught up in political reform movements. The National Liberals were gaining political influence; in the wave of popular uprisings sweeping across Europe, a liberal constitution was granted in 1849, with a weak elected legislature, religious tolerance, and an end to censorship (Eagleton, 1990: 190–191). Kierkegaard sharply opposed every aspect of reform. *The Present Age,* published in 1846 simultaneously with his major philosophical work, attacks the leveling of modern mass society which he discerned in the movements around him. Here Kierkegaard seems to have been acting not so much on his personal class interest as against the liberalizing movement in his own class. The stance he had discovered, and that powered his creativity, was opposition as a value in itself. His political position, like Nietzsche's, would be downplayed or forgotten when the oppositional movement of a later day focused on his literary-philosophical message.

Isolation of the individual forms part of the content of these proto-existentialist philosophies. Its corresponding reality is partly in career bases, partly geographical. Both Kierkegaard and Nietzsche prepared for academic careers, then dropped out. Both went through phases of despair, not unmixed with pride, at their lack of recognition. Their hybrid qualities between literary and philosophical bases made them, initially, successful in neither. Both too were provincials, far from the centers of intellectual life; more exactly, they were provincials who had been at the center, connected with its main networks, who then retired to the periphery to work out their unique positions.[4] There was another commonality in the way their reputations were finally made. Kierkegaard was publicized in the 1880s by the Danish critic and Berlin sojourner Georg Brandes, who also first discovered Nietzsche (Bretall, 1946: xviii; Kaufmann, 1950: 16, 106). As a result Kierkegaard was translated into German around the turn of the century, publicized in the same circles that welcomed Nietzsche.

Nietzsche portrayed himself as the lonely explorer of the frontiers of thought. During most of his creative life he was unknown; just when his fame began (around 1888), he went mad, removing the possibility of having to live with a public persona. He worked in isolation, in tourist hotels in Italy and the Alps, having resigned his academic post at Basel in 1879, before his great series of writings in the 1880s. Is he an exception to world network patterns, an isolated creator of the first rank? But no; Nietzsche had excellent connections from early in his career. He studied at Leipzig with the preeminent academic philologists of the time, who sponsored him for a chair at the early age of 24. From his days in the *Gymnasium* at Pforta, he was a friend of Paul Deussen, who went on to introduce Hindu Vedanta into Europe (1883) at the same time Nietzsche was writing his *Zarathustra,* idealizing yet another non-Christian religion.[5] At Basel the young Nietzsche audited the lectures of the Renaissance historian Burckhardt, and from 1868 onward he was a close follower of the composer Richard Wagner, whom he often visited in nearby Lucerne. To be sure, these are not the ordinary connections of his philosophical contemporaries; the German network by his generation had become dominated by academic lineages. Yet Wagner and Burckhardt are in the network too; Wagner had been an early friend of the anarchist Bakunin, who, like Burckhardt, had attended Schelling's lectures at Berlin in the 1840s. Nietzsche culminates the lineage of Schelling and the Idealist circle: his vitalism is a radical extension of *Naturphilosophie,* while his anti-Christianity carries further the *Atheismusstreit* that surrounded Fichte, just as his connections with Deussen and Overbeck relate him to the Tübingen historical theologians and those who widened philosophical history to include non-Western traditions.

The rebels inhabit the same network neighborhood. If we trace the indirect ties in Nietzsche's network, we see that he is three links away from Kierkegaard (his existentialist network cousin, so to speak), two links from Bakunin's anarchism, three links from Marx.[6] Nietzsche was by no means a follower of the ideas found nearby in his network. Creativity is a transformation of the surrounding cultural capital, often by opposition. It is characteristic that Nietzsche found his own direction when he broke with Wagner, and that he developed a position in opposition to Marxian socialism and to its Hegelian background as well, that is, to the key topics in the network a few links away. Creativity consists in just such sensitivity to the direction of argumentative slots open in the intellectual field.

Nietzsche wrote his first work, *The Birth of Tragedy from the Spirit of Music* (1872), by combining his classical scholarship with Wagner's idealization of music, thereby initiating critique of the received image of the Greeks as rationalists. Just as Kierkegaard was sparked off by Schelling, Nietzsche became creative after making contact with Wagner, just then at the height of promoting his musical ideology. Eminent composers have networks of their own, which have been almost completely independent of philosophers' networks; Wagner illustrates a rare instance where the networks touch. He was the most philosophical of composers. Wagner attempted to elevate opera into music drama with deep layers of meaning—including, according to Shaw ([1898] 1967), revolutionary political ones, influenced by Wagner's friendship with Bakunin. He wrote to educate his listeners and polemicize against his enemies. He explicitly adopted Schopenhauer, both in general terms and specifically as exalting music for its access to the will as thing-it-itself.[7] The sociological key is that Wagner was the biggest independent star on the musical marketplace; his enormous egotism went along with the liberation from patronage that came with the expansion of the commercially based middle-class opera audience. Wagner continuously raised his ambitions, and the costs of his grandiose productions (as well as of his personal lifestyle as artist-king), and thus was in need of a patron as well as market supports. Like Goethe in the literary sphere, Wagner found his niche by combining all the sources of material support—a royal patron who was willing to treat him as a status equal,[8] together with a mass fund-raising arm that became the organizational core of the Wagnerian movement. At the moment when the young philology professor was attracted to the Wagner camp, he encountered a social transformation of artistic publicity onto an unprecedented plane.

The Wagner discipleship soon weighed on Nietzsche's creative independence, not unlike the depression of John Stuart Mill under the guidance of his father. Wagner corrected Nietzsche's manuscripts. Nietzsche broke with him, ostensibly in disagreement over the turn Wagner was taking in the mid-1870s with the *Ring* cycle and especially with his religious outlook in *Parsifal* (1882). The Wagner connection was a crucial part of Nietzsche's creative field, and the time of the break (January 1878) was just the time when Nietzsche developed physical ill health (eyes, head, stomach), which led him to resign his chair in 1879 (*EP*, 1967: 5:504–510). Whatever other causes may have contributed to Nietzsche's health problems and to his eventual insanity (syphilis is suspected), his symptoms also fit the pattern of stress reactions to his break with his charismatic mentor. Nietzsche found the path of greatest creative energy with an outburst of his best books right after the break: *The Dawn* (1881) and *The Gay Science* (1882), then *Zarathustra,* with its radical attacks on religion and on Wagner, patterned in a four-act drama to resemble the *Ring*. Nietzsche was not a network isolate but a rebel among rebels; he made and unmade new combinations on the fringes where the philosophical networks of his day overlapped the popular markets opening up for religion, science, and entertainment. The personal stress and the iconoclasm were alike facets of his creative energy and the central content about which he wrote.

The Retrospective Literary Canon

Existentialists labeled as their own the novels of the previous two generations which best fit the philosophical-literary hybrid. Dostoyevsky's fame outside of Russia began to grow in the same time and place as the reputations of Kierkegaard and Nietzsche. The takeoff point for all these writings was Germany just before World War I, which shows that the literary fashion was not caused by postwar disillusionment. Kafka's stories too were written before the war (published 1913–1916), and came into vogue along with his posthumous novels, published in 1926–27. The philosophical interpretation of this body of literature was the work of the Sartre circle, and in this guise reached its peak as a publishing phenomenon in the anglophone world of the 1940s and 1950s.

Dostoyevsky seems a sudden intrusion from a peripheral region never before significant in European culture. Nevertheless, his works reflected back to the intellectuals of core European networks a dramatized version of their own ancestral ideas. For political reasons, the bases of intellectual production in Russia were concentrated on the new middle-class market for novels which opened around 1860. The universities, newly founded in the Westernizing reforms of the 1700s, were forbidden to teach philosophy after the Decembrist uprising in 1825; in a slight liberalization from 1863 until 1889 only commentaries on Plato and Aristotle were allowed (*EP*, 1967: 7:258). The role of the general-purpose intellectual, the philosopher's traditional slot in intellectual space, was taken by the journalist-critic, then increasingly with the expansion of the market, by the novelist—all the more so because, under political censorship, fiction was the only mode in which general ideas could be expressed.

With commercialization and ties to the world market, Russia became an importer of European culture; intellectually, it fell into the export zone for the German universities, the dynamo of world intellectual production. To the extent allowed under Russian conditions, German academic structures and contents were imported, with some notable results in mathematics and science. Emulation of German cultural production was of course not confined to Russia, but it was especially pronounced there because, unlike in England or France, there was little indigenous organization of intellectual production to act as rival. Russian intellectuals sojourned in the West and became links in the German network: most notably Bakunin (in the Schelling-Marx-Wagner networks; see Figure 14.2) and the former Hegelian Herzen, a central node of the Russian exile community since fleeing to the West in 1847. Turgenev, educated in Berlin, depicted in his novel *Smoke* (1867) the Russian intellectuals in Baden, with their mixture of German philosophy and political plots for their homeland.

Each current of German philosophy was quickly taken up in Russia. Under the ban on university teaching and the censorship of translations, texts acquired by sojourners passed from hand to hand in student discussion circles. This mode of organization maximized ritualism and emotional commitment to the text; intellectual life itself became a form of political action, since the penalty for illicit writing or even reading was imprisonment and exile to Siberia, frequently exacted upon intellectuals around midcentury. In the 1830s, Schelling and Fichte came fanatically into vogue; in the 1840s, Hegel. German cultural capital was adapted to the factions of Russian underground politics; both Westernizers and nativist Slavophiles drew abstract justification from universalist or Romanticist strands of German Idealism. The materialist controversy of Germany in the 1850s was transmuted into the Russian nihilism of the 1860s. Drawing political implications undreamed of in the West, Chernyshevski and Pisarev mingled Feuerbach, Moleschott, and Büchner with British reform Utilitarianism to conclude that morality means nothing beyond rational egotism, and that the sacrifice of lives in political action, even terrorism, is justified by the greater good of the future populace. Still later, as soon as Marxism became established in Germany through the journals and publishing houses of the Social Democratic Party of the 1880s and 1890s, Russian intellectuals adopted the doctrine to their already existing style of underground radicalism.

Dostoyevsky came from the student generation of the 1840s, with its Idealist loyalties. Arrested, sentenced to death, and then commuted to a decade of imprisonment in Siberia during the 1850s, he returned just in time to confront the new generation of materialist radicals. Turgenev had already pioneered the description of his intellectual compatriots as material for novels; *Fathers and Sons* (1862) became famous for contrasting the political sensibilities of previous and current generations, and popularized the term "nihilist" for the younger one. Dostoyevsky now resumed his writing career with a series of anguished portraits of the new radicals. *Notes from Underground* (1864) attacks the scientism and materialist determinism of Chernyshevski. *Crime and Punishment* (1864), which made Dostoyevsky's reputation, depicts a student revolutionist who justifies a murder on Pisarev's reasoning. The plot of *The Possessed* (1871) fictionalizes a famous incident: Nechaiev, sent by Bakunin from the exile community in Switzerland to set up an underground cell in Russia, had ordered the murder of one of its student members in a Machiavellian exercise of revolutionary discipline. *The Brothers Karamazov* (1877–1881) again centers on a revolutionary intellectual, this time afflicted with guilt over the consequences of his doctrines.

Dostoyevsky's own explicit doctrines, no doubt sincerely held but serving also to make his materials palatable to government censorship, extol a religious doctrine of passive suffering; but it is his villains who drive the drama and provide the atmosphere of impassioned philosophy that would appeal internationally to intellectuals. What made Dostoyevsky a literary success was that he combined this material with the style of the mass market novel, often taking the form of a murder mystery or police thriller. Dostoyevsky exploited the intellectual's self-examination made successful by Turgenev, purged of its polite drawing room qualities and transposed into the melodrama of popular fiction. This too fitted Dostoyevsky for the deliberately déclassé literary tastes of French intellectuals in the 1930s.

Kafka started out even closer to the mainstream of the German philosophical networks. He was educated in the early 1900s in the German university of Prague; among his teachers were Marty, from the Brentano lineage, and Christian von Ehrenfels, who descends from Meinong (see Figure 13.8). Ehrenfels conveyed with charismatic energy the main movements of the time: he was a pioneer of Gestalt psychology and a friend of Sigmund Freud; he also advocated Weltanschauung philosophy to replace lost religious faith.[9] Kafka started out in an intellectual milieu not far removed from phenomenology and Freudian dream symbolism. When existentialism was explicitly launched in Sartre's circle, such works were now relabeled as a canon leading up to themselves. Sartre strove for a Kafkaesque tone of fatal inescapability as in *No Exit* (1944). The sinister quality which Kafka gives to ordinary life is explicitly subjected to philosophical reflection in *Nausea* (1938) through a protagonist who applies phenomenology to study his own alienation. Camus contrives a murder story in *The Stranger* (1942) in order to set up a Kafka-reprise trial in the second part.

Camus did the most explicit work in redefining an ancestral literary canon. His philosophical essays, *The Myth of Sisyphus* (1942) and *The Rebel* (1951), depict a lineage of "metaphysical rebels": the Romanticists with their Byronic gestures of defying God; the Symbolist poets at their most iconoclastic, especially Rimbaud and Lautréamont, active in the period of the Paris Commune of 1871; the nose-thumbing of the dadaists and surrealists of the 1920s, who were the existentialists' immediate literary predecessors. Sartre was more concerned to define his philosophical ancestors (Hegel, Husserl, Heidegger); he also appropriated Freud—a popular market success in nonfiction, branching off from the Brentano philosophical lineage—for a version of existential psychoanalysis,[10] and made the novelist-playwright Genet into an existentialist "saint" (1952). Sartre's and Camus's dramas of the 1940s, in allegorical form suitable for conveying rebellious messages under Nazi occupation, were stylistically continuous with the modernist theater pioneered by Pirandello and Anouilh in the 1920s and 1930s; they were joined with the plays of Beckett and Ionesco in the 1950s under the Camusian label "theater of the absurd."

In literature, the existentialists continued a well-established trajectory. In ideologizing it with their philosophy, they disguised its social common denominator. The alienated stance which they depicted as their tradition arose with the independence of the writers' market. To be sure, not every market-oriented writer conveyed a worldview bereft of values other than those of the sensitive intellectual-creator; Scott, Balzac, and Dickens hit a vein of popularity based on colorful entertainment while turning out novels as fast as they could write them. These differences reflect the split between two forms of the writers' market which emerged after the decline of patronage: between the work of "highbrow" literary elitists writing to their own standards and "middlebrow" writing for the middle-class public, with a morally respectable tone, moderately reformist in politics, but withal entertaining for a leisure audience.[11] It was the inwardly oriented, professionally self-contained writers who produced the lineage of "metaphysical rebellion." What Camus recounts is the history of intellectual movements within this elite, who adopt successively aesthetic Idealism, Romanticist individualism and pessimism, the art-for-art's-sake aestheticism of technical formalism and symbolism, and still later the *épater-le-bourgeois* gestures of the dadaists and their successors.

Economically, the highbrow segment rarely has been able to support itself on returns from the market. It arises where writers turn inward upon their professional connections within the network of peers; the audience which alone is given legitimacy to set standards of judgment are other elite writers. Such an elite can survive only with external financial support. Occasionally this happens by bootlegging avant-garde materials into works for the middlebrow market; this is one reason for the adulation of Dostoyevsky, who unconsciously carried off this fusion by making his topic the rebellious Russian intellectuals of his day. Similarly in the 1930s, the admiration of French intellectuals went to Hemingway, for his amalgamation of adventure story, stylistic severity, and quasi-metaphysical code of meaning. More commonly highbrow writers survive by patronage, sometimes the self-patronage of wealthy inheritors (Flaubert and Proust), reinforcing the self-image of the artist as the true aristocrat. Some highbrow writers hold alternative jobs (Baudelaire as journalist-critic, T. S. Eliot as bank clerk), the despising of which usually figures into the theme of artistic alienation from the ordinary commercial world which fails to support their art. Another common external niche is an academic job, which bruises the writer's self-esteem because its bureaucratic routine contrasts with the freedom and creative exaltation which the writers' market holds out as its ultimate reward. Most common of all is economic failure.[12] This gives rise to the image of the artist starving in a garret, melodramatically ending as a youthful suicide rather than be forced back into the mundane world. In fact, most highbrow writers (perhaps middlebrow writers as well) spend only a youthful episode in writing, like Rimbaud from 17 to 19, before economic realities force them back into a conventional career.

The best chances of success for highbrow writers exist where many aspiring and part-time writers are concentrated in a community. Sheer size is the crucial variable in making a critical mass which can support at least a few technically oriented esoteric writers on the proceeds of their works. Paris has been the modern archetype. Building over several generations, it reached the critical mass (perhaps already by the 1830s) by the overlap of various intellectual communities: the concentration of aspiring students not yet funneled though the selection of the *lycées* and the competitive examinations; the universities, libraries, and research institutes; the publishing business; the national newspapers and magazines; professionals and aspirants in music and fine arts.[13] This concentrated mass of intellectual aspirants, together with failures who had not yet given up their highbrow identities and their network contacts with the culture production business, made up a local market supporting viable careers for a few pure intellectual creators, whose lives became emblems for the rest. Such was the market structure in which the Sartre circle forged a brief episode of high-level creativity merging philosophy and literature.

Sartre as Movement Emblem

For all its ideology of solitary individual choice, existentialism was a phenomenon of group success. Once again we witness tight personal connections starting at an early age, the progressive intensification of emotional energy and accumulation of cultural capital, building up to creative originality and dominance of the intellectual attention space. Sartre, Nizan, and Canguilhem are already close friends in the early 1920s, at the elite Paris Lycée Louis le Grand and in the cram courses preparing for the entrance examination for the ENS. They enter the ENS in the same class as Raymond Aron, who becomes Sartre's roommate; Aron takes first place in the *agrégation* in 1928, Sartre first place the next year; this time around Sartre crams with Simone de Beauvoir, who comes in second. Merleau-Ponty, entering the ENS slightly later, by 1929 is in the same group of friends. De Beauvoir, Sartre's longtime intimate, eventually becomes famous in her own right, using the life story of the group as material for her novels.[14]

They mutually support one another's career chances. Aron, who lectures on French philosophy at the University of Cologne soon after Scheler's death, introduces Sartre to phenomenology and gets him a visiting scholarship in Berlin to study the German philosophers. Nizan, who makes an early success with his literary-political writings and his eminence in French Marxism, recommends Sartre to his own publisher, Gallimard. The way is facilitated by the presence on staff there of some of Sartre's own former *lycée* pupils. Later on, at the end of the 1940s, Sartre would tout Genet and prepare the way for his theatrical success. All of Sartre's major works, literary and philosophical, are published by Gallimard (from 1938 onward), as are the works of Camus (from 1942), Merleau-Ponty, and de Beauvoir, and the key early works of Gabriel Marcel and Aron. Gallimard is a network center in its own right. Camus comes to work there as a reader in 1943. The intellectual director of the Gallimard staff, Bernard Groethuysen, a friend of Scheler, had been instrumental in introducing Hegel, Nietzsche, Heidegger, Freud, and Kafka into French intellectual life in the 1920s and 1930s.[15] The firm makes a publishing breakthrough not only in content, especially importing the German modernists, but also in form: in the 1930s Gallimard pioneered cheap paperback editions, and explicitly bills itself publisher of the modern canon in the literature of ideas.

In the case of existentialism, the confluence of networks and the mutual support within a group that underlies all creativity is heavily documented and easy to trace. Why then should it take the form of glorifying a single individual, the literary-philosophical genius Sartre? In fact this is a bit exaggerated. Camus, who comes from outside the main group, though approaching along intersecting pathways (Paris avant-garde theater, Gallimard publishing) and then joining it at its moment of initial creativity, is for a few years a dual figurehead with Sartre. Nevertheless, the estrangement that commences in 1946 (Cohen-Solal, 1987: 332), and the bitter and open break which takes place in 1952, seem to have been fated by the structure. Sartre or Camus, one commands most of the loyalty and is glorified as the totemic emblem. The circulation and mutual enhancement of creative energies among a circle of persons is characteristic of the peak years—so often compressed into less than a decade—of a creative movement; so too are the eventual splits. Fichte, Schelling, or Hegel; Camus, Merleau-Ponty, or Sartre: several may be supremely energized, but there is space for only one to personify the group.

In retrospect, Sartre's personality stands out from his childhood, his schooldays, his long years in the provinces. It is easy to portray him as predestined for intellectual success of one sort or another. Fanatically writing, he produces as many as 80 pages a day, volunteering for extra guard duty while on military service so that he won't be disturbed. It is always the group focus that brings him into the local center of attraction; he blossoms in the German prisoner-of-war camp in 1940–41, putting on camp theatricals and organizing discussions, acting again like the popular class clown that he played at the ENS. Sartre is the energy vortex of his network, reading and writing about everything that comes into its purview. He has so much cultural capital that it explains little of his pathway; the pre-success Sartre writes voluminously in all directions, and it is only when a social mechanism, in the form of the Gallimard staff, selects for him the central tracks of the attention space that he becomes a star. Later Sartre would do the same thing again with the topics of the day: postwar politics, theater of the absurd, Marxism. Sartre is indeed a "nothingness" of vital energy, not so much negating and rebelling—which was already the dominant style of French intellectuals decades before—as a blank, ready to fill itself with whatever is available and to transform it into the attention center of the future.

How many other rabid young readers and writers were about during Sartre's youth who could have taken the same path? It is impossible to know. But France in the 1920s was structurally set up to generate just such energies, and to select from among these youths in an organization which focused maximal attention upon the most successful. Sartre represents the extreme product of the centralized French educational system, with its years of preparation for competitive examinations, its *khâgne* and *hypokhâgne* (the student slang reflecting the tribalism of the informal group) cram courses at the elite *lycées,* its make-or-break examination points—the *concours* for admission to the ENS, the *agrégation* for the teaching certificate—with their publicly announced rankings. The organizational structure concentrated the most ambitious and cultural capital–accumulating youths in one place and threw them into intense group interaction with palpable barriers to mere mortals outside the bounds. This is the formula for the totemic group at its most intense.[16]

The philosophical capital which flowed through the larger network into France came from Germany. The links are multiple and cumulative: Groethuysen and Aron, with their direct and indirect links to Scheler; Koyré, a former pupil of both Bergson and Husserl (he had lived in Husserl's house as a student), who introduced Neo-Kantian Weltanschauung analysis into the French historical critique of modern science;[17] Aaron Gurwitsch (former pupil of Husserl, Scheler, and the Gestalt psychologists Wertheimer and Kohler at Berlin), whose lectures on phenomenology at the Sorbonne during 1928–1930 inspired his hearer Merleau-Ponty; Kojève (a Russian émigré Marxist and former pupil of Jaspers), whose lectures on Hegel during 1933–1939 were heard by Aron, Merleau-Ponty, Lacan, and many others, including Breton and the remains of the surrealist movement. From the Strasbourg phenomenologists, former members of the Husserl circle, Levinas entered Sartre's circle and later became the French promoter of phenomenology in the late 1940s. Sartre had missed Husserl's own lectures at the Sorbonne in 1929, but the latest rage reached him via his multiple links with the intermediary network. Others became French Hegel experts (such as Hippolyte, a slightly younger compatriot of Sartre at the ENS). Sartre put the ingredients to new use, combining his own fanaticism for phenomenology (dating since Aron converted him in 1931) with Kojève's new revelation of Hegel, not as a closed system but as the dialectic of slave and master in the *Phenomenology of the Spirit*. The final ingredient came in 1938, when Sartre added Heidegger to the mix. *Sein und Zeit* was already the most heavily read volume in the ENS library from 1928 to 1934, but Sartre at the time was overloaded with projects in every direction; only after he had his own phenomenology in place, and his publishers had set him into the Kafkaesque line, could Heidegger's material become not a distraction but an ingredient for his own system, and now could be redefined as existentialism.

Sartre used phenomenology as a springboard for creative originality by reversing its metaphysical implications. His key article on intentionality, published in *Nouvelle Revue Française* in 1939, evokes the doctrine with which Brentano had launched the new psychology 60 years earlier. Sartre's tack is that consciousness's intending an object threatens the basic character of the self; if it tries to grasp itself, suppressing the intentionality which locks it to the world, it annihilates itself. This is something like Husserl's *epochê* in reverse: not objects of consciousness without concern for their existence, but the character of existence, beyond objects.[18] Intentionality is the great coverup: although humans are constituted so as to intend objects, they are ultimately contingent, without reason why they, or indeed anything, should exist, rather than nothing at all. Sartre is closer to Hegel, endorsing his bifurcation of being, between the determinate being-something, and the undetermined being-as-such. Being as "pure indeterminativeness and vacuity" is the condition of privation which drives the world into activity. Sartre detaches the Hegelian metaphysic from its world-historical system and blends it with the angst of modern literature and theology.

Through Hegel, Sartre rediscovered Fichte's focus on negation and freedom.

Fichte's self is above all reflexive; there is a self which is "an object for myself," as well as a "self-in-itself," which displaces the old object-like thing-in-itself overthrown by Idealism (Fichte, [1794–1797] 1982: 10). Fichte describes the logical dialectic of the "striving" of self and the counter-striving of the not-self.[19] The revival of the original élan of the Idealist revolution by the existentialists, ostensibly anti-Idealist in their immediate surroundings, makes sense when we recall that German Idealism was not merely a halfway house in the secularization of dogmatic religion, but the ideology of the intellectuals at the moment they struck for control of their organizational base. Fichte's themes of will, self-consciousness, and freedom are the manifesto of academic intellectuals in their autonomy to create for themselves; their Idealism is a tacit recognition that only in the realm of ideas do they reign supreme. It was this perennial tool of creation via meta-critique that the German Idealists bequeathed to the generations of their successors. Sartre and the existentialists wielded it in the moment of their own special opening in the philosophical-literary marketplace of their time.[20]

Fichte's statements are not far from Sartre's "futile passion" of the human being striving to posit itself as absolutely founded, to become God (Sartre, 1943: 708). But the religious and valuational stance has drastically shifted. For the existentialist the dialectic of unfoundedness is a tragic impulse to impossibility propelling the doomed projects of human life; for the Idealist it was a revelation of one's individual participation in a glorious cosmic outflow. The Idealists were transforming dogmatic Christianity into lay spirituality, assuring a pantheist version of immortality. Conservative theologians, pioneered by Kierkegaard and burgeoning to a full-fledged movement in the 1920s, had struck back, reasserting a distinctive religious turf by making immortality and salvation not cheap and automatic but difficult and anguishing. Heidegger had provided an up-to-date philosophical underpinning for this theological stance; but he continued the essential strand of theological hope, making Being full of meaning, however elusive it is to grasp. Sartre radicalizes the religious tone; with the full force of the modernist tradition of *les poètes maudits,* he declares that the world is meaningless, and being is empty. The only meaning is that which is created through human freedom.[21]

Sartre's accomplishment was to put the accepted postures of literary nihilism and theological angst on the footing of technical philosophical argument, built from the central themes of the great metaphysicians. It is not just that some beings are empirically contingent while others are essences. Being itself is profoundly contingent; there is no reason why anything should exist at all. Christian theology, paralleling Buddhist and Hindu mysticism, had confronted this issue in the unanswerable question why God (or primal reality) had created the world in the first place. Sartre rejects all transcendent and mystical justifications; not only the world but any metaphysical ultimates whatever are arbitrary. Even Heidegger had not gone this far, noticing only that it is the human being who is thrown into the world. Sartre notes that the world itself, the existence or non-existence of God, being itself, are "thrown" down from nowhere. It is this realization that Sartre dramatizes in his fictional alter ego staring at the ugly roots of a tree, stripping away words and concepts which hide the brute existent like the Buddhist stripping bare *sunyata* beneath "name and form," recognizing that there is no ultimate reason for *this,* or for anything else. Sartre's character, like the author himself, has long had a sense of nihilistic malaise, which he calls nausea; only at length does his phenomenological diagnosis lead him to identify, with an emotional jolt corresponding to a Buddhist counter-enlightenment, his nausea with the world itself in its metaphysical unfoundedness.[22]

Once an atheist existentialist movement became formulated, the term was retrospectively applied to neoconservative theologians. Parallel to the German lineages which energized and welcomed Heidegger was a movement of French theologians of the 1920s through the 1940s. In France too the flow was from the disillusioned religious liberals into the conservative camp. Maritain came from a liberal Protestant background, but associated with the Catholic social activists Charles Peguy and Léon Bloy and studied with Bergson and with the vitalist Driesch at Heidelberg. Maritain converted to Catholicism in 1906 and joined its most politically reactionary branch, the Action Française, growing out of the Dreyfus controversy and the final disestablishment of the French Catholic Church. Gabriel Marcel came from an agnostic family; was active in secular altruism with the Red Cross during the war; became increasingly disillusioned with rationalist philosophy; associated with Scheler on his French visits and with the Berdyaev circle of conservative émigré theologians in the 1920s; and eventually converted to Catholicism in 1929. The works of Maritain and Marcel, which became "existentialist theology," date from the late 1920s and 1930s, although the terminology did not become explicitly existentialist until the late 1940s, at the height of Sartre's popularity.[23]

The movement grew out of the vitalism represented by Bergson; but whereas vitalism was a halfway house combining popular science with liberalized religion, the next generation of theologians and philosophers took science as part of the alienating rationalism of the modern world. Instead of an ally, science became an opponent against which more emotionally exalting positions could energize themselves. For vitalism, too, reason was not necessary to give value to life, which surges with its own joyous *élan.* In the next generation, the mood was repudiated, and nature became nothing but a march toward death.[24]

Sartre's philosophy is resolutely atheist, but it retains the concept of God as a crucial metaphysical foil. This stance of anti-theism, even more strongly than atheism, is especially marked in Camus. Rebellion against religion is central in all of Camus's writings. His first work, the play *Caligula,* written in 1938 but not produced until the "existentialist year" 1945, depicts rebellion against the gods because life entails death and unhappiness. The success of the theme demands a delicate balance; for if God does not exist, metaphysical rebellion is a rather adolescent gesture. Ambivalence between religion and disillusioned secularism is the requisite turf, which Camus plays from the atheist side, in counterpoint to the existentialist theologians. Where Camus came into his own was in asserting the equivalence between God and the modern state. Camus's novel *La Peste,* written during World War II and published in 1947, borders on ludicrousness in its discussions by an atheist in a quarantined city blaming God for a plague; but it strikes a resonant chord as a metaphor of Nazi occupation and the Resistance, the style in which Sartre had made his theatrical mark under German censorship in *The Flies* (1943).[25]

Camus's career channel was a mixture of academics, theater, journalism, and politics. He started in the conventional path of *lycée* and university; deflected by illness from sitting for the philosophy *agrégation* leading toward a schoolteachers's career, he became an actor, playwright, and newspaper reporter (Lesbesque, 1960; Lottman, 1979). The newspaper chain sent him to Paris in 1940, where he rapidly assimilated current intellectual topics. In 1943 he was back again, working for Gallimard and editing the underground resistance paper, mixing in avant-garde theater and in Sartre's intimate circle. In the centralized French educational system, Camus was exposed to much the same curriculum as Sartre; his initial selection from this material, however, was its Greek classics, which he wields in time-honored fashion as a secular value system with which to attack Christianity. Camus has much in him of the provincial French schoolteacher, the stalwart of the secularist campaign and enemy of the Catholics, with whom control of the school system had been contested only a generation previously.

Camus strikes an anti-academic note: "There is but one truly serious philosophical problem, and that is suicide . . . All the rest—whether or not the world has three dimensions, whether the mind has nine or twelve categories—comes afterwards" (Camus, [1942] 1955: 3). It is the specifically Kantian issues of the dominant school curriculum which he singles out here. Nevertheless, his tools are those of the academic curriculum; he uses the Neo-Kantian style of argument to show that to judge life to be absurd, one must assume a prior value standard (a Kantian would say "transcendental") in terms of which to judge it. In his most ambitious treatise, *The Rebel* (1951), Camus adopts an explicitly Cartesian logic, asserting that the value revealed by rebellion is a universal and collective one. "I rebel—therefore we exist."[26]

In fact, Camus spends most of his discussion not on the question whether an ordinary person should commit suicide, but on the preceding lineage of "existential" thinkers as the philosophical equivalent of suicide. Kierkegaard and Jaspers (and, in a forced interpretation, Husserl) are charged with giving up the tension between the human demand for reason and meaning and the meaninglessness of the world, taking the leap toward metaphysical transcendence and thereby losing the honest affirmation of absurdity. Camus devotes most of his two major philosophical essays to presenting a lineage of existentialist predecessors. They are selected from the classical French school curriculum, updated and integrated with the literary modernists of the current publishing explosion. Camus dresses them in their most Romanticist poses: Epicurus walling himself in his garden to shut out death, the revolutionist Saint-Just working out his philosophy of the guillotine in a shuttered room with black walls spangled with white teardrops, and (since Camus does not distinguish fictional characters from historical ones) Ivan Karamazov confronting the Grand Inquisitor. Camus's "metaphysical rebels" are a popularized enticement to philosophy, and his essays serve as an existentialist pedagogy.

By 1951 Camus was ready to appropriate for himself Sartre's central philosophical resource: Hegel. In Camus's reconstruction of modern intellectual and political development, Hegel is the arch-villain, the betrayer of the impulse to rebel by turning it into the supremacy of the absolute and the victory of the totalitarian state. At the same time, Camus mimics Hegelian history, presenting his own stages of the logic of rebellion; he arranges his canon from Rousseau and de Sade onward, claiming at every step that an inevitable logical impulse causes rebels to overstep their bounds and negate the value of the earlier steps. In fact it is little more than a device for organizing Camus's poets, philosophers, and revolutionists in a series; there is no real chain of logical negations from one period to the next. For Camus, references to logic serve largely for their rhetorical force: "There are crimes of passion and crimes of logic" (Camus, [1951] 1956: 3). As a Hegelian he is an amateur. The beauty of his style, and its infusion with passion and political relevance, carried his readers over the thinness of his argument.

Camus's split with Sartre came ostensibly on political grounds. Camus's Cartesian proof of collective morality went a step beyond Sartre's exit-less individualism, and was a justification of the moral standards of political activism. But in fact both men had long been committed political activists; even in 1951 they remained in the same faction, the segment of French intellectuals attempting to establish a non-communist party of the left. The larger dynamic of political conflict doomed the effort; as world geopolitical blocs realigned and the cold war and the nuclear arms race began their polarization, neutralist intellectuals were forced to choose between ineffectuality and giving in to the pressure for alliance with the most active partisans. Malraux ended up going with de Gaulle; Camus, for all his claims to represent the heritage of rebellion, stood paralyzed on the sidelines by the rebellion in his Algerian homeland, and formulated a stance of political philosophy that became an archetype for cold war anticommunism. On the other side, Sartre, deeply committed to the autonomy of a third force, ineluctably shifted into the camp of Marxism. Merleau-Ponty, who originated the quarrel with Camus in 1946 over their attitude toward the communists, eventually split with Sartre during 1952–1955 because now he too found Stalin's communism insupportable, while Sartre came to its defense.[27]

Such pressures belong to the external political environment. A central theme of this sociological analysis is that the distinctive contents of intellectual creativity are no mere reflection of what everyone believes, but derive from the inner struggle for attention in the intellectual space. The split between the two stars of the existentialist movement was fated by the dynamics of creative energy in a necessarily enclosed space. Politics provided the occasion for the break; but the break itself, and its intellectual form, came from the oppositional structure of creativity.

Envoi: Into the Fog of the Present

Here the manuscript breaks off . . . as it says in copies of old texts. In fact, we could trace the networks further, on into our own day. Some of the links are easy enough: in America, from Quine and Reichenbach to Putnam, Carnap to Rorty, Popper to Feyerabend; in France, Merleau-Ponty to Foucault to Derrida, Aron to Bourdieu; in Germany, from Heidegger via Oscar Becker to Habermas. The trouble is that we don't know where to focus; there are many pupils and seminar interlocutors proceeding down from the main chains of the past, and perhaps new chains of eminence starting up. But we have no way of knowing who if anyone will be remembered as a major or secondary figure; even the names which stir the center of controversy for a decade may do well if they fade only to a minor mention in the intellectual histories written in the future. Such is the nature of the intellectual attention space. It is intrinsically shaped by the flow of conflicts and realignment across the generations, and our significance as puny human nodes in this long-term network is given not by ourselves, but by the resonances that make some names into emblems for what has happened at memorable turning points in the flow.

In this chapter we have already been drifting dangerously into the fogs of the near-present. The generation before us is enveloped in a fog which we might better call the steam of polemics too close for us to penetrate; that is why in the 1990s we have just been beginning to get some scholarly perspective on the disputes of two generations back, between the logical positivists and phenomenologists of the 1920s and 1930s. And the long-term significance of that generation and even the one before it no doubt remains to be seen.

Nevertheless, there is some structural unity in the whole period since the university revolution. The triumph of the research university has had several overlapping effects on intellectual life. There is inevitably some trend toward scholasticism, toward the curatorship of texts and compiling commentaries on them. This is one route toward the stagnation which we have seen in other periods of academicized philosophy in world history. The stagnation too may be only a matter of perspective; inside the network of academic specialists there may be creativity of a highly technical kind, which does not travel well outside. But histories are written for the most part about the larger attention space of general issues and broad-ranging disputes, and this viewpoint swallows up the technical creativity in fine print.

A second result is peculiar to the academicization of the period after 1960: the huge expansion in numbers of universities in every wealthy society, and indeed around the world. There is a population explosion of professors and of texts. This puts unprecedented pressure on the law of small numbers. To survive, intellectuals must divide the attention space into smaller and smaller specialties. The larger arenas of conflict are crowded with huge numbers of contenders. Pan-intellectual movements across the specialties have the only chance for full-scale fame, but the choppiness of this vast ocean makes it heavy going.

Yet with all this proliferation of specialties, there are still some structural sources of first-class innovation in philosophy. This is so even though the space of philosophy, which is that of the most general questions, is just the territory which would seem to have the greatest difficulty in an age of specialization and large-scale intellectual populations. But these have existed on a lesser scale in the German universities since the 1830s, and elsewhere since about 1900. What has kept philosophy alive, even fostering some spectacular developments in the periods we have just reviewed, has been the impetus to border disputes.

Academic structures foster these in many directions. Some movements, such as Neo-Kantianism, arise to adjudicate the knowledge claims that specialized disciplines put forward in their own self-aggrandizement, especially new fields when they first capture a university chair or separate themselves off from an older department. Physicists disputing the status of findings generated by their new research technologies made border alliances with psychologists and mathematicians, and eventually produced the Vienna Circle. Mathematicians' disputes over their methodological foundations spilled over onto philosophical terrain and philosophical careers, with ramifications that reached as far as phenomenology. Existentialism emerged from further twists in these networks, in part because they entwined with border disputes between orthodox theology and its philosophical hybrids. In France, another version of existentialism became famous because it mediated the border between academic philosophy and the self-dramatization of literary intellectuals on the writers' market.

There is no reason to expect that such border issues will come to an end. The growing density of intellectual networks drives them to form groups and disciplines, and just as inevitably makes their borders into topics. Borders shift within academic fields, and between academic thought communities and those outside. The edges of things have always made deep troubles for philosophers. Such troubles are intellectuals' hidden treasure, the philosophers' stone that keeps philosophy alive.

META-REFLECTIONS

CHAPTER 15

❀

Sequence and Branch in the
Social Production of Ideas

The long-term tendency of an active intellectual community is to raise the level of abstraction and reflexivity.

The Continuum of Abstraction and Reflexivity

In China, the ancient *Book of Poetry* contains the yin and yang graphs, but only in the concrete sense of shadow and light. It was the philosophers around 265 B.C.E. who took such terms in the sense of generalized phenomena beyond everyday concrete objects. From these building blocks the next three generations of Chinese intellectuals constructed a cosmological system, with its cycles and correspondences between the natural and the political world. Confucians had begun by formulating abstract concepts for the moral realm, beginning with *li,* proper ritual behavior, and abstracting into a generalized notion of social and moral propriety. Further levels of abstraction emerged when philosophers turned their explicit attention to the nature of such concepts per se. The "Pure Conversation school," ca. 235–300 C.E., was regarded as engaged in "dark learning" because its adherents subjected Taoist and Confucian texts to analysis, not for the familiar purposes of asserting the primacy of favorite cosmological and moral positions, but for rising to a metaphysical level in discussing being, non-being, and substance.

After the lapse of such discussions for many centuries, the Neo-Confucians revived the level of abstraction. Ch'eng Hao gave new meaning to *li* as "principle," explicitly recognizing levels of abstraction. Chu Hsi identified *li* with the cosmological origin *T'ai Chi* (Supreme Ultimate), while distinguishing it from the master substance *ch'i* (ether/energy), and recognizing the distinction between logical and factual priority. Still later, in Tokugawa Japan at the time of Ito Jinsai and Ogyu Sorai, Neo-Confucian metaphysics was subjected to yet further dissection. The fusion among moral principle and the cosmological and abstract senses of *li* was now critiqued, the several realms explicitly separated and opened for independent investigation.

Reflexivity, the self-consciousness of intellectual operations, comes increasingly to the fore as the intergenerational sequence lengthens. Levels of intellectual self-consciousness are potentially endless. Changes in the content of what is reflected on change the form of possible reflexivity. There is some incipient reflexivity in the recognition by the Greek Sophists that concepts are names given by human thought. More refined reflexivity occurs in Kant's transcendental critique of the categories of the understanding. Building rapidly on this step, Fichte and Hegel's dialectic made the process of increasing reflexivity into a self-conscious topic. Even that recognition does not bring the sequence to an end. There have been post-Hegelian philosophies aplenty; the postmodernism of the 1980s was only one more signpost along this route. Such hyper-reflexivity is not merely the decadence of a particular branch of philosophy. Modern mathematics too exemplifies the abstraction-reflexivity sequence. The logical formalist philosophy following from Frege's revolution in logic similarly feeds on itself, as we see from the subsequent history of Russell's theory of types.

The abstraction-reflexivity sequence has occurred in every part of the philosophical world. It is produced by a basic dynamic of intellectual communities, on which are superimposed several other processes. The abstraction-reflexivity sequence does not run off of its own accord as a self-propelling Hegelian dialectic. In some world intellectual networks, the abstraction-reflexivity sequence extended further than in others; there have been periods when the sequence is arrested at a constant level of abstraction, and times when it retrogresses to lower levels of concreteness and reification. There have been side-branches, among them naturalism and empirical science, which at a certain point cut against the grain of the abstraction-reflexivity sequence. Let us observe a large caveat. The abstraction-reflexivity sequence is not to be identified with a single dimension of intellectual "progress," taking the form of the emergence of empirical-discovery science. My analysis is neutral regarding the value of the upper levels of the abstraction-reflexivity sequence. It is merely a predominant feature of the natural history of intellectual communities.

A second general point may be made about long-run intellectual tendencies. The abstraction/reflexivity sequence can grow from any materials on which intellectuals focus attention. Philosophy has diverse starting points: issues of ritual propriety in ancient China, cosmological myths in India and Greece, theological disputes in early Islam. Philosophical abstraction shifts attention from the original questions and transforms them into other matters. Higher or "pure" philosophy emerges as a focus on abstraction and reflexivity in their own right. Techniques arising as tools ancillary to disputes become ends in themselves. Sub-topics become specialized branches of attention. Epistemology, arising in disputes over substantive questions, turns away from answering those questions and into its own arena of dispute, raising the complaint made by a critic of neo-Kantianism about the "endless sharpening of the knife which is never used to cut anything." This is the distinctiveness of the philosophical field: as the purest form of the abstraction-reflexivity sequence, philosophy is constantly re-digging its foundations, moving not forwards but backwards, deepening its questions by digging the ground out from under them.

Not every form of intellectual life does this. The philosophical mode is based in the oldest and most central intellectual community, but many specialties have branched off from it, some of which remained more resolutely focused on their substantive questions. Instead of constantly re-digging their foundations, fields of empirical-discovery science and other arenas of scholarship—such as the study of history—have accumulated facts and principles by doggedly sticking to a fixed level of abstraction. Analytically, the several modes of intellectual life may overlap; and there are special conditions, to be considered in their due place, when a field can evade the abstraction-reflexivity sequence, as well as when it is subject to it.

The second major theme of philosophical networks, then, is goal displacement. Here is one of the sources of conflict in intellectual life. There is disgruntlement, frustration about being unable to solve questions, or rather about seeing their meaning fade away before one's eyes. It is part of a perennial conflict among traditionalists and progressives, conservatives and radicals—not necessarily in the lay senses of these terms as they might be applied to religion or politics, but among intellectuals taking their stand on a higher or lower level of the abstraction-reflexivity sequence. Sniping takes place across the levels: the disparagement of higher levels as "logic-chopping" or useless subtleties, "angels dancing on the head of a pin"; and name-calling in the opposite direction, a lineage in which postmodernist charges of "foundationalism" take their place. Each side accuses the other of hindering insight; the process of intellectual history is merciless toward both. Their conflict is one more manifestation of the very general process of conflict which drives intellectual change. Neither conservatism nor radicalism at any one level is a guide to what will emerge as their positions are transformed at later levels of the abstraction-reflexivity sequence. Goal displacement means that, from the point of view of the participants, subsequent intellectual history is always a matter of rude surprises.

What causes the abstraction-reflexivity sequence? Durkheim theorized that a trend toward abstractness and universalism takes place in the collective consciousness as the social division of labor increases. As evidence he cites trends in religion and law. In isolated tribal societies, religious symbols are concrete and specific; rules are reified and their violations expiated by punitive ritual. As societies grow larger, more stratified, organizationally and economically differentiated, the spiritual entities of religion become less localized, expanding in their scope, and eventually leaving the concrete worldly level entirely for a transcendent realm. Still further on this continuum, the "modernism" of Durkheim's day regarded God as a symbol of the universal moral order, and explained the anthropomorphic traits of earlier belief as reification, mistaking a symbol for a concrete entity. The Durkheimian explanation cannot be straightforwardly adopted because of two difficulties. The mechanical solidarity of small enclosed groups does not disappear in differentiated modern societies; concrete symbols subsist along with various levels of abstraction characterizing the many realms of public and professional life. And the networks of intellectuals are not identical with the society at large; the insulation of an intellectual community from lay conceptions is the key to the existence of distinctively intellectual topics. With proper amendment, the Durkheimian explanation can be applied to conceptual trends within the intellectual community itself.

An intellectual network is a community of implicit awareness among its members: opposing stances within the attention space structure one another through their arguments; intergenerational transmission of concepts and topics makes up the basic sense of what the community is about. As Durkheim held, abstraction develops so as to maintain unification across diverseness. As more members are included in the intellectual network, its collective consciousness is strained to encompass their distinctiveness. G. H. Mead's generalized other, which plays the part of the audience for the internalized conversation of individual thinkers, increases in scope. Ideas are emblems of group membership; to keep up the sense of membership across the generations, under conditions of repetitive creativity, the collective consciousness becomes more abstract. The *nomos-physis* debate at the time of the Sophists was transcended by moving to the stance of a higher abstraction, from which particular concepts of morality (and of cosmology as well) could be seen as sub-realms within a more encompassing realm of Form. Debates at one level of abstraction are resolved by moving to a higher level of abstraction from which they can be judged and reinterpreted. This never brings the process of debate itself to an end; the intellectual world lives on debates, and each new conceptual level provides terrain on which new oppositions can be staked out.

The Durkheimian model helps explains the increase in abstraction. Reflexivity can be explained as a further consequence of expanding the scope of the generalized other. The mind of a "sophisticated" intellectual, heir to a historically complex network of oppositions and changes in level, internalizes an invisible community of diverse viewpoints, unified by looking on them from a yet more encompassing standpoint. Reflexiveness grows more intense as there is more history of the network to incorporate. Awareness grows that the individual positions are constructed as parts of a web of oppositions. Eventually the meta-concept emerges that there are higher-order concepts, and that there is an error—a narrower sphere of awareness—in treating a symbol as if it were a concrete existent. Reflexivity is the growing self-exploration of relations among standpoints within this increasingly complicated network-generated mind.

The argument so far explains why the diversity of positions within an intellectual community should drive upwards the abstraction-reflexivity sequence, but it leaves open a prior question: What causes the diversity of positions in the first place? Here I bring in two of the basic principles of intellectual creativity, used throughout this book: the law of small numbers, which shapes the internal struggles within the intellectual attention space; and the two-step model of causality, through which external social conditions operate indirectly by rearranging the material base for intellectual life.

Creation by Negation and by External Shock

Intellectual life proceeds by horizontal tensions among contemporaries as well as by vertical sequence among the generations. Let us avoid the retrospective fallacy, the explanatory complacency which comes from taking for granted what the positions will be because we already know the history, say, of Greek philosophy from Thales to Epicurus. Visualize a small number of particles—three to six—moving through a tunnel of time; each draws energy from its past momentum, renewed and accelerated by repulsion from the other particles. This tunnel is the attention space of the intellectual world; indeed the tunnel is created by the movement of the particles and the tensions that connect them. The tunnel's walls are not fixed; it extends forward in time only so long as the negative interplay of the particles keeps up a sufficient level of energy. As arguments intensify, the tunnel becomes brighter, more luminous in social space; and as positions rigidify, going their own way without reference to one another, the attention space fades.

Surrounding the tunnel are the ordinary concerns of the lay society. Persons on the outside notice the intellectual tunnel only as much as the glow of its debates makes it visible from a distance. Intellectual stratification is represented by distance from the core of the tunnel. The walls of the tunnel are no more than a moving glow generated from within. The trajectories of the particles and the borders between light and shadow are seen most sharply at the center, by viewers situated on the main energy lines. The farther one is from the central zone, the harder it is to see where the walls are, this membrane of relevance for the controversialists inside it. In the half-light of semi-focused regions, it is easy to mistake residues of old arguments for the central issues that will generate the forward thrust of the attention space. Provincials, latecomers, and autodidacts flail in the wake of past disputes but do not catch up with the bright center of energy.

The forward movement in time, if continued at a high level of creative energy, traverses the abstraction-reflexivity sequence. At each point in creative time, the current level of abstraction is divided by the three to six factions allowed by the law of small numbers. Negation at the forefront occurs along the dimensions stressed most strongly in the arguments of the leading school—the most brightly glowing particle—as opposing particles formulate negations to it which preserve or raise the level of abstraction. Thus occurs the multiplication of positions, providing the tensions on which moves can be made to higher levels of abstraction.

Consider now the external conditions driving creativity. The abstraction-reflexivity sequence does not run off automatically; there are periods when intellectual life stagnates at a fixed level of abstraction, or even retrogresses to a lower level. The famous periods of creativity are those when the abstraction-reflexivity sequence is moving forward most rapidly. These flareups in the time tunnel are set off against the periods of mild, steady light when nothing much seems to be happening, and against the twilights when sophistication is lost. The two-step model of causality applies: when external conditions disrupt the intellectual attention space, internal realignment takes place; and this in turn unleashes the creativity for formulating new positions, new tensions among the privileged arguers at the core of the attention space. When the material base for one cluster of intellectual factions is destroyed, their space in the field is opened up to be occupied by a new set of positions. When a large particle disappears from the field of oppositions, new particles veer and fragment to take its place, lighting up the tunnel in an episode of famous creativity. In India, when the religious base for Buddhism was destroyed, the victorious Hindus led by Shankara subdivided to take over the range of philosophical positions once held by their rivals. Conversely, the side experiencing the collapse of its external base huddles together into a defense alliance, sometimes imploding in a brilliant moment, as in the grand coalition of pagan philosophies led by Plotinus against the rise of Christianity. When a new material base for intellectuals springs up, new factions appear simultaneously in a rush to fill this new arena of attention with the three to six opposing positions available under the law of small numbers. We have sees this repeatedly: following the invention of higher education in the generation of Plato and his rivals; with the reform of the Chinese examination system in the Sung dynasty, undergirding the outburst of Neo-Confucianism; in the rise of the medieval Christian university; yet again with the German university revolution, which set off a new terrain for research specializations.

Once the shock in the external base subsides and the internal rearrangement of factions in the attention space runs its course (a process which takes several generations), intellectual life settles into a routine. Continuous movement in the abstraction-reflexivity sequence depends on repeated shocks to the external base. The dynamism of intellectual life which characterizes Europe rather continuously in the 30 generations from 1000 c.e. onward, is due indirectly to the amount of institutional change in the surrounding society, resulting in a large number of shifts in the bases which have supported intellectuals.

Textual Scholasticism and Arrested Sequences

In periods when there are no shocks rearranging the material base, the internal division of the attention space remains static. What then are the intellectuals doing to fill up their time and the attention of their colleagues and pupils? The problem strikes us most forcefully in the case of "scholastic" periods, when intellectuals are primarily curators of old texts. Nevertheless, even a backwards-looking textual mode is not necessarily stagnant. We find here another analytically separable strand: a textual scholastic sequence which may unfold either in isolation—totally dominating the intellectual space—or in combination with the abstraction-reflexivity sequence.

There is a temptation to identify this textual-scholastic mode with Asian modes of thought; we see it prominently in Confucianism, in both Indian and Chinese Buddhism, and within the Hindu *darshanas*. Yet it is not a matter of regional mentality; there is similar textual-scholasticism in Hellenistic and Roman antiquity, among the Arabic Aristoteleans, and in medieval Christendom. A textual-scholastic mode becomes prominent again in the university scholarship of the 1800s and 1900s, within both philosophy and other disciplines. The study and commentary on classic texts of "dead Germans" is a large part of contemporary sociological theory; and in the contemporary academic world more generally there is polemic over the attention paid to the canon of "white European males"—a polemic whose principal results are to enlarge the canon, not to move away from the textual commentary mode.

It is not the activity of preserving texts and writing commentaries per se that makes a philosopher unoriginal. The textual commentary is employable in the mode of scholastic conservatism but adaptable as a means of publishing new ideas. The copyist takes the opportunity to add clarifying commentaries, which become all the more acceptable as the growing antiquity of a text brings a demand for explaining archaic language or cryptic modes of expression grown incomprehensible with time. We are inclined to regard a string of super-commentaries as the essence of scholasticism, but they can also be cases of cumulative development to progressive levels of sophistication. The advantage from the point of view of the writer is that if one attaches one's commentary to a famous text, one's own work can be assured of wide circulation. The great works of Chinese philosophy are to a large extent commentaries on earlier classics, from the *Yi Ching* appendices and the *Great Learning* attached to the *Book of Rites,* through the "Dark Learning" attached to the *Tao Te Ching* and the Confucian classics. The works of the Neo-Confucian school are largely in the form of compilations and commentaries on classic texts.

We see much the same thing in India. The great work of the Nyaya school is Vatsyayana's commentary on the *Nyaya-sutras,* and an analogous position for the Vaisheshika is held by Prashastapada's commentary on the *Vaisheshika-sutra.* Among the Buddhists, the growth of the scholasticizing *Abhidharma* literature occurs simultaneously with the development of new philosophical positions: it is a vehicle for creativity from the early Sarvastivada realists through the Yogacara Idealists; schools which transcended the *Abhidharma* compilations replaced them with accretions of commentaries on other texts, such as the logic treatises which were vehicles for the metaphysical systems of Dignaga and Dharmakirti.[1] Composition of commentaries should be regarded as a mode of publication, in the absence of an open market for books, and where religious education provided the main place where texts could be physically reproduced. What was propagated in this way was determined not by the mode of publication, but by the general conditions of opposition and synthesis within the intellectual networks.

The Christian "scholastics" of the medieval universities, whose name was given to this style, used the commentary mode of publication, but they were not predominantly traditionalistic in the content of their work. The university scholars from Abelard to Scotus constituted one of the most intensely creative periods in the history of world philosophy, exemplary of the abstraction sequence at its most dynamic. The pejorative connotation of "scholastic" was applied to them by their enemies and successors, the Renaissance Humanists. Ironically, the latter were more "scholastic" in the narrow sense of the term, adulators of past classics, attempting to recover original meanings rather than innovating on abstract philosophical terrain.

In the Confucian, Buddhist, and Hindu networks, textual scholasticism was supported by an ideology that venerated ancient texts and denigrated departures from them. The effect was not necessarily to stifle innovation; new high-status texts, in order to be regarded as religiously inspired, were produced anonymously or pseudonymously and attributed to as great antiquity as possible. The *Tao Te Ching,* probably written around 240 B.C.E., was projected backwards to a mythical sage antedating Confucius, no doubt to claim rank over contemporary Confucian rivals. Successive Mahayana sutras, like their Jaina sutra contemporaries, were attributed to earlier incarnations of their respective religious lineage heads; competition over "more ancient than thou" expanded the calendrical framework, escalating the eons of cosmic time within which their founders are situated. It is almost a rule of thumb that the more ancient a text claims to be, the more recently it falls in the sequence of composition. This "archaizing strategy" is itself a form of innovation; rather than claiming creativity moving forward in time, one projects the edge of creativity backwards.

There was plenty of room for creativity within the textual commentary mode. Rival camps could choose their favorite text on which to expound. We see this in full force in the high period of Tokugawa Japan, when rival schools attached their views to old texts which served as vehicles, while denouncing the views of their rivals as later accretions. The Ancient Learning school of Yamaga Soko, Ito Jinsai, and Ogyu Sorai dismissed the previously dominant Neo-Confucian school as merely the learning of the Sung dynasty, while using its newfound independence for drastic conceptual innovations. The still more archaizing National Learning school of Kamo Mabuchi and Motoori Norinaga, turning to the Japanese poetic-religious classics, exemplifies another path along which textual commentary acquires its own mode of innovation. There is a cumulative development of the techniques of scholarship, the sharpening of the critical tools, and the accumulation of knowledge about historical sequences. The claims of Neo-Confucians to propound eternal verities were punctured by rival scholars who could marshal a better historical apparatus. The claim to uncover a "true" tradition is an innovative move against prevailing conventions. The battle among Japanese scholars over the distant past moved to a higher level of the abstraction-reflexivity sequence, creating a sophisticated neoconservative epistemology about the limits of rationality in order to argue about the nature of historicity and the accessibility of tradition. Again the dynamic is not confined to Asian textual scholars; a similar sequence is traced out in biblical scholarship in the German universities after 1820, from the figurative interpretations by liberal "higher criticism" to Barthian neo-orthodoxy.

The textual commentary mode contains several possibilities for innovation, including the use of commentaries as publication vehicles for new ideas, the development of historical scholarship and reflexivity about one's historical situatedness, and eventually about the abstract conception of historicity itself. The emergence of self-conscious historical standards marks a level of sophistication above the blind adulation of texts for their claimed antiquity. But sharpening technical standards of historical scholarship does not necessarily bring an upward move in the overall sequence of philosophical abstraction and reflexivity. The "Old Text school" arose in the Han dynasty as a movement of librarians and textual scholars attacking the pseudo-ancient texts of the Han Confucians, and branding them as a phony "New Text school." Modern scholars tend to regard the members of the "Old Text school" as progressives, rationalists who punctured the occultist cosmologies promulgated by their "New Text" rivals. Nevertheless, this kind of "rationalism" may be sterile for philosophical innovation. To insist on the letter of old texts is less innovative than to produce new metaphysical constructions, even if the latter is done is the false guise of promulgating fake ancient texts. A comparative proof is that India never had anything like an "Old Text school" of scholars puncturing the archaizing claims of the predominant publication practice. Indian Buddhist and Hindu philosophies alike were dominated by their own version of the "New Text school," and it was via this vehicle that both proceeded much further in the abstraction-reflexivity sequence than did Chinese philosophy.

The textual-scholastic mode is a vehicle within which the creativity of network competition may take place, to the extent that the usual dynamics of internal opposition and external shock are present. There is another version, which we might call "classificatory scholasticism," which is a genuine arresting of movement at a constant level of the abstraction-reflexivity sequence. In this case there is no creativity, at least not of the sort which makes famous names in the long-term histories; here we find lineages filled with names remembered as minor at best. Nevertheless, there is a dynamism of classificatory scholasticism as well, making it an activity that takes up its own modicum of creative energy and focuses attention on the inner rankings of the intellectual network during these periods.

Consider the later Neoplatonists of the Roman period. They rely on authorities, above all Plato, Aristotle, the Chaldean Oracles, the Orphic hymns; their constant reference is "as the gods say," "the theurgists say," and the like (CHLG, 1967: 280–282).[2] Their method is the textual commentary, unimaginative, hair-splitting, full of repetition and jargon. But they are not stagnant in the sense of lacking movement from one scholar to the next. Over time there builds up a tendency to argue for conclusions in an explicit chain of deductive argument, demonstrated in formal Euclidean proofs. The Neoplatonist cosmology, a hierarchy of emanations from the highest unity down through the plurality of the lower spheres, is constantly expanding. Later members of the school multiply levels, introducing further hypostases into the three expounded by Plotinus, subdividing into further triads, inserting demons and heroes among gods and disembodied souls. These cosmologies become increasingly concrete and particularistic, regressing in the abstraction-reflexivity sequence; this regression is combined with innovativeness in the sheer quantitative expansion of complexity within these systems.

The dynamics of this intellectual game are to classify and to list. The Vedic traditions are full of numbered lists. Buddhist texts of the early period list the four kinds of insight, the four kinds of Right Effort, five Moral Powers, seven

Qualities of Wisdom, the eightfold Noble Path, and so on. It is tempting to interpret these rubrics as simply mnemonic devices from the period of oral recitation; but the list motif continues into the period of written texts as well. Moreover the lists keep expanding in both periods, making the mnemonic task even more difficult. The classificatory mode is pervasive in Indian scholarship, through the Hindu *darshanas* as well as the period of the Buddhist metaphysical systems. The major Hindu cosmological systems, Samkhya and Vaisheshika, derive from names for "classification" or "making distinctions." The number of the various kinds of things becomes the topic of dispute, the frame in which philosophical issues are raised. The Hindu schools are concerned with how many kinds of knowledge there are, and in the Nyaya school, which specializes in rules of debate, how many kinds of fallacies and how many parts of the syllogism.

This is the pathway toward the sub-discipline of logic. This "scholastic" impulse within Greek philosophy, as early as Aristotle's school, leads to a classification of types of predicate and of the figures and moods of the syllogism, just as it is scholasticism within Greek mathematics that leads to the axiomatic classification system culminating in Euclid's geometry. This classification game is a goal displacement in the abstraction-reflexivity sequence, turning away from the substance of arguments to the formal rules of the argumentation process; nevertheless, it opens an arena in which creativity can take place, if in a technical guise difficult for outsiders to penetrate. We are inclined to view the classificatory activities of the Hellenistic and the later Islamic logicians as mere droning scholasticism; and indeed this was the view of many philosophers nearer to them in time. Creative activity sometimes went on within the technical schools of logic in these times, but such work does not travel well, nor does it propagate its intellectual energy widely. Avoiding value judgments, we may say merely that the classificatory mode is generally looked down on by intellectuals who work on more widely appealing ethical and metaphysical issues. The long-term attention that constitutes the historical self-image of the community drops the technical classifiers into the background in favor of more spectacular moves in the abstraction sequence, labeling as stagnant the periods in which the technicians dominate.

The classificatory mode can also take the form of hierarchic classifications. This was especially prominent in medieval Chinese Buddhism. The most successful schools, T'ien-t'ai and Hua-yen, engaged in the practice called *p'an-chiao,* arranging the various Buddhist doctrines in ordered lists from the most naive up through the most sophisticated. Classification served several purposes. It introduced bibliographic order, important for Chinese Buddhism as a foreign-based religion subservient to the importation and translation of texts from a morass of sects formulated in India. Classification also constituted a turf in its own right on which the intellectual division of the attention space could go on, not with spectacular changes in the level of abstraction, but by trying out various modes of classification of texts (by content, chronologically, by mode of exposition), giving rise to many minor puzzles to establish consistency among the various modes. Classification served the purposes of religious politics, simultaneously maintaining the alliance among various proponents of the doctrine while asserting superiority for one's own sect. Later, as scholarly Buddhism weakened under political pressure, the classification mode allowed for syncretistic alliances. The last great Hua-yen syncretizer, Tsung-mi, went so far as to include Confucianism as the first step in the Buddhist hierarchical sequence, and to work out elaborate correspondences among the numbered Buddhist precepts and the various rubrics of Chinese cosmology: the Five Agents, five emperors, five sacred peaks, five colors, five virtues, and so forth (Gregory, 1991: 282). Tsung-mi appealed simultaneously to the last surviving strong Buddhist sect by extending classification to Ch'an (Zen) doctrines (even though Ch'an itself, at this time in its expansive phase, was militantly anti-scholastic), while extending a bridge to enemy Confucian and Taoist tenets.

The classificatory mode with numbered lists sometimes overlaps with numerology. Here numbers are regarded as a system of occult correspondences, linking the world into a net of symbols. Such a system can be used for divination or magical manipulation. The Cabalism of the Hellenistic period parallels in this respect the correlative cosmology formulated in the Han dynasty, which remained such a significant part of the Chinese repertoire down through the Neo-Confucians (and which we see the syncretizer Tsung-mi introducing into Buddhism via the *p'an-chiao* textual classifications). Here it is important to bear several distinctions in mind.

Numerology is not per se a form of the development of mathematics; that is to say, mathematics has its own sequence of abstraction and reflexivity, in relation to which the practice of numerology is a diversion into a side-channel at a lower, more concrete level.[3] Nor should we regard numerology as a continuation of primordial or popular magic. Numerology appears not at the beginning of the intellectual sequences in China, India, and Greece, but after a phase of abstract development. Numerology is an offshoot of the scholastic path of development, the textual-scholastic sequence. It is scholasticism itself, combined with the concreteness that comes from appealing to lay audiences rather than specialized intellectuals, which produces the upsurge of sophisticated occultism.

Numerology and the divination games of correlative cosmologies are a kind of busywork of intellectuals, a way of playing the game in the attention space at times when the external conditions driving creativity on the "mainline" of the abstraction-reflexivity sequence are in abeyance. It is a version of the "normal science" of philosophy, played at a level of reified abstractions, providing a fund of small-scale puzzles rather than the deep troubles around which philosophy makes its more spectacular moves.

The same may be said in a more general sense about textual scholasticism. The causes of scholasticism are to be found in the normal conditions of any community of teachers, curators of past knowledge to be passed along to subsequent generations. Scholasticism is the baseline of intellectual life; it is one analytically distinct process along with whatever other sequences, abstraction-generating or otherwise, happen to take place. In the absence of external shocks to the material base and of internal rearrangements under the law of small numbers, scholarship settles down to a routinized activity. The quantitative extension of classifications and commentaries is the bureaucratization of intellectual life.

Reversals and Loss of Abstraction

What then of periods in which there is an actual slippage, a retrogression in the abstraction-reflexivity sequence? We find several instances of this pattern. In China, the abstraction reached by the Mohists and the School of Names is reversed into the concrete reifications of Han Confucianism; the revival of abstract philosophy in the "Dark Learning" period lasts only a few generations before Confucianism (and all the more so Taoist religion) returns to a concrete level for many centuries, until the abstract sequence is resumed again with the Sung Neo-Confucians. In late Greco-Roman Neoplatonism, there is a tendency to lose abstraction as concrete deities are inserted into the austere metaphysics of Plotinus' emanations. In late Indian Buddhism, tantrism marks a collapse in abstraction, a movement toward magical forces and their concrete manifestations. Again in later Hindu philosophy, the acuteness of earlier argument collapses after 1600 in the combination of *bhakti* theist devotionalism with the Advaita "leap-philosophy" beyond conceptual distinctions. Advaita becomes a united front against the political dominance of Muslim invaders, and later the emblem of Indian nationalism in the face of European colonialists. In each case the material base for intellectual production gets squeezed; it is the defensive move in time of weakness that produces the loss of abstraction and reflexivity.

We need to treat this process with some care. Not every weakening of the external base of an intellectual position results in retrogression of the abstraction-reflexivity sequence; after all, there are also the great synthetic positions in times of weakness, which push up the level of abstraction in the grand combination. Plotinus is the best example. We should avoid confusing the kind of synthesis which occurs in response to overcrowding in the attention space—

the grand syntheses of Aristotle, Aquinas, Dharmakirti—with the syncretism which occurs when there is external pressure to put together disparate positions because of a radical collapse of their external base. The defensive syncretism in which intellectuals ally themselves predominantly with lay audiences has a strongly retrogressive effect on abstraction. Buddhism tantrism in India, Taoist popular religion, Confucianism as a state cult: all of these make an alliance which eliminates the internal attention space of intellectuals and thereby undercuts their professional drive toward acuteness of abstraction. It is not the contents of the doctrine per se that is the key to the loss of this acuteness. The shift to a cosmology of energy forces in tantrism is part of a de-differentiating, lay-oriented movement in the death period of Indian Buddhism, but the same doctrines in the hands of the growing movement of Hindu thinkers (above all the Kashmir Shaivites) become platforms for raising the level of metaphysical abstraction and logical refinement.

In general, the externally driven pressures for alliance tend toward syncretism rather than synthesis. The "four Vedas" became a standard package in the period when the ancient sacrificial cult was in decay, an arbitrary compilation. Indeed, they survived textually for intellectuals above all because they served as a publication vehicle for the commentaries attached to them. The original alliance had no overall consistency, all the more so when Upanishadic interpretations were attached. It was a "lumpy alliance," sheer masses of undigested material, held together by the external politics of the situation. Such "lumpy alliances" are the result of conditions which reduce the internal autonomy of the intellectual attention space. External conditions promoting such loss of autonomy determine most of the historical episodes of retrogression in the abstraction-reflexivity sequence.

Three Pathways: Cosmological, Epistemological-Metaphysical, Mathematical

We come now to the ways the abstraction-reflexivity sequence has worked out in historical cases. Three sub-sequences are visible. First, there is a shift from mythological to philosophical cosmologies; an example is the takeoff into abstract argument in India and Greece. Second, there is an interplay between epistemological and metaphysical arguments pushing toward higher levels of abstraction and reflexivity. This sequence followed and built on the mythological-cosmological sequence in India and Greece; Islamic, Christian, and European philosophies generally built further upon this sequence. In ancient China, the argumentative sequence began with very different materials than in India and Greece, then proceeded intermittently along much the same path; here the mythological-cosmological sequence was not initial, but cut into the Chinese epistemological sequence later on, around the seventh or eighth generation, and thereafter tended to swamp it. Finally, there is a version of the abstraction-reflexivity sequence which takes place on the specialized terrain of mathematics, playing back into philosophy and driving its abstraction and reflexivity to new grounds. This sequence is found mainly in Europe, beginning in the 1600s and playing a dominant role in the generations around 1900. Our "modern" or "Western" philosophy has gone especially far in the abstraction-reflexivity sequence because it has built on all three sequences.

Why did the various world regions start their sequences with argument around their distinctive questions? Initial contents of discussion were given by external conditions. Chinese philosophy arose in the context of political discussions over the legitimating rituals of the state cult. In Greece the background was the decentralization of cults and temples, which reduced the significance of religious legitimation, together with the secularization of political and legal argument in the emerging city-states. In India it was the decline of the Vedic priestly powers and the competition of rival religious movements. In Islam it was a tribal coalition administering its conquests and legitimating succession disputes by forming schools of religious law. Once the argumentative community is constituted, causal dynamics within each sequence work much the same way: oppositions splitting the network within each generation, together with the periodic overcoming of those oppositions on a new level of abstraction.

The Cosmological Sequence

FROM RELIGIOUS MYTHOLOGY TO WORLD INGREDIENT COSMOLOGIES
The cosmological sequence proceeds along a series of steps. First there are mythologies, tales recounted by popular storytellers and reworked by semiprofessional reciters and poets.[4] Next the components of the world are classified as provinces of specialized gods, and stories are told explaining their origins. There follows a period of rationalizing these fragmentary world explanations by systematizing into genealogies or pantheons. This shades over into more abstract concepts in answer to the explicit question, what is the world composed of: at first mixed lists of gods, elements, physical and psychological processes, followed by discussions of which ingredient or ingredients are dominant. Eventually discussion moves to the level of metaphysical and epistemological abstractions; questions are raised about conceptual paradoxes and logical consistency, which are resolved by making the step to an explicitly abstract level of philosophy.

In India, the mythological period begins in pre-Vedic times, followed by a certain amount of systematizing of the Vedic pantheon under the organization of the Vedic priests. In the Upanishadic period argument centers on the elements or ingredients which make up the world; the transcendent monism identified with the self, picked out of these texts some 30 to 40 generations later by highly abstract Advaita philosophers, is only one of many elements in a morass of competing and, for the most part, pluralistic worldviews. The non-Vedic sages in the same period make themselves the center of debate by transmuting these world ingredient discussions onto the level of coherent systems of abstract concepts. Rivals at the time of the Buddha propound various cosmologies of four elements, or seven; still further unification occurs by focusing on a thread that runs through all the world components, karma or fate. Gautama Buddha captures the center of the attention space by systematizing the various world ingredients into a chain, grouping together psychological and physical elements into the aggregations *(skandas)* which make up the world of experience. There is now an antithesis between a world-transcending "ultimate ingredient" (nirvana) and the constituents of the world itself, bridged by rising to the level of a master concept, causality, ordering the relations of constituent parts.

The center of action in the intellectual community has now shifted to an abstract philosophical discourse, even if it remains surrounded for centuries longer by mythology in the Buddhist sutras, the Hindu *Puranas* and epics. Metaphysical and eventually logical and epistemological issues arise, leading into the second of our sequences. Cosmological issues however can also continue for a long time, and in some respects the world ingredient sequence is never outdated. There is a borderline between world ingredient cosmology and more analytical metaphysical questions; for a long period the chief Buddhist and Hindu schools—the various factions of *Abhidharma* scholasticism, of Samkhya and Vaisheshika—proceed from systematizing lists of world ingredients. In another direction, the search for world ingredients takes the form we may call empirical science (although not its rapid-discovery version); doctrines such as the *chakra* scheme of medical physiology and systems of astrological divination mix explanations of the material world with occultism and magic.

In Greece, mythologies are systematized into a pantheon by Homer and Hesiod. The nature-function gods are already a cosmological classification system, and Hesiod's genealogies are a version of causal sequence among world elements. The discussion that breaks out in the generation of Thales now directly expounds the originating or primal elements by reinterpreting myths or postulating basic substances. The lineup of competing ingredients, as in India, is conceptually motley: water, air, fire, number, the unbounded, together with various notions of natural transformations in the vein that "all things are full of gods." Three generations after Thales there is a break to abstract metaphysical conceptions with Heraclitus and Parmenides, leading into the epistemological sequence.

The Greeks traverse the cosmological sequence rapidly, arriving at the metaphysical level in many fewer generations than in the Indian network. The cosmological part of the Greek sequence does not thereby come to an end, but continues alongside the metaphysical level. Part of the philosophical community is no longer concerned with cosmology, such as the Sophists; but their contemporaries, Anaxagoras and more influentially Empedocles, with his four-element scheme, successfully keep up the focus of attention on the lineage of cosmological issues. Plato's generation attains more abstract conceptions, giving a standpoint from which to revise cosmological heritages. Aristotle coordinates metaphysical and cosmological levels; he is rivaled by the atomism of Democratus, which is institutionalized into a long-standing position by the Epicurean school. The Stoics too have a strong cosmological component. As in India, the Greek cosmological sequence continues for a long time alongside other philosophical discussions. In one branch it is concretized, both de-mythologized and de-metaphysicized in empirical science, such as in the various systems of the medical schools; in another direction, abstract ontology fuses with magical occultism in Middle Platonism, the occultist numerologies, and late Neoplatonism. In both sequences, Indian and Greek alike, we find not merely a linear trajectory of cosmological abstraction finally sublated into metaphysics, but branching sequences expanding into niches on the intermediate levels of concreteness and abstraction.

In China the earliest sequence of philosophical argument is not cosmological but political. The first issue on which the attention space divides is the character of human nature; the chief rival positions are Confucian familistic-hierarchical obligation, Yang Chu's selfishness, and Mohist universal altruism; a few generations later they are Mencius' human-heartedness, Hsun Tzu's innate evil, and the political repressiveness advocated by the Legalists. The Chinese route into philosophical abstraction proceeds not by competition among cosmological alternatives, but by the growth of procedural logic and conceptual investigation; this is visible in the sixth and seventh generations of the argumentative community, with Hui Shih's paradoxes and Kung-sun Lung's "School of Names."

The Chinese cosmological sequence takes off when the materials of primitive religion are drawn into this argumentative community. Around 270 B.C.E. in the generation of Kung-sun Lung, just when the core network is at the transition point to the metaphysical level of debate, the Yin-Yang scheme and Tsou Yen's Five Processes cosmology enter the field and rapidly take the center of attention. Both are divination schemes, presumably nurtured in provincial places and drawing on the mythological stratum of popular magical practice. Tsou Yen makes a great success by systematizing the Five Agents (water, fire, wood, metal, earth) in such a way that they line up with current philosophical debates, as well as appealing to lay interests in political prediction and dynastic

legitimation. In the next generation, the long-standing network of elite philosophers answers with the *Tao Te Ching,* blending a Confucian concept of
behavior and propriety, the way *(Tao),* with abstract issues of the significance
of nominalism, into a cosmology whose core ingredient is nameless natural
spontaneity.

From now on the cosmological systems sweep to domination in Chinese
philosophy, derailing the secularized tone of moral and political discussion, as
well as turning back the short-lived trend into epistemology and metaphysics.
In the next two generations (the eighth and ninth after Confucius), the main
intellectual events are the formulation of new cosmologically oriented texts
within the Confucian school: *The Great Learning,* which takes a naturalistic
stance toward the "investigation of things"; *The Doctrine of the Mean,* which
interprets the Confucian Superior Man as a mystical sympathy with the cosmic
Way. At this time also is composed a Confucian appendix to the old *Yi Ching*
divination text, thereby bringing it into the Confucians' professional canon.
The takeover by the cosmological schemes is sealed in the twelfth generation
by Tung Chung-shu, who systematizes Confucianism as a synthesis of Yin-
Yang, Five Agents, and *Yi Ching* divination systems into a grand scheme of
counterparts between cosmology and the political and moral order. Tung
Chung-shu's contemporary is the *Hui-nan Tzu* group of scholars, who produce
a rival cosmology of nature elements, divination practices, and political resonances, drawing together a mixture of non-Confucian cultural capital now
becoming identified as Taoism.

China ends up by the time of the Han dynasty in much the same place as
Greece about the time of the late Presocratics or India at the time of the
Buddha's older contemporaries, although with a stronger political component.
Confucian cosmology becomes relatively impervious to intellectual change now
that its carriers are the curators of canonical texts and simultaneously ritual
specialists administering the cult which legitimates a strongly centralized state.
From now on, even in downward times of the dynastic cycles when the empire
disintegrates, the Confucians are ideologists of centralization and imperial
legitimacy. Competition among intellectuals loses its autonomy from political
faction fighting and falls to a particularistic level: the various cosmological
elements and colors, along with the phenomena of climate and natural disaster,
are taken as correlated with the rise and fall of dynasties, and their discussion
is equivalent to political prognostication favoring one state faction or another.[5]
Confucianism becomes a religious pantheon, engaged in particularistic disputes
with the rival pantheons of Taoism and popular Buddhism; intellectual debate
drops to the level of arguing whether Lao Tzu, Confucius, or the Buddha
taught the others first.

When external conditions of intellectual production change, the cosmological sequence is resumed in China. In the period 1030–1200, Neo-Confucianism is created out of a revival of Han dynasty cosmologies infused with Taoist divination schemes. The discussion picks up again at a more abstract level, formulating the overarching cosmic-metaphysical concepts of the world substance *ch'i* and the *logos*/principle *li*. After a detour, during which Confucian philosophy is largely static and cut off from the much more abstract terrain of medieval Buddhism, Chinese metaphysics reemerges at approximately the point reached by the Greek Stoics.

OCCULTISM AND NATURAL SCIENCE: TWO SIDE-CHANNELS

Comparing China with the rest of the world shows that the several versions of the abstraction-reflexivity sequence are indeed analytically distinct, and can be combined in different orders in time. How far each world intellectual network progresses in the sequence is variable. So are the starting times and the length of the periods of arrested movement. In all three indigenous cases, India, Greece, and China, the cosmological sequence branches after it reaches the level where metaphysical abstraction is first reached. One branch continues further into ontological questions, blending with the metaphysical abstraction reached by the sequence of epistemological discussion; this happens most notably in India, as well as in Greece and its textual continuations in Islam and Christendom. A second branch turns aside to systematic speculation and empirical investigations of the natural world, which eventually become science. This branch was very active in China, as well as in Greece and its Western offshoots, formulating the specialized cosmologies of astronomy, medical physiology, chemistry, and so forth. A third branch, a blend between concrete empiricism and conceptual abstraction treated in a reified mode, leads into occultism, a system of portents and correspondences combining the natural and the symbolic, the human moral-political-psychological realm with a cosmology of concrete nature.

The cosmology sequence may run straight through to high levels of philosophical abstraction. The other two branches pose the likelihood of arresting or reversing the level of abstraction and reflexivity. The occultist path does so by holding to a lower-middle range of reified abstraction; occult forces, portents, and significances make sense precisely because they come from a level of conceptual abstraction that could only have been reached by the accumulation of intellectual sophistication across the generations. At the same time, its adherents link it to practices which appeal to lay audiences and concerns, sometimes for political faction fighting or state legitimation, sometimes in the retail sale of popular magic. In either case, the autonomy of the internal intellectual discussion space is lost; the abstraction-reflexivity sequence is prevented from moving further.

The sub-sequence which leads into empirical science would seem to be the opposite of the occultist branch; and indeed the proponents of these two paths have often been explicit enemies. Wang Ch'ung and the "rationalists" of the Old Text school were energized and focused by their oppositional space carved out against the Han Confucian occultists. But this path too can be retrograde on the abstraction-reflexivity sequence. To be opposed to occultist reification does not necessarily lead onward into further philosophical creativity, nor for that matter into empirical-scientific discovery. To puncture stories of ghosts and portents with mundane "rational" explanation, as Wang Ch'ung did, is to be tied to the occultists through the very process of conflict, much in the same way that twentieth-century opponents of parapsychology are locked into debates that do not produce anything to move the forefront of discovery. Periods when a naturalistic, anti-occultist movement dominates tend to be periods of opposition to metaphysics generally, as we see in both the European Enlightenment of the 1700s and its contemporary, the rationalism of the Jinsai and Sorai schools in Tokugawa Japan.

Science per se does not constitute the main path upward on the abstraction-reflexivity sequence; it emerges from a particular point on that sequence, but it is a separate branch.[6] From this point of view, the vexed question of the relations between science and magical occultism may be briefly addressed. Science originates within the intellectual networks whose central concern has been philosophy, and is subject to many of its dynamics.

Empirical science throughout most of history has been a version of classificatory scholasticism: not so much as applied to texts (although it may be that too) but applied to natural observations, travelers' tales, collections of minerals and gems, and so on. Intellectual action and competition take the form of quantitative extension, much like what textual scholars do with their categories, but consisting now in accumulating facts and imposing rubrics upon them. As in the textual classificatory mode, the level of abstraction generally remains constant. Naturalistic treatises ranging from Pliny to Albertus Magnus have this shape; classificatory scholasticism continues after the "scientific revolution" adds another mode of doing science, both in the "cabinet of wonders" popular among aristocratic science buffs in the 1600s and 1700s, and in Linnaean-style taxonomic enterprises.

Naturalistic observations overlap with occultism, since the latter takes the form of correspondence schemes among the different realms of reality, including the natural world. Occultism too is a version of classificatory scholasticism, differing from the pure form, so to speak, by mixing concepts derived from intellectual abstraction with the concrete interests of lay audiences in applied magic.

The "scientific revolution" in Europe around 1600 changes not the naturalistic focus of traditional science but its social dynamics. I have called this dynamic rapid-discovery science (Chapter 10). By linking intellectual networks to genealogies of research equipment, a stream of new phenomena is produced on which theoretical interpretations may be constructed. Innovation and hence intellectual reputations no longer depend on moves in the abstraction-reflexivity sequence, as in philosophy, but on manipulating the forefront of research technology, the offspring of Galileo's telescope and Boyle's air pump.[7]

The question of occult influence in the scientific revolution arises because the takeoff of rapid-discovery science took place in the same networks which included an upsurge of interest in occultism: Paracelsus, Bruno, Kepler, and Newton are famous examples of the overlap. Occultism did not cause rapid-discovery science; the one is a mode of thought (and a long-standing traditional one at that), the other a reorganization in social practice and material possessions. In mathematics, where the rapid-discovery mode took off a generation or so before it did in physical science, the new "machinery" for setting up and manipulating equations was quite distinct from the methods of occultist numerology, which underwent no revolution.[8]

There is, however, a similarity in the social milieux which constituted both occultism and rapid-discovery science. Both brought together lay interests with the higher abstractions of the inwardly oriented arguments of the intellectual network. Rapid-discovery science emerged when a branch of the philosophical network fused with commercial and other practitioners who had been developing the genealogies of physical equipment such as lenses and pumps. Occultism is the use of higher abstraction schemes from the intellectual world as an invisible world of correspondences, by which practitioners appeal to lay interests in magical manipulation and prognostication. The late Renaissance–post-Reformation period, with its upheaval in the material bases of intellectual production and its cracking of religious-political legitimation schemes, promoted the reshuffling of networks in both these respects. Occultism did not cause the rapid-discovery scientific revolution, but there is an underlying resemblance in the causes of both.

The Epistemology-Metaphysics Sequence

We enter now the second of the major pathways of rising abstraction and reflexivity.

ASSERTIVE, DESCRIPTIVE, AND CRITICAL EPISTEMOLOGIES

The world ingredient cosmologies, especially in their early periods, are asserted, not argued for. They are left to carry the day by their impressiveness as striking imagery, and later by the comprehensiveness and coherence of the world vision that they offer. They are pre-epistemological. In disputes between rival positions, commonsense standards are relied on, along with rhetorical devices such as argument by analogy. It is much the same when philosophical argument begins on religious, ethical, or political issues rather than cosmological ones. When the acuteness of argument intensifies as the intergenerational chains of intellectual specialists lengthen, the subject of knowledge itself becomes a topic—a notch upward in the sequence of reflexivity. Here too the initial statements are dogmatic assertions about the proper form of knowledge. The early *Nyaya sutras* simply list the kinds of knowledge: sense perception, inference, analogy, textual authority. On a similar level is the first classification of types of knowledge by al-Baqillani (965 C.E.), about eight generations into the Islamic sequence. The Neo-Confucians declare that knowledge comes from the investigation of things, but the reasons why this should be the preferred form of knowledge are not articulated. Whenever a new epistemological direction emerges, it tends at first to be baldly asserted: Roger Bacon—after a period of acute discussion over knowledge of universals—propagandizes for experiment and experience by declaring that they bring complete certitude.

Assertive epistemologies may be elaborated into descriptive epistemologies. The nature of knowledge is described in an ontological or psychological mode. In India the Jainas regarded ignorance as a substance, a kind of dust clinging to the soul and obscuring its original purity of knowledge. The early Samkhya school held knowledge to be based on a beam carrying a physical impression from an object to the eye. Neoplatonists and Platonizing Aristoteleans, from late Greek antiquity through their medieval Islamic, Jewish, and Christian successors, treated knowledge descriptively as a realm of ideas emanating from God or the highest principle; taking this for granted, they debated instead whether the human intellect was part of a single world-soul. Logic emerged everywhere as a specialized kind of descriptive epistemology; on this turf a version of the scholastic classification game was pursued much as on the terrain of world ingredient ontologies.

None of these descriptive epistemologists raises critical questions about whether these forms of knowledge are indeed really knowledge. Critical epistemology arose in an antagonistic vein. In the Islamic world, it was forwarded by anti-rationalist Sufis or theological conservatives, such as al-Ghazali, who rejects the entire Greek corpus, along with the rational theology of Islamic *kalam,* by exposing their lack of epistemological foundations; and Ibn Taymiyah, who critiques syllogistic reasoning as empty because of its glib assumption of universal premises and self-evident propositions. The impulse to critical epistemology is episodic, rising at certain periods (e.g., the times of Socrates, Descartes, Kant) and often falling back into a further round of descriptive epistemology. Ibn Taymiyah's criticisms did not stick; despite the victory of theological conservatism, logic, almost alone of the Greek heritage, survived as a staple of the curriculum in the orthodox *madrasas*. Hume's acute epistemological standards were superseded in popular estimation for several generations thereafter by Scottish common-sense philosophy, which hypothesized a faculty of common sense (a descriptive epistemology) as if it were a solution to critical difficulties. Such retrogression in the level of epistemological analysis is common. It is obscured by the high prestige of epistemological questions in the twentieth century, and the resulting tendency to read the history of our classics selectively as a movement from one peak of critical epistemology to another.

The epistemology-metaphysics sequence is itself a version of the abstraction-reflexivity sequence. It is driven by the same general process of opposition within the intellectual attention space and reorganization at a higher level of abstraction. Critical epistemology is a higher order of reflexivity; it is second-order epistemology, structured by conscious reflection on the first-order knowledge methods of previous generations.

Epistemology entwines with successive levels of metaphysical abstraction. Critical epistemology is a highway to higher metaphysical schemes. The Sophists' controversy, culminating in Socrates and Plato explicitly formulating the question of standards of objective knowledge, soon resulted in the creation of new ontologies: Plato's universe of Forms, Aristotle's more complex mixture of Forms and the world ingredient cosmologies, along with several rival metaphysical systems. Similarly in India, the grander metaphysical abstractions, from the successive Buddhist systems through the Hindu Advaita and its dualist rivals, were produced with the tools of immediately preceding epistemological acuteness. Even in China, where the epistemology sequence did not get very far, the epistemological querying of the School of Names was soon followed by the appropriation of namelessness as an ontological category in the *Tao Te Ching*.

At times the development of epistemology threatens to bring metaphysics to a halt. Francis Bacon, setting knowledge on the path to empirical accumulation, aims to destroy philosophical abstraction. Bacon's is an asserted epistemology, not a critical one. Descartes sets up explicitly critical standards with a similar aim of replacing old philosophy with new science. Nevertheless, the result is not to end abstract philosophy but to underscore the separation of science and philosophy as distinct branches, and within philosophy to provide tools by which metaphysics undergoes a spectacular revival. We see this repeatedly. Modern Europe, where critical epistemologies become increasingly central, goes through a consequent series of new and esoteric metaphysical constructions. Kant, who makes the notion of "critical" philosophy and theory of knowledge central to the enterprise of philosophy, does not succeed in his avowed intention to fence off the sphere of forbidden speculation, but provides a tool by which Idealist constructions might proceed onto that terrain. Frege, who aims to clear up confusions by introducing a new and very general logical formalism, and Brentano, who proposes to induce logic from empirical psychology, are followed immediately by metaphysical constructions such as Meinong's realm of "subsistence" containing Golden Mountains and round circles, and Husserl's phenomenological hierarchy of essences and transcendental ego.

Russell's militancy in wielding the new logical tools illustrates a general process of the abstraction-reflexivity sequence. The brain-wracking paradoxes which he uncovers in the theory of sets are resolved by moving to the vantage point of a higher level of abstraction; the theory of types gives him a reflexive position from which to look down on the confusion among heterogeneous types of statements at the source of the contradictions. Nevertheless, Russell's new tools quickly become the grounds for constructing bizarre new metaphysical systems, such as Wittgenstein's *Tractatus*. It is not ironic for the antimetaphysical movement of logical positivism and analytical philosophy to be followed by a renewed outburst of metaphysics;[9] it is part of the normal epistemology-metaphysics sequence.

If epistemologies provide food for metaphysics, the reverse is also the case. Aquinas derives his epistemology from metaphysical assumptions; since humans cannot apprehend the angelic world of universals, their knowledge must proceed by way of particulars. Duns Scotus, attacking both the Augustinians' primacy of the knowledge of universals and Aquinas's primacy of knowledge of particulars, comes to the conclusion that the first knowledge is that of univocal being, beyond this division. Here epistemology fuses with ontology; critical questions of the bases of knowledge become inseparable from discussions of what exists.

In recycling back onto metaphysical terrain, epistemological critique tends to subside, and epistemology is pursued again in a descriptive vein. Locke's empiricism, with its attack on innate ideas and its studied distance from the uncritically asserted materialism of the corpuscular philosophy, comes out of the epistemological debates of the Cartesian network. Some followers treat this as a descriptive epistemology and seek the principles of knowledge concretely in empirical psychology. Locke's immediate successor, Berkeley, however, converts the same empiricist tools into an extreme Idealist metaphysics. Hume starts out along the more conventional Lockean route by attempting to build an empirical system of the human sciences, but is diverted into what for him are side-channels of epistemological conundrums. These in turn provide the puzzle space for Kant. The richness of modern European philosophy is this recurrent recycling between epistemology and metaphysics.

We have now to consider the causes of the epistemology-metaphysics sequence. Three analytically distinct, sometimes historically overlapping causes are discernible: (1) skepticism as a catalyst (among the classic counter-moves it provokes is the cogito); (2) the sheer intensity and continuity of debate, resulting in epistemological reflexivity; and (3) the epistemological tensions produced by anthropomorphic monotheism.

SKEPTICISM AS CATALYST

An early and recurrent form of contested epistemology occurs in the form of skepticism. One way in which this arises is that the intellectual attention space is overcrowded: multiple factions violate the upper limits of the law of small numbers, and there is a chaotic sense of lack of clear positions. Not only is there no agreement on what is true, but even the alternatives are muddy.[10]

Skepticism emerges in times of rapid expansion of the intellectual community at venues for multi-sided debate. Athens at the time of the Sophists, when all the networks converged and the level of competition over the originality of ideas was at its height, is one famous case. In the following generations, this skepticism was raised to the level of a school with Pyrrho and Timon. Another case is India in the late Upanishadic period, with the inchoate breakdown of Vedic schools and the multiple sects of the *shramanas*. Some critical positions deny karma, others deny morality. The Buddha's contemporary Sañjaya was a full-fledged skeptic, denying knowledge in general. Yet another parallel is China during the late Warring States, when centers such as the Chi-hsia Academy promoted a network of "the hundred schools." Specialists in debate appear who argue on both sides of a question; the style of paradoxical argument became famous from Hui Shih down through the *Tao Te Ching*. In the crucial founding periods for these three great regional traditions, the center of attention was disturbed by expounders of paradoxes and claims that truth does not exist.[11]

Militant skepticism proclaims the intellectual community as a whole a dead end. Nevertheless, skepticism arises only in an oppositional field of forces. It is striking that opponents are never convinced by skeptical arguments, nor derailed from continuing their positions. Skepticism is one faction among many within an array of oppositions; it is parasitical on its enemies, and dies out with them. The skepticism of Arcesilaus' Academy was tied to refutation of the Old Stoics, and disappeared with the changing doctrine of its opponents (Reale, 1985: 334).

Skepticism is a step in the sequence of oppositions driving toward higher levels of abstraction. The Greek Sophists were followed by the emergence of explicit epistemological standards with Socrates and Plato. The debating stance was institutionalized in a dialectical logic by the Megarian school, followed by the less contentious logic of the Aristoteleans and the Stoics. The epistemological concerns of Greek philosophy were kept alive by the continual presence and challenge of the Skeptics. In Greece, the strongest development of skeptical traditions goes along with the strongest of the ancient developments of epistemological argument.

In India, the omni-skeptical stance is put forward by Sañjaya. The response of the intellectual network, crystallized by Gautama Buddha, is not so much epistemology per se as a fusion of epistemology and ontology in the general conception that the world of ordinary objects is an illusion. Buddhism incorporates an extensive, but not unlimited, skepticism into its basic stance, directed against the material world and against any reification of absolute transcendence, and especially against the permanence of the self; but the karmic causal chain, and the religious pathway out of it, are not illusory. This doctrine of world illusion becomes the foil against which future generations of Indian philosophers, on both the Buddhist and Hindu sides, would develop more explicit epistemologies.

In China, the skepticism of the Warring States debaters is not very sharply formulated; we have no records of an omni-skeptical doctrine that truth does not exist. Nevertheless, in the latter part of this period we find the strongest development toward Chinese epistemology. This sequence is the high point for many centuries of the Chinese push toward higher abstraction. In these generations occur the sole development of Chinese logic, the Mohist *Canon*, which may be interpreted as a move to overcome the paradoxes of Hui Shih and the School of Names by more careful abstract statement. This epistemological standard is largely lost as the result of the dominant synthesis of Han Confucianism. A more enduring result is an epistemological-metaphysical fusion in the *Tao Te Ching* ontology of the Nameless. Unlike in India, where world illusion holds up an explicitly epistemological criterion, Taoist namelessness proclaims not the non-truthfulness of ordinary objects, but only the futility of articulating them. Implicitly it is a statement of the end of epistemological debate, and of the abstraction sequence in Chinese philosophy generally.

The initial appearance of skepticism in all these world arenas occurs in situations where the intellectual attention space first undergoes a crisis of overcrowding. Thereafter, as the networks accumulate concepts on a higher level of abstraction, skepticism is periodically revived, sometimes in its classic guise of "a plague on all houses," but sometimes deliberately invoked as a surgical tool by those who wish to separate their own brand of truth from the accretions of the field. In Hellenistic Greece and the "Second Sophistic" of competing rhetors in the Roman Empire, skepticism is an institutionalized school, counterpart to the morass of the Middle Platonist syncretisms, while the seeming imperviousness of Stoicism and Epicureanism to resolving their debates reinforces the mood that there can be no agreement on knowledge. In the later centuries of medieval Christendom, the endless and unconvincing debates of Thomists and Scotists feed an increasingly critical mood among the nominalists. The mood intensifies by the late 1500s, with the piling of position on position as Renaissance Humanists revive ancient philosophies; the result is another period in which the law of small numbers does not structure attention and the energy of intellectual life flows in no clear channels. External political conditions compound the situation; the splits and subsplits among Lutheran, Calvinist, and sectarian Protestantism, and the machinations of secular lords between these and Counterreformation Catholicism, add up to a vast intellectual weariness of debate, which provides the setting in which Montaigne, Sanchez, and Charron appear. In our own times, the massive expansion of the university professoriate resulting from the inflationary educational marketplace from the 1960s onward has brought about the reappearance of skepticism in the relativistic anti-foundationalism of cultural historicists and postmodernists.

These are the skepticisms of overcrowding the attention space. Other conditions give rise to less encompassing uses of skeptical tools. One is a fideist use of skeptical arguments, not as omni-skepticism but to counterattack the critics of religious tradition. Here we find Catholics using skeptical arguments to undermine Protestant reformers' reliance on the Bible; Christian conservatives undercutting scientific materialism or sensory empiricism; or again Jacobi defending scriptural faith against Kantian Idealism. Once the skeptical argument is prominently advanced in the attention space, it can be used in later generations for various, more limited purposes, in combination with the main doctrines of other factions in the field. The most striking of such uses of skepticism is the cogito.

RECURRENCE OF THE COGITO

The "cogito ergo sum" is a dialectical move, building on omni-skepticism to establish a criterion of knowledge and hence a critical epistemology; by applying skepticism to itself, one establishes what cannot be doubted. The cogito is a classic example of an upward step in the reflexivity hierarchy. Some of the greatest figures in the histories of their respective traditions—Augustine, Shankara, Ibn Sina, Descartes, Fichte—made use of the cogito; that is to say, great reputations were made thereby as the result of opening up a new expanse of the abstraction-reflexivity sequence.[12]

Augustine wrote in the late 300s C.E., in the generation of the Christian "Fathers of the Church," when its doctrines were definitively codified. As a professional teacher of rhetoric, a convert from the last pagan profession, Augustine was in a position to ground Christian doctrine in the accumulated sophistication of the philosophical networks. Skepticism, however, was a long-standing position in Greek philosophy, going back some 20 generations. So why should the cogito maneuver appear now for the first time? The defense that skepticism undermines itself, that the doubter cannot doubt his own doubt, had been urged by opponents since the early period of this school; and indeed it had been incorporated into the sophisticated skepticism of Aenesidemus (ca. 65 B.C.E.), the position that the skeptic withholds judgment on everything, even on skepticism itself. In this lineup of intellectual factions, the arguments and counter-arguments leave the field static; the skeptics find a way to hold to their basic position, and anti-skeptics find reasons to their own satisfaction for rejecting skepticism and continuing with their systems.

Augustine was motivated to do something else: he adopted skepticism to clear the ground of rival philosophies, then built upon it a secure system of his own—in this case to show that Christian doctrine is the superior of pagan philosophies, by their own best criterion. Doubt extinguishes everything but one great truth, the existence of the doubter. The self which is thereby proven—the very awareness which receives this realization—is illuminated by the clear light of consciousness, and this transcendent standard comes from God. Augustine became father to the many versions of Christian Neoplatonism which were to dominate down to the High Middle Ages and even beyond; he also established a tradition of critical epistemology with which the most intense standards of argument had henceforth to contend.

In the Islamic networks, skepticism appears relatively late; the political power of religion allows no true omni-skepticism, and what does appear is the fideist skepticism put forward by al-Ghazali (ca. 1065 C.E.), rejecting Greek-oriented *falsafa* (the Arabic translation of "philosophy") and the rational theology of Islamic *kalam* to bolster the rising third party, Sufism. Here the Islamic cogito appears several generations before skepticism rather than in response to it. The matrix is the formation, in the early 900s, of a full-fledged array of philosophical positions: rationalistic *kalam* is confronted with Greek *falsafa*; Arab-Islamic nationalism is growing, and tolerance of non-Islamic religions is disappearing in a wave of campaigns for religious conversion. In the Ash'arite school, which blends *kalam* with the more conservative theological tendencies, the codifier of doctrine al-Baqillani (late 900s) systematizes, in a scholastic manner, the various sources of knowledge. Among others he lists knowledge of self, which he notes cannot be doubted. This is not yet a critical epistemology, and it is not based in confrontation with skepticism; knowledge from the senses and from reports of other persons is listed on the same level with al-Baqillani's cogito.

In the next generation concern for epistemology is invoked in a much more consequent way by Ibn Sina. He is fully aware of the external pressures building up against imported Greek philosophy. Ibn Sina's fame-making project is to amalgamate this alien heritage with the key dispute within Islamic rational theology, the relation between God's creative power and the fleeting substances of the world. Ibn Sina's cogito is a move to sharpen the sheer contingency of created being, and thereby to produce a proof of God at hitherto unknown levels of philosophical abstraction and reflexivity. Ibn Sina's thought experiment of a man flying in the dark, doubtful of everything about the bodily world, is designed to show that being itself is always known, even if there is doubt as to what kind of being it is. This sets the stage for Ibn Sina's distinctions among the sub-types of necessary, possible, and contingent being, leading to a proof of God as being purely necessary in itself alone.

The case of Ibn Sina shows that the systematic use of doubt can be deliberately fostered in the clashes of intellectual life in order to uncover new levels of abstraction. Until the revival of Aristotle in the mid-1200s, Augustine and Ibn Sina (under the name Avicenna) were the two most influential imports in medieval Christian philosophy. This is not surprising, given that they form the two high points of the dominant Neoplatonic tradition, honed to epistemological acuteness by hostile confrontation with militant monotheism. Ibn Sina's use of doubt would be emulated even after the triumph of Christian Aristoteleanism; Duns Scotus drives beyond both Aquinas and Avicenna to yet higher levels of metaphysical abstraction by pointing to univocal being, that which we conceive of even if we are in doubt as to whether it is existence or essence.

Generally speaking, the rationalistic lines of Islamic and Christian philosophy have no use for omni-skepticism; Duns Scotus's use of doubt is quite limited and specific. A full-blown skepticism, together with the cogito, does appear with the outburst of the nominalist movement in the 1300s. Here the situation is more like the classic conditions for skepticism as a plague on all houses, which typically arises when the attention space is crowded, and the lines of rivalry have become set and show no sign of going away. Jean of Mirecourt, in the height of the action at Paris in the 1340s, takes to an extreme the nominalist tactic of undercutting Thomist and Scotist positions, and indeed any rational propositions of theology. Mirecourt hits on the cogito, but as a residual, the one item of knowledge that is secure because it passes the test of resisting self-contradiction. Mirecourt was an offbeat character in medieval Christian philosophy; his books were burned, and his doctrine was without influence. Here the cogito acquires no fame because it has no system-generating consequences. Mirecourt's use is purely destructive.

In India, Shankara established a dominant reputation for the entire period of post-Buddhist philosophy by a constructive use of the cogito. His is a full-fledged use of omni-skepticism, to clear the decks of all worldly knowledge.

Then: doubt proves the existence of the doubter and of a luminous ground of consciousness; this is the highest reality, beyond dualism and its opposite as well. There had been no tradition of omni-skepticism in Indian philosophy for a very long time (since Sañjaya in the generation before the Buddha), and Shankara was not reviving its memory. But this is not quite a case of Shankara creating both the skepticism and the cogito which overcomes it at the same time. He has two key ingredients in his network of antecedents: the debates among his immediate masters in the Mimamsa school of realists, who had raised an acute question of epistemological standards and the necessary role of consciousness in knowledge, and the entire Buddhist tradition, which had held the Idealist side of the field that Shankara now took over for Hindu philosophy. Buddhist philosophy had incorporated an institutionalized skepticism about the world of name-and-form, extending even to the emphasis that nirvana should not be reified. Shankara could use the heritage of this skepticism to overthrow the worldly-sensory realism which was widespread among the other Hindu *darshanas*. At the same time, a cogito move was attractive to him because the non-existence of the self was one central item of Buddhist dogma. A proof of the self as the pathway to the highest reality enabled Shankara to keep himself orthodoxly non-Buddhist while appropriating Buddhist turf and building a Hindu Idealism.

The cogito as a system-founding move allows various kinds of edifices to be constructed upon it. Augustine, Ibn Sina, and Shankara used it to ground Idealism. Descartes used the cogito so that he could clear away scholastic philosophy and the Humanists' revival of the Greeks alike, trumpeting a fresh start for the new science with an ontology of extended substance. In this case, Descartes emerged from a network where skepticism already flourished; he is only a few links away from Montaigne, who used skepticism to urge disengagement from the polemics of the religious wars. Descartes's own teacher, Veron, was a Catholic fideist who used skeptical arguments against Protestant reliance on the Bible. For those of us educated in the tradition of modern European philosophy, Descartes's is *the* famous cogito, because the system-generating tasks for which he used it, and the multifarious branches which followed, constitute the framework within which we think.

The importance of the system-building trajectory is made plain in the aftermath. Descartes's philosophy was construed both broadly and narrowly, the latter by specific Cartesian and anti-Cartesian movement. Descartes's cogito was the topic of dispute among these circles in the 1670s; opponents raised issues such as whether the cogito itself means anything more than "I thought, therefore I think I was." Despite this acuteness, Huet and Régis are minor figures in their long-term influence; criticism in the absence of constructive alternatives does nothing to open up further developments of the attention space.

Yet among the most powerful tactics in setting off new intellectual movements are broadenings of the cogito approach. Kant's transcendental method of searching for the necessary grounds implied in any judgment is a generalization of Descartes's self-limiting doubt. Fichte's version drops out the Cartesian step of proving the existence of the empirical self; the most undeniable proposition A = A implies a permanent self for which it is true. By a series of similar steps, Fichte derives the existence of the external world and the unfolding of a dialectic in which self-undermining statements lead onward to the elaboration of the whole system. Two generations later, when Idealism appears in the American universities, Royce formulates a version of the cogito which combines the Cartesian and Fichtean moves: the existence of error implies the existence of a standard in terms of which it is error; to doubt something implies that there is something which is apprehended in some way, by a deeper self beyond our momentary consciousness. Kant and Royce did not spring up in situations where skepticism was a significant living faction in the intellectual world; both invoked skepticism because they had uses for it in constructing their own systems.[13] If skepticism did not exist, it would have had to be invented. As it happens, they went looking for what sources of skepticism they could find.

The fame of the Cartesian cogito gave rise to a number of adaptations in France, where Descartes became nationalistically enshrined in the educational curriculum. Maine de Biran (ca. 1815) substitutes the formulation "I will, therefore I am." This is not an argument from the self-limitation of skepticism, but a means of breaking free from the empirical associationist psychology until then dominant in France. Invoking Hume, Maine holds that external sensations give no necessary causal connections; it is the inner experience of will overcoming resistance that reveals the immediate certainty of causality. A more explicit analogy to Cartesian omni-skepticism is Camus's existentialism (ca. 1940–1950), which transfers the cogito from epistemology to the sphere of values. In his dramatized language, the only fundamental issue is suicide, because this calls into question all values of living. But the very impulse to nihilism reveals its limits: I reject the world as meaningless; therefore a standard of meaning exists. Breaking through to the social dimension, Camus goes on: I rebel, therefore we, a moral community, exist.

The cogito is found in many world networks but not all. There is no famous use of the cogito in China; this is not surprising, given the fact that its networks did not progress very far in the epistemology-metaphysics sequence. Nor do we find the cogito in Greek philosophy (at least as far as we know, which is to say that it never made an important part of the attention space); it occurs only with Augustine, at the very end, about 1,000 years (30 generations) after Thales. In India there is no notable use of the cogito during the time span that corresponds to the Greek networks; if we count from the time of the Upanishadic world ingredient philosophers, Shankara appears in about the fortieth generation. This is somewhat later than Augustine but on a par with Ibn Sina, insofar as we count Islamic *falsafa* as a continuation of the Greek network. The cogito is a development fairly deep into the medieval segment of the sequence, which is not to say it became outdated thereafter; the sophisticated abstractions attained in medieval religious garb became permanent acquisitions for later secularist versions.

A thoroughgoing omni-skepticism is a deep trouble, the counterpart to the regulative ideal, the most central sacred object of intellectual life, the ideal of absolute truth.[14] That is why skepticism is repeatedly revived, even though hardly anyone is ever convinced by it. The "great philosophers" are those who find a variant on the same reflexive deep troubles; hence the kinship in the solutions which they pose to them, even though these too are not uniform, but fall into the oppositional pattern characteristic of intellectual space.

LONG-TERM FRACTIONATION OVER THE CATEGORIES OF REALITY

Over the long term, the major intellectual driving force is the dynamics of organizationally sustained debate. Factions which keep their identities during many generations of argument become locked into a long dance step with one another; increasingly impervious to outside influences and turned inward upon their mutually constituted argumentative identities, they drive the collective conscience of the intellectual attention space repeatedly to new heights of abstract self-reflection. To illustrate how this unfolds the epistemology-metaphysics sequence, let us sketch the sequence in India.

The Indian Sequence. We can distinguish five periods:

1. *From about 700 to 400 B.C.E., the breaking apart of the Vedic schools into multi-sided competition among Upanishadic and heterodox sages.* The intellectual content consists in rival claims as to the cosmological ingredients underlying the visible world. At the end of this period, Buddhism becomes the dominant school. The Buddha's winning stroke is to explain that the seeming permanence of objects and of the self are transitory aggregates, and to identify spiritual liberation with detachment from the illusory. The strand of skepticism which had emerged in the overcrowded attention space is incorporated into the Buddhist synthesis as an intellectual motivation to detach oneself from the world through meditation. The dominance of Buddhism during the formative period of Indian abstract philosophy made Sañjaya's skepticism into its ruling frame; with the external decline of Buddhism, Advaita took over its basic stance for the Hindu side.

From the point of view of Western thought, the premise that the world is an illusion tends to reduce Indian philosophy to merely sectarian or historical interest. To approach Indian philosophy in this way is to miss its technical sophistication, which is transposable outside the religious frame. The same can be said about medieval Islamic and Christian philosophy, where the concept of God is not merely a matter of dogma; it is philosophically fruitful because it operates as an epistemological ideal (perfect knowledge), and an ideal of metaphysical ultimates (infinite causal power, ultimate ontological foundation, and so on).

In the dominant Buddhist and Hindu schools, the critique of illusion holds prestige as the path to higher religious insight. This is also the driving force of the epistemology-metaphysics sequence in Indian philosophy. The premise of world illusion is the basic challenge, the locus of arguments. It can be regarded as an institutionalized skepticism about the reality of objects. At first discussion concerns the underlying ingredients which undercut surface appearances; subsequent debate goes on to critique the reality of the ingredients as well. Indian realists, Idealists, and those who held that metaphysical ultimates are inexpressible all had to deal with the challenge of this institutionalized skepticism, this perennially available weapon wielded against any assertions whatever. An assertion as to the reality of *anything* could always be met by the charge that it was a move away from religious enlightenment.

Freed from the religious animus—and there were times, especially at the height of cosmopolitan debates, when philosophers seemed only nominally religious—the same skeptical claim held up an abstract standard as to how the philosophical game would be played. In point of fact, considerable portions of Indian philosophy have *not* regarded the world in general as illusory. All of the Hindu *darshanas* before the rise of Advaita non-dualism rested valid knowledge on sensory perception of material objects. The *Abhidharma* wing of Buddhist philosophers also generally accepted various world elements as real, denying only the mentally imposed reifications of permanent objects and of the self—a position which is not so different from that of a modern physicist. Even after Shankara, Advaita opponents flourished by taking their stand on the reality of the world. Intellectual life plays out by oppositions. The world illusion issue in the Indian debates meant that realist positions too would be explicated with epistemological sharpness.

The question of illusion required all of Indian philosophy to grapple with epistemology. That is why, once we abstract it from its religious garb, Indian philosophy is so rich in the themes that characterize the deepest puzzles of the Greek-Christian-European sequence.

2. *From about 400 B.C.E. to 200 C.E., the philosophical splits among Buddhist sects, culminating with the rise of Mahayana and Nagarjuna's dialectical negation.* Extending the time period to about 350 C.E., still keeping within the unfolding of Buddhist sectarian rivalries, we can include the rise of Yogacara, making Buddhism a full-fledged idealism.

It will be convenient to combine this period with the next.

3. *From about 100 to 500 C.E., the growth of the main Hindu darshanas (Nyaya, Vaisheshika, Samkhya, Yoga, Mimamsa, all except late-blooming Advaita);* this is also the time of Buddhist-Hindu confrontation, the debates across a now-unified attention space.

Several explicitly epistemological-metaphysical themes now become the object of debate. Typically the issue is raised first between the Buddhist sects, then crops up within the Hindu *darshanas,* through confrontations that drive initially inchoate schools of thought into increasingly polarized positions on philosophical turf.

Nominalism and *realism, universals* and *particulars* arose as issues among the early Buddhist schools. How do the lists of world ingredients in the *Abhidharma* compilations stand the test of illusion? The Sarvastivada, the "everything-exists-theory," holds that all the *dharma* elements are real, by warrant of the intentionality of consciousness: the mind never has a true cognition without an object. The Sarvastivadins' debating partners, the Sautrantikas, pointed to an inconsistency in treating non-concrete categories on the same level as material substances; they supported a nominalism of abstract categories on a non-referential aspect of mind. As the notion of universals emerged, other Buddhist schools attacked it, declaring that the only reals are particulars, indeed the inexpressible suchness *(tathata)* which was to become a hallmark of certain forms of Buddhist mysticism. Carrying this argument to an extreme, Nagarjuna held that all *dharmas* (world constituents) are void; none contains any self-essence at all.

The Hindu schools crystallized on a similar level of abstraction. The Nyaya school of logic took a nominalist stance, holding the conventionalism of world meanings. The Vaisheshika category scheme lists substance and quality, plus a hierarchy of universals and particulars of various levels of generality paralleling Aristotle's genera and species. Now debate with the Buddhists kicked in, raising critical questions: How can bare substances exist without any qualities? How can there be relations between substances and their qualities without an infinite regress of intermediating connectors? By around 550, the Nyaya-Vaisheshika alliance had backed off from early nominalism and was taking a stance of increasingly intransigent realism: relations are real; relations among relations are real; even non-existence is real. Debate was polarizing into positions of world illusion and pluralist realism.

Causality and *potentiality* became sites of argument over the reality and plurality of substance. Nagarjuna had pointed up the problem by defining the real as that which is causally efficacious. Therefore, since everything is linked in a chain of causes, nothing is independently real, possessing its own nature. There are no universals and no substance. Out of this stance the Yogacara school propounded a full-fledged Idealism: what appear to be world objects are supplied by the mind, which imposes the relation of externality on subjective ideas.

Parallel problems over causality arose on the Hindu side. Samkhya was hit by Buddhist criticism of conundrums in its dualistic metaphysics. If a material world substance is posited, along with a pure detached witness consciousness looking down upon it, how are these separate and distinct substances related? Samkhya seems to have made repairs by making the witness consciousness ever more detached, and incorporating the empirical and dynamic aspects of mind in the material substance. Critics attacked this too: If substance is permanent and at rest, why does it ever set itself in motion? This is equivalent to the deep trouble uncovered by Parmenides, the turning point to higher abstraction in Greek philosophy. Samkhya responded with a solution parallel to Aristotle's: substance includes latency or potentiality; the world substance periodically extrudes the visible world, like a tortoise putting out its claws.

A deep trouble locates a fruitful spot, where layers of debate build up. These arguments echo throughout Indian philosophy. Positions are taken on the side of *satkaryavada,* which holds that the effect preexists in the material cause, and *asatkaryavada*—that causes and effects are distinct entities, and these cannot be connected, because that would reduce one substance to another. The Vaisheshika pluralists took the latter position, holding that latency does not exist, and that new combinations of ingredients lead to completely new entities. The division cropped up on the Buddhist side as well: an early inter-sectarian dispute was whether past, present, and future exist independently, or whether all are contained in the earlier existent. Nagarjuna eliminated time and substance entirely, opting in effect for monism, whereas Yogacara Idealism held that all plurality derives from seeds of potentiality in the storehouse consciousness. Later, after the big realignment of positions removing both Samkhya and Buddhism from the field, Advaita ("non-dualism") took over the Samkhya *satkaryavada* stance (effects preexist in the cause), eliminating the embarrassment of dual substances and elevating Parmenidean immutability to a purer monism. Debate did not end here; the deep troubles of plurality and change were exploited repeatedly in each subsequent round of Indian philosophical creativity. The same deep troubles were exploited in the West: Spinoza and Leibniz, later Bradley and Russell, worked through the facets of the *satkaryavada* puzzle; the occasionalist question, raised both in Islamic theology and in post-Cartesian Europe, is another variant on the plurality of substances problem.

4. *The height of the Buddhist-Hindu confrontation, when their networks cross and their positions mix and transform (500–800 C.E.).* The deep troubles of the previous generations are recombined. Again the nominalism versus universals controversy provides fertile grounds. Bhartrihari—a cosmopolitan

Hindu in the Buddhist camp—attacked Nyaya-Vaisheshika pluralist realism and its identification of each word with a self-subsistent reality. Rather, he held, there is a transcendent unit of meaning behind the spoken word; words make merely artificial distinctions within a wordless, undifferentiated reality. Bhartrihari was a professional grammarian, for whom language was no mere collection of names but a processual system. Combining grammar with a primal religious ground, Bhartrihari depicts the world as constituted by Brahman speaking, introducing differentiation into the undifferentiated; time emerges in the eternal through grammatical tenses. Expanding far beyond static nominalism, grammar is ontologized. Bhartrihari's language-centered philosophy contrasts with the Platonic emanation of the world from Forms in the highest One. In the case of the Greeks, the technical inspiration comes from geometry, thereby giving a static and eternal image of the Forms, whereas Bhartrihari's model is based on syntax, giving a dynamic slant to the formal aspect of reality while his religious motivation is to identify language with world illusion.

Bhartrihari was followed up on the Buddhist side by Dignaga, who continued the attack on the realist and sensory epistemologies of the Hindu schools. Sense perception is always of particulars; names are universals, and universals do not exist. Dignaga continued to defend Buddhist turf, dissolving the reality of ordinary objects by revealing them as mere "name-and-form." Language is the source of illusion, making permanences out of evanescent particulars. Dignaga introduced negation as the central process of world construction. Concepts are universals, encompassing all their instances; but the all can never be shown. Hence words only demarcate one thing from another by negation; a cow is at best a "not-not-cow." The undifferentiated unity of reality is divided into illusory concretenesses by the negation inherent in verbal thought.[15]

The last great Buddhist philosopher, Dharmakirti, combines themes from Nagarjuna and Dignaga into an epistemological-metaphysical synthesis. Reality is that which is causally efficacious. Entities are differentiations imposed by the mind, and are unreal because the causal chain cannot be broken into bits. The world really exists and is not constructed by the mind, but it is not to be identified with ordinary objects, which are mental constructs. Dharmakirti uses a variant of the argument against the reality of relations (something like Leibniz's labyrinth of the continuum) to arrive at a position which parallels Kant's inconceivable thing-in-itself; but the ontological emphasis is shifted, in the Buddhist point of view, to deny any validity to the categories of the understanding. Time and space are unreal; the categories are the source of illusion.

On the Hindu side of the field, upgrading to a high level of abstraction and reflexivity came about as a previously ultra-conservative school, the Mimamsa, entered the debates. Mimamsa defended the old Vedic rituals against the newer meditative and theist religions. In order to explain how rituals could have magical effects—and simultaneously to deny the efficacy of any other religious practice—around 600 c.e. the Mimamsa philosophers formulated a magical-religious version of the causality argument, holding that each person has a soul substance, which accumulates karmic potentialities through ritual action. This led the Mimamsa leaders onto the territory of current debates over the nature of substance. Kumarila held that abstractions are real; negation, made central by Dharmakirti, is itself a real entity. A dissident in the Mimamsa camp, Prabhakara held that reality is always positive, and negation is not ontological but only a logical inference; there is no negation in general, but only of particulars. From these discussions Indian philosophy broke into the territory of critical epistemology.

Like other Indian schools, Mimsaka accepted sensory perception as a valid source of knowledge; since the school was concerned to show that long-distance causal processes (such as the accumulation of karma) are also valid, it became an important issue to show how errors in perception occur. The general issue of validity was explicitly raised: since everything is known through consciousness, there is no criterion of valid knowledge outside of consciousness. Prabhakara held that a perceptual illusion (mistaking a coiled rope for a snake) shows not that perceptual consciousness is false, but only that one's second look (seeing the rope) reveals that the first look (seeing the snake) was not a simple perception but the intrusion of memories or inferences. The validity of cognition cannot be undermined, as its validity is given only by itself. (A version of the argument was later used by G. E. Moore against the abstract entities postulated by the logical formalists as in Russell's mathematical set theory or Wittgenstein's *Tractatus*.) Kumarila by contrast held that perceptual error comes from the imposition of a non-presence (a snake-memory) on a reality (the rope); since negations are also real, even errors are perceptions of reality, leaving to be specified only what form the reality takes.

Debate between Prabhakara and Kumarila led to the formulation of an Indian version of "cogito ergo sum." The former held that the "I" is subject, never an object, and thus cannot be the object of knowledge. The latter held that the "I" emerges from inference, and thus is a valid form of knowledge. Reflexivity becomes an explicit topic. Shankara now turns the Mimamsa maneuvers in defense of worldly realism into a pathway to secure a transcendent reality. Taking over Prabhakara's self-validity of cognitive experience, he notes that even doubt over reality implies a ground from which the doubt is formulated; this self-luminescent ground at the root of consciousness is behind all differentiations of worldly experience.

Shankara's cogito opens up simultaneously a new metaphysics and an epistemology. The ground of consciousness is the highest metaphysical and religious reality. Adopting the position that the effect preexists in the cause (i.e., following Nagarjuna and Dharmakirti in opposing a plurality of causally efficacious substances), Shankara holds that the Absolute is undifferentiated from the world. We cannot say that the world holds any duality. But what of the duality of the Absolute vis-à-vis the ordinary world of experience? Shankara elaborates an epistemology of levels of truth. Nagarjuna, encountering the problem from the point of view of his omni-skepticism, had called his own position a theory of no-theory. To put it another way, there is two-fold truth: the worldly level on which arguments are made, and the level of ultimate reality, which is inexpressible. Shankara elaborates this into three-fold levels: the inexpressible Absolute, about which we can only say that it is non-dual; the ordinary world, which is an illusion only from the standpoint of the Absolute; and finally the level of perceptual errors (snakes which are really ropes), as seen from the worldly standpoint.

5. *From 800 C.E. through the 1500s: the post-Buddhist period of debates among the victorious Hindu schools.* This is the most neglected period of Indian philosophy, with a reputation for religious sectarianism and anti-rational bhakti faith. The sectarian trend was real enough; during a time when European networks were separating theology from philosophy and then undergoing radical secularization, Indian philosophy was increasingly absorbed into disputes on behalf of particularistic theological positions. After 1600 a "lumpy syncretism" sets in, in opposition to Muslim conquerors and European colonialists, amalgamating every position under the banner of a bhaktized Advaita aconceptualism. Nevertheless, down through the 1300s at least, intellectual competition among the schools remains sharp. Even when new theist cults are established, they usually advertise their presence in the attention space by disputing the metaphysical tenets of their established rivals. For a while the shift toward sectarianism acts as a series of shocks to the external base, stimulating philosophical creativity. If we take the pains to seek it out beneath the theological trappings, we find in this period the mature phase of Indian philosophy, its highest level of acuteness of the epistemology-metaphysics sequence.

In the Advaita camp, Shri Harsha and Chitsukha took the offensive against realists, mustering arguments paralleling Berkeley, Hume, and Kant. There can be no knowledge of an object apart from the act of knowing it; to assume independent reality lands one in the contradiction of knowing before one knows. Substances are never perceived, but only qualities; yet how can qualities act upon one another? There followed an argument made famous in the West by Bradley: substance and quality cannot be related, since the relations of any relation to its terms leads to an infinite regress. All concepts—being, cause, relation, quality—lead to contradictions. Chitsukha embraced solipsism, since the self is the only item not reduced to illusion. Later, in the 1500s, Prakashananda formulated Advaita as a Berkeleyesque subjectivism, in which objects come into existence only when they are perceived.

The Advaita opponents responded by extending the heritage of disputes over nominalism and realism. Shri Harsha's anti-conceptualism rested on destruction of categories, that is, of universals; Madhva countered that everything, even God, is particular. The basic feature of reality is the power of everything to be itself, paralleling Duns Scotus's *haecceitas* formulated in the medieval Christian debate over universal and particular being. Madhva asserted that the universals of non-transient entities are themselves transient, elevating particularism to the highest ontological level. Again this parallels the position of Scotus and Ockham, that universals are only a filter through which limited human consciousness sees the world; the perfect epistemological standpoint, God, sees everything in its particularity.

Other Indian philosophers rang a series of changes on the tensions within the concept of fundamental substance, here formulated as God or the world ground. Ramanuja invoked the epistemological arguments that inner experience is self-validating, and that consciousness always intends an object, concluding that consciousness always involves a real plurality. The one reality, Brahman, includes plurality as the relation between substance and its attributes. Nimbarka responded that duality cannot be an attribute of non-duality because attributes distinguish a substance from other substances, yet only one substance exists. His solution is a version of Spinoza's dual-aspect monism, transposed from mental and material into a self-identical aspect and an energizing-potentiality aspect.

The apex of Indian philosophy around 1100–1300, including Shri Harsha, Chitsukha, Ramanuja, Madhva, and Nimbarka, includes many points parallel to European thought from Duns Scotus through Spinoza, Leibniz, Berkeley, Hume, Kant, Idealists such as Bradley, even Bergson and Heidegger—a period from about 1200 to 1900.[16] Obviously there is no strict parallel in the unfolding of these arguments in chronological sequence. This is only to be expected, since there are multiple social causes of ideas, and different combinations of internal oppositions and external shocks occurred in India and Europe. Some of the sequence of external causes were running in reverse: European intellectual life was becoming more secularized, India more absorbed in sectarian religion; hence the territory of Idealism, which is a halfway house between universalistic and particularistic religious stances, was traversed in different directions. What we see is a complex of ideas on the same general level of abstraction and reflexivity, which are shared out among the opposing intellectual factions in the network.

Nominalism versus Realism of Universals. Certain topics emerge in every world network during the epistemology-metaphysics sequence. The issue of universals arises early in both India and Greece, as soon as the cosmology sequence has been upgraded to abstract consideration of epistemology. In China, too, where the epistemology-metaphysics sequence does not get very far, the School of Names at the climax of the intense debates during the ancient Warring States appears to raise the nominalist-realist issue for a brief period. To postulate universals is explicitly to recognize abstraction; thus it is not surprising that the topic should arise virtually everywhere as one of the first metaphysical questions. For how many generations debate continues on this territory varies considerably, owing to external social conditions.

In India, universals are formulated noncontroversially as an item in the Buddhist *Abhidharma* lists. Debate arose as abstract entities were attacked within the Buddhist schools, first as nominal, then by an argument for radical particularism: that the "suchness" of reality is inexpressible. The attack on universals occurs repeatedly down through the medieval period of Indian philosophy. As the attention space was divided between Buddhist and Hindu schools, the former staked its turf ever more sharply on the destruction of any realist position, including mild ones encompassing both universals and particulars. The Hindu schools played their part in the polarization by taking increasingly intransigeant stances, reifying virtually every new abstraction as it was discovered. After Buddhism disappeared and its cultural capital was re-divided on the Hindu side, the theological disputes between Advaita and the theist schools resurrected the issue of universals and particulars as tools for arguing over the tensions inherent in the concept of a single highest substance.

In Greek philosophy, the concept of universals emerges early, but opposition to it is neither very prolonged nor radical. The limited nominalism of the Sophists was directed not against concepts in general, but against the more specific concepts of the ethical virtues. This debate catalyzed Plato to formulate the very general concept of abstract Form. Antisthenes and his successors the Cynics for a while opposed universal forms with a version of nominalism, but more generally from distrust of all intellectual constructions; these schools faded away into skepticism, holding no doctrines at all. Aristotle's compromise arranged a hierarchy of generality from the most encompassing universal down through those of more limited scope to concrete particulars, and identified particular beings with primary substance, universals with secondary substance which cannot exist apart from particulars.

The question as to the relative reality of one pole or the other becomes moot in the Hellenistic period. Aristoteleanism was generally absorbed into the Middle Platonist systems, which identified the hierarchy of abstraction with the cosmology of emanations from the highest universal to the lowest particular. In the Neoplatonism of late antiquity, the reality status of the bottom sensory realm was so low that it was barely regarded as having any being at all. Plotinus formulated a new level at the top of the hierarchy, above the highest Form of the Middle Platonists, transcending intellect and being. This was the first philosophical Greek mysticism in the sense of Buddhist radical ineffability; but the mystical ground was still the fount from which emanate the Forms. Universals continued to be regarded as the closest approach to the religious peak, the opposite of the Buddhist view of universals as the source of worldly illusion.

Here we see how important Christianity is in changing the direction of Western philosophy. The challenge to Neoplatonism mounted by Christianity tended to break the identification of universals with reality, opening the way to the nominalism-realism debate. We see a first flurry at the end of the pagan era, when Christian thinkers emphasized the concrete reality of the material world and Jesus' incarnation, and rejected the purely intellectual conception of salvation in pagan Neoplatonism. Aristoteleanism, which in its original form provided at least a moderate opposition to the dominance of Platonic universals, was revived, and questions of the relative standing of universals and particulars was raised, first by Alexander of Aphrodisias (ca. 200 C.E.), then most influentially in Boethius's textbook (about 510).

With the collapse of literate culture at the end of the Roman Empire, the Neoplatonic amalgamation of Plato and Aristotle sweeps over Christian philosophy. The reviving waves of learning in the Christian Middle Ages reopened the tensions. The first debates we hear about in the Carolingian period were disputes between mild nominalism and extreme realism of universals. Again after a decline in external conditions, when intellectual life came alive after 1000, the wandering debaters (Lanfranc, Berengar, Roscelin, the immediate predecessors of Anselm and Abelard) established their turf on the question of nominalism and universals; these debates culminated with Abelard, who proposed a compromise doctrine ("conceptualism") giving a more complex version of the epistemological process of formulating abstractions.

Then Christian philosophy switches gears. The nominalism-realism debate was the field warming up; now the level of abstraction was pushed upward to more elaborate metaphysical systems. Since these mostly built on Neoplatonic materials, universals became predominant again for three generations, and nominalism dropped out. This had nothing to do with the external pressures of Christian doctrine. Some nominalists got into heresy trouble for interpreting the three Persons of the Trinity as merely nominal, but so did their opponents who treated the Trinity as three abstract reals. The nominalism-realism dispute was driven by purely internal dynamics of intellectual networks. When the issue reemerged, it was because conflicts over metaphysical turf had come to the point of pushing beyond Neoplatonism.

Aquinas disowns the implication that salvation occurs through the intellect by participation in the sphere of general ideas. He leaves intact the hierarchy of spheres of abstraction, but undercuts their importance by separating onto-logical and epistemological grounds, arguing that humans lack the ability to apprehend directly the world of universals, and instead know things only through particulars. Aquinas was a compromiser, but his new mixed formula-tion overthrew the Platonist ontological hierarchy and gave primacy to exist-ence over essence (i.e., universal form). It was in response to this move that Henry of Ghent (see note 15) formulated his doctrine that individuality is merely a web of negations, against the backdrop of the higher reality of positively existing Forms. Duns Scotus, in turn, trumped all the rival positions by declaring that the essence of a thing is neither universal nor particular, but depends on a general principle of particularity, what he calls *haecceitas,* "this-ness." By this route Christian philosophy, having cast off the Neoplatonic position which identified highest religious reality with universals, finally came into parallel with Nagarjuna, Dharmakirti, and the Buddhists with a concep-tion of radically inexpressible particularity. The way was opened to an acon-ceptual Christian mysticism, and at the same time to the revival of radical nominalism such as that of William of Ockham.

In the Islamic sequence, debate over the question of nominalism and realism breaks out via clashes between indigenous Muslim theologians and the Neo-platonists—the equivalent of the clash between Christian anthropomorphism and the Greek heritage. Al-Farabi (early 900s) imported these conceptions into the branch of Islamic philosophers who continued the Greek traditions, but these Muslim *falasifa* were generally Neoplatonists and followed the party line on the superior reality of universals; what al-Farabi added was to formulate the issue as a distinction between existence and essence. In the same generation as al-Farabi, the theologian al-Ash'ari argued that there are no universal essences but only concrete and particular facts. Three generations later, the themes of Neoplatonism and Islamic rational theology were brought together by Ibn Sina, who formulated the concept of contingent being, merely possible in itself but made necessary as the result of an external cause. That is to say, the lower world participates in the necessity characteristic of the realm of logical universals, but only in a derivative way, through the causal operation of the one being necessary in itself, namely, God.

Ibn Sina's contingency sharpens the sense in which the realm of particular being is real. Seizing the advantage, the Ash'arite lineage continued to hammer away against the notion that reality is structured by universals or forces operating according to universal principles. Al-Juwayni argued that if an object has particular characteristics but could have had others, there must be something causing it to be particularized. This cause, which al-Juwayni identified with God, may be regarded as an abstraction on the concept of particularity, equivalent to Duns Scotus's *haecceitas* or Buddhist "thusness." Al-Ghazali, al-Juwayni's pupil, went on to refute Ibn Sina by arguing against the notion of necessary cause, using arguments against causality parallel to Hume's: Ibn Sina's notion of contingency is not radical enough, and needs to be extended to the point where we see that even causality is particular, the sheer acts of God's will. The arbitrary power of God to establish or disestablish any general principles at all, stressed by both Duns Scotus and al-Juwayni, is a very high-level claim about fundamental ontology; the same assertion would resurface in Heidegger's "thrown-ness" of the world and Sartre's point that the nature of being is to be unfounded, without any reason for anything to exist in the first place.

This radical conception of particularity emerges at various times in the world networks, in sequences of debate against systems which make universals into the ontological centerpiece.[17] But radical particularity too is never sustained for long without answering strokes in the intellectual field. It is an extreme, anchored against an opposing extreme of realism of universals, and disappears along with its enemy. Buddhist Madhyamika, made popular by Nagarjuna, sustained its radical "thusness" only as long as it had Hindu realists as a foil, and even so was answered on its own side by Yogacara Idealism, whose seeds in the mind are the equivalent of universal forms. Scotism, encircling its radical *haecceitas* in a bastion of high-level abstractions, faded from focus in the intellectual attention space of the 1300s and 1400s.

In Europe, the history of nominalism-realism picks up once again in the 1600s, but in much moderated form. Extreme claims for either transcendent universals or inexpressible particulars gave way to compromises which attempted to show how experience of particular things allows persons to formulate names, or general ideas, which stand for the resemblance among things. The terminology changed along with the center of ontological gravity; "realism" now meant the reality not of universals but of the material world. Since all issues are driven by conflict, proponents of universals were a crucial part of the field of oppositions which set off the debate. Neoplatonism had made a comeback during the Renaissance, when the metaphysical advances of the medieval Schoolmen were rejected in the name of reviving classical antiquity; once again in a revolt against Neoplatonism, the nominalist critique came to the fore.

Hobbes attaches his nominalism to the ontology of material substance; this in turn opens still further controversies. The Cambridge Platonists sprang to the defense of religion by attacking belief in a material reality, as if it could be known without going through subjective ideas. Locke in turn (who appears at the intersection of the networks of both the Cambridge Neoplatonic circle and the Hobbesian-Cartesian materialists) put forward a moderated version of sensory empiricism. Locke recognized not only particular sensory experiences but also particular ideas which come from them, followed by general ideas which arise by abstracting the resemblances among particular ideas. The difficulties which Locke opened up (as to in what sense resemblance may be understood) became fruitful ground for a number of other philosophies in the next generations of his network, including those of Berkeley (who rejected the realist underpinnings entirely) and Hume (who ended with the defense of commonsense realism as resting on nothing but psychological propensities). Difficulties in accounting for the universal aspect in experience have remained unsolved; after Hume the attention space of Western philosophers generally turned to other disputes.

We could make another set of world comparisons about recurrent deep troubles found in the Indian sequence, such as the relations among multiple substances. Such issues are even more obviously entwined with the dynamics of religious positions. This brings us to the third major cause driving the epistemology-metaphysics sequence.

MONOTHEISM AS PHILOSOPHERS' PUZZLE
A long-standing tradition holds theist religion inimical to intellectual advance. The historical consciousness of liberal anglophone philosophy takes its signposts from a series of disputes along this divide, from Abelard's condemnation for heresy, down through the triumphantly secularized schools of the 1930s and thereafter. This conception makes for poor sociology of ideas, reducing a multi-dimensional process of structured oppositions into a single-line evolution, and all too glibly identifying that line with rationality and with empirical science.

The onset of rapid-discovery science in Europe provided a jolt leading to a renewed round of philosophical creativity, but this was essentially a separation of networks and a shift in the organizational base, leading to internal realignment in the philosophical attention space; contrary to the ideologies of contemporary philosophers, it was not the substitution of scientific method for core philosophical tools and puzzles. The revolution of rapid-discovery science happened to coincide with the period of European secularization in the stalemate of religious conflicts; and still later the wresting of control of the university base from theologians into the hands of research scholars—philosophers, scientists, and humanists alike—generated a united front ideology of the forces of "reason" against those of theological traditionalism. These were alliances of convenience, ephemeral over the long run, and their ideologies held no insight into the deeper oppositional pattern that drives philosophical creativity.

The disputes recurring in the West along the lines of faith versus reason were by no means a battlefront of progressive and traditionalistic forces, whatever their conscious self-identifications. The abstraction-reflexivity sequence is driven by conflict and by the discovery of deep troubles. Rationalism by itself is often glib and in its own way traditionalistic, for instance, in the attachment of medieval Averroists to their aging texts, or in the backward-looking stance of the Renaissance Humanists. It was the reemergence of the cultural capital of high scholasticism in the era of Descartes and Leibniz that got philosophy moving again. It is the *dispute* between faith and reason that is crucial for philosophical and especially epistemological advance, not the victory of one side or the other.[18] The pattern occurs repeatedly: Kant's creation of a new level of critical epistemology happened in the heart of battle over theological control of the organizational base of intellectual life. This was not the extreme rejection of metaphysics by Enlightenment-style secular intellectuals, but a move within the contested terrain of faith and reason, a deep puzzle played through again fruitfully on a higher level of abstraction. Again in very recent times, Heidegger's existentialism comes from tension between neo-orthodox theology and the "rigorous science" of phenomenology.

Contrary to the ideologies of both its proponents and opponents, conservatism cannot help being dynamic. Conservatism is a recurrent mediating moment in the epistemology-metaphysics sequence, whenever conditions allow competition among intellectual factions. A community of curators of the canonical texts always produces a faction of rationalists, pursuing the normal scholastic tendency toward systematic classification and conceptual consistency. Conservatism is not primordial. The emergence of a conservative consciousness, explicitly aware of the particularity of tradition, is a response to the prior existence of rationalists. This split is part of the normal dynamics of the intellectual life.

The battle between faith and reason is an impetus to epistemology, since it raises explicitly the question of the nature and source of knowledge. Often it is the conservatives, the theological particularists, who push toward critical epistemology, attacking the confidently taken-for-granted tools of the constructive metaphysicians. In Islamic philosophy, it was from the theologically conservative camp that al-Ghazali and Ibn Taymiyah raised acute questions about the bases of reason and Ibn Khaldun attacked the scholasticism of syllogistic method. In India, it was the most conservative school, the Mimamsa, literalist curators of the Vedic texts, who made the most explicit moves into epistemology and set off the higher flights of Hindu philosophical abstraction.

The tensions which drive upward the epistemology-metaphysics sequence come out most strongly when religious orthodoxy is politically enforced monotheism. In this context appear the entwining of epistemology and metaphysics in proofs of metaphysical arguments, and the opening up of the basic questions of substance and relation, causality and free will, being and contingency. This is why there is such a gulf in the level of abstraction between Chinese thought and that of the West (including both Islamic and Christian branches). In China, where state-enforced supremacy of a monotheist church never took place, a major pathway to metaphysical development is missing. In India, state-supported religious monopoly was usually absent, and the decentralizing structures which promoted meditative mysticism had the effect of turning philosophical argument in different directions than in the monotheist West. As Indian philosophy, from the medieval period onward, became increasingly theist, epistemological and metaphysical parallels to the West increased as well.

Proofs of God. Anthropomorphic monotheism produces high levels of tension in intellectual argument and leads to theological proofs. This process raises the level of philosophical abstraction and generates movement in the epistemology-metaphysics sequence. As comparative evidence, we may note the virtual absence of proofs of God in Chinese philosophy. The gods of the Taoist pantheon, and the popular deities sponsored under the umbrella of the Confucian state rites, have no qualities of infinite perfection nor world-creating power, and call for no abstract argument as to their existence. The cosmos-generating Supreme Ultimate of Neo-Confucianism is not the object of proof either; and Chu Hsi rejects both immortality and existence of spirits. As in other respects, early Chinese philosophy had an opportunity to take a different path. The Heaven cult of the early Confucians had already transcended anthropomorphic qualities (even the conception of the Mandate of Heaven is an impersonal cosmic rightness of political rulership); its fusion with the divination cosmologies in the Han dynasty reinforced its impersonal quality and its identification with the cosmos rather than its transcendence. The Mohists, as usual, could have made a difference. Against the impersonal cult of Heaven and Destiny they exalted a personal God, rewarding the righteous and punishing sinners, with ghosts as avengers of evil. The Mohists critiqued the Heaven-Destiny conception for its fatalism, opening an early argument for free will. It is possible that in the obscure middle period of the Mohists, the five generations between Mo Ti and the formulation of the *Mohist Canon,* the basics of Mohist logic arose from conflicts over religious faith and mutual accusations of heresy among its schismatic factions. Mohist monotheism and formal logic went together. Both were cut off by the destruction of the Mohist school in the Han, a turning point in the history of Chinese philosophy.

The great development of proofs of God occur in three periods: Greek philosophy from the pre-Socratics down through the Hellenistic Skeptics; the showdown between late Neoplatonism and Christianity in the 400s C.E.; and the growth of Islamic (and in parallel to it Jewish) philosophy from the early Baghdad and Basra schools of the 700s through 1200, culminating in the positions of Ibn Sina, al-Ghazali, Ibn Rushd (Averroës), and Maimonides. The classic Greek period mixed together arguments pro and con polytheism, monotheism, and pantheism, without focus on a transcendent world-creating God. The first carefully articulated proofs on this terrain emerged with Proclus, at the end of the Neoplatonic school, who argued against Christianity for the eternity of the world. His grandpupils Simplicius and John Philoponus, converts to Christianity, refuted Neoplatonic arguments from the monotheist side. It was the synthesis between the networks of abstract philosophy and anthropomorphic Christian monotheism that generated these first comprehensive proofs.[19]

Islamic philosophy was no mere passive transmission belt for Greek philosophy. The first community of abstract argument comprised the indigenous development of *kalam,* rational theology, in the Mu'tazilite school. It was only after Islamic philosophy experienced a turning point, the rising power of scriptural conservatives after 835, that Mu'tazilite creativity went on the defensive, leaving a vacuum in the attention space into which Greek imports were now welcomed. The first rounds of Muslim philosophy centered on questions of free will and predestination, and of proofs of the unity and justice of God, arising directly from indigenous theological controversy. There developed an acute consciousness of what is proven and not proven. Various kinds of proofs of the existence of God were recognized, and distinguished from proofs of the unity of God and of the creation of the world ex nihilo. Formation of a conservative opposition raised the level of abstraction, leading to acute discussions of primary and secondary accidents, of the contingency of creation, of particularity as opposed to universals, and of causality. Ibn Sina created his version of the cogito in the competition over rising standards of proofs, adding his distinctions of necessary, possible, and contingent being, to come up with a proof of God as being purely necessary in itself alone. Al-Ghazali is a response to Ibn Sina's rationalism, Averroës a response to al-Ghazali. The mainline of the epistemology-metaphysics sequence in Islamic philosophy is a series of moves along the debating space of proofs of God. In the Greek networks, and for later Christian philosophy, Simplicius and Philoponus are minor figures, receiving little attention; in medieval Muslim and Jewish philosophy, it is the formulators of the proofs of God who are the stars.

When intellectual life came alive in medieval Christendom, proofs of God became a standard turf for tests of philosophical skill, not primarily for converting unbelievers but for precedence in the intellectual community. It was a pure intellectual game; there was no premium on accepting proofs, and rejection of inadequacies of rival argument was taken as a mark of superiority. The philosophers of the High Middle Ages were no beginners in the abstraction-reflexivity sequence. They started off by appropriating what ancient capital was available, but turned it toward the distinctive puzzles of anthropomorphic monotheist theology. Anselm, a law-trained debater, won the first great medieval reputation by raising the standards of argument, seeking a perfect proof contained in itself, without appeal to any empirical premise. The acuteness of philosophical abstraction was raised thereafter in conjunction with refinements in the concept of God. The proofs marshaled by Aquinas, refined by Duns Scotus, and rejected by Ockham and the nominalists were entwined with the metaphysical game. Although the arguments seemed to press the borders of heresy and sometimes outraged traditional relations between faith and reason, there was no question of jettisoning Christian theology for a purely secular philosophy; the reasoned conception of God, opened up and dramatized by the proof game, is the deep trouble space on which metaphysical advance is made.

The same holds true in much of the secularizing period of European philosophy. From Descartes to Leibniz and Berkeley, God is a central item in the reasoning contests of philosophy, played with new standards of argument. Anthropomorphic qualities are transcended on this refined level of abstraction; what is retained, and what makes the path to further abstract construction possible, are the standards of perfection embodied in the concepts of infinite perfection. Secular science and the philosophies of pure reason and freedom eventually became movements for overthrowing theology. But this is a case of the offspring devouring the parent; the standards of omniscience, omnipotence, infinite freedom, and goodness explored by theology provide the conceptions taken over by the scientific and philosophical goals of totally comprehensive explanation, perfect and complete causality, and the various ultimates of Idealist and post-Idealist philosophy. Even the skeptical and anti-foundational positions were formulated against this yardstick. Arguments over God are not atavisms in modern European philosophy, but the main pathway of the epistemology-metaphysics sequence.

The most important comparison for testing the importance of anthropomorphic monotheism is ancient Greece. Here was no political pressure to adhere to a sole God, much less a personalistic one; yet there were some developments of theological proofs. The early development of cosmological philosophy took place by critiquing polytheism or reinterpreting the multiple gods as natural elements. A second version of rationalizing mythologies was forwarded by the Stoics, who conceived of divinity in a generalized sense as one of the world ingredients, developing arguments that the universe itself is an animate, rational being with an intelligent soul.

A third direction was that taken by Plato, the tendency to conceive of a transcendent God on a metaphysical level above the empirical world, not immanent within it, with human-like qualities of intelligence and provident foresight. Plato is only vacillatingly monotheist; as in Aristotle's sharply delimited proof from motion for the Unmoved Mover, Plato endows God with only limited powers, at best shaper or controller of the world, creator of neither the world substance nor the eternal Forms. The Middle Platonists moved closer to constructing a monotheism of reason, and tried various models by which forms emanate from the primal One; but these are generally ontological descriptions rather than proofs, and slip off into pantheism.

The inner arguments of the Greek philosophical network are one of the sources of the concept of monotheism. In general, the trend of the abstraction-reflexivity sequence produces some components of monotheism, including the concepts of metaphysical unification and transcendence of the empirical, and of epistemological and moral perfection. Greek philosophy developed a strand capable of blending with the full-blooded anthropomorphic monotheism of Christianity, and may even have promoted its spread. But there is no single religious tendency of philosophical networks; left to itself, Greek philosophy was just as likely to emphasize sheer naturalism (for a while), omni-skepticism, or pantheism.[20]

The Greek networks are notable in world comparison for the popularity of counter-proofs against the existence of the gods or God. In fact, the negative proofs were first on the ground, and their continued instigation prodded much of the successive development of positive proofs. There were famous atheists, especially in the Megarian and Cyrenaic schools. The Academy, during its skeptical phase (down through Carneades), made a staple out of arguments against the religious proofs of the Stoics; this in turn stimulated still further counter-proofs from the Middle Stoics. The Skeptic school took ammunition from the balance of inconclusive arguments on both sides. These arguments contributed modestly to sharpening the level of conceptual abstraction, for instance, as the Megarians forced the Stoics to distinguish a dimension of relative and absolute perfections.

On the whole, these arguments did not drive philosophical development with anything like the centrality that proofs of God had for Islamic, Jewish, and Christian philosophy. As late as Sextus Empiricus (200 C.E.), arguments over the polytheist gods were mixed indiscriminately with those concerning monotheism. Even concerning the latter, arguments were often at a low level of abstraction, as in the anti-Stoic arguments that the proof from motion makes the Divine into a material body sharing the imperfect qualities of the material world. This concreteness was due to the continuing political presence of polytheism. The main external pressures against philosophical arguments came from affronts to the polytheist cults, both early (the charges for which Socrates died, as well as the scandals of the Sophists and Cyrenaics) and late (the polytheist defense against Christianity in the later Roman Empire). Not until Christianity became politically dominant did high-order metaphysical proofs of God begin to drive the epistemology-metaphysics sequence.

India provides another useful comparison. Proofs of the existence of God were not prominent until the 700s C.E., notably with Shankara. This was the period when Buddhism was declining and its place in the abstract regions of the philosophical attention space was being taken by the Hindu schools. The occasion has some analogy to the takeover of philosophy by Christianity in the 400s from the Neoplatonists; both of the previously dominant philosophical schools were non-anthropomorphic transcendental mysticism, which in the case of Buddhism was explicitly atheist. Shankara, who took the lead within Hinduism, is a network offshoot of the Mimamsakas. This school of scriptural literalists, in their struggle against the non-traditional cults of Hindu theism, had denied the reality of the gods as more than mere names in the Vedic texts. It is the Vedas which are eternal, and thus play a part like the eternity of matter in the classic Greek cosmologies. Kumarila, in the generation before Shankara, sharpened the argument to deny that a transcendent God would have a motive for creating the world (a point also argued by Greek Skeptics cited by Augustine). Shankara turned Mimamsa epistemology to a different purpose, in effect splitting the difference between Buddhist atheism and popular Hindu realist polytheism. Since doubt presupposes a standard by which to judge, the existence of the highest standpoint is proven; this is Brahman, the inexpressible non-dual reality, in contrast to which the world is illusory.

Once Advaita had taken control of the attention space from Buddhism, all the remaining Hindu schools were forced to readjust. Nyaya-Vaisheshika, the only one to remain active outside the Advaita ranks, abandoned its early atheism and expanded its pluralist realism to include God as another metaphysical entity in its list. Udayana (1000s C.E.) produced a compendium of proofs; one variant of these (that right knowledge requires an external source, which can only be God) is reminiscent of Shankara's epistemological proof, although without the acuteness of Shankara's argument from doubt and begging the question as to whether right knowledge does in fact exist. Udayana's other arguments include versions of the cosmological argument from causal dependence (Radhakrishnan and Moore, 1957: 379–385). The compendium form implies that these arguments were current in previous generations of the Nyaya-Vaisheshika school. Udayana ostensibly argues against Buddhism; but Buddhist atheism was no longer a living school, and the only Buddhist survivors at that date were magical-theistic tantrists. What we see instead is a parallel to medieval Christianity, where proofs of God become a game in its own right for the display of intellectual skills.

Between 1000 and 1400, as theist schools (Ramanuja, Madhva, Nimbarka) challenged Advaita on philosophical turf, arguments focused not on the existence of a creator-God, but on the degree of reality of the world, and on how the undifferentiated Absolute could give rise to this lower realm. It was in this context of dispute that the Advaita dialecticians Shri Harsha and Chitsukha subjected every concept to analysis which dissolved it in the unreality of contradictions, leaving the non-dualist Absolute as the sole reality. The epistemology-metaphysics sequence was propelled to considerable heights as monotheism grew in medieval India. The angle of approach is different than in the Islamic and Christian West, where the reality of the world is the starting point from which proofs of God are mounted. In India, because the dominant school in the post-Buddhist period is an impersonal transcendent mysticism, proofs of the world become the crucial question. In either case, the tension for philosophical argument is generated by the strength of anthropomorphic monotheism.

Deep Troubles: Free Will and Determinism, Substance and Plurality. A deep trouble is a doctrine containing a self-propagating difficulty. Alternative paths open out, each of which contains further puzzles. Exploration of such conundrums becomes a chief dynamic on the medium to higher reaches of the philosophical abstraction-reflexivity sequence. Intellectual life gets its energy from oppositions. It thrives on deep troubles because these provide guaranteed topics for debate. Once a deep trouble is discovered, it tends to be recycled through successive levels of abstraction. The recognition of deep troubles enables us to reformulate with greater precision a basic principle of intellectual creativity: oppositions divide the attention space under the law of small numbers, not merely along the lines of greatest importance to the participants, but along the lines of the available deep troubles.[21]

Monotheism is fruitful for advance along the abstraction-reflexivity sequence because it is a major source of deep troubles. One of the simplest of these is the issue of free will. The question of free will arises only at a level of abstraction capable of generating contradictions within a pair of opposing concepts. On one side there must be the generalized notion of omni-causality, on the other side an equally abstract and general notion of moral principle. Anthropomorphic monotheism is virtually defined by the combination of these two abstractions: God's unity and power is exalted to the extreme; at the same time, the apotheosis of human virtues makes God into the essence of righteousness and justice. The issue does not arise in polytheism, nor in transcendent mysticism, nor under an immanent cosmic world principle. That is why the issue of free will is an important one for Islam and Christianity (and in the secular philosophy that follows after it), but not in Chinese, Indian, or Greek philosophy.

A version of the free will deep trouble does arise in the non-monotheist sequences. In China, India, and Greece alike, fairly early in the abstraction-reflexivity sequence there arose the question of fate or destiny. This was a major objection for the early Mohists against the early Confucian cult of Heaven or Destiny. It crystallized among the Buddha's contemporaries in the concept of karma, which the Ajivikas called an inescapable Fate, and which the Buddha and the Jaina founder, Mahavira, proposed to overcome by meditative detachment and by asceticism, respectively. In Greece, soon after the conception of logical necessity was formed, the Megarian logician Diodorus Cronus, and after him the Stoic school, argued that every statement about the future is either true or false, and hence everything that will happen is already logically determined. Debaters countered that this would leave the world to fate, and undermine the motivation of the individual to do anything at all; to which the Stoic Chrysippus made the rejoinder that the actions of the individual are also determined.

As soon as the generalized notion of causality was formed, it became an object of debate because it promoted the formulation of an equally abstract concept of morality. Thus the oppositional path taken by the Mohists drove in the direction of monotheism, which can be regarded as the projection of a generalized human morality onto the supernatural plane of a God personality. In India several philosophers who denied karma were attacked for denying morality by the Buddha, who thereby promoted a moral standard not previously heard in this intellectual community.

These debates were fairly quickly resolved, as a philosophical conception of morality was created which eliminated the tension with omni-causality: in China, human moral action was identified with either ritual and social tradition, or harmony with the cosmic *tao;* in India, causality was identified with the world-order of illusion, which the highest morality lies in transcending; in Greece (leaving aside the polytheist position which had no moral or cosmic tension), the predominant philosophical ethics were based on skeptical withdrawal from all judgments, cosmic and moral alike, or on Stoic harmonization of self with an immanent world principle governing the universe. For the Greeks, the moral argument for free will was never strong, and the issue focused on the more generalized question of determinism versus indeterminism. Plato and Aristotle influentially identified freedom with acting in harmony with reason (which was identified with cosmic order) and unfreedom with being in thrall to the passions.

In all these cases, the tension dissipated as the abstraction-reflexivity sequence hit its middle ranges. Under monotheism the tension increased; in fact it became the driving force for development of higher abstraction in what began as positions that had no use for intellectual abstraction, and developed major factions explicitly hostile to it as their indigenous philosophies appeared.

Free will is only a semi-deep trouble; it arises from tensions which derive from accepting a particular theology. Over a period of generations, exploration of free will uncovers more generic deep troubles built into concepts themselves. This is the problem of relations among unlike substances, or more generally the problem of ontological plurality; this leads to the issues of causality and occasionalism. At a still higher level of metaphysical acuteness, the deep trouble becomes reformulated as one of being and contingency. We see this driving force clearly in the case of Islamic philosophy.

The first important issue around which intellectual networks formed in the early 700s was a dispute over reconciling the omnipotence of God with responsibility for moral evil. The faction of rational theology *(kalam)* elaborated a conception of God as having a rational nature, and therefore adhering to an ultimate standard of good; evil was thereby attributed to human free will. The opposition of scriptural literalists who arose in response took the stance that free will is a limitation on the power of God, and concluded for predestination. These same circles of argument launched proofs of the unity and power of God as omnipotent world creator, sharpening anthropomorphic monotheism to where the deep trouble came out in full bloom. On this problem space emerged the first set of famous Islamic intellectuals.

The Mu'tazilite faction which emerged in the third and fourth generations of *kalam* moved onto metaphysical grounds in order to defend simultaneously free will and the proofs of God's unity and power. The result of this combination was the occasionalist doctrine of divine intervention in a world composed of time-atoms. The free will argument led to a refined theory of causality, the modes by which God intervenes in the world; while the proofs of God's unity led to breaking apart the concepts of substance and its attributes. Dirar rejected bodily substance; the body is only a collection of attributes, with some attributes built on others (e.g., being round is built on having a shape, and so on). There is no distinction of substance and attribute, since every substance is infinitely divisible (a line of argument reminiscent of Buddhist nominalism). Dirar's rival Mu'ammar took a stance somewhat like Buddhist *Abhidharma* realism: attributes are only the aggregation of underlying bodily atoms; but in keeping with Islamic monotheism, Mu'ammar held that God creates human bodies by creating the atoms of which they are composed. This allowed a defense of free will and of God's justice, since God is only indirectly responsible for the attributes of human bodies, and is not responsible for their good or evil qualities. Abu-l-Hudhayl went on to distinguish which kinds of attributes exist only momentarily in time, and which ones are relatively permanent; among the latter must be will and motion, life and knowledge, which are necessary if there is to be a responsible human entity existing across time. These Muslims did not wish to dissolve the person into a fleeting aggregate, in effect an illusion, since they were aiming not at a Buddhist nirvana, but at anthropomorphic moral salvation.

The next round pushed further into the ontological status of existence and change. Bishr took the realist side. Everything exists only as a series of atomic instants in time, which God overseeing the world repeatedly creates and destroys. But every existent is real during the time when it is there. Furthermore, Bishr—probably goaded by debates, similar to those in which the Buddhists pressed their Vaisheshika opponents onto increasingly extreme realist territory—held that destruction too is a real action, and even the "nothing" out of which God creates time-atoms is a real "something" too. Against this extreme realism, true to the pattern of intellectual polarization, al-Nazzam developed a Heraclitus-like extreme processualism. Substance does not exist, since it can be infinitely subdivided. Attributes too dissolve, since all other attributes reduce to motion, and motion is inherently transitory. Al-Nazzam's opponents replied by raising Eleatic-like difficulties: Since any distance is made up of an infinity of points, how is it possible for infinitely divisible time-atoms to traverse them?

Dirar and Mu'ammar, Abu-l-Hudhayl, Bishr and al-Nazzam are not famous names; the debates within Islamic rational theology have never had a major place within the historical consciousness of philosophers, even in the Islamic world, where either Greek-oriented *falasifa* (al-Farabi, Ibn Sina, et al.) or the more conservative orthodoxy of a later period reaped the long-term attention. Nevertheless, the early Mu'tazilites show the metaphysical driving power of monotheism and its capabilities for generating from its own resources (this was a period before Greek philosophy had penetrated the Islamic world, and there is no serious reason to slough off these debates as imports of Buddhist or Christian ideas) some key positions in the medium ranges of the abstraction-reflexivity sequence, colored by a distinctively monotheist problematic.

The occasionalism first formulated by the Mu'tazilites, and continued by the theologically more conservative Ash'arites, is a religiously specific version of the deep trouble in the concept of substance and plurality. For the Muslims, it was a question of invoking God to ensure the continuity from one instant to the next among a plurality of time-atoms. Radical plurality calls for an equally radical higher presence to explain the experience of continuity. The problem arises more generally in world philosophy, in the issue of relations among plural substances, or in the related issue of relationships among any kinds of ontological differences. In the Western tradition, this is the classic problem of Parmenides: the very concept of being contradicts any sort of change or plurality. Being, the truly existing substance, is always itself; how can it become any other thing without contradicting its nature? Simultaneous with Parmenides, Heraclitus formulated the other side of the issue: change implies that there is no substance, no river into which one can step twice. Parmenides' follower Zeno of Elea turned the infinite divisibility of motion into a set of paradoxical arguments against the reality of change; the same kind of arguments came up among the Muʿtazilites when the divisibility and reality of substance were debated. Both networks were working the same deep trouble space.

In Greece, the generations immediately after Parmenides responded with an array of solutions: one was Democritus' atomism, in which the atoms were taken as Parmenidean ultimates, incapable of modification, with plurality and change shunted to a level of the aggregations of atoms. Other solutions were Platonic forms, upgrading the qualities of ontological permanence to the level of abstraction and downgrading the experienced world to non-reality; another was Aristotle's distinction of potentiality and actuality. As we know from the long run of intellectual history, none of these solutions was in principle impervious to new assaults of deep trouble: Can the Democritean atoms truly aggregate without giving rise to the problems of plurality and relation? Can the plurality of Platonic Forms be reconciled with the premise that true reality exists only in unity, the Form of all Forms? In Greece, the deep troubles were not probed much further; halfhearted solutions held sway for many centuries without bringing additional changes in metaphysical conceptions.[22] The most acute standards were those held up by the Skeptics; but since their stance was to cast doubt on all positions and to abstain from any positive constructions, they too became part of the fixity of positions in Hellenistic philosophy. One conclusion is that the absence of monotheism kept Greek philosophy from probing these troubles more deeply, and thereby advancing further in the abstraction-reflexivity sequence.[23]

In India, the deep trouble of substance-relation, or of plurality in general, was much more central. This shows us that the issue does arise independently of monotheism; monotheism only gives it a specific form. The issue of *satkaryavada* and *asatkaryavada,* arising in Buddhist critiques of Samkhya dualism, focuses on the same deep trouble in both its major forms. How can an immutable material substance suddenly launch itself in motion to emanate the universe? And how can it be related to a totally unlike substance of pure consciousness, which does nothing but witness unperturbed what transpires on the material plane? The Indian solution was to distinguish the concept of potentiality from ontological actuality. In this case, the Aristotelean move was countered by a further series of deep troubles: Is potentiality itself real? If not, are we not back at the same dilemma? If, however, potentiality is real, how is this additional substance related to the substance in which it inheres?

Indian philosophers pushed fairly early through the further levels of this deep trouble. The Buddhists, whose initial stance in the field was to destroy the reality of the self and of other aggregates, moved onward to the destruction of all substances and all reals. Nagarjuna attacked the intelligibility of any kinds of relations in general; taking as the mark of reality the capacity of causing something, he argued that the endless link of causes makes everything unreal; causality dissolves substance. The argument was wielded not only by medieval Buddhists such as Dignaga and Dharmakirti, dissolving substances into a web of conceptual negations, but also on the Hindu side. Shankara generalized the critique from causality into a critique of any relations whatsoever: any cause-and-effect relation implies that the relation must be linked at each end to the cause and to the effect, and that in turn implies another relation between the relation and the relata, and so on infinitely. Shri Harsha and the other Advaita dialecticians employed similar arguments against the reality of any concepts. Among the earlier Indian thinkers, the deep trouble was exploited mainly from the Buddhist side, that is to say, by a militantly atheistic mysticism.[24] The growth of philosophical theism on the Hindu side was stimulated by antagonism to Buddhism. The point at which the higher levels of the substance-relation deep trouble are brought out, with Shankara and his Advaita followers, is the point when theism begins to acquire a presence on the philosophical field itself. Shankara's Brahman was not very anthropomorphic, but it opened the gates to philosophical respectability for more explicitly theist philosophies. Accordingly, it is in the debates of later Hindu philosophy between Advaita and the variants of theist metaphysical pluralism that Indian intellectual life produces the most parallels to European themes.

Occasionalism is the version which the substance-relation deep trouble takes when religious dogma presents philosophy with an anthropomorphic God transcending both material and spiritual worlds. Occasionalism does not arise when there is a graduated hierarchy of matter and spirit (as in Neoplatonism), or where spirit is regarded as form immanent within matter. Islamic occasionalism invokes God to connect the temporal splinters of the material world together; Christian occasionalism invokes God as a bridge between the material and spiritual substances, now taken as coeval in their reality. A similar complex of philosophical side-issues was discussed in the periods when occasionalism was most central. For the Muslims, invoking God as a bridge was part of a stance that no natural causality occurs among the atomic instants of the world. Causality and contingency came increasingly to the fore as issues at the apex of Islamic philosophy between al-Ash'ari and al-Ghazali. Al-Baqillani, in the Ash'arite school of the late 900s, held that there are no natural laws; each atomic instant is uniquely created by God, under no necessity of repetition. From this lineage three generations later, al-Ghazali produced his famous Hume-like refutation of causality.

In Europe, the four generations leading up to Hume were energized by working through a similar family of deep troubles. The similarity in the context is that here too a rationalized monotheism was confronted with a conception of an independently existing—that is, created, not emanated—material world.[25] In Islam, the naturalism was already present in the commonsensical religious texts of anthropomorphic monotheism, while the rationalism grew with philosophical debate. In Europe, philosophical rationalism was long-standing from the first textual imports onward, while naturalist materialism came to the fore with the overthrow of Neoplatonism and Aristoteleanism around 1600. Descartes now brought out the two-substance problem in full force. Debate, which always takes off from a successful new focus of the attention space, flamed up over fruitful inconsistencies in Descartes's position. The result was an array of solutions: Malebranche and Geulincx formulated an occasionalism of time-instants constantly re-created by God; Spinoza avoided two-substance dilemmas by positing a single substance with mental and material aspects; Leibniz formulated a plurality of self-enclosed monads linked by a pre-established harmony. Concentrated in this generation are parallels to positions laid out in Buddhist, Hindu, and Islamic philosophy at points where the same deep trouble was confronted.

The same circle of problems in Islamic and European networks results in the distinction between primary and secondary qualities. Locke reconciles the plurality of substances by translating them into ideas originating in the senses. Instead of material substance there are simple ideas containing the relations of extension and motion. From these in turn the mind generates the secondary qualities characterizing the visible world. The Ash'arites had come to a similar conclusion: primary attributes of motion, rest, and location always accompany substance, while other attributes are derivative of these. The Ash'arites arrived at this conception through the theological debates of the Mu'tazilites, from whom they had split. Locke's primary-secondary distinction is often interpreted as an early formulation of the scientific standpoint, in which physics generates the subjective qualities of human experience. The Islamic comparison shows us something deeper: much the same distinction can be produced by theological issues; and in fact the same range of theological-philosophical deep troubles were the context in which Locke's formulation emerged as well.

Locke's solution was unstable, which is to say, the deep troubles it contained were taken up again in the following generation. Berkeley (along with several figures overshadowed by him, Collier and Norris) stressed that there is no direct evidence of any substance at all underlying the visible qualities of experience, nor of bare primary qualities shorn of secondary qualities such as color. The order of the world can be attributed instead to the constant intervention of God. This is a version of the occasionalist position, except that instead of intervening to establish the connection between physical and mental events or substances, God intervenes to connect the succession of subjectively experienced qualities. This position is equivalent to that of al-Nazzam in the Muʿtazilite debates. (We might notice that Berkeley and al-Nazzam both failed to acquire followers for their positions; both were regarded as taking debates to an absurd extreme—in effect, testing the limits of what can be said about a deep trouble in this particular direction).

Still further down this road, Hume followed out the implications of Locke and Berkeley to note that from a purely empirical stance, there is no evidence of necessary causes or patterns of regularity in the phenomenal stream. Hume culminated this series of debates much in the same way that al-Ghazali did for this period of the Islamic sequence.

The problem of substance and plurality resurfaces in later revivals of metaphysics in European philosophy. One prong was to raise the issue at a higher level of abstraction, in the very general question of relations. Bradley's version of Idealism was based on showing the incoherence of any kind of relation; using the same kind of argument as Shankara and Nagarjuna, Bradley pointed to an infinite regress of relations connecting relations with their relata. This problem stimulated yet a further step in the abstraction-reflexivity sequence when Russell distinguished external and internal relations. To hold that all relations are internal (as did Bradley, Leibniz, and Spinoza) is to hold that a thing's properties are so closely connected that to change one would make it a different thing (we recognize here an explicit point from Nyaya-Vaisheshika, upholding *asatkaryavada*). To hold that relations are external is to say that the essential properties of a thing are intrinsic to it, and would remain the same no matter how its relations with the rest of the world might change. The latter position allows for plurality but makes mysterious just what constitutes the properties of the plural things of the world; the former position reduces the world into a single substance, something like Indra's net in Hua-yen Buddhism. Russell's distinction aimed to overthrow Bradleyan Idealism by showing that it rested upon a confusion; but the clarification reopened the problem in new form, into the depths of which Wittgenstein's *Tractatus* soon plunged.

The other prong of this issue in modern philosophy followed the line that the deep trouble is built into the structure of reality itself. That is to say, reality is both plural and single, relations are both coherent and incoherent; it is this contradiction within metaphysical substance that generates time and drives change. This was the position worked out by Fichte and Hegel. It is the classic deep trouble treated at a higher level of reflexivity; the sequence of philosophers comes to recognize explicitly the existence of the deep trouble, and instead of trying to solve it by taking one side or the other, makes an ontological category out of it on which further constructions can be built. The period of these dialectical Idealist systems was succeeded in turn by anti-Idealist philosophies.

But the basic deep trouble remained, to be re-exploited whenever the motivation arose to construct a new metaphysical system. The existentialists, for all their hostility to Idealism, reworked the dialectics of Fichte and Hegel in a version which denies the priority of substance and gives primacy to negation as the paramount human reality. The anti-essentialism of the postmodernist generation continues to work that terrain in another fashion. No doubt future philosophies will be created upon this long-standing deep trouble.

Mathematical Networks and the Distinctiveness of European Philosophy

Let us summarize where we are so far. If external conditions keep up creativity in intellectual networks for many generations, the content is driven beyond cosmological descriptions of the world to reflexive questions about the nature of knowledge itself. Epistemology entwines with metaphysics proper, opening for exploration the realm of abstract properties of what there is. This epistemology-metaphysics sequence is propelled by several different social processes, of which I single out the following.

First, the sheer density and continuity of debate raises the issue of what knowledge is, initially on the level of bald assertion, then description. Formulating rules of debate leads to the rules of logic as the mechanics of truth. As usual, there is danger that a side-sequence will set in, making classificatory scholasticism an end in itself. But if conditions exist to keep the abstraction-reflexivity sequence going even across this classificatory tendency, logic will entwine with ontology and become part of the abstract framework of what exists in general.

At times the density of debating factions floods the attention space with contending positions; this excess of horizontal density is fateful for the abstraction-reflexivity sequence too, because it generates epistemological skepticism. This faction takes the meta-stance of "a plague on all houses," denying on reflexive grounds the very possibility of knowledge. This in turn provides a foil for a cogito move, providing new transcendental grounding for epistemological-metaphysical systems. This "horizontal" crowding of the network's collective conscience has a counterpart in the "vertical" crowding which takes place if continuing factional wars are kept up across the generations. Such long-term debates drive up the abstraction-reflexivity sequence by raising the level of reflexivity concerning the categories of argument: names, universals, particulars, radical contingency.

Debate is most fruitful when it discovers deep troubles. An especially intense journey to high-level abstraction leads through monotheism, because this is a primary source of deep troubles. From relatively superficial or particularistic deep troubles about the Trinity or free will, the network reaches deeper troubles about plurality and substance, causality and relation. Mono-theism is not the only way some of these questions can be reached, but it makes them especially acute, and produces abstract philosophy even quite early in a network's history, as in the case of early Islamic thinkers. A monotheistic argumentative community generates proofs of God, rising to acute levels about just what is proved and not proved; the proof game becomes freed up as an intellectual terrain in its own right.

The network dynamics just outlined have occurred throughout the literate civilizations of the world, with some variations in emphasis: China did not go far in the epistemology-metaphysics sequence and, after the Han dynasty, focused on a cosmology-ethics fusion on a moderate level of abstraction; Islam, Judaism, Christendom, and Europe reaped the strongest consequences of the monotheist impetus, which is found also to some extent in later medieval Indian philosophy. Besides the cosmological and epistemology-metaphysics sequences, there is a third major pathway in world philosophy: mathematics. This has been most important in modern Europe, where the takeoff in modern mathematics coincided with that of modern philosophy. Its effects are most visible in the networks around Descartes, Leibniz, and Newton, and again with Frege, Husserl, Carnap, and Gödel on the Continent, and the British lineage from Boole to Russell and Wittgenstein. If we add the anti-mathemati-cal side of these same networks (e.g., Berkeley, Heidegger, Moore, and the later Wittgenstein), creating their positions by opposition, we can say modern European philosophy is driven by mathematics.

Let us be careful to understand what this means. European philosophy is not driven *only* by mathematics; it combines all of the major processes just outlined. It has continued a series of high-density debates and is heir to monotheism, going through the period of religious secularization at just this time and thereby traversing again the territory of deep troubles in the God concept. In fact it went through this terrain twice: in the 1600s, at the end of the religious wars, and again in the 1800s with the spread of the German university revolution which seized secular control of the bastion of religious education, setting off the Idealist metaphysics which served as a halfway house for philosophers on religious turf. The revolutions of modern mathematics were superimposed upon all this. The social conditions for the other routes are present elsewhere; in medieval India and Islam there are many parallels to European thought from Descartes to Bradley, because there were high-density communities of debate which also traversed, if in different directions, the terrain between sheer religion of reason and anthropomorphic monotheism. Mathematics is the ingredient which makes European philosophy unique, driving it to especially high levels of abstraction and reflexivity.

Is mathematics just a contingent external intrusion upon philosophy? Not so; nor should we regard it as a tendency of philosophy to become "scientific" in its maturity. Mathematics is not identical with science; and as we have seen, empirical-discovery science per se does not drive up the abstraction-reflexivity sequence but tends to hold it constant on a given level, at least for long periods of time, so that "lateral" exploration can take place. Mathematics has an intimate effect on the structure of the intellectual community because it reveals some of the innermost qualities of that community to itself.

A key social determinant of this influence is the connection between mathematical and philosophical networks. Mathematics has existed in all world civilizations. It reached some fairly elaborate developments in China (especially the algebra of the Sung dynasty) and Japan (the calculus during the Tokugawa), with bits of development in India, more in medieval Islam, and of course ancient Greece. As we have seen, the network patterns have varied widely. In China and India, mathematical and philosophical networks were totally separate, whereas there was considerable network overlap in all four Western cases. This is most notable in Greece and in modern Europe, where not only do the networks overlap in regard to minor figures, but also the stars or network centers in each are closely linked, and sometimes even coincide in the same person.

In Greece, crucial developments in the content of philosophy and mathematics were influenced by this connection. The Sophists, who catalyzed the jump to higher abstraction in philosophy, were also the circle that popularized mathematical puzzles. The Pythagoreans began as cosmologists based on the primitive conceptions of mathematics; out of their ranks emerged the specialized mathematicians, as well as the key deep troubles such as the incommensurability problem of irrational numbers. It was through the combination of the networks and concepts of the Sophists and the Pythagoreans that Plato created the philosophy of abstract Forms. Philosophy also played back into mathematics. Aristotle's formalized logic became the basis for axiomatic systems which culminated in Euclid's synthesis of geometry. In the Hellenistic period, technical mathematics tended to become separate; the philosophy-mathematics overlap continued, shifting into numerology, blending a classificatory scholasticism with lay-oriented occultism and the cosmology of world emanations. After the classic period, the mathematics-philosophy overlap no longer contributed to the abstraction-reflexivity sequence; we might even say that it was their overlap for a few generations which made the period "classic" in both fields.

In modern Europe, the mathematical revolution of the 1500s produced both a new form of mathematics and an impetus to modern philosophy, involving the fusion for a while between the most creative mathematical and philosophical networks. Why should the network fusion have this effect? The answer requires a sociology of mathematics. The history of mathematics is the purest case of the abstraction-reflexivity sequence. The objects which mathematicians investigate are intellectual operations. It took many generations of continuous intellectual competition before the community came to recognize this. At first mathematics was regarded as a realm of objective objects—the Pythagoreans' number pebbles and the Platonic Forms. It took successive layers of self-reflection for the network to discover that it could create new operations, new modes of manipulating its symbolism, and investigate their consequences. Higher mathematics consists in exploring this reflexivity of mathematical operations.

Since thinking is internalized from communication within a social network, mathematics is the investigation of the pure, contentless properties of thought as internalized operations of communication per se. This will become clearer if we review the two great revolutions in modern mathematics.

MATHEMATICIANS DISCOVER THE PURE
REFLEXIVENESS OF INTELLECTUAL OPERATIONS

The takeoff of modern mathematics in the 1500s and early 1600s occurred by turning mathematics into a problem-solving machine. The verbal methods by which mathematical argument previously had been carried out were replaced by a pervasive symbolism, and even more important, by an apparatus for manipulating symbols according to rules. Mathematics became a technology of symbols on paper, lined up in equations; the principles of how to move symbols about so as to transform one into another mechanically became both the means of solving particular problems and an arena in which reliable generalizations were discovered. Methods were found for solving lower-order problems (e.g., algebra gives general principles for classes of problems in arithmetic). These methods in turn could be taken as lower-order patterns about which still higher-order principles can be discovered. That is to say, the lower-order operations can be collected under a symbol (numbers are symbolized as algebraic unknowns x, y, and so on; adding, subtracting, and so forth can be symbolized as a function; functions can be collected under functions of functions), and the rules for operating with those higher-order symbols can in turn be explored. As earlier problems were solved, extensions were suggested (e.g., from rules for solving algebraic problems involving cubic equations, new challenges were posed by competing mathematicians to solve quartic and quintic equations, and so on). Suddenly there was an outpouring of mathematical discoveries. This intellectual network began to pulsate with energy as it explored a widening turf: the general features of algebraic equations and trigonometry, which in turn cross-fertilized older areas of mathematics such as geometry, giving increasing attention to the more difficult problems of solid figures, and the conic sections which turned out to yield representations of motion and open the way to the calculus.

Descartes was the network member who reaped the first great fame for this revolution. He set out the general methods for what henceforth became the standard forms for setting up equations and symbolizing unknowns and the rules for manipulating them. His algebraic geometry unified all the field of mathematics into a single conceptual realm; it also brought to the center of attention a meta-space on which points, lines, squares, and dimensions higher than those of the physical universe could all be combined in a single process of mathematical manipulation. Descartes made the intellectual world aware of a meta-level of abstraction, expounding not only his particular results but also a general theory of equations, and pointed to a higher dimension of mathematics. Most important, he trumpeted it abroad that the mathematical community now possessed a method for producing a stream of new and reliable results, a machine for making discoveries.

Exploring the turf opened up by this discovery-making machine made up the first wave of modern mathematics. Around 1800 a second wave of mathematical abstraction and discovery took off. This time it proceeded by heightening reflexiveness about what mathematicians themselves were doing, a growing self-consciousness which led up to the realization that mathematics itself is a study not of things but of its own operations. This wave of higher mathematics was set off by an organizational shift, the emergence of academic positions, networks, and publications in which mathematics could be pursued independently of the physical sciences and their applications. The machinery of mathematics began to be scrutinized in its own right, apart from the results it gave for generalizations about the world of nature. The practical methods of the previous period, when the various territories of calculus were explored, now began to be criticized for their lack of rigor, for operations such as discarding terms and dividing by zero, and for assuming concepts such as series which are never seen to converge.

Rigor became a new standard for the competitive game, now played on its own abstract turf. Conceptually sloppy methods could no longer be justified merely because they brought good results in physics or engineering; at the same time, new standards of proof were held up in the competitive challenges between one mathematician and another. This purposely involuted game turned out to be a success; rather than being a needless refinement, rigor opened up a vast new realm of abstract mathematics to be explored. The discovery-making machinery took off again, this time on a higher plane. The method of axiomatization, carefully laying out the rules of operations, was applied not only to geometry (where a set of restricted, physically commonsensical principles had been standard since Euclid), but also to algebra, and then to still more abstract realms such as the theory of groups.

The march into this realm was made exciting by the recurrent experience of discovering paradoxes: patterns which seemed absurd from the point of view of previously accepted concepts of mathematical reality, strange mathematical beasts which outraged traditionalists. A self-generating cycle was set in motion: the conflicts over paradoxes energized stronger efforts to overcome them by more careful re-digging of axiomatic foundations and by making clear the operations of the mathematical machinery which produced them. Further axiomatization and rigor made it possible to examine still other kinds of axiomatic sets, and to discover still more comprehensive layers of abstract space, within which could be found still more of the paradoxical breed. Not only spatial intuition but any acceptance of self-evident procedures or concepts came under suspicion.

Vast new realms of higher mathematics opened up. At the same time, conflict grew acute between the most enthusiastic explorers of those realms of free mathematical invention—such as Georg Cantor, with his multiple levels of transfinite numbers—and opponents who declared that rigor must ground itself upon firmly intuited reality. Mathematics, the time-honored standard of absolute certainty and consensual agreement, now split into a foundational conflict. At this point some mathematicians reached a meta-turf resembling a branch of philosophy, and a new hybrid of mathematical philosophy arose.

MATHEMATICIAN-PHILOSOPHER HYBRIDS
FROM DESCARTES TO RUSSELL

The key points of modern philosophy come when the mathematical network spills over into philosophical terrain. This happens naturally because any topics pursued at a sufficiently high level of abstraction and reflexivity leave the specific problems of the original practitioners and encounter philosophical turf. In his own interests and intentions, Descartes was a mathematician and (what we would call) natural scientist. He was a key figure in proclaiming and consolidating the takeoff of the mathematical revolution, synthesizing the notational tools developed by his predecessors, and turning them into an explicit machinery for the manipulation of equations. His famous analytical geometry, published in conjunction with his *Discourse on Method,* displays how even the most traditional parts of mathematics can be pushed forward with this new machinery. In his larger philosophical statements, Descartes extends to the entire realm of knowledge the confidence of the scientific and mathematical revolutions, the feeling that rapid discovery and certainty are linked through the use of the new methodological machinery. Mathematics was his inspiration and standard for attempting the comprehensive deduction of all certain knowledge; his goal was to deduce all scientific principles from the properties of extended substance or matter, which now replaced the Neoplatonist and Aristotelean cosmologies.

The philosophical attention space was rejuvenated by the preliminary parts of Descartes's system; issues of the cogito and of the relations among dual substances became the deep troubles on which specifically philosophical creativity took off. A second key intrusion from mathematics came when Leibniz, the most aggressive developer and purveyor of the calculus, used his command of the new mathematical sophistication—now a quantum leap higher than in Descartes's generation—to solve these metaphysical problems. Leibniz's approach to the two-substance conundrum was to reinstate a scholastic doctrine: that essence contains all its predicates. His calculus provides a respectably up-to-date analogy: each substance contains its past and future states, just like a point moving along mathematical coordinates; since in geometrical representation a moving point looks like a point at rest, the point must contain an additional mathematical quality (later called "kinetic energy") which generates the motion from past to future. The infinitesimal calculus had opened the way to conceiving of second-order (and higher) relations among first-order relations. Leibniz used this to solve an issue which had arisen over both Descartes's extended substance and the rival materialist doctrine of atomism, namely, that all material substance is infinitely divisible, and thus ultimately fades away into nothing. From the point of view inspired by Leibniz's calculus, there is a transcendent order which arises from examining the pattern of infinite subdivision, which shows how infinitesimals nevertheless make up a solid continuum. Leibniz's monadology combines an infinite array of independent substances, each of whose essence logically contains all its predicates or qualities, including its causal and time-space relations. It is a mathematician's vision of the universe.[26]

The next big leap in metaphysics and epistemology comes with Kant. He is not a star mathematician on the level with Descartes and Leibniz, but he taught mathematics and science early in his career, and his first interests—and his most prominent network contacts—were in science and mathematics. He also inherited Leibniz's position within philosophy, as part of the Wolffian school which dominated the Prussian universities; Kant's creativity was the response of that network as it met the challenges posed both on the religious side and by the Newtonians, who constituted a counter-wave to the Descartes-Leibniz lineage throughout this period. Again with Kant, consideration of the abstract properties of mathematics was the key to his philosophy. His key discovery was the concept of the synthetic a priori. Up to this time the conventional view was that mathematics epitomizes analytical knowledge, the investigation of the implications of definitions and axioms. But such knowledge is merely tautological; Kant wanted a version of knowledge which is synthetic, non-tautological, amplifying what we know rather than merely clarifying what we already knew.

Kant took his crucial step by arguing that mathematics is in fact not analytical but synthetic, while remaining a priori. It follows that there does exist a form of knowledge which is both certain and informative, going beyond mere knowledge of concepts. Kant went on to investigate what are the categories of synthetic a priori understanding, concluding that time, space, and causality are categories through which all experience is necessarily filtered, and in whose necessary regularities all valid scientific knowledge can be formulated. Kant's transcendental method opened up a whole new playing field—in fact two such fields—for philosophers, quite apart from whatever science can be grounded in this way. One is the path into Idealism, constructing all of reality from the working out of consciousness. The other path, which has proven to be more enduring, is the critical aspect of Kant's transcendental method. It is a method of working backwards, investigating in any field of experience what is necessarily presupposed for that experience to be formulated.

This method makes critical epistemology into the central philosophical question. At the same time—a point that was to provide grounds for a huge neo-Kantian movement in the burgeoning university system—it makes the philosopher the arbiter of the knowledge conditions of every other intellectual discipline. In Kant's own generation this method spread like wildfire because it proclaimed the autonomy of philosophical intellectuals over theology, indeed giving philosophy the position of pronouncing on the conditions for knowledge claims in theology as in every other field. This Kantian critical epistemology was the ideology of the university revolution. And since the research university has been the key organizational base for intellectuals ever since, we are all post-Kantians, ever since anchored around the centrality of critical epistemology.[27]

These movements from Descartes to Kant were parts of one wave, spilling over from the first round of the mathematical revolution. The second wave of higher or reflexive, self-consciously abstract mathematics was the catalyst for the philosophies of the turn of the 1900s. It started off with persons who pursued (at least initially) mathematical careers—Frege, Husserl, Russell—and ramified into the movements not only of logical positivism, the Vienna Circle, and analytical philosophy generally, but also into phenomenology and existentialism. The mathematical movement toward rigor, reflexivity, and the deliberate creation of higher-order formal systems stimulated philosophy in several ways. Reflexivity and higher-order abstraction became topics for discussion in their own right, leading to devices such as Russell's theory of types and Husserl's layers of phenomenological reduction or *epochê*. Higher mathematics encourages the formulation of new languages, which Frege pioneered in logic, and his followers attempted for all the verbal realms. And it turned up its own deep troubles, in the debate over the foundations of mathematics which generalized to philosophical turf and energized the action at Cambridge, Göttingen, and Vienna.

The history of higher mathematics is a piling on of levels of abstraction as the search for greater generalization goes on. In effect, arithmetic was created as a generalization of the principles of counting, summarizing in rules what the result would be of various kinds of operations (adding things together, removing some, partitioning, recombining). Algebra gives higher-order generalizations about whole classes of operations that might be carried out in arithmetic (thus it is always possible to check an algebraic equation with a specific numerical example). The takeoff of modern mathematics around the time of Tartaglia and Cardano was in formulating higher-order principles as to how to solve whole classes of equations; these in turn gave rise to still further questions as to whether general solutions were possible in various areas (e.g., the famous question of the general solution of the quintic equation, a flashpoint for abstract mathematics in the 1820s). The revolution of higher mathematics was the formulation of still higher levels of abstraction for dealing with these meta-issues, such as the theory of groups. This turned revolutionary as it dawned on mathematicians that they were in the business of exploring successive levels of abstraction, and that they could create abstract systems at will in order to solve their problems, or indeed just for the free creativity of exploring these realms. The non-Euclidean geometries took off when it was recognized that there was no longer any need to connect them with plausible physical representations; at the same time, alternative algebras were invented by deliberately varying the axiomatic sets of operations which underlie conventional algebra.

The increasing reflexivity that went along with this movement had a double direction: piling on still higher levels of abstraction, and also delving backwards into the concepts which were used in a taken-for-granted, non-reflexive manner earlier in the history of mathematics. Higher algebra was created when it was realized that the set of axioms underlying elementary algebra were only one of the possible abstract combinations possible. Plunging still further back, one arrives at arithmetic, and then at the concept of number itself. Here the conservative mathematics drew the line, Kronecker declaring, "God made the integers, man created all the rest!" and blasting the more extreme forms of revolutionary mathematicians for its monstrosities and paradoxes. Nevertheless, this terrain too was aggressively opened up, by Cantor and Frege. Extrapolating the path of previous revolutionary reconstructions, Frege recognized that numbers are not primitive things, but emerge in systems of operations, and indeed there are multiple dimensions of these operations. In the same way that Cantor distinguished several orders of infinity by several methods of counting, Frege distinguished cardinal and ordinal properties of numbers. More generally, by examining the operations that are implied in using the equal sign (=) in an equation, he uncovered multiple dimensions in our taken-for-granted concept of equality; with greater generality this became the distinction between sense and reference. In this spirit Frege undertook a reform in the entire system of notation and operations which made up traditional logic, replacing the taken-for-granted concepts of subjects and predicates, modeled on language, with a formal system which makes explicit the multiple dimensions of operations brought out in the mathematics of numbers. It was this machinery which Russell saw could be as revolutionary in the realm of philosophy as was the machinery of equations with which Descartes had promoted the takeoff of modern mathematics.

Once again, the straightforward path toward solving all problems with a new tool became displaced into a fanning-out of creativity at the newly exposed ground level. What made the Frege-Russell movement philosophically fruitful was not so much its avowed intention, the technical exercise of translating philosophical problems into the new formalism and thereby clearing away confusion forever, as that it uncovered deep troubles. Russell became more famous for his theory of types, his device for repairing a deep trouble, than for his logicist program itself. The real fame of the movement came with Wittgenstein, who built a meta-system by wrestling with the general difficulties in hierarchical programs such as the theory of types, and with the Vienna Circle, who promoted Russellian logicism as the revolution which was to sweep away all the fallacies of philosophy. After the fireworks of the initial phases of combat, what settled out as the new philosophical turf was the exploration of what kinds of things are sayable in various sorts of systems of notation or symbolism. In a sense Wittgenstein amplified Kant's discovery about the synthetic a priori: what had previously been taken as merely arbitrary and tautological symbols turned out to be a realm with its own contours, an unknown land to be explored, and in which discoveries might be made far beyond the taken-for-granted of past history or "common" sense. This is much the same as what higher mathematics does, in full reflexive consciousness; this is why we can say that the mathematical abstraction-reflexivity sequence has been the instigator of the philosophical abstraction-reflexivity sequence in modern Europe.

OPPOSITIONS OF HIGHER REFLEXIVITY: FORMALISM AND
ANTI-FORMALISM TO HUSSERL AND WITTGENSTEIN

A large segment of modern European philosophers would have been surprised to hear mathematics described as the driving force of modern philosophy. Nevertheless, the intellectual world is structured by oppositions; there is not merely a non-mathematical philosophy in the modern attention space but a wing of militantly anti-mathematical philosophers. The weapons of modern anti-mathematical philosophies have owed more to their enemies than the anchorage which enemies always provide for one another. The reflexivity of higher mathematics has been central to the various branches of anti-positivists; the postmodernism of the late 1900s loudly echoes the themes of the mathematical foundations crisis, for those who have ears to hear.[28]

The drive of the mathematical networks into higher abstraction and reflexivity is what gives the distinct edge to the philosophy of the modern West. Of course, the abstraction-reflexivity sequence in general also drives up the level of reflexivity, but this has become hyper-accelerated in the West by the long-term tendencies of two disciplinary networks. It is this which has produced the latest round of self-consciousness about symbol systems that seems to be cutting away the very ground beneath one's feet.

The intellectual situation since about 1700 in this respect is historically unique. An anti-mathematical stance of this sort would have been inconceivable to most Greek, Islamic, and medieval Christian philosophers,[29] for whom mathematics would have been not seen as a bringdown to mundane calculation but as the essence of the transcendental, even mystical hierarchy. Mathematics was the ally of religion and faith. It was only after the great reversal of alliances, at the time of the secularization of the intellectual world in the late 1600s, that an anti-science and anti-mathematical front appeared. Moreover, this front consisted not merely of religious reactionaries, but of a secular opposition to the main line of philosophical development.

The break began as an opposition formed to the Cartesian-Hobbesian ontology of extended substance. Newton, a hero for the scientific movement, was nevertheless anchored in the anti-Cartesian–anti-Hobbesian network, the Cambridge Platonists; the quarrel between Newtonian action-at-a-distance ("occult qualities" to its enemies) and the Cartesian physics of solidly filled space was the opening clash on the new battle lines. It was philosophers flowing from Newton's network—Berkeley, Hume—who went on to do the most damage to the claims of mathematical science as a comprehensive philosophy. Henceforward every development in the mathematically driven sequence of higher abstraction and reflexivity had a counterpart on the anti-mathematical side: Kantian transcendentalism promoted aesthetic Idealism as well as Hegel's denigration of mathematics as an outmoded and superficial consciousness on the level of mere calculation. Mathematical and anti-mathematical inspiration became the deep troubles of philosophical creativity.

The struggle for and against mathematical formalism became the chief dividing line in philosophy after 1900. Husserl put forward phenomenology as "rigorous science" in order to solve the crisis of modern thought, by which initially he meant the foundations crisis just then bursting into the open in the programmatic battles of formalists and intuitionists. The phenomenological movement then migrated en masse to the other side of the field, as the later Husserl himself, and his existentialist offshoots, came to see formalization as the dead hand of technique. Against this we get the anti-technicism of Heidegger, and Sartre's identification of existence with sheer logical unfoundedness. A similar oppositional dialectic took place within the logicist camp, the immediate network offspring of Frege and Russell. Ordinary language philosophy was formulated in reaction to the search for a logically perfect language. Wittgenstein, a dominant figure in the attention space because of the way he battened on deep troubles, managed by a series of switches to be a major player in almost every camp.

Has the mathematical impetus spent itself? Since mathematics is another version of the abstraction-reflexivity sequence, albeit the one that strips abstraction and reflexivity down to purest essentials, one might well say that the two streams merge once again at the point where a self-conscious meta-mathematics becomes mathematically inspired philosophy. And since mathematics continues to have its distinctive turf—the lineage of operations deriving primitively from counting and measuring—the trajectory of meta-mathematics can be seen as a balloon which has slipped its moorings and now is floating away on the high level of generality which is the hereditary turf of philosophy.

The Future of Philosophy

Will philosophy have a future? And why would it not? To say that philosophy is coming to an end is tantamount to saying that the abstraction-reflexivity sequence is coming to an end. It is to say that there are no more deep troubles to drive oppositions, no more law of small numbers dividing the attention space, no more rearrangements of the networks in reaction to shifts in the organization bases of intellectual life.

It is a partisan theme which announces that the era of foundational questions is over, a move within the normal oppositions of struggle over intellectual attention space. The call for the end of philosophy is recurrent, a standard ploy in intergenerational rearrangements, usually a prelude to a new round of deep troubles and new creativity. The version popular in the 1980s and 1990s is couched in the terms of heightened reflexivity of this era. It fails to take sociological reflexivity far enough to perceive the nature of philosophical turf. The search for permanent foundations is another recurrent ploy, the standard terminology of staking a claim on a certain region of the intellectual battleground. Neither side perceives that philosophy is the terrain of struggle, and that deep troubles, not permanent solutions, are the treasures which are the implicit focus of the struggles for possession of the attention space. Philosophy is the turf of intellectuals who perpetually re-dig their conceptual foundations. Foundations are their terrain, not because they are bedrock, but because they are the ever-receding apex of the abstraction-reflexivity sequence—receding not upward to the heavens but downward and inward. This endless digging no more dissolves philosophy into nothingness than Leibniz's infinitesimal calculus made an unreality out of the continuum.

The same can be said for the diagnosis that philosophy becomes exhausted as its contents eventually split free to become empirical sciences. This conception rests on dim awareness that there are branching paths of the abstraction-reflexivity sequence, a polemical awareness that identifies philosophy with the cosmological sequence alone. This misperceives the character of the philosophical attention space, and fails to see that sciences find their niche at a lower level of abstraction. The social practices of modern rapid-discovery natural science are not those of intellectual networks in philosophy, and their niches in attention space to do not supplant one another. The end of philosophy was proclaimed yet again when the modern social sciences split off from philosophical networks. As we have seen, there have been substantive repercussions of both these breaks within the contents of modern philosophy. It would be the wrong inference to see in this anything more than the energizing flows that happen in intellectual networks when their surrounding material bases are changed, opening up the factional space for creative realignments.

Most recently, the organizational revolution of the modern university made it possible to expand the number of specialized disciplines, and each new alignment provides new topics for argument on the most abstract intellectual space. Philosophy is more than the womb of disciplines, and there is no danger of its emptying out to find nothing left of its own. On the contrary, the splitting off of specific empirical disciplines has laid bare the core topics and deep troubles of the abstraction-reflexivity sequence.

As long as there are intellectual networks capable of autonomous action to divide their own attention space, there will be philosophy. If we but knew the social structure of the intellectual world from now until the end of human-like consciousness in the universe, we could chart as long a sequence of future generations of philosophers.

Epilogue:
Sociological Realism

It is often supposed that social constructivism undermines truth. If reality is socially constructed, there is no objectivity and no reality. I deny the conclusion. Social constructivism is sociological realism; and sociological realism carries with it a wide range of realist consequences.

The Sociological Cogito

The philosophically strongest argument is traditionally that which is self-grounding, certain in itself, without appeal to empirical observation. The classic argument of this kind, the cogito, seeks irrefutable truths by passing statements through the acid bath of doubt. "I am thinking" is irrefutable because "I am not thinking" nevertheless displays oneself thinking.

The familiar conclusion from the cogito is the existence of the self. This is not the most useful path of argument. The self which is proven is ambiguous, conceivably only momentary and insubstantial. Consider what else is proven by the cogito. First of all, time exists. To doubt this ("time does not exist") is to make a statement in time. Conscious thinking occupies the saddleback of the present, merging imperceptibly with past and future.

Second, thinking exists. This thinking which is irrefutably proven takes place in language; it constitutes a kind of conversation, myself saying something to myself.[1] The cogito reveals a speaker and an audience. Denial proves it. To think to oneself "there is no one speaking" is uttered by a speaker; "there is no audience for this statement" is received by an audience. Thinking has a social form.

We have not yet proved the existence of other people. This too is given by verbal thinking. Language takes place in words which carry meaning, and follows a grammar which is to a large degree inescapable if statements are to make sense. I do not invent my own language; my thinking depends on forms which have come to me ready-made, from beyond the present moment of consciousness. The constraints of language use, along with its capability for conveying meaning, imply the existence of communicative beings beyond my self. To deny that other people exist—in this specific sense—is to deny the communicability and objectivity, indeed the meaningfulness, of one's own sentences.

The reality of other people also may be derived from another aspect of the language in which we think. Words are to a large extent universals. Concepts (except for indexicals) transcend particulars; they enable one to refer to an object or a quality as appearing over again in time and in different contexts; in short, they are generalized. Apply the test of doubt: "Universals do not exist" is a statement making use of universals. But a general concept implies a generalized viewpoint. A merely fragmentary, temporal sliver of consciousness cannot refer to an experience as "a tree," or even as "that tree again"; it must be a consciousness which involves both continuity and generality. How can my particular fleeting experience give rise to the idea of universals? It must come to me from outside.

The existence of universals implies the existence of society. A concept carries with it a social stance: not merely of some one other person, but an open and universalizing viewpoint of a plurality of other persons. Just how many people this implies is not given. It is more than two; in fact it must be explicitly *unspecified* how many it comprises, since concepts imply meaningfulness for any and every personal stance at all. The concepts which go through one's mind are more than fleeting, having significance over and above my particular moment of thinking. Generality of perspective is at the core of our capacity to think; and this generality implies a collective, omnipresent social viewpoint.

Third, space exists. Although space is not one of the items primordially given through the sociological cogito, it may be quickly derived. If there are other people, not identical with one another in their particularity, they must exist outside one another. This existing outside cannot be merely in time, since time is a single dimension which does not itself provide room for simultaneous plurality. There must be some other dimension in which the multiplicity of selves exists; and we can call this dimension *space.*[2]

We now have the existence of the time-space world as a firm reality. This is the material world of obdurate objects in ordinary experience, externally resistant to one another. One of these objects, the most certain of all, is one's own body. A plurality of selves exists, outside one another in space. There are divisions between me and them; this barrier, as experienced from the inside, is my body. Another argument to the same effect (courtesy of Maine de Biran): I feel resistance to my will; this resistance is the materiality of time-space existence, which meets me first of all as the presence of my body.

The sociological cogito thus gives us assurance of several items of reality: thinking, language, other people, time and space, material bodies. This is not to say that illusions do not exist, or that mistakes cannot be made about particular things of this kind. But perceptual illusions and other mistakes can be discovered and rectified in the usual ways; particular errors occur within a framework of social language, time, and space, and do not call the reality of the framework into question. This can be demonstrated by the method of Cartesian doubt. To say "this is not a real person but a showroom dummy (or a computer)" is nevertheless to affirm that language exists, with its social basis and so forth. The possibility that I am dreaming when I make these statements is nevertheless formulated in sentences, with the same consequences; whether I am dreaming or not at this particular moment, language and society nevertheless exist.[3]

We seem to have drifted beyond the borders of strictly a priori argument. My arguments as to what is beyond doubt, what survives its own refutation, have led to asserting the existence of the realm of empirical experience. This seems inevitable. The distinction between purely conceptual thinking and empirical experience is not absolute, and indeed is hard to pin down precisely. Especially when one affirms a sociological view of thinking, there are regions where the empirical and the conceptual fuse; for example, this fusion takes place in every particular moment of the experience of thinking. The procedure of Cartesian doubt is a methodological game; we use it for the sake of argument, granting one's imaginary skeptical opponent the maximal possible concessions, to show what can be established at the highest level of certainty. Peirce held that Cartesian doubt is impossible, since in fact one never really doubts everything, but only focuses the beam of a targeted doubt on some specific points. Peirce meant that the Cartesian philosopher is already immersed in a stream of language. I have been drawing out the sociological realist implications of this immersion.

Let us now pass beyond the methodological cogito. A second methodological principle can guide us: we are always in medias res, in the middle of things. We always find ourselves in the midst of time, space, discourse, other people. In medias res means that our thinking is always preceded by other thinking, our own and other people's. Wherever we are is always a region from which space stretches out toward an indefinite horizon. In medias res is a primal experience, before we begin to probe for precision. The history of philosophy, and of mathematics, is full of deep troubles which arise in the search for precise borders and for outer limits. Difficulties arise with the infinitesimal and the infinite in time and space, and conceptually with the foundational, the first principle and the ultimate argument. Troubles appear because these formulations too arise in medias res.

In medias res can be taken as an empirical observation. It nevertheless is of a high order of generality, since there appear to be no exceptions. In medias res seems also to be part of an inescapable conceptual framework, a region in which the empirical and conceptual fuse.[4]

Consider then from the empirical side the argument which I have been making for sociological realism. Whence did I get the ideas of the preceding paragraphs, to mount just this line of argument about a sociological cogito? Obviously, from the preceding chapters of this book, and from the empirical and theoretical work of the networks of philosophers and sociologists which have been its materials. I have not crawled into a stove, like Descartes, suddenly and inexplicably resolving to doubt everything, then spontaneously discovering that I cannot doubt that I am thinking in a social language. I have constructed this argument by assimilating the arguments of intellectual networks whose history stretches back for generations. It would be artificial to deny the existence of those historical networks, not only as ideas unfolding in time, but also as bodies of real human beings living in material space. Since I take my own argument seriously, I must agree that I am thinking an internal conversation which attempts to construct a coalition of intellectual audiences, and that the emotional energies which animate my writing come from my own experiences in intellectual networks. The immediate reality of my own activity implies the reality of a larger world of discourse, society, and bodily existence.

And there is no justification for drawing any sharp borders as to what realities are supported by this admission. I cannot deny the reality of intellectual networks; and I can find no reason for supposing that these networks alone have existed, a thin band of historical existence threading back across the centuries, without a wider social and material world surrounding them.

The social constructivist theory of intellectual life, far from being anti-realist, gives us an abundance of realities. Social networks exist; so do their material bases, the churches and schools and the audiences and patrons who have fed and clothed them; so do the economic, political, and geopolitical processes which constituted the outer sphere of causality. These successive layers of context for the minds of philosophers display no sharp borders. There is no criterion for arbitrarily stopping, for declaring that "I concede that social reality exists; but the world of material nature does not." It is all of a piece, all on the continuum in medias res.

The conclusions that we arrive at by following the empirical pathway of in medias res reinforce the a priori conclusions of the sociological cogito. In both directions, social constructivism leads to sociological realism.

Virtually no one actually doubts the reality of the world of ordinary experience. It is only within specialized intellectual networks that the question has arisen whether this banal reality can be proven to a high standard of argument; and even intellectuals, when they are "off duty," go back to assuming the reality of the ordinary time-space world. Sociological realism shows that even within intellectual contention at its most reflexive, it is possible to support banal realism. It does not follow that every kind of ontological reality is thereby supported. There are several kinds of realism and anti-realism; let us see now what sociological realism implies for some of these non-ordinary realms.

Sociological realism affirms mental and physical realities in human-sized time and space. Problems arise when statements are made about realities beyond the human-sized world. These include the objects of science, insofar as these are entities or structures which are not observed by the naked eye or acted upon by the unaided limbs; the concepts of mathematics; conceptual or abstract reality per se, ideas and especially universals; the mind, taken as an entity or substance. A variety of positions have been taken as to these things, either to deny their reality or to affirm that they have a higher reality than ordinary experience. These positions, denying or transcending banal reality, have been produced by intellectual networks, whose struggles for innovation in their argumentative attention space have repeatedly pushed beyond the human-sized world.

Mathematics as Communicative Operations

Mathematics is social discourse. The fact is inescapable if we straightforwardly examine what is given. Here is a mathematical argument of slight technical complexity:

$$(1) \quad a = bx + cy$$
$$(2) \quad a - bx - cy = 0$$

The sequence of statements is true, and meaningful, for me only because I know what the symbols mean, and I know the acceptable procedures for manipulating them, so that equation (1) becomes equation (2). The symbols, like any other form of discourse, imply communication. This modest statement of mathematical abstraction implies that I have had contact with a network of teachers, no doubt many links removed from those who originated this mathematics. Let us take an example from a higher level of abstraction (Kline, 1972: 1128):

If $\mathbf{A_{ik}}$ is a component of a covariant tensor of rank 2, then its covariant derivative with respect to x^l is given by

$$A_{ik,l} = \frac{\partial A_{ik}}{\partial x^1} - \sum_{j=1}^{n} \{il,j\}A_{jk} - \sum_{j=1}^{n} \{kl,j\}A_{ij.}$$

The network of mathematicians now becomes more restricted; at some level it is limited to the network of active mathematicians who are creating the research front of mathematical truths.

For comparison, consider a statement made in the Chinese mathematics of the Sung dynasty algebra in Figure E.1. The difficulty is not merely that we (if we are Westerners) do not know the individual symbols in the same way that Westerners usually cannot understand the equation $4 + 5 = 9$ if it is written

$$四 + 五 = 九$$

but that we do not know the operations determining how these markers are to be manipulated. Chinese mathematics was performed on a counting board divided into squares (depicted in this text as a series of 3×3 or 3×4 matrices, depending on how much of the counting board was used). The Sung algebra, called the "celestial element method," was a set of procedures for representing expressions of constants and unknowns raised to various degrees by placing number signs in particular places on the board surrounding the central element. For example, in conventional modern European notation, the frame in the middle of the first column on the right can be stated as $xy^2 - 120y - 2xy + 2x^2 + 2x$. The Chinese ideographs between the frames are an argument in words (read from top to bottom and right to left), explaining how one algebraic expression is to be transformed into another. This is a verbal rendition of mathematical results; in actual practice, the mathematician uses a set of stand-ard procedures for manipulating the counters on the board and thereby trans-forming one expression into another. The physical operations and the symbolic structure (not just the individual symbols) are different from the Cartesian rules for moving expressions from one side an equal sign ($=$) to another; the similarity is in the overall form of the practice, which allows derivation of strings of mathematical expressions from one another.

A Platonist would say that the form of statement is irrelevant; that the derivation from one mathematical expression to another is true, no matter if it is written in verbal argument in Latin, in post-Cartesian symbolism, in Sung algebra, or anything else. But Platonism is merely a theory; it assumes what has to be proven, that mathematical truths exist somewhere in a realm that has nothing to do with the human activities of making mathematical state-ments. One may show this with a mathematical quasi-cogito: if I deny that a mathematical statement must exist in the form of some particular kind of

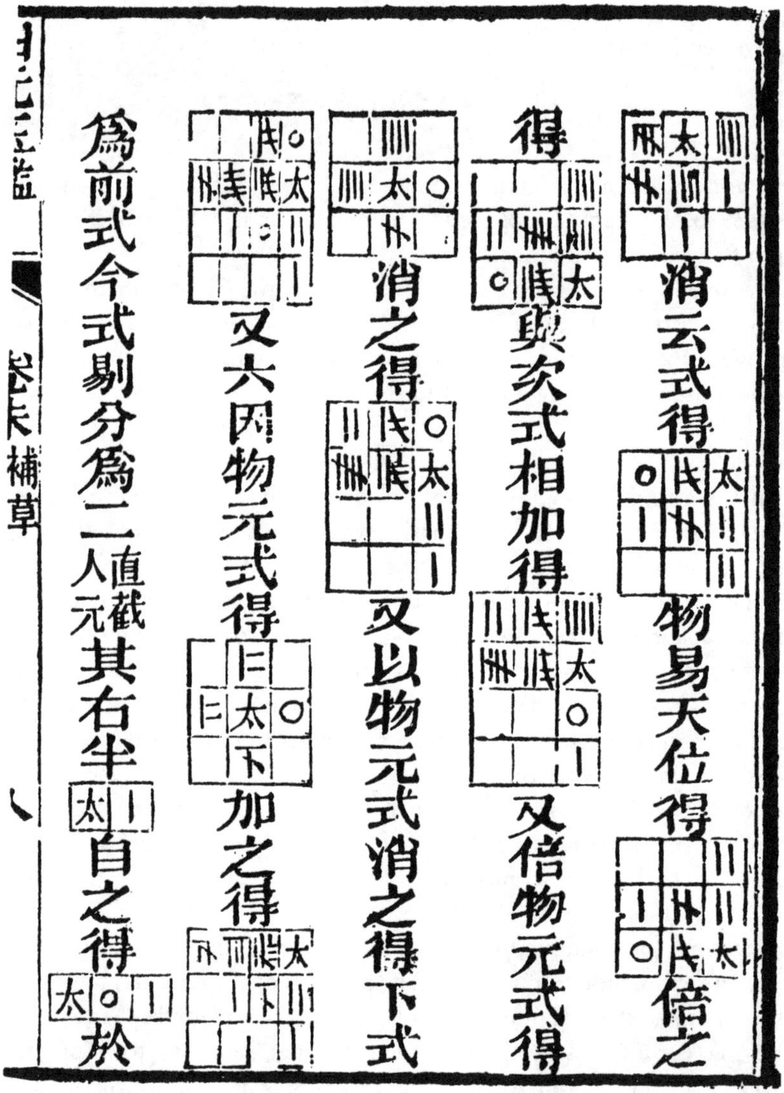

FIGURE E.1. SUNG DYNASTY CELESTIAL ELEMENT ALGEBRA
(Source: Needham, 1959: 131)

discourse, in the very saying I display a statement in a discourse. If I fall back on asserting that mathematics must be transcendent because it can be translated from one language to another, I rest my claim on the existence of translations, operations which connect several discourses together; this not only does not escape from discourse but adds yet another kind of discourse.[5]

Mathematics has a social reality in that it is inescapably a discourse within a social community. This might seem a minimal kind of reality. We should not assume, however, that social discourse has no objective, obdurate quality, the kind of strong constraint that answers the concept of "truth." To show why mathematical discourse has this quality, we must explore the distinctive character of mathematical networks.

Mathematical networks are historically linked backwards to previous mathematicians. This is so not merely in the genealogical sense typical of all creative intellectuals, that the central network of famous creators in one generation typically spawns the next generation of discoverers. Mathematicians are distinctively focused on their history, insofar as the main path of mathematical discovery is to make a topic out of the methods used in a previous level of mathematics, to formulate a symbolism which makes explicit some operations previously tacitly assumed, and to explore the implications of the higher order of abstract symbolism. Algebra generalizes the rules of arithmetic, formulating methods whereby entire classes of arithmetical problems can be solved. Successively higher levels of algebra produce general rules about the solvability of various kinds of algebraic equations. Similar sequences have occurred in analysis, number theory, geometry, and their various hybrids.

Over the course of such sequences, new concepts are created which abstract and summarize whole classes of previous work. The conventional algebraic symbols for unknowns, x, y, stand for any number whatsoever; at a higher level, the function sign $f(x)$ stands for entire expressions of whatever form. Functions of functions abstract still further; so do groups, rings, fields, and so forth. It matters not if what is abstracted is taken to be a number, an unknown, or an operation; on a higher level, the operations of conventional arithmetic are abstracted into a class of operations, which may be selected and elaborated in various ways to give rise to alternative arithmetics, alternative algebras—in short, the pathway to higher mathematics.

Mathematics is the most historical of disciplines in the sense that its central topic is digging backwards into what is taken for granted in its previous work. Algebra not only implies arithmetic; and higher levels of algebra, of analysis, and so forth, not only imply the previously investigated lower levels of abstraction in these fields. The symbolism of mathematics at any point in its history refers to the kinds of operations which were carried out in the earlier mathematics. It is impossible to escape from the historical accumulation of previous results, embedded in the meaning of any particular mathematical expression. The history of mathematics is embodied in its symbolism.

After Descartes, the machinery of manipulating equations has consisted in procedures for transferring symbols from one side of the equal sign to the other, and for rearranging terms until the equation takes the form of what was to be proven. A key to this method is reversibility. The results of operations may be taken as starting points, by assigning them symbols which can be manipulated in the equation. The symbols for unknown numbers x, y which satisfy particular equations are treated as if they were already known; in the same way, any other class of expressions, including those yet to be discovered, are represented as placeholders in the equation. The machinery is not impeded by our ignorance of any particular fact; by the method of symbolizing whole classes, including both past results, future results, perhaps even unattainable or impossible results, it is possible to set in motion the procedures of manipulating equations, and to come to conclusions which reveal how its terms are related.

In one sense the symbolism is a reification. It treats items as if they were things, by symbolizing them in a thing-like way; it gives apparent solidity to this x, or this $f(x)$, which is yet another temptation to treat the objects of mathematics as if they were Platonic realities. But this reification is provisional only, for the sake of proceeding with the technology of manipulating equations. The symbolism belongs to an ongoing history. It points both backwards and forwards: backwards because the most obvious referent of a symbolic placeholder is something of the kind which has already been found on a more concrete level. The x may be replaced with a number which solves an arithmetic problem; the $f(x)$ may be exemplified by some particular algebraic expression. And because the symbolism is abstract and general, it points forward to larger classes of mathematics: not only to all the particular unknowns which might be substituted for a symbol, but outward toward the space of abstract possibilities in a cognate family of operations. In this way the formulation of new symbolism—which always means new systems of practice, procedures for manipulating a collection of symbols—opens up new areas of discovery, higher orders of mathematics to be investigated. Successive orders of symbolism thus point not only backwards to previous work in which they are grounded, but also onward to new kinds of problems.

Mathematics is social, then, in two successively stronger senses: Anyone who performs mathematics even to the extent of understanding an equation in elementary arithmetic is engaged in a form of social discourse and a network of teachers and discoverers. And symbols and procedures which make up mathematics reflexively embody the history of that creative network all the way back to its earliest links; self-reflection on its own prior operations is itself the edifice of higher mathematics.

Let us underline a further aspect which demonstrates that mathematics is thoroughly social. The topic of mathematics is operations, not things. It is not a field which examines what kinds of things exist in the world, or somehow in a world beyond the world. Return to the ground zero of mathematics, numbers. Because a number may be treated as a noun in a sentence, it is easy to assume it is a thing. But the primitive of number is simply counting; it consists in making gestures, verbal or otherwise, toward something while telling off a sequence, "1, 2, 3 . . ." The answer to "How many?" is the number that one stops with when one's gesturing to each in turn is complete. Numbers are primordially the activity or operation of numbering.

In this respect, numbers are like other symbols which make up human discourse. Their universality comes from their universal use, not from any character of the objects on which they are used. Numbering is a process of dividing and pointing. It may be applied to anything: to material objects which may have obvious separations among them, but also to things whose outlines are vague and shifting (clouds, for instance), or indeed to "things" which are not things at all, which may be operations or abstractions or imaginations. Numbering is the operation of making items equivalent by counting them off; they become items because they are treated as such. This does not mean that numbers are illusions. They are real, as operations carried out by human beings, activities carried out in time and spatial location. They are also generalizable, transferable from one situation to another, because they are operations which we can apply over and over again. Their generality comes from their being operations of human discourse.

The operations of mathematics are social, from the primitive level of counting on up. It is not merely that we learn to count by being taught by others, and that the skill of counting is extremely widespread in most societies. The principles of the sociology of mind apply. Counting can be an overt social activity: I count these things in front of us, I invite you to count them as well, or to accept my count because if you follow the same procedure, you will come to the same conclusion.[6] Since conceptual thinking is internalized from external discourse, and takes its meaning only because it implies an external audience, counting which I do for myself alone is also an operation within a social frame. And the conclusion reached earlier may be repeated in this instance: counting produces universals because it takes a universal stance, the stance of anyone at all who follows this convention of discourse.

What has been said about counting may be said again about each of the successively more abstract forms of mathematics. Arithmetic generalizes the results of counting: adding gives rules or shortcuts as to what will happen if one counts first one group, then another, then counts them both, and so forth. Elementary algebra generalizes the results from various kinds of arithmetic problems. There is a generalizing, and reflexive, chain from one form of mathematics to another, from the operations of counting up through the study of operations upon operations which are raised to intricate degrees in abstract math. At each level mathematics investigates and classifies operations. It makes operations equivalent to one another by treating them as equivalent, by subjecting them to a systematic set of higher-order operations. We make the numbers of a counting system equivalent by imposing the conventions of adding and subtracting them. For mathematics, there are no problems of mixing apples and oranges; the mathematician coins a new concept of that which is equivalent among them. Nor need that equivalent be a "natural kind," a concept *in rebus* (e.g., fruit), but just that equivalence which is given by the operation imposed on them. If counting consists in making a series of gestures which thereby constitutes something as a series, arithmetic consists in making gestures toward number operations, elementary algebra in making gestures toward arithmetic operations, higher algebra in making gestures toward elementary algebraic operations which treat them as equivalent.

These gestures are made in common with others in the community of mathematicians. One becomes a member by adopting its conventions of communication. The social structure of mathematics is pyramid-shaped. Across the base, there is the huge community of those who use the conventions of counting and of arithmetic. Building step-wise upon this are the communities of increasingly specialized and esoteric mathematicians, networks which have taken the lower-level communicative operations, the lower-level conventions, as topics for abstraction and reflexive generalization.

Mathematical objects are real in the same sense that human communication is real. It is the reality of activities of real human beings, carried out in time, located in space. And it is the doubly strong, obdurate reality of the social: of widespread conventions of discourse, which is to say activities carried out in common, and which constitute a community out of just those persons who adopt these conventional operations. We may even say it is triply strong, since the network of mathematicians is that which has grown up around the central activity of constructing techniques of building meta-operations which take as content the previous operations of the community.

The long-standing view of mathematics as a realm of Platonic ideals is mistaken. Some Greeks philosophers and mathematicians argued that the objects of mathematics must be ideal because the truths they proved about geometric figures referred to ideal circles and lines, not to the imperfectly drawn lines on the sand.[7] Others have argued for the ideality of mathematics by using empiricism as a foil; numbers are not the things we observe in the world, since it is by numbers that we can enumerate things. Both lines of argument make the same mistake (and so does that which holds that mathematics arises by induction from experience of things): assuming that reality must consist either in substantive things or in self-subsistent ideas. But mathematical concepts are neither; they are emblems for actions, for operations of mathematical discourse. Universals and ideals are activities of social discourse; they are as real as that discourse, which is to say as real as the ordinary human-sized world of action. There is no need to assign them to another world.

Another mistake is to interpret mathematics as consisting in tautologies. The identity between those items on opposite sides of the equal sign in a mathematical equation is not the same kind of identity as that established by giving something a name; it is not the empty tautology exemplified by explaining "gravity" as "the propensity to fall." Mathematical equivalence and verbal tautology are embedded in different language games, in different systems of operations. The arbitrary tautologies of ordinary language lead nowhere; mathematical procedure is a discovery-making machine. The machinery of mathematical equations operates in multiple directions, as Frege noted in distinguishing sense and reference. The equivalence-making conventions of mathematics open up successive classes of abstract operations whose properties can be investigated. Conventions are arbitrary, but discovery in mathematics consists in exploring the patterns opened up by adopting various kinds of conventions. Mathematics is a special field of empirical discovery, insofar as "empirical" means investigation of experience in time; it is the experience of the mathematical network of investigating what is implied in the symbolic conventions it adopts.

The theories that mathematics must be a transcendent realm of Platonic objects, or at least the a priori truths inherent in tautologies, are attractive because they help explain the feeling that mathematics is certain, that its results are as high and irrefutable a level of truth as humans can attain. This certainty can be explained by the special social character of mathematical networks. Because the contents of mathematics are chained together over time, from the most rarefied abstractions back to the ordinary operations of counting, the edifice is tied together at an awesome level of tightness. It is not simply that results are lazily passed along from one generation to the next, as a long-standing traditional paradigm which no one bothers to question. On the contrary, the linkage is deep and inescapable, since the topics of successively more abstract mathematics have been the underlying patterns of the operations of previous mathematics. Mathematics embodies its history, in its procedures for using symbolism, to a degree found in no other field. The most naive practitioner produces the same results as everyone else, because anyone who learns to follow the conventions can repeat the chain of argument. Mathematics is certain because it is repeatable and reliable, and these consist in the repeatability of a chain of social conventions.

The Objects of Rapid-Discovery Science

Social constructivism in the sociology of science is generally associated with an anti-realist position as to the entities of science. Let us see to what extent this is justified. The activity of natural science, if not the name, has existed in intellectual networks in many parts of the world since ancient times. Throughout most of history (as Chapter 10 has described) these networks were subject to the law of small numbers, dividing into opposing positions within astronomy, medical physiology, even mathematics. The entities of science constituted multiple and competing realities for the networks that conceived them. In the European generations between 1500 and 1700, a branch of intellectual networks reorganized in such a way that science changed its character: it became rapid-discovery science, which eventually acquired a high degree of consensus. The network shifted attention toward a train of forward-moving discoveries. Disputes became more short-lived, rarely lasting beyond a generation. The division among opposing positions under the law of small numbers was truncated into a temporary disagreement at the research front, which was repeatedly put behind as attention moved onward to the next round of discoveries.

What I have just described is on the level of the social reality of these networks of scientists; it refers to the entities of science only insofar as they are contents asserted, disputed, accepted, and passed along by the network. The network of scientists at the time of the rapid-discovery revolution was largely a branch of the long-standing philosophical network. Gradually splitting off from the philosophers, the scientific network became in its own sphere a double network: on one side a network of intellectuals, chains of masters and pupils; on the other side chains of research equipment, modified from one generation to the next.

The genealogies of research technology are carried along by the human network; it is living persons who modify lenses into telescopes and microscopes, and thence into the laboratory equipment of optics and spectrography. Both kinds of networks are parasitical on one another. The rapid movement of research equipment from one modification to the next is the key to the mode of rapid discovery in which scientists have so much confidence; they feel that discoveries are there to be made along a certain angle of research because the previous generation of equipment has turned up phenomena which are suitable for the intellectual life of the human network. The favored part of the scientific network is that part which has closest access to the previous generation of successful discovery-making equipment; these persons are in a position to refine or modify the equipment to extend past lines of discovery-making. This applies both to the accretion of small discoveries within a successful paradigm, which generally takes place by small modifications or extensions of the application of existing technique, and to major new lines of discovery, which typically arise by the cross-breeding of lines of equipment or by the invention of radically new research technology: the development of the electrical battery and its combination with the equipment of chemical experiment, and thence with the equipment of astronomy, and so onward.[8] There is no apparent limit to this process in time; the combinatorial cross-breeding of research equipment genealogies will apparently continue to generate phenomena for scientific discoveries as long as social networks exist to promote the equipment genealogies.

The lineages of research equipment are real, in the sense in which the world of human-sized objects in time and space is real. They are lineages of material things. The interpretation is sometimes made that scientific experiments are embodied theories, that research equipment has a primarily mental reality. This seriously overstates the case. The genealogy of equipment is carried along by a network of scientific intellectuals who cultivate and cross-breed their technological crops in order to produce empirical results which can be grafted onto an ongoing lineage of intellectual arguments. This is not to say that scientists always experiment in the light of theories which give a supportable interpretation of what their equipment is doing. Tinkering with the equipment, cross-breeding it, or initially inventing it may be done with very little sense of the theoretical issues that later develop out of it and provide a retrospective theoretical interpretation of what the equipment is doing. Whether scientific intellectuals have a clear and defensible theoretical conception of their equipment or not, they engage in practical bodily action whenever they use equipment. The network of scientists acts in the banal material time-space world, and the theoretical entities which they discuss and pass along as the contents of their science are grounded in this human-sized world of human bodies and research equipment.

What then is the reality of the theoretical entities of science? As invisible structures or substances they are prey to all the philosophical troubles which arise whenever one attempts to step out of in medias res and into a realm of perfect precision and enduring substantiality. Nevertheless, this does not make them necessarily illusory or unreal. Theoretical constructs can acquire an obdurate quality like that of the world of banal reality because they are linked with it in at least two ways. They are a real focus of attention and, over time, of consensus within a real network of scientists. This social consensus is of a distinctive kind, oriented toward a lineage of discoveries about obdurate reality, because scientific entities are also grounded in the material genealogies of research equipment; though scientific entities have an intellectual side, they also have a non-intellectual side, phenomena which arise from the ways in which this equipment behaves.

Both of these links to banal reality of human-sized material experience extend outward in time; both have generations of predecessors, and both carry along the prior experience of past generations; both imply what practices will work again in the future. This is particularly strong in the equipment genealogy; research technologies have been manipulated and modified just so that they give repeatable results. The stability of scientific entities is the counterpart on the intellectual plane of the stability which has been created in practice in the equipment of research. One can regard this as stability in the interaction between the bodies of experimenters and the equipment. The perfection of the equipment, and the stabilization of a theoretical entity (an electron, let us say), rests on the way in which the genealogy of equipment has become successively easier to manipulate. This reaches a very high degree when the standardized equipment, or some offspring of it, is shipped out of the laboratory; electric circuits become wiring manipulated by millions of people in everyday life; electromagnetic wave detectors become radio receivers. When this occurs, the human social network which hosts the theoretical entity gives it a seemingly irreproachable reality. The specialized intellectual network, prone to creating the esoterica of the non-ordinary world, fades from presence; electricity becomes so closely tied to the unquestionable realities of human bodies and the human-sized things that surround them that it comes to seem continuous with ordinary reality.

And indeed in a sense it is. Although we are rarely conscious of the fact, the electric switches, batteries, wave detectors, and so forth are the current generation of a long trail of previous equipment whose youth was spent in the genealogies of laboratories. It is this long train, extending backwards and forwards through time, that makes some scientific entities so obdurate; they are so tightly and multiply linked to ordinary reality that it is hard to separate them from it.

The obdurate reality acquired by some entities of science comes more from their material grounding in equipment than from their theoretical conceptualization. Electricity has had a widespread practical reality since about 1850,[9] while its theoretical interpretation within the core of the research network has changed several times. In the same way, modern conceptions of the elementary components of chemistry and physics have changed over the generations from atoms to electron orbits to successive reorderings of families of subatomic particles and anti-particles to strings; an examination of the standard textbooks at intervals of 30 years suggests a pattern of ongoing evolution and no reason to suppose that today's entities will be accepted as more than crude approximations at some time in the future.[10] This historical fluidity of the conceptual constructions of science is what we should expect from competitive intellectual networks. The stability and obdurate reality of "electricity," "bacterial infection," and other now familiar entities are guaranteed by their embeddedness in genealogies of material practice which have spread among non-intellectuals. The superior reality accorded to the conceptions of rapid-discovery science comes from the way in which the dual, mutually parasitical networks of that community, the equipment genealogies and the human intellectuals, have spawned a third branch, equipment genealogies, which have found a home apart from the incessantly frontier-seeking idea contest of the intellectuals. It matters not how the esoteric intellectual frontier at the moment interprets "electricity"; the unexamined word serves as a marker for an obdurate reality of everyday life.

The social construction of scientific entities leads to at least quasi-realism. Although not all scientific entities, as intellectual constructs, have the same claim to be regarded as real, some of them are so closely entwined with human-sized banal reality that the borderline is difficult to draw. Although their epistemological justification is more complex than the irrefutable realities of immediate social experience, they are at least close kin.

How is it possible that mathematics is so often found applicable to the natural, non-human, non-symbolic world? Why has it become so useful in science? It is not so mysterious once we see the force of the point that mathematics arises in social networks which are part of the natural world. The distinctiveness of the network of mathematical practitioners is that they focus their attention on the pure, contentless forms of human communicative operations: on the gestures of marking items as equivalent and of ordering them in series, and on the higher-order operations which reflexively investigate the combinations of such operations. The primal operations—counting, measuring—begin as gestures toward the ordinary human-sized bodily objects and activities of time-space reality. Such activities have the same quality of reality as anything else on the level of this ordinary banal world. The abstract mathematics which arises reflexively on these operations remains part of the natural world; in fact it is an empirical investigation of an aspect of that natural world, the part which consists in the communicative activities of mathematicians as they create new forms of operating on their prior operations. Mathematics arises in medias res, and it maintains a smooth continuity from one level of its own abstraction to another. There is no sharp boundary between the objects of mathematics and the world of natural science. The scientific applicability of mathematical procedures should not be surprising.

High consensus over the objects of science arises only in rapid-discovery networks; and these in turn are composed of mutually parasitical relationships between genealogies of research equipment and the argumentative network of scientific intellectuals. Mathematical rapid-discovery science adds a third network, the lineage of techniques for manipulating formal symbols representing classes of communicative operations. Mathematics does not provide a magical eye by which we see the transcendently existing objects behind the phenomenal surface of experience, the invisible entities of scientific theories. Mathematics is connected to the other two networks in the phenomenal world of experience.

On one side, the measurements given by the research equipment are made into mathematical realities because humans use them as markers, in the same sense that the primitive mathematical operation of counting is the social procedure of gesturing toward (and thereby setting equivalent) items of experience. As Searle (1992) would say, there is no homunculus in the research equipment; it is the human mathematicians who use equipment as extensions of their own capacity for making gestures. These are gestures simultaneously toward the non-human world and toward the social community, which has built up a repertoire of reliable methods of transforming one set of symbolic gestures into another.

On the other side, the genealogy of mathematical techniques connects to the network of scientific intellectuals, which constructs the meaningful objects and arguments which make up the humanly familiar contents of science. Equipment genealogies produce phenomena in the world of experience; scientific intellectuals turn these phenomena into interpretations, useful for winning arguments and setting off the network onto yet further topics of investigation. The "invisible" world of scientific entities comes from the intellectuals, not directly from the equipment. Mathematical technique becomes important for scientists because it enables them to give an especially obdurate character to at least parts of their arguments; but this is the obdurate reality of certain chains of reflexive communicative operations, which it has been the business of mathematicians to investigate. The crystal-hard social reality of mathematics gives backbone to the socially negotiated arguments of scientific coalitions.

Mathematics is a bridge: it shares with the scientific network the character of being social; it shares with equipment genealogies the character of being a lineage of techniques. Since the lineage of mathematical technique is a lineage of discoveries about processes in time-space reality (i.e., about mathematical operations), it meshes well with equipment-generated phenomena which are multi-dimensional processes, whose form cannot be interpreted on the low levels of abstraction and reflexivity encountered in ordinary noun-adjective-verb grammar or ordinary arithmetic. (That is why the investigation of higher algebras—quaternions, vectors, matrices—was so fruitful for the development of modern physics.) Here again we find the social reality of mathematics blending seamlessly with the non-human natural reality of equipment-generated phenomena.

The core social network in science remains that of the human intellectuals. Science, to be successful, ultimately issues in words and imagery. A purely mathematical enterprise such as string theory does not acquire full, socially accepted "reality" until there is a verbal interpretation of its main points, which translates them into the familiar noun-like "entities" which count as paramount reality in ordinary language. But here we should note that mathematics too is embedded in words.[11] This reminds us that "mathematics" is two networks in one, a genealogy of techniques and a human network which both knows how to work the techniques and engages in the usual intellectual contest of setting arguments for one another. Verbal discourse is the most encompassing frame, the home ground of intellectual life. If mathematics is an important bridge among the human and non-human networks which constitute science, it is because mathematicians are hybrids sharing all the traits of humanness, from verbal discourse to their own special form of formal reflexiveness.

Mathematics is simultaneously empirical and conceptual. It encompasses both the observation of experience in time and space, which is always particular and situationally located. But it deals with the universal and general, indeed with patterns which are irrefutably found among universal concepts, because its topic is the pure generality of human communicative operations. These are the activities of making things equivalent, of transposing them for one another. The topic is universal because it comprises the operations of treating things as universals. It is simultaneously empirical, arising within experience and applicable to experience, because doing mathematics is an activity taking place in time and within a social network. The universal features of mathematics are empirically discovered, by the work of mathematicians investigating various systems of operations. The topic of mathematics is their system of communicative conventions. What they discover about this is objective, obdurate reality. If we say it is socially constructed, it is an empirical investigation of the obdurate qualities of social construction. It is so real because it is so thoroughly socially constructed.

Why Should Intellectual Networks Undermine Themselves?

A social constructivist theory of the intellectual world affirms several inescapable realities: other people and their intercommunication, the time-space world, and human-sized material things with our own bodies among them. Mathematics makes discoveries about the obdurate realities of intellectual operations, the nested chains of gestures by which we designate equivalences and transform abstract statements into one another. Genealogies of scientific research equipment have become part of inescapable banal reality. The effectiveness of this equipment in producing and reproducing special phenomena in ordinary time-space, which the network of scientific intellectuals interprets, ties the non-immediate entities of scientific theories closely, if not immediately, to ordinary reality as well.

How then does far-reaching doubt arise about so many of these realities? In part it simply continues the main dynamic of creativity, the law of small numbers. Intellectuals thrive on disagreement, dividing the attention space into three to six factions, seeking lines of creativity by negating the chief tenets of their rivals, rearranging into alliances or fanning out into disagreements as the material base for one faction or another is strengthened or weakened. Conflict over the attention space is a fundamental social fact about intellectuals. It follows that intellectuals produce multiple competing views of reality. And this disagreement will go on in the future, as long as intellectual networks exist.

Disagreement over fundamental realities has been normal in the intellectual world ever since specialized networks appeared in ancient times; it is only in the last dozen generations of modern European networks that a social structure has arisen producing intellectual consensus on some topics. The network of intellectuals has split into several branches: philosophers and general-purpose intellectuals, whose dynamics continue to be determined by the law of small numbers; rapid-discovery science, which developed out of a technique for evading the law of small numbers; and mathematicians, whose niche is a cumulative, self-entwining investigation which builds a core of virtual certainty in its lineage of knowledge. Besides these, in a limbo between rapid-discovery science and philosophy, are the disciplines of social science and humanistic scholarship; they resemble the natural sciences in taking topics of empirical (including historical) investigation, but share with philosophy the social organization which produces intellectual fractionalization under the law of small numbers.

As intellectual networks have continued to branch, especially with the accelerating expansion of academic populations since 1900, criticism of the reality of the objects studied by particular branches has entered a new phase. Some branches take one another for their topics of investigation. These disciplinary overflows are a normal source of the expansion of knowledge. Creativity in philosophy since the academic revolution of the 1800s has been largely stimulated by the adjudication of new disciplinary boundaries. The emergence of history of science, sociology of knowledge, the literary theory of textuality, along with many other actual and potential combinations, heightens the reflexivity of the intellectual community as a whole. The search for problems, for energizing points of attention and contention, which is the life of intellectual networks, has turned to exposing the inner truth claims of the various specialized branches to the alternative perspectives of different branches.

Much of the intellectual action now comes from cross-disciplinary clashes, but this sociological point is not yet an epistemological judgment on the reality of the objects that particular fields are studying. Analysis is not the same as critique. Reflexivity per se is not necessarily self-undermining. To say "I am lying" is paradoxical; but to say "I am telling the truth" is not. Why then is it so easily assumed that sociological reflexivity undermines the truth of whatever socially produced knowledge it focuses upon?

The widespread assumption is that truth is determined by reality; a statement is true because it meets the criteria of truth, not because of any other reason. If truth is socially determined, then it cannot be determined by truth itself. This is like saying that one sees things accurately only if one sees without eyeballs, as if knowing must take place without any human apparatus for knowing.

Truth characterizes statements. Reality is that which makes statements true, but reality itself is neither true nor false; it simply is. Statements are inevitably human; truth, when it exists, is inevitably a phenomenon of the human world. The abstract truths we are concerned with, found in the statements of intellectuals, arise in the specialized discourse of social networks. The very conception of truth, and the criteria by which truth is recognized, arise within human communities, and have been changed, abstracted, and refined over the generations of intellectual networks. That is merely a historical fact. That conceptions of truth are human, and historical, does not automatically divorce true statements from reality.

Truths do not arise in isolated brains or disembodied minds. The message of this book is that mind is not a substance or an entity; the verbal thinking we are concerned with is an activity of overt and internal conversations. Thought is always linked in a flow of verbal gesture from human body to body, among mutually focused nervous systems, reverberating with shared rhythms of attention. Its symbols represent general and abstract viewpoints because they are communicable markings, activities of taking the stance of all the members of the network. Its arguments are energized by the emotional energy arising from the ritual density of interactions in the core of the intellectual networks, where disagreements are focused and alliances are made. The individual thinker, closeted in privacy, thinks something which is significant for the network only because his or her inner conversation is part of the larger conversation and contributes to its problems. If a brain flickers and brightens with statements which are true, this happens only because that brain is pulsing in connection with the past and anticipated future of a social network. Truth arises in social networks; it could not possibly arise anywhere else.

The social construction of science does not undermine scientific truths. Intellectual networks are part of the time-space physical world; to say that social networks produce science is only to say that the natural world gives rise to knowledge about the natural world. The social network of mathematicians investigates the pure properties of human communication; human communication is part of the natural world; again a part of reality investigates and discovers something about itself. Sociology and the other social and humanistic research disciplines, for all the layers of reflexivity that went into constructing their objects, nevertheless study something real precisely because their objects are social.

Social reflexivity outrages our assumptions only when we conceptualize Truth as existing apart from people, or as the relation between a disembodied, featureless observing Mind and a sharply separate Reality. We have made knowledge the equivalent of God in a transcendent religion. Durkheim puts this into perspective: the highest sacred object, symbolized as God, is society. For intellectuals, the society which matters above all, which gives them their creative energy and is the fount and arena of their ideas, is their own social network. The concept of transcendent Truth is an expression of the felt autonomy of the inner activities of the intellectual network.[12]

The intrusion of sociological reflexivity is taken as an affront to a sacred object of truth. This affront is felt most sharply by members of particular intellectual communities whose work is itself not very reflexive. As the disciplines have differentiated, philosophy has taken as its terrain the discovery of deep troubles, which drive them along a sequence of increasing abstraction and reflexivity; the natural sciences have taken as their terrain the investigation of empirical topics with conceptions on moderate levels of abstraction. Since their level of abstraction stays fairly constant, scientists are unconcerned with problems of reflexivity, especially the deep troubles of high degrees of self-consciousness which have been reached in philosophy since 1900. Sociologists of knowledge have been hybrids from the philosophical networks, and thus have shared their reflexivity, since the time of Scheler, Lukács, and Mannheim in the 1920s, through the Wittgensteinian and ethnomethodological influence on sociology of science in the 1970s and 1980s.[13] This reflexivity clashes with the relatively more concrete conceptions of scientists. Many scientists, especially as they display their findings to lay audiences (including politicians and industries who fund their research), speak about their theoretical objects as if they were natural objects on the same level as the banal realities of everyday life. Sophisticated and pragmatically adept within their own research communities, scientists often adopt the stance of naive realism, amounting to reifying complexly mediated abstractions, when they communicate with outsiders.

Some heat of the argument comes from embarrassment, above all in the case of the high-prestige wing of contemporary intellectuals, the scientists. Sociologists of science have stripped away the idealizations with which scientists have traditionally presented their results, hiding their actual investigation and negotiation, as if they produced scientific truths untouched by human hands. It does not necessarily follow that the dirty work of science, its ordinary constructive activities, undermines its truth. On the other side of the conflict, many sociologists have pursued the investigation of other disciplines in a debunking mood, again not sociologically surprising in that the social energies of intellectual life come from uncovering lines of disagreement. To repeat the conclusions arrived at: social construction per se does not necessarily undermine truth, for there is no other way that true statements could arise than by the activities of social networks. And since social constructivism is itself a form of realism, it can ally itself with realism in science and mathematics.

This leaves a region of the intellectual world in which sociological realism may not take us very far. The law of small numbers continues to determine the pattern of creativity in philosophy, sociology, and other humanistic and social research disciplines. Does this mean that there is no single reality, no truth, in these fields?

One way out of this conclusion is the possibility that multiple realities and competing truths will turn out to be complementary. We may hope that the situation is that of the many blind men touching different parts of the same elephant; more appropriately, since that image is too static, we may hope that the competing factions of philosophers or sociologists are pursuing multiple paths of advance into the same wilderness. But it is also possible that this will not be the case; a unified map may never be filled in because the paths may never intersect.

The social processes of intellectual life imply that the future will consist in still further fanning out rather than convergence. New topics are constructed by combining previous chains of intellectual work. The research topics and theoretical perspectives of the previous generation can always be combined to yield new studies.[14] Crossing disciplinary boundaries expands the possibilities still further. Reflexive methods, treating a topic from the viewpoint of its history, of feminist critique, of its social production, of textual rhetoric, and other standpoints, results in further fanning out in the pattern of permutations and combinations. Still more topics can be created as higher levels of abstraction and reflexivity, taken over from the long-term sequence of philosophical life, make it possible to re-study earlier problems at successive levels of the abstraction-reflexivity sequence. The endless fanning out of intellectual combinations does not happen mechanically, and does not exclude work that will be received as striking and insightful. There is a premium on being able to crystallize new gestalts which bring ingredients together. And throughout, the law of small numbers dividing the attention space motivates creativity, sometimes of genuinely new positions, by negating key premises of opposing positions.

In practical reality there is no danger that future intellectuals will run out of topics for creativity. No matter how much mass higher education expands in the future, with the rising tide of credential inflation, no matter how many professors need to write articles and books for academic promotion, there will always be topics to write about. The inverted pyramid of publications building on previous publications has no intrinsic limit.

Does the widening combinatorial fan of intellectual productions mean that the humanities and social sciences of the future will diverge infinitely into multiple realities? Social processes imply that intellectual atomization may not go very far. Within any particular intellectual community, the law of small numbers limits how many positions can receive widespread attention. This still could leave us with half a dozen hermetically sealed viewpoints in each specialty. But borders will not be sharp, precisely because so many publications are constructed by combining ingredients from several previous lines of work. The larger the number of intellectuals all under pressure to publish original work, the more incentive there will be to range widely across borders in search of new combinations.

The sense of a common reality is fostered where the patches of intellectual production are stitched together piece by piece into a multi-patterned quilt. This does not produce the object-like reality in which all the intellectuals in a given faction share a single world frame, or posit the same kind of world substance whose characteristics they are all investigating. Combinatorial construction of intellectual topics, if unmitigated by other social features of the intellectual world, produces neither a central conception nor a limiting frame around what they believe they are studying. It nevertheless leads not to infinitely fragmenting individual realities, but to a decentered network of overlapping realities.

In philosophy, because its central terrain remains conceptual rather than historical or empirical, the construction of multiple realities seems fated to an especially strong form of divisiveness. Philosophy takes as its terrain the discovery of deep troubles, self-propagating difficulties. These deep conceptual troubles are the hidden treasures of first-rate philosophical creativity, the discovery of which brings fame to those who bring them to light. To cultivate deep troubles is to court disagreement. It is to keep the law of small numbers operating, thereby bringing the focus of hard-fought argument which energizes conceptual advance.

Yet even in the heart of philosophy there is a shared reality. The very concept of a deep trouble combines an element of realism with its inevitable consequence of splitting realities. Deep troubles are discovered by the network, not merely contrived; they are obdurate and unmalleable; they constrain and shape the path of the philosophical network across the generations. In the same way, the sequence of abstraction and reflexivity, which socially undermines itself at high levels of self-reflection, also is an obdurate reality, a constraint which shapes the long-term pathway of the network. Abstraction and reflexivity, the terrain explored by this most acutely self-conscious and inwardly turning of all networks, are real because they are activities arising through the historical existence of the social network itself. Even philosophy, the archetypal conflictual discipline under the law of small numbers, the field whose creativity battens on self-propagating difficulties, makes discoveries about a reality of its own.

APPENDIX 1

The Clustering of
Contemporaneous Creativity

The typical pattern throughout world networks is for philosophers of a similar level of creative eminence to cluster in the same generations. For China, the main exceptions are the following:

Major	Year	Secondary
Confucius	480 B.C.E.	
	450	Tseng Tzu
Mo Ti	420	
	380	Yang Chu
	80 C.E.	Wang Ch'ung
	950	Ch'en T'uan
	1480	Ch'en Hsien-Chang
Wang Yang-ming	1520	Lo Ch'in-shun

Cases are not counted as mismatches which arise only through arbitrary placement of borderlines in ranking or between generations.

The most important isolates are the two earliest major philosophers on the chart, Confucius and Mo Ti, and the last, Wang Yang-ming. These are truly major figures; especially the first two, whose names dominated Chinese thought in one case for several thousand years, in the latter case several hundred. But here we may be victim of a retrospective illusion. As I have discussed in Chapter 4, the philosophical work of these two men was rudimentary; it was their lineages which gradually built up their towering reputations. Confucius and Mo Ti are more important as founders of organizations and symbolic figure-heads than as intellectual creators. Thus in the next generation after Confucius the most noted name is Tseng Tzu (listed as borderline minor), who is merely the best remembered of the leaders of some seven or eight organizational lineages which branched off at that point. Confucius, Tseng Tzu, and the other minor figures of this time ought to be taken as a movement, none of whose reputations would have survived without the others.

Mo Ti, who branches off from one of these Confucian schools another generation later, was building intellectually upon his opposition to the Confucian "establishment." The case of Mo Ti's eminence is structurally similar to Confucius', especially since in both cases it is unclear which parts of their doctrines—and their canonical texts—are the work of the founders and which are the work of followers. There is reason to believe that much of the philosophical refinement of the older part of the *Mo Tzu* is the work of Mo's principal pupil, Ch'in Ku-li (28 in Figure 4.1). This casts light on the position of Yang Chu, who appears in this generation as an isolated secondary figure. But Yang Chu stirred up great controversy in his day with his doctrine that the Way of Heaven is to nourish the vital needs of the individual, rather than assume social obligations. Moreover, Yang Chu is structurally locked in antagonism with the Confucians, and especially the Mohists, as he is known to have debated with Ch'in Ku-li. In view of the likelihood that "individualist" or "agriculturalist self-sufficiency" doctrines branched off from the Mohist lineage around this time (e.g., Hsu Hsing in the next generation after Ch'in Ku-li), it appears that we have here another case where creative alternatives are being formulated in counterpoint with one another.

The main cases of horizontal isolation that remain consist of one major figure and several secondary ones. The major philosopher is Wang Yang-ming, who enlivened the dead orthodoxy of the Ming dynasty. But even though he lacks a rival of major stature, he belongs to a cluster in his youthful and mature generations (i.e., 1465–1500 and 1500–35) which includes several secondary figures both from the dominant Ch'eng-Chu Neo-Confucians and in opposition, in addition to those who branch off from Wang's own school. Here there is at least partial eminence against his major eminence. This leaves two secondary figures: Ch'en T'uan is a borderline minor figure, a Taoist cosmologist ca. 950 C.E., a time when not much is happening apart from minor figures of the Ch'an lineages. Ch'en T'uan is not a vertical isolate, since he leads into what eventually becomes the neo-Confucian cosmologists four generations later.

The most isolated figure in the entire Chinese chart is Wang Ch'ung, the only name of any significance for four generations of the Later Han (i.e., the entire period from 35 to 165 C.E.). Wang Ch'ung is also among the most unusual intellectually as well, an outspoken rationalist and enemy of superstition. In his themes he continues the critical scholarship of the Old Text school, which had arisen in opposition to the occultism, false antiquarianism, and downright forgeries of the so-called New Text school. That is to say, this was a battle within Confucianism between the occultist synthesis which Tung Chung-shu had brought to prominence around 130 B.C.E., and the movement of critical textual scholars which had come to prominence with Liu Hsin around 1 C.E. (Fung, 1952–53: 2:133–167). But Wang Ch'ung lacks an important contemporary rival on the occultist side. Here we encounter a seeming exception to the pattern of contemporary rival creativity.

Among the Greeks, the apparent exceptions are as follows:

Major	*Year*	*Secondary*
Carneades	180 B.C.E.	
	120 C.E.	Calvenus Taurus
	220	Origen
Plotinus	250	Mani
Porphyry	280	
Proclus	450	

Once again I do not count mismatches based only on small differences in ranking or timing. Pythagoras and Plato, although having no contemporaries in their maturity to match their truly eminent stature, nevertheless have quite a bevy of rivals. Not only is Plato the most eminent of the Greeks, but also he lived in the generation richest in new developments, matched against six philosophers listed as secondary in Figure 3.4. Arcesilaus and Chrysippus both overlapped in time and personally debated; Carneades, the great Academic Skeptic, comes close on Chrysippus' heels. What we have here is a succession of overlapping generations, the Academic and Stoic schools, counterpunching at a pace of about thirty years. Carneades himself recognized this: "If there were no Chrysippus, there would be no me" (Tarrant, 1985: 127).

Plotinus seems a mismatch against Gnostic Mani, a secondary figure for philosophy, and Porphyry in the next generation lacks important rivals. But the parallel is closer when we realize that Mani is founder of the Manichaean heresy, which was to receive great philosophical attention within Christianity just as Plotinus was founding a religious version of Platonism that was to become the philosophical rallying point for pagans in their struggle against Christianity. Moreover, Origen, Plotinus, and Porphyry overlap and take off on one another's turf, and Porphyry turns up the anti-Christian note into an explicit polemic, for the first time in the Neoplatonist tradition. The close personal contact among these builders of rival positions confirms their mutual orientation to a common division in the field. Augustine is contemporary in the west with the great Church Fathers of the east, Gregory of Nyssa and Gregory Nazianzen, although Augustine's work in philosophy lacks the rival counterpart it has in theology. Proclus still eludes the structural generalization: a major figure without significant rivals or contemporaries. Although he is connected to all the important chains of adjacent generations, these include only minor figures in terms of long-run importance.

It is worth briefly comparing the lists of horizontal isolates from contemporary creativity with lists of major or secondary philosophers who are vertical isolates from significant master-pupil chains:

China:
Shen Pu-Hai
Shang Yang
Tao Te Ching author
Wang Ch'ung

Greece:
Melissus
Lucretius
Numenius of Apamea
Mani
Pseudo-Dionysius

The *Tao Te Ching* author may not belong on this list. That person, I would conjecture, was probably in the network of the followers of Chuang Tzu and those around Kung-sun Lung, most likely at the court of Wei; but I will not press the point. The anonymous *Mohist Canons,* however, were surely produced in the network of known figures of the Mohist schools.

There are relatively few and unimportant figures who are isolated from significant master-pupil chains or other personal ties among well-known intellectuals. Lucretius is perhaps the most notable exception here.

The network patterns of Greek and Chinese philosophers are representative of what we find throughout world history. In medieval Islam, Judaism, Christendom and modern Europe, episodes of creativity occur among contemporary rivals and in significant intergenerational chains. There are relatively few exceptions. Among philosophers listed as major, we find only the following:

Horizontal isolates (lack of significant rivals):
Ibn Sina (Avicenna)   1120 C.E.   Iran
Al-Ghazali   1180   Iraq, Iran

Vertical isolates (lack of intellectual network ties):
None

The major Jewish philosopher-scientist Levi ben Gerson (early 1300s), as far as we know, was not directly connected with the minor Jewish philosophers in southern France of his day; but he was connected with the papal court at Avignon at just the period when it was the center for numerous Christian philosophers, and thus probably had an indirect connection to the latter network (*DSB,* 1981: 8:279–280).

Even these may not be so very exceptional. Ibn Sina lacks significant philosophical contemporaries other than the secondary figure Miskawayh, but he is matched with scientific stars, and his own work is to a considerable extent in science (see Figure 8.2 and the discussion in Chapter 8). Al-Ghazali lived in a time when the Islamic intellectual world was closing down into religious dogmatism; nevertheless, very close to him in time and space is the famous mathematician and philosophical poet 'Umar Khayyam.

There are more exceptions among secondary philosophers:

Horizontal isolates (lack of significant rivals):

Hasan al-Basri	720 C.E.	Iraq
Abu Hanifa	750	Iraq
Ibn Taymiyah	1320	Damascus
Ibn Khaldun	1380	Algeria, Egypt
Bassui	1380	Japan
Ikkyu	1450	Japan
Alan of Lille	1180	Paris
Cusanus	1450	Germany, Italy

Vertical isolates (lack of significant network ties):

Bahya ibn Paquda	1050 C.E.	Spain
Ibn Hazm	1080	Córdoba
Ibn Khaldun	1380	Algeria, Egypt
Bassui	1380	Japan
Peter Damiani	1050	Italy
Lull	1280	Spain, France
Bruno	1580	Italy, England, Germany
Boehme	1620	Germany
Vico	1720	Italy
Paley	1780	England
Mach	1880	Prague

Bruno may not belong on this list if in fact he is connected to the network at Naples deriving from Telesio in the previous generation, or with the other radical Dominicans from whom Campanella emerged (see Figure 9.6 in Chapter 9).

On the whole, there are relatively few philosophers in world history who are isolates of either kind. In six long-term networks (Greece, China, Japan, Islam, Christendom, Europe), 114 philosophers are listed as major figures; of these between 4 and 8 (Confucius, Mo Ti, Wang Yang-ming; Carneades, Porphyry, Proclus; Ibn Sina, al-Ghazali) have no important contemporary rivals (the lower figure if we admit the importance of nearby figures for Wang Yang-ming, Carneades, Ibn Sina, and al-Ghazali). There are even fewer network isolates at this level of eminence: only 1 of 114, the *Tao Te Ching* author, and even in this case, as indicated, a plausible network connection can be conjectured.

India is omitted because dating is often obscure and information on network ties is missing. Figures 5.1 through 5.5 list figures by century only rather than by generation. Even here, there are apparently only 2 horizontal isolates, and those among the secondary figures, lacking corresponding rivals in their century (Aryadeva 200s C.E., Raghunatha Shiromani, 1400s C.E.). The first two important Upanishadic philosophers appeared together and debated each other; the founders of the three great organized lineages of ascetics, Gautama Buddha, Mahavira, and Makkali Gosala, emerged simultaneously in a network of debates; later Buddhist and Hindu philosophers are generally quite tightly matched. Vertical linkages from one important figure to another, however, are much sparser in India than elsewhere. Although such ties are fairly dense on the Buddhist side, and at certain key periods among the Hindu philosophers (as in the key Mimamsa and Advaita Vedanta thinkers around Shankara), a considerable portion of the Hindu philosophers are not known to connect to significant networks, or any networks at all.

For secondary philosophers we have a total of 313 names from six world networks; 14 of these are horizontal isolates, 18 or 19 network isolates. The isolates from rival contemporary creativity include a number from the early generations when philosophical traditions were just building up; this includes some of the early figures in China (Tseng Tzu, Yang Chu, similarly situated to the more important Confucius and Mo Ti), and Islam (Hasan al-Basri, Abu Hanifa), as well as philosophers isolated in the afterwash of a network which had disintegrated (Ibn Taymiyah, Ibn Khaldun in the later period of Islamic philosophy; Alan of Lille in the one-generation interregnum between the two great networks at medieval Paris, Cusanus in the mid-1400s). Network isolates are more likely to appear on the periphery in crowded periods, often from deviant backgrounds: the wandering knight Raymond Lull among the university theologians at Paris; the mystical shoemaker Boehme in a small town in Silesia; Vico at Naples at a time when philosophy was dominated by freethinking networks in France and England while Italy was under a conservative Catholicism. Still there are horizontal coincidences in both creativity and contents; Vico's *Scienza Nuova* of 1725 is not so far away in materials and theme from Montesquieu's far more successful *L'Esprit des Lois,* written 1731–1748. The network-isolated Utilitarian-Deist theologian Paley is overmatched by his contemporary Bentham, who centers one of the most important intergenerational networks. Such isolates tend to pay the structural price of being outcompeted for attention in the long run by better-connected thinkers.

If we collate the two charts of isolates, horizontal and vertical, we find almost no one who is isolated on both dimensions. In all of world history there are only three significant philosophers who fill this description: Wang Ch'ung in China; Bassui Tokusho in Japan; and Ibn Khaldun in Islam. All are secondary figures in the influence they have exerted in the history of their respective philosophical communities. Bassui is one of the few notable Zen monks during a period (1365–1600) when the spiritual innovativeness of Japanese Buddhism was in decline. Wang Ch'ung stands out as an oasis in the desert of intellectual networks of the Later Han dynasty. There is some thematic competition nevertheless, in that his aggressively secularizing rationalism is structured in counterpoint to the occultism of his times, and carries on the battles of the Old Text school of a few generations earlier. Ibn Khaldun is somewhat similar, an opponent of the scholasticizing curriculum which by his day had dominated the Islamic *madrasas* for several centuries. Both Wang Ch'ung and Ibn Khaldun were advocates of empirical methods; Ibn Khaldun implemented this with a wide-ranging achievement as historian and comparative sociologist. Under these structural circumstances their successful creativity is mysterious. But it may be partially understandable in theme. Without philosophical networks and important contemporary rivals, it appears impossible to carry on work at higher levels of metaphysical abstraction; criticism and empiricism may be the only direction open in which something notable could be done.

APPENDIX 2

〻

The Incompleteness of Our Historical Picture

Historical sources, especially for remote periods, are often fragmentary, and the whole enterprise of reconstructing intellectual communities may seem like looking for landmarks in the mist. But history itself was not mist but structure, however it may sometimes seem to us trying to catch a glimpse in the distance. For all the failings and biases of our sources, I am nevertheless moderately confident of having included most of the creative philosophers in my pool, with a fair sense of the more routine or ephemeral intellectuals who made up the surrounding communities. For one slice of history, for example, Liu Hsin's catalogue of the imperial library ca. 20 B.C.E. gave a total of 198 authors (53 classified as *ju*, or "scholars"—i.e., Confucians—37 as "Taoist," 21 Yin-Yang, 10 Legalist, 6 Mohist, 7 Logicians, 64 others; Knoblock, 1988: 65–66). About a quarter of these books survive today. My networks for this period of ancient China, covering about 15 generations, include some 75 names, something more than one third of those who had enough distinction for their works to last that long.

More complete historical data (and more patience in working through the details of what is available) could add hundreds more figures to the kinds of networks I have presented; in an ideal situation of unlimited data, we might imagine charting the networks among all active intellectuals (maybe on the order of thousands in some epochs). But as Price ([1963] 1986: 69, 107–108, 257) has demonstrated for modern citation and publication data (extending back to scientists of the 1600s), the proportion of publications by and citations to (and hence the influence of) intellectuals falls off rapidly as one leaves the central core. This kind of work would add only to the tails of the distribution, further demonstrating the disproportionate success of the tiny sector at the center. Many figures lapsed into oblivion because they were indeed minor.

For these reasons I am doubtful that new archaeological discoveries would drastically revise our view of the main events of intellectual history. To be sure, we would love to have additional information. Who wrote the *Tao Te Ching,* in the midst of what network ties, and how did the work get put into circulation? Who wrote the Mohist *Canons,* and what precisely was the process of debate among the three "heretical" factions of Mohism that went on at this period? Perhaps these names are already on our chart (numbers 57–61 in the key to Figure 4.2), but it would be wonderful to pin down the circumstances of producing this high point of Chinese rationalistic logic and mathematical philosophy. Who precisely, within the Confucian schools, was responsible for the *Doctrine of the Mean* and the "Great Appendix" to the *Yi Ching?* For India we would even more like to pin down the life of Nagarjuna, to know more about Asanga, the two Vasubandhus, to add some of the richness of secondary and minor figures that we have for other regions; we would like to be able to explore what is behind the scattered names of philosophers in the Upanishads, and to know when and by whom were composed the Buddhist sutras, which often foreshadowed technical philosophical doctrines in a scriptural form.

For Greece and the West generally (including the Islamic philosophers), anonymity is less of a problem; despite the cult of antiquity that sometimes emerged, creative work was usually propagated under the author's own name. Our main problem of this kind is the Christian-occultist syncretist Pseudo-Dionysus, a secondary figure ca. 450 C.E. We would like to be able fill in more about certain mysterious figures: Ammonius Saccas, who taught both Plotinus and the Christian Origen (could he have been a "gymnosophist" from the orbit of India? although scholars think not); the Alexandria Skeptic Aenesidemus; the milieu of Philo of Alexandria, popping up out of nowhere onto a major position on the chart; Lucretius, the great Roman Epicurean, whose life is completely unknown. We would like to know more about the early figures, to know what Thales really did and what was legend; what were Pythagoras' own contributions, and what went on inside the Pythagorean organization. And of course we would like to have full texts of Heraclitus' book, of Parmenides' and Empedocles' famous poems, and other works of the pre-Socratics.

It would also be useful to know more about missing network ties of eminent persons. Who were the teachers of Hui Shih or Chuang Tzu? From whom if anyone did Heraclitus get his learning? But the lack of information about these figures implies that the persons in question were minor indeed; perhaps they might provide an incidental link to some other milieu of importance. This information might confirm the initial impression that a few creative figures "come out of nowhere," apart from existing chains of eminence, although I suspect that the tendency would be to add connections to yet further minor figures. On the downstream side, such information might strengthen my claim about secondary eminence being the result of the transmission of cultural capital. If we knew, for instance, who were the anonymous followers who compiled the *Chuang Tzu*, we could assign them a portion of the reputation which has accrued instead for the book.

Still, we must ask ourselves if having this information would drastically revise our picture of intellectual structures. Would it cause us to change our rankings of particular philosophers? Democritus, who wrote many books, all lost, would probably be further enhanced in our eyes (perhaps especially casting light on the early development of mathematics); but we rank him as a major figure in any case. Similarly Chrysippus, who has the reputation as the most acute technical thinker of the Stoic school. Or in China, Hui Shih, whose "books filled five carts"; or Kung-sun Lung, the other famous logician. We would clearly be enriched, but the pattern of eminence in the network chart would not change. It is conceivable that some figures might be elevated: such as Leucippus, reputed founder of atomism, but who receives only ancillary mention, from earliest sources onward, as a predecessor of Democritus. We would perhaps be full of admiration for the lost works of the logicians of the Megarian school, and some of the Chi-hsia Academicians might rise to greater heights in our eyes, which is to say, some secondary figures might move to borderline major, or some minor figures up to secondary. Still, our indications of what these figures did do already seem reflected in their remembered reputations. Within broad categories, I believe that we already understand the stratification of creativity that actually existed.

Keys to Figures

The following abbreviations are used throughout this appendix (see special notation listed for Figure 10.2 only):

number	=	minor philosopher listed in corresponding figure
+	=	person omitted from network diagram because of lack of known network ties; such persons are listed here to indicate the prevalence of particular philosophical positions in each time period
i	=	incidental person (not known independently of recorded contact with a known philosopher)
(no. in parentheses)	=	non-philosopher
[name or no. in brackets]	=	foreigner, listed in another network (e.g., in Figures 7.1 through 7.3, Chinese philosophers connected to Japanese network)
?	=	precise date unknown
"name in quotes"	=	possibly mythical
f.	=	founder of
tr.	=	translator
cm.	=	textual commentator
st.	=	studied at
crit.	=	critic of
{ }	=	scientist or mathematician
*	=	major scientist
astron	=	astronomy
astrol	=	astrology
alc	=	alchemy
alg	=	algebra
geom	=	geometry
theol	=	theology
phil	=	philosophy

Figure 2.1. Network of Chinese Philosophers, 400–200 B.C.E.

10	Tzu-yu (f. school of Confucian disciples)
11	Tzu-chang (f. school of Confucian disciples)
19	Tzu-ssu (Confucius' grandson; f. school of disciples)
21	Tuan-kun Mu (Confucian)
28	Ch'in Ku-li (major disciple of Mo Ti)
30	Yi Chih (Mohist)
35	Kung-tu Tzu (disciple of Mencius)
39	Shunyü Kun (debater)
43	P'eng Meng
45	Chieh Tzu
46	Huan Yuan
47	Wei Mou (hedonist/individualist)
49	Yo-chêng Tzu-chun (school of Tsêng-Tzu, Confucian)
50	K'ung Chuan (descendant of Confucius)
54	Ch'imu Tzu (Kung-sun Lung disciple)
56	Fan Sui (diplomat, debater, prime minister of Ch'in)
57	Wu Hou (leader of Mohist faction)
58	Hsiang-li Ch'in (leader of Mohist faction)
59	T'eng-ling Tzu (Mohist faction of the south)
62	Tsou Shih (Chi-hsia Acad.)
63	Yü Ching
64	Lü Pu-wei (prime minister of Ch'in)

Figure 2.2. Network of Greek Philosophers from Socrates to Chrysippus

39	Nessos of Chios (atomist)
40	Metrodorus of Chios (atomist, Skeptic)
48	Antipater of Cyrene (Cyrenaic)
49	Arete (Cyrenaic)
50	Epitimides of Cyrene (Cyrenaic)
51	Parabates of Cyrene (Cyrenaic)
52	Aristippus the Younger (Cyrenaic)
53	Anchipylus (school of Elis)
54	Moschus (Elis)
55	Plistenos of Elis (Elis)
57	Anaxarchus of Abdera (atomist, Skeptic)
58	Nausiphanes (atomist)
62	Alexines (Megarian)
68	Pamphilus (Academic)
78	Polemarchus (math)
80	Autolycus of Pitane (math)
87	Crantor (Academic)
88	Crates (Academic)
91	Philo of Megara (Megarian)
97	Lacydes (Academic)

Figure 3.1. Forming the Network of Greek Philosophers, 600–465 B.C.E.

600 B.C.E.

(1)	Alcman (cosmological poet)
(2)	Pittacus (one of the "Seven" or "Ten Sages")
(3)	Cleobulus (same)
(4)	Periander (same)
(5)	Myson (same)
(6)	Epimenides (same)
(7)	Anacharsis (same)
(8)	Bias (same)
(9)	Chilon (same)

10	Democedes of Croton (medicine)
i 11	Ameinas (Pythagorean)

500 C.E.

12	Epicharmas
13	Hippasus (Pythagorean)
(14)	Hecataeus (geographer)

Figure 3.2. Centralization of the Greek Network in Athens, 465–365 B.C.E.

465 B.C.E.

15	Corax (orator)
16	Tisias (same)
17	Oenopides of Chios (math, cosmol)
18	Cleidemos (cosmol)
i 19	Heraclides (medicine, father of Hippocrates)
i 20	Herodias (medicine, Cnidus)
i 21	Aegisidemus
22	Hippon (eclectic)
23	Hicetas (Pythagorean, astron)
24	Ecphantus (Pythagorean)
25	Eurytas (Pythagorean)
26	Echecrates (Pythagorean)
i 27	Simmias (Pythagorean)
i 28	Cebes (Pythagorean)
29	Alcidamas (Sophist)
30	Lycophron (Sophist)
32	Idaeus of Himera (eclectic physicist)
33	Thrasymachus
34	Xeniades (Sophist)
35	Theodorus (math)
36	Critias (patron of Sophists)

400 B.C.E.

37	Diagoras of Melos ("atheist")
38	Cratylus
i 39	Nessos of Chios (atomist)

40	Metrodorus of Chios (atomist, Skeptic)
41	Theaetetus (Academic, math)
42	Menaechmus (Academic, math)
43	Philip of Opus (Academic)
i 44	Hemodorus (Academic)
i 45	Histaeus (Academic)
46	Theudus (Academic)

Figure 3.4. Proliferation and Recombination of the Greek Schools, 400–200 B.C.E.

365 B.C.E.

i 47	Aethiops of Ptolemas (Cyrenaic) +
i 48	Antipater of Cyrene (Cyrenaic)
49	Arete (Cyrenaic, daughter of Aristippus)
i 50	Epitimides of Cyrene (Cyrenaic)
i 51	Parabates of Cyrene (Cyrenaic)
52	Aristippus the younger (Cyrenaic systematizer, son of 49)
53	Anchipylus (Elis/Eretria school)
54	Moschus (same)
55	Plistenos of Elis (same)
i 56	Diogenes of Smyrna +
57	Anaxarchus of Abdera (atomist, Skeptic)
58	Nausiphanes (atomist)
59	Apollonus (Megarian)
60	Apollonus Cronos (Megarian)
61	Anneceris (Cyrenaic)
62	Alexines (Megarian)
63	Philiscus (Cynic)
64	Onesicritus (Cynic)
i 65	Asclepediades (Elis/Eretria school)
66	Bryson (Megarian, math)
67	Polyxenus (Megarian)

i 68 Pamphilus (Academic)

i 69 Spintharus

70 Nicharchus (medicine) +

71 Praxagoras (medicine, Cos) +

72 Aristoxenus (Aristotelean)

73 Eudemus (same)

74 Dicaerchus (same)

75 Metrodorus of Athens (medicine) +

76 Diocles (medicine) +

77 Clearchus (Aristotelean, occultist)

78 Polemarchus (math)

79 Callipus (math)

80 Autolycus of Pitane (math)

81 Metrocles (Cynic)

82 Hipparchus (Cynic, wife of Crates)

83 Monimus (Cynic)

84 5 minor followers of Aristotle

300 B.C.E.

85 14 minor followers of Theophrastus

(86) Demetrius of Phalerum (politician)

87 Crantor (Academic)

88 Crates (Academic *scholarch*)

89 Bion (Cynic)

90 Evemerus of Messina

i 91 Philo of Megara

92 Dionysius the Renegade (heterodox Stoic)

93 Herillus (heterodox Stoic)

i 94 Apollophanes (Stoic) +

96 Aratus of Soli (Stoic, astron poet)

97 Lacydes (Academic)

(98) Ctesibus (mechanics)

(99) Aristarchus of Samos (math, astron)

100 Hieronymus of Rhodes (Aristotelean)

101 Lyco (same)

102 Ariston (same)

(103) Eratosthenes (math, literary criticism)

104 Phylotimus (medicine, Cos) +

105 Plistonicus (same) +

106 Xenophon (same) +

107 Herophilus (medicine, Alexandria) +

108 Erasistratus (medicine, f. school Cos, Alexandria Museum) +

109? Menippus of Gadara (Cynic)

110 Sphaerus (Stoic)

111 Polyaenus of Cyzicus (Epicurean, from school of Eudoxus)

i 112 Zopyrus (medicine, Alexandria)

i 113 Metrodorus of Lampsacus (Epicurean)

114 Hermachus of Mytilene (Epicurean first successor)

i 115 Leonteus of Lampsacus (Epicurean financial patron) +

i 116 Idomeneus (same) +

117 Timocrates (Epicurean renegade, brother of Metrodorus)

118 Leontion (Epicurean, Athens *hetaera*) +

119 Colotes (Epicurean)

120 Menedemus (Cynic)

121 Cercidas (Cynic)

122 Teles of Megara (Cynic)

123 Polystratus (Epicurean *scholarch*)

i 124 Hippoclydes (Epicurean)

125 Dionysius (Epicurean *scholarch*)

i 128 Hegesius (Academic)

Figure 3.5. Realignment of Schools in the Roman Conquest, 200 B.C.E.–1 C.E.

200 B.C.E.

126   Basilides (Epicurean *scholarch*)
127   Zeno of Tarsus (Stoic)
129   Critolaus (Aristotelean materialist, neo-Pythagorean)
130   Diogenes of Babylon (Stoic *scholarch*)
131?   3 Stoics after Chrysippus (Eudromus, Crinus, Basilides)
132?   5 Aristoteleans (Sotion, Satyrus, Antisthenes of Rhodes, Heraclides Lembus, Agatharchides)
133?   Cratippus (Aristotelean, changed from Academic) +
134   Diodorus of Tyre (Aristotelean, eclectic materialist, Epicurean)
135?   Callipho, Dinomachus (Aristotelean/Epicurean syncretism)
136   Phormio (Aristotelean)
137   Aristobolus of Alexandria (Jewish theol, allegorized Greek myths) +
138   Boethus (Stoic)
(139)   Apollodorus of Seleucia (Stoic, rhetor)
(140)   Apollodorus of Athens (same)
141   Archedemus of Tarsus (f. Stoic school, Babylon)
142   Antipater of Tarsus (Stoic *scholarch*)
143–144   Alceus, Philiscus (Epicureans at Rome)
145   Protarchus of Barghilia (Epicurean)
146   Demetrius of Laconia (Epicurean)
147   Apollodorus "the Tyrant of the Garden" (Epicurean)
148   Philonides of Laodicea (Syria Epicurean, math)
149   Clitomachus (Academic/Skeptic)
150   Metrodorus of Stratonicea (Academic, from Epicurean school)
151?   Meleagra of Gadara (Cynic) +
152   Charmadas (Academic/rhetor)
153   Mnesarchus (Stoic)
(154)   Polybius (historian)

100 B.C.E.

i 155   Heraclides of Tarentum (empiricist medicine)
156   Dio of Alexandria (Academic)
i 157   Aristus (Academic, brother of Antiochus of Ascalon, successor)
i 158   Theomnestus (Academic) +
159   L. Aelius Stilo (Stoic, rhetor)
160   Varro (eclectic, Stoic)
(161)   Lucullus (politician, patron)
162   Rutilius Rufus (Stoic)
163   Alexander Polyhister (Pythagorean, eclectic)
164   Nigidius Figulus (Pythagorean)
165   Asclepiades of Bythynia (medicine, Epicurean, Rome)
166   Zeno of Sidon (Epicurean, math)
167   Phaedrus (Epicurean, Rome)
168   Patronus (same)
169   Amalfinus (Epicurean, Italy)
170   Sciro (Epicurean, Rome)
(171)   Calpurnius Piso (Julius Caesar's father-in-law)
i 172   Philostratus (rhetor, skeptic, Academic-Sophist)
173   Tyrranio (edited Aristotle's manuscripts)

174 Andronicus of Rhodes (same)
175 Xenarchus (Academic)
176 Arius Didymus
     (Academic/Stoic/Aristotelean)
i 177 Athenodorus Cananites (Stoic)
178 Strabo (Stoic, geographer,
     historian)
179 Boethus of Sidon (Aristotelean)

Figure 3.6. Syncretisms and Skepticism, 1–200 C.E.

1 C.E.

180 Eudorus (Platonist,
     neo-Pythagorean, Alexandria)
181 Anaxilaus of Larissa
     (Pythagorean, occultist) +
182 Quintus Sextus (Stoic)
183 Sotion (Stoic,
     neo-Pythagorean, eclectic
     doxographer, Alexandria)
183a? Agrippa (Skeptic, ca. 1–200
     C.E.)
184 Thrasyllus
     (neo-Pythagorean/Platonist)
185 Potamo of Alexandria
     (Platonist, eclectic)
186 C. Musonius Rufus (Stoic)
i (187) Epaphroditus (Nero's
     secretary, Epictetus' owner)
188 Dio Chrysostom (rhetor/Stoic)
189 L. Annaeus Cornutus (Stoic)
(190) Perseus (poet)
(191) Lucan (poet)
192 Demetrius (Cynic) +
i 193 Agathinos (medicine)
194 Archigenes (medicine, eclectic,
     Stoic)
195 Simon Magus (Gnostic) +
196 Apollonius of Tyana
     (Pythagorean, occultist) +
i 197 Ammonius of Alexandria
     (Platonist)
198 Lucius (Pythagorean)

199 Nicostratus (Platonist, Stoic,
     rhetor, anti-Aristotelean)

100 C.E.

i 200 Flavius Arrianus (Stoic)
201 Magnus Ephesius (medicine)
202 Soranus of Ephesus
     (Methodist medicine)
203 Favorinus (rhetor, Skeptic)
i 204 Stalilius Attalius (medicine)
205 Theodas (Empiricist
     medicine) +
206 Menodotus of Nicomedia
     (Skeptic, Empiricist medicine)
207 Heroditus of Tarsus
     (Empiricist medicine)
208 Aristocles (Aristotelean, Stoic,
     Platonist)
209 Gaius (Aristotelean)
i 210 Numisianus
i 211 Satyrus (medicine)
i 212 Pelops (medicine)
(213) Hadrian of Tyre (rhetor)
(214) Demetrius of Alexandria
     (rhetor)
i 215 Diognetus (Stoic)
216 M. Cornelius Fronto (rhetor,
     anti-phil)
i 217 Athenagoras (Christian)
i 218 Demonax (Stoic)
219 Lucian of Samosata
     (Skeptic/eclectic)
220? Saturninus of Antioch
     (Gnostic) +
221? Carpocrates of
     Alexandria(Gnostic) +
222? Cerdon the Syrian
     (Christian/Gnostic) +
223? Cerinthus (Christian/
     Gnostic) +
224 Basilides of Syria (Gnostic,
     Alexandria) +
225? Demonax of Cyprus (popular
     Cynic) +

226? Oenomaus of Gadara
(same) +

227? Perigrinus Proteus (same,
ex-Christian) +

228? *pseudo-Pythagorean texts*
1–200 C.E. +

229? *Corpus Hermeticum* (anon.
text) +

230? Cronius (neo-Pythagorean) +

231 Nicomachus of Gerasa (math,
neo-Pythagorean) +

232 Theon of Smyrna (math,
Platonist) +

233 Aulus Gellius (Platonist,
Athens)

234 Celsus (Platonist,
anti-Christian) +

236 Tatian (Christian) +

237? Aristides (Christian
apologist) +

238 Melitto of Sardis (same) +

239? Apollinaris of Hieropolis
(same) +

240 Marcion (Christian/Gnostic,
Rome) +

i 242 Panaenus (ex-Stoic, Christian)

243 Theophilus (Christian)

244 Iranaeus (Christian,
anti-Gnostic)

245 Hippolytus (same, Rome)

246 Julianus (Gnostic, occultist,
forged *Chaldean Oracles*) +

247 Bardesanes of Mesopotamia
(Gnostic) +

248 Marcus (Gnostic, occultist,
disciple of Valentinus)

249 Theodotus (Gnostic, disciple
of Valentinus)

250 Ptolemaeus (same)

(251) Aelius Aristides (rhetor)

252 Harpocration of Argos
(neo-Pythagorean/eclectic)

253 Maximus of Tyre
(rhetor/Platonist/Aristotelean/
eclectic) +

254 Severus (Platonist/Stoic
anti-Aristotelean) +

Figure 3.7. Showdown of Neoplatonists and Christians, 200–400 C.E.

200 C.E.

i 255 Saturninus (Skeptic, medicine)

256 Tertullian (Christian,
anti-phil, anti-Gnostic)

257 Minucius Felix (Christian) +

258 Diogenes of Oenoanda
(Epicurean) +

(259) Diogenes Laertius
(doxographer) +

260 *On the World* anon. text
(Stoic/Aristotelean
syncretism) +

261 Ammonius Saccas
(neo-Pythagorean? Platonist?
eclectic, Alexandria)

i 262 Herennius +

263 Cassius Longinus (rhetor,
Platonist, Athens)

264 Origen the Pagan (Platonist)

i 265 Olympus of Alexandria (star
magic)

266 Amelius Gentilianus
(expositor of Plotinus)

i 267 Typho (Stoic, Platonist)

268 Anatolius of Alexandria
(Christian/Aristotelean/math)

i 269 Lucian (Christian, Antioch)

300 C.E.

270 Arnobius (Christian) +

271 Lactantius (Christian) +

272 Eusebius (Christian,
anti-Porphyry)

273 Gedalius (Neoplatonist)

274 Chrysaorinus (Neoplatonist)

275   Doxippus (Platonist/Aristotelean/pagan theol, Syria)

i 276   Eugenius (father of 278)

277   Theodorus of Asine (Platonist, Athens)

278   Themistius (Aristotelean/Platonist, Constantinople)

279   Sallustius (Syrian Neoplatonist, pagan catechism, Pergamum)

280   Sosipatra (occultist, Pergamum, woman)

281   Aedisius (Neoplatonist, occultist, Athens)

282   Maximus (occultist)

(283)   Libanius (rhetor)

i 284   Himerius (rhetor)

285   John Chrysostom (Christian, Origenist, Antioch/Constantinople)

286   St. Basil of Cappadocia (Christian/Platonist)

287   Apollinaris (Christian, opposite heresy from Arius) +

288   Simplicianus (Christian/Neoplatonist)

289   Macrobius (Platonist/neo-Pythagorean) +

290   Martianus Capella (Platonist, encyclopedist) +

293   Heraiscus (religious syncretism, Alexandria)

294   Asclepiades (same, brother of 293)

Figure 3.8. Neoplatonists under Christian Triumph, 400–600 C.E.

400 C.E.

292   Theon of Alexandria(math, Platonist)

295   Isidorus (Neoplatonist, Alexandria)

296   Hypatia (math, Neoplatonist, woman)

297   Synesius (math, Platonist, later Christian)

298   Plutarch of Athens (Neoplatonist/Aristotelean)

i 299   (daughter of 298, theurgy)

300   Syrianus (Platonist/Neoplatonist, Aristotelean, Athens)

301   Domninus of Larissa (math/occultist/Neoplatonist)

302   Hierocles (intro Neoplatonist at Alexandria)

303   Marinus (math, Neoplatonist scholarch, Athens)

304   Ammonius, son of Hermias (Platonist/Aristotelean/math/astron)

305   Damascius (Neoplatonist, Athens)

306   Simplicius (Neoplatonist, Athens)

307   Olympiodorus

308   Aeneas (Christian/Platonist, Gaza)

500 C.E.

309   George of Scythopolis (Christian, anti-heresies) +

310   John of Scythopolis (same) +

311   Zacharias (Christian/Platonist, anti-304)

312   Procopius

313   Cassiodorus (Christian, handbook writer, Italy)

i 314   Leander

315   Isidore of Sevelle (encyclopedist)

316   Stephanus of Alexandria. (Aristotelean/occultist/math, Byzantium)

317   St. Maximus
       (Platonist/Christian,
       Byzantium)

Figure 4.1. Emergence of Chinese Network, 500–365 B.C.E.: Rival Confucian Lineages, Mohists, Primitivists

500 B.C.E.

1   Têng Hsi (lawyer/debater)
2   Yen Hui (Confucian)
3   Tzu-lu (Confucian)
4   Tzu Kung (Confucian,
       diplomat)
i 5   Jan Yu (politician)
i 6   Chung Kung (Confucian)
i 7   Yu Tzu (soldier)
i 8   Tseng Hsi (Confucian)
9   Tzu-hsia (f. school of
       Confucian disciples)
10   Tzu-yu (same)
11   Tzu-chang (same)
i 12   Mi Tzu-chien (Confucian)
i 13   Tzu-ch'ih (Confucian)
i 14   Tzu-hua (Confucian)
15   Shih Shih (Confucian)
16   Ch'i Tiao-K'ai (f. school of
       Confucian disciples)
17   Kung-sun Ni-tzu (Confucian)
18   Fu Tzu-chien (Confucian)
19   Tzu-ssu (Confucius' grandson;
       f. school of disciples)
19a?   Chung-liang (f. school of
       Confucian disciples)
i 20   T'ien Tzu-Fung (Confucian,
       instructor of kings)
i 21   Tuan-kun Mu (same)
i 22   Wu Ch'i (Confucian general)
i 23   Kung-meng Tzu (Confucian)
23a   Li K'uei ("agriculturalist"
       politician)
i 24   Ch'eng-tzu (Confucian)
25   Kêng Chu (Mohist)
26   Sui Ch'ao Ti (Mohist)

400 B.C.E.

27   Wü Lu ("agriculturalist"
       self-sufficiency)
28   Ch'in Ku-li (major disciple of
       Mo Ti)

Figure 4.2. Intersecting Centers of the Warring States, 365–200 B.C.E.

365 B.C.E.

29   Tzu Hua Tzu (Yang Chu
       follower)
i 30   Yi Chih (Mohist)
31   Hsu Fan (from Mohist
       school; neo-Confucian,
       possibly identical w Hsü
       Hsing)
32   Ch'en Hsiang
       ("agriculturalist" primitivist)
i 33   Ch'en Liang
34?   Shih Ch'iu (individualist like
       Ch'en Chung)
i 35   Kung-tu Tzu (disciple of
       Mencius)
i 36   Wan Chang (same)
i 37   Meng Chi Tzu (same)
i 38   Kungsun Ch'ou (same)
39   Shunyü Kun (debater at Wei
       court, then Chi-hsia Academy)
40   Ch'en Chung
       ("agriculturalist" primitivist;
       of Ch'i royal house)
43   P'eng Meng
45   Chieh Tzu (Chi-hsia Acad.)
46   Huan Yuan (Chi-hsia Acad.)
47   Wei Mou (Prince of Wei,
       hedonist/individualist)
49   Yo-chêng Tzu-chun (school of
       Tsêng-Tzu, Confucian)
50   K'ung Chuan (descendant of
       Confucius)

300 B.C.E.

51   Huan T'uan
52   T'ien Pa

i 53   Mao Kung (Kung-sun Lung disciple)

i 54   Ch'imu Tzu (same)

i 55   Chan Tzu

56   Fan Sui (Wei diplomat, debater, prime minister of Ch'in)

57   Wu Hou (leader of Mohist faction)

58   Hsiang-li Ch'in (leader of Mohist faction)

59   T'eng-ling Tzu (Mohist faction of the south)

60   Ku Huo (same)

61   Chi Ch'ih (same)

62   Tsou Shih (Chi-hsia Acad.)

63   Yü Ching (prime Minister of Pingyuan court; patron of *Yü's Spring and Autumn Annals*)

64   Lü Pu-wei (prime minister of Ch'in; patron of *Lü's Spring and Autumn Annals*)

65   Fü-ch'iu Po

66   Mao Heng (textual scholar)

Figure 4.3. Han Dynasty Transition and Forming of Official Confucianism, 235 B.C.E.–100 C.E.

200 B.C.E.

67   Meng Ch'ing (Lanling school of Hsun-tzu)

68   Shen Pei (teacher of numerous Han officials and Erudites)

68a   Kung-yang Chiu (transmitted interpretation of *Spring and Autumn Annals* from Confucian family chain)

69   Liu Chiao

70   Mao Chang (textual scholar)

71   Chang Ts'ang (Yin-Yang, calendar, Han court)

72   Fu Shang (textual scholar; restored destroyed texts from memory)

73   Chang Liang ("Taoist" immortality magic, Han court)

74   Chia I (Yin-Yang; famous poet)

75   Hsiahou Shih-Ch'ang

76   Hsiahou Sheng

77   Hsiahou Ch'ien

78   Ouyang Shêng (Five Agents; occult portents; New Text school)

79   Ouyang Kao (same)

80   Hu K'ang (textual scholar: *Annals, I Ching*)

80a   Hu-wu Cheng (*Annals*, Erudite)

80b   Kung-sun Hung (head of Erudites, prime minister of Emperor Wu)

i 80c   Lu P'ou-chou (disciple of Tung Chung-shu; prosecuted Liu An)

81   Shu Kuang (same as 80)

82   Meng Hsi (same as 78 and 79, Lanling school)

83   K'ung An-kuo (descendant of Confucius; began study of old texts)

84   Ts'ou Pa (*Book of History*)

85   Shu-sun Tung (Confucian court ritual)

86   Li Shao-chün ("Taoist" magic, Han court)

87   Min Chi (same)

100 B.C.E.

88   Liu Pi-chiang

i 89   Liu Te

91   Ssu-ma Ch'ien (historian)

92   Chiao Kan (divination)

93   Ching Fang (same)

94   Yen Chün-ping (diviner; *Tao Te Ching* and *Chuang Tzu* scholar)

1 C.E.

95   An-ch'iu Wang-jih (shaman/physician, *Tao Te Ching* scholar)
96   Chia K'uei (eclectic cm., Old Text school)
97   Ts'ao Pao (numerology group leader)

Figure 4.4. Later Han Dynasty Disintegration and the Dark Learning, 100–300 C.E.

100 C.E.

98   Ma Jung (Confucian cm., Old Text school, anti-occult skeptic)
99   Wang Fu (Confucian political phil, anti-occult skeptic)
100   Wei Po-Yang (Taoist, first alchemy book) +
101   Yü Chi (pop. Taoist cult)
102   Chang Tao-Ling (Taoist healing cult, military org., Szechuan)
103?   Ho Shang Kung (*Tao Te Ching* cm.) +
i 104   Chang Heng (same as 102)
105   Chang Lu (f. Taoist church)
(106)   Chang Chüeh (*Tao* of Great Peace, Yellow Turban uprising)
107   Ho Hsiu (Confucian religion) +
107b   Yü Fan (Confucian, *Yi Ching* cm., numerology) +
108   Hsün Shuang
109   Hsün Yüeh (Confucian, anti-Taoist, anti-occult skeptic)
110   Ts'ai Yung (anti-occult skeptic, astronomer)

i 111   Wang K'ai (bequeathed library to son, 117)
i 112   Liu Pao (patron of Ching-Chou Academy Old Text scholars)

200 C.E.

113   Wang Lang (anti-occult skeptic) +
114   Tso Tzu (Taoist magician)
115   Ko Hsüan (religious Taoist, south China)
i 116   Wang Ts'an (inherited library of 110)
i 117   Wang Yeh (father of Wang Pi)
118   Ouyang Chien
119   Wang Tao
120   Yin Jung (or Hsün Jung)
121   Hsia-hou Hsuan
122   Wang Su (Confucian, high Wei official; Old Text school, *K'ung-Ts'ung Tzu* author?)
123   Juan Chi (poet, Seven Sages of the Bamboo Grove)
124   Shan T'ao (statesman, general, Seven Sages)
125   Juan Hsian (Seven Sages)
126   Wang Jung (same)
127   Liu Ling (same)
128   Wang Têng (Pure Conversation, nudist circle)
129   Wang Yen (same)
130   Juan Chan (same)
131   Hsu Kun (same)
132   Humu Yen-Kuo (same)
133   Pi Cho(same)
134   Yueh Kuang (Name/Principle doctrine)
134a   Hsieh Hsuan (same)
135   P'ei Wei (skeptic, anti-nihilist)
135a   Ssu-ma P'iao (cm. *Chuang Tzu*, Mohist *Canons*) +
136   Juan Fou (libertine, Pure Conversation)

137   Wei Chieh (Pure Conversation)

138?   Lu Shêng (cm. Mohist
       Canons)

139   Chueh Kung-tse (Buddhist
       Pure Land) +

140   Wei Shih-tu (same) +

141   Dharmaraksha (Buddhist at
       Tun Huang, central Asia) +

Figure 5.1. Indian Network, 800–400 B.C.E.: The Founding Rivalries

800–600 B.C.E.

In *Brihadaranyaka Upanishad:*

(1)   King Janaka

2   King Ajatashatru

In *Chandogya Upanishad:*

3   King Pravehana Jaivali
       (defeated Aruni in debate)

4   King Ashvapati (debated
       Aruni &11–15)

5   Sanatkumara +

6   Shandilya +

7   Raikva +

8   Satyakama Jabali +

9   Chakrayana Ushasti +

10   Ghora Angirasa +

11   Aupamanayava

12   Prachinayogya

13   Vaisyagrahpadya

14   Sharkarakshya

15   Budila

16   Parshvanatha (last of 24 Jaina
       predecessors, some mythical)

600–400 B.C.E.

17   Brihaspati (pre-Buddhist
       skeptic/Lokayata materialist?)

18   Sañjaya (skeptic)

19   Alara Kalama (meditation
       master)

20   Uddaka Ramaputta (ascetic)

(21)   King Bimbisara of Magadha

22   Buddha's followers (debated
       Mahavira)

23   Mahavira's followers (debated
       Buddha)

24   Purana Kashyapa (or
       Kassapa; skeptic, denied
       karma and morality;
       converted by Buddha)

25   Pakudha Kaccayana (or
       Kakuda Katyayana; 7
       elements; denied karma)

26   Ajita Keshakambala (4
       elements; Lokayata materialist)

27   Payasi (Lokayata materialist)

28   "Kanada" (early Vaisheshika)

29   Sariputra (Buddha's major
       disciple)

30   Moggallana (Maudgalyayana)
       (same)

31   Devadatta (early revolt within
       Buddhism)

Figure 5.2. India, 400 B.C.E.– 400 C.E.: Age of Anonymous Texts

400–200 B.C.E.

32   Moggaliputta-tissa (organized
       Buddhist missions)

33   Nagasena (Buddhist
       debater) +

34   Katyayana (Katyayaniputra)
       (predecessor of
       Sarvastivada) +

35   Dharmatrata (early devel. of
       Sarvastivada) +

In Middle *Upanishads:*

36   Nachikitas (in *Katha Up.*)

37   Shvetashvatara (in
       Shvetashvatara Up.)

38   "Kapila" (same)

39   "Asuri" (converted from
       Lokayata and Ajivikas) +

40 Varuna (in *Taittiriya Up.*)
41 Mahachamasya (same)
42 Pippalada (in *Prashnopanishad*)
43 Pratardana (in *Kaushitaki Up.*)

200 B.C.E.

44 Mahadeva Buddhist (f. Chaitiya sect, stupa worship) +
45 Kumaralabdha (f. Sautrantika?) +

1 C.E.

46 Upatissa (Pali Theravada compendium) +
47 "Pañchashikha" (early Samkhya figurehead?) +

100 C.E.

48 Kumaralata (Sarvastivadin)
49 Matracheta (Buddhist court poet)
50 Buddhadeva (Sarvastivadin) +
51 Bhadanta Ghoshaka (Sarvastivadin) +
51a "Gautama" (Mithila? f. Nyaya) +
52 Upavarsha (Vedanta/Mimamsa, 1st *Brahmasutra* cm.) +
(53) Charaka (compiled medical text) +
54 Lakulisha? (f. Shaiva dualism) +

200 C.E.

55 Dharmashri (Sarvastivadin) +
56 Upashanta (Sarvastivadin) +
57 Paurika? (earliest distinctive Samkhya) +
58 Pañchadhikarana (same) +
59 Pantañjali (not Yogin; early Samkhya) +

60 Varshaganya? (crystallized Samkhya) +
61 Shabara? (Mimamsa, cm. "Jaimini") +

300 C.E.

62 Harivarman (Sautrantika) +
63 Saramati (Yogacara) +

Figure 5.4. Conflict of Buddhist and Hindu Schools, 400–900

Persons listed here and for Figure 5.5 include philosophers of Kashmir Shaivism and continuation of all Indian networks to 1500–1800 not shown in Figures 5.4 and 5.5.

400

64 Sanghamitra (Shri Lanka, crit. Theravada) +
65 Buddhadatta (Shri Lanka) +
66 Dhammapala (Shri Lanka) +
66a Shrilabdha (Sautrantika) +
i 67 Buddhamitra (Sautrantika)
68 Vindhyavasin (revised older Samkhya, debated 67)
69 Madhava (Samkhya "heretic," debated 73)
i 70 Vasubandhu's pupil (brother-in-law of 71)
i 71 Vasurata
72 Chandramati (unorthodox Vaisheshika) +

500

73 Gunamati (Sarvastivadin, crit. Samkhya, Vaisheshika, and Jainism)
74 Ashvabhava
74a Vasuvarman (Sarvastivadin) +
75 Guñaprabha (converted from Yogacara to Sarvastivada, attacked Mahayana) +

76 Arya-Vimuktasena
    (Yogacara) +
77 Bhadanta-Vimuktasena
    (Yogacara) +
78 Bhavivikta Nyaya
    (reputational rival of
    Dharmakirti) +

600

79 Shilabhadra (Brahman,
    Nalanda head, Yogacara)
80 Yashomitra (Sarvastivadin,
    crit. Vasubandhu II as
    Sautrantika) +
81 Samathadeva
    (Sarvastivadin) +
82 Purnavardhana
    (Sarvastivadin) +
83 Jñanaprabha (Svatantrika) +
84 Gunabhadra? (Mahayana) +
85 Simhabhadra (Mahayana) +
86 Prajñagupta (Mahayana) +
87 Jñanachandra (at Nalanda) +
88 Ratnashimha (Mahayana) +
89 Divakaramitra (Mahayana) +
90 Tathagatagarbha
    (Mahayana) +
91 Nagabodhi (Vajrayana tantrist
    sutra) +
92 Jina (Yogacara, logic) +
93 Jinendrabuddhi (Buddhist
    logic) +
i 94 Ishvarasena
95 Devendrabuddhi (Buddhist
    logic)
96 Yogasena (Sammitiya
    personalist school) +
97 Purandhara (last-known
    Lokayata materialist) +
98 Bhamana (grammarian crit.
    Buddhist logic)
99 Shankarasvamin (Nyaya cm.
    Dignaga logic) +

100 Pritichandra (Nyaya "rival to
     Dharmakirti") +
101 Aviddhakarna (Nyaya) +
i 102 Govinda
103 "Vyasa"? (1st great cm.
     Yogasutras) +
104 Bhartriprapañcha (1st
     Bhedabhedavada
     dualism-cum-nondualism) +

700

105 Haribhadra
     (Yogacara/Madhyamika/
     Svatantrika) +
106 Vajrabodhi (Vajrayana
     tantrism)
107 Amoghavajra (tantric/sexual
     rites; to China court)
108 Dombi Heruka (sexual-Yogic
     tantrism) +
109 Anandagavajra? +
110 Jñanagarbha
     (Yogacara/Madhyamika &
     Vajrayana tantrism; to
     Tibet) +
111 Karnakagomin (Madhyamika
     or Yogacara, Buddhist logic) +
112 Archata (Madhyamika or
     Yogacara, Buddhist logic) +
113 Jinendrabuddhi (cm.
     Dignaga) +
114 Patrakesari (refuted
     Dharmakirti logic)
115 Shakyamati (Buddhist cm.
     Dharmakirti logic)
116 Vinitadeva (Buddhist logic
     cm. Dharmakirti)
117 Shakyabuddhi (Buddhist) +
118 Prabhabuddhi (Buddhist) +
119 Shubhakara (Buddhist logic,
     tantrist anti-Idealist; to China)
120 Akalanka (major Jaina logic,
     crit. Dharmakirti)

121 Mallavadin (Jaina, cm. Buddhist logic) +

122 Haribhadra Suri? (Jaina formulated "6 *darshanas*") +

123 Shalikanatha (Mimamsa crit. Dharmakirti logic)

124 Mahodadhi (Mimamsa)

125 Umveka (Mimamsa, cm. Mandana)

126 Totaka (grammarian, Mimamsa, converted to Advaita) +

127 Vasugupta (Kashmir Shaiva) +

800

128 King Indrabuddhi (Bengal tantrist) +

129 Lakshminkara Devi (sister of 128; sexual-Yoga) +

130 Pandita Ashoka (Buddhist logic, Madhyamika or Yogacara) +

131 Durveka (Buddhist logic) +

132 Vidyananda? (Jaina logic) +

133 Yashovija (Jaina logic) +

134 Vishvarupa (Nyaya) +

135 Dhairyarashi (Nyaya) +

136 Chandrananda? (Vaisheshika) +

137 Bhasarvajna (Kashmir Nyaya)

138 Somadeva (1st systematized Kashmir Shaivism) +

139 Ugrajyoti (crit. monistic Shaivism) +

140 Sadyojyati (dualistic Shaiva, Kashmir) +

141 Brihaspati (Kashmir Shaiva) +

142 Shankarananda (Kashmir Brahman, Shaiva; cm. Buddhist logic) +

143 Bhatta Kallata (Kashmir Shaiva) +

144 Anandavardhana (Kashmir Brahman; poetics, cm. Buddhist logic) +

Figure 5.5. Hindu Oppositions, 900–1500: Nyaya Realists, Advaita Idealists, Vaishnava Dualists

900

145 Prajñakaragupta (Buddhist logic, tantrist, layman, Vikramashila [Bengal]) +

146 Ravi Gupta (Buddhist layman, tantrist, Bengal, to Kashmir) +

147 Jina II (Buddhist logic, tantrist, layman; crit. 146) +

148 Jñanashri (Buddhist logic, tantrist, layman; Kashmir Brahman) +

149 Jitari (Buddhist, crit. Vaisheshika, Mimamsa, Jainism; Bengal court) +

150 Chandragomin (Buddhist logic, Bengal court) +

151 Prajñakaramati (Madhyamika, crit. Yogacara Idealism) +

152 Vidyakarashanti (Buddhist logic) +

153 Ratnavajra (Buddhist) +

154 Dharmadeva (Buddhist, Nalanda; to China) +

155 Trilocana (Nyaya)

156 Sanatani (Nyaya, Bengal?) +

157 Vyomashiva (Nyaya-Vaisheshika Shaiva, Kashmir?) +

158 Adhyayana (Nyaya) +

159 Vittoka (Nyaya) +

160 Narasimha (Nyaya) +

i 161 Lakshmanagupta (Utpala's pupil, teacher of Abhinavagupta) +

162 Bhatriraja (grammarian, Kashmir) +

163 Helaraja (same) +

164 Ramakantha (Shaiva dualist, Kashmir) +

165 Devabala (Shaiva dualist) +

In Kashmir:

Major: ABHINAVAGUPTA (Shaiva, Shakti pan-energy phil.) +

Secondary: Utpala (Shaiva, astron, crit. Buddhists) +

1000

166 Jñanshrimitra (Buddhist logic, tantrist, layman; last of Kashmir school, to Vikramashila [Bengal]) +

167 Ratnakarashanti (classified all Buddhist sects into Vajrayana tantrism) +

168 Ratnakirti (Buddhist, embraced solipsism) +

169 Abhayakara-gupta (abbot of Nalanda & Vikramashila; tantrist) +

170 Sarahapada (sexual-Yoga, poems) +

171 Advayavajra (Buddhist tantrism to Tibet) +

172 Devachandra (Mahamudra sect of Vajrayana tantrism) +

173 Manorathanandin (Buddhist logic) +

174 Mokshakaragupta (Buddhist logic) +

175 Anuruddha (Shri Lanka, Theravadin) +

176 Sariputta? (Theravadin) +

177 Prabhachandra (Jaina logic) +

178 Anandabodha? (Advaita solipsism) +

179 Kularka Pandita (Advaita *mahavidya* logic formalism) +

180 Bhavadeva (Mimamsa, Bengal?) +

181 Shrivatsa (Nyaya, Mithila?)

182 Aniruddha (Nyaya) +

183 Uttuñga (Shaiva dualist) +

184 King Bhoja (cm. Yoga, Samkhya; polymath, Shaiva dualist) +

185 Bhaskara? (with 186, greatest names of Shaktism) +

186 Lakshmidhara +

187 Vidyakantha (son/pupil of 164) +

188 Narayana Kantha +

189 Ramakantha II (refuted grammarians) +

190 Yadavaprakasha (Vaishnava, theistic dualism-cum-nondualism) brother-in-law of 192

i 191

i 192 Ramanuja's father

1100

193 Hemachandra (encyclopedic Jaina, poet, grammarian, logic) +

193a Shri Harsha's father

i 194 brother of 195

195 Meghanadari (Ramanuja sect; refuted objections vs. self-validity of intuition, crit. Nyaya)

196 Aghorashiva (Shaiva dualist) +

197 Basava (Vira Shiva sect/phallic symbols; dualism-cum-nondualism) +

198 Revana (Vira Shiva; crit. nihilistic monism, Jainism, Buddhism, & Lokayata) +

199 Upamaya (voluntaristic Shaiva monism, crit. nihilistic monism) +

200 Someshvara (Mimamsa) +

201 Aparakadeva (Nyaya) +
202 Shrikantha (Nyaya) +
203 Vadaraja (Nyaya, Kashmir?) +
204 Vallabha (Nyaya-Vaisheshika, Mithila)
205 Shivaditya (Nyaya-Vaisheshika; *mahavidya* syllogisms combo. w Advaita)

1200

206 Shri Rama Chandrabharati (only Buddhist bhakti poet; Shri Lanka) +
207 Mallisena (Jaina logic) +
208 Parthasarathi Mishra (Mimamsa crit. Dharmakirti logic) +
209 Vadindra (Nyaya, refuted over-elaborate *mahavidya* syllogisms)
210 Bhatta Raghava (Nyaya) +
211 Divikara (Nyaya Mithila) +
212 Keshava Mishra (Nyaya-Vaisheshika Mithila)
213 Vadi Vagishvara (Nyaya) +
214 Narayana Sarvajña (Nyaya) +
215 Anandahubhava (Nyaya) +
216 Anandajñana (Advaita, crit. Vaisheshika atomism) +
217 Vimuktatman (Advaita, crit. Mandana, dualism-cum-nondualism & Bhartrihari) +
218 Vatsya Varada (Ramanuja theist, refuted Shriharsha world illusion) +
219 Pillai Lokacharya (led faction in Vaishnava split) +
220 Marua (Vira Shiva) +
221 Ekorama (same) +

1300

222 Rajashekhara Suri (Jaina cm. 6 *darshanas*) +
223 Vidya Tilaka (same) +
224 Prabhakarapadya (Nyaya) +
224a Varhamana (neo-Nyaya, Gangesha's son)
225 Abhayatilaka (Nyaya, Mithila)
226 Sondadopadhyaya (Nyaya)
227 Manikantha Mishra Nyaya
228 Shashadhara (Nyaya)
229 Tarami Mishra (Nyaya) +
230 Jagadguru (Nyaya) +
231 Nyayabhaskarakara (Nyaya) +
232 Ravishvara (Nyaya) +
233 Ramadvaya (Advaita) +
i 234 Anandatman
235 Shankarananda (*Upanishads* cm.)
236 Madhavacharya (or Vidyaranya; Advaita, Mimamsa cm.; compendium of all schools)
237 Sayana (Mimamsa, cm. early Vedas; brother of 236)
238 Anubhavananda
239 Amalananda (Advaita)
i 240 brother of 241
241 Shaila Shrinivasa (defended Ramanuja sect vs. Advaita crit)
242 Shripati Pandita (Vira Shiva sectarian; crit. all schools) +

1400

243 Gunaratna Suri (Jaina, cm. Haribhadra's 6 *darshanas*) +
244 Aniruddha (compiled *Samkhyasutras*) +
245 Sadananda Vyasa (Advaita; cm. Samkhya, *Gita*) +
246 Shankara Mishra (neo-Nyaya)

246a Vacaspati Mishra II
(neo-Nyaya)

247 Vasudevasarvabhauma (intro.
neo-Nyaya to Bengal)

248 Madhava Mukunda
(Vishishtadvaita qualified
non-dualism, crit. monism &
world illusion) +

Continuation, 1500–1800 (not shown in Figure 5.5)

1500

Secondary:

Vijñanabhikshu (syncr., cm. Mimamsa,
Yoga, Vedanta; turned Samkhya to
theism)

Appaya Dikshita (from Mimamsa;
synth. Advaita sub-schools)

Prakashananda (Advaita, subjectivist)

Vyasa-tirtha? (Madhva pontiff, crit.
Advaita monism using Nyaya
epistemology)

Madhusudana Sarasvati? (Advaita,
refuted Vyasa-tirtha)

Chaitanya (Vaishnava bhakti, Krishna
emotionalism)

Vallabha (Vaishnava Vedanta theist,
bhakti, pure nondualism)

249 Bhavaganesha (cm. Samkhya)

250 Annambhatta
(Nyaya-Vaisheshika, cm.
Advaita, Mimamsa)

251 Narayana Bhatta (Mimamsa
theist)

252 Narayana Bhatta II (same;
refuted Appaya Dikshita)

253 Langakshi Bhaskara (same)

254 Nrisimhashrama Muni
(Advaita)

255 Jiva Gosvami (Chaitanya
follower)

1600

256 Mahadeva Vedantin
(Samkhya)

257 Svayamprakashayati
(Samkhya)

258 Apadeva (Mimamsa)

259 Khandadeva (Mimamsa)

260 Mathuranatha Bhattacharya
(extreme neo-Nyaya
formalism)

261 Jagadisha Bhattacharya
(important late neo-Nyaya)

262 Gadadhara Bhattacharya
(same)

263 Vishvanatha
(Nyaya-Vaisheshika)

263a Radhomohana Gosvami
Bhattacharya (Nyaya)

264 Narayanatirtha
(Nyaya-Vaisheshika-
Samkhya-Vedanta syncretism)

265 Dharmaraja (Advaita)

266 Shrinivasacharya (Ramanuja
sect)

1700

267 Yasovijaya (Jaina)

268 Nagoji Bhatta (Samkhya)

269 Vamshidhara Mishra
(Samkhya/Nyaya)

270 Sadananda Yati (Advaita
syncretism)

271 Baladeva (Vedanta Vaishnava,
unthinkable-nondifference-
indifference, Bengal)

272 Rangaramanuja (Ramanuja
sect)

Figure 6.1. Taoist Church and Imported Buddhist Schools, 300–500

300

142	"Pao Ching-yen" (Taoist radical, mythical?)
143	Wang Pao (Taoist magician)
144	Wei Hua-Ts'un (woman; "revelations" of Taoist scriptures)
145	Tu Ching (Taoist church leader)
146	Sun Tai (f. Taoist sect)
(147)	Sun En (Taoist rebel, south coast)
148	Yang Hsi ("revelations" of Taoist scriptures)
149	Hsü Mi (Taoist theologian)
150	Hsü Hui (Taoist)
i 151	Hsü Mai (father of 149)
(152)	Wang Hsi-chih (1st great calligrapher)
153	"Pure Conversation" circle
154	Yin Hao (Buddhist layman)
155	Sun Ch'o (Buddhist, sync. w Taoism and Confucianism)
156	Wang Pan-chih (Confucian, criticized Taoism)
157	Ko Ch'ao-fu (Ko family; estab. Taoist scriptures)
158	Ts'ui Hao (Confucian, Taoist, Northern Wei minister; persecuted Buddhism)
159	K'ou Ch'ien-chih (Taoist "pope" in Northern Wei state)
160	Mao Hsui-chih (Taoist disciple)
161	Ch'eng-Kung Hsing (Buddhist)
162	Shih T'an-ying (Buddhist)
163	Fa-hsian (Buddhist pilgrim, tr. *Lotus sutra*)
164	Chih-yen (Buddhist traveler to Kashmir)
i 165	Buddhabhadra (Buddhist monk from Kashmir)
166	T'an-chi (Madhyamika "Three Treatise school")
167	Seng-tao (Sautrantika school)
168	Seng-sung (Sautrantika school)
169	Seng-jui (Buddhist)
170	Hui Kuan (Buddhist, debated Tao Sheng vs. sudden Enlightenment)

400

171	Fa-yen (Pure Land)
172	Fa-hao (Pure Land)
173	Chu Fa-t'ai (Pure Land)
174	T'an Chi
175	Seng-lang (Madhyamika, separated from Sautrantika)
176	Fa-yao (pop. Nirvana sutra preacher, south China)
177	Ro-ling (same)
178	Seng-yu (continued Tao-An's catalogue of Buddhist texts)
179	Fan Chen (skeptic anti-Buddhist, south China)
180	Hsün Chi (same)
181	Ku Huan (anti-Buddhist, compiled Taoist scriptures)
182	Lu Hsin-ch'ing (Taoist reformer, compiler, alc)
183	Sun Yu-yueh (Taoist, Southern capital)
184	T'ao Hung-ching (f. Taoist sect; occultist, alc)
185	Chou Yung (Buddhist syncretizer w Taoism and Confucianism)
186	Chang Jung (same)
187	Meng Ching-I (same)

**Figure 6.2. T'ien-t'ai, Yogacara, Hua-yen, 500–800; *and*
Figure 6.3. Cascade of Ch'an (Zen) Schools, 635–935**

500

188 Wang Yuan-chih (Taoist charms, talismans)
189 Chou Tzu-liang (Taoist scripture "revelations")
190 P'an Yüan-wen (Taoist)
191 Buddhasanta (Buddhist fr. India)
192 Seng-ch'ou (Buddhist meditation master)
193 Sun Wen-ming (estab. Taoist pantheon, monasteries)
194 Hui-chiao (Buddhist biogs. of famous monks) +
195 Liu Chou (sync. Buddhism, Taoism, Confucianism)
196 Hsin-hsing (f. Buddhist apocalyptic sect of Three Stages) +
197 Bodhiruci (fr. India, tr. Vasubandhu, Pure Land)
198 Ratnamati (same)
199 Hui Kuang (Buddhist Store-consciousness)
200 T'an Luan (f. Pure Land sect; converted fr. magic Taoism)
201 Fa-shang (Store-consc. and Pure Land)
202 Tao-chung (Store-consc., Northern branch)
203 Chêng Tao-chao (Buddhist, replied to Taoist attacks by 179)
204 Lo Ch'un-chang (same)
205 Fan-yun (Sautrantika text scholar)
206 Chih-tsang (same)
207 Sêng-min (same)
208 Hui-wen (*Lotus sutra*)
209 Seng-chuan (Madhyamika)
210 Fa-lang (same; crit. Sautrantika/Sattyasidhi school)
211 Paramartha (st. India; tr. *Abhidharma* realism & Mahayana idealism)
i 212 20 minor disciples of Hui-K'o
213 Seng-ts'an (alleged Ch'an 3rd patriarch)
i 214 minor disciple of Hui-K'o

600

215 Hui-kuan (transmitted Madhyamika to Korea, Japan)
216 Tao-cho (T'ien-T'ai monk, Pure Land proselytizer)
i 217 Kuang-ting (recorded Chih-I's lectures)
218 Shan-tao (Pure Land)
219 Fa-chung (Buddhist)
220 Tao-hsin (Ch'an)
221 Fa-shun (Hua-yen, imperial patronage)
222 Yüeh Tai (ed. *Mo Tzu*) +
223 Wei Chêng (Confucian, imperial librarian) +
224 Wang T'ung (Confucian) +
225 Kung Ying Ta (cm. 5 Agents, *Yi Ching*) +
226 Lü Ts'ai (5 Agents, skeptical preface on divination) +
227 Fu Yi (Confucian, won court debate vs. Buddhist thaumaturge) +
228 Chih-Yen (Hua-yen)
229 Siksananda (fr. Khotan, tr.)
230 Divakara (fr. India, tr.)
231 Divaprajña (same)
232 Li T'ung-hsuan (Hua-yen, Buddhist salvation)
233 Kuei-chi (completed *Abhidharma* realist system; systematized Yogacara)

234 Tao-hsüan (Buddhist, f. Vinaya disciplinary school)

235 Fa-min

236 Hui-ming

237 Fa-ju (Ch'an)

238 Fa-jung (f. Oxhead school? Ch'an & Madhyamika)

239 Lao-an (Ch'an Northern school)

240 Fa-chih (f. Oxhead school? meditation master; Amitabha devotee)

240a Chih-wei (Oxhead school)

240b Hsuan-Chih (Ch'an Szechuan school, meditation on Buddha's name, close to Pure Land)

241 Chieh-hsien (Ch'an Szechuan school)

242 Chih-ta (Ch'an Northern school)

243 Hsiang-mo Tsang (same)

244 I-fu (same)

245 P'u-chi (same)

246 Ching-hsien (same)

247 Hsuan-tse (Ch'an, Northern school)

700

248 Shên-Hsiang (propagated Hua-yen to Japan)

249 Dharmagupta (fr. India; presided at Nalanda university)

250 Subhakarasinha (fr. India; tantrist, Chang-an court)

251 Vajrabodhi (st. Nalanda; at Chang-an; tantrist)

252 Chih-yen (tantrist)

253 I-hsing (tantrist, math/astron; Hua-yen temple)

254 Amoghavajra (st. Ceylon; tutor of emperors; tantrist, rainmaker)

255 Chih-yen (tantrist)

256 Wên-Ku (same)

257 Yen Chen-Ch'ing ("mystic theses" on logic of Kung-sun Lung)

i 258 Chang Chih-Ho (Taoist)

259? *Kuan Yin* (text by Taoist author) +

260 Ssu-ma Ch'eng-Chêng ("Taoist" naturalist) +

261 T'ien T'ung Hsu (same) +

262 Li Ch'uan (same) +

263 Hui-yuan (Hua-yen sectarian split)

264 Ch'eng-kuan (Hua-yen; refuted 263)

(265) K'uei discussion group members (reformers of politics, economic, lit.)

i 266 Han Hui (brother of Han Yü)

i 266a Han Chung-ch'ing (father of Han Yü)

267 Chan-jan (revived T'ien-tai; universal salvation)

268 Tzu-min (Pure Land, polemic vs. Hui Neng)

269 Tao-sui (T'ien-T'ai)

i 270 4 minor followers of Ch'an Northern school

271 Fa-chao (Pure Land; National Preceptor; Heaven/Hell doctrine; attacked universal salvation)

272 Nan-yüeh Huai-jang (Ch'an)

274 Yüeh-shan Wei Yen (Ch'an)

275 T'ien-huang Tao-wu (Ch'an)

276 Nan-chüan Po-yüan (Ch'an)

277 Chao-chou (Ch'an)

i 278 Yün-yen (Ch'an)

800

278a Yang Liang (Confucian cm. on *Hsün Tzu*)

278b Lü Yen (Taoist reformer, spiritual alchemy, Buddhist-style meditation)
279 Kuei-Shan Ling-yu (Ch'an; f. Kuei-Shan sect)
280 Hsueh-fêng (Ch'an)
281 Ta-Yu (Ch'an)
i 282 Mu-chou (Ch'an)
283 Yang-shan Hui-chi (Ch'an, f. Kuei-Yang sect: meditation on circular symbols)
284 Hsiang-yen Chih-hsien (Ch'an)
285 Shih-pei (Ch'an)
286 Ts'ao Shan Pen-Chi (f. Ch'an Ts'ao-Tung sect; incorp. Hua-yen, doctrine of "5 Ranks")

900

287 Ts'ao-shan Hui-Hsia
288 Chin-feng Ts'ung-chih
289 Fa Yen (Ch'an, f. Fa-yen sect; incl. Hua-yen)
290 Nan-yüan Hui-yung (1st used koan)
291 Yung-ming (sync. Ch'an & Pure Land, scriptures)
292 T'ien-tai Te-shao (sync. Ch'an & T'ien-t'ai)

Figure 6.4. Neo-Confucian Movement and the Winnowing of Zen, 935–1265

935

293 Fen-yang
294 Ta-yang
295 Chih-yuan (Buddhist, Taoist/Confucian syncretism)
296 Ch'ung Fan (Taoist numerologist)
297 T'an Ch'iao (Taoist naturalist) +
298 Hsing Ping (Confucian) +

1000

299 Mu Hsin (Taoist numerologist)
300 Li Chih-tsai (numerologist)
301 Li Kai (same)
302 Fan O-ch'ang (same)
303 Liu Mu (same)
i 304 Shou Yai (Buddhist)
305 Hsüeh-tou (koan compiler and poet)
306 Shih-shuang
307 Yang-chi Fang-hui (f. Ch'an sect)
308 Huang-lung Hui-nan (f. Ch'an sect)
309 T'ou-tzu (revived Ch'an Ts'ao-Tung [Soto] sect, Hua-yen)
310 Ch'i-Sung (Buddhist monk, Taoist/Confucian syncretism)
i 311 Ch'eng Hsiang (father of Ch'eng brothers)
312 Ch'eng Pen (Taoist) +
313 Fan Chung-yen (political reformer, orthodox Confucian)
314 Ouyang Hsiu (politician, historian, poet)
315 Sun Fu (Confucian)
(316) Mei Yao-Ch'en (poet)
317 Su Hsun (poet, father of 319 and Su Shih; all in Szechuan faction, anti-reform and anti–Neo-Confucian)
318 Chang Po-tuan (f. Taoist sect, spiritual alchemy) +
319 Su Ch'e (poet and politician; polit. tolerance)
320 Shih Chieh (poet, anti-Buddhist and anti-Taoist)
321 Fan Tsu-yü (Confucian textual cm.)
322 Lü Ta-lin (moved fr. Chang Tsai school to Ch'eng school after death of Chang Tsai)

323 Su Chi-ming

324 Hou Ch'ung-liang

325 Wang P'in

326 Liu Hsüan

327 Hsieh Liang-tso (disciple of Ch'eng brothers)

328 Yu Tso (same; anti-Shao school polemic)

329 Yin T'un

330 Ch'i Kuan (popularized Chou Tun-i diagram)

1100

331 Shao Po-wên (Shao school, rival of Ch'eng school)

332 Ch'ao Yüeh-chin (same)

333 Shao Po (same)

334 Chu Chên (numerology, cm. *Yi Ching;* popularized Chou Tun-i diagram)

335 Tung-lin Ch'ang-tsung (Ch'an monk)

336 Lo Ts'ung-yen

337 Hu An-Kuo (Hu school of Neo-Confucianism, rival to Chu Hsi)

338 Hu Hung (same; circulated Chou Tun-i's numerology)

339 Hu Yin (same)

340 Chang Shih (same; 1st printed Ch'eng bros. mss, criticized by Chu Hsi)

341 Liu Kung (same)

342 Hu Chi-sui

343 Li Tung

344 Wu Yu (Confucian textual historian) +

345 Cheng Chia (same) +

346 Wang Che (f. Taoist Perfect Realization sect in north Khitan conquest state)

347 Hui-t'ang Tsu-hsin (Ch'an)

348 Ling-yüan Wei-ch'ing (same)

349 Wu-tsu Fa-yen (Ch'an *Blue Cliff Record*)

350 K'ai-fu Tao-ning (Ch'an)

351 Tan-hsia

352 Hung-chih Cheng-chueh (Silent Illumination Ch'an, Hua-yen, anti-koan meditation)

353 K'ai-hsi Tao-ch'ien (Ch'an)

354 Fo-chao Te-kuang (same)

1200

355 Wu-men Hui-k'ai (koan collection)

356 T'ien-t'ung Ju-ching (Buddhist, opposed Confucian/Taoist syncretism)

357 Li Po-mien

358 Liu Tse-chih

359 Lin Ti

360 Ts'ai Chi-tung

361 Huang Hsün

362 Ts'ai Ch'en

363 Chang Hsi

364 Ch'en Fu-liang

365 Ts'ao Shu-yuan

366 Ch'ang Ch'un (Taoist sect chief)

367 Li Chih-Ch'ang (Taoist sect chief)

368 Hsü Lu-Chai

369 Li Ching-tê

370 Yeh Ts'ai

371 Wei Liao-Ong

372 Wu Lin Ch'uan +

372a Wu Ch'eng (compromise Lu Chiu-yüan & Chu Hsi phils) +

Figure 6.5. Neo-Confucian Orthodoxy and the Idealist Movement, 1435–1565

1300

373	Liu Chi (astron/astrol, skeptic anti-superstition) +
374	Hsieh Ying Fang (skeptic) +
374a	Cheng Yü (same as 372a) +

1400

375	Ts'ao Tuan (skeptic, anti-Buddhist) +
376	Yang P'u +
377	Hsieh Hsuan (cm. Neo-Confucian texts) +
378	Wu Yü-pi +
379	Hu Chü-jen (faithful Neo-Confucian)

1500

380	Lou Liang
381	Chan Jo-shui
382	Hsü Ai
383	Huang Wan
384	Ku Yin-hsing
385	Ch'ien Te-hung (split in Wang Yang-Ming school)
386	Ch'en Ching-lan (orthodox Neo-Confucian, crit. Lu Chiu-yuan and Wang Yang-Ming as Ch'an Buddhism) +

Figure 7.1. Network of Japanese Philosophers, 600–1100: Founding of Tendai and Shingon

600

1	Kwalluk (Buddhist fr. Korea) +
2	Hui-Kuan (Korean, transmitted Buddhist Satyasiddhi & Madhyamika schools) +
3	
4	
5	

635

	Chisu (Japanese priest, transmitted *Abhidharma*)
	Chitatsu (same)
	Dosho (Japanese priest, transmitted Yogacara)

700

6	Gyogi (shamanistic Buddhist) +

735

7	Kibi-no-Makibi (transmitted Confucianism fr. China) +
8	Gembo (Japanese priest, st. China) +
9	Bodhisena (Indian Buddhist monk) +
10	Tao-hsüan (transmitted Vinaya) +
11	Shen-huiang (China, transmitted Kegon [Hua-yen]) +
12	Chien-chien (Chinese Vinaya master) +
[13]	Amoghavajra (tantrist, from China; 254 in Fig. 6.2)

765

[14]	Hsiu-jan (Zen, China)
[15]	Shun-chia (mantra doctrine [tantrism], China)
[16]	Tao-sui (T'ien-t'ai, China; 269 in Fig. 6.2)
[18]	Hui-kuo (tantrist, China)

835

19	Ennin (systematized Tendai [T'ien-t'ai]) +
20	Enchin f. Tendai esotericism/magic

865

21 Shobo (Shingon [tantrist] patriarch, Mtn. Priesthood fr. Shinto) +

22 Sugawara no Michizane (Confucian) +

935

23 Fujiwara no Arihira (Confucian) +

24 Kuya (Tendai, popularized Amida devotion) +

25 Ryogen (Tendai abbot, Amida faith)

965

26 Geshin (Pure Land) +

27 Kancho (Shingon split) +

1000

(Sei Shonagon) *Pillow Book*
(Lady Murasaki) *Tale of Genji*

1035

28 Ninkai (Shingon split) +

29 Eicho (Yogacara) +

1100

30 Ryonin (traveling priest, Pure Land) +

Figure 7.2. Expansion of Pure Land and Zen, 1100–1400

1135

31 Kukaban (syncretized Shingon & Amida recitation) +

1165

32 Fujiwara no Jien (Tendai, Buddhist phil of history) +

[33] Tou-Ts'ung (China, minor pupil of Chu Hsi)

[34] Te Kuang (Lin-chi lineage; 354 in Fig.6.4)

1200

35 Jokei (Yogacara, incorp. Zen, Pure Land *nembutsu* chanting)

36 Ryohen (sync. Yogacara, Zen, *nembutsu*, Tendai)

37 Ryozen (or Myozen, Zen)

38 Myoe (Kegon, incorp. Zen, *nembutsu*)

39 Kosai (Pure Land sub-split)

40 Ryukan (same)

41 Bencho (same)

42 Shoku (same)

43 Shakuen Eicho (Zen synchr. w Shingon rituals, Tendai)

44 Taiko Gyoyu (esoteric Zen)

45 Kakuen Zen

[46] T'ien-t'ung Ju-ching (Soto Zen, China; 356 in Fig.6.4)

[47] Wu-men Hui-K'ai (koan collection; 355 in Fig.6.4)

[48] Wu-chan Shih-fan (Zen, China)

[49] Wu-ming Hui-hsing (Zen, China)

1235

50 Shinchi Kakushin (Shingon, f. Fuke Zen sect, transmitted koan collection)

51 Kakuzen Ekan (Soto)

52 Shotatsu (Pure Land)

[53] Hsü-t'ang Chih-yü (Lin-chi Zen, China)

1265

54 Lan-hsi Tao-lung (transmitted Rinzai [Lin-chi] Zen)

55 Wu-hsüeh Tsu-yüan (Chinese immigrant, Rinzai Zen)

56   Koho Kennichi (son of
      emperor, sync. Zen and
      Shingon)
57   Gien (Soto Zen)
58   Kangan Giin (same) +
59   Kakushin-ni (Shinran's
      daughter, f. True Pure Land
      headquarters, Kyoto)
60   Chozen (Sanron, encyclopedia
      of all Buddhist schools) +
61   Shusho (Kegon, biogs of
      priests) +
62   Shocho (Shingon, encyc. of
      ceremonials) +
63   Kakuzen (Tendai, same) +
64   Gyonen (Buddhist history) +

      1300

65   Gen-e (Neo-Confucian)
66   Watarai Tsuneyoshi (Ise
      Shinto school)
67   Kokan Shiren (Rinzai Zen,
      history of Japanese
      Buddhism) +
68   Shinkyo (Ippen successor)
69   Kakunyo (Shinran's grandson,
      unified Ikko Pure Land)

      1335

70   Watarai Iyeyoki (Ise Shinto)
71   Gido Shushin (Zen koans and
      poetry)
72   Jakashitsu Genko (wandering
      monk, Rinka Zen) +

      1365

73   Imbe-no-Masamichi
      (Shinto/Buddhist syncretism) +

Figure 7.3. Zen Artists and Tea Masters, 1400–1600

      1400

74   Mansai (Shingon, adviser to
      shogun) +
75   Hoshu (Neo-Confucian) +

      1435

78   Ichijo Kanera (Shinto
      monotheism) +

      1465

80   Keian (Zen, adopted
      Confucianism) +

      1535

81   Minamimura Baiken (f.
      Shikoku Neo-Confucian
      school) +

Figure 7.4. Tokugawa Confucian and National Learning Schools, 1600–1835

      1600

82   Tenkai (Tendai, govt. adviser)
83   Ishin Suden (Rinzai Zen,
      adviser to shogun)
84   Nichio (Fuju-fuse sect of
      Nichiren Buddhism) +
(85) Yagyu Munenori (sword
      master)

      1635

86   Tani Jichu (Shikoku
      Neo-Confucian school)
87   Hayashi Gaho (official
      Neo-Confucian school, Edo)
88   Matsunaga Sekigo (taught
      Confucian classics)
[89] Fai-yin T'ang-jing (China,
      Buddhist)

90	Tao-che Ch'ao-yüan (Zen, from China)
91	Gudo Toshoku (Rinzai Zen)

1665

92	Mu-an Hsing-T'ao (Zen)
93	Kao-Ch'uan Hsing-tun (Chinese émigré, Zen)
94	Dokyo Etan (Rinzai Zen)
95	Keichu (Shingon, pioneer of Japanese classics, Shinto)
96	Yoshikawa Koretaru (Shinto compromise with Neo-Confucianism)
97	Watarai Nobuyoshi (rebirth of Ise Shinto) +
98	Chu Shun-sui (Chinese émigré Confucian, Mito school)
99	Asami Keisai (Yamazaki disciple)
100	Sato Naokata (same)
101	Hayashi Hoko (hereditary head of Edo school)
(102)	Oishi Kuranosuke (leader of 47 *ronin*)
104	Kinoshita Junan (Kyoto school, liberal Neo-Confucian)
105	Ando Seian (Kyoto Chu Hsi school) +

1700

106	Ito Togai (son of Ito Jinsai, systematizer)
107	Goi Jiken (Ito school)
108	Miyake Sekian (1st head Kaitokudo merchant school, Osaka)
109	Nakai Shuan (Kaitokudo merchant school)
110	Miwa Shissai (Edo, supported Kaitokudo school) +
112	Kada no Azumamaro (National Learning; Edo court poetry)

113	Miwa Shosai (Wang Yang-Ming school [Neo-Confucian Idealism]) +
114	Amenomori Hoshu (Kyoto Chu Hsi Neo-Confucian school) +
115	Hori Keizan (Neo-Confucian)
116	Hattori Nankaku (philologist)
117	Dohi Motonari (Neo-Confucian)

1735

118	Kada Arimaro (National Learning)
119	Yamagata Shunan (Sorai school, public policy)
120	Ando Toya (Sorai school, literary studies)
121	Usami Shinsui (same)
122	Hirano Kinka
123	Watanabe Keian (Sorai school)
124	Aoki Konyo (ordered by shogun to learn from Dutch) +
125	Tayasu Munetake (shogun's son, patron of court poetry)
126	Goi Ranju (Kaitokudo merchant school, naturalism)

1765

127	Inoue Kinga (eclectic Sorai & Jinsai schools)
127a	Katayama Kenzan (same)
128	Hosoi Heishu (same)
129	Minagawa Kien
130	Yoshida Koton
131	Yamamoto Hokuzan
132	Gasan Jito (Zen movement)
133	Hiraga Gennai (Dutch Learning, Nagasaki) +
134	Isobe Dosai
135	Asada Goryu (astron)
137	Minagawa Kien (eclectic Chu Hsi & Wang Yang-Ming) +

(139) Matsudaira Sadanobu (head of shogunal council; prohibited non-Confucian teachings)

140 Nakai Chikuzan (head of Kaitokudo merchant school)

141 Nakai Riken (Kaitokudo school)

142 Waki Guzan (scientist, Kaitokudo school)

143 Hoashi Banri (same)

1800

144 Nakai Sekka (Kaitokudo school)

145 Oshio Heihachiro (Wang Yang-Ming Idealist)

146 Kusama Naokata (history of money)

147 Yamagata Banto (Osaka merchant; astron)

148 Naka Tenyu (science)

149 Hashimoto Sokichi (science)

150 Sugita Gempaku (*daimyo*'s doctor, Dutch Learning) +

i 151 Motoori Ohira (son of Norinaga)

152 Ban Nobutomo (Norinaga school)

154 Sato Nobuhiro (reformer, Dutch Learning) +

155 Omura Mitsue (disciple of Kamo Mabuchi)

156 Daigu Ryokan (Zen poet-monk, popular Soto)

Figure 7.5. Meiji Westernizers and the Kyoto School, 1835–1935

1835

157 Ogata Koan (f. school of Dutch Learning, Osaka)

158 Takeno Choei (summarized Western phils) +

159 Ninomiya Sontoku (Shinto, Buddhist, Confucian syncretism) +

161 Yoshida Shoin (reformer, Wang Yang-Ming school) +

162 Sato Issai (official neo-Confucian at Edo, privately taught Wang Yang-Ming activism) +

(163) several leaders of Meiji Restoration

1865

164 Fukazawa Yukichi (transmitted Western liberal positivism)

165 Nishi Amane (transmitted Brit. Util., Mill, Kant) +

166 Tsuda Mamichi (transmitted Comte positivism) +

168 Kato Hiroyuki (materialist evolution)

169 Inoue Tetsujiro (1st Japanese phil chair, Tokyo; German Idealism)

170 Onishi Hajime (T. H. Green Idealist ethics) +

171 Kiyozawa Manshi (sync. Hegel & Amidaist Buddhism) +

172 Nanjo Bunyu (st. Sanskrit; taught Indian phil, Tokyo)

173 Raphael von Koeber (E. von Hartmann disciple, taught Tokyo)

174 Ernest Fenollosa (H. Spencer evol., taught Tokyo)

175 Ludwig Busse (Lotze disciple, taught Tokyo)

176 Inouye Enryo (True Pure Land) +

1900

177   Takakusu Junjiro (Buddhist scholar) +

178   Kuwaki Gen'yoku (neo-Kantian) +

180   Tanaka Odo (Dewey instrumentalism)

Figure 8.1. Islamic and Jewish Philosophers and Scientists, 700–935: Basra and Baghdad Schools

735

1   John of Damascus. (Christian theol, Ummayad court) +

2   al-Awza'i (Syria, f. school of law) +

3   Yazid ibn-Aban al-Raqashi (theol)

4   'Amr ibn 'Ubayd (Basra; *kalam* rational theology)

5   al-Muqaffa (Basra, tr., Aristotelean logic) +

6   Wasil ibn 'Ata (Basra; *kalam*)

7   Jahm b. Safwan (theol, denied free will) +

8   Ja'far al-Sadiq (Shi'ite 6th Imam; allegorist, *hadith*) +

9   Ibrahim b. Adham (pre-Sufi, pious ritualist ascetic)

10   Muqatil ibn Sulayman (allegorical interp. of Qur'an) +

765

11   Shaqiq al-Balkhi (mystic) +

12   Jabir b. Hayyan (Shi'ite; mystic, alc) +

13   Rabi'a al-'Adawiya (Basra, freed slave girl; mystic)

{14}   'Umar Ibn al-Farrakhan (Baghdad; astron, astrol)

{15}   Kanaka al-Hindi (India, Baghdad; astron, astrol)

{16}   Ya-'qub Ibn Tariq (Baghdad; Hindu astron)

{17}   al-Fazari (Kufa, Baghdad; astron)

{18}   Masha'allah (Baghdad; astrol)

19   Timotheus (Baghdad; Nestorian Christian patriarch; tr.) +

20   al-Shaybani (Baghdad jurist)

21   Abu-Yusuf (Baghdad jurist; crit. 23 for using *kalam*)

22   Hisham ibn al-Hakam (Kufa, Basra; scriptural literalist)

800

23   Bishr al-Marisi (Kufa, Basra, Baghdad; *kalam*)

24   Husayn al-Najjar (followed Dirar)

25   Hafs al-Fard (Egypt, Basra; Dirar spokesman vs. Abu-l-Hudhayl)

26   Hisham al-Fuwati (Basra Mu'tazilite, atomist)

27   Thumama b. Ashras (Baghdad Mu'tazilite; agnostic re. freedom and determinism)

28   Abu Musa al-Murdar (Baghdad Mu'tazilite)

29   'Ali al-Aswari (same)

30   Abu Bakr al-Asamm (Basra Mu'tazilite)

{32}   Habash al-Hasab (head Baghdad astron observatory; trigonometry)

{33}   Al-Khwarizmi (Baghdad House of Wisdom; encyclopedia of sciences, *algebra)

{34} Yahya ibn Abi Mansur (Zoroastrian convert to Islam; Baghdad court astrologer; astron tables)

{35} al-Jawhari (Baghdad court astron, math)

{36} al-Farghani (Baghdad court astron/astrol)

37 Ibn al-Qasim al-Raqqi (Sabian star worshipper, logic) +

38 Jibril b. Bakhtishu (Jundishapur, medical doctor to Baghdad caliph)

39 al-Barmaki (Baghdad court astrol/astron; tr.)

40 Theodore (Christian tr.) +

42 Dhu'l-Nun al-Misri (Egypt Sufi, alc, Coptic Neoplatonist)

43 al-Kharkhi (Baghdad Sufi) +

44 Mansur b. Ammar (same) +

45 Bishr b. al-Hati (same) +

46 Abu 'Ali al-Sindi (Hindu convert, mystic)

47 Benjamin al-Nah'awendi (Jew, f. karaite rational theol)

835

48 Daniel al Qumisi (Jerusalem, Jew, karaite)

49 Habbib ibn Bahriz (Christian bishop of Harran, northern Iraq) +

50 'Abd-al-Azzis al-Makki (Baghdad; conserv. *hadith*, *kalam* methods for debate)

51 Abu Ya'qub al-Shahham (Basra Mu'tazilite head)

52 al-Kashini *(kalam)*

53 'Abbad b. Sulayman (Basra Mu'tazilite; atomist)

54 'Amr al-Jahiz (Basra Mu'tazilite; master of Arabic prose; religious essays, nat hist)

55 al-Iskafi (Baghdad court Mu'tazilite; crit. Nazzam)

56 Ja'far ibn-Harb (Baghdad court Mu'tazilite)

57 Ahmad b. Abi Du'ad (Baghdad Mu'tazilite; chief magistrate of Inquisition)

58 al-Qasim ibn-Ibrahim (Imam; infl. by Mu'tazilite)

59 Ja'far ibn Mubashshir (Baghdad Mu'tazilite)

60 Ibn Na'imah al-Himsi (Christian, worked for al-Kindi; tr. Plotinus as "Theology of Aristotle")

61 Yahya ibn al-Bitriq (Baghdad tr.)

{62} Banu Musa (3 brothers; Baghdad House of Wisdom; astron, astrol, math; organized Greek tr.)

{63} Abu Ma'shar (astrol)

64 Yuhanna ibn Masawaih (Jundishapur Christian, 1st head of Baghdad House of Wisdom; tr.)

65 al-Harish al-Muhasibi (Basra, Baghdad; *kalam* combined with law; changed Sufism from asceticism to mysticism)

i 66 al-Saqati (Junayd's uncle; initiated him into mysticism)

67 Ibn-Karram (Nishapur; f. Karramite sect, anthropomorphic compromise) +

68 al-Bukhari (main *hadith* collection) +

69 Muslim (same) +

70 Hayuye (Hiwi) al-Balkhi (Jew, Manichaean dualist) +

{71} al-Tabari (Baghdad; medicine, nat sci, theol)

72 Ibn Kallub (*hadith*/Mu'tazilite compromise)

865

73 Khalif al-Isfahani (f. legal school, literalist; crit. *kalam*)

74 al-Qalanisi (moderate *kalam* within *hadith* literalists)

75 Abu'l-Husain al-Salihi (Basra Mu'tazilite)

{76} Ibn Khurradadhbih (Medina; geog, music)

76a David al-Mukammas (Nisibus/Mesopotamia Jew, Rabbinite, Mu'tazilite)

77 al-Khayyat (Baghdad Mu'tazilite head)

79 Ibn al-Rawandi (Baghdad freethinker)

80 al-Sarakhsi (Baghdad court astrol; attacked prophecy)

81 Abu Yahya al-Marwazi (Syrian Christian, Baghdad; logic)

82 Yuhanna ibn Hailan (Baghdad Christian logic; taught al-Farabi at Harran)

83 Ibrahim Quwairi (Baghdad Christian logic)

85 Hubaish ibn al-Hasan (Baghdad Christian tr.)

86 Ishaq ibn Hunayn (Nestorian Christian, medical doctor to caliph; logic)

87 'Isa ibn Yahya (Baghdad Christian; tr medicine)

88 Qusta ibn Luqa (Baghdad Christian medical doctor, visited Byzantium; main rival to Hunayn, tr. Greek math, medicine)

{89} al-Battani (Albatenius) (same home as Thabit ibn Qurra; converted fr. Sabian star worship; greatest Islamic astron*)

90 Ibn Zahrun (Sabian star worshipper, logic, medicine)

{91} al-Mahani (Baghdad; math, astron)

{92} Ibn Qutayba (Baghdad; astron collection)

93 'Amr al-Makki (Basra, Baghdad Sufi)

94 al-Shibli (intoxicated Sufi)

95 Sahl al-Tustari (Sufi; God is light)

96 Ibn Salim (Sufi)

97 al-Hakim al-Tirmidhi (biog. of early Sufis; saint upholds universe) +

98 Abu Sa'id Karraz (Sufi)

900

100 Abu Sahl al-Nawbakhti (Shi'ite doctrine of hidden Imam)

101 al-Hasan ibn-Musa al-Nawbakhti (Imamite)

102 al-Kulini (canonical Imami Shi'i law and *hadith*)

{103} al-Nayrizi (Baghdad; geom, astron; Euclid) +

{104} Ibn Wahshiyya (Baghdad; medical doctor, biol, alc) +

{105} Sinan ibn Thabit (Baghdad court medical doctor; Sabian forced convert to Islam; astron, math)

106 al-Iranshari (Indian transmigration doctr.?)

107 Ibrahim ibn 'Abd Allah (Baghdad Christian, logic)

107a Abu 'Uthman al-Dimashqi (Baghdad medical doctor, Christian convert to Islam; logic)

108   Abu Saʿid al-Sirafi (jurist, grammarian; public debate vs. Matta's logic)
109   al-Kaʿbi (Baghdad Muʿtazilite head; atomism)
110   al-Tabari (sum. Qurʾan interp.)
111   Ibn-Mujahid (definitive Qurʾan texts)
112   Ibn al-Ayadi (Muʿtazilite; metaphorical attributes of God)
{114}   Ahmad Ibn Yusuf (Egypt; math)
{115}   Abu Kamil (Egypt; *algebra)

Figure 8.2. Ashʿarites, Greek *Falasifa,* and the Syntheses of IbnSina and al-Ghazali, 935–1100

935

{116}   al-Uqlidisi (Damascus, India travel; arith)
{117}   al-Wabisi (Syria; astrol)
{118}   al-Hamdani (geog, nat sci)
119   Abu Sahl al-Suʾluki (Nishapur; Ashʿarite)
120   Abuʾl-Hasan al-Bahahi (Basra; Ashʿarite)
121   Ibn Mujahid (Basra, Baghdad; Ashʿarite)
124   al-Ajuni (Baghdad Hanbali) +
125   Ibn Batta al-ʿUkbari (Baghdad, Mecca; Hanbali preacher) +
126   Ibn al-Samh (Baghdad Christian logic)
{127}   Ibrahim ibn Qurra (Baghdad medical doctor; son of 105; math)
{128}   Ibn Hibinth (Iraq; astrol)
{129}   Abu Jaʿfar al-Khazim (Rayy court; astron, math)
{130}   al-Tabari (Rayy court; medicine)

131   al-Niffari (wandering darvish intoxicated Sufi) +
132   Al-Hakim al-Samarqandi (moderate *kalam*)

965

133   Abuʾl-Layth al-Samarqandi (moderate *kalam*)
134   al-Sarraj (Sufis as branch of ʿulama legalists) +
135   Ibn Samʿun (Baghdad pop. Hanbali preacher, Sufi) +
135a   Ibn Butta (Hanbali) +
{136}   al-Majusi (Shiraz; medicine, nat sci) +
137   Abu Sahl al-Masihi (Christian medical doctor; Baghdad, Khwarizm court) +
138   al-Mufid (Baghdad, Imamite head)
139   Ibn-Babawayh (Baghdad, Rayy; Imamite/Muʿtazilite canon)
140   Sahib Ibn-ʿAbbad (Rayy vizier; Muʿtazilite, Imamite)
141   ʿAbd-al-Jabbar (Basra, Baghdad; Rayy chief judge; Muʿtazilite)
142   al-Muʿayyad (Imam, Rayy; Muʿtazilite)
{143}   al-Khujandi (Transoxiana court, Rayy; math, astron)
144   Ibn al-Khammar (Jacobite Christian medical doctor; Baghdad, Khwarizm, Afghanistan)
{145}   al-Sufi (Rayy; astron)
{146}   al-Quhi (Baghdad; math, astron)
{147}   Abuʾl-Wafa al-Buzjani (Baghdad; *Diophantine alg)
148   Abuʾl Hasan (Basra; author of *Brethren of Purity?*)

149 Abu Ahmad al-Nahrajuri (same)

150 al-'Aufi (same)

151 Zaid b. Rifa'a (member or friend of Brethen)

152 Ibn al-Nadim (Baghdad bookseller, logic)

153 al-Tawhidi (Baghdad; "arch-heretic of Islam")

154 Ibn Zur'ah (Baghdad; medical doctor, tr., logic; accord of philosophy & Christianity)

156 Ibn Furak (Basra, Baghdad; Nishapur; Ash'arite attacked karamite anthropomorphists)

{157} Ibn Hauqal (upper Mesopotamia; geog) +

158 Japheth b. Ali ha-Levi (al-Basri) (Iraq, Jerusalem; Jew, karaite biblical exegesis; tr. Bible into Arabic)

{159} Ibn Yunus (Cairo; one of greatest Islamic astron*) +

1000

{160} Ibn al-Haitham (Alhazen) (Basra, Cairo; *optics)

160a Ibn Badr (Spain, exiled to Cairo; logic, math)

161 Ibn al-Tayyib (Baghdad; Christian medical doctor, Western [al-Farabi] logic)

162 Abu-l-Husayn al-Basri (Mu'tazilite attacked Imamites)

163 al-Murtada (head Baghdad Mu'tazilite)

164 Abd al-Molitian (Baghdad Mu'tazilite) +

165 al-Natiq Abu Talib (Zaydite Imam, Mu'tazilite)

166 Manekdim (Imami, Mu'tazilite)

167 Abd-al-Qahir al-Baghdadi (Nishapur; Ash'arite, attacked anthropomorphists; math)

169 al-Sulami (Nishapur; 1st register of Sufis)

169a Abu'l-Qasim al-Qushayri (Nishapur; scholastic Sufi)

{170} al-Karaji (Baghdad; *algebra)

{171} Abu Nasr Mansur ibn Iraq (Khwarizm, Afghanistan; math, astron)

{172} al-Sijzi (Iran, Baghdad; geom, astron, astrol)

{173} al-Biruni (Khwarizm, Ghazna; *astron, geog) +

{174} Kushyar (astron, math) +

175 Abu Ishaq al-Kazaruni (Persia; pop. Sufi preacher) +

176 Abi'l-Khayr (Sufi)

177 Ibn Hamid (Baghdad; Hanbali)

1035

178 al-Tusi (Baghdad; Mu'tazilite head)

179 Abu-Rashid (dispute betw. Baghdad & Basra Mu'tazilites)

180 Ibn al-Walid (Baghdad; logic) +

181 Ibn Butlan (Cairo; Christian, medical doctor, logic)

182 Ibn Ridwan (Cairo; Ibn Sina medicine)

183 al-Mubashshir (Alexandria; medicine, logic) +

184 Joseph al-Basir (Mesopotamia; Jew, karaite/Mu'tazilite)

185 Jeshua b. Judah (Palestine; Jew, karaite, Mu'tazilite exegete)

186 Abu-Ya'la (Baghdad; Hanbali, *kalam* method)

187   Abu-Ja'far (Baghdad; Hanbali, mob inciter vs. Mu'tazilites)

188   Abu-Nasr al-Qushayri (Nishapur; Ash'arite *kalam*)

{189}   al-Nasawi (Baghdad; geom, Hindu arith) +

190   al-Hujwiri (routinized Sufi theol, biogs.) +

191   al-Farmadhi (Sufi)

192   Ibn al-Marzuban (disciple of Ibn Sina)

193   minor disciples of Ibn Sina

194   Bahmanyar (Persia, Zoroastrian)

195   al-Bayhaqi (Nishapur; Ash'arite/Mu'tazilite; sync. Karramite anthropomorphism & Mu'tazilites) +

1065

196   'Abdullah al-Ansari (Afghanistan; f. Sufi order; anti-*kalam*) +

198   al-Tabrisi (Imamite theol) +

201   Ibn 'Aqil (Baghdad, Hanbali moderate)

202   Abu-l-Faraj (f. Hanbali school in Damascus, *kalam*)

203   Abu-l-Yasr al-Pazdawi (Bukhara, *kalam*) +

Figure 8.3. Mystics, Scientists, and Logicians, 1100–1400

1100

204   Najm al-Din al-Nasafi (Maturidite *kalam*) +

205   Abu-Mu'in al-Nasafi (Maturidite creed, *kal.*) +

206   Ibn Barraja (eastern Persia; Sufi) +

207   Yusuf al-Hamadani (f. Sufi order, Transox.) +

208   al-Zamakhshari (Baghdad, Khwarizm; Mu'tazilite/philology) +

209   Zain al-Din al-Jurjani (Persia; medicine, logic; wrote Persian) +

{210}   al-Khazini (Iran Seljuk court; astron, *mechanics) +

211   Ahmad al-Ghazali (Sufi, Platonist)

{212}   Ibn al-Tilmidh (Baghdad; medicine, pharmacy, logic) +

1135

213   al-'Ainzarbi (Baghdad, Cairo; medicine, logic)

{214}   Ibn al-Salah (Baghdad, Damascus; medicine, astrol, astron, math)

215   Ibn-Hubayra (Baghdad; Hanbali)

216   Ibn al-Jawzi (same, polymath)

217   Ahmad al-Yawavi (Anatolia; f. Sufi order, dancing darvishes) +

218   'Abd al-Qahir al-Suhrawardi (Sufi)

219   Ahmad al-Rifa'i (Iraq; f. fanatical Sufi order) +

220   'Abdulqadir Gilani (al-Jilani) (Sufi ecstatic)

{221}   al-Samaw'al (Baghdad, Jew, medicine, math)

i 222   Isaac ibn Ezra (son of Abraham ibn Ezra of Spain [Fig. 8.5]; Jew, convert to Islam)

223   al-Sawi (Persia; defended Ibn Sina logic vs. Abu-l-Barakat)

224   al-Gawnawi (Persia; astron, crit. Abu-l-Barakat logic)

225   Majd al-Din al-Jili

i 226   father of Fakhruddin Razi (st. Nishapur)

227 San'ai (1st great Sufi poet; Afghanistan) +

1165

228 al-Ushi (Maturidite creed, *kalam*) +

229 Abu-Hafs al-Suhrawardi (f. Sufi "monastic" order) +

230 al-Qatta (Baghdad; logic, geom) +

{231} al-Jazani (Baghdad court; machinery) +

1200

232 Abu al-Hasan al-Shadhili (Tunis, Alexandria; f. Sufi order) +

233 Saif al-Din al-Amidi (Baghdad, Cairo, Damascus; logic, theol) +

(234) Ibn al-Farid (Egy; Sufi poet) +

235 Najmuddin Kubra (Bukhara; f. Sufi order)

i 236 Rumi's father

237 Sa'ddudin Hammu'i (Sufi)

(238) Sa'di (Baghdad, Shiraz; Sufi, most pop. Persian poet)

239 Yaqut al Hamawi (Baghdad bookseller, encyclopedist) +

i 240 Dia al-Din Mas'ud (Shiraz medical doctor)

241 'Abd al-Latif (Baghdad, Cairo; deserted eastern for western logic)

242 Kamal al-Din ibn Yunus (Baghdad; eastern [Ibn Sina] logic, math)

i 243 Qutb al-Din al-Masri

(244) 'Attar (Nishapur; major Sufi poet) +

245 al-Kashi (Persia; western logic) +

246 Mu'in al-Din Chisti (India; Sufi) +

{247} al-Samarqandi (medical doctor) +

1235

248 al-Abhari (st. Mausil, Arbela; eastern [Ibn Sina] logic)

249 Sadr al-Din al-Qunyawi (chief disciple of Ibn al-'Arabi)

250 Hafiz al-Din al-Nasafi (Persia; Hanafite)

251 Shams-e Tabriz (wandering Sufi radical)

252 al-Nakhjuwani (Aleppo; medicine, eastern logic) +

253 Ibn al-Lubudi (Aleppo; medicine, eastern logic, astron, math) +

{254} al-Maghribi (Syria; astron, astrol, trig) +

255 Ahmad al-Badawi (Egy; f. pop. Sufi order) +

256 Ibn al-'Assal (Cairo; eastern logic)

257 al-Khunaji (Cairo; judge, western logic)

258 al-Urmawi (Mausil, Persia; handbook western logic)

{259} al-Tifashi (Cairo; phys, minerology)

{260} Baylak al-Qibjaqi (Cairo; clocks, minerology)

1265

261 Ibn Kammunah (last Jewish phil. in east, converted to Islam; driven from Baghdad by pop. disturbance; medicine, logic)

262 Ibn Wasil al-Hamawi (Syria, Cairo; western logic)

263 Butrus ibn al-Rahib (Cairo; Coptic Christian, anti-logic) +

264 Ibn al-Nafis (Damascus, Cairo; medicine, western logic vs. Ibn Sina) +

265 Ibn al-Hanhas (Aleppo, Cairo; logic) +

266 Bar Hebraeus (Syria; converted Jew, Christian bishop; logic) +

{267} Ibn al-Quff (al-Karaki) (Damascus; medicine, physiol)

268 'Iraqi (ecstatic Sufi poet) +

269 al-Astarabadhi (grammarian, logic)

270 Shams al-Din al-Samarqandi (Persia; assimilates eastern logic to disputation)

271 al-Qazwini al-Katibi (Persia; eastern logic, cosmol, geog)

272 al-Shahrazuri (Persia; logic) +

273 al-Hilli (Iraq, theol, eastern logic)

274 al-Baydawi (Shiraz, Tabriz; theol)

1300

275 Nizamuddin Awliya (India, Persia, f. Sufi order) +

276 Hajji Bektash (f. Sufi order, Anatolia) +

277 al-Simnani (f. Sufi order Iran, central Asia) +

278 al-Tustari (reconciled eastern & western logic)

{279} Kamal al-Din al-Farisi (Tabriz; *optics, math)

280 al-Qunawi (Persia; eastern logic)

{282} al-Umawi (Damascus; arith) +

283 al-Juzjani (Cairo; logic, language, jurisprudence) +

1335

284 Aaron ben Elija (Cairo, Constantinople; Jew, karaite, atomist) +

285 Muhammad ibn Ahmad al-Tilimsani (N. Africa, logic) +

286 Ibn Qayyim al-Jawziyah (Damascus, jurist; attacked logic)

{287} Ibn al-Shatir (Damascus; astron) +

{288} al-Khalili (Damascus; astron) +

289 al-Tahtani (Persia, reconciled eastern & western logic)

290 al-Iji (Shiraz; theol handbk.)

1365

291 Sayyid Haydar al-Amuli (Iraq, Iran; Shi'ism/ Sufi) +

292 Ibn Mubarakshah (Persia, Egypt; astron; logic handbks.)

293 'Ali ibn Muhammad al-Jurjani (Shiraz; theol, logic)

294 Bahauddin Naqshband (f. Sufi secret order, Iran, central Asia) +

295 al-Taftazani (Samarqand; Ash'arite logic handbooks)

296 al-Khidri (theol, logic)

297 al-Harawi (Persia; logic)

1400

298 Qadi Zadah (Samarqand; math, astron, logic)

{299} al-Kashi (Samarqand; *astron, trig)

{300} Ulugh Beg (Samarqand ruler; *astron)

301 Muhammad ibn Marzuq al-Tilimsani (logic, theol) +

302 Shams al-Din al-Husaini (logic)

303 Muhammad al-Husaini (Persia, logic) +

304 al-Fanari (Persia, theol, logic)

305 Nur al-Din al-Jurjani (logic handbk)

306 Hajji Pasha al-Aidini (Egypt, medicine, logic)

307 Ibn al-Shihnah (Aleppo, Damascus; Hanbali logic) +

Continuation to 1500 (not shown in Figure 8.3)

1435

308 al-Sanusi (western Algeria; Sufi; theol, logic textbk.)

{309} al-Qalasadi (Granada, Tunis; arith, alg)

310 Mulla Khusraw al-Tarasusi (Ottoman adviser, logic)

311 'Ala al-Din al-Tusi (Anatolia, Persia; logic; isolated attempt to mediate Averroës's rebuttal of Ghazali)

312 'Abdulkarim Jili (Sufi systematizer)

313 al-Bitlisi (logic)

314 Da'ud al-Shirwani (Persia; theol, logic)

315 al-Rikabi (Persia; logic)

316 al-'Ajami (same)

317 al-Hanafi (theol, logic)

318 al-Nisaburi (theol, logic)

319 al-Kafiyaji (theol, logic)

320 Jalauddin Davani (al-Dawwani) (Shiraz; Sufi; logic cm.)

1465

321 al-Maibudi (Persia; logic)

322 Mahmud al-Shirazi (Persia; logic; theol controversy)

323 Jami (Afghanistan; last great Sufi poet; theosophy)

324 al-Ansari (jurist; logic)

325 Mulla Lutfi (Ottoman official, logic)

326 al-Shirwani al-Rumi (sterile logic cm.)

327 al-Talishi (logic)

328 al-Shaf'i al-Biqa'i (Persia; encyclopedist, logic)

329 Sadr al-Din al-Shirazi (Persia; theol, logic)

330 al-Abiwardi (Persia; logic)

331 al-Farisi (same)

332 al-Tabrizi (same)

333 'Abd al-Ghafur al-Lari (Persia; theol, philol, logic)

Figure 8.4. Islamic and Jewish Philosophers in Spain, 900–1065

935

1 Ibn-Massara (f. Almeria school; Mu'tazilite, Sufi, numerology) +

(2) Hasdai ibn Shaprut (Córdoba court official, medicine; patron of Jewish intellectuals)

(3) Menahem b. Saruq (Córdoba; Jew; poet, Hebrew grammarian)

(4) Dunash b. Labrat (Jew; st. Babylon; Córdoba; new grammar & poetic style)

965

(5) Judah ibn Seset (Jew; disciple of 4)

(6) Isaac b. Capron (Jew; Córdoba; poet, grammarian)

7 Moses b. Enoch (Jew; fr. Babylon Acad.; f. Córdoba rabbinical acad.)

{8} Ibrahim ibn Yaqub (Jew, merchant traveler, geog) +

9 al-Majriti (Córdoba; astron, geom, magic)

10   Muhammad ibn ʿAbdun (st. Baghdad; medical doctor to Córdoba caliph; western logic)

{11}   Ibn Juljul (Córdoba; medicine, pharm) +

{12}   al-Zahrawi (same) +

1000

13   al-Hammar (logic; exiled) +

14   Ibn Badr (exiled to Cairo; logic, math) +

15   Ibn al-Baghunish (st. Córdoba; Toledo medicine; western logic, geom)

{16}   Ibn al-Samh (astron, astrol)

{17}   Ibn al-Saffar (same)

{18}   Ibn al-Khayyat (same)

20   Rabbi Hanok b. Mose (Córdoba Jew)

(21)   Judah b. David Huyyuy (Córdoba Jew; Hebrew grammarian)

22   al-Kirmani (transmitted Pure Brethren texts to Saragossa)

1035

(23)   Johan ibn Yanah (st. Lucena; Saragossa; peak of Hebrew grammar)

24   Samuel ibn Negrella (Córdoba Jew; Granada vizier; poet, theol)

{25}   Ibn Muʿad al-Jayyani (Córdoba; *math & astron)

26   al-Darimi (medicine, western logic, geom)

{27}   Ibn Wafid (Toledo; pharmacy) +

Figure 8.5. Spain, 1065–1235: The Hinge of the Hinge

1065

{28}   al-Zaqali (Toledo, Córdoba; astron, instrument maker) +

29   Isaac al-Fasi (Fez, Córdoba; Jew; head Lucena Academy)

30   Isaac b. Baruq (Córdoba, Seville Jew; astron, theol)

31   Isaac ibn Gayyat (Jew; head Lucena Acad.)

32   Joseph ibn Samuel (son of 24)

1100

33   Abu al-ʿAbbas b. al-ʿArif (Almeria Sufi) +

34   Rabbi Joseph Ibn Sahl (Córdoba Jew; judge)

35   Moses ibn Ezra (Granada, Lucena, Córdoba; Jew; eclectic Neoplatonist; poet)

(36)   Judah Levi (Córdoba Jew; poet)

37   Joseph ibn Megas (Jew; head Lucena Acad.)

38   Baruc b. Isaac al-Balia (Lucena Jew; son of 30; sci, phil)

39   Ibn Hasdai (Spain, Egypt; medicine, logic)

40   Abu'l-Salt (Seville, Cairo; medicine, logic)

41   Abraham bar Hiyya (Barcelona Jew; astron/astrol, Neoplatonist/Arist; tr. Arab sci into Latin) +

1135

43   Plato of Tivoli (Barcelona; Christian tr.) +

45   Ibn al-Imam

46   Ibn Zuhr (or Avenzoar) (Seville; medicine, logic, phil)

{47} Jabir ibn Aflah (or Geber) (Seville; revised Ptolemy)

48 Meir b. Joseph ibn Megas (Jew; migrated to Toledo after Almohad conquest; son of 37)

1165

i 48b son of 47

49 Judah ibn Tibbon (Jew; southern France; tr.)

50 Joseph ibn Aknin (Fez Jew; favorite disciple of Maimonides)

{51} al-Bitruji (or Alpetragius) (Seville; *astron, alternative to Ptolemy)

52 Ibn Bundud (Córdoba jurist, logic; cm. Averroës)

53 Ibn Tumlus (Córdoba medical doctor to caliph; western logic)

54 Abu Madyan (Morocco Sufi) +

1200

55 Abraham b. Moses Maimonides (Egypt; son of Maimonides; relig. pietist)

56 Samuel ibn Tibbon (Jew, southern France, Toledo, Barcelona, Alexandria; Maimonidist)

1235

57 Ibn Sab'in (Granada court; Aristotelean turned Sufi) +

Figure 9.3. Christian Philosophers, 1000–1200: Forming the Argumentative Network

1000

1 Gerbert of Aurillac (Catalonia, Rome; pope; math)

2 Fulbert (f. Chartres school)

4 Anselm of Besate (Parma, Burgundy, Germany) +

5 Gerard Czanad (Italy, France; anti-phil)

1035

3 Berengar of Tours

6 Otloh of St. Emmeran (Regensburg; anti-phil)

7 Constantius Africans (tr. medicine; Monte Cassino)

1065

8 Bruno of Segni (Monte Cassino)

9 Manegold of Lautenbach (Paris; anti-phil)

10 Gilbert Crespin (England)

11 Ralph of Laon

12 Anselm of Laon

13 Gaunilo (monastery near Tours)

14 Garlandus Composita (dialectician; Liege, England, Besançon)

15 John the Sophist (Tours)

16 Yves of Chartres (canon lawyer)

17 Odo of Tournai +

1100

18 Adelard of Bath (tr.; Tours, Laon, Sicily, Toledo?)

19 Walter of Mortagne (Paris)

20 Josselin of Soissons

21 Arnold of Brescia (Paris)

22 Honorius of Autun

23 William of St. Thierry (Cistercian)

24 William of Conches (Paris)

25 Thierry of Chartres

26 Isaac of Stella (Cistercian)

27 Rupert of Deutz

28   Adam of St. Victor (hymn
      writer)
29   Otto of Freising

1135

30   Alcher of Clairvaux
      (Cistercian)
31   Hermann Judaeus
32   Irenerius (Bologna; law) +
33   Gratian (Bologna; canon
      law) +
34   Bandino (Italy) +
35   Gandolfus (Bologna) +
37   Peter of Poitiers (Paris)
38   Simon of Tournai (Paris)
39   Peter Comester (Paris)
40   Odo of Soissons (Paris)
41   Robert of Melun (near Paris)
42   Robert Pullen (Oxford)
43   Adam of Petit Pont (Paris)
44   Nicolas of Amiens
45   Jean Beleth
46   Bernard Silvestris (Tours)
47   Clarembald of Arras
48   Hermann of Carinthia (tr.,
      Toulouse, Toledo?)
49   Gerard of Cremona (tr.,
      Toledo)
50   John of Seville (tr., Toledo)

1165

51   Raoul Ardent (Paris)
52   Peter the Chanter (Paris)
53   Alexander of Neckham (Paris,
      Oxford, nat sci)
54   Walter of St. Victor
55   Prévostin of Cremona +
(56) Joachim of Floris (Cistercian
      abbot, Calabria;
      eschatological prophecies)
57   Godfrey of St. Victor
      (historian)
58   Amaury of Bènes (Paris,
      pantheist)

Figure 9.4. Franciscan and Dominican Rivalries, 1200–1335

1200

59   David of Dinant (materialist
      pantheist)
60   Ralph of Longo Campo
61   Jacques de Vitry (Augustinian
      friar)
62   Stephen Langton
63   Thomas Gallo of Vercelli (St.
      Victor; mysticism)
66   Michael Scotus (Toledo
      Palermo, Rome; astrol; tr.
      Averroës)
(67) Jordan of Saxony (Padua,
      Bologna; Dominican general)
68   Gerard of Abbeville (Paris,
      theol) +
69   Adam Marsh (Oxford,
      Franciscan)
70   Thomas of York (Oxford,
      Franciscan)
71   Peter of Maricourt (Paris)
72   Richard of Cornwall (Paris,
      Oxford)
73   John of Rochelle (Paris)
74   William of Auxerre (Paris
      theol)
75   Robert of Curcon (Paris; univ.
      chancellor) +
76   Philip of Greve (Paris; theol) +
77   Johannes Pagus +
78   Alfred of Sareschel (nat sci,
      England) +
79   Adam Pulchrae Mulieri (nat
      sci) +

1235

80   Richard Fishacre (Oxford,
      Dominican, Aristotelean) +
81   Robert Bacon (Oxford,
      Dominican) +

82 John of Garland (Paris, grammar) +

83 Nicolas of Paris (logic) +

84 Eustachius of Arras (Franciscan)

85 Walter of Bruges (Paris, Franciscan)

86 William of Hothun (Paris, Oxford; Dominican Thomist) +

87 Richard of Clapwell (Paris, Oxford; Dominican Thomist)

88 William of Shyreswood or Sherwood (Oxford, Paris? logic)

89 Lambert of Auxerre (Paris; Dominican; logic) +

90 William Arnauld (Toulouse; logic)

91 Raymond of Pennaforte (Bologna, Barcelona; Dominican general)

92 Thomas of Chantimpré (Louvain, Paris; Dominican, sci encyclopedia)

93 William of Moerbeke (tr.; papal court, Viterbo; Greece)

94 Witelo (Paris, Padua, Viterbo; nat sci)

95 Henry Bate of Malines (nat sci; secretary of princes)

96 Barthomaus Anglicus (encyclopedist) +

97 Vincent of Beauvais (Paris, Beauvais; Dominican encyclopedist) +

98 Roland of Cremona (Dominican) +

99 Hugh of St. Cher (Dominican) +

100 John Pungens-Asinum (Dominican) +

101 Peter of Tarantaise (Dominican; Pope Innocent V) +

102 Bombolognus of Bononia (Dominican) +

103 Romanus of Rome (Dominican) +

1265

104 Campanus of Novara (Bologna, Paris, Rome; math)

105 Ulrich of Strasbourg (Cologne, Strasbourg; Dominican Neoplatonist)

106 Dietrich of Freiberg (Cologne, Paris; Dominican)

107 Hugh Ripelin of Strasbourg (Cologne; Dominican Neoplatonist)

108 John of Fribourg

109 John of Geneo (Italy; Dominican Thomist) +

110 Durandellus (Italy; Dominican Thomist) +

111 Humbert of Frulli (Italy; led Cisterians into Thomist camp) +

112 Peter of Auvergne (Paris rector; secular Thomist) +

113 Bernard of Treilles (France; Dominican Thomist) +

114 Bernard of Auvergne (France; Dominican Thomist) +

115 Bernard of Claremont (France; Dominican Thomist) +

116 Hannibaldus of Hannibaldus (Italy; Dominican Thomist)

117 Remigio dei Girolami (Italy; Dominican Thomist; alleged teacher of Dante)

118 William de la Mare (Franciscan)

119 John of Paris (Dominican, Thomist)

120 Giles of Lessines (Dominican, Thomist)

121 Bernier of Nivelles (Averroist)

122 Roger of Marston (Oxford, Cambridge, Franciscan primate of England)

123 Boethius of Dacia (Paris, Averroist)

124 Jacob of Viterbo (Paris, Naples; Thomist)

125 Richard of Middleton (Paris, Oxford; Franciscan; anti-Thomist)

126 William of Ware (Oxford)

127 Gonsalvus of Spain (Franciscan general)

128 Radulphus Brito (Paris; logic)

129 Hervé Nedellec (Hervaeus Natalis) (Dominican Thomist)

130 Jacques of Metz (Dominican)

131 Gerhard of Bologna (Paris; Carmelite; Thomist anti-Scotist)

132 John of Naples (Avignon; Dominican Thomist)

133 Tolomeo di Lucca (Naples; Dominican Thomist)

134 Berthold of Mosburg (Cologne)

1300

135 Peter of Palude (Avignon; Dominican Thomist)

136 James of Lausanne (Paris; Dominican Thomist)

137 Guido Terreni (Carmelite; Thomist anti-Scotist)

(138) Michael of Cesena (Paris, Avignon; Franciscan general)

139 Francis of Marchia (Paris, Avignon, emperor's court; Franciscan; nat sci)

140 Thomas Wylton (Oxford, Merton; Paris)

141 Henry of Harclay (Paris; Oxford chancellor; atomist)

142 William of Alnwick (Scotist)

143 Francis of Meyronnes (Paris, England, Avignon; Franciscan, leading Scotist)

144 John of Basel (Scotist and Nominalist)

145 Thomas of Sutton (Oxford; Dominican Thomist, anti-Scotist)

146 William of Macklesfield (Dominican Thomist)

147 Walter Chatton (Oxford, Avignon; Franciscan; atomist)

148 Gerard of Odo (Paris; Franciscan general)

149 Vital du Four (traditional Augustinian)

150 William of Falgar (Franciscan) +

151 Nicholas of Ockham (Franciscan) +

152 Robert of Orford (Oxford; Dominican Thomist) +

153 Simon of Favesham (Oxford) +

154 Geoffrey of Hasphall (Paris, Oxford; logic) +

155 Bartholomy of Bologna (Paris theol; Bologna) +

156 James of Douai (Paris Aristotelean) +

157 Martin of Dacia (Paris theol) +

158 Adénulfe of Agnani (Paris logic) +

159 Richard of Winchelsea (England; nat sci) +

160 Henry of Wile (England; nat sci) +

161 Gilbert of Seagrove (England; nat sci) +

162 Roger Swineshead (Benedictine, Glastonbury) +

163 Siger of Courtrai (Paris; logic) +

164 Nicolas Trivet (Oxford; Dominican Thomist) +

165 Hugh of Castro Novo (Scotist) +

166 Antonius Andreas (Scotist) +

167 John of Reading (Oxford; Franciscan; Scotist anti-Ockham) +

168 Richard Rolle of Hampole (mystic hermit poet) +

169 Nicolas Bonet (Paris; nat sci) +

170 Siegbert of Beck (Carmelite; Thomist) +

171 John of Jandun (Paris; quasi-Averroist)

172 Peter of Abagno (Padua, Paris; medicine, Averroist?)

173 William Peter of Godin (Avignon; Dominican Thomist) +

174 Armand of Belvezer (France; Dominican Thomist) +

175 Bernard Lombardi (France; Dominican Thomist) +

176 Durand of Aureliaco (France; Dominican Thomist) +

177 Augustinus Triumphus (Paris, Padua; Augustinian; Thomist) +

178 Angelo of Arezzo (Bologna; Averroist) +

179 Taddeo of Parma (Bologna; medicine; Averroist) +

180 Michael of Massa (Augustinian; nat phil) +

181 John of Sterngasse (Cologne Albertist Neoplatonist) +

182 Gerhard of Sterngasse (Cologne Albertist Neoplatonist) +

183 Nicolas of Strasbourg (Cologne Albertist Neoplatonist) +

184 John of Lichtenberg (Cologne; Dominican Thomist) +

185 Henry of Lubeck (Cologne; Dominican Thomist) +

186 Thomas of Erfurt (grammarian) +

187 John Aurifaber (Erfurt, logic) +

Figure 9.5. Jewish Philosophers within Christendom, 1135–1535: Maimonidists, Averroists, and Kabbalists

1135

1 Yehuda ben Barzilai (Barcelona)

2 Abraham ben Isaac of Narbonne (Provence)

3 Samuel the Hasid (Speyer, f. Hasidism)

1165

4 Jehudah the Hasid (Worms Hasidist)

5 Abraham ben David (or Rabad) (f. Kabbalah school, Provence)

6 Jacob ha-Nazir

[49 Fig. 8.5] Judah ibn Tibbon (fled Spain in Almohad invasion to southern France; tr.)

1200

7 Isaac the Blind (Narbonne school of Kabbalah)

8 Eleazar ben Jehudah (Worms Hasidist)

[56 Fig. 8.5] Samuel ibn Tibbon (Toledo, Barcelona, southern France, Alexandria; tr. Maimonides into Hebrew)

1235

9   Moses ben Nahman (Nahmanides) (Gerona, near Barcelona; Kabbalah)
10   Ezra Ben Solomon (Catalonia; Kabbalah)
11   Azriel (Catalonia; Kabbalah)
12   Jacob ben Makhir Ibn Tibbon (Marseille/Montpellier, tr., astron)
13   Joseph Anatoli (Naples, tr.)
14   Hillel ben Samuel (Italy; Maimonidist, Thomist)

1265

15   Moses Ibn Tibbon (Jew; Montpellier, Naples; Averroist)
16   Isaac Albalog (Catalonia; Averroist)
17   Shentob Falaquera (Jew; tr.; Maimonidist)
18   Salomon Ibn Adreth (Barcelona; Kabbalah)
19   Joseph Gikatila (Spain; Kabbalah)
20   Todros Abulafia (Toledo; Kabbalah)

1300

21   Joseph ibn Wakkar (Toledo, reconciled Kabbalah and phil)
22   Meir ben Solomon Ibn Sahula (Barcelona; Kabbalah)
23   Joseph ibn Kaspi (Spain, Maimonidist, Averroist)
24   Judah ibn Tibbon (Montpellier; Maimonidist)
25   Yeda'ya Bedersi (southern France; Scotist)

1335

26   Moses of Narbonne (tr.; Maimonidist, Averroist)

1365

27   Themo Judaei (Nominalist, nat sci)

1400

28   Simon Duran (Maimonidist)
29   Shentob ibn Shentob (Spain; anti-phil, anti-Maimonidist)

1435

30   Joseph ben Shentob (Spain; Aristotelean, Maimonidist)

1465

31   Shentob ibn Shentob (Spain; defended Maimonides vs. Crescas)
32   Isaac Aburbanel (Spain; defended Maimonides vs. Crescas & Albo; attacked rationalism of Gerson & 26)
33   Isaac Arama (Spain; Kabbalah)

1500

34   Judah Leo Aburbanel (Italy; Platonist)

Figure 9.6. Scholastics, Mystics, Humanists, 1335–1465

1335

188   Richard Fitz-Ralph (Oxford Balliol, Ireland; Averroist/Augustine sync.)
189   Richard Kilvington (Oxford)
(190) Richard de Bury (bishop of Durham; London patron)

191 Walter Burley (Oxford Merton, Paris, Avignon; realist, anti-Nominalist; logic, nat sci)

192 William Heytesbury (Oxford Merton; Nominalist logic, kinematics)

193 Richard Swineshead (Oxford Merton; logic, math)

194 Ralph Strode (Oxford Merton; Nominalist logic)

195 Richard Billingham (Oxford Merton; Nominalist)

196 John Dumbleton (Oxford Merton; mechanics)

197 John Bode (Oxford Merton)

198 Richard of Campbell (Oxford Merton; logic) +

199 Richard Brinkley (Franciscan; Nominalist) +

200 Robert Fland (Oxford) +

201 John of Baconthorp (England; anti-Averroist) +

202 Adam Woodham (Oxford, London; Franciscan; Ockhamist)

203 Robert Holkot (Cambridge Dominican; Ockhamist Nominalist)

204 Peter of Aquila (Scotist) +

205 Landolphe of Carraciolo (Scotist) +

206 André de Neufchateau +

207 Peter Ceffons (Paris; Cistercian) +

208 John of Ripa (Paris; Franciscan; indep. Scotist, Nominalist) +

209 Thomas of Strasbourg (Augustinian general; indep. Thomist)

210 Henry Suso (Constance, Cologne; mystic, Dominican)

211 John Tauler (Cologne; mystic, Dominican)

212 John Ruysbroeck (Netherlands; mystic)

213 Barotolus of Sassoferato (Italy) +

214 Hugolin of Orvieta (nat sci; anti-phil) +

215 Guy of Rimini (Bologna) +

216 Paulus Perusinus (Averroist) +

1365

217 Walter Hilton (England; Augustinian; mystic) +

218 Richard of Lavenham (Oxford; Carmelite) +

219 Marsilius of Inghen (Paris, Heidelberg; Nominalist)

220 Henry of Hainbuch (Paris, Toledo; Nominalist)

221 Henry of Oyta (Paris, Toledo; Nominalist)

222 Peter of Candia (Paris, Oxford; Franciscan; Pope Alexander V; eclectic tolerance) +

223 Baldus of Ubaldus (Bologna, Pisa, Padua; law) +

224 Bonsembiante of Padua +

225 John of Legnano (Bologna; law, theol) +

(227) Gerhard Groot (Netherlands; f. Brethren of Common Life)

(228) Florentinus Radevynszoon (same)

229 St. Catherine of Siena (mystic raptures) +

(230) Giovanni di Conversino (Padua; Humanist)

(231) Manual Chrysoloras (Byzantium, Florence; Humanist)

252 John Rodington (Oxford; Franciscan; Scotist) +

253 John Capreolus (Paris,
Toulouse; Dominican revived
Thomism; crit. Scotism
Nominalism) +
254 Raymond Sebond (Toulouse;
Lullist) +
255 Henry of Gorkum (Cologne;
Dominican Thomist) +

1400

256 John Schoonhoven (defended
Ruysbroeck's mysticism)
259 Jerome of Prague
260 Theodore of Gaza (Italy, tr.
Aristotle) +
261 Gemistus Pletho (Humanist,
Byzantium, Florence, revived
Platonist religion)
262 Guarino of Verona
(Constantinople, Padua,
Florence, Ferrara; Humanist
Greek tr.)
263 Vittorino da Feltre (Mantua,
Humanist educ reform)
264 Paul of Venice (Oxford, Paris,
Padua; Averroist, sci, logic)

1435

265 Paul of Perugia (Padua,
Venice; Averroist) +
266 Gaetano di Tiene (Padua,
Averroist) +
267 Henry of Kamper (Cologne;
Dominican Thomist)
268 Denis the Carthusian
(Cologne; Thomist,
Neoplatonist mystic,
anti-Nominalist, anti-Scotist)
269 Hendrik Herp (Netherlands,
mystic theol) +
270 St. Catherine of Bologna
(mystic vision Scotist) +
(271) Enea Silvio de Piccolomini
(imperial official, pope;
Humanist)

272 Lorenzo Valla (papal
secretary; Humanist
anti-Aristotelean,
anti-scholastic)
273 George Trebizond
(Byzantium, Italy; Humanist,
Aristotelean)
274 Cardinal Bessarion
(Byzantium, Italy; Humanist,
Platonist)
276 St. Antoninus (Florence;
Dominican Thomist)
277 Dominic of Flanders (Italy;
Dominican Thomist) +
278 Serafino Capponi de Porrecta
(same) +
279 Bartholomew of Spina
(same) +
280 Chrisostomo Javelli (same) +
281 Johan Versoris (Dominican
Thomist) +
282 Gerhard von Elten (same) +
283 Gerhard de Monte (same) +
284 Lambert de Monte (same) +.
{285} Georg Peurbach (Vienna,
math)
{286} Regiomontanus (Vienna, math)

Figure 9.7. Reformers, Metaphysicians, Skeptics, 1465–1600

1465

287 Argyropoulos (Byzantium,
Florence, Rome; Humanist)
288 St. Catherine of Genoa
(mystic) +
289 William of Vaurouillon
(Franciscan Scotist) +
290 Nicolas of Orbellis (Scotist) +
291 Antonius Serectus (same) +
292 Bonetus of Venice (same) +

293 George of Brussels (same) +
294 Samuel de Cassinis (same) +
295 Thomas Bricot (Paris; Scotist/Nominalist)
296 Nicolas Tinctor (Paris, Tübingen; Scotist) +
297 Stephen Brulefer (Paris, Mainz; Scotist)
298 Scriptoris (Tübingen, Scotist)
299 Peter Tartaretus (Paris rector; Scotist)
300 Gabriel Biel (Heidelberg, Tübingen; leading Nominalist) +
301 Petrus Nigri (Cologne, Thomist, anti-Nominalist) +
302 Gerhard von Hardenwyck (Cologne; Albertist/Thomist)
303 Arnold of Lugde (same)
304 Rudolph Agricola (Germany, Netherlands; Humanist, Aristotelean, anti-scholastic) +
305 Ermolao Barbaro (Venice; "Alexandrist" Aristotelean)
306 Nicoletto Vernias (Padua; Averroist Aristotelean)
307 Alexander Achillini (Bologna; Averroist)
308 Elija Delmedigo (Crete; Jew)
309 John Reuchlin (Tübingen, Heidelberg, France, Italy; Humanist, Cabalist) +
313 Francis Lychetus (Scotist) +

1500

314 John Mair (Paris, St. Andrews; Scotist/Nominalist, logic, math)
315 Dullaert of Ghent (Paris; nat phil; edited Aristotle, Buridan)
317 Jacques Lefevre (France; Humanist Aristotelean) +
318 Charles Bouillé (France; Humanist, nat phil) +

321 Agrippa von Nettesheim (occultist; Cologne, France, Italy, England)
324 Francisco Silvestri of Ferrera (Bologna, Italy; Dominican; modified Thomist)
325 Cardinal Cajetan, Thomas di Vio (Bologna, Padua; Dominican Thomist)
326 Agostino Nifo (Bologna; Averroist)

1535

327 Simon Porta (Italy; Aristotelean)
328 Gasparo Contarini (same)
329 Franco Zorzi (Italy; occulist) +
330 Andreas Osiander (Germany; f. Protestant sect) +
331 Caspar Schwenckfeld (same)
332 Sebastian Franck (Germany, Protestant, Humanist, mystic)
332a Michael Servetus
333 Julius Scaliger (France)
334 Marius Nizolius (Humanist eclectic, anti-scholastic logic) +
335 Peter Crockoert (Paris, Salamanca; Thomist)
336 Bartolomé de las Casas (missionary to Amerindians; natural law)
(336a) George Buchanan (religious reformer, Latin poet; Scotland, Paris, Coimbra)
(336b) Marc-Antoine Muret (Latin anti-Ciceronian stylist; Paris, Toulouse, Padua)
337 Francisco de Vitoria (Salamanca; Thomist; f. internatl. law)

338   Melchior Cano (Spain; Dominican Thomist; sci anti-mystic, anti-Jesuit)

1565

339   Martin de Ledesma (Spain; Dominican Thomist; moral theory)

340   Dominic de Soto (Dominican Thomist, f. internat. law; Alcala, Paris)

341   Bartholomew de Medina (same) +

342   Dominic Bañez (Salamanca; Dominican Thomist)

343   Luis de Molina (Spain, Coimbra, Evora; Jesuit)

346   Valentine Weigel (Germany, Lutheran mystic) +

347   Joseph Scaliger (Geneva, Leyden)

348   Lelio Sozzini (Sienna; anti-Aristotelean)

349   Fausto Sozzini (Sienna, Poland; Socinianism/Unitarianism)

352   Jacobo Zabarella (Padua, Aristotelean) +

353   Andreas Cesalpinus (Italy; Aristotelean) +

354   Jacobo Cremonini (same) +

355   Nicolaus Taurellus (Basel; Protestant anti-Aristotelean) +

356   Joest Lipsius (Louvain, Leyden; Humanist revived Stoicism, sync. w Christianity)

357   Francisco Sanchez (Bourdeaux, Toulouse; medicine; skeptic, Montaigne's cousin)

358   Pierre Charron (France; skeptical fideist, anti-Calvinist)

Figure 10.1. European Network: The Cascade of Circles, 1600–1735

1565

{A}   Maestlin (Tübingen theol)

i {B}   Ostilio Ricci (math)

i (C)   Galileo's father

i (D)   Descartes's father

{E}   della Porta (Accademia Segreti, Naples; Accademia Lincei, Rome)

{F}   Fabricus (Padua, physiol)

G   Jesuit team (Coimbra, summa Thomist phil)

(H)   Spenser (Sidney circle)

1600

1   Cardinal Bellarmine (Jesuit, Rome; Thomist)

2   Sarpi (Venetian state theologian, nat phil)

3   Carmelite team (Alcala, summa Thomist phil) +

4   Vanini (Padua, Naples, Toulouse; medicine; Averroist/pantheist) +

{5}   Harriot (math, astron, geog)

{6}   Napier (Scotland; logarithms)

{7}   Briggs (geom, Gresham College, London)

{8}   Oughtred (math notation)

(9)   Ben Jonson

(10)   John Donne

(11)   George Herbert (younger brother of Cherbery)

12   Andrae (Tübingen; publicized "Rosicrucians") +

13   Alsted (Herborn; anti-Arist; Lullist; chiliast theol)

14   Veron (Jesuit teacher at La Flêche; anti-Calvinist debater)

(15)   Cardinal Bérulle (anti-Calvinist leader; f. Oratorians)

{15a} Mydorge (Descartes's friend; conic sections; optics)

i 16 Montaigne's daughter

(17) Maurice of Nassau (Dutch general)

i (17a) Huygens family

18 van Helmont (Louvain, medicine, Paracelsian chemistry) +

19 da Costa (Acosta) (Jew, st. Coimbra, fled to Amsterdam; religion as human creation)

{20} Cavalieri (Milan, Jesuit; calculus)

1635

{21} Torricelli (Rome, Florence; math, physics)

{22} Viviani (barometer)

(23) Haak (London agent of Palatine Elector; sci correspondence)

(24) Hartlib (Silesia merchant, London; sci correspondence)

{25} Pell (Cambridge, London, Holland; math)

(26) Palatine Elector

27 Bisterfeld (Heidelberg, Leipzig, diplomat; church reunification)

{28} Roberval (Paris, math)

{29} Desargues (math)

{30} Fermat (Toulouse)

31 La Peyrère (Bordeaux, Paris, Amsterdam; pre-Adamite)

32 La Mothe de Vayer (skepticism basis of Christianity; led Libertins Érudits)

33 Naudé

34 Patin

(35) Corneille

(36) Molière

37 Cyrano de Bergerac (freethinker, satirist)

38 Jungius (medical doctor, st. Padua; "Hamburg logic") +

i 39 Grotius's son

40 Erhard Weigel (Leipzig; taught ethics geometrically)

i 41 Jakob Thomasius (father of Christian Thomasius)

42 Rabbi Menasseh ben Israel (Spain; Jew, Amsterdam printer; predicted messianic age)

43 Ribera (Amsterdam Jew, excommunicated w Spinoza)

44 Boreil (hosted Amsterdam Jewish/interdenominational circle)

45 Fisher (Amsterdam Quaker)

46 Nicole (Port-Royal logic; Jansenist polemic)

47 La Rochefoucauld

48 Mme. Sablé (collab. with La Rochefoucauld)

49 Jacques Esprit (same)

{50} Ent (medical doctor, Padua, London; defended circulation of blood)

{51} Glisson (Cambridge, med.)

(52) First Earl Shaftesbury

(53) Oldenburg (Bremen, England, correspondence)

{54} Wilkins (London chaplain to Elector Palatine; Oxford meetings became Invisible College)

{55} Wallis (geom, Oxford)

{56} Wren (Oxford, astron, Gresham College; geom)

{57} Hooke (Oxford, Royal Society curator)

{58} Petty (Oxford, hosted Invisible College; professor of anatomy)

{59} Sprat (Oxford, King's chaplain)

{60} John Collins (math, London, correspondence)

60a Glanvill (propagandist for Royal Society)

61 Whichcote (led Cambridge Platonists)

62 Culverwel (Calvinist moral phil)

63 John Smith (liberal theology)

64 Worthington

64a Anne Conway (More's pupil; spiritual monism)

{65} Barrow (Trinity, Cambridge, math)

66 Gracian (Spain, Jesuit; Machiavellian advice) +

67 Luke Wadding (Lyons, edited Scotus works) +

68 John of St. Thomas (Coimbra, Louvain, Alcala; last creative Thomist) +

69 Sallo (Paris f. *Journal des Scavans,* 1st scientific journal)

70 Clerselier (Descartes admirer, disseminated mss)

(71) Montmor (patron, Paris circle)

(72) Thévenot (organized Académie des Sciences)

1665

80 Rohault (Paris, Cartesian phil and nat sci)

81 Sorbière (Paris, Cartesian circle)

82 Régis (same)

83 Geulincx (st. Louvain; professor at Leiden; occasionalism)

84 Tschirnhaus (German count; math, optics, epist.)

85 Simon Foucher (Paris chaplain)

86 Fontenelle (defended moderns vs. ancients)

87 La Bruyère (Paris lawyer, epigrams)

(87a) Racine

88 Richard Simon (Oratorian)

89 Huet (Dauphin tutor, priest)

90 Fénelon (Paris court; love of God apart fr. salvation)

90a Cordemoy (reader to Dauphin; occasionalism)

90b La Forge (occasionalism)

91 Mme. Guyon (quietism, mysticism)

92 Pufendorf (st. Leipzig; Berlin court historian; natural law)

93 Spener (Strasbourg, Frankfurt; f. Pietism)

{94} Jakob Bernouilli (Basel, math)

{95} Marquis de L'Hospital (math)

96 LeClerc (Geneva, Holland exile; Locke disciple)

97 Orobio de Castro (Amsterdam; rational defense of Judaism)

98 Juan de Prado (Amsterdam; natural religion)

i 99 Lady Masham (Cudworth's daughter)

100 Antoine Goudin (Milan, Thomist) +

101 Frances Macedo (Scotist encyclopedia) +

102 Claudius Frassen (Paris, Scotist) +

{103} Halley (Oxford; astron)

{104} Flamsteed (astronomer royal)

{105} William Molyneux (Dublin, London; astron, optics)

106 Norris (Oxford, village rector; crit. Deism)

107 Toland (st. Edinburgh, Leiden; Oxford; Deist)

108 Syndenham (medicine, Oxford)

109	Blount (noble, Deist)
(110)	Dryden
(110a)	Thomas Herbert (grandson of Herbert of Cherbury, patron)
(110b)	Sir William Temple (diplomat; ancients vs. moderns)
(110c)	Viscount Molesworth (patron)
(110d)	Castares (co-conspirator w Shaftesbury and Locke; principal of Edinburgh Univ.)

1700

111	Anthony Collins (st. Cambridge, rural justice of the peace; Deist)
112	Tindal (st. Oxford, fellow; anti-clerical)
(113)	Bentley (royal librarian; Greek textual crit.)
114	Samuel Clarke (queen's chaplain; controversy w Leibniz)
114a	Catherine Cockburn (defended Locke, crit. Shaftesbury, Hutcheson)
115	Balgny (vicar; crit. Shaftesbury, Hutcheson)
116	Woodston (Cambridge fellow; Deist) +
117	William Law (Cambridge anti-Deist, devotional mystic)
(118)	Mandeville (st. Leiden, medical doctor, London) +
119	Collier (st. Oxford; rural vicar; Idealism)
{120}	Samuel Molyneux (son of 105; Dublin; astron)
121	Jerome of Monteforlino (Scotist/Thomist) +
{122}	Maclauren (Edinburgh math chair)
(122a)	Mackie (nephew of 110d; taught civil law, Edinburgh)
(123)	Addison

(124)	Steele
(125)	Pope
(126)	John Gay (poet)
(127)	Congreve
(128)	Arbuthnot (medical doctor to queen; satires)
129	Lord Bolingbroke (Tory leader, Deist)
(130)	Lord Chesterfield
{131}	Johan Bernouilli (Basel, calculus)
{132}	Goldbach (Königsberg, math)
{133}	de Moivre (Huguenot, fled to London; probability)
134	Comte de Boulainvilliers
135	Meslier (village curé, Champagne; radical crit. of religion) +
136	Budde (Wittenberg, Halle, Jena; eclectic)
137	Rudiger (Leipzig, Halle; Thomasian)
138	A. F. Hoffman (Leipzig, reformed Pietism)
139	August Francke (Pietist; Halle, Strasbourg)
140	Saint-Hyacinthe (Holland, moral nihilism) +

1735

(140a)	Genovese (Naples, econ)
157	Maupertuis (Paris, Berlin; Newtonian science)
{158}	Euler (Basel, St. Petersburg, Berlin; math)
161	Bilfinger (Wolffian/Leibnizian)
162	Crusius (Leipzig; Pietist attacked Wolffianism)
163	Baumgarten (Halle Wolffian, aesthetics)

Figure 10.2. Network Overlap of Greek Mathematicians and Philosophers, 600 B.C.E.–600 C.E.

Note: Figure 10.2 follows a notation different from all other figures. For this figure only:

() = non-mathematician

[] = number in Figures 3.1 through 3.8, network of Greek philosophers

underlined = major or secondary philosopher in Figures 3.1 through 3.8

1	Ameristus
(1a)	Stesichorus (poet)
2	Naburianos (Chaldean astron)
(3)	Leucippus
4	Anaximander
5	Phaeinus (astron)
6	Bryson (Sophist)
7	Meton (astron)
8	Euctemon (astron)
8a	Antiphon (Sophist)
8b	Hippasus of Metapontum (Pythagorean)
8c	Theodorus of Cyrene (Pythagorean)
9	Oenopides of Chios [17]
11	Andron
12	Zenodotus
13	Hicetas of Syracuse [23] (Pythagorean astron)
14	Eurytas [25] (Pythagorean)
15	Echecrates [26] (Pythagorean)
16	Thymaridas (Pythagorean)
18	Leo
20	Theaetetus [41]
21	Leodamos of Thasos +
22	Kidenas (astron, Babylon)
23	Polemarchus [78]
23a	Helicon
24a	Dinostratus
24b	Aristaeus
25	Speusippus

26	Theudius of Magnesia [46]
27	Ecphantus [24] (Pythagorean)
28	Philippus Medmaeus (Philip of Opus) [43]
29	Heraclides Ponticus
31	Spintharus [69]
32	Aristoxenus [72] (harmonics)
33	Dicearchus of Messina [74]
34	Eudemus of Rhodes [73]
35	Theophrastus
36	Xenocrates
37	Autolycus of Pitane [80]
38	Callipus [79]
39	Arcesilaus
40	Aratus of Soli [96] (astron, poet)
41	Crantor of Soli
42	Strato
(43)	Ariston of Chios
44	Bion [89] (Cynic)
45	Callimachus
46	Conon of Samos
47	Dositheus
i 48	Phidias (astron, father of Archimedes)
i 49	father of 50 (Epicurean)
50	Dionysodorus
51	Eudemus of Pergamum
52	Sudines (Chaldean astron & astrol at Seleucid court, Pergamum)
53	Philonides (Epicurean, Pergamum court)
54	Zenodorus
55	Diocles
i 56	father of 58
57	Basilides of Tyre [126] (Epicurean)
58	Hypsicles of Alexandria
59	Seleucus of Selucia (same as 52)
60	Theodosius of Bythinia
61	sons of 60
63	Zeno of Sidon [166]

63a	Phaedrus [167] (Epicurean)
65	Perseus
65a	Hermotinus of Colophon
66	Aristyllus (astron)
67	Philo of Byzantium +
68	Nicomedes
69	Pseudo-Petosiris (astrol) +
70	Clemedes (astron) +
71	Dionysidorus
72	Diodorus Siculus
73	Stilo [159]
(74)	Antiochus of Ascalon
75	Sosigenes of Alexandria (astron)
76	Varro [160]
78	Nigidius Figilus [164] (Neo-Pythagorean occultist)
79	Strabo [178]
80	Columella (astron, surveying)
81	Marcus Manlius (astrol)
82	Pliny (encyclopedist)
83	Theodosius of Cyrene
84	Hyginus (surveying)
85	Balbus (surveying)
86	Marinus of Tyre (geog) +
87	Dorotheus of Sidon (astrol)
88	Junius Nipsus (surveying)
89	Epaphroditus
90	Censorius (astrol)
91	Adratus (astron)
93	Theon of Smyrna [232]
94	Alexander of Aphrodisias
95	Philo of Gadera
96	Sporus of Nicea
(97)	Dionysius (Christian bishop of Alexandria)
98	Anatolius of Alexandria [268]
99	Serenus
100	Peithon
101	Theon of Alexandria [292]
102	Hypatia [296]
103	Synesius of Cyrene [297] (astron)
104	Paul of Alexandria (astrol)

105	Firmus Maternus (astrol)
106	Martinus Capella [290] (encyclopedist)
107	Macrobius [289]
108	Syrianus [300]
109	Plutarch of Athens [298]
110	Victorius of Aquitania
111	Domninus of Larissa [301]
112	Marinus [303]
113	Ammonius [304]
114	Eutocus of Ascalon
115	Anthemius of Trelles
116	Isidorus of Miletus
117	Simplicius [306]
118	Cassiodorus [313]

Figure 11.1. French and British Network during the Enlightenment, 1735–1800

Connections from Fig. 10.1

(52)	First Earl Shaftesbury
86	Fontenelle
(110c)	Viscount Molesworth (patron)
(110d)	Castares (co-conspirator with Shaftesbury and Locke; principal of Edinburgh Univ.)
{122}	Maclauren (Edinburgh math chair)
(122a)	Mackie (nephew of 110d, taught civil law, Edinburgh)
129	Lord Bolingbroke (Tory leader, Deist)
130	Lord Chesterfield
134	Comte de Boulainvilliers

1735

141	Thomas Morgan (dissenting minister; Christian Deist)
144	Hartley (st. Cambridge; medical doctor, London; associationism)
145	John Gay (st. Cambridge; rural vicar; Utilitarianism)

146   Lord Kames (Henry Home) (Edinburgh judge; nat relig)

148   Tucker (association basis of moral sense)

(149)   Dr. Samuel Johnson

151   Helvetius (Paris, materialism)

(152)   Turgot (Paris, Limoges; minister of finance)

{153}   Marquise de Châtelet (patron, sci cm)

{154}   Boerhave (Leiden; medical doctor, chemistry)

155   La Mettrie (Leiden; army doctor, Berlin exile; materialism)

156   Marquis de Vauvenarges (Deist)

157   Maupertuis (Paris, Berlin; Newtonian science)

1765

184   Robinet (French; Amsterdam; Spinozaist)

185   Naigeon (*Encyclopédie* assistant; atheist)

188   Mme. Helvetius (Auteuil circle hostess)

(189)   Comte de Volney

{190}   Lavoisier

{191}   Laplace

{192}   Franklin

(193)   Jefferson

(194)   Blackstone (chair, English law, Oxford)

{195}   Priestly (Nonconformist minister)

(196)   Burke

197   Richard Price (London, Calvinist minister; crit. Hutcheson common sense)

{198}   Erasmus Darwin (st. Cambridge, Edinburgh; medical doctor; Lamarckian)

199   Beattie (Aberdeen; Reid common sense)

200   Campbell (Aberdeen, prof. divinity; common sense)

201   Ferguson (Edinburgh)

202   Dugald Stewart (Edinburgh, moral phil)

203   Destutt de Tracy

204   Cabanis (led Idéologues)

1800

205   Thomas Brown (Edinburgh; crit. Reid)

206   James Mill (Edinburgh, London)

Notes

Introduction

1. See the theory-group model developed by Mullins (1973), and Griffith and Mullins (1972), based on studies of molecular biologists and sociologists during the period 1930–1970.
2. Tibetan, by contrast, contains a natural distinction between existential and copula; the distinction is less clear in Sanskrit, and completely lacking in Greek (Halbfass, 1992: 39). The pre-philosophical propensity of the language does not correlate well with the direction that thought took in each of these regions.
3. Although I do not pursue the networks of philosophers up to the current generation, Chapters 13 and 14 show the connections of many of their predecessors, including Durkheim, Freud, Wittgenstein, and Husserl.

1. Coalitions in the Mind

1. Hence the well-established relationship between frequency of interaction and conformity of belief (Homans, 1950). Scheff (1988) shows how tightly focused group interaction results in cognitive conformity by generating pride, the positive emotion of what I would call the ritual bond, or shame, the negative emotion of being excluded from the focus of interaction.
2. Note that to negotiate the next in a chain of situations, using the symbolic capital accumulated in previous rituals, is not the same as following a set of meta-rules. Symbols, like rules, are idealized cognitive constructs which participants may focus on within situations and thereby impose a subjective interpretation of what is going on. But the cognitive meaning of the symbols is not what is guiding the interaction ritual; they are precipitates of the more basic coordination of action which determines the ritual intensity of the encounter. Ritual practices do not happen because people are following rules on how to carry out IRs; the ingredients listed as 1–6 are naturally occurring forms of social interaction.
3. It has been calculated that 10 percent of all articles in some fields are never cited, perhaps never read (Price, 1986: 108; Hagstrom, 1965: 229). As we shall see, there is an enormous differential in intellectual exposure between the small numbers of publications with many readers and the large numbers with few.

4. The term is Pierre Bourdieu's ([1979] 1984; Bourdieu and Passeron, [1970] 1977). There are some similarities between my approach and Bourdieu's. Both of our works derive from empirical studies of education's effects on stratification and of the inflationary market for educational credentials. In early work (Collins, 1971) I used the term *status group culture* for what I now call *cultural capital*. I disagree with Bourdieu's principle that the intellectual field is homologous to the social space of non-intellectuals, however; the dynamics of struggle over the intellectual space is shaped in a distinctive way by the law of small numbers; and the cultural capital specific to the forefront of intellectual competition is not the cultural capital of educated persons generally, and it is not directly transposable with economic capital, in either direction.

5. The short-term, disruptive emotions are best explained as departures from a baseline of emotional energy, and thus are affected by the EE trajectory at any particular time. A full theory of emotions must include both levels. See Collins (1990); and on the sociology of emotions more generally, Kemper (1990); Scheff (1990).

6. A writing style is the precipitate of a particular kind of emotional energy flow. A crabbed and involuted style, full of false starts and shaky transitions, comes from a weak and hesitant EE flow. The writer who hides the speaker's voice behind an unbroken wall of abstractions and technicalities is clinging to his or her identity inside the community of intellectual specialists, not at its creative core but near enough the outer boundary to be concerned mainly with marking oneself off from the lay world of non-specialists outside. The distinctive styles of successful intellectuals, too, are tracks of their dominant EE flows. The sonorous periods of Gibbon bespeak his membership in a world where leading writers could be parliamentary orators, and belonged to an aristocracy of pomp and circumstance. The social sources of Russell's and Wittgenstein's ultra-confident styles are analyzed in Chapter 13.

7. In Sung China, there are the Ch'eng brothers, studying and discussing together from an early age, then spearheading the Neo-Confucian movement. In France of the late 1920s, there was the student circle of future literary and philosophical eminences Jean-Paul Sartre, Paul Nizan, Raymond Aron, Simone de Beauvoir, and Maurice Merleau-Ponty (Cohen-Solal, 1987: 74–75). In London of the early 1850s, a youthful group of friends comprised Herbert Spencer, T. H. Huxley, Mary Ann Evans (George Eliot), John Tyndall, and G. H. Lewes, their important creativity still in the future. There was the youthful friendship of Marx and Heine, or for that matter Marx and Engels. Centuries earlier we find the schoolmates Descartes and Mersenne. This structure seems to burst forth across various fields of creativity, again suggesting that what is being circulated is not so much cultural capital as emotional energy. We could add the friendship of future novelist F. Scott Fitzgerald, critic Edmund Wilson, and poet John Peale Bishop during their student days at Princeton University (Mizener, 1959: 36–55); or the youthful Bloomsbury circle which nurtured the incipient creativity across a range of literary, artistic, and scholarly fields that became famed as the work of Virginia Woolf, Lytton Strachey, John Maynard Keynes, and others (Bell, 1972).

8. The issue is not one of motivation. When an individual enters the intellectual field, the structural problem is where one will fit into the apportionment of attention. This cannot be evaded, whatever one's values of modesty, self-effacement, or commitment to intellectual virtues.

9. Strictly speaking, for a successful IR, participants should match similar CCs, so that they have something to talk about. For creative intellectuals, CCs cannot be completely similar, but should overlap enough so that one or another participant can contribute new CC to the others, and CCs can be recombined to produce new ideas. Participants do not match EE levels the same way. What is necessary for a successful IR is that at least one person have relatively high EE, to take the initiative in getting the interaction flowing and bring the available CC into the conversation. The law of small numbers suggests that one person tends to get the most attention in each intellectual group; two persons with very high EEs would tend to negate each other by competing over attention. The formula for a successful IR is: matching CCs, complimentary EEs.

10. We can be even more definitive. Being calculating is a particular kind of conscious thinking. Insofar as thought is itself determined by CC, EE, and surrounding network opportunities, there are structural conditions under which individuals will have sentences going through their minds such as "What will happen if I do this? Wouldn't it be better if I . . ." We could also specify the conditions under which individuals think nothing of the sort but merely go with the flow. In circumstances of steady energy flow, whether high or low, persons tend to follow their path without reflecting about it. It is when energy flows are sharply contradictory, owing to network locations which pull one way and another, that conscious calculation is more likely. At the extreme, low success in IRs leading to low EE, combined with a multiplicity of unattractive interactional opportunities, can lead to paralyzing self-reflectiveness. The IR chain model expanded in this direction would constitute a sociological psychiatry.

11. In the United States, the number of published writers of commercial (trade) books is estimated at 45,000 (Kingston and Cole, 1986: 36).

12. Kuhn's theory asserts that there are fundamental differences between those fields (sciences) which possess paradigms and those which do not (humanities and social "science"). But stratification of creativity and recognition appears to be rather similar in all fields. Analysis pointing to similar structures underlying artistic careers is given in White (1993); see also Kaufer and Carley (1993); for mathematicians and sociologists, see Crane (1972).

13. Chambliss (1989) gives a compelling image of the differences among ranks of achievement in any competitive field, intellectual, athletic, or professional. The reality for those in the successful inner circle is simply "the mundanity of excellence": a smoothly applied routine of using finely tuned resources with the confidence that one knows how to make them pay off. To those in the outer tiers, even those in the second competitive rank, there seems to be some mysterious quality that the successful possess, and this sense of difference generates a barrier of anxiety which makes it all the more impassable.

14. This sketch of a conversational artificial intelligence is amplified in Collins (1992).

On the levels of rhythmic coordination in conversation, see Sacks, Schegloff, and Jefferson (1974); Gregory (1994).

15. This should not be taken too literally. Thinking is carried out with ideas deriving from past conversations, which come into consciousness to the extent that they are carried on the emotional loadings deriving from the social solidarity they have been associated with in past conversations. Verbal thinking does not depend on visualizing oneself talking to an audience. One should not suppose that some people (i.e., "intellectuals") have vivid imaginations, whereas most of the rest of us prosaically go about our business of thinking without imagining audiences. The social sense of ideas constitutes the very possibility of human thought.

2. Networks across the Generations

1. Sources for Chinese rankings (Fung, 1952–53; Needham, 1956; Chan, 1963; Ch'en, 1964; Schwartz, 1985; Kuo, 1986; *CHC*, 1979, 1986; Dumoulin, 1988; Graham, 1989). Sources for Greek rankings (*DL*, 1925 [orig. ca. 200 C.E.]; Sextus Empiricus, 1949 [orig. ca. 200 C.E.]; *Suidae Lexicon*, 1937 [orig. ca. 950 C.E.]; Zeller, 1919; Guthrie, 1961–1982; *EP*, 1967; *CHLG*, 1967; Rist, 1969; Dillon, 1977; Kirk and Raven, 1983; Long, 1986; Reale, 1985, 1987, 1990). Additional information on network connections among Chinese philosophers (Ariel, 1989; Chang, 1957–1962; Cleary, 1983; Gernet, 1982; Graham, 1958, 1978; Knoblock, 1988; Kodera, 1980; Liu, 1967; McMullen, 1988; McRae, 1986; Odin, 1982; Pulleybank, 1960; Smith et al., 1990; Takakusu, [1956] 1973; Welch, 1965; Welch and Seidel, 1979). Additional network connections among Greek philosophers (*CHLG; DSB; OCCL;* Frede, 1987; Hadas, 1950, 1952, 1954; Jonas, 1963; Tarrant, 1985; Rawson, 1985).

2. I assume three active generations per century, corresponding to the typical period of creative maturity within an individual lifetime. Hence each individual typically overlaps the lifetimes of the creative generations immediately before and after: until age 33 or thereabouts, as pupil or protégé of the elder; thereafter as mentor or obstacle to the younger. Corroborating my use of 33 years as a generation, succession charts of Buddhist lineages show an almost exact correspondence to the figure of three generations per century. See Kodera (1980: 98), which gives a succession of 39 generations in 1,300 years; and the Ch'an lineages in Dumoulin (1988: 328–335).

3. The Chinese average is affected by some long empty spells: 21 generations out of 63 in which there are neither major nor secondary figures, although there are minor figures scattered throughout. Leaving aside these empty generations, as well as the 6 empty generations in the Greek networks, gives us averages which are almost identical: 0.6 major philosophers and 1.5 secondary ones per generation for China, 0.6 major and 1.6 secondary for Greece.

4. One might suppose that creativity is based on a randomly distributed trait, a rare trace element of human physiology or psychology; hence it should occur more frequently when populations are larger. But neither in China nor in Greece is creativity regularly related to population size. We might restrict this finding by

assuming that creativity can come out only in the literate population; but wide historical variations in the literacy rate do not correlate with creativity (estimates from McEvedy and Jones, 1978; *CHC*, 1986, 1979; Rawson, 1985; Havelock, 1982; Jones, [1964] 1986: 874–879, 910–912, 930–934, 992; Mann, 1986: 206–207, 253–256, 269, 313–316, 336). And we shall see that the concentration of creativity continues even within the massive highly educated populations of modern times.

5. These initial ratings are relative to any given history: comprehensive volumes treat more individual figures; specialized histories of particular eras or schools of thought offer comparisons only within their scope; longer books allow lengthier treatments of particular philosophers. Sources include both ancient and modern ones. There are, of course, differences: Sextus Empiricus, Diogenes Laertius (both ca. 200 C.E.), and the *Suidas* (ca. 950 C.E.) have somewhat different priorities than we do. Diogenes Laertius gives 75 pages to Epicurus and 71 to Zeno of Citium but only 49 to Plato. Aristotle is treated as a distinctly secondary figure, receiving 19 pages—the same as Aristippus and less than Pyrrho's 22 pages (Greek text, 1925 Loeb edition). Diogenes' relatively modest assessment of Plato was a minority position in his day, and Diogenes' preference for Epicureanism was something of a last gasp for that philosophy. The *Suidas* (Byzantium) shows virtually no interest in Latin authors, and does not even mention Lucretius, Seneca, or Augustine. It also shows little interest in Christian or heretic philosophers, ignores most of the Middle Platonists, and is very spotty on the Presocratics, giving Heraclitus only 1 reference, compared to 32 for Aristotle and 75 for Plato. Among the Neoplatonists, Plotinus gets a surprisingly low 3 references, Porphyry 13, Proclus 26. Diogenes Laertius, writing some 15 generations after the classic age of Greek philosophers, was of course no more of a contemporary than we are, and the *Suidas* is 20 generations later than that. My method averages together reputations from different periods, using generous cutting points so that persons who had major reputations for any extended period of time are listed as at least secondary in the overall scheme.

6. Not to be confused with Euclid the Alexandrian geometer, 100 years later.

7. In the Confucian school, the canon had an especially privileged position; from the Han dynasty onwards, it comprised the books which were officially recognized by the state, and which in later dynasties were used as texts for civil service examinations.

8. Compare the figures to whom Sorokin gives most attention in his *Contemporary Sociological Theories* of 1928 (in rank order from the top): LePlay, Huntington, Pareto, Marx, Durkheim, Coste, Engels, De Roberty, and LaPouge. Weber ranks in the next group of secondary figures along with Winiarsky, Hobhouse, Gumplowicz, Ammon, and Gobineau. Our current pantheon members Simmel, Toennies, Comte, Cooley, and Thomas are treated as minor figures; George Herbert Mead is not mentioned at all.

9. In the Greek networks, a couple of important incidental figures connect the great Roman Stoics Seneca and Epictetus: the emperor Nero and Epaphroditus (187 in Figure 3.6), Nero's secretary and owner of the slave Epictetus. Incidental persons

also figure in our representation of formally organized schools; because of the care with which lineage transmission records were treated by the Buddhist sects, we usually know the names of sect leaders for generations, even if there is nothing significant to be said about their own doctrines.

10. The periphery is the world of the autodidact, and home of the myth of posthumous glory. Though one might hope to find "closet creativity" here, untrammeled by conformity to the fashions of the center, the reality is almost the reverse. Peripheral intellectuals may combine ideas in different ways from what the intellectuals of the current core are doing, yet they depend on cultural capital transmitted from the past, only with a greater lag. I recall an undergraduate student—older than the others, someone who had come back to school on his own—coming up to me excitedly after a sociology class, proclaiming his discovery: social change is neither a straight-line evolution nor a cycle but their combination in a spiral. I hadn't the heart to tell him that he was working on the ideas of Vico and Condorcet, more than half a dozen generations behind his time.

11. Where formal schools constitute probable connections among known individuals via unknown intermediaries (marked "x"), they are indicated as dotted lines. This dotted-line symbolism is also used for connections which are likely but not certain. In some cases, these formal school connections run through persons labeled "i": those whose names are known incidentally because of their connection to a more eminent philosopher rather than mentioned because of notable accomplishments in their own right (for example, see the Ch'an lineages in Figures 6.3 and 6.4). The problem of incomplete information, especially as it affects our view of ancient networks, is considered in Appendix 2.

12. To avoid misunderstanding, it is worth underlining what the network chart is about. Everyone has a social milieu that is much larger than the ties shown on the chart, including many persons who are not intellectuals as well as some who are. What this network displays are ties among philosophers who have achieved at least some minimal degree of eminence in intergenerational memory.

13. Incidental figures are excluded from these calculations of immediate connections, since they are listed only because they are known from their connection to a more famous figure rather than in their own right. They are however, included in subsequent calculations where they mediate links to more distant philosophers of higher rank.

14. Once again let us understand the substantive significance of my methodology. If we could add links to a chain indefinitely, and we included any persons in these chains whatsoever as long as they eventually link up to someone of eminence, we could undoubtedly connect anyone to anyone else in the history of the world. The "small world" studies on social networks in the 1960s (Travers and Milgram, 1969) show that many Americans can communicate with a high-status person unknown to them within about six links or so. To guard against this possibility, I allow "incidental" figures (those marked "i") into the networks only as one-link connections between members of the well-known intellectual community. Moreover, experimental studies of message transmission show that communications tend to become garbled after a few links. What this implies for our intellectual networks

is that two-link connections may be providing cultural capital as well as emotional energy, and four-link connections are important mainly because of the structural effects of belonging to a dense creative chain or community; they may shape creative energy but do not significantly transmit cultural capital.

15. The chart might scatter major and minor figures about with no ties among them; this, of course, would mean not that they had no social contacts at all, but that their immediate circles, teachers, and pupils are too unimportant to appear on the chart. The isolates actually appearing in the network charts are given in Appendix 1.

16. On various lists, down through late antiquity, the number of sages varies, sometimes to 10, and the membership fluctuates. Thales, along with Solon, is the most constant across all lists.

17. Confucius (fl. 480 B.C.E.) was deified in the mid-Han dynasty, and his cult received official recognition from around 60 C.E. until the end of the dynasty (200 C.E.), and again from the mid-Tang (ca. 700) onwards. Mencius (fl. 320 B.C.E.) was worshiped in Confucian temples after about 1100 C.E., Chu Hsi after 1241 and again following political interruptions from 1313 onwards (Fung, 1952–53: 2:534; Needham, 1956: 31).

18. Undoubtedly later figures also have had their reputations swollen by the success of their long-term followers. Socrates is so celebrated because many schools branched off from him, and his fame was highest during the time when those schools flourished. Plato's dominant standing, above other major philosophers, is partly due to the Neoplatonic school, which used him as a legitimating figure for doctrines that diverged fairly substantially from his own emphases. But here we are just adding glory to glory. Socrates, Plato, and other cases of this sort that one could mention—for instance Mencius, Chu Hsi, and the *Tao Te Ching* author—are unquestionably major creators of new ideas; they mark turning points in the networks of their own day, and are not merely emblems for turning points which happen later, although this is also true.

19. See the cases cited in Chapter 1, note 7; or the section "A Cascade of Creative Circles" in Chapter 10. In European philosophy, where biographical data are most abundant, there are relatively few connections which consist only in a "clubbing together" of the famous. For instance, Hume brought Rousseau to England in 1766, at the end of both their creative lives. But both Hume and Rousseau had other important network connections earlier, noted in Figure 11.1. Where contacts consist only of this "club of the famous," I have not included such ties in the network charts.

20. Chinese books at this time were written on pieces of bamboo tied together with cords, and hence were rather bulky.

21. Guthrie (1961–1982: 2:388); Hadas (1954: 64–67). Anaxagoras' book was on sale in Athens for a drachma, relatively cheap at about a day's wage for a skilled worker. There were professional copyists at Athens, and by 50 B.C.E. at Rome; in Cicero's day one way to acquire a book was to borrow it from someone else and set one's slaves to copying it (Rawson, 1985: 42–45). Libraries began to be collected, at first within the philosophical schools themselves, at the time of Aristotle. The Hellenistic

kings competed over possession of great libraries, first at Alexandria (soon after 300 B.C.E.), at Pergamum (190 B.C.E.) and Rhodes (100 B.C.E.), and thereafter in the houses of wealthy Romans (*OCCL*, 1937: 64; Rawson, 1985: 39–42). In China there is mention of bookshops in the Han capital Loyang ca. 50 C.E., which provided the impoverished young Wang Ch'ung his learning (*CHC*, 1986: 1:633–64). Imperial libraries existed from the first unified dynasty, the Ch'in, onwards.

22. The prevalence of personal ties among creative intellectuals is documented in many other modern fields besides philosophy (Griffith and Mullins, 1972; Crane, 1972). Zuckerman (1967) shows that Nobel Prize–winning scientists are most likely to have been trained in the laboratories of previous Nobel Prize winners.

23. Later in the book I will occasionally zoom in on individuals whom we know a great deal about, attempting to show how their trajectory through micro-sociological networks shaped their personality, (e.g., Peirce, in Chapter 12; Wittgenstein in Chapter 13; Sartre in Chapter 14). At least two of the three, I dare say, might well have admitted the validity of this kind of analysis.

24. Detailed analysis, including the pattern of apparent exceptions to this general rule, is given in Appendix 1.

25. These figures can hardly be taken as exact. For reasons discussed in Chapter 12, our ability to judge the long-term reputations of intellectuals becomes less reliable as we near our own generation; totals after 1835 are probably inflated, and after 1900 are surely unrealistic. On the one hand, the Japanese network may overstate the number of secondary figures by including some who are publicized only in histories of Zen Buddhism; on the other hand, the total of minor figures could be expanded by including more from Buddhist sources. For India, the number of important thinkers is no doubt understated owing to the large amount of creativity before 400 C.E. which took the form of anonymous or pseudonymous religious texts. In general, information on which the Indian network was based is sparser, and dating more conjectural, than for the other world networks. The world total is also incomplete insofar as several of the networks are truncated, justified by the lesser influence of philosophers of recent centuries; for example, I have traced the Chinese network only through 1565 C.E. In my view the most important omissions are the networks of Buddhist philosophers in Tibet and Korea (although some of the founders of the Tibetan lineages are found in the Indian network in the key to Figures 5.4 and 5.5).

3. Ancient Greece

1. We thus see why, as Holton ([1973] 1988) documents, the themata of intellectual discourse usually come in opposing pairs or trios. Holton lists a large number of opposing themata from the history of scientific theories. The fact that Holton's list of oppositions is much larger than the three to six positions specified in the law of small numbers implies that what is constant is not a set of deep-rooted cognitive schemata repeating throughout history but rather the structural condition of splitting.

2. These external conditions are prominent in historical and sociological accounts of the emergence of Greek philosophy (Lloyd, 1987, 1990; Bryant, 1996).

3. From Latin *calculus,* Greek *chalix:* pebble.

4. The family migrated to Boeotia, a rather backwoods region of mainland Greece. Hesiod is known to have read a poem at a festival at Chalcis, on the island of Euboea. But he wrote in the cosmopolitan language Ionian, not Boeotian (*OCCL,* 1937: 207–208).

5. For this reason I have included probable connections in Figure 3.1 for several persons: Pythagoras' youth coincided with Anaximander's maturity and fame at nearby Miletus; given Pythagoras' reputation for wide travels, it seems likely that he would have heard the latter personally, although the sources do not mention it. Hecataeus of Miletus, an exact contemporary of Heraclitus, played a major role in organizing the Ionian revolt of 499–494 B.C.E. and traveled widely. He must have been at the neighboring city of Ephesus, and in his public capacity could hardly have been unacquainted with Heraclitus, an official of the local temple. Hecataeus was known as a geographer; given the connection of cosmology with geography at this time, Hecataeus likely connects with the chain of cosmological philosophers at Miletus (Guthrie, 1961–1982: 1:74, 173; *DSB,* 1981: 6:212).

6. Similarly, ancient sources attributed the origins of the atomist Leucippus to both Miletus and Elea (Guthrie, 1961–1982: 2:384). Elea was an Ionian colony, and Miletus was the most actively colonizing city of Ionia (Barraclough, 1979: 75).

7. Plato is reputed to have paid the princely sum of 40 minas (about 4,000 drachmas) for this book (Kirk, Raven, and Schofield, 1983: 324).

8. There was a chain of teachers at Cos down through 280 B.C.E.; after that point its leaders, such as Herophilus (107 in the key to Figure 3.5) and Erasistratus (108), migrated to Alexandria (*DSB,* 1981: 4:104, 382; 6:316). This was reorganization rather than intellectual death; medical doctrines were simultaneously appearing at Athens, branching off from Aristotle's school, especially that of Diocles (76), who formalized Hippocratic materials using the categories of philosophy. Within a generation medicine, as well as natural science, was firmly institutionalized at Alexandria in the Museum (von Staden, 1989).

9. The Library was begun under Ptolemy (r. 323–283) and greatly expanded under his son Ptolemy II (r. 285–246), who is said to have purchased Aristotle's collection of books (*OCCL,* 1937: 22, 138, 241, 281; Hadas, 1954: 21–24). The Museum, founded under Ptolemy II, supported literary scholars and also scientists. It is likely that both Ptolemy patronized individual scholars even before this formal institution was created; Strato was the tutor of Ptolemy II before returning to Athens as head of the Lyceum.

10. Epicurus had taught earlier at Lampsacus (on the Hellespont) and Mytilene (in the northeastern Aegean), where he formed his first community of followers. Other early branches were established at Antioch and Alexandria (Long, 1986: 17). The Epicurean community was organized into ranks, with the wise man at the top (Epicurus himself and his successors), followed by associate leaders, assistants, and pupils (Rist, 1972: 9–12). Probably the subordinate communities and lower ranks

of membership included persons in lay life who provided material support for the intellectual elite.

11. The master-pupil chains, which we can trace down to 50 B.C.E. in the case of the Academics, Stoics, and Epicureans, break up after 200 B.C.E. in the case of the Aristoteleans, although there are scattered names of notable members of the school through the next three generations, and the *scholarch* of the Peripatos was part of the delegation of Athenian ambassadors to Rome in 156–55 B.C.E., along with the heads of the Academy and the Stoa.

12. The old Academy was physically deserted; Antiochus of Ascalon (d. 68 B.C.E.) lectured at a gymnasium near the Agora, the original property having apparently lapsed (Dillon, 1977: 60, 232). After 50 B.C.E. the Epicurean Garden was sold and the school became defunct at Athens (Reale, 1985: 183–184, 413).

13. The higher numbers apply if we count the medical schools and the Alexandria Museum.

14. Zeno of Elea, for example, was famous for taking part in democratic political movements; he was allegedly killed by a tyrant of Elea or Syracuse (*DSB*, 1981: 14:607–608). Empedocles was active both in politics and in practicing medicine (Guthrie, 1961–1982: 2:131).

15. But Gorgias, Prodicus, Hippias, and others also served as ambassadors of their native cities, and Protagoras was entrusted by Pericles with drafting legal codes (Guthrie, 1961–1982: 3:264, 270, 274, 281).

16. There were many scandalous stories, such as of Crates and his wife, Hipparchia, who mated under their cloaks in public, gave away their daughter for a 30-day trial marriage, and—a violation of sexist convention—attended (all-male) dinner parties together (DL, 1925: 6:97; Reale, 1985: 381–382, 30–34).

17. There is no indication that the Pythagoreans themselves had connected their mathematics with their transmigration doctrine. It was left for Plato to do this, because he was using their cultural capital in a different context: the competition against an active intellectual field of relativists armed with self-conscious logical standards of argument. The classical Pythagoreans, by contrast, apparently did not confront epistemological issues (cf. Morgan, 1990; Burkert, 1972).

18. Aristotle was not consistently hostile to mathematics, since he contributed to the formalization of proofs by pointing out the role of definitions, hypotheses, and axioms (in *Posterior Analytics*). The trajectory of his split probably developed as the religious cult of mathematics grew up around his rival for the succession as *scholarch*, Speusippus. Conversely, the Aristotelean school later returned to mathematics, after the Academy repudiated its number religion and turned to skepticism.

19. Three if we count the Alexandrian Library and Museum; this, however, was connected at first with the Aristotelean school and provided an alternate base which kept the school alive during the political upheavals after Alexander's death.

20. As we see in Figure 3.4, Zeno emerged from extremely wide connections, as pupil of Academics, Megarians, Cynics, Eretrians, and even studying medicine in Alexandria (Frede, 1987: 230). His syncretism comes from this confluence of diverse cultural capitals.

21. Archimedes studied at Alexandria; though he resided in Syracuse, he "published" his results in letters to his Alexandrian mathematical friends ca. 240 B.C.E.

22. Eudoxus had moved at least part of his mathematical school from Cyzicus to Cnidus a generation or two previously (*DSB*, 1981: 4:465–467); it is possible that the mathematics at Alexandria was fostered by a further migration of the remnants of that school, at the same time as the medical scholars.

23. "The logic of propositions, which [the Stoics] studied, is more fundamental than the logic of general terms, which Aristotle studied . . . Aristotle's syllogistic takes its place as a fragment of general logic in which theorems of primary logic are assumed without explicit formulation, while the dialectic of Chrysippus appears as the first version of primary logic" (Kneale and Kneale, 1984: 175–176). "When Clement of Alexandria [late 100s C.E.] wishes to mention one who is master among logicians, as Homer is master among poets, it is Chrysippus, not Aristotle, whom he names" (ibid., 116).

24. The Epicurean Philodemus had a school at Naples around 50 B.C.E., but the enterprise lapsed with his death (Rawson, 1985). Epictetus taught Stoicism in exile at Epirus (the backwoods of northwestern Greece) after 100 C.E., but his successful school was not perpetuated.

25. Later, the most famous developers of Empiricist medical doctrine, Menedotus and Theodas (100s C.E.), were also the main representatives of skepticism, leading up to Sextus Empiricus. The connection is further supported by the fact that medical Empiricism and philosophical skepticism both disappear together after 200 C.E.

26. This was not strictly accurate. There were a few Epicurean renegades, such as Timocrates in the founding generation (who wrote a scathing exposé of the community's practices), and Metrodorus of Stratonicea, who joined the Academy in Carneades' generation (Frischer, 1982: 50–51; Tarrant, 1985: 94). But this is nothing like the shifting of personnel among the other schools: Zeno himself, Arcesilaus, and Chrysippus all built up their cultural capital through such moves.

27. Both circles were concerned with poetry, a high-prestige art in Rome at this time. Epicurean doctrine survived mainly because it was embodied in Lucretius' Latin masterpiece. In the other school, as Figure 3.5 indicates, one of Philodemus' pupils was Virgil.

28. When Platonists reappeared at Athens from 50 C.E. onwards, they were not described as *scholarch* or *diadochos* (successor), although some of them (such as Calvenus Taurus, ca. 100–165 C.E.) had their own private schools (Dillon, 1977: 232–233, 237–239).

29. A handsome sum, since a day's wage for a skilled workman was about one drachma, and a year's salary for a Roman legionary about 1,000 sesterces, roughly equivalent to 250 drachmas (*OCCL*, 1937: 277–278; Finley, 1973: 79–80, 104).

30. On the social role of the rhetorician (who often doubled as legal advocate) and of the grammarians who prepared students for the rhetoric schools, see Kaster (1988).

31. The organizational weakness of pagan cults was that they had few if any full-time priests (Jones, [1964] 1986: 933). Their upkeep was usually tied to the local gentry; for instance, Plutarch of Chaeronea was among other things a priest of nearby

Delphi. The Gnostics, although nontraditional in doctrine and elitist in membership, shared this traditional organization style of part-time leaders with merely local roots. The traditional Egyptian temples with their extensive property were an exception to this amateur pattern, but their circles were very parochial.

32. Another pro-Christian emperor, Gallienus, who called off the Decian persecutions, vetoed Plotinus' project for the religious community "Platonopolis" (*CHLG*, 1967: 202).

33. This is not to deny that there were external organizational and political factors involved in the heresy disputes, but rather to stress that there were internal intellectual issues involved as well, which had their own *sociological* impetus inside the intellectual community. The heresies emerged when there was a coordination of the two levels of struggle.

34. The tendency of Middle Platonism to become relatively more associated with Christianity may well be another reason why Plotinus formulated a rival Neoplatonist doctrine for the anti-Christian coalition.

35. Of the eight great Latin and Greek doctors recognized by the church, seven worked in the generation of the 360s to the 390s: Ambrose, Augustine, Jerome, Basil of Cappadocia, Gregory of Nazianzus, Gregory of Nyssa, and John Chrysostom (Attwater and John, 1983: 41, 107, 194). This is the period immediately after the failure of Julian's restoration of the pagan cults in 362–363. The only major church father not in this generation is Pope Gregory the Great, active 575–604.

36. Once inside the church, it was not difficult to choose a winning faction. In 386 the Manichees were purged at Carthage; in 388 a Donatist bishop was executed; in 391 the emperor issued a general edict against paganism; in 399 imperial agents closed pagan shrines in Africa (Brown, 1967: 74, 184, 187). Carthage, a land of organizational struggle among Catholics, Donatists, and Manichees, was just the place to produce a thinker like Augustine. An ingredient of his greatness was the opportunity to define the doctrinal content of orthodoxy for the victorious organizational faction.

37. It was about this time that Neoplatonism had its last upsurge, with the formal reestablishment of the Academy at Athens and Alexandria. Neoplatonism made a useful religion for educated pagans under Christian power, since it favored inner worship approached via philosophy rather than exterior cult practices at just the time when the latter were being abolished.

4. Ancient China

1. Historical sources are often vague regarding the lives of intellectuals of early China, as they are for Greece and India. What follows here is an attempt at coherent reconstruction of how the oppositions of the intellectual community unfolded. It should be understood throughout, without repeated caveats in the text, that an interpretation is being offered. Occasional footnotes cite evidence in regard to controversial points about the dating. Network sources for Chapters 4 and 6 are those given in Chapter 2. On Chinese social history, see Eberhard (1977); Gernet (1982); *CHC* (1986).

2. Han Fei Tzu mentions eight schools (Han Fei Tzu, [sect. 50], 1964: 118), Hsün Tzu mentions 5 major schools of Confucian *ju* (scholars), although perhaps only a smaller number survived down into contemporary times (250 B.C.E.) (Knoblock, 1988: 214–220, 224–229).

3. Mo Ti himself led 180 soldiers. All the Mohists in the state of Ch'u—a total of 83—were wiped out in a siege in 381 B.C.E. (Fung, 1952–53: 1:82). By 280 the major armies were perhaps on the order of 100,000 men (Knoblock, 1988: 8); Eberhard (1977: 49), however, suggests only around 10,000.

4. A parallel development occurred in Europe during the 1600s: the international network of diplomats, religious emissaries, and soldiers of fortune became for several generations the base of the new intellectual community which formed outside traditional positions in the church (see Chapter 10).

5. This collection of intellectuals also produced what was becoming the prestige intellectual product: an encyclopedia of knowledge under the standard title, *Spring and Autumn Annals* (in this case) *of Master Lü* (the prime minister). *Spring and Autumn Annals* was the title of a Confucian text, attributed to Confucius himself.

6. There remained for a while groups such as the augurs in Rome, but even in this religiously conservative city-state the college of *pontifices* was monopolized by politicians (*OCCL*, 1937: 65, 342; Rawson, 1985). There were some hereditary priests in Greece as late as 500 B.C.E. who played an occasional role in philosophy; Heraclitus came from such a priestly family in the cult center of Ephesus, and his imprecations upon the new secular philosophers were probably related to their professional challenge. There are also shamanistic aspects to figures such as Empedocles and Heraclides Ponticus and in the medical cult of the Asclepiades. But even they were not especially concerned to restore the ancient rites, which would have seemed outside the realm of political possibility.

7. Plato is the principal exception here. Of all the Greek philosophers, he is closest to the Chinese pattern of centering his analysis on political projects, and in the *Laws* he proposes an ideal state centered on a compulsory but non-traditional cult. But this political interest was confined to Plato's own lifetime; the Academy, in both its phases of astral religion and skepticism, quickly fell back into the mainstream pattern of Greek intellectuals in focusing on the inner lives of individuals. If there is a tradition of "Western individualism," it originated in the autonomy of political struggle from religious legitimation.

8. In the absence of Hui Shih's own texts and with minimal survivals of Kung-sun Lung's, there have been widely divergent interpretations of their positions. Fung Yu-lan (1952–53: 192–220) regards Hui Shih's as a metaphysics of particulars in ceaseless change, Kung-sun Lung's as a realism of universals. Graham (1989: 82–83) argues that all philosophers of this period took nominalism for granted, and interprets the paradoxes as explorations of part-whole relations. Farther afield, Reding (1985) suggests that Hui Shih's statements derive from political arguments. The most extreme position is that of Hansen (1983), that classical Chinese language lacks abstractions and thus constrains thought into channels totally different from those of the West. This linguistic determinism is rejected by Schwartz (1985: 12, 165, 168) and moderated by Graham (1989: 389–428).

9. The *Canons* refute positions of all the rival schools, including the Five Agents of Tsou Yen, but do not mention doctrines of the *Tao Te Ching* or the Legalists (Graham, 1978: 61). This implies a date before Han Fei Tzu popularized legalism, but at least contemporary with Tsou Yen.

10. Empedocles had four elements (fire, water, earth, air) ordered by opposing principles of strife and love. It is generally agreed that *wu hsing* should be rendered not as "five elements" but as "five processes" or "five agents"; *hsing* is "walk" or "move" with the connotation "put into effect" (Knoblock, 1988: 216–217). Major (1976) proposes "five phases." But three of the five (wood, metal, earth) are concrete substances, conceivable as processes only under interpretations imposed later.

11. These comprised the *Odes, Documents, Rites, Changes (Yi Ching),* and *Spring and Autumn Annals.* This culminated a struggle over precedence among a wide range of earlier texts, each supported by their own specialists.

12. During the T'ang, relatives of the imperial house were executed or impeached for consulting diviners (*CHC,* 1979: 334, 379–381; Fung, 1952–53: 16; Woo, 1932).

13. It is notable that the word *yi* (change), and the cosmological opposites yin and yang appear for the first time in this Appendix rather than in the original divination texts or the earlier Appendices commenting on the interpretation of particular hexagrams (Legge, [1899] 1963: 38, 43). The argument is not very abstract; overall the tone is more one of worldly advice than of cosmological system. The text of the third Appendix "makes plain the nature of anxieties and calamities, and the causes of them" (Legge, [1899] 1963: 399), extols the superior man, and sprinkles references to ancient sage-kings who were allegedly inspired in their technological inventions by the hexagrams. This is another indication that this Appendix dates from the time of the burning of the books, when works on technology and other practical lore remained in favor.

14. The Han dynasty produced considerable work in science and mathematics, although generally in other branches of the official bureaucracy than the Confucians (Needham, 1959: 19–30, 199–200, 216–219; Mikami, 1913; Sivin, 1969).

15. In 37 C.E. the descendants of Confucius were ennobled, and in 59 annual sacrifices to Confucius were instituted at all schools. Wang Ch'ung wrote soon after.

16. Recall that in the comparative analysis of networks in Chapter 2, Wang Ch'ung is one of the most unusual figures in all of the world history of philosophy: an individual of at least secondary importance in the long-term attention space who has no contemporary rivals of equal eminence, and who is not only a horizontal but also a vertical isolate from chains of historically significant intellectuals.

17. We find a similar situation in Japan during the Sengoku period, the "country at war" (1470–1580). Vociferous public debates took place among the rival branches of Pure Land Buddhism, but these generations are devoid of intellectual innovation. At this time the monasteries were major political powers, and their debates were an immediate part of the struggle for public prestige and military alliance.

18. The *Chuang Tzu* (chap. 6) speaks rhapsodically about death as a natural and even desirable process.

19. Members of the "Five Pecks of Grain" movement, a health cult for the peasantry,

for example, memorized the *Tao Te Ching* but gave it a vulgar interpretation. "'The Tao that can be Tao'd,' this is to eat good things in the morning: 'the Tao that is not eternal,' this is to have a bowel movement in the evening" (Welch, 1965: 119).

20. Kuo Hsiang's major work is his commentary on the *Chuang Tzu,* which was in part a continuation—and perhaps a plagiarism—of the unfinished commentary by Hsiang Hsu in the previous generation. As Figure 4.4 indicates, Hsiang Hsu probably took part in the discussions of the Seven Sages of the Bamboo Grove, and is indirectly linked to Wang Pi and the rationalistic interpreters of Taoism. Kuo Hsiang probably had some contact with Hsiang Hsu's son, reportedly careless in scattering his father's treatise about (Fung, 1952–53: 206). Whatever the individual contributions, the "philosophy of Kuo Hsiang" is very much a product of the core intellectual factions around Loyang in the late 200s.

5. India

1. There were eight such swings: (1) Consolidation of the numerous small kingdoms in the middle Ganges into 16 major states around 600 B.C.E., then down to 4 contenders 100 years later, culminating in the Maurya Empire over almost all of India ca. 300–185 B.C.E., and disintegrating thereafter. The two leading states around 500, Magadha and Kosala, were the first patrons of Buddhism and Jainism. (2) A three-way split among leading states, peaking around 150 C.E., including the south-central Andhra kingdom, another Buddhist patron. (3) The Gupta Empire in the north, from 335 C.E. to the late 400s. (4) Harsha's reconquest of Gupta territory around 600–650. (5) In the late 800s another three-way struggle in the north, including the last great patron of Buddhism, the Pala kingdom in Bengal, expanding westward into the ancient Magadha heartland. The last three cycles prior to the British Empire involve Muslim invaders from the northwest; in counterpoint, Hindu kingdoms in the far south attain their maximal size. (6) Around 1000, the Ghaznavid Muslim empire centered in Iran and central Asia conquered the northwest; meanwhile the Chola Empire expanded in the south. (7) Another Muslim conquest in the late 1100s, expanding by 1335 to almost all of India except the far south, then disintegrating rapidly after 1340. In the south the kingdom of Vijayanagar attains its greatest size in the 1500s. (8) The Mogul conquest from Afghanistan in the 1560s, spreading south in the 1600s; its disintegration after 1770 leaves the power vacuum filled by European overseas empires (Davies, 1949; *OHI,* 1981; Dutt, 1962; Thapar, 1966; Craven, 1975; Zürcher, 1962; Gombrich, 1988; Chandler and Fox, 1974).

2. The centralizing Maurya dynasty arose on the basis of a succession of parricide kings. The *Arthashastra,* or classic of statecraft, composed at this time, advocated the most blatant tactics of treachery and espionage as the path to *artha,* worldly success.

3. Hence the lower Ganges province takes its name, Bihar, from *vihara,* monastery. On Buddhist support, see *OHI,* (1981: 169–173); Dutt (1962: 331; 225–230).

4. Sharma (1965); Mann (1986: 356–357); *OHI,* (1981: 112–113, 178–179, 206–208). An exception to this pattern apparently occurred in coastal states of the south

and west, where overseas trade gave an alternative basis for state revenues. The importance of this pattern for state-building in the European context is shown by Tilly (1990). This may be a reason why the Jainas, associated with merchants, were major contenders for state alliance in these regions. Conversely the Buddhists, with their agrarian monastic base, fit Tilly's alternative pattern of state formation: landed revenues. Hence Buddhism declined in the south as the trade-based states rose.

5. It is worth underlining that the so-called "six *darshanas*" or "orthodox philosophies" (Nyaya, Vaisheshika, Yoga, Samkhya, Mimamsa, Vedanta), which are the standard rubrics in virtually all general histories of Indian philosophy, were by no means static or primordial positions. The notion of "six *darshanas*" was not created until fairly late in the medieval period, and they developed, much as philosophical schools did elsewhere, out of debates both among their own ranks and across the attention space with non-Hindu rivals. The ideology of the *darshanas* is part of the static bias which it is necessary to break through in order to reconstruct the actual history of Indian intellectual life.

6. Sources for the networks which follow (*EIP*, 1977, 1981, 1987, 1990; Halbfass, 1991, 1992; Isayeva, 1993; Potter, 1976; Dasgupta, 1922–1955; Chattopadhyaya, 1972, 1979; Basham, 1989; Raju, 1985; Pandey, 1986; Nakamura, 1980; Dutt, 1962; Hirakawa, 1990; Conze, 1962; Kalupahana, 1992; Lamotte, 1958; Stcherbatsky, 1962; Phillips, 1995).

7. Nakamura (1973: 33–35); Chattopadhyaya (1972: 32–40); Gonda (1975); Stutley (1980). For a position stressing the long-term unity of orthodox Hinduism since the early Vedas, see Smith (1994). On the other side, see Krishna (1991).

8. These separate groups of teachers were recognized outside the Vedic texts as well. The Buddha himself refers to followers of the *Samaveda, Rigveda,* and the two *Yagurvedas* (Barua, 1974: 284). Krishna (1991: 83–84) argues for even more sub-splits within the schools of the Vedas.

9. It is not clear when the Upanishads actually became standard parts of the Vedic transmission schools; as we shall see, the early and middle Upanishads depict freelance sages who are quite critical of Vedic priestcraft. The reorganization of Upanishadic lore into a broad pan-Vedic coalition may have occurred in the early centuries of the Common Era.

10. E.g., *Chand. Up.* 7.1.2; *Brihad. Up.* 1.5.5 and 4.1.2 (700–500 B.C.E.). Somewhat later the *Aitareya* (1.3.9), about 500 B.C.E., mentions only the three Vedas. The Buddhist Jataka tales, ca. 300 B.C.E., similarly refer to the three Vedas; so does Kautilya's *Arthashastra,* which itself draws on spells from the Atharva, as from a separate tradition, as "secret means" for spying and destroying enemies (bk. 14). The earliest to list all four as Vedas is the *Mundaka Upanishad* (1.5), ca. 350–300 B.C.E. But the late *Maitriyana* (6.32) still lists only three Vedas and calls the Atharva "hymns," indicating that the canon was not settled as late as 200 C.E. Dates from Nakamura (1973: 77–78); see also *OHI*, (1981: 86–87, 107).

11. Krishna (1991: 95–109) points out that the "Upanishads" are an inchoate category of texts, selected under that label from a wide variety of sources and time periods. Far from constituting "the end of the Vedas," they were often selected from

chapters in the midst of *Brahmanas* and *Aranyakas,* or expanded from such texts, while others were added later. Most of them originally did not use the term "Upanishad," which in the *Arthashastra* (300 B.C.E.) still meant "secret weapon" rather than a religious doctrine.

12. Chakravarti (1987); Mizuno (1980); Hirakawa (1990); Jacobi (1884); Dutt (1962: 46–51). The Videha land, whose king sponsors debates involving such sages as Yajñavalkya, is a scene of the Buddha's life too. Both kinds of sources show kings striving to attract famous sages to their courts by material patronage (e.g., *Brihadaranyaka Upanishad* 2.1.1).

13. Cf. *Chandogya Upanishad* 5.11 and 17; 6.1; *Brihad. Up.* 3.7; 6.2; *Kaushitaki Upanishad* 1.1. This probably indicates the rivalry of the Samavedists to which Uddalaka's Upanishad was attached, against the White Yagur, allied to Yajñavalkya's lore, as well as against the Rigvedists of the *Kaushitaki.*

14. *Brihad. Up.* 3.6.1; 3.9.27; cf. *Chand. Up.* 1.8; 10.10–11, where the threat that "your head will fall off" invokes a magical punishment for singing a hymn without knowing its meaning. The implication is that winning a debate sequence was regarded as a demonstration of superior magic.

15. Akin to this may be the famous lesson of Uddalaka Aruni about breaking a seed into infinitesimal pieces to find the invisible essence (*Chand. Up.* 6.12). Ruben (in Chattopadhyaya, 1979: 141–156) points out that Uddalaka's sequence of arguments (*Chand. Up.* 6.1–16) indicates a kind of hylozoist materialism of living matter; for instance, he instructs his son to abstain from eating for fifteen days in order to show that this impairs one's memory, concluding that "mind comes from food" (6.7.6). The ultimate lesson, that one's self is part of the invisible essence of the universe, does not so much imply that the universe is spiritual, as that the human self, too, is produced from the hylozoic essence. Given the lack of distinction between levels of abstraction, what later philosophers interpreted as a transcendental monism may just as well have been a claim for one physical element underlying the others, in much the same sense that Thales posited water as the primal element. Similarly, Uddalaka's experiment with salt invisibly pervading water (*Chand. Up.* 6.13) is primitive physics as much as it is transcendental philosophy.

16. *Brihad. Up.* 6.3; this magic is attributed to Uddalaka Aruni, who gives it to his "pupil" Yajñavalkya. Similar worldly magical claims are made in some of the most "philosophical" Upanishads, e.g., *Chand. Up.* 2.1–29; *Kaush. Up.* 2.6.4–10.

17. Only one of the classic Upanishads, the *Maitrayani* (1.3–4), equates life with suffering, and it uses words identical with classic Buddhist phrases; this is a late Upanishad from around 200 C.E.. (Nakamura, 1973: 77–78). Its contemporary, the *Mandukya Upanishad* includes phrases found in the *Prajñaparamitasutras* of Mahayana Buddhism.

18. O'Flaherty (1980: xi–xxiv, 3–13). The clearest formulation of the karma doctrine appears again in the late *Maitrayani Upanishad* (3–4), in virtually Buddhist language; this is also the only Upanishad which links karma and rebirth to the performance of caste duties (4.4.3). In the pre-Buddhist *Brihad. Up.* (3.2.13), a debate is described in which one question has to be discussed privately. The

narrator then tells us at the end of the chapter that the interlocutors talked of karma. This may be a late interpolation, since the lines appear at the end of a chapter. If not, it implies that karma—in whatever version at that time—was a secret doctrine, not a view that would be accepted as religiously binding by most hearers. As late as the *Bhagavad Gita,* a series of interpolations in the *Mahabharata* influenced by the new Hindu philosophical schools ca. 100–500 C.E., there is a mixture of conflicting doctrines about reincarnation and other forms of life after death (e.g., 1.42.44; 8.6.23–25; 9.25). The thread which is retrospectively emphasized, that favorable reincarnation depends on performance of one's duties under caste law, becomes the dominant religious interpretation still later, in the final onslaught against Buddhism around 700 C.E..

19. For debates on these dates, see Hirakawa (1990: 22–23).

20. The futile questions which the Buddha tells his followers to avoid are similar to Kant's antinomies: the beginning and end of the universe, the difference between body and soul, life after death. These are favorite debating topics among the Upanishadic sages; by denying their solubility, the Buddha claims a superior level of reflexive sophistication.

21. For various translations and sources, see Nakamura (1980: 66–69; Kalupahana (1986: 10–16).

22. The Ajivikas too received royal patronage, for instance, under the Maurya dynasty. Mahavira and Makkhali Gosala were close associates until their debates led to a sharp break between their respective sects. Mahavira and Shakyamuni competitively proselytized some of the same lay patrons. But Shakyamuni's strongest enemy, in tactical struggles in the lay community as well as in debate, was Makkhali Gosala (Mizuno, 1980: 120–141; Basham, 1951; *OHI,* 1981: 77, 130). This rivalry probably resulted from the fact that Shakyamuni was both appropriating and negating Makkhali's key doctrine in proposing a method to overcome karmic fate.

23. Mizuno (1980: 99, 104). The Jainas also preached, although not as aggressively as the Buddhists.

24. Chakravarti (1987: 122–149). This recruitment base continued throughout the lifetime of Indian Buddhism.

25. The range of meditation techniques includes one-pointed concentration, observing one's breath, stilling the inner dialogue, focusing on consciousness itself apart from its objects (Buddhist and Yoga techniques); visualizing energies or lights within one's own body, especially in the genitals; raising inner heat and moving it about one's body (tantric techniques); inwardly visualizing symbols, gods, the experience of one's own death, the letters in the name of God, and so on (Tibetan Buddhist, Sufi, Taoist, Kabbalist techniques); outwardly focusing on visual symbols (mandalas, crucifixes, etc.); chanting mantras (pure sounds) or sutras (holy texts), singing verbal hymns; rhythmic dancing (Sufi darvish sects, medieval Japanese Amidaists); physical activities to the point of exhaustion, or self-torture (Sufis, *shramanas,* Christian ascetics, shamans, tribal vision-seekers); verbal prayer or communication with a personified deity (Christianity); counting, slowing, or holding breaths (Buddhists, Taoists); blowing and spitting (Chinese *Huai-nan Tzu*);

intellectual "investigation of things" (Neo-Confucians), or analysis of concepts into emptiness (Buddhists); koan paradoxes, sometimes together with receiving shouts and blows from one's teacher (Ch'an); enlightenment during preaching (T'ien-t'ai and Amida Buddhism, Sufism, enthusiastic sectarian Christianity). The resulting experiences range from tranquillity to weeping and emotional enthusiasm, from "bright light" to "divine dark" to "clear glass consciousness," from floating detachment *(zazen)* to deep trance *(samadhi)* to sudden enlightenment *(satori).*

26. Results of meditation have been conceived to involve both detachment from the world and action in it. Detachment may be interpreted as an end in itself, or an end to individual suffering (Buddhism); as contact with God or salvation from sins (Sufism, Christianity, Mahayana); as individual psychotherapy (post-1950 Western secularism). Worldly results aimed at include health and longevity (Taoism); magical powers such as clairvoyance, levitation, and spells over other living beings (shamanistic and folk beliefs, incorporated in most mystical traditions as lesser side effects); political power to regulate the state (Taoism); shelter from political persecution (medieval Jewish Kabbalism); motivation of millennial political movements, ranging from nationalist particularism (Sufism, Imamism, Kabbalism) to universalistic trans-sectarianism (Rosicrucianism, Masonism).

27. In later historical cases, monasteries become organizational vehicles for settling frontier areas or introducing capitalist accumulation, especially in a rural economy. This is most notable in China ca. 400–800 C.E., and again in Christian Europe 1050–1300 and in Japan 1200–1600. The key advantage of the monastic mode of organization is its ability to free up and reinvest resources in a society otherwise dominated by kinship organization of production.

28. Nakamura (1973: 77–79). The *Mandukya Upanishad,* which Gaudapada (ca. 500–600) used as a basis for developing Advaita, is not attached to a Vedic school and does not exist independently of Gaudapada's commentary (Isayeva, 1993: 50). A good many Upanishads may have originated in this independent fashion before acquiring a connection with a Brahmanical lineage and canonical status from later scholars. Some Upanishads became attached to more than one Veda (e.g., the *Katha,* attached to Black Yajur, Sama, and Atharva; the *Kena,* attached to both Sama and Atharva; Muller, [1879–1884] 1962: 1:xci; 2:xxi). This implies that at some period the schools competed over possession of this new high-prestige intellectual property.

29. The *Manu Smriti* collected earlier ritual duties and prohibitions, beginning after 200 B.C.E., reaching its final form about 100 C.E. The *Yajñavalkya Smriti* shows a more systematic treatment of law, ca. 100–200 C.E. Its attribution to the sage implies that the Upanishads were being taken into Brahmanical orthodoxy at this time. Still other rival law books were created around this time by the Vishnu sect and others. There was an outpouring of law texts in the medieval period, 700–1200, when Hinduism definitively triumphed over Buddhism (Basham, 1989: 101–103). *Manu* became regarded as the definitive book of Hindu caste law only during the British Empire in the 1800s; before that time other works were more widely used in Hindu legal circles (Doniger, 1991: lx–lxi).

30. *Manu Smriti* 2:3. In contrast, ca. 150 B.C.E. Panini's grammar (4:6) had merely defined *nastika* as a non-believer in the other world, excluding only the materialist element philosophers.

31. The *Ramayana* depicts the Buddhists in the guise of demons inhabiting Sri Lanka, who are defeated by an expedition to the island, headed by a warrior-hero who is identified with one of the gods of the Hindu pantheon.

32. See the accounts of Lamotte (1958: 571–606); Conze (1962: 119, 123, 195); Hirakawa (1990: 110–118); Raju (1985: 147, 154–156); Nakamura (1980); Dutt (1962).

33. Theological issues are those of concern only to believers in particular religious tenets; these may be highly particularistic, such as the name and distinctive identity of God, or local traditions of stories, rituals, and memberships; for instance, the Christian dispute over the immaculate conception of the Virgin Mary, or Hindu arguments over the relative standing of Shiva or Vishnu. Theological issues may also develop more abstract questions, such as the relations among the Trinity, or the existence of cosmic bodies of the Buddha. Philosophical issues are those which, although they may arise in a theological context, are potentially detachable from it and of interest to a wider range of argument. Many issues entwine between theology and philosophy; this is one reason why theological controversies give rise to philosophy, even if the theologians are opposed to it, as was the case in early Buddhism, Christianity, and Islam alike.

34. Hirakawa (1990: 302–303). Mahayana emerged at the same time (100 B.C.E.–100 C.E.) that scribes were taking the place of the oral reciters who specialized in memorizing particular classes of texts (Dutt, 1962: 30, 149).

35. Willis (1979: 52–53). There seem to have been two Vasubandhus, the Yogacara in the mid-300s (designated Vasubandhu I), and the Sarvastivadin a century later (Vasubandhu II). This interpretation is supported by Frauwallner (1953–56), Dutt (1962: 270, 281–282), Potter (1976), and Nakamura (1980: 109), although the traditional identification of the two is maintained by some scholars.

36. Conze (1962: 166–171); Nakamura (1980: 129); Guenther (1972: 59, 132). A thousand years later, a similar inflation of enlightenment took place in the Zen school in its late scholasticizing phase in Japan.

37. Cut off from these developments in the north was a flurry of Buddhist philosophy in Sri Lanka in the mid-400s, where Buddhaghosa combined all the schools into a Theravada master text (Conze, 1962: 203; Kalupahana, 1992: 206–216). It was a syncretism characteristic of defensive periods, at a time when Buddhism was closing down in south India. Its survivors migrated to Sri Lanka, where the king fought off a Tamil invasion from the mainland.

38. Old geopolitical bases reappeared in the newer religious-intellectual rivalries. Mithila was apparently in old Videha, the rival of the Magadha capital in the time of the Buddha and Mahavira (*OHI*, 1981:77).

39. The *Samkhya-sutras,* however, were not manufactured until around 1400, during the period when the "six *darshanas*" rubric was adopted among orthodox Hindus (*EIP*, 1987: 327).

40. A brief guide to this entire period appears in Chapter 15 under the heading "The

Indian Sequence" (pages 818–826). There is no overall narrative history of Indian philosophy as a sequence of ongoing arguments; most histories segregate Buddhist and Hindu developments from each other, and within each camp divide the exposition among separate schools as isolated rubrics. The volumes of the *Encyclopedia of Indian Philosophy (EIP)* provide corrective material at a high level of detail; and partial sketches of overall dynamics and interactions among the schools exist in Stcherbatsky's (1962) and Frauwallner's (1953–1956) classic works; see also Rubin (1954). A recent exception is Phillips (1995), which concentrates primarily on the interaction between Nyaya and Advaita.

41. These included lengthy classifications of fallacies, which the Greeks tended to ignore; that is to say, the Indians treated logic as the science of argument rather than the study of valid inference. See Potter, (1976: 56–92); Stcherbatsky (1962); *EIP* (1977); on the development of Indian logic and its conflictual interaction with Buddhist logicians, see Shastri (1976); and generally Matilal (1986, 1990).

42. In this ecumenical mood Bhartrihari interpreted the Vedic *aum* as identical to the Madhyamika *shunyata;* in the succeeding generations, Bhavaviveka (500s) and Chandrakirti (600s) accepted Hinduism as propaedeutic to Buddhism (Halbfass, 1991: 66). Grammar became among the most intersectarian of disciplines. Bhartrihari's grammar was commented upon by the Yogacarin Dharmapala, the head monk of Nalanda, in the 500s.

43. The details of Bhartrihari's argument are connected with discussions by his grandteacher Vasubandhu about the nature of time in the Buddhist *Abhidharma* (*EIP*, 1990: 41–44, and Potter, 1976: 130–134) as well as with issues then debated between the rival Hindu substance philosophies Samkhya and Vaisheshika.

44. Dignaga's doctrine is something like Saussure's structuralist theory of language, in which words take their meaning not by indicating instances but by marking differences from one another. As the later commentator Dharmottara (700s) puts it: pure sensation is all that exists; thought makes it definite by negation; negation is the essence of thought, not of reality (Stcherbatsky, 1962: 1:536).

45. Dignaga here expresses the equivalent of the position of Duns Scotus and William of Ockham that God—the ideal condition of knowledge—perceives everything in its radical particularity, its *haecceitas,* without the distorting lens of universals.

46. *EIP* (1987: 4); an early version was known simply as the "sixty topics." A rather similar activity is implied in the name of the Vaisheshika, which originally seems to have meant "those who make distinctions" (Halbfass, 1992: 272–273). Samkhya lists paralleled in many details the Buddhist *Abhidharma.* Samkhya as the philosophy of "enumeration" seems to have made its turf the coordination of various lists of this sort, setting up parallels, and deriving further categories from more basic generative ones. Later lists were created by cross-classifying, resulting in mega-systems of 28 or 50 items or more.

47. *Purusha* is the older concept. In the *Rigveda* it is the primal Man from whose body the universe was divided; in the *Brihadaranyaka Upanishad,* it is identified with atman, which divides itself into man and woman, from whose copulation were created the living species. *Prakriti,* material nature, is eventually identified with the female side, while *Purusha* becomes a plurality of individual soul substances. In

the tantric Yoga cult that became popular after 800 C.E., the naked woman who copulates with the yogi (in inner visualization or in the flesh) is regarded as an incarnation of *Prakriti* (Eliade, 1969: 259).

48. The *Yoga-sutras,* compiled around 500 C.E., differed from previous sutra collections on meditative practice by incorporating an explicit metaphysics from Samkhya, and by adding Hindu theism. Classic Samkhya culminating in Ishvarakrishna was atheistic, following the tendency toward a naturalistic cosmology which comes from raising the level of abstraction on a mythological tradition of anthropomorphic world elements. The Yoga-Samkhya combination heightened the Hindu identity of both positions. Before this time, Yoga meditation was more typically identified with Buddhism; the Yogacara school simply meant "those who meditate." Philosophical intellectuals looked down on this rather eclectic Hindu syncretism. Yoga is not counted as one of the "six *darshanas*" by Haribhadra in the 700s; by the time it gets standard mention (around 1400), it is usually lumped in a rubric of positions that are no longer intellectually alive. Shankara in the 700s considered Yoga meditation beneficial mainly for "persons of slower understanding," and regarded its plurality of souls, and its progression through which the meditator rises from matter to atman, as obstacles to understanding the true non-dualist reality (Halbfass, 1991: 226).

49. It is worth stressing, insofar as the image of Indian philosophy is so heavily colored retrospectively by the later dominance of Advaita, that all five *darshanas* that existed before 700 C.E. were at least partially materialist, and included sense perception among the valid sources of knowledge.

50. *EIP* (1981: 15–16, 177, 346). As usual there is debate over the authenticity of these connections. I follow Potter (*EIP*, 1981) in dating Shankara in the early 700s rather than the traditional 788–820. See also Wood (1990: 38, 47); Isayeva (1993: 83–87).

51. Gaudapada's famous commentary was on one of the most Buddhist-influenced Upanishads, the *Mandukya* (ca. 200 C.E.). This Upanishad was also devoted to the cult of the mantra *aum,* which we have seen Bhartrihari advocating across Buddhist-Hindu lines a few generations earlier. In his commentary on this text, Shankara blatantly inserted the terminology of Brahmanistic Vedanta (Isayeva, 1993: 61). On the composite nature of the *Gaudapadiya-Karika* and its relationship to Buddhism, see King (1995).

52. Halbfass (1991: 301–310). The complexities of how a sacrifice could bring about its consequences became a fertile ground for debate among the Naiyayikas, from Uddyotakara in the 500s to Jayanta in the 800s. They raised issues such as how a sacrifice gave merit to the sponsor who merely paid the Brahmans to carry it out, or how deficiencies in the karma of the sacrificer could offset the potency of the ritual.

53. After Prabhakara's Mimamsa had disappeared as an active school, this structural conflict was repeated 400 years later: Prabhakara's extreme epistemological realism was reappropriated by Ramanuja as part of the differentiation of Advaita intellectual space.

54. For Shankara, the self cannot observe itself, just as "even hot fire cannot burn

itself, and even the most able actor cannot climb on his own shoulder" (*Brahma-sutra-bhasya* 3.3.54). Shankara also takes over Prabhakara's argument for the self-validity of knowledge, while transferring its conclusion from the empirical world to the self, which is in the nature of the case not delimited by any of the concepts which apply to objects. In addition, Shankara cuts short any infinite regress of consciousness observing consciousness, since its knowledge is immediately self-revealing (Isayeva, 1993: 126, 184–185).

55. For instance, in opposing the Mimamsa doctrine of karmic action through ritual, Shankara defends salvation by insight alone, which was the mark of the Madhyamika school. Shankara engages in his lengthiest polemics with the Yogacara school (Isayeva, 1993: 172). This is in keeping with the sociological principle that conflict is most intense when it occurs over close identities (Coser, 1956: 67–71).

56. Shankara's disciple Sureshvara formulated the argument: "No doubts can arise in relation to the Self, since its nature is pure immediate consciousness" (Deutsch, 1969: 19).

57. Orthodox scholars count between 10 and 14 Upanishads as fundamental, out of the hundred created by this time. Shankara established 11 as classic by citing them in his commentary on the *Brahma-sutras,* and wrote commentaries on 10 of them (*EIP,* 1981; Nakamura, 1973: 77–79). Badarayana had referred to 6 of these; Gaudapada's Advaita commentary had publicized yet another Upanishad, the Buddhist-influenced *Mandukya,* which Shankara (if his surviving commentary is authentic) added to the canon.

58. Shankara's home *math* at Sringeri in south India was probably founded on the site of a Buddhist monastery (Eliot, 1988: 209–211).

59. Basham (1951: 284). Time is the only unextended substance the Jainas recognize, and that too is a substance. On Jaina philosophy generally, see Raju (1985: 106–123); Potter (1976: 115, 145–149).

60. Although Buddhist texts disappeared from India as Hindu triumphed, Sanskrit texts by Shantarakshita and Kamalashila were preserved in Jaina collections, further testifying to the cosmopolitanism and the marginality of Jaina observers in this period (Dutt, 1962: 239).

61. Nakamura (1980: 309–311, 332–341); Stein (1972: 72–74, 165, 224); Dutt (1962: 350–351). Prominent sexual-yogic tantrists in the 800s included the Bengal king Indrabuddhi and his sister.

62. The Shaiva movement became philosophically creative when it came into contact with a long-standing network of Nyaya logicians in the midst of declining Buddhism in Kashmir. The Shaivas' mythology of their god of death and destruction was the ideological counterpart of their practices of overturning orthodox Hindu taboos through ritual orgiasticism and even violence. The Shaiva order branded their bodies with the mark of a phallus, inhabited charnel yards, carried skulls, and daubed their bodies with ashes. Theirs was the charisma of emotional shock; nevertheless it entered the field of intellectual argument when Shaivas began to convert the Nyaya and Buddhist logicians. The emotion-centered mythology was rationalized into a cosmology in which the universe is composed not of consciousness, substance, or even nothingness but of the energy of creation and destruction.

Contacts and debates with Advaitins resulted in identifying the pan-energy cult with metaphysical monism. A variant on this position, Shaktism, identified this energy with metaphysical potentiality (Pandey, 1986; Eliot, 1988: 2:211–222; Muller-Ortega, 1989). The internal debates of this network cannot be followed here. Leading thinkers were in a network from about 900 to early 1000s C.E. passing from Utpala to Abhinavagupta and Shri Kantha, including the minor figures listed as 137–134, 161–165, and 185–189 in the key to Figures 5.4 and 5.5, but not depicted in these network diagrams.

63. The story goes that Udayana defeated Shri Harsha's father in a public debate; the son exacted revenge (Phillips, 1995: 75).

64. Shri Harsha was in Bengal, and thus in the sphere of whatever Buddhist networks survived in India during these generations of Buddhism's death.

65. Potter (1976: 181); Halbfass (1992: 235). A Buddhist philosopher ca. 1090, Ratnakirti, had also taken the step of refuting the existence of other minds. Culminating earlier debates of Advaitas and Buddhists, which seem to have treated any solipsistic conclusion as a reductio ad absurdum, Ratnakirti let the argument for solipsism stand on its own merits. The Buddhist criterion of being—Dignaga's standard, that which is causally effective—underlies all other conceptions of being; the resulting primacy of momentariness further entails the non-existence of other minds and other experiences (Halbfass, 1992: 24; Nakamura, 1980: 310). Ratnakirti, coming as the very last gasp of Buddhist thought in India, was an isolate indeed; his boldness gained him no following among the unphilosophical tantrists of his own camp, and his reputation was swallowed up in the Hindu tide. The same matrix of argument, in the following generations would lead again to an extreme with Chitsukha.

66. The sect claimed a succession of at least three previous leaders, including the philosopher Yamunacharya, a relative of Ramanuja's father. Ramanuja codified the rituals and hymns of prior south Indian poet-saints, while bringing the lineage onto philosophical turf by providing a comprehensive theology. Ramanuja was the great organizer, founding some 700 *maths* and establishing monastic rules. Unlike Buddhists and Shaivites, Ramanuja monks were allowed to marry, and abbotships were hereditary, a feature which was imitated by several other Vaishnava sects, and which no doubt added property interests to sectarian barriers and hostilities (Eliot, 1988: 2:231–237, 316; Dasgupta, 1922–1955: 3:63–165).

67. Phillips (1995: 145) regards Ragunatha's Neo-Nyaya as similar to the ontology of David Armstrong. See also Potter (1976: 122); Phillips (1995: 142–144).

68. Gangesha, the creative founder of Neo-Nyaya, acquired a reputation as impenetrably scholastic; for example, in his major work he considers the merits and defects of 35 definitions of veridicality (Phillips, 1995: 130).

69. Phillips (1995: 145) argues that Neo-Nyaya is an unrecognized contribution that will eventually become part of the forefront of world philosophy: "It is inevitable that on-going work in [Western] ontology embrace eventually the Nyaya-Vaisesika tradition, i.e. when its most astute contributors, Raghunatha, Jagadisa, and Gadadhara, have been recognized by the broad philosophical community [of the future] as the great philosophers they are."

70. See 251–253 in the key to Figure 5.5; and Raju (1985: 61).

71. Potter (1976: 252–254). This pattern is particularly prominent in modern thinkers such as Ramakrishna who represent India to the West.

6. Buddhist and Neo-Confucian China

1. At the end of the Northern Wei (about 534 C.E.) there were 2 million monks and nuns, and 30,000 temples. The size of the Buddhist church fluctuated widely during battles for political favor with Taoists and Confucians. In 574–577, the Northern Chou emperor, at the instigation of Taoist advisers, confiscated the property of the Buddhist temples and returned as many as 3 million monks to lay life. After reunification, the Sui emperor in 601 drastically curtailed the Confucian schools and promoted Buddhism; during his reign 230,000 monks and nuns were converted. In the mid-T'ang dynasty (713–741), a time of violent shifts in the political popularity of Buddhism, there were 125,000 monks and nuns; in 830 as many as 700,000 monks were officially registered. In the great persecution of 845 the census indicated 260,000 monks and nuns to be returned to secular life, 4,600 monasteries and 40,000 temples and shrines destroyed, and several million acres of fertile lands confiscated. Even these numbers do not indicate the full extent of Buddhism; they do not include novice monks, who may have been far more numerous than the fully ordained monks. In addition, the monasteries at this time possessed 150,000 slaves, who were turned into tax-paying peasants. Data from Ch'en (1964: 136, 155, 158, 190–191, 200–201, 204, 232, 242, 244, 250–251, 259, 401). On Chinese population growth, see McEvedy and Jones (1978). On Chinese social history in these periods, see Eberhard (1977); Gernet (1982, 1962); *CHC* (1986, 1979). On the development of Buddhism, see Ch'en (1964); Demiéville (1986); Zürcher (1959); Weinstein (1987). Network sources are cited in Chapter 2.

2. On economic growth in medieval China, see Elvin (1973); Jones (1988). On the role of Buddhist institutions in economic growth, see Gernet (1956); Ch'en (1964); and the theoretical model in Collins (1986: 19–76), and Collins (1997).

3. Loyang in the east and Ch'ang-an (Sian) in the west were the two great capital cities of northern China; the seat of government often changed between them, while the other remained the secondary capital.

4. In fact, the Yogacara doctrine of Consciousness-Only had already been in existence in China, previously imported from India by Paramartha around 550; Hsüan-tsang himself had studied with these masters before going to Nalanda. Chinese intellectuals did not fail to understand these doctrines; the school had survived already for three generations. And the Hua-yen philosophy that displaced Consciousness-Only was fully as abstract and technical.

5. Hsüan-tsang's travels to India became the subject of the most popular novel of medieval China, *Journey to the West* (or *Monkey*). It is a comic fairy tale of supernatural demons and protectors, featuring the monkey with magic powers who accompanies Hsüan-tsang. The basket of scriptures which is the object of the trip is a kind of magical precious object; there is no sense that it has intellectual contents. This reflects the way Hsüan-tsang was received by the emperor and the

populace when he returned to Ch'ang-an. Earlier, the translator Kumarajiva was reputed to be a great magician, and was even forced to mate with court concubines to propagate his magic powers.

6. Gregory (1991); Weinstein (1987: 63, 149); Dumoulin (1988: 45–49, 225–235, 284–285). The influence of Hua-yen within the Ch'an lineages is noted in Figures 6.3 and 6.4 from the time of the great innovators Shih-t'ou and Ma-tzu, ca. 750, down to Ta-hui, ca. 1150.

7. In Figure 6.3 we see the Ch'an lineages already starting to split at the time of Hung-jen's contemporary Fa-jung (238), the alleged founder of the Oxhead school, who syncretized Ch'an meditation with the old Three Treatise school. Obviously there was no strong anti-intellectualism here, but the splitting was a structural harbinger of things to come. The most prominent Oxhead master was Hung-jen's pupil Fa-chih (240), who combined meditation with the Amidaist practice of invoking the name of the Buddha. The Oxhead school lasted through seven generations of masters, although it never had any of the famous "Zen"-style paradoxers (McRae, 1985; 1986: 241–242). Hung-jen's pupils included three more who originated their own lineages: the "Northern school" patriarch Shen-hsiu; his rival Hui-Neng; and Hsuan-Chih (240a), who founded a Szechuan school which practiced meditation on the Buddha's name, another syncretism of Ch'an with the Pure Land school. Hui-Neng in turn was not only master of the contentious Shen-Hui but propagator of several other lineages as well, including those of the "Zen" radicals Ma-tzu and Shih-t'ou. It is apparent that Hui-Neng did not make an isolated doctrinal breakthrough, but was in the midst of an organizational transformation as Ch'an lineages split off all around him.

8. Consciousness-Only, with its great intellectual difficulty, was highly elitist; the route to enlightenment culminated in mastery of the philosophy, with the highest religious status reserved for advanced scholars. T'ien-t'ai had already made a similar claim, with its hierarchy of doctrines to be mastered before enlightenment. At the opposite end of the field, the Pure Land sects made salvation as easy as possible, with the Amidaists taking it to the extreme of demanding only chanting a holy name. In the mid- and late 700s this conflict became explicit, as T'ien-t'ai and Pure Land monks polemicized between intellectual and anti-intellectual, hard and easy routes to peak religious status. Hui-neng himself was subject of polemical attack by Tzu-min (268 in Figure 6.3) of the Pure Land school; and Tzu-min is a lineage predecessor of Fa-chao (271), who preached the prospect of damnation in hell and condemned the easy paths to enlightenment, including universal salvation. The Ch'an route, however, was at neither of the two Pure Land poles, which applied essentially to laypeople, and differed over the rigorousness of faith required. The Ch'an innovation concerned the restrictedness or availability of high religious status among the elite of meditation specialists.

9. We see this clearly by comparing Figures 6.3 and 6.4: in the former the Ch'an lineages fan out across the page, taking the place of all other Buddhist factions; in the latter, from 900 through 1200, we see the Ch'an lineages winnowing down, the surviving branches amalgamating with one another and finally disappearing, while the neo-Confucians fan out across their side of intellectual space.

10. This effort to rewrite the Confucian lineage is reminiscent of Shen-hui's claims for an esoteric lineage which were announced at the time of the Zen revolution 60 years earlier, and might have been inspired by it. Hartman (1986) points out parallels between Ch'an and the philosophy of Han Yü's *ku wen* movement; both movements were challenges to the state-supported popular Buddhism of the capital. Late in life Han Yü was friendly with a monk from Shih-tou's Ch'an lineage (275a in Figure 6.3). On Li Ao, see Barrett (1992).

11. "Han Yü's bold equation of *wen* and *tao,* which is perhaps related to his philosophical equation of thought and action, constituted a dramatic lift for the status and role of literature in a Confucian society. It demanded for the writer a position on par with the administrator. Artistically valid literary expression was no longer a polite accoutrement of the civil servant but rather became a basic requisite for great political success" (Hartman, 1986: 14). Han Yü himself had repeatedly failed the examinations under the older system.

12. It is only at this point that Chou Tun-I was retrospectively made a founder of Neo-Confucianism, although his ideas had been seeping among the Ch'eng disciples after the Shao lineage disappeared around 1130 (Graham, 1958: xix, 168). At the same time, Chang Tsai's system, based on the Supreme Void, lost influence to the Ch'eng focus on principle. Chu Hsi rewrote the earlier history of these movements, obscuring the central formative influence of the Ch'engs by ascribing the origins to Chou Tun-I; whereas Chou was not a militant Neo-Confucian but a Confucian-Taoist syncretist who added only the Supreme Ultimate to his system.

13. Plato's idealism, centered on mathematics, emerged within the first seven generations of the Greek intellectual community, and his immediate successors took it in the direction of a rather particularized religion of star worship. But Plato himself explored a variety of positions, and what became known as "Platonism" did not settle into a pervasively religious idealism until the Roman period; in the interim, the Academy was predominantly in the skeptical camp. For India, it is conventional to interpret the philosophy of the Upanishads as idealist; in Chapter 5 I argued that this tendency has been exaggerated.

14. In fact, Ch'an paralleled Hua-Yen as a highly reflexive philosophical consciousness, but the Neo-Confucians were building from too concrete a level to see this. What Ch'an cultural capital could produce in abstract philosophy was demonstrated in virtually the same generation (the early 1200s) in Japanese Zen with Dogen's system. Figure 7.2 in Chapter 7 shows that Dogen was both a direct and indirect pupil of Chinese Ch'an networks, and also a great-grandpupil of Chu Hsi.

7. Japan

1. As before, philosophers are divided into major (listed in all capitals), secondary (listed by name), and minor (listed by number in the key to Figures 7.1 through 7.5). Criterion for ranking is the relative amount of space devoted to them in a combination of sources (*EP,* 1967; Piovesana, 1963; Kitagawa, 1987, 1990; Dumoulin, 1990; Dilworth, 1989; Maruyama, 1974; Najita and Scheiner, 1978; Tsunoda, de Bary, and Keene, 1958; Totman, 1993; Akamatsu and Yampolsky,

1977; Harootunian, 1989; *CHJ*, 1988: chap. 14). Not listed are persons who receive less than a minimal amount of citation in these sources, who fail to appear in more than one source, or who receive only minor mention in these texts. (Additional sources used for network information are Najita, 1987; Nosco, 1990; Ooms, 1985; Bellah, 1957; Weinstein, 1977). It should be stressed that the criterion for inclusion in this network is relative ranking in the attention space; the network does not simply reproduce the lineage charts which were used as a mode of organizational legitimation (and transfer of rights of office) in Chinese and Japanese Buddhism, and which were imitated by the Neo-Confucian, Ancient Learning, and National Learning schools. Similarly, my criterion for network contact is not simply listing in one of these official lineages as a pupil or successor; it is significant direct personal contact (including written correspondence) between individuals, whether they are listed as doctrinal followers or not. As we see repeatedly throughout the world, innovation typically breaks off from within an established school of thought. Thus, Ogyu Sorai was a student at the Hayashi school of official Neo-Confucianism, although he became its most vehement critic; Kamo Mabuchi, the promoter of National Learning, is linked by intermediaries of acquaintanceship as well as pupilship to Sorai's lineage of Ancient Learning. It is the same in the Buddhist period: Honen the Pure Land founder and Eisai the patriarch of Japanese Zen were taught by the same Tendai masters.

2. Sources on Japanese institutional and historical development (Yamamura, 1990; McMullin, 1984; Anderson, 1974: 435–461; Kitagawa, 1990; Sansom, 1958, 1961; Morris, 1964; Frédéric, 1972; Ikegami, 1995).

3. Once again eminence arises from the center of the prior network. Saicho began by studying with all the main Nara orders; in China his ordination came from Tao-sui (269 in Figure 6.2), a grandpupil of Chan-jan (267), who had revived the T'ien-tai doctrine during the mid-700s. Saicho, a typical importer, eclectically collected other ordination certificates, from Zen as well as Vinaya and mantra (tantric) masters.

4. Kukai was ordained by a grandpupil of Amoghavajra (254 in Figure 6.2), a Ceylonese tantrist who had been tutor and rainmaker to emperors.

5. A popular saying of the Kamakura period went: "Tendai for the imperial court, Shingon for the nobility, Zen for the warriors, Pure Land for the common people" (Dumoulin, 1990: 31).

6. This syncretism had already set in by the mid-900s, when the Zen master T'ien-tai Te-shao revived the old center on Mount T'ien-t'ai; among his pupils were Tao Yüan, who edited the Zen chronicles, *Record of the Transmission of the Lamp* (1004, formulating a Zen orthodoxy), and Yung-ming Yen-shou, who compiled a huge syncretist overview of all teachings, emphasizing compatibility between Zen and the sutras. In a parallel branch of the same lineage, Ch'i-sung (1007–1072) even incorporated Confucianism into Zen by composing a work on the classic *Doctrine of the Mean*.

7. See Dumoulin (1990: 8–15, 54). Nonin's pupils made contact with Te-kuang, a disciple of Ta-hui, of secondary stature in Figure 6.4, from the Lin-chi line. These pupils brought back a rich reliquary from China, including Ta-hui's dharma robe, implying that the Chinese lineages encouraged the Japanese as continuers of a

visibly dying tradition. Genealogical documents of lines of succession were preserved in monasteries as precious treasures.

8. Eisai was already middle-aged. He had been to China 20 years earlier, at which time he had merely returned with Tendai texts; on his later trip he studied Zen and Vinaya as well. Upon his second return to Japan, Eisai founded the first Zen monasteries, but he continued to be very compromising toward the established schools. His monasteries at first remained a branch of the Enryaku-ji on Mount Hiei; they continued to practice ceremonial, sutra reading, and Shingon, even developing a version called tantric-magical Zen. Such eclecticism was nothing new. Eisai also brought back with him Neo-Confucianism from a very minor pupil of Chu Hsi. His visit coincided with a compromising mood in Chinese Zen, the height of its contact with the Neo-Confucian networks (as we see in Figure 6.4).

9. In all, 46 Rinzai lineages were founded in Japan, along with several other Zen sects; the official Zen history included the lives of 1,600 important monks (Dumoulin, 1990: 8, 36). These numbers far exceed the upper limits of the attention space; by the law of small numbers only a few lineages could become eminent. It was by building on a successful vector of attention that a small set of Rinzai and Soto lineages produced virtually all the famous masters, whose names appear as major and secondary figures in Figure 7.2 (as well as most of the names in the key to that figure which meet the criterion of sufficient historical attention to be listed as "minor").

10. The tea master Murata Juko, in the late 1400s, created the famous Zen stone garden of the Daitokuji in Kyoto. This monastery became a center for the tea ceremony and for the most worldly aspect of Zen. Other outstanding Kyoto temple rock gardens were built around 1500 by Soami, a samurai and government official who simultaneously excelled as poet, tea master, and ink painter (Kidder, 1985: 222–236; Kitagawa, 1990: 126; Dumoulin, 1990: 20, 151–153, 248; Varley, 1977).

11. "This is the great watershed, a point of demarcation in Japanese cultural history remarkably similar to that in the West between the arts of the Renaissance and those of Medieval Christianity from which they emerged" (Rosenfield, 1977: 207).

12. The inflation of religious currency was also promoted in the interests of raising money from the laity. One of the targets of Ikkyu's scorn was the Zen abbot Doso, who raised money among the wealthy merchants "by granting certificates of enlightenment to lay people who attended mass meditation sessions at which *koan* were 'solved' by esoteric transmission rather than through rigorous self-directed meditative enquiry" (Collcutt, 1990: 614).

13. Collcutt (1990: 604–609, 613). The situation was similar to that which arose in T'ang and Sung China, when certificates of monastic ordination (as ordinary monks, not as abbots) were sold in official revenue-raising campaigns; in the later period these certificates came to circulate for private resale. In the Chinese case, these certificates became used as a paper currency, and were items of investment on a speculative market (Ch'en, 1964: 241–244). The Sung dynasty economy was probably the world's first breakthrough into full-scale market capitalism, outgrowing the sector of monastic entrepreneurship which had pioneered rationalized structures of market production and reinvestment. In subsequent dynasties the

market was asphyxiated by governmental regulation, confined to local exchanges which never regained the dynamic of rationalized economic growth. When this structural complex was transferred to Japan through the Buddhist movements, market growth resumed. On the sociological model of the Chinese and Japanese Buddhist economies (Collins, 1986: 58–73; and Collins, 1997). On Japanese economic growth (Hanley and Yamamura, 1977; Nakane and Oishi, 1990; Totman, 1993; Nakai and McClain, 1991; Smith, 1959; Collcutt, 1981; McMullin, 1984; Yamamura, 1990.)

14. "There is no *satori*. Your mind is the original Buddha. Is there anything lacking in the Buddha mind? Can one attain enlightenment from outside oneself?" "Even when enlightenment is present, it is not good to simply stay with it, for the most important thing comes afterwards," (quoted in Dumoulin, 1990: 323).

15. The full force of official establishment developed gradually. In 1640 an Office of Inquisition was established to check that families were registered with a temple; at first directed only against Christians, in 1661 its activities were extended to the entire population (McMullin, 1984: 243–245).

16. Hakuin described his experience as follows: "Night and day I did not sleep; I forgot both to eat and rest. Suddenly a great doubt manifested itself before me. It was as though I was frozen solid in the midst of an ice sheet extending tens of thousands of miles. A purity filled my breast and I could neither go forward nor retreat . . . Although I sat in the lecture hall and listened to the master's lecture, it was as though I were hearing a discussion from a distance outside the hall. At times it felt as though I were floating through the air . . . The state lasted for several days. Then I chanced to hear the sound of the temple bell and I was suddenly transformed. It was as if a sheet of ice had been smashed or a jade tower had fallen with a crash" (Dumoulin, 1990: 370). Hakuin remained egotistically proud of his experience and was not awarded the dharma seal. Months later, while he was begging in a village, his mind filled by working on a koan, a peasant woman knocked him down with a broom. When he regained consciousness, he suddenly found that the koan had been solved, sending him into dancing, clapping, and shouts of laughter. This time his master recognized the experience as valid (Dumoulin, 1990: 372).

17. Dumoulin (1990: 157 186, 194, 204, 331). Bankei Yotaku in 1647, after two years of extreme asceticism had left him close to death, experienced his own sickness as the shock of realization: "So I was ready to die, and at the time I felt no remorse. There was nothing special left for me. My only thought was that I was going to die without fulfilling my long-nourished desire. Then I felt a strange sensation in my throat. I spat against a wall. A mass of black phlegm, large as a soapberry, rolled down the side . . . Suddenly just at that instant . . . I realized what it was that had escaped me until now" (quoted in Dumoulin, 1990: 312).

18. "One night during *zazen* practice the boundary between before and after suddenly disappeared . . . It was as if I had arrived at the ground of the Great Death, with no memory of the existence of anything, not even of myself. All I remember is an energy in my body that spread out over ten times ten-thousand worlds and a light that radiated endlessly . . . I forgot that my hands were moving in the air and my

feet were dancing" (Dumoulin, 1990: 408). The account is from a Zen master of the mid-1800s.

19. Preston's (1988) ethnography of a Zen meditation center concludes that the Zen experience is socially constructed by the focused setting and rituals of inward attention. What is constructed, however, is not a particular "culture" but an attitude set free from the contents of verbal cultures. The rituals of Zen practice are, so to speak, counter-rituals, which de-reify and disenchant the objects of ordinary social life. Buddhism recognizes a deep version of the social construction of reality; the institutions and paramount realities of the ordinary world (samsara) are mere "name and form." The path pursued by Zen is not to escape into another realm but to transform into another key; instead of living focused on cognitive constructions, to live focused on the flow of wordless practices.

20. Kitagawa (1990: 143). Ooms (1985) points out that the shogun was more interested in promoting a cult, centered on the lavishly baroque Tokugawa mausoleum at Nikko, which elevated Ieyasu personally into a reincarnation of the national deity, the sun goddess Amaterasu. This cult, promoted vigorously in the 1640s, was no great success against the better-organized religious and educational institutions; indeed, Ieyasu had to rely on the Tendai abbott Tenkai to work out the theological justification of the reincarnation doctrine. Razan's hostility to Buddhism was not a general propensity of the Tokugawas, but rather a stance in the struggle among intellectuals, which did not shift decisively in an anti-Buddhist direction until the opening of the successful proprietary schools in the 1660s.

21. Takuan was the teacher of Hoshina Masayuki, Lord of Aizu, who became central in the patronage network of the following generation (Ooms, 1985: 197). Takuan represents the height of fusion between samurai culture and Zen. Takuan was friendly with the shogun's sword master, Yagyu Munenori, and was connected with a very famous swordsman, Miyamoto Musashi, author of *A Book of Five Rings,* on the spiritual dimension of combat. Takuan wrote for Munenori a text applying Buddhist doctrine of non-attachment to the technique of the sword fight. The connection is not merely to show fearlessness in the face of death; it is to avoid clinging to one's opponent's movements or to the sword itself, to flow through everything without distinction and without consciously directing one's mind (Dumoulin, 1990: 285–287; Kammer, 1969).

22. Nakamura (1967); Dumoulin (1990: 341–344). It would be more accurate to say that Suzuki integrated Buddhist subduing of the body into the spirit of samurai military discipline, but universalistically, without caste distinctions among social ranks. Suzuki was close to official power and was given *bakufu* appointments, including restoration of provincial temple properties as a means of exerting control over local samurai. He was entrusted with a mission to pacify the peasants after a major provincial rebellion in 1637–1638 (Ooms, 1985: 123–139).

23. The network of tea masters in Figure 7.3 originated at the shogun's court in the mid-1400s. The famous iconoclast Ikkyu Sojun, though not himself a tea master, connects this network with the religious elite, as teacher of Murata Shuko, a Zen monk who returned to the world as a tea master. The several branches of the lineage culminate in the most famous of all, Sen no Rikyu, in the late 1500s. Sen

no Rikyu became tea master to Hideyoshi, and the social arbiter of good taste in the 1580s. The tea ceremony became a lavish display and a criterion of elite standing; in 1587 a huge gathering of 800 devotees was held at Kyoto, at which Hideyoshi was upstaged by his tea master. Sen no Rikyu's claims to status precedence apparently provoked the dictator to demand in 1591 that he commit ritual suicide (Dumoulin, 1990: 239–241; Varley, 1977).

24. Sources on Tokugawa education (Rubinger, 1982; Dore, 1965; Totman, 1993: 161–168, 301–302, 349–354, 429–435, 469–471; Passin, 1965; Najita, 1987).

25. As Ikegami (1995) notes, Zen was not the source of the samurai ethos; samurai codes went back to a distinctive warrior culture of the medieval period, and these were transformed during the Tokugawa under conditions of pacification into the "tamed" and refined manners which became anachronistic emblems of samurai identity. The networks of leading Zen and samurai masters overlapped at just this time, because the underlying social bases of both career paths were crumbling simultaneously.

26. In 1682 came the first non-religious "best-seller," Ihara Saikaku's *Life of an Amorous Man,* a novel which was something of a cross between Defoe and the *Memoirs of Casanova.* This marks the point at which it became possible for a writer to support oneself purely off the market (Nosco, 1990: 27).

27. Sources on Tokugawa intellectuals (*EP,* 1967; Maruyama, 1974; Piovesana, 1963; Tsunoda, de Bary, and Keene, 1958; Totman, 1993; Sansom, 1963; Bellah, 1957, 1978; Harootunian, 1970, 1988; Matsumoto, 1970; Najita and Scheiner, 1978; Naita, 1987; Nosco, 1990; Ooms, 1985; Tucker, 1989; Wakabayashi, 1986; Koschmann, 1987; de Bary, 1979; Dilworth, 1979; *CHJ,* 1988: chap. 14).

28. In a passage which shows the rising tide of rejection of both Zen and Zen-like meditative practices prominent in religious Neo-Confucianism, Banzan declares: "My name is vacuity. How with this name can I make a pretense of learning and serve as a teacher of others?" (Maruyama, 1974: 42).

29. De Bary (1979). Ansai's declaration of loyalty—"If a person errs by studying Chu Hsi, he errs with Chu Hsi. He has nothing to regret"—echoes the famous loyalty of Shinran to his master during the founding of the Pure Land movements: "Even though, having been persuaded by Honen Shonin, I should go to Hell through the Nembutsu, I should not regret it" (quoted in Maruyama, 1974: 37; Kitagawa, 1990: 115).

30. Shikoku is the large island south of the inland sea. The Neo-Confucian school there had an independent beginning already in the mid-1500s with Minamimura Baiken, supported by the local *daimyo*'s clan. Ansai went there to study following his Buddhist training at the old centers, at Mount Hiei and at a Rinzai temple in Kyoto (Ooms, 1985: 199).

31. Both were grandsons of Tokugawa Ieyasu, and held domains in the innermost circle of shogunal alliances.

32. In other words, the samurai becomes a policeman, although Soko formulates this as a more academic role: "The three classes of the common people make him their teacher and respect him" (quoted in Tsunoda, de Bary, and Keene, 1958: 399).

33. Soko's pronouncements have an anti-Zen tone, which can be applied equally to

the puritanism of Ansai's sage religion: "Those who eliminate all human desires are not human beings; they are no different from tiles and stones. Can we say that tiles and stones can comprehend the Principle of Heaven?" (quoted in Maruyama, 1974: 46). In contrast, Ansai's chief disciple, Sato Naokata, explicitly extolled Zen as the basis for discipline within government bureaucracy. Here we have a rival legitimation for the same shift toward the peacetime samurai role which Soko was concerned with. Rival intellectual alliances approached the same issue with different resources.

34. Ito came from a branch of the lineage of Fujiwara Seika parallel and rival to Razan, via his teacher Matsunaga Sekigo. The Kogido initially took the form of a discussion group at Ito's home, where his wealthy family entertained court nobles, doctors, Confucian scholars, poets, and painters. From this gathering developed regularly scheduled lectures with debates and grading (Rubinger, 1982: 50–51). By this route Ito became the first successful teacher from the merchant classes, breaking into the samurai educational monopoly.

35. Tetsugen was the most eminent member of the new Obaku Zen sect; he edited a comprehensive edition of the Buddhist scriptures of every sect, representing an equivalent on the Buddhist side of the tendency toward pure scholarship that was building up among the Confucians at this time, as well as the tendency to syncretism in a weakening movement.

36. In Sorai's words, the samurai class "lived like guests at an inn," where "even a single chopstick had to be paid for" (Maruyama, 1974: 132).

37. At Sorai's school, pupils were required to sign an agreement which included this clause, in regard to studying the laws of the Ming dynasty: "These laws are the institutions of a different era and a different country. One must not simply employ them in the present era and destroy the existing laws" (quoted in Maruyama, 1974: 97).

38. Economics was emerging as a recognized discipline in the generation of the early 1800s, explicitly known as *keizai* (Najita, 1987: 8). In 1815, following the work of Kaiho, another Kaitokudo product, Kusama Naokata, produced a history of money, the central subject of economic controversy since the time of Arai Hakuseki and Sorai.

39. Here Sorai was directly challenging the Bushido school of Yamaga Soko, which defended the action of the *ronin*. Oishi Kuranosuke, the leader of 47 *ronin,* was a direct disciple of Yamaga Soko (Kitagawa, 1990: 159).

40. "Although *li* seems to be the Ultimate Principle, it is not so. Since it is an abstract principle, it can be used in any way whatsoever. It is like being able to call a white thing black or any other color" (quoted in Maruyama, 1974: 146).

41. During the crisis of the 1320s–1330s, when Go-Daigo tried to restore imperial rule, we find in Figure 7.2 the first significant Shinto branch of the intellectual network. The leaders of the Watarai family, priests at the national Ise shrine, excluded Buddhist emblems from its precincts while emulating Buddhism by stressing moral purity rather than merely ceremonial offerings for fertility and protection magic (Bellah, 1957: 65). The court intellectual Kitabatake Chikafusa now joined the Shinto cause, in part because of its usefulness in legitimating the Go-Daigo

restoration; at the same time, Chikafusa relied on Buddhist metaphysics to give a larger significance to the conception of Japan as a divine nation under the *kami*. It should be noted that this took place two generations after the rise of Nichiren's Hokke movement, which had made the same claim for Japan as the world's Buddha-land. Again in the 1480s, when feudal combat in the aftermath of the Onin War destroyed any semblance of shogunal government, Kanetomo, a priest of the Yoshida shrine, promoted a syncretist Shinto which reversed previous rankings and made Buddhas and Boddhisatvas manifestations of the *kami* instead of the other way around (Kitagawa, 1990: 160).

42. Under Shingon auspices, the *kami* had been reduced to a dualism corresponding to Buddhist tantrism: matter and mind, male and female, dynamic and potential aspects of things (Maruyama, 1974: 155). We are reminded here that Keichu, the adumbrator of National Learning, was a Shingon monk in the camp of Shinto supporters.

43. The Shinto–National Learning movement was not the only religious reaction against (and split in the ranks of) the Sorai network. In 1729 (overlapping with the height of Kada no Azumamaro's activity), the Kyoto teacher Ishida Baigan founded the Shingaku movement. It took an opposing position both to the Shinto fundamentalists and to Sorai's naturalist utilitarianism. Shingaku preached that the spiritual reality behind Buddhism, Neo-Confucianism, and Shinto were the same; its main practice, however, was meditation, not ceremonialism, thus putting it closer to the Zen–sage religion tradition that was now disappearing from the upper-class intellectual space. Shingaku was preached successfully among the popular classes, but using the vehicle of the educational marketplace rather than the traditional evangelist. Baigan's network connections shaped the direction of his innovation. He was the pupil of a lay teacher of the Obaku sect (i.e., the most syncretist of the Zen sects) as well as of a neo-Confucian; his early religious activity was in the Ise-pilgrimage movement; and he formulated his distinctive doctrine soon after engaging in argument with a disciple of Sorai. The term *shingaku* itself had been used by Sorai in his attack on Neo-Confucian philosophy (Bellah, 1978: 139; 1957: 134–138).

44. "What they call *li* is not something clearly fixed, it is not something readily comprehensible to the human intellect. Hence a Confucian should define *li* in terms of the theories of the ancient Sages, and a Buddhist should do so by using the theories of the Buddha . . . It is a Way based not on any objective criteria, but arbitrarily established by individuals" (quoted in Maruyama, 1974: 159).

45. The schools devoted exclusively to Japanese studies *(kokugaku)* never reached mass proportions. Only 9 such schools are known in the entire period before 1872, making up less than 1 percent of all proprietary schools. The vast majority (70 percent) remained those with curricula of Chinese studies or calligraphy (Rubinger, 1982: 13). The sheer number of schools, however, is not the source of intellectual movement on the creative edge. Under the law of small numbers, the 200 *shijuku* (proprietary schools) founded during 1789–1829, and the additional 800 founded during 1830–1867, were outside the center of intellectual attention; they propa-

gated older culture, and this period of mass expansion of schooling was not the time when the main intellectual innovations took place.

46. In France, the conservative monarchy following the 1815 restoration broke into factions because of divergence between ultramontane Catholics and the administrators of the state bureaucracy, especially over educational policy; the result was a series of liberalizing and conservatizing swings leading up to the Orleanist revolution of 1830. Again in 1860s, splits between Catholic traditionalists and statist officials undermined conservative control; in this case the dominance of the secularistic officials motivated the Catholics to join the anti-monarchist forces in pushing for liberalized rights (*CMH*, 1902–1911: 10:40–100; 11:295–297, 469–474).

47. The first non-religious work was printed in Japan in 1591. Religious texts continued to be major items on the market until 1680–1700 (Nosco, 1990: 26). This was much the same time the transition occurred in European publishing.

48. Tokyo University was founded in 1877 with European teachers. In 1893 chairs were opened to Japanese professors and the Europeans were gradually replaced. The same model developed elsewhere: Waseda University originated in 1882; Kyoto University, the second imperial foundation, was established 1897 (*EP*, 1967: 252–253; Kitagawa, 1987: 305). Sources on post-Meiji intellectual life (*EP*, 1967; Kitagawa, 1987, 1990; Dilworth, 1989; Ketelaar, 1990; Najita and Scheiner, 1978; Tsunoda, de Bary, and Keene, 1958; Blacker, 1964; Gluck, 1985; Havens, 1970; Nishitani, 1982).

49. See Chapter 8, Coda: "Are Idea Imports a Substitute for Creativity?"

50. The attack on Christianity as an alien philosophy could be directed toward other contemporary aims as well. Inouye Enryo, a True Pure Land priest, in 1887–1890 attacked Christianity as irrational and irreconcilable with science; playing to the prestige of positivism, he argued that Buddhist religion is in greater harmony with rationality (Kitagawa, 1990: 230).

51. In other words, the network connection comes first. It was apparently via Suzuki that Zen's appeal to the philosophical networks of the West came home to Nishida and stimulated his own creativity.

52. The central experience consists in "acts of consciousness," which are also the "place of nothingness," and the "historically formative act" (quoted in Dilworth, 1989: 149). Paralleling Buddhist dialectics is the puzzle in Aristotelean logic of how the individual can be reached by specification of the universal; a *principium individuationis*, Nishida suggests, points beyond itself to the ultimate emptiness of the things of conventional experience. A further resource is Kant's unity of transcendental apperception, which Nishida takes as referring to a place where subject and object are united (Nishitani, 1982; xxxi). Nishida synthesizes a selection of Western concepts with a position rather like that of Nagarjuna and Dharmakirti: there is neither God/transcendence beyond phenomena nor substance to the phenomena themselves. Samsara is *sunyata;* the world is ultimate reality, as Emptiness.

53. In the 1890s Nakae Chomin attempted to revive Sorai's naturalism as the explicit Japanese counterpart of Bentham's Utilitarianism (Najita, 1987: 35). Thereafter

the Kyoto school did not reign in Japanese philosophy without opposition. For a period in the 1920s there were some advocates of Marxism, but no indigenous creativity came from this.

8. Islam, Judaism, Christendom

1. The strong 'Abbasid caliphate lasted long enough so that the period of redaction of *hadith* was closed before Islam began to fragment politically. Similarly, Catholic and Greek Christianity established its canon during the height of the Roman Empire, and its adoption as state religion allowed heterodox variants to be forcibly excluded.

2. The conflict between religious orthodoxy and independent intellectual concerns is one, but not the only, route to epistemology. Long-term processes in the development of epistemology and logic will be considered more fully in Chapter 15.

3. One point of substantive difference that was argued, however, was the unity of God, upheld by the Muslim theologians against Zoroastrian and Manichaean dualists. Even here Muslim theologians were more interested in turning the argument against anthropomorphists in their own ranks. A comparison with China and India implies that multi-religious competition in itself does not lead to proofs of the existence and nature of God. See Chapter 15.

4. It lacked only Muslim Spain, conquered between 711 and 759, which broke free in the name of the Umayyad caliphate, which had been overthrown by the 'Abbasids in the civil war of 744–750. General sources for Islamic political, religious and social history (Hodgson, 1974; Lapidus, 1988; McEvedy, 1961; Humphreys 1991).

5. This account of philosophers and biographical data draws generally on numerous sources (Watt, 1973, 1985; Fakhry, 1983; Hodgson, 1974; Wolfson, 1976; Rescher, 1964; de Boer, 1903; individual essays in *DSB*, 1981, and *EP*, 1967). I have included scientists and mathematicians in the networks, since their pattern is intimately connected with that of the philosophers. The methodology of ranking philosophers into major, secondary, and minor figures is the same as that used in Chapter 2. Islamic philosophers are ranked according to the relative amount of reference to them in the cited sources. Jewish philosophers are ranked in relation to one another, based on Sirat (1985); Husik (1969); Guttman (1933); Pines (1967); *EP* (1967). These histories are all recent and largely European; earlier historical accounts on which they draw include Ibn al-Nadim (ca. 990), al-Baqillani (1000), al-Baghdadi (1030), al-Ghazali (1090), al-Sharastani (1130), Maimonides (1190), and Ibn Khaldun (1380).

6. Intellectual historians have tended to ascribe most kalamite positions to foreign influences (summarized in Wolfson, 1976: 58–79) and to downplay indigenous lines of development. The principal Mu'tazilite arguments, however, were formed before 830, and it was in the next two generations that most of the translation of Greek texts took place. The early Mu'tazilites knew something of the categories of Aristotelean logic, which seem to have come from secondhand accounts of

Greek philosophy then beginning to circulate (Fakhry, 1983: 8–9; Watt, 1973: 154–155, 205, 249); but they turned the concepts of substance and accident into a quite different direction through the dynamics of their own disputes. Democritus' atomism is mentioned in Aristotle's refutation of it in the *Physics;* but a translation was probably not available in the formative period of Arabic atomism. Most important, Mu'tazilite atomism is far from Democritean or Epicurean; the durable and spatial physical atoms of the Greeks are not the time-instants of the Mu'tazilites. When the genuinely Greek-oriented *falasifa* (philosophers) did appear, they polemicized against Mu'tazilite atomism (Peters, 1968: 144). Alternatively, Fakhry (1983: 33–34) suggests that this point-atomism came from Buddhist, Hindu, and Jaina schools in India existing by 500 C.E.; he mentions an anonymous treatise, "Religious Beliefs of India," circulated in Arabic by the late 700s, contemporary with the Mu'tazilite founders. The Jainas, however, combined atomism with very un-Mu'tazilite doctrines in which everything is a substance, including motion, action, and time. The Nyaya-Vaisesika school of the Hindus combines atomism of material things with the reality of universals, plus the substances of infinite spirit (atman) and infinite mind *(manas)*. The Buddhist Sarvastivadins had a time-atomism which was closest to the Mu'tazilites, but held very un-Muslim doctrines that the self is an unreal void, that God does not exist, that past and future as well as the cessation of existence all exist (Raju, 1985: 53, 121, 253–262). It is implausible that the Arabs would have extracted just the relevant aspects of atomism from these closely knit systems, even if they had access to these kinds of philosophical texts. Karl Potter (*EIP,* 1977: 17) concludes that there is little evidence of explicit East-West borrowing of doctrines in either direction.

7. In part Mu'tazilite political policy set in motion this course of events. Initially the Mu'tazilites were aggressive primarily toward the dualists rather than against the *hadith* faction; their alliance with the 'Abbasids involved the suppression of the Zoroastrian religion of the old Persian regime and its Manichaean offshoot, which had flourished in Mesopotamia and the Christian Mediterranean since the 200s C.E. (Hodgson, 1974: 1:385). This aspect of kalamite religious policy continued, even with the reversal of caliphal favor toward *hadith;* it appears that Zoroastrians may have made up 20 percent of the population of Baghdad in al-Ma'mun's time, but were down to perhaps 2 percent two generations later (Massignon, 1982: 241). The religious pluralism of the early Islamic Empire was closing down at the same time that a conservative orthodoxy was taking control.

8. Mu'tazilites still existed in the early 1100s (the last Mu'tazilite notable enough to appear in the Figure 8.3 key is 208), and their position was carried on by Jewish Karaites even longer.

9. From the late 700s there were already court astronomers and astrologers at Baghdad, including foreigners from India, Persia, and Central Asia (see 14 through 18 and 32 through 36 in Figure 8.1).

10. On the Nestorians and Jacobites, see Latourette (1975: 167–169, 282–283). The Nestorian headquarters was at Baghdad. Islam had acquired an empire not through a holy war to spread the faith, but because its effort to convert the Arabs had

spilled over into border clashes with surrounding states; then it fell heir to a geopolitical vacuum owing to the mutually destructive wars of the Byzantine and Persian empires (Lapidus, 1988: 38–43). There was little effort initially to convert conquered peoples, and outside of Arabia, most Muslim cities had very large non-Muslim populations. The reversal of this religious policy began to pick up strength after 900.

11. Jewish philosophers are ranked relative to one another, separate from the ranking of Muslim philosophers. Hence it is not implied that Saadia ben Joseph is of the same order of importance in this intellectual field as his most dominant Muslim contemporaries.

12. I refer to him by his Latin name, Rhazes, to distinguish him from Fakhr al-Din al-Razi (Fakhruddin Razi), who lived eight generations later.

13. Rescher (1964). Aristotle's had been a logic of classes, the Stoics' a logic of propositions. The Baghdad school recovered these from Galen and from Aristotelean commentaries and extended their scope. The nature of possibility was debated. Matta and al-Farabi developed conditional syllogisms; al-Farabi dealt with general and particular predication and the quantification of predicates. He and Yahia ibn-ʿAdi took up from Alexandrian logic the question of universals, and attempted to reduce Aristotle's 10 categories to substance and various species of accidents.

14. This was not necessarily due to al-Ashʿari personally. There are indications that his position was already laid out in the previous generation by al-Qalanisi (74 in Figure 8.1), a moderate rational theologian among the *hadith* literalists; during his lifetime he was as famous as al-Ashʿari. The latter's fame resulted from a retrospective reinterpretation by his lineage two generations later of its own origins (Watt, 1973: 287–288, 311); by the time of al-Baqillani, there was a vehement polemic against Muʿtazilites as well as against Christians and Jews, and al-Ashʿari's public break with the Muʿtazilites made him an appropriate emblem of their distinctiveness. Once again we see that it is the lineage and its conflicts more than the individual which generates intellectual fame; and the structural crunch of intellectual attention deprives credit from someone like al-Qalanisi while giving it to another like al-Ashʿari.

15. Wolfson (1976: 355–454; 1979). Davidson (1987) emphasizes that arguments for creation based on the impossibility of traversing an infinity go back to the Christian critic of Aristotle, John Philoponus, while arguments for God as the unmoved mover come from Aristotle. Philoponus was being cited by the Muslims by the time of al-Farabi in the early 900s; in the mid-800s al-Kindi was making arguments very similar to those of Philoponus (Davidson, 1987: 92–95, 106). Yet the early Muʿtazilites' proofs emerged a generation before this, and some of them (such as Abu-l-Hudhayl's) are not obviously dependent on Philoponus; even those which are similar may have come from the kalamites' own discussions of divisibility and atomism. In any case, the issues did not become important for the Muslims out of passive imitation of the Greeks. Greek philosophy had been only marginally concerned with the existence of God in anything approaching a religious sense. Aristotle's unmoved mover is unrelated to Providence, creation, or immortality.

The Neoplatonists, who developed as a pagan rival to Christianity, eventually produced a full-fledged religious conception of God; but since their synthesis included Aristoteleanism, the One is very unlike a creator or Providence. Philosophical arguments over God finally became focused when the Neoplatonists had to make their peace with victorious Christianity. The Patristic writers were content with the argument from design—the order of the world implies a creator—but as Averroës later said, this is an argument for laypeople, not one argued at the level of formal philosophical consideration (Davidson, 1987: 219, 236). The more sophisticated level emerged with Proclus (mid-400s), the last gasp of the pagan Neoplatonist school at Athens. He was the first to recognize that Aristotle's proof of an unmoved mover from the motion of the spheres is not a proof of a cause of the existence of the spheres; Proclus added an argument that the existence of the heavens requires an eternal being to sustain their existence, and compiled 18 proofs for the eternity of the world (Davidson, 1987: 51, 281–282). Proclus' pupil was Ammonius (304 in Figure 3.8), who abandoned Neoplatonism for Christianity; he was the teacher of both Simplicius (306 in Figure 3.8) and John Philoponus. Simplicius was the first to take the impossibility of an infinite regress of causes as a proof of God (Davidson, 1987: 338). And Philoponus based his arguments explicitly on a refutation of Proclus *(Contra Proclum)*; in converting to Christianity, he reconverted the cultural capital of his school into a reasoned philosophical theology which Christianity had previously lacked. With the ending of his lineage, however, Philoponus' arguments were not taken up in Christian philosophy. They survived largely because similar lines of argument emerged among Muslim theologians. Less particularistically, the ancient struggle between an anthropomorphic monotheism and a defensive religion of philosophical syncretism (i.e., Christianity versus Neoplatonism) eventually brought about reasoned arguments over the fundamental items of the religious cosmology; and these arguments were picked up again when another monotheistic anthropomorphism (Islam) developed its own intellectual networks.

16. Davidson (1987: 214–215, 309–310), however points out that Ibn Sina did not produce a pure ontological proof, based on concepts alone, as Anselm did in Europe two generations later. Ibn Sina included reference to the fact that something exists. But he raised philosophical analysis toward the ontological level, although most of the further development was to take place after his texts were transmitted into Christian philosophy.

17. As compared to Descartes, Ibn Sina did not lay stress on the existence of self in the "cogito ergo sum," but emphasized instead the modality of being which is thereby revealed.

18. Ibn Sina is the high point of Islamic logic; he contributes a theory of categorical propositions involving quantification of the predicate; of hypothetical and disjunctive propositions; of singular propositions; and a theory of definition and classification (Rescher, 1964: 154–155). A rather sterile debate between proponents of Ibn Sina's "eastern" logic and the "western" logic of the Baghdad and Cairo schools supplied what focus of attention there was within intellectual life from the mid-1100s down through the mid-1300s.

19. In the key to Figures 8.2 and 8.3, 196 in Afghanistan, 207 in Transoxiana, 217 in Anatolia, 229 in Baghdad, 232 in North Africa, 235 in Khwarazm–Oxus River valley, 246 and 275 in India, Rumi's order of darvish dancers in Anatolia, 255 in Egypt, 276 among the Anatolian lower classes, 277 in Persia, 294 in Iran and central Asia. Sources on these movements (Hodgson, 1974: 2:192–234; Corbin, 1969; Massignon, 1982: 36–51; Lapidus, 1988: 168–172).

20. After writing the *Muqaddimah,* Ibn Khaldun migrated to Egypt and finished life as a Malikite judge. Figure 8.3 shows that Egypt too had had no significant intellectual life at this point for several generations.

21. In fact, al-Kindi's protégé Ibn Ha'imah (60 in Figure 8.1) translated Plotinus as "Theology of Aristotle." Plotinus himself was not translated by name, and was very seldom mentioned (Fakhry, 1983: 20).

22. Similarly, in Christian Europe, the translations of Aristotle which were made directly from the Greek by James of Venice and others in the mid-1100s were interpreted within the Neoplatonic framework. Slightly later in the century, Gerard of Cremona, translating Arabic texts in Toledo, translated not only Aristotle but also Proclus' *Elements of Theology*—the arch-Neoplatonic system—as the *Liber de Causis,* which also was attributed to Aristotle. The so-called "Theology of Aristotle" was also translated from the Arabic at this time. Europeans could see no difference between Aristotle and Plotinus, since they were apparently unaware of the latter until Ficino translated the *Enneads* in 1492 (*DSB,* 1981: 1:270–273; 11:42; Weinberg, 1964: 10–11, 95, 100).

23. Sources on Jewish philosophy generally (Sirat, 1985; Husik, 1969; Guttman, 1933; Wolfson, 1979; Pines, 1967, and individual articles in *EP,* 1967, and *DSB,* 1981).

24. Only rabbinical writings were in Hebrew. Thus Maimonides produced his rabbinical code in Hebrew, but his *Guide for the Perplexed,* a philosophical reconciliation with religion, was written in Arabic but using Hebrew characters, a kind of code for members combining the cosmopolitan and the ethnic religious communities. Bahya ibn Paquda, among others, also wrote in this way, in Arabic with Hebrew characters (Pelaez del Rosal, 1985: 106). Even the nationalist anti-cosmopolitans among the Jews, such as Judah Halevi, wrote in Arabic. Arabic was the language of the Jewish intellectual community, and even the critics of that community used it. The only philosophers who wrote in Hebrew before 1200 were Bar Hiyya and Abraham Ibn Ezra; both were in the Christian orbit, the former in Barcelona, while the latter traveled in Italy, France, and England (Sirat, 1985: ix; Hodgson, 1974: 1:357, 452, 468–469). Sources for this period generally (Husik, 1969; Sirat, 1985; Pelaez de Rosal, 1985; Cruz Hernandez, 1957).

25. This is the network of Jewish poets and grammarians (beginning with 2 and 3 in Figure 8.4) which was prominent at Córdoba down through 1100, and which branched off to form the great Jewish rabbinical academy at Lucena (30 miles from Córdoba), connecting to Ibn Zaddik, Judah Halevi, Abraham Ibn Ezra, and Maimonides. The early Spanish Muslim scientists were virtually all at Córdoba; we may note especially al-Majriti (9 in Figure 8.4), who apparently traveled in the east before 1000 and not only returned with astronomy and geometry, but also propagated magic and the numerology of the Pure Brethren texts, which

had been formulated in this generation at Basra. Al-Majriti's pupils were astronomers and astrologers at Córdoba; one of them (22 in Figure 8.4) propagated the Pure Brethren system to Saragossa (one of the independent Muslim states of the north), where this astrological occultism was passed along to the first important Jewish philosopher in Spain, Ibn Gabirol (Sirat, 1985: 97). Ibn Gabirol is the creative individual at the intersection of the networks, connecting also to the Jewish network of poets and grammarians at Córdoba and Lucena; he became a famous religious poet in his own right. Another famous contemporary, perhaps also at this cultural center Saragossa, was the Jewish philosopher Bahya ibn Paquda. A second network worthy of note (10, 15, and 26 in Figure 8.4) begins with a follower of al-Sijistani in Baghdad, and continues the tradition of logic and mathematics first at Córdoba, then at Toledo (where also appear such scientists as 27 and 28; see key to Figures 8.4 and 8.5). The first scientific star is the mathematician-astronomer al-Jayyami (25 in Figure 8.4) at Córdoba in the mid-1000s.

26. Barcelona had been ruled by the Christians since the 800s; in the 1100s it became one of the first places for translation from Arabic into Latin. Bar Hiyya is notable for the first Hebrew exposition of the Ptolemaic astronomy and for the first complete solution in Europe of the quadratic equation (*DSB*, 1981: 1:23), while his philosophy is a mixed Neoplatonism reminiscent of the Pure Brethren influence propagated by Ibn Gabirol at Saragossa. The two cities are 150 miles apart, and for centuries were the major outposts between which influences flowed across the Muslim-Christian frontier.

27. Maimonides himself (1956: 164) reports that he was acquainted with Jabir's son. The *Guide for the Perplexed* (pt. 2, chaps. 4–12) contains a section on astronomy.

28. See *EP* (1967: 4:267); *DSB* (1981: 5:591–592). Ibn Daud is sometimes identified with John of Seville; but John translated in Toledo about 1133–1143, whereas Ibn Daud and Gundissalinus came a generation later, in the 1160s (*DSB*, 1981: 15:174, 190).

29. Ibn Daud never mentions him, but it is unlikely that they did not know of each other, as they represented the opposing wings of the Jewish community on the reconciliation of philosophy and scripture.

30. At Saragossa, Muslim scientists and Jewish grammarians had had important networks in the previous century; here too was where Ibn Gabirol apparently brought Neoplatonism and astrological occultism from the Islamic network into Jewish philosophy, and where Bahya ibn Paquda probably flourished.

31. Meir ibn Megas (48 in the key to Figure 8.5), from the main Jewish academy of Lucena, was reputed to be Maimonides's teacher (Pelaez de Rosal, 1985: 137); like Ibn Daud, Meir had migrated to Toledo as the academy broke up under the Almohad conquest in 1148. If the young Maimonides studied with Meir at Toledo, it is not unlikely that he would have known Ibn Daud as well.

32. Note that Ibn Zaddiq was an official in Córdoba during Ibn Rushd's youth.

33. For instance, the existence of God; God's unity, perfection, and justice; the creation of the world; validity of prophecy; and survival of the soul after death (Fakhry, 1983: 281–283). Ibn Rushd goes on to argue, for example, that the Qur'an

nowhere says that creation did not take place from preexisting matter or in pre-existing time; creation consisted only of giving form to the world.

34. Ibn Daud states that he wrote his *Exalted Faith* in order to defend free will; this would make a sharp opposition to Ibn Gabirol's emanationism, in which everything is a manifestation or even an embodiment of the will of God. In countering this position, Ibn Daud produces a lengthy exposition of an Aristotelean universe (Sirat, 1985: 142–154).

35. Gilson (1944: 358); Fakhry (1983: 275, 292). Ibn Rushd's *Incoherence of the Incoherence,* against al-Ghazali, was known in the east; his Aristotle commentaries were not (Watt, 1985: 119).

36. When he was sent into exile in 1195, it was to Lucena, the old Jewish intellectual center (Fakhry, 1983: 272). Was this a deliberate slap on the part of his funda-mentalist Malikite enemies?

37. This connection to the Christian philosophers is even more direct in the case of Ibn Daud, who was the first to bring forth Aristoteleanism as an alternative to Neoplatonism. Ibn Daud apparently began his intellectual career by collaborating at Toledo with Gundissalinus on translating the Neoplatonists, Ibn Sina, and possibly Ibn Gabirol; this intimate familiarity with their texts, as well as with the Christian demand for idea imports, could then have motivated him to go on to criticize the Neoplatonist position and put forward Aristotle as an alternative.

38. One can see the change in the way linguistic lines shifted with the growing nationalism of the times. Virtually all of the Jewish philosophers wrote in Arabic up through Ibn Daud and Maimonides. The first step in nationalist reaction was to translate the Jewish philosophers into Hebrew: Judah ibn Tibbon (49 in Figure 8.5, father of Maimonides's translator Samuel ibn Tibbon, 56), fled the Almohads to southern France, and translated Bahya ibn Paquda, Halevi, and Gabirol into Hebrew (Sirat, 1985: 213). After 1200 the Jews composed their original works in Hebrew, or occasionally in Latin or a secular European language.

39. Like most of the historians of world philosophy, I am guilty of slighting the Byzantine philosophers. The consensus is that they were "scholars and exegetes rather than creative thinkers" (*EP,* 1967: 1:436). Kazhdan and Epstein (1985) do little to upset this judgment.

40. It is dangerous to draw parallels to our own day, since we lack the perspective of future generations on what philosophical movements mark important turning points in the long-run attention space. Imports of French and German philosophies into the anglophone world have brought local reputations for their importers; the effects on indigenous creativity remain to be seen. On the side of the exporters, see Lamont (1987) for evidence that Derrida's reputation was constructed more outside France than within its home network.

9. Medieval Christendom

1. On the organizational dynamics of the medieval church, see Southern (1970). For the papacy in the early period, see Morrison (1969: 205–360). On the monasteries, see Butler (1962); Knowles (1949).

2. Popes Innocent III (r. 1198–1216), Gregory IX (1227–1241), and Innocent IV (1243–1254) were especially powerful vis-à-vis secular rulers. Sources on papal organizational growth (Southern, 1970; Ullman, 1970; Kelley, 1986; Poole, 1915; Waley, 1961).

3. Ranking of philosophers into major, secondary, and minor is done according to their long-term influence, indexed by the amount of reference to them in numerous sources (Windelband, [1892] 1901; Geyer, 1928; Gilson, 1944; de Wulf, 1934–1947; Copleston, 1950–1977; Knowles, 1962; Weinberg, 1964; *EP*, 1967; *CHLMP*, 1982). The account of philosophical positions draws generally on these and other sources (Pieper, [1950], 1960; Evans, 1980; Paré, Brunet, and Tremblay, 1933; Southern, 1995; individual articles in *EP*, 1967, and *DSB*, 1981).

4. The debate over the Forms goes back to Plato's *Parmenides* and Aristotle's *Metaphysics*. Nominalism was upheld by Socrates' contemporary and rival Antisthenes, and later by some of the Stoics, who incorporated materials from the Cynic position flowing from Antisthenes (Weinberg, 1964: 80). The early medievals picked up the most prominent puzzle in the literature available to them, the texts on ancient logic.

5. In Figure 9.4 and the key these are 66, the translator and astrologer Michael Scotus; as well as 78, 79, 94, 95, 96, 97, and Albert's Dominican protégé, 92.

6. The number of Dominican houses by this time was equal to that of the Cistercians, while the Franciscan total was much greater (Southern, 1970: 285).

7. A few of the leading philosophers were Augustinian monks, such as Giles of Rome. The Cistercians reversed their anti-intellectual stance and established colleges at Paris and elsewhere from the 1240s, although they had no notable philosophers until the idiosyncratic Jean of Mirecourt a century later. There were also substantial numbers of Benedictines at the universities; to judge from the figures at Oxford (Cobban, 1988: 318–319), they were about two thirds of the friars' total, but they played no part in intellectual leadership. It was the Franciscans and Dominicans specifically, not the monks in general, who provided the creativity of this period. And they were a minority of the university students; again judging from Oxford, the friars made up about 10 percent of the total. They are important in philosophy in part because they almost all concentrated in theology, whereas two thirds of the secular clergy were studying canon or civil law (Cobban, 1988: 214–215).

8. The curriculum within the arts faculty (later to become known as the philosophical faculty), consisted of the *trivium* (grammar, rhetoric, logic) and the *quadrivium* (arithmetic, geometry, music—i.e., arithmetical theory of tones—and astronomy). The Christian schools had begun by taking over the compendium of knowledge at the end of the Roman era, combining respectively the contents of the rhetoric schools with the scientific curriculum of the Neo-Pythagoreans. The higher faculties derived from the distinctive structures of licensed professions which emerged in medieval Europe. Within Christendom, the messy and conflictual overlap between church and state made for separate professions of lawyers and theologians not found in China or Islam, nor in the pagan Greek and Roman schools, where lawyer-rhetorician was the primary profession but theologians did not exist in the

absence of a bureaucratic church. In Christendom medicine became a learned subject claiming the licensing privileges of the university corporation, again unlike in China and India, where it was a practice of private individuals or guilds of healers and magicians, and in Islam, where medicine was not admitted to the theological/legalist–dominated *madrasas*. As we shall see in Chapter 12, this differentiation of disciplines within the university was later to shape European intellectual life in a distinctive pathway, after the establishment of the research university in Germany around 1800.

9. The apex of papal power was during 1235–1248, when the German emperor was successfully excommunicated, defeated in war by papal allies, and deposed. The Germans were finally evicted from northern Italy in 1268 by a French army financed by the pope. In the 1270s the French king began to claim the right to tax the clergy for war expenses, which led to an open break in 1296–1303. This time the pope lost. In 1305 the new pope was a Frenchman, compliant with French policies, and in 1309 the Curia had moved to Avignon (Keen, 1968: 170–177, 207–221; Boase, 1933).

10. From here through the discussion of Ockham, we enter a progressively rarefying level of philosophical abstraction. The reader is invited to scan the section "Nominalism versus Realism of Universals" in Chapter 15 (pages 826–830) to keep tabs on the chess game of move and countermove in intellectual space.

11. Duns is a close parallel to Aquinas in this respect. Although there was opposition in the Dominican order, Aquinas was clearly the favorite of its dominant faction. As Albert's star pupil, Thomas was named the Dominicans' teacher at the papal Curia in Rome; the Minister General of the order personally directed him to write his great *Summa contra Gentiles*. When the Averroist controversy broke out in full force in the 1270s, Aquinas was sent back to Paris to combat it (Gilson, 1944: 526). Duns similarly came from the inner circles of his order. His family had been benefactors of the Franciscans for generations; his uncle was their Vicar General for Scotland, and young John Duns was taken into his uncle's priory. Extensively educated at Oxford and Paris in the 1280s and 1290s, he was personally sponsored by Gonsalvus of Spain, the Minister General of the Franciscan order. During these years he must have been exposed to the teaching and debates of Giles of Rome, Godfrey of Fontaines, and Henry of Ghent, and would have personally known fellow Franciscans Richard of Middleton and Peter John Olivi (Bettoni, 1961: 2–6). Scotus was a strong supporter of the pope in his struggles against the kings; in the major theological movement of the time, Scotus helped the pope in establishing the dogma of the Immaculate Conception of the Virgin Mary.

12. Ockham was likely a pupil, or at least a hearer, of Henry of Harclay (141 in Figure 9.4) at Oxford, who in turn probably heard Scotus at Paris. Harclay criticized Duns from a nominalist direction that Ockham was to radicalize. At Avignon, Ockham apparently lived in the Franciscan house with another critical philosopher, Walter of Chatton (147), with whom he carried on a continuing controversy. He also would have encountered there Duns Scotus's major disciple (143), Francis of Meyronnes (Gilson, 1944: 633–634; *EP*, 1967: 3:476–477; *CHLMP*, 1982: 863, 891).

13. Dante, from the anti-papal faction in Florence, was sympathetic to the Averroist worldview.

14. It contained stranger combinations yet, such as Fitz-Ralph (188 in Figure 9.6) of Balliol, who propounded a syncretism of Averroism and Augustinianism. Positions which had lost ground in the struggle for attention became a grab bag, alliances of the weak.

15. This network also ties to non-academic religious reformers such as Thomas More and Sebastian Franck. A generation back, the network was fed by Italian Humanist circles; Reuchlin derived his cultural capital from the Florence group, and the young Colet had corresponded with Ficino (*EP*, 1967: 2:138).

16. Popkin (1979: 37–43, 360–361); *EP* (1967: 5:366–368). Wuthnow (1989: 97–98) points out that the presence of a local *parlement* in Bordeaux kept the city orthodox, since the dominant nobility throughout Europe generally had an interest in maintaining the traditional status order of Catholicism. In Toulouse, where Montaigne probably had studied, an insurrection had been put down in 1562, and hundreds of Protestants were executed.

17. This is emphasized throughout *CHLMP* (1982). The creativity of the nominalists apparently lasted two generations, dissipating by the late 1300s. It is possible that later advances occurred but have been ignored by historians, since this period of late scholasticism has not been much studied. In any case, this obliviousness to nominalist innovation started very early, with its contemporaries.

18. The sheer complexity of argument tended to bury it. The works of Dullaert of Ghent (315 in the key to Figure 9.7), at Paris in the early 1500s, "summarize in great detail (and usually with hopelessly involved logical argument) the teachings of Oxford 'calculatores' such as Thomas Bradwardine, William Heytesbury, and Richard Swineshead; of Paris 'terminists' such as Jean Buridan, Albert of Saxony, and Nicole Oresme; and of Italian authors such as James of Forli, Simon of Lendenaria, and Peter of Mantua—while not neglecting the more realist positions of Walter Burley and Paul of Venice. The logical subtlety of Dullaert's endless dialectics provoked considerable adverse criticism from Vives (Dullaert's student) and other humanists" (*DSB*, 1981: 9:237). Two generations later, the leading Aristotelean in Italy, Zabarella (352), at the great University of Padua, discussed Aristotelean physics in complete ignorance of the work of the Merton College and Buridan groups (*EP*, 1967: 8:366).

19. The failure rate for the 1200s is skewed upward by several failures in the 1290s; prior to that point the success rate was quite high. Estimates of undercounting of "paper universities," which received charters but failed to come into existence, probably make the failure rate for the 1400s 10 to 15 percent too low; see Rashdall (1936: 2:325–331). Enrollment data from Rashdall (1936: 2:149, 171, 178–191); Stone (1974b: 91); Simon (1966: 245).

20. The military and political struggle between pope and emperor during the 1200s probably explains why there were no universities chartered there during that period. The Italian ambitions of the emperor finally collapsed in the 1340s, as the papacy weakened as well. Soon thereafter Prague University was founded, with charters from both emperor and pope.

10. Cross-Breeding Networks and Rapid-Discovery Science

1. When not otherwise cited, biographical and network information throughout Chapters 10–14 comes from the relevant articles in *DSB* and *EP* as well as other basic sources (Copleston, 1950–1977; Merz, [1904–1912] 1965; Heer, [1953] 1968; *Chambers Biographical Dictionary;* 1984; Popkin, 1979; Johnston, 1972; Schnädelbach, 1984; Toews, 1980, 1993; Köhnke, 1991; Willey, 1978; Lindenfeld, 1980; Ben-David and Collins, 1966; Dickey, 1993; Ayer, 1982; Coffa, 1991; Waismann, 1979; Dummett, 1981; Wang, 1987; Kline, 1972; Boyer, 1985; Levy, 1981; Spiegelberg, 1982; Gadamer, 1985; Fabiani, 1988; Cohen-Solal, 1987; Boschetti, 1985).

2. Michael Mahoney (private communication) points to a number of overlapping Parisian circles, in addition to the Mersenne-Montmor groups, around Le Pailleur, Thévenot, and Bourdelot, and materially sponsored by the royal minister Colbert; collectively these became in 1666 the basis of the Académie des Sciences. Figure 10.1 omits most purely scientific academies and circles.

3. As in previous chapters, the ranking of philosophers as major, secondary, and minor is based on their long-term influence; this is estimated by the relative space which they receive in various histories (Hegel, [1820–1830] 1971; Windelband, [1892] 1901; Lévi-Bruhl, 1899; Bentley, 1939; Heer, [1953] 1968; Copleston, 1950–1977; Marias, [1941] 1966; *EP,* 1967; Passmore, 1968; Kneale and Kneale, 1984). On the growth of the European philosophical canon as viewed by anglophone scholarship, cf. Kuklick (1984).

4. Structurally this is the same condition I noted in Chapter 9 in comparing stagnant with creative periods: an intersection of overlapping and rival circles. The material improvement of transportation and communications in the 1600s broadened the geographical zone in which such an intersection of circles could take place.

5. It is impossible to avoid some anachronism in terminology. "Science" took on its restricted modern meaning in English after 1847. Latin *scientia* was equivalent to Greek *episteme,* knowledge in any realm. Some term is needed for making historical comparisons, precisely so that we can see what is distinctive about certain activities in various periods. "Science" enables us to focus jointly on the several activities of collecting information by observations of nature, especially in the well-defined occupations of astronomy and medicine, and the equally distinctive activity of mathematical calculation and measurement.

6. Price (1986). Sources for discussion of various methods by which speed of scientific discovery may be measured (Cole, 1983; Griffith, 1988; Cozzens, 1989; Leydesdorff and Amsterdamska, 1990; Collins, 1994). The rapid-discovery mode set in earlier in some scientific fields than others, and the rate appears to have accelerated several times, most recently since the 1920s. On differences in consensus, see Cole, Cole, and Dietrich (1978); Hargens and Hagstrom (1982).

7. Highly accurate calculations of pi made between 220 and 500 C.E. were variously and often inaccurately recorded in the standard textbooks of the T'ang and Sung, which sometimes gave the traditional value of pi as 3 (Institute, 1983: 86–87, 35,

38; Mikami, 1913: 45–58; Qian, 1985: 62–63; Ho, 1985: 125–127; Chen, 1987: 77–85; Li and Du, 1987). Algebra reached sophisticated methods in the solution of higher-order equations between 1200 and Chu Shih-chieh's work in 1303; fifty years later textbooks had reverted to an elementary level of arithmetic (Ho, 1985: 106). In the 1500s those who still recorded the Sung "celestial element" algebra were no longer able to understand it (Mikami, 1913: 110). For other instances of loss of advanced work, see Ho (1985: 72, 77); Needham (1959: 31, 33); Mikami (1913: 37–39).

8. In India, Aryabhata I (late 400s C.E.) expounded two astronomical systems; shortly thereafter Varahamihira (ca. 500 C.E.) described five systems, one based on Vedic astrology and four on Greek models (*DSB*, 1981: 15:533–632). Chinese astronomy was always divided among competing models. In the Han dynasty there was a struggle between advocates of the *kaitian* (hemispherical dome) and *huntian* (celestial sphere) cosmologies; in addition, two other systems were known. The *huntian* model became dominant in the astronomical bureaus of dynasties after 550 C.E., but there continued to be advocates of a rival model as late as the Sung. During the T'ang dynasty, there were three different schools of Indian astronomers employed at the imperial observatory, but without influence on Chinese astronomers. In the Yuan and Ming dynasties, there were Arab astronomers in official service, but Chinese astronomers ignored the Arab-Ptolemaic epicyclic planetary theory (Needham, 1959: 171–436; Sivin, 1969; Ho, 1985: 82, 129, 161–168; Mikami, 1913: 101–106).

9. There is evidence of around five competing research groups in a scientific specialty (Price, [1963] 1986: 130–133).

10. Thus Boyle's vacuum pump could not be successfully imitated by anyone who had not physically used an earlier exemplar (Shapin and Shaffer, 1985: 229–230, 281). Harry Collins (1974) emphasizes that tacit knowledge of how to do research must be transmitted by a personal network of craft-like apprenticeship, since it cannot be encoded in purely verbal instructions. Latour's (1987) depiction of science as a network of human plus non-human actors may well anthropomorphize the natural world, but it has this much justification: research-front science includes an ongoing network of scientists together with the genealogy of machines on which they are parasites, and vice versa.

11. Many examples are given in Braudel ([1967] 1973: 244–324) in which technologies stagnated for hundreds of years, including during the European centuries of the scientific revolution. And even where there were periods of technological innovation, they did not spill over into lineages of scientific research technology unless they were carried by intellectual networks. Thus the periods of innovation in weaponry, shipping, and construction engineering at various times in the history of Hellenistic Greece, the Islamic world, and medieval Christendom did not connect to intellectuals or become rapid-discovery science. See references in Collins (1986: 77–116).

12. The number of mathematicians treated in *DSB* (1981) active in each third of a century is as follows:

1200s: 3–4–7
1300s: 5–6–0
1400s: 2–3–10
1500s: 17–18–26
1600s: 37–44–23
1700s: 19–39–34

Moreover, before 1500, most of the names listed are persons who recorded any mathematics even without originality; the criterion for listing shifts over in the 1500s to original contributions.

13. The first use of the equal sign (=) was in Recorde's 1551 book on elementary commercial arithmetic; what would become the modern notation for operations was popularized in England by Harriot's 1621 textbook. Neither book contained any original mathematics. On the history of notation generally, see Cajori (1928).

14. See Figure 10.1. The other major philosophers are Bacon, Hobbes, Spinoza, and Locke. If we look not at overlaps between the scientific and philosophical networks but at personal contacts among their members, we find that all of the major philosophers are within one link of a significantly creative scientist, and 12 of 14 secondary philosophers are within two links of a scientist. The only major philosopher who is not an active scientist, Locke, is a medical doctor, directly connected with 2 scientific stars and a host of other scientists. The fact of their working in science does not imply that the work of these philosophers is itself a significant contribution; Bacon's experiments, for example, led to no important discoveries. Here I use the strong criterion, indicated in note 19, for identifying scientists. I will often use the term *science* to include both science and mathematics; it should be obvious from the context when I am using it in a more restricted sense, exclusive of the activities of mathematicians.

15. During 1700–1900, 5 of 13 major philosophers were active in science (Berkeley, Kant, Schelling, Peirce, James), and 10 of 13 are within one link of an important scientist. Of secondary philosophers, 14 of 46 are scientists, and 33 are within two links of one.

16. We see this by comparing Figure 10.2 (network of Greek mathematicians) with Figures 3.1 to 3.8 (network of Greek philosophers). Sources for Greek mathematicians (Heath, [1921] 1981; Smith, 1951; Ball, [1908] 1960; Cajori, 1928; Knorr, 1975; Neugebauer, 1957; Boyer, 1985; Kline, 1972; van der Waerden, 1975; *DSB*, 1981).

17. This may be traced in the key to Figure 3.4 by noting the figures marked "medicine," beginning with the merging of the Hippocratic lineage with the network around Aristotle and the Alexandria schools (71, 75, 76, 108). These connections are not depicted in Figure 3.4 itself to avoid overcomplicating the diagram.

18. As we saw in Chapter 8, the creativity of this original Baghdad group derived not simply from Greek imports but from the cosmopolitan situation which combined these with materials from Babylonian sects and Indian astronomers, resulting in al-Khwarizmi's encyclopedic synthesis in the early 800s. By the generations of

965–1035, this elementary algebra had been developed to the high points of world mathematics at the time, al-Buzjani's Diophantine equations and al-Karaji's theory of algebraic calculation and algebra of polynomials, breaking with geometrical representations into an arithmeticized algebra. The Spanish network began around 965 with migrants from the Pure Brethren, numerological cosmologists branching from the Baghdad scientific network. Within a few generations this spread to the Jews (initially via numerology); it blossomed simultaneously into creative astronomy (e.g., al-Bitruji's revision of the Ptolemaic system in the late 1100s) and the work of the major Jewish and Muslim philosophers. The scientific-philosophical network was disrupted in the eastern region around 1100. It was reestablished by Jewish travelers back from Spain: Abraham Ibn Ezra and Maimonides, who linked to the network around the Jewish doctor and astronomer Abu-l-Barakat and onward to the major astronomer al-Tusi and his lineage. The Jews played the role of cosmopolitan transmitters twice, not only to Christian Europe but also to the high point of Iranian Muslim science.

19. If we use the loose criterion of writing on some aspect of natural science, we would have to include 8 of 11 major philosophers (72 percent) and 19 of 48 secondary (40 percent) in medieval Christendom. By a stricter criterion (formulating principles in astronomy or physics, collecting naturalistic observations, or making at least crude calculations), we still find 45 percent of major and 23 percent of secondary Christian philosophers active in science. For comparison let us use a strong criterion: contributing actively to astronomy, mathematics, medicine, or naturalist observation. In Greece, 14 of 28 major philosophers were themselves scientists; in medieval Islam (including Jews), 5 of 11; in Europe, 1600–1900, 10 of 19. The percentages are similar in all four places: Greece, 50 percent; Islam/Jews, 45 percent; Christendom, 45 percent; Europe, 53 percent. Throughout the West, the most influential philosophers tend to be more interested in science than less influential philosophers. Among secondary philosophers, the percentages of overlap are lower everywhere: Greece, 28 percent (19 of 68); Islam, 20 percent (8 of 41); Christendom, 23 percent (11 of 48); and Europe, 28 percent (17 of 60). If we extend the perimeter to two links from the scientific network, the pattern is similar everywhere: for major philosophers, Greece, 82 percent; Islam, 82 percent, Christendom, 73 percent, Europe, 89 percent; for secondaries, Greece, 50 percent, Christendom, 44 percent, and Islam, 44 percent though here Europe stands out with 76 percent within the periphery of scientists.

20. Eminence among scientists and mathematicians is measured in the same way as for philosophers: by the relative amount of space devoted to them in histories of those periods.

21. In China, of 25 major philosophers, 6 (24 percent) were involved in some way in mathematical science, for the most part very tangentially. Among secondary philosophers, 7 of 61 (11 percent) were involved in astronomy, and only one of them, Liu Hsin in the Han dynasty, was an important astronomer. An additional 6 names of astronomers overlap the list of minor philosophers, making up less than 2 percent of the total. Extending the network outward, we find a mathematical

scientist within two links for 16 of 25 major philosophers (64 percent) and for 15 of 61 secondaries (25 percent). If we start from the side of the mathematicians and astronomers, of the 12 major figures, none has any direct contact with philosophers important enough to be listed even as minor figures, and only 1 (the state astronomer Shen Kua, during the Sung dynasty) is within two links of a known philosopher. Of 9 mathematical scientists of secondary importance, only 1 has any philosophical contacts. By comparison, 63 percent of major Islamic scientists (12 of 19) are within two links of a known philosopher. Sources on Chinese mathematicians (Mikami, 1913; Needham, 1959; Sivin, 1969; Libbrecht, 1973; Nakayama and Sivin, 1973; Swetz and Kao, 1977; Graham, 1978; *CHC*, 1979, 1986; *DSB*, 1981; Institute, 1983; Ho, 1985; Qian, 1985; Chen, 1987; Li and Du, 1987).

22. The exception which proves the rule is the Buddhist monk I-hsing, the only important Buddhist mathematician and astronomer. He worked for the emperor at the time of the abortive Buddhist near-theocracy in the early 700s, and in the same temple where the great Hua-yen philosophy was created in the previous generation.

23. The method was revived and extended in Tokugawa Japan, leading to indigenous development of the calculus (Smith and Mikami, 1914). Here again we see a brief confluence of networks. Mathematics was carried in a network of samurai, bureaucratic officials of the shogun, and other high-ranking lords in positions concerned with accounts, astronomy, and other practical administration. By itself this was not conducive to intellectualized mathematics; but by the 1670s, these mathematician-officials were also running private schools in Edo and Kyoto, similar to the competitive expansion of Confucian schools which underpinned the philosophical outburst of the same period. Merely practical considerations were transcended by social competition over prestige; much as in Italy during the time of Tartaglia and Cardano, leading mathematicians attracted pupils by publishing problems and challenging others to solve them. Topics went far beyond practical problems, beginning with magic squares and circles, escalating to solving equations of very high degree. The most important developments from circle measurement problems to an integral calculus were made in the school of Seki Kowa from the 1670s through the early 1700s. Methods were kept secret, although occasionally spilled out in publications during the late 1700s. In the key period of innovation, the mathematical networks connected with the philosophical centers. Seki worked for the same Edo lord who employed the somewhat younger Ogyu Sorai; a Seki grandpupil became head of the Mito school. The mathematical lineages continued down through the early 1800s, but the connection with philosophy was not taken further; mathematics did not become invoked as an epistemological ideal, and mathematical methods were not generalized as abstract principles. Mathematical innovation stagnated after the mid-1700s; most likely the increasing bureaucratization of education in the later Tokugawa had a restricting effect on mathematics just as it did on philosophy. The wide expansion of low-status practical training schools for commercial mathematics, stimulated by the growth of the commercial

economy, remained separate from the samurai schools, and had no effect on innovation in abstract mathematics (Dore, 1965).

24. We see this in the surrounding conditions of several episodes of takeoff in *intellectual* mathematics: Athens established a monetized retail market in the late 400s B.C.E., and from 330 to 100 B.C.E. the international grain trade, centered on Alexandria, broke out of the usual government-administered exchange into the only competitive price-setting markets in antiquity (Polanyi, 1977: 238–251; Finley, 1973). Tokugawa Japan was a period of commercial capitalist boom; Italian and German cities of the 1400s and 1500s were commercial and banking centers. In the latter two cases we know explicitly that numeracy spread widely in the urban population, and there were many commercial schools teaching practical mathematics. Swetz (1987) and, in a Marxian version, Sohn-Rethel (1978) argue on the basis of this correlation that capitalism produced the mathematical worldview.

25. In Tokugawa Japan a rapidly expanding capitalist market, based on Weberian structural conditions, had very little innovation in machinery but a great deal of innovation in refinements of production for specialized market niches (Morris-Suzuki, 1994).

26. Rheticus in turn visited Cardano in 1545, and Cardano dedicated his great mathematical work *Ars Magna* to Osiander. The work was published in Nuremberg by the printer of *De Revolutionibus* (Blumenberg, 1987: 340). Cardano, in contact with virtually every innovative network, was also a friend of Vesalius. Historical sources on mathematicians of this period (*DSB*, 1981; Kline, 1972; Boyer, 1985; Smith, 1951; Cardan, [1575] 1962).

27. Michael Mahoney (personal communication) suggests that Copernicus's new model was worked out within the long-standing Ptolemaic tradition of astronomy, eliminating some spheres and thereby better preserving Aristotle's cosmology; thus Copernicus belongs to a "reestablished classical tradition." Copernicus differs from Oresme in that he actually worked out the mathematics in detail; along the way, as I noted earlier, he took part in developing new trigonometric tables to speed up calculations.

28. Brunelleschi and Alberti became concerned with the geometry of perspective in the early 1400s, and Piero della Francesca treated the subject in a mathematical treatise in 1478. The painters too were raising their status by connecting their manual craft to an academic field; the result was to widen audiences and increase the focus of attention all around.

29. Notice that Descartes met Beeckman in 1618, before either of them did the work that would make them famous: yet another case of a network forming a node which promotes the later success of its members.

30. The intention is plain despite continuities in terminology. The new science is variously referred to as "natural" or "mechanical philosophy," or sometimes merely "philosophy" (e.g., Bacon *De Dig.* 1.3). As did others, Descartes (in *Principles*) distinguished his "Philosophy" from "that which is taught in the schools" (Descartes, [1644] 1983: xxvi).

31. Here we see one of the weaknesses of the Burtt-Koyré thesis that the scientific

revolution derives from the metaphysical assumptions of a Neoplatonic cosmology. It is not only that many of the scientific innovators were not following this particular metaphysics, or were more concerned with the adequacy of technical matters (Hatfield, 1990). The numerous competing strands of late scholastic, Humanist, and occultist philosophies between 1400 and 1600 constituted an intellectual field without a focus of attention; these are structural conditions for stagnation rather than for the dynamism of discovery. The main effect of philosophy on the mathematical and scientific revolutions was on the level of social structures; math and science networks were stimulated to make their arguments on a higher level of generality when they intersected with the networks of theologians and philosophers. The importance of this contact is not primarily through the transmission of philosophical capital into math and science, but in transmission of the emotional energy of intellectual competition characteristic of the philosophical networks.

32. Kangro (1968). Like Harvey, Jungius was a medical doctor from the Padua network.

33. Upheaval in the material bases of intellectual life fosters creativity in several directions at once. The last glory of Latin stylistics sprang up in the generations just before Bacon and Descartes: the anti-Ciceronian and Attic prose movements, which encompassed Montaigne and his teachers and lasted until the time of Milton (Croll, 1966). Descartes and especially Bacon were noted Latin prose stylists, along with their other accomplishments. As we have seen in the case of Greek philosophy, there is creativity in the moment of closing down an intellectual structure as well of opening one up.

34. Viète and Descartes's father were both members of the Parlement of Brittany, and Viète was counselor at Tours in the 1590s, near Descartes's home (*DSB*, 1981: 4:51, 14:52). The fame of Viète's mathematics may have made an impression on Descartes in this way. Notice the parallel instances showing the public prestige of mathematical puzzle-solving: in 1593 the Dutch ambassador put a mathematical challenge to the French court involving an equation of the forty-fifth degree, which Viète solved. Descartes first became interested in mathematics through a challenge to solve a geometrical problem announced on a public placard in Breda, Holland, in 1618. It was on this occasion that he met Beeckman (Gaukroger, 1995: 68).

35. As Michael Mahoney (personal communication) puts it, Descartes's symbolism "was essentially different from earlier systems of notation. It was *operational*. That is, the symbols revealed through their structure the operations being carried on them, so that one did the mathematics by manipulating the symbols . . . Moreover, unlike cossist algebra, Viète's and Descartes' systems symbolized both knowns and unknowns, making it possible then to unfold the structure of equations viewed as general relations." Descartes had a "drive for generality."

36. Hatfield (1990: 159). Descartes does have a place for empirical observation, in the sense that "the truths that can be deduced from . . . Principles" include many which will not be noticed until "certain specific observations" are made. For the advancement of science, experiments must be made by those who know how to unite their results with a deductive system (Descartes [1644] 1983: xxvii).

11. Secularization and Philosophical Meta-territoriality

1. Compare the general model of political revolutions in Skocpol (1979) and Gold-stone (1991).
2. In Figure 9.7, this is the lineage of prominent Scotists and nominalists (see 295 and 299 in the key), of whom the most notable was John Mair (314), the teacher of the reformer John Knox; Mair's successors include Dullaert of Ghent (315), Thomist natural philosopher and editor of Buridan; Vives; and the leading Thomists of the period—all of whom were now teaching in Spain—Crockoert, Vitoria, Cano, de Soto, and Medina (335, 337, 338, 340, 341).
3. Aquinas had held that only in God are existence and essence united. Suarez held that this is true of finite beings as well. This sharpens the problem of how to characterize contingency, which led Leibniz to his distinction among kinds of necessity, logical and physical (Funkenstein, 1986: 118–121, 198).
4. Kagan (1974); Collins (1979: 4, 92). By comparison to Spain, consider the fact that England also was in an educational boom period during 1580–1670, when university students were about 1 percent of the late teen population, according to Stone's (1974a) calculations, a ratio which dropped back to one third this level in the 1700s. In both Spain and England, the educational boom went along with an outburst of intellectual activity.
5. Bérulle is one of the main connections to Spanish movements. He was ambassador to Spain, and introduced the Carmelites—Saint Teresa's order—into France. The conflict of the Oratorians versus the Jesuits structurally continued earlier battles in Spain (*EP*, 1967: 2:345–355; Ariew, 1990). See 31, 88, and 134 in the key to Figure 10.1.
6. Truchet (1967). The contemporary Spanish Jesuit, Balthazar Gracian, whose *Art of Prudence* (1647) is a manual on how to survive in a treacherous world by using deceit, had provided a model admired by Mme. de Sablé. Here we see the inner affinity of Jansenists and Jesuits beneath their surface antagonism.
7. In the same way the Cambridge Platonists, who published most of their works during this time, were absorbed in the flux of attention by more striking formulations of spiritual primacy. Henry More's tutee Lady Anne Conway formulated a monistic ontology of spirits emanating from God, with matter at the lowest level as congealed spirit (Audi, 1995: 162, 513). Conway made little impact on the attention space: in part from sexist disregard of women, in part from her conversion to Quakerism, and above all because this Neoplatonist-sounding position was upstaged. On the other side, Locke produced the most defensible version of the primacy of extended matter, which eclipsed the earlier efforts on this side of the turf: those of Gassendi, who was not wholeheartedly modernist or secularist, and Hobbes, whose reputation survives because of his political philosophy rather than his ontology.
8. In Figure 10.1, note in the network 19, 31, 43–45, 97–98 and their ties. On the episodes recounted in the text, see Popkin (1979) and the relevant articles in *EP* (1967). The first round of controversy began with the arrival of Uriel da Costa, a crypto-Jew (i.e., forced convert to Christianity) who had studied at Coimbra, which

had been the Portuguese base for the Jesuit philosophers Molina and Suarez. In 1624 da Costa interpreted religion as a human creation. For this he was excommunicated by the Jews and his books burned by the Dutch; he committed suicide in 1640.

9. On the gradual development of Spinoza's monism; see Funkenstein (1986: 81–87).

10. Brown (1984: 15–31); Funkenstein (1986: 118–123). The intellectual energy generated by this Leipzig milieu is shown in Figure 10.1: Leibniz's teacher Weigel had previously taught Pufendorf, who became a famous legal philosopher and, like Leibniz, proponent of universal law. Another of Leibniz's teachers was the father of the other notable German philosopher of this generation; this was Thomasius, who began as a natural lawyer, converted to Pietism in 1694, and produced a philosophy of mystical vitalism. Again there was a structural rivalry; the Pietists, who were the equivalent of the Catholic fideists in the context of Protestant Germany, became the main opponents of Leibniz's lineage, including Wolff and his followers.

11. Broad (1975: 43); Mahoney (1990). Leibniz was publishing his "calculus of transcendent qualities" and his new dynamics between 1684 and 1694, just the years in which he worked out his philosophical system: *Discourse on Metaphysics* (1684–85); correspondence with Arnauld (1686–1690); *New System* (1695).

12. "Space is nothing but the order of co-existing things and time the order of successive things" (quoted in Brown, 1984: 147; see also 115). In keeping with this point, Leibniz criticizes Newton's physics for assuming a frame of empty space, just as he rejects his theory of gravity as action-at-a-distance, since a vacuum does not exist in Leibniz's metaphysics.

13. Hobbes's important works were all produced at a rather advanced age: his contribution to Descartes's *Meditations on the First Philosophy* in 1641 (age 53); *De Cive*, his first published treatise on political power, 1642 (54); *Leviathan* 1651 (63); *De Corpore*, containing his most thorough scientific materialism, 1655 (67). As in other cases, creativity had nothing to do with age, but with the moment of contact with the central intellectual networks. On Hobbes's career trajectory, see Macpherson (1968); Shapin and Schaffer (1985); Lynch (1991).

14. Locke took over some of Cudworth's arguments straightforwardly. His argument in the *Essay* (4.10) for the existence of God is identical to Cudworth's: that nothing can come from nothing, and the existence of something implies the existence of an eternal creator (Copleston, 1950–1977: 5:58; Locke, [1690] 1959: bk. 4.10). This is the only point, along with the self-evident existence of the self, on which Locke admits knowledge derived other than from the senses.

15. Juan de Prado, who had been excommunicated from the synagogue in 1656 along with Spinoza, supported natural religion and was attacked by Orobio de Castro, who defended Jewish orthodoxy with Cartesian and Spinozaist weapons, a geometric sequence of proofs. Orobio wielded the same weapons against Christianity, and Locke was present at a debate in Amsterdam in 1684 on this topic, which he reviewed in one of his earliest publications (*EP*, 1967: 5:552). Bayle, not yet famous at the time when Locke met him, was similarly stimulated by the milieu of Jewish controversies over natural religion.

16. Leibniz stresses the argument for innate ideas in his *Discourse,* written in 1686 but left unpublished; Locke's *Essay* was completed the following year.

17. Lord Herbert of Cherbury, who had been English ambassador to France during the religious maneuvers of the 1620s, had argued for a minimalist religion based on common notions and the common consent of mankind; this argument was put forward in 1645, amidst the fervors of the Civil War, as a critique of religious authoritarianism. Locke has a network contact here too; Locke's friend at the time he wrote the first draft of his *Essay* (during his stay in France in the late 1670s) was Cherbury's grandson Thomas Herbert, who as earl of Pembroke was to receive the dedication of the publication (Fraser, [1894] 1959: xxviii). Pembroke later received the dedication of Berkeley's *Principles of Human Knowledge* in 1710—an indication of the emerging split within the network of Locke's successors.

18. An exemplary figure is Dryden (110 in the key to Figure 10.1). A supporter of Cromwell in the 1650s, he shifted to the Royalist court thereafter and was made poet laureate and court historian. In the early 1680s he wrote poetic satires defending the king's party against the Whigs; in 1685 he followed court fashion and converted to Catholicism. Even with the Glorious Revolution he landed on his feet; in the 1690s he launched the dramatic career of Congreve (later recipient of Whig sinecures), and protected the Deist Blount.

19. These writers not only gave prestige to their political patrons but propagandized on their behalf as well. Swift in London during 1710–1714 edited the Tory party magazine. In the opposing literary circle, Addison made his reputation for poems celebrating Whig military victory and wrote the Whig attack on the Treaty of Utrecht which brought down the Tory ministry in 1714. Steele started as a gazeteer for Lord Harley, and edited Whig periodicals including *Tatler* and *Spectator.* Addison was rewarded by becoming secretary of state; Steele received a parliamentary seat.

20. The lineage of Boulainvilliers's teachers goes back to the controversies over natural religion at Amsterdam in the 1650s. After La Peyrère's scandalous pre-Adamite thesis got him arrested, he recanted and took refuge in the Oratorian college at Juilly. There Richard Simon continued La Peyrère's project, producing in 1678 a historical critique of the Old Testament, which was in turn banned by Bossuet. In the next generation Simon's student was Boulainvilliers. In Boulainvilliers's philosophy the cogito implies a universal Being wider than matter; on this Boulainvilliers erects a natural religion, in which the body after death returns to universal matter while the soul remains an idea in the infinite mind (*EP,* 1967: 1:354; Roger, 1964: 6–7; Heer, [1953] 1968: 188).

21. Burrage (1993); Ariès (1962: 195–237); Heilbron (1994). The same collapse of enrollments and loss of professional credentialing is characteristic of the universities in England after 1670. In both places intellectuals operated in secular life and scorned the formalities of university lectures and examinations as "silly and obsolete," "childish and useless exercises" (Green, 1969: 50; Stone, 1974b).

22. Condillac, the one member of the circle of Encyclopedists who came from a university background in theology, was the one who took up a traditional philosophical topic, although he did it using the new anti-metaphysical capital imported

from Britain by his network fellows, building a theory of mind on Locke and Newton.

23. I place "modern" in quotes to indicate that this is a historically relative usage. The alliance among religious and political liberalism and science, and among their opposites on the conservative side, was at its height in the Enlightenment and in the 1800s. The alliance has been breaking down in our own times, beginning with the existentialists and continuing through the postmodernists.

24. *DSB* (1981: 10:42–102); Westfall [1981]. Newton had early contacts with the main mathematical network too. His teacher Barrow had been a Royalist, unlike the Oxford scientists; ousted from his Cambridge fellowship in 1655, he toured the Continent and met the leading mathematicians, likely including Fermat and Roberval. Although Barrow's substantive influence may not have been great, Newton was thereby made aware of the forefront of mathematical problems, and it was upon this terrain that he made his youthful contributions in the mid-1660s to the calculus and infinite series. Barrow recommended Newton as his successor when he gave up the Lucasian professorship of mathematics in 1669 to take the professorship in divinity. This suggests the order of precedence at Cambridge at this time: theology was regarded as more significant than science, and Newton shows the same priorities in his own work before 1684.

25. Berkeley was very young compared to other philosophers at their height of creativity: 25 years old when he published his masterwork, *Principles of Human Knowledge.* A similar case is Schelling, who burst on the philosophical scene in Germany at the age of 20. In both cases there was early contact with a core network, at a time when the structural situation was rapidly changing. For contrast there are the aged Hobbes and Locke. Young or old, whoever gets onto the central turf at those moments reaps the fame.

26. See Hume's *Letters* (Greig, 1932: 23). Hume presents himself in the Introduction of his *Treatise* as a follower of Locke, Shaftesbury, Butler, and the other Deists. In a private letter in 1737, however, he points to Descartes, Malebranche, Bayle, and Berkeley as keys to his *Treatise,* suggesting the wider intellectual sphere at which he was aiming. This was just the time when Newton's calculus of fluxions was coming under attack for its glib assumptions about infinitesimals. In 1734 Berkeley joined the fray with an extended critique, following the points he had raised against mathematics in his *New Theory of Vision.* Hume studied at Edinburgh with Newtonian mathematicians, probably including Colin Maclauren (122 in the key to Figure 10.1), who had extended Newton's geometrical proofs and gotten his chair at Newton's recommendation, and who led the Newtonian response to Berkeley in 1742 (Kitcher, 1984: 232–240; Jesseph, 1993). Hume picked up the theme of Berkeley's attack; in the beginning of his *Treatise* he devotes considerable attention to arguing against the infinite divisibility of time and space (i.e., against the Maclauren-Newton position) and in favor of indivisible points, which must be matters of experience if they are to exist at all. He criticizes geometry (Maclauren's specialty) as a science of no great certainty, since it must proceed via induction from the senses, and concludes that all knowledge, including that of mathematics, is only probable (Hume, [1739–40] 1969: 74–75, 176).

27. By the 1770s and 1780s, these included Hutton, whose geology overturned biblical chronology, and Lord Monboddo, who produced early speculations on the evolution of humans from the apes. Sources on the social history of Scotland (*CMH*, 1902–1911: 6:117; Daiches, Jones, and Jones, 1986; Sher, 1985; Camic, 1983).

28. Hume was only in his mid-twenties when he wrote his *Treatise* in the 1730s. Once again, age is important only as it coincides with structural opportunity.

12. The German University Revolution

1. These are Bergson, Dewey, Moore, Russell, Wittgenstein, Carnap, Husserl, and Heidegger; at least another 12 are in the running for secondary: Croce, Schlick, Meinong, Scheler, Cassirer, Rickert, McTaggart, Whitehead, Alexander, Santayana, G. H. Mead, and C. I. Lewis. For sources, see Chapter 10, notes 1 and 3. Comparing Figures 10.1 and 11.1, we see that the number of major philosophers in any one generation in Europe is never more than 3—a pattern in keeping with that for medieval Christendom, Islam, India, China, and Greece. By my standard method of ranking by amount of attention given in comprehensive histories, for 1865–1900 the number of major philosophers is 5 (Peirce, James, Frege, Bradley, and Nietzsche). For secondary philosophers, the number calculated rises for 1835–1865 to 12, for 1865–1900 to 9, and 1900–1935 to 12. These numbers are as high as or higher than those for even the most active generations in all of past history—the generation of 335–300 B.C.E. in Greece, when there were 8 secondaries, and 1265–1300 in medieval Christendom, when there were 9. It appears that we are gradually losing perspective on the fifth generation back from our own, that of 1835–1865, and almost certainly on the 1865–1900 generation. Within the next few generations of our future, some of these major figures will fall to secondary historical influence, and some secondaries to minor.

   Unlike earlier network figures in the book, those in Chapters 12–14 list everyone by name and thus do not distinguish rankings by capitalization and key numbers. For convenience, what follows is a list of European philosophers ranked major (all capitals) and secondary by generation: 1600: BACON, Suarez, Campanella, Herbert of Cherbury, Boehme, Grotius; 1635: DESCARTES, HOBBES, More, Cudworth, Arnauld, Mersenne, Gassendi, Pascal; 1665: SPINOZA, LEIBNIZ, LOCKE, Malebranche, Bayle, Thomasius; 1700: BERKELEY, Shaftesbury, Hutcheson, Wolff, Vico; 1735: HUME, ROUSSEAU, Voltaire, Montesquieu, d'Holbach, Diderot, d'Alembert, Condillac, Butler, Adam Smith, Reid; 1765: KANT, FICHTE, Hamann, Lessing, Herder, Jacobi, Schiller, Paley, Bentham, Condorcet; 1800: SCHELLING, HEGEL, SCHOPENHAUER, Schleiermacher, Herbart, Maine de Biran, Cousin, Saint-Simon; 1835: J. S. MILL, Spencer, Huxley, Newman, Kierkegaard, Emerson, Comte, Renouvier, Marx, Engels, Lotze, Fechner, Boole; 1865: PEIRCE, JAMES, BRADLEY, NIETZSCHE, FREGE, Green, Bosanquet, Royce, Wundt, Mach, Brentano, Dilthey, von Hartmann, Hermann Cohen.

2. In anglophone philosophy, the canonical reputations of Berkeley and Hume were not established until the 1870s; until then Reid and Dugald Stewart were better known (Kaufmann, 1966: 277–278; Kuklick, 1984).

3. Intellectual movements in this respect resemble other social movements (Marwell and Oliver, 1993).

4. Goethe on his travels in 1774 sought out Lavater, and it was on their voyage together down the Rhine, when Goethe was flushed with new fame from publishing *Werther,* that both first met Jacobi. The custom of the day was for travelers to visit the famous, and conversely for famous travelers to be greeted by literary aspirants along the way. The pattern recurs throughout Goethe's autobiography ([1811–32] 1974).

5. Herder, another friend of both sides of the network, took from Jacobi's publicity the cue to become an ardent Spinozaist. His *Gott: Einige Gespräche* (1787) rejected Kant as dry scientific rationalism and extolled the flowing impulses of nature as Spinozaist penetration by the infinite attributes of the divine (Zammito, 1992: 243–245). Herder's vitalist philosophy sounds superficially like Schelling's *Naturphilosophie* of a decade later, except that the latter would perform the task with post-Kantian tools: the synthetic a priori, the categories of the understanding, and the dialectic of the transcendental self. Kant himself probably goaded his old pupil into this split by his own review in 1784 of Herder's *Philosophie der Geschichte der Menschheit,* in which he rejected on critical grounds Herder's particularistic philosophy of history.

6. By 1802, publications on Kant numbered 2,832 items (Guyer, 1992: 449; Beiser, 1987).

7. About the same time, Fichte fell in love with a relative of the famous poet Klopstock. He eventually married her after the success of his book in 1793 made it economically possible.

8. In 1790 the French clergy were turned into elected civic functionaries; in 1794 Christianity was replaced with an official Deist cult, complete with a new calendar beginning with the Year One. The civic church lasted until Napoleon's 1801 Concordat with the pope restored Christianity as the state church.

9. The atmosphere of Idealism, electrical science, and sexual liberation that surrounded Schelling is expressed in Mary Wollstonecraft Shelley's *Frankenstein,* written in 1816 in a Swiss castle to entertain her companions Byron and Shelley. Mineralogy, another new field of scientific discovery, was also the site of Romantic speculation; in the context of the time, it was not incongruous that the most extreme member of the Romantic circle, Novalis, was a mining engineer. Swedenborg held the same occupation in a previous generation.

10. Born in 1770, Hegel did not make his independent mark until he was 37, with his *Phenomenology of Spirit*. In contrast, Schelling (born in 1775) was precocious, a famous leader of Idealism by the age of 20, and progenitor of three different systems by age 28—a forcible illustration that what counts is not biological age but time of centrality within the active network. Kant was a prolific publisher from 1781 (age 57) through 1798 (age 74), the years when he was maximally energized by being the center of attention.

11. Hölderlin was finally recognized as one of the greatest German poets through the attention of Rilke and Stephan George after the complete edition of his works came out in 1913.

12. The famous incident when Schopenhauer was sued for throwing a seamstress out of his anteroom occurred in Berlin in 1821, at just the time when it became apparent that he would have no success lecturing in competition with Hegel (Safranski, 1989: 271–273).

13. Arthur Schopenhauer is not the only one who was inducted into creativity by these contacts; his widowed mother, Johanna Schopenhauer, began to write essays and novels in 1813, virtually simultaneously with Arthur's philosophy, and became by the 1820s the best-known woman writer in Germany. She had also hosted Mme. de Staël—the other famous woman writer of the day—when the latter was an émigrée from the French Revolution. The Schopenhauer family, heirs to a merchant fortune, nicely exemplify the investment of money in the single-minded pursuit of cultural eminence: not as consumers, but for social contacts as means of cultural production.

14. "If I am asked where the *most intimate knowledge* of that inner essence of the world, of that thing in itself which I called the *will to live,* is to be found . . . then I must point to the *ecstasy in the act of copulation*" (Schopenhauer's journal, quoted in Safranski, 1989:269).

15. Another distinctive strand in Schopenhauer's cultural capital, the knowledge of Upanishadic philosophy, which was just beginning to be translated in 1799–1802, was made available by his wide network contacts in the old Romanticist camp. In just these years Friedrich Schlegel began to promote Sanskrit philology (1808), and August Schlegel in 1818 at Bonn occupied the first German chair of Indology (Halbfass, 1988: 63–107).

16. Hegel's immediate background was not particularly distinguished in comparison to Schopenhauer's: after leaving Jena in 1806, he had been a newspaper editor in Bamberg for two years, headmaster of a *Gymnasium* at Nuremberg for eight years, finally becoming professor at Heidelberg in 1816 (succeeding Fries, who went to Jena) two years before his invitation to Berlin (Gregory, 1989: 32–33; Kaufmann, 1966: 227–230; Safranski, 1989: 252).

17. In France, a mixture of various non-academic bases existed throughout the century. Voltaire and Rousseau, although popularized and eventually enriched by the new publishing market, relied for material support during most of their lives on old-fashioned individual patronage. Voltaire at one point also received some collective patronage at Frederick the Great's academy. Montesquieu, Helvetius, d'Holbach, and Turgot were self-supporting aristocrats, although their intellectual interests were shaped by contacts with the circles around the new publishing enterprises. On the publishing market in Germany and its associated careers, see Bruford (1965, 1962); Brunschwig (1947); Wuthnow (1989: 228–251).

18. Johan Heilbron (1994: 26–46) shows that in France, where aristocratic salons in the period from 1650 to 1790 brought together status-conscious courtiers with the most ambitious intellectuals, the hegemony of the literary style was taken to an extreme. The standards of polite and entertaining face-to-face conversation produced an emphasis on aphoristic wit and superficial cleverness of expression, and a denigration of sustained argument or erudition as pedantic. In this milieu, disdain for the traditional university subjects was especially strong.

19. Sources on the movement to abolish the university (Lilge, 1948: 2–3; Schnabel, 1959: 408–457; Weisz, 1983: 18). On German education and its reform (Paulsen, 1919; Bruford, 1965; Brunschwig, 1947; Ben-David and Zloczower, 1962; Hammerstein, 1970; Turner, 1974; McClelland, 1980; Mueller, 1987).

20. The first educational administration independent of the church was founded in Prussia in 1787, a council composed of legal administrators, university professors, and rectors of the chief Latin schools. In 1794 the Prussian legal code made all schools and universities state institutions. The reforms in place by 1820 gave the philosophical faculty a further career basis: teaching in a secondary school was professionalized under the requirement of three years of university study in the philosophical faculty. In the 1700s most secondary school teachers were theology students waiting for a pastorate to open up. Prussian reforms after 1787 simultaneously raised the pay of secondary teachers to the point where they could compete with pastorates (Mueller, 1987: 18–26).

21. For example, the University of Berlin expanded from 28 chairs for full professors in 1810–1819 to 115 chairs by 1909; total teaching staff expanded from 54 to 540. In German universities as a whole, total faculty (including the ranks of *Ordinarius, Extraordinarius,* and *Privatdozent*) grew from 890 in 1796, to 1,200 in 1835, to 3,000 in 1905 (McClelland, 1980: 80, 258–259, 266).

22. I put aside some cases which further complicate the argument. A few non-academic individuals became famous in philosophy even after the academic revolution in their nation: Schopenhauer, Marx, Nietzsche, Sartre, Camus. But most of these were academic hybrids, dropouts from academic careers (Sartre teaching in a *lycée* was pursuing a typical French academic career, like that of Bergson). And we generally see in their work a shift back toward a literary mode, a de-differentiation of the intellectual role and a revolt against the technical level of philosophy along with this distancing from an academic base.

23. Emerson's network ties, before his creative work began in 1836, were literary: Goethe, Coleridge, Wordsworth, Carlyle. The Transcendentalists purveyed a mélange of Goethesque pantheism, Plotinine emanationism, Platonic Ideas, and the adulation of geniuses such as Shakespeare. Kant was often invoked but his distinction of critical versus dogmatic philosophy ignored; epistemological issues were dismissed in favor of direct intuition of higher Truth. The St. Louis Hegelians were more rigorous but unoriginal in the fashion typical of idea importers. Their arena for innovation was to apply the dialectic to current events. For example, in the Civil War, the slave-owning states represented "abstract right," the North "abstract morality," and the victorious Union was Hegel's ethical state (Pochmann, 1948: 32).

24. How then did earlier non-academic philosophers such as Descartes and Spinoza create metaphysical systems? Generally speaking, it was against their expressed intentions. They were part of the scientific revolution, that is to say, the movement of rapid-discovery scientists which their general arguments were intended to justify. These intellectuals were unable to replace philosophy with science, because the very act of arguing for the foundations of science, and any continuation of these arguments by their successors, re-creates the turf of philosophy. Why thinkers like

Descartes stayed on the abstract level whereas the philosophes of the 1700s or the Utilitarians of the 1800s limited their issues to topical lay concerns, cannot be explained by this aspect of their material bases, since all of them were non-academics. The thinkers of the 1600s were inwardly oriented toward their own network, especially the part of it which was carrying out the autonomous researches of physical and mathematical science, whereas later non-academic philosophers were much more lay-oriented because of their bases in popular literary media and political movements.

25. "Religion on the strength of its sanctity, and law, on the strength of its majesty, try to withdraw themselves from [criticism]; but by so doing they arouse just suspicions, and cannot claim that sincere respect which reason pays to those only who have been able to stand its free and open examination" (Kant, [1781] 1966: A.xi).

26. "For if God actually spoke to man, man could still never *know* that it was God speaking. It is quite impossible for a man to apprehend the infinite by his senses, distinguish it from sensible beings, and *recognize* it as such" (Kant, [1798] 1991: 115).

27. A quasi-experimental validation of this point is the fate of the Karlsschule, founded by the duke of Württemberg at Stuttgart in the early 1770s, and upgraded from a *Gymnasium* to a university in 1781 (*DSB*, 1981: 7:366–368; Schnabel, 1959: 424). Here the culture was heavily secular, focusing on the Enlightenment program of practical sciences (especially medicine and public administration) plus vernacular languages. Its notable early graduates (all with medical training) included Schiller (posted as an army surgeon) and the biological scientists Cuvier and Kielmeyer. The Karlsschule was suppressed in 1794, at the height of educational failures during the crisis of the revolutionary wars. The structural weakness which it illustrated was that reform in too secular a direction eliminated the main career attraction of the traditional university: its credentialing claim on careers in the church and in law, the two occupations on which the bureaucratizing state was building. The Enlightenment culture left education dangling too much on its popular appeal to withstand shocks in material support.

28. Kant was the son of a harness maker, who happened to grow up in a university town; Fichte, son of a poor ribbon peddler, was educated by the charity of a neighboring landowner; Herder, son of a schoolmaster, was so poor that Kant remitted his lecture fees; Schelling's and Hölderlin's fathers were pastors. Hegel's father was in the upper civil service of one of the small states, but Hegel too had to find support as a tutor and secondary school teacher. The literary intellectuals, by contrast, were typically from wealthy families; they were much less dependent on low-paying academic or clerical careers, and had greater access to aristocratic connections for becoming higher officials. Goethe, Jacobi, and Friedrich Schlegel were university-educated in law, the faculty favored by aristocrats. Schopenhauer, the only one of the major Idealists who was independently wealthy, could afford to be a maverick; by the same token he was uninterested in educational or religious reform.

29. The very availability of tutoring jobs was due to the widespread unfashionableness

of formal education at this time. The leaders of educational reform all had personal experience of one of the main alternative systems, and were strongly motivated to escape this alternative as a degradation of the autonomy of the teacher. The only remaining career path would have been to become a schoolmaster while waiting for a pastorate to open up; such positions were extremely low paying and isolated from most intellectual networks, whereas tutoring at least held out the possibility of contact with cultivated circles of aristocratic or upper-bourgeois society.

30. Despite periods of stagnation in enrollments, notably 1830–1860, in general the German university system was on a solid footing after 1810, quite the opposite of its precarious position in the 1700s. Similarly, the criterion that professors' career advancement depended on their research publications built up gradually, becoming dominant throughout Germany by around 1850 (Jarausch, 1982; McClelland, 1980: 148, 171–172, 242–247).

31. Success on Kant's intellectual development (Beiser, 1992; Ameriks, 1992; Werkmeister, 1980; Guyer, 1987). For positions and network details of the Wolffians, Pietists, and Berlin Academicians, see *DSB* (1981) and *EP* (1967).

32. In his *Metaphysical Foundations of Natural Science* (1786). Kant continued this project to the end of his life, leaving work from the early 1800s to be published posthumously (Friedman, 1992: 185–191, 199; Werkmeister, 1980: 101–128). The maturity and validity of a science depended on how far it moved along this path. Kant held that chemistry, especially in the version of Stahl, presented only empirical principles, not yet necessary ones; with the development of quantitative chemistry in the 1790s, Kant gave his endorsement to Lavoisier's system.

33. Fichte described the fundamental method of Idealism: "It shows that what is first set up as fundamental principle and directly demonstrated in consciousness, is impossible unless something else occurs along with it, and that this something else is impossible unless a third something also takes place, and so on until the conditions of what was first exhibited are completely exhausted, and this latter is, with respect to its possibility, fully intelligible" (Fichte, [1794–1797] 1982: 25).

34. "There is no need for premature alarm at the fact that this proposition expressly contradicts the first principle . . . It is sufficient that this conclusion follows by correct inferences from established premises, no less than that which it contradicts. The ground of their unity will emerge in due time" (Fichte, [1794–1797] 1982: 153; cf. pp. 98 and 226): "All contradictions are reconciled by more accurate determination of the propositions at variance; and so too here. The self must have been posited as infinite in one sense, and as finite in another."

35. Fichte's own summary of "the essence of transcendental idealism" states: "The concept of existence is by no means regarded as a *primary* and *original* concept, but is viewed merely as *derivative,* as a concept derived, at that, through opposition to activity, and hence is a merely *negative* concept. To the Idealist, the only positive thing is freedom; existence, for him, is a mere negation of the latter" (Fichte, [1794–1797] 1982: 69). The identification of one's personal self with freedom and with the Eternal and Absolute is stressed particularly strongly in Fichte's popular manifesto *The Vocation of Man,* written in 1800 at the height of his identification with the Romantic movement. The theme was carried on by the other Idealists at

this time, such as in Schelling's *Philosophical Inquiries into the Nature of Human Freedom* (1809).

36. The first history of philosophy to go beyond Greek models based on Diogenes Laertius and to give some attention to relatively recent philosophy was that of Brucker (5 vols., 1742–1767) at Leipzig (*EP*, 1969: 6:227; Santinello, 1981). Brucker remained traditional in form, listing in parallel the opinions of various schools rather than attempting to explain why philosophers had developed their arguments. The first efforts to develop the chronological history of philosophical ideas coincided with the German university revolution: Tiedemann (6 vols., 1791–1797) at Marburg, and Tennemann (11 vols., 1789–1819) at Leipzig. Hegel drew on their pathbreaking work, while illustrating that one needs a philosophy of one's own to write the history of philosophy in a philosophical manner. In Hegel, too, the emphasis shifts to a modern canonical sequence, rather than remaining preponderantly with the Greeks. Hence Hegel shares with Aristotle, who made a similar move in the historiography of ancient Greek philosophy, a focus on a synthesizing system mediating all the extremes, and on dynamic potential as the prime substance. On Hegel's intellectual development, see Harris (1972, 1983, 1993). Marx, who parallels Hegel in many ways during the following generation, also began by specializing in ancient philosophy, writing his dissertation on the Epicurean materialists.

37. Hegel sets out the critique at the beginning of his system, in the Introduction to the *Phenomenology* ([1807] 1967: 100–107), and repeats it in his *Logic* ([1812–1816] 1929: 2:251–252). Hegel is not unprecedented here; in the 1750s the Pietist Crusius in polemics against the Wolffians had also rejected mathematics. Hegel claims, more damningly as an academic modernist, that mathematical method in science "belongs to a stage of mental culture that has now passed away" (Hegel, [1807] 1967: 106).

38. Fries and Hegel had become *Privatdozenten* at Jena in 1801, leading to a publications race in which Fries pulled ahead early. Fries got a chair at Heidelberg in 1805; this was later to be Hegel's first chair, when Fries vacated it in 1816 to take the professorship at the old Jena center. Both competed for the Berlin job after Fichte's death in 1814; but now in the period of growing conservatism, Fries's activities in the radical student movement got him into trouble with the authorities and made Hegel more acceptable.

39. Schelling too had the pragmatic sense to abandon *Naturphilosophie* before its first burst of enthusiasm in the early 1800s wore off, leaving the field for minor disciples to exploit, himself moving into the more congenial humanistic field of comparative mythology.

40. MacGregor (1992). Here again Hegel followed Fichte's path, especially in the latter's quasi-socialist blueprint, *The Closed Industrial State* (1804).

41. It is instructive to compare Spinoza, whose monist system bears some resemblance to Idealist metaphysics. But Spinoza denied freedom of the will, while the Idealists exalted it to a metaphysical extreme. It is not the surrounding political situation which makes the difference in these views. During Spinoza's youth, the United Provinces had won final recognition of its revolutionary struggle for independence

from Spain (1648), and the Dutch Republic in the 1660s and 1670s was the freest state in the world. Spinoza's own political activities were on behalf of freedom of private religious belief, whereas the German Idealists were wresting control of the educational system from the theologians and proselytizing the creative freedom of the philosophical faculty. The difference in the immediate organizational bases for intellectual life, rather than the political context as a whole, explains the divergent positions on freedom in these philosophical systems.

42. Sources on the history of English university reform (Rothblatt, 1981; Engel, 1982; Green, 1969; Richter, 1969); for international comparisons, see Rothblatt and Wittrock (1993).

43. Bradley sardonically expressed his attitude toward religious authority by parking his bicycle in the Merton College chapel; upon protest that it was desecrating the holy place, Bradley replied that he was willing to have it consecrated (Richter, 1969: 36–38).

44. To see bare particulars in the world is not primitive or simple, but an advanced accomplishment resting on many intellectual distinctions. We ourselves, as well as children and animals, Bradley declares, first perceive universals. Even indexicals ("this," "here") are in some respect universals, words invocable across situations. To be sure, there is an indexically inexpressible aspect of every experience, but it resides not in the particularity of that moment, but in the fact that every "this" has for its subject reality as a whole; it is the whole which is indexical and inexpressible. Bradley hints at metaphysical consequences by pointing out that "this," unlike other ideas, can never be a symbol of something else. If we could find all ideas whose contents cannot be used as adjectives of something else, this would open the way to a new Anselmian ontological proof (Bradley, [1883] 1922: 27, 35, 69, 98).

45. A foreign member was William James, who founded the American Society for Psychical Research in 1884, during the time when he was working on his psychology. Peirce and Royce participated in the 1880s and 1890s in research on haunted houses and table turning (Myers, 1986: 11; Brent, 1993: 209, 215, 223).

46. Bradley's *Logic* (1883: 53–55) had started a somewhat similar argument: the fiction of the atomic now is due to the combination of *presence* (two events marked as simultaneous) plus *existence* (a real appears in the time series, but is not *in* time). Bradley concluded that presence is the negation of time. For Bradley, time is mere appearance, and there may be any number of time-sequence equivalents in the Absolute.

47. It was formulated in the Gifford Lectures, 1916–1918, and published in 1920 as *Space, Time, and Deity*. Whitehead's *Process and Reality* (1929) was from the Gifford Lectures for 1926–1928. James's *Varieties of Religious Experience* was from the lectures for 1902. The Gifford Lectures on Natural Religion, endowed at the Scottish theological strongholds of Edinburgh and Glasgow, were a principal promoter of Idealist philosophy.

48. Russell (1967). Perhaps because German Idealism was acquiring a bad name under the influence of Russell's polemics, Whitehead pretended that his system was a development of themes in the classical tradition from Descartes to Locke and

Hume; in fact Whitehead's discussion of these thinkers largely focuses on the flaws of their sensationism and intellectualism. Leibniz, the thinker whom he most closely resembles, receives relatively few explicit references. Whitehead and Alexander in effect recapitulate the positions of Leibniz and Spinoza in terms of twentieth-century scientifically oriented Idealism.

49. A phenomenon noted for all historical periods by sociologists of religion (Stark and Bainbridge, 1985; Finke and Stark, 1992).

50. Kuklick (1977: 135–136; 234–235). Royce had come as a graduate student to Hopkins from Berkeley, where Gilman had been president before Hopkins; he was introduced to Idealism by Hopkins's G. S. Morris, who also taught John Dewey. During the customary sojourn in Germany, Royce studied with Lotze, Wundt, and Windelband. Characteristically for the Americans of this period, his own philosophy was more Idealist than that of his German professors.

51. James's changing disciplinary identification may be traced in his successive titles: assistant professor of physiology in 1876, assistant professor of philosophy in 1880, and professor in 1885; professor of psychology in 1889; back to professor of philosophy in 1897 (Boring, 1950: 510–511).

52. For this reason Peirce regarded mathematics as the investigation of the consequences of hypotheses; he himself innovated mathematical notation similar to the work of Dedekind and Cantor (*DSB*, 1981: 10:484).

53. Buchler (1955: 354, 356). Peirce pointed out that an infinite regress results when one attempts to analyze certain kinds of relations: a statement of relation must always characterize the relation of relations to their subjects, and so on. The argument parallels Bradley, except that from Peirce's mathematical viewpoint, such nested series of relations fit the definition of the continuum "as that in which every part is of the same nature as the whole" (*EP*, 1967: 6:76).

54. Brent (1993: 311, 300, 209); Buchler (1955: 323). Eisele (*DSB*, 1981: 10:485) summarizes: "Nature syllogizes, making inductions and abductions."

55. This is confirmed by the pattern of the various European analogues to pragmatism. In Germany, Mach interpreted scientific laws as practical fictions; and indeed James met and admired Mach during a visit to the Continent in 1882, long before formulating his own pragmatist doctrine (Johnston, 1972: 181). Vaihinger's *Philosophy of As-If* (1911) similarly resonates with James. But the aims are quite different from James's religious concerns. Mach's positivism is purely scientific, and Vaihinger is a Neo-Kantian concerned with the validity of the forms of experience in the absence of a thing-in-itself. Pragmatism never became a self-conscious movement in Germany as it was in the United States. In the German university orbit the generations of Idealists had long since passed, and there was no demand for such a stepping-stone between religious Idealism and secularism. Where we do find the analogue to the United States is in Italy, where a pragmatist movement, led by Calderoni, arose soon after the zenith of Idealism. Here the timing was like that in America: the university system was under reform, as secularizers wrested it from the hands of the church and installed a German-style educational system. The Italian pragmatists were a halfway house between positivism and Idealism, criticizing both schools while borrowing elements from both.

56. Peirce's 1868 argument resonates both with his semiotic chains and with the later maneuvers of Idealists such as Royce. Peirce holds that Cartesian doubt is an impossibility; whereas Royce concludes that a larger Self is behind the activity of doubting, Peirce specifies that the very thoughts in which the doubt is formulated are composed of signs, whose meaning is in the system of signs and in the social community which uses them.

57. Peirce's life is often depicted as a melodrama illustrating the moralistic prejudices of his day and the failure of America to honor genius. Alternatively, Brent (1993) gives a reductionist explanation for Peirce's career difficulties as the result of chronic neuralgia, which drove him to drugs, and in turn to episodes of financial and professional irresponsibility, outbursts of anger, and violence against his wives and servants. Yet it appears that Peirce's episodic afflictions, like his propensity for personal conflicts, coincided with times of uncertainty and strain in his intellectual career; he himself finally recognized that his sicknesses were set off emotionally by adversity (Brent, 1993: 294). A more sociological interpretation is that Peirce's network position gave him high ambitions and resources, but placed insuperable obstacles in the way of creating a clear-cut intellectual position.

58. Peirce was another of Dewey's teachers, whose energy must have given some indication of what could be done at the interface of Idealism and science; but Peirce's formal semiotic did not favorably impress the unmathematical Dewey at all.

59. Experimental psychology in its academic origins stressed the overlap of physiology and philosophy because the discipline was created by the migration of medical physiologists into philosophy chairs—James in the United States, Wundt in Germany—motivated by the shortage of positions in science faculties and the surplus of positions in philosophy (Ben-David and Collins, 1966). Most American psychologists of this generation had been sojourning pupils of Wundt.

60. Ruckmick (1912). The first independent psychology department in the world was founded by G. Stanley Hall, Dewey's old mentor, at Clark University in 1889. In Germany experimental psychologists, ensconced in philosophy departments in a university system which was no longer differentiating new chairs, never developed behaviorism, but continued the philosophical focus on consciousness with introspectionist psychology (1870s–1910) and then Gestalt psychology (1910s). I examine the origins of experimental psychology within the German university system in Chapter 13.

13. The Post-revolutionary Condition

1. Kline (1972: 623). The point was repeated as late as 1810 by Delambre, secretary of the mathematics and physics section of the Institut de France.

2. Abel had five papers in the first issue of Crelle's journal (including his resolution of the long-standing puzzle of the general solution of quintic equations), and Galois's general theory of the solvability of algebraic equations by means of the theory of groups appeared in Liouville's journal in 1846.

3. Practicing mathematicians, such as Euler, Lagrange, and Gauss, did occasionally

attempt to clarify disreputable issues such as divergent series (Boyer, 1985: 562, 566), but as an exploration of particular issues rather than a general methodological concern.

4. This helps explain why innovations in basic axiomatic systems now came from schoolteachers on the periphery of the mathematical world, such as Lobachevsky in Russia, Bolyai in Hungary, and Grassmann while teaching at a German *Gymnasium*. I explore this further in the section on England, "The Advantages of Provinciality."

5. This is not to say that physical interpretations of non-Euclidean geometry were not offered; for example, elliptic geometry can be considered the geometry of a surface of a sphere. Gauss around 1820 attempted to measure angles among mountain peaks in order to test which geometry fit (Kline, 1972: 867–880). Non-Euclidean geometry was more a flashpoint of public recognition than an underlying shift in the way mathematicians worked. N-dimensional geometries, which had been used occasionally in purely technical manipulations by d'Alembert and Lagrange, broke the connection with the physical world even more decisively by the 1840s. Older mathematicians such as Gauss had anticipated some of these conceptions by following out pathways available in existing mathematical practice; but they failed to see the potential significance because they were still operating in a frame of reference, grounded in the lack of differentiation between mathematics and scientific application, in which mathematical concepts must have intuitive meaning. Gauss's unwillingness to publish many of his ideas, in contrast with Cauchy's ambitious rush into print in the new attention space of pure math, shows the key part the social context plays in selecting ideas from an unfocused background and putting them into the center of attention.

6. All categorical propositions are to be analyzed into propositions asserting or denying existence; "all men are mortal" becomes "an immortal man does not exist," and "all triangles have 180 degrees" becomes "there exists no triangle that does not have 180 degrees" (Johnston, 1972: 292–293; Lindenfeld, 1980: 48–53).

7. This parallels Brentano's doctrine, developed around the same time, that the mind intends objects; the object in general is, so to speak, a slot to be filled with particular objects. In Brentano, the doctrine is mixed with empirical psychology; Husserl, a network offshoot of both Brentano and Frege, extracts from their concepts a general phenomenology.

8. To put it another way: an entire functional statement may be taken as content for a second-order statement; thus, existence may be treated as a second-order concept, but it is invalid to collapse the levels and treat them as an attribute of a first-order concept within the nested statements. This is the error Descartes made when he argued that divinity implies existence just as the concept of a triangle implies truths about its angles. In the same way, the universal quantifier ("all") is a second-order concept whose complexities are hidden in ordinary language (Kneale and Kneale, 1984: 504; Coffa, 1991: 73).

9. This is the Leibnizian problem of identity of indiscernibles again. Frege points out that it cannot be solved by distinguishing different positions in space or time, since the issue arises once again in this context.

10. Cantor originated the method of one-to-one correspondence; Cantor's concept of the power or cardinal number of a set is similar to Frege's Platonic object-numbers.

11. Here Frege converges rather surprisingly with Bradley, who also held in his very different logic of 1883 that all true statements are about a single object, the universe. The British Idealist and the German logical formalist pursue a similar path insofar as they are rebounding off a common enemy, empiricist logic in the manner of J. S. Mill.

12. When the full-blown logicist movement widened the search for predecessors, Bolzano was also added retrospectively to the pantheon. Beginning in the 1810s as a mathematician-philosopher in the pre-disciplinary mode of an old-fashioned university (Prague) on the periphery of the German system, Bolzano set out to refute Kant with a combination of Leibnizian metaphysics and infinitesimal calculus (Coffa, 1991: 26–32; Boyer, 1985: 564–566). The result included various distinctions resembling those of Frege and his successors. Bolzano was ignored, owing in part to his isolation in the networks of the time; his work lacked the drive to omni-symbolism which became the mark of the later movement, and his innovations were buried in a metaphysical system of archaic cast. As in other cases where adumbrations were recognized only in retrospect, Bolzano points up the importance of a full-scale intellectual movement to raise details from their surroundings and focus attention on them as landmarks of a new worldview.

13. Almost simultaneously, in 1844 Grassmann produced an even wider generalization of complex numbers, connected to n-dimensional geometry, and dropping not only the commutative but also the associative law. Grassmann's work was little recognized until the 1860s. The difference in fame was due to the fact that Hamilton's work came as the climax of controversy around the fundamentals of British mathematics; whereas Grassmann was working in a side area far from the topics on which German and French mathematicians were focusing attention. Grassmann originated not in the network of leading German mathematicians, but as a theology pupil of Schleiermacher. Under prevailing conceptions of mathematics, such nonnaturalistic innovations were likely seen in a theological rather than a strictly mathematical context. Hamilton too had German Idealist connections as an intimate of Coleridge; he claimed quaternions had cosmic rather than merely mathematical significance (Hankins, 1980).

14. Sir William Hamilton and Bolzano (see note 12) are structural parallels: both were philosophical conservatives at provincial universities who found their stimulus in opposing the influx of fashionable Kantianism. In both cases fundamental innovations in logic were set in motion in the 1830s which were not recognized until later.

15. Again in 1863 Mill was to promote his systematic philosophy by using Sir William Hamilton as a foil. Hamilton was especially well known in America, where Scottish faculty psychology dominated the colleges; there he became the subject of discussions from which emerged yet another innovation in logic, that of Peirce in the 1870s. As we saw in Chapter 12, Peirce's starting point in mathematics, via his father's work, was an extension of Cayley and Sylvester's method for inventing

alternative algebras, which they had generalized from Hamilton's quaternions. Peirce was an American import of British mathematical and philosophical networks, who brought together their controversies into a full-fledged system.

16. There is even a personal connection to the core of the Utilitarians: John Stuart Mill was Russell's godfather. This could hardly have produced any direct intellectual or emotional influence, since Mill died when Russell was one year old. But it exemplifies how central Russell was in the late Victorian network structure, a fact which must have shaped his intellectual trajectory. He was raised by his grandparents, Lord Russell, the introducer of the Reform Bill in 1832 and subsequent prime minister, and Lady Russell, an outspoken political liberal and promoter of Utilitarian causes.

17. Kline (1972: 1031–33). At this time Whitehead was purely a mathematician; his shift into philosophy did not occur until the 1920s.

18. Kline (1972: 1197–1208; *DSB*, 1981: 14:613–616; Peckhaus, 1990). Zermelo's basic idea, showing the existence of relations by which every set in an infinite system corresponds to one of its elements, was already formulated in 1900–1901 lectures. It burst into prominence in 1904 in the aftermath of Russell and in tandem with Hilbert's announcement of his formalist program. This was the formalist network in action; Zermelo was a *Dozent* at Göttingen, a colleague of Hilbert and Husserl, and a former pupil at Halle of Cantor, whose set theory Zermelo defended. At the same moment, Hilbert proposed his drastic new program to cure mathematical paradoxes, including these newest ones, by treating mathematical symbols as nothing more than arbitrary but consistent sets of marks on paper. Dramatic developments of this kind are not mysterious and sudden insights. Typically they happen in the course of long and intense concentration on problems focused by network conflicts. In this case Russell found his paradox, and Zermelo his axiom of choice, by wrestling with dubious points in Cantor's system. Russell describes how he tried out every conceivable approach to his problems, just as W. R. Hamilton discovered quaternions in a sudden insight after 15 years of working on the problem (Coffa, 1991: 103, 115; Kline, 1972: 779).

19. Wedberg (1984: 139–141). Because of his emphasis on the independence of logical elements, Russell for a while endorsed Meinong's 1904 doctrine of the types of reality of all mental and extra-mental objects. Russell could vacillate among various forms of realism—Platonist, sensory, and others—because his principle of acquaintance covered very generally every kind of item that might be directly known.

20. Wittgenstein also rejects Neo-Kantianism, which he otherwise somewhat resembles. The space-form is not merely a kind of spectacles through which we see the world; it involves a "multiplicity of relations" which we have had to discover through exploration of uses of symbol systems (*Tractatus* 4.0412). Wittgenstein seems to have in mind that a fact such as space having three dimensions rather than something else is not explained by Neo-Kantian a priority; logic permeates the world, including its "empirical" aspects.

21. Russell himself, who declared that his brain had been burned out by the struggle

to break through old gestalts in the theory of types, had an inkling of the importance of symbolism in Wittgenstein's breakthrough (Russell, 1967: 228–229, 247). Referring to Wittgenstein's notion of unsayability, in the introduction to the *Tractatus* (Russell, 1922: xvii–xviii) Russell says: "This view may have been originally suggested by notation, and if so, that is much in its favor, for a good notation has a subtlety and suggestiveness which at times makes it seem almost like a live teacher. Notational irregularities are often the first sign of philosophical errors, and a perfect notation would be a substitute for thought."

22. Frege had already shown the way in pointing out that his distinction between asserting a function and the content asserted—a predecessor of the hierarchic theory of types—reveals the error in Anselm's ontological proof.

23. "Vienna Circle" is a loose term for an entire movement. In the narrower sense, the circle was the personal seminar conducted by Schlick from 1924 to 1936; as the movement grew, it became formalized through the leadership of Neurath with its manifesto in 1929 and its own journal, *Erkenntnis,* in 1930 (Ayer, 1982; Popper, 1976; Quine, 1985; Waismann, 1979; Johnston, 1972). Overlapping were other sub-factions and discussion groups, as well as a pared-down circle of those Wittgenstein allowed to meet with him during 1927–1932. These circles are interconnected by visitors with the Berlin circle of Reichenbach, and with the Warsaw school of logicians; another node at Prague via the physicist Philip Frank, becoming more central when Carnap gets a chair there in 1931; and in the 1930s a widening network of young philosophers who spread the message abroad: from Oxford, Ryle's pupil Ayer; from Harvard, Whitehead's and C. S. Lewis's pupil (and thereby James's grandpupil) Quine.

24. Schnädelbach (1984: 87); Willey (1978: 155, 173); Johnston (1972: 189). Vaihinger began to formulate his doctrine in the 1870s after studying with the militant Neo-Kantian Lange. Vaihinger was strongly identified with Kantian scholarship; he founded the journal *Kant Studien* in 1896 and the Kant Society in 1904, the major channels for the proliferation of Kantian publications at the turn of the century. It was in this journal that Schlick delivered his attack on Cassirer's Neo-Kantian physics in 1921. The Vienna Circle journal *Erkenntnis* was a successor to another of Vaihinger's journals, *Annalen der Philosophie.*

25. Coffa (1991: 189–201). Einstein overthrew Newtonian space as an absolute container of motion; as late as 1920, Reichenbach regarded Einstein's argument as providing support for Neo-Kantianism. Einstein himself came to dislike the Neo-Kantian interpretation, holding instead that time-space has physically objective existence. In 1921 Einstein wrote to Schlick in support of the latter's critique of Cassirer's interpretation of relativity theory. But Einstein's opinion was hardly decisive for the changing philosophical atmosphere. His own sympathies were mixed and highly variable (Holton, [1973] 1988: 237–278). Early (around 1905) Einstein regarded himself as sympathetic to Machian phenomenalism, though drawing crucial components from Planck's opposing position; in the 1910s he shifted toward theory-accessible realism; by 1922—just after his contact with Schlick—he was publicly attacking the Machians as overly empiricist. When the

Vienna Circle was developing in the 1920s, Einstein was going in the opposite direction. The fact is Einstein's special relativity was taken as support by all the major philosophical positions alike: Neo-Kantian, positivist, realist, pragmatist, and even religious Idealist.

26. We have seen this in the endless critiques by ancient Greek Academics pointing out contradictions in the doctrines of Stoics, and in the imperviousness of Epicureans to attack. In ancient India the Ajivikas were ridiculed for their inconsistency between believing in all-encompassing Fate and their personal striving for liberation. In medieval India the Nyaya-Vaisheshika school responded to acute Buddhist and Advaita attacks on paradoxes in their position not by backing away from their realism but by extending it. These schools lasted many generations without changing their positions.

27. Popper states in his autobiography that he had had the basic idea already in 1919, as the result of disgust with Marxist politics and the enthusiastic claims of the Freudian and Adlerian psychoanalytic factions. This was at about the same time Schlick was invoking falsification against the Neo-Kantians; but neither Schlick nor Popper made much further use of the idea in these years. Popper's family and personal connections brought him in contact with a wide range of the avant-garde political, musical, and social science movements in Vienna during the 1920s; these connections also kept his career interests scattered until 1930, when he began to focus on developing the philosophical implications of a falsification criterion in terms of the debates that were now splitting the Vienna Circle. Although he retrospectively portrays himself as the destroyer of logical positivism, Popper became famous through his connection with the Vienna Circle (Popper, 1976: 36–38, 78–90, 107).

28. Kuhn's originating network overlaps with that of Quine: both were members of the Harvard Society of Junior Fellows, and early in their careers both were personally connected to Conant, who built up the program in history of science at Harvard. Kuhn's work is the best-known result of the confluence of two major organizational developments: the differentiation of the academic discipline of history of science, together with the foundation-of-science issues generated by cross-disciplinary border flows of mathematics and physics into philosophy which constituted the Vienna Circle.

29. Moore however remained oblivious to the revolt against the subject-predicate form being carried out by Frege and Russell; small wonder Wittgenstein despised the book.

30. See the genealogical charts in Levy (1981: 22–25); Bell (1972: xviii–xix). There is nothing to match this elsewhere. In Germany, Brentano came from a family of famous writers, and Fichte's son had some reputation among theological Idealists; but in general German linkages are purely academic ones. In America, James and Peirce were born into families of famous intellectuals, but overall the intellectual network has few kinship ties. Nor were British philosophers usually tied together by kinship, except in these few generations. Under previous conditions, most intellectuals were either celibate clerics or recipients of patronage in aristocratic

households who could not afford to marry; after the Humboldtian university revolution, professors were middle-class specialists segregated in alliance networks by their careers.

31. For instance, in his Introduction to Wittgenstein's *Tractatus*, (1922: xxii) Russell comments: "As one with long experience of the difficulties of logic and of the deceptiveness of theories which seem irrefutable, I find myself unable to be sure of the rightness of a theory, merely on the ground that I cannot see any point on which it is wrong."

32. The doctrine of Stevenson (Quine's pupil) that ethical statements are emotional expressions (1944) had a similar effect in the United States.

33. Mauthner, who explored the philosophy of language during Wittgenstein's youth in Vienna, is sometimes regarded as an early influence or predecessor. Nevertheless, Mauthner's "critique of language" did not set the pathway Wittgenstein followed from mathematical logic into a theory of propositions. The case of Mauthner shows that the philosophical resonances of language were noticed from time to time—as is to be expected in the increasing consciousness of symbol systems in fields ranging from Neo-Kantianism to Freud. The movement to turn all of philosophy into the study of ordinary language was a more specific and militant move within the philosophical discipline, and that is where its structural causes are found.

34. Wittgenstein was merely an undergraduate at Cambridge during his period of discipleship with Russell, never took a formal degree, although he was given a Ph.D. pro forma upon returning in 1929. Russell and Moore also had enough independent wealth (and, especially in the case of Russell, social eminence) to dedicate themselves to their intellectual interests, even during periods without academic support. Wittgenstein made ostentatious gestures of despising material wealth, for instance, keeping no furniture in his college rooms during the 1930s, so that his pupils had to bring their own chairs. It was the kind of sacrifice of wealth for status of which the satiated rich are capable; in a more conventional version, Wittgenstein cultivated entrée with the artistic elite upon his return to Vienna in 1914 by donating a large amount of money to them (Monk, 1990: 109). Something of the same self-confident eliteness was expressed in Russell's insouciant style. At the age of 27 he could treat the famous mathematician Poincaré in debate as follows: "M. Poincaré requests a definition . . . Perhaps he will be shocked if I tell him that one is not entitled to make such a request since everything that is fundamental is necessarily indefinable . . . Since mathematicians almost invariably ignore the role of definitions, and since M. Poincaré appears to share their disdain, I will allow myself a few remarks on this topic" (Coffa, 1991: 130). Russell's polemical style was a form of mocking, often with an undertone of class consciousness, as when he derided the Idealist conception of sensory experience as parts of a whole by imagining the professor calling his college servant to testify what the "plain man" thinks: "Well, sir, greenness is to me the name of a complex fact, the factors of which essentially and reciprocally determine one another. And if you, sir, choose to select one factor out of the complex, and to call it greenness, I will not dispute about the term, for I know my place, sir" (Coffa, 1991: 96).

35. The organizational setting too played a role. Göttingen had been the main center

for programs of unification in mathematics since Riemann's generalization of non-Euclidean geometries in the 1850s; Klein's unification of geometry around the theory of groups and their invariants beginning in the 1870s and developing into an encyclopedic movement at Göttingen from 1886 until 1913; and Hilbert's efforts at formal unification of vast areas of mathematics at the turn of the century (*DSB*, 1981: 7:396–397; Paukert, 1990). Husserl created an even broader program to unify science on its most general basis.

36. Lipps was a former pupil of Stumpf, and thus another network grandpupil of Brentano, whose act-psychology Lipps's position resembled. Lipps was known for his theory of empathy, as the active project of the self into external objects. His psychological version of phenomenology was upstaged by the more radical object-bracketing phenomenology of Husserl.

37. Though publicly supportive of Scheler, Husserl referred to his work privately as "fool's gold"; later he would call Scheler and Heidegger his "antipodes" (Spiegelberg, 1982: 269).

38. Heidegger overdramatized the extent to which the question of being had been forgotten since the time of Duns Scotus. In fact, it had become a hot issue among his own immediate network predecessors. Husserl bracketed the question of being in order to study essences; Meinong multiplied the kinds of being. Heidegger took the opposite direction from his teacher's rival, searching for the univocal meaning of being underlying all varieties.

39. From Husserl's viewpoint this was a merely naturalistic use, which he nevertheless encouraged when meeting Jaspers in 1913. At this point Husserl was still looking for allies (Natanson, 1973: 160). A key network contact in Jaspers's development was Erich Frank, a pupil of Rickert and Windelband, who in 1914 discovered the virtually unknown Kierkegaard and shared this enthusiasm with Jaspers. In 1919 Frank's *Wissen, Wollen, Glauben,* along with Jaspers's *Psychologie der Weltanschauungen,* launched German existentialism (*EP*, 1967: 3:218–219). By 1923, Heidegger was personally acquainted with Jaspers.

40. In the pattern typical of creative groups, the personal relationships had formed before either of them did the creative work which made them famous. Out of this same period came a generation of younger scholars later to be famous in German thought: Heidegger's assistants Gadamer, Löwith, and Marcuse. Another of Husserl's assistants, Oscar Becker, forms the intermediary link as teacher of Apel and Habermas (Gadamer, 1985: 141, 171).

41. In the 1960s and again in the 1980s, there were controversies over Heidegger's involvement with Nazism in the early 1930s (Bourdieu, [1975] 1991; Farias, 1987). None of these makes a convincing case that Heidegger's politics determined his philosophy. Bourdieu's analysis, the most sociological, rests on the assertion that the intellectual field is homologous to the surrounding social and political field. Hence Heidegger did not need to be conscious that he was expressing in the concepts specific to the philosophical field the same stance of the resentful provincial middle class which gave rise to Nazism in the political field. But in fact the intellectual field is not homologous to the social and political world; the one is governed by the struggle for attention under the law of small numbers, with its

limit of a half dozen effective factions and its structural pressures for oppositions and regroupings; whereas the social and political worlds do not operate by this kind of struggle over attention space, and do not have the same numbers of factions and oppositions. Bourdieu posits a further homology between the factions within philosophy and the structure of relations within the intermediate level constituting the academic field of the universities in general. Nevertheless, the overcrowding of candidates for faculty positions after 1900, and a huge influx of students in the 1920s (Bourdieu, [1975] 1991: 123, citing Ringer, 1969), are not phenomena unique in the history of modern education, and do not account for the range of opposing positions in philosophy of this time. Similar overcrowding occurred in the 1830s and 1840s, but the result was not anti-modernist conservatism but the radicalism of the Young Hegelians (Toews, 1980: 213–216, 1993: 389–392; McClelland, 1980). The external resonances of Heidegger's philosophy were not specific to (or even primarily with) the Nazis; its greatest popularity was among Protestant and Catholic theologians, and among the French existentialists of the anti-Nazi underground, and it received its widest fame in France in the years immediately after the liberation. The attempts to discredit Heidegger by means of his Nazi phase are part of the intellectual maneuvers of a later period.

42. Husserl followed Kant in taking time as the basic form of experience, since all experience is temporal but not spatial. For Kant, all categories are configurations of time: substance is permanence through time; causality is lawful succession in time; and so on. But in this Kantian approach, being itself is not temporal. Husserl kept changing his mind as to whether time flows from the pre-temporal transcendental ego or vice versa, or indeed whether subjectivity and temporality are identical (Dostal, 1993: 147–149).

43. There is an additional reason why Heidegger reverses Husserl's position. Husserl identified being with the naturalistic level, distinguishing being from the essences revealed by bracketing. Heidegger's being is univocal across all levels; therefore he eliminates bracketing.

44. The intermediary between Schutz and Husserl was Felix Kaufmann, a Viennese whose interests in mathematics, physics, and economics were fostered in the periphery of the Vienna Circle. Kaufmann had visited Husserl from 1922 on, and introduced Schutz to him in 1932. Schutz, an economist, took up the phenomenological method in order to clarify debates over the foundations of social science, and especially Max Weber's categories of *verstehen* and rational action. Schutz's followers, like the later phenomenologists in general, became known as violent antagonists of the logical positivists. Not uncharacteristically in the growth of intellectual movements, opposing movements tend to split off from a common center: in the network, Schutz is only two links away from Schlick, Carnap, and von Mises. Harold Garfinkel, a pupil of Schutz at the New School for Social Research in New York during the early 1950s, went on to develop the sociological research program of ethnomethodology, inventing methods for breaching the taken-for-grantedness of everyday life which are something like experimental equivalents of the phenomenological *epochê*. Garfinkel's movement in U.S. sociology during the 1960s and 1970s resurrected some qualities of Heidegger's preach-

ing, emphasizing the moral resonances of uncovering the merely constructed nature of the social world while pessimistically recognizing the inevitability of such constructions.

45. It was this phase of Heidegger that gave him a philosophical point of contact—apart from whatever temporizing and bandwagon jumping was involved—for greeting the Nazi rise to power in 1933.

46. Projecting this back into medieval Christendom, William of Ockham is supposed to be a typical Anglo philosopher, but Duns Scotus is not; in fact both of these Britons spent most of their careers in France and Germany. The archetypal metaphysician, Saint Anselm, was archbishop of Canterbury.

47. Hoch (1991) suggests that the Vienna Circle shifted from a militant program of replacing philosophy with unified science to a reforming movement within philosophy because of their migration to the United States. At this time their base shifted predominantly from physics chairs to philosophy departments. Carnap's chair at Prague had been in philosophy, but it was housed, unusually, in the natural science faculty; as in Vienna, the philosophy chairs had been split into one for inductive science or natural philosophy, another for traditional humanistic philosophy. The organizational background of the Vienna Circle was a European movement to absorb philosophy academically into the natural sciences. Nothing like this existed in the United States or Britain. Hence when the Vienna Circle migrated, it had to accommodate, becoming a reform movement within academic philosophy and eventually a technical specialty among others.

48. This may be one reason why Wittgenstein—apart from his usual cantankerousness—refused to go along with the Vienna Circle's condemnation of Heidegger (Janik and Toulmin, 1973: 288).

14. Writers' Markets and Academic Networks

1. Sources on the institutional structure of French education (*CMH*, 1902–1911: 8:52, 752; 9:126–129; 10:73–93; 11:23–26, 297; 12:92–93, 114–118; Weisz, 1983; Fabiani, 1988; Burrage, 1993; Ringer, 1992).

2. Politician-philosophers included not only the Idéologues but also Royer-Collard, who led the "Doctrinaires" faction, deriving politics from immutable self-evident principles (in fact taken largely from the Scottish philosophy of Reid, who held against Hume that man has a faculty of common sense); on the conservative side, de Maistre and de Bonald with their self-conscious traditionalism; Mme. de Staël, the daughter of the pre-Revolutionary finance minister, and emblem of the vacillating loyalties of the Royalist exiles; and Chateaubriand, like Destutt and Maine de Biran a former army officer, prominent after 1800 in the politics of Royalist opposition to Napoleon. Chateaubriand made his reputation in 1802 with his *Genius of Christianity*, written in opposition to Cabanis. The emergence of the political assemblies as the focus of attention went along with an underlying shift in the bases of intellectual production in the Revolutionary/Napoleonic period.

3. For instance, he was pictured on the cover of *Time* magazine in 1946 while on a publicity tour of the United States (Cohen-Solal, 1987: 271). The nearest approach

to such publicity would have been Kant, who was widely discussed in German magazines of the late 1780s; but the large-scale mass media did not exist yet in the twentieth-century sense. Sartre was the equivalent in philosophy of the publicity which elevated into media figures, among scientists, Einstein in the 1920s, and among writers, Hemingway in the 1940s. Within France, André Malraux had achieved some of this standing of front-page publicity in the 1930s with his exotic adventure-cum-writing exploits (Lacouture, 1975).

4. We see the same thing again with Sartre, whose first major production, *Nausea,* takes its surface content from his own situation as a provincial *lycée* teacher in Le Havre.

5. Deussen became a pupil of Zeller, and thus connects Nietzsche indirectly to the main Hegel network (Figure 13.1). Pforta had been Fichte's secondary school as well. A younger schoolmate of Nietzsche, Ulrich Wilamowitz-Moellendorf, who later became the preeminent classicist of his day (and grandteacher of the hermeneutic philosopher Gadamer), made his first statement by critiquing Nietzsche's *Birth of Tragedy* of 1872. Pforta was in fact the only *Gymnasium* which offered a truly elite curriculum in the 1850s–1870s; it selected most of its students for scholarships, and more than 30 of its pupils went on to become full professors at German universities, including Liebmann (originator of Neo-Kantianism) and Paulsen (Mueller, 1987: 29). Nietzsche was a product of the cutting edge of education in the German school system.

6. Although Nietzsche hated the anti-Semitic movement, he is within two links of it through two different connections: via Wagner to the latter's son-in-law Houston Stewart Chamberlain, and via his own sister to his brother-in-law Foerster, who was an anti-Semite politician. From a network point of view, it is no surprise that Nietzsche's philosophy became associated with this movement.

7. Wagner was in the first wave of those who recognized Schopenhauer in the mid-1850s, sending him the *Ring* libretto, as yet musically unscored, with a dedication. Schopenhauer replied politely but preferred, as a musical traditionalist, Mozart and Rossini; he suggested that Wagner had more genius as a poet (Safranski, 1989: 347).

8. The king of Bavaria had inherited in 1864 a palpably weak state in the geopolitics of the day, soon to be swallowed up in the unified German Empire through the wars of 1866–1871. His status equalization with Wagner is a case of aristocracy on the downward track meeting the market star on the upward slope. Wagner on his side was vituperatively scornful of musicians who let the popular market dictate their musical style, singling out Meyerbeer for connivance with the cliques and even bribery associated with his success at the Paris Opéra. Wagner's anti-Semitism originated in this rivalry with the commercially more successful Meyerbeer.

9. Lindenfeld (1980: 115–116). Ehrenfels also was an ardent Wagnerian and a member of the Wagner network (thereby linking Kafka indirectly to Nietzsche), and a friend of Wagner's son-in-law, the social Darwinist–racist H. S. Chamberlain. Given the oppressiveness of anti-Semitism in Kafka's milieu, Ehrenfels showed his idiosyncrasy by concluding that the solution to racial decadence was free-breeding sexuality by means of polygamy.

10. Lacan, in the Sartre literary circle of the 1940s, went on to become a leading figure of the 1970s and 1980s with his further synthesis of psychoanalysis with literary theory.

11. Another literary niche, lowbrow entertainment for the working class, had always existed, but was never a prestige motivator for intellectuals. Under modern market conditions, aspirants for the highbrow market have lumped together everything beneath their own standards, denigrating middle-class audience-oriented writings as if they were indistinguishable from penny dreadfuls.

12. Contemporary evidence too shows that most professional writers make very little income, and support themselves from other jobs; only a small fraction make a decent living by writing (Kingston and Cole, 1986).

13. Once a critical mass is attained, the visible production of avant-garde works, together with the palpable social milieu where intellectual values are held in high esteem by concentrated groups, makes such a center a mecca for international migrants. Other cities which locally passed the critical mass and became intellectual centers within their own language zone—London, St. Petersburg, Vienna, New York City, San Francisco—generally have been attractors only from their national hinterlands. This operated for Paris too; aspirant Frenchmen such as Rimbaud made the trek from the provinces. Paris alone became an international attractor for literary intellectuals: Germans such as Heine and Marx in the 1830s and 1840s; Russians such as Turgenev and Herzen in the 1850s; the Uruguayan Isidore Ducasse, who published under the French pseudonym Lautréamont in the 1870s; and a veritable lemming movement of American and British writers in the 1920s, not to mention Spaniards (Unamuno, Picasso), Latin Americans, and Russian exiles. It is notable that Germany has had less literary- geographical concentration than other language zones. German intellectual production was dominated by universities since their reform, and these kept up a decentralized network of competition among some 20 centers. International sojourners in Germany had no very central target, but wandered throughout the system.

14. Cohen-Solal (1987: 52–75); Biemel (1964). De Beauvoir's pioneering feminist work, *The Second Sex* (1949), comes at the height of the existentialist group's fame and its period of most intense political activity. Independent credit for creativity goes only to those individuals who mark out a distinctive turf; de Beauvoir, who had long contributed anonymously to the energy of the Sartre circle, now finds a niche in which its themes of authenticity and rebellion can be applied without forcing her into a break with her friends. Camus and Merleau-Ponty, by contrast, find the path to independence only at the cost of splitting from the group.

15. This account is drawn from numerous sources (Boschetti, 1985: 88; Lacouture, 1975: 163–165; Lebesque, 1960: 165; Cohen-Solal, 1987: 111–116). Groethuysen, originally Dutch, had studied under Dilthey at Berlin, and from the 1920s directed Gallimard's pacesetting literary magazine, *Nouvelle Revue Française;* he was an intimate friend of the chief literary figures of the 1920s and 1930s, Gide and Malraux, and acted as political-intellectual inspiration to the latter. It was the Gallimard intellectuals who shaped Sartre's path, turning the manuscript of his first novel from a naturalistic shocker in the style of Céline, full of raw sexuality,

into a metaphysical novel. Sartre's original psychological title, *Melancholia,* was changed to *Nausea* by the Gallimard staff to play up the theme of ontological unfoundedness.

16. Perhaps it is no surprise that Durkheim, who first formulated the general theory of the group worshipping sacred symbols of itself, was also a product of the ENS.

17. It was in Koyré's journal, *Recherches philosophiques* that Sartre published his first philosophical work, "The Transcendence of the Ego," in 1936. Within the main line of French academic philosophy, Sartre, Merleau-Ponty, Aron, and most others in the group had been taught by Léon Brunschwicg (who earlier had also taught Koyré and Piaget). Brunschwicg had a career similar to Bergson's: a pupil of Boutroux at the ENS, he spent 19 years teaching at one of the elite Paris *lycées* and was active in the group involved in academic reform in the early 1900s, before arriving at the Sorbonne. Brunschwicg taught the French lineage of spiritualism and Idealist epistemology descending from Renouvier, Maine de Biran, and Ravaisson; it was against the Idealism of this position that Sartre's generation rebelled. Sources on these network connections (Wagner, 1983: 156, 161; Lindberg, 1990: 14–18; Boschetti, 1985: 83–92, 210; Fabiani, 1988: 20, 100, 116; *EP*, 1967: 2:545, 7:482; Spiegelberg, 1982).

18. Merleau-Ponty ([1945] 1962: xiv) makes the same point in his existential revision of phenomenology: "The most important lesson that reduction teaches us is the impossibility of a complete reduction."

19. "The result of our inquiry so far is therefore as follows: *in relation to a possible object,* the pure self-reverting activity of the self is a *striving;* and as shown earlier, *an infinite striving* at that. This boundless striving, carried to infinity, is the *condition of the possibility of any object whatsoever:* no striving, no object" (Fichte [1794–1797] 1982: 231). Immediately preceding, Fichte had stated that the self never can conform to the not-self, since that would overturn the original negation.

20. Another version of this dialectic had been enunciated in France only a few years before Sartre. Meyerson, a German-trained scientist whose circle included Brunschwicg, Lévy-Bruhl, and Koyré, in well-known works published in 1908 and 1921 had argued that science expresses the inexhaustible drive of the human mind to make reality intelligible, although nature always remains independent; the empirical is ultimately irrational. Furthermore, the essence of rational explanation is causality, the principle of sufficient reason; and "the principle of causality is simply the principle of identity applied to the existence of objects in time" (quoted in Copleston, 1950–1977: 9:282). To establish causality fully would be to deduce every phenomenon from its antecedents, which would be equivalent to removing the independent standing of entities and reducing them to a timeless Parmenidean immutability. (Thus far Meyerson resembles Dharmakirti's Buddhist dissolution of entities through omni-causality.) But this is impossible; the human mind, expressed in its most rational form in science, strives for an unattainable unity. In his 1921 work Meyerson explicitly relates his argument to Hegel's philosophy of nature.

21. Here too Sartre betrays his conviction that only the artist lives a life of authentic freedom and meaning; it is beauty and art which is the union of essence and existence, and thus the only equivalent to God (Sartre, 1943: 244).

22. "It was unthinkable: to imagine nothingness you had to be there already, in the midst of the World, eyes wide open and alive; nothingness was only an idea in my head, an existing idea floating in this immensity: this nothingness had not come *before* existence, it was an existence like any other and appeared after many others. I shouted 'filth! what rotten filth!' and shook myself to get rid of this sticky filth, but it held fast and there was so much, tons and tons of existence, endless: I stifled at the depths of this immense weariness. And then suddenly the park emptied as through a great hole, the World disappeared as it had come, or else I woke up." (Sartre, [1938] 1964: 134). Camus's *Myth of Sisyphus* explicitly refers to Sartre's nausea as the absurd, following Sartre's lead (Sartre, [1938] 1964: 129), and succinctly sums up the nub of Sartre's position (without attributing it to him): "These two certainties—my appetite for the absolute and for unity and the impossibility of reducing this world to a rational and reasonable principle—I also know I cannot reconcile them" (Camus, [1942] 1955: 38). This was published in 1942, before Sartre had finished his 1943 masterwork, and before Camus personally knew Sartre. The materials for combining the literary and philosophical traditions must have been in the air. Sartre had already formulated the literary version of metaphysical omni-contingency and unfoundedness in his 1938 novel, before he had acquired the Hegelian and Heideggerian tools worked out in *L'Être et le Néant*. For both authors, subsequent creativity was a matter of working out further consequences from this starting point: for Camus, a lineage of literary and political rebellion; for Sartre, a full-scale phenomenological dialectic of self-deception and authenticity.

23. Maritain's 1948 *Existence and the Existent* (which he published at age 66) argues that Thomism is the only authentic existentialism (Herberg, 1958: 26–28, 155–157; *EP*, 1967: 5:153–155, 160–164; Boschetti, 1985: 89; Friedmann, 1981–1983). Among the theologians retrospectively labeled "existentialist," Buber is the most idiosyncratic. His academic parentage was mainline, as pupil of Brentano and Dilthey at Vienna and Berlin at the turn of the century. As editor of a Zionist journal during 1901–1926, he promoted Hasidism as the distinctively Jewish contribution to universal religious experience. Buber balanced uneasily between political Zionists and the secular Jewish assimilationists, writing in a universalistic vein on the classics of Eastern and Western mysticism. After 1913 he converted from mysticism to a religion of everyday *Existenz* (what Weber would call "inner-worldly mysticism"), then shifting to the dialogue of *I and Thou*, which Buber drafted in 1916 and published in 1923. Again, it was only in the late 1940s that Buber became famous as an existentialist, and published in his old age works (*Between Man and Man*, 1947; *Eclipse of God*, 1952) which brought out that identification. Originally Sartre branched off from the network of this same theological transformation. Raised by his maternal grandparents, of the Alsatian Schweitzer family of liberal Protestants involved for generations in secular pedagogy, Sartre would have known from childhood of the family's intellectual star, his cousin Albert Schweitzer. Schweitzer's *Search for the Historical Jesus* in 1906 had demolished the liberal interpretation of Jesus as an ethical teacher in favor a historical picture of Christ as apocalyptic prophet. Schweitzer was trained by the

main German networks in theology and philosophy, as pupil of Windelband at Strasbourg and of Harnack, Simmel, Paulsen, and Stumpf at Berlin. Like his younger cousin, Schweitzer was a hybrid across fields, combining academic scholarship with eminence as a musician and as a medical missionary.

24. "There were those idiots who came to tell you about will-power and the struggle for life. Hadn't they ever seen a beast of a tree? This plane-tree with its scaling bark, this half-rotten oak, they wanted me to take them for rugged youthful endeavour surging towards the sky . . . Impossible to see things that way. Weaknesses, frailties, yes. The trees floated. Gushing towards the sky? Or rather a collapse; at any instant I expected to see the tree-trunks shrivel like weary wands, crumple up, fall on the ground in a soft, folded, black heap. *They did not want* to exist, only they could not help themselves . . . For every existing thing is born without reason, prolongs itself out of weakness and dies by chance" (Sartre, [1938] 1964: 133).

25. The balance between unbelief and religion comes off best in Beckett's *Waiting for Godot,* a popular production in 1956 when existentialism was dying. Beckett, who came from the old anglophone émigré circle of James Joyce, suppressed existentialist political resonances in favor of religious nostalgia. Sartre's protégé Genet exploited Camus's track in the other direction, making metaphysical rebellion a primarily political theme in *The Balcony* (1958), *The Blacks* (1959), and *The Screens* (1961), which plays up the Algerian rebellion, a subject that Camus had avoided.

26. Camus ([1951] 1956: 22). He comments (p. 8) that the experience of the absurd is "the equivalent, in existence, of Descartes' methodical doubt."

27. Separation between Sartre and Merleau-Ponty, too, came ultimately from divergent interests in intellectual space. Both discovered the same cultural capital, Husserlian phenomenology; in extracting opposite uses from it they were able to create distinctive pathways for themselves. "One day, [Merleau-Ponty] discovered what he had been looking for, *intentionality* . . . The same year, in Berlin, I also came across *intentionality* in [Husserl's] *Ideen,* but what I wanted from it was more or less the opposite of what Merleau-Ponty had been looking for: I wanted it to rid consciousness of all its slags, of all its 'states'" (Sartre, quoted in Cohen-Solal, 1987: 343). Merleau-Ponty, by contrast, used intentionality as grounds for his own conception of human spontaneity, a rival to what would become Sartre's dialectic of freedom through negation. Merleau-Ponty's chief phenomenological works were published in 1942 and 1945, very close to the appearance of Sartre's masterwork in 1943. Merleau-Ponty came into fully independent standing in the attention space only after he ceased collaborating with Sartre in editing *Les Temps Modernes,* with his *Adventures of the Dialectic* (1955) and *Signs* (1960).

15. Sequence and Branch in the Social Production of Ideas

1. Dharmakirti describes a student learning philosophy by reading a text at his teacher's house, repeating it, and learning it by heart (Stcherbatski, [1930] 1962:

523); this method of teaching was going on at the height of innovation in Buddhist philosophy.

2. Gibbon, with characteristic eloquence and bias, puts it: "A cloud of critics, of compilers, of commentators, darkened the face of learning, and the decline of genius was soon followed by the corruption of taste" (*The Decline and Fall of the Roman Empire;* Gibbon, [1776] 1956: 52).

3. The arithmetic formulated in the early Roman Empire, at the same time as numerology, and indeed connected with the concerns for occult divination in a universe of numerological correspondences, also made substantive advances in number theory. This shows that there was a combination of two processes; their overlap in the case of Nicomachus led to some mathematical discovery, whereas in other parts of the Greek Cabalistic world and in the correlative cosmologies of China, the result was primarily occultist classification.

4. There are processes of conceptual development within mythology which I will make no attempt to deal with here. Lévi-Strauss's structuralism emphasizes interactions across the border between humans and animals. These themes are characteristic of relatively unstratified, kinship-structured tribal and band societies, in which totemic animals are emblems of group membership. The mythologies of high gods, as in the Vedic and Greek pantheons, are typical of politically organized societies with ruling kings. Here the fragmentary and episodic narratives of tribal myth give way to longer coherent narratives stressing the psychological motivations of their characters, implying the working of professionalized entertainers, whose minds are made sophisticated by the frontstage Goffmanian settings on which they perform (Schneider, 1993: 83–113). Thus a degree of abstraction and reflexivity emerges already within the sequence of mythologies, although we know little about what kinds of networks among mythology specialists were responsible.

5. The notorious burning of the books which took place just before the founding of the Han dynasty is an extreme example of external political forces intruding to deny the autonomy of the intellectual attention space. It is no surprise that Han intellectuals responded by moving in a particularistic direction.

6. As I noted in Chapter 10, note 5, the use of the modern term "science" is anachronistic. But all abstract terms which we use for analyzing history are to some degree anachronistic. The point is to be clear on what we are talking about. The present discussion makes the relevant distinctions.

7. That is not so say that developments in scientific theories never change the level of abstraction. Most Kuhnian paradigm shifts (Ptolemaic to Copernican astronomy, phlogiston to oxygen chemistry) stay at the same level of abstraction; but some new theories shift to higher abstract levels and occasionally introduce reflexivity (Maxwell's non-representational electromagnetic equations, Einsteinian relativity, Heisenberg quantum mechanics). This kind of shift occurs primarily when scientific theories are based on higher mathematics, a field which has its own abstraction-reflexivity sequence.

8. This is one of the characteristics of occultism: once formulated, it remains fixed at

a constant level of the abstraction-reflexivity sequence, changing if at all by accretion of concrete contents in its systems of divination and correspondence.

9. Cases emerging from the analytical camp include Robert Nozick's *Philosophical Explanations* (1981) and David Lewis's *On the Plurality of Worlds* (1986), which turns possible-worlds logic into a metaphysics of "modal realism"—all possible worlds really exist.

10. I am using the term "skepticism" in the specific sense of an omni-critical view against the possibility of knowledge, a stance often manifested in the display of unresolvable paradoxes. I do not use "skepticism" in the loose sense of opposition to magical superstition or religious supernaturalism; it is better to reserve the term "secular rationalism" or "naturalism" for such attitudes.

11. Krishna (1991: 42) notes that the conception of doubt, as it arises in debates, is integral to the very definition of philosophy in the Indian tradition. "Doubt or *samshaya* arises because there is *vipratipatti,* i.e. two opposite positions seem to be supported by equally weighty arguments. It is true that the word 'philosophy' is not a Sanskrit word, but there is no reason to suppose there is no Sanskrit analogue to it in the Indian tradition."

12. The question of possible transmission of influences is not a significant one for our purposes, since the cogito is used in different contexts and for different purposes.

13. In Kant's case, the backdrop is Hume's more limited skepticism regarding causality. In Royce's, the catalyst is Peirce's criticism that Cartesian doubt is impossible, since human consciousness is always in the midst of a chain of sensations and signs, within which clear-cut doubt is an artificial construction.

14. Unlike other deep troubles, especially the problems of being and plurality, or substance and its relations, which are discovered quite early in the network sequences and recycle repeatedly thereafter at each higher level of abstraction, the cogito starts off in the mid-periods of these sequences. That is because the cogito hinges on the recognition not merely of abstract concepts, but of a considerable degree of reflexivity.

15. This is a theme not much explored in the West, where Platonic influence labeled negation mere privation of being. After the collapse of Neoplatonic influence, negation was finally made prominent in the dialectic of Fichte and Hegel, paving the way for the ontological use of negation by Heidegger's and Sartre's existentialism. An episodic parallel to Dignaga is the medieval Christian philosopher Henry of Ghent, who in order to avoid using matter as the source of individuation described individuation as a double negation: negation of all differences within the particular thing, and negation of identity with other things. A generation later Eckhart made negation central to his non-Platonic formulation of Christian mysticism: God is so far above being that we can say nothing about him; human existence is so low that it is virtually nothing; and these two nothings converge in a divine spark. Apart from these ontological uses of negation, a parallel to Bhartrihari's and Dignaga's theories of language shows up in the structuralism of Saussure, in which words are arbitrary markers of difference within a system of language. (There is a further parallel insofar as Bhartrihari gives ontological precedence to what Saussure called *parole,* the acts of speaking, over *langue,* the

formal system of oppositions, which Bhartrihari and Dignaga regard as the source of illusion.) The structuralist-postmodernist emphasis on "difference" adds an ontological tone that is not far from the original Buddhist conception of world illusion arising through name-and-form.

16. In other words, Indian intellectual life incorporated into about 200 years a range of arguments that spread over 600–700 years in Europe. This should cast doubt on our image of the West as uniquely dynamic intellectually. Everywhere the pace of argument on the abstraction sequence is stalled from time to time by external factors. Such periods occur not only in the East (e.g., in India, the period after 1500) but in the West as well, where the Renaissance period, 1400–1600, is largely a diversion from the abstract philosophy of the medieval Christian universities. European philosophy after 1600, its own ideological assertions to the contrary notwithstanding, to a large extent revived and continued the higher levels of abstraction attained by medieval scholasticism. We can add to this interruption the 1300s, when the higher levels of scholasticism were obscured from being transmitted further by conditions which are explained in the Coda to Chapter 9. To make the comparison fair, we should take account of the fact that the parallels to modern European philosophy begin in India around 550–750, the time of Bhartrihari, Dignaga, Dharmakirti, Prabhakara, and Shankara. Indian philosophy from about 800 to 1100 seems in a slowdown compared to the half-dozen generations preceding and following, probably owing to external conditions affecting the base of intellectual life (discussed in Chapter 5 in relation to the conditions for the popularity of tantric magic). If we could subtract the dead spots from both sequences, we might say that the parallel between India around 500–1300 and Europe about 1200–1900 boils down to a comparable number of generations in each during which the networks had enough continuity to keep the abstraction-reflexivity sequence moving.

17. Thus Heidegger's and Sartre's radical particularism was constructed in reaction to Husserl's radical realism of universals, so to speak—Husserl's program of searching for the deepest levels of formal ontological structures framing experience. This is a typical case of innovation by split within a creative network, and of creation by negating a rival's central premise.

18. The question of the sincerity of faith sometimes raised about famous figures on the religious-philosophical divide is doubly useless. To ask whether Ockham or Descartes was sincere in his professions of religious faith or only adopting a protective mask is to ignore the structural situation which such individuals occupy: it is precisely because they are transforming the deep troubles of the argument space that they are not easily categorized on one side or the other. From a micro-sociological viewpoint, the question of sincerity is naive. Thinking takes place by the flow of emotional energies focused in intellectual networks, recombining within a thinker's mind ideas representing membership in particular camps. The creative thinker is making and transforming alliances in the realm of symbols. In struggles of faith versus reason, creative developments fuse concepts which cut across both sides of the struggle. It is possible, of course, that a philosopher's internal conversation might include discussions about what it would be politic to say

in public. But prolonged hiding of one's inner thoughts is difficult, above all in the intellectual world, where rituals of communication are the taps controlling its energy flow. When the philosopher publicly states a position—such as the double truth, or the compatibility of conceptual innovations with religious orthodoxy— the ritualistic process of repeating it before an audience generates further emotional energy, which makes these ideas still more dominant in the internal conversation. Successful thinkers cannot be Machiavellian about their creativity for very long; as their ideas become publicly known, the result is self-indoctrination.

19. There are seven often-used types of proofs of God, together with proofs of another six auxiliary questions (Davidson, 1987; *EP*, 1967: 2:147–155, 232–237, 324–326, 3:345–348, 6:538–541, 7:84–87; Sextus Empiricus, 1949: 1:13–194). Their distribution throughout world history confirms the importance of the monotheist context. There are two lay-oriented proofs. *Common consent of mankind:* Cicero, Seneca, Clement of Alexandria; widely used in the 1600s by Cherbury, Gassendi, Grotius, Hooker, and the Cambridge Platonists. In India it appears in the Nyaya-Vaisheshika commentary of Udayana (1000 C.E.). This is a popularistic argument for the laity; it has been applied to defending both polytheism and monotheism, and was attacked as early as the Greek Sophists, Stoics, and Skeptics. *Teleology or design* (the harmonious order of the world implies a maker): Socrates (as recorded by Xenophon), Plato, the Christian Fathers; included by Saadia, Maimonides, and Aquinas in their compendia; especially emphasized in Europe of the 1700s with Butler and Paley. It has been most prominent in the context of reconciling science and religion. This type of argument does not arise in Asia, as it implies an anthropomorphic God and is senseless in connection with mysticism, which declares the lower world an illusion, or in connection with an immanent world order as in the Chinese cosmologies. Both of these proofs are metaphysically limited, implying nothing about God's perfection and unity, or about creation of the world ex nihilo.

There are three metaphysical proofs. *Cosmological,* whose subtypes include *from motion:* Aristotle's proof of the existence of an unmoved Mover, Stoics; and *from causality:* allied with auxiliary arguments, used as proofs of God by medieval Muslims and Jews, Aquinas, Descartes, Locke. *From relative perfection* (comparative degrees of perfection implies a superlative): early Stoics, Augustine, Anselm, Aquinas, Descartes; Shankara gives an epistemological version. *Ontological:* Ibn Sina (arguing from contingency); Anselm's version was widely used, discussed, and rejected in medieval Christian philosophy, revived by Descartes, Spinoza, and Leibniz, and critically discussed down through Frege and Russell. Technical philosophers have found this the most metaphysically stimulating proof because it acutely raises the issue of reflexivity. The ontological proof does not appear in India, owing to the anti-conceptual stance toward the highest reality dominant since the rise of Advaita.

There are two post-metaphysical proofs. *Moral:* Kant (the ideal of the highest good implies a source outside the human individual). *From religious experience:* Schleiermacher, James. These arguments result from Kant's critique cutting off metaphysical arguments, especially the cosmological and ontological proofs.

Auxiliary proofs: of the unity, perfection, infinity, incorporeality of God; of creation ex nihilo (rejecting the eternity of the world substance); of the immortality of the soul. These proofs are the key to distinguishing arguments for transcendent monotheism from arguments for polytheism and pantheism. Some of these proofs began with the late Christian Neoplatonists; they developed most widely in medieval Islamic and Jewish philosophy.

20. Monotheism is not a primordial concept of popular religion; nor does it come from professional priests, whose politics tends toward compromise into pantheons. It takes the drive toward abstraction in a competitive intellectual community to purify the concept of divinity into ontological monotheism. This is why monotheism tends to appear well into the middle generations of an intellectual sequence. But there is nothing within intellectual dynamics to stabilize at the point of anthropomorphic monotheism. Where it occurs, such monotheism is the result of the combination of internal intellectual trends with external social conditions of the kind noted by Weber and Durkheim. These are, respectively, the dominance of an imperial state (or in the case of the war confederation of ancient Israel, aspiration to such a state), which raises the primary god of a pantheon above the others (Weber), and the universalization which goes with increasing social differentiation (Durkheim). Comparative evidence is presented by Swanson (1962).

21. A deep trouble like the Indian *satkaryavada* versus *asatkaryavada,* however, would divide the attention space into only two positions, whereas the law of small numbers provides room for three to six. Deep troubles are the most important of the factors dividing the attention space, but not the only one.

22. For instance Epicureans, dropping to a lower level of concreteness, solved the problem of causal relations among independent atoms by fiat, asserting that the atoms swerved into one another's courses, thereby setting off the formation of the visible universe.

23. A shift is visible at the point where Christianity began to formulate a theology at a generalized level. The disputes about the relations among the parts of the Trinity, which took up much of the attention between 190 and 530 C.E., were a version on the moderately abstract plane of theology of the deep trouble of the plurality of substances. The first of these disputes, the Monarchian heresy, may be regarded as the discovery of a puzzle space on which an intellectual community of Christian theologians could form. In this light, the outburst of heresy fights was an indication not of the weakness of Christianity, but of its institutionalization.

24. Buddhism also developed a theist side. Mahayana added the worship of Boddhisattavas plus a sequence of future and past incarnations of the Buddha, including the doctrine of the Buddha's three bodies, one of which is the body of the universe. But these movements toward anthropomorphism did not produce the conception of a creator God; and the doctrines of Mahayana philosophies denied that there was any world-substance to be created.

25. The traditional practice of intellectual historians when noting parallels among ideas is to search for ways that influence could have been transmitted (e.g., ways in which Hume could directly or indirectly have heard of al-Ghazali's discussion of causality). For reasons argued earlier (Chapter 8, notes 6 and 15), such influences

are usually overstated; this approach also omits consideration of why intellectuals in one community would be motivated to pay attention to arguments from elsewhere. We should notice the difference in the intellectual organization of two scholarly enterprises: historians typically operate on a fairly modest level of the abstraction-reflexivity sequence, with a concrete conception of intellectual causality (an idea is transmitted from one person to another). Sociological analysis operates at a somewhat more abstract level, looking for the general principles which explain intellectual production, and hence taking similarities in ideas as a challenge to find similarities in conditions within intellectual life.

26. A foreshadowing of this came with Cusanus in the mid-1400s, at the very beginning of the mathematical revolution. Cusanus describes the world by extending geometrical forms to infinity, where all forms merge into one another; hence the famous formulation that the universe is a sphere whose circumference is nowhere and its center everywhere. Leibniz turns every physical and logical quality into positions along a continuum: rest is infinitely slow motion; equality is infinitely small differences.

27. Despite the many parallels between the higher levels of the abstraction-reflexivity sequence in India and in Europe, there are no distinctions made between a priori and a posteriori, and between analytical and synthetic, in Indian philosophy (Potter, [1963] 1976: 259). This is a consequence of the divergence between mathematical and philosophical networks in India, and their convergence in Europe.

28. It is more than straws in the wind that Derrida comes from the later generations of the Husserl network and that his first publication (Derrida, 1962) was on Husserl's work on the philosophy of geometry.

29. There have been no specifically anti-mathematical philosophies in the traditions of China and India because mathematics was never a significant part of those philosophical networks.

Epilogue

1. There are other kinds of thinking, such as in imagery, but these are not at issue here; it is thinking in verbal statements which yields some irrefutably true statements.

2. What this argument does not prove is that space must have three dimensions. The various numbers of dimensions conjectured in physics such as string theory are compatible with the argument so far developed.

3. And since thinking depends on the meaning of concepts, it is impossible to formulate the notion of dreaming unless one is embedded in a discourse which distinguishes dreaming from waking experience. Dreaming could not exist if non-dreaming did not exist.

4. In medias res passes the test of Cartesian doubt. To deny in medias res is still to affirm an instance of it in the very act of thinking the denial.

5. I am not disputing here whether such translation can in fact always be carried out; the point is merely that translation does not escape from discourse. In social

experience, translation is a merging between two networks. Quine's argument, that there is a multiplicity of different possible translations among languages, may well not be applicable to mathematical translations, for reasons that will become apparent.

6. If we do not in fact arrive at the same total, we assume that someone has made a mistake, has carried out the operation wrongly; this is to say that we did not both follow the convention.

7. The comparative sociology of networks casts light on how this conception of mathematics arose. Plato's faction within the Greek networks was an alliance between mathematicians and philosophers, whose creativity came from tension with opposing factions of empiricists, materialists, and skeptical relativists. Subsequent Platonic and Neoplatonic religions made mutually supporting arguments out of the conception of a transcendent God, a hierarchy of degrees of universality, and mathematical Platonism. This combination of concepts was later taken over by the mainstream of Christian, Islamic, and Jewish philosophers, and has remained available as a tradition for philosophy of mathematics into the secularizing period of European thought. In India and China no such mathematical Platonism arose, even with the prevalence of Idealist philosophy in India in the post-Buddhist period. This is due to the fact (documented in Chapter 10) that the networks of mathematics and of philosophers had very few overlaps in China and India, unlike in Greece and the West.

8. Since mathematics is also a genealogy of techniques, which took off in its own rapid-discovery revolution in the generations between Tartaglia and Descartes, the development of mathematical-experimental paradigms in modern science has been yet another kind of hybridization among genealogies of techniques. The lineages of mathematics have branched and recombined among themselves, giving rise to a rich ecology of mathematical "species" which have cross-bred in various ways with the similarly cross-breeding "species" of research equipment genealogies.

9. That is, since the telegraph (first in 1837), and subsequently electric motors, telephones, lighting, and so on made it part of banal reality. Electricity had had a more restricted laboratory reality for researchers since the Leiden jar was invented in the 1740s, and especially since the voltaic cell (1799), which produced a reliable continuous current. During the intervening period before laboratory equipment was widely exported into everyday life, there were many popular interpretations of the reality of electricity (e.g., Mesmer's, as well as religious interpretations), which lacked the sense of banal normalcy electricity was later to acquire.

10. There is a family continuity between one generation of such concepts and the next, although just what constitutes such continuity does not appear to be specifiable in general and in advance. Kuhn (1961) has argued that even in the massive conceptual shifts which he calls paradigm revolutions, the mathematics is preserved. As we have seen in the previous section, mathematics should be regarded as a practical technique for making discoveries about formal intellectual operations; this means that once again what is preserved across the generations is not the ideas per se but the continuity of yet another genealogy of research "equipment." Mathematical continuity and groundedness of scientific entities is another case of the continuity

of practical time-space activity. Again we see an epistemological gap between this reliable, materially existing but tacit practice and the verbal constructions and human-sized imagery which include the reified nouns and imputed substances of theoretical scientific entities.

11. Every mathematical article starts off with a verbal title and engages in verbal explanations, however cryptic, of its problems before plunging into manipulating its symbolism; at the other end, successful mathematics becomes part of the verbal discourse by which mathematicians summarize and point toward past accomplishments and future topics. Data illustrating this point for mathematical journals are given in Collins (1984).

12. One version of the sociology of knowledge or sociology of science attempts to reduce knowledge produced by intellectuals to the ideological claims of external groups outside the network, for example, as reflection of class interests in the surrounding society. Knowledge is sometimes constructed in this way. But lay influence is not the main source of the social construction of specifically intellectual knowledge. The ideas of ordinary social discourse are on a lower level of abstraction than ideas produced by intellectuals; and the creativity of intellectual networks comes from creating topics and problems which arise not in the lay world at all but primarily through the dynamics of attention-seeking within their inner social space. The externalist sociology of knowledge began with the conception of ideology, and thus with the tendency to regard sociology as explaining the source of false beliefs. As sociology has begun to study the internal social communities of intellectuals, it has come to encompass the social construction of true beliefs. The suspicion lingers that sociology means reducing true beliefs to false beliefs, although this flatly contradicts what is asserted: the social construction of true beliefs is about true beliefs.

13. Bloor's "strong programme" (1978) is that of a Wittgensteinian philosopher; the local social constructivism of laboratory studies (e.g., Latour and Woolgar, 1983) derived from a network which branched from the phenomenologists to ethnomethodology, via Schutz and Garfinkel. The earlier sociology of knowledge of Marx and Engels came from the Hegelian circle of the 1840s; Durkheim's came from his personal confrontation between the neo-Kantianism and empiricist psychology of his immediate predecessors.

14. In one batch of manuscripts for journal review, I have read of the intersection between the conceptions of Max Weber and Dostoyevsky, and between those of Durkheim and Schopenhauer. Further cross-combinations of these and others are obvious. And each generation of literature makes possible new combinations in the following generation.

References

Afnan, Soheil M. 1958. *Avicenna: His Life and Works.* London: Allen and Unwin.

Akamatsu, Toshihide, and Philip Yampolsky. 1977. "Muromachi Zen and the Gozan System." In Hall and Toyoda, 1977.

Aland, Kurt, and Barbara Aland. 1987. *The Text of the New Testament.* Leiden: Brill.

Alexander, Samuel. 1927. *Space, Time, and Deity.* London: Macmillan.

Ameriks, Karl. 1992. "The Critique of Metaphysics: Kant and Traditional Ontology." In Guyer, 1992.

Anderson, Perry. 1974. *Lineages of the Absolutist State.* London: Verso.

Anselm. 1962. *Basic Writings.* La Salle, Ill.: Open Court.

Ariel, Yoav. 1989. *K'ung-Ts'ung-Tzu: The K'ung Family Masters' Anthology.* Princeton: Princeton University Press.

Ariès, Phillipe. 1962. *Centuries of Childhood.* New York: Random House.

Ariew, Roger. 1990. "Descartes in Social Context." Unpublished Paper.

Attwater, Donald, and Catherine Rachel John. 1983. *The Penguin Dictionary of Saints.* New York: Viking Penguin.

Audi, Robert (ed.). 1995. *The Cambridge Dictionary of Philosophy.* Cambridge: Cambridge University Press.

Ayer, A. J. 1982. *Philosophy in the Twentieth Century.* New York: Random House.

Bacon, Francis. 1965. *A Selection from His Works.* New York: Macmillan.

Balazs, Étienne. 1964. *Chinese Civilization and Bureaucracy.* New Haven: Yale University Press.

Ball, W. W. Rouse. [1908] 1960. *A Short Account of the History of Mathematics.* New York: Dover.

Barbagli, Marzio. 1982. *Educating for Unemployment: Politics, Labor Markets, and the School System—Italy, 1859–1973.* New York: Columbia University Press.

Barnes, Barry. 1977. *Interests and the Growth of Knowledge.* London: Routledge and Kegan Paul.

Barraclough, Geoffrey. 1979. *The Times Atlas of World History.* Maplewood, N.J.: Hammond.

Barrett, T. H. 1992. *Li Ao: Buddhist, Taoist, or Neo-Confucian?* Oxford: Oxford University Press.

Barua, Beni Madhab. 1974. *Studies in Buddhism.* Calcutta: Saraswat Library.

Basham, A. L. 1951. *History and Doctrines of the Ajivikas.* London: Luzac.

—— 1989. *The Origins and Development of Classical Hinduism.* New York: Oxford University Press.

Beiser, Frederick C. 1987. *The Fate of Reason: German Philosophy from Kant to Fichte.* Cambridge, Mass.: Harvard University Press.

—— 1992. "Kant's Intellectual Development: 1746–1781." In Guyer, 1992.

—— (ed.). 1993. *The Cambridge Companion to Hegel.* Cambridge: Cambridge University Press.

Bell, Quentin. 1972. *Virginia Woolf: A Biography.* New York: Harcourt Brace Jovanovich.

Bellah, Robert N. 1957. *Tokugawa Religion.* New York: Free Press.

—— 1978. "Baigan and Sorai: Continuities and Discontinuities in Eighteenth-Century Japanese Thought." In Najita and Scheiner, 1978.

Ben-David, Joseph. 1960. "Roles and Innovations in Medicine." *American Journal of Sociology* 65:557–568.

—— 1971. *The Scientist's Role in Society.* Englewood Cliffs, N.J.: Prentice-Hall.

Ben-David, Joseph, and Randall Collins. 1966. "Social Factors in the Origins of a New Science: The Case of Psychology." *American Sociological Review* 31:451–465.

Ben-David, Joseph, and Awraham Zloczower. 1962. "Universities and Academic Systems in Modern Societies." *European Journal of Sociology* 3:45–85.

Bennett, Ralph F. 1971. *The Early Dominicans.* New York: Russell and Russell.

Bentley, John Edward. 1939. *Outline of Philosophy.* New York: Longmans, Green.

Bergmann, Gustav. 1967. *Realism: A Critique of Brentano and Meinong.* Madison: University of Wisconsin Press.

Berkeley, George. [1709] 1925. *Essay Towards a New Theory of Vision.* New York: Dutton.

Berman, Harold. 1983. *Law and Revolution: The Formation of the Western Legal Tradition.* Cambridge, Mass.: Harvard University Press.

Bernard, Luther L., and Jessie Bernard. 1943. *Origins of American Sociology.* New York: Crowell.

Bernstein, Basil. 1971–1975. *Class, Codes, and Control.* London: Routledge.

Bettoni, Efrem. 1961. *Duns Scotus: The Basic Principles of His Philosophy.* Washington, D.C.: Catholic University Press.

Biemel, Walter. 1964. *Sartre.* Reinbek bei Hamburg: Rohwolt.

Blacker, Carmen. 1964. *The Japanese Enlightenment: A Study in the Writings of Fukazawa Yukichi.* Cambridge: Cambridge University Press.

Bloch, Marc. 1961. *Feudal Society.* Chicago: University of Chicago Press.

Bloor, David. 1976. *Knowledge and Social Imagery.* New York: Columbia University Press.

—— 1983. *Wittgenstein: A Social Theory of Knowledge.* Chicago: University of Chicago Press.

The Blue Cliff Record. 1977 [orig. 1128 c.e.]. Translated by Thomas and J. C. Cleary. Boulder: Shambala.

Blumenberg, Hans. 1983. *The Legitimacy of the Modern Age.* Cambridge, Mass.: MIT Press.

——— 1987. *The Genesis of the Copernican World.* Cambridge, Mass.: MIT Press.

Boase, T. S. R. 1933. *Boniface VIII.* London: Constable.

Bodde, Dirk. 1991. *Chinese Thought, Society, and Science.* Honolulu: University of Hawaii Press.

Borgman, Christine L. (ed.). 1990. *Scholarly Communication and Bibliometrics.* London: Sage.

Boring, Edward G. 1950. *A History of Experimental Psychology.* New York: Appleton-Century-Crofts.

Borkenau, Franz. 1981. *End and Beginning. On the Generations of Cultures and the Origins of the West.* New York: Columbia University Press.

Boschetti, Anna. 1985. *Sartre et "Les temps modernes."* Paris: Éditions de Minuit.

Bourdieu, Pierre. [1975] 1991. *The Political Ontology of Martin Heidegger.* Oxford: Polity Press.

——— [1979] 1984. *Distinction.* Cambridge, Mass.: Harvard University Press.

——— [1984] 1988. *Homo Academicus.* Stanford: Stanford University Press.

Bourdieu, Pierre, and Jean-Claude Passeron. [1970] 1977. *Reproduction: In Education, Society, and Culture.* London: Sage.

Boyer, Carl B. 1985. *A History of Mathematics.* Princeton: Princeton University Press.

Bradley, F. H. [1883] 1922. *The Principles of Logic.* Oxford: Oxford University Press.

——— 1893. *Appearance and Reality.* Oxford: Clarendon Press.

Braudel, Fernand. [1967] 1973. *Capitalism and Material Life, 1400–1800.* New York: Harper and Row.

——— [1979] 1984. *The Perspective of the World.* Vol. 3 of *Civilization and Capitalism, Fifteenth–Eighteenth Century.* New York: Harper.

Brent, Joseph. 1993. *Charles Sanders Peirce: A Life.* Bloomington: Indiana University Press.

Brentano, Franz. [1862] 1975. *On the Several Senses of Being in Aristotle.* Berkeley: University of California Press.

Bretall, Robert (ed.). 1946. *A Kierkegaard Anthology.* New York: Random House.

Broad, C. D. 1975. *Leibniz: An Introduction.* Cambridge: Cambridge University Press.

Brooke, Rosalind B. 1959. *Early Franciscan Government.* Cambridge: Cambridge University Press.

Brown, Peter. 1967. *Augustine of Hippo: A Biography.* Berkeley: University of California Press.

——— 1982. *Society and the Holy in Late Antiquity.* Berkeley: University of California Press.

Brown, Stuart. 1984. *Leibniz.* Minneapolis: University of Minnesota Press.

Bruford, W. H. 1962. *Culture and Society in Classical Weimar, 1775–1806.* Cambridge: Cambridge University Press.

——— 1965. *Germany in the Eighteenth Century: The Social Background of the Literary Revival.* Cambridge: Cambridge University Press.

Brunschwig, Henri. 1947. *Le crise de l'état prussien à la fin de XVIIIe siècle*. Paris: Presses Universitaires de France.

Bryant, Joseph M. 1986. "Intellectuals and Religion in Ancient Greece." *British Journal of Sociology* 37:269–296.

—— 1990. "Enlightenment Psychology and Political Reaction in Plato's Social Philosophy: An Ideological Contradiction?" *History of Political Thought* 11:1–19.

—— 1996. *Moral Codes and Social Structure in Ancient Greece: A Sociology of Greek Ethics from Homer to the Epicureans and Stoics*. Albany: SUNY Press.

Buchler, Justus (ed.). 1955. *Philosophical Writings of Peirce*. New York: Dover.

Burkert, Walter. 1972. *Lore and Science in Ancient Pythagoreanism*. Cambridge, Mass.: Harvard University Press.

—— 1985. *Greek Religion*. Oxford: Oxford University Press.

Burrage, Michael. 1993. "From Practice to School-Based Professional Education: Patterns of Conflict and Accommodation in England, France, and the United States." In Rothblatt and Wittrock, 1993.

Burschell, Friedrich. 1958. *Schiller*. Hamburg: Rowohlt.

Butler, Edward C. 1962. *Benedictine Monachism*. New York: Barnes and Noble.

Cajori, Florian. 1928. *A History of Mathematical Notations*. La Salle, Ill.: Open Court.

Cameron, Euan. 1991. *The European Reformation*. Oxford: Clarendon Press.

Camic, Charles. 1983. *Experience and Enlightenment: Socialization for Cultural Change in Eighteenth-Century Scotland*. Chicago: University of Chicago Press.

Camus, Albert. [1942] 1955. *The Myth of Sisyphus*. New York: Knopf.

—— [1951] 1956. *The Rebel*. New York: Knopf.

Canfora, Luciano. 1990. *The Vanished Library: A Wonder of the Ancient World*. Berkeley: University of California Press.

Cannon, Susan. 1978. *Science in Culture: The Early Victorian Period*. New York: Dawson Scientific History Publications.

Caputo, John D. 1993. "Heidegger and Theology." In Guignon, 1993.

Cardan, Jerome. [1575] 1962. *The Book of My Life*. New York: Dover.

Caron, Jean-Claude. 1991. *Générations romantiques, 1814–1851: les étudiants de Paris et le quartier latin*. Paris: Colin.

Chadwick, Henry. 1967. *The Early Church*. Baltimore: Penguin Books.

Chadwick, Owen. 1966. *The Victorian Church*. New York: Oxford University Press.

Chaffee, John W. 1985. *The Thorny Gates of Learning in Sung China*. Cambridge: Cambridge University Press.

Chakravarti, Uma. 1987. *The Social Dimensions of Early Buddhism*. Delhi: Oxford University Press.

Chambers Biographical Dictionary. 1984. Edinburgh: Chambers.

Chambliss, Daniel F. 1989. "The Mundanity of Excellence." *Sociological Theory* 7:70–86.

Chan, Wing-Tsit. 1963. *A Sourcebook in Chinese Philosophy*. Princeton: Princeton University Press.

—— 1970. "The Ch'eng-Chu School of Early Ming." In *Self and Society in Ming Thought,* ed. William Theodore de Bary. New York: Columbia University Press.

Chandler, Tertius, and Gerald Fox. 1974. *3,000 Years of Urban Growth.* New York: Academic Press.

Chang, Carsun. 1957–1962. *The Development of Neo-Confucian Thought.* New York: Bookman Associates.

Chappell, David W. 1987. *Buddhist and Taoist Practice in Medieval Chinese Society.* Honolulu: University of Hawaii Press.

Chattopadhyaya, Debiprasad. 1972. *Indian Philosophy.* Delhi: People's Publishing House.

—— 1979. *Studies in the History of Indian Philosophy.* 3 volumes. Calcutta: K. P. Bagchi.

Chauvin, André. 1991. *Les Jesuits à la Flèche.* La Flèche: Prytanée National Militaire.

CHC = The Cambridge History of China. 1986. Vol. 1. *The Ch'in and Han Empires, 221 B.C.–A.D. 220.* 1979. Vol. 3. *Sui and T'ang China, 581–906.* 1988. Vol. 7. *The Ming Dynasty. 1368–1644.* Part 1. Cambridge: Cambridge University Press.

Chen, Cheng-Yih (ed.). 1987. *Science and Technology in Chinese Civilization.* Singapore: World Scientific Publishing Company.

Ch'en, Kenneth. 1964. *Buddhism in China.* Princeton: Princeton University Press.

Ch'ien, Edward. 1982. "The Neo-Confucian Confrontation with Buddhism." *Journal of Chinese Philosophy* 9:307–328.

—— 1986. *Chiao Hung and the Restructuring of Neo-Confucianism in the Late Ming.* New York: Columbia University Press.

Ching, Julia (ed.). 1987. *The Records of Ming Scholars by Huang Tsung-shi.* Honolulu: University of Hawaii Press

CHJ = The Cambridge History of Japan. 1990. Vol. 3. Kozo Yamamura (ed.), *Medieval Japan.* 1991. Vol. 4. John W. Hall (ed.), *Early Modern Japan.* 1989. Vol. 5. Marius B. Jansen (ed.), *The Nineteenth Century.* 1988. Vol. 6. Peter Duus (ed.), *The Twentieth Century.* Cambridge: Cambridge University Press.

CHLG = Cambridge History of Later Greek and Early Medieval Philosophy. 1967. Cambridge: Cambridge University Press.

CHLMP = The Cambridge History of Later Medieval Philosophy. 1982. Cambridge: Cambridge University Press.

Cleary, Thomas. 1983. *Entry into the Inconceivable: An Introduction to Hua-yen Buddhism.* Honolulu: University of Hawaii Press.

Cleary, Thomas (trans.). 1986. *The Inner Teachings of Taoism by Chang Po-tuan.* Boston: Shambala.

Clooney, Francis X. 1990. *Thinking Ritually: Rediscovering the Purva Mimamsa of Jaimini.* Vienna: Publications of the de Nobili Research Library.

CMH = The Cambridge Modern History. 1902–1911. 13 volumes. Cambridge: Cambridge University Press.

Cobban, Alan B. 1975. *The Medieval Universities: Their Development and Organization.* London: Methuen.

———— 1988. *The Medieval English Universities*. Berkeley: University of California Press.

Coffa, J. Alberto. 1991. *The Semantic Tradition from Kant to Carnap*. Cambridge: Cambridge University Press.

Cohen-Solal, Annie. 1987. *Sartre: A Life*. New York: Pantheon.

Cole, Stephen. 1983. "The Hierarchy of the Sciences." *American Journal of Sociology* 89:111–139.

Cole, Stephen, Jonathan R. Cole, and Lorraine Dietrich. 1978. "Measuring the Cognitive state of a Scientific Discipline." In *Toward a Metric of Science,* ed. Yehuda Elkana et al. New York: Wiley.

Collcutt, Martin. 1981. *Five Mountains: The Rinzai Zen Monastic Institution in Medieval Japan*. Cambridge, Mass.: Harvard University Press.

———— 1986. "Buddhism: The Threat of Eradication." In *Japan in Transition: From Tokugawa to Meiji,* ed. Marius Jansen and Gilbert Rozman. Princeton: Princeton University Press.

———— 1990. "Zen and the *Gozan*." In Yamamura, 1990.

Collins, Churton. 1908. *Voltaire, Montesquieu, and Rousseau in England*. London: E. Nash.

Collins, Harry M. 1974. "The TEA Set: Tacit Knowledge and Scientific Networks." *Science Studies* 4:165–186.

———— 1985. *Changing Order: Replication and Induction in Scientific Practice*. London: Sage.

Collins, Randall. 1971. "Functional and Conflict Theories of Educational Stratification." *American Sociological Review* 36:1002–19.

———— 1975. *Conflict Sociology: Towards an Explanatory Science*. New York: Academic Press.

———— 1979. *The Credential Society: An Historical Sociology of Education and Stratification*. New York: Academic Press.

———— 1981. *Sociology since Midcentury*. New York: Academic Press.

———— 1984. "Statistics versus Words." In *Sociological Theory 1984*. San Francisco: Jossey-Bass.

———— 1986. *Weberian Sociological Theory*. New York: Cambridge University Press.

———— 1990. "Stratification, Emotional Energy, and the Transient Emotions." In Kemper, 1990.

———— 1992. "Can Sociology Create an Artificial Intelligence?" In Randall Collins, *Sociological Insight: An Introduction to Non-obvious Sociology*. New York: Oxford University Press.

———— 1994. "Why the Social Sciences Won't Become High-Consensus, Rapid-Discovery Science." *Sociological Forum* 9:155–177.

———— 1997. "An Asian Route to Capitalism: Religious Economy and the Origins of Self-transforming Growth in Japan." *American Sociological Review* 62.

Collins, Randall, and Sal Restivo. 1983. "Robber-Barons and Politicians in Mathematics: A Conflict Model of Science." *Canadian Journal of Sociology* 8:199–227.

Conze, Edward. 1959. *Buddhism: Its Essence and Development*. New York: Harper.

———— 1962. *Buddhist Thought in India*. Ann Arbor: University of Michigan Press.

—— (ed.). 1973. *The Perfection of Wisdom in Eight Thousand Lines*. Bolinas, Calif.: Four Seasons Foundation.

Coomaraswamy, Ananda K. [1927] 1965. *History of Indian and Indonesian Art*. New York: Dover.

Copleston, Frederick. 1950–1977. *A History of Philosophy*. 9 volumes. New York: Doubleday.

—— 1979. *On the History of Philosophy*. New York: Harper and Row.

Corbin, Henry. 1969. *Creative Imagination in the Sufism of Ibn ʿArabi*. Princeton: Princeton University Press.

Coser, Lewis. 1956. *The Functions of Social Conflict*. New York: Free Press.

Courcelle, Pierre. 1969. *Late Latin Writers and Their Greek Sources*. Cambridge, Mass.: Harvard University Press.

Cozzens, Susan E. 1989. "What Do Citations Count? The Rhetoric-First Model." *Scientometrics* 15:437–447.

Crane, Diana. 1972. *Invisible Colleges: Diffusion of Knowledge in Scientific Communities*. Chicago: University of Chicago Press.

Craven, Roy C. 1975. *A Concise History of Indian Art*. New York: Oxford University Press.

Croll, Morris W. 1966. *Style, Rhetoric, and Rhythm: Collected Essays*. Princeton: Princeton University Press.

Cruz Hernandez, Miguel. 1957. *Filosofia hispano-musulmana*. Madrid: Asociation Española para el Progreso de las Ciencias.

Cumont, Franz. [1912] 1960. *Astrology and Religion among the Greeks and Romans*. New York: Dover.

Daiches, David, Peter Jones, and Jean Jones. 1986. *A Hotbed of Genius: The Scottish Enlightenment, 1730–1790*. Edinburgh: Edinburgh University Press.

Dardess, John W. 1983. *Confucianism and Autocracy: Professional Ethics in the Founding of the Ming Dynasty*. Berkeley: University of California Press.

Dasgupta, Surendranath. 1922–1955. *History of Indian Philosophy*. 5 volumes. Cambridge: Cambridge University Press.

Dauben, J. W. 1979. *Georg Cantor: His Mathematics and Philosophy of the Infinite*. Cambridge, Mass.: Harvard University Press.

Davidson, Herbert H. 1987. *Proofs for Eternity, Creation, and the Existence of God in Medieval Islamic and Jewish Philosophy*. New York: Oxford University Press.

Davies, C. Collin. 1949. *An Historical Atlas of the Indian Peninsula*. 2nd ed. Oxford: Oxford University Press.

Dear, Peter. 1988. *Mersenne and the Learning of the Schools*. Ithaca, N.Y.: Cornell University Press.

—— 1995. *Discipline and Experience: The Mathematical Way in the Scientific Revolution*. Chicago: University of Chicago Press.

de Bary, William T. 1979. "Sagehood as a Secular and Spiritual Ideal in Tokugawa Neo-Confucianism." In de Bary and Bloom, 1979.

—— 1988a. *East Asian Civilizations*. Cambridge, Mass.: Harvard University Press.

—— 1988b. *The Message of the Mind in Neo-Confucian Thought, 1200–1850*. New York: Columbia University Press.

de Bary, William T., and Irene Bloom (eds.). 1979. *Principle and Practicality: Essays in Neo-Confucianism and Practical Learning.* New York: Columbia University Press.

de Boer, T. J. 1903. *The History of Philosophy in Islam.* London: Luzac and Company.

Degler, Carl. 1991. *In Search of Human Nature: The Decline and Revival of Darwinism in American Social Thought.* New York: Oxford University Press.

Demiéville, Paul. 1986. "Philosophy and Religion from Han to Sui." In *CHC*, 1:808–872.

Derrida, Jacques. [1962] 1978. *Edmund Husserl's Origin of Geometry: An Introduction.* Lincoln: University of Nebraska Press.

Descartes, René. [1637] 1954. *Geometry.* New York: Dover.

—— [1644] 1983. *Principles of Philosophy.* Dordrecht: Reidel.

—— 1985. *The Philosophical Writings of Descartes.* Cambridge: Cambridge University Press.

Deussen, Paul. 1912. *The System of Vedanta.* Chicago: Open Court.

Deutsch, Eliot. 1969. *Advaita Vedanta.* Honolulu: University of Hawaii Press.

De Vogel, C. J. 1971. "Boethiana, I." *Vivarium* 9:49–66.

de Wulf, Maurice. 1934–1947. *Histoire de la philosophie médiévale.* 3 volumes. Paris: Vrin.

Dickey, Laurence. 1993. "Hegel on Religion and Philosophy." In Beiser, 1993.

Di Giovanni, George. 1992. "The First Twenty Years of Critique: The Spinoza Connection." In Guyer, 1992.

Dillon, John. 1977. *The Middle Platonists.* London: Duckworth.

Dilworth, David A. 1979. "Jitsugaku as an Ontological Conception: Continuities and Discontinuities in Early and Mid-Tokugawa Thought." In de Bary and Bloom, 1979.

—— 1989. *Philosophy in World Perspective.* New Haven: Yale University Press.

DL = Diogenes Laertius. 1925 [orig. ca. 200 C.E.]. *Lives of Eminent Philosophers.* 2 volumes. Loeb Classical Library. London: Heinemann.

Dodds, E. R. 1951. *The Greeks and the Irrational.* Berkeley: University of California Press.

Doniger, Wendy. 1991. "Introduction." In *The Laws of Manu.* Baltimore: Penguin.

Dore, Ronald P. 1965. *Education in Tokugawa Japan.* Berkeley: University of California Press.

Dostal, Robert J. 1993. "Time and Phenomenology in Husserl and Heidegger." In Guignon, 1993.

Douglas, Mary. 1966. *Purity and Danger.* London: Routledge and Kegan Paul.

—— 1973. *Natural Symbols.* Baltimore: Penguin Books.

Douie, Decima 1932. *The Nature and Effect of the Heresy of the Fraticelli.* Manchester: The University Press.

DSB = *Dictionary of Scientific Biography.* 16 volumes. 1981. New York: Scribner's.

Dummett, Michael. 1978. *Truth and Other Enigmas.* Cambridge, Mass.: Harvard University Press.

—— 1981. *The Interpretation of Frege's Philosophy.* Cambridge, Mass.: Harvard University Press.

Dumont, Louis. 1980. *Homo Hierarchicus. The Caste System and Its Implications.* Chicago: University of Chicago Press.

Dumoulin, Heinrich. 1988. *Zen Buddhism: A History.* Vol. 1. *India and China.* New York: Macmillan.

—— 1990. *Zen Buddhism: A History.* Vol. 2. *Japan.* New York: Macmillan.

Durkheim, Émile. [1912] 1961. *The Elementary Forms of the Religious Life.* New York: Collier.

Dutt, Sukumar. 1962. *Buddhist Monks and Monasteries of India.* London: Allen and Unwin.

Eagleton, Terry. 1990. *The Ideology of the Aesthetic.* Oxford: Blackwell.

Eberhard, Wolfram. 1977. *A History of China.* Berkeley: University of California Press.

EIP = *Encyclopedia of Indian Philosophies.* 1977. Vol. 2. *Indian Metaphysics and Epistemology. The Tradition of Nyaya-Vaisesika up to Gangesa.* 1981. Vol. 3. *Advaita Vedanta up to Samkara and His Pupils.* 1987. Vol. 4. *Samkhya: A Dualist Tradition in Indian Philosophy.* 1990. Vol. 5. *The Philosophy of the Grammarians.* Princeton: Princeton University Press.

Eisele, Carolyn. 1979. *Studies in the Scientific and Mathematical Philosophy of Charles S. Peirce.* The Hague: Mouton.

Eliade, Mircea. 1969. *Yoga: Immortality and Freedom.* Princeton: Princeton University Press.

Eliot, Charles. 1988. *Hinduism and Buddhism.* 3 volumes. Delhi: Indian Books Centre.

Elison, George, and B. L. Smith (eds.). 1981. *Warlords, Artists, and Commoners: Japan in the Sixteenth Century.* Honolulu: University of Hawaii Press.

Elliott, J. H. 1970. *Imperial Spain, 1469–1716.* Baltimore: Penguin Books.

Elvin, Mark. 1973. *The Pattern of the Chinese Past.* London: Methuen.

Engel, Arthur J. 1982. *From Clergyman to Don: The Rise of the Academic Profession in Nineteenth-Century Oxford.* Oxford: Oxford University Press.

Enros, Philip C. 1981. "Cambridge University and the Adoption of Analysis in Early Nineteenth-Century England." In *Social History of Nineteenth-Century Mathematics,* ed. Herbert Mehrtens, Henk Bos, and Ivo Schneider. Boston: Birkhauser.

EP = *The Encyclopedia of Philosophy.* 8 volumes. 1967. New York: Macmillan.

Evans, G. R. 1980. *Anselm and a New Generation.* Oxford: Clarendon Press.

Fabiani, Jean-Louis. 1988. *Les philosophes de la République.* Paris: Éditions de Minuit.

—— 1989. "Sociologie et histoire des idées: l'épistemologie et les sciences sociales." In *Les enjeux philosophies des années cinquante,* ed. Christian Descamps. Paris: Éditions du Centre Pompidou.

Fakhry, Majid. 1983. *A History of Islamic Philosophy.* New York: Columbia University Press.

Farias, Victor. 1987. *Heidegger et le nazisme*. Lagrasse: Verdier.

Ferguson, John. 1970. *The Religions of the Roman Empire*. Ithaca, N.Y.: Cornell University Press.

Ferruolo, Stephen C. 1985. *The Origins of the University. The Schools of Paris and Their Critics, 1100–1215*. Stanford: Stanford University Press.

Fichte, Johann Gottlieb. [1794–1797] 1982. *The Science of Knowledge*. Cambridge: Cambridge University Press.

——— [1800] 1965. *The Vocation of Man*. Chicago: Open Court.

——— [1808] 1922. *Addresses to the German Nation*. Chicago: Open Court.

Finke, Roger, and Rodney Stark. 1992. *The Churching of America, 1776–1990: Winners and Losers in Our Religious Economy*. New Brunswick, N.J.: Rutgers University Press.

Finley, M. I. 1973. *The Ancient Economy*. Berkeley: University of California Press.

Flower, Elizabeth, and Murray G. Murphey. 1977. *A History of Philosophy in America*. New York: G. P. Putnam's Sons.

Fontenrose, Joseph. 1978. *The Delphic Oracle*. Berkeley: University of California Press.

Forke, Alfred. [1927] 1964. *Geschichte der alten chinesischen Philosophie*. Hamburg: Cram.

——— [1934] 1964. *Geschichte der mittelaltlichen chinesischen Philosophie*. Hamburg: Cram.

Forster, Michael. 1993. "Hegel's Dialectical Method." In Beiser, 1993.

Fowden, Garth. 1986. *The Egyptian Hermes: A Historical Approach to the Late Pagan Mind*. Cambridge: Cambridge University Press.

Fowler, D. H. 1987. *The Mathematics of Plato's Academy: A New Reconstruction*. Oxford: Clarendon Press.

Fraser, Alexander Campbell. [1894] 1959. "Prologemena: Biographical." In Locke, 1959.

Frauwallner, Erich. 1953–1956. *Geschichte der indischen Philosophie*. 2 volumes. Salzburg: O. Muller.

Frede, Dorothea. 1993. "The Question of Heidegger's Project." In Guignon, 1993.

Frede, Michael. 1987. *Essays in Ancient Philosophy*. Cambridge: Cambridge University Press.

Frédéric, Louis. 1972. *Daily Life in Japan at the Time of the Samurai, 1185–1603*. London: Allen and Unwin.

Frege, Gottlob. [1883] 1980. *The Foundations of Arithmetic*. Evanston, Ill.: Northwestern University Press.

Friedman, Maurice S. 1981–1983. *Martin Buber's Life and Thought*. 3 volumes New York: Dutton.

Friedman, Michael. 1992. "Causal Laws and the Foundations of Natural Science." In Guyer, 1992.

Frischer, Bernard. 1982. *The Sculpted Word: Epicureanism and Philosophical Recruitment in Ancient Greece*. Berkeley: University of California Press.

Fuller, Steve. 1988. *Social Epistemology*. Bloomington: Indiana University Press.

Fung Yu-lan. 1948. *A Short History of Chinese Philosophy*. New York: Macmillan.

——— 1952–53. *A History of Chinese Philosophy.* 2 volumes. Princeton: Princeton University Press.

Funkenstein, Amos. 1986. *Theology and the Scientific Imagination from the Middle Ages to the Seventeenth Century.* Princeton: Princeton University Press.

Gadamer, Hans-Georg. 1985. *Philosophical Apprenticeships.* Cambridge, Mass.: MIT Press.

Galison, Peter. 1987. *How Experiments End.* Chicago: University of Chicago Press.

Garber, Daniel. 1992. *Descartes' Metaphysical Physics.* Chicago: University of Chicago Press.

Garcin, Jean-Claude. 1988. "The Mamluk Military System and the Blocking of Medieval Moslem Society." In *Europe and the Rise of Capitalism,* ed. Jean Baechler, John A. Hall, and Michael Mann. Oxford: Blackwell.

Garfield, Eugene. 1979. *Citation Indexing.* New York: Wiley.

Gatti, Hilary. 1989. *The Renaissance Drama of Knowledge: Giordano Bruno in England.* London: Routledge.

Gaukroger, Stephen. 1995. *Descartes: An Intellectual Biography.* Oxford: Oxford University Press.

Geiger, Roger. 1986. *To Advance Knowledge: The Growth of American Research Universities, 1900–1940.* New York: Oxford University Press.

——— 1993. "Research, General Education, and the Ecology of American Universities." In Rothblatt and Wittrock, 1993.

Gentile, Giovanni. [1916] 1922. *The Theory of Mind as Pure Activity.* London: Macmillan.

Gernet, Jacques. 1956. *Les aspects economiques du Bouddhisme dans la societé chinoise du Ve au Xe siècle.* Saigon: École française d'Extreme-Orient.

——— 1962. *Daily Life in China on the Eve of the Mongol Invasion, 1250–1276.* Stanford: Stanford University Press.

——— 1982. *A History of Chinese Civilization.* Cambridge: Cambridge University Press.

Gersch, Stephen. 1986. *Middle Platonism and Neoplatonism: The Latin Tradition.* Notre Dame, Ind.: Notre Dame University Press.

Geyer, Bernhard (ed.). 1928. *Die patristiche und scholastische Philosophie.* In *Friedrich Ueberwegs Grundriss der Geschichte der Philosophie.* Vol. 2. Berlin: E. S. Mittler.

al-Ghazali. 1951 [orig. ca. 1110] *The Faith and Practice of al-Ghazali.* Translated by W. M. Watt. London: Allen and Unwin.

Gibbon, Edward. [1776] 1956. *The Decline and Fall of the Roman Empire.* Vol. 1. New York: Modern Library.

Gilbert, Martin. 1969. *Jewish Historical Atlas.* New York: Macmillan.

Gilson, Étienne. 1944. *La philosophie au moyen âge des origines patristiques à la fin du 14e siècle.* Paris: Payot.

Gimpel, Jean. 1976. *The Medieval Machine.* New York: Penguin Books.

Girouard, Mark. 1978. *Life in the English Country House.* New Haven: Yale University Press.

Gluck, Carol. 1985. *Japan's Modern Myths: Ideology in the Late Meiji Period.* Princeton: Princeton University Press.

Glucker, John. 1978. *Antiochus and the Late Academy.* Göttingen: Vandenhoeck and Ruprecht.

Goethe, Johann Wolfgang von. [1811–1832] 1974. *Dichtung und Wahrheit.* Chicago: University of Chicago Press.

Goffman, Erving. 1959. *The Presentation of Self in Everyday Life.* New York: Doubleday.

———— 1967. *Interaction Ritual.* New York: Doubleday.

———— 1971. *Relations in Public.* New York: Basic Books.

———— 1974. *Frame Analysis.* New York: Harper and Row.

———— 1981. *Forms of Talk.* Philadelphia: University of Pennsylvania Press.

Goldstone, Jack. 1991. *Revolution and Rebellion in the Early Modern World.* Berkeley: University of California Press.

Gombrich, Richard F. 1988. *Theravada Buddhism.* London: Routledge.

Gonda, Jan. 1975. *Vedic Literatures.* Wiesbaden: Otto Harrassowitz.

Goodman, L. E. 1992. *Avicenna.* London: Routledge.

Goodspeed, E. J. 1937. *Introduction to the New Testament.* Chicago: University of Chicago Press.

Goody, Jack, and Ian Watt. 1968. "The Consequences of Literacy." In *Literacy in Traditional Societies,* ed. Jack Goody. Cambridge: Cambridge University Press.

Grabiner, Judith. 1986. "Is Mathematical Truth Time-Dependent?" In *New Directions in the Philosophy of Mathematics,* ed. Thomas Tymoczko. Boston: Birkhäuser.

Grabmann, Martin. 1909–1911. *Die Geschichte der scholastischen Methode.* Freiburg im Breisgau: Herdersche Verlagshandlung.

Graham, A. C. 1958. *Two Chinese Philosophers: Ch'eng Ming-tao and Ch'eng Yi-Ch'uan.* London: Lund Humphries.

———— 1978. *Later Mohist Logic, Ethics, and Science.* Hong Kong: Chinese University Press.

———— 1989. *Disputers of the Tao: Philosophical Argument in Ancient China.* La Salle, Ill.: Open Court.

———— 1991. "Reflections and Replies." In *Chinese Texts and Philosophical Contexts,* ed. Henry Rosemont. La Salle, Ill.: Open Court.

Grant, Edward. 1986. "Science and Theology in the Middle Ages." In *God and Nature: Historical Essays on the Encounter between Christianity and Science,* ed. David C. Lindberg and Ronald L. Numbers. Berkeley: University of California Press.

Grant, Michael. 1985. *Atlas of Ancient History, 1700 B.C. to 565 A.D.* New York: Dorset Press.

Grayeff, Felix. 1974. *Aristotle and His School.* New York: Harper and Row.

Green, V. H. H. 1969. *The Universities.* Baltimore: Penguin Books.

Gregory, Frederick. 1989. "Kant, Schelling and the Administration of Science in the Romantic Era." *Osiris,* 2d ser., 5:17–35.

Gregory, Peter N. 1986. *Traditions of Meditation in Chinese Buddhism*. Honolulu: University of Hawaii Press.

——— 1991. *Tsung-mi and the Sinification of Buddhism*. Princeton: Princeton University Press.

Gregory, Stanford W. 1994. "Sounds of Power and Deference: Acoustic Analysis of Macro Social Constraints on Micro Interaction." *Sociological Perspectives* 37:497–526.

Greig, J. Y. T. (ed.). 1932. *Letters of David Hume*. Oxford: Clarendon Press.

Grendler, Paul F. 1989. *Schooling in Renaissance Italy: Literacy and Learning, 1300–1600*. Baltimore: Johns Hopkins University Press.

Griffith, Belver C. 1988. "Derek Price's Puzzles: Numerical Metaphors for the Operation of Science." *Science, Technology, and Human Values* 13:351–360.

Griffith, Belver C., and Nicholas C. Mullins. 1972. "Coherent Groups in Scientific Change." *Science* 177:959–964.

Griffiths, Paul J. 1986. *On Being Mindless: Buddhist Meditation and the Mind-Body Problem*. LaSalle, Ill.: Open Court.

Guenther, Herbert V. 1972. *Buddhist Philosophy*. Baltimore: Penguin Books.

——— 1976. *Philosophy and Psychology in the Abhidharma*. Berkeley: Shambhala.

Guignon, Charles B. (ed.). 1993. *The Cambridge Companion to Heidegger*. Cambridge: Cambridge University Press.

Guthrie, W. K. C. 1961–1982. *A History of Greek Philosophy*. 6 volumes. Cambridge: Cambridge University Press.

Guttman, Julius. 1933. *Die Philosophie des Judentums*. Munich: Reinhardt.

Guyer, Paul. 1987. *Kant and the Claims of Knowledge*. Cambridge: Cambridge University Press.

——— (ed.). 1992. *The Cambridge Companion to Kant*. Cambridge: Cambridge University Press.

Hadas, Moses. 1950. *A History of Greek Literature*. New York: Columbia University Press.

——— 1952. *A History of Latin Literature*. New York: Columbia University Press.

——— 1954. *Ancilla to Classical Reading*. New York: Columbia University Press.

Hagstrom, Warren O. 1965. *The Scientific Community*. New York: Basic Books.

Halbfass, Wilhelm. 1988. *India and Europe*. Albany: SUNY Press.

——— 1991. *Tradition and Reflection: Explorations in Indian Thought*. Albany: SUNY Press.

——— 1992. *On Being and What There Is: Classical Vaisesika and the History of Indian Ontology*. Albany: SUNY Press.

Hall, A. R. 1980. *Philosophers at War: The Quarrel between Newton and Leibniz*. Cambridge: Cambridge University Press.

Hall, John Whitney, and Toyoda Takeshi (eds.). 1977. *Japan in the Muromachi Age*. Berkeley: University of California Press.

Hall, John Whitney, Keiji Nagahara, and Kozo Yamamura (eds.). 1981. *Japan before Tokugawa: Political Consolidation and Economic Growth, 1500 to 1650*. Princeton: Princeton University Press.

Hammerstein, Notker. 1970. "Zur Geschichte der deutschen Universität im Zeitalter der Aufklaerung." In *Universität und Gelehrtenstand, 1400–1800,* ed. Hans Roessler and Georg Franz. Limburg: Starke Verlag.

Han Fei Tzu. 1964. *Basic Writings.* Translated by Burton Watson. New York: Columbia University Press.

Hankins, Thomas L. 1980. *Sir William Rowan Hamilton.* Baltimore: Johns Hopkins University Press.

Hanley, Susan B., and Kozo Yamamura (eds.). 1977. *Economic and Demographic Change in Preindustrial Japan, 1600–1868.* Princeton: Princeton University Press.

Hansen, Chad. 1983. *Language and Logic in Ancient China.* Ann Arbor: University of Michigan Press.

Hargens, Lowell, and Warren O. Hagstrom. 1982. "Scientific Consensus and Academic Status Attainment Patterns." *Sociology of Education* 40:24–38.

Harootunian, Harry D. 1970. *Towards Restoration: The Growth of Political Consciousness in Tokugawa Japan.* Berkeley: University of California Press.

——— 1988. *Things Seen and Unseen: Discourse and Ideology in Tokugawa Nativism.* Chicago: University of Chicago Press.

——— 1989. "Late Tokugawa Thought and Culture." In *CHJ,* 1989.

Harris, H. S. 1972. *Hegel's Development.* Vol. 1. *Toward the Sunlight, 1770–1801.* 1983. Vol. 2. *Night Thoughts. Jena, 1801–1806.* New York: Oxford University Press.

——— 1993. "Hegel's Intellectual Development to 1807." In Beiser, 1993.

Harris, Horton. 1975. *The Tübingen School.* Oxford: Oxford University Press.

Hartman, Charles. 1986. *Han Yü and the T'ang Search for Unity.* Princeton: Princeton University Press.

Hatfield, Gary. 1990. "Metaphysics and the New Science." In *Reappraisals of the Scientific Revolution,* ed. David C. Lindberg and Robert S. Westman. Cambridge: Cambridge University Press.

Havelock, Eric A. 1982. *The Literate Revolution in Greece and Its Cultural Consequences.* Princeton: Princeton University Press.

——— 1986. *The Muse Learns to Write: Reflections on Orality and Literacy from Antiquity to the Present.* New Haven: Yale University Press.

Havens, Thomas R. H. 1970. *Nishi Amane and Modern Japanese Thought.* Princeton: Princeton University Press.

Heath, Thomas. [1921] 1981. *A History of Greek Mathematics.* 2 volumes. New York: Dover.

Heer, Friedrich. [1953] 1968. *The Intellectual History of Europe.* New York: Doubleday.

Heesterman, J. C. 1985. *The Inner Conflict of Tradition: Essays in Indian Ritual, Kingship, and Society.* Chicago: University of Chicago Press.

Hegel, G. W. F. [1807] 1967. *The Phenomenology of Mind.* New York: Harper and Row.

——— [1812–1816] 1929. *Science of Logic.* New York: Macmillan.

——— [1820–1830] 1971. *Vorlesungen über die Geschichte der Philosophie.* Frankfurt am Main: Suhrkamp.

Heilbron, Johan. 1994. *The Rise of Social Theory.* Oxford: Polity Press.

Heine, Heinrich. [1833] 1986. *Religion and Philosophy in Germany.* Albany: SUNY Press.

Helbig, H. 1961. *Universität Leipzig.* Frankfurt am Main: Weidlich.

Henricks, Robert G. 1983. *Philosophy and Argumentation in Third-Century China: The Essays of Hsi K'ang.* Princeton: Princeton University Press.

Herberg, Will. 1958. *Four Existentialist Theologians.* New York: Doubleday.

Herbert, P. 1959. "Creativity and Mental Illness." *Psychiatric Quarterly* 33:534–547.

Hermann, A. 1966. *An Historical Atlas of China.* Chicago: Aldine.

Heyting, Arend. 1983. "Disputation." In *Philosophy of Mathematics,* ed. Paul Benacerraf and Hilary Putnam. Cambridge: Cambridge University Press.

Hirakawa Akira. 1990. *A History of Indian Buddhism: From Sakyamuni to Early Mahayana.* Honolulu: University of Hawaii Press.

Ho Peng Yoke. 1985. *Li, Qi, and Shu: An Introduction to Science and Civilization in China.* Hong Kong: Hong Kong University Press.

Hoch, Paul K. 1991. "Between Central European Physics, American Philosophy and Scientific Sociology: A Social Epistemology of the Inter-national, Inter-institutional and Inter-disciplinary Migrations of the Vienna Circle." Paper delivered at International Congress of Logic, Methodology, and Philosophy of Science, Uppsala, Sweden.

Hochberg, Leonard. 1984. "The English Civil War in Geographical Perspective." *Journal of Interdisciplinary History* 14:729–750.

Hodgson, Marshall G. S. 1974. *The Venture of Islam.* 3 volumes. Chicago: University of Chicago Press.

Hofmann, J. E. 1972. *Leibniz in Paris, 1671–76.* Cambridge: Cambridge University Press.

Holton, Gerald. [1973] 1988. *Thematic Origins of Scientific Thought.* Revised edition. Cambridge, Mass.: Harvard University Press.

Holtzman, Donald. 1976. *Poetry and Politics: The Life and Works of Juan Chi, A.D. 210–263.* Cambridge: Cambridge University Press.

Homans, George C. 1950. *The Human Group.* New York: Harcourt.

Huff, Toby E. 1993. *The Rise of Early Modern Science: Islam, China, and the West.* Cambridge: Cambridge University Press.

Hume, David. [1739–1740] 1969. *A Treatise of Human Nature.* Baltimore: Penguin Books.

Humphreys, R. Stephen. 1991. *Islamic History: A Framework for Inquiry.* Princeton: Princeton University Press.

Husik, Isaac. 1969. *A History of Medieval Jewish Philosophy.* New York: Atheneum.

Hylton, Peter. 1993. "Hegel and Analytic Philosophy." In Beiser, 1993.

Hyman, Arthur, and James J. Walsh (eds.). 1983. *Philosophy in the Middle Ages.* Indianapolis: Hackett.

Ikegami, Eiko. 1995. *The Taming of the Samurai.* Cambridge, Mass.: Harvard University Press.

Impey, Oliver, and Arthur McGregor (eds.). 1985. *The Origins of Museums: The*

Cabinet of Curiosities in Sixteenth- and Seventeenth-Century Europe. Oxford: Oxford University Press.

Inden, Ronald B. 1992. *Imagining India.* Oxford: Blackwell.

Institute = Institute of the History of Natural Sciences, Chinese Academy of Sciences. 1983. *Ancient China's Technology and Science.* Beijing: Foreign Languages Press.

Isayeva, Natalia. 1993. *Shankara and Indian Philosophy.* Albany: SUNY Press.

———— 1995. *From Early Vedanta to Kashmir Shaivism.* Albany: SUNY Press.

Jacob, E. F. 1963. *Essays in the Conciliar Epoch.* Manchester: Manchester University Press.

Jacobi, Hermann (trans. and ed.). 1884. *Jaina Sutras.* Oxford: Clarendon Press.

Janik, Allan, and Stephen Toulmin. 1973. *Wittgenstein's Vienna.* New York: Simon and Schuster.

Jarausch, Konrad H. 1982. *Students, Society, and Politics in Imperial Germany.* Princeton: Princeton University Press.

Jardine, Lisa. 1983. "Lorenzo Valla: Academic Skepticism and the New Humanist Dialectic." In *The Skeptical Tradition,* ed. Myles Burnyeat. Berkeley: University of California Press.

Jencks, Christopher, and David Riesman. 1968. *The Academic Revolution.* New York: Doubleday.

Jesseph, Douglas M. 1993. *Berkeley's Philosophy of Mathematics.* Chicago: University of Chicago Press.

Joas, Hans. 1985. *George Herbert Mead: A Contemporary Re-examination of His Thought.* Oxford: Polity Press.

Johnston, William M. 1972. *The Austrian Mind: An Intellectual and Social History, 1848–1938.* Berkeley: University of California Press.

Jonas, Hans. 1963. *The Gnostic Religion.* Boston: Beacon Press.

Jones, A. H. M. [1964] 1986. *The Later Roman Empire, 284–602: A Social, Economic, and Administrative Survey.* Baltimore: Johns Hopkins University Press.

Jones, Alexander. 1991. "The Adaptation of Babylonian Methods in Greek Numerical Astronomy." *Isis* 82:441–453.

Jones, Eric L. 1988. *Growth Recurring: Economic Change in World History.* New York: Oxford University Press.

Jones, Ernest. 1963. *The Life and Work of Sigmund Freud.* New York: Doubleday.

Joy, Linda Sumida. 1987. *Gassendi the Atomist.* Cambridge: Cambridge University Press.

Kagan, Richard L. 1974. "Universities in Castile, 1500–1800." In Stone, 1974b.

Kaltenmark, Max. 1969. *Lao Tzu and Taoism.* Stanford: Stanford University Press.

Kalupahana, David J. 1986. *Nagarjuna: The Philosophy of the Middle Way.* Albany: SUNY Press.

———— 1992. *A History of Buddhist Philosophy.* Honolulu: University of Hawaii Press.

Kammer, Reinhard. 1969. *Die Kunst der Bergdämonen: Zen-Lehre und Konfuzianismus in der japanischen Schwertkunst.* Weilheim: O. W. Barth.

Kangro, Hans. 1968. *Joachim Jungius' Experimente und Gedanken zur Begrundung der Chemie als Wissenschaft.* Wiesbaden: F. Steiner.

Kant, Immanuel. [1781] 1966. *Critique of Pure Reason.* New York: Doubleday.

———— [1798] 1991. *The Conflict of the Faculties.* New York: Abaris Books.

Kantorowicz, E. H. 1938. *Studies in the Glossators of the Roman Law.* Cambridge: Cambridge University Press.

Kaster, Robert A. 1988. *Guardians of Language: The Grammarian and Society in Late Antiquity.* Berkeley: University of California Press.

Kaufer, David S., and Kathleen M. Carley. 1993. *Communication at a Distance. The Influence of Print on Sociocultural Organization and Change.* Hillsdale, N.J.: Erlbaum.

Kaufmann, Walter. 1950. *Nietzsche: Philosopher, Psychologist, Anti-Christ.* Princeton: Princeton University Press.

———— 1966. *Hegel: An Interpretation.* New York: Doubleday.

———— 1980. *Discovering the Mind: Goethe, Kant, and Hegel.* New York: McGraw-Hill.

Kazhdan, A. P., and Ann Wharton Epstein. 1985. *Change in Byzantine Culture in the Eleventh and Twelfth Centuries.* Berkeley: University of California Press.

Keen, Maurice. 1968. *The Pelican History of Medieval Europe.* Baltimore: Penguin Books.

Kelley, J. N. D. 1986. *The Oxford Dictionary of Popes.* New York: Oxford University Press.

Kemper, Theodore D. (ed.). 1990. *Research Agendas in the Sociology of Emotions.* Albany: SUNY Press.

Keohane, Nannerl O. 1980. *Philosophy and the State in France: The Renaissance to the Enlightenment.* Princeton: Princeton University Press.

Kerford, G. B. 1981. *The Sophistic Movement.* Cambridge: Cambridge University Press.

Ketelaar, James E. 1990. *On Heretics and Martyrs in Meiji Japan: Buddhism and Its Persecution.* Princeton: Princeton University Press.

Kidder, J. Edward. 1985. *The Art of Japan.* Milan: Mondadori Editore.

Kierkegaard, Soren. [1843] 1959. *Either/Or.* Vol. 1. Princeton: Princeton University Press.

Kinder, Hermann, and Werner Hilgemann. 1968. *Atlas historique.* Paris: Stock.

King, Richard. 1995. *Early Vedanta and Buddhism.* Albany: SUNY Press.

Kingston, Paul, and Jonathan R. Cole. 1986. *The Wages of Writing.* New York: Columbia University Press.

Kirchhoff, Jochen. 1982. *Schelling.* Reinbek: Rowohlt.

Kirk, G. S., J. E. Raven, and M. Schofield. 1983. *The Presocratic Philosophers.* 2d edition. Cambridge: Cambridge University Press.

Kisiel, Theodore. 1993. *The Genesis of Heidegger's Being and Time.* Berkeley: University of California Press.

Kitagawa, Joseph M. 1987. *On Understanding Japanese Religion.* Princeton: Princeton University Press.

———— 1990. *Religion in Japanese History*. New York: Columbia University Press.

Kitcher, Philip. 1984. *The Nature of Mathematical Knowledge*. New York: Oxford University Press.

Kline, Morris. 1972. *Mathematical Thought from Ancient to Modern Times*. New York: Oxford University Press.

Kneale, William, and Martha Kneale. 1984. *The Development of Logic*. Oxford: Clarendon Press.

Knoblock, John. 1988. *Xunzi: A Translation and Study of the Complete Works*. Vol. 1. Stanford: Stanford University Press.

Knorr, Wilbur R. 1975. *The Evolution of the Euclidean Elements*. Dordrecht: Reidel.

———— 1982. "Infinity and Continuity: the Interaction of Mathematics and Philosophy in Antiquity." In *Infinity and Continuity in Ancient and Medieval Thought*, ed. Norman Kretzman. Ithaca, N.Y.: Cornell University Press.

Knowles, David. 1949. *The Monastic Order in England*. Cambridge: Cambridge University Press.

———— 1962. *The Evolution of Medieval Thought*. New York: Vintage.

Kodera, Takashi James. 1980. *Dogen's Formative Years in China*. Boulder: Great Eastern Book Company.

Kohn, Livia. 1992. *Early Chinese Mysticism: Philosophy and Soteriology in the Taoist Tradition*. Princeton: Princeton University Press.

Köhnke, Klaus Christian. 1991. *The Rise of Neo-Kantianism*. Cambridge: Cambridge University Press.

Kolakowski, Leszek. 1978. *Main Currents in Marxism*. New York: Oxford University Press.

Koschmann, J. Victor. 1987. *The Mito Ideology*. Berkeley: University of California Press.

Krishna, Daya (ed). 1978. *What Is Living and What Is Dead in Indian Philosophy?* Waltair, India: Andhra University Press.

———— 1991. *Indian Philosophy: A Counter Perspective*. New York: Oxford University Press.

Kuhn, Thomas S. 1961. "The Function of Measurement in Modern Physical Science." In *Quantification: A History of the Meaning of Measurement in the Natural and Social Sciences,* ed. Harry Woolf. Indianapolis: Bobbs-Merrill.

Kuklick, Bruce. 1972. *Josiah Royce: An Intellectual Biography*. Indianapolis: Bobbs-Merrill.

———— 1977. *The Rise of American Philosophy: Cambridge, Massachusetts, 1860–1930*. New Haven: Yale University Press.

———— 1984. "Seven Thinkers and How They Grew: Descartes, Spinoza, Leibniz; Locke, Berkeley, Hume; Kant." In *Philosophy in History: Essays on the Historiography of Philosophy,* ed. Richard Rorty, J. B. Schneewind, and Quentin Skinner. Cambridge: Cambridge University Press.

———— 1985. *Churchmen and Philosophers: From Jonathan Edwards to John Dewey*. New Haven: Yale University Press.

Kuo, You-Yuh. 1986. "The Growth and Decline of Chinese Philosophical Genius." *Chinese Journal of Philosophy* 28:81–91.

———— 1988. "The Social Psychology of Chinese Philosophical Creativity: A Critical Synthesis." *Social Epistemology* 2:283–296.

Lacouture, Jean. 1975. *André Malraux*. London: Deutsch.

Lai, Whalen, and Lewis R. Lancaster (eds.). 1983. *Early Ch'an in China and Tibet*. Berkeley: University of California Press.

Lamont, Michèle. 1987. "How to Become a Dominant French Philosopher: The Case of Jacques Derrida." *American Journal of Sociology* 93:584–622.

Lamotte, Étienne. 1958. *Histoire du Bouddhisme indien*. Louvain: Publications Universitaires.

Lapidus, Ira M. 1988. *A History of Islamic Societies*. Cambridge: Cambridge University Press.

Latour, Bruno. 1987. *Science in Action* Cambridge, Mass.: Harvard University Press.

Latour, Bruno, and Steve Woolgar. 1983. *Laboratory Life: The Social Construction of Scientific Facts*. Beverly Hills, Calif.: Sage.

Latourette, Kenneth Scott. 1975. *A History of Christianity*. Vol. 1. New York: Harper and Row.

Lavopa, Anthony J. 1988. *Grace, Talent, and Merit: Poor Students, Clerical Careers, and Professional Ideology in Eighteenth-Century Germany*. Cambridge: Cambridge University Press.

Leaman, Oliver. 1985. *An Introduction to Medieval Islamic Philosophy*. Cambridge: Cambridge University Press.

Lebesque, Morvan. 1960. *Camus*. Reinbek bei Hamburg: Rohwolt.

Legge, James (trans.). [1899] 1963. *The Yi Ching*. New York: Dover.

Leventhal, Robert S. 1986. "The Emergence of Philological Discourse in the German States, 1770–1810." *Isis* 77:243–260.

Lévi-Bruhl, Lucien. 1899. *History of Philosophy in France*. Chicago: Open Court.

Lévi-Strauss, Claude. [1962] 1966. *The Savage Mind*. Chicago: University of Chicago Press.

Levy, Paul. 1981. *Moore: G. E. Moore and the Cambridge Apostles*. New York: Oxford University Press.

Lewis, David. 1986. *On the Plurality of Worlds*. Oxford: Blackwell.

Leydesdorff, Loet, and Olga Amsterdamska. 1990. "Dimensions of Citation Analysis." *Science, Technology, and Human Values* 15:305–335.

Li Yan and Du Shiran. 1987. *Chinese Mathematics: A Concise History*. Oxford: Clarendon Press.

Libbrecht, Ulrich. 1973. *Chinese Mathematics in the Thirteenth Century*. Cambridge, Mass.: MIT Press.

Liberman, Kenneth. 1992. "Philosophical Debate in the Tibetan Academy." *Tibet Journal* 17:36–67.

Liedman, Sven-Eric. 1993. "In Search of Isis: General Education in Germany and Sweden." In Rothblatt and Wittrock, 1993.

Lilge, Frederic. 1948. *The Abuse of Learning*. New York: Macmillan.

Lindberg, David C. 1990. "Conceptions of the Scientific Revolution from Bacon to Butterfield." In *Reappraisals of the Scientific Revolution,* ed. David C. Lindberg and Robert S. Westman. Cambridge: Cambridge University Press.

——— 1992. *The Beginnings of Western Science: The European Scientific Tradition in Philosophical, Religious, and Institutional Context, 600 B.C. to A.D. 1450.* Chicago: University of Chicago Press.

Lindberg, David C. (ed.). 1978. *Science in the Middle Ages.* Chicago: University of Chicago Press.

Lindenfeld, David F. 1980. *The Transformation of Positivism: Alexius Meinong and European Thought, 1880–1920.* Berkeley: University of California Press.

Liu, James T. C. 1967. *Ou-yang Hsiu: An Eleventh-Century Neo-Confucianist.* Stanford: Stanford University Press.

——— 1973. "How Did a Neo-Confucian School Become the State Orthodoxy?" *Philosophy East and West* 23:483–505.

Lloyd, G. E. R. 1987. *The Revolutions of Wisdom: Studies in the Claims and Practice of Ancient Greek Science.* Berkeley: University of California Press.

——— 1990. *Demystifying Mentalities.* Cambridge: Cambridge University Press.

Locke, John. [1690] 1959. *An Essay Concerning Human Understanding.* New York: Dover.

Loewith, Karl. [1941] 1967. *From Hegel to Nietzsche.* New York: Doubleday.

Long, A. A. 1986. *Hellenistic Philosophy.* Berkeley: University of California Press.

Lottman, Herbert R. 1979. *Albert Camus: A Biography.* New York: Doubleday.

Lowrie, Walter. 1942. *A Short Life of Kierkegaard.* Princeton: Princeton University Press.

Loy, David. 1988. *Nonduality: A Study in Comparative Philosophy.* New Haven: Yale University Press.

Luce, A. A. 1934. *Berkeley and Malebranche: A Study in the Origins of Berkeley's Thought.* London: Oxford University Press.

——— 1968. *The Life of George Berkeley.* New York: Greenwood Press.

Lynch, J. P. 1972. *Aristotle's School: A Study of a Greek Educational Institution.* Berkeley: University of California Press.

Lynch, William T. 1991. "Politics in Hobbes' Mechanics: The Social as Enabling." *Studies in History and Philosophy of Science* 22:295–320.

MacGregor, David. 1992. *Hegel, Marx, and the English State.* Boulder: Westview Press.

Macpherson, C. B. 1968. "Introduction." In Thomas Hobbes, *Leviathan.* Baltimore: Penguin Books.

Mahoney, Michael S. 1980. "The Beginnings of Algebraic Thought in the Seventeenth Century." In *Descartes. Philosophy, Mathematics, and Physics,* ed. Stephen Gaukroger. Brighton, Sussex: Harvester.

——— 1990. "Infinitesimals and Transcendental Relations: The Mathematics of Motion in the Late Seventeenth Century." In *Reappraisals of the Scientific Revolution,* ed. David C. Lindberg and Robert S. Westman. Cambridge: Cambridge University Press.

Maimonides, Moses. 1956 [orig. ca. 1190]. *The Guide for the Perplexed.* New York: Dover.

Major, John S. 1976. "A Note on the Translation of Two Technical Terms in Chinese Science, *Wu hsing* and *Hsiu.*" *Early China* 2:1–3.

Makdisi, George. 1981. *The Rise of Colleges: Institutions of Learning in Islam and the West.* Edinburgh: Edinburgh University Press.

Malraux, André. 1953. *The Voices of Silence.* New York: Doubleday.

Mandonnet, Pierre. 1937. *St. Dominique: l'idée, l'homme, et l'oeuvre.* Paris: de Brouwer.

Mann, Michael. 1986. *The Sources of Social Power.* Vol. 1. New York: Cambridge University Press.

Marcuse, Herbert. 1960. *Reason and Revolution.* Boston: Beacon Press.

Marias, Julian. [1941] 1966. *History of Philosophy.* New York: Dover.

Marrou, H. I. 1964. *A History of Education in Antiquity.* New York: New American Library.

Martin, James J. 1963. "Introduction." In Max Stirner, *The Ego and His Own.* New York: Libertarian Book Club.

Martin, Julian. 1992. *Francis Bacon, the State, and the Reform of Natural Philosophy.* Cambridge: Cambridge University Press.

Martin, Luther H. 1987. *Hellenistic Religions.* Oxford: Oxford University Press.

Maruyama, Masao. 1974. *Studies in the Intellectual History of Tokugawa Japan.* Princeton: Princeton University Press..

Marwell, Gerald, and Pamela Oliver. 1993. *The Critical Mass in Collective Action. A Micro-social Theory.* New York: Cambridge University Press.

Maslow, Abraham H. 1970. *Motivation and Personality.* New York: Harper and Row.

Massignon, Louis. [1975] 1982. *The Passion of al-Hallaj. Mystic and Martyr of Islam.* Princeton: Princeton University Press.

Mather, Richard B. 1979. "K'ou Ch'ien-chih and the Taoist Theocracy at the Northern Wei Court, 425–451." In Welch and Seidel, 1979.

Matilal, B. K. 1985. *Logic, Language, and Reality: An Introduction to Indian Philosophical Studies.* Delhi: Motilal Banarsidas.

——— 1986. *Perception: An Essay on Classical Indian Theories of Knowledge.* New York: Oxford University Press.

——— 1990. *The Word and the World: India's Contribution to the Study of Language.* New York: Oxford University Press.

Matsumoto, Shigeru. 1970. *Motoori Norinaga, 1730–1801.* Cambridge, Mass.: Harvard University Press.

McClelland, Charles E. 1980. *State, Society, and University in Germany, 1700–1914.* Cambridge: Cambridge University Press.

McCormack, Gavin, and Yoshio Sugimoto (eds.). 1984. *The Japanese Trajectory: Modernization and Beyond.* Cambridge: Cambridge University Press

McEvedy, Colin. 1961. *The Penguin Atlas of Medieval History.* Baltimore: Penguin Books.

——— 1967. *The Penguin Atlas of Ancient History.* Baltimore: Penguin Books.

——— 1972. *The Penguin Atlas of Modern History.* Baltimore: Penguin Books.

McEvedy, Colin, and Richard Jones. 1978. *Atlas of World Population History.* Baltimore: Penguin Books.

McLellan, David. 1973. *Karl Marx: His Life and Thought.* London: Macmillan.

McMullen, David. 1988. *State and Scholars in T'ang China*. Cambridge: Cambridge University Press.

McMullin, Ernan. 1990. "Conceptions of Science in the Scientific Revolution." In *Reappraisals of the Scientific Revolution*, ed. David C. Lindberg and Robert S. Westman. Cambridge: Cambridge University Press.

McMullin, Neil. 1984. *Buddhism and the State in Sixteenth-Century Japan*. Princeton: Princeton University Press.

McRae, John R. 1985. "The Ox-Head School of Chinese Ch'an Buddhism." In *Studies in Ch'an Buddhism*, ed. Robert M. Gimello and Peter N. Gregory. Honolulu: University of Hawaii Press.

—— 1986. *The Northern School and the Formation of Early Ch'an Buddhism*. Honolulu: University of Hawaii Press.

Mead, George Herbert. 1932. *The Philosophy of the Present*. LaSalle, Ill.: Open Court.

—— 1938. *The Philosophy of the Act*. Chicago: University of Chicago Press.

Merleau-Ponty, Maurice. [1945] 1962. *The Phenomenology of Perception*. New York: Humanities Press.

Merz, John Theodore. [1904–1912] 1965. *A History of European Thought in the Nineteenth Century*. 4 volumes. New York: Dover.

Mikami, Yoshio. 1913. *The Development of Mathematics in China and Japan*. New York: Chelsea Publishing Company.

Miller, David L. 1973. *George Herbert Mead: Self, Language, and the World*. Austin: University of Texas Press.

Mills, C. Wright. [1942] 1969. *Sociology and Pragmatism: The Higher Learning in America*. New York: Oxford University Press.

Milner, Murray, Jr. 1994. *Status and Sacredness: A General Theory of Status Relations and an Analysis of Indian Culture*. New York: Oxford University Press.

Mizener, Arthur. 1959. *The Far Side of Paradise: A Biography of F. Scott Fitzgerald*. New York: Random House.

Mizuno, Kogen. 1980. *The Beginnings of Buddhism*. Tokyo: Kosei.

Mohanty, J. N. 1982. *Husserl and Frege*. Bloomington: Indiana University Press.

—— 1993. *Essays on Indian Philosophy Traditional and Modern*. New York: Oxford University Press.

Monk, Ray. 1990. *Ludwig Wittgenstein*. Baltimore: Penguin Books.

Moore, Barrington, Jr. 1966. *Social Origins of Dictatorship and Democracy*. Boston: Beacon Press.

Moraw, Peter. 1984. "Humboldt in Giessen: Zur Professorenberufung einer deutschen Universität des 19. Jahrhunderts." *Geschichte und Gesellschaft* 10:47–71.

Morgan, Michael L. 1990. *Platonic Piety: Philosophy and Ritual in Fourth-Century Athens*. New Haven: Yale University Press.

Morris, Ivan. 1964. *The World of the Shining Prince: Court Life in Ancient Japan*. Oxford: Oxford University Press.

Morris-Suzuki, Tessa. 1994. *The Technological Transformation of Japan: From the Seventeenth to the Twenty-first Century*. Cambridge: Cambridge University Press.

Morrison, Karl F. 1969. *Tradition and Authority in the Western Church, 330–1140.* Princeton: Princeton University Press.

Mossner, E. C. 1954. *The Life of David Hume.* Austin: University of Texas Press.

Mueller, Detlef K. 1987. "The Process of Systematization: The Case of German Secondary Education." In *The Rise of the Modern Educational System,* ed. Detlef K. Mueller, Fritz Ringer, and Brian Simon. Cambridge: Cambridge University Press.

Mueller, Hans-Eberhard. 1983. *Bureaucracy, Education, and Monopoly: Civil Service Reforms in Prussia and England.* Berkeley: University of California Press.

Müller, F. Max (trans. and ed.). [1879–1884] 1962. *The Upanishads.* 2 volumes. New York: Dover.

Muller-Ortega, Paul. 1989. *The Triadic Heart of Siva: Kaula Tantricism of Abhinavagupta in the Non-dual Shiva Traditions of Kashmir.* Albany: SUNY Press.

Mullins, Nicholas C. 1973. *Theories and Theory Groups in Contemporary American Sociology.* New York: Harper and Row.

Murphey, Murray G. 1961. *The Development of Peirce's Philosophy.* Cambridge, Mass.: Harvard University Press.

Murray, Alexander. 1978. *Reason and Society in the Middle Ages.* Oxford: Clarendon Press.

Myers, Gerald E. 1986. *William James: His Life and Thought.* New Haven: Yale University Press.

Nagao, Gadjin M. 1991. *Madhyamika and Yogacara.* Albany: SUNY Press.

Najita, Tetsuo. 1987. *Visions of Virtue in Tokugawa Japan: The Kaitokudo, Merchant Academy of Osaka.* Chicago: University of Chicago Press.

Najita, Tetsuo, and Irwin Scheiner (eds.). 1978. *Japanese Thought in the Tokugawa Period, 1600–1868.* Chicago: University of Chicago Press.

Nakai, Nobuhiko, and James L. McClain. 1991. "Commercial Change and Urban Growth in Early Modern Japan." In *The Cambridge History of Japan.* Vol. 4. *Early Modern Japan,* ed. John W. Hall. Cambridge: Cambridge University Press.

Nakamura, Hajime. 1973. *Religions and Philosophies of India.* Tokyo: Hokuseido Press.

——— 1980. *Indian Buddhism: A Survey with Bibliographical Notes.* Osaka: KUFS.

Nakane, Chie, and Shinzaburo Oishi (eds.). 1990. *Tokugawa Japan: The Social and Economic Antecedents of Modern Japan.* Tokyo: University of Tokyo Press.

Nakayama, Shigeru. 1984. *Academic and Scientific Traditions in China, Japan, and the West.* Tokyo: University of Tokyo Press.

Nakayama, Shigeru, and Nathan Sivin (eds.). 1973. *Chinese Science: Explorations of an Ancient Tradition.* Cambridge, Mass.: MIT Press.

Nakosteen, Mehdi. 1964. *History of Islamic Origins of Western Education.* Boulder: University of Colorado Press.

Natanson, Maurice. 1973. *Edmund Husserl: Philosopher of Infinite Tasks.* Evanston, Ill.: Northwestern University Press.

Needham, Joseph. 1956. *Science and Civilization in China.* Vol. 2. *History of Scientific Thought.* Cambridge: Cambridge University Press.

———— 1959. *Science and Civilization in China.* Vol. 3. *Mathematics and the Sciences of the Heavens and the Earth.* Cambridge: Cambridge University Press.

———— 1965. *Science and Civilization in China.* Vol. 4. *Physics and Physical Technology.* Cambridge: Cambridge University Press.

Neugebauer, O. 1957. *The Exact Sciences in Antiquity.* New York: Dover.

Nicholson, Peter P. 1990. *The Political Philosophy of the British Idealists.* Cambridge: Cambridge University Press.

Nishitani, Keiji. 1982. *Religion and Nothingness.* Berkeley: University of California Press.

Nosco, Peter. 1990. *Remembering Paradise: Nativism and Nostalgia in Eighteenth-Century Japan.* Cambridge, Mass.: Harvard University Press.

Nozick, Robert. 1981. *Philosophical Explanations.* Cambridge, Mass.: Harvard University Press.

Obeyesekere, Gananath. 1980. "The Rebirth Eschatology and Its Transformations: A Contribution to the Sociology of Early Buddhism." In O'Flaherty, 1980.

OCCL = *The Oxford Companion to Classical Literature.* 1937. Compiled by Paul Harvey. Oxford: Oxford University Press.

Odin, Steve. 1982. *Process Metaphysics and Hua-yen Buddhism.* Albany: SUNY Press.

O'Flaherty, Wendy Doniger. 1975. *Hindu Myths.* Baltimore: Penguin Books.

———— (ed.). 1980. *Karma and Rebirth in Classical Indian Traditions.* Berkeley: University of California Press.

Ofuchi, Ninji. 1979. "The Formation of the Taoist Canon." In Welch and Seidel, 1979.

OHI = *The Oxford History of India.* 1981. 4th edition. Edited by Percival Spear. Oxford: Oxford University Press.

O'Malley, John W. 1993. *The First Jesuits.* Cambridge, Mass.: Harvard University Press.

O'Meara, Dominic J. 1989. *Pythagoras Revived: Mathematics and Philosophy in Late Antiquity.* New York: Oxford University Press.

Ooms, Herman. 1985. *Tokugawa Ideology: Early Constructs, 1570–1680.* Princeton: Princeton University Press.

Pagels, Elaine H. 1979. *The Gnostic Gospels.* New York: Random House.

Pandey, Kanti Chandra. 1986. *An Outline of History of Shaiva Philosophy.* Delhi: Motilal Banarsidass.

Paré, Gerard., A. Brunet, and P. Tremblay. 1933. *La Renaissance de XIIeme siècle: les écoles et l'enseignement.* Paris: Vrin.

Passin, Herbert. 1965. *Society and Education in Japan.* Berkeley: University of California Press.

Passmore, John. 1968. *A Hundred Years of Philosophy.* Baltimore: Penguin Books.

———— 1980. *Hume's Intentions.* London: Duckworth.

———— 1985. *Recent Philosophers.* London: Duckworth.

Peckhaus, Volker. 1990. *Hilbertprogramm und kritische Philosophie: Das Göttinger Modell interdisziplinärer Zusammenarbeit zwischen Mathematik und Philosophie.* Göttingen: Vandenhoeck & Ruprecht.

Paulsen, Friedrich. 1919. *Geschichte des Gelehrten Unterrichts*. Leipzig: Verlag Von Veit.

Pelaez del Rosal, Jesus. 1985. *The Jews of Córdoba, X–XII centuries*. Córdoba: Ediciones El Almendro.

Pelikan, Jaroslav. 1978. *The Christian Tradition*. Vol. 3. *The Growth of Medieval Theology (600–1300)*. Chicago: University of Chicago Press.

—— 1984. *The Christian Tradition*. Vol. 4. *Reformation of Church and Dogma (1300–1700)*. Chicago: University of Chicago Press.

Peters, F. E. 1968. *Aristotle and the Arabs: The Aristotelean Tradition in Islam*. New York: New York University Press.

Phillips, Stephen H. 1995. *Classical Indian Metaphysics: Refutations of Realism and the Emergence of "New Logic."* Chicago: Open Court.

Pieper, Josef. [1950] 1960. *Scholasticism*. New York: Pantheon.

Pines, Shlomo. 1967. "Jewish Philosophy." In *EP*, 1967: 4:261–277.

Pingree, David. 1981. "History of Mathematical Astronomy in India." In *DSB*, 1981.

Piovesana, Gino K. 1967. "Japanese Philosophy." In *EP*, 1967.

—— 1963. *Recent Japanese Philosophical Thought, 1862–1962*. Tokyo: Enderle Books.

Pochmann, Henry A. 1948. *New England Transcendentalism and St. Louis Hegelianism*. Philadelphia: Carl Schurtz Memorial Foundation.

Polanyi, Karl. 1977. *The Livelihood of Man*. New York: Academic Press.

Poole, R. L. 1915. *Lectures on the History of the Papal Chancery*. Cambridge: Cambridge University Press.

Popkin, Richard H. 1979. *The History of Skepticism from Erasmus to Spinoza*. Berkeley: University of California Press.

Popper, Karl. 1976. *The Unended Quest: An Intellectual Autobiography*. LaSalle, Ill.: Open Court.

Potter, Karl H. [1963] 1976. *Presuppositions of India's Philosophies*. Westport, Conn.: Greenwood Press.

Preston, David L. 1988. *The Social Organization of Zen Practice: Constructing Transcultural Reality*. Cambridge: Cambridge University Press.

Price, Derek J. de Solla. 1975. *Science since Babylon*. New Haven: Yale University Press.

—— 1986. *Little Science, Big Science, and Beyond*. New York: Columbia University Press.

Pulleybank, Edwin G. 1960. "Neo-Confucianism and Neo-Legalism in T'ang Intellectual Life, 755–805." In *The Confucian Persuasion*, ed. Arthur F. Wright. Stanford: Stanford University Press.

Qian, Wen-yuan. 1985. *The Great Inertia: Scientific Stagnation in Traditional China*. London: Croom Helm.

Quine, W. V. 1985. *The Time of My Life: An Autobiography*. Cambridge, Mass.: MIT Press.

Radding, Charles M. 1985. *A World Made by Men: Cognition and Society, 400–1200*. Chapel Hill: University of North Carolina Press.

———— 1988. *The Origins of Medieval Jurisprudence: Pavia and Bologna, 850–1150.* New Haven: Yale University Press.

Radhakrishnan, Sarvepalli, and Charles A. Moore (eds.). 1957. *A Sourcebook in Indian Philosophy.* Princeton: Princeton University Press.

Raju, P. T. 1985. *Structural Depths of Indian Thought.* Albany: SUNY Press.

Ramirez, Francisco, and John Boli-Bennett. 1982. "Global Patterns of Educational Institutionalization," In *Comparative Education,* ed. Philip Altbach. New York: Macmillan.

Rashdall, Hastings. 1936. *The Universities of Europe in the Middle Ages,* ed. F. M. Powicke and A. B. Emden. 3 volumes. Oxford: Oxford University Press.

Rawson, Elizabeth. 1985. *Intellectual Life in the Late Roman Republic.* London: Duckworth.

Reale, Giovanni. 1985. *A History of Ancient Philosophy.* Vol. 3. *The Systems of the Hellenistic Age.* Albany: SUNY Press.

———— 1987. *A History of Ancient Philosophy.* Vol. 1. *From the Origins to Socrates.* Albany: SUNY Press.

———— 1990. *A History of Ancient Philosophy.* Vol. 4. *The Schools of the Imperial Age.* Albany: SUNY Press.

Reding, Jean-Paul. 1985. *Les fondemonts philosophiques de la rhétorique chez les sophistes grecs et chez les sophistes chinois.* Berne: Peter Lang.

Rescher, Nicolas. 1964. *The Development of Arabic Logic.* Pittsburgh: Pittsburgh University Press.

———— 1966. *Studies in Islamic Philosophy.* Pittsburgh: Pittsburgh University Press.

Resnik, Michael D. 1980. *Frege and the Philosophy of Mathematics.* Ithaca, N.Y.: Cornell University Press.

Richards, Joan L. 1980. "The Art and Science of British Algebra: A Study in the Perception of Mathematical Truth." *Historia Mathematica* 7:343–365.

———— 1988. *Mathematical Visions: The Pursuit of Geometry in Victorian England.* Boston: Academic Press.

Richter, Melvin. 1969. *The Politics of Conscience: T. H. Green and His Age.* Cambridge, Mass.: Harvard University Press.

Ringer, Fritz K. 1969. *The Decline of the German Mandarins: The German Academic Community, 1890–1933.* Cambridge, Mass.: Harvard University Press.

———— 1987. "On Segmentation in Modern European Educational Systems: The Case of French Secondary Education, 1865–1920." In *The Rise of the Modern Educational System,* ed. Detlef K. Mueller, Fritz Ringer, and Brian Simon. Cambridge: Cambridge University Press.

———— 1992. *Fields of Knowledge: French Academic Culture in Comparative Perspective, 1890–1920.* Cambridge: Cambridge University Press.

Rist, J. M. 1967. *Plotinus: The Road to Reality.* Cambridge: Cambridge University Press.

———— 1969. *Stoic Philosophy.* Cambridge: Cambridge University Press.

———— 1972. *Epicurus: An Introduction.* Cambridge: Cambridge University Press.

Roberts, Julian. 1992. *The Logic of Reflection: German Philosophy in the Twentieth Century.* New Haven: Yale University Press.

Robinson, Richard H. 1967. *Early Madhymika in India and China.* Madison: University of Wisconsin Press.

Robles Garcia, José A. 1991. "The Mathematical Ideas of George Berkeley." Unpublished ms.

Roger, Jacques. 1964. Preface to Montesquieu, *Lettres persanes.* Paris: Flammarion.

Rose, Paul L. 1975. *The Italian Renaissance of Mathematics.* Geneva: Droz.

Rosenberg, Hans. 1958. *Bureaucracy, Aristocracy, and Autocracy.* Cambridge, Mass.: Harvard University Press.

Rosenfield, John M. 1977. "The Unity of the Three Creeds." In Hall and Toyoda, 1977.

Roth, Harold. 1991. "Who Compiled the *Chuang Tzu?*" In *Chinese Texts and Philosophical Contexts,* ed. Henry Rosemont. La Salle, Ill.: Open Court.

Rothblatt, Sheldon. 1981. *The Revolution of the Dons: Cambridge and Society in Victorian England.* Cambridge: Cambridge University Press.

Rothblatt, Sheldon, and Bjorn Wittrock (eds.). 1993. *The European and American University since 1800.* Cambridge: Cambridge University Press.

Rubin, Walter, 1954. *Geschichte der indischen Philosophie.* Berlin: Deutscher Verlag der Wissenschaften.

Rubinger, Richard. 1982. *Private Academies in Tokugawa Japan.* Princeton: Princeton University Press.

Ruckmick, C. A. 1912. "The History and Status of Psychology in the United States." *American Journal of Psychology* 23:517–521.

Ruegg, David Seyfort. 1989. *Buddha-Nature, Mind, and the Problem of Gradualism in a Comparative Perspective: On the Transmission and Reception of Buddhism in India and Tibet.* London: School of Oriental and African Studies.

Rump, Ariane, and Wing-tsit Chan (trans.). 1979. *Commentary on the Lao Tzu by Wang Pi.* Honolulu: Hawaii University Press.

Russell, Bertrand. 1922. "Introduction." In Ludwig Wittgenstein, *Tractatus Logico-Philosophicus.* London: Kegan Paul.

———— 1967. *The Autobiography of Bertrand Russell.* London: Allen and Unwin.

Sacks, Harvey, Emanuel A. Schegloff, and Gail Jefferson. 1974. "A Simplest Systematics for the Organization of Turn-Taking for Conversation." *Language* 50:696–735.

Safranski, Rudiger. 1989. *Schopenhauer and the Wild Years of Philosophy.* Cambridge, Mass.: Harvard University Press.

Samson, George B. 1961. *A History of Japan, 1334–1615.* Stanford: Stanford University Press.

———— 1963. *A History of Japan, 1615–1867.* Stanford: Stanford University Press.

Samuel, Richard H., and R. Hinton Thomas. 1949. *Education and Society in Modern Germany.* London: Routledge and Kegan Paul.

Santayana, George. 1920. *Character and Opinion in the United States.* New York: Norton.

Santinello, Giovanni. (ed.). 1981. *Storia delle storie generali della filosofia.* Brescia: La Scuola.

Sartre, Jean-Paul. [1938] 1964. *Nausea.* New York: New Directions.

—— 1943. *L'être et le néant.* Paris: Gallimard.

Scharfstein, Ben-Ami. 1980. *The Philosophers: Their Lives and the Nature of Their Thought.* New York: Oxford University Press.

Scheff, Thomas J. 1988. "Shame and Conformity: The Deference-Emotion System." *American Sociological Review* 53:395–406.

—— 1990. *Micro-sociology: Discourse, Emotion, and Social Structure* Chicago: University of Chicago Press.

Schelsky, Helmut. 1963. *Einsamkeit und Freiheit: Idee und Gestalt der deutschen Universität und ihrer Reformen* Reinbek bei Hamburg: Rowohlt.

Schnabel, Franz. 1959. *Deutsche Geschichte im neuzehnten Jahrhundert.* Vol. 1. Freiburg: Verlag Herder.

Schnädelbach, Herbert. 1984. *Philosophy in Germany, 1831–1933.* Cambridge: Cambridge University Press.

Schneider, Herbert W. 1963. *A History of American Philosophy.* New York: Columbia University Press.

Schneider, Mark A. 1993. *Culture and Enchantment.* Chicago: University of Chicago Press.

Schneider, Ulrich Johannes. 1993. "The Teaching of Philosophy at German Universities in the Nineteenth Century." *History of Universities* 12:197–338.

Scholem, Gershom G. 1946. *Major Trends in Jewish Mysticism.* New York: Schocken.

—— 1990. *Origins of the Kabbalah.* Princeton: Princeton University Press.

Schultz, Uwe. 1965. *Kant.* Reinbek bei Hamburg: Rowohlt.

Schuster, John A. 1980. "Descartes' *Mathesis Universalis, 1619–1628.*" In *Descartes: Philosophy, Mathematics, and Physics,* ed. Stephen Gaukroger. Brighton, Sussex: Harvester.

Schwartz, Benjamin I. 1985. *The World of Thought in Ancient China.* Cambridge, Mass.: Belknap Press.

Searle, John R. 1992. *The Rediscovery of Mind.* Cambridge, Mass.: MIT Press.

Sedley, David. 1977. "Diodorus Cronos and Hellenistic Philosophy." *Proceedings of the Cambridge Philological Society* 203:74–120.

Segal, Alan F. 1986. *Rebecca's Children: Judaism and Christianity in the Roman World.* Cambridge, Mass.: Harvard University Press.

Sextus Empiricus. 1949 [orig. ca. 200 C.E.]. *Against the Professors and Against the Dogmatists.* Loeb Classical Library. London: Heinemann.

Shah, Idries (ed.). 1970. *The Way of the Sufi.* New York: Dutton.

Shapin, Steven, and Simon Schaffer. 1985. *Leviathan and the Air-Pump: Hobbes, Boyle, and the Experimental Life.* Princeton: Princeton University Press.

Sharma, R. S. 1965. *Indian Feudalism, c. 300–1200.* Calcutta: Calcutta University Press.

Shastri, Dharmedra Nath. 1976. *The Philosophy of Nyaya-Vaisesika and Its Conflict with the Buddhist Dignaga School.* Delhi: Bharatiya Vidya Prakastan.

Shaw, George Bernard. [1898] 1967. *The Perfect Wagnerite.* New York: Dover.

Sheehan, Thomas. 1993. "Reading a Life: Heidegger and Hard Times." in Guignon, 1993.

Shepard, W. R. 1964. *Historical Atlas*. 9th edition. New York: Barnes and Noble.

Sher, Richard B. 1985. *Church and University in the Scottish Enlightenment*. Princeton: Princeton University Press.

Simon, J. 1966. *Education in Tudor England*. Cambridge: Cambridge University Press.

Simonton, Dean Keith. 1976. "The Sociopolitical Context of Philosophical Beliefs: A Transhistorical Causal Analysis." *Social Forces* 54:513–523.

—— 1984. *Genius, Creativity, and Leadership: Historiometric Inquiries*. Cambridge, Mass.: Harvard University Press.

—— 1988. *Scientific Genius: A Psychology of Science*. Cambridge: Cambridge University Press.

Sirat, Colette. 1985. *A History of Jewish Philosophy in the Middle Ages*. Cambridge: Cambridge University Press.

Sivin, Nathan. 1968. *Chinese Alchemy: Preliminary Studies*. Cambridge, Mass.: Harvard University Press.

—— 1969. *Cosmos and Computation in Early Chinese Mathematical Astronomy*. Leiden: Brill.

—— 1978. "On the Word 'Taoist' as Source of Perplexity." *History of Religions* 17:303–330.

—— 1987. *Traditional Medicine in Contemporary China*. Ann Arbor: University of Michigan Center for Chinese Studies.

Skocpol, Theda. 1979. *States and Social Revolutions*. Cambridge: Cambridge University Press.

Smart, H. R. 1962. *Philosophy and Its History*. La Salle, Ill.: Open Court.

Smith, Brian K. 1989. *Reflections on Resemblance, Ritual, and Religion*. New York: Oxford University Press.

—— 1994. *Classifying the Universe: The Ancient Indian Varna System and the Origins of Caste*. New York: Oxford University Press.

Smith, D. E. 1951. *History of Mathematics*. New York: Dover.

Smith, D. E., and Yoshio Mikami. 1914. *A History of Japanese Mathematics*. Chicago: Open Court.

Smith, Kidder, Jr., Peter K. Bol, Joseph A. Adler, and Don J. Wyatt. 1990. *Sung Dynasty Uses of the I Ching*. Princeton: Princeton University Press.

Smith, Thomas C. 1959. *Agrarian Origins of Modern Japan*. Stanford: Stanford University Press.

Snodgrass, Anthony. 1980. *Archaic Greece*. Berkeley: University of California Press.

Sohn-Rethel, Alfred. 1978. *Intellectual and Manual Labor*. London: Macmillan.

Sorabji, Richard. 1982. "Atoms and Time Atoms." In *Infinity and Continuity in Ancient and Medieval Thought*, ed. Norman Kretzmann. Ithaca, N.Y.: Cornell University Press.

Southern, R. W. 1963. *St. Anselm and His Biographer*. Cambridge: Cambridge University Press.

—— 1970. *Western Society and the Church in the Middle Ages*. Baltimore: Penguin Books.

—— 1992. *Robert Grosseteste*. 2d edition. New York: Oxford University Press.

———— 1995. *Scholastic Humanism and the Unification of Europe.* Oxford: Blackwell.

Spiegelberg, Herbert. 1982. *The Phenomenological Movement: An Historical Introduction.* The Hague: Nijhoff.

Sprung, Mervyn. 1979. *Lucid Exposition of the Middle Way. The Essential Chapters from the Prasannapada of Candrakirti.* Boulder: Prajña Press.

Srinivas, M. N. 1952. *Religion and Society among the Coorgs of South India.* Oxford: Clarendon.

Staal, Frits. 1988. *Universals. Studies in Indian Logic and Linguistics.* Chicago: University of Chicago Press.

Stark, Rodney, and William Sims Bainbridge. 1985. *The Future of Religion.* Berkeley: University of California Press.

———— 1987. *A Theory of Religion.* New York: Peter Lang.

Staude, John Raphael. 1967. *Max Scheler, 1872–1928: An Intellectual Portrait.* New York: Free Press.

Stcherbatsky, Theodore. 1962. *Buddhist Logic.* New York: Dover.

Stein, R. A. 1972. *Tibetan Civilization.* Stanford: Stanford University Press.

———— 1979. "Religious Taoism and Popular Religion from the Second to the Seventh Centuries." In Welch and Seidel, 1979.

Stone, Lawrence. 1967. *The Crisis of the Aristocracy, 1558–1641.* New York: Oxford University Press.

———— 1974a. "The Size and Composition of the Oxford Student Body, 1580–1900." In Stone, 1974b.

———— 1974b. *The University in Society.* 2 volumes. Princeton: Princeton University Press.

Streng, Frederick J. 1967. *Emptiness: A Study of Religious Meaning.* Nashville: Abington Press.

Strickmann, Michel. 1979. "On the Alchemy of T'ao Hung-ching." In Welch and Seidel, 1979.

Stutley, Margaret. 1980. *Ancient Indian Magic and Folklore.* Boulder: Great Eastern Books.

Suidae Lexicon. 1937 [orig. ca. 950 C.E.]. Ed. Ada Adler. Leipzig: B. G. Teubner.

Sulloway, Frank J. 1996. *Born to Rebel: Family Dynamics and Creative Lives.* New York: Pantheon.

Swanson, Guy E. 1962. *The Birth of the Gods.* Ann Arbor: University of Michigan Press.

Swetz, Frank J. 1987. *Capitalism and Arithmetic.* La Salle, Ill.: Open Court.

———— 1992. *The Sea Island Mathematical Manual: Survey and Mathematics in Ancient China.* University Park: Pennsylvania State University Press.

Swetz, Frank J., and T. I. Kao. 1977. *Was Pythagoras Chinese? An Examination of Right Triangle Theory in Ancient China.* University Park: Pennsylvania State University Press.

Takakusu, Junjiro. [1956] 1973. *The Essentials of Buddhist Philosophy.* Westport, Conn.: Greenwood Press.

Tarrant, Harold. 1985. *Scepticism or Platonism? The Philosophy of the Fourth Academy.* Cambridge: Cambridge University Press.

Telfer, William. 1962. *The Office of a Bishop.* London: Darton, Longman and Todd.

Thapar, Romila. 1966. *A History of India.* Baltimore: Penguin Books.

Tilly, Charles. 1990. *Coercion, Capital, and European States,* A.D. *990–1990.* Oxford: Blackwell.

Titze, Hartmut. 1990. *Der Akademikerzyklus.* Göttingen: Vandenhoeck and Ruprecht.

Toews, John. 1980. *Hegelianism.* Cambridge: Cambridge University Press.

——— 1993. "Transformations of Hegelianism, 1805–1846." In Beiser, 1993.

Totman, Conrad. 1993. *Early Modern Japan.* Berkeley: University of California Press.

Tragesser, Robert S. 1984. *Husserl and Realism in Logic and Mathematics.* Cambridge: Cambridge University Press.

Travers, Jeffrey, and Stanley Milgram. 1969. "An Experimental Study of the Small World Problem." *Sociometry* 32:425–443.

Truchet, Jacques. 1967. "Introduction." In La Rochefoucauld, *Maximes.* Paris: Garnier.

Tsunoda, Ryusaku, Wm. T. de Bary, and Donald Keene (eds.). 1958. *Sources of the Japanese Tradition.* New York: Columbia University Press.

Tu Wei-ming. 1976. *Neo-Confucian Thought in Action: Wang Yang-Ming's Youth (1472–1509).* Berkeley: University of California Press.

Tucker, Mary Evelyn. 1989. *Moral and Spiritual Cultivation in Japanese Neo-Confucianism: The Life and Thought of Kaibara Ekken.* Albany: SUNY Press.

Turner, R. Steven. 1974. "University Reformers and Professional Scholarship in Germany, 1760–1806." In Stone, 1974b.

Ullman, Walter. 1970. *The Growth of Papal Government.* London: Methuen.

Van Buitenen, J. A. B. 1973. "The Mahabharata: Introduction." In *The Mahabharata.* Chicago: University of Chicago Press.

van der Waerden, B. L. 1975. *Science Awakening.* Vol. 1. *Egyptian, Babylonian, and Greek Mathematics.* Dordrecht: Kluwer.

Varley, H. Paul. 1977. "Ashikaga Yoshimitsu and the World of Kitayama: Social Change and Shogunal Patronage in Early Muromachi." In Hall and Toyoda, 1977.

Verger, Jacques. 1986. *Histoire des universités en France.* Toulouse: Bibliothèque historique privat.

Vesey, Lawrence R. 1965. *The Emergence of the American University.* Chicago: University of Chicago Press.

von Ferber, Christian. 1956. *Die Entwicklung der Lehrkörpers der deutschen Universitäten und Hochschulen, 1864–1954.* In *Untersuchungen zur Lage der deutschen Hochschullehrer,* ed. Helmuth Plessner. Gottingen: Vandenhoeck & Ruprecht.

von Staden, Heinrich. 1989. *Herophilus: The Art of Medicine in Early Alexandria.* Cambridge: Cambridge University Press.

Vuillemin, Jules. 1986. *What Are Philosophical Systems?* Cambridge: Cambridge University Press.

Wagner, Helmut. 1983. *Alfred Schutz: An Intellectual Biography.* Chicago: University of Chicago Press.

Waismann, Friedrich. 1979. *Wittgenstein and the Vienna Circle.* New York: Harper and Row.

Waithe, Mary Ellen (ed.). 1987–1995. *A History of Women Philosophers.* 4 volumes. Dordrecht: Nijhoff.

Wakabayashi, Bob Tadashi. 1986. *Anti-Foreignism and Western Learning in Early Modern Japan.* Cambridge, Mass.: Harvard University Press.

Waley, Arthur. 1958. *The Way and Its Power. A Study of the Tao Tê Ching and Its Place in Chinese Thought.* New York: Grove Press.

——— 1970. "Introduction." In Lady Murasaki, *The Tale of Genji.* Tokyo: Tuttle.

Waley, Daniel P. 1961. *The Papal State in the Thirteenth Century.* London: Macmillan.

Wallace, William A. 1984. *Galileo and His Sources: The Heritage of the Collegio Romano in Galileo's Science.* Princeton: Princeton University Press.

Wang, Hao. 1987. *Reflections on Kurt Gödel.* Cambridge, Mass.: MIT Press.

Watt, W. Montgomery. 1973. *The Formative Period of Islamic Thought.* Edinburgh: Edinburgh University Press.

——— 1985. *Islamic Philosophy and Theology.* Edinburgh: Edinburgh University Press.

Weber, Max. [1916] 1951. *The Religion of China.* Glencoe, Ill.: Free Press.

——— [1916–1917] 1958. *The Religion of India.* Glencoe, Ill.: Free Press.

——— [1917–1919] 1952. *Ancient Judaism.* Glencoe, Ill.: Free Press.

——— [1922] 1968. *Economy and Society.* New York: Bedminster Press.

——— [1923] 1961. *General Economic History.* New York: Collier-Macmillan.

Wedberg, Anders. 1984. *A History of Philosophy.* Vol. 3. *From Bolzano to Wittgenstein.* New York: Oxford University Press.

Weinberg, Julius R. 1964. *A Short History of Medieval Philosophy.* Princeton: Princeton University Press.

Weinstein, Stanley. 1977. "Rennyo and the Shinshu Revival." In Hall and Toyoda, 1977.

——— *Buddhism under the T'ang.* Cambridge: Cambridge University Press.

Weisz, George. 1983. *The Emergence of Modern Universities in France, 1863–1914.* Princeton: Princeton University Press.

Welch, Holmes. 1965. *Taoism: The Parting of the Way.* Boston: Beacon Press.

Welch, Holmes, and Anna Seidel (eds.). 1979. *Facets of Taoism: Essays in Chinese Religion.* New Haven: Yale University Press.

Werkmeister, W. H. 1980. *Kant: The Architectonic and Development of His Philosophy.* Chicago: Open Court.

Westfall, Richard S. 1981. *Never at Rest: A Biography of Isaac Newton.* Cambridge: Cambridge University Press.

Westman, Robert S. 1980. "The Astronomer's Role in the Sixteenth Century." *History of Science* 18:105–147.

White, Harrison C. 1993. *Careers and Creativity: Social Forces in the Arts*. Boulder: Westview Press.

Whitehead, Alfred North. 1929. *Process and Reality*. London: Macmillan.

Whitley, Richard. 1984. *The Intellectual and Social Organization of the Sciences*. Oxford: Clarendon Press.

Wijayaratna, Mohan. 1990. *Buddhist Monastic Life*. Cambridge: Cambridge University Press.

Willey, Thomas E. 1978. *Back to Kant: The Revival of Kantianism in German Social and Historical Thought, 1860–1914*. Detroit: Wayne State University Press.

Willis, Janice Dean. 1979. *On Knowing Reality: The Tattvartha Chapter of Asanga's Bodhisattvabhumi*. New York: Columbia University Press.

Wilson, Daniel J. 1990. *Science, Community, and the Transformation of American Philosophy, 1860–1930*. Chicago: University of Chicago Press.

Wilson, Edmund. 1931. *Axel's Castle: A Study in the Imaginative Literature of 1870–1930*. New York: Scribner's.

Windelband, Wilhelm. [1892] 1901. *A History of Philosophy*. New York: Macmillan.

Wolfson, Harry A. 1976. *The Philosophy of the Kalam*. Cambridge, Mass.: Harvard University Press.

——— 1979. *Repercussions of the Kalam in Jewish Philosophy*. Cambridge, Mass.: Harvard University Press.

Woo Kang. 1932. *Les trois théories politiques du Tch'ouen Ts'ieou, interpretées par Tong Tchong-Chou*. Paris: Ernest Leroux.

Wood, Thomas E. 1990. *The Mandukya Upanishad and the Agama Sastra*. Honolulu: University of Hawaii Press.

——— 1991. *Mind Only: A Philosophical and Doctrinal Analysis of the Vijñanavada*. Honolulu: University of Hawaii Press.

Wuthnow, Robert. 1989. *Communities of Discourse: Ideology and Social Structure in the Reformation, the Enlightenment, and European Socialism*. Cambridge, Mass.: Harvard University Press.

Yamamura, Kozo (ed.). 1990. *The Cambridge History of Japan*. Vol. 3. *Medieval Japan*. Cambridge: Cambridge University Press.

Yates, Frances A. 1972. *The Rosicrucian Enlightenment*. London: Routledge.

Zaehner, R. E. 1960. *Hindu and Muslim Mysticism*. New York: Schocken.

Zammito, John H. 1992. *The Genesis of Kant's Critique of Judgment*. Chicago: University of Chicago Press.

Zeller, Eduard. 1919. *Die Philosophie der Greichen in ihrer geschichtlichen entwicklung*. 5th edition, revised by Wilhelm Nestle. Leipzig: O. R. Reisland.

The Zen Teachings of Rinzai. 1976. Berkeley: Shambala.

Zimmer, Heinrich. 1951. *Philosophies of India*. Princeton: Princeton University Press.

Zuckerman, Harriet. 1967. "Nobel Laureates in Science: Patterns of Productivity, Collaboration, and Authorship." *American Sociological Review* 32:391–403.

Zürcher, Erik. 1959. *The Buddhist Conquest of China*. Leiden: E. J. Brill.

—— 1962. *Buddhism: Its Origin and Spread in Words, Maps, and Pictures*. London: Routledge.

Index of Persons

1102 · *Index of Persons*

Index of Subjects

Neoplatonism, 108, 116, 124, 127, 130, 430–432, 435–437, 440–445, 449, 596, 796, 799, 828, 829, 958n34, 958n37

Neo-Pythagoreans, 109, 111, 114, 125, 126, 128, 442, 448, 847

Netherlands, 496, 529, 567, 575, 585, 589–591, 598

Networks, theory of, 2, 5–6, 64–68, 71–76, 379

Neutral monism, 724

New Text School, 157–158, 794–795, 806, 884

Nominalism, 221, 238, 259, 269, 465–466, 487–490, 497, 518–519, 555, 820, 821, 826–830. *See also* Names, school of; Name and form

Non-Euclidean Geometry, 699

Numerology, 101, 109, 312, 416, 550, 552, 798–799

Nyaya, 188, 228–233, 244, 257, 262, 269–270. *See also* Nyaya-Vaisheshika

Nyaya-Vaisheshika, 226, 232, 237, 241–242, 249, 252, 256, 259–262, 266, 822, 836

Occasionalism, 398–401, 411–413, 587, 612, 652, 821, 840, 842–843

Occultism and spiritualism, 805–807; in Greece, 120–127; in China, 152–158; in Europe, 610, 669, 731, 748. *See also* Numerology

Ockham's razor, 485–486

Old Text School, 157–158, 169–170, 173, 794–795, 884

Ontology, 89, 97, 125, 236–240, 244–245, 255, 263–267, 419, 469, 555, 654–655, 713, 720, 810

Opposition, division of attention space by, 6, 137, 379, 792, 811

Oratorians, 524, 583

Organizational bases of intellectuals. *See* Academies; Courts; Libraries; Medicine; Monasteries; Patronage; Publishing; Religions *(specific entries)*; Schools; Translation bureaus; Universities

"Oriental logic," 375

Papacy, 445–446, 455–458, 460, 462–463, 479, 497, 518, 743

Paris, 73, 528–529, 531, 583; critical mass for intellectual market, 774; as international literary center, 1023n13. *See also* Christendom, intellectual centers in

Pascal's wager, 586

Patronage: in Greece, 88, 95, 113; in China, 169; in India, 180–191; in Islamic world, 410, 434, 453; in Europe, 497, 554, 585, 595, 598, 601–602, 605, 608, 638–640, 754–755

Peripatetics, Peripatos. *See* Aristotelean school

Phenomenology, 688, 737–751, 777–779, 831

Philosophical Radicals (London), 530

Pietism, 625, 639, 650–652, 654

Platonism, 59, 101, 109, 596–597, 500, 600, 610, 675, 716, 957n28; Middle Platonism, 125, 128, 812, 827, 958n34. *See also* Neoplatonism

Pneuma, 106, 107; Pneumatist physicians, 112

Political philosophy, 152–153, 523, 525, 596, 608–609, 660, 803. *See also* Legalists

Port-Royal, 529, 585–586

Positivism, 684, 688, 693, 690, 696; logical, 262, 268, 717–730, 750

Postmodernism, 10–13, 789, 750, 756, 834, 845

Potentiality, 236–237, 820–821, 841

Pragmatism, 675, 678–683, 718

Presocratics, 82–87, 95, 147, 319, 744, 804

Protestantism, 524; similar organization in Taoism, Hinduism, and Japanese Buddhism, 167–168, 227, 323; and scientific revolution, 553–554, 570–571; early authoritarianism in, 570–572, 575; liberal, 746–748, 769. *See also* Calvinism; Evangelicals; Pietism

Psychology, experimental, 669, 670, 674, 681–682, 689–693

Publishing, 72, 355, 370, 528–531, 601–602, 608, 627, 639, 645, 754, 770, 773–774, 775; textual commentaries as form of, 793–794

Pugdalavadins, 215, 253

Pure Brethren, 410, 415–418, 420

CPSIA information can be obtained
at www.ICGtesting.com
Printed in the USA
JSHW040936090622
26859JS00003B/35

9 780674 001879